THE FACTS ON FILE
COMPANION TO

WORLD
POETRY

1900 to the Present

THE FACTS ON FILE
COMPANION TO

WORLD POETRY

1900 to the Present

R. VICTORIA ARANA

Facts On File

An imprint of Infobase Publishing

The Facts On File Companion to World Poetry, 1900 to the Present

Facts On File, Inc.
An imprint of Infobase Publishing
132 West 31st Street
New York NY 10001

Library of Congress Cataloging-in-Publication Data

Arana, R. Victoria.
    The Facts on File companion to world poetry, 1900 to the present / R. Victoria Arana.
        p. cm.
    Includes bibliographical references and index.
    ISBN 978-0-8160-6457-1 (hc : alk. paper)
    1. Poetry—20th century—History and criticism—Handbooks, manuals, etc. 2. Poetry—21st century—History and criticism—Handbooks, manuals, etc. I. Title.
    PN1271A73 2008
    809.1'04—dc22   2007001831

Text design adapted by James Scotto-Lavino
Cover design by Salvatore Luongo

Printed in the United States of America

VB Hermitage 10 9 8 7 6 5 4 3 2 1

This book is printed on acid-free paper.

In honor of my teacher and mother, Marie Elverine Arana,
who taught me to love the literature of the world

CONTENTS

PREFACE

The Facts On File Companion to World Poetry, 1900 to the Present provides a comprehensive introduction to 20th- and 21st-century world poets and their most famous, most characteristic, or most influential poetic works. The hundreds of entries found in this book encompass the globe and represent the most prominent writers from each continent and many of the world's islands. Only poets from Britain, Ireland, and the United States have been excluded: Their lives and works are found in other volumes, published or forthcoming, in the Facts On File Companion to Literature series.

This *Companion to World Poetry* is conceived, as its title suggests, to serve as a "friendly associate" of many books of poetry already on our library shelves. It complements the collected poems in English translation of hundreds of the world's poets, and it is meant to lead interested readers to them. It relates to and supplements the selections available in today's most popular anthologies of world literature and poetry. The entries are designed to cast bright light on the backgrounds and surroundings of the poets we have included as well as to invite closer and better informed readings of their major poetic works. The many cross-references bring to life the connections among the world's writers, whether they were friends and associates or merely admirers at a distance of one another's works. Cross-references are indicated in SMALL CAPITAL LETTERS. Only poems with published English translations have entries in this book, but we have often found it necessary to mention works that have not yet been translated.

Because this volume is designed to be as accessible as possible to English-speaking readers, entries on poems are alphabetized according to the title of the poem's most common published English translation.

Because the nature of poetry is to be concise and sometimes allusive or otherwise mysterious, it helps to possess a reference such as this, a compilation of tips about what to notice about particular writers and their works. Understanding the poetic idiom is not always easy, and the difficulties are compounded when the material is foreign. It is for this reason that we have endeavored to engage African scholars to write on African poets, Arabic scholars to write on Arabic poetry, Chinese scholars to write on Chinese poetry, and so on. This way, the troublesome challenges of responding to works in translation are somewhat alleviated. Readers of our entries are in good hands: Our contributors have been alert and sensitive to the problems of translation and often comment on them, where comments are warranted. The entries on specific poems or poetic sequences treat their themes, forms, special qualities, and significance within the larger body of their author's works. Wherever necessary to clarify a point, contributors quote from both the original poem and its best translation.

We have tried to keep a reasonable balance of poets and poems profiled in this volume so that each continent and decade is fairly represented. It has not been an easy task deciding whom to include, especially since the last 100 years saw a surge of interest in experimental poetic expression and a stunning proliferation in formats of publication. Thousands upon thousands of writers from every part of the world have made their poems available in magazines, local periodicals, slim volumes of verse, and group anthologies—and, in more recent years, on CDs, DVDs, and Internet sites.

Making the process of selection even more difficult, each national or linguistic tradition has preserved a strong sense of which poets are its giants; in more cases than one might imagine, there may be hundreds of "stellar poets" presenting themselves for inclusion from any one region, nation, or language group from which we have been able to select, sometimes, only two or three exemplars. To compensate, however, our entries on individual poets situate them in their literary contexts and widen the scope of our treatment by referencing other relevant poets too numerous to highlight in a volume of this type. Each biographical entry and most of the entries on individual poetic works include a bibliography to steer users toward further reading on the lives of the poets, as well as to outstanding recent editions, especially bilingual editions and translations.

In selecting our entries, we have been guided by research into what is being taught in world literature courses in anglophone high schools and colleges. We have also taken into consideration which poets and poems are included in the major anthologies of world literature currently available to teachers and students and the general public. Finally, we have focused on those poems for which one or more excellent translations into English are available.

In addition to the entries on individual poets and poems or poetic sequences, we include a number of substantial entries on aesthetic movements of particular importance to this period of poetic creativity, such as Arab rap and hip hop culture, colonialism, ecopoetics, *écriture,* field Poetics, French rap, modernism, *négritude,* and "poetry beyond the page." These essays on important avant-garde movements define their characteristics and identify their principal figures, and they also provide lists of books for further reading and even some dynamic Internet resources (some with video streaming).

The contributors (listed at the back of the book) all have special expertise and academic credentials in the areas about which they have written their entries. Because so many of them are scholars and teachers with cultural backgrounds in common with their subjects, they have brought extremely valuable cultural and historical insights to the poets and poems they have profiled. This factor, in particular, is what makes our *Companion to World Poetry* an essential new resource for students and readers of world literature.

R. Victoria Arana

INTRODUCTION

No grand narrative could possibly weave a unified story that encompasses all of the historical, cultural, social, and literary developments covered by the contents of this book. The works produced by the world's poets over the past century and into this one are representative of an enormous wealth of distinct, even wildly divergent literary traditions. Moreover, to complicate matters, most of the world's poets of this period were very aware of literary and artistic movements in other times and places, or were rebels of various sorts, and they absorbed and exploited their knowledge of the artistic works of others from around the world as they labored to express insights about their own lives and, more generally, about the human experience.

The 20th century is, nevertheless, remarkable in literary history for being a time of universal upheavals, punctuated by two world wars and many more regional and international conflicts that resulted in the deracination or death of millions all over the planet. The spiritual consequences of the century's massive migrations across the world's landmasses and oceans were profound and transformative. Empires grew and collapsed, totalitarian governments emerged out of the chaos that ensued, colonies everywhere gained independence, local regimes contended for control of precious natural resources, indigenous populations explored their cultural traditions and prospects for the future, and multinational corporations pursued global markets. Poets worldwide, many of them dislocated, also, responded to these events and produced bril-

liant responses to the social and cultural upheavals that they lived through. The 20th century was also a period, for some poets, of more leisurely intercontinental travel—for pleasure, business, or the pursuit of education or jobs in foreign lands. Historians, sociologists, philosophers, psychologists, and pundits have recorded their observations on the significant events of the century and commented on the public personalities and momentous transactions that now constitute our sense of the past, but it is to the poets that we must look to find deeper spiritual responses to the recent history of our planet.

Many individual poets were inspired by those shifts and the foreign influences in their lives to create startlingly original works of art. Others explored ways of rescuing cultural traditions and poetic forms and endowing them with contemporary relevance and significance. One by one, they gave voice to some of the most moving and enduring works of the human imagination that have ever been fashioned out of words. They captured everything from the finest nuances of devotional experience to prophetic pronouncements on the ecological state of planet Earth. In their creative engagement with the challenges of their lives, as poets have always aspired to do, the world's poets since 1900 have captured and preserved for later generations a broad range of human experiences—intellectual, sensual, nostalgic, amatory, ethnic, familial, political, revolutionary, cosmic, and religious, to mention just some. They have articulated feelings of surprise, amusement, respect, desolation, hatred, love, anger, disgust, and transcendent joy. And they have done so in many languages and diverse verbal shapes and poetic forms. Most important, they have produced a body of works so vast, so diverse, and so modern that we can hardly call ourselves well informed without an awareness, partial at least, of its brilliance, range, and magnificence.

Amid all the turbulence and trauma caused by the historical developments of the 20th century, children were born and became writers zealous about living meaningfully. Their growth into artistic maturity, their aesthetic and other insights, and their passionately crafted responses to their natural and social environments are the true topics of this book. This *Companion to World Poetry, 1900 to the Present* features biocritical accounts of the lives of over 200 greatly beloved and critically esteemed world poets, as well as close readings of and commentaries on hundreds of their most important or characteristic works.

R. Victoria Arana
Potomac, Maryland, U.S.A.

A

ABANI, CHRIS (1966–) Born Christopher Uchechukwu Andrew Abani on December 27, 1966, in Afikpo, Nigeria, to an Oxford-educated Igbo father and a white English mother, Abani is a prolific author of poetry, novels, drama, and literary criticism in English. A long-time resident of three world cities—Lagos, London, and Los Angeles—and an active participant in their literary circles, he writes at the transnational nexus of the developing and developed world, an embodiment of African, European, and American connections.

In the second half of the 20th century, Nigeria produced one of the world's most impressive literatures in English. Abani is part of a third generation of such writers, many of whom write outside the country as part of the Black British or African American literary scene. They have turned from their predecessors' concern about the impact of colonialism on traditional society to 21st-century concerns over the global urban space. Abani adds to this a focus on the intertwined violence of international capital and the patriarchal family, particularly the conflicted, ambivalent, brutal, and wounded nature of modern masculinity.

Abani published his first short story when he was 10 and wrote his first novel, *Masters of the Board* (Delta, 1985), when he was 16. Since that novel had some minor plot points in common with a real-life coup attempt against the Nigerian government, Abani was arrested and imprisoned for six months. He emerged as a political radical and was arrested twice again for guerrilla street theater work, spending two and a half years in prison, much of it on death row, some of it in solitary confinement. Abani enrolled at Imo State University (1987–91), and after he finished a B.A. in English and literary studies there, he moved to London.

There he became involved with the Centerprise Black Literature Project, funded by the Arts Council, where he taught community literature workshops and was part of the Black British writing scene during the 1990s. He was emerging with authors Roger Robinson, Kadija George Sesay, Lemn Sissay, Biyi Bandele-Thomas, and Bernardine Evaristo and getting to know more established writers, including Ben Okri, Ferdinand Dennis, and Caryl Phillips. Abani continued to write, churning out novel after novel, none of which was published despite his vigorous efforts. Abani was struggling to forge a new style, attempting to switch from the pulp fiction and agitprop writing he had done in Nigeria to a more philosophical and conceptual style. During this period, Abani spent a great deal of time reading and was especially impressed by Ishiguro's *The Unconsoled,* Ayi Kwei Armah's *Fragments,* Ben Okri's *Famished Road,* Salman Rushdie's early work, and the writing of Julian Barnes, Bruce Chatwin, and Ian McEwan. Abani took an M.A. in gender and cultural studies from Birkbeck College, part of the University of London (1993–95), and began to reference postcolonial and feminist theory in his work. He also began to speak for Amnesty International and PEN, the international writers' society, to raise awareness about writers in prison, work that he continues today.

In December 1996 Abani was urged to turn from the theoretical and to face the specific horrors of his life. He poured out more than 100 poems over the next two weeks, writing about everything he experienced in prison: rape, torture, friends' deaths, their comic book heroes, the movies they endlessly discussed. Abani then took the poems, unedited, to the Jamaican poet Kwame Dawes, in whose poetry workshop Abani was studying. Dawes recommended that the poems be pared to their essence. Abani did so and, 15 years after his first published book, he published his second book, *Kalakuta Republic* (Saqi, 2001). This harrowing and transcendent book quickly garnered Abani international attention, selling thousands of copies and winning him a number of awards, including the PEN USA Freedom-to-Write Award for 2001, the Prince Claus Award for 2001, and the 2002 Imbonge Yesizwe Poetry International Award (South Africa).

Not long after its publication, Abani moved to Los Angeles, where, in 2001 he joined the University of Southern California's new doctoral program in literature and creative writing, hoping to find a place to hone his craft further. There, too, he began working with African-American novelist Percival Everett and the poets Carol Muske-Dukes and David St. John, who encouraged the tenderness of his style and helped shape his form; and with Ron Gottesman, who insured that he always had a sounding board for his thoughts and a roof over his head. In quick succession, Abani wrote two well-received books of poems, including *DAPHNE'S LOT* (Red Hen 2003), a book-length poem about his mother and the Nigerian-Biafran civil war. He was then awarded the 2003 Lannan Literary Fellowship for his developing body of work and its engagement with the world. *DOG WOMAN* (Red Hen 2004) followed a year later, a historical exploration of race, gender, and memory. His simultaneous work on a novel resulted in *GraceLand* (Farrar, Straus and Giroux, 2004), about a teenage Nigerian Elvis impersonator who hopes to escape poverty and his alcoholic father's physical abuse. *GraceLand* was a critical and popular favorite, listed as one of the best books of the year by many critics and winning several awards. Abani continues to write at a prodigious rate: *Hands Washing Water* (Copper Canyon, 2006), a book of poetry; *Becoming Abigail* (Akashic Books, 2006), a novella about a 15-year-old prostitute; and *The Virgin of Flames,* a novel about Los Angeles, immigration, and the ambiguity of masculine sexuality.

Abani received a Ph.D. from the University of Southern California in 2005 and teaches at the University of California, Riverside. He is the founder of the Black Goat poetry series with Red Hen Press.

BIBLIOGRAPHY
Abani, Chris. Chris Abani's homepage and links. Available online. URL: http://www.chrisabani.com/. Accessed on April 20, 2007.

Wendy Belcher

ACHEBE, CHINUA (1930–   )

African novelist and poet Chinua Achebe was born in Nigeria to parents active in Anglican missions. He grew up in Ogidi, an Igbo village in the eastern part of the country, an area that inspired the setting of his most famous work, the novel *Things Fall Apart* (1958). Achebe went to parochial schools in Ogidi and read the primers and theological works in his father's library, but also heard traditional Igbo tales from his mother and sister. Thus, while adopting the European language and religion brought by the British, Achebe also absorbed the traditional beliefs and culture of his people—elements of Nigerian life robustly portrayed in his novels and poetry.

As an adolescent, Achebe attended a prestigious government-run secondary school in the town of Umuahia, which had an excellent library, unlike the typical private secondary schools. Achebe credited the government school for providing more resources and noted that many early postcolonial African writers had the advantage of state-supported educations to assist them in their academic development. In 1948 Achebe entered University College in Ibadan on a medical scholarship, but he switched to liberal arts a year later and focused on English, history, and religion. During that period, Achebe read several European works featuring African settings and realized that the portraits created by British authors, such as Joyce Cary and Joseph Conrad, distorted and demeaned African culture. This inaccurate depiction of Africans impelled him to start writing stories from the viewpoint of African characters, and he published a few of these in *University Herald,* a campus publication.

After receiving a B.A. in 1953, Achebe began working in radio for the Nigerian Broadcasting Service (NBS). He made his first trip to Europe in 1956 when he traveled to London to attend the British Broadcasting Corporation's training for employees. When he returned to Nigeria, he quickly became an influential figure in the NBS, eventually attaining the position of director of External Services in 1961. While his work with NBS allowed him to create programs emphasizing Nigerian culture and identity, he harnessed his frustration with European attitudes toward Africans as the inspiration for a series of novels written over the next three decades: *Things Fall Apart* (1958), *Arrow of God* (1964), *A Man of the People* (1966), and *Anthills of the Savannah* (1987). Achebe's fiction describes the conflict between native cultures and the European colonial powers, as well as the internal strife rampant in postcolonial Nigeria.

Achebe's efforts within Nigeria toward developing a healthy cultural identity paralleled the country's independence movement, which achieved Nigerian sovereignty from Britain in 1960. When internal ethnic and religious divisions soon began to dominate Nigerian politics, Achebe sided with the Igbo of eastern Nigeria, whose attempt to establish the independent state of Biafra led to the bloody Nigerian civil war (1967–70). The conflict also forced Achebe into exile in Europe and North America, where he became an outspoken advocate against the repressive measures of the various Nigerian military regimes that have largely controlled the country from the mid-1960s onward. Since the mid-1970s Achebe has spent most of his time teaching and writing. He has made several brief visits to his homeland and to South Africa. He currently resides in New York State, where he teaches at Bard College.

Though he is chiefly known and admired as a novelist, Achebe was a joint recipient of the first Commonwealth Poetry Prize in 1972 for his book *Christmas in Biafra and Other Poems,* written during the Nigerian civil war (see "CHRISTMAS IN BIAFRA"). His 1964 novel, *Arrow of God,* won the New Statesman–Jock Campbell Award, and *Anthills of the Savannah* was a finalist for the prestigious Booker Prize in 1987. Achebe has also been awarded numerous honors around the world, including an Honorary Fellowship of the American Academy of Arts and Letters, and he has been granted Foreign Honorary Membership in the prestigious American Academy of Arts and Sciences, along with some 30 honorary doctorates from universities across North America, Europe, and Africa. In addition, he was awarded Nigeria's highest intellectual award, the National Order of Merit, and Germany's Friedenpreis des Deutschen Buchhandels (both in 2002).

Achebe's singular achievement, though, is the tremendous cultural inspiration he gave to African writers with his first novel, *Things Fall Apart,* which describes the life and times of Okonkwo, an Igbo tribesman who fights to preserve his people's cultural identity against the encroaching Europeans who threaten to destroy the Igbo way of life. In addition, the novel describes the internal forces and conflicts that exist within the Igbo culture and demonstrates that African culture, unlike the simplistic depictions of European writers, is dignified and complex, with intricate relationships that provide a solid social structure for its members. The novel also demonstrates that European missionaries were particularly adept at exploiting weaknesses in the Igbo system that eventually undermined and suppressed it, thereby allowing them to impose their own sociopolitical institutions on the native peoples.

Achebe's poetry, though less well known than his novelistic endeavors, is credited for its simplicity, attention to detail, and rich intermixture of individual and national consciousness that emphasizes the individual's precarious position in the larger movement of events in the nation's history. Achebe's poetic treatments—which include the Nigerian civil war, Igbo myth and legend, and religious speculation—capture the juxtaposition of Christian and traditional Igbo viewpoints in the lives of contemporary Nigerians.

BIBLIOGRAPHY

Ohaeto, Ezenwa. *Chinua Achebe: A Biography.* Bloomington: Indiana University Press, 1997.

Innes, C. L. *Chinua Achebe: A Biography.* London: Cambridge University Press, 1990.

Sallah, Tijan, and Ngozi Okonjo-Iweala. *Chinua Achebe, Teacher of Light: A Biography.* Trenton, N.J.: Africa World Press, 2003.

Joseph E. Becker

"ADMONITION TO THE BLACK WORLD"

CHINWEIZU (1986)   "Admonition to the Black World" begins with four prose paragraphs that summarize 25 centuries of foreign assault on Africa. CHINWEIZU thus gives his spectacular, 21-page prophetic harangue a historical and ideological context. Before the poem proper, readers are reminded that since 525 B.C., when parts of Africa were conquered by "white Persians," the African peoples have endured an uninterrupted series of invasions—by Greeks, Romans, Arabs, western Europeans, Russians, and (most recently) "the agents and money-lenders of the West."

The poem itself is divided into four numbered and subtitled sections. Overall, the tone of the poem is ominous, acrimonious, and oracular. The voice is that of an inspired prophet whose premonitory vision includes images of Africa as a "manacled bitch / Tied to a post and raped / By every passing white dog" (ll. 3–5). The poem's first stanza ends with the lines "Listen! Listen to the pack / Of scavenger dogs from white heartlands / Snarling in their gang rape of Africa!" (ll. 9–11). That urgent, monitory temper is sustained to the end of the poem.

The poem's first section ("I: Scatterbrained Land") is composed of 10 free-verse stanzas of varying lengths. In stanza 2, we learn that Africa is not the "bitch" that the dogs consider her, but a "Black Lady" forced to wear "A white turban of shame" as she is violated. Stanza 3 sees Africa as male as well as female, calling the continent the "father of sciences" and exclaiming how "unlucky in its rulers" it has been: "Like an eagle / Shot in soaring flight" and "dropped . . . / Into the lightless ooze / Of a mangrove ravine" from which it cannot free itself. Stanza 4 gives the African ancestry of the world's religions, symbolized by "Tablet, Cross, Crescent and Red Star," and asks the reader (or auditor) to "Behold" the "venerable land / Assaulted, dismembered". . . "By the mongrel progeny" of the god Aten, whom Africa "discarded!" Stanza 5 compares Africans to whales, their brains polluted by infections, "beached . . . on white shores" and "panting for white theologies." Stanza 6 mocks the African who "claims he is an Arab." Stanza 7 ridicules the Christian African who in assembly "Lustily chants / The [blond] identity of his desire." Stanza 8 conveys the warped ideology of the socialist African, who ("deracialized . . . denationalized . . . purified") abhors the "taint" of "black identity" and prays to the "Prophet Marx" for "assimilation / Into the Universal!" Stanza 9 relays a bit of dialogue between a white boy and an African who complains that the white boy does not relate to him as an equal, despite the African's efforts to bleach his body, mind, and faith—to which the white boy responds: "Who would treat his mimic as an equal? / Do you think I am dotty like you?" The final stanza of the first section begins with the expostulation, "O terrible, terrible, terrible! / What meningitis of the soul / Has twisted their identity spines?" Africans are, the prophet intones, "Like yam tendrils fleeing earth damp" and groping "For any genealogical tree / With white bark."

In the first of three stanzas that constitute Section II of the poem ("The Anger of Ancestors"), the prophet asks the reader to "Behold the ancestors!" and their "volcanic anger" over the "circus of absurdities" displayed before them—ancestors "thirsting for the new black man" who would know how to resist being "trampled by shined boots spiked with dollars." The second stanza of this section catalogs—fiercely and at length—the unreasonable desires of Africans bombarded with inferiorizing propaganda and drowning in "elixirs of mad modernity / sold by titillation" and "from the podia of academia." The final stanza of the section asks Africans to "Behold our new notables," drunk "Trans-civilized idolators all / Craving a white massage!"

Section "III: If You Let Them" begins "O Blacks, hear and heed!" This section hammers the message that the "white predators" will not readily be driven from Africa and will, instead, drug, lie to, and hack their enemies to death. The last stanza of this section (which begins, "If you let them, if you let them, / They will use your fears against you") addresses the African soul and contains an extensive list of the insolent psychological tactics the "white foes" will use "against you" to get their way. It ends with the soothsayer's warning: "Woe to them who forget their history / And drug their hearts with false memories."

Section "IV: The Pyramid Is Our Icon" constitutes the longest part of the poem. In 24 stanzas of varied lengths, it chronicles the feats of the "Grand lords of the Land of Khemet . . . the founding fathers / Of Black civilization." In impassioned tones the poet praises the ancestral geniuses who built up whole civilizations and filled them with wonders. In stanza 20 the poet exclaims: "Look what their minds conceived! / Look what they taught the world! / Look what their hands had wrought!" After designating the pyramid as the "Venerable symbol of Black Civilization," the poet questions why Africans have abandoned their true icon (the pyramid) to "kneel and bow" and to "adore" the Cross, Crescent, and Red Star. In the poem's last two stanzas the poet prophet commands the "Demented, delirious black sheep" to return to the Nile and "Drink deep of its waters of wisdom" (st. 23) and to "douse the acid of humiliations / From your anciently merry eyes" (st. 24).

BIBLIOGRAPHY
Chinweizu. *Invocations and Admonitions: 49 Poems and a Triptych of Parables.* Lagos, Nigeria: Pero Press, 1986.

R. Victoria Arana

ADONIS (ALI AHMAD SAʻID; ADUNIS)
(1930–) Arguably the most important contemporary Arab poet, Adonis (pen name for Ali Ahmad Saʻid) was born in Qassabin—a small town in Syria—into a modest, traditional, but learned home. His poetic gift and critical intelligence, recognized early in his life, helped him secure grants for his education in Damascus, Beirut, and Paris. Later as a well-known poet and intellectual, Adonis taught in universities in Paris and Geneva and lectured in several European and American universities. With a philosophical bent and academic specialization, solid knowledge of classical Arabic thought and poetry, and commitment to radical change, Adonis became the emblem of modernism and cultural renaissance in the Arab world.

A prolific author with dozens of poetic collections, Adonis set his poetic innovation by complementing his creative works with critical works that embodied his cultural vision, his innovative poetics. In his *An Introduction to Arab Poetics,* he argued for modernizing Arabic literature from within, calling on the sublime language of the Quran, Sufi texts, and medieval poets he named as precursors of the Arab literary modernist movement as he viewed it. Adonis argued for the affinities and parallelism between European modernism as exemplified in 19th-century French symbolism and early 20th-century surrealism, on the one hand, and on the other Arab heritage in its philosophical, mystical, and lyrical dimension. Thus, he presented Arab modernism as a transformation from within, rather than simply an imported and alien artistic movement. Adonis located the seeds of innovation in classical Arabic culture.

Adonis lived for three decades (1956–86) in Beirut and became a Lebanese national. Beirut in those years was the cultural capital of the Arab world, open to experimental writing and welcoming winds of change. Beirut was then also the intellectual capital of the Arab world, where debates over cultural change were fermenting in a context of a relatively free press. In Beirut in 1957, Adonis along with other like-minded writers founded the self-styled avant-garde journal *Shiʻr* (Poetry)—the first literary periodical to espouse the prose poem in Arabic, among other innovations mostly influenced by Western modernism. Later, Adonis left this journal and established his own, *Mawaqif* (Positions), which was involved with broad cultural issues and was more than a strictly literary periodical. The political agenda of Adonis has always been a secular one, based on cultural interaction with the rest of the world, even though he has been called sectarian and accused of seeking the destruction of Arab culture by breaking with traditions.

Since the mid-1980s Adonis has lived in Paris and has become well known in European literary circles. He travels frequently to the Arab world and was recently honored in his own country, Syria. He remains a controversial figure in the Arab world, both demonized and revered. He is definitely a cultural icon and a seminal figure.

Adonis uses figures from Arabic history in his poetry as poetic masks. Mihyar al-Dimashqi is one of many. His choice of such personae to embody his own ideology is rooted in his view that Arab culture is not monolithic, but has had two major trends: the institutional and hegemonic versus the radical and marginalized. Adonis has sought to revive historical characters who have dared question the dominant discourse and who thus established viable norms of religion, politics, culture, and literature. Adonis turns to these premodern revolutionaries to transform them into forces that can challenge a rigid system. He affiliates himself to them, creating what Jorge Luis Borges called the precursor selected by a contemporary to establish his literary and intellectual genealogy.

Adonis's three-volume *Al-Thabit wa'l-mutahawil* (The Invariant and the Variant)—based on his doctoral dissertation at St. Joseph's University in Beirut and published in 1974—has a significant subtitle: "A Study in Subservience and Creativity among the Arabs." It indicates Adonis's commitment to change and innovation, which he identifies with creativity, in contrast to fixed order and its production of dependents who follow authority. His 1961 poetic collection *Aghani Mihyar al-Dimashqi* (Songs of Mihyar the Damascene), with its sociopolitical concerns and powerful lyricism, made Adonis a prominent poet in the Arab world. Since then he has continued to experiment with poetic forms, turning at times to aphorisms.

Adonis has admitted that he came to discover innovation in Arab heritage indirectly—through reading French modernists and symbolists. He states in *An Introduction to Arab Poetics* that it was French poet Charles Baudelaire who made him discover Abu Nuwas; Stéphane Mallarmé who made him see the layers of meaning in Abu Tammam; and Arthur Rimbaud, Gérard de Nerval, and other surrealists who made him grasp the extraordinary texts of Sufis like al-Nifarri. However Adonis came to it, he insisted on digging into the Arab legacy and isolating the counter-discourse and subaltern voices, making of them his intellectual and poetic ancestors.

Among the later works of Adonis is *Al-Kitab* (The Book), published in 1995, designed to be read on different levels by bringing together the text with the marginalia and notes. In it he impersonates the 10th-century al-Mutanabbi, Arab bard par excellence. The book is ambitious in its layout and content. It makes use of the traditional form of an Arabic manuscript with its annotations, on the one hand, and, on the other, its use of Mallarmé's different fonts in his "Un coup de dés jamais n'abolira le hasard" (A toss of the dice never will abolish chance). More and more Adonis moves into more complex and cerebral work, losing some of his earlier lyricism along the way.

Essentially an urban poet who thrives on the heterogeneity of cities, Adonis has written powerfully of the cityscape, poeticizing the metropolis. Arab cities as well as European and American cities are lyricized, evoking place and history: Beirut (see "Desert, The"), Damascus, Petra, Paris, Sanaa, Cairo, Marrakesh, Granada, and New York (see "A Grave for New York"), among others. In a beautiful edition published by UNESCO, his bilingual *Kitab al-mudn/Le livre des villes* (The Book of Cities), published in 1999, includes his city poems in the original Arabic translated into French by Anne Wade Minkowski, with prints by Ziad Dalloul.

In his concern for Arab culture to change and modernize instead of remaining isolated and living off its past glory, Adonis deconstructed the view of one monolithic Arab legacy by highlighting counter and iconoclastic voices. He also produced translations of French works that he felt would inject new ideas and modes of writing, notably those of Saint-John Perse, Georges Schehadeh, and Jean Racine. Adonis takes liberties in his translations when rendering them in Arabic, as he is more concerned about the target language.

Adonis also edited and introduced (along with his wife, Khalida Sa'id) a series of selected works by poets and thinkers. The series included varied figures from a progressive Iraqi writer such as Sudqi Al-Zahawi, who defended women's rights and questioned religious dogma, to Muhammad Abdul-Wahab, the founder of the Wahabi movement in the Arabian Peninsula, a strict and literal form of Islam. His poem "A Mirror to Khalida" simultaneously celebrates his relationship with his wife and the eternal.

Adonis continues to be a driving force on the Arab literary scene. His impact on Arab poets and Arab thought is immense, but so are the attacks on him. He remains a controversial figure. Nevertheless, Adonis continues to produce poetic and critical works and is ever-present to the public through his weekly column in the London-based Arab daily *Al-Hayat*.

BIBLIOGRAPHY

Adonis. *The Blood of Adonis*. Translated by Samuel Hazo. Pittsburgh: University of Pittsburgh Press, 1971.

———. *Transformation of a Lover.* Translated by Samuel. Hazo. Athens: Ohio University Press, 1983.

——— et al. *Victims of a Map: A Bilingual Anthology of Arabic Poetry.* Translated by Abdullah al-Udhari. London: Al Saqi Books, 1984.

———. *If Only the Sea Could Sleep.* Translated by K. Boullata, Susan Einbinder, and Mirène Ghossein. Los Angeles: Green Integer, 2003.

———. *An Introduction to Arab Poetics.* Translated by Catherine Cobham. Austin: University of Texas Press, 1990.

———. *Sufism and Surrealism.* Translated by Judith Cumberbatch. London: Al Saqi Books, 2005.

Adonis: Le feu souterain. Special issue of *Détours d'écriture* 16 (1991): 105–117.

Adonis: Un poète dans le monde d'aujourd'hui 1950–2000. Paris: Institut du Monde Arabe, 2000.

Faddul, Atif Y. *The Poetics of T. S. Eliot and Adunis.* Beirut: Al-Hamra, 1992.

Ferial J. Ghazoul

"AFRICA" DAVID MANDESSI DIOP (1956)

This is the most frequently anthologized of DIOP's poems, and it is also his most representative poem. Its enduring appeal comes from both the passion that it expresses and the voice it gives to Diop's vision of his ancestral land. As a Negritude poem, "Africa" celebrates Africa, albeit indirectly. It emphasizes the alienation of the poet-persona from his homeland. The separation from the continent intensifies the sense of loss that permeates the poem.

In this poem the persona identifies with an Africa that he has not known personally. The Africa that one encounters in the poem is largely a product of the poet-persona's imagination, because Diop wrote the poem before he had been to Africa. The only reason he claims to have an association with Africa is that the continent is his "ancestral" homeland. His knowledge of Africa in this poem is based on secondhand information and his idea of his own identity ("your blood flows in my veins"). But the most important aspect of the poem is its sense of history.

The poem presents three different phases in African history. The first six lines describe an Africa that is only an imagined space—and that is also romanticized. The poet can retrieve Africa's glorious past ("of proud warriors in ancestral savannahs") only by imagining it. This image is also necessary to enable him to establish a contrast between it and colonized Africa. The next nine lines paint the pathetic picture of the era of enslavement and colonial subjugation. The section comes to its emotional climax with a set of rhetorical questions, in which the personified Africa is asked by a shocked and emphatic son about her agony ("Is this you"). The last section hints at the imminence of reconstruction and restoration. The speaker represents the new Africa as a young tree "of splendid loveliness" that is springing up anew and "grows again patiently obstinately."

The poem transforms as it grows: It uses apostrophe and visual imagery effectively. In the first part of the poem, Africa is an identifiable physical space. In the second it is a person. In the last it assumes the symbolic image of a young but resilient tree that holds a lot of promise. The tone of the poem shifts from the nostalgic through the emphatic to the optimistic.

Oyeniyi Okunoye

AKHMATOVA, ANNA (1889–1966)

Akhmatova stands with OSIP MANDELSTAM, MARINA TSVETAEVA, and BORIS PASTERNAK as the greatest Russian poets of the 20th century. They were well acquainted with one another: Pasternak proposed marriage to Akhmatova more than once, though he was already married; Tsvetaeva called her the "weeping muse" and "Anna of All the Russias"; Mandelstam was her Poets' Guild and acmeist colleague. It is Mandelstam who told her, during the visit memorialized in her poem "VORONEZH," that "Poetry is power" (Mandelstam 170). Her powerful poem cycles REQUIEM and POEM WITHOUT A HERO and her well-known poem "IN THE FORTIETH YEAR" stand as witnesses to both political and literary history. ALEKSANDR BLOK was a significant influence on her early work, and even *Hero* from her later work shows the symbolist impact, achieving what the symbolists "had preached in theory, but had never been able to realize in their creative work" (Zhirmunsky, quoted in Hemschemeyer 8). She was revered by JOSEPH BRODSKY along with Dmitry Bobashev, Anatoly Naiman, and Evgeny Rein, other young poets of the next generation, and has been called "the true heir of Pushkin" (Reeder, *Complete Poems* 33).

Anna Andreevna Gorenko was born one of five children near Odessa on the Black Sea and raised at Tsarskoye Selo, near St. Petersburg. She began writing poetry as a child and took her pseudonym Akhmatova from a maternal great-grandmother in response to her father's admonition not to bring shame on the family name with her poetry. She completed secondary schooling and briefly studied law in Kiev, but could not forsake poetry as her vocation. Her first publications were in the journal *Sirius* in 1907; she married the editor, poet, and cofounder of the Poets' Guild, Nikolay Gumilyov in 1910. On their Paris honeymoon, she became friends with the artist Amadeo Modigliani, for whom she sat for many portraits. She and Gumilyov had one child together, Lev, who was raised by his paternal grandparents after Akhmatova and Gumilyov divorced in 1918. Gumilyov was executed by the Bolsheviks in 1921, and is *Requiem*'s "husband in the grave." Akhmatova married Vladimir Shileiko, a poet and Assyriologist in 1918, divorcing in 1926, and had a prolonged affair with Nikolai Punin, during which they maintained an unconventional living arrangement with his former wife and daughter and Akhmatova's son when he was 16 years old. There were other lovers, but no more marriages.

Lev Gumilyov suffered repeated arrests and imprisonments over a period of 20 years, primarily for the crime of being his parents' child. It is he for whom Akhmatova "spent seventeen months in the prison lines," "stood for three hundred hours," "three-hundredth in line, with a parcel" (*Requiem*, 1963). His first arrest came in 1935, but unlike Punin, he survived Stalin's purges. Punin died in prison in 1953. After one of Lev's later arrests, Akhmatova briefly compromised herself in 1950 by writing Stalin's praises in hopes that she could secure her son's release. The tactic did not work. Akhmatova herself was never arrested, but her work was unofficially banned from the mid-1920s until 1940. She was subsequently denounced by Stalin's cultural enforcer, Andrey Zhdanov, for subverting socialist realism and was expelled from the Union of Soviet Writers in 1946. Ironically, she became president of the union 18 years later. Earlier, Leon Trotsky had declared her irrelevant to the new state, and the futurist poet VLADIMIR MAYAKOVSKY considered her "a

relic" (Reeder 25)—she considered him "a genius, not a great poet but a great literary innovator . . . a destroyer, a blaster of everything" (Berlin 49).

In the period before she fell from favor, she published five books: *Evening* (*Vecher,* 1912); *Rosary* (*Chyotki* 1914); *White Flock* (*Belaya staya,* 1917); *Plantain* (*Podorozhnik,* 1921); and *Anno Domini MCMXXI* (1922). During her forced absence from creative publication, she wrote a series of articles on her much-loved Pushkin and translations of the early 19th-century Italian poet Giacomo Leopardi, India's Nobel laureate RABINDRANATH TAGORE, and the French political exile Victor Hugo. Then *From Six Books* (*Iz shesti knig*) was published in 1940 but soon ordered withdrawn from the shelves. Akhmatova, who periodically had to take rests to deal with tuberculosis, responded to this blow by having a heart attack. Subsequent books published during her lifetime were rigidly censored; a 1946 collection was completely destroyed. During her evacuation from Leningrad to Tashkent during World War II, she took in Mandelstam's widow, Nadezhda, (not for the last time) and mother-in-law to live with her. In spite of all her troubles, she never considered emigrating, believing that it is the poet's responsibility to remain and document what happens.

During all these years she continued to write, with friends such as Lidiya Chukovskaya keeping notebooks and memorizing poems too dangerous to print. Akhmatova herself burned some of the poems, writing later how they had "wanted to live" and "feared the acrid flame" (*Poems and Long Poems* [*Stikhotvoreniya I poemy*] 1979). Late in life, after Stalin's death in 1953, her situation eased considerably, and she was rehabilitated and published once again. Censored collections of selected poems appeared in 1958 and 1961. She was allowed to travel and accepted the Etna-Taormina International Prize in Poetry in Italy in 1964 and an honorary doctorate from Oxford University in England in 1965, the same year that *The Flight of Time* (*Beg vremeni*) appeared. It was the last publication in her lifetime.

The opening poem of her first book describes "Love" as "like a little snake" that can "coo like a dove" and "Drowse like a gillyflower" (*Evening*, 1912). Written in 1911, the poem shows that its young speaker has been seduced by love's trickery. Akhmatova never turned away from love lyrics, in spite of learning early, as she wrote in November 1910, that a woman could be the wife of a man who had three loves—"Evensong, white peacocks / And old maps of America"—and she was none of them (*Evening,* 1912). She was an autobiographical poet, and the events of her life are the events of her poems: war, revolution, illness, love. She also could be gracious to the memory of the man who had dismissed her as a "relic." A decade after his suicide, she wrote "Mayakovsky in 1913" (*Poems and Long Poems* 1979) to say she had not known him in his "glory," but to acknowledge that he had been "constructing formidable scaffolding," in a time when he had an "unheralded name" that later would "ring out like a battle cry." Similarly, in the ninth part of "Secrets of the Craft" (*Poems and Long Poems* 1979) she writes to Mandelstam two decades after his death, describing the lines of his poems as "the black, tender news / Of our bloodstained youth" and assuring him that they are his "pass to immortality."

Akhmatova was recovering from a heart attack when she learned of Pasternak's death in 1960. She wrote that he was "a life-giving ear of grain," a poet "who conversed with the groves" (*Poems and Long Poems* 1979). A few years earlier, she mused that she had "been sitting alone in the prisoner's dock / for almost half a century" in a time that could have been "invented by Kafka / And played by Chaplin" (*Poems and Long Poems* 1979). It had indeed been an absurdist's dream, and now she was left alone in it, the other great Russian voices of the century having been quieted. She observed near the end of her life that "Torment proved to be [her] muse" and that they had found themselves in "The place where nothing is permitted" (*Poems and Long Poems* 1979). After more than half a century of writing and repression, Akhmatova died in Moscow in March 1966 and is buried in Komarovo near St. Petersburg.

BIBLIOGRAPHY
Akhmatova, Anna. *The Complete Poems of Anna Akhmatova.* Expanded edition. Edited and with an introduction by Roberta Reeder. Translated by Judith Hemschemeyer. Boston: Zephyr Press, 1997.
———. *My Half Century: Selected Prose.* Evanston, Illinois: Northwestern University Press, 1992.
Berlin, Isaiah. "Anna Akhmatova: A Memoir." In *Complete Poems of Anna Akhmatova.* Expanded edition, edited and introduced by Roberta Reeder, translated by Judith Hemschemeyer, 35–55. Boston: Zephyr Press, 1997.
Feinstein, Elaine. *Anna of All the Russians.* London: Wiedenfeld & Nicolson, 1988.
Ketchian, Sonia I., ed. *Anna Akhmatova 1889–1989.* Oakland, Calif.: Berkeley Slavic Specialties, 1993.
Mandelstam, Nadezhda. *Hope Against Hope: A Memoir.* New York: Atheneum, 1970.
Nayman, Anatoly. *Remembering Anna Akhmatova.* New York: Henry Holt, 1991.
Reeder, Roberta. *Anna Akhmatova: Poet and Prophet.* New York: St. Martin's Press, 1994.
Rosslyn, Wendy, ed. *The Speech of Unknown Eyes: Akhmatova's Readers on Her Poetry.* 2 vols. Nottingham, U.K.: Astra Press, 1990.

Mary Murphy

ALBERTI, RAFAEL (1902–1999)
Rafael Alberti, a Spanish poet and painter, was one of the leading members of the "Generation of '27," a prolific group of avant-garde poets who revitalized the Spanish poetic tradition, which had remained quiescent since the 17th century. Like many of his peers, Alberti searched for new ways of expression in modernist aesthetics, Spain's own once rich poetic heritage, and the country's eclectic folklore. The longest-living member of the group, Alberti stands out for the painterly quality of his images and his relentless experimentation with poetic language.

Alberti was born on December 16, 1902, in Puerto de Santa Maria, a town on the Atlantic coast of the Spanish province of Andalusia. In 1917 his family moved to Madrid, where Alberti developed a passion for art, trained as a painter, and, in 1920, exhibited his first works in a Madrid art salon. Shortly thereafter, he left the capital for Guadarrama to recuperate from tuberculosis and there, for the first time, dedicated serious effort to writing poetry. *Sailor on Dry Land* (*Marinero en Tierra*), Alberti's first collection, appeared in 1925. The book won that year's National Prize in Literature, established Alberti as a powerful new poetic voice, and determined his vocation. Although Alberti never gave up painting, poetry became the main outlet for his creative talent, an uneasy decision that left the poet grappling with what he later described as "pena enterrada de enterrar el dolor de nacerse un poeta por morirse un pintor" (the buried sorrow of burying the pain of one's birth as poet by one's death as painter).

Upon returning to Madrid, Alberti lived in the Residencia de Estudiantes (Student Residence), a vibrant center of Spain's intellectual life. There, he met other young poets, including Pedro Salinas, JORGE GUILLÉN, VICENTE ALEIXANDRE, Damaso Alonso, and, most important, FEDERICO GARCÍA LORCA, whose work, life, and tragic death would have a deep impact on Alberti. He also became friends with the filmmaker Luis Buñuel and artist Salvador Dalí, who fueled his interest in the surrealist aesthetic that manifests itself strongly in the collection *Cal y Canto* (Passion and Form) (1927) and especially in *Sobre los ángeles* (Concerning the Angels) (1929), whose tragic tone marks a striking contrast to the optimism of his first volume.

Spanish avant-garde poetry developed in the complex political climate with which Alberti fully engaged. A devoted Republican, and since 1931 a member of the Spanish Communist Party, Alberti throughout his life saw in literature and art powerful political media. *Fermín Galán,* for example, one of Alberti's first dramatic works, portrays a Republican hero killed for the cause. The poet's own commitment to the opposition made it impossible for him to remain in Spain. After Franco came to power in 1939, Alberti, like many other Spanish intellectuals, left the country for what amounted to nearly 40 years of exile. After a brief stay in Paris, he and his wife, the writer María Teresa León, settled in Argentina. There Alberti began writing *Arboleda Perdida* (The Lost Grove), a lyrical memoir about life in Madrid's turn-of-the-century intellectual circles. He continued to paint and write. In *A la pintura, 1947–1967* (To Painting: Poems), Alberti reconciled his two great passions: poetry and painting. The book—with poems devoted to colors, painting materials, and techniques as well as to artists from Giotto to Picasso—represents a true tribute to art, but also to poetry, that offers a means to paint images with words. He also continued to write for the theater, exploring the relationship between art and politics in *Noche de guerra en el Museo del Prado* (Night of War in the Prado Museum) (1956). In 1963 Alberti left Argentina for Rome, where he spent the next 15 years. *Roma, peligro para caminantes* (Rome:

Danger to Pedestrians) recaptures the poet's complex relationship with this monumental city that in 1988 named Alberti an honorary citizen. After Franco's death Alberti returned to Spain in 1977, where he remained until his death in October 1999.

Alberti's vast oeuvre mirrors closely the different periods in the poet's life. What remains constant, however, is his love for and devotion to language, whose limits Alberti never tired of testing. As in his poem "PICASSO," his poetry blurs images and words into what resembles the harmonies of impressionistic painting. Like the classical poets of the Spanish Golden Age, Alberti takes to an extreme the possibilities of wordplay and stretches the boundaries of grammar and syntax, surprising the reader by suddenly revealing the intimate connections between the most unrelated words. The extraordinary linguistic richness of his poetry poses challenges for translators and accounts partly for the relative paucity of Alberti's work in translation.

BIBLIOGRAPHY
Alberti, Rafael. *Concerning the Angels.* Christopher Sawyer-Laucanno, trans. San Francisco: City Lights Books, 1995.
———. *The Lost Grove.* Gabriel Berns, trans. and ed. Berkeley: University of California Press, 1976.
———. *The Other Shore: 100 Poems by Rafael Alberti.* Bilingual edition. Edited by Kosrof Chantikian, translated by José A. Elgorriaga and Martin Paul. San Francisco: Kosmos, 1981.
———. *The Owl's Insomnia.* Selected and translated by Mark Strand. New York: Atheneum, 1973.
———. *To Painting: Poems.* Translated and introduced by Carolyn L. Tipton. Evanston, Ill.: Northwestern University Press, 1997.

Alina Sokol

ALEGRÍA, CLARA ISABEL (CLARIBEL) (1924–)   Claribel Alegría is the most prolific Central American writer today, with over 50 books of poetry, testimony, fiction, translations into Spanish, and anthologies, produced alone or in collaboration with her late husband, Darwin J. Flakoll (1923–95). Like numerous American intellectuals born south of the Río Grande, this poet, peace activist, and outspoken defender of human rights around the world has lived in exile and faced death threats against her and her children. Although· she resided outside Central

America for over 30 years, Alegría is claimed by two countries: her parents were from El Salvador and Nicaragua; she was born in Nicaragua but taken to El Salvador as a baby and grew up there; she returned to Nicaragua after the overthrow of dictator Anastasio Somoza Debayle in 1979, and now considers it her home. Alegría is internationally renowned, especially in the United States, where she studied (she earned a B.A. from George Washington University), married, and lived for several years and where the University of Pittsburgh Press and Curbstone Press have published superb bilingual editions of many volumes of her poetry (*Flowers from the Volcano, Woman of the River, Fugues, Thresholds, Sorrow, Casting Off*).

As a young writer, Alegría was mentored by the Spanish poet JUAN RAMÓN JIMÉNEZ, who was then living in exile in Washington, D.C. Her first poetry collections reflected his influence, but she soon charted her own path, oriented instead toward the new Latin American human metaphysics of Peruvian poet CÉSAR VALLEJO that evolved into a poetics of pain and suffering. She later explained: "The blood-drenched reality of Central America over the past two decades [the 1970s and 1980s] has been such a traumatic spectacle that no self-respecting human being in the area can avoid taking sides. Any artist who avoids commitment in this struggle is guilty at least of ivory tower escapism and at worst of complicity with the Squadrons of Death and the total militarization of society" (Alegría, "Our Little Region" 45). Alegría cites two moments of profound personal change that redirected her philosophy and writing: the 1959 Cuban revolution, which awakened her to politics and the possibility of an end to U.S. interference in Central America, and the assassination of Archbishop Oscar Romero in San Salvador (in 1980), which led Alegría and other writers to renew the political activism of the literary "Committed Generation" of the 1950s and 1960s and to replace Romero's silenced "voice for the voiceless" with their own. Thus, they reclaimed for themselves the long tradition of Latin American poet-activists.

Alegría acknowledges her evolution from upper-class, self-absorbed poet "contemplating her navel" to creator of "testimonial," or witness, poetry (e.g., "Woman of the River"), a new genre that incorporates the real-life stories of victims of oppression such as those recorded in *They Won't Take Me Alive.* The rescue of history from official oblivion is prominent in her coauthored, groundbreaking novel *Ashes of Izalco,* as well as in *Luisa in Realityland,* a genre-bending "fictionalized autobiographical collection of prose poems" and poetry that "reaches beyond any canonic concept of literature and its genres" (Agosín). Like oppositional writing by other Central American women, Alegría's work must be viewed in the context of what Hussain calls the four interlocking sites of systemic oppression: patriarchy, capitalism, colonialism, and racism. So incendiary were Alegría's denunciations of the political situation in El Salvador and of the bourgeois class into which she was born that the first printing of *Ashes of Izalco* was bought up and burned by her own family, and subsequent editions were torched by the military during its destruction of the University Press in San Salvador. In one of those ironies of history, the book later became required reading for secondary school students in El Salvador and has had some 20 reprints.

Alegría made a commitment to "name the dead" in her works and to embrace the legacy of struggle of fallen poet-revolutionaries and, in so doing, created a new literary form: "With others of her generation, she has helped define a New World elegiac tradition, individual and collective, unmediated and profound, a poetry 'for and about everyone's humanity'" (Engelbert 197). As in the poem "PERSONAL CREED," death is not the final stage but an opportunity for rebirth; a hallmark of Alegría's poetry is the juxtaposition of intense, seemingly oppositional emotions: Hope springs from anguish, joy from pain, life from death (McGowan, "Claribel Alegría" 1).

Alegría's work reflects a political imagination that "goes beyond protest to articulate an *artistry* of dissent," aligned with the contributions of other American poets, such as Walt Whitman, PABLO NERUDA, Jack Hirschman, ERNESTO CARDENAL, Roque Dalton, Leonel Rugama, DAISY ZAMORA, and GIOCONDA BELLI (Espada). In her latest books that focus on aging and invoke mythological figures (*Thresholds, Sorrow, Fugues, Casting Off*), poet-visionary Alegría reexplores an early theme, death, but with a new awareness that in the "nationless cemetery," as she once called herself, the dead provide support, strength, and inspiration; she unburies the dead and, in naming them, keeps their struggle alive (Saporta Sternbach). Alegría and others define a new paradigm of the contemporary writer creating a homeland, a new "countryless" world community, through a transnational vision grounded in the homelessness of exile (Longo).

Alegría has received many honors, including Cuba's prestigious Casa de las Américas poetry award in 1978 for *Sobrevivo* (I Survive) and, more recently, the U.S. Independent Publisher Book Award for Poetry (2000), France's Ordre des Arts et Lettres (2004), and honorary doctorates from Eastern Connecticut State University (1997) and the University of León, Nicaragua (2005). In contrast to the generalized dismissal of poetry in the United States, in Latin America poetry "belongs to the people," and Alegría gives readings there to enormous crowds, affirming her belief in the organic relationship between poetry and social transformation (McGowan, "Closing the Circle" 238).

Although in Central America Alegría is celebrated as a poet and was the first woman admitted into the Salvadoran literary canon, relatively little criticism in English focuses on her poetry. Engelbert, Hussain, and Longo demonstrate potentially rich approaches. The worldwide implications of her work have yet to be explored, as Zimmerman says: "The materialization of the feminist intervention and its effect in transforming the literary system is indeed present in all of Alegría's work and marks her overall contribution to Central American, Latin American, and now, through translation, overall American and world literature" (224–225). (See Alegría, "The Writer's Commitment" for her philosophy; Boschetto-Sandoval for an interview, biography, and publications to 1991; Engelbert for indigenous elements; Moyers for a 1995 PBS interview; Puleo for an excellent synthesis; *Scholastic Magazine*'s "The Poetry of Claribel Alegría"; Hussain for poems with comments; and Zimmerman's suggestions for further research.)

On October 28, 2005, Claribel Alegría was awarded the 2006 Neustadt International Prize for Literature, an honor conferred by an international jury representing eight countries and administered by the University of Oklahoma and its international magazine, *World Literature Today*.

BIBLIOGRAPHY

Agosín, Marjorie. "Claribel Alegría." Translated by Ruth Morales. *Americas* 51, no. 1 (1999). Academic Search Premier. Downloaded on Aug. 31, 2005.

Alegría, Claribel. *Casting Off/Soltando amarras*. Translated by Margaret Sayers Peden. Willimantic, Conn.: Curbstone, 2003.

———. *Flowers from the Volcano/Flores del volcán*. Translated by Carolyn Forché. Pittsburgh: University of Pittsburgh Press, 1982.

———. *Fugues/Fugas*. Translated by Darwin J. Flakoll. Willimantic, Conn.: Curbstone, 1993.

———. *Luisa in Realityland*. Translated by Darwin J. Flakoll. Willimantic, Conn.: Curbstone, 1987.

———. "Our Little Region." *Being América: Essays on Art, Literature, and Identity from Latin America,* edited by Rachel Weiss, with Alan West, 41–50. Fredonia, N.Y.: White Pine, 1991.

———. *Sorrow/Saudade*. Translated by Carolyn Forché. Willimantic, Conn.: Curbstone, 1999.

———. *Thresholds/Umbrales*. Translated by Darwin J. Flakoll. Willimantic, Conn.: Curbstone, 1996.

———. *Woman of the River*. Translated by Darwin J. Flakoll. Pittsburgh: University of Pittsburgh Press, 1989.

———. "The Writer's Commitment." *Lives on the Line: The Testimony of Contemporary Latin American Authors,* edited by Doris Meyer, 306–311. Berkeley: University of California Press, 1988.

Alegría, Claribel, and Darwin J. Flakoll. *Ashes of Izalco.* Translated by Darwin J. Flakoll. Willimantic, Conn.: Curbstone, 1989.

———. *They Won't Take Me Alive: Salvadoran Women in the Struggle for National Liberation.* Translated by Amanda Hopkinson. London: Women's Press, 1987.

Boschetto-Sandoval, Sandra M., and Marcia Phillips McGowan, eds. *Claribel Alegría and Central American Literature: Critical Essays.* Athens: Ohio University Center for International Studies, 1994.

Engelbert, Jo Anne. "Claribel Alegría and the Elegiac Tradition." In *Claribel Alegría and Central American Literature: Critical Essays,* edited by Sandra M. Boschetto-Sandoval and Marcia Phillips McGowan, 183–199. Athens: Ohio Center for International Studies, 1994.

Espada, Martin. "Poetry Like Bread: Poets of the Political Imagination." *Peacework* (1999). Available online. URL: http://www.afsc.org/pwork/0799/0713.htm. Downloaded on Aug. 31, 2005.

Hussain, Melissa. "Revolutionary Women Writers of Central America: Poetics, Praxis, and Politics." *Megabarta* 6, no.

4 (2005). Available online. URL: http://www.megabarta.org/2005/September/gender.html. Downloaded on Sept. 9, 2005.

Longo, Teresa. "Migrancy, Exile and the Hybrid Landscapes of Homelessness." *Peace Review* 13, no. 2 (2001): 167–175.

McGowan, Marcia Phillips. "Claribel Alegría: A Tribute." *Curbstone Ink* (Fall 1999): 1+.

———. "Closing the Circle: Interview with Claribel Alegría." In *Claribel Alegría and Central American Literature: Critical Essays,* edited by Sandra M. Boschetto-Sandoval and Marcia Phillips McGowan, 213–227. Athens: Ohio Center for International Studies, 1994. 228–245.

Moyers, Bill. "Claribel Alegría." *The Language of Life: A Festival of Poets.* New York: Broadway Books, 1995, 4–16.

"The Poetry of Claribel Alegría." *Literary Cavalcade* 52, no. 4 (2000). Academic Search Premier. Downloaded on Aug. 31, 2005.

Puleo, Gus. Review of *Claribel Alegría and Central American Literature: Critical Essays,* edited by Sandra M. Boschetto-Sandoval and Marcia Phillips McGowan. *Hispanic Review* 66, no. 1 (1998). Academic Search Premier. Downloaded on Aug. 31, 2005.

Saporta Sternbach, Nancy. "Claribel Alegría." In *Spanish American Women Writers: A Bio-Bibliographical Source Book,* edited by Diane E. Marting, 9–13. New York: Greenwood, 1990.

Zimmerman, Marc. "Afterword." In *Claribel Alegría and Central American Literature Critical Essays,* edited by Sandra M. Boschetto-Sandoval and Marcia Phillips McGowan, 213–227. Athens: Ohio Center for International Studies, 1994.

María Roof

ALEIXANDRE, VICENTE (1898–1984)

Nobel laureate Vicente Aleixandre was one of the most important Spanish writers of the 20th century. A central figure in the country's celebrated Generation of 1927, Aleixandre emerged in the wake of the Spanish civil war as a voice of inspiration for a new group of young poets writing under the Franco dictatorship.

Aleixandre was born in Seville in 1898, the only son of a middle-class family. After spending his childhood in Málaga, he moved in 1909 with his parents and sister to Madrid. In 1914, after a rigorous, traditional Catholic education, Aleixandre began university studies in law. Although he eventually became a professor of mercantile law, a friendship with the poet and fellow scholar Dámaso Alonso led the young academic to an ever-increasing interest in verse. Bedridden by health problems in 1925, Aleixandre turned his full energies to poetry. His first book of poetry, *Ambito* (Ambit) (1928), reflected the modernism of JUAN RAMÓN JIMÉNEZ, as well as the recent revival of baroque formalism. A growing interest in Freud and surrealism influenced the free-verse collections *Pasión de la tierra* (Passion of the Earth) (written in 1928–29 but not published until 1935) and *Espadas como labios* (Swords Like Lips, 1929). The relationship among love, sex, and death, an emergent theme in *Espadas como labios,* became the focus of Aleixandre's next work, *La destrucción o el amor* (1933). The collection, with its dreamlike fusion of erotic and violent images, won the National Literary Prize and elevated its writer to the forefront of Spain's poetic vanguard. The next 10 years, however, proved to be the most difficult of Aleixandre's life. In 1934 his mother died. Shortly after the outbreak of the Spanish civil war in 1936, pro-fascist forces murdered his close friend FEDERICO GARCÍA LORCA. That same year, a kidney operation left Aleixandre incapacitated and trapped in the capital for the duration of the conflict. The destruction of his family's home and the death of his father, both in the waning months of the war, deepened the poet's sense of loss. The cessation of hostilities did not improve Aleixandre's situation. Distrusted by the Franco regime, his works banned, he was not permitted to publish until 1944. When he was finally allowed to release *Sombra del paraíso* (Shadow of Paradise) in 1944, it became his most widely acclaimed collection. Inspired by childhood memories of Málaga, *Sombra del paraíso* contrasted a luminescent "paradise lost" with a tenebrous, sterile present. Unlike the disturbing surrealist imagery of his earlier work, *Sombra del paraíso* (see "CITY OF PARADISE") created a world of fragile beauty teetering on the precipice of destruction. The theme resonated with young postwar poets such as José Hierro and Carlos Bousoño, struggling under a repressive dictatorship; and they embraced Aleixandre as their leader. His Madrid home became a meeting place for a new generation of Spanish writers. *Mundo a solas* (World Alone, 1950), a collection of despondent poems written in the late 1930s, was followed by his election to the Royal Spanish Academy. Nearly imprisoned by the regime in 1951, the poet remained a steadfast voice of antifascist resistance in his next collection, *Historia del corazón* (History of the Heart, 1954). Extolling the redemptive powers of love, personal dignity, and human solidarity in a cruel universe, its message was understood as a metaphor for life in Spain under Franco. In *Un vasto dominio* (In a Vast Domain, 1962), Aleixandre's humanistic vision shaped a historical context. Poor health restricted his production in the final decades of his life. *Poemas de la consumación* (Poems of Consummation, 1968), a nostalgic contemplation on human mortality, and *Diálogos del conocimiento* (Dialogues of Insight, 1973), a dialectical interrogatory of optimistic and pessimistic worldviews, were the last major works he produced before his death in 1984.

Although his selection for the 1977 Nobel Prize in literature has frequently been interpreted as a symbolic gesture toward the entire Generation of 1927, Aleixandre's contribution to his country's prewar literary renaissance and his unquestionable influence during the Franco dictatorship establish him as a unique and vital figure in 20th-century Spanish poetry. Among the few available English translations of Aleixandre's poetry, the best are Lewis Hyde's bilingual anthology *Longing for Light: Selected Poems of Vicente Aleixandre* (Port Townsend, Washington: Copper Canyon Press, 1985) and Hugh Harter's bilingual edition of *Sombra del paraíso, Shadow of Paradise* (Los Angeles: University of California Press, 1987). A good introduction to the writer's work is Santiago Daydí-Tolson's *Vicente Aleixandre: A Critical Appraisal* (Tempe, Arizona: Bilingual Review Press, 1981).

Eric Reinholtz

ALTAZOR, OR, A VOYAGE IN A PARACHUTE: POEM IN VII CANTOS (1919)

VICENTE HUIDOBRO (1931)　*Altazor,* a coinage derived from *"alto"* (high) and *"azor"* (hawk), the work identified by its recent English translator as HUIDOBRO's masterpiece, interrogates both the nature of the modern poet and his lofty aspirations. Despite its importance, however, *Altazor* is also one of Huidobro's most problematic works.

Fluent in both Spanish and French and living for a long time in Paris, Huidobro wrote in both languages—and he wrote *Altazor* in both languages. The book itself is not bilingual, but different parts of the same (original) text exist in French and in Spanish, complicating its translation. A version of the work was published in Spanish in Madrid—finally—in 1931; however, Huidobro had begun *Altazor's* composition in 1919.

Huidobro, whose unique poetic movement, creationism, regarded the poet as a "little god," explores the heights and the depths of poetry and poetic creation in *Altazor*. In the preface to the poem, the speaker observes that he came into the world on the same day Christ left it, already 33 years old. But the world the speaker enters is recognizably the modern world, complete with planes and cars and mechanical inventions. It is also a highly imaginative world in which the speaker passes through fanciful dreams and encounters realistic and impossible creatures and places. By the first lines of Canto I, Altazor, the figure of the poet, has begun to fall, descending through worlds, suspended from a parachute.

The meaning of the parachute changes throughout the cantos, as does the significance of the fall itself. So, too, does the idea of the poet change. When the poem refers to God, as it does in Canto I, speaking of him as "todo y nada" (all and nothing), a God of the Mind and the Breath, a God both young and old, a "Dios pútrido" (putrid God), the poem might as well be referring to the poet. In many ways, the book is a search for a modern poet, an examination of the poet's new identity and continued relevance in a modern world. Indeed, *Altazor* interrogates the very nature of poetry, questioning its potency and its ability to shape truly new, real worlds from the imagination. *Altazor* also investigates words themselves; it is a work consciously poetic, and its language changes as the cantos progress. Ultimately, the poem's language devolves into—or restores—meaningless, imitation words, vocalizations, perhaps, of the poet's interior state. Canto VII, then, represents language without ascertainable public meaning: poetry derived from sound rather than sense. It is also Altazor's last expression, a scream of sorts—either the poet's howl of relief or joy as his feet touch solid ground, or the splat of language, as his parachute fails.

BIBLIOGRAPHY
Huidobro, Vicente. *Altazor, or, A Voyage in a Parachute: Poem in VII Cantos (1919)*. Translated by Eliot Weinberger. Middletown, Conn.: Wesleyan University Press, 2003.

Winter Elliott

AMICHAI, YEHUDA (1924–2000)

When the late Yitzhak Rabin won the Nobel Peace Prize in 1995, he asked poet Yehuda Amichai—often described by the Israeli press as the spokesperson for his fellow citizens—to join the official Israeli delegation and read one of his poems, *Pirhei Bar* (Wild Flowers). Moreover, in his acceptance speech, Rabin quoted from Amichai's "GOD HAS PITY ON KINDERGARTEN CHILDREN" ("*Elohim Merachem al yaldey hagan,*" 1955), Amichai's signature poem. Although he repeatedly rejected the appellation, Amichai was recognized by general agreement as Israel's poet laureate, and he was considered by many literary critics as one of the half dozen leading poets in the world. Called the most widely translated Hebrew poet since King David and "Israel's Citizen No. 1," he was the country's best-known poet internationally. American commentator Jonathan Wilson wrote that Amichai "should have won the Nobel Prize." In the many eulogies that followed his passing, he was lauded by the Speaker of the Israeli parliament as "the foundation stone of Israeliness" and by former Israeli prime minister Ehud Barak as "one of the greatest artists of Israel and the Jewish world." A master craftsman whose elegant poetic style was always accessible and widely read, Amichai explored the possibility of coexistence in antipodal relationships—in the union of tradition and modernity and of beauty and bloodshed—that have punctuated Israel's history.

Born in Würzburg, Germany, in 1924, Amichai grew up in a middle-class, religious family of ardent Zionists and learned both Hebrew and German. In 1936 the family fled the Nazis and settled first in Petach Tikvah (Palestine), then in Jerusalem, where he lived for most of the rest of his life in the Yemin Moshe neighborhood (the first Jewish neighborhood to be built outside of the Old City walls).

As a 12-year-old boy, Yehuda began secondary studies at the Ma'aleh High School and later graduated with a B.A. in literature and biblical studies from the Hebrew University in Jerusalem. He served in the Jewish Brigade of the British army in World War II, but joined the Palmach (the fighting force of Jewish settlements) during the British Mandate and helped smuggle arms and illegal immigrants into Palestine. He fought in Israel's War of Independence in 1948 and later served in three subsequent wars. Although he was an active soldier, his writings about his wartime experiences reveal a profound distaste for nationalistic fervor and a concern for the bereaved in the aftermath of battle, as in his 1976 poem "Seven Laments for the War-Dead."

After graduating with a teacher's degree, he taught Hebrew literature at the Chaim Greenberg College in Jerusalem and elsewhere. He won several literary awards, including the Shlonsky Award (1957), the Bialik Award (1975), and the country's most distinguished award, the Israel Prize, in 1981. In 1986 he was made an honorary member of the American Academy of Arts and Sciences and won the Agnon Award. Alongside his 16 volumes of poetry, Amichai also published tales for children, one-act plays, short stories, and a novel, *Lo Meachshav, Lo Mikan* (Not of This Time, Not of This Place, 1963). Precipitated by a return in 1959 to his hometown and later dramatized in a play, *Bells and Trains* (*Pa'amonim Ve-Rakavot*, 1967), the novel was a fictionalized account of that visit and of the author's exploration of the Holocaust and its effects on the present generation. Indeed, the role of remembrance and man's tendency to traverse the same roads of history was a persistent motif in his canon.

Amichai's first collection, *Now and in Other Days* (*Achshav u-beyamim acherim*) (1955), transformed Israeli poetry by shunning the formal tone of pre-1948 poets and by employing slang and modern vernacular. With this and succeeding collections, Amichai liberated Hebrew poetry from its deep immersion in biblical phraseology, making it more concordant with modern realities. Still, for all his iconoclasm, Amichai borrowed heavily from the scriptures, overlaying the archaic with a contemporary patina, as in a sequence describing a man under a fig tree calling to another standing under a vine. The early poems also deal with his father's death and their complex emotional relationship. Yet for all the modernity that shimmers through the poems, Amichai possessed a multivalent Jewish sensibility that braids the very personal with the mythic. The Jewish past is often alluded to, both in theological meditations and in its reverberations through the life of Israeli society. For instance, one of his longest poems—*Binyamin mitudela* (Benjamin of Tudela), about the great medieval Jewish traveler of the second half of the 12th century—was penned while Amichai was living on Benjamin of Tudela Street in Jerusalem and is full of self-referential elements. Amichai's canvas is characterized by colloquial language, self-deprecating humor, irony, and the autobiographical, showcasing a depth of emotion that is raw and introspective. With just a few words and images, he delivered special insights and evocative associations on a breadth of such weighty issues as the Holocaust, God, loss, love, idealism, war, and national destiny, unlocking a world enriched by allusions to both the Old Testament and the quotidian. Typically he probed (at times with a prophetic voice) the nexus between bipolar tropes—natural forgetting and the burden of memory, faith and doubt, personal and public history—tropes that acutely characterize life in Israel. He once noted that the metaphor was the greatest invention since the wheel.

A substantive portion of his vigorous writing zeroed in on Jerusalem's political and religious undercurrents, reflecting his profound admiration for and exasperation with the city as an epicenter of history and conflict that transcends the imagination. The magisterial cycle of poems *Jerusalem 1967* embodies the special interconnectedness that he felt existed between the capital and the Jewish people. In one poem he wryly comments on the gravity of living in Jerusalem, warning embracing lovers to be careful since every display of love can turn into a new religion. As a result, a *Newsweek* critic called him "The Walt Whitman of Jerusalem." Amichai wrote that the Jews, rather than being a historical people, were a geological nation, tied to their land by vows and oaths. His poems have been translated into over 37 languages, including Catalan and Korean, whose speakers are not likely to be Jewish but who do respond to Amichai's geological thematics. So monumental was his accessibility and so beloved was Amichai that when Israeli university students were called up for duty prior to the 1973 Yom Kippur War, they went back to their rooms and packed their gear, a rifle, and a book of his poems. Although his art transcended politics, Amichai frequently urged harmony with Israel's Arab neighbors and backed former prime minister Yitzhak Rabin's initiative to make peace with the Palestinians.

He was married twice—first to Tamar Horn, with whom he had one son, then to Chana Sokolov; they had one son and one daughter. He died, after a long battle with cancer, on September 22, 2000, at the age of 76.

BIBLIOGRAPHY

Abramson, Glenda, ed. *The Experienced Soul: Studies in Amichai.* Modern Hebrew Classics. Boulder, Colo.: Westview Press, 1997.

———. *The Writing of Yehuda Amichai: A Thematic Approach.* SUNY Series in Modern Jewish Literature and Culture. Albany: State University of New York Press, 1989.

Alter, Robert. *Hebrew and Modernity* Bloomington: Indiana University Press, 1994.

Bloch, Chana, and Stephen Mitchell, eds. *The Selected Poetry of Yehuda Amichai.* Berkeley: University of California Press, 1996.

Cohen, Joseph. *Voices of Israel: Essays on and Interviews with Yehuda Amichai, A.B. Yehoshua, T. Carmi, Aharon Appelfeld, and Amos Oz.* Albany: State University of New York Press, c. 1990.

Ramras-Rauch, Gila. "Remembering Yehuda Amichai 1924–2000." *World Literature Today* 75, no. 1 (January 1, 2001): 68.

Dvir Abramovich

"AMOR AMERICA (1400)" PABLO NERUDA (1950)

NERUDA begins all of *Canto General* with "Amor America (1400)," in the opening section titled "A Lamp of Earth." The significance of the year 1400 is that it marks a time before the arrival of Christopher Columbus or any other European explorers, "before the wig and the dress coat" (l. 1). This poem is Neruda's first punch thrown in the ring, boxing against the gloved fist of colonial imperialism. The reader is invited to celebrate the original people of America, who lived in organic harmony with the land that created them. Once "Man was dust," the speaker intones, naming tribes native to the soil: "he was Carib jug, Chibcha stone, / imperial cup of Araucanian silica" (ll. 9–10).

Even if the poem wants to stay with these "tender and bloody" people (l. 11), time pushes us onward.

Soon an implied narrative struggle shapes the literal page: The text of line 14 is abbreviated, and when the partially broken stanza picks up on line 15, a battle seems to have been waged in the gap of text. The cool, mercantile reason of explorers has defeated the hot-blooded passions of native inhabitants—their land exploited, their races diluted—and "No one could / remember them afterward: the wind / forgot them, the language of water / was buried, the keys were lost / or flooded with silence" (ll. 15–19).

So far, the speaker has been unspecific, as if it were the voice of historical record. Now the poet introduces himself, and boldly assures that "Life was not lost, pastoral brothers . . . I am here to tell the story" (ll. 20, 24). Neruda describes the search for his heritage across extremes of climate, "from the peace of the buffalo / to the pummeled sands" (ll. 25–26); in tracing his lineage to a "copper" father, a "nuptial plant" mother, the poet claims kin to the original, organic people of America. Because silence has been equated to death, the poet's ability to unearth their language becomes a power of metaphysical resurrection. His ultimate promise is a toast to "my land without name . . . your aroma climbed my roots up to the glass / raised to my lips, up to the slenderest / word as yet unborn in my mouth" (ll. 43–47). Neruda often associates his origins with the potent motif of *raíces* ("roots"), which both nourish and bind. Just as someone drinking a fine wine can taste the influence of lavender that was planted in vineyard soil, so Neruda tastes America in every word he may come to speak.

Although the *Canto General* does not satisfy the formal constraints of a narrative epic, the collection is epic in terms of its scale—in length as well as geographical and chronological scope—and its dedication to the themes of war and homeland. Every epic opens with an invocation to the muse, and Neruda had no dearer muses than the ghosts of his native people. "Amor America" serves as a summoning of long-dead spirits. The poet relights their "lamp of earth," (l. 23), once extinguished by the crush of invaders, and holds the lamp high so as to illuminate the path to a story waiting to be told.

Sandra Beasley

ANCESTORS Kamau Brathwaite (2001) Kamau Brathwaite's poetic trilogy *Ancestors* (2001) consists of three poems, "Mother Poem" (1977), "Sun Poem" (1982), and "X/Self" (1987). Brathwaite began "Mother Poem" while back in Barbados for the first time in almost 20 years. He recounts the realization that in looking back on his first trilogy, The Arrivants, "there is an absence of my family . . . I made the link between Barbados and my mother" (Dawes 35). The structure of *Ancestors* thus roughly corresponds to the fertile landscape / the poet's mother ("Mother Poem"), life-giving power / his father ("Sun Poem"), and finally the poet's self ("X/Self"). Brathwaite has suggested that the *Ancestors* trilogy also connects with his previous trilogy, *The Arrivants,* to which pair he plans to add a final trilogy, thus creating from the three long poems a larger composition with a macro "tidealectic" structure, in "rejection of the notion of dialectic" (Naylor 145; Mackey 13–14). "X/Self" takes a long historical view of the European history that leads to the conditions that gave rise to the poet's existence. The poetic refrain "Rome burns / & our slavery begins" suggests the first link in a causal chain by which cultural erosion and the displacement of power among European powers competing for domination leads inexorably to colonial contests and the economics of slavery that drove expansion (393).

Ancestors employs Brathwaite's "Sycorax Video Style" (derived from "Sycorax," Caliban's mother, banished for practicing witchcraft)—in which experimentation with layered fragments and physical layout, such as typeface and spacing, works to create the poem's aural feel (Dawes 37). If the figure of Sycorax represents for Brathwaite the mystical maternal core of Caribbean sensibility, this technique enlists technology to generate an organic form through which, Brathwaite explains, "the fonts take me across Mexico to Sisqueiros and the Aztec murals and all the way back to ancient Nilotic Egypt to hieroglyphics—allowing me to write in light and make sound visible as if I am in video" (Dawes 37).

BIBLIOGRAPHY
Brathwaite, Kamau. *Ancestors.* Oxford: Oxford University Press, 2001.

Dawes, Kwame, and Neville Senu, eds. *Talk Yuh Talk: Interviews with Anglophone Caribbean Poets.* Charlottesville: University of Virginia Press, 2001, 22–37.

Mackey, Nathaniel. "An Interview with Kamau Brathwaite." In *The Art of Kamau Brathwaite,* edited by Stewart Brown, 13–32. Mid Galmorgan: Poetry Wales Press, 1995.

Naylor, Paul. *Poetic Investigations: Singing the Holes in History.* Evanston, Ill.: Northwestern University Press, 1999.

Rohlehr, Gordon. "The Rehumanization of History: Regeneration of Spirit: Apocalypse and Revolution in Brathwaite's *The Arrivants* and *X/Self.*" In *The Art of Kamau Brathwaite,* edited by Stewart Brown, 163–207. Mid Glamorgan: Poetry Wales Press, 1995.

Williams, Emily. *The Critical Response to Kamau Brathwaite.* Westport, Conn.: Greenwood Press, 2004.

Alex Feerst

"ANCESTRAL WEIGHT" ALFONSINA STORNI (1919)

"Ancestral Weight" ("*Peso ancestral*"), published in ALFONSINA STORNI's second poetry collection and sometimes translated as "Ancestral Burden," provides a historical dimension to the expression of tensions between the genders evident in her early works, even as it belies the claim that her poetry disparages men. This poem shows that strict gender stereotypes define, confine, and victimize both genders, not just women.

Absent is the romantic movement's individualistic "I" struggling alone in a hostile world. Here, the weight of historical forces has created a patriarchal system that defines proper, limited roles based on gender. Handed down from generation to generation of male descendants is the prohibition against expressing emotions, the entrapment of men who must appear to be "made of steel" ("*de acero*") and live a machinelike existence without the option of feeling or expressing pain. Storni is clear that restrictions on one gender can poison relations with the other, since the woman sheds a tear that is part of her heritage too, a "soft" sign that cues her gendered difference from her progenitors and signifies her exclusion from society's "strong." It is not just the contemporary form of social conditions that separates the genders and impedes communion between them; the male-female divide is the legacy of centuries.

Yet, the insistent "You said . . . You said . . ." ("*Tú me dijiste . . . / Tú me dijiste . . .* ") signals that a female breaks her silence, although she speaks only of the "other" (and not of herself) to signal her pain, which is fully expressible only in a tear. Communication between females can eschew the male-dominated (phallologocentric) world of words in favor of the nonverbal, physical, body-linking sharing of a tear, shed by one, absorbed and understood by another. In this expression of the collective concerns of women, a legacy of silent grief, accepted by one as destiny and inheritance, is rejected, however, by the speaker, who can no longer tolerate that historical determinism. By implication, what is historically defined as the human condition is not God-given but, rather, what we today would call a social construction that can be dismantled and reconstructed. The poem, then, actually stands firm in rejecting the historically dualistic definitions and divisions of people and is generally considered to reflect Storni's comprehension of (but distancing from) her mother's generation.

In this often anthologized poem, the first two lines are almost identical, a familiar technique in oral and popular literature to engage the listener/reader's attention. Storni employs a rigid four-line stanza of three unrhyming lines of 12 syllables (*abc*), followed by a short (five-syllable) fourth line in assonant "*b*" rhyme (*abuelo, acero*); likewise, the following 2 stanzas maintain the same assonant "*b*" rhyme (an unaccented "oh": *veneno, pequeño; beberlo, peso*). This structural element, in contrast to "free verse," for example, reinforces the poem's message of conformity to predefined patterns. However, the short fourth line of each stanza, as against more classic quatrains, leaves the reader/listener with a mental sort of *dot-dot-dot,* or ellipsis, as if to invite questioning.

BIBLIOGRAPHY
Storni, Alfonsina. "Peso ancestral"/"Ancestral Burden." Translated by Andrew Rosing. In *Twentieth-Century Latin American Poetry: A Bilingual Edition,* edited by Stephen Tapscott, 106–111. Austin: University of Texas Press, 1996.

María Roof

ANIARA: A REVIEW OF MAN IN TIME AND SPACE HARRY MARTINSON (1956)

It may seem strange that a poet known primarily for his nature writing would win a Nobel Prize in 1974 for a long narrative poem that narrates the nuclear destruction of the world and its aftermath. But HARRY MARTINSON's literary epic *Aniara: En revy av människan i tid och rum* (Aniara: A Review of Man in Time and Space) is designed to illustrate, in 103 haunting and compelling individual songs, the consequences of humankind's unexamined faith in technology and its consequent alienation from nature. While a number of famous dystopic science fiction novels were published in the early 20th century, among them Yevgeny Zamyatin's *We*, Aldous Huxley's *A Brave New World*, KARIN BOYE's *Kallocain*, and George Orwell's *1984*, Martinson's *Aniara* is considered the first great poem of the Space Age and the Atomic Age. Martinson has said that the inspiration for Aniara came from one night when he was studying the Andromeda galaxy through his home telescope, and the galaxy seemed to be shining so much brighter than before that he woke his wife, Ingrid, to come look. This experience sparked his imagination about what it would be like to travel to the galaxy in a spaceship. Martinson's subsequent publication of the first 29 songs in 1953, under the title "The Song of Doris and Mima" in his collection *Cicada*, happened the same year the Soviet Union tested a hydrogen bomb and preceded by four years the Soviet Union's launch of *Sputnik*, which started the space race between the world's two superpowers, the USSR and the United States. Through this poem Martinson offers the world a dystopic vision of what could happen if both the space race and the nuclear arms race continued to accelerate unchecked.

Aniara is on one level a compelling, fantastical travel narrative told through a sequence of poems, recalling ancient epics such as Homer's *The Odyssey*. It depicts the fallout of a nuclear war that destroys Earth and forces its survivors to flee on spaceships to colonies on neighboring planets. One of these ships, *Aniara*, is knocked off course by an asteroid and is lost in outer space, predicting by several decades the premise of the popular 1990s American television show *Star Trek: Voyager* (the first song describes being knocked off course). The refugees onboard *Aniara* panic when they realize they are doomed to drift in space forever, but an empathetic telecommunications console known as the mima, which culls the galaxy for audio and video

feeds of their lost home and projects them for the refugees, restores their hopes: "The mima tuned us into signs of life / spread far and wide. . . . We pull in traces, pictures, landscapes, scraps of language / being spoken someplace, only where?" (Song 6). The mima becomes a goddess figure for those onboard, and most of the poem's songs are narrated by the mimarobe—the mechanic who maintains the mima. But the mimarobe and everyone else soon realize that the mima is no longer mere machine but, by becoming humanity's vessel of hope, has developed human qualities such as empathy: "the mima had invented half herself" (Song 9). Thus when the mima receives the horrifying images of the nuclear destruction of Earth, she is overwhelmed with sorrow and dies (Songs 2 through 29). For the remainder of the doomed journey, the mimarobe and his travel companions first try to repair the mima, then to re-create their harsh reality by creating a world of visions (Songs 30 to 68), then to take refuge in memories of life on Earth (Songs 69 to 80). In the fourth and final phase of the journey, which begins, "The dark in our minds neared its worst," the mimarobe's songs become especially despairing and haunting (Songs 81–101). The final two songs are the concluding comments of the mimarobe, whom Martinson clearly intends to be society's poet, trying to make sense of the whole calamity: "I had meant to make them an Edenic place, / but since we left the one we had destroyed / our only home became the night of space / where no god heard us in the endless void" (Song 102).

Martinson's long poem is distinctive for its depth of emotion, its compelling female characters throughout, its skillful use of neologisms (to suggest futurist technology and experience), its evocation of Norse and Greek myth and legend, its breathtaking poetic imagery, and the rich variation in its lyrical form. These qualities made it ideal for musical adaptation, and it was transformed into a successful opera, which premiered in 1959, with music composed by Karl-Birger Blomdahl.

Like many works of science fiction, *Aniara* has its own distinctive vocabulary. Earth is named Doris (after a district of ancient Greece just north of Mount Parnassus, expressing "both the natural and intellectual beauty found upon Earth"), the telecommunications console-goddess is "mima," the mima's mechanical processes are a "gyrospin," the spaceship is called a "goldonder," and the chief pilot—a woman—is named Isagel, suggesting Isis, the Egyptian goddess associated with the cosmic order. Although the poem was written in Swedish, because Martinson invents this fantastical vocabulary from words with Latin and Greek roots familiar to English speakers, Klass and Sjöberg were able to translate Martinson's distinctive vocabulary very skillfully in their English version.

As all good science fiction does, Martinson's poem easily transcends the historical moment in which it was written to become a universal tale for all ages. In addition, Martinson used the distinctive qualities of lyrical poetry to depict the beauty of nature and humankind, even in its most devastated, compromised state.

BIBLIOGRAPHY
Broman, Lars. "Aniara: On a Space Epic and its Author." *Planetarian* 27, no. 2 (June 1998).
Hall, Todd. "Introduction to Aniara." *Just the Other Day: Essays on the Suture of the Future,* edited by Luk Vos, 383–386, Antwerp: EXA, 1985.
Martinson, Harry. *Aniara: A Review of Man in Time and Space.* Translated by Stephen Klass and Leif Sjöberg. Ashland, Oreg.: Story Line Press, 1999.

Ursula A. L. Lindqvist

"THE ANSWER" BEI DAO (1976)

"The Answer" was written in 1976 and was soon taken as a representative poem of the Chinese Democracy Movement. According to Eliot Weinberger, BEI DAO's English translator, this seven-stanza poem is the movement's "Blowin' in the Wind" (Weinberger 108). It is also regarded as the poet's affirmation of freedom and independent thinking.

The poem is rich in metaphors, and the tone is direct and determined, enhanced by a strong sense of loss, anger, and disbelief. The first stanza encapsulates pairs of contrasting metaphors: debasement and nobility, the inhuman and the human. Each meets its different outcome in the chaotic situation. When debasement survives, nobility suffers from perished fate. Based on the description of the previous, infuriating stanza, the poet raises his question: Why are indifference, ignorance, and darkness still in control when "the Ice Age is over" and "The Cape of Good Hope has been discovered"? "The Ice Age" can be taken metaphorically as cruelty, and the "Dead Sea" as the situation of China at that time. The poet presents himself in the third stanza as a man of responsibility, a representative voice for the people who otherwise lack a means of expression. The phrase "Paper, rope and shadow" refers, respectively, to the poet's poem, his means of survival, and his physical self. The next stanza is full of doubt when the poet declares that he is skeptical about what is preached and overtly challenges, with defiance, whatever comes up. The emphatic line "I—do—not—believe!" is a rejection of brainwashing. It is made more specific in the next stanza, where the poet utters his refusal to follow blindly the dictates of propaganda. The implication is clear: Social reality is bleak, authority may not remain powerful all the time, the dream of democracy is not a dream in vain, and revenge is on the way. The next stanza foresees the coming storm and shows the poet's determination and expectation: As an individual he would rather endure all suffering and let there be a choice and a change for a better, more democratic life. The last stanza embodies a sign of promise. There comes an opportunity, an awakening; and history and tradition help to make possible such a change. What happens today will be a meaningful lesson to generations to come.

Bei Dao's poems are known for their "intensely compressed images and cryptic style" (http://www.kirjasto.sci.fi/beidao.htm). As an example of his early poetry, "The Answer" shares what translator Bonnie S. McDougall characterizes as "a revelation of the self inhabiting two unreal universes: a dream world of love, tranquility and normality, that should exist but does not, and a nightmare of cruelty, terror and hatred, that should not exist but does" (McDougall 10).

BIBLIOGRAPHY
Anonymous. "Bei Dao (1949–   )" Author's Calendar. Available online. URL: http://www.kirjasto.sci.fi/beidao.htm. Accessed on April 20, 2007.
Bei Dao. *The August Sleepwalker.* Translated by Bonnie McDougall. New York: New Directions, 1988.
Weinberger, Eliot. "A Note on the Translation." In Bei Dao's, *Unlock,* translated by Eliot Weinberger and Iona Man-Cheong. New York: New Directions, 2000.

Shan Xuemei

ANTHEM OF THE DECADES MAZISI KUNENE

(1981) MAZISI KUNENE's *Anthem of the Decades: A Zulu Epic Dedicated to the Women of Africa* exemplifies several of the qualities that have made Kunene one of the most significant among South African poets—and, indeed, among African poets—of the 20th century. As with all Kunene's work, *Anthem of the Decades* is grounded in Zulu cosmology, or philosophical and religious beliefs. Like another of his most famous works, *Emperor Shaka the Great, Anthem* is an epic poem and, at approximately 12,000 lines, a gargantuan work. This sense of massive scope extends to the subject matter as well, which is the creation of human beings by the gods and the ensuing debate about their proper role in the universe. Since understanding the story depends on a certain degree of familiarity with basic concepts from Zulu cosmology, Kunene explains these briefly in the introduction. The poem comprises three parts, each of which contains five books.

In the first part, "Age of the Gods," the two gods Sodume and Somazwi debate the merits of creating the new species of human beings. Sodume rejoices at the idea of new creation, while Somazwi argues that humans will be continually unhappy because of the difficulty of life on Earth. Both are reasonable positions, but Nomkhubulwane, the Princess of Heaven and daughter of the divine Creator, Mvelinqangi, ultimately sides with Sodume, and the gods set about creating humans. The newly created humans impress the gods by taming wild dogs, and the gods send a chameleon as messenger to let humans know that they will live eternally. In part two, "Age of Fantasy," the chameleon is led astray by Somazwi's wife, Nofuka, who wants humans to be destroyed. The gods then send a salamander, who reaches the humans. The humans, nevertheless, embrace death, displeasing the gods. Lost in the realm of individual fantasy, humans fail to act in their community's best interests. Finally, after a brutal war between humans who side with the chameleon (or forces of creation) and those who side with the salamander (or forces of destruction), both sides surrender, and balance between the two forces is restored. In part three, "Age of the Ancestors," the spirits of humans who have died begin to play a more active role in the lives of human beings, meeting with the gods on their

behalf and conveying knowledge and a sense of continuity to the human race. The ancestors and the gods join together to protect the Sun, which is necessary for human life, from Nofuka, who still seeks to destroy humanity. After an epic battle, Nofuka is finally defeated, and the continued life of humans is ensured. The poem demonstrates that a balance among different views reached through community consensus is crucial for humanity's survival. Because, as Sodume says, "True wisdom is only of a woman / She alone holds the balance between opposites / She nourishes the forces that bind day and night together," it is fitting that Kunene dedicates the poem to the women of Africa.

BIBLIOGRAPHY

Kunene, Mazisi. *Anthem of the Decades: A Zulu Epic Dedicated to the Women of Africa.* London: Heinemann, 1981.

Emily S. Davis

ANYIDOHO, KOFI (1947–)

Born in the coastal town of Wheta in the Volta region of Ghana, Kofi Anyidoho shares a common birthplace with KOFI AWOONOR, an older Ghanaian poet with whom he also shares the Anlo-Ewe poetic heritage. He is best known for promoting a type of poetry that is performance-oriented. Though initially constrained by his poor background, he realized his dream of acquiring formal education with the support of his uncle and by weaving the traditional kente cloth and farming. After his primary education, which was truncated at different points due to lack of adequate financial support, he attended a middle school and later attended the Accra Teacher Training College. He made up for his inability to attend secondary school by studying for the General Certificate of Education by correspondence while at the training college and also wrote the advanced-level exams. He taught for two years at the Wenchi District of the Brong Ahafo Region of Ghana before proceeding to the Advanced Teachers Training College, Winneba. After graduating he taught at the famous Achimota College. He was later admitted to the University of Ghana, Legon, where he studied English and linguistics and won a scholarship for a master's degree at Indiana University. He did his doctoral work on comparative literature at the University of Texas at Austin.

His interest in theorizing African oral traditions is evident in his doctoral research, "Oral Poetics and Traditions of Verbal Arts in Africa." He returned to the University of Ghana after completing his studies in 1983 and has been on the staff of its Department of English. He is currently a professor of literature and head of the Department of English.

It is impossible to appreciate the growth and orientation of Kofi Anyidoho as a poet without situating his work within the cultural, national, and intellectual circumstances that shaped his outlook and aesthetic preferences. Anyidoho, very much like Awoonor, has drawn extensively on the poetic practices of the Ewe, who are found mainly in Ghana and Togo. Interestingly, he has also devoted much of his scholarly attention to studying these traditions. This explains why his cultural environment has substantially fed his creative practice and scholarly pursuits. His work draws, although in a creative and often subversive manner, from his cultural background, using such poetic forms as the *halo*—the song of abuse—and the dirge. These have become, in his handling, fresh and versatile forms for articulating experiences and realities that transcend the personal and the ethnic. His debt to the tradition of his people is most glaring in his increasing retrieval of the atmosphere of performance, which characterizes the experience of poetry in the African context. Though he nods to the practice of performance that Atukwei Okai introduced on the Ghanaian poetic scene in the 1970s, Anyidoho has since built on Okai's initiative by disseminating the performance of his own work in up-to-date technology. His most recent collection of poetry, *Praise Song for The Land,* is accompanied by an audio CD that presents his reading of the entire collection. He has, in addition, produced Ewe songs *GhanaNya* (performed with his mother) and *Agbenoxevi* on CD and audio tapes.

Anyidoho's creative imagination draws inspiration from ethnic, national, and racial memories. His earliest work represents an attempt at re-creating the Ghanaian experience, and his work articulates the pervasive disillusionment of the Ghanaian people with the hypocrisy of the military adventurers who claimed to be on a redemptive mission. He finds the elegiac idiom appropriate for re-creating the entire experience. His later work also celebrates the intervention of Jerry Rawlings and the hopes his coming held for the nation. In representing the Ghanaian experience, Anyidoho constantly inscribes a longing for realizing the dreams of the nation. In this sense, he seems to subscribe to the hopes that Kwame Nkrumah, the founder of the Ghanaian nation, gave in its formative years. Like Nkrumah, Anyidoho does not see the story of his nation as separable from the story of black communities worldwide, especially as the tragedy of slavery and the crisis of self-definition that it has created for people of African descent all over the world regularly feature in the notion of Pan-Africanism, a cultural philosophy to which Anyidoho subscribes. There is in his recent poetry, therefore, a sustained engagement with the experiences associated with the forced dispersal of black peoples from Africa and a longing for meaningful ties among people of African descent, and that emphasis is consistent with his personal involvement in media, cultural, and academic activities and institutions associated with sustaining Pan-Africanism. He participates in the W. E. B Du Bois Memorial Centre for Pan African Culture, designing and teaching literature courses around the black diasporic experience and serving as director of the African Humanities Institute based at his university.

The growth of Anyidoho as a poet is best appreciated in relation to his immersion in the tradition of singing, but many others have contributed to his development. His mother, Abla Adidi, and his uncles, Kwadzovi and Agbodzinshi Yortuwor, were singers. Besides absorbing the poetry of Awoonor, Anyidoho studied the works of Heno Domegbe, an elegist, and of Vinoko Akpalu, the influential Ewe singer whose work circulated widely beyond Eweland. Anyidoho's talent was first recognized in his student days. He has since drawn on his training in linguistics and English. He exhibits the playful manipulation of language and constantly articulates prophetic projections animated by a longing for the fulfilment of the collective aspirations of the Ghanaian people in particular and of African peoples in general. As a much traveled writer, he gives expression to his various encounters and associations. Many of his recent poems are dedicated to those who inspired them—and, thus, require contextual information for fullest understanding.

Anyidoho's poetry exhibits a profound sense of historical awareness, is very African in its technical properties, and deploys homely imagery in unique ways. It is a poetry of lived experience, conscious of the primacy of attending to the peculiar needs of a developing society and deriving its energy from an enduring sense of patriotism and commitment to the common good. He has acquired a personal poetic idiom that is unpretentious, performative, and linguistically subversive. If we recognize three major phases (or generations) in the development of modern Ghanaian poetry of English expression, beginning with the works of the nationalist poets such as J. B. Danquah and R. E. G. Armattoe and transitioning with the work of Atukwei Okai, the work of Kofi Anyidoho falls within the third generation of modern Ghanaian poets. His contemporaries include Kwabena Eyi Acqua, Kwadwo Opoku-Agyemang, Kojo Laing, and Lade Wosornu.

He has published five collections of poetry: *Elegy for the Revolution; A Harvest of Our Dreams; Earthchild, with Brain Surgery; Ancestrallogic and CarribeanBlues;* and *Praise Song for the Land.* An honorary member of the international writing program of the University of Iowa, Anyidoho is a recipient of several awards, including the Valco Fund Literary Award for Poetry, the Langston Hughes Prize, the BBC Arts and Africa Poetry Award, the Fania Kruger Fellowship for Poetry of Social Vision, and the Ghana Book Award, in addition to being declared poet of the year in Ghana. He has performed his poetry in different parts of the world and has held visiting professorships at many American universities, and his poetry has been translated into Italian, Dutch, German, and several Slavic languages.

BIBLIOGRAPHY

Angmor, Charles. *Contemporary Literature in Ghana 1911–1978: A Critical Evaluation.* Accra, Ghana: Woeli Publishing Services, 1996.

Anyidoho, Kofi. *A Harvest of Our Dreams* with *Elegy for the Revolution.* London: Heinemann, 1984.

———. *Ancestrallogic and Caribbeanblues.* Trenton, N.J.: Africa World Press, 1993.

———. *Elegy for the Revolution.* New York: Greenfield Review Press, 1978.

———. "Poetry as Dramatic Performance: The Example of Ghana." *Research in African Literatures* 22. no. 2 (Summer 1991).

———. *PraiseSong for The Land.* Accra, Ghana: Sub-Saharan, 2003.

Anyidoho, Kofi, and James Gibbs, eds. *Fontonfrom: Contemporary Ghanaian Literature, Theater and Film.* Amsterdam and Atlanta: Matatu/Rodopi, 2000.

Deandrea, Pietro. *Fertile Crossings: Metamorphosis of Genre in Anglophone West African Literature.* Amsterdam: Rodopi, 2002.

Fraser, Robert. *West African Poetry: A Critical History.* Cambridge: Cambridge University Press, 1986.

Okunoye, Oyeniyi. "'We Too Sing': Kofi Anyidoho and Ewe Poetic Practices in *Elegy for the Revolution.*" *Journal of Commonwealth Literature* 40, no. 1 (2005): 91–111.

Priebe, Richard K. *Ghanaian Literatures.* New York and Westport, Conn.: Greenword, 1988.

Oyeniyi Okunoye

APOLLINAIRE, GUILLAUME (WILHELM APOLLINARIS DE KOSTROWITZKY) (1880–1918)

Poet, critic, dramatist, and journalist Guillaume Apollinaire occupies a significant place in literature of the early 20th century. Apollinaire was a transitional figure between traditionalists and modernists, and his experimental and innovative works set the stage for new forms of writing. He also helped shape the modern artistic landscape by influencing avant-garde movements such as cubism, surrealism, and dadaism. Among his friends were Pablo Picasso, Georges Braque, Henri Rousseau, and Gertrude Stein.

Wilhelm Apollinaris de Kostrowitzky was born in Rome, Italy, in 1880 to Angeliska Kostrowitzky, the daughter of a Polish aristocrat living in the Vatican. The identity of his father is unknown, but speculation has ranged widely—from a military officer or a cardinal to the pope himself. More likely, however, his father was the gambler and man-about-town Flugi d'Aspermont, with whom his mother had a long-standing affair and probably a second son. Apollinaire's mother further confused the issue by recording his name in a variety of ways on various legal documents. When d'Aspermont abandoned Angeliska in 1882, she took her sons and settled on the French Riviera.

Apollinaire and his younger brother were enrolled in Catholic school in Monaco. Apollinaire was an excellent student there and won a wide circle of friends with his playful personality and ability to create fantastic stories.

Further education was arranged for him at the Collège Stanilas in Cannes, then at the Lycée de Nice; however, the young man was by then more interested in writing than in his studies. He left the Lycée without completing his course of study and moved to Paris, where he was employed as a bank clerk, a job he found boring and low paying. To supplement his income, he wrote erotica, which brought him more fame than money.

It was in Paris, however, that Apollinaire became acquainted with a number of young avant-garde artists and writers whose work he encouraged. In 1903 he secured funds to begin publishing *Le Festin d'Esope*, a magazine devoted to literature, art, and ideas. It was here that Apollinaire's collection of short stories *L'Enchanteur pourissant* (The Rotting Enchanter) was published before being published in book form in 1909. These short stories demonstrate the author's ability to create extraordinary characters and situations. After trying his hand at publishing and then writing for several magazines, Apollinaire became editor of *Chronique des grands siècles de la France* in 1912, a vehicle through which he continued to disseminate his thoughts on modern art.

Apollinaire created a number of significant works in 1913. In addition to writing for magazines and newspapers, he is credited with introducing the term *cubism* in his book *Les Peintres cubistes* (The Cubist Painters). He also published a landmark discussion of progressive art in *L'Antitradition futuriste: Manifesto-synthèse* (The Futuristic Antitradition: Manifesto-Synthesis). Furthermore, *Alcools: Poèmes 1898–1913* was published that year. One of Apollinaire's best-known works, this volume of poems presents a series of nostalgic images and reflections on a one-day procession through the streets of Paris, in all its glory and its squalor. The collection includes traditional formal verse forms and rhyme schemes juxtaposed with unrhymed, irregular, experimental verses. One of the innovations in *Alcools* is the use of a collage, or fractured images. The works of 1913 added to Apollinaire's growing reputation but did little to solve his financial problems.

In 1914 Apollinaire joined the French army and was eventually sent to the front lines. There he received a severe head wound from which he never fully recovered. Returning to Paris in 1916, he staged his play *Les mamelles de Tirésias: Drame surréaliste,* the first use of the word *surrealist,* later adopted by a group of writers and artists. The next year Apollinaire presented a lecture in which he called for artists to throw off the conventions of the past and to risk using inspiration and invention to achieve a different reality. This lecture, "L'Esprit nouveau et les poètes," has been called the manifesto of modern art.

Making use of his wartime experience, Apollinaire published his most innovative and memorable collection of poems, *Calligrammes: Poèmes de la paix et de la guerre 1913–1916* (CALLIGRAMMES: POEMS OF LOVE AND WAR, 1918). The title comes from the use of calligrams—that is, shaped, concrete poems, or ideograms: the arrangement of lines on the page to create pictures. The first poems, written before Apollinaire experienced the war front, are playful and see war as a pleasant game. Later poems present a more realistic view of war and its *"effroyables boyaus"* (horrifying trenches).

Guillaume Apollinaire married Jacqueline Kolb a few months before his death. Still weakened from his war injury, he succumbed to the Spanish influenza during the epidemic of 1918; he was 38. Apollinaire left behind a remarkable body of literature in many genres, some of which was published posthumously. While his name is not so well known in the United States as those of many of the artists he influenced, Apollinaire's example and his support for modernism made it possible for other avant-garde artists to succeed.

BIBLIOGRAPHY

Apollinaire, Guillaume. *Alcools: Poèmes 1898–1913.* Edited by Tristan Tzara. Paris: Deplanche, 1913. Published in English as *Alcools. Poems 1898–1913.* Translated by William Meredith. New York: Doubleday, 1964.

———. *Le Bestiaire; ou, Cortège d'Orphée.* Paris: Deplanche, 1911. Published as *Le Bestiaire.* New York: Metropolitan Museum of Art, 1977.

———. *Calligrammes: Poèmes de la paix et de la guerre.* Paris: Deplanche, 1918. Published as *Calligrammes: Poems of Peace and War.* Translated by Anne Hyde Greet. Berkeley: University of California Press, 1991.

———. *Century of Clouds: Selected Poems from the French of Guillaume Apollinaire.* Translated by Geoff Page and Wendy Coutts. Canberra: Leros, 1985.

———. *Les Peintres cubistes.* Paris: Deplanche, 1913. Published as *The Cubist Painters.* Translated by Peter Read. Berkeley: University of California Press, 2004.

————. *Selected Poems*. Edited and translated by Oliver Bernard. London: Anvil Press Poetry, 1986.

Jean Hamm

APPROXIMATE MAN Tristan Tzara (1931)

This book-length poetic work was published in the same year that Tristan Tzara's critical "Essay on the Situation of Poetry" (Essai sur la situation de la poésie) ran in the Marxist journal *Surréalisme au service de la révolution* (Surrealism in the Service of the Revolution). In this essay, which stirred much debate among the contemporary Parisian literati, Tzara proposes that the primary contribution of surrealist art to communist struggle is surrealist art's ability to transcend the conventions and judgments that enslave the mind in bourgeois modes of thought. Surrealist art, according to Tzara, does not express or represent a material reality, but rather disrupts such expectations and representations through surprising and spontaneous images that do not adhere to accepted modes of logic. In the essay Tzara distinguishes poetry as a means of expression (*poésie-moyen d'expression*) from poetry that is an activity of the mind (*la poésie-activité de l'esprit*). Such poetry as mental activity is not purely aesthetic, Tzara insists, but rather supra-aesthetic; the laws of aesthetics no longer apply. He writes: "It is not the recent lubrications concerning *poésie pure* that will situate the debate." What results from such spontaneous mental activity, Tzara believed, was a shift from a focus on *quality*—i.e., categorical judgments and classifications by the "qualified" critics of the bourgeoisie—to a focus on *quantity*, as the "poetry-activity of the mind increases quantitatively and progressively over time" (Harris 97).

The poem *Approximate Man* represents the kind of creative evolution Tzara advocates, as he wrote it over a six-year period and published several excerpts at different times before finally publishing it as a book in 1931. (One such excerpt appeared in *Surréalisme au service de la révolution* in 1930.) The poem comprises 19 separate parts, designated by roman numerals, and in its 1931 book form fills 158 pages. (The poem was reissued in book form in French in 1968, published in English translation in 1973, and reissued in English in 2006.) The poem's considerable length, its liberal use of refrains to provide cohesion within individual parts

and throughout the poem as a whole, and its allegorical function of creating the new man have drawn comparisons with the modern narrative epic, such as Walt Whitman's *Leaves of Grass* (1855) or T. S. Eliot's "anti-epic" *The Waste Land* (1922). Similarly to Whitman's poem, which narrates the story of an entire people (America) through the voice of a single poet-speaker, Tzara's poem features a speaker whose individual struggles represent those of all humanity. But the comparisons to Whitman and Eliot end there, as Tzara does not attempt to narrate the human condition, but rather to illuminate it in flashes of constantly shifting images and sounds. Tzara's poetry does not recognize established rules of grammar and punctuation and instead links words primarily by their sound—a process that scholar Mary Ann Caws describes as "knotting"—in order to produce spontaneous, illogical, and "associative" (*non-dirigé*) images. Thus, sound and image take the place of grammatical structures in propelling poetry forward in an interrupted and often chaotic stream. Because the internal creative force of both man and poetry are constantly in motion, Tzara believed, it can be sensed only in fleeting and spontaneous moments. This is why man, like poetry, is always "approximate," since the motion of this creative life force never pauses long enough to declare any of its rapidly evolving forms finished. In the poem's seventh part, Tzara writes: "words are spinning / leaving a faint trail majestic trail behind their meaning scarcely a meaning"; and in the ninth part, he says: "oh powers I have glimpsed only in rare flashes / and that I know and feel in the tumultuous encounter." Tzara's poetry remains stubbornly committed to the perpetual independence of individual elements, which join with other elements only for an instant and never long enough to form a pattern.

Where patterns appear in *Approximate Man*, they represent the banality and monotony of everyday life, in which Tzara believed humans unthinkingly rejoice, rather than forge a desired unity. One pattern that pervades the opening three parts of Tzara's poem and establishes the seductive monotony of everyday life is the ringing of the church bells that summon people to Sunday services. Tzara's poem begins: "the bells ring for no reason and we too / ring bells for no reason and we too / we rejoice at the sound of the chains / that we set ringing in us with the bells." Such repetition both creates and disrupts the ringing of the bells. The repetition of the words for "bells" and "sound" in French—*cloches* and *sonnent/sonnez*—produces both the sound and the image of a bell swinging in a church tower. The bells ring "for no reason": They serve a practical purpose, but that purpose is to summon human beings to partake in a hollow ritual that does not lead to enlightenment. The people ring along with the bells ("and we too"). The speaker constructs ironic distance between the speaking self and the observed self, which are both contained in the collective "we," representing humans generally. This ironic distance opens up a moment of resistance in which "we" can consider whether we really should be rejoicing in the unity of sound between our "chains" and the "bells," but rather rattling them in noisy rage as a defiant prisoner would. This brief moment of sensing the bells' activity embodies Tzara's idea that while the central functions of language are to organize, assimilate, and enslave, language's individual elements—words, sounds, and images—can force open spontaneous sites of resistance that propel both creator and audience (conjoined in "we") beyond the limits of language and into the liberating realm of poetry.

BIBLIOGRAPHY

Harris, Steven. *Surrealist Art and Thought in the 1930s: Art, Politics, and the Psyche.* New York: Cambridge University Press, 2004.

Tzara, Tristan. *Approximate Man and Other Writings.* Translated by Mary Ann Caws and Peter Caws. Boston: Black Widow Press, 2006.

Ursula A. L. Lindqvist

ARAB RAP AND HIP-HOP CULTURE

Since the 1990s, with the seemingly unending cycle of violence that has defined the Second Palestinian Intifada and the current war in Iraq, Western media outlets have bombarded their viewers with the stark imagery of disaffected Arab youth. Terms like *jihadi, mujahadeen,* and *martyr* have become commonplace nomenclature for commentators and audiences alike in their attempts to make sense of why the region's young

people adopt such drastic measures to cope with their dismal prospects. Yet while donning a hidden explosives belt or making a covert border crossing to join the ranks of like-minded insurgents are very real options for some, there are still many uncelebrated groups in the Middle East for whom artistic expression has become a preferred outlet for resistance. Among these, hip-hop communities have emerged, and their outspoken orators, the rappers, are at the forefront, leading the way as the "new-style troubadours" (Pinn 13) of the globalized ghetto.

To the conscientious observer it comes as little surprise that hip-hop is flourishing around the world. With the export of MTV and the proliferation of international music labels, scarcely anyone anywhere remains outside of McWorld's grasp. As one author stated, "U.S. popular culture has become global popular culture" (Wermuth 153). Nearly every country has a rap music scene of one form or another, although the local variants frequently diverge to reflect indigenous concerns accordingly. The composite is a global phenomenon embedded at the community level but reworked and retooled by its recipients. The resulting product of this intersection between the global and the local is a "regionalization of rap" (Prévos 15), a style that lecturer Tony Mitchell has appropriately termed "glocal" (11, 32).

However, no matter how far hip-hop travels or how "glocalized" it becomes, its constituent elements remain intact. These include the graffiti artwork of taggers, the acrobatics of break-dancers, and the musical menagerie created by DJs and MCs working separately or in unison. Moreover, each of these roles is outwardly united by the fashion statements that symbolize one's membership in the hip-hop community, the "oversized, baggy pants, sloppy T-shirts, baseball caps" (Levy 134), athletic apparel, and other requisite accessories. Hip-hop style is a cultural force that seeks to create its own niche in the public consciousness while simultaneously remaining outside of orthodox institutional frameworks. This feature provides the distinction between hip-hop's real adherents versus its commercialized wannabes or poseurs.

Notwithstanding hip-hop's multifaceted articulation, its most prominent feature is its music, popularly known as rap. In the United States today, every rap single is performed by an individual or crew and typically takes the form of a three to five-minute narrative interspersed with a chorus. Combined with the lyricists' linguistic manipulations and wordplay are the DJ's technological arrangements of sound layering, breaks, and volume switching. Although this musical structure may appear obvious, one must stress this intermixed lyrical and sound formula for the sake of clarity because it is the standard by which U.S. rap has been defined and categorized. Also, due to the lack of scholarship on rap outside of the United States, we have used many of these same criteria to classify rap's manifestations in the Middle East, despite the absence of any such indigenous uniformity. One component may be found to exist without the other, yet either may be called "rap" by locals. For instance, DJ electronica with no lyrical accompaniment or vocalized rhythmic flows unaided by a DJ's skills can both separately qualify in the region as rap.

While this may appear as a conceptual inconsistency for stateside observers, there is a significant rationale at work here that underscores the principal not only of Middle Eastern rap, but the entire rap genre worldwide. Whereas stateside rap today is produced according to the aforementioned blueprint of DJing and MCing, with a few notable exceptions, it has traditionally been not the format but rather the content that distinguished rap and set it apart as a musical genus. As a textual agent, rap is a verbose challenge to the oppression that supplements the status quo. And just like Malcolm X's "jihad of words" was marked by its "talking back at white America" (Floyd-Thomas 50), the same analogy can be invoked for rap's lyrical mission. Rap mobilizes local voices and gives them an expressive conduit by which they can channel their frustrations and anxieties. In the face of global capitalism and the resultant economic trauma, social alienation, and political inequalities that are fervently guarded by police, rap becomes more than a form of entertainment; it becomes an urban "survival tactic" (Dimitriadis 63).

Hence, rap music and the hip-hop community exist as points of identity for their adherents; they are simultaneously fabrications of the self and others, as in-group or out-group affiliates. And while U.S. corporate rap has been largely commodified into a state of territorial ambiguity or disembodiment, its overseas counterparts have yet to reach this condition. There is still among rap's foreign variants a very distinct sense of place-boundedness, where the local neighborhood or district prevails as the site of emphasis. This "ghetto-centricity" (Silverstein 55) or "tribalization" prioritizes the local, often much to the chagrin of the nation-state, and elevates the plights of the community. Rap's local-level commitments serve not only to preserve the values, histories, and traditions of marginalized communities; it also validates and re-creates these locales by bringing them under the spotlight of performance politics. The irony of rap's localization is that the genre's arrival on the scene has been made possible only through the efforts of global agents. Furthermore, many MCs and DJs are keenly aware of their place in the international hip-hop arena—a self-realization that truly underscores hip-hop's "glocal" nature.

Consequently, despite the claims of numerous lyrical protagonists, there is simply no clear-cut way to determine when rap first emerged on the Middle Eastern musical landscape. In fact, the efforts of local journalists, not to mention the egos of musicians, appear to be mainly reconstructive, retrospective, and partisan, and their arguments can be summarized in the following manner: "although hip-hop is gaining popularity in Arab countries today, it all began in our country." Each state has its own hip-hop pioneer, and in some cases, there are multiple actors or groups vying for that distinction. For instance, Egypt's Shaaban Abd al-Rahim has been heralded in the country's media as the father of Arab rap. Although illiterate and, some would argue, crude, this former ironer has gained quite a following in Egypt. And though his music may not fit the Western model of synthesized rap, his simple repetitive lyrics, street dialect, and content (with songs like "I Hate Israel," "America," and "The War in Iraq") have established Shaaban as a leading voice for the Egyptian ghetto and the Cairene masses. While Shaaban, in interviews and songs, eschews rap as a genre along with Westernization, even he was caught in the grip of McWorld a few years ago when he wrote a jingle for a new delicacy: the McDonald's McFalafel.

In addition to Shaaban's folk-type chants, other troupes in the region are producing very recognizable rap compilations, though the messages of resistance, urban disenchantment, and social critique remain the same. As Takki (of the Egyptian crew MTM) surmised in 2006 after his group won the prize for best modern Arabic act at the Arabian Music Awards, "The best thing about rap is that it is a form of music that criticizes, so it discusses the issues of young people. . . . We really need this in the Arab world" (Al Jazeera 2004). Similarly, Tamar Nafer (of Da Arabian MCs, an ensemble of Israeli Arabs) expressed his group's approach to rap as "protest music" and explained why this global export resonates so profoundly for young Arabs today: "Black people in America were oppressed for hundreds of years—that's why we feel connected to this music" (Winder 2004). The members of DAM (the crew's acronym means "blood" in both Arabic and Hebrew) have become Palestine's preeminent ghetto reporters, taking on such topics as the Israeli occupation, poverty, drugs, and the ineptitude of Arab regimes to alleviate the suffering. In their own words, they are the "CNN of Palestine" (Rush 2004). To spread their message, DAM has toured Israel and Europe, and they have been featured on the BBC and in *Rolling Stone Magazine*. Yet their documentary-style videos offer the most poignant examples of their music; their visual integration of the local vividly endorses their allegiance to a neighborhood struggle where military checkpoints and forced evictions at the end of a bulldozer regularly scar daily life.

While the Middle East's homegrown hip-hop phenomenon is rapidly establishing its fan base among the region's youth, its most appealing component, the controversial rhetoric, is troubling for authorities. As Al Jazeera (2004) recently reported, rap is widely feared to be a corrupting Western influence. Just a few years ago, in a desperate attempt at preemption, *Islam Online* published "A Hip-Hop Parental Guide" (2001), followed by an article titled "Hip Hop and the 'New Age' of Ignorance" (2002), in which the author warned of rap's harmful effects. In Algeria, now home to at least 160 rap groups, local crew "Intik" has successfully fused Western and traditional compositional motifs with penetrating Arabic and French lyrics. However, the group's brusque commentaries on conditions in their native land quickly attracted the attention of government censors, and in 2000 a communiqué informed the public that Intik's songs and performances were forbidden in Algeria. Not to be deterred, Intik has since prospered in France, and their references to the Peoples' Democratic Republic of Algeria as the "Peoples' Republican Dictatorship of Algeria" (Original UK HipHop 2000) is an assurance that there will be no heartfelt reconciliations.

Some observers have noted that the contemporary urban Middle East is quite the appropriate environment for this nascent hip-hop movement, if it can be said that somehow poverty and upheaval represent the perfect ghetto. But we must be wary of this approach, lest we fall into the myth of "expressive causality" (Krims 32). Instead, it is important to appreciate the multiple global and local variables that have given birth to the Middle East's hip-hop communities and the struggles they confront as they stake their claims to the "glocal." Indeed, Da Arabian MCs promises, "We'll reach you all" (Rush 2004).

BIBLIOGRAPHY

"Arabs Rap to a Different Beat." Al Jazeera.Net. Available online. URL: http://english.aljazeera.net/NR/exeres/ 7185A83E-1CDC-4589-90AB-434C194BAF9.htm. Accessed on May 16, 2004.

Banjoko, Adisa. "A Hip-Hop Parental Guide!" Islam Online. Available online. URL: http://www.islam-online.net/ english/ArtCulture/2001/06/article11.shtml. Accessed on June 26, 2001.

———. "Hip Hop and the 'New Age' of Ignorance." Islam Online. Available online. URL: http://www.islamonline. net/English/artculture/2002/02/article14.shtml. Accessed on February 2, 2002.

Barber, Benjamin R. *Jihad vs. McWorld*. London: Corgi Books, 2003.

Danielson, Virginia. "New Nightingales of the Nile: Popular Music in Egypt since the 1970s." *Popular Music* 15, no. 3 (Oct. 1996): 299–312.

Daoudi, Bouziane. "Algerian Rappers Sing the Blues," UNESCO Courier. Available online. URL: http://www. unesco.org/courier/2000_07/uk/doss23.htm. Accessed on July 2000.

Dimitriadis, Greg. *Performing Identity/Performing Culture; Hip Hop as Text, Pedagogy, and Lived Performance*. New York: Peter Lang, 2001.

Espiner, Mark. "Comment & Analysis: Hip-hop on the Frontline: Globalised Rap Music May Have Lost Its Bite, But in the Middle East It's Giving Voice to Both Sides in the Conflict." *The Guardian,* October 26, 2004, 22.

Floyd-Thomas, Juan M. "A Jihad of Words; The Evolution of African American Islam and Contemporary Hip-Hop." In *Noise and Spirit; The Religious and Spiritual Sensibilities of Rap Music,* edited by Anthony B. Pinn, 49–70. New York: New York University Press, 2003.

Gordon, Joel. "Singing the Pulse of the Egyptian-Arab Street: Shaaban Abd al-Rahim and the Geo-Pop-Politics of Fast Food." *Popular Music* 22, no. 1 (2003): 73–88.

Gross, Joan, David McMurray, David, and Ted Swedenburg. "Rai, Rap, and Ramadan Nights: Franco-Maghribi Cultural Identities." *Middle East Report* no. 178 (September–October 1992): 11–16, 24.

Hakam, Mohamad. "Yo! Hip Hop Is in Da Middle East House . . ." MusicDish Industry e-Journal Available online. URL: http://www.musicdish.com/mag/index. php3?id=9722. Accessed on August 30, 2004.

Hazan, Jenny. "Moved by Music." *Jerusalem Post,* June 3, 2003, 8.

Hesmondhalgh, David, and Melville, Caspar. "Urban Breakbeat Culture; Repercussions of Hip-Hop in the United Kingdom." In Tony Mitchell, ed., *Global Noise; Rap and Hip-Hop Outside the USA,* 86–110.

Howeidy, Amira. "Shaaban Against Israel." Classic Cairo Live, 2000. Available online. URL: http://www.cairolive. com/newcairolive/dardasha/shaaban.html. Accessed on April 20, 2007.

Hudson, David. "Martyrs' Militant Rap Brings Pop Sound to Jihad Soundtrack." *Vancouver Sun,* Aug. 21, 1995, C. 1.

"Intik Interview." Original UK HipHop. Available online. URL: http://www.ukhh.com/features/interviews/intik. html. Accessed on October 10, 2000.

Keyes, Cheryl L. *Rap Music and Street Consciousness.* Urbana: University of Illinois Press, 2002.

Krims, Adam. *Rap Music and the Poetics of Identity.* Cambridge: Cambridge University Press, 2000.

Levy, Clair. "Rap in Bulgaria; Between Fashion and Reality." In *Global Noise; Rap and Hip-Hop Outside the USA,* edited by Tony Mitchell, 134–148. Middletown, Conn.: Wesleyan University Press, 2002.

Loza, Pierre. "Hip-Hop on the Nile." *Al-Ahram Weekly On-Line,* No. 723. Available online. URL: http://weekly. ahram.org.eg/2004/723/fe2.htm. Accessed on December 30, 2004–January 5, 2005.

Mitchell, Tony. "Introduction; Another Root—Hip-Hop Outside the USA." In *Global Noise; Rap and Hip-Hop Out-side the USA,* edited by Tony Mitchell, 1–38. Middleton, Conn.: Wesleyan University Press, 2001.

Orlando, Valérie. "From Rap to Raï in the Mixing Bowl: Beur Hip-Hop Culture and Banlieue Cinema in Urban France." *Journal of Popular Culture* 36, no. 3 (January 2003): 395–415.

Osumare, Halifu. "Beat Streets in the Global Hood: Connective Marginalities of the Hip Hop Globe." *Journal of American & Comparative Cultures* nos. 24, 1–2 (Spring 2001): 171–181.

Pinn, Anthony B. "Introduction; Making a World with a Beat: Musical Expression's Relationship to Religious Identity and Experience." In *Noise and Spirit; The Religious and Spiritual Sensibilities of Rap Music,* edited by Anthony B. Pinn, 1–26. New York: New York University Press, 2003.

Prévos, André J. M. "Postcolonial Popular Music in France; Rap Music and Hip-Hop Culture in the 1980s and 1990s." In *Global Noise; Rap and Hip-Hop Outside the USA,* edited by Tony Mitchell, 39–56. Middletown, Conn.: Wesleyan University Press, 2002.

———. "Two Decades of Rap in France: Emergence, Developments, Prospects." In *Black, Blanc, Beur; Rap Music and Hip-Hop Culture in the Francophone World,* edited by Alain-Philippe Durand, 1–21. Lanham, Md.: Scarecrow Press, 2002.

Rush. "Interview with Da Arab Mc's–D.A.M." AfricasGateway.com. Available online. URL: http://www.africasgateway.com/article609.html. Accessed on May 7, 2004.

Shiloh, Dina. "Young, Palestinian and Proud; Dina Shiloh Meets Angry Young Rapper Tamer Nafar." *Jewish Quarterly* 196 (Winter 2004). Available online. URL: http://www.jewishquarterly.org/article.asp?articleid=56. Accessed on April 20, 2007.

Silverstein, Paul A. "'Why Are We Waiting to Start the Fire?': French Gangsta Rap and the Critique of State Capitalism." In *Black, Blanc, Beur; Rap Music and Hip-Hop Culture in the Francophone World,* edited by Alain-Philippe Durand, 45–67. Lanham, Md.: Scarecrow Press, 2002.

Sisario, Ben. "Hip-Hop from the Middle East Comes to Brooklyn." *New York Times,* July 8, 2004, E. 1.

Urla, Jacqueline. "'We are all Malcolm X!' Negu Gorriak, Hip-Hop, and the Basque Political Imaginary." In *Global Noise; Rap and Hip-Hop Outside the USA,* edited by Tony Mitchell, 171–193. Middleton, Conn.: Wesleyan University Press, 2002.

Veash, Nicole. "Pop Crooner Hits Sour Note With Egyptian Elite." *Christian Science Monitor* 94, no. 39 (Jan. 18, 2002): 1.

Wermuth, Mir. "Rap in the Low Countries; Global Dichotomies on a National Scale." In *Global Noise; Rap and Hip-Hop Outside the USA,* edited by Tony Mitchell, 149–170. Middleton, Conn.: Wesleyan University Press, 2001.

Winder, Rob. "Rival Rappers Reflect Mid-East Conflict." BBC News World Edition. Available online. URL: http://news.bbc.co.uk/2/hi/middle_east/4039399.stm. Accessed on November 26, 2004.

DISCOGRAPHY

Aks al-Seir. 2002. *Aks al-Seir.* Chich/Aks al-Seir.
————. 2002. *Khartoush.* Chich/Aks al-Seir.
Clotaire K. 2003. *Lebanese.* Nocturne.
DAM. n.d. Available online. URL: http://www.dam3rap.com/. Official Web site.
Intik. 1999. *Intik.* Sony Music Entertainment (France).
————. 2001. *La Victoire.* Sony Music Entertainment (France).
MTM. 2003. *Ommy Mesafra.* EMI Music Arabia.
MBS. 1998. *Ouled El Bahdja.* Blue Silver/Virgin.
————. 1999. *Le Micro Brise le Silence.* Island/Universal.
MWR. n.d. Available online. URL: http://www.mwr-rap.com/. Official Web site.
Rayess Bek. 2003. *Am Bihki Bil Skout.* Chich.
Shaaban Abd al-Rahim. 2001. *Amrika ya Amrika.* Al-Wadi lil-Intaj (Cairo).
————. 2001. *Ma Tidarsh.* Al-Wadi lil-Intaj (Cairo).
Various Artists. 1999. *Algerap.* Virgin France.
————. 2003. *ArabRap.Net Volume 1.* ArabRap.Net.

James Redman

ARAGON, LOUIS (1897–1982)

The poet, novelist, and essayist Louis Aragon founded surrealism with PAUL ÉLUARD, ANDRÉ BRÉTON, and LUIS BUÑUEL among others. With concerns ranging from dadaism and surrealism to communism, the French Resistance, and a "religion of love," his works reflect the principal trends of thought and theory of the 20th century.

Louis Aragon, illegitimate child of Marguerite Toucas and the politician and former police prefect Louis Andrieux, was born in Paris on October 3, 1897, in the elegant 16th arrondissement (the "Beaux Quartier" of one of his novels), where his family ran a pension. After completing his studies at the Lycée Carnot in Paris in 1916 and earning a baccalaureate, he entered the army as a medical aide and later participated in the occupation of the Saar and the Rhineland. At Val-de-Grâce, a military

hospital, he met André Bréton, who was also serving in the medical corps and through whom Aragon was introduced to dadaism, an art cult rejecting all conventions. Aragon's first collection of 29 poems, *Feu de joie* (Bonfire, 1920), echoes the proposal of the dadaists to destroy all traditional institutions and values. *"Le monde à bas, je le bâtis plus beau"* (Down with the world, I will make it more beautiful), he cries in his poem "Secousse" (Shock), thereby echoing the absolute nihilism of the dadaists in a world destroyed by the horrors of war. Gradually the group that had filled the pages of the journal *Littérature,* edited by Bréton and Aragon, turned away from the sterility of dada and moved toward surrealism.

Aragon's first novel, *Anicet; ou, Le panorama* (Anicet, or the Panorama, 1921), is a picaresque story and a philosophical tale that attempts to define the revolt of the young generation and to denounce the hypocrisy of traditional society. His second collection of poems, *Le Mouvement perpétuel* (Perpetual Movement, 1926), includes poems written between 1920 and 1924 that describe the hypnotic trances cultivated by the surrealists in their effort to explore the world of dreams and the hidden recesses of the mind. Although many of the images in these poems may have been the product of automatic or trance-state writing, Aragon always stressed the importance of conscious artistry and used not only free verse, but also regular verse forms.

Aragon's most famous surrealist novel, *Le paysan de Paris* (Paris Peasant, 1926), is a celebration of Paris, in which he compares the love of the poet for his city with the emotions felt by a peasant for his land. The novel is a quest for surreality, for the unusual and mythical in the streets, parks, and cafés of Paris. Love features as the basis of a metaphysical, absolute state of mind, the confusion of the real and the marvelous, of consciousness and the unconscious. The cult of the mythical woman later became the cult of a real woman, his Russian-born wife, Elsa Triolet (sister-in-law of the poet Vladimir Mayakovsky), who became the source of and inspiration for most of his work after he met her in 1928.

Gradually the surrealists realized that a revolution in the field of ideas was impossible without a change in the social structure. In 1927 Aragon joined the French Communist Party, sharing its opposition to the Moroccan War of 1925, which was being waged by France against a colonial people seeking its freedom. Aragon's condemnation is expressed in the poem *"Front rouge"* (Red Front), in which he attacked the French establishment and called for the assassination of its leaders. As a result he was convicted in January 1932 of inciting soldiers to mutiny and of provocation to murder and was given a suspended five-year prison sentence. After a journey to the Soviet Union in 1932, Aragon's political commitment resulted in a break with the surrealists and increased support of the communists.

Aragon's novels in the 1930s and 1940s, *Persécuté persécuteur* (Persecuted Persecutor, 1931) and *Hourra l'Oural* (Hurrah, the Urals, 1934), were more political manifestos than poetical works. His massive fresco, the cycle of long novels *Le monde réel* (The Real World, 5 volumes, 1934–51), draws a vivid picture of the bourgeoisie from 1880 to the end of the 1920s; in this opus, Aragon sought to interweave the individual destinies of his characters with the broader lines of the Marxist interpretation of history.

From 1937 on he was codirector of the Communist newspaper *Ce Soir,* a post he occupied until the paper was suppressed after the Nazi-Soviet pact of 1939 by order of the French government. In the Spanish civil war (1936–39), Aragon fought against the Nationalists, and when the Germans occupied France in World War II, he was a member of the Resistance. Mobilized in 1939, he served as an auxiliary doctor with warrant officer rank. He helped build up the National Writers' Committee, a network of writers who contributed to Resistance journals. The six collections of poetry he wrote during the war years cover a wide range of emotions, from the first bitterness and distress of war to the joy of liberation. *Le crève-coeur* (Heartbreak) (1941), published in Canada, Algeria, and London, was the first collection that showed that the spirit of France was still alive under the German occupation. In the collection *Les yeux d'Elsa* (Elsa's Eyes, 1942) Aragon expressed his despair and fear that France would never be freed from the nightmare of German occupation, while at the same time identifying his love for Elsa with his love for France and exhorting all the French to fight against their oppressors. Further resistance collections were *Brocéliande* (1942), *Le musée Grévin* (1943), and *La Diane française* (1944).

In 1944, after the liberation of France, Aragon decided to reconcile and unite the patriotic poet and the revolutionary by working for the French Communist Party. He maintained that German imperialism had been replaced by the social domination of the bourgeoisie, and his collection *Le nouveau crève-coeur* (The New Heartbreak) targets the abuses of the bourgeoisie. In 1947 he became director of the revived *Ce Soir,* and in 1948 he was deprived of his civil rights for 10 years as a result of an editorial he wrote in that paper. In 1949 he joined the staff of the newspaper *Les lettres françaises* and became its director in 1953 (until 1972), after the demise of *Ce Soir.* In *Les Communistes* (The Communists) (1949–51) Aragon played with a new kind of novel, one that gave the effect of a series of newspaper reports, editorials, and Communist Party speeches. He was elected to membership on the Central Committee of the French Communist Party in 1950 and received the Lenin Peace Prize in 1957.

Aragon's ongoing support for Soviet leader Joseph Stalin (despite a deep personal crisis when he learned about Stalinist atrocities) met the disbelief and outrage of other writers such as Albert Camus, who criticized him in his *L'Homme révolté* (1951). After Stalin's death in 1953, Aragon celebrated the dictator in *Les lettres françaises* under the headline "What We Owe to Stalin" and later embarked upon his four-volume *Histoire parallèle* (Parallel History) of the United States and the USSR. He did not join with other French intellectuals in condemning the Soviet intervention in Hungary in 1956. It was the Soviet trial of the writers Andrey Sinyavsky and Yuli Daniel that finally brought him to speak out, and he condemned the Soviet-led 1968 invasion of Czechoslovakia, finally repudiating Soviet aggression and Stalinism, even though not communism. After 1960 his works combined the subjective idealism of his early surrealist works with the socialist realism of subsequent texts. In 1965 he began a new series of novels, including *La mise à mort* (Putting to Death, 1965), *Blanche; ou l'oubli* (Blanche; or Forgetfulness, 1967), and *Théâtre/Roman* (Theatre/Novel, 1974), as well as autobiographical poems, critical works, and the historical novel *La Semaine sainte* (Holy Week, A Novel, 1958). *Les yeux et la mémoire* (Eyes and Memory, 1954), a series of long autobiographical poems, combined political events with the expression of his love for Elsa. *Le roman inachevé* (The Unfinished Novel, 1956), which was influenced by Elsa's own novels, is an autobiographical poem turning his love of Elsa into a religion. The following collection of poems, *Les poètes* (1960), mingles poems on love and friendship with an essay on poetics, paying homage to the poets of the past. Death is ever present in the 1964 collection *Le voyage de Hollande* (1965), which was inspired by a trip to the Netherlands. In *Le fou d'Elsa* (Elsa's Madman), published in 1963, we find the highest expression of the poet's adoration of Elsa. After the death of his wife (June 16, 1970), Aragon came out as a bisexual, appearing at gay pride parades and publicizing his relations with the writer Jean Ristad. Aragon died on December 24, 1982, in Paris.

BIBLIOGRAPHY

Auster, Paul, ed. The *Random House Book of Twentieth Century French Poetry*. New York: Vintage Books, 1982.

Adereth, Maxwell. *Elsa Triolet and Louis Aragon: An Introduction to Their Interwoven Lives and Works*. Lewiston, N.Y.: Mellen Press, 1994.

Bauer, Jerry. *Louis Aragon*. Paris: Marval, 1997.

Becker, Lucille Frackman. *Louis Aragon*. New York: Twayne, 1971.

Caws, Mary Anne. *The Yale Anthology of Twentieth-Century French Poetry*. New Haven, Conn.: Yale University Press, 2004.

Heike Grundmann

"ARCHAIC TORSO OF APOLLO" RAINER MARIA RILKE (1908)

This sonnet by RAINER MARIA RILKE consists, in the original German, of an introductory line, a series of 12 lines, and a final line. The atypical form, wherein the sonnet itself is segmented in an unusual way, emphasizes the broken, ruined character of the sculpture that the speaker is examining. Paradoxically, the very fragmented nature of the torso is what lends it special strength, attractiveness, and beauty in that viewers will endlessly speculate about what the missing portions may have looked like.

In the initial line of the sonnet, the speaker bemoans that viewers will never know what the head of the statue looked like and will not experience the light of its eyes. Yet in the following lines, the speaker remarks that the power and physical beauty of the torso is emphasized by that lack—something that might not have occurred had the sculpture's head been intact. So the statue's destruction, instead of being a negative event, is seen as revealing beauty in unexpected portions of the stone from which the torso, from breast to loins, is carved. The speaker implies that those who look upon the ancient torso of Apollo cannot help noting that their appreciation of this artwork is an interchange of sorts; they learn from this experience to view things in a new way. In the poem's final line, the speaker addresses the reader directly as "you." Speculating that each viewer of the torso will feel, in turn, strangely gazed at by the (faceless) torso, the speaker declares: "You must change your life." The implication is that viewers henceforth will seek beauty that may be hidden by the dominant features of any object. The value of art reaches beyond that which catches the eye.

Joseph E. Becker

THE ARRIVANTS KAMAU BRATHWAITE (1988)

KAMAU BRATHWAITE's poetic trilogy, *The Arrivants* (1988), consists of three previously published long poems, *Rights of Passage* (1967), *Islands* (1968), and *Masks* (1969), each comprised of many constituent parts. Critic Pamela Mordecai labels the trilogy's structural elements in descending order as "books," further divided into "sequences," "statements," and "sections." Structurally, the three books suggest the transatlantic flow of bodies, ideas, and images that Brathwaite has called "tidalectic." Reversing the direction of New World settlement, the poem begins in the Caribbean, moves to Africa, then returns to the Caribbean, synthesizing preserved African myths and practices into a vision aware of the African elements embedded in Caribbean culture.

Brathwaite's use of "nation language" draws on the cadence, vocabulary, and diction of Caribbean speech, creating layers of internal rhymes, puns, and subtle cultural references. For example, in a characteristically deft play on the commonplace of the black Caribbean diaspora, that the islands' chief imports are Caribbeans, he observes "so the boy now nigratin' overseas" (50). A recurrent motif is the image of Caribbean islands as pebbles sprinkled across the sea: "The stone had skidded arc'd and bloomed into islands" (48). Brathwaite's rocks are a complex symbol, alternately fertile "Jewels" in the sea and at other moments barren stones from which no water can be wrung (205). Brathwaite sardonically observes the economic realities of life under plantation economics ("The rat / in the warehouse is as much king / as the sugar he plunders"), and he harshly criticizes the rise of tourism as a key industry in continuity with more candid forms of past colonial power: "Unrighteousness of Mammon / hotels for tourists rise on sites / of the old empire's promenades of cannon" (204, 216). In exploring African elements in the history and culture of Caribbean life, the poem represents a kind of answer, Brathwaite has remarked, to basic questions of self-scrutiny necessary for self-determination: "Where were we coming from, and why are we not going where we should!" (Dawes 34).

BIBLIOGRAPHY

Mordecai, Pamela. "Images for Creativity and the Art of Writing in *The Arrivants.*" *For the Geography of a Soul: Emerging Perspectives on Kamau Brathwaite.* Edited by Timothy J. Reiss. Trenton, N.J., 21–42. Africa World Press, 2001.

Morris, Mervyn. "Overlapping Journeys: *The Arrivants.*" *The Art of Kamau Brathwaite.* Edited by Stewart Brown, 117–131. Mid Glamorgan: Poetry Wales Press, 1995.

Rohlehr, Gordon. *Pathfinder: Black Awakening in* The Arrivants *of Edward Kamau Brathwaite.* Tunapuna, Trinidad: Gordon Rohlehr, 1981.

Williams, Emily. *The Critical Response to Kamau Brathwaite.* Westport, Conn.: Greenwood Press, 2004.

Alex Feerst

"ARS POETICA" VICENTE HUIDOBRO (1916)

Found in the 1916 volume *El espejo de agua* (The Mirror of Water), *"Arte poética"* ("Ars Poetica") expresses both VICENTE HUIDOBRO's artistic vision and his concept of the poet. It is one of his best-known shorter poems. Founder of his own literary movement, creationism, Huidobro imbued the poet with radical tendencies and tremendous power. *"Que el verso sea como una llave / Que abra mil puertas"* (Let poetry be like a key / Opening a thousand doors), Huidobro says in the opening lines of *"Arte poética."* Poetry, Huidobro suggests in keeping with his own philosophies, should be generative and exploratory, the key not to the known, but to the unknown. He advises the poet to seek out new worlds, but to exercise caution; poetry has the ability to create—and to kill. Thus, poetry is possessed of real power: not just the power of the imagination, but the power to transform reality.

Huidobro, however, is intent on shifting the location of reality. Recognizing that his is a generation of "nervios," or nerves, Huidobro emphasizes in contrast a mental or spiritual strength: *"El vigor verdadero / Reside en la cabeza"* (True vigor / Resides in the head.). The age of the purely physical muscle, he claims, is dead: *"El músculo cuelga, / Como recuerdo, en los museos"* (The muscle hangs, / Like a memory, in museums). The poet is the logical inheritor of Huidobro's vision of power. Possessed of a kind of ultimate mental strength or vigor, the poet has the ability not only to explore experience, but to create it. Only in the poet's imaginative power, Huidobro says, are all things possible: *"Sólo para nosotros / Viven todas las cosas bajo el Sol"* (For us alone / Do all things live beneath the Sun).

The poem's last line, however, is its most telling. In words perfectly evocative of Huidobro's concept of a poet, he claims, *"El poeta es un pequeño Dios"* (The poet is a little God). With supreme confidence, Huidobro elevates the poet to godlike status as both a creator and a destroyer, defining him or her as a shaper of both interior and exterior reality.

BIBLIOGRAPHY

The Selected Poetry of Vicente Huidobro. Translated by Stephen Fredman and David M. Guss. New York: New Directions, 1981.

Winter Elliott

"ARS POETICA" PABLO NERUDA (1933)

"Ars Poetica" is one of PABLO NERUDA's earliest significant poems and appears in the first volume of *Residencia en la Tierra* (Residence on Earth). He wrote it when he was in his late twenties, had just taken up the post of consul in an unfamiliar land, and was struggling to redefine his voice in the wake of *Veinte poemas de amor y una canción desperada's* immense success. He paints a self-portrait of a man caught between the official burdens of a bureaucrat and the temptations of a poet, "between shadow and space, between harnesses and maidens" (l. 1). Like a martyr kneeling before his god, the poet lays himself before the altar of Art, and the poem becomes a litany of humiliations—he is "like a bell gone a bit hoarse" (l. 11)—and of deprivations: "Alas, for every drink of invisible water I swallow drowsily . . . I feel the same missing thirst" (ll. 5, 7).

But are these injuries just self-inflicted forgery? The sudden entrance of truth as "the wind that lashes my chest" (l. 16) suggests that these previous sufferings were trivial distractions, a way for the poet to escape his greater, more exhaustive duties: New experiences and "the noise of a day burning with sacrifice / demand what there is in me of the prophetic" (ll. 18–19). The poem offers no resolution to the poet's plight, only "ceaseless movement"; in an explicit nod to the "Ars Poetica" tradition, Neruda reflects this psychic state on the page by using the extraordinary structure of a single sentence enjambed over 21 lines of free verse.

An older Neruda rejected the self-centered and depressed abstraction of *Residencia en la Tierra*. Compare the complaint "there's an odor of clothes on the floor, and an absence of flowers" (l. 14) to his eventual proclamations that poetry should be "impure as old clothes, as a body, with its food stains and its shame." Even within this poem, though, there are stirrings of a forthcoming critical self-consciousness, as in the parenthetical aside that immediately follows line 14: "—or maybe somehow a little less melancholic—" (l. 15). As an "Ars Poetica," the poem addresses not only the art of poems being written, but also the situation of a poet poised at the cusp of what he will come to write. Though, as he says, for now "there is a swarm of objects that call without being answered" (l. 20), in later years the "bewildered man" would answer their call, and Neruda would be revived by the song of everyday objects, notably in his *Odas elementales*. He would find new purpose in writing of the struggles of the people, not of the poet.

Sandra Beasley

ARTAUD, ANTONIN (1896–1948)

Genius, madman, or both? This is the question that surrounds Antonin Artaud's life and work. The most significant contribution Artaud made to modern literature was his willingness to explore his own psyche, to expose his total existence in his writing. It is impossible to separate Artaud the man from his works, whether they are the insights of genius or the ravings from a madhouse. Artaud is best known for his influence on modern theater, creating "theater of cruelty," experimenting in staging, and revolutionizing dramatic theory. Artaud was also an actor, director, playwright, and journalist. Along with his interest in theater, poetry provided a creative outlet for Artaud from childhood to death. The poems he wrote during the last three years of his life are considered some of his best work.

That Artaud survived to adulthood is remarkable in itself. His father, also Antonin, and his mother, Euphrasia, were affluent citizens of Marseilles, France. Four of the nine Artaud children were stillborn and two more died in childhood. Antonin was born in 1896 and at five contracted spinal meningitis. This disease had no cure, but after a long struggle including a comatose period, a severely weakened Antonin survived. Antonin's father was largely uninterested in his children, so the boy was reared in a household of women who lavished their attention on him. Because of his physical and mental illness, Artaud's schooling was haphazard at best. The young Antonin was deeply attached to his devout Catholic mother and sister and attended Catholic school at the Collège du Sacré Coeur in Marseilles. For a brief period he even considered becoming a priest. He later denounced God and the repression that he felt was part of organized religion, and still later claimed to be Christ. These early experiences may have resulted in Artaud's lifelong ambivalence toward religion and sexuality.

When Artaud was 19, he began to suffer severe headaches and bodily pain and at times had difficulty speaking clearly, delayed effects of his meningitis. Within a few months, he started to use laudanum for pain and developed an addiction that lasted the remainder of his life. In 1916 he joined the army but was discharged within a few months because of his addiction and mental instability. Shortly thereafter, Artaud committed himself to a sanatorium in Switzerland, where he stayed for two years.

At 24 and still under psychiatric care, Artaud decided to seek his fortune in Paris. Here, as a result of his study with actor and director Charles Dullin, he became intensely involved in theater. He found a variety of jobs as set and costume designer and as stage actor. Soon he also appeared in a number of films. Along with Roger Vitrac and Robert Aron, Artaud founded the Théâtre Alfred Jarry in 1927 to produce experimental and progressive works.

When Artaud first came to Paris, his psychiatrist Édouard Toulouse recognized Artaud's troubled genius and suggested he compose poetry as a means of therapy. Toulouse printed many of these poems in a small literary magazine he published. The doctor also suggested readings and discussed these with Artaud and introduced him to members of Parisian literary circles. Artaud also published several of his poems in other French literary magazines. Then he took a selection of his poems to noted editor and critic Jacques Rivière, who, although he rejected the poems, recognized the genius in Artaud. The two men began a correspondence in which Artaud opened himself completely to the other man, discussing his mental torment, creative theory, fantasies, and hopes. These remarkable letters were published in Rivière's *Nouvelle revue française* in September 1924. The letters were published in a separate volume in 1927.

In 1937 Artaud was lecturing in Brussels when he had a complete breakdown and began screaming at his audience. That same year, his famed *Théâtre et son double* (The Theater and Its Double) was published to great critical success. He also visited Ireland on a personal religious quest. From there, when he began to claim that he was Jesus Christ, he was sent back to France in a straitjacket. He spent the next nine years in sanatoriums where he was diagnosed as a schizophrenic and received electric shock treatments at least three times. During these years Artaud continued to write, especially poetry. When he was released from the mental hospital after the end of World War II, Artaud's admirers staged a benefit performance and auction to help provide his financial support. In Paris he secured a room at a private clinic where he wrote and drew continuously. He carried notebooks in which to write as he walked through Paris. He wrote and drew on the walls of his room. He would nail his poems to posts and trees. And most of all, he suffered

from his addiction and from his delusions and fantasies. In 1948, still living in the private clinic, Artaud died from cancer.

If one has read Antonin Artaud, the style and character of his work is easily recognizable, yet difficult to define. In spite of the diversity of genre and topic, there is a strong consistency in the writing. Dark humor, startling images, experimentation in form, clearly autobiographical poetry exploring the author's consciousness, the juxtaposition of disparate images and ideas, and the transcendent power to draw the reader into the work are all present in Artaud's poetry. Some of these works reveal Artaud questioning his own madness or sanity, but all expose an author in deep self-reflection on his own life's events. And so the question remains, Did Artaud's madness enhance or hamper his genius? Did he have a greater grasp of the turmoil of the post–World War I world because of his own inner turmoil? What would his genius have been without the insanity? Readers can only appreciate the genius and pity the madness of a writer so terrifyingly brilliant.

BIBLIOGRAPHY

Artaud, Antonin. *Artaud Anthology*. Edited by Jack Hirschman. San Francisco: City Lights Books, 1965.

————. *Antonin Artaud: Four Texts*. Translated by Clayton Eshleman and Norman Glass. Los Angeles: Panjandrum Books, 1982.

————. *Antonin Artaud: Selected Writings*. Edited by Susan Sontag. Translated by Helen Weaver. New York: Farrar, Straus and Giroux, 1976.

————. *Collected Works*. 4 vols. Translated by Victor Corti. London: Calder and Boyars 1968–1975.

————. *Correspondance avec Jacques Rivière. Nouvelle Revue Française,* 1927. Republished as *Artaud-Rivière Correspondence* in journal *Exodus,* 1960.

————. *L'Art et la mort.* Paris: Denoel, 1929. Published as "Art and Death" in *Antonin Artaud: Selected Writings.* Berkeley: University of California Press, 1988.

————. *Le Pèse-nerfs.* In the collection *Pour vos beau yeux* (Paris: Gallimard, 1925); published with *Fragments d'un journal d'enfer,* Cahiers du Sud (Marseilles), 1927; published as "The Nerve Meter" and "Fragments of a Diary of Hell" in *Antonin Artaud: Selected Writings.*

————. *L'ombilic des limbes. Nouvelle Revue Française,* 1925. Published as "The Umbilicus of Limbo" in *Antonin Artaud:*

Selected Writings. Edited by Susan Sontag. New York: Farrar, Straus and Giroux, 1976.

———. *Tric-trac du ciel*. Paris: Galerie Simon, 1923.

Jean Hamm

"AT A FUNERAL" Dennis Brutus (1963) As a highly mannered poem that combines lavish figurative language with precisely recorded images to protest the apartheid system in South Africa, "At a Funeral" provides an excellent example of Dennis Brutus's early poetry. Dedicated to Valencia Majombozi, a young African doctor who died an untimely death, it begins as an elegy for lost hopes and ends as a defiant call to arms. "At a Funeral" is neatly divided into two stanzas made up of six loosely rhymed lines of varying length. The first stanza sets the scene for the poem by describing the funeral as a mass rallying point. The political significance of this event is immediately made clear through reference to "Black, green and gold" (l. 1), the colors of the African National Congress (ANC). Observing the ministrations of the nurses dressed like nuns, the speaker acknowledges the martyred status of the deceased. But he seems deeply ambivalent about this sacrifice, as he refers to the spectacle of the funeral as a "hollow panoply" (l. 5). Moving beyond the immediate scene of the funeral, the second stanza calls on "powers tombed in dirt" (l. 10), attempting not only to resurrect those who have already fallen in the struggle against oppression but also to revivify the spirit of freedom that inspired them. According to the speaker, this spirit is held in check by "carrion books of birth" (l. 8), perhaps alluding to the pass books that black South Africans were required to carry at all times and that governed their movements. Tyranny takes the place of Death here to prepare "narrow cells of pain, defeat and dearth" (l. 11), as much a reference to government housing as to burial chambers. Such personification points to the influence of 17th-century metaphysical poetry on Brutus as a young poet. Certainly, "At a Funeral" could be categorized with Claude McKay's "If We Must Die" as a protest poem that draws heavily on the English poetic tradition. At the same time, of course, it is enlivened by a wealth of journalistic details that make clear its South African birthright. "At a Funeral" originally appeared in *Sirens, Knuckles, Boots* (1963), Brutus's first volume of poetry. It was also included in *A Simple Lust* (1973), a compilation of the poet's earliest work. Since then, the poem has been widely anthologized, most recently in the fourth edition of Penguin's *Modern African Poetry* (1998), edited by Gerald Moore and Ulli Beier.

BIBLIOGRAPHY

Brutus, Dennis. *A Simple Lust: Collected Poems of South African Jail and Exile including "Letters to Martha."* London: Heinemann, 1973.

———. *Sirens, Knuckles, Boots*. Ibadan, Nigeria: Mbari Productions, 1963.

Moore, Gerald, and Ulli Beier, eds. *Modern African Poetry*. 4th ed. London: Penguin, 1998.

Alexander B. McKee

"AUTUMN DAY" Rainer Maria Rilke (1902) Rainer Maria Rilke composed "Autumn Day" in fall 1902. The poem is a meditative lyric on the passing of time and the seasons—an image underscored by the rhyme scheme of the poem (a-b-a—c-d-d-c—e-f-f-e-f). The irregularities of the meter and rhythms, however, suggest that a human being's experience of time and its seasonal cycles is subject to unexpected frustration. In the first stanza the speaker addresses the Lord ("Herr"), indicating relief that the long summer is over, that the seasonal shadows are growing longer on the sundials, and that the autumn wind is beginning to blow. The second stanza asks the Lord to allow the seasonal weather to hold on a bit longer—enough for the harvest of the wine grapes to be completed (and this stanza, which asks for "two more southerly days," is one line longer than the first). The third stanza indicates that the time for outdoor activities, such as house building, is at an end when the solitary practices of winter begin—letter writing and melancholy wandering in the blustery streets. A certain existential atmosphere is evident in the poem: The speaker seems world-weary, thankful that summer and its fullness are over, but not particularly looking forward to winter and its long and lonely emptiness (the feeling of extended loneliness is mirrored in this stanza's augmented size). Overall the rhyme scheme and irregular stanza length parallel the poem's content by lending an air of uncertainty to the speaker's somber mood and thoughts—summer was long ("the summer was immense"), but will winter seem longer? The melancholy reflections seem to be about human life in general.

Joseph E. Becker

"AUTUMN MANEUVER" INGEBORG BACHMANN (1953)

In her first collection, *Die gestundete Zeit* (Mortgaged Time, in *In the Storm of Roses*), INGEBORG BACHMANN grapples with the lingering effects of fascism after World War II. "Autumn Maneuver" ("Herbstmanöver") is one of the best illustrations of the theme of this volume, as its title suggests military tactics as well as images of movement, particularly that of seasonal progressions. The combination of the image of the natural world's progression toward winter with that of the human activity of warfare suggests an "apocalyptic final winter" (Boa 272). In such an apocalyptic vision, the urgency of Bachmann's poem becomes evident. The first line of the poem, "I don't say: that was before," clearly expresses the speaker's inability to separate the atrocities of the recent past from the actions one takes in the present. In the postwar period there is no escaping recent history, and even "flight to the South, / where the birds fly, won't help us."

The second stanza continues the poem's theme of inability to "spare yourself an unpleasant sight," to forget the destruction that resulted from war. The references to newspapers, refugees, and murderers all evoke specifically human phenomena and elicit emotional responses to the death and dislocation inherent in war. These images, however, are mingled with "myriads / of ice-flows," a natural image that seems to herald a "new ice-age" (Boa 272). In the apocalyptic vision of both human and natural events, Bachmann reveals that, though in the postwar period "there is peace," one is unable to avoid "the joyless dying of leaves" that heralds autumn.

Similarly, Bachmann's poem argues that one cannot ignore the human "beggar" and those who have "slam[med] the door in his face." This image of the beggar in "Autumn Maneuver" evokes the biblical tale in the book of Hebrews of an angel disguised as a destitute who is repeatedly turned away from townspeople's doors when he seeks shelter. The biblical passage serves as a moral reminder of human beings' responsibility toward one another; similarly, Bachmann's reference to the beggar can be understood as an exhortation for postwar responsibility for human death and in some sense for the death of humanity itself.

BIBLIOGRAPHY

Bachmann, Ingeborg. *In the Storm of Roses: Selected Poems.* Edited and translated by Mark Anderson. Princeton, N.J.: Princeton University Press, 1986.
Boa, Elizabeth. "Reading Ingeborg Bachmann." *Postwar Women's Writing in German,* edited by Chris Weedon. Providence: Berghahn Books, 1997.

Jennifer Perrine

AWOONOR, KOFI NYIDEVU (1935–)

Kofi Awoonor—poet, novelist, diplomat, and cultural critic—was born in 1935 in Wheta, Gold Coast (now Ghana), of Ewe parentage. His grandmother was a village dirge singer, and this may have influenced the poet's earliest creative works, among them "The WEAVER BIRD," arguably his most famous lament. The dirge, an oral performance that employs an insistent beat and emphatic repetitions of plaintive phrases of mournful wretchedness, becomes in Awoonor's hands the poetic genre most appropriate for describing postcolonial Africa and the fate of Africans dislocated from their birthplace by historical forces. Much of Awoonor's early work expresses in chantlike rhythms his sorrow that "Returning is not possible / And going forward is a great difficulty" because "The affairs of this world are like the chameleon faeces / Into which I have stepped" and that cannot be cleaned off ("Songs of Sorrow"). In "Songs of Sorrow," for instance, the speaker laments: "I have no sons to fire the gun when I die / And no daughters to wail when I close my mouth" . . . "I have no kin and no brother . . . And strangers walk over our portion."

Awoonor (formerly George Awoonor-Williams) was educated in Ghana, London, and New York. A self-described socialist and strong supporter of Kwame Nkrumah, Awoonor fled Ghana in 1966 when Nkrumah, Ghana's first president, was overthrown by a military coup d'état (supported by the U.S. CIA). Awoonor in due course enrolled in a doctoral program in literature at the State University of New York and earned a Ph.D. there in 1972. His dissertation, published in 1975 as *The Breast of the Earth: A Survey of the History, Culture and Literature of Africa South of the Sahara,* launched him as a respected reviewer of African literature; but in December of that year, he was arrested on the campus of Cape Coast University, just west of Accra, Ghana, and jailed at the Ussher Fort Prison for assisting a fugitive and holding subversive political views, an experience he relates in *The House by the Sea* (1978) and *Until the Morning After* (1987). His career as a diplomat began when he became Ghana's ambassador to Brazil in 1985 and, after that, to Cuba in 1989. From 1990 to 1994, Awoonor represented Ghana as its ambassador to the United Nations, where he joined collective efforts underway there to eradicate South African apartheid. Awoonor has since then served as president of the African Literature Association (1998–99). He received the National Book Council Award (for poetry) in 2001.

BIBLIOGRAPHY

Awoonor, Kofi. *Rediscovery and Other Poems.* Ibadan, Nigeria: Mbari, 1964.
————. *Night of My Blood.* Garden City, N.Y.: Doubleday, 1971.
————. *The House by the Sea.* Greenfield Center, N.Y.: Greenfield Review Press, 1978.
————. *Until the Morning After: Collected Poems.* Greenfield Center, N.Y.: Greenfield Review Press, 1987.
————. *Praise Song for the Land: Poems of Hope and Love and Care.* Accra, Ghana: Sub-Saharan Publishers, 2002.

R. Victoria Arana

B

"BABI YAR" YEVGENY YEVTUSHENKO (1961) This poem begins with the observation that no marker preserves the memory of the Jews and others whom the Germans killed at Babi Yar, a ravine outside the Ukrainian capital of Kiev, on September 29, 1941. YEVTUSHENKO's words (and the part of Dmitry Shostakovich's Symphony no. 13 based on them) have become that memorial. The poem briefly describes in plain yet evocative language the landscape around the site but centers on the speaker's identification with the Jews, who have suffered collectively and individually throughout history. The early part of the poem refers to the Jews' flight from Egypt, the Passover, which in Russian Orthodox theology is integral to humankind's salvation history, and to the Crucifixion, which suggests a link between Jewish and Christian suffering as well as an echo of VLADIMIR MAYAKOVSKY's view of the artist as a Christ-like sufferer. Other significant allusions name individual Jews—Alfred Dreyfus and Anne Frank—who are symbols of the world's injustice to the Jews. This section of the poem also mentions a 1905 pogrom at Białystok, Poland, that typified attacks on the Jews in czarist Russia, but Babi Yar was different: The Jews defended themselves, and a young Russian student joined them and was killed. The speaker of the poem here identifies with an anonymous Jew, just as he has identified with Captain Alfred Dreyfus, scandalously convicted of treason, Anne Frank, and all the unnamed people who were shot at Babi Yar. He then addresses the greater part of the Russian people, whom he knows to be better than the anti-Semitic minority and who tarnish Russian's reputation. They, he says, embrace the brotherhood of man. The poem makes this point more explicitly at the end with an allusion to the anthem The Internationale, which also brings to mind Lenin's condemnation, in a pamphlet, of the Białystok pogrom. Anne Frank is also a symbol of hope and love, and the imagery in the poem changes to that of renewal as the poem evokes the sounds of spring coming to a place where the trees stand like harsh judges to condemn the anti-Semites, as the Philistines earlier in the poem condemned the Jews. The speaker is aware of the silent screams that fill Babi Yar, and the poem gives voice to the pain that permeates it and to the life of the Jewish people, as well as to the hope that others will follow his example: Even though no Jewish blood mixes with his Russian blood, he is nevertheless an idealist like the Russian student in Białystok and hence the representative of all that is truly Russian.

BIBLIOGRAPHY

Mass, Francis. *A History of Russian Music from Kamarinskaya to Babi Yar*. Translated by Arnold J. and Erica Pomerans. Berkeley: University of California Press, 2002.

Yevtushenko, Yevgeny. "Babi Yar." Translated by George Reavey. *Modern European Poetry*, edited by Willis Barnstone, 450–452. Toronto and New York: Bantam Books, 1966.

Karen Rae Keck

BACHMANN, INGEBORG (1926–1973)

After publishing just two volumes of poetry, Ingeborg Bachmann was the recipient of much critical acclaim both in her native Austria and abroad during her short career as a poet. Despite the accolades, after the publication of her second collection Bachmann found poetry increasingly problematic, and by 1967 she had turned from poetry altogether in favor of other genres. While Bachmann completed several radio plays and short story collections as well as a novel, she is perhaps still best known for her allusive lyrical poems, which confronted the legacy of Nazism and fascism in post–World War II Europe.

Born on June 25, 1926, in Klagenfurt, Austria, Bachmann was keenly aware of the complexity of her Austrian heritage, which enabled her to write in German but bestowed on her a sense of being outside the traditions of German literature. Bachmann's poetry was deeply influenced by her doctoral study in philosophy at the University of Vienna from 1946 to 1950, where she encountered the work of Ludwig Wittgenstein. Her first volume of poetry, *Die gestundete Zeit* (Mortgaged Time), published in 1953, combines this philosophical interest with her earlier sense of national and linguistic exclusion to create a poetry that constantly questions the limitations of language as it critiques the remains of Germany's Nazi past. The poems in this collection, including "AUTUMN MANEUVER," stress that fascism did not disappear with the end of World War II; rather, as she writes in "Every Day," "War is no longer declared, / only continued."

Later in 1953 Bachmann was awarded the prestigious Group 47 prize and moved to Italy, where she remained until 1957. Living in a Mediterranean landscape profoundly influenced her second collection, *Anrufung des Großen Bären* (Invocation of the Great Bear), published in 1956. The images of this volume frequently draw on juxtapositions between the cold, wooded atmosphere of her native Austria and the light, vivacity, and beauty of her newly adopted home, to suggest Bachmann's literary search for hope amid the destruction of war.

Bachmann continued to live outside Austria, periodically residing in Munich, Zurich, and Berlin, but remaining primarily in Rome. While she published no more poetry collections, for several years she continued to write poetry sporadically, becoming increasingly frustrated by critical receptions that lauded the aesthetics of her poems while ignoring their moral and philosophical import. By 1968, when her native country awarded her the Great Austrian State Prize, she had abandoned poetry's "plotted word operas" ("No Delicacies"), choosing other genres that she felt would allow access to a wider audience and could better achieve her social and political ends. Bachmann died on October 17, 1973, after accidentally having set fire to herself in her Rome apartment several weeks earlier.

BIBLIOGRAPHY

Achberger, Karen R. *Understanding Ingeborg Bachmann.* Columbia: University of South Carolina Press, 1995.

Bachmann, Ingeborg. *In the Storm of Roses: Selected Poems.* Edited and translated by Mark Anderson. Princeton, N.J.: Princeton University Press, 1986. (This volume includes *Mortgaged Time* and *Invocation of the Great Bear*.)

Brokoph-Mauch, Gudrun. *Thunder Rumbling at My Heels: Tracing Ingeborg Bachmann.* Riverside, Calif.: Ariadne Press, 1998.

Jennifer Perrine

"BACKBONE FLUTE, THE" VLADIMIR MAYAKOVSKY (1915)

Written shortly after MAYAKOVSKY's first meeting with Lily Brik in 1915, this poem takes its tone from Catullus's "I love, and I hate" and its mood from the gothic tales of E. T. A. Hoffmann, to whom the poem alludes in its first stanza. The composition has four parts, a prologue and three stanzas, each of which communicates the agony the speaker endures for love of this fiend in womanly shape. In addition to foreshadowing the despair expressed in the poem, the prologue expresses in flamboyant words and images Mayakovsky's sense that his poetry sprang from the torments of his body: In a macabre gesture he offers to the complacent reader a skull-full of verse, rather like the skull Byron used as a wine glass, and adds that he plays on the flute of his backbone. Other images of verse making also hint at the difficulty of this task: He must shape his words like a jeweler cutting a diamond. Furthermore, writing his poem is like drinking poison, and the words of the poem crucify him. The prologue also speaks of the joy that comes from weddings, a joy seemingly at odds with the pain the ensnared lover fights throughout the poem but cannot conquer. His language at times sounds like that of the Psalms that begin with a sense of abandonment, but the poet finds no relief or reassurance in human or divine love. He speculates that God, whom he views as an inquisitor, has created this she-devil as punishment for his failure to believe, and he begs for any penalty but the one he has received. He describes himself as an apostle not of God but of his beloved, and as her disciple, he, who was accustomed to gladness, must suffer and travel the world, like the Wandering Jew, without ever escaping her attraction and the pain it brings him. He compares his defeated helplessness to that of Napoléon on St. Helena, and he compares her, a married woman, to unattainable women, Gretchen in *Faust* and Violetta in *La Traviata*. In the prologue's statement that he may end his life with a bullet, critics find a hint of Mayakovsky's eventual suicide; however, this image is consonant with later references in this poem to war and with the crazed desperation he expresses as he considers joining the army in the hope that death will end the suffering he endures for the sake of this red-haired, painted woman.

BIBLIOGRAPHY

Brown, Edward J. *Mayakovsky: A Poet in the Revolution.* Princeton, N.J.: Princeton University Press, 1973.

Charters, Ann, and Samuel Charters. *I Love: The Story of Vladimir Mayakovsky and Lily Brik.* New York: Farrar, Straus and Giroux, 1979.

Liukkonen, Petri. "Vladimir Mayakovsky." *Pegasos* (1999). Available online. URL: http://www.kirjasto.sci.fi/ majakovs.htm. Accessed on April 21, 2007.

Mayakosky, Vladimir. *The Bedbug and Selected Poetry.* Edited by Patricia Davis, translated by Max Hayward and George Reavey. Bloomington: Indiana University Press, 1960.

Terras, Victor. *Vladimir Mayakovsky.* Boston: Twayne, 1983.

Karen Rae Keck

"BANALATA SEN" JIBANANANDA DAS (1935)

JIBANANANDA DAS's famous love poem "Banalata Sen" was first published in the journal *Kavita* (Poetry) in 1935 and later anthologized in a 1942 collection to which it gave its name. It is widely regarded as one of Das's finest poems and is certainly his most popular work. Of great historical expanse, the poem conjures up the splendor of classical antiquity through an invocation of the names of the august Indian kings Vimbisar and Asok and the fabled cities of Vidarbha, Vidisa, and Sravasti. From such grandiosity the poet returns with each refrain to the ordinariness of Banalata Sen, a woman from Natore, a small town in the Indian state of Bengal. Such down-scaling parallels the movement from distinguished kings such as Asok to the unknown Banalata Sen and from past millennia to the present moment and a much-diminished modern world.

Like its historical complement, the geography of the narrator's travels is also cast on the grandest possible scale, covering the Indian subcontinent from cities in north and central India, to the seas in the south, and finally, to Bengal in the east. For a long time critics assumed that "Malay Sea," in the first stanza, was a reference to the waters around the Malay Peninsula in Southeast Asia, so that the poet somewhat inexplicably had in this single case referred outside the Indian subcontinent. However, a recent study by Clinton Seely argues convincingly that "Malay" actually refers to the Malabar region, or the southwestern coast of India, so that both "Malay Sea" and "Ceylon waters" refer to the southern seas surrounding the Indian subcontinent. (Ceylon is present-day Sri Lanka). Thus does the poet suggest that all of Indian history and geography somehow culminate in the beauty of a girl from a nondescript village.

The reference to Banalata Sen recurs in the last line of each stanza of the poem. She is presented with few specifics beyond her full name, place of origin, and some details of her person—her face and dark hair, both of which evoke past perfection for the narrator, and her eyes. She speaks in no elevated rhetoric, but simply greets the narrator with the rather quotidian "Where were you so long?" It is an expression of Das's modernism that he integrates in this way Banalata Sen's colloquial speech with the narrator's more poetic language.

"Banalata Sen" is an 18-line poem divided into three sestets. It is composed in the Bengali *payar* meter, and the rhyme scheme is *ababcc / dedecc / fgfgcc,* so that the last line of each sestet ends with "Banalata Sen." Opulent and sensuous imagery creates scenic spaces: dark nights over ancient cities, a mariner lost in stormy seas, islands redolent of cinnamon, and so on. Surprising metaphors characterize Das's poetry, and "Banalata Sen" is no exception. For instance, the last line of the second stanza makes an unconventional comparison between a woman's eyes and a bird's nest. Still, the simile is perhaps intelligible if we shift from a literal reading of visual resemblance to a more philosophical one. A "nest," as a home for a bird at the end of the day, suggests shelter and repose. Similarly, Banalata Sen, in the tired narrator's mind, promises tranquility; and if her soul is mirrored in her eyes, as the saying goes, the simile no longer seems quite so strange. Both a bird's nest and her eyes come to symbolize restfulness. The phrases "the sound of dew" or the "scent of sunlight," which occur in the third stanza, combine two different sense perceptions and thus also form one of Das's more favored figures of speech, synesthesia. Repeated references to darkness evoke a general melancholy throughout the poem, but it ends on a note of hope, ripe with the assurance of rest and the companionship of Banalata Sen.

BIBLIOGRAPHY

Chaudhuri, Sukanta. "Introduction." *A Certain Sense: Poems by Jibanananda Das.* Translated by various, edited by Sukanta Chaudhuri. New Delhi: Sahitya Akademi, 1998.

Seely, Clinton B. *A Poet Apart: A Literary Biography of the Bengali Poet Jibanananda Das.* Newark: University of Delaware Press, 1990.

Seely, Clinton. "Shifting Seas & 'Banalata Sen.'" Paper presented at the Centre for Studies in the Social Sciences, Kolkata, and Bangiya Sahitya Parishat (Bengal Council of Literature), Kolkata, 2004.

Debali Mookerjea-Leonard

BARAHENI, REZA (1935–)

Reza Baraheni is an important, exiled Iranian poet and intellectual. He is best known for his dissident political writing (incisive critiques of Iranian political repression) and austere and hard-hitting poetry. He is also internationally recognized as a novelist, prolific essayist, cultural critic, and professor of comparative literature. He has written in many languages and published over 55 books, including *The Crowned Cannibals: Writings on Repression in Iran,* a collection of prose and poetry; *Les Saisons en Enfer du Jeune Ayyaz* (translated into English by Carter Harrison Bryant as The Infernal Days of Aqa-ye Ayaz), a novel; and *GOD'S SHADOW: PRISON POEMS* on Baraheni's imprisonment and torture in Tehran in 1973, a collection originally written in Iranian that Baraheni himself translated into English.

The son of Mohammad-Taghi (a worker) and Zahrasoltan Baraheni, Baraheni was born on April 7, 1935, in Tabriz, one of the most ancient urban centers of the world, a sprawling and pretty city nestled between mountains in a fertile valley in the northwestern part of Iran. His family, of Azeri (not Persian) ethnicity, is Muslim.

When he was a child the Iranian government was taken over by Persian ethnics who ruled that all education was henceforward to take place in Farsi (the language of the Persian group). Baraheni's Azeri language, kin to Turkish, was expressly forbidden. Baraheni tells of mortifying punishment he suffered as a child, forced by his teacher to lick the words off the page that he had written in Turkish, the only language he knew how to write, and laughed at by the children of Farsi-speaking government officials. It was only the first of a series of abuses he suffered for asserting his cultural heritage in the land of his birth. This shaped his conviction to fight, whenever necessary, for freedom of speech and artistic expression.

Baraheni earned a B.A. from the University of Tabriz in 1957. He married Angela Marangozidi in 1959, when he was 24, and earned a Ph.D. from the University of Istanbul in 1960. From 1961 until 1974 he was a member of the faculty of the University of Tehran, rising through the ranks to associate professor of English literature and serving for three years as dean of students (1965–68). In 1966 he divorced his first wife; five years later he married Sanaz Sihhati, a teacher. During his tenure at the University of Tehran, he took leaves of absence to accept prestigious visiting professorships abroad. He held the post of distinguished visiting professor at the University of Cairo in 1971; he was visiting associate professor at the University of Texas at Austin in 1972 and at the University of Utah in 1973. When he returned to Iran in 1973, he was arrested, detained for 102 days by SAVAK, the secret police, and severely tortured for his published analyses of the regime's political oppression of Iran's huge population of ethnic minorities.

In 1974 he escaped from Iran and was offered a position as poet in residence by the University of Iowa—Iowa City. The following year he was named visiting professor of creative writing at the University of Indiana at Bloomington. In 1997 he moved to Bard College in New York State and, from 1977 to 1979, taught at the University of Maryland in Baltimore. After the Islamic revolution in Iran that toppled the shah, Baraheni returned to the University of Tehran as a professor of English and comparative literature. He was twice rearrested (in fall 1981 and winter 1982) and tortured by the secret police of the Islamic Republic of Iran for speaking out about conditions of life in Iran under the rule of the ayatollahs. When he was released, he was barred from teaching at the university but responded to the gag order by founding an underground fiction and poetry workshop in Tehran, which he ran out of his basement for over a decade until he managed once again to escape the country. He was welcomed by Canada and offered a visiting professorship at the University of Toronto (for 1997), followed by an appointment as writer-in-exile at the University of Toronto's Massey College (1997–98). Since then he has acquired tenure and a full professorship there, as well as Canadian citizenship. In his course in comparative literature, he features the poetry of JORGE LUIS BORGES and others, and compares and contrasts the experiments of early MODERNISM to present-day exilic literature.

Baraheni is a prolific translator, working in Farsi, Arabic, Turkish, English, and French. His scores of renditions into Persian include many classics of world literature, e.g., Shakespeare's *Richard III* and the poetry of FAIZ AHMED FAIZ (from its original Urdu). Baraheni's works have been translated into Arabic, Armenian, French, German, Polish, Russian, Spanish, and Turkish.

BIBLIOGRAPHY

Baraheni, Reza. *God's Shadow: Prison Poems.* Bloomington: Indiana University Press, 1976.

R. Victoria Arana

"BARBARITY" AIMÉ CÉSAIRE (1947)

Initially one might read the opening line of this four-stanza poem as a reference to AIMÉ CÉSAIRE's own recourse to barbarity as a means of violent rebellion: "This [barbarity] is the word that sustains me / and smacks against my brass carcass." The reader comes to realize, however, that it is the barbarity of others, of the unjust and dishonest, that feeds the poet's desire to resist and rebel against "the barbarous / bones of the cowardly prowling beasts of the lie." The powerful frankness of the poem lies in its clear imagery and its absence of rhyme and fixed meter. The barbarity of colonizers has died, and yet it resurrects itself in the present at various times, deaf to voices of protest, including the poet's, as he put it: "Barbarity of the dead circulating in the veins of the earth / who at times come and break their heads against the walls of our ears / and the screams of revolt never heard." In the poem's final stanza there is a warning to those who might forget the prevalence of barbarity in the world. Barbarity is evoked as a series of fierce animal images: "barbarity I the spitting cobra / awakening from my putrefying flesh / suddenly a flying gecko / suddenly a fringed gecko."

In the ominous final lines of the poem, the entity of barbarity personified warns that the only means of escape is by death: "I adhere so well to the very loci of strength / that to forget me you must / cast the hairy flesh of your chests to the dogs." This final image, of the human corpse become carrion, is the obverse of the more hopeful image of the living resister of barbarity in the poem's beginning, whose "brass carcass" cannot be penetrated.

BIBLIOGRAPHY

Césaire, Aimé. *The Collected Poetry of Aimé Césaire.* Translated and edited by Clayton Eshleman and Annette Smith. Berkeley and Los Angeles: University of California Press, 1983.

Patrick L. Day

"BARGAIN" LÉON DAMAS (1937)

"Bargain" ("Solde"), from DAMAS's first collection, *Pigments* (1937), reveals the effects of centuries of exploitation by white European colonials. Damas's message is even more direct in this poem than in "HICCUP"; the speaker is an adult who has fully assimilated white European customs and is forced to continue the farce as he makes his way in the world, dispiritedly repeating the refrain, "I feel like an awful fool." The poem—devoid of rhyme, and of varying meter and stanza length—furnishes a list of the ridiculous customs of white colonial society that the speaker finds so alien: clothing ("in their dinner jacket / in their shirt front / in their monocle / in their derby hat"); social practices ("in their mannerisms / in their bowings and scrapings / in their endless need for affectation"); perceived intellectual superiority ("with theories that they season / to the taste of their needs"). Finally, the judgment that the speaker passes on himself is harsh and unforgiving, for unlike the child in "Hiccup," he is not an innocent participant, but rather an active agent in the continued exploitation of his less fortunate countrymen. He has struck a "bargain" with colonialist whites, and he has sold out his own culture to succeed in white society. He is thus complicit in the injustice perpetrated by "them" (white Europeans) for centuries: "I feel like an awful fool / accomplice among them / panderer among them / cutthroat among them / my hands hideously red / with the blood of their ci-vi-li-za-tion." The irony of the poem's final word, *civilization,* is felt in its emphatic division into syllables, forcing readers to slow their reading and ponder the implications of the word in light of the speaker's bitter, cynical conclusion.

Patrick Day

BAXTER, JAMES K. (1926–1972)
James Keir Baxter was born in Dunedin, Otago, New Zealand, into a farming family of Scottish and Polynesian descent. Baxter's father was a pacifist and a conscientious objector to World War I; his mother was an educated, left-wing daughter of a university professor. In childhood Baxter imbibed his parents' ethical principles, and they reinforced their strong moral influence over their son by enrolling him in Quaker schools in England and New Zealand, an interesting background for an artist who would later become a social activist, a Catholic, and a participant in the political life of his country.

Always an avid reader, even as a failed academic, an alcoholic, and a school dropout, the young adult Baxter sought refuge in the writings of Arthur Rimbaud, W. B. Yeats, Dylan Thomas, and Hart Crane. In 1948 he began his vocation as a teacher and laid the foundations for his poetic career in the widely acclaimed publication *Blow, Wind of Fruitfulness.* That same year (1948), Baxter was accepted into the Church of England and married the poet Jacqueline Strum, one of the first Māori women to receive a university degree.

After graduating with a B.A. from Wellington Teachers College in 1955, Baxter joined the Catholic Church in 1957. The well-documented, highly significant event of his mature life—his trip in 1958 to Asia to research educational standards and methodology—provided material for Baxter's poetry for the next decade. His central subject had earlier been the dehumanization of the individual, but his reflections on the human condition were to be magnified by his journey to Asia and the poverty that he witnessed there. The experience was comparable to that of New Zealand poet Robyn Hyde (1906–39), who visited China in 1934 as a journalist during the Sino-Japanese War. Whereas Hyde returned to New Zealand with neuroses, opium addictions, and a radically expanded vision of her poetry, Baxter returned charged with new-found zeal and changed his poetic subject matter—from his earlier focus on the repressed, tortured individual to the poetic treatment of a radically expanded and politicized sense of selfhood. This new consciousness developed into a concept of poverty as virtue: poverty seen *not* as the deprivation of the commodities of modernity, but as a positive force for (and within) community. Upon returning to New Zealand, Baxter saw—in the triviality of the city and its representations of materialism—blind obedience and injustice; this disgust energized his poetry and crystallized his desire to ensure that art contain moral truth. His *In Fires of No Return,* published in 1958, reflected his new awareness of the relation of art to the human spirit. Thus awakened, Baxter kicked his alcoholism and began a period of prolific writing, which lasted through the 1960s. In this period he moved away from British romantic and modernist influences while reworking the quality of the personal, subconscious, and mythical underpinnings of his early work. In his new poems he began to confirm the modern world's degradation of love, God, and the soul—a view that he conflated into a treatise on the natural and social orders. These conceptualizations evolved for Baxter into the principles that underscored his ultimate idea of the poet. This figure, rather than being out of time and place in the economy of a detached and nonspiritual world, would be "poverty-stricken" and all the richer for it.

Between the mid-1940s and the 1960s, New Zealand looked to find an identity and a national literature different from the British sense of "home." While models of pragmatism and stoicism informed this literature to a considerable degree, writers like Hyde and Baxter—although dismissed at first during this period—were working at representing the deepest spiritual experiences of New Zealand, writing a new sort of poetry that would soon be noticed and celebrated in both New Zealand and Great Britain. Baxter's conviction, however, was unique; his authentic readings of Māori culture enabled him to connect and be accepted within their communities. He worked the border between the materialistic and directionless *Pākeha* (foreign, nonindigenous) culture and that of the *Pākeha*'s spiritual elder, the *Māoritanga* (or natural and indigenous Māori ways), as the site for his poetry. Baxter's desire to learn from the different side of things as presented by Māori culture should not be read as a retreat into primitivism, for he recognized that Māori culture had always maintained a highly developed social conscience. Additionally, during a time when the Māori were increasingly alienated from their own culture, Baxter provided them an opportunity to relearn their values and to relate Māori values to the Catholicism that was then central to his own selfhood. This entwining of faiths was a move forward for him into a place where individual and nation were situated within the larger context of the world.

In 1966, coinciding with his publication of *Pig Island Letters,* Baxter was honored as Burns fellow at the University of Otago, an almost inconceivable homecoming after the failures of 20 years earlier. The honor provided the poet with a scaffold for his increasingly assured self-belief. His work from this period, while frequently revisiting his earlier thoughts on his family and first home, began to take on a new poetic configuration, now watermarked by the figure of death. The abstractions of his earlier poetry were shifting into haunting authenticity in lyrics that examined the conditions and the frailty of human life from a direct and unashamedly personal perspective. The poetry from this period realizes simple and austere forms, ostensibly naked sounds, and shapes that form the baseline for his late works.

In 1969 Baxter moved to Jerusalem, a Māori settlement near the Wanganui River on the west coast of the north island of New Zealand. The relocation was an attempt to share the deprivation of people whom he wanted to rally, and it was, at the same time, part of a personal plan to reconstruct, in their ambience, the myths of humanity—so as to aid the poor, the needy, and the destitute. There Baxter meant to practice his philosophy of social relationship—a movement summed up by the word *Arohanui,* which can be translated as "the love of many," encompassing God, humanity, and the living Earth. But problems with the authorities and local residents plagued his (misjudged) project to settle a peaceable commune.

Autumn Testament (1972), his third collection of poetry, records Baxter's time in Jerusalem and his philosophy of community and spiritual life. Following *Jerusalem Sonnets* (1970) and *Jerusalem Daybook* (1971), this final book harnesses the duality of anger and compassion in the poet's psyche, fusing them into a courageous poetics born from simplicity and unparalleled integrity.

> So simple, tree, star, the bare cup of the hills,
> The lifelong grave of waiting
> As indeed it has to be.
> —from *"Te Whiori O Te Kuri"*
> (The Tale of the Dog)

These three lines from the final movement of the concluding poem of *Autumn Testament* are framed by Baxter's contemplation of the Earth as "human shelter" and his knowledge of the body as "a meeting house." Moving thematically from last things and the soul to natural objects exposed to the elements and the shifting shapes of the landscape through time, this poem revisits the theme of place and the idea of dwelling. Characteristic of his later style, the poem offers the reader a place to sit from which to contemplate the assonance of *bare* and *grave.* Baxter's effortless list and metaphoric punctuation works to soothe any disquiet brokered in the preceding verses; moreover, this echo folds the notions of body and shelter into a sense of being: We are left feeling that nature and humanity are gathered into a singular dimension of existence or shared destiny.

In 1972 Baxter left north New Zealand for a commune in Auckland, to revitalize his energies, but he died in October of that year. He was buried on Māori tribal land in Jerusalem.

As the author of over 30 books, Baxter still exerts a remarkable influence over New Zealand's literary culture. He is foremost a figure of biculturalism: a visionary thinker able to understand his country's colonial history and its modern and progressive aspirations. W. H. Oliver writes that Baxter was a man of many paradoxes, none more remarkable than his desperate need to live in isolation, yet compulsively drawn to communicate and to externalize his beliefs. Thinking of the poet's gift, Oliver commented that Baxter's personality exhibited "the innocence of the dove and the guile of the serpent" (Oliver 1983: 146). The axiom reminds us of the poet's role as suppliant and student of the dispossessed, but it also throws Baxter's troubled human vision into relief, for its simple contradiction fails to do justice to Baxter's spiritual and poetic journey, pursued in full awareness of the planet's future and the probable challenges of our new and fragile century.

BIBLIOGRAPHY

Doyle, Charles. *James K. Baxter.* Twayne's World Authors Series. Boston: Twayne, 1976.
Journal of New Zealand Literature. Vol. 13, 1995. Special issue on J. K. Baxter.
McKay, Frank. *Life of James K. Baxter.* Auckland, New Zealand: Oxford University Press, 1990.
Minehan, Mike. *O Jerusalem: James K. Baxter an Intimate Memoir.* Christchurch, New Zealand: Hazard Press, 2002.
Oliver, W. H. *James K. Baxter: A Portrait.* Wellington, New Zealand: Port Nicholson Press, 1983. Reprinted 1994, Godwit Press/Bridget Williams Books.
O' Sullivan, Vincent. *James K. Baxter.* Wellington, New Zealand: Oxford University Press, 1976.
Weir, John. *The Poetry of James K. Baxter.* Wellington, New Zealand: Oxford University Press, 1970.
Weir, John, and Barbara Lyon, eds. *A Preliminary Biography of Works by and Works about James K. Baxter.* Christchurch, New Zealand: University of Canterbury, 1979.
McKay, Frank. *James K. Baxter as Critic.* Oxford: Heinemann Educational Books, 1978.

Tom Bristow

BEI DAO (1949–   )   Bei Dao, meaning literarily "North Island," is the pseudonym of Zhao Zhenkai, the Chinese poet who now writes and teaches in the United States. Recognized as the leading figure of the Misty Poets, who were popular in the late 1970s and 1980s, Bei Dao is frequently related to the Democracy Movement in China and mentioned as a potential Nobel Prize candidate. Those links refer to two aspects of his life: his political activism and his literary achievements.

Born in August 1949, the same year that the People's Republic of China was founded, Bei Dao has led a life inevitably tied to the ups and downs of his native land. His father was an administrator and his mother a doctor. He became a worker at a construction company after he graduated from Number Four Middle School in Beijing in 1968, in the third year of the 10-year-long Cultural Revolution. Propelled by a strong sense of responsibility and disillusionment, he started writing poetry in the early 1970s and founded the underground poetry journal *Today* (*Jintian*) with Mang Ke in 1978. "THE ANSWER," one of his most famous poems, was well received during the Democracy Movement of 1976, published in the first issue of *Today,* then formally published in 1979 in the official literary *Journal of Poetry.* Since then Bei Dao has become a primary figure among the Misty Poets, acting as a catalyst for ideological and literary transformation. However, the group's efforts for a more subjective and individualistic literary voice aroused heated discussions, and *Today* was closed down in 1980.

Bei Dao was invited to Great Britain in 1987 for a year's appointment as a visiting scholar. He went to Europe in April 1989 for a visit, but—as a result of the student protest and police brutality at Tiananmen Square—he did not immediately return to China. As Bei Dao reveals in his book of prose *The Book of Failure* (2004), he moved 15 times and lived in seven different countries between 1989 and 1995.

Bei Dao was officially allowed to spend time with his relatives in Beijing during the Spring Festival of 2002 and in 2004 was asked to introduce a number of famous foreign poets in *Shouhuo* (Harvest), an official Chinese journal.

Bei Dao's poetry mirrors the harsh realities of his time, and some of his poems are replete with social criticism. The frustrations, sense of loss, and awakening consciousness of the younger generation found a voice in his poetry—with its marked, strong sense of reason, deep concern for humanity, portrayal of alienation, moments of disbelief, and meaningful reflections. "Declaration" and "An End or a Beginning" are good examples.

Wide reading and his translation of Western literary works during his literary apprenticeship helped to shape Bei Dao's poetic style, which has close ties with Western modernism. As Bei Dao admits, "The use of metaphor, symbol, synesthesia, changing of the point of view or perspective and breaking the continuity of time and scene, etc., provide new possibilities for us" ("On Poetry"). Metaphor and symbolism are indeed two important devices with which Bei Dao expresses his understanding of reality, society, and humanity.

Over the years Bei Dao's friendships with internationally famous poets and writers—including Allen Ginsberg, Gary Snyder, Eliot Weinberger, Jonathan Spence, OCTAVIO PAZ, and TOMAS TRANSTRÖMER—have shown his popularity in the international literary arena. He has been awarded various prizes, including the Aragana Poetry Prize from the International Festival of Poetry in Casablanca, Morocco, and a Guggenheim Fellowship. He was also named an honorary member of the American Academy of Arts and Letters. In addition in 2002 Bei Dao visited Israel and the Palestinian territories as a member of the delegation for the International Parliament of Writers.

Over the years numerous translations of Bei Dao's poems and texts have been published in English, including *Notes from the City of the Sun* (1984), *The August Sleepwalker* (1988), *Old Snow* (1991), *Forms of Distance* (1994), *Landscape Over Zero* (1995), *At the Sky's Edge: Poems 1991–1996* (1996), and *Unlock* (2000). Bei Dao is also the author of novels and prose. Being a wanderer has enriched his experiences. He started writing prose in 1996, and his first book of prose in English is *Blue House* (2000). His more recent publications of prose in Chinese include *The Rose of Time* (2005) and *The Book of Failure* (2004).

BIBLIOGRAPHY

Barnstone, Tony, ed. *Out of the Howling Storm: The New Chinese Poetry.* Hanover, N.H.: Wesleyan University Press, 1993.

Bei Dao. "On Poetry." Translated by Gordon T. Osing and De-An Wu Swihart. The Meng Long Shi Series. *Salt Hill Journal* 5 (1998).

Klein, Lucas. "Alphabets Upside-down: the Voice of Bei Dao". Rain Taxi online. Edition Spring 2003. Available online. URL: http://www.raintaxi.com/online/2003spring/beidao.shtml. Accessed on April 21, 2007.

McDougall, Bonnie, trans. *The August Sleepwalker.* New York: New Directions, 1988.

Saussy, Haun. "Bei Dao and His Audiences." Available online. URL: http://prelectur.stanford.edu/lecturers/dao/daoaudience.html. Accessed on April 21, 2007.

Shan Xuemei

BELLI, CARLOS GERMÁN (1927–)

Carlos Germán Belli is one of the most technically accomplished Latin American poets of the post–avant-garde period. Alongside his compatriot José María Eguren, Belli's neoclassical verse provides an intriguing nexus between poetry of social concerns, such as the work of PABLO NERUDA or Juan Gelman, and more aesthetically oriented works, such as those of OCTAVIO PAZ and the so-called *neobarroco* poets such as the Argentine Néstor Perlongher. The son of Italian immigrants, Belli was born in Lima, Peru, in 1927 and, like many of his generation of poets, formed part of the growing urban middle and lower middle classes. He studied at the University of San Marcos in the Peruvian capital, where he later earned a doctorate in literature. Early dreams of joining the diplomatic service were thwarted, and Belli began a career in repetitive and mediocre civil service jobs that marked his outlook and poetic production. His earliest poems deal with unhappy amorous experiences, and a tone of frustration and disappointment is present in much of his work. In the vein of Neruda's *Residencia en la tierra,* Belli combined surrealist and even dada elements with a thematic presentation of the drudgery, poverty, and social injustice of contemporary existence. He published *Poemas* (Poems) in 1958, and his oeuvre includes more than 10 collections. Much of his work is characterized by a profoundly bitter, even grotesque, presentation of everyday life. Belli's tortured poet-narrator is not the idealized and windswept figure of romanticism or Latin American *modernismo*, but rather that of the *Don Nadie* (Mister Nobody) of modern urban life. Migration, industrialization, labor rights, and racism appear strongly as themes in his works. Typical of Belli's outlook is his description of the world as an *"alimenticio bolo, mas de polvo"* (a nutritive ball, but of dust).

What sets Belli apart from other socially engaged poets is the formal aspect of his verse. He has spoken of the importance of poetic borrowing, rewriting, and outright plagiarism, but this is to underplay the skill with which Belli's work draws on, for example, Spanish Golden Age poetry, creating pieces that meld ornate construction and conceits to contemporary themes and colloquial language, including Lima slang. We find in his work long disregarded forms such as the *silva*, a combination of seven- and 11-syllable lines prominent in Luis de Góngora's 17th-century poetry. Many of his symbols, particularly those of the female beauties for whom his narrator-protagonist longs, are based on Golden Age or *dolce stil nuovo* staples, and this symbolic archive is used to make personal and private pain public. Such a portrayal of social inequality and frustration is illustrated by his remarkably accomplished *"Sextina de los desiguales"* ("Sestina of the Unequals") (1970), which takes the troubadour's sestina form with its unrhymed but interlaced sestets and final tercet to explore the gulf between emotional expectations and social reality. In addition Belli has coined new symbolic figures, such as his *Hada Cibernética*, or Cybernetic Fairy (1961), a benign technological spirit who would free humanity from frustration and oppression, within a cosmology that sees human beings as victims of modern society's false promises of plenitude and happiness. Despite his pessimism, there are two sources of hope in Belli's poetry: first, the poet-everyman's quixotic or Sisyphean refusal to give in to his circumstances; and second, the notion of poetry as a form of redemption for the lives of the mediocre, something close to a popular version of the Horacian monument against the ages. In Belli's later poetry, for example, the collection *El buen mudar* (The Good Move, 1986), there are touches of mysticism. In an *ars poetica, Asir la forma que se va* (To Grasp the Form That Flees, 1982), Belli calls poetic form a source of pleasure as well as a guard against the abyss, form being innate in the continent and even in the makeup of the human body. Form is offered as a consolation against time and its corollary, death. His later poetry, which draws on the work of the troubadour Arnaut Daniel and his *sestina* form and on Petrarch's *Canzoniere*, is further proof of this technical mastery.

In 1962 Belli won Peru's National Poetry Prize, and more recently he has worked as a university professor. Although he has been widely translated into English, Italian, and French, many of his works have resisted translation into English, perhaps because of their precise use of forms more suited to the Romance languages. Several of his earlier poems, however, are included with translations in *Peru: The New Poetry*. Paul W. Borgeson Jr. edited a good, fairly recent Spanish-language selection.

BIBLIOGRAPHY
Aherne, Maureen, and David Tripton, eds. *Peru: The New Poetry*. London: London Magazine Editions, 1970.
Borgeson, Paul W. Jr. *Los Talleres del Tiempo. Versos escogidos de Carlos Germán Belli*. Madrid: Visor, 1992.

Ben Bollig

BELLI, GIOCONDA (1948–   ) Erotic and boldly feminist, Gioconda Belli first published poetry that shocked polite society in 1970 Managua, which considered it "vaginal poetry . . . shameless pornography," after which her engineer husband ordered her to submit future poems to him for editing (Belli, *The Country* 38). Born into a wealthy family accustomed to country clubs, debutante balls, and rubbing shoulders with the rich and powerful, Belli at first conformed to traditional social roles but soon rejected them as too confining. Like several other Nicaraguan women with similar Catholic upbringing—DAISY ZAMORA, Michèle Najlis, VIDALUZ MENESES—Belli explored in her writings a growing sense of identity as an independent woman that went hand in hand with a commitment to social reform and political action. She became a militant in the insurgent movement to overthrow the Somoza dynasty, which had initiated its stranglehold on the country in the early 1930s.

Ironically it was precisely the deference accorded to members of her social class that allowed Belli to lead a double life after 1970, when she became a clandestine member of the revolutionary Sandinista National Liberation Front (FSLN). By the mid-1970s, however, class privilege no longer could protect her, and she was spirited out of the country just days before her arrest order was issued. Between 1975 and 1979, she worked for the revolution from exile in Mexico and Costa Rica, distanced for long periods from her children while she served as international spokesperson for the FSLN, while a Nicaraguan military court tried her in absentia and condemned her to prison. She returned to her homeland immediately after the 1979 triumph of the revolution, to work first as head of Sandinista television and later in other high-level positions appropriate to her training and experience in advertising. She later distanced herself from FSLN party politics and now divides her time between Managua and Santa Monica, California.

As in "And God Made Me Woman"—from her first collection, *Sobre la grama* (On the Grass) (1974), which won a prestigious national poetry award—Belli's early poetry expressed a new pride in celebrating femaleness from a woman's point of view: "God dug into me, / made a workshop in me for human beings, / . . . / everything God gently created / with hammering whispers / and the drilling motion of love / the thousand and one things that make me woman every day, / that make me proud every morning / when I arise / and bless my sex" (*De la costilla de Eva* [From Eve's Rib], 15). Her female identity is "based on a celebration of women's power, both creative and procreative," yet the contemporary Central American context is evident in her "erotic celebrations" grounded in the reality of war, death, and separation (Barbas-Rhoden 54–55).

Belli's poetry interweaves feminism, womanhood, motherhood, eroticism, cultural activism, militancy, and political commitment in all her collections: *Sobre la grama; Línea de fuego* (Line of Fire, 1978), winner of Cuba's acclaimed Casa de las Américas award; *Truenos y arco iris* (Thunder and Rainbow, 1982); the *Amor insurrecto* anthology (Insurrectional Love, 1984); *De la costilla de Eva* (1986); the anthology *El ojo de la mujer* (Woman's Eye, 1991); and *Apogeo* (Apogee, 1997). By

1988 anthologist Amanda Hopkinson was calling Belli "perhaps the greatest love poet" in Central America (xxii).

Surprisingly few critical assessments of Belli's poetry have come out in English. U.S. critics tend to emphasize her novels, especially *La mujer habitada* (The Inhabited Woman, 1988) and the gripping narration of her life-changing experiences of love, war, motherhood, exile, and politics in *El país bajo mi piel* (The Country under My Skin, 2001), which is the best introduction to her life. Pilar Moyano and Oralia Preble-Niemi give insightful readings of her poetic themes. Curbstone Press's *From Eve's Rib* (1989) is an excellent bilingual introduction to Belli's poetry. The title is from her *De la costilla de Eva*; however, this volume is an anthology selected from many of her published works, not a translation of that one book.

BIBLIOGRAPHY
Barbas-Rhoden, Laura. *Writing Women in Central America: Gender and the Fictionalization of History.* Athens: Ohio University Press, 2003.
Belli, Gioconda. *The Country Under My Skin: A Memoir of Love and War.* Translated by Kristina Cordero and the author. New York: Anchor, 2003.
———. *From Eve's Rib.* Bilingual edition, translated by Steven F. White. Willimantic, Conn.: Curbstone, 1989.
Hopkinson, Amanda. Introduction. *Lovers and Comrades: Women's Resistance Poetry from Central America.* London: Women's Press, 1989, xv–xxv.
Moyano, Pilar. "The Transformation of Nation and Womanhood: Revisionist Mythmaking in the Poetry of Nicaragua's Gioconda Belli." In *Interventions: Feminist Dialogues on Third World Women's Literature and Film,* edited by Bishnupriya Ghosh and Brinda Bose. New York: Garland, 1997, 79–95.
Preble-Niemi, Oralia. "Gioconda Belli." *Modern Spanish American Poets: Second Series,* edited by María A. Salgado. Detroit: Gale, 2004, 26–33.

María Roof

BENN, GOTTFRIED (1886–1956)

Gottfried Benn, whose singular influence on German poetry and poetics is still felt into the 21st century, eludes succinct description. Benn invited his readers time and again to grasp his person and works in terms of irreconcilable dichotomies. The titles of his autobiographical sketch

"Doppelleben" (Double-Life, 1950) and his poem *"Teils-Teils"* (Half-and-Half, 1954) illustrate Benn's sense of a divided self—a recurring theme throughout his literary corpus. Critics have grasped this notion of oppositions as an elemental aspect of understanding Benn: his parentage (German father and French-Swiss mother), his career choices (medical doctor and poet), his personality (socialite and loner), and, perhaps most provocatively, his wavering political stance during World War II. As much as this dialectical framework serves to describe Benn's exceptional life and choices, it also aptly characterizes his contributions to 20th-century German poetry, giving voice to both a passionate expressionistic style and to a rapturous yet remote aesthetic.

Gottfried Benn was born on May 2, 1886, in Mansfeld (Westprignitz), Germany, the son of a strict yet politically progressive German Protestant minister and a French-Swiss governess. After receiving a first-rate education at the Friedrich Gymnasium in Frankfurt an der Oder, which fortified his knowledge of the classics and natural sciences, he began studies in Marburg in theology and German philology. In 1905 the young Benn abandoned his university studies and moved to Berlin, where he was admitted to the Kaiser Wilhelm Academy of Army Medicine, an institution that provided largely free medical training in exchange for a specified period of service as an army doctor. As a medical student, Benn's wide-ranging interests initially included psychology and neurology. Soon, however, his expertise expanded to include the fields of venereal and skin diseases. During these early years in Berlin, the young doctor Benn was assigned to various hospitals, which not only afforded him his first professional experience, but also revealed to him a world of misery and suffering. At the same time Benn entered Berlin's vibrant arts scene, frequenting the city's cafés, where he befriended avant-garde artists and poets. The objects of his knife became in turn the objects of his pen, giving rise to cynical, ironic, and even grotesque renderings of Berlin's unsavory realities, as in his acclaimed volume *Morgue* (1912), emblematic of the German expressionist style. His ecstatic, vivid verse would continue to capture drug-induced euphoria and melancholic despair during these early years.

After receiving a doctorate in 1912, Benn served as an army physician, including during World War I in Belgium, where he met his future wife, the actress Edith Brosin. He produced his plays during this period. In 1917 Benn returned to Berlin with Edith, opening a private practice as a specialist in skin and sexually transmitted diseases. After the sudden death of his wife in 1922, Benn faced frequent bouts of depression. Despite this period of alienation and loneliness, his literary production continued to flourish. Following the war he emerged not only as a significant poet, but also as a prose writer and essayist, producing texts dealing with history, philosophy, and the role of the artist in contemporary life. His initiation into the highest circles of authorial acclaim occurred in 1932, when he was admitted to the poetry section of the Prussian Academy of Arts, among such luminaries as Thomas Mann and Alfred Döblin. Yet this accomplishment was soon followed by decisions that tainted Benn's reputation for years to come. He stood by unflinchingly and watched the removal or resignation of several members of the academy in the wake of Hitler's rise in 1933, failing to speak up on their behalf. Benn's position was not merely a passive one. In radio broadcasts and essays, he lauded the new reich and its führer—even as it began to expel and to persecute many of the very artists who had so influenced and supported him, including fellow expressionist poet and former lover ELSE LASKER-SCHÜLER.

Soon, though, the tables turned on Benn, when his own racial purity was brought into question by the Nazis. As early as 1934, Benn began processing the brutal ideology of the regime and withdrew his support for it. Perhaps counterintuitively, Benn reenlisted as an army doctor in 1935, seeking sanctuary from the chaos around him. By 1938 the regime issued to him a *Schreibverbot* (writing ban). Nonetheless, Benn recorded the atrocities he witnessed and the existential questioning they triggered; the volume was titled simply *Zweiundzwanzig Gedichte* (22 Poems). As the war came to a close in early 1945, Benn's seven-year marriage to Herta von Wedemeyer ended in tragedy when she committed suicide in her countryside refuge as the Red Army approached.

Benn returned to the publishing scene in 1948 with his collection *Statische Gedichte* (Static Poems) and in

1949 issued the anthology of poetry *Trunkene Flut* (Drunken Flood)—volumes that voiced Benn's growing affinity for the autonomous aesthetic. Despite persistent charges that he had been a traitor and opportunist, Benn found an audience and received much critical acclaim, culminating in his being awarded the Georg Büchner Prize (1951). In his 1951 seminal lecture, *Probleme der Lyrik* (Problems of Poetry), delivered in Darmstadt, Benn posited the notion of an "absolute poetry"—a departure from his evocative, impassioned expressionist style of old. Instead this new concept comprised a renewed attention to form, an emphasis on the substantive, and an invocation of the remote and primeval, finding inspiration from symbolist and modernist poets including T. S. Eliot and Stéphane Mallarmé. Having revived his private medical practice in West Berlin in 1945, Benn shared his final years with his third wife, Ilse Kaul. He died of cancer on July 7, 1956, in West Berlin.

BIBLIOGRAPHY

Benn, Gottfried. *Poems.* Edited by Michael Lebeck and Rosemarie Beck. Mendelheim, Germany: Three Kings Press, 1967.

———. *Primal Visions: Selected Writings of Gottfried Benn.* Edited by E. B. Ashton. New York: New Directions, 1960.

———. *Prose, Essays, Poems.* Edited by Reinhard Becker and Volkmar Sandor. New York: Continuum, 1987.

———. *Poems 1937–1947.* Edited by Simona Draghici. Washington, D.C.: Plutarch Press, 1991.

Dierick, Augustinus. *Gottfried Benn and His Critics: Major Interpretations, 1912–1992.* Columbia, S.C.: Camden House, 1992.

Ritchie, J. M. *Gottfried Benn: The Unreconstructed Expressionist.* London: Wolff, 1972.

Roche, Mark William. *Gottfried Benn's Static Poetry. Aesthetic and Intellectual-Historical Interpretations.* Chapel Hill: University of North Carolina Press, 1991.

Michele Ricci

"BESIDE A CHRYSANTHEMUM" SUH JUNG-JU (1947)

"Beside a Chrysanthemum" (1947) is one of SUH JUNG-JU's most famous poems. It was originally published in his third collection of poetry, *Selected Poems* (1955), in which Suh tries to revisit traditional Korean sensibility, distancing himself from the Baude-lairean art-for-art's-sake vision of his first volume, *Hwa-Sa-Jip* (Flower and Snake Collection, 1941). Thus the tone of serene contemplation and deep meditation prevails in this collection. In particular, in "Beside a Chrysanthemum" Suh, looking at a chrysanthemum, attains an intimation of the cosmic principle of life.

Traditionally, a chrysanthemum has been a familiar symbol of integrity for a male Confucian scholar. A yellow chrysanthemum symbolized a golden principle, the loyalty to his ruler, that a scholar must exhibit no matter what. Thus most scholars during the Chosun period of Korean history spent their leisure time drawing chrysanthemums with a calligraphic brush or composing poems about them. Like his predecessors, Suh crafts a poem about a chrysanthemum; but, unlike Confucian scholars, he compares it to the female qualities of perseverance and maternal love. Thus looking at a chrysanthemum, he is not reminded of a scholar's promise of loyalty, but instead of his elder sister's maturity. Recalling Confucius's dictum that 40 is an age of spiritual maturity that enables an individual to overcome the raging hormones of the twenties and the anxiety and frustration of the thirties, Suh finds a chrysanthemum—which has finally bloomed after the coldness of winter, the freshness of spring, and the heat of summer—to be suggestive of his sister's spiritual firmness. Like the flower, he imagines, she reached her full-flowered maturity only after she survived hope, dejection, fear, anger, and frustration.

At the same time, in the presence of the chrysanthemum Suh is reminded of the Buddhist principle of cause and effect. In other words, for him the flower's bloom seems to be the end result of a collaboration of all related forces, here represented by a cuckoo who cried in the spring, the rolling thunder that rumbled in dark gray clouds in the summer, and the early frost that fell in the fall. Realizing that all these forces cooperated in giving a flower its transient but beautiful life, the poet suspects that his sleepless night might have also somehow participated in the flower's bloom. With his sister's life and the cosmic power surrounding a chrysanthemum thus overlapped, Suh cannot help feeling awe toward the cosmic principle of life that connects all visible forms (appearances) and all invisible forces (reality) one to another. In the end, feeling humble in the presence of life, he cautiously hopes that he and his poetry do have a part in the immense network of life.

BIBLIOGRAPHY
McCann, David R., ed. *Selected Poems of Sŏ Chŏngju*. New York: Columbia University Press, 1989.
Suh Jung-ju. "Beside a Chrysanthemum." Translated by Peter Lee. In *The Silence of Love: Twentieth-Century Korean Poetry*, edited by Sammy E. Solberg, 122. Honolulu: University of Hawaii Press, 1990.

Han Ji-hee

BIALIK, HAYYIM NAHMAN (1873–1934)

Regarded as one of the greatest Hebrew poets of modern times, Hayyim Nahman Bialik was instrumental in the revival of the Hebrew language and in expressing the Jewish people's pain and yearnings in a time of great change. Born on January 11, 1873, in the Ukrainian village of Radi, in Volynia, Russia, Bialik experienced childhood as dappled with tragedy and pathos, although in later years he viewed his formative days with sentimental fondness, which he portrayed in his musings. He was intoxicated by the mysteries of nature, a theme to which he returned frequently in his poems, recapturing and idealizing the hours he spent roaming the woods. His father, Yitzhak Yossef, was a timber merchant whose business failings forced the family to relocate to the town of Zhitomir, where Bialik's grandfather, a sternly religious man, also lived. The sojourn in Zhitomir left an indelible mark on the young man, who at the age of seven was devastated when his father, then a tavern owner, fell ill and died. That sudden loss would soon come to occupy a central place in the poet's personality and poetic productions—and was all the more significant, because the familial trauma was set to continue. Before long, his mother, Dinah (née Priveh), incapacitated by her husband's death and unable to support her children, sent Bialik and his sister to live with her elderly in-laws. The poet paints a picture of the pain of life in his mother's house in poems such as "Almenut" (Widowhood, 1933) and "Shirati" (My Song, 1900–1) describing with pathos the scanty Sabbath meals, the chilly evenings, and his mother's grief. Bialik had to contend as well with his puritanical grandfather, Yaakov Moshe Bialik, who shackled the boy to a rigorous program of learning and prayer. Nonetheless, this laborious study regime did not diminish the 13 year old's enthusiasm for Talmudic inquiry, as he would often retreat on his own to the *bet hamidrash* (Jewish house of study) to dissect the intricacies of Halacha (Jewish law). At 17 he convinced his grandfather to allow him to study at the Great Yeshiva in Volozhin, Lithuania, under the tutelage of Rabbi Naftali Zvi, where he not only began his poetic activity, composing in Hebrew, but also gradually came to be influenced by the polemical writing of the father of spiritual Zionism, Ahad Ha'am. Later, Bialik became a supporter of the effluent Zionist movement Hovevei Tzion (Lover of Zion) and its backing of a Jewish homeland in Palestine. Growing impatient with the deadening and myopic regimen of yeshiva study, Bialik left for Odessa, the hub of Hebrew literary activity. Although his hopes for a university degree were not actualized, the stay in Odessa proved fruitful. After meeting with his mentor Ahad Ha'am and J. H Ravnitzky, one of his poems, "El Hatzippor" (To the Bird, 1892), was included in a collection of Hebrew literature, cementing his place as one of the most capable young poets of his time writing in Hebrew. Still, the bard had to return to Zhitomir to tend to his gravely ill grandfather, who died shortly after he arrived.

In 1893 Bialik married Manya Averbuch, the daughter of a wealthy timber merchant, for whom Bialik reluctantly worked. During this period he produced a series of national poems, which in their despairingly bleak overtones condemned the passivity of the Jewish people in the face of the tragedies befalling them. In 1900 Bialik returned to Odessa with his wife, at first teaching Hebrew and then becoming the literary editor of *Hashiloh*. In 1901 his first collection of poems appeared to critical acclaim, and Bialik was lauded as the poet of the national renaissance. The first volume was followed by Bialik's magnum opus, the historical prose poem *Metei Midbar* (The Dead of the Desert, 1902). In 1921 he and a cadre of Hebrew writers were allowed to leave the Ukraine. Besides publishing his first collected poems that year, he established (jointly with Ravnitzky) the Moriah Publishing Company, with the aim of generating Hebrew pedagogical materials for schools. Following his move to Germany, he reestablished the publishing venture and increased its capacity, at the same time opening Dvir Publishing. After three years in Berlin and Hamburg, Bialik emigrated to Palestine, settling in Tel Aviv, where he founded again his Dvir Publishing in 1924. From the time he arrived, Tel Aviv became his beloved hamlet, and his house today contains the Bialik Museum, frequented by thousands of visitors every year.

In Palestine his creative output took a backseat to his public and cultural activities. Inevitably he was called on to serve on countless boards (of the Hebrew University, the Hebrew Writer's Association, the literary magazine *Moznaim,* and so forth), and he was sent abroad by the Zionist Organization to solicit financial aid from diaspora Jews. Though he authored only a single opus while in Israel, *Yatmut* (Orphanhood, 1928), he assembled into contemporary editions the medieval work of Solomon ibn Gabirol and Abraham ibn Ezra and compiled several anthologies of legends for children. Dear to Bialik's heart was his enterprise of *kinnus* (ingathering), his project to find and collect hundreds of scattered poems from hard-to-find books and manuscripts and make them more widely available. His swansong, *Yatmut,* a moving account of his forced separation from his mother and the death of his father, was completed shortly before his untimely death from a heart attack on July 4, 1934, in Vienna, where he had traveled for a prostate operation.

Translated into more than 30 languages, Bialik's canon can be divided formally into verse articulating the national revival, interior poetry anchored in the personal, and songs of nature. Radically experimenting with linguistic configurations and meters, Bialik fused symbolist poetry with romanticism, making modernist Hebrew verse accessible for future poets. Today Bialik is seen as a "modern prophet," especially as many of his poems served as springboards for the revival of the Hebrew language and enshrined it as the culture's representative tongue. It is of particular significance that Bialik deployed the classical Hebrew of the founding books, with its theological weight, to hew a poetry that in effect challenged and disrupted the historical authority of Orthodox Judaism. The fact that Bialik forged religious visions out of the coherent qualities of biblical words and phrasings, encasing within their midst multiple ironic meanings, was not lost on later Hebrew poets, who followed his route in displacing the original meaning of the founding texts. The writer's dramatic focus was the process of change that affected the world of eastern European Jewry, transforming it from one of fierce tradition to one of secular values. Instead of recycling the biblical rhetoric of his predecessors, Bialik devised a fresh and expansive linguistic canvas that reflected the new, vibrant national and linguistic reality and allowed Hebrew poetry to depict the youthful pioneering revolution sweeping through Palestine. Earning the title "national poet," Bialik set his imprimatur on an entire generation by combining the personal with the collective and intermingling his responses to national catastrophes and aspirations with his intimate sense of sorrow and orphanhood. The generation of poets that followed Bialik, including such luminaries as Yaakov Fichman, Yaakov Steinberg, and Zalman Shneur, to name a few, were labeled the "Bialik Generation" in recognition of the enormous artistic and spiritual influence Bialik wielded on their ars poetica.

BIBLIOGRAPHY

Bialik, Hayyim Nachman. *Chaim Nachman Bialik: Selected Poems.* Translated by Ruth Nevo. Jerusalem: Dvir and *Jerusalem Post,* 1981.

Feinstein, Sara. *Sunshine, Blossoms, and Blood: H.N. Bialik in His Time: A Literary Biography.* Lanham, Md.: University Press of America, 2005.

Halkin, Simon. *From the Enlightenment to the Birth of the State of Israel: Trends and Values.* New York: Schoken, 1970.

Klasuner, Joseph. *A History of Modern Hebrew Literature (1785–1930).* Westport, Conn.: Greenwood Press, 1932.

Roskies, David, ed. *The Literature of Destruction: Jewish Responses to Catastrophe.* Philadelphia: Jewish Publication Society, 1988, 1989.

Shaked, Gershon, ed. *Bialik: Critical Essays on His Works.* Jerusalem: Mossad Bialik, 1974.

Silberschlag. Eisig. *From Renaissance to Renaissance.* New York: Ktav, 1975.

Dvir Abramovich

"BIRTHDAY" ALFREDO GIULIANI (1961) ALFREDO GIULIANI's unrhymed free-verse poem *"Compleanno"* (Birthday) was first published in *I novissimi: poesie per gli anni '60* (1961), the famous and influential anthology of

neo-avant-garde poetry that Giuliani himself edited, containing his own poetry and that of four other poets, including the more celebrated EDOARDO SANGUINETI. "Birthday" contains four stanzas of free verse: The first has 10 lines, the second five, the third 27, the last six. Its subject, appropriately enough, is Giuliani's 13th birthday, and the poem addresses Giuliani himself. Peculiar to the poem and the anthology as a whole are the editor's notes (Giuliani's) explaining allusions and authorial intentions. It is vital to know that this poem is "almost completely dreamlike," that the birthday is a "journey," first leading to sleep, then to the final "rising." Giuliani glosses the passage "the holy garden was enclosed in the iron cage, the tongue [language] pressed between a wall and a coin" as referring to Ezra Pound imprisoned in the cage at the concentration camp in Pisa. But this reference, as Giuliani writes, goes beyond Pound to signify "the condition of the poet in the modern world." The poet must deal with the "Enemy" who forebodingly lurks behind the syllables and "lacerates" or "slashes." The enemy is in language. For Giuliani (and other avant-garde poets) language must be purified of all the encrustations of capitalism and consumerism; the focus on the ego must be diminished; objects must be endowed with presence. And yet this poem rises above ideology, or specific theories, to become a mosaic of riddling and lovely images in which the poet recites with thunder in his veins. This poem in particular shows the influence of surrealists and of the Welsh poet Dylan Thomas and is quite different from the majority of Giuliani's less imagistic poems. Here we do not sense so much a struggle with language as a struggle with poetic inspiration and the existential course of life.

BIBLIOGRAPHY

Eco, Umberto. *Open Work*. Translated by Anna Cancogni. Cambridge, Mass.: Harvard University Press, 1989.

Giuliani, Alfredo. *I Novissimi: Poetry for the Sixties*. Translated by David Jacobson, Luigi Ballerini, Bradley Dick, Michael Moore, Stephen Sartarelli, and Paul Vangelisti. Los Angeles: Sun & Moon Press, 1995.

Wagstaff, C. "The Neo-avantgarde." In *Writers and Society in Contemporary Italy*, edited by M. Caesar and P. Hainsworth, 35–62. London: Palgrave, 1984.

Jacob Blakesley

BJØRNVIG, THORKILD (1918–2005) Thorkild Bjørnvig is one of the greatest Danish poets. He debuted with *The Star Behind the Gable* (*Stjaernen bag Gavlen*) in 1947, followed in 1955 and 1959 with *Anubis* (Anubis) and *Figur og Ild* (Figure and Fire), and the book-length poem *Ravnen* (The Raven), published in 1968. All four collections marked high points in Danish poetry.

Bjørnvig's art and thought influenced every facet of Danish political, intellectual, and artistic life. Born in Aarhus, Jutland, on February 2, 1918, he earned a masters in comparative literature in 1947 and a Ph.D. in 1964, both from the University of Aarhus. He was invited to join the Danish Academy in 1960. He authored multiple essays on ecological and political issues, as well as works of criticism, personal memoirs, and multiple translations. Bjørnvig founded and served as editor of the literary journal *Heretica* (1948–50), and translated the German poets RAINER MARIA RILKE and Friedrich Hölderlin into Danish. His most famous prose works are memoirs of his unhappy childhood and *The Pact: My Friendship with Isak Dinesen* (1974), an account of the intense, master-acolyte relationship between the young poet and the older, world-famous Danish author.

The poet Bjørnvig started as a conscious modernist, experimenting with prosody, rhythm, and tone. After his second marriage, to teacher Birgit Nielsen, he embraced prose poetry concerned principally with the environment. Acutely aware of the fragility of the ecosystem, Bjørnvig's later poems are frequently angry protests about the rape of the Earth. Bjørnvig also said his childhood inspired his respect for nature. A sickly boy, he often stayed indoors while others played outside. One such rainy afternoon, half asleep, young Thorkild imagined all the animals of the forest gathered before his window, proclaiming their autonomy from man. A childhood spent as the school scapegoat, alternately beaten and shunned, further convinced him of the importance of defending helpless nature against the brutality of mankind.

Bjørnvig's mature verse explores the mysteries of the cosmos, ruminates on life and death, and questions man's relationship to his surroundings, as in the late poem "WATER, RUSHES AND THE MOON." It has been said that Bjørnvig made himself nature's advocate. Poems concerned with the depletion of the Earth's resources have titles such as "Can We Afford It?" (*"Har Vi Raad?"*) and "What About the Earth?" (*"Hvad med Jorden?"*).

When Thorkild Bjørnvig died on March 4, 2005, on the small island of Samsø, Denmark was a country in mourning. Himself a "religious atheist" (a title he coined to describe a fellow writer), Bjørnvig left over 50 published works and a legacy of absolute faith that dignity and art are the twin compasses of human existence.

Annette Olsen-Fazi

"BLACK HERALDS, THE" César Vallejo (1918)

"The Black Heralds" (also published as "The Black Messengers") expresses the metaphysics of human pain and suffering that informed much of César Vallejo's poetry. In contrast to romantic writers who considered poetry a means to commune with the sublime, Vallejo disrupts poetry's "beauty" to force poetry to express doubt, hesitation, and disbelief, not in abstract but in physical, bodily terms. In this poem the violence of life's "bloodstained blows" slashes "the fiercest face" and "the strongest back" and is as "barbaric" as the infamous Huns.

More than expressing philosophical angst, this poem paints life as a series of unprovoked, disconcerting, incomprehensible misfortunes. The source of the assaults might even be God himself in his hatred of humanity, and the poet says "I don't know"—that is, this all makes no sense to me. Life itself, then, makes no sense, and that is one of Vallejo's main poetic themes, that there is no rational design to life; we are destined to suffer and will never know why, since rationality, in seeking to define causes and effects, provides no answers. Religion is of even less use than reason, when "some adored faith" can be negated or "blasphemed by Destiny." Because the blows are undeserved, humanity is pictured as a passive victim, unable to provide self-protection, even through faith, and this destiny might reflect God's will. Death holds no hope for escape or salvation, because the blows could be an announcement of what death has in store for us.

This poem is a scream, a crying out, but expressed in mainly colloquial language ("I don't know!") and common images, such as the bread burning in the oven (also, perhaps, an allusion to lack of salvation through Christ). Vallejo turns on its head the traditional metaphor of life flowing like a river; and, here, the water is repeatedly stopped in its course: "undertow," "suffering welled up in the soul," "everything lived wells up, like a pool of guilt," expressed in man's crazed, frightened eyes. The fourth stanza in Spanish is a deep wailing, repeating the *"o"* vowel equivalent to the English "oh": *"Y el hombre . . . ¡Pobre . . . pobre! Vuelve los ojos como / cuando por sobre el hombro nos llama una palmada,"* followed by 13 other *"o"* sounds in the next two lines. The ". . ." slow the presentation and suggest hesitation, doubt, and fear.

BIBLIOGRAPHY
Vallejo, César. "The Black Heralds." Originally published in Vallejo's collection *Los heraldos negros* (1918). Translated by Clayton Eshleman and published in English in *American Poetry Review* 34, no. 3 (May–June 2005): 25.

María Roof

"BLACK SNAKE" Raul Bopp (1931)

"Cobra Norato," written in 1928 and first published in 1931, is considered not only Raul Bopp's masterpiece, but also one of the most important literary works of Brazilian modernism. In this long poem Bopp develops a dramatic epic with fairy-tale–like episodes and sequences. The work describes the adventures of a young man in the Amazon jungle who strangles a large black snake and enters its body to travel through the jungle to the Amazonian city Belem do Pará, in search of a queen's daughter whom he wishes to marry. In many ways the poem is a love story, but the value of the poem lies in Bopp's skillful use of the Amazonian geographical background to capture and focus on indigenous myths, cultural practices, and rituals in that region of Brazil. Using the folklore of the region, Bopp creates, through striking metaphors and unexpected imaginative images, a text that uncovers and rediscovers elements of Brazilian national identity embedded in indigenous myths.

Bopp was not a native of the Brazilian Amazon region, but he spent many years there during his political exile during the 1920s. That period deeply influenced his artistry and themes as a poet. In that regard, "Black Snake" is also a manifestation of the poet's belief in the need to preserve the natural and ecological integrity of Amazonia. Using the mythical past and referencing the "primitive," Bopp plunges the reader into thinking about "modern" Brazilian and universal concerns. The mythical and symbolic journey—through the dense Amazon—of the poem's protagonist is fraught with complications and solutions. The dilemma of the protagonist is the same one that human beings have endured in all times and spaces. "Black Snake" remains one of Brazil's most important works for its enduring universal message. Bopp's creative and ingenious use of poetic language also added to the definitive literary importance of this work.

BIBLIOGRAPHY

Bopp, Raul. "Black Snake." In *Twentieth-Century Latin American Poetry: A Bilingual Anthology,* edited by Stephen Tapscott, 133–137. Austin: University of Texas Press, 1996.

James J. Davis

"BLACK WOMAN" NANCY MOREJÓN (1979)

One of Cuban writer NANCY MOREJÓN's most anthologized and best-known works is "*Mujer Negra.*" According to the author, this compelling poem came to her in a dream of a woman appearing at her bedroom window. The next morning Morejón recorded the voice of the spirit she had dreamed about. The speaker is the black woman throughout Cuba's history, from when she was brought to the island as a slave to the recognition of her personhood after the 1959 revolution. In spite of the terrible circumstances of her existence, the black woman is not simply a victim of colonialism; she is a resilient actor in the drama of history and is in fact a protagonist in the postrevolutionary society. Although Morejón herself says she was not writing a feminist poem, the fact that the main character is a woman who is at the center of the struggle for racial freedom and whose role is essential to the history of her nation leads critics to read the work as feminist.

The chronological arrangement of the poem provides a woman's perception of the price history has extracted from her. The first, free-verse stanza tells of her being taken by men who "left me here and here I've lived," with only the memories of her West African homeland to sustain her. Sold into bondage, the

woman becomes "His Worship's" mistress. As her slavery continues, she builds the nation but cannot share in the benefits of its growth. Escaping the cruelty of slavery, the woman enters the long struggle for freedom, from the 1895 revolution led by the black Cuban Antonio Maceo against Spanish rule to the revolution of 1959 led by Fidel Castro.

Each section of the poem ends with an affirmation of action on the part of the speaker. In the face of each adversity, the black woman proudly says, "I rebelled . . . I walked . . . I rose up . . . I worked . . . I left . . . [and] I came down." Each deed is an act of both self-preservation and defiance. Significantly, when the black woman comes "down from the Sierra," it is to join others; the *"my"* at the beginning of the poem has become the *"our"* of the revolution that made it possible for all, especially Cubans of African descent, to become full participants in the new society.

"*Mujer Negra*" is representative of recurring concerns in Morejón's poetry: the strength and determination of women, pride in African and Cuban history and culture, and support for the revolutionary Marxist regime. The poem was first published in *Parajes de una época* (Places of an Epoch) in 1979. An English translation by Kathleen Weaver is found in *Where the Island Sleeps like a Wing* (a dual-language edition published in 1985).

BIBLIOGRAPHY

Morejón, Nancy. "Mujer Negra." Translated by Kathleen Weaver. In *Where the Island Sleeps Like a Wing: Selected Poetry.* Oakland, Calif.: Black Scholar Press, 1985.

Jean Hamm

"BLACK WOMAN" Léopold Sédar Senghor (1945)

Published in his first collection of poetry, *Chants d'ombre* (Songs of Darkness or Shadow Songs), "Black Woman" is a short praise song to the beauty of black women. Moreover, like other poems in *Chants* and throughout the canon of LÉOPOLD SÉDAR SENGHOR, the poem celebrates blackness itself, as well as African landscape and culture, thereby revising pejorative evaluations. It is therefore characteristic of Senghor's early poetry and of the manner in which it undertakes the projects of the NEGRITUDE MOVEMENT that Senghor helped to found and define, and it remains widely anthologized.

"Black Woman" is divided into four short stanzas that alternately begin "Naked woman, black woman" and "Naked woman, dark woman." Throughout the poem the persona speaks directly to the title subject, the "black woman," using imagery and metaphorical language (particularly mixed metaphors) to depict both her and her blackness as beautiful. The black woman is "[d]ressed in" a "color that is life" (Stanza 1, l. 2) and has a "form that is beauty (1. 2). She is "discover[ed]" as a "Promised Land" (1. 5) and is a "[r]ipe fruit with firm flesh, dark raptures of black wine" (2.2). Such language simultaneously pays homage to the beauty of black women and also (re)defines blackness itself as beautiful, life-giving. In fact, even in death, while her "passing beauty" has been "fix[ed] . . . for all Eternity" (4.2) by the poet, the black woman is "reduce[d] to ashes to nourish the roots of life" (4.3).

In addition to such poetic technique, Senghor also uses imagery of African land, culture, and fauna to depict the beauty of black women. The black woman is a "savanna quivering to the fervent caress / Of the East Wind, sculptured tom-tom, stretched drumskin" (2.4–5); she is "oil soothing . . . the thighs of the princes of Mali / Gazelle with celestial limbs" (3.2–4). Such imagery concurrently etches the beauty of black women while also valuing and valorizing Africa and African culture, which here situates the black woman within a broader cultural milieu and also becomes the touchstone for the poet's very definition of beauty, thereby rendering in poetic form the African aesthetic that Senghor strove to define in his essays. Moreover, in a broader metaphor, the black woman may be seen as Africa itself.

At the same time, while "Black Woman" celebrates its subject, it also clearly depicts black womanhood through a perspective coded as male by the language of the poem. Though the speaker "grew up in [her] shadow" (1.3), as the "promised land" "discover[ed]" by the speaker, as the "drumskin / Moaning under the hands of the conqueror" (2.5–6), as the "oil soothing . . . princes," the black woman depicted here is viewed by, acted upon by, or acts for a male figure who, in the imagery of the poem, is colonizer, "conqueror," ruler. Her beauty, while it is potentially maternal in early

lines (1.3–4), is highly eroticized throughout the piece. In addition, even though imagery evokes the voice of the black woman—who is "[m]outh that gives music" (2.3) and whose "voice is the spiritual song of the Beloved" (2.7)—her voice is not heard in the poem, and the larger portion of the imagery pertains to her physical body (skin, hair, eyes). Such a reading, however, does not mitigate the negritude ideals expressed by the poem.

BIBLIOGRAPHY
Senghor, Léopold Sédar. *The Collected Poetry.* Translated by Melvin Dixon. Charlottesville: University Press of Virginia, 1991.

Yasmin Y. DeGout

BLAGA, LUCIAN (1895–1961)

Lucian Blaga was born on May 9, 1895, in the large household of the parish priest of the village of Lancram in Transylvania (in present-day Romania). Though the early death of his father hampered his secondary education, Lucian showed promise as a teenage poet with a romantic, spiritual, and philosophical bent of mind. At the age of 25 he took a Ph.D. degree in philosophy at the University of Philosophy in Vienna. During these green years was laid the foundation for the growth of a great national poet—"maybe the most original creator of images in Romanian literature" (Eugen Lovinescu)—one who was denied his laurels from the world at large, but not by those who revered him. As a poet he is placed in the company of Mihai Eminescu and Mihail Sadoveanu, on the one side, and Ion Barbu, on the other. His originality incorporates a resurrection of national (and related) mythologies, marking "a return of the house-gods, the forest spirits and a national historicity" (Don Eulert).

Blaga's close identification with nature is revealed in his series of poems on the folk archetypal figure of Pan. These view nature from the inside in a pristine litany that evokes the diverse and palpable domains of the senses in an elemental setting, drawing a fine line between life and death, Dionysian wholeness and Apollonian individuation. Pan expresses his passion to the Nymph: "I would tear you like warm bread / your movement casts sweet moments into my blood" (*The*

Death of Pan). And Pan's loneliness—in Pan Sings—highlights, perhaps, Blaga's own: "I am alone and covered with burrs. / Master once of a sky of stars / and to the worlds / I sang through my pipes." In Self-Portrait he declares himself as being "silent as a swan" searching for "the water / from which the rainbow drinks its beauty and its non-being." To Blaga, "no suffering is too great / to be changed into song" (Quatrain). He sees himself as a poet who "translates" into the Romanian language only those songs that nature whispers to him, "softly murmured, in her own language" (Versifier), recalling the Muse of oral poetry investing the mind of the bard with divine knowledge of human mutability.

Blaga has been seen as an anti-intellectualist and agnostic, open to spiritual revelations from various quarters of life. As Constantin Ciopraga has observed, the trajectory of Blaga's poetry is seen as "essentially reaching out towards the transcendent" and as embodying a state of "self-contemplation."

In his lifetime Blaga gathered experience as poet, philosopher, playwright, journalist, and librarian. He was elected to the Romanian Academy in 1936. Two years later he was appointed professor of the philosophy of culture at the University of Cluj; and his works On Philosophical Cognition (1947) and Anthropological Aspects (1948) emerged as publications from lectures prepared for the courses he taught there. From the 1920s, for four decades Blaga penned numerous treatises on culture, history, art, and language, plays (e.g., Noah's Ark, 1944), memoirs, aphorisms, a novel (Charon's Ferry, 1990), and seven collections of poetry. In 1983 his Posthumous Poems were published.

In 1956 unfounded political allegations against Blaga by the prevailing communist government in Bucharest (it was said) scuttled his nomination for the Nobel Prize in literature. On May 6, 1961, he died of cancer and was buried in his village of Lancram under the cool shade of the goronul trees he loved. Romanians look upon him not only as one of the greatest of poets that Romania has produced, but as a universal seer with a cosmic vision whose poetry "constitutes as a body an exceptional document of the human condition in general" (Constantin Ciopraga).

BIBLIOGRAPHY

Blaga, Lucian. Poems of Light. Translated and introduced by Don Eulert, with a preface by Constantin Ciopraga. Bucharest: Minerva, 1975.

Rupendra Guha Majumdar

BLOK, ALEKSANDR A. (1880–1921)

Aleksandr Blok, a prolific poet, dramatist, and essayist, is the most widely known representative of Russian symbolism. The son of a law professor at Warsaw University, Aleksandr Blok grew up in the family of his mother, many of whom were respected members of the Petersburg intelligentsia. Aleksandra Beketova-Blok was a translator and writer who provided a stimulating atmosphere for her son, acquainting him with literature and music from an early age. Blok began to devote himself to poetry during his student years, first at law school and then at the Historical-Philological Faculty of St Petersburg University. His early poems were later published as a collection, Ante Lucem.

Russian symbolism (embodied in the works of Dmitry Merezhkovsky, Konstantin Dmitrievich Bal'mont, Valery Briusov, Fyodor Sologub, Zinaida Gippius)—a neoromantic reaction against the earlier realist and positivist trends—had existed as a poetic school since the 1890s. Blok began to associate with the symbolists in 1903, together with the poets Andrey Belyi and Vyacheslav Ivanov. In that same year Blok made his literary debut in the symbolist journal Novyi Put' (The New Way). The teachings of the religious philosopher Vladimir Solovyov left a clear mark on Blok's early verse, and Blok's first collection in book form, Stikhi k prekrasnoi dame (Verses to the Beautiful Lady, 1904), brought him wide critical recognition. The Beautiful Lady is an elusive feminine presence modeled on the Solovyovian idea of the Eternal Feminine or Divine Wisdom, who is supposed to appear on Earth after the Apocalypse and herald the Kingdom of God. The metaphysical plane overlaps with reality, as the poems are also a celebration of Blok's love for Lyubov Mendeleeva, who became his wife in 1904 and onto whom the poet projected his ideas, calling her in a diary entry from 1902 "the earthly incarnation of the Eternal Feminine." The poems are permeated by a premonition of doom characteristic of many fin de siècle works and in places reminiscent of the liturgy as a result of their melodious quality and elaborate incantatory repetitions.

Blok's second collection, *Nechaiannaia Radost'* (Inadvertent Joy), came out in 1906. In the wake of the 1905 revolution, the early, romantic mood of symbolism gradually changed to a more skeptical attitude. At the time Blok often undertook long nightly strolls through Petersburg, visited the dens, and participated in drunken excesses. The epitome of his poetic creation in this period is the poem *Neznakomka* (The Stranger), indicating that Blok had found a new female source of inspiration. The elusive eternal feminine was replaced by a stranger in black, whose quiet dignity makes her stand out among the nightly crowd. As in the case of the beautiful lady, Blok found an incarnation of the stranger in a real woman, the actress Natalia Volkhova, with whom Blok had a passionate affair. To her the poet dedicated the collection *Snezhnaia Maska* (The Snow Mask, 1907). Here the unfettered aspect of the blizzard engulfing the poet symbolizes the dynamics of their relationship.

Blok had always been interested in the theater. In 1906 he wrote four plays in verse. The staging of *Balaganchik* (The Puppet Show) by the famous director Vsevolod Meyerhold was a key event both for symbolism and for avant-garde theater. The other plays are *Neznakomka* (The Stranger), *Korol' na plohchadi* (The King in the Square), and *Pesnya Sud'by* (The Song of Fate). In 1912–13 he wrote the verse play *Roza i krest* (The Rose and the Cross).

Blok abandoned both the mystical exaltation of his early poetry and the despair of the urban poems around 1910, when he turned his attention toward Russia and its destiny. At this time symbolism as a unified movement began to fall apart and was increasingly losing out to the upcoming poetic schools of acmeism (see ANNA AKHMATOVA, OSIP MANDELSTAM) and futurism (Khlebnikov, MAYAKOVSKY, PASTERNAK). In the collection *Rodina* (Motherland, 1910) Russia emerges as a new female source of inspiration. Russia as a mother is a widely used metaphor in Russian literature, but here Russia turns into a gentle wife, an image that alludes to the intuitive qualities of the Russian soul. Within that collection it is above all the cycle *Na pole Kulikovom* (On Kulikovo Field) that deserves attention. The battle

on Kulikovo Field, where Dmitry Donskoi defeated the Tartars in 1380, is an established symbol of national identity. Blok's poem focuses not on the precise moment in history but rather on the symbolic significance of the event. The last poem of the cycle ends with the words "The clouds have gathered for a purpose. Your hour has come. Pray!" Influenced by Friedrich Nietzsche (1844–1900) and his idea of eternal recurrence, the poet is convinced that Russia is once again facing a time of battle and tribulation, from which it will emerge strong and victorious. The events of World War I and the October Revolution (1917) confirmed Blok's vision of impending struggle as a sombre prophecy.

In an essay written in 1918, *Intelligentsia i revoliutsia* (The Intelligentsia and the Revolution), he writes: "The artist has to see, the artist is *obliged* to see *that which* is conceived, and to hear the music with which the 'air torn by the wind' is resounding." To Blok music was the most important element in poetry, and he greeted the revolution as an essentially creative event resounding with the music of the "universal orchestra of the nation's spirit." His dark premonition had come true, but the poet was confident that the revolution would make life "more just, clean, happy, and beautiful." "What did you think? That revolution is idyllic? That creation does not bring destruction?" he exhorted his compatriots in *The Intelligentsia and the Revolution*.

Blok "heard" his possibly greatest work during this period. The 12-poem cycle *Dvenadtsat'* (The Twelve) was composed in the wake of the dissolution of the short-lived democratically elected Constituent Assembly in January 1918. *The Twelve* is a narrative depicting the march of 12 marauding revolutionaries through wintertime Petersburg, overarched by an attempt at a metaphysical interpretation of the events, but it is above all an intensely musical poem, picking up on street slang and weaving folk song forms into the stanzas. This poem, one that Blok refused to read or to interpret publicly, was rejected by Blok's former symbolist friends as well as by the authorities. The ending, in which Jesus Christ leads the procession of the Twelve under the red flag, is to the present day the subject of scholarly controversy. A few days after he completed *The Twelve*, Blok conceived *Skify* (THE SCYTHIANS), a passionate poem celebrating Russia's double nature as both Asian and European and warning Europe to embrace the new world order coming from Russia or perish as the ancient civilizations before had done.

Blok wrote no new poetry after *The Twelve* and *The Scythians,* reportedly because he could "no longer hear the music of the world." He continued to write essays and lectures and to edit his poems. Increasingly disillusioned with the course of political events, Blok died in 1921.

BIBLIOGRAPHY
Pyman, Avril. *The Life of Aleksandr Blok.* 2 vols. Oxford and New York: Oxford University Press, 1979–1980.
Hackel, Sergei. *The Poet and the Revolution: Aleksandr Blok's "The Twelve."* Oxford: Clarendon Press, 1975.
Reeve, F. D. *Aleksandr Blok: Between Image and Idea.* 1962. Reprint, New York: Columbia University Press, 1980.
Berberova, Nina. *Aleksandr Blok: A Life.* Translated from the French by Robyn Marsack. New York: Carcanet, 1996.

Josephine von Zitzewitz

BOBROWSKI, JOHANNES (1917–1965) No

modern German poet has articulated eastern European (pre-)history, landscapes, and mythologies so extensively and acutely as Johannes Bobrowski. Sharing thematic and stylistic affinities with poems by Sappho, Friedrich Klopstock (1729–1802), and Friedrich Hölderlin (1770–1843), Bobrowski's poems fuse concise evocations of nature with erotic and religious motifs. Demanding and exemplifying remembrance of obliterated eastern European ethnic groups and cultures, many of Bobrowski's short apostrophic and prosopopoeic texts suggest an immediate, if unanswered, attempt at dialogic exchange with forgotten voices.

Born in Tilsit, East Prussia, in 1917, Bobrowski spent his childhood and early adulthood in East Prussia. The son of a railroad administrator and medical officer, Bobrowski received his early education in Königsberg (today Kaliningrad), Immanuel Kant's hometown on the Baltic Sea. From his early teens Bobrowski was an active member of an independent Protestant church alliance, and in 1936, together with his whole family, he joined the Bekennende Kirche (Confessing Church), an independent Protestant organization that resisted the Nazi dictatorship's instru-

mentalization (or political use) of religion. In 1937, immediately after receiving his high school diploma, Bobrowski was drafted into the military. During World War II he was stationed in Poland, France, and the USSR. In late 1941 and early 1942 he was allowed to leave the front in order to study art history in Berlin for one semester. During a brief home visit in 1943, he married Johanna Buddrus. From the end of the war until December 1949, he was held as a prisoner of war in the Soviet Union. In early 1950, shortly after his release, Bobrowski became an editor in East Berlin. Two years later his daughter Juliane was born, followed by his sons Justus in 1957 and Carl-Adam in 1964.

During the cold war Bobrowski kept a low political profile as a member of the Christian Democratic Party in the German Democratic Republic (GDR), an officially tolerated opposition party. Throughout the 1950s several of his poems and prose pieces were included in various literary magazines and anthologies in both West and East Germany, most important in the East German journal *Sinn und Form,* whose main editor, the poet Peter Huchel, was later put under house arrest by the GDR regime. Bobrowski's first book of poetry, *Sarmatische Zeit* (Sarmatian Time), was published in two competing editions in the Federal Republic of Germany (FRG), or West Germany, and in the GDR in 1961. In the same year two of his poems appeared in English translation in the *Times Literary Supplement,* and several poems and novellas appeared in Czech translation. In 1962, when his second volume of poetry, *Schattenland Ströme* (Shadow Land Streams), was published, Bobrowski's achievements began to be recognized internationally; *Schattenland Ströme* includes the important poem "EXPERIENCE." In the same year Bobrowski received the Alma-Johanna-Koenig award in Vienna, as well as the Gruppe 47 award in Berlin. In 1965, shortly before his death, he was honored with the Heinrich Mann Award and the International Charles Veillon Prize for his novel *Levin's Mühle* (Levin's Mill, 1964). Bobrowski died in East Berlin in 1965. In 1966 his second novel, *Litauische Claviere* (Lithuanian Pianos), came out; and in 1967 Bobrowski's third volume of poetry, *Wetterzeichen* (Weather Signs), was published. In the same year he was posthumously honored by the Berlin Academy of the Arts with the F.C. Weiskopf Prize.

BIBLIOGRAPHY

Bobrowski, Johannes. *From the Rivers.* Translated by Ruth Mead and Matthew Mead. London: Anvil Press, 1975. Reprinted and rearranged by the same translators in *Shadow Lands: Selected Poems.* New York: New Directions Press, 1994.

Scrase, David: *Understanding Johannes Bobrowski.* Columbia: University of South Carolina Press, 1995.

Wieczorek, John P. *Between Sarmatia and Socialism: The Life and Works of Johannes Bobrowski.* Amsterdam and Atlanta: Rodopi, 1999.

Olaf Berwald

"BOILED DUMPLINGS" SHAUL TCHERNI-CHOVSKY (1902)

SHAUL TCHERNICHOVSKY's first idyll, "Boiled Dumplings" (Levivot Mevushalot), was composed in Heidelberg, Germany, in 1902 and has been celebrated for its coherence, vibrancy, bittersweet humor, and multiplex form, as well as for its engagement with weighty matters significant at the time of its writing. Set among the pastoral fields of the Ukraine, it opens with a lyrical description of a bright spring morning as the sun breaks through, the lark awakes, and Gittel, the old rabbi's widow, rises from her warm bed. It is as if the universe, enveloped by a "dreamy calm," has risen and is stunned by the splendor of the world: "It seemed as if the universe greeted her now with a charming smile / As if everything was glad, rejoicing at life's abundant beauty." Gittel recites the morning prayer, observes the cat licking the milk, and descends to the basement to fetch the cheese and jugs of buttermilk essential for the dumplings she intends to make. Before long this tranquil atmosphere is shattered with the appearance of the gentile Domaha, who hints at the crumbling of the old world and the emergence of a new order that the two women struggle to understand. Domaha, who laments the disintegration of Christianity (". . . faith has disappeared in the people. / Who comes to the monastery service / Two old men, three old women, while they are still alive . . . ?"), empathizes with Gittel's grief over the dwindling of the Jewish generation. Domaha remarks that the Jews of the day are heretics, eating pigs, smoking on the Sabbath—in sharp contrast to when she was a child and the Sabbath was honored. The gentile woman tells Gittel that she feels guilty patronizing a Jewish shop on the Sabbath and reproaches Zalman, the Jewish trader, for daring to sell on that holy day. The Jewish trader responds, good-naturedly, by telling Domaha's son that his mother should become their rabbi. When Domaha leaves and Gittel sifts the flour, we realize that the epic serenity of the first lines is merely an outer one, concealing an elegiac core. Watching the specks of flour fall through the sieve, Gittel recalls the ups and downs, the suffering, hard labor, and moments of bliss she has experienced. The poem's second section illustrates the effects of dwindling faith by narrating the tragic fortunes of Razeleh, Gittel's granddaughter. Gittel's son leaves the small town for St. Petersburg, where his Jewish way of life is weakened by his having to adjust to the urban milieu. He stands in awe of the enormous developments encircling him. Affected by the overpowering metropolis, the rabbi's son enrolls his daughter (Razeleh) in a Russian high school. His wife, too, accepts the break with tradition and delights in seeing their daughter excel in her studies. Soon the poems of Aleksandr Pushkin (1799–1837) instead of the scriptural and midrashic texts are what Razeleh imbibes. The poem here draws clear parallels between Gittel's preparation of the dumplings and her ruminations about her granddaughter. Gittel's dumplings, she notes, come out uniform like the students in the Russian gymnasium, who evolve into revolutionaries. In short, Razaleh over time had become quiet, forlorn, and noncommunicative. In the end embodying the defiant generation, stripped of nationalistic ideals, and removed from the traditional anchor of home and faith—Razaleh had broken away from her studies and been swept up by the Russian Revolution. Razaleh's doom—as the old woman learns from a letter sent from prison—is incarceration for opposing the oppressive regime of the czar. Shocked by the terrifying reality of this dismal result, Gittel faints. As she lies unconscious on the floor, the room is bathed in rays of light that caress her cheeks and stir her into waking. Opening her eyes, she hears the boiling of the water in the pot and spies the dumplings nestled amongst the bubbles. The sunlight and the traditional cooking, we perceive, endure.

BIBLIOGRAPHY

Ha'efrati, Yosef, ed. *Saul Tchernichowsky, A Selection of Critical Essays of his Writings.* Tel Aviv: Am Oved, 1976.

Sha'anan, Avraham. *Saul Tchernichowsky: Monograph.* Tel Aviv: Hidekel, 1984.

Yaniv, Shlomo. *The Hebrew Ballad.* Haifa: Haifa University Press, 1986.

Dvir Abramovich

BOPP, RAUL (1898–1984)

Raul Bopp was born on August 4, 1898, in Vila Pinhal in the Brazilian state of Rio Grande do Sul. He studied law in various Brazilian cities from 1918 to 1925, the year he received a law degree. During the 1920s he spent a great deal of time traveling throughout the Amazon region to become familiar with all aspects of Brazil's culture and life. In 1922 he participated in the Week of Modern Art (São Paulo), which officially launched the Brazilian Modernist Movement. Bopp would later become a member of the Anthropophagic Movement (O Movimiento Antropofágico) and Brazilian Wood (Pau Brazil), whose basic tenet was to break away from European and North American hegemony in the arts and culture. In 1932 he published his first volume of poetry, *Cobra Norato* (Black Snake), which would become one of the most important works of Brazilian modernism. The long poem entitled *"Cobra Norato"* ("BLACK SNAKE")—which constitutes the entire volume—demonstrates the poet's conscious effort to break away from traditional forms and poetic sources. In *"Cobra Norato"* Bopp draws on Brazilian myths and legends while utilizing indigenous and African words and phrases to capture the essence of what Brazil was in the past and what it is today: a culture that comprises significant influences from indigenous and African cultures. *Twentieth-Century Latin American Poetry: A Bilingual Anthology* includes an excellent translation of sections of *"Cobra Norato"* (133–137).

Bopp later worked as a journalist and diplomat, which provided him the opportunity to travel extensively through almost every continent and become familiar with many world cultures. This undoubtedly expanded his vision and the themes in his poetry, although his topics were consistently about Brazil, and he remained a profound nationalist throughout his life.

In addition to his poetic works, Bopp published, between 1942 and 1973, several volumes in prose. Some of the titles give an indication of the poet's literary and cultural concerns: *América* (America); *Notas de Viagem: Uma Volta ao Mundo em Trinta Dias* (Trip Notes: A Tour around the World in Thirty Days); *Memorias de um Embaixador* (Memories of an Ambassador); *Movimentos modernistas no Brasil: 1922/1928* (Modernist Movements in Brazil: 1922/1928); *Caminho para Brasil* (Road to Brazil); *Vida e morte da antropofagia* (Life and Death of Anthropophagy); and *Livro do nenê antropofágico* (Book of/on the Anthropophagic Child). Before his death on June 2, 1984, Raul Bopp witnessed the production of a film about his life, *Raul Bopp* (1975), and the staging of a dramatic play based on his most popular work, *Cobra norato por e para Raul Bopp* (Black snake by and for Raul Bopp, 1979).

BIBLIOGRAPHY

Madureira, Luís. *Cannibal Modernities: Postcoloniality and the Avant-Garde in Caribbean and Brazilian Literature.* Charlottesville and London: University of Virginia Press, 2005.

Tapscott, Stephen, ed. *Twentieth-Century Latin American Poetry: A Bilingual Anthology.* Austin: University of Texas Press, 1996.

James J. Davis

BORGES, JORGE LUIS (1899–1986)

Jorge Luis Borges's poems have long been obscured by his celebrated short stories. His fame as a prose writer notwithstanding, Borges produced an extensive body of verse that includes some of the most important metaphysical poetry of the 20th century.

Borges was born in Buenos Aires, Argentina, on August 24, 1899, the son of a highly educated, patrician family. Owing to his mother's British ancestry and his father's anglophile tendencies, "Georgie" was educated from an early age in the English language and its literature. When the family traveled to Europe in 1916, Borges came in contact with French symbolism, German expressionism, and especially Spanish ultraism. The latter association led to his first book of poetry, *Fervor de Buenos Aires* (1923). Borges's use of free verse and his stark urban imagery placed him at the vanguard of South American *ultraismo,* but he soon lost interest in the movement's strictly minimalist tenets against narrative elements and any sort of effusion. With *Luna de enfrente* (Moon Across the Way, 1925) and the short *Cuaderno San Martín* (San Martín Notebook, 1929), Borges continued his poetic mapping of Buenos Aires, but with a greater willingness to employ traditional poetic forms from a more personal perspective. He also began to explore the themes that would come to dominate his mature writing: death, memory, history, and aesthetics. From 1929 to 1960 Borges worked as a municipal librarian while writing many of the short stories that would come to earn him international renown. As a result of this ever-growing prominence, he was appointed director of the National Library in 1955 and, a year later, professor of English literature at the University of Buenos Aires. It was also at this point that Borges's chronically poor eyesight degenerated to virtual blindness. His literary and economic status assured, but his short story writing inhibited by seriously impaired vision, Borges returned to writing poetry with the collection *El hacedor* (The Maker, 1960). A mixture of prose poems and classical verse forms, *El hacedor* is a meditation on the nature of artistic creation within the labyrinthine metaphysics most commonly associated with Borges's prose. The collection is also characterized by the extensive use of philosophical, literary, and historical conceits—a distinguishing element of Borges's mature poetry. In 1961 Borges shared the International Publishers Prize with Samuel Beckett. The worldwide recognition that followed led to extensive travel throughout the United States, Europe, and Japan. His neobaroque union of traditional form and philosophical content attained its fullest expression with his exploration of human destiny in *El otro, el mismo* (The Self and the Other, 1964). In 1967 the lifelong bachelor, who had lived much of his adult life with his mother, Leonor, married Elsa Astete Millán. Although the couple had been friends for years, the marriage ended after three years, and Borges took up residence with his mother once again. His next collection, *Elogio de la sombra* (In Praise of Darkness, 1969), was a poignant and highly personal meditation on blindness and the inevitability of death. In the last two decades of his life, Borges continued to expand his enigmatic poetic universe in collections that include *El oro de los tigres* (The Gold of the Tigers,

1972), *La moneda de hierro* (The Iron Coin, 1976), and *Historia de la noche* (History of the Night, 1977). Shortly before his death in 1986, Borges married his Japanese language translator, María Kodama.

Today Borges's poetry has emerged from the shadow of his prose. While his early ultraist production remains an important part of Latin American literary history, it is his mature work that has assured Borges a place in Hispanic literature alongside Quevedo and Unamuno in the tradition of great metaphysical poets. Alexander Coleman's bilingual edition of Borges's *Selected Poems* (Penguin, 2000) constitutes the best available single-volume edition. An outstanding collection of critical essays is *Borges the Poet,* edited by Carlos Cortínez (Fayetteville: University of Arkansas Press, 1986).

Eric L. Reinholtz

BOSE, BUDDHADEVA (1908–1974)   Buddhadeva Bose has been acknowledged as one of the most significant poetic figures of Indian and Bengali modernism. A prolific writer, a noteworthy critic, and a renowned academic, Bose was also the founder-editor of *Kavita* (Poetry), the earliest Bengali journal devoted solely to poetry. The firstborn child of Bhudebchandra and Binoykumari Basu, Bose was born in Comilla in eastern India, a town that in 1947 became part of East Pakistan and in 1972 part of Bangladesh. Binoykumari died within a day of giving birth to her first son, and Buddhadeva was brought up by his maternal grandparents with a love and affection that he remembered fondly in his writings. Bose was educated in Dhaka at Dhaka Collegiate School, Dhaka Intermediate College, and finally at Dhaka University, where he received B.A. and M.A. degrees in English literature. His literary career also began in Dhaka; his first collections of stories, poetry, and his first novel were published and his first play staged while he was a student at Dhaka University. He launched—with his friend and fellow poet Ajit Dutta—a literary journal, *Pragati* (Progress), the first few issues of which were distributed in manuscript format. In 1931, shortly after writing the final examination for an M.A. degree, Bose moved permanently from Dhaka to Calcutta. Even though the capital of the British Indian Empire had moved from Calcutta to New Delhi in 1911, Calcutta

in 1931 was still the great metropolitan city of the East, the center of great literary, cultural, and political momentum. Bose was eager to find a stimulating atmosphere for his writing career, and Calcutta provided him with that. In 1934 he married Protiva Shome, then an acclaimed singer, who became a prolific and popular writer of fiction soon afterward. Protiva shared Bose's literary enthusiasm and stood by him during the years of financial and professional struggle and hardship. In 1935 Bose founded *Kavita* (Poetry) as a quarterly magazine. It soon became the leading Bengali poetry magazine of its time, contributing not only to the showcasing of works by both established and emerging poets, but also to the discussion, review, and criticism of contemporary poetry. From 1934 to 1945 Bose earned his living teaching English literature at Ripon College, in Wisconsin, to a body of mostly unconcerned students, and did freelancing and editorial work for *The Statesman* newspaper. In 1953 he traveled to the United States on a Fulbright grant to teach for a year at the Pennsylvania College for Women. On his return to India he began the work of setting up a department of comparative literature at Jadavpur University, Calcutta, and joined the department as its head in 1956. Bose traveled abroad in 1961 and again in 1963 on lecture and teaching tours. He was awarded the Sahitya Akademi Award in 1967 (the highest Indian literary prize), the Ananda Prize in 1972, and a posthumous Rabindra Prize in 1974. He suffered a major stroke and died on March 18, 1974.

Bose had begun his literary career with a mission to define Bengali modernism in the shadow of the Nobel laureate RABINDRANATH TAGORE (1861–1941), whose versatility had made it impossible for younger writers to assert their creative independence. Like many of his contemporaries, Bose had sought the antidote for Tagorean style and diction in French symbolism and modernism. The influence of the poetry and ethos of Charles Baudelaire on Bose's poetic enterprise could not be overemphasized. His early collections *Bandir Bandana* (A Prisoner's Song of Praise, 1930) and *Kankabati* (1937) broke free from the contemporary Bengali romantic poetry, both in style and content, and drew inspiration from Baudelaire, as, for example, in his well-known poem "HILSA." Later in life, Bose would take on the translation of Baudelaire's poems into Bengali as a labor of love. Even as he endeavored all his life to break free from Tagore's creative influence, Bose remained an enchanted admirer of his great literary predecessor. He wrote a fond memoir of time spent in Shantiniketan, Tagore's university, titled *Sab-peyechhir Deshey* (Country of Fulfilled Wishes, 1941). In his first significant novel, *Tithidor* (The Moment's Bond, 1949), the principal male and the female characters meet for the first time on the day of Tagore's death as they join thousands of mourners in the poet's funeral procession in Calcutta. Bose continued to write successfully in different genres. In between the publication of his books of poetry—*Draupadir Sari* (Darupadi's Cloth, 1948), *Sheeter Prarthana: Basanter Uttar* (Winter's Prayer: Spring's Answer, 1955), *Je Andhar Alor Odhik* (The Darkness That Is Greater Than Light, 1958), and *Morche-para Pereker Gan* (Song of a Rusty Nail, 1966)—he wrote several plays, one of them based on the Electra myth: *Kolkatar Elektra* (The Electra of Calcutta, 1968). One of his later novels, *Raat Bhorey Brishti* (Rain through the Night, 1967), was accused of obscenity, but the civil suit filed against Bose was dismissed. The novel was translated into English by Clinton B. Seely (1973).

BIBLIOGRAPHY

Bose, Buddhadeva. *An Acre of Green Grass: A Review of Modern Bengali Literature.* Calcutta: Orient Longmans, 1948.

Dasgupta, Alokeranjan. *Buddhadeva Bose.* New Delhi: Sahitya Akademi, 1977.

Dyson, Ketaki Kushari, ed. and trans. *Selected Poems of Buddhadeva Bose.* New Delhi: Oxford University Press, 2003.

Rini Bhattacharya Mehta

BOUCHET, ANDRÉ DU (1924–2001)

The son of Russian immigrants, André du Bouchet was born in Paris and left France as a teenager, when his family moved to the United States at the outbreak of World War II. He studied at Amherst College and Harvard University. After his return to France, du Bouchet published his first volume of poetry, *Air,* in 1951, followed by *Cette surface* (1956), and in 1961 by *Dans la chaleur vacante*—translated by David Mus as *Where Heat Looms* (Los Angeles: Sun and Moon Press, 1996). In 1967 du Bouchet cofounded the literary magazine

L'Éphémère, together with literary critics and fellow poets, including JACQUES DUPIN, YVES BONNEFOY, and PAUL CELAN.

Du Bouchet's poetry explores the materiality of seeing and rehearses variations on blindness and absence. Immediate sense perceptions and aesthetic reflections are inextricably fused in his work. An idiosyncratic typography (most pages give room to vast empty spaces) adds a concrete visual layer to his lyrical discussions of lacunae. The sparse syntax is part of a slow and spiraling textual movement. Du Bouchet's precise and perceptive work can be read as one continuous set of self-modifying parallel drafts that form an unprecedented auto- and intertextual process. In lyrical prose fragments that defy genre definition, du Bouchet considered classical and 20th-century works of visual art, from a 1959 text that examines Poussin's *Blind Orion* to essayistic responses to the modernist works of Alberto Giacometti and Pierre Tal-Coat, with whom he occasionally collaborated. Du Bouchet's later volumes of verse include *Peinture* (Painting) (1983), *Matière de l'interlocuteur* (1992), and *D'un trait qui figure et défigure* (About a Trace that Shapes and Disfigures, 1997). A prolific translator, he composed French versions of the works of, among others, William Shakespeare, Freidrich Hölderlin, Gerard Manley Hopkins, OSIP MANDELSTAM, James Joyce, and William Faulkner. His sympoetic friendship with Celan is manifest in mutual translations of each other's poetry and in their unpublished correspondence, available in the Deutsches Literaturarchiv in Marbach, Germany. Paul Auster's translations of du Bouchet's works, collected in his du Bouchet anthology *The Uninhabited* (New York: Living Hand, 1976), are thorough and lucid. It is time for a bilingual edition of du Bouchet's complete works.

Olaf Berwald

BOYE, KARIN (1900–1941)

The poetry of Karin Boye enjoys an honored place not only in the Swedish literary canon but also in popular Swedish language and culture. Newspaper reporters quote freely from her verse, confident in their frame of reference, and seven decades after her death her collected poems continue to be sold in state-subsidized, paper-

back form at train station kiosks. In October 2000, on the centennial of the poet's birth, Swedish poet Marie Silkeberg wrote in the culture pages of *Dagens Nyheter,* Sweden's largest-circulating daily newspaper: "Few poets are as read and loved as Karin Boye. Her poems have succeeded in living their own life. Perhaps they have become so incorporated into our culture and language, circulated so many revolutions, that they have been worn down and now exist there as a nearly anonymous source." Many consider Boye's language and ideas to be quintessentially Swedish in their melodic simplicity and moral tenor. Some of her most-quoted lines take the form of proverbs or aphorisms, such as the famous opening couplet *"Den mätta dagen, den är aldrig störst. / Den bästa dagen är en dag av törst"* (The fulfilled day is never greatest / The best day is a day of thirst) of her poem *"I rörelse"* (In Motion), from her collection *Härdarna* (The Hearths, 1927). These lines also demonstrate the enormous difficulty of rendering her verse adequately in English translation. While the Swedish couplet rhymes perfectly and only a single comma alters the rhythm from the first line to the second, the English equivalent lacks the melodiousness of the original, making these lines sound dogmatic rather than poetic. For this reason, the two poems from her later collections highlighted in this volume, "I WANT TO MEET . . ." and "PRAYER TO THE SUN," exemplify Boye's free verse and as such do not depend so heavily on the particular tonal patterns of the Swedish language. But Boye's masterful use of the particular tonal patterns of the Swedish language is exactly what has made her lyrical poetry so beloved to Swedes and popular among speakers of other Nordic languages that are close to Swedish, such as Danish and Norwegian.

In addition Boye is known for her extensive and groundbreaking work as a literary critic, translator, editor, and author of prose fiction during a crucial time in the development of literary modernism in Sweden. The radical breakthrough period of literary experimentation known as modernism began early in the 20th century elsewhere in Europe, spawned at least in part by the inescapable horrors of World War I and the mechanisms of the Industrial Revolution. But in agrarian and geographically remote Scandinavia, modernism was slow to develop and did not fully blossom until the 1940s. Boye's work as a poet and critic in the 1930s is considered instrumental in introducing modernist discourses in Sweden's still traditional and insulated cultural milieu.

Boye was born in the western coastal city of Gothenburg, Sweden's second-largest city, to parents of German descent and was proficient in German from a young age. When she was eight years old, her family moved to Stockholm, Sweden's capital. As a child Boye began writing poetry and exploring religious and existential questions. For her these tasks were interlinked, and as early as elementary school she held sessions with playmates in which they read and discussed religious and philosophical texts and wrote poetry. As an adolescent Boye famously declared to her schoolteacher that she was a Buddhist, and by young adulthood she had consciously embraced Christianity. Her early influences ranged from Rudyard Kipling's *Kim* to the philosophy of Rudolph Steiner. Once she enrolled at Uppsala University, north of Stockholm, she became a key figure in a radically pacifist student group known as Clarté, which fused communist and Freudian philosophies. Psychoanalysis became a cornerstone life philosophy for Boye, and she underwent psychoanalysis with the first Swede to be trained in Freud's method, a woman named Ahlfrid Tamm. Boye translated and wrote commentaries on a number of contemporary psychoanalytical texts from Germany and Austria for Clarté's journal, which she edited in the late 1920s. In 1928 she traveled with other Swedish Clartéists to the Soviet Union to study the fruits of the Bolshevik Revolution there and to interact with Soviet intellectuals and artists. In 1930 she and two other Clartéists, Erik Mesterton and Josef Riwkin, founded the groundbreaking cultural journal *Spektrum,* which published for a little more than two years but had an enormous impact on the development of literary modernism in Sweden. The editors published both original work, including polemical cultural commentary and experimental work by Swedish writers, and translations of previously published modernist and radical philosophical writing by contemporary Slavic, German, French, English, and Spanish writers. *Spektrum*'s most celebrated contribution was its 1932 publication, in Swedish translation, of the full text of the most famous English modernist

poem to date, *The Waste Land* (1922), by T.S. Eliot, who would win the Nobel Prize in literature in 1948. Boye and Mesterton's masterful cotranslation of the long poem, in Swedish *Det öde landet,* has entered the Swedish canon as a modernist literary text that Swedes consider more important for their literary history than the original. Boye also translated a number of important and difficult German modernist texts into Swedish for the first time, such as Thomas Mann's *Der Zauerberg* (The Magic Mountain, 1922).

For a brief period in the late 1920s, Boye was married to fellow Clartéist Leif Björk, an economist. The marriage was relatively short-lived as Boye struggled to come to terms with her own sexual identity, which was shaped by encounters with both male and female lovers. From 1932 to 1934, when Boye was living in Berlin and undergoing psychoanalysis there, she met a much younger woman, Margot Hanel, who would become Boye's long-term companion. When Boye returned to Sweden in 1934, she published her novel *Kris* (Crisis), which documents a young woman's struggle to come to terms with her homosexuality in a society that strictly interprets Christian doctrines to declare such love sinful. Boye had become increasingly alarmed by the rise of fascism in Germany, and Hanel, who was Jewish, soon joined Boye in Stockholm. Boye's final novel, *Kallocain* (1940), depicts a dystopic and totalitarian society in which individual creativity and humanism has no place. While Boye is most celebrated for her poetry, her novels also demonstrate her mastery of poetic language in prose fiction and are still read today. As World War II raged on the continent and Boye struggled to deal with the impending loss of a very close childhood friend to cancer, she became increasingly depressed. Boye committed suicide in 1941 by taking a walk in the countryside in subzero temperatures and taking an entire bottle of pills while sitting near a stream. Her body was not discovered for several days, and the search for her made the national news in Sweden. Once she was found, her death was mourned by many in Sweden, and fellow poet Hjalmar Gullberg published a now famous elegy to Boye titled "Död amazon" (Dead Amazon) in a leading literary journal the following month.

Poetically, among Boye's strongest influences were Swedish-Finnish EDITH SÖDERGRAN, the German modernists, and the southern Swedish poet Vilhelm Eke-lund, whose volume of poetry *Melodier i skymningen* (Melodies in Twilight, 1902) had been the first Swedish poetry published in free verse. While Ekelund's poetry never became popular in Sweden, it was required reading among Sweden's budding modernist poets. Boye, who studied history and ancient Greek and Nordic mythology at Uppsala University, appreciated how Ekelund anchored his figurative language in Nordic myth and legends. Boye's first volume of poetry, *Moln* (Clouds) was published when she still was a student at Uppsala University in 1922. This was followed by the collections *Gömda land* (Hidden Lands, 1924) and *Härdarna* (The Hearths, 1927). In student circles Boye had become known for her mesmerizing public readings of her poetry, and once her work became better known—and national radio came to Sweden in 1925—she began reading her poetry on Sveriges Radio's broadcasts. Recordings of her readings are frequently rebroadcast on present-day culture programs, and many Swedes are very familiar with Boye's charismatic voice. Following *Härdarna* Boye took a leave from publishing poetry and began publishing novels, starting with her award-winning *Astarte* (1931), an ironic fictional account of the idolization of a department store mannequin. Her engagement with Eliot's poem had a deep impact on her own work, and her next published volume of poetry, *För trädets skull* (For the Tree's Sake, 1935) was not only considered her most modernistic to date, but also reflected many tropes similar to those Eliot favored. Public reaction to this volume was mixed; it contained far more free verse than her earlier collections and reflected a deepening engagement with psychoanalysis, sexuality, and morality. Readers who had come to love Boye's work for its simple and harmonious lyricism felt betrayed by this new modernistic bent, and some of her colleagues accused her in reviews of kowtowing to continental trends. Such criticism wounded Boye, who considered this volume to reflect her most mature work to date. She did not publish another volume of poetry. The fifth and final collection, *De sju dödssynderna och andra efterlämnade dikter* (The Seven Deadly Sins and Other Posthumous Poems) was published following her death in 1941. Ironically Boye's most canonized poem

originally appeared in the 1935 collection: *Javisst gör det ont* (Of Course It Hurts), which she wrote to honor friend and fellow writer Elin Wägner. This poem demonstrates the mastery of Swedish melody, rhythm, and rhyme that marks her early poetry, as well as reflects the trope of cyclical rebirth featured in her later work. It has yet to be translated adequately, although David McDuff makes a valiant attempt in his *Complete Poems* (1994). McDuff's volume represents the only set of Boye's poems currently available in English translation.

BIBLIOGRAPHY
Abenius, Margit. *Drabbad av renhet: en bok om Karin Boyes liv och diktning* [Afflicted by Purity: A Book about Karin Boye's Life and Creative Work]. 3rd ed. Stockholm: Bonniers, 1965.
Boye, Karin. *Complete Poems.* Translated and introduced by David McDuff. Newcastle-upon-Tyne, U.K.: Bloodaxe Books, 1994.
Boye, Karin. *Ett verkligt jordiskt liv: brev* [A Real and Earthbound Life: Letters]. Collected and annotated by Paulina Helgeson. Stockholm: Bonniers, 2000.
Domellöf, Gunilla. *I oss är en mångfald levande: Karin Boye som kritiker och prosamodernist* [In Us a Multiplicity Lives: Karin Boye as a Critic and Modernist Prose Writer]. Ph.d. diss., University of Umeå, Sweden, 1986.
Karin Boye Society Web site. Available online. URL: http://www.karinboye.se/index-en.shtml. Accessed on December 23, 2005.
"Nordic Authors: Karin Boye." Projekt Runeberg online Nordic literary database. Available online. URL: http://runeberg.org/authors/kboye.html. Accessed on December 23, 2005.

Ursula A. L. Lindqvist

BRATHWAITE, EDWARD KAMAU (LAWSON EDWARD BRATHWAITE) (1930–)   Lawson Edward Kamau Brathwaite was born in Bridgetown, Barbados, and attended Harrison College in Barbados and Pembroke College, Cambridge University, from which he received a B.A. with honors in history in 1953 and a teaching certificate in 1954. He worked for the Ministry of Education in Ghana from 1955 to 1961. He began teaching at the University of the West Indies in 1962, first as a resident tutor at the St. Lucia campus and the following year at the Mona campus in Kingston, Jamaica, where he taught

in the History Department for nearly three decades. Brathwaite received a Ph.D. from the University of Sussex in 1968, publishing his dissertation in 1971 as *The Development of Creole Society in Jamaica, 1770–1820*. While living in England from 1965 to 1968, Brathwaite, along with Andrew Salkey and John LaRose, founded the Caribbean Arts Movement in 1966 and coedited its journal, *Savacou*. In 1972 he taught at Nairobi University, at which time he received the name "Kamau." Brathwaite has taught at Harvard and Yale Universities and since 1991 has been a professor of comparative literature at New York University.

Kamau Brathwaite is among the most influential figures in Caribbean letters. He has been instrumental in conceiving, formulating, and developing many ideas and practices that have been central in creating and understanding Caribbean art. Among these is the idea underwriting his poetry of "nation language," which he formulated directly in critical and historical essays, for example, *History of the Voice* (1984). His early practice of reciting over drums and music presaged "dub" poetry. Most recently, his "Sycorax Video Style" has employed experiments in material presentation to simulate an aural dimension of his poetry. Emphasizing the vernacular roots of Brathwaite's work, Ngugi wa Thiong'o has commented that Brathwaite "gropes for the word in its oral purity . . . for the voice of the peasant, the submerged voice of the many who toil and endure" (*World Literature Today*).

Brathwaite's extensive body of work includes poetry, short stories, plays, novels, history, and literary criticism. His more than 20 poetry collections include two landmark trilogies, *The Arrivants* (1988, first published separately in the late 1960s) and *Ancestors* (2001, first published separately in the late 1970s and 1980s); other volumes include *Middle Passages* (1992), *Roots* (1993), *The Zea Mexican Diary* (1993), *Barabajan Poems* (1994), *Trenchtown Rock* (1993), *Words Need Love Too* (2000), and *Born to Slow Horses* (2005). Brathwaite's many honors include the Cholmondeley Award (1970), Guggenheim Fellowship (1971), Fulbright Fellowship, Casa de las Americas Award, Commonwealth Poetry Prize, Bussa Award, Neustadt Prize (1994), and the Pride of Barbados Award (1998). He holds honorary doctorates from Oxford University, the Sorbonne, and the University of the West Indies.

BIBLIOGRAPHY

Bobb, June. *Beating a Restless Drum: The Poetics of Kamau Brathwaite and Derek Walcott*. Trenton, N.J.: Africa World Press, 1998.

Brathwaite, Kamau, and Chris Funkhouser. *ConVERSations with Nathaniel Mackey*. Minneapolis: We Press & XCP, 1999.

Brown, Stewart, ed. *The Art of Kamau Brathwaite*. Brigdend, Mid Glamorgan, Wales: Poetry Wales Press, 1995.

Reiss, Timothy J., ed. *For the Geography of a Soul: Emerging Perspectives on Kamau Brathwaite*. Trenton, N.J.: Africa World Press, 2001.

Walmsley, Anne. *The Caribbean Artists Movement, 1966–1972: A Literary and Cultural History*. London: New Beacon Books, 1992.

Williams, Emily. *The Critical Response to Kamau Brathwaite*. Westport, Conn.: Greenwood Press, 2004.

World Literature Today. Vol. 68, no. 4 (Autumn 1994). Special issue on Brathwaite.

Alex Feerst

BRECHT, BERTOLT (1898–1956)

An uncompromising adherent to socialist principles, Bertolt Brecht has been called the most influential playwright of the 20th century. His philosophical insistence that plays should educate, inform, and inspire social action in audiences complements his insistence on the need to distance an audience from any sentimental attachment to characters represented on stage. Taken together, this dual stress on the theater as a political tool and on drama as a self-conscious, artificial construct has had an impact on every major Western playwright since World War II. Even in ideological or aesthetic opposition to Brecht, dramatists must acknowledge the German's towering, ubiquitous presence. Several of Brecht's many plays remain seminal both on stage and in the study; Brecht's poetry, however, is less well known, even though many of the plays are enlivened with pointed, self-reflexive poems. Brecht asserted that his poetry was of only secondary importance to his main pursuit of politically transformative drama. This seems an appropriate judgment when it is considered that Brecht made little effort to publish the majority of the 1,000-plus poems that he wrote. Many were published posthumously, and hitherto unknown texts are still being uncovered by Brecht scholars. Brecht's poems, though, were often written for specific events such as radio broadcasts, for local political affairs, or for ephemeral publication in periodicals with sometimes only a tiny circulation. That Brecht made little effort to publish hundreds of his poems does not detract from their important place in the history of 20th-century political poetry. So many committed, serious Brechtian poems exist that they necessarily form a major part of his canon.

Despite Brecht's sometimes casual attitude toward his poetry's publication, the poems have always enjoyed a high reputation in western Europe and in America. For instance, the critic and philosopher Hannah Arendt—who was bitterly opposed to Brecht's apologies for absolute socialist rule—announced in an important essay: "I have no doubt that Bertolt Brecht is the greatest living German poet." There have been two important editions of Brecht's poems in English. In 1947 Brecht himself collaborated with H. R. Hays to facilitate the publication of his *Selected Poems* in English. And in 1976 John Willett and Ralph Manheim, after many years of research, presented over 500 of Brecht's poems (translated by many different translators) in the crucial English-language volume *Poems, 1913–56*.

Brecht wrote poems in many different genres: He excelled particularly in ballads, elegies, laments, satires, and sonnets. In these Brecht rejects any romantic notion of the transcendent; instead, his poetry is contrived to pursue pressing issues of the times directly. Given the vast scale of Brecht's poetic output, it is unproductive to attempt to define a "typical" Brecht poem. However, one generalization about Brecht's major, mature poetry is piquant: Brecht's significant poems are rooted firmly in the precise context of the poet's perception of current political issues.

Brecht wrote poems throughout his life. Even in adolescence his output was prolific; he was still writing poems in 1958, the year of his death. Brecht's poetry appeared in a hugely piecemeal fashion. Censorship—whether from Nazis, from East Germany's postwar Communist hegemony, or from other sources—prevented many poems from being published promptly. Many were published decades after they were written.

But a chronology of Brecht's poetry has been established, in part because the poems are easily dated by their frequent references to contemporary events. An introductory guide to Brecht's poetry is best supported by a complementary account of his biography because the major cycles of Brecht's poetry slot in conveniently to specific periods. Brecht's poems, then, fit neatly into three main phases of his life: his residence in urban Germany before Hitler, from 1917 to 1933; his exile from Nazi and postwar Germany, from 1933 to 1948; and his East German years, from 1948 to 1956.

Brecht was born in Augsburg, Germany, in 1898. He studied and worked in Munich for seven years after 1917, then moved to Berlin in 1924. The traumatic move from (relatively) rural Augsburg to urban Germany—"to the asphalt cities / From the black forests"—is described (with self-effacing exaggeration) in Brecht's early ballad, "Of Poor B B." Brecht's first important poems were written in Munich and then in Berlin, particularly after his political consciousness was raised by his literary and personal involvement with many committed Marxists. It is not known whether he was ever actually a member of the Communist Party, but his ideological devotion to a program for workers' emancipation was total and consistent. Brecht's poems from this period often criticize German self-deception about World War I losses, and they warn of the dangers of a rising attraction to right-wing nationalism. His first major collection of poems, *Hauspostille* (Manual of Piety), was published in Germany in 1927. The 50 poems, many of them acerbic satires on bourgeois greed and self-interest, are disguised satirically as family prayers. Many of Brecht's poems from this period caused offence and could not be published, even in Germany's supposedly liberal Weimar Republic. For example, one poem, "Legend of the Dead Soldier," satirized mercilessly what Brecht saw as a German propensity for military aggression. The soldier, who metonymically represents a defeated kaiser-led Germany, has been killed in battle, but must still be dug up and cheered as he goes off to battle again. The moral of the poem is clear: Whatever catastrophes Germany suffers through war, there will always be a malign number of Germans who pursue self-evidently doomed, aggrandizing martial adventures.

Brecht, like many other left-wing intellectuals and artists, was forced to flee Germany in 1933, as soon as Hitler's Communist-hating Nazis established absolute power in Germany. Brecht lived in peripatetic exile for a number of years, spending periods in Denmark, England, Finland, France, and Sweden. Poems from this time of crisis reflect Brecht's despair at Germany's slide into fascist totalitarianism. Also poems from this period of exile were often set to music by committed comrades, including Hanns Eisler and Kurt Weill. One collaborative venture, the 1934 Brecht-Eisler volume *Lieder, Gedichte, Chöre* (Songs, Poems, Choruses) includes seminal anti-Hitler poems, including "GERMANY." Another 1934 poem, "Solely Because of the Increasing Disorder," constitutes one of Brecht's most explicit poetic assertions that poetry must assist in the struggle for "class justice." Brecht was living in exile during a peace-threatening, Nazi-inspired emergency: therefore, pleasant but ideologically irrelevant poems about "ripe apples" and "the senses of the flesh" (art for art's sake) were, he thought, unforgivable; instead, the needs of Europe's threatened workers must be addressed urgently. Brecht's scabrous humor during these disastrous years for Germany can be seen in the satire on Nazi censorship, "The Burning of the Books." That poem was one of several written for anti-Nazi radio propaganda in the late 1930s. Here a writer is upset because the Nazis do not publicly burn his books. Convinced that his books report "the truth," he writes vituperatively to the authorities, demanding that they destroy his books publicly. Hatred from the Nazis, Brecht implies, is a sign of both artistic merit and moral sense. Other poems bludgeon the reader with more bitter, withering attacks on mendacious, power-hungry, militant, right-wing governments.

After much traveling to escape encroaching fascism, Brecht moved to the United States in 1941. Wherever Brecht went, he wrote films, plays, poems, and other forms of politically committed entertainment. During the World War II years, Brecht's poems of exile often betray a sense of guilt that he was able to escape the Nazis while millions were not. One poem written in America, "I, the Survivor," rejects through the conceit of a remembered dream the notion that there is "survival of the fittest." The speaker realizes that mere "luck" has saved him from Nazi brutality. Brecht's communism was always treated with alarm by American authorities, and soon after he was investigated for un-American activities, he left America, returning to Europe. After a brief period in Switzerland, in 1948 he settled permanently in Berlin. There, the East German Communist government allowed Brecht to set up a permanent theatrical company, the Berliner Ensemble. Despite, in effect, being paid to be a state poet, one loyal to the one-party diktat, Brecht was often critical of the rulers whom he (quietly) accused of perpetuating a tyranny that he saw as a travesty of socialism.

After his 1948 return to Berlin, Brecht's poems became, arguably, more adventurous in terms of form and genre. He wrote adaptations of Chinese left-wing poetry and sonnet-form "studies" that critique literary classics from a Marxist viewpoint. In the 1953 sequence "BUCKOW ELEGIES," Brecht assumed an unusually personal, reflective tone. Despite retaining a discreet disdain for many policies of the East German government, Brecht was effectively patronized as a servant of the state. He wrote impersonal poems for the state, including "The Nurture of Millet" (1951). This long, Soviet Union–inspired poem, which details the improvements made by reformed agricultural techniques, was memorably satirized by Martin Esslin as a "rare attempt" to "extract the lyrical possibilities from the statistics of increased yields per hectare." Most of Brecht's other poems are less easy to mock: The commitment to socialism and workers' advancement is dated, but the attacks on government cruelty and myopia remain clear and rousing. Quite exhausted after a stress-filled life of much traveling, fear of arrest or assassination, and compulsive agitating, directing, producing, and writing, Brecht died of a heart attack in 1956.

BIBLIOGRAPHY

Arendt, Hannah. "The Poet Bertolt Brecht." In *Brecht: A Collection of Critical Essays,* edited by Peter Demetz. Englewood Cliffs, N.J.: Prentice Hall, 1962, 43–58.

Brecht, Bertolt. *Journals, 1934–1955.* Edited by John Willett. New York: Routledge, 1996.

———. *Letters.* Edited by John Willett. New York: Routledge, 1990.

———. *Poems, 1913–56.* Edited and translated by John Willett and Ralph Manheim. London: Eyre Methuen Ltd., 1976.

———. *Poems and Songs from the Plays.* Edited by John Willett. London: Methuen, 1990.

———. *Selected Poems: Translation and Introduction by H. R. Hays.* New York: Reynal and Hitchcock, 1947.

Brooker, Peter. *Bertolt Brecht: Dialectics, Poetry, Politics.* London: Croom Helm, 1988.

Cook, Bruce. *Brecht in Exile.* New York: Holt, Rinehart, and Winston, 1982.

Esslin, Martin. *Brecht: A Choice of Evils.* London: Eyre Methuen, 1980.

International Brecht Society. Useful, accurate information. Available online. URL: http://www.brechtsociety.org. Downloaded on April 4, 2006.

Speirs, Ronald, ed. *Brecht's Poetry of Political Exile.* Cambridge: Cambridge University Press, 2000.

Thomson, Philip. *The Poetry of Brecht: Seven Studies.* Chapel Hill: University of North Carolina Press, 1989.

———. "Brecht's Poetry." In Peter Thomson and Glendyr Sacks, eds. *The Cambridge Companion to Brecht.* Cambridge: Cambridge University Press, 1994, 201–217.

University of Wisconsin Digital Collections. "Brecht's Works in English: A Bibliography." Available online. URL: http://digital.library.wisc.edu/1711.dl/BrechtGuide. Downloaded on April 4, 2006.

Völker, Klaus. *Brecht: A Biography.* London: Marion Boyars, 1979.

Whitaker, Peter. *Brecht's Poetry: A Critical Survey.* Oxford: Clarendon Press, 1985.

Kevin De Ornellas

BRETON, ANDRÉ (1896–1966)

French poet, essayist, critic, and editor André Breton was one of the founders of the surrealist movement, with PAUL ÉLUARD and LOUIS ARAGON, among others. Breton's manifestos of surrealism were the most influential statements of the movement, and he remained surrealism's chief proponent throughout his life. Breton left an impact on psychoanalysis and feminism through Jacques Lacan, on politics through Herbert Marcuse, and on criticism through Roland Barthes.

André Breton was born the son of a shopkeeper on February 18, 1896, in Tinchebray, in Normandy, France. He later changed his birth date to February 19 for superstitious reasons. He started early to write poems, admiring Stéphane Mallarmé and the symbolist poets, and in 1913 he met the poet PAUL VALÉRY, who became his model. Complying with his parents'

wishes, Breton studied medicine and in 1915, during World War I, was drafted into the army as a medical aide. He served in the neurological ward in Nantes, began to read Arthur Rimbaud and Sigmund Freud (whom he would meet once in 1921 in Vienna), and made some attempts to psychoanalyze his patients, collecting their disturbed dream images. In Nantes he got to know the wounded soldier Jacques Vaché (who committed suicide in 1919), a rebel who defied all values and conventions and who was a living example of dadaism. Breton joined the dadaist group in 1916, but after various quarrels left the group in 1922 and went his own way. He established contact with GUILLAUME APOLLINAIRE and, after he was transferred to a hospital in Paris, also met Philippe Soupault, Louis Aragon, and Paul Éluard and became acquainted with the work of Lautréamont. Together they explored the unconscious through automatic writing, hypnosis, and dream protocols, which led to the publication of *Les champs magnétiques* (Magnetic Fields, 1919).

After the war Breton did not resume the study of medicine but became a freelance writer. In 1919 he cofounded with Aragon and Soupault the review *Littérature*. Dadaism soon turned into surrealism, and in 1924 the organ of the group became the journal *La révolution surréaliste* (1924–29), which was later renamed *Le surréalisme au service de la révolution* (1930–33). In 1924 his first *Manifeste du surréalisme* was published, in which he defined surrealism as a "pure psychic automatism, by which an attempt is made to express, either verbally, in writing or in any other manner, the true functioning of thought. The dictation of thought, in the absence of all control by reason, excluding any aesthetic or moral preoccupation." Growing political concerns brought Breton and the other surrealists close to the communists, and in 1927 Breton, Aragon, Éluard, Benjamin Péret, and Pierre Unik became members of the French Communist Party. In 1935 tensions led to Breton's final break with the party in protest against Stalinist atrocities, yet he remained committed to Marxism.

In 1928 Breton wrote his successful experimental novel *Nadja,* about his relationship with a mysterious and "mad" young woman whom he regarded as his soul mate. Breton's first-person narrative is supplemented by photographs of places and objects that inspired the author or are connected to Nadja. In 1930 he redefined surrealism in his *Seconde Manifeste du surréalisme* as a social-revolutionary movement, claiming that personal freedom and social liberation were to be achieved through the liberation of the unconscious mind, synthesizing the social and psychological revolution. In the same year he wrote together with Éluard *L'Immaculée Conception* (The Immaculate Conception), in which they attempted the simulation of moments of madness from Freudian psychoanalysis. Breton expressed his fascination with the opposition of dream and waking in his collection *Les Vases communicants* (The Communicating Vessels, 1932), which includes a short letter exchange with Freud. In the image of vessels Breton explores the constantly widening circle of possibilities of the self, but also the divisions within the self, between a waking and a sleeping, dreaming personality, between visionary states and immersion in everyday life. The collection *Le Revolver a cheveux blancs,* also published in 1932, includes poems of passionate self-analysis (see "VIGILANCE"). They express faith in a new sort of unified vision through intensive awareness and openness toward moments of spontaneous union of the interior and exterior worlds.

The hallucinatory collection *L'Air de l'eau* (1934) is a celebration of woman, love, and life. It expresses the surrealist belief that love is the source of supreme unity where all contradictions are resolved. In spring 1934 Breton met Jacqueline Lamba, who became his second wife in August and with whom he had one daughter, Aube. Breton celebrated their love in the collection *L'Amour fou* (Mad Love, 1937), which declared woman to be the incarnation of irrationality and therefore the eternally marvelous. Mad love, absolute love without moderation or constraints, is man's only guarantee that his endeavors are not undertaken in vain, and earthly salvation can come only through the redemptive power of woman.

In 1938 Breton met Leon Trotsky in his exile in Mexico at Diego Rivera's home. Together they wrote the manifesto on the civil liberties of the artist *Pour un art révolutionnaire indépendant* (For an Independent Revolutionary Art) and founded the Fédération de l'Art Revolutionnaire Independant. Surrealism was by now an international movement with groups and manifestos in Brussels, Barcelona, London, and Prague. In 1938 Breton organized the first International Exhibition of Surrealism in Paris. When France was occupied by Nazi Germany in 1940, Breton fled to Marseille. From there he and his family went to the Antilles and then to New York, where he met many other exiled artists and writers, such as Marcel Duchamp and Max Ernst. While in New York he held a broadcasting job and arranged a surrealist exhibition at Yale University in 1942. Breton met the anthropologist Claude Lévi-Strauss on a boat ride to Martinique in 1941 and began to work on pre-Columbian America and the history of early socialism, especially Charles Fourier.

In *Les Etats-Généraux* (1942) he suggests the actual insignificance of the individual personality, since memory may be only a product of the imagination. He sees the individual from a wider perspective, arguing for the equality of all people and a harmony of universal dependence. His marriage to Jacqueline disintegrated in 1943, when she left him. Shortly afterward he met Chilean-born Elisa Claro-Bindhoff, who meant for him the liberation from depressing exile and loss. They traveled to Canada, Arizona, New Mexico, and Haiti, where his political ideas were greeted enthusiastically by the students whose rebellion led to a change of government. In the collection of poems *Arcane 17* (1945), he celebrates their love in occult and mythological images, using, for example, the Osiris myth of dismemberment and rebirth.

He returned with Elisa to Europe in 1946, but his hopes for a new political and social beginning were disappointed, as parts of the surrealist group, including Aragon and Éluard, were pro-Stalinists. Together with Jean Dubuffet, Breton founded in 1947 the Compagnie de l'Art Brut to support art made by mad people, inmates of prisons, and other marginalized groups, but they fell out with each other in 1951. The opposition of the Stalinists in France made it difficult for him to find an audience after the war, but this changed with the great Surrealist Exhibition in 1947 (Paris) that he organized together with Marcel Duchamp. In 1960 he was active against the war in Algeria. In the following decade the much criticized "pope of surrealism" kept the movement alive through collections such as *L'Art magique* (1957), *Le Surréalisme et la Peinture* (1965), and the organization of several international exhibitions on surrealism, e.g. *E.R.O.S.* (1959–60) and the last great exhibition, *L'écart absolu* (The Absolute Divergence, 1965). Breton's last poetic work, *Constellations* (1959), paralleled a series of poems with gouaches by Joan Miró. André Breton died in Paris on September 28, 1966, of lung disease and was interred at the Cimetière des Batignolles near Paris. His three-room studio at 42 rue Fontaine became a research center, preserved by his third wife, Elisa.

BIBLIOGRAPHY

Brandon, Ruth. *Surreal Lives: The Surrealists 1917–1945.* New York: Grove Press, 1999.

Breton, André. *Œuvres complètes.* Vols. 1–3, edited by Marguerite Bonnet. Paris: Bibliothèque de la Pléiade, 1988–1999.

Balakian, Anna. *André Breton: Magus of Surrealism.* New York: Oxford University Press, 1971.

Ballabriga, Michel. *Sémiotique du surréalisme: André Breton ou la cohérence.* Toulouse, France: Presses Universitaires du Mirail, 1995.

Béhar, Henri. *André Breton: le grand indésirable.* Paris: Calmann-Lévy, 1990.

Bonnet, Marguerite. *André Breton: naissance de l'aventure surréaliste.* Paris: Corti, 1988.

Caws, Mary Ann. *The Poetry of Dada and Surrealism: Aragon, Breton, Tzara, Éluard and Desnos.* Princeton, N.J.: Princeton University Press, 1970.

———. *Surrealism.* London: Phaidon, 2004.

———. *André Breton.* Updated edition. New York: Twayne, 1996.

Fotiade, Ramona, ed. *André Breton: The Power of Language.* Exeter, U.K.: Elm Bank Publications, 2000.

Polizzotti, Mark. *Revolution of the Mind: The Life of André Breton.* London: Bloomsbury, 1995.

Heike Grundmann

BREYTENBACH, BREYTEN (1939–   ) As a writer, painter, and political activist, Breyten Breytenbach has consistently used his art to explore the ambiguous position that he occupies as both a privileged, white South African and a vocal critic of apartheid, the system of racial segregation that was in place in his country until the last decade of the 20th century. Although he has written numerous well-received works of prose in English, he is most highly regarded for the poetry he produced in the white South African language of Afrikaans. Born in Bonnievale, South Africa, Breytenbach grew up as part of an old Afrikaner family whose ancestors were among the first Dutch settlers of the 17th century. He studied art at the University of Cape Town until 1959, when he decided to leave for Europe, reacting in part to the increasingly pervasive regulations of the apartheid regime. In Paris Breytenbach was exposed to the surrealist movement of the 1960s, which significantly influenced much of his subsequent work both on canvas and in print in terms of its deliberately provocative use of imagery. In Paris he also met Yolande Ngo Thi Hoang Lien, the Vietnamese artist who became his wife. The two of them were effectively barred from visiting South Africa as a couple because interracial relationships had been outlawed there at the start of the apartheid era. Early in his exile, Breytenbach gained prominence as a poet within South Africa through his association with the Sestigers (literally, the Sixties generation), a group of nonconformist Afrikaans writers that also included the novelist André Brink. It is perhaps not surprising, therefore, that Breytenbach's earliest published poetry is characterized by an attitude of defiance not only to the South African political order but also to earlier writers in the Afrikaans tradition (see, for example, "BREYTEN PRAYS FOR HIMSELF"). Somewhat ironically, this rebellious stance earned Breytenbach such an ardent following among Afrikaans readers that the South African government was prevailed upon to let him and his wife enter the country as part of a literary tour in 1973. Breytenbach took advantage of this opportunity to deliver a searing address at the University of Cape Town, in which he excoriated himself and his white listeners for not taking a stronger stand against apartheid. Back in Paris, he answered his own charge by forming Okehla ("spark" in Zulu), a group of white South Africans living abroad that had links to the African National Congress (ANC) liberation movement. In 1975 Breytenbach returned to South Africa on a clandestine mission to establish connections between Okhela supporters and black activists. Betrayed by an unknown source, the poet was arrested and put on trial for conspiracy and terrorism. Despite a controversial courtroom confession, he was sentenced to nine years in prison, seven of which he

served. During this period of incarceration, Breyten-bach was not allowed to paint. But he did gain permission to write after a series of pleas were lodged on his behalf by members of the Afrikaner literary establishment. Seeking to protect his own thoughts from official scrutiny, the poet developed an elusive and fragmentary style in the work he produced at this time. Writing under the watchful eyes of the prison censors also encouraged him to reflect further on the uses of language as a political tool (see, for example, "THE STRUGGLE FOR THE TAAL"). Breytenbach was released from prison in 1982, thanks in part to efforts by French president François Mitterrand. By then he had emerged as an international literary figure, since his case had become a minor cause célèbre. Two collections of his poems in translation, *And Death White as Words* (1978) and *In Africa Even the Flies Are Happy* (1978), had also made his work more readily available to an English-speaking audience. Over the next few years Breyten-bach continued to gain widespread attention as he set about publishing all he had written in prison. Four volumes of poetry in Afrikaans came out in rapid succession. Drawing on this series of poems, known together as *Die ongedanste dans* (The Undanced Dance), the poet eventually put together a collection of his own translations into English under the title *Judas Eye* (1988). Alongside this poetry Breytenbach also produced *Mouroir: Mirrornotes of a Novel* (1984), an experimental work of fiction in both English and Afrikaans, and *The True Confessions of an Albino Terrorist* (1985), an autobiographical work written only in English. All of these works make clear that the poet's opposition to the South African government had only grown stronger during his imprisonment. To some extent Breyten-bach's critical stance remains unchanged today, even though the apartheid system has been dismantled. He continues to raise concerns about the situation in South Africa, most recently in the memoir *Dog Heart* (1999). His relationship with Afrikaans still seems fraught, as evidenced by his latest volume of poetry, *Lady One: Of Love and Other Poems* (2002). There is no question that Breytenbach remains something of a controversial figure, both within South Africa and abroad. The transparent attempts that he has made to fashion himself as a literary provocateur within his own poetry

have not played well with some critics, including Terence Des Pres. But others, like J. M. Coetzee, see in such posturings the potential for genuine transgression. Among all of these critics, there seems to be a consensus that Breytenbach has done more than any other writer to win international attention for Afrikaans as a literary language. Breytenbach himself may continue to feel ambivalent about his own heritage as an Afrikaner. But his name will forever be associated with the language of his birth.

BIBLIOGRAPHY

Coetzee, J. M. "Breytenbach and the Censor." *Raritan* 10 (Spring 1991): 58–84.

Des Pres, Terence. "Rimbaud's Nephews." *Parnassus* 11 (Fall–Winter 1983–84): 83–102.

Lütge Coullie, Judith, and J. U. Jacobs, eds. *A. K. A. Breyten Breytenbach: Critical Approaches to His Writings and Paintings.* Amsterdam: Rodopi, 2004.

Weschler, Lawrence. "An Afrikaner Dante." *The New Yorker,* 8 November 1993, 78–100.

Alexander B. McKee

"BREYTEN PRAYS FOR HIMSELF" BREYTEN BREYTENBACH (1964)

This early composition (*"Breyten bid vie homself"*) perfectly captures BREYTEN-BACH's irreverent tone, as it deliberately parodies a poem by the renowned Afrikaans poet N. P. Van Wyk Louw, "Ignatius Prays for His Order" ("Ignatius bid vir sy orde"). Speaking on behalf of privileged, white South Africa, Breytenbach transforms the unselfish prayer of St. Ignatius into a selfish protest against pain to highlight the moral failure of apartheid. "Breyten Prays for Himself" comprises nearly 30 unrhymed lines of varying length, divided unequally into four stanzas. In the first stanza the speaker demonstrates that pleasure can exist separate from pain by observing that "A flower has no teeth" (l. 3). Although he pays tribute to death in the second stanza, he indicates his preference for life by asking God to grant him good health. The bizarre similes that Breytenbach employs here to describe the vigor of youth point to his own debt to French surrealism. There is a hint of remorse in the third stanza when the speaker begs God to pardon "our mouths our bowels our brains" (l. 8), as if he regrets not raising his voice out of cowardice and ignorance.

Even so he remains determined to eliminate this nagging sense of guilt so that he can enjoy the sensuous pleasures of life without reservation. The fourth stanza makes clear that the speaker would prefer God to visit pain upon others rather than himself. He welcomes the sacrifice of those "taken into custody" (l. 15) and persecuted by various means, cataloged here in a long list of passive participial adjectives printed separately on the page. But at the same time the speaker denies his own complicity in the crimes committed against these people. As he says, "we never give Pain or complain" (l. 29). The ironic stance that underlies "Breyten Prays for Himself" comes fully into focus in these words. Although this poem was included in Breytenbach's first collection of Afrikaans poetry, *Die Ysterkoei Moet Sweet* (The Iron Cow Must Sweat), it did not appear in English before the release of *And Death White as Words* (1978). The original translation by Denis Hirson for this volume remains the standard one. It was published most recently in *The Vintage Book of Contemporary World Poetry* (1996), edited by J. D. McClatchy.

BIBLIOGRAPHY
Breytenbach, Breyten. *And Death White as Words: An Anthology of the Poetry of Breyten Breytenbach.* Edited by A. J. Coetzee. London: Rex Collings, 1978.
McClatchy, J. D., ed. *The Vintage Book of Contemporary World Poetry.* New York: Vintage, 1996.

Alexander B. McKee

BRINKMANN, ROLF DIETER (1940–1975)

Rolf Dieter Brinkmann, often referred to as the greatest rebel talent in postwar German poetry, can be considered one of the main representatives of the German literary Pop Art movement in the late 1960s. Born in Vechta, a small town in northern Germany, on April 16, 1940, Brinkmann left secondary school at the age of 19 and, in Essen, started a bookseller's apprenticeship. Without finishing he moved to Cologne in 1962 to pursue a career as a writer. That year some of his prose, influenced by the French *nouveau roman,* was published in an anthology of young urban writing and instantly propelled him onto the German literary scene. Brinkmann's writings—his essays, short prose, and poems—are characterized by his attempt to dispose of the boundaries between "high prose" and "mere liter-

ary writing" (his terms). Texts by Jack Kerouac and other American Beat poets opened his eyes to the possibilities of literature, and Brinkmann strove to introduce their new approaches to Germany. He became one of the most prolific translators and editors of American Beat literature in Germany (e.g., *Acid: Neue amerikanische Szene* [Acid: New American Scene], 1969).

The central themes of Brinkmann's texts are drawn from daily life and the difficult, often confusing, existence of human beings in the metropolis. Although influenced by German literary traditions, such as neoromanticism's search for sensuousness, Brinkmann understood his poems to be a protest against the elitist aestheticism of the literary establishment in Germany, which he found tiresome and limiting. By focusing on trivial items and taboo topics—such as shutters, laundry, trash, and other everyday objects, as well as sexuality—and by his seemingly reckless treatment of serious subject matter, he hoped to free himself and the reader from the stifling demands of societal and cultural conformity. He advocated creative spontaneity, authenticity of reactions, and actuality in literary production as a way to subvert existing and old-fashioned aesthetic norms and to create a dynamic countercultural literary movement.

However, at a time when German literature was preoccupied with the dissemination of certain moral values whose previous lack had contributed to the rise of the Third Reich and the Holocaust, Brinkmann's purported antipolitical approach was snubbed by a majority of the reading public and fellow writers. Eventually, through the support of literary critics who recognized his talent, he received a number of awards and fellowships, among them the prestigious position as a writer-in-residence in 1971 and 1972 at the Villa Massimo in Rome. At the beginning of the 1970s, disappointed by the politicization of culture and society in the wake of the civil rights and student movements that had swept Europe and the United States, Brinkmann alienated some of his supporters with repeated elitist comments and, at the same time, even expressed a growing loss of confidence in his own earlier artistic convictions. He withdrew from the public literary landscape and focused his work on radio plays and poems, many of which were published only posthumously. In spring

1975 Brinkmann was killed in London when he was struck by a car as he was leaving a public reading of his poems.

Over a dozen collections of Brinkmann's poems and stories were ultimately published. The two best-known and critically acclaimed collections, *Westwärts 1 & 2* (Go West 1 & 2), which includes the controversial "MOURNING ON THE WASHING-LINE IN JANUARY," and *Rom, Blicke* (Rome, Views), were printed after his death. Although Brinkmann did not succeed in changing the German literary scene, his poetry can certainly be considered a precursor to the German "Hip-Hop poetry" movement that, coming from the United States, began to take hold in Germany in the early 1990s (see ARAB RAP AND HIP HOP CULTURE and FRENCH RAP). The only available collection of Brinkmann's poems in English translation was published in 2001 by Mark Terrill with the title *Like a Pilot*.

BIBLIOGRAPHY
Brinkmann, Rolf Dieter. *Rolf Dieter Brinkmann*. Sound recording. Kansas City, Mo.: New Letters, 1978.
Brinkmann, Rolf Dieter. *Rom, Blicke*. Reinbek bei Hamburg: Rowolth, 1979.
Brinkmann, Rolf Dieter. *Westwärts 1 & 2*. Reinbek bei Hamburg: Rowolth, 1975.
Brinkmann, Rolf Dieter, and Ralf-Rainer Rygulla, eds. *Acid. Neue amerikanische Szene*. Reinbek bei Hamburg: Rowolth, 1983.
Gemünden, Gerd. *Framed Visions: Popular Culture, Americanization, and the Contemporary German and Austrian Imagination*. Ann Arbor: University of Michigan Press, 1998.
Terrill, Mark. *Like a Pilot: Rolf Dieter Brinkmann, Selected Poems 1963–1970*. Austin, Tex.: Sulphur River Literary Review Press, 2001.
Woolley, Jonathan. "Beyond the Beats: An Ethics of Spontaneity in the Poetry of Rolf Dieter Brinkmann." *College Literature* 30, no. 4 (2003): 1–31.

Peter C. Weise

BRODSKY, JOSEPH (1940–1996)

Joseph Brodsky is considered the most significant Russian writer of his generation. Best known for his lyrics and elegies in Russian and for his prose in English, he was awarded the Nobel Prize in literature in 1987. Yet during his lifetime, he saw his work censured in the Soviet Union, and in 1972 he was coerced into exile.

Born Iosif Brodskii to Jewish parents in Leningrad shortly before the city was laid seige to by Germany, Brodsky became disillusioned with Soviet education early and left school at the age of 15. At 18 he began writing poetry, and although his early work garnered praise from many established Russian writers, particularly ANNA AKHMATOVA, it also drew unwanted attention from Soviet officials. Largely influenced by the Russian poets Gavriil Derzhavin, Evgeny Baratynsky, and OSIP MANDELSTAM, Brodsky's poems are characterized by their metaphysical and biblical allusions—themes once taboo in Soviet letters.

In 1964, on exaggerated charges of social parasitism, Brodsky was sentenced to five years' hard labor in northern Russia for refusing proper employment. It was during this time that his first collection, *Stikhotvoreniia i poemy* (Poetry and Narrative Verse, 1965), was published in the United States; and even though his sentence was commuted, he was later forced to leave the Soviet Union. With the help of English poet W. H. Auden, he secured a teaching position at the University of Michigan, and, in 1973, Auden wrote the introduction to *Joseph Brodsky: Selected Poems*.

In 1977 Brodsky became a naturalized U.S. citizen and was awarded many honors in the United States: an honorary doctor of letters from Yale University (1977), a MacArthur Foundation Award (1981), the Andrew Mellon Professorship in Literature at Mount Holyoke College (1981), and the National Book Critics' Circle Award for *Less than One* (1986), a collection of essays written in English. But his life and work continued to be deeply influenced by his exile.

Despite many efforts, Brodsky's parents were never allowed to visit their son, and it was not until the mid-1990s that Brodsky was reunited with his son, Andrey, whose mother was the Russian artist Maria Basmanova. The moving lyric "ODYSSEUS TO TELEMACHUS" captures the isolation of a father forced into separation from his son, while many of Brodsky's poems address the psychological effects of exile. Formally, his poetry exhibits a highly syllabic, complex system of metrics often difficult to capture in English. Of the translations in *A Part of Speech* (1980), those by Richard Wilbur, DEREK WALCOTT, and Anthony Hecht are some of the best.

In 1990 Brodsky married the translator Maria Sozzani. Throughout the 1990s, as both poet laureate of the United States (1991–92) and cofounder of the American Poetry and Literacy Project, he worked to make poetry ubiquitous in American culture. In 1995 he approached the mayor of Rome to establish a Russian Academy for writers and artists. To realize that vision, shortly after Brodsky died of heart failure in 1996, his friends created the Joseph Brodsky Memorial Fellowship Foundation.

BIBLIOGRAPHY
Poetry
Brodsky, Joseph. *Collected Poems in English.* New York: Farrar, Straus and Giroux, 2000.
———. *Elegy for John Donne and Other Poems.* London: Longmans, 1967.
———. *Nativity Poems.* New York: Farrar, Straus and Giroux, 2001.
———. *A Part of Speech.* New York: Farrar, Straus and Giroux, 1981.
———. *So Forth.* New York: Farrar, Straus and Giroux 1996.
———. *To Urania.* New York: Farrar, Straus and Giroux, 1988.

Prose
Brodsky, Joseph. *On Grief and Reason.* New York: Farrar, Straus and Giroux, 1995.
———. *Watermark.* New York: Farrar, Straus, and Giroux, 1992.
Brodsky, Joseph, Seamus Heaney, and Derek Walcott. *Homage to Robert Frost.* New York: Farrar, Straus and Giroux, 1996.
Brodsky, Joseph, Cynthia L. Haven, and Richard Avedon. *Joseph Brodsky: Conversations.* Jackson: University Press of Mississippi, 2003.

Drama
Brodsky, Joseph. *Marbles: A Play in Three Acts.* New York: Farrar, Straus and Giroux, 1989.

Stacy Kidd

"BROOKLYN BRIDGE" VLADIMIR MAYAKOVSKY (1925)

A hymn of praise to the Brooklyn Bridge, MAYAKOVSKY's poem (*Bruklinskii Most*) expresses the awe that he, as an artist and a technophile, feels when he experiences the sight of this symbol of New York City and American ingenuity. The work, written and recited in New York before its publication in the Soviet Union, is unusual among his American poems in that its focus is not the condemnation of capitalism, although a few hints of criticism appear in the poem. It begins with a jocular call for Calvin Coolidge—who was the U.S. president when Mayakovsky visited the country in 1925—to share the poet's amazement at this web of metal so breathtaking that even a fervent Russian communist, an enemy of the United States and of capitalism, must pay it tribute. Mayakovsky's offering is a single long stanza of 169 lines, in sequentially indented patterns, some lines only one word long, with occasional rhymes. The poet conveys a nearly thunderstruck fascination with the structure that towers over the East River, with one footing in Manhattan and another in Brooklyn; the engineering wonder also pulls together the various parts of the United States and allows the Old World entry into the New. In addition to being of utilitarian design, the bridge possesses a dazzling style that epitomizes the futurist aesthetic of a union of function and grace; in it the poet sees his own artistic visions realized. The bridge inspires the same feelings in him as those experienced by a worshipper entering a magnificent church or a painter viewing an exquisite masterpiece. This impressive work, the bridge itself, dwarfs every other technological wonder in the city, and after the inevitable destruction of Western civilization, the remnants of the Brooklyn Bridge will be the dinosaur bones from which future geologists will reconstruct our age. Although the speaker acknowledges that no one will ever know the true sufferings of the laborers who erected the bridge (and from which the unemployed now commit suicide), he remains proud to have become a part of its history and continues to wonder at it in slangy amazement.

BIBLIOGRAPHY
Brown, Edward J. *Mayakovsky: A Poet in the Revolution.* Princeton, N.J.: Princeton University Press, 1973.
Haw, Richard. *The Brooklyn Bridge: A Cultural History.* New Brunswick, N.J., and London: Rutgers University Press, 2005.
Mayakovsky, Vladimir. *The Bedbug and Selected Poetry.* Edited by Patricia Davis, translated by Max Hayward and George Reavey. Bloomington: Indiana University Press, 1960.

———. "Brooklyn Bridge." Available online in Russian and English translation. Available online. URL: http://ww2.lafayette.edu/~noblea/russian.htm. Accessed on April 21, 2007.

Karen Rae Keck

BRUTUS, DENNIS (1924–   )

Commonly recognized as one of the most important South African poets of the 20th century, Dennis Brutus has sought through his writing to call attention to injustices in his own country and around the world. Until fairly recently, however, his work was virtually unknown in South Africa, where it was banned under the repressive regime that was in power there for nearly half a century.

Brutus was born in Salisbury, Southern Rhodesia (known today as Harare, Zimbabwe). His South African parents, who were classified as "coloreds" within their country's system of institutionalized racism, moved to the coastal city of Port Elizabeth soon after their son's birth. Upon receiving a bachelor's degree in English at Fort Hare (later University) College, Brutus took his first job as a high school English and Afrikaans teacher in 1948. In the same year the conservative Afrikaner National Party won the all-white elections in South Africa, thanks in part to a platform that emphasized "apartheid," an Afrikaans word that literally means "separateness." Over the next 10 years Brutus became increasingly involved in the antiapartheid movement as he continued to teach at different South African high schools. He worked briefly with antiapartheid activist Nelson Mandela on the National Convention organized by the African National Congress (ANC) following the Sharpeville massacre of demonstrators by South African police in 1960. But he devoted most of his energies as an activist to the conflict over race in sports. As the founding secretary of the South African Non-Racial Olympic Committee (SANROC), he played a central role in the movement to ban South Africa's segregated sports teams from international competition. If Brutus found in this cause an outlet for his anger at the system, he found another one in the political poetry that he began to write at this time.

Heavily influenced by the metaphysical poetry of John Donne, Brutus's early work is remarkable for the way it combines elaborate figurative language with precisely observed journalistic details to produce vivid and harrowing accounts of oppression in apartheid South Africa (see, for example, "AT A FUNERAL"). In 1961 Brutus lost his job as a teacher when he was banned under the Suppression of Communism Act from participating in gatherings of any kind. A separate order was issued in 1962 to prevent his writings from being reproduced. Brutus attempted to flee the country in 1963 after being arrested for attending a sports meeting in defiance of his ban. But he was apprehended at the Mozambique border and returned to South African custody. He was shot in the stomach when he tried to escape a second time. Upon his recovery Brutus was sentenced to 18 months of hard labor, part of which he spent on Robben Island, the notorious prison facility off the coast of South Africa where many political prisoners were held. During this period of incarceration his first volume of poetry, *Sirens, Knuckles, Boots* (1963), was published. Brutus was placed under house arrest in Port Elizabeth when he got out of prison in 1965. Banned from writing anything for publication, he secretly composed poems in the form of letters to his sister-in-law. Many of these were eventually published abroad in Brutus's second collection, *Letters to Martha, and Other Poems from a South African Prison* (1968). This volume of poetry marks a significant departure from the first one in terms of both style and content. Brutus aims in these poems for a greater simplicity to reach a much wider audience. By addressing the hardships of prison life, he also introduces one of the major themes of his later work (see, for example, his "ROBBEN ISLAND SEQUENCE"). In 1966 Brutus was allowed to leave South Africa with an exit permit that prohibited him from reentering the country. He settled first in England, where he worked as both a journalist and a teacher. But he moved permanently to the United States after visiting the country on a one-year visa in 1970. Since then, he has taught at several American institutions of higher learning, including Northwestern University and the University of Pittsburgh. He has also published a number of volumes of poetry. Writing under the pseudonym John Bruin, Brutus outwitted the censors with *Thoughts Abroad* (1970), a collection of poems about exile and alienation, which circulated freely in South Africa for some time. He further contemplated his status as an exile in *A Simple Lust* (1973), a compilation of his earlier works that included some new poems as well. Looking beyond South Africa, Brutus sought in *Stubborn Hope* (1978) to raise awareness of the plight of the oppressed in other parts of the world. In *Salutes and Censures* (1984) and *Airs and Tributes* (1989), he worked further to educate the American public about apartheid. His devoting so much attention to political concerns has led some critics to question the aesthetic value of his poetry. FRANK CHIPASULA, for one, suggests that Brutus's reputation as a poet is built largely on his status as a freedom fighter. Other critics maintain that Brutus found in poetry an appropriate means of protest. Among these, Jasper Onuekwusi argues against those who claim that Brutus is too passionate in his poetry, by emphasizing the urgent political purpose behind it. In the end, of course, no matter how one defines Dennis Brutus's achievement as a poet, there is no question that his voice has been a powerful one for change over the past 50 years.

BIBLIOGRAPHY

Brutus, Dennis. "Through the Bars: The Prison Experience in Poetry." In *The Word Behind Bars and the Paradox of Exile,* edited by Kofi Anyidoho, 210–225. Evanston, Ill.: Northwestern University Press, 1997.

Chipasula, Frank M. "A Terrible Trajectory: The Impact of Apartheid, Prison and Exile on Dennis Brutus's Poetry." In *Essays on African Writing: A Re-evaluation,* edited by Abdulrazak Gurnah, 38–55. Oxford: Heinemann, 1993.

McLuckie, Craig W., and Patrick J. Colbert, eds. *Critical Perspectives on Dennis Brutus.* Colorado Springs: Three Continents Press, 1995.

Onuekwusi, Jasper A. "Pain and Anguish of an African Poet: Dennis Brutus and South African Reality." *Literary Criterion* 23, no. 1 (1988): 59–68.

Richard, Lee. "Activism from Elsewhere: An Interview with Dennis Brutus." *Exit 9: The Rutgers Journal of Comparative Literature* 1 (Fall 1993): 5–22.

Alexander B. McKee

"BUCKOW ELEGIES" BERTOLT BRECHT (1953)

The "Buckow Elegies" are 22 poems that BERTOLT BRECHT wrote during summer 1953, when he was staying at a country house that he had bought early the previous year. The poems were published gradually over the next two decades. The sequence includes the most significant late poems of Brecht, renowned for being controlled, short, and formally tight. Elegies are, by definition, backward looking. Many of the "Buckow Elegies," then, look back to the past, with Brecht indulging in unusually lyrical, personal remembrances. In "Firs," for example, the speaker (who can be equated unproblematically with Brecht in all of the "Elegies") sees the trees as stable, constant presences during a century of unparalleled turbulence: The trees are unchanged, but the speaker is marked by age and by the constant memories of "two world wars."

The title "Eight Years Ago" looks back to 1945, to the end of the war that destroyed Nazi Germany; the poem is concerned with the current whereabouts of the Nazis who caused Germany's downfall. The speaker suspects the "gait" ("erect") of a postman and wonders about what "the electrician" did during the war. In other words, the past affects the present: The legacy of Hitler is alive and dangerous because men who served his destructive ideology are still at liberty in Germany. Another poem, "The One-Armed Man," actually imagines a Nazi Gestapo officer ("The dreaded S. S. man") being exposed in the present. Despite the poems' inclination to retrospection, as is apparent in these reflections, there is also a strong engagement with issues pertinent to 1953.

A number of the poems deliver a lacerating critique of what Brecht saw as the state-led malaise on his side of partitioned Germany, communist East Germany. Many of these poems could not be published in East Germany during Brecht's lifetime because they were so critical of the one-party state. "The Solution," for example, is renowned for its bitterness and withering sarcasm about what Brecht viewed as the malign state apparatus that misruled East Germany. On June 17, 1953, the East German authorities had used Soviet tanks to crush a rebellion staged by workers who protested against increased productivity quotas. Brecht supported the workers (with some reservations) and wrote in his journal in August of that year that the workers were "exposed to the class enemy again, to the capitalism of the fascist era in renewed strength." For

Brecht the East German communist government acted as selfishly and brutally as any Western capitalist or even fascist government. Brecht attacks this betrayal in "The Solution": He sarcastically imagines a state that would rather solve all of its problems by destroying the people rather than face censure or challenge—"dissolve the people" rather than improve the nation. For such courage Brecht was regarded by many East Germans as a poet of the state. The poet's anger over being associated by the East German government with the betrayal of the workers fully invests another poem, "Nasty Morning," where the first-person speaker describes an anxiety dream in which some people point at him as if he were "a leper." Ultimately Brecht was very conscious that he was not a major political player, but merely a poet writing verses in a rural retreat. "Changing the Wheel" best encapsulates Brecht's sense of marginality. The speaker is an impotent passenger who must watch a driver "changing the wheel": He can only watch "with impatience" as society struggles against the botched application of socialism by the East German government.

A low-budget German film released in 2000, *The Farewell: Brecht's Last Summer,* dramatizes a sensitive fictional account of Brecht's writing of the "Buckow Elegies." In this dramatization Brecht's disillusionment and fatigue reflect eloquently the poems' resigned disappointment at the apparent failure of Brecht's art to contribute to a dynamic, just Germany.

BIBLIOGRAPHY

Brecht, Bertolt. *Journals, 1934–1955.* Edited by John Willett. New York: Routledge, 1996, 454–455.

———. *Letters.* Edited by John Willett. New York: Routledge, 1990, 674.

———. *Poems, 1913–56.* Edited by John Willett and Ralph Manheim. London: Eyre Methuen, 1976, 439–446, 514–515, 600–603.

The Farewell: Brecht's Last Summer (2000). Artificial Eye, DVD, 2001.

Thomson, Philip. "Brecht's Poetry". In *The Cambridge Companion to Brecht,* edited by Peter Thomson and Glendyr Sacks. Cambridge: Cambridge University Press, 1994, 201–217, especially 215–216.

Völker, Klaus. *Brecht: A Biography.* London: Marion Boyars, 1979, 371–372.

Kevin De Ornellas

"BUDDHA IN THE GLORY, THE" RAINER MARIA RILKE (1908) This poem, a short free-verse lyric by German poet RAINER MARIA RILKE, describes the speaker's understanding of the Buddha's existence in the state of nirvana—the place beyond time, space, and being that the Buddha strove to attain. In the first stanza the speaker indicates that the Buddha exists at the "center of centers" and is also coexistant with the universe itself. In the second stanza the speaker affirms that the Buddha's being expands throughout the universe but is not subject to disturbance, and all of space/time flows about and through his being. The final stanza notes that swarms of stars fill the skies above the Buddha's head, and a distinct sense of the immensity of time and space is evoked by the image. Nonetheless, the inner peace and stability of the Buddha will be what really survives and will exist beyond the end of the stars themselves.

In many respects the poem reflects the mysticism of the East as well as the momentous discoveries being made in astronomy and physics (especially quantum physics) during the first years of the 20th century when Rilke composed the work. Albert Einstein was just becoming famous for his theory of relativity, and physicists, including Max Planck and Niels Bohr, were making some of their first important contributions to our understanding of the universe's structure and laws. Rilke saw the parallels between the new discoveries in Western science and the ancient wisdom of the East. The Buddha epitomized the centered, immovable human spirit that was ultimately unconcerned about the vastness of space, time, and being because the human imagination—especially the artistic imagination of the poet—could encompass it all.

Joseph E. Becker

BUTTERFLY VALLEY: A REQUIEM INGER CHRISTENSEN (1991) The final (15th) sonnet, the magisterial sonnet, of INGER CHRISTENSEN's sonnet sequence *Sommerfugledalen—et requiem* (Butterfly Valley: A Requiem) consists of the first lines of the sequence's preceding 14 sonnets. *Butterfly Valley* describes the speaker's vision of a swarm of butterflies in Brajčino Valley, a vision that evokes memories of the speaker's life, from childhood to adulthood, and inspires philosophical questions about the meaning of life—and of death.

The names of the more than 30 different kinds of butterflies in *Butterfly Valley* both refer to the speaker's visual experience of the "flickering of wings" (sonnet I) and carry symbolic meanings. The admirals, blues, mourning cloaks, and peacock butterflies mentioned in the magisterial sonnet are symbols of states of being and emotions: the elevated feeling of being admired implicit in the word *admiral,* the sadness implied by the word *blues,* and the mourning specifically referred to in *mourning cloaks.* The symbolic image of the peacock points to a fascination with the aesthetic and beautiful, but possibly superficial, experiences in life.

The speaker of *Butterfly Valley* questions the nature and origin of the vision of the butterflies: "And who has conjured this encounter forth . . ."? Is the vision a creation of the subconscious, symbolically referred to as "acrid caverns underground"? Or is it just the play of light and dust, "a shoal of light particles, a quirk of perception"—as the speaker asks in the first sonnet of the sequence? Is the vision of "a life that does not die like anything" an empty display, a delusion for "the universe's fool?"

The answer is a "deafened ringing." The final lines of the sonnet—"This is a death that looks through its own eyes / regarding you from wings of butterflies" (as well as the sequence's subtitle: *A Requiem*)—suggest that the vision is experienced in the face of death, an existential condition of life. *Butterfly Valley* expresses a psychologically insightful and thus modern view of life. Using a traditional poetic form, Christensen in this lyrical sequence brings together old and new, past and present, life and death in an extraordinarily beautiful and symbolic poetic language.

Jan H. K. Nielsen

C

CABRAL DE MELO NETO, JOÃO (1920–1999)

João Cabral de Melo Neto wanted to be a literary critic. By the age of 17, considering himself too immature, he started writing poetry to kill time while he prepared to become a critic. This pastime became a lifelong passion that confirmed his initial career plan. Cabral de Melo Neto wrote poems that expressed strong criticisms—of literature, of artists, of Brazilian society. Together with CARLOS DRUMMOND DE ANDRADE, Cabral de Melo Neto is considered to be the most important voice of Brazilian poetry in the 20th century. Author of 20 books of poems, he is frequently described as a "difficult" and "unclassifiable" poet. Fighting against both the idea of the inspired, spontaneous poet and an overemphasis on academic rationalism, Cabral belongs to the heterogeneous Brazilian literary Generation of 45, among writers whose characteristics range from the subjectivism of Clarice Lispector to the artistic re-creation of language in Guimarães Rosa's prose. Strongly influenced by the modernist architect Le Corbusier, Cabral de Melo Neto, who was known as a "poet engineer," did not believe in poetic inspiration but in vigilance and lucidity. As the author describes in the poem "*Catar feijão*" ("CULLING BEANS")—one of his numerous poems that touch on the writing process—attention and persistence are among the most desirable attributes in a poet. For Cabral beauty does not stem from a poet's feelings but from the reality created by a poem. This attack on subjectivism, however, does not translate into a lack of emotion. Precise words and symmetry are, in his opinion, means to achieve a text capable of creating emotion by itself: in Cabral's words, a "poem-machine."

João Cabral de Melo Neto was a privileged child. Raised on his family's sugar plantation in the interior of the state of Pernambuco, in a region known as Mata, he suffered no privation, nor was he from the dry backlands, known as *Sertão*. But he could see close up the privation of the migrants who escaped droughts toward the coast. As a child he used to read to illiterate sugar mill workers from *literatura de cordel* (string literature), verse narratives published in pamphlet form and sold in the marketplace, a genre that later strongly influenced his poetry. In 1930 political unrest forced his family to move to Recife, a city whose landscape is dominated by the Capibaribe River. The trajectory of the Capibaribe through Recife is a recurrent theme in *O cão sem plumas* (Dog without Feathers, 1950), a long poem marked by descriptive images. In 1942 Cabral de Melo Neto moved to Rio de Janeiro, where he published his first book of poems, *Pedra do sono* (Stone of Sleep), strongly influenced by French surrealism's emphasis on the unconscious. This book, which includes a poem on Picasso in his cubist period and another on the French surrealist André Masson, revealed Cabral's passion for painting. In 1950 Cabral published a book-length essay on the Spanish painter Joan Miró. In Rio Cabral met Joaquim Cardozo, a poet and mathematician who would become his intellectual mentor. After working as a civil service employee

Cabral joined the Brazilian foreign service in 1945. In the same year he published his programmatic poetry volume *O Engenheiro* (The Engineer). In 1946 he married Stella Maria Barbosa de Oliveira—with whom he had five children (she died in 1986). In 1947 he became vice consul in Barcelona. The author's desire to eliminate chance and to affirm the importance of attention and patience in the writing process characterizes his third book of poems, *Psicologia da composição* (Psychology of Composition, 1947). Over the next years Cabral de Melo Neto worked in various diplomatic positions in England, Spain, France, Switzerland, Paraguay, Senegal, Ecuador, Honduras, and Portugal. In the poems of *Paisagens com figuras* (Landscapes with Figures), published in *Duas Águas* (Two Waters, 1956), the geographical settings of the poems alternate between Pernambuco and Spain. Both landscapes are described as dry, empty, and rough, and the characters that inhabit them are mostly dead or destitute.

During an administrative investigation in 1952, Cabral de Melo Neto was accused of subversion. While he waited for the decision on this matter, he traveled throughout Pernambuco, following the Capibaribe River in a sort of geographic-sentimental investigation that resulted in the long poem "O rio" (The River, 1953), in which the personified Capibaribe River describes its journey from its source, the dry backlands of the Northeast to the coastal city of Recife. In 1954 "O rio" received a prize during the celebrations of the fourth centennial of São Paulo. In the same year Cabral was rehabilitated, and he moved to Seville, Spain. In 1956 he published the comprehensive volume *Duas Águas*. Its subtitle, "Poetry of reflective concentration and poetry for wider audiences," suggests a division in Cabral's poetry. The first category includes *Paisagens com figuras,* as well as *"Uma faca só lamina"* (A Knife All Blade), a long poem in 11 sections revolving around three images—a knife, a clock, and a bullet—that evoke aggression and privation as weapons to use against daily oppression and alienation. The latter category, "poetry for wider audiences," encompasses *O cão sem plumas,* "O rio," and the verse drama *Morte e vida severina* (Death and Life of a Severino, 1956). The adjective *severino* (meaning both "severe" and "characteristic of a person named Severino," a common name

in the Northeast) refers to the desperate *sertanejo,* an inhabitant from the backlands who migrates to the coast to escape the droughts. In 1966 *Morte e vida severina* was staged with music by the Brazilian composer and singer Chico Buarque de Hollanda, and it became the most performed play in Brazil. It brought Cabral international renown when he received the prize for best living author at the Nancy Theater Festival. In 1967 Cabral received the silver Order of Merit of Pernambuco and in the following year the golden one. In 1968 he received three other awards in Brazil, all for the book of poems *Educação pela pedra* (Education by Stone, orig. 1966; trans. 2005). The intricately woven poems of this book are formulated like theorems, with recurrent plays of oppositions. In the homonymous poem ("Education by Stone"), Cabral de Melo Neto describes the influence of a dry and stony landscape on its inhabitants' survivor personalities and their concise use of language.

Cabral became a member of the Brazilian Academy of Letters in 1969. In the 1980s *Morte e vida severina* was adapted for TV. The success of this play—which combined poetry, music, and dance, following the northeastern popular tradition of verse plays—would overshadow his other works, including *O cão sem plumas, A educação pela pedra,* and *Museu de tudo* (Catchall Museum, 1975), the latter a collection of miscellaneous poems that comment on a diversity of themes, from writers and artists to places and soccer (the poet's passion from adolescence, when he was a champion player). Cabral considered *Morte e vida severina* one of his less well-crafted works, but he recognized the importance of its connection to the reality of Pernambuco, not only thematically but also formally. The state of Pernambuco reappears in the autobiographical *A escola das facas* (The School of Knives, 1980), with poems that are reminiscences of the author's upbringing. The poems are mostly written in the first person and are set entirely in Pernambuco.

Returning to his "poetry for wider audiences," Cabral published *Auto do Frade* (The Friar, 1984), a long poem comprising seven dialogues between a chorus—consisting of the people of Recife—and Frei Caneca, a Carmelite friar who had played an important role in an antimonarchic movement in Pernambuco in 1824 and who was for this reason condemned to death by the Portuguese court. In 1985 Cabral published *Agrestes* ("Agreste" refers to the region between the coast and the interior of Brazil's Northeast), consisting of 90 poems with themes ranging from Pernambuco to places where the author served as a diplomat. In the book one can also find poems on Cabral's favorite writers and artists, including the painter Paul Klee and the poets Elizabeth Bishop, Marianne Moore, and the Brazilian Augusto de Campos. With the publication of *Crime na Calle Relator* (Crime on the Calle Relator, 1987), a collection of 16 poems of tales and anecdotes, his poetry moves toward storytelling. Half of the poems take place in Seville, which is presented as an exuberant world, with its women, Flamenco music, dancing, and bullfighters. In his last book of poems, *Sevilha andando* (Seville Walking, 1989), Cabral de Melo Neto explores an ideal of woman closely connected to the Andalusian landscape, a theme he had already elaborated in *Quaderna* (Four-Spot, 1959). Cabral retired from the foreign service in 1990. He was the first Brazilian to receive the Camões Prize, the most important Portuguese-language literary prize. In 1992 he received the prestigious Neustadt International Prize for Literature from the University of Oklahoma and the Spanish Reina Sofia Award for his collected works. Suffering from a degenerative eye disease since the early 1990s, Cabral became reclusive and stopped writing. He died on October 9, 1999. The bilingual edition of his *Selected Poetry, 1937–1990* (University Press of New England, 1994), which includes translations by Elizabeth Bishop, is the best among translations of his work into English.

Moving from surrealism to social concerns, from Pernambuco to Spain, João Cabral de Melo Neto prized careful work with language as a means to stir in his readers their own—in opposition to the poet's—emotion. The themes of his poems range from the suffering of the northeastern migrants due to long droughts to his own recurrent pain caused by migraine (see "Num monumento à aspirina" [On a Monument to Aspirin] in *A Educação pela pedra*). Living abroad, Cabral de Melo Neto could write about what he had always seen. When he became blind, the poet-engineer stopped building new poem-machines. The old ones, however, are still working.

BIBLIOGRAPHY
Cabral de Melo Neto, João. *Education by Stone: Selected Poems.* Translated by Richard Zenith. New York: Archipelago Books, 2005.
———. *A Knife All Blade: Or, Usefulness of Fixed Ideas.* Translated by Kerry Shawn Keys. Camp Hill, Pa.: Pine Press, 1980.
———. *Selected Poetry, 1937–1990.* Edited by Djelal Kadir. Hanover, N.H.: Wesleyan University Press / University Press of New England, 1994.
Parker, John M. "João Cabral de Melo Neto: 'Literalist of the Imagination'." *World Literature Today* 66 (Autumn 1992): 609–616.

Luciana Namorato

CADENAS, RAFAEL (1930–   )

Born in Barquisimeto, Venezuela, in 1930, Rafael Cadenas is one of the most influential writers in contemporary Venezuelan literature. Cadenas's celebrity as a poet began with his second book of poems, the highly symbolist *Cuadernos del destierro* (Notebooks from Exile), written during the Venezuelan dictatorship of Marcos Perez Jimenez, while Cadenas was exiled in Trinidad (1957–59). His following work, published after Perez Jimenez's fall, was a long poem titled *Derrota* (Defeat, 1960). This poem was of capital importance among the Venezuelan poets of the 1960s. Although its political connotations are few, it became a sort of emblem for those young artists who felt betrayed by the newly installed democracy and its politicians. *Derrota* also opened fresh options for the new Venezuelan poetry of the 1960s: a concise and direct style, distant from symbolist and surrealistic experiments, in which the poetic voice claims no special qualities and conditions such as aesthetic or ethical authority, nor even a particular lucidity for the task of writing.

The next collection of poems, *Falsas maniobras* (Failed Maneuvers), was also written in a straightforward, almost confessional tone. But these poems created a more complex, articulated image of an uncentered, unsettled self whose diverse and contradictory social roles and vain illusions were adrift but reproducing a vicious cycle. After *Falsas maniobras* another major change took place in Cadenas's poetry with the publication in 1977 of *Intemperie* (In the Open) and *Memorial* (Memorial). *Memorial* contains three sections, or gatherings, of poems written in different years: *Zonas*

(Zones) composed in 1970, *Notaciones* (Notes) in 1973, and *Nupcias* (Wedlock) in 1975. *Intemperie* and *Zonas* expressed the discovery of a new and assertive consciousness, which from 1977 to the present seems to have moved into position as the very source of Cadena's lyric voice(s). That new consciousness manifests itself unattached to political or social ideologies, aware of the illusions and vanities of the ego, and critical of literary conventions. *Intemperie* and *Zonas* demonstrate the extraordinary efforts of Cadenas's creative process to reach that consciousness, a consciousness initially defined in a negative way—in terms of what it is not—and as something volatile, since reaching it was not a matter of will, but of a trained perception and disposition.

That sort of training, present in Cadenas's writings since 1970, one decade later rendered a more deeply spiritual expression of consciousness in the volume titled *Amante* (Lover, 1980). *Amante* is usually interpreted as a secular collection of love poems. But since its models are Solomon's Song of Songs and the mystic work of Saint John of the Cross, *Dark Night of the Soul, Amante* can also be interpreted as the poet's pursuit of an experience of a purely spiritual love. *Notaciones* and *Nupcias* were already moving toward a poetry of celebration, offering, and contemplation; therefore, *Amante* appears as the book where the spiritual union between the *I* and the *other* (or *others*) finally succeeds, consummated through poetic language. The humble recognition of love as the single condition sufficient to erase the apperception of distance between people becomes, in this work, a celebration of language itself because language shapes thought. If the new consciousness appeared in *Intemperie* mainly as ethical, in *Amante* it shows its extraordinary loving nature and desire to celebrate the present as well as the unrepeatable moment of an utterance.

Gestiones (Moves, 1992), Cadenas's latest book of poetry, adopts the same concise lyrical style that began taking shape in 1970, as well as the complexity involving the construction of a nonalienated yet very human poetic voice. In *Gestiones,* however, the urge to search, to learn, and to train the self disappears. A seasoned and grateful acceptance of what reality offers and what the poet is and can accomplish is at the center of this book of poems.

Cadenas has written essays of considerable importance, such as *Realidad y literatura* (Reality and Literature, 1970), *En torno al lenguaje* (On Language, 1985), and *Apuntes sobre San Juan de la Cruz y la mística* (Notes on St. John of the Cross and Mysticism, 1995), and also two volumes of epigrams, thoughts, and reflections: *Anotaciones* (Short Notes) and *Dichos* (Sayings). Cadenas's essays and reflections pose similar problems to those that his poems enunciate. Using philosophical, psychological, and sociological resources, Cadenas underlines in them the responsibility of writers to remain lucid and independent from the controls exerted by those groups who claim to have intellectual authority—and independent, also, from the vortex of mass products and their devastating effects on the language. Cadenas enjoys a large audience in his native country, due not only to his works but to his integrity as an intellectual.

BIBLIOGRAPHY

Cadenas, Rafael. *Lover.* Translated and edited by Rowena Hill. Caracas, Venezuela: BidCo, 2004.
———. *The Space of Silence.* Translated by Brian Evenson and Trenton Hickman. Grimsby, U.K.: Goldeneye Books, 1995.

Amelia Mondragón

CALLIGRAMMES: POEMS OF PEACE AND WAR, 1913–1916   GUILLAUME APOLLINAIRE (1918)

As the title indicates, the series of poems published in *Calligrammes* was written over several years, but the volume was not published until after the author's death. As one of France's avant-garde writers, Apollinaire experimented with new forms of expression, and his deliberate visual arrangement of words on the page in *Calligrammes* uses images to convey an immediate impact extended through, and frequently complicated by, the words themselves. The title, a combination of *calligraphy* and *pictogram* and meaning "picture writing," illustrates what Apollinaire forced his reader to do in some of the poems: recombine the fragmented structure and language of poems to achieve a unified understanding.

Deemed by many critics as Apollinaire's most significant work, the collection is divided into six sections:

Waves, Banners, Flutchel, Flash of Gunfire, Moon-Colored Shells, and The Starry Head. Apollinaire's subjects in *Calligrammes* range from the novel to the traditional. Ideas such as the effects of technology on modern life had not been treated extensively in avant-garde poetry. However, even when Apollinaire chose more conventional subjects such as love or war, he regarded them with a fresh perspective.

The poem "Lettre-Ocean" from the first section, Waves, presents a global vision of modern culture through a series of radiating lines and disjointed phrases. Instead of one linear progression through the poem, readers must follow numerous pathways. Yet the poems placed immediately following this disorderly view of life are coherent and arranged in shapes that are immediately identifiable. These simple shapes do not mean that the poems are simple and can be comprehended through the visual experience alone. The initial visual recognition leads to an examination of the poet's contemplation of the idea, then to a return to the image with new understanding. Arrangements such as this suggest the attempts by Apollinaire and other modernists to find graphic means of reconciliation between the order and disorder of the world.

The collection's fourth section, Flash of Gunfire, deals not so much with war as with love and sexual desire. The speaker in "In the Dugout" directly addresses his love and creates an illusory idyllic landscape. Amid this landscape his "soul that's hollow and empty" is nevertheless crowded with "ugly beings that hurt / me" and recognizes both the reality of war and the ephemeral nature of love.

With this collection Apollinaire challenges the traditional boundaries of poetry with new forms of expression and avant-garde concepts. The ordeals facing the modern individual must be met with confidence and vision and with a willingness to reach across borders to establish new understandings. This is the task Apollinaire sets for himself and for his readers in *Calligrammes*.

BIBLIOGRAPHY

Apollinaire, Guillaume. *Calligrammes: Poems of Peace and War (1913–1916)*. Translated by Anne Hyde Greet. Berkeley: University of California Press, 1980, 2004.

Jean Hamm

CARDENAL, ERNESTO (1925–   )   Poet, priest, sculptor, humanitarian, and activist, Ernesto Cardenal is regarded as one of the foremost Latin American poets of the 20th century. Born in Granada, Nicaragua, on January 20, 1925, he spent his childhood and adolescence in his native land. Later he attended the National Autonomous University of Mexico and graduated with a degree in arts in 1947. His master's thesis (1946) later became the introduction to an anthology of Nicaraguan poets of the mid-20th century, *Nueva poesía de Nicaragua* (1949). During his years of study, he published poetry in journals and formed part of a group of Latin American writers including Ernesto Mejía Sánchez, Carlos Martínez Rivas, and Rosario Castellanos. The following year (1947–48) he studied North American literature at Columbia University in New York. Later, while traveling in Spain, Mexican poet OCTAVIO PAZ offered to send selections of Cardenal's poetry to the noted journal *Sur* in Buenos Aires. After traveling in Europe, Cardenal returned to Nicaragua, where he began writing "historical poetry"—a poetry whose style and content would come to be associated with his particular brand of verse. He also founded a bookstore and publishing company, El Hilo Azul (The Blue Thread) as he worked on translations of North American poetry with fellow poet José Coronel Urtecho.

In the 1950s Cardenal's commitment to overthrowing the U.S.-backed Somoza dictatorship inspired political epigrams. In writing these poems Cardenal was greatly influenced by the epigrammatic style of American poet Ezra Pound and by the Latin poets, especially Catullus and Martial. PABLO NERUDA published some of these poems in the *Gaceta de Chile*, but due to their criticism of Somoza, they were published anonymously. In 1954 Cardenal helped to plan a failed attempt to overthrow Somoza. Cardenal recalls this event, the "April Rebellion," in one of the sections of his poem "*Hora 0*" ("ZERO HOUR," 1957). He also composed love epigrams that were inspired by his amorous relationships of the time.

Cardenal experienced what he refers to as his "epiphany," after which he decided to become a priest, in 1956. The next year he traveled to the U.S. State of Kentucky, where he became a novice at Our Lady of

Gethsemani, a Trappist abbey. Cardenal's spiritual mentor at Gethsemani was the world-renowned poet and religious scholar Thomas Merton. For health reasons Cardenal left the abbey in 1959 to spend two years at the Benedictine monastery of Santa María de la Resurrección in Cuernavaca, Mexico. In 1961 he continued his studies at the seminary of Cristo Sacerdote in La Ceja, Colombia. Cardenal was ordained a priest in Managua in 1965.

That same year Cardenal founded the spiritual and utopian commune Nuestra Señora de Solentiname, on an island in Lake Nicaragua, a project he had planned with several of his peers. Although Solentiname initially adhered to the ideals of nonviolence, over the next decade this Christian-based community of peasants, fishermen, and artists became committed to the cause of the Sandinista National Liberation Front. Because of its links to this revolutionary movement, Somoza's national guard destroyed the commune in 1977. A few years earlier, in 1970, Cardenal's uniting of politics and religion took on a new form when he visited Cuba and experienced what he considered a "second conversion." At that point he became a Marxist Christian—a social and spiritual paradigm that in his formulation resembled early Christian communities. For his commitment to the Sandinista cause, Cardenal was sentenced in absentia to prison by Somoza and later publicly admonished by Pope John Paul II. During these years Cardenal traveled extensively to win international support for his cause, the struggle for human rights in Nicaragua.

With the Sandinista's victory over Somoza in 1979, Cardenal was named minister of culture (1979–88). In that capacity he promoted the democratization of culture through poetry workshops and was honored with a variety of national and international honors for his poetry and humanitarian efforts. He received an honorary doctorate from the University of Granada and Valencia and another from the Latin-American Autonomous University in Colombia. Cardenal was named by the government of France Chevalier de l'Ordre des Artes et des Lettres (1985) and elected to the former East Germany's Academy of Fine Arts (1986). Nicaragua awarded him the RUBÉN DARÍO cultural prize (1982) and membership in the Order of Augusto César Sandino (1985).

Since the electoral defeat of the Sandinistas in 1990, Cardenal has continued to publish both poetry and prose (including his memoirs) and to participate actively in cultural and humanitarian causes. His life and works were celebrated in May 2005 in honor of his 80th birthday. He is currently an honorary president of the Casa de los Tres Mundos, a cultural organization in Granada, Nicaragua.

Cardenal is most often identified with *exteriorismo,* a movement that employs a language and syntax that are prosaic in nature and contain a narrative and even testimonial quality. The poet has stated that in writing he tries to create poetry that is understandable and inspires his audience to action, to change the world. According to Robert Pring-Mill, this style of poetry uses techniques similar to those of documentary filmmakers, such as the treatment of factual information, cross-cutting, montage (juxtaposition), and contrast. Cardenal's poetry is also typographically inventive, resembling the graphic field techniques of vanguard movements. He incorporates a variety of what have been traditionally considered "nonliterary" sources in his poetry. This inclusiveness of content as well as its connection to the *canto* and praxis may be seen in the poetic theory of Ezra Pound. For its political, epic, and encyclopedic character, Cardenal's poetry could best be compared to that of PABLO NERUDA's *Canto general* (1950).

Cardenal's extensive publications include anthologies and translations into many languages. Only his poetic works are listed here. Cardenal began writing in the 1940s, and some of his first poems were published in the 1950s. His first collection of poems, *Gethsemani Ky* (1960), is based on his reflections while a novice in the seminary of that name. That same year he published "Hora 0," in which he critiques the Somoza dictatorship and the international intervention and exploitation of Central America.

Although they were written between 1952 and 1956, Cardenal published his *Epigramas* (Epigrams), which included both political and amorous themes, in 1961. Taking on the title and form of the Old Testament's book of Psalms, in *Salmos* (Psalms, 1964) the poet modernizes the content of biblical songs to discuss questions of justice and oppression in the 20th century. In 1965 Cardenal published *Oración por Marilyn Monroe y otros poemas* ("Marilyn Monroe" and Other Poems). As Tamara Williams explains, this collection rejects the spread of American cultural values and critiques the effects of materialism and consumerism on the human spirit (ix). *El estrecho dudoso* (The Doubtful Strait, 1966) uses "exteriorist" techniques to document the turbulent history of oppression and exploitation in Nicaragua and elsewhere in Central America. In this epic Cardenal recounts this region's discovery, conquest, and colonization. In 1969 his *Homenaje a los indios americanos* (Homage to the American Indians) incorporates anthropological and historical research to document the indigenous societies of the Americas. The poet juxtaposes his poetic portraits of these societies with those of their conquerors and Western society in general.

Vida en el amor (To Live Is to Love; Abide in Love, 1970) is a prose poem that celebrates love as the center of the universe. *Canto Nacional al F.S.L.N.* (Nicaraguan Canto, 1972) is an epic poem dedicated to the Sandinistas in which the poet openly declares his commitment to overthrow the Somoza dictatorship. *Oráculo sobre Managua* (Oracle over Managua, 1973) evidences a change in the poet's political commitment in supporting revolution and commemorating the life of a seminary student turned guerrilla fighter. This poem also critiques Somoza's greed after Managua's devastating 1972 earthquake.

Vuelos de victoria (Flights of Victory, 1984) celebrates the triumph of the Sandinistas and the construction of a new society in Nicaragua. Some of the poems included in the collection predate 1979 and consequently provide a perspective of Nicaragua before and after the revolution. *With Walker in Nicaragua and Other Early Poems 1949–1954* (1984) offers a historical perspective of Nicaragua and Central America. In *Los Ovnis de oro* (Golden UFOs, 1988), Cardenal continues his historical documentation of the native tribes of the Americas, and in 1992 the poet combined *Homenaje* and *Los Ovnis de oro* to create *Los ovnis de oro (poemas indios)* (Golden UFOs: The Indian Poems). *Cántico Cósmico* (Cosmic Canticle, 1989) is an epic poem of over 600 words that contemplates the history of the universe from its cosmic beginnings, the "Big Bang," to the 20th century. Topics included in this collection of "cantos" are the Nicaraguan revolution, capitalism,

oppression, and Gaia theory. In a manner similar to his 20th-century version of the Psalms, in *Telescopio en la noche oscura* (1993) Cardenal nods to Saint John of the Cross's *The Dark Night of the Soul* in a modern mystical poem.

BIBLIOGRAPHY

Benedetti, Mario. "Ernesto Cardenal: Evangelio y Revolución." *Casa de las Américas* 63 (1970): 174–183.

Dawes, Greg. *Aesthetics and Revolution: Nicaraguan Poetry, 1979–1990.* Minneapolis: University of Minnesota Press, 1993.

Pring-Mill, Robert. "The Redemption of Reality Through Documentary Poetry." In *Zero Hour and Other Documentary Poems by Ernesto Cardenal.* Translated by Paul W. Borgeson Jr. New York: New Directions, 1980.

Salmon, Russell O. "Introduction." *Los Ovnis de oro: poemas indios/Golden UFOs: The Indian Poems by Ernesto Cardenal.* Translated by Carlos and Monique Altschul. Bloomington: Indiana University Press, 1992.

White, Steven F. "Ernesto Cardenal and North American Literature: The Formulation of an Ethical Identity." In *Modern Nicaraguan Poetry: Dialogues with France and the United States.* Lewisburg, Pa.: Bucknell University Press, 1993. 158–187.

Williams, Tamara R. Introduction to *The Doubtful Strait/El estrecho dudoso by Ernesto Cardenal.* Translated by John Lyons. Bloomington: Indiana University Press, 1995.

Analisa E. De Grave

"CATAMARAN" Henrik Nordbrandt (1995)

This poem appeared in a poetry collection titled *Worms at the Gate of Heaven* (*Ormene ved himlens port*) in 1995, four years following a deep personal tragedy in Henrik Nordbrandt's life that had an indelible impact on his poetics. Nordbrandt had married and divorced twice by the time he met Ingrid, a woman 18 years his junior. According to Nordbrandt's biographer, scholar Thomas Bredsdorff, Nordbrandt had planned to settle down with his love, culminating a life of wanderlust among various Mediterranean countries. But Ingrid died suddenly of thrombosis at age 28, turning Nordbrandt's world upside down. Four years following her death, he still clearly was working through the loss in the poems of this collection, the highlight of which is "Catamaran." The poem features Nordbrandt's signature theme of absence serving as a precondition for presence, but as Bredsdorff points out, this poem "seemed, for the first time, to turn 'absence' from an aesthetic and philosophical category into an existential one" (Bredsdorff 315). In the poem the speaker recalls a trivial argument he once had with his beloved, who had insisted that a large black object in the water was a catamaran. When the speaker later travels alone over the object in a plane and discovers it is not, in fact, a catamaran, he makes a note to call and tell her. But when he calls, she does not answer. The poem's most understated and powerful line blends the banal—a failure to answer the phone—with the existential: "You didn't pick up, I later learned, / because you had died some hours before." The poem concludes with the speaker once again flying over the object that is not a catamaran, and the speaker's tone underscores his loss in an ironic, unsentimental way: "I wanted the plane to go down, but it wouldn't. / You and your catamaran!" In this poem the initial absence of the speaker's lover from the plane, when he first discovers that the catamaran is not a catamaran, ironically makes him feel her presence more strongly. As deeply connected lovers often do, he writes this observation down on a list of many things to share with her when they communicate next. Then, even when her sudden death makes such communication impossible, it ironically makes the poem possible; her permanent physical absence from the speaker's life results in a poignant form of communication that immortalizes a moment that once seemed quite trivial. This kind of ironic tension pervades much of Nordbrandt's poetry. While the body of Nordbrandt's poetry reveals a deep cynicism about whether lasting love is possible in the real world, Nordbrandt makes it clear in this poem that love, in all of its collected trivial moments, is immortal in poetry.

BIBLIOGRAPHY

Bredsdorff, Thomas. "Henrik Nordbrandt." In *Twentieth-Century Danish Writers.* Edited by Marianne Stecher-Hansen. Detroit: Gale Group, 1999, 311–316.
Nordbrandt, Henrik. *The Hangman's Lament: Poems, A Bilingual Edition.* Translated by Thom Satterlee. Los Angeles: Green Integer 95, 2003.

Ursula A. L. Lindqvist

CAVAFY, CONSTANTINE P. (1863–1933)

Constantine Cavafy, who is considered the greatest Greek diasporic poet of the 20th century, lived an uneventful life whose bareness attests not only to the poet's withdrawal from public life, but also hints at the esoteric quality of his verse. Described by E. M. Forster, one of his most ardent admirers, as "a Greek gentleman in a straw hat, standing at a slight angle to the universe," Cavafy was a solitary individual with a cosmopolitan heritage and upbringing. He grew up in Alexandria, Liverpool, London, and Constantinople, spoke Greek, English, French, Italian, and Arabic, and was raised an Orthodox Christian in prevailing Muslim and Protestant environments. His poetry focused on marginal historical figures, furtive sexual desires, delusional aspirations, irreversible disappointments, solitude, mortality, and unexpected turns of fortune and was influenced by the same aesthetic asceticism that kept him from publishing a single volume of poetry during his lifetime. He was described by Lawrence Durrell, John Fowles, and Marguerite Yourcenar as *the* great poet of Alexandria, the city to which he returned at 22 and in which he lived for the rest of his life. Cavafy's first volume of collected poems (the 154 poems that constitute his "canon" to this day) was not published in Greece until 1935, two years after his death.

Constantine P. Cavafy (Konstantinos Kavafis) was the last of nine children born into a wealthy family from Constantinople that had settled in Alexandria in 1854 and remained there until the father, Petros Cavafy's, death in 1870, when Constantine was only seven. The family's subsequent travels across three continents were accompanied by (if not directly related to) the mismanagement of the father's business and its steady decline. The financial anxiety and repeated dislocation Cavafy experienced in his formative years affected both his formal education (of which few records exist—and those account only for one year of high school in Alexandria) and his sensibility. The seven years that Cavafy spent in England, between the ages of nine and 16, were important in introducing him to English literature and in shaping his poetic orientation, but the absence of financial security and guidance for his early interest in literature led Cavafy to pursue temporary jobs, first as a journalist, then as a broker at the Egyptian stock exchange. At the age of 29 he acquired a permanent post as a clerk at the Irrigation Service, a job that offered him relative economic security and that he kept for 30 years.

His daily life was the humdrum routine of working at an uninteresting job, living simply at the home he shared with his mother, Haricleia, and having few intellectual associations, but Cavafy dedicated his afternoons and evenings to the pursuit of pleasure—studying literature, history, and archaeology, working on his poetry, and pursuing secretive and transitory homosexual affairs. Between 1891 and 1904 Cavafy completed several prose works, including an editorial written in English and published in *Rivista Quindicinalen* that argued for the return by Britain of the "Elgin Marbles," removed in 1806 from the Parthenon in Athens. During this period Cavafy also produced 180 poems, out of which he circulated only six to his close friends and relatives in the form of a self-published pamphlet produced in 1904—when he was 41. Included in this early production are some of his best-known poems, including "Walls," "Candles," "The City," "Waiting for the Barbarians," and "Che fece . . . il gran Rifiuto," among others. It is also in this period (1903) that on one of his few trips to Greece, Cavafy met Gregorios Xenopoulos, a prominent man of letters who published the earliest Greek article to recognize the value of Cavafy's poetry.

By 1907 the limited dissemination of Cavafy's work had come to the attention of literary circles in Alexandria and Athens, though the latter city never granted him wide acknowledgment in his lifetime. Nea Zoe (New Life), a literary group comprised of young Alexandrians, picked up Cavafy's poetry and promoted it by publishing it in their journal, while other poems were published in *Grammata* (Letters), another important literary journal of the period. It was also in 1907, eight years after his mother's death, that Cavafy moved to the famous house on Lepsius Street in Alexandria, from whose windows he could see a brothel, a hospital, and a church—according to Cavafy the three cornerstone institutions of society.

Cavafy claimed that the year 1911 marked a turning point in his poetry, the production of the preceding years reduced to the "pre-Cavafy" works. During this year, at the age of 48, he wrote two of his best-known poems, "Ithaka" and "The God Abandons Anthony," and it was from this point forward that he began to distribute his poetry to a greater number of readers in folders of collected offprints. He wrote "In the Month of Athyr" in 1917, and in this period Cavafy began to surround himself with his intellectual equals (his future heir Alekos Sengopoulos, Nikos Kazantzakis, Penelope Delta, Sir John Forsdyke, Robin Furness, and Filippo Marinetti among others) and began to receive international recognition, especially when in 1924 Forster encouraged T. S. Eliot to publish several of Cavafy's poems in *The Criterion*, a year after Forster himself had published a selection of Cavafy's works in *Pharos and Pharillon*. Slightly later, in 1926, Cavafy received the only public recognition that Greece would bestow on him in his lifetime, when the Greek dictator Theodoros Pangalos awarded him the Order of the Phoenix. The award was seen as compromising by many, who advised Cavafy to decline it, but the apolitical Cavafy gratefully accepted it in the name of honoring his beloved and revered Greek state. Some of Cavafy's best poems were composed after he received those awards, for instance, "Myres, Alexandria, a.d. 340" (1929), "He Was Asking about the Quality" (1930), and "Days of 1908" (1932).

The literary activity that embellished Cavafy's later life came to an abrupt end in 1932 when he was diagnosed with cancer of the larynx and, following a tracheotomy in Athens, lost his ability to speak. In the last year of his life, which he spent at his home in Alexandria, Cavafy completed one last poem, "On the Outskirts of Antioch." Cavafy died on his birthday, April 29, 1933.

BIBLIOGRAPHY

Bien, Peter. *Constantine Cavafy*. New York: Columbia University Press, 1964.

Cavafy, C. P. *Collected Poems*. Translated by Edmund Keeley and Phillip Sheppard and edited by George Savidis. Princeton, N.J.: Princeton University Press, 1975; London: Hogarth Press, 1975.

———. *Passions and Ancient Days*. Translated by Edmund Keeley and George Savidis. New York: Dial Press, 1971; London: Hogarth Press, 1971.

Jusdanis, Gregory. *The Poetics of Cavafy: Textuality, Eroticism, History*. Princeton, N.J.: Princeton University Press, 1987.

Keeley, Edmund. *Cavafy's Alexandria: A Study of a Myth in Progress*. Princeton, N.J.: Princeton University Press, 1976.

Liddell, Robert. *Cavafy: A Biography*. New York: Schocken Books, 1974.

Yianna Liatsos

CELAN, PAUL (1920–1970)

Regarded as one of the most complex and introspective poets of the 20th century, Paul Celan has been highly acclaimed by critics, including George Steiner, who called Celan "almost certainly the major European poet of the period after 1945."

Celan was born Paul Antschel (also transliterated as Ancel) in 1920 in Chernivtsi (now in Ukraine), the capital of Bukovina (annexed by Romania), on the eastern edge of the Austro-Hungarian Empire, to a semitraditional, German-speaking Jewish family. The region, labeled "Little Vienna," was heavily Jewish. His father, Leo, an ardent Zionist, wanted his son to imbibe the Jewish tradition, so he pulled the boy, at the age of six, from an elementary school where subjects were taught in German and placed him in the Hebrew school Safa Ivria, run by the Jewish Socialist Bund. Feeling that he was compelled to learn Hebrew, Paul resisted his father's beliefs and embraced leftist, antifascist politics. His mother, Friederike Schrager, with whom he mostly identified (and to whom he addresses many of his tragic poems), taught him to love the German language. His first romantic sonnet, "Mother's Day 1938," crafted when he was 17, is devoted to his mother. Other works radiate with her symbolic presence. At night she read him German lullabies and fairy tales, instilling in her son a fondness for Goethe and the poetry of Schiller. In 1938 he traveled from Chernivtsi to Tours, France, to study medicine but returned the following summer just before the outbreak of World War II. Between 1939 and 1941 he studied Romance languages and literature in Chernivtsi until he was pressed into labor by the Germans in July 1941. On June 27, 1942, he arrived home after hiding with his friends to discover the house boarded up and his parents missing (the ghetto had been swept). He never saw them again. He later learned that they had been deported along with hundreds of other Jews to the labor camp of Transnistria in German-occupied Ukraine. Among the conflicting historical accounts (Celan did not provide a clear version), one assumption is that his father died from typhus in fall 1942 in the Michailowka camp (in Ukraine) and that his mother was shot by the German Schutzstaffel when it ruled that she could not longer work as a slave laborer. Other accounts say that his father was shot too.

From that fateful day on, the legacy of the Nazi genocide was to haunt Celan until his death. Celan himself was sent to a Romanian-administered forced labor camp in Tabaresti, in Wallachia (now Romania), 400 miles south of his hometown. He spent two years there "shoveling" (from July 1942 until early 1944). In 1945 he took up residence in the Romanian capital, Bucharest—where he wrote prodigiously and worked concurrently as an aide in a psychiatric clinic, as a translator of Romanian newspaper articles into Ukrainian, and as a reader of manuscripts. When reports of the horrors of the concentration camps began to filter through and were printed, Celan—after meeting former classmates who, with their families, had survived the horrors that had claimed his parents—reportedly underwent a violent psychic shock from which he never entirely recovered. In 1947 he moved to Vienna, after Romania fell to communism, and in July 1948 relocated to Paris, where he lived for the rest of his life, becoming a naturalized French citizen in 1955. At that point, in essence, his familial and geographical points of origin had been obliterated. In Paris he adopted the pen name Celan, an anagram of his surname.

His first volume of poetry was published in Vienna in August 1948. Disappointed by its poor sales (only 20 copies), he had the book pulped. Meanwhile, he earned a living translating various authors (Shakespeare, Emily Dickinson, Henri Michaux, OSIP MANDELSTAM, Arthur Rimbaud); and after obtaining his B.A. (Licence ès lettres) from the University of Paris, he taught German literature at its École Normale Supérieure. In Christmas 1952 he married the French Catholic graphic artist Gisèle de Lestrange, despite her family's displeasure at the poor poet's meager salary. Their first child, born in 1952, died that same year; and their second, Eric, was born in June 1955. In 1952 "DEATH FUGUE" (Todesfugue) was published and instantaneously won wide critical acclaim and popular recognition; the poem is still arguably the most famous of Holocaust poems. Celan became a celebrity in Germany and was invited to deliver lectures and give readings to packed halls. He won the prestigious Buechner Prize in 1960, awarded by the West German Academy of Language and Literature.

In 1967 he left his wife to live alone. Tormented by survivor guilt, as were many of his contemporaries, he suffered constant spells of acute depression that led to his hospitalization a number of times and to shock therapy. A spurious accusation of plagiarism in the 1960s by Claire Goll, the wife of the Jewish poet YVAN GOLL, whom Celan had translated, exacerbated his recurrent melancholy and loneliness. Likewise, the realization that anti-Semitism was still widespread in Europe deeply shook the manic-depressive poet. In September 1969 he traveled to Israel, where he delivered several readings and seemed to be happy. In April 1970, at the age of 49, back in Paris, he jumped into the Seine River from the Mirabeau Bridge and was found by a fisherman on May 1, 1970, 11 kilometers downstream and 10 days after he had gone missing. He left a biography of Freidrich Hölderlin on his desk, open at a page with a highlighted passage: "Sometimes this genius goes dark and sinks down into the bitter well of his heart."

Celan, who began writing poetry in the labor camps, saw poems as "messages in a bottle" that might or might not be picked up. He once wrote that poems are gifts "to the attentive—fate bearing gifts." Searching for meaning in a meaningless life, Celan found solace in surrealism. He managed to make sorrowful art out of loss, writing torturous poems that these days, as John Felstiner puts it, "are so cryptic as to seem like signals from another planet." Though he wrote that no one witnesses for the witnesses, Celan (deep within) carried the onerous weight of having borne witness to the unspeakable, and he attempted to revive, along with the German language, a treasured human presence lost in the whirlpool of death. But as his work became more and more insular, he absolutely insisted that it was not hermetic.

An alchemist of the word, Celan wanted to unshackle German from its recent history and overlay it with a new patina that would integrate what had been demol-ished—as a monument, a tombstone, for the unburied dead. He also wanted to sever the German language from its Nazi past so that it might be possible to speak that language again in a humane manner. He sought to transform and purify the German language by blending ancient German with neologisms, reworking syntax, and borrowing from other languages. Although he was proficient in many tongues—Romanian, Russian, Yiddish, Hebrew, Portuguese, Italian, and English—he elected to compose in German, his endeavor to rescue his mother's tongue from the depths of his own sorrow. For although the German Nazis had killed his mother and stained the language she loved and taught him, Celan found it impossible to renounce the German tongue, for abjuring it would have meant rejecting his mother's legacy. In 1948, shortly after settling in Paris, Celan told a friend that "there is nothing in the world for which a poet will give up writing, not even when he is a Jew and the language of his poems is German." This paradox rested on his shoulders as a heavy affliction.

Clearly German remained for Celan the most intimate configuration of living speech. His verse was an undertaking to shatter and refit the syntax and morphology of the language that "had to walk through its own loss of answers, through its terrible silence, through the thousand darknesses of death-bringing speech." Celan's artistic purpose was to reestablish the erstwhile integrity of the German language after its degradation by the Third Reich, because, like Celan's childhood and like Judaism, the German language was an inextricable part of his heritage. But the language, savaged by genocidal Nazis who employed German euphemisms (for *action, special treatment, resettlement,* and so on) to dehumanize and ultimately to annihilate European Jewry, was an agonizingly painful medium for him.

Celan's poetry resonates with Jewish themes, a brick by brick, dense maze of copious linguistic elements and biblical allusions that lament the Almighty's absence. One poem concerns dead angels and a blind God, while another speaks of people who do not praise the Creator because he has allowed their abasement, and still another presents a mortally wounded God watching a blood tent (see Leviticus 4:1–21) brutalized by the Nazis, impotent to save the collapsing tent.

Building on the romantic tradition of Friedrich Hölderlin and RAINER MARIA RILKE, Celan's total oeuvre included nonsectarian and non-Holocaust themes, though such subjects took a back seat to his colossal preoccupation. Now 35 years after his death and despite an oeuvre of 700 poems, Paul Celan is still an enigmatic poet whose gaunt, elliptical poems baffle readers and critics alike.

BIBLIOGRAPHY

Bernstein, Michael Andre. *Five Portraits: Modernity and the Imagination in Twentieth-Century German Writing.* Evanston, Ill.: Northwestern University Press, 2000.

Chalfen, Israel. *Paul Celan: A Biography of His Youth.* Translated by Maximilian Bleyleben, introduction by John Felstiner. New York: Persea Books, 1991.

Colin, Amy. *Holograms of Darkness.* Bloomington: Indiana University Press, 1991.

DeKoven Ezrahi, Sidra. *By Words Alone: The Holocaust in Literature.* Chicago: University of Chicago Press, 1980.

Del Caro, Adrian. *The Early Poetry of Paul Celan: In the Beginning Was the Word.* Baton Rouge: Louisiana State University Press, 1997.

Emery, George. "Language and Holocaust: Reflections on the Poetry of Paul Celan." *Michigan Quarterly Review* 36. no. 1, (Winter 1997): 475–483.

Felstiner, John. *Paul Celan: Poet, Survivor, Jew.* New Haven, Conn.: Yale University Press, 1995.

Fioretos, Aris, ed. *Word Traces: Readings of Paul Celan.* Baltimore: Johns Hopkins University Press, 1994.

Glenn, Jerry. *Paul Celan.* New York: Twayne, 1973.

Roselfeld, Alvin. *A Double Dying.* Bloomington: Indiana University Press, 1980.

Rosenthal, Bianca. *Pathways to Paul Celan: A History of Critical Responses as a Chorus of Discordant Voices.* New York: P. Lang, 1995.

Samuels, Clarise. *Holocaust Visions: Surrealism and Existentialism in the Poetry of Paul Celan.* Columbia, S.C.: Camden House, 1993.

Steiner, George. *After Babel: Aspects of Language and Translation.* London: Oxford University Press, 1975.

Szondi, Peter. *Celan Studies.* Translated by Susan Bernofsky with Harvey Mendelssohn, edited by Jean Bollack et al. Stanford, Calif. : Stanford University Press, 2003.

Dvir Abramovich

CENDRARS, BLAISE (FRÉDÉRIC-LOUIS SAUSER) (1887–1961) Poet, novelist, and *"bourlinguer"* (knockabout), Blaise Cendrars (né Frédéric-Louis Sauser) identified deeply with ordinary people. He was born on September 27, 1887, at La Chaux-de-fonds, Switzerland. His innovative writing maps multiple responses to modern life. A literary sensation and succès de scandal upon its publication in 1913, his most widely read poem is *La Prose du Transibbérien et de la Petite Jehanne de France* (The PROSE OF THE TRANS-SIBERIAN AND THE LITTLE JOAN OF FRANCE). A collaboration with the Russian avant-garde painter and graphic artist Sonia Delaunay, the text draws on Cendrars's experiences as a boy apprenticed to a jewelry merchant in Russia between 1904 and 1907. Celebrated during his lifetime as a cubist poet in the school of GUILLAUME APOLLINAIRE, his *Le Panama ou les aventures de mes sept oncles* (Panama or the Adventures of My Seven Uncles) and *Dix-neuf poèmes élastiques* (Nineteen Elastic Poems) are remarkable instances of avant-garde poetry. Poems of this period, conceived often in conjunction with innovations in the visual arts, can be distinguished from surrealism's address to the unconscious in that they are collages of observed or lived experiences, opaque, antipoetic (in the same sense that dada is an anti-art or Pablo Picasso's cubism is "a sum of destructions"). The artists with whom Cendrars collaborated on these projects include Marc Chagall, Ferdinand Léger, Georges Braque, Robert and Sonia Delaunay, and Picasso.

Fortunately for the speaker of English, Ron Padgett's *Blaise Cendrars: The Complete Poems* offers excellent translations and the complete French texts of all Cendrars's poems. For Jay Bochner, writing in the introduction to this volume, *Nineteen Elastic Poems* offers a primer of found, cubist, assemblage, and collage techniques and constitutes an act of "decolonizing perception" (xxvii). Cendrars disliked coterie poetics, pitting his personal integrity against the false sophistication of *"Paris et ses chapelles littéraires"* (Paris and Its Literary Chapels) (quoted in Miriam Cendrars 55). Happily embracing adventure, he adopted what anthropologists identify as the participant-observer point of view. Both his poetry and his prose bridge the gap between high culture and mass culture, finding the spiritual in everyday observations such as those described in his *Profond aujourd'hui: "Phénomènes de cette hallucination congénitale qu'est la vie dans toutes ses manifestations et l'activité continue de la conscience. Le moteur tourne en spirale. Le rythme parle. Chimisme. Tu es.*" (Phenomena of that congenital hallucination that is life in all of its manifestations and the continuous activity of awareness. The motor turns in a spiral. Rhythm speaks. Body chemistry. You are.) (quoted in Perloff 42).

Cendrars's first language was German. He attended primary school in Italy and traveled to Russia after high school, where his literary ambitions first formed. In the poem "*Au coeur du monde*" (At the Heart of the World), Cendrars dates his coming of age poetically to the year 1910, when he discovered Rémy de Gourmont's *Le Latin mystique*. At that time Cendrars and Fela Poznanski, his fellow student, future wife, and mother of his three children, shared a small room in the Hôtel des Étrangers at 216 rue St. Jacques, opposite the house where the 14th-century courtly poem *Le Roman de la Rose* was written. A freeing or jovial irony marks his style, manufacturing for himself, in this instance, a literary tradition reflecting exceptional personal ambition. Invoking diverse associations, the poet invents a place for himself beside that of Jean de Muen (c. 1250–c. 1305) and that predecessor roustabout and libertine François Villon (1431–1463). Living in New York City in 1912 to be near Fela, he sought refuge from the winter cold in the New York Public Library, where he went daily to write. The experience was crucial to Cendrars's developing persona, a birth that he proclaimed for himself in adopting his pen name, the name that he would identify with for the rest of his life, Blaise Cendrars (literally "blaze cinders"), a reference to the cold and poverty of this period. In 1917 he met the actress Raymone Duchâteau, his life-long companion.

During World War I Cendrars served with the French foreign legion, suffering the loss of his right arm in combat on the western front. Adjusting to that loss (and coping with the associated phantom pain) is undoubtedly a source of his ironic enthusiasm for modern technology. In *Kodak,* a volume of poems published in 1924 with a cover by Francis Picabia, Cendrars pioneered a documentary-based style of composition. Following legal proceedings by the American corporation of that name, the volume was renamed *Documentaire.* After 1923 novels and journalism became his main creative outlets. In his novel *Moravagine,* the most col-

lagelike and fantastic of these endeavors, Cendrars describes the airplane as the most beautiful product of the human imagination, "*la plus belle projection du cerveau*" (162), a message consistent with his poetic engagement with the "*profond aujourd'hui*" (profound present day). His documentary fiction is a precursor of the *nouveau roman.* In this postwar period he also worked with the important French film director Abel Gance, both as an assistant director and in the role of a crippled veteran, leading the dead who return to life in the climactic scene of *J'accuse.*

As an editor he was one of the first to compile anthologies of African folklore, his *Anthologie nègre* (1921) being a crucial source of the emergence of NÉGRITUDE literatures in Africa and the Caribbean. Indicative of his range, in 1923 he wrote the scenario for French composer Darius Milhaud's *Creation du monde.* Between 1924 and 1929 he made five separate trips to Brazil, where he deeply influenced the *modernista* movement. Both *Moravagine* and the poem *Feuilles de routes* (written onboard a transatlantic steamer during his first trip to Brazil) contain reflections on the seriousness with which Cendrars undertook the writing process, mapping the different stages from inspiration to copyediting.

A disciplined and productive talent of enormous achievement, he nevertheless pursued the libertine ethos until his demise, both in rejection of rules and authority and in his embrace of sensuality. During World War II Cendrars lived in isolation in Provence, devastated by the German invasion after which his Paris apartment was appropriated and many of his belongings were destroyed. Yet, these were productive years during which he pursued, according to his own account, 33 different projects, including *L'Homme foudroyé* (The Astonished Man, 1945), in which a ghostly avatar of Cendrars revisits the trenches of World War I and the jungles of South America—a rhapsodic text that enacts a form of eternal return. A similar heady mélange of real trauma and hardship with invoked and imagined backgrounds of exotic travel marks Cendrars's poetry and his fiction. In 1961, confined to a wheel chair, only three days before his passing, Cendrars received the Grand Prix for literature from the city of Paris. He died on January 26, 1961, in Paris.

BIBLIOGRAPHY
Bochner, Jay. *Blaise Cendrars, Discovery and Re-creation.*
Toronto: University of Toronto Press, 1978.
Cendrars, Blaise. *Blaise Cendrars: Complete Poems.* Translated
by Ron Padgett, with an introduction by Jay Bochner.
Berkeley: University of California Press, 1992. Appendix
with *Poesies complètes.*
———. *Moravagine.* Paris: Bernard Grasset, 2002.
———. *Œuvres complètes.* 16 vols. Edited by Raymond
Dumay and Nino Frank. Paris: Le Club français du livre,
1968–71.
———. *Poésies complètes avec 41 poèmes inédits.* Paris:
Denoël, 2001.
Cendrars, Miriam. *Blaise Cendrars: L'or d'un poète.* Paris: Gal-
limard, 1996.
Chefdor, Monique. *Blaise Cendrars.* Boston: Twayne, 1980.
Perloff, Marjorie. *The Futurist Moment.* Chicago: University
of Chicago Press, 1986.

Donald Wellman

CÉSAIRE, AIMÉ (1913–)

Aimé Césaire—poet, playwright, essayist, and political leader—was born in 1913 in Basse-Pointe, a small coastal town in northeast Martinique, then under French colonial rule. The second of six children, Césaire was raised in poverty, but his father and mother aspired to the middle class. With the aid of his grandmother Eugénie, Césaire learned to read and write in French by the age of four. At age 11 he moved with his family to the capital, Fort-de-France, where he attended the colonial high school, Lycée Schoelcher. Eschewing Creole, the language spoken by the majority of Martinicans, Césaire's father exposed his children to French classics of prose and poetry, which led Césaire to prefer standard French to Creole as a means of artistic expression of Martinican culture. Césaire attended the prestigious Lycée Louis-le-grand and later the École Normale Supérieure in Paris.

Along with LÉON DAMAS (Guiana) and LÉOPOLD SENGHOR (poet and future president of Senegal), Césaire helped found the NÉGRITUDE MOVEMENT in the 1930s. This movement was inspired by the Harlem Renaissance of the United States—an artistic flowering in the 1920s celebrating African-American writers, musicians, and artists. Césaire was particularly influenced by Jamaican-born Claude McKay, whose Harlem Renaissance novel *Banjo* (1928) served as a cautionary tale for African Americans who try to assimilate white, bourgeois culture to the detriment of their own distinctive cultural heritage. The Harlem Renaissance represented for Césaire the possibility of a wider black artistic and cultural movement (*négritude*), powerful in its collectivity and scornful of the inferiority complex caused by white supremacist attitudes. Like the Harlem Renaissance, the Négritude Movement was an affirmation of black artistic achievement and pride in the wake of French colonization of Africa, the West Indies, and Guiana. The Négritude Movement took its name from the pejorative French term for blacks (*nègres*) and defused its power as an offensive racial slur, while simultaneously investing it with the dignity of a movement that would give voice to oppressed artists whose works had been previously ignored by white Europeans. Césaire is generally credited with coining the term *negritude*: It appears in his poetic masterpiece *Cahier d'un retour au pays natal* (NOTEBOOK OF A RETURN TO THE NATIVE LAND) (1939), but some scholars dispute the term's provenance.

Through his association with Damas and Senghor, who had started the Paris newspaper *L'Étudiant noir* (The Black Student) in 1934, Césaire became acquainted with other writers from Africa and the West Indies who would form the nexus of the Négritude Movement. It was also at this time that he met Suzanne Roussy, a Martinican whom he married in 1937 and with whom he later collaborated.

While still a student in Paris, Césaire began writing in 1935 what would become his masterpiece, the epic poem in free verse, *Notebook of a Return to the Native Land.* He continued to write and revise the poem throughout the remainder of his student days in Paris, publishing the first version of it in the Paris literary journal *Volontés* in 1939. Relying on strange imagery and a stream-of-consciousness style, Césaire wrote *Notebook* in the surrealist vein. The surrealist movement in Europe, begun in France by ANDRÉ BRETON in the 1930s, emphasized the subconscious and eschewed traditional metaphors and imagery. Surrealist poets practiced "automatic writing," a technique in which the poet does not reflect in detail before writing, but rather writes spontaneously as thoughts manifest themselves in his or her mind. The effect produces strange images, associations, and metaphors; and although this is true of Césaire's *Notebook,* the principal theme of the poem is clear—that the poet's native Antilles have been degraded through French slavery and colonization, which left in their wake poverty, racism, and the loss of native culture. However, the poet's ultimate message is one of hope rather than despair, for his *négritude*—his "blackness"—is a source of strength and dignity, and not a reason to feel inferior in spite of decades of slavery and racial prejudice. As he put it, "my negritude is not a stone, its deafness hurled against the clamor of the day / my negritude is not a leukoma of dead liquid over the earth's dead eye . . . it takes root in the red flesh of the soil / it takes root in the ardent flesh of the sky / it breaks through the opaque prostration with its upright patience."

After completing an advanced university degree (Diplôme d'Études Supérieures), Césaire returned with his wife to their native Martinique, where both taught at the Lycée Schoelcher. In 1939 they started the literary review *Tropiques,* whose mission was to blend the artistic ideals of *négritude* with European modernism; for if Césaire was determined to give a voice to black writers of francophone countries, he was equally influenced by the surrealist movement in France, as evidenced in his stream-of-consciousness style and strange, dreamlike imagery in *Notebook.*

In 1944 Césaire visited Haiti, where he gave a series of lectures. There he began to deepen his interest in politics, heartened by the belief that Haiti represented the most promising possibility for an independent Caribbean nation. Césaire wrote a historical study, *Toussaint L'Ouverture* (1960), about the life of the general who had fought against France for Haitian independence. In 1945 Césaire began his own political career when he was elected mayor of Fort de France and deputy in the Constituent Assembly on the French Communist ticket. He would henceforth divide his time between his literary and political careers. In 1956 he resigned from the French Communist Party and began the socialist Parti Progressiste Martiniquais (Martinican Progressivist Party). Already established as one of the major poets in 20th-century literature, Césaire was a playwright as well, publishing, among other plays, *A Season in the Congo* (1968) and *A Tempest* (1968)—a daring adaptation of

Shakespeare's *The Tempest.* All of his poetry, plays, and essays have as their central themes power, black identity, and decolonization.

See also "BARBARITY," "IT IS THE COURAGE OF MEN WHICH IS DISLOCATED," "ON THE STATE OF THE UNION," and "A PROPHECY."

BIBLIOGRAPHY

Césaire, Aimé. *The Collected Poetry of Aimé Césaire.* Translated and edited by Clayton Eshleman and Annette Smith. Berkeley and Los Angeles: University of California Press, 1983.

Davis, Gregson. *Aimé Césaire.* Cambridge: Cambridge University. Press, 1997.

Patrick L. Day

CHAR, RENÉ (1907–1988)

Born in L'Isle-sur-la-Sorgue in the Provence region of France that would inform so much of his poetry, René Char is one of the major poets of 20th-century French literature. His literary career spans 60 years, from *Les cloches sur le cœur* (Bells on the Heart, 1928) to *Éloge d'une soupçonnée* (Praise for a Suspect, 1988) and reflects much of French literary history of that period. Often elegiac in tone, Char's poetry, like that of his contemporaries Francis Ponge and SAINT-JOHN PERSE, usually takes the form of *vers libre,* prose poems, or simple aphorisms. Hermetic without being recherché, pastoral without being folksy, and imbued with an unmistakable moral weight, Char's oeuvre stands among the work of such literary luminaries as PAUL CELAN, OSIP MANDELSTAM, and CZESŁAW MIŁOSZ.

Char was influenced early by Arthur Rimbaud (1854–1891), particularly *Les illuminations* (Illuminations, 1886) and, to a lesser extent, by Stéphane Mallarmé (1842–98). In the late 1920s he fell in with the surrealists, in particular ANDRÉ BRETON, PAUL ÉLUARD, and LOUIS ARAGON. Typical of this early period are his collections *Ralentir travaux* (Slow Under Construction, 1930), written with Breton and Éluard, and *Le tombeau des secrets* (The Tomb of Secrets, 1930), which contains photographs, à la Breton's *Nadja.*

Char began to hit full stride with his collection *Le marteau sans maître* (The Masterless Hammer, 1934), which included some material published from 1927 through 1934. The influence of surrealism is noticeable in the volume, particularly in the early poems. In "Commune présence" (Common Presence, 1936), the final poem of the collection *Moulin premier* (First Mill), appended later to *Le marteau sans maître*, the act of writing stands against a disintegrating world: *"Quartier suivant quartier la liquidation du monde se poursuit / Sans interruption / Sans égarement"* (Quarter after quarter the liquidation of the world continues / Without interruption / Without distraction). Against this fragmentation the writer who is addressed in this poem stands unified and whole. Char published two more collections in the next few years—*Placard pour un chemin des écoliers* (Placard for a Path for Schoolchildren, 1937) and *Dehors la nuit est gouvernée* (The Night Is Governed Outside, 1938)—but critics date Char's mature work from World War II.

Char did not publish during the war, but instead served in the Resistance in a *maquis,* or underground unit, in southern France, where his nom de guerre was Capitaine Alexandre. For this service, for his fight against the German occupation as well as for not working with the collaborationist Vichy government, Char enjoyed moral authority in the later part of his career. Even though he did not publish during the war, he never stopped writing. He kept a lyric diary from 1941 to 1944, which was later published as *Feuillets d'Hypnos* (Leaves of Hypnos, 1946), and dedicated to French novelist Albert Camus. It is a collection of aphorisms—recalling Blaise Pascal's lonely and philosophical musings—that range from the personal (*"Comment m'entendez-vous? Je parle de si loin . . ."* [How can you hear me? I speak from so far away . . .]), through the philosophical and telegramatic (*"L'acte est vierge, même répété"* [The act is virgin, even repeated] and *"Devoirs infernaux"* [Infernal duties]), to the simply enigmatic (*"Épouse et n'épouse pas ta maison"* [Marry and don't marry your house]). *Feuillets d'hypnos* was reissued as part of the collection *Fureur et mystère* (Furor and Mystery, 1948), which would become his most famous collection (and includes his "The METEOR OF AUGUST 13TH"). The juxtaposition in the title is indicative of the energy that characterizes the collection and of the play of opposing forces that extends through all of Char's work. His next collection, *Les Matinaux* (The Dawn Breakers, 1949), as the title indicates, revealed a calmer mood as Char recovered from the war

and began to portray the morning after the storm, as it were. There is a return to Char's native Vaucluse, but as with all of his work the specific and local gives way to the universal.

Char continued to write steadily, producing a collection every year or two. His next collection, *La Parole en archipel* (The Archipelago Word, 1960), included six books written over eight years. Striking here is his use of the cave drawings of Lascaux in the series *La Paroi et la prairie* (The Partition and the Prairie): *"Cerfs, vous avez franchi l'espace millénaire, / Des ténèbres du roc aux caresses de l'air."* (Deer, you have crossed millennial space, / From the shadows of the rock to the caresses of the air.) *Le Nu perdu* (Nakedness Lost, 1970) was Char's last major collection, followed by smaller books including *Aromates chasseurs* (Herb Hunters, 1975), *Chants de la Balandrane* (Songs of the Balandrane, 1977), and *Loin de nos cendres* (Far from Our Ashes, 1982). These later works, covering the last 24 years of Char's life, would not drastically change the trajectory of his work. The same moral uprightness is evident, as is the important role of writing in a rudderless world (see "Baudelaire mécontente Nietzsche" [Baudelaire Annoys Nietzsche]) and the rural landscape of the Vaucluse ("Contre une maison sèche" [Against a Dry House]). *Aromates chasseurs* even returns to the aphoristic format of *Feuillets d'hypnos.*

Char used his moral authority to support certain political and especially environmental goals—goals inseparable from the poems themselves. Most notably, Char wrote the essay *"La Provence point oméga"* (Ground Zero Provence, 1965) protesting the installation of nuclear missiles within sight of his beloved Mt. Ventoux. Char's environmental concerns are probably most clearly seen in one of his four plays, *Le Soleil des eaux* (The Sun of the Waters, 1967; reworked for television in 1968). His thoughts on things political as well as artistic are collected in *Recherche de la base et du sommet* (Searching for Base and Summit, final edition 1971). He also has one ballet to his credit, *L'Abominable Homme des neiges* (The Abominable Snowman, 1952), cowritten with Nicolas de Staël. In addition Char maintained close ties with many contemporary artists and musicians, some of whom are featured in his poetry. His penultimate book was entitled *Les voisinages de Van*

Gogh (Van Gogh's Neighborhoods, 1985). He wrote on Picasso, Braque, and Giacometti. Some of his collections feature prints by, among others, Braque, Miró, and Kandinsky. Char died of a heart attack on February 19, 1988, five months after his second marriage. His final collection, *Éloge d'une soupçonnée* (In Praise of One Suspected), was published posthumously in 1988.

BIBLIOGRAPHY

Caws, Mary Ann. *The Presence of René Char.* Princeton, N.J.: Princeton University Press, 1976.

———. *René Char.* Boston: Twayne, 1977.

Char, René. *Leaves of Hypnos.* Translated by Cid Corman. New York: Grossman, 1973.

———. *This Smoke That Carried Us.* Translated by Susanne Dubroff. Buffalo, N.Y.: White Pine Press, 2004.

———. *Selected Poems.* Edited by Mary Ann Caws and Tina Jolas. New York: New Directions, 1992.

La Charité, Virginia A. *The Poetics and the Poetry of René Char.* Chapel Hill: University of North Carolina Press, 1968.

Piore, Nancy Kline. *Lightning: The Poetry of René Char.* Boston: Northeastern University Press, 1981.

Tom Dolack

CHEDID, ANDRÉE (1920–   )

Born to Lebanese parents in 1920 in Cairo, Egypt, Andrée Chedid is today regarded as one of France's literary gems. She has been writing since the age of 18, and her vast oeuvre encompasses novels, plays, short stories, and especially poetry, which has brought her the most acclaim. Chedid considers poetry to be the essential source of her writing (Laurentine) and her most cherished form of expression (Leca). Her poetry often carries a mystical resonance, as illustrated by "LANDSCAPES."

Chedid attended a Catholic boarding school while growing up and later studied at the American University in Cairo. After marriage, she and her husband, Louis Chedid, spent three years in Beirut, Lebanon, before making Paris their permanent home in 1946. Talent runs in the family. In France today the name Chedid is also widely associated with the author's son Louis and grandson Matthieu, who are both well-known musicians. Matthieu's hit number *Je dis aime* (Love, I Say) was written by Andrée Chedid. Chedid's first book, published in 1943, was a volume of poetry in English titled *On the Trails of My Fancy,* after which French was her preferred artistic medium.

Chedid's writing, in which reality appears under the guise of myth, is impregnated with images from Lebanon and the Orient. Her works do not have the sentimentality or nostalgia of a transplanted writer, but instead reflect a cosmopolitanism grounded in her profound knowledge of and affiliation with two civilizations: the Western and the Mediterranean Middle Eastern. The clarity and economy of her style; the absence of dogma, ideology, and religion in her writing; the temporal and spatial universality of the emotions and situations highlighted in her writing; her quest for humanity and for the essence of things; her questioning at the deepest level; her exploration of the human condition through the prism of the sociopolitical reality of the Middle East; her choice of subjects marked by tragedy and hope; her belief in the mysterious essence within humanity that is greater than humans; her avoidance of all forms of labeling and classification; and her indifference to transient literary trends and innovations—these are some of the salient characteristics of her writing that situate her within a classical, humanistic paradigm. Even though Chedid often depicts women and their struggles, critics hesitate to label her as a feminist writer in the militant sense of the term. The poet declares that when she writes, she does not proceed from the premise that she is a female. Her writing comes from a perspective involving a meditation on our relationship to the world, individual liberty, the human condition, and the mystery of life. The great themes of her oeuvre are life, death, and love. Some of her works, like her novel *The Return to Beirut* (*La Maison sans racines*) and her poems in *Rituals of Violence* (*Cérémonial de la violence*), are important for their denunciation of the 1976 civil war that ravaged Lebanon.

Among the various awards and prizes Chedid has received are the following: Le Prix Louise Labé (1966), Le Prix de L'Académie Mallarmé (1976), La Bourse Goncourt de la Nouvelle (1979), Le Grand Prix de la Société des Gens de Lettres (1990), Le Prix des Quatre Jurys (1994), Le Prix Albert Camus (1996), and Le Prix Goncourt de la Poésie (2003).

BIBLIOGRAPHY
Chedid, Andrée. *Cérémonial de la violence.* Paris: Flammarion, 1976.
———. *On the Trails of My Fancy.* Cairo: Horus, 1943.
———. *The Return to Beirut.* London: Serpent's Tail, 1989.
Cochran, Judy, trans. *Selected Poems of Andrée Chedid.* New York: Edwin Mellen Press, 1995.
Laurentine, Renée. "Andrée Chedid et le pouvoir de l'écriture." *Points de vue sur l'écriture.* Available online. URL: http://ecrits-vains.com/points_de_vue/renee_laurentine01.htm. Downloaded on September 12, 2005.
Leca, Martine. "'An inner freedom.'—interview with poet, novelist and playwright Andrée Chedid-Interview." *UNESCO Courier,* November 1997. Available online. URL: http://www.findarticles.com/p/articles/mi_m1310/is_1997_Nov/ai_20099668. Downloaded on September 12, 2005.

Shonu Nangia

CHENEY-COKER, SYL (1945–)

Born to Christian Creole parents in Freetown, Sierra Leone, on June 28, 1945, Syl Cheney Coker spent his childhood in Sierra Leone and received his earliest education there. He traveled to the United States in 1966 to attend the University of California at Los Angeles and continued his studies of literature and journalism at the University of Oregon and the University of Wisconsin. He hyphenated his last name (as Cheney-Coker) in 1970. Upon completing his education he worked as press secretary to the prime minister of Sierra Leone, Siaka Stevens, for a short time, then in 1975 took a faculty position at the University of the Philippines. There he met his wife, Dalisay, a Filipina. They moved to Nigeria in 1977, where he held a teaching position at the University of Maiduguri for many years. He returned to Sierra Leone in 1985 to establish a fortnightly newspaper in Freetown, *The Vanguard.* In 1988 he accepted the post of writer-in-residence at the University of Iowa. Back in Freetown he was threatened from 1991 to 1997 by members of the United Revolutionary Front for his outspokenness about freedom of speech. When his home was attacked during the 1997 coup d'état, he was forced to seek asylum in the United States. Since then he has held faculty positions in various American cities, including Las Vegas, Nevada, and Charlotte, North Carolina, and he has been invited to speak and read from his works at literary events worldwide. His works have been translated into many languages, including Dutch, Filipino, French, German, Greek, Italian, Portuguese, Spanish, and Russian.

Cheney-Coker's early poetry was inspired by the Negritude discourse of LÉOPOLD SÉDAR SENGHOR. His first book-length publication, *Concerto for an Exile* (1973), exposes his deeply conflicted feelings about growing up the child of privilege within a financially well-to-do family descended from freed slaves who, having returned to Freetown, came to dominate Sierra Leonean political affairs and ways of life. The martyr-like figure who is the speaker of the poems in *Concerto* differs in spirit from the persona that dominates the next volume, *The Graveyard Also Has Teeth* (1980), where exile and self-torment are not the main themes—but, rather, the desire to become a national poet and to sing the country's Creole history. His "ON BEING A POET IN SIERRA LEONE" typifies the poems of that collection. For his third book, *The Blood in the Desert's Eyes* (1990), Cheney-Coker assumes a prophetic posture, stridently condemning injustices and blazoning out a critique of the brutality of those who hold or try to usurp political power. *The Last Harmattan of Alusine Dunbar* (1990), Cheney-Coker's novel, won the 1991 Commonwealth Writers Prize (Africa Region) and features one character who embodies the Creole consciousness that Cheney-Coker has always striven to express. All together Cheney-Coker's works transmit one of Africa's most clamorous voices, an elegiac howl full of fervor and rage. It is not, however, a particularly "African" body of writing in the customary sense. Breaking with the practices of traditional poets and more recent ones, including Ngugi wa Thiong'o and CHINUA ACHEBE, it owes more to the styles of French and South American writers whom he has studied, including the Beats and Gabriel García Márquez. Cheney-Coker returned to Sierra Leone in 2003, declaring that "after a while, exile is neither justifiable nor tolerable" (Morrison).

BIBLIOGRAPHY
Cheney-Coker, Syl. *Concerto for an Exile: Poems.* London: Heinemann, 1973.
———. *The Graveyard Also Has Teeth.* London: Heinemann, 1980.

————. *The Blood in the Desert's Eyes: Poems*. London Heinemann, 1990.

————. *The Last Harmattan of Alusine Dunbar*. London: Heinemann, 1990.

Morrison, Jane Ann. "Symbol of Freedom: Exiled Writer: Time Is Right to Go Home." *Las Vegas Review Journal* (January 17, 2003).

R. Victoria Arana

CHIEKO COLLECTION, THE TAKAMURA KŌTARŌ (1941)

Chieko Shō is TAKAMURA KŌTARŌ's best-known book. The collection consists of 31 poems and three essays. *Chieko Shō* is a unified collection and a poetry sequence in the true sense, chronicling Takamura's life together with his wife, Chieko. The sequence begins in 1912 with his courtship of Chieko and ends in 1940, two years after her death. Early poems, such as "To Someone (Not to Play)," record their youthful and exuberant love for each other. Others, such as "Deep Night Snow," show a deep-seated and mature love. All of the poems of this period, however, emphasize their unique relationship. In a time of arranged marriages, their marriage, based on love and gender equality, was unusual for the time. These early poems also focus on Chieko's spiritual role in Takamura's life. Throughout his life Takamura looked upon Chieko as having rescued him from a life of decadence. He saw Chieko as having a close connection with nature, and for Takamura Chieko was a spiritual guide and the means to a purifying communion with nature. These early poems also express the couple's isolation from society, which seems to have resulted largely from their unique relationship. *Chieko Shō* goes on to record their poor but content existence together until Chieko's depression and attempted suicide in 1931 and her diagnosis of schizophrenia the following year. The close connection between the couple chronicled in the earlier part of the book heightens the poignancy of the series of poems that records Chieko's journey from madness into death. As Chieko drifts ever further from him, tender poems, such as "Chieko among the Plovers" and "Two of the Foothills," chronicle both Takamura's sadness at Chieko's plight as well as his loneliness at losing someone who had become woven into the fabric of his existence. The most touching part of the sequence occurs in the last few poems, beginning with "Lemon Dirge," in which Chieko, on her deathbed, momentarily returns to sanity and to Takamura just before she passes away. "Bleak Homecoming" follows, a poem in which Takamura expresses his extreme isolation both during Chieko's funeral arrangements and after she is gone, when he finds himself alone in his studio. The sequence moves on to a note of consolation in "To One Who Died" and "Plum Wine." In the former Takamura comes to see himself communing once again with Chieko as her spirit becomes one with nature, and in the latter Takamura later discovers a bottle of plum wine that Chieko had made many years earlier and then sits sipping the wine and feeling once again connected to Chieko. The sequence concludes with "Six Songs," a series of six vignettes of their life together. The latter part of the book includes three essays: a biography of the last half of Chieko's life, a short essay about Chieko's time living near Kujūkuri Beach while Takamura tried to care for her in her illness, and a short essay about Chieko's cut paper art.

BIBLIOGRAPHY
Takamura Kōtarō. *The Chieko Poems*. Translated by John G. Peters. Los Angeles: Green Integer Books, 2005.

John G. Peters

"CHILD OF EUROPE" CZESŁAW MIŁOSZ (1946)

When accepting the Nobel Prize in literature in 1980, CZESŁAW MIŁOSZ said, "I am a *child of Europe,* as the title of one of my poems admits, but that is a bitter, sarcastic admission." Miłosz composed "Child of Europe" during a diplomatic posting in New York, as the poet looked back at his homeland with increasing cynicism. The poem asserts that the only inheritance Europe offers its children is moral decay. Miłosz's poem is bold in its vitriol, yet nuanced in its craft—using polyphonic voices that shift between the second and third person, an imperative tone, and a form reminiscent of Alexander Pope's verse-essays—and its multiple sections presage subsequent book-length poems.

In the sardonic and swaggering latter sections, the speaker's commands outline an egocentric path: "Love no country: countries soon disappear. / Love no city:

cities are soon rubble . . . Do not love people: people soon perish." What is even more of an inconvenience, people "are wronged and call for your help" (vi, ll. 1–2, 5–6). In the course of World War II Europe had already traveled far along this path to self-destruction. A founder of the catastrophist movement, Miłosz believed that humankind's penchant for self-fulfilling prophecy would lead to annihilation: "Learn to predict fire with unerring precision. / Then burn the house down to fulfill the prediction" (iii, ll. 11–12). The poet ironically employs couplets reminiscent of Pope's to describe the death of critical wit, as his speaker swears that "Stern as befits the servants of a cause, / We will permit ourselves only sycophantic humor" (vi, ll. 5–6). The culminating section is a wicked vision of a world without recognized truth: "Tight-lipped, guided by reasons only, / Cautiously let us step into the era of unchained fire" (vi, ll. 6–8).

How did it come to this? The anonymous "we" of the first section speaks in disquieting but not abominable tones, as celebration of survival creeps delicately toward righteousness: "We, whose lungs fill with the sweetness of day . . . are better than those who perished" (i, ll. 1, 3). The speaker, part of this unified second person, inspects the slippery moral slope of sinning for the sake of self-preservation: "Having the choice of our own death or that of a friend, / We chose his, coldly thinking: let it be done quickly" (i, ll. 14–15). From these flawed but understandable origins comes hubris; and in the second section Miłosz creates a linguistic and ethical schism between speaker and body: "You have a clever mind which sees instantly / The good and bad of any situation. / You have an elegant, skeptical mind which enjoys pleasures / Quite unknown to primitive races" (ii, ll. 7–10). The seed of pride has morphed into the flowery language of eugenics. Miłosz was fascinated by a good man's ability to lose himself in a greater evil, which he described as a schizophrenia of the public self and the private. He said, "utopian expectations, projected on historical reality, could become justification for totalitarianism." A few years later Miłosz incorporated the issues examined in this poem into his seminal philosophical volume, *The Captive Mind*.

Sandra Beasley

"CHILDREN OF THE LAND" KOFI ANYIDOHO (1993)

"Children of the Land (A Sequence for African Liberation)" is from KOFI ANYIDOHO's third collection of poems, *Ancestrallogic and Caribbeanblues* (*sic*). It is representative of his freedom poetry and was composed at the request of the Ghana Commission on Children for a performance commemorating the flag-raising ceremony at the Organisation of African Unity (OAU) in Accra in July 1984.

The poem was originally performed by five groups of school children (symbolically representative of the five regions of the continent—North Africa, East Africa, West Africa, Central Africa, and Southern Africa). The work exists in two versions. The original version is longer, with child-speakers representing each country making an appearance, while the revised version preserves only the sequence of regions. The two versions appear in the collection.

As an occasional poem, "Children of the Land" celebrates the shared aspiration of African freedom and seeks to invent a common dream from the diverse struggles for self-determination in Africa. It promotes the ideals of African liberation and the spirit of brotherhood that the Organisation of African Unity (now the African Union) stood for. It celebrates the beauty that comes from the various cultural and historical experiences in the different parts of the continent and creates an admirable vision of Africa by carefully evoking its beauty as revealed in its physical and cultural geography and in the resilience with which it has withstood external intrusions and internal crises. It consequently underscores the paradox that underlies the African identity: the reality of its unity and diversity.

This poem, essentially Pan-Africanist, celebrates Africa through its children, as symbolizing the hopes and possibilities that exist for the continent. In a sense it is the dreams that the children hold for Africa that inspire hope. Otherwise, there will be little or nothing to celebrate about contemporary Africa, whose leaders must take responsibility for its many failures and woes. Positive legacies exist to inspire them. In this sense the poem must not be read as pretending that all is well with Africa. It relies on an effective adoption of imagery drawn from the common historical, cultural, and geographical indexes of identity in the five regions of

Africa that it identifies in imagining Africa and the possibilities that exist for it. The five movements logically coincide with the appearances of the five groups representing the various regions. The beauty of this poem is most apparent in performance, where the closing lines at the end of each movement are chorused by children holding flags of the various countries they represent.

Oyeniyi Okunoye

CHINWEIZU (1943–)

Chinweizu—the name is one he invented and adopted—is among the most visible, prolific, and influential public intellectuals writing and speaking about Africa today. He has published contentious poetry, contemporary history, literary criticism, cultural critiques, and trenchant analyses of African economics and current events. His writing, most of which is highly polemical, derives its revolutionary edge from Ghanaian politician Kwame Nkrumah and Martinique-born revolutionary thinker Frantz Fanon, but Chinweizu adds a good measure of scathing satire to his socially conscious poetry and prose. His particular brand of postcolonial critique, when compared with that of his contemporaries, could well be considered ultraradical. He has contended, at different moments and for various reasons, against CHINUA ACHEBE and CHRISTOPHER OKIGBO, WOLE SOYINKA and J. P. CLARK, and W. E. B. Du Bois and South African civil rights leader Nelson Mandela—calling them infected by "Blancophilia" and, thereby, indirect contributors to "Negro Negrophobia." Alluding to Edward Said's critique of the West's "Orientalism," Chinweizu has called himself (maybe not tongue in cheek) "an occidentalist" (Energy Crisis, back matter). It is his sardonic way of asserting not only that he knows he sometimes overgeneralizes but also that he enjoys the tit-for-tat of abridging his depiction of Westerners and their predatory social and cultural ways—for his own particular political purposes. Chinweizu's oral and written deliberations of what is wrong with Africa are multidisciplinary, hard-hitting, and boldly rhetorical. His writings promote a spiritual and moral regeneration of African culture, which he calls self-reparation. The ideology he endorses is anti–World Bank, anti–International Monetary Fund, anti–United Nations, anti-Nigeria,

anti-Islamic, anti-Arab, anti-Western (European, white, Christian), and pro-resistance to foreign imperial exploitation of all types. He is also a severe critic of contemporary African politics and politicians, current African educational systems, and the scandalous waste of African natural resources by Africans themselves.

Chinweizu was born on March 26, 1943, in Eluama-Isuikwato, a town in eastern Nigeria. His parents—Obediah Dimgba and Oluchi Akuji (Ejinwa) Ibekwe—belonged to the Igbo tribe. His father was a successful businessman. Chinweizu attended schools in Nigeria but received all of his postsecondary education in the United States. He studied philosophy and mathematics at the Massachusetts Institute of Technology (MIT), from which he earned a bachelor of science degree in 1967, the year of the outbreak of civil war in Nigeria. He was 24 and living in Cambridge, Massachusetts, at the time. His response to the war at home was to found and edit the Biafra Review (Cambridge, 1969–70). Next he enrolled at the State University of New York at Buffalo, where he specialized in history and American studies. After earning an M.A. (1975) and a Ph.D. (1976) at SUNY-Buffalo, he was awarded a Rockefeller Foundation scholarship in 1976 and returned to MIT to do postdoctoral work in economics. Even before that (in 1971) he had begun the research for one of his most famous publications, The West and the Rest of Us: White Predators, Black Slavers, and the African Elite, a book published in 1975 by American novelist Toni Morrison when she was senior editor at Random House. At this time Chinweizu was serving as an associate editor of Okike, a journal of the arts and criticism based in Nsukka, Nigeria (a post he held for many years). Okike published many of his essays between 1973 and 1978. They were followed by Toward the Decolonization of African Literature (1980), which Chinweizu coedited with O. Jemie and I. Madubuike. In 1987 Chinweizu published two book-length essays: The Black World and the Nobel and Decolonizing the African Mind, arguably his most celebrated arguments in favor of disavowing and discounting non-African traditions, agendas, and honors. His grumbling Anatomy of Female Power: A Masculinist Dissection of Matriarchy appeared in 1990 and drew attention because its author had sided with and quoted approvingly some of the most virulently reactionary critics of 20th-century feminism.

Chinweizu's reputation as a poet rests primarily on his two volumes: *Energy Crisis and Other Poems* (1978) and *Invocations and Admonitions: 49 Poems and a Triptych of Parables* (1986). These collections contain rich poetic versions of his standard messages in prose. Often the poems are delightfully satirical, sometimes exploiting a carefully calibrated double entendre. The title poem of his first volume, "Energy Crisis," for instance, records a conversation between a woman desperate to fill her gas tank and a gas station attendant who claims he cannot do so because of the national energy crisis, which has left him depleted due to an inordinate demand for his goods. The sexual subtext is cleverly managed so that the poem seems to refer all at once to the world's mismanagement of natural resources, to Nigeria's cupidity and political culpability for the shortages, and to the insatiable sexuality of women (the man cannot service the pleading woman because she has been preceded by vast numbers of fashionable clients with large gas tanks, and they have left him "exhausted").

Invocations and Admonitions contains many acerbic poems that praise a footloose and fancy-free masculinity and excoriate the possessive female, who is used and discarded in poem after poem. In "Hard Mean Woman," for instance, the speaker says: "You could shovel into your maul / All the pain, all the anger, all the stubbornness in the world, / stoke it down your vulcanized chute, / and it wouldn't jam your diamond gizzards" (57). In "The Vow," the speaker promises: "I shall indulge my pubic charities; / I shall loll in the laps of damsels; / I shall not be diverted from bottle, bosom and prattle, / Till white hairs and wilted limbs / Compel it. / . . . and I like it so" (60–61). The collection also contains a number of longer poems: his powerful "Lament for a Dauntless Three," which commemorates heroes of the Biafran conflict (the poet Christopher Okigbo and two other leaders of the revolt against political oppressions in Nigeria); his "Invocation on a Day of Exile," a heady prayer to ancestral gods asking them to conserve the poet, innocent of the crimes of those who have driven him from home; and Chinweizu's panoramic "ADMONITION TO THE BLACK WORLD."

The collection also contains poems that question religious and political hypocrisy (e.g., "Monks, Nuns and Orphans" and "The Warmonger's Beatitudes"), colonial recidivism ("Colonizer's Logic"; "Law and Order"), and the challenges of science ("Sex in Space"; "This Rational Animal, Man!"). His poem "PROFESSOR DERRIDA ESHU" makes fun of deconstructionist literary critics. "The Penis of a God" (a rare poem for Chinweizu in that its persona is a likable woman) renders a biting critique of postcolonial African men and their notions of patriarchal entitlement, voiced from the perspective of a wife who sees through the foolish self-aggrandizement of her pompous husband and upbraids him for his airs. While some readers may interpret the poem as evidence that Chinweizu was not such a virulent misogynist as he sometimes can seem, it must be remembered that Chinweizu has devoted many feisty essays and an entire book to his verbal combat against what he calls the fantastic Euro-feminist premise that women have been dominated by men over the ages and throughout the world. To read Chinweizu is to realize that he can be counted on, time and again, *not* to accept anyone else's view of current realities at face value.

BIBLIOGRAPHY
Chinweizu. *Energy Crisis and Other Poems.* New York and Lagos, Nigeria: NOK, 1978.
———. *Invocations and Admonitions: 49 Poems and a Triptych of Parables.* Lagos, Nigeria: Pero Press, 1986.
———. *The West and the Rest of Us: White Predators, Black Slavers, and the African Elite.* New York: Random House, 1975; New York and Lagos, Nigeria: NOK, 1980.
Dunton, Chris. "Chinweizu." *Dictionary of Literary Biography,* Vol. 157, Twentieth-Century Caribbean and Black African Writers, third series, edited by Bernth Lindfors. Sumter, S.C: Bruccoli, Clark Layman. Detroit: Gale, 1996, 36–48.

R. Victoria Arana

CHIPASULA, FRANK MKALAWILE (1949–)
Frank M. Chipasula is easily one of the best of the known writers in the discourse of Malawian letters. His impressive efforts place him in an admirable space in historicizing a literary tradition that also produced such engaging voices as Steve Chimombo (b. 1945), Jack Mapanje (b. 1945), and Lupenga Mphande

(b. 1947), among others. Born in Luanshya, Zambia, on October 16, 1949, Chipasula received his early education in Zambia. He later studied at the Universities of Malawi and Zambia before proceeding to the United States, where he pursued postgraduate programs at Brown and Yale Universities. In spite of his long stay in the United States, where he has taught black literature and creative writing in several universities, Chipasula's poetry demonstrates that for the diasporic African, "home" is never forgotten. Home in this sense is the writer's specific nationality in Africa. While sojourning in Europe and America, the African writer who finds himself or herself in either "forced" or "voluntary" exile carries the burden of his or her community at "home." The recent history of Malawi is a constant reminder of the dictatorial hangovers to which a number of African countries have suffered at the hands of such despots as Kamuzu Banda, Sani Abacha, Idi Amin Dada, and P. W. Botha, to mention a few. This state of affairs raises the recurrent question concerning artistic responsibility and the allied question of creative medium and its accessibility.

Chipasula has shown commitment to addressing these questions in his creative writing and in his scholarship. Among his publications are *Visions and Reflections* (1972), *O Earth, Wait for Me* (1984), *Nightwatcher, Nightsong* (1986), *Whispers in the Wind* (1991), and *Whispers in the Wings: New and Selected Poems* (2007). But where a number of African poets are simply satisfied with publishing their collection of poems, not many of them have taken on the challenge of engaging poetry as a creative form whose aesthetic and utilitarian identities need be subjected to critical inquiry. Chipasula is among the few poets who have addressed this basic question of definition—a mission so brilliantly addressed in poetic form by poets as varying as NIYI OSUNDARE and Ezenwa Ohaeto. Chipasula's efforts become particularly interesting because, like Osundare and Ohaeto, he does not embrace the Euro-modernism whose obscurantist tradition was subject to long debate by poets and scholars of decolonization in several African universities.

Chipasula's forte is evident in his lyrical presentation of what he labels "Manifesto on *Ars Poetica*." Notwithstanding his allusions to the classical and neoclassical defense of aesthetic theory and praxis that we find in Horace, Longinus, Cicero, Philip Sidney, and so on, Chipasula's "Manifesto" outlines his aesthetic and his mission as a poet in a concise, lyrical, yet engaging manner. Implicit in his poetic engagements is a sacramental imperative—a confessional attitude—that authorizes the telling of a *truth*. If there is any conflict in the poetry emanating from many parts of Africa, it is one arising from how to locate the nexus or the creative points of convergence between ethics and aesthetics. But Chipasula is not insensible of the dilemma arising from a self-indulgent poetry that idolizes itself without regard to the demands of social responsibility, just as he is not comfortable with poetic forms defined primarily by their dominant political content. For him there must be a nexus in the creative process that takes into account the need to construct a functionalist poetry not devoid of aesthetic embellishments.

In "Manifesto on *Ars Poetica*" Chipasula eloquently proclaims his poetic sensibility. His poetry "exacts" a confession, and the ethical imperative of his profession as a poet compels him to tell the whole truth: "I will not bar / the voice undressed by the bees / from entering the gourd of my bow-harp / I will not wash the blood of the image / I will let it flow from the gullet / slit by the assassin's dagger through / the run-on line until it rages in the verbs of terror" (*The Fate of Vultures* 19).

Such lines remind the reader not to lose sight of the historical and political contexts that inform Chipasula's poetry. Malawi, his native country in southern Africa, was for a long time presided over by one of the continent's most infamous despots, Kamuzu Banda. Many writers were subjected during his regime to all forms of censorship, torture, and exile, and they were sometimes killed. The Banda government banned the works of a number of influential African writers, especially those by Achebe and Soyinka. Chipasula's experience was not totally different from those of many writers across the continent. The implication is that emergent writers in Malawi were frustrated by Banda's draconian policies, and many were too intimidated to develop their talents. For Chipasula, Banda's policies were better confronted than ignored. It was against this background that Chipasula vowed in his "Manifesto on *Ars Poetica*": "I will pierce the silence around our land with sharp metaphors / And I will point the light of my poems into the dark / nooks where our people are pounded to pulp / I will not coat my words in lumps of sugar / I will serve them to our people with the bitter quinine. . . ." (*The Fate of Vultures* 19–20).

Apart from poetry Chipasula has also written fiction, short stories, and plays. His scholarship spans journal contributions to edited anthologies of African letters. He edited *When My Brothers Come Home: Poems from Central and Southern Africa* (1985), and with Stella P. Chipasula he edited *The Heinemann Book of African Women's Poetry* (1995). He has continued to write from his base in America, where he has taught African-American literature for years—at the University of Nebraska at Omaha, Howard University in Washington, D.C., and the University of Southern Illinois at Carbondale.

BIBLIOGRAPHY

Chipasula, Frank M. "Manifesto on *Ars Poetica*." In Anyidoho, *The Fate of Vultures: New Poetry of Africa,* edited by Peter Porter Kofi and Musaemura Zimunya, 19–20. London: Heinemann, 1989.
———. *Whispers in the Wings: New and Selected Poems.* Devon, England: Mallory, 2007.
Chipasula, Frank M., and Stella P., eds. *The Heinemann Book of African Women's Poetry.* London: Heinemann, 1995.

Osita Ezeliora

CHIRIKURE, CHIRIKURE (1962–   )

Chirikure was born in Gutu, a rural district of Zimbabwe, in 1962. He is a graduate of the University of Zimbabwe and an honorary fellow of Iowa University. Recognized as an important performance (POETRY BEYOND THE PAGE) poet in Zimbabwe, Chirikure worked with one of Zimbabwe's leading publishing houses as an editor/publisher for 17 years, until 2002. Currently he runs a literary agency and also works as a performance poet, cultural consultant, and translator.

Chirikure has published three volumes of poetry: *Rukuvhute* (1989), *Chamupupuri* (1994), and *Hakurarwi—We Shall Not Sleep* (1998). He has also written and translated a number of children's stories and published textbooks. Combining poetry, storytelling, proverb, and anecdote in both Shona and English, Chirikure's performances are rich and diverse. He has recorded an album of poetry and music, *Napukeni* (2002), with his colleagues, the DeteMbira Group. He has also written lyrics for a number of leading Zimbabwean musicians and occasionally performs with some of these musicians.

Through his collaborations with bands and musicians, Chirikure maintains a connection with the ancient partnership between music and poetry. Whether solo or in collaboration with his DeteMbira music ensemble or other Zimbabwean musicians, Chirikure entertains as well as informs. In spite of the violence perpetrated against poets who resist the current Zimbabwean president Robert Mugabe and his government, Chirikure maintains a commitment to performance, believing that staying silent is as impossible as resistance: "I have to speak out; it is my duty to my people." Strongly invested in Shona oral culture, Chirikure's poems attack political corruption, social malfeasance, sycophancy, poverty, pessimism, and ideological confusion. Despite their provocative portrayals of postcolonial disillusion and their bitingly satirical tone, all of Chirikure's volumes of poetry have received first prizes in the annual Zimbabwe writer-of-the-year awards. His first volume, *Rukuvhute,* also received an honorable mention in the Noma Awards for Publishing in Africa in 1990. His third volume, *Hakurarwi—We Shall not Sleep,* was selected as one of the "75 Best Zimbabwean Books of the 20th Century" in a competition run by the Zimbabwe International Book Fair (2004); it was then also awarded the distinction of being one of the best five Shona publications of the 20th century.

BIBLIOGRAPHY

Chirikure, Chirikure. *Rukuvhute.* (Poetry in Shona). Harare, Zimbabwe: College Press, 1989.
———. *Chamupupuri* (Poetry in Shona). Harare, Zimbabwe: College Press, 1994.
———. *Hakurarwi—We Shall not Sleep.* (Poetry in Shona, with English translations) Harare, Zimbabwe: Baobab Books, 1998.
———. *Mavende aKiti* (Children's Stories). Harare, Zimbabwe: College Press, 1989.
———. *Zviri Muchinokoro.* (Poetry anthology) Harare, Zimbabwe: ZPH Publishers, 2005.

Discography/Audio Recordings
Napukeni. (Album of mbira music and poetry) Tuku Music/ZMC, Harare, Zimbabwe, 2002.

Ray of Hope, (Compilation album of AIDS awareness music) Harare, Zimbabwe: Rooftop Promotions, nd.

Jayne Fenton Keane

CHRISTENSEN, INGER (1935–) Inger

Christensen is one of the most celebrated contemporary Danish poets. Born 1935 in Vejle, Christensen trained to be an elementary school teacher and taught at the College for Arts in Holbæk (1963–64) before becoming a freelance writer. She married the critic and poet Poul Borum in 1959, and they had a son, Peter, in 1973. In 1976 the couple divorced. Christensen has written poetry, novels, short stories, plays, children's books, and essays and has translated among others PAUL CELAN, Max Frisch, and Virginia Woolf, but she is most famous for her poetry. Her work has been translated into numerous languages, and she has received several international literary awards, including the Nordic Prize of the Swedish Academy (1994), Der Österreichischen Staatspreis für Europäische Literatur (1994), Preis der Stadt Münster für Europäische Poesie (1995), Grand Prix de Biénnales Internationales de Poésie (1995), and Horst Bienek Preis der Bayerischen Akademi (1998). In 1978 she was appointed to the Danish Academy and in 1996 to the Académie Européenne de Poésie. She lives in Copenhagen.

She published her first poetry collection, *Lys* (Light), in 1962, followed in 1963 by the collection *Græs* (Grass). Two novels, *Evighedsmaskinen* (The Eternity Machine) (1964) and *Azorno* (1967) followed before Christensen's third collection of poetry, *Det* (It), came out in 1969. *Det* is a groundbreaking poetic work in modern Danish poetry, thematizing a broad range of modernistic themes: creation, nature, language, life, death, alienation, and modern society in a philosophically organized poetic structure with three main parts termed Prologos, Logos, and Epilogos, and subheadings with titles inspired by the linguist Viggo Brøndal such as Symmetries, Transitivities, Continuities, and so on.

Christensen challenges and channels her poetic voice by using complex compositional structures and systems. Like *Det, Alfabet* (Alphabet), Christensen's next major collection of poetry from 1981, is highly structured, based on the alphabet and the Fibonacci sequence 1-2-3-5-8-13-21-44-etc. (each number being

the sum of the previous two numbers). Each number designates the number of poem lines and corresponds to a letter of the alphabet; for example, the third poem in the work consists of three lines with words beginning with the letter c:

> cicadas exist; chicory, chromium
> citrus trees; cicadas exist;
> cicadas, cedars, cypresses, the cerebellum

The system also governs individual stanza lengths. *Alfabet* ends with the letter *n*, as the number of lines required by the system makes it impossible to continue within the structure. Mirroring the occurrence of Fibonacci structures in nature, the lines of *Alfabet* grow out of the system of the Fibonacci sequence. A recurring word in *Alfabet* is the verb *exist(s)*, and like *Det, Alfabet* thematizes a broad range of phenomena in existence: the natural life, human life, modern life, and the technology of destruction that threatens all life. *Alfabet* is available in English in Susanna Nied's translation, which was awarded the 1982 American-Scandinavian Foundation PEN Translation Prize.

With her next major poetic work, the collection *Sommerfugledalen—et requiem* (BUTTERFLY VALLEY: A REQUIEM) from 1991, Inger Christensen turns to a classical poetic structure, the sonnet. *Butterfly Valley* is a sonnet sequence, a crown of 15 sonnets, in which the last line of each sonnet is repeated as the first line in the following sonnet. The final (15th) sonnet of the sequence, the magisterial sonnet, consists of the first lines of the preceding 14 sonnets. In *Butterfly Valley* Christensen infuses a traditional form with new poetic life. Questions about life and death, memory, and word and phenomenon make *Butterfly Valley* a distinctly modern work. *Butterfly Valley* is an event in modern European literature and already a classic. Nied's excellent translation is available in a bilingual edition (Dedalus Press, 2001) as well as in an edition also containing the works "Watersteps," "Poem on Death," and "Meeting" (New Directions Books, 2004).

Jan Nielsen

"CHRISTMAS IN BIAFRA (1969)" CHI-NUA ACHEBE (1971) This is the title piece for ACHEBE's collection *Christmas in Biafra and Other Poems,*

a joint winner of the first Commonwealth Poetry Prize (1972). The poem graphically depicts the suffering endured by civilians during the bloody Nigerian civil war (1967–70) (also known as the Biafran War), which began when the eastern, predominately Igbo section of Nigeria attempted to secede and form an independent state. The ensuing conflict proved disastrous for the nation and led to great loss of life from Nigerian military attacks on Biafran civilian populations, disease, and famine.

The poem's first stanza depicts a figure stumbling into a village on or near Christmas Day. The stanza portrays a nightmarish scene of warfare (bombs and gunfire are implied) that ironically is taking place during the festive Christmas season, when Christians are supposed to celebrate the birth of the Prince of Peace. The second stanza describes the meticulous detail with which a group of Catholic nuns has set up a traditional manger scene outside a hospital. Here the ironic contrast between the peaceful manger scene and the previous stanza's description of the stumbling figure wandering into the village is further heightened. The third stanza depicts the figure, now identified as a destitute mother. She is holding a starving child—quite the opposite of the plump Christ child depicted in the second stanza—and standing before the Christmas scene. She has nothing to offer—not even the practically worthless aluminum coins that other worshipers have deposited at the outdoor crèche. The Biafran child lies motionless on his mother's shoulder, staring glassy-eyed into the distance. The final stanza—in which the woman tries in vain to interest her child in his surroundings—strikes a symbolic chord. The child only glances at the Nativity scene for a moment before reverting to his former position and gazing into the distance. The mother, shrugging, venerates the religious statuary, then walks away with her stricken child.

"Christmas in Biafra (1969)" finds Achebe utilizing his poetic gifts to craft a complex signifying system from the few, well-chosen images he composes into the poem's brief series of visionary scenes. For instance, the European-made Nativity scene, which features the serene Holy Mother and a well-fed Christ child, stands in sharp contrast to the real and despondent African mother and her starving infant. Additionally, the final two stanzas—portraying the mother's failed attempt to interest her son in the Christmas scene and her subsequent departure—could well represent the evident failure of European ideologies to provide an adequate solution to Africa's problems.

Joseph E. Becker

ÇIRAK, ZEHRA (1960–   )

The Turkish-German poet Çirak was born in Turkey and moved with her family to West Germany in 1963, when she was three years old. Since 1982 she has lived in Berlin, together with her partner, the sculptor and installation artist Jürgen Walter, with whom she continues to give internationally renowned audiovisual performances.

Çirak, who writes exclusively in German, published her first poetry collection, *Flugfänger* (Flight Catcher), in 1987. Four years later the volume *Vogel auf dem Rücken eines Elefanten* (Bird on an Elephant's Back) followed. In 1994 Çirak's third book of poetry, *Fremde Flügel auf eigener Schulter* (Alien Wings on Your Own Shoulder), was published; it includes "WOMEN—PORTRAIT I." In the same year she received the Friedrich Hölderlin Award for young poets. In 2000 her poetry volume *Leibesübungen* (Body Exercises) was published. She received the Chamisso Award in 2001.

Offering playful fusions of linguistic explorations and social observations, Çirak's poems are highly accessible. Thematic threads of her popular work include the body, memory, multiethnicity, and feminism. Echoing the ludic reflective spontaneity of ELSE LASKER-SCHÜLER, Çirak combines acute perceptiveness with a textual desire for synesthesia. The visual, the tactile, and the corporeality of the spoken word complement each other and co-create fruitful tensions. In a 1987 interview with scholar-translator Marilya Veteto-Conrad, Çirak defined her work as the invention of bicultural *"Sprachbilder"* (speech pictures/images) and emphasized the authorial productiveness of embodying German as well as Turkish cultures, or what she describes with a neologism that is reminiscent of the poet Rose Ausländer, *"[m]eine Zweiatmigkeit"* (my dual way of breathing).

BIBLIOGRAPHY

Oehlkers, Elizabeth Ann. "Where Germany begins: Translations from the German of the poetry and prose of Zehra

Çirak, Zafer Senocak, and Yoko Tawada." MFA thesis, University of Arkansas, 1996.

Veteto-Conrad, Marilya. "'Innere Unruthe?' Zehra Çirak and Minority Literature Today." Available online at the Rocky Mountain Modern Foreign Language Association Web site. URL: http://rmmla.wsu.edu/ereview/53.2/articles/veteto.asp. Accessed on April 22, 2007.

Olaf Berwald

"CITY JOHANNESBURG" MONGANE WALLY SEROTE (1972)

In this justly famous poem, which runs to nearly 40 lines, MONGANE SEROTE ironically pays tribute to the city of Johannesburg, where black South Africans were allowed to work but not live during the apartheid era. Like much of the poet's work, "City Johannesburg" fits into the free-verse tradition of American poets Walt Whitman (1819–92) and Langston Hughes (1902–67), but it also employs elements of the African panegyric form. Thus the speaker salutes— at the very start of this poem—the city that rules over him. But instead of raising his hand in a show of respect, he lowers it to search through his pockets for "my pass, my life" (l. 4), the reference book that is a key to his survival as a black South African. There is something desperate in this motion, as the speaker's hand moves "like a starved snake" (l. 6), suggesting that he has been dehumanized by this daily routine. After saluting Johannesburg a second time, the speaker goes on to describe the world in which he lives outside of the city. He has mixed feelings about his home in the township, to which he refers as both "my love" (l. 14) and "my death" (l. 16). At the same time, however, he cannot help appreciating the personal connection he has to this place, which distinguishes it from the cold and distant city. The speaker imagines Johannesburg as a giant machine that sucks people in and spits them out as part of the "thick iron breath" (l. 20) of its commuter traffic. According to him there is nothing natural about this lifeless place where "neon flowers" (l. 26) glow on "cement trees" (l. 27). But even so, the speaker cannot deny the city's powerful hold on his life, as it has enforced upon him a sense of "feebleness" (l. 31) that is utterly debilitating. The "frozen expressions" (l. 38) worn by other township dwellers make it clear to him that many people have been worn down by the city in the same way. From this the speaker concludes that Johannesburg itself is to blame for the degradation of the township. In the end, therefore, Serote uses this poem to highlight the intimate connection between working conditions in the city and living conditions in the township. Originally published in *Yakhal'inkomo* (1972), "City Johannesburg" appeared in Serote's *Selected Poems* (1982) as well. The poem has also been widely anthologized, most recently in *The New Century of South African Poetry* (2002), edited by Michael Chapman.

BIBLIOGRAPHY

Chapman, Michael, ed. *The New Century of South African Poetry.* Johannesburg: Ad Donker, 2002.
Serote, Mongane Wally. *Yakhal'inkomo.* Johannesburg: Renoster Books, 1972.
———. *Selected Poems.* Edited by M. V. Mzamane. Johannesburg: Ad Donker, 1982.

Alexander B. McKee

"CITY OF PARADISE" VICENTE ALEIXANDRE (1944)

"Ciudad del paraíso" ("City of Paradise"), from the collection *Sombra del paraíso* (1944), typifies the style that established VICENTE ALEIXANDRE as the seminal poetic voice in Spain after the Spanish civil war (1936–39). An homage to Málaga, where the poet spent his childhood, "Ciudad del paraíso" is a nostalgic meditation on the fragile beauty of an irretrievable past, a theme with great meaning for Spaniards living under the Franco dictatorship in the wake of the country's bloody civil war. Written in free verse, the beginning of the poem is replete with images of Málaga as a utopia lying precariously on the edge of destruction. The city is *"colgada del imponente monte, apenas detenida / en tu vertical caída a las onda azules"* (hanging from the towering mountain's side and scarcely in your headlong plunge from the sea detained). Streets, gardens, walls, and beaches are light and diaphanous, reflecting the blissful innocence of *"mis días alegres"* (my happy days). Aleixandre's use of synesthesia in *"palmas de luz"* (palms of light), *"rutilantes paredes"* (sparkling walls), and *"el brillo de la brisa"* (the brilliance of the breeze) reinforces the idealization of the subject as purity embodied. The apotheosis of Málaga as an *"angélica ciudad"* (angelic city) is made complete through the

neobaroque conceits of angel-like *"palmas . . . aladas"* (winged palm trees) and clouds as *"labios celestiales"* (celestial lips) above the archetypal virgin mother: *"ciudad madre y blanquísima"* (mother city of a purest white). Within this textual cosmology, the speaker, ambiguously the child of both human and divine mothers, recalls being *"conducido por una mano maternal"* (guided by a maternal hand) through a sensual world of *"reja florida"* (flowered window) and *"guitarra triste"* (sad guitar). However, as if re-creating the act of remembering itself, and returning to the poem's central theme, the guitar's song is *"suspendida en el tiempo"* (suspended in time). The antithesis of *"la luna eterna"* (the eternal moon), a single moment in time is transitory (*"instantánea transcurre"*). The next stanza continues this ontological dialectic. The polyvalent phrases *"soplo divino"* (divine breath) and *"soplo de eternidad"* (breath of eternity) suggest both genesis and apocalypse. The same stanza is dominated by the antithetical assonant rhyme of *"destruirte"* (destroy you)/ *"emergiste"* (you emerged) and the repetition of *"vivieron, no vivieron"* (lived, did not live). In the final two stanzas the poem reveals its dialectical synthesis. Through memory, the Málaga of the speaker's youth is transformed into a *"ciudad no en la tierra"* (city not upon this earth), spared destruction as if it were a *"pájaro suspenso / que nunca arriba"* (bird in flight that never comes to land). Antithetical images are made harmonious: *"Pie desnudo en el día./ Pie desnudo en la noche. Luna grande. Sol puro"* (Barefoot in the daytime. Barefoot in the night. Full moon. Pure sun). No longer a part of the corruptible world, Málaga rises with outspread wings to become one with the heavens: *"el cielo eras tú, ciudad que en él morabas"* (you were the sky, the city where you dwelled). A metaphor for the fragile Spanish Republic destroyed by fascism, Aleixandre's transcendent Málaga endures inviolable in the memories of its children.

Eric Reinholtz

"CLAIMING AN IDENTITY THEY TAUGHT ME TO DESPISE" MICHELLE CLIFF (1980) MICHELLE CLIFF's first book, *Claiming an Identity They Taught Me to Despise,* is a collection of what can best be described as "proems" in both the intuitive and the official meanings of the word. The pieces combine prose and poetry and also serve as a preface to Cliff's later longer works. The title poem signifies on Creole Caribbean women with whom Cliff identifies in claiming her black and Jamaican heritage, and incorporates many of the concerns of Cliff's collection and later works: mixed racial identity, stifling gender roles, early immigration, and female sexuality. It has eight verses, and six of the eight begin with quotations from other works, three of which are from *Wide Sargasso Sea* and two from *Jane Eyre.* Cliff is clearly calling on Charlotte Brontë's Bertha Mason and Jean Rhys's Antoinette Cosway as inspirations. In Section I, she blends both characters through the idea of confinement, interweaving phrases from both novels as she imagines Bertha's entrapment and escape. Despite acknowledging *Wide Sargasso Sea* as a separate text, Cliff soon begins to treat Bertha and Antoinette as one continuous character, envisioning sisterhood with the resulting fusion. In Section II Cliff imagines a similar kinship with another Creole woman—Annie Palmer, the legendary "White Witch" of Rosehall. Cliff provides a short "history" of Annie Palmer, but only through the words of others. She peppers her description with attributives, "they told me" or "they indicated," which serve, like the quotation marks around "White Witch," to question the history she has been handed of this woman who could run a plantation on her own in the 19th century, when white women rarely even visited Caribbean plantations. Through Cliff's continuous invocations of Annie Palmer and Bertha Rochester in this poem, these fictional characters become for Cliff's poetic persona both historical and familial. The speaker begins the poem with her mother, claims sisterhood with Annie Palmer and Bertha Rochester, and ends with her father. Her sister also makes an appearance at the table of a "white-haired" woman who belongs to a branch of the family. Family is not only emphasized but also extended. Cliff's poetic persona wishes to claim the part of her family—the black part of herself—that has been denigrated. But she is also claiming her white father and the white-haired woman. Just as she weaves the words of *Wide Sargasso Sea* with the words from *Jane Eyre* to create a picture of a single character, so Cliff is attempting to weave together the different sides of her identity

to create a whole that encompasses a larger Caribbean authenticity.

Kelly Josephs

CLARK-BEKEDEREMO, JOHN PEPPER

(1935–   ) John Pepper Clark-Bekederemo (long known as John Pepper Clark) was born on April 6, 1935, in Delta State, Nigeria. One of the makers of modern African writing, he is a poet, dramatist, and literary scholar, although he is best known as a poet. He belongs to the generation of university-educated poets who invented modern African poetry of English expression in the second half of the 20th century—and whose works dominate the canon of modern African poetry. His contemporaries include WOLE SOYINKA, CHRISTOPHER OKIGBO, KOFI AWOONOR, and DENNIS BRUTUS. He attended Government College, Ughelli, before attending the University College, Ibadan, where he was a leading figure in the literary awakening that the undergraduates of the university stirred in the late 1950s. He founded and edited *The Horn,* the student magazine that first published the poems of many of his contemporaries. He also coedited *The Black Orpheus,* another magazine started by Janheinz Jahn and Ulli Beier, in addition to identifying with the Mbari Writers and Artists Club, an Ibadan-based society that brought together writers, artists, and literary enthusiasts from Nigeria and other countries. Mbari Press was to release later the early works of many African poets, including Clark-Bekederemo's *Poems* (1962). His early poems were included in *Nigerian Student Verse* (1959), an anthology of poems from *The Horn* that Martin Banham, who had inspired the founding of the magazine in 1957, edited.

On graduation in 1960 Clark-Bekederemo worked as an information officer in the civil service of the old Western Region of Nigeria and later as features editor for the *Daily Express.* His career at the university started with his appointment as a research fellow at the Institute of African Studies of the University of Ibadan. He spent the rest of his working life in the Department of English, University of Lagos, from where he retired as a professor of English in 1980. He established the Pec Repertory Theatre in 1982 and has lived in Lagos since then.

Clark-Bekederemo is a major figure within the African literary scene and enjoys considerable critical attention as one of the most studied African poets. Apart from representing a major phase in the development of African poetry, his work has also inspired younger poets. It is ironic that the most representative of his poems are among his earliest works. Like those of many of his contemporaries, especially Christopher Okigbo, some of his earliest poems were modeled on the works of the poets that they studied as undergraduates—T. S. Eliot, W. E. B. Yeats, and G. M. Hopkins. Much of his earliest poetry is, therefore, derivative. "Ibadan Dawn" best exemplifies his enthusiastic imitation of Hopkins. His best poems do not show traces of imitation of European poets but rather demonstrate an awareness of nature and physical landscape.

Some of Clark's early poems—including his frequently anthologized "NIGHT RAIN"—are set in his native Delta country, and they reveal his interest in exploring the close relationship between nature and humankind. This aspect partly explains why his poetry relies mainly on visual imagery and is remarkable for its evocative charm. He also draws attention to his alienation as an educated African from traditional society, in addition to reacting to the crisis created by the colonial engagement. The preoccupation of his poetry later shifted, from an earlier obsession with personal reflection inspired by a keen observation of the immediate physical world, to an engagement with shared experiences and incidents.

His first volume of verse, *Poems,* brings his earliest works together. Some of these are also included in *A Reed in the Tide,* a collection remarkable for utilizing imagery drawn from the poet's physical and cultural environment in the Delta country. He shares this consciousness of the cultural and physical environment of his birthplace with the older Gabriel Okara and TANURE OJAIDE, who are also from the Niger Delta. But while Okara is Ijaw and Ojaide is Urhobo, Clark-Bekederemo has both Ijaw and Urhobo roots. His poems on the Nigerian civil war, published as *Casualties,* attracted negative critical reception from critics and younger poets because of the perceived failure of its craft and its supposed lack of social vision. In *State of the Union* the poet engages the pervasive decadence in his nation, and this feature hints at a near pessimistic vision of Nigerian society. His concern widens in *Mandela and Other Poems* as he celebrates heroism and indicts man's capacity for inhumanity. In his recent collections—*A Lot from Paradise* and *Of Sleep and Old Age*—he has increasingly retreated into introspection and self-writing. In recognition of the privileged space that his work occupies in the canon of contemporary African writing, Clark-Bekederemo was honored in 1991 with the Nigerian National Merit Award.

BIBLIOGRAPHY
Banham, Martin. *Nigerian Student Verse*. Ibadan, Nigeria: Ibadan University Press, 1959.
Clark, J. P. *A Decade of Tongues: Selected Poems 1958–1968*. London: Longman, 1981.
———. *A Lot from Paradise*. Lagos, Nigeria: Malthouse, 1997.
———. *A Reed in the Tide*. London: Longman, 1965.
———. *Casualties, Poems: 1966–1968*. London: Longman, 1970.
———. *Poems*. Ibadan, Nigeria: Mbari, 1962.
Wren, Robert. *J. P. Clark*. Lagos, Nigeria: University of Lagos Press, 1984.
———. *Those Magical Years: The Making of Nigerian Literature at Ibadan: 1948–1966*. Boston: Three Continents Press, 1991.
Okunoye, Oyeniyi. "Captives of Empire: Ibadan Poets and Poetry." *Journal of Commonwealth Literature* 34, no. 2 (1999): 105–116.

Oyeniyi Okunoye

CLAUDEL, PAUL (1868–1955)

Paul Claudel was a French poet, dramatist, and diplomat and the brother of the sculptor Camille Claudel. He was born in Villeneuve-sur-Fère, a town in northern France. His father was a banker, and his mother was from a devout family of farmers and Catholic clergy. He grew up in Champagne and first attended *lycée* (school) at Bar-le-Duc and later at the Lycée Louis-le-Grand when his family moved to Paris. He was not religious in his youth, but he experienced a sudden conversion at a vespers service on Christmas Day, 1886, while listening to the church choir. He became a devout Catholic and remained so for the rest of his life. His religious fervor caused him to consider seriously entering a Benedictine monastery (he was an oblate and remained in an abbey for a time). But his failed four-year affair with Rosalie Vetch—a married Polish woman who became pregnant with his child and who is said to have inspired both his *FIVE GREAT ODES* and *THE SATIN SLIPPER*—disturbed him deeply. He nearly abandoned his faith and was suicidal for a period. In 1906 he married Reine Sainte-Marie Perrin, with whom he had five children. As a French career diplomat he served at various consular posts around the world, including New York, Shanghai, Tokyo, and Washington, D.C.

Claudel's first poetic endeavors were heavily influenced by the French symbolists, but he eventually developed a distinctive versification that was markedly influenced by the Latin Vulgate Bible's psalm meter. His famous *Five Great Odes (Cinq Grandes Odes),* which focuses on the spiritual gifts that allow the poet to convey the mystery of the universe in words, clearly displays the erotic fervency of Claudel's faith and its influence on his poetics. These poems also display the intense lyricism and emotional power that Claudel instilled in his most famous works.

In 1901 he produced his first drama, *Tête d'Or* (Golden Head), in verse, and he continued developing his craft in the genre, culminating in what many critics consider his finest verse drama, *L'Annonce faite à Marie* (The Tidings Brought to Mary, 1910). The play focuses on a medieval peasant girl, Violaine, who contracts leprosy and becomes a saint through her suffering. The play clearly indicates that Violaine's situation is analogous to the sufferings of Mary, the mother of Jesus, who must ultimately witness the self-sacrifice of her only child for the salvation of the world. The drama's lyricism and juxtapositions of biblical narrative with the medieval tale convey great strength as well as the Catholic conviction that typifies Claudel's worldview.

As he aged Claudel's religiously flavored writings predominated. The stirring works he produced impressed critics and general readers alike, and he was eventually awarded numerous prestigious national titles. In addition to his diplomatic work, which he continued to do around the world, he was elected to membership in the French Academy in 1947 and in 1950 was honored by Pope Pius XII in a public ceremony. These honors capped a life spent in the service of his country and the Roman Catholic Church. Although he might be considered by some readers to have been a misogynist, an Islamophobe, and an anti-Semite, he is generally credited in France with having produced some of the most important spiritual writings of the 20th century to have been published in the French language. In 1955, at the age of 86, he died in Paris.

BIBLIOGRAPHY

Chiari, Joseph. *The Poetic Drama of Paul Claudel.* London: Harvill, 1954.

Knapp, Bettina. *Paul Claudel.* New York: Ungar, 1982.

Paliyenko, Adrianna M. *Mis-reading the Creative Impulse: The Poetic Subject in Rimbaud and Claudel, Restaged.* Carbondale: Southern Illinois University Press, 1997.

Joseph E. Becker

CLIFF, MICHELLE (1946–) Born in Kingston, Jamaica, Michelle Cliff is equally accomplished as a poet and a prose writer. She often mixes the two in her writings, noting in an interview with Judith Raiskin that writers outside the dominant culture "can be much more experimental, you can mix styles up, you don't have to be linear, you don't have to be dichotomous, and believe it's either poetry or prose or whatever." Cliff immigrated to New York during her early teens, and her writings reflect the loss and discomfort she felt in her new home. The aspect of being an outsider—in respect to race, gender, nationality, and sexuality—continuously marks her work. She attended public schools in New York City and graduated from Wagner College (N.Y.) in 1969 with a B.A. in European history. She worked in publishing at W. W. Norton but left in 1971 to attend the Warburg Institute in London. After earning a M.Phil. in 1974 with a concentration in Italian Renaissance studies, she returned full-time to Norton, where she edited *The Winner Names the Age: A Collection of Writing by Lillian Smith* in 1978. Cliff left Norton in 1979 to devote more time to her own writing. Her first published piece, "Notes on Speechlessness" (1978), appeared in *Sinister Wisdom,* a feminist journal she eventually coedited with Adrienne Rich (1981–83). Cliff's first book, a prose poetry collection, soon followed (in 1980), boldly announcing in its title what would become the major theme of her works— CLAIMING AN IDENTITY THEY TAUGHT ME TO DESPISE. The identity that Cliff begins to claim here is primarily black and Jamaican, but inextricably interlaced with these are her concerns with gender and sexuality. Portions of *Claiming an Identity* are reprinted in *The Land of Look Behind,* a mix of essays and poetry published in 1985, which Cliff describes in the preface as her effort to "depict personal fragmentation and describe political reality, according to the peculiar lens of the colonized." Cliff published her first novel, *Abeng,* in 1984. Like her earlier work, the novel is quasi-autobiographical, and readers of *Claiming an Identity* will recognize some of the experiences of Clare Savage, the young protagonist. Cliff followed with a second novel, *No Telephone to Heaven,* in 1987, which focuses on Clare's return to Jamaica in her thirties. Although Clare travels to America and Europe, the first two novels are primarily set in Jamaica, which Cliff identifies as her main inspiration. But her third novel, *Free Enterprise* (1993), is set in 19th-century America. As with the first two novels and her poetry, in *Free Enterprise* Cliff interweaves history with fiction to present a multidimensional narrative. Cliff has also published two collections of short stories: *Bodies of Water* (1990) and *The Store of a Million Items* (1998).

BIBLIOGRAPHY

Raiskin, Judith "The Art of History: An Interview with Michelle Cliff." *Kenyon Review* 15 (1993): 57–71.

Kelly Josephs

"COLLISION" MIROSLAV HOLUB (1982) "Collision" was first published in a collection of poems— *Interferon, or on Theater* (1982, United States; 1986 Czechoslovakia)—that, as the title suggests, takes immunology and theater as the central realms from which the poet draws his metaphors. The action in this poem takes place in the moments before death occurs. The poem is a striking example of the way Holub interweaves the two domains (immunology and theater) through the whole collection and suggests how their interconnectedness can enrich human understanding of life. As David Young puts it, "[i]nterference on the cellular level corresponds to the presence of theater in our lives; both are attempts to arrest and mesmerize destructive forces, disease and history."

Formally and stylistically, "Collision" features devices for which Holub was well known, such as litany, irony, the documentary narrative style, free-versification, technical and scientific expressions, and occasional unexpected line breaks that interrupt the otherwise straightforward narrative. Like several other poems in the collection, it employs a personal tone, something virtually nonexistent in Holub's earlier poetry.

The poem reports the last thoughts of a dying victim of a car accident who lies bleeding on the ground. By means of the persona of the speaker, the poem also comments on the world beyond the collision. By using the two closely related perspectives, the poet further expands the already large themes presented in the poem, such as death, the meaning of life, human existence, and the representation of life (and death) in art. The first line announces grimly and matter-of-factly, "I could have been dead by now." As it turns out, while the first-person-singular vocalization is of the person who has been hit, it is not this speaker who becomes an omniscient observer of the scene. While the "I" is immediately displaced in the second line by the narrative voice saying, "he said to himself," the personal perspective stays with the reader as a reminder of the actual person/character who is allowed to comment on his own tragedy. The "I" comes back in the last stanza to speak one more time before the narrator cuts him off with a straightforward and unemotional statement, "[a]nd then he died."

The realistic-fantastic descriptions of the collision create a sense of unreality that can be experienced only by a person as close to death as the protagonist: "what was left / of the car was a funny pretzel / bitten by the dentures of a mad angel." But the most memorable moments in the poem are the skillful metaphors of its speaker while observing the scene, because though he recognizes the inescapable fact of death and suffering, he also recognizes life's will to endure. These metaphors range from "the giant molecular cloud complexes" that deliver "embryonic stars" after the Big Bang, to "dried starfish . . . grasping the bottoms / of vanishing seas." Therefore, despite the protagonist's inevitable death and the severe reminder about the profound insignificance of a human life, the reader is left with a sense that human beings are endowed with life for a reason, even if the reason is just to witness such stark beauty.

Daniela Kukrechtová

COLONIALISM, POETRY AND   The term *colonialism* has been variously defined, but most definitions agree that the word refers to processes for the extension and safeguarding of control by one nation or empire over the land, economic resources, and culture of another (and often very different) group of people. The associated imposition of sovereignty includes forcible dominance of labor, markets, educational systems, and sometimes elaborate reward structures for complicitous members of the occupied society. To qualify as bona fide colonialism, the period of political rule by the colonizing power cannot be of short duration. It takes time for the sorts of changes that a colonizing power effects to be institutionalized in the overpowered region. Some of these changes involve transformations in the attitudes of people in the occupied territories toward the culture of the colonizer—e.g., the colonized society's capitulation concerning language use and its adoption of the colonizers' language for the schooling of children and the daily business of acquiring goods, services, and social status; deference, however begrudging, toward the government and officers assigned to rule over the colony; and accommodation to economic realities resulting from technologies imported by the colonizing power into the colonized landscape (roads and railroads, motor vehicles and air transport, communication systems, weaponry, electronic technology, and so forth). With educational programs that emphasize the superiority of the colonizing power's culture over that of the colonized, changes in domestic arrangements, health care, indigenous problem solving institutions, fashion, and aesthetic norms often take place as well. So widespread and deep can the influence of the colonizing power become that traditional ways of living are called into question, compromised, or simply abandoned. The result of colonialism on the personal level can be devastating to individuals who value their ancestral religions and cosmologies, traditional systems of exchange, time-honored customs and mores, and general cultural heritage.

Historians have studied with zeal the growth and collapse of many major colonial regimes: the empire of Alexander of Macedonia; the Roman Imperium; the Persian Empire; the kingdoms of Mali and Benin; the Holy Roman Empire; the Ottoman Empire; the Moguls' conquest and dominion over the Indian subcontinent; the Islamic Ummah's conquest of the Arabian Peninsula, the Near East, North Africa, the Mediterranean Sea, and Spain; the conquest and dominion of Japan over China and Manchuria at the turn of the century; the Iberian dominion over South and Central America; and the British Empire.

By the beginning of the 20th century, European colonial domination of the world's landmasses and seaways had reached historical record. But the vast extent of European dominions around the globe was not a sudden achievement. European regimes had begun the process of competing for the world's economic resources as early as the Middle Ages—with the Crusades' militant excursions into geographic areas to the east and south of the Mediterranean Sea. During the so-called European Renaissance (1492–1700), England, Spain, and Portugal entered into competition for domination of the Western Hemisphere and the African coastlines, establishing and defending their new trade routes. By the 16th century Holland had begun its colonization of Indonesia. During the 17th century Britain and France were energetically vying for North America, the Caribbean, the Middle East, and parts of Africa. The British actively pursued military and hegemonic dominion over India from the 17th century onward—a vastly profitable enterprise for the English that did not end until the middle of the 20th century. By the 18th century the British had successfully colonized New England, Maryland, Virginia, and Georgia and set down permanent roots in Australia and New Zealand. By the 19th century Britain was interested in China and other areas of the Far East and had deployed diplomatic delegations, spies, financial operatives, and naval forces to that region of the world. Also in the 19th century European countries began a vigorous race to explore, conquer, and appropriate parts of Africa. By the turn of the 20th century, European kingdoms and principalities had gained control of nearly the whole African continent—contended

areas of which were claimed and fought over by Belgium, Portugal, Britain, France, Spain, Germany, the Netherlands, and Italy.

The history of the world's colonial adventures bears in crucial ways on the development of 20th-century poetry. First, the upheavals caused by the colonial wars themselves made lasting impressions on poets in every part of the world. There is hardly a poet in this volume who was not affected either directly or indirectly by cataclysmic local events having their sources in the jostling for supremacy of colonial powers. The two world wars as well as the interwar and postwar eras of dislocations, burgeoning totalitarian regimes, and nationalist insurrections form the background for virtually all of the personal histories recorded in the entries on individual poets. Because colonialism forced the movement of individuals from imperial centers to imperial margins and vice versa and required the mastery of multiple languages and cultural practices, writers everywhere experienced opportunities to transcend local poetic traditions and experiment with and absorb influences from many other lands and cultures. The richness of poetry produced by writers from Asia, Europe, Central America, the world's great islands, and South America is especially due to the cross-pollination of poetic practices resulting from the transoceanic travels of so many, who were thereby inspired to forge new expressive languages and poetic idiom with which to communicate their feelings and thoughts about contemporary life.

Nevertheless, 20th-century poets do not record a merely secular history of colonialism and its aftermath. Their works describe or contend with the impact of colonialism and its global repercussions on the human spirit. In this respect whole movements of poetry have arisen since 1900 whose purposes have been to restore to humanity something of its latent dignity and spiritual health. Among those movements one may count the various MODERNISMS, the NEGRITUDE MOVEMENT, FRENCH RAP, ARAB RAP AND HIP-HOP CULTURE, not to mention nearly all of the poetry emerging from Africa, the Caribbean, and the Middle East.

A reliable scholarly resource for ongoing contemporary scholarship on this subject is the *Journal of Colonialism and Colonial History,* published by Johns Hopkins University Press.

BIBLIOGRAPHY

Boahen, A. Adu. *African Perspectives on Colonialism*. Baltimore: Johns Hopkins University Press, 1987.

Canny, Nicholas, and Anthony Pagden, eds. *Colonial Identity in the Atlantic World, 1500–1800*. Princeton, N.J.: Princeton University Press, 1987.

Curtin, Philip D. *The World and the West: The European Challenge and the Overseas Response in the Age of Empire*. Cambridge: Cambridge University Press, 2000.

Eagleton, Terry, Fredric Jameson, and Edward W. Said. *Nationalism, Colonialism, and Literature*. Minneapolis: University of Minnesota Press, 1990.

Fanon, Frantz. *A Dying Colonialism*. Translated by Haakon Chevalier, introduction by Adolfo Gilly. New York: Grove Press, 1967, 1965.

Hogan, Patrick Colm. *Colonialism and Cultural Identity: Crises of Tradition in the Anglophone Literatures of India, Africa, and the Caribbean*. Albany: State University of New York Press, 2000.

Horvath, Robert J. "A Definition of Colonialism." *Current Anthropology* 13, no. 1 (Feb. 1972): 45–57.

Loomba, Ania. *Colonialism-postcolonialism*. London and New York: Routledge, 1998.

Makdisi, Saree. *Romantic Imperialism: Universal Empire and the Culture of Modernity*. Cambridge: Cambridge University Press, 1998.

Nasta, Susheila, ed. *Motherlands: Black Women's Writing from Africa, the Caribbean, and South Asia*. New Brunswick, N.J.: Rutgers University Press, 1992.

Ngugi wa Thiong'o. *Decolonising the Mind: The Politics of Language in African Literature*. London and Portsmouth, N.H.: J. Currey; Heinemann, 1986.

Pagden, Anthony. *Lords of All the World: Ideologies of Empire in Spain, Britain and France c. 1500–c. 1800*. New Haven, Conn.: Yale University Press, 1995.

Said, Edward W. *Orientalism*. New York: Pantheon, 1978.

Sartre, Jean-Paul. *Colonialism and Neocolonialism*. (Originally in French. Paris: Gallimard, 1964.) Translated by Azzedine Haddour, Steve Brewer, and Terry McWilliams. London: Routledge, 2001.

R. Victoria Arana

"CONQUEST OF THE GARDEN" FORUGH FARROKHZAD (1962)

"Conquest of the Garden" ("Fath-e Bagh") appeared in FARROKHZAD's fourth collection, *Another Birth*. An early translator and proponent of Farrokhzad's poetry, Ahmad Karimi-Hakkak, argued that this publication was "perhaps the most significant single document of contemporary Persian letters" (*Anthology of Modern Persian Poetry* 18). Farrokhzad herself prized *Another Birth* above earlier volumes as her most fully developed articulation of style and thematic concerns. She believed contemporary literature necessitated concrete vocabulary, fresh imagery, and structural innovation. "Our poetry," she claimed, "requires a great deal of harshness and unpoetical words in order to be vitalized and live anew." Innovative poets of Farrokhzad's generation countered the classical canon in several ways. Traditional metric patterns were loosened; the poetic voice became more colloquial, confessional, and psychological; and old symbols gained new identities. Farrokhzad's signal contribution was her authenticity of expression. The sexual explicitness of her poems was unprecedented. Her transgression was to unveil the intimate female self, hitherto cloaked and silent. She wrote so unequivocally outside the masculine tradition that it was impossible not to approach her poetry on its own terms. It is important to note that auto/biography as it exists in the West was not found in the Persian literary tradition. Similarly, Iranian society is still very private and guarded, especially as it relates to women. Farrokhzad's feminist challenge becomes clear when one realizes the enormous, complex, and even dangerous pressures opposing her candid self-expression.

In "Conquest of the Garden," two lovers escape to the countryside for privacy. Figured as Adam and Eve, the couple plucks an apple. But they resist the biblical and Koranic narrative with blissful communion: There is no Fall in this Paradise. Farrokhzad puts language at issue in this poem. The talk in town is condemning, and it contrasts with the language of love transmitted in "the burning peonies of your kiss, / of our candid bodies in playfulness." The lovers refuse the speech of convention, and they seek answers in nature. Love's journey leads to the mystic state of the Phoenix. The experience depersonalizes and joins Being to the cosmic everlasting, such that the lovers discover "existence in one infinite moment / when two suns gazed at one another." "Conquest of the Garden" is an eloquent and defiant poetic argument for emancipated union over contractual coupling. What becomes satanic are the narrow and oppressive judgments of society.

BIBLIOGRAPHY
Farrokhzad, Forugh. *Another Birth,* translated by Hasan
  Javadi with Susan Sallee. Emoryville, Calif.: Albany Press,
  1981.
Karimi-Hakkak, Ahmad, comp. and trans. *An Anthology of
  Modern Persian Poetry.* Boulder, Colo.: Westview, 1978.

Anett Jessop

"CORRESPONDENCE" LÉOPOLD SÉDAR SENGHOR (1990)

"Correspondence," a short poem by LÉOPOLD SÉDAR SENGHOR, was first published in *Poèmes perdus* (Lost Poems), included in his final collection of original poetry, *Oeuvre poétique.* However, "according to the author's preface, these poems are not new as such, but were previously unpublished" (Dixon xxxviii). While many of Senghor's poems are easily related to the theme of the NEGRITUDE MOVEMENT, some of those in *Poèmes perdus* are not but "offer valuable evidence of . . . his debt to a wide range of French and American poets." According to Melvin Dixon, "[t]he rhyme and quatrain form of 'Correspondence' reveal Senghor's early interest in the prosody of the truncated sonnet" (Dixon xxxvii–xxxviii). "Correspondence" conveys the introspective emotional landscape of its persona and the author's experimentation with language and his discourse on its capacity to communicate.

"Correspondence" is written in three stanzas, two quatrains, and a final couplet, with each pair of lines rhymed in the original French. The first stanza situates the speaker in a "friendly vigil night" (Stanza 1, l. 1) in which he undertakes the "correspondence" indicated by the title of the poem. The act of writing draws the addressee closer to the letter writer: His or her "nimble presence softens the light" (1.2). The act of writing "[o]n paper white as a beach" (1.3)—"beach" suggesting a distance separated by water—is imaged as an attempt to touch the addressee; the persona's "hands search" through writing "to reach" the "dream hands" (1.4) of the one who is present only in memory.

The second stanza makes use of mixed metaphors and introduces the reader to three additional images in the poem—all conveying the distance between the writer and the addressee and commenting on the act of writing. The writer and his "[d]ear one" here "travel by the express train's silent leap" (2.1)—images suggesting

distance and the prospect that the act of corresponding will allow the writer to travel *with* the one who is far away, collapsing the distance between them. The "unknown eyelashes" that "peep / On the night of [the addressee's] wide eyes" (2.2–3) convey the movement of the train and indicate not only that the act of correspondence allows the writer to enter into and look upon the addressee but also that the act of writing (taken in by the "wide eyes" of the reader when received) can collapse time as well as space. Writing is imaged here as an act of "waving scarves on the horizon skies!" (2.4)—allowing even sight across a vast distance.

The final couplet of the "Correspondence" adds a second layer of meaning to the poem: "Will I ever again see the bleeding city / Where rises the endless lament of minarets?" (3.1–2). Here (and in other poems) imagery links people to landscapes and physical places. Yet shifting from second person (the direct address of the "you" for whom the correspondence is intended), these lines may imply that what the writer longs for is not a person, but a place. The image of the towers of Muslim temples suggests a possible longing for Senegal, Senghor's homeland, which is more than 90 percent Muslim. But the personification of the city and the imagery of "bleeding" and of "endless lament" may suggest more than a projection of the writer's emotions onto the city. Depending on the time of its composition, such imagery may refer to the political turmoil concurrent with the independence of French colonies in Africa such as Algeria and Tunisia.

BIBLIOGRAPHY
Senghor, Léopold Sédar. *The Collected Poetry.* Translated
  and with an introduction by Melvin Dixon. Charlottesville: University Press of Virginia, 1991.

Yasmin Y. DeGout

"CULLING BEANS" JOÃO CABRAL DE MELO NETO (1966)

The poem *"Catar feijão"* ("Culling Beans") from *Educação pela Pedra* (Education by Stone, 1966) is one of JOÃO CABRAL DE MELO NETO's various poems that explore the process of writing. Dedicated to the Portuguese poet Alexandre O'Neill, this poem reaffirms its author's preference for the use of simile instead of metaphor through the unusual comparison between writing and culling beans ("Culling beans is not unlike writing"). As in other poems from the same book, "Culling Beans" is formulated like a theorem, and it is divided into two parts of eight lines. The first part points to the similarities between culling beans—an apparently mechanical and thoughtless task—and writing, therefore emphasizing the importance of physical work—as opposed to pure inspiration—to the process of writing poetry. According to the poem the success of both procedures presupposes careful separation of the light, unwanted superficial elements—redundant words, hollow beans—from the heavy, essential components—meaningful words, fresh beans. The last four lines of the first part of the poem refer to the differences between the two terms of the comparison (in order to perfect a sentence, one cannot toss out all the words that float since "all words will float on the paper") and anticipate the second part of the poem, which focuses on the limitations of such comparisons. Culling beans, on the one hand, involves the risk of leaving an unchewable grain among fresh beans. When dealing with words, on the other hand, attention is required in order not to avoid, but to select a "tooth-breaker." According to the poem, stonelike words are responsible for anchoring a sentence in reality and, as a result, for inducing the reader's feelings. To give "the phrase its most vivid seed," careful selection and the precise location of words are required. The unexpected usage and the unusual positioning of words are responsible for a productive interruption of the readers' expectations. Such an interruption alerts readers to the meaning of words, which had been dampened by their constant use. In "Culling Beans," Cabral de Melo Neto makes use of assonant and consonant rhymes. Among his play—and work—with words in this poem, one can point to the presence of neologisms—*fluviante* and *flutual,* translated as "flowing" and "floating"—created through the exchange of suffixes between the words *flutuante* (floating) and *fluvial* (fluvial). By emphasizing the stem of adjectives and reminding readers of the arbitrariness of their formation, the poet recovers the sonorous and graphic materiality of words and brings their concrete referents closer to readers. Cabral de Melo Neto's understanding of writing as a rational fight against any excess is also developed in other poems,

such as "A lição de poesia" (The Lesson of Poetry) and "O engenheiro" (The Engineer) in *O engenheiro* (1945) and "Psicologia da composição" (Psychology of Composition) in *Psicologia da composição (1947).*

BIBLIOGRAPHY
Cabral de Melo Neto, João. *Selected Poetry, 1937–1990.* Edited by Djelal Kadir. Hanover, N.H.: Wesleyan University Press / University Press of New England, 1994.

Luciana Namorato

"CURVE OF YOUR EYES, THE" PAUL ÉLUARD (1926)

PAUL ÉLUARD was not only one of the major proponents of surrealism, but also one of the greatest love poets of the 20th century. His poetry stands in a long tradition of adoration of the beloved woman, indebted to the early Provençal troubadour poetry, to Petrarch's sonnets to Madonna Laura, and to Dante's sacred love of Beatrice. Éluard's own love experiences were in turmoil when he published his first major collection of poems in 1926, *Capitale de la douleur* (Capital of Pain). His love for his Russian-born wife, Gala, was undermined by her affair with surrealist artist Max Ernst in 1924, which sent Éluard on a seven-month trip around the world to get over his marital unhappiness. Gala later left him for the artist Salvador Dalí, whom she married while retaining a friendly relationship with her former husband. Éluard's two most beautiful and most famous love poems, *"L'Amoureuse"* and *"La Courbe de tes yeux,"* were published in this anthology "of pain," but both poems rather seem to celebrate the happiness of mutual, shared love instead of its betrayal. *"La Courbe de tes yeux,"* the penultimate poem in the collection, is in many ways characteristic of Éluard's poetry. It abounds in musicality through assonance and alliteration, uses a network of surreal but coherent images throughout, and celebrates the eyes of the beloved woman, which can be regarded as *the* central motif of his entire oeuvre.

The poem develops around images of roundness and circularity: *"La courbe de tes yeux fait le tour de mon cœur, / Un rond de danse et de douceur, / Auréole du temps, berceau nocturne et sûr"* (The curve of your eyes embraces my heart / A ring of sweetness and dance / halo of time, sure nocturnal cradle). The curved form of the eyes is taken up by *tour* (tour), *cœur* (heart), *rond* (round), *auréole* (halo), and *berceau* (cradle)—terms that imply love as well as divinity and maternity. The impression of an encirclement of man by woman is heightened by the sound structure, which depends heavily on *o* and *ou* sounds, with assonances ([*eur/ur/u*], [*é, ère, eur*]) also being used instead of regular rhymes. The evocation of the eyes (here the curve of the eyes) of a beloved woman is a topos that goes back to the blazon techniques of the above-mentioned traditions of the *amour courtois* (courtly love). The naming of physical details of the woman's face (which stand metonymically for the entire person) and the adoration of the woman as a deity are characteristic elements, as well as the helpless dependence of the lover on the beloved: *"Et si je ne sais plus tout ce que j'ai vécu / C'est que tes yeux ne m'ont pas toujours vu"* (And if I no longer know all I have lived through / It's that your eyes have not always been mine). The mirror image of the beloved's eyes is necessary to confirm the identity of the speaker.

The second stanza extends the symbolism of the eyes by including wider and wider phenomena in the chain of images associated with the curve of her eyes. These images appear to be independent, as they are not connected to the eyes by a term of comparison (*comme*, like), a characteristic of Éluard's surrealist technique. As in a cubist or impressionist painting, particles of associations are juxtaposed, going from tangible objects to more abstract, surreal images: *"Feuilles de jour et mousse de rosée, / Roseaux du vent, sourires parfumés, / Ailes couvrant le monde de lumière, / Bateaux chargés du ciel et de la mer, / Chasseurs des bruits et sources des couleurs"* (Leaves of day and moss of dew, / Reeds of breeze, smiles perfumed, / Wings covering the world of light, / Boats charged with sky and sea, / Hunters of sound and sources of color"). Éluard combines spontaneous, oneiric (dreamlike) images that express his feeling but are not connected in the visible world as it presents itself to a waking consciousness. The reader is free to associate these images with the eyes of the beloved: "leaves of day" could refer to her eyelids, the "moss of dew" and "reed" to her wet eyelashes, "wings" and "boats" again take up the idea of roundness of the eyes as well as evoking the maternal

protection of the womb. The synesthesia of "smiles perfumed" and the idea of woman as the source of sounds and colors evoke the all-encompassing metaphysical presence of the beloved as well as her appeal to all the senses. Her eyes are not only the source of the life of the poet, but the source of all life and beauty (sounds, smells, images, feelings) in the world. For Éluard love derives from the inner recesses of the subconscious and is immediately accessible through an abandonment of reason, a truth he attempts to demonstrate by his surrealist technique.

The last stanza celebrates the woman's beauty and metaphysical significance by even more daring images. She is *"Parfums éclos d'une couvée d'aurores / Qui gît toujours sur la paille des astres"* (Perfume enclosed by a covey of dawns / That beds forever on the straw of stars). Again, Éluard uses traditional images, associating the beloved with the "dawn" and "stars," images still connected to the physicality of her eyes but also with moral implications: The woman stands for the purity and innocence of the divine, on the one hand, and the maternal, life-spending force, on the other. The speaker finally invokes his utter dependence: *"Le monde entier dépend de tes yeux purs"* (The whole world depends on your pure eyes). Éluard renews the courtly and Petrarchan tradition by combining the idea of woman as maternal protectress and pure virgin with the sensuality of the subconscious, the daring imagery of dreams.

BIBLIOGRAPHY

Éluard, Paul. *Capitale de la douleur, suivi de L'amour la poésie.* Paris: Gallimard, 2003.

———. *Capital of Pain.* Translated by Richard M. Weisman, etchings by John Thein. New York: Grossman, 1973.

Boulestreau, Nicole. *La Poésie de Paul Éluard: la rupture et le partage.* 1913–1936. Paris: Klincksieck, 1985.

Decaunes, Luc. *Paul Éluard: L'amour, la révolte, le rêve.* Paris: Balland, 1982.

McNab, Robert. *Ghost Ships: A Surrealist Love Triangle.* New Haven, Conn.: Yale University Press, 2004.

Nugent, Robert. *Paul Éluard.* New York: Twayne, 1974.

Perche, Louis. *Paul Éluard.* Paris: Éditions Universitaires, 1963.

Heike Grundmann

DABYDEEN, DAVID (1955–) David Dabydeen was born in Berbice, Guyana, grew up in New Amsterdam, and from the age of 10 lived and attended school in Georgetown. He moved to London in 1969 and received a B.A. in English from Cambridge University (1978) and a Ph.D. from the University of London in 18th-century literature and art (1981). Dabydeen was a junior research fellow at Wolfson College, Oxford, a resident fellow at Yale University's Center for British Art in 1982, and a postdoctoral fellow at Oxford from 1983. He is currently professor at the Centre for British Comparative Cultural Studies and director of the Centre for Caribbean Studies at Warwick University.

Dabydeen has published three collections of poetry. *SLAVE SONG* (1984) consists of poems written in Guyanese vernacular (with translations into conventional English) about plantation life in the colonial era. Poems in this collection had earlier received the Commonwealth Poetry Prize and Cambridge's Quiller-Couch Prize (in 1978). *Coolie Odyssey* (1988), written in more conventional orthography, focuses on Indian diasporic experience in the Caribbean. The long poem *TURNER* (first published in 1993) narrates the scene of J. M. W. Turner's renowned painting *Slavers Throwing Overboard the Dead & Dying* from the perspective of a drowning African in the foreground. Dabydeen's novels include *The Intended* (1991), which won the Guyana Prize for Literature; *Disappearance* (1993); *The Counting House* (1996), which was shortlisted for the

IMPAC Dublin Prize; *A Harlot's Progress* (1999); and *Our Lady of Demerara* (2004).

Dabydeen's scholarly and artistic work has been influential in restoring the black presence to the factual and imaginative records of British history. His nonfiction work includes the edited collection *The Black Presence in English Literature* (1985), *Hogarth's Blacks: Images of Blacks in Eighteenth Century British Art* (1985), *Hogarth, Walpole, and Commercial Britain* (1987), *Handbook for Teaching Caribbean Literature* (1988), and (with Brinsley Samaroo) *Across the Dark Waters: Ethnicity and Indian Identity in the Caribbean* (1996). A fellow of the Royal Society of Literature (one of two West Indian writers, along with V. S. Naipaul), he received the Raja Rao Award in 2004. He has served as Guyanese ambassador-at-large, ambassador to the United Kingdom, and ambassador to the United Nations Education, Scientific, and Cultural Organization (UNESCO).

BIBLIOGRAPHY
Dabydeen, David. "David Dabydeen: Coolie Odyssey." Interview in *Frontiers of Caribbean Literature in English*. Frank Birbalsingh, ed. New York: St. Martin's Press, 1996, 167–182.
Dawes, Kwame, and Neville Senu, eds. *Talk Yuh Talk: Interviews with Anglophone Caribbean Poets*. Charlottesville: University of Virginia Press, 2001.
Grant, Kevin, ed. *The Art of David Dabydeen*. Leeds, U.K.: Peepal Press, 1997.
Hornung, Alfred, and Ernstpeter Ruhe. *Postcolonialism and Autobiography*. Amsterdam: Rodopi, B.V., 1998.

Parry, Benita. "Between Creole and Cambridge English: The Poetry of David Dabydeen." *Kunapipi* 10 (1988): 1–14.

Stein, Mark. "David Dabydeen Talks to Mark Stein." *Wasafiri: Journal of Caribbean, African, Asian, and Associated Literatures and Film* 29 (1999): 27–29.

Thomas, Sue. "Liberating 'contrasting space': David Dabydeen." In *England Through Colonial Eyes in Twentieth-Century Fiction,* edited by Ann Black, Leela Gandhi, and Sue Thomas. New York: Palgrave, 2001, 171–182.

Williams, Emily A. *Poetic Negotiation of Identity in the Works of Brathwaite, Harris, Senior, and Dabydeen: Tropical Paradise Lost and Regained.* Lewiston, N.Y.: Edwin Mellen Press, 1999.

Alex Feerst

DADIÉ, BERNARD BINLIN (1916–   ) One

of the most important West African Francophone poets, patriots, and politicians, Bernard Dadié has always served two passions, his writing and his country. A poet, essayist, storyteller, journalist, novelist, and playwright, Dadié is as famous for a lifelong commitment to the freedom and progress of his native Ivory Coast as for his important contributions to literature.

Born in 1916 to a one-eyed mother and a politically active father in the seaside village of Assiéné near Abidjan (the historical capital of Ivory Coast), young Bernard was sent to live with relatives. Having lost her first three children in infancy, Dadié's mother feared she carried a curse that could also kill Bernard. While living with his storytelling Uncle N'dabian, Dadié was first introduced to the rich folklore of his ancestral Baoulé tradition. Dadié attended Catholic school in Grand Bassam and Bingerville, becoming involved in local drama and folklore as a youth. In Dakkar, Senegal, Dadié passed the highly competitive French civil service exam in 1939 and was hired by the Institut Français d'Afrique Noir (IFAN, later known as the Institut Fondamental d'Afrique Noir).

Dadié's first play, *Asémien Déhylé,* was performed in 1936 by fellow students in Dakkar and later was part of the 1937 Colonial Exposition in Paris. While all Dadié's work expresses his commitment to the ideals of democracy, theater has perhaps been the strongest vehicle for his idealism. Especially noteworthy are the plays *Monsieur Thogo-gnini,* performed in Abidjan in 1963 at a time of enormous postindependence unrest; *Béatrice du Congo,* 1970; *Les Voix dans le Vent* (Voices in the Wind), 1969; *Îles de Tempête* (Stormy Islands), 1973; and *Mhoi-Ceul* (a "petit-nègre" transcription of the French *Moi-Seul,* Me Alone), 1979.

A friend and kindred spirit of the future president of Senegal and member of the French Academy, LÉOPOLD SÉDAR SENGHOR, Dadié was part of the NÉGRITUDE MOVEMENT that sought a divorce from the European tradition and a return to an authentic African voice using French as the language of expression.

Returning to Ivory Coast from Senegal in 1947, Dadié wrote for *Le Reveil* (The Awakening), the official organ of the Parti Democratique de Côte d'Ivoire, the political movement to which his father had also belonged. A passionate fighter for his country's independence, Dadié was jailed for 16 months by French colonial authorities for leading a demonstration, an experience related in *Carnet de prison* (Prison Notebook), 1981.

In 1950, shortly after his release from prison, Dadié gained both fame and notoriety (fame among like-minded intellectuals; notoriety among members of the colonial elite) for *Afrique debout* (Africa Standing/Africa, Stand!), a collection of verse exhorting Africa to liberate itself from the yoke of European oppression. Other collections of poetry are *La Ronde des jours* (The Round of Days, which includes the poem "I THANK GOD"), 1956; and *Hommes de tous les continents* (Peoples of All Continents), 1967. Ever conscious of the rich culture of his country, Dadié founded the Cercle Culturel et Folklorique de la Côte d'Ivoire (Ivorian Circle for Culture and Folklore) in 1953. That same year he published his first novel, *Climbié,* a story about traditional village life. Dadié was also the first Ivorian to publish short stories. *"Mémoires d'une rue"* (Memories of a Street), *"Ablation"* (Ablation), and *"Vive qui?"* (Long Live Who?), all vociferously anticolonial texts, appeared in the magazine *Présence Africaine* in 1948.

Dadié's novels, each dealing with an aspect of African identity, are *Un Nègre à Paris* (An African in Paris), 1959; *La Ville oy nul ne meurt* (The City Where No One Dies), 1986; *Commandant Taureault et ses nègres* (Commander Taureault and His Blacks), 1980; and *Patron de New York* (One Way: Bernard Dadié Observes America), 1994. Dadié also writes traditional African stories such as those in *Le pagne noir* (The Black Cloth: A Collection of African Folktales), 1955.

Since the independence of Ivory Coast in 1960, Dadié has been involved in building his nation, eventually serving as minister of culture between 1977 and 1986. The recipient of multiple Ivorian and foreign decorations and honors, Bernard Binlin Dadié today is a vocal critic of a world ruled by the "hegemony of money," a global system where the international market, controlled by the Northern Hemisphere, condemns young nations in the Southern Hemisphere to a future without hope.

BIBLIOGRAPHY

Dadié, Bernard Binlin. *An African in Paris.* Translated by Karen Hatch. Champaign: University of Illinois Press, 1994.

———. *One Way: Bernard Dadié Observes America.* Translated by Jo Patterson. Champaign: University of Illinois Press, 1994.

Annette Olsen-Fazi

DAMAS, LÉON-GONTRAN (1912–1978)

Léon-Gontran Damas—poet, statesman, activist, educator—was one of the first black writers to achieve prominence in Francophone literature. He was as well one of the founders of the NEGRITUDE MOVEMENT, a literary and cultural movement begun by black writers of French colonies who sought to proclaim pride in their "blackness" and eliminate the racial inferiority complex imposed on them through centuries of white European colonization of their native countries.

Damas was born in 1912 in Cayenne, French Guiana. His mother died in 1913, and he was raised by his aunt, Gabrielle Damas. He attended primary school in Cayenne and high school at the Lycée Schoelcher in Martinique, where he was a classmate of Martinican writer-statesman AIMÉ CÉSAIRE. Damas completed secondary school in Meaux, France, in 1928 and remained in France to complete his university education in Paris, where he studied Russian, Japanese, law, and ethnology.

While a student in Paris Damas was subjected to the racial discrimination that was to affect his future writing. In the 1930s he became interested in the newly postrevolutionary Russia and witnessed the rise of fascism in Europe. He was concerned with the civil rights struggles of African Americans as well and became acquainted with American writers of the Harlem Renaissance, including Countee Cullen, Langston Hughes, and Claude McKay. In 1935, with Aimé Césaire and LÉOPOLD SENGHOR (Senegal), he cofounded the newspaper *L'Etudiant noir* (The Black Student), which served as a forum of ideas for the Negritude Movement.

In 1937 Damas published his first and most renowned collection of poetry, *Pigments,* which was the earliest major work to be published by a black writer in France, and its critical acclaim was immediate, as it received wide praise from white French writers, such as Robert Desnos, who had written an introduction to the work. The collection's title makes clear the concerns of much of Damas's poetry—that the color of one's skin ("pigment") has for too long served as a means of determining human worth. From this notion Damas planted the seeds of the Negritude Movement. By appropriating and using in his poems the pejorative term for blacks in France (*nègre*), Damas did more than defuse its power to denigrate. On the contrary, he championed its use as a way of showing other blacks that they should be proud of their "blackness" and the unique cultural traditions that had thrived in Africa and the Caribbean before French colonization. Damas's compatriot Aimé Césaire would be credited with coining the term *négritude* in his seminal epic poem *Cahier d'un retour au pays natal* (NOTEBOOK OF A RETURN TO THE NATIVE LAND), first published in 1939. In the poem Césaire describes the ravages of his native Martinique at the hands of French colonials but retains hope and strength in his *négritude*—his unique racial and cultural heritage that will reassert itself one day when his compatriots overcome centuries of slavery and European colonization.

In 1938 Damas published a second collection of poetry, *Retour de Guyane* (Return from Guiana), and strengthened his reputation as one of the preeminent voices of *négritude*. His interest in equality for blacks of all nations led him to take an increased interest in politics, and in 1948 he was elected deputy from Guiana to the French National Assembly, a post he held until 1951. During this time he met and married Martinican Isabelle Victoire Vécilia Achille and wrote for political and social newspapers, including *La Revue du monde noir* and *Légitime Défense*. Damas continued to write poetry, publishing the collection *Graffiti* (1953) and *Black Label* (1956), which contained not only Damas's usual themes of race, religion, language, and nationality, but which were also infused with the spirit of American jazz and the spirit of the American Harlem Renaissance. Damas, who along with French writers Robert Desnos and Marguerite Duras, had taken part in the French Resistance against the Vichy government and the German occupation of France, included a decidedly antimilitaristic tone in his poetry, commiserating with soldiers of all lands who must do the bidding of powerful regimes.

The 1960s saw Damas spending much of his time studying ethnology with French writers Jacques Roumain and Michel Leiris at Paris's Institut de l'Ethnologie. From 1964 to 1969 Damas served as a researcher for the United Nations Educational, Scientific and Cultural Organization (UNESCO), which promotes peace among nations and encourages the sharing of knowledge. He traveled extensively during this time, visiting the United States, the Caribbean, and Brazil, where he met his second wife, Marietta Campos, whom he married in 1969. During this period, he established a division of *Écrits français d'outre-mer* (French Writings from Overseas) for the prestigious Paris publishing house Éditions Fasquelle. Damas continued to write poetry, publishing two collections—*Névralgies* (1966) and *Veillées noires* (1972)—before his death. He was also named distinguished professor of African literature at Howard University in Washington, D.C.—a post occupied until his death from cancer in 1978.

BIBLIOGRAPHY

Rochelle M. Smith. "Leon Damas: Poet of Negritude." Postcolonial Studies at Emory University. Available online. URL: http://www.english.emory.edu/Bahri/Damas.html. Downloaded on April 22, 2007.

Shapiro, Norman R., trans. and ed. *Négritude: Black Poetry from Africa and the Caribbean*. New York: October House, 1970.

Patrick Day

D'ANNUNZIO, GABRIELE (1863–1938) A

highly controversial individual, especially for his association with fascist ideology, D'Annunzio—poet, dramatist, and novelist—is among the Italian authors less frequently translated into English. During the second half of the 20th century more attention was directed to his worldly lifestyle, his glamorous love affairs, and his military undertakings than to his literary achievements. Nevertheless, he has to be recognized as one of the major exponents of turn-of-the-century European decadence.

He was born in Pescara, in the region of Abbruzzi, into a family of landowners. He studied in one of the most prestigious schools and made his debut on the literary scene when he was only 16 with the volume of verse *Primo vere* (1879), soon to be followed by a second, *Canto novo*, in 1882. His first poetic production, together with tales that appeared in the same period, already revealed the sensual and naturalistic inspiration that would characterize his work. He lived in Rome for several years, collaborated with different newspapers, and took part in the aristocratic life of the capital, becoming an aesthete always in search of refined pleasures, erotic adventures, and intellectual sensuality. From the poets of European decadence he absorbed a particular sensibility for verbal refinement reflected in the work of this period in a wealth of technique. He continued publishing volumes of verse and several novels, the most widely known of which, *Il piacere* (The Child of Pleasure, 1889), mirrors his own sensual and aesthetic experience.

A second phase in his production began in 1894 with the novel *Il trionfo della morte* (The Triumph of Death), followed by several poetry collections and plays, all inspired by the myth of the Nietzschean hero, a fascination with adventure and power that eventually developed into an exaggerated nationalism and finally led to his association with the Italian fascist movement. In this period of full artistic maturity he produced his best poetry. The three first books of the *Laudi* (*Maia, Elettra,* and *Alcyone*) appeared in 1903. Of those, only the third has recently been made available in English (as *Halcyon*). In 1910, to escape debts, D'Annunzio fled to France and returned to Italy only to participate with fervent enthusiasm in World War I. He contributed to the rise of fascism but was eventually set aside by the regime. In his old age he devoted himself to autobiographical writing. He died in his home on Lake Garda in 1938 and was given a state funeral by Italian leader Benito Mussolini.

D'Annunzio's egocentric character, his taste for sensuous pleasure, and his exasperated patriotism are fully reflected in his work. He enacted the decadent fusion of art and life and represented both the elegance and the authoritarian ideology of the Italian upper classes of the time. Nevertheless, his best verses reveal a profound love for nature and a sensibility for the deepest secrets of the self, as in "The Rain in the Pinewood" and "The Shepherds of Abruzzo." Through the senses D'Annunzio seeks a physical and spiritual communion with the primal forces of life—a spirit that has come to be known as "D'Annunzian panism," a total immersion of the self into the harmony of the world beyond the mediation of the intellect. In that spirit he offers a beautiful poetic transfiguration of reality.

BIBLIOGRAPHY

Becker, Jared M. Nationalism and Culture: Gabriele D'Annunzio and Italy after the Risorgimento. New York: Peter Lang, 1994.

D'Annunzio, Gabriele. Halcyon. Translated and with an introduction by J. G. Nichols. New York: Routledge, 2003.

Klopp, Charles. Gabriele D'Annunzio. Boston: Twayne, 1988.

Spackman, Barbara. Decadent Genealogies: The Rhetoric of Sickness from Baudelaire to D'Annunzio. Ithaca, N.Y.: Cornell University Press, 1989.

Valesio, Paolo. Gabriele D'Annunzio: The Dark Flame, New Haven, Conn.: Yale University Press, 1992 (English translation by Marilyn Migiel).

Woodhouse, John. Gabriele D'Annunzio: Defiant Arcangel. Oxford: Clarendon Press, 1998.

Sabrina Brancato

DAPHNE'S LOT Chris Abani (2003) Chris

Abani's second published book of poetry, Daphne's Lot, is a book-length free-verse poem about his mother's life and its shaping by the violence of family and war. A reworking of the epic tradition that both subverts and uses its devices, the poem centers a woman and sacrificial love against the epic's traditional backdrop of war, a quest, and a heroic journey. In Abani's epic men are the backdrop, civilians are the focus, and history is a story told by the vanquished. It is in couplets with rhythmic structures that vary from the standard English pentameter, employing instead cadences that reflect the African rhythms of highlife, reggae, and blues.

In these poems Abani attempts to imitate his mother's act of creating him. He creates her on the page from what is left of their past—faded photographs, poor memories, and her silence about his father's hostility—recognizing from the outset that his creation can never live in the literal sense. By trying to imagine the limits of his mother's life, he hopes to find them both redemption. The poems alternate between telling the story of Daphne's life as a girl growing up in an English village during World War II (mid-1930s to mid-1940s) and her life as a woman in a Nigerian village during the Nigerian-Biafran civil war (mid-1960s to mid-1970s), where she moved after marrying a Nigerian student she met while he was attending Oxford.

In England she both accepted the stringencies of women's lives of the time (turning down a scholarship to work as a secretary) and rejected them (by leaving home without being married and falling in love with a black man). In Nigeria life involved fewer choices. She had to convert to Catholicism, learn to cook without electricity, bear five children, and endure her husband's growing violence, fed by her mother-in-law's disdain for her uselessness. Meanwhile the Igbo people, her husband's group, were engaged in ethnic conflicts with the Nigerian government. In 1967 the Igbo republic of Biafra seceded from Nigeria, and government forces supported by the United States and Britain quickly struck back, bombing villages and cutting off food supplies. In the two and a half years following, over a million Igbos died, many of them of starvation. Daphne's family quickly abandoned their homes to avoid being killed. In the epic arc of the poem their experiences as refugees, rather than as warriors, are detailed. The book (published by Red Hen) concludes with poems about various figures from the war and its aftermath.

Wendy Belcher

DARÍO, RUBÉN (1867–1916) Born in Nicaragua as Felix Rubén García Sarmiento, Rubén Darío is one of the better-known Latin American poets of the

turn of the century. He is considered the leader of Spanish American *modernismo,* a movement influenced by romantic, Parnassian, and symbolist French poets such as Charles Baudelaire and Paul Verlaine. According to Cathy Jrade, Darío himself baptized the *modernismo* movement in 1888 "to designate the shared orientations of Spanish American authors writing toward the end of the 19th century" (1). The year 1888 is also significant for Darío because it was when the first edition of *Azul* (Blue) appeared. Enlarged and updated editions of this important book appeared in 1890 and 1905.

Many scholars have described Spanish American *modernismo* as both an evolution from Spanish American romanticism and, at the same time, a reaction against it. Alberto Acereda has described it as "a cultural and artistic attitude that dominated Spanish and Spanish American art and letters toward the end of the 19th and the early 20th century." Among the literary movement's predominant characteristics are the focus on form, use of new rhythms and verses, imagery of elegance and refinement, exoticism and cosmopolitanism, and an interest in fantasy. The literary critic Orlando Gómez-Gil describes four phases in this literary movement's evolution: a precursor stage led by José Martí, Julián del Casal, Manuel González Prada, and José Asunción Silva; in the second phase, the writers' preoccupation with aestheticism (where the emphasis was on evasion and exoticism) and the creation of the "ivory tower" (where poets would escape their own realities); in the third phase, a concern for the problems facing Spanish America; finally, the poets' reaction against the aesthetic phase of the movement itself (405). Darío was a major figure in all four phases.

Darío's early life was lived in poverty. He was educated by Jesuits in Nicaragua, who taught him Latin and Greek and exposed him to peninsular literature. He was the illegitimate son of Manuel García and Rosa Sarmiento, and "Darío" became his artistic surname, which was also his father's nickname. At the age of 13 he published his first poem in *El ensayo,* in the city of León, and he became known as the "child poet." His first verses were homage, in terms of style, to poets such as Victor Hugo, José Zorrilla, José de Espronceda, and Gustavo Adolfo Bécquer—romantic writers. As he was

developing an interest in politics without clearly knowing his own political leanings, Darío become a liberal, believing in the union of the countries of Central America. This political interest continued to develop throughout his voyages to various Latin American nations, among them Argentina and Chile. In 1892 he was appointed secretary to the Guatemalan delegation to Madrid for the events commemorating the anniversary of the "discovery" of the Americas. In 1893 he was named general consul for Colombia in Argentina.

Aside from being a diplomat and a poet, Darío was also a journalist, having directed the newspapers *La unión* in 1889 in San Salvador and worked as a reporter for *La nación* and *La tribuna* in Buenos Aires in 1898. In 1894, with Ricardo Jaime Freyre, Darío cofounded the literary magazine *Revista de América* (Journal of America). Darío was married twice. In 1889 he married Rafaela Contreras, who died two years later. In 1893 he married Rosario Murillo. It is believed that her family forced him to marry her.

His first book of poems, *Epístolas y poemas: Primeras notas* (Epistles and Poems: First Notes) was published in 1885, which according to Acereda he reissued in 1888. His trip to Chile in 1886 led to the publication of his second book of poems, *Abrojos* (Difficulties), in 1887. The poems that appeared in that volume all focused on his experiences in Chile, including *"Canto épico a las glorias de Chile"* (Epic Song to the Glories of Chile), for which he shared an award in a poetry contest sponsored by a Chilean millionaire. When *Azul* was first published in 1888, the Spanish writer Juan Valera, while somewhat critical of his poems, exalted Darío's stories for their style and catapulted Darío's reputation as a talented and gifted poet, prompting the poet to publish two more editions of *Azul,* each time including poems more daring and modernist.

In 1896 Darío published *Prosas profanas y otros poemas* (Profane Prose and Other Poems), which, many critics claim marked the height of *modernismo* since it confirmed a new concept of art, as well as a revolutionary literary endeavor. Acereda and Derusha state that this book of poems "represents Darío's poetic eruption, one that continues practically until the end of his life" (19). A second edition was published in 1901. The next two books Darío published were *Cantos de vida y* esperanza: Los cisnes y otros poemas (Songs of Life and Hope: The Swans and Other Poems) in 1905 and *El canto errante* (The Wandering Song) in 1907. *Cantos de vida* established Darío as a mature poet whose focus now turned to those metaphysical preoccupations that most affect man. "A Roosevelt" (To Roosevelt) appears in this volume. His style is here simpler and profound, but Darío does not abandon his established poetic expression. *El canto errante,* while not so popular, confirmed his status as an important and prolific poet. Although Acereda and Derusha claim that the poems for that book were put together to make ends meet, they state that *El canto errante* honors "the poet roving through a world that is not overly concerned with art and poetry" (27). Darío's final volumes, *Poemas del otoño y otros poemas* (Autumn Poems and Other Poems) and *Canto a la Argentina y otros poemas* (Song to Argentina and Other Poems) were published in 1910 and 1914, respectively.

Many of Darío's poems reflect his anguish and despair. He was brilliant in his adaptation of Spanish and foreign styles, which he cultivated and made his own. His contribution to the arts in the Americas elevated the quality of literature, and in Spanish America specifically he set the standards for those 20th-century artists who were to follow.

BIBLIOGRAPHY
Acereda, Alberto, and Will Derusha. *Selected Poems of Rubén Darío: A Bilingual Anthology.* Lewisburg, Pa.: Bucknell University Press, 2001.
Gómez-Gil, Orlando. *Historia crítica de la literatura hispanoamericana, desde los orígenes hasta el momento actual.* New York: Holt, Rinehart and Winston, 1968.
Jrade, Cathy L. *Modernismo, Modernity and the Development of Spanish American Literature.* Austin: University of Texas Press, 1998.

Enrique Morales-Díaz

"DARK ROOM, THE" Enrique Lihn (1963)

The title poem of Enrique Lihn's 1963 collection *La pieza oscura* (The Dark Room) uses dense description and rich symbolism to communicate the problematic division between childhood and adulthood. The setting of *La pieza oscura* gives the poem its title. In a dark room four children—the speaker, his sister Paulina, and his cousins Ángel and Isabel—engage in a ritualistic battle. Mimicking the more consciously sexual interactions of adults, the two pairs of children struggle, rolling around on the floor, their game at once innocent and provocative. The poem repeatedly recalls *"la vieja rueda"* (the old wheel), an image it blatantly associates with life and the transition from childhood to adulthood and between generations. The wheel turns as the children's game becomes less and less of a game, as they grow more aware of the sexual act that their mock battle could precipitate.

On the verge of tumbling into adulthood, the wheel rotating faster and faster, the speaker in the poem suddenly pulls away, releasing Isabel, afraid to move too fast into the unknown. The lights come back on as the speaker wonders where their childhoods have fled, even as the four children hurry to behave properly once the adults arrive. Ultimately the poem suggests the dark period bridging childhood and adulthood, but it also investigates the shadow self, the *"fantasma,"* or ghost, of the child speaker, permanently petrified before the *"imposibles presagios,"* the unbearable omens, of a future his naive mind cannot imagine.

Both the depth of imagery and the psychological exploration of the poem are typical of Lihn's work. The images of *"La pieza oscura"* are often surprising and occasionally violent. For example, the poet describes *"la crueldad del corazón en el fruto del amor, / la corrupción del fruto y luego . . . el carozo sangriento, afiebrado y seco"* (the heart's cruelty in the fruit of love, the fruit rotting / and then . . . the bloody pit, feverish and dried out). United by the cyclic symbol of the wheel, the speaker's former self, the innocent boy, and his mature presence are able to recall this important moment of transition perfectly.

BIBLIOGRAPHY
Lihn, Enrique. *The Dark Room and Other Poems.* Edited by Patricio Unger, translated by Jonathan Cohen, John Felsteiner, and David Unger. New York: New Directions, 1978.

Winter Elliott

DARWISH, MAHMUD (1942–)

Mahmud Darwish was born in Palestine when it was a British mandate. At the age of six he experienced the dispersal of his people upon the birth of the state of Israel (1948). The Palestinians had to flee or accept subjugation. Darwish's family left their village, al-Birwa (near Acre), for Lebanon to avoid the violence in the expectation that they would be able to return when the conflict was over. When they did return a year later, they found their village destroyed by the new Zionist state, and they had become internal refugees in their own country, denied the status of citizens.

Darwish studied in schools in Galilee and was harassed and imprisoned several times for asserting Arab identity and Palestinian rights, but he remembers gratefully teachers who encouraged him—both Arabs and Israeli Jews. He started writing poetry at an early age. His first collection of poetry, 'Asafir bila ajniha (Birds without Wings), was published in 1960. His second collection, Awraq al-Zaytun (Olive Leaves), published in 1964, made him known widely as a resistance poet. His confrontational poem in this collection, "Identity Card," asserted Palestinian Arab identity despite Israeli efforts to suppress it.

In 1961 Darwish joined Rakah, the Communist Party of Israel—arguably the only political organization that recognized Palestinians as equals. Darwish published articles and poems in Arabic newspapers and magazines in Israel and became a coeditor of al-Fajr.

In 1970 he left his occupied country and lived in different cities: Moscow, Cairo, Beirut, Tunis, and Paris. In Beirut in the 1970s he worked as editor of the monthly Shu'un Falastiniyya (Palestinian Affairs) and as director of the Research Center of the Palestinian Liberation Organization (PLO). He founded the acclaimed literary and cultural journal Al-Karmal in 1980 and continues to be its editor in chief. At present he lives between Amman, Jordan, and Ramallah, in the occupied West Bank of Palestine.

In summer 1982 Israel invaded Lebanon and laid siege to Beirut, where Darwish resided. Darwish wrote poems that depicted the situation and circulated widely in the decade that followed. He also wrote the prose work Dhakira lil-Nisyan (Memory for Forgetfulness) about besieged Beirut and the Palestinian catastrophe known as nakba. Following that Darwish had to leave Beirut, thus adding another exile. He lived in various cities in Europe and the Middle East. In 1987 he was selected as a member of the PLO Executive Committee, but he resigned later in protest against the Oslo Accords of 1993, which did not restore their legitimate rights to the Palestinians.

A prolific author with about 20 collections of poetry and more than half a dozen prose works, Darwish is both a poets' poet and a national bard. Popular as he is among general readers, he is also a sophisticated and multilayered poet whose works attract intellectuals and critics. He is also known as a significant voice in Third World literature and is one of the few Arab poets who has a global readership. When Darwish recites his poetry at literary festivals, thousands of people attend what is considered a momentous cultural event. He communicates intimacy and profundity even when reading to crowds in huge halls. His poetry has been discussed in the Israeli Knesset,—including "Passing among Passing Words," which commemorates the Palestinian uprising known as the Intifada. In 2000 Yossi Sarid, the Israeli minister of education, proposed including Darwish's poems in the secondary school curriculum, but there was strong opposition against allowing a Palestinian voice to surface.

Darwish's poetry combines lyricism with symbolism while staying close to historical events and everyday concerns. His poems have since developed from the earlier confrontational statements and explicitly political works to a more reflective and philosophical poetics. Darwish is an educated poet, well-read in different fields and familiar with various poetic traditions and trends. He admires great poetry whether of the ancients or the moderns (see, for instance, his "LESSON FROM THE KAMA SUTRA"). But his favorite poet is Federico García Lorca, who like Darwish defended the cause of an oppressed people. In Darwish's Jidariyya (Mural), published in 2000 following a serious heart operation, his poetry reached the heights of the epical with its echoing of human history and existential questions. In its focus on the self, Jidariyya inevitably reminds one of those renowned, long autobiographical poems—Walt Whitman's Song of Myself and John Ashbery's Self-Portrait in a Convex Mirror, for example. Whitman presents an imperial self with its all-encompassing optimistic drive, looking brightly at the future. Ashbury presents a convoluted self delving ironically and torturously into the nexus between the past and the present. *Jidariyya,* however, presents a vulnerable self. The confessional element in Darwish's long poem stems from admitting human weakness, physical deterioration, and reluctance to bid farewell to the world.

There is a humanistic strain in Darwish's poetry where resistance is divorced from chauvinism, and where peace is the other face of justice. His longings for his country are often akin to the lyrical outpouring of an unrequited lover. His poetry can be read as a patriotic song for Palestine (see "DIARY OF A PALESTINIAN WOUND") or a love poem for an unnamed beloved.

Darwish, unlike other modernist poets, has not broken ties with the long tradition of Arabic poetry. He continues to savor prosodic musicality, and his lexicon is rich and compelling. Yet his concerns are thoroughly modern and contemporary. His writing articulates eloquently the frustrations and dreams of his silenced people, and by extension it expresses those states of mind of the oppressed and displaced everywhere. His poems have expressed the tragedy and aspirations of other people as well as his own. He has written about the struggle of colonized Africans as well as of North American Indians. A famous poem that incarnates the persona of an American Indian, Chief Seattle, addressing the white man, "Speech of the 'Red Indian,'" contrasts different philosophies of being, one that believes in harmony with nature and another that attempts conquering nature. His poem about the Hoopoe, with its rich intertextual references, partakes of the vision of Farid al-Din Attar, the 12th-century Persian poet and author of the allegorical narrative poem *Mantiq al-Tayr* (The Conference of the Birds). Darwish has also been able to go under the skin of Israeli soldiers, not to denounce and condemn as in "A SOLDIER DREAMS OF WHITE TULIPS," but to represent the pacific streak that is repressed in them by military logic. Darwish's humanist drive makes him a poet who listens to the wretched of the Earth and articulates their agony. His universal appeal stems from his universal concerns. Rather than turning the political into the ideological, he weaves it into a tragic lyricism. Yet hope and passion never desert his writing. Having lost his physical homeland, he turned his native language—Arabic—into a homeland of sorts.

Many of Darwish's poems have been set to music and sung by the well-known Lebanese singer associated with the resistance, Marcel Khalife. The Palestinian-American critic and theorist Edward W. Said analyzed the poetry of Darwish and compared it to that of William Butler Yeats, PABLO NERUDA, FAIZ AHMED FAIZ, and AIMÉ CÉSAIRE. A documentary film entitled *Mahmud Darwich* was produced by French television and directed by Simone Bitton in 1997. In 2004 Darwish invited a delegation of internationally renowned writers (including two Nobel laureates) to occupied Palestine to see for themselves what Israeli rule meant for indigenous people. The writers included Russell Banks (United States), BEI DAO (China), José Saramago (Portugal), and WOLE SOYINKA (Nigeria). The visit was recorded in a documentary film directed by Samir Abdallah and José Reynes and entitled *Writers on the Borders.*

Mahmud Darwish has received many awards in the Arab world as well as having been awarded international honors including the Lotus Prize (1969, Union of Afro-American Writers), the Lenin Prize for Peace (1983, USSR), the Knight of the Order of Arts and Letters (1993, France), the Lannan Foundation Prize for Cultural Freedom (2002, United States), and the Prince Claus Fund Principal Award (2004, Netherlands).

BIBLIOGRAPHY

Abou-Bakr, Randa. *The Conflict of Voices in the Poetry of Dennis Brutus and Mahmud Darwish.* Wiesbaden, Germany: Reichert Verlag, 2004.

Darwish, Mahmud. *Selected Poems.* Translated by Ian Wedde and Fawwaz Tuqan. Cheadle Hulme, U.K.: Carcanet Press, 1973.

———. *Splinters of Bone.* Translated by B. M. Bennani. Greenfield Center, N.Y.: Greenfield Review Press, 1974.

———. *The Music of Human Flesh: Poems of the Palestinian Struggle.* Translated by Denys Johnson-Davies. London: Heinemann, 1980.

———. *Sand and Other Poems.* Translated by Rana Kabbani. New York: KPI (distributed by Routledge & Kegan Paul), 1986.

———. [Darwich, Mahmoud]. *Palestine mon pays: L'affaire du poème.* Paris: L'Édition de Minuit, 1988.

———. *Psalms: Poems.* Translated by Ben Bennani. Colorado Springs, Colo.: Three Continents Press, 1994.

———. *Memory for Forgetfulness: August, Beirut 1982.* Translated by Ibrahim Muhari. Berkeley: University of California Press, 1995.

———. *The Adam of Two Edens: Poems.* Edited by Munir Akash and Daniel Moore. Syracuse, N.Y.: Syracuse University Press, 2000.

———. *Unfortunately, It Was Paradise.* Translated by Munir Akash and Carolyn Forché. Berkeley: University of California Press, 2003.

Hafez, Sabry. *Mahmud Darwish* (in Arabic). Cairo: Dar al-Fata al-'Arabi, 1994.

Jayyusi, Salma Khadra. "Introduction: Palestinian Literature in Modern Times." Edited by Salma K. Jayyusi, *Anthology of Modern Palestinian Literature.* New York: Columbia University Press, 1992, 1–80.

Said, Edward. "On Mahmud Darwish." *Grand Street* 12 (Winter 1994): 12–15.

Saith, Ashwani. "Mahmud Darwish: Hope as Home in the Eye of the Storm." *ISIM Review* 15 (Spring 2005): 28–29.

Ferial J. Ghazoul

DAS, JIBANANANDA (1899–1954)

Jibanananda Das is acknowledged as the premier poet of the post-TAGORE era in India. On November 6, 1949, in an article entitled "Bengali Poetry Today" published in the Calcutta daily *The Statesman,* Das wrote, "[T]he most significant of the post-Tagoreans . . . have effected in our poetry a healthy change." Although Tagore's work continued to enjoy wide popularity, in Bengal in the 1930s a distinctly new literary movement had consolidated itself—modernism. With Das as its finest exemplar, the modernism of the 1930s and 1940s ultimately transformed the Bengali poetic idiom.

Jibanananda Das was born on February 18, 1899, in Barisal in eastern Bengal (now in Bangladesh). While he was proficient in Bengali classical and folk literary traditions, like other poets of his generation—BUD-DHADEV BOSE, Amiya Chakravarty, Sudhindranath Datta, and Bishnu Dey—Das cultivated English literature in college and beyond. For him and others English gave access to the new literary turn in the West associated with Yeats, Pound, and Eliot. After graduating with a master's degree from Calcutta University, Das accepted a teaching position in the English Department at City College in Calcutta, only to be dismissed from the post six years later, in 1928. Although the institution's financial cutbacks might have contributed to his discharge, it is popularly held that an allegation of obscenity—a mention of "breast" in one of his poems—was at the root of the college authority's displeasure. Charges of obscenity, cultural inauthenticity, and abstruseness would haunt Das's work for a long time.

In August 1946 while he was on a visit to Calcutta, riots between Hindus and Muslims broke out in the city. The tumult continued for a full year, culminating in independence and the partition of British India into India and Pakistan in August 1947. During this period Das was unable to return to Barisal—his hometown and place of employment. And since Barisal, after the partition, fell within the territory of the newly created Pakistan (after 1971, Bangladesh), the Das family relocated to Calcutta. He passed away on October 22, 1954, eight days after he was hit by a tramcar while crossing the street.

After the rather amateurish *Jhara Palak* (Fallen Feathers, 1927), Das's first mature collection of verse, *Dhusar Pandulipi* (The Grey Manuscript), appeared in 1936. It was followed in 1942 by BANALATA SEN, an anthology generally thought to contain some of his finest work. Its expanded 1952 edition received a literary award from the Nikhil Banga Rabindrasahitya Sammelan (All-Bengal Rabindra Literary Conference) in 1953. His next two books—*Mahaprithibi* (The Great Earth, 1944) and *Satti Tarar Timir* (The Darkness of Seven Stars, 1948)—emerged out of the social and political ferment of the 1940s: the Bengal famine, the riots, and the partition. This engagement with history and society was continued in *Bela Abela Kalbela* (Time Wrong Time Inauspicious Time, 1961), a collection whose press copy the poet himself had prepared but whose publication he did not live to see. The bitterness in the tone and the urban setting of *Mahaprithibi, Satti Tarar Timir,* and *Bela Abela Kalbela* were far from the tranquility of the *Rupasi Bangla* (Beautiful Bengal) poems that celebrated the beauty of the Bengali countryside. These poems were written in the 1930s, but Das had withheld publishing them. When they were published posthumously in 1957, the collection became an immediate favorite and was especially cherished by Bengali nationalists fighting in 1971 for Bangladeshi secession from Pakistan. While he is most famed for his poetry, Das was also an accomplished writer of prose fiction, though his novels and short stories were published only long after he had passed away. At the time of his death he was just beginning to win recognition beyond the small circle of his literary friends and colleagues. The year after his death he was awarded the first annual Sahitya (Literature) Akademi's Bengali Prize, a prestigious seal of critical approval.

Marxist critics during his lifetime censured Das's work for what they perceived to be its nihilism and subjectivism, citing what they thought was the poetry's detachment from the political and social struggles of the time. Yet if the radicals were vexed, the conservatives too were wary of his fresh poetic idiom. The arch-conservative critic Sajanikanta Das regularly deprecated Jibanananda Das on the pages of his weekly literary journal, *Sanibarer Chithi* (The Saturday Letter). Other critics too were bewildered by the poet's uneven diction, his mixing of high and low styles, his unusual and seemingly rustic vocabulary, his sensuous imagery, and, especially, his thoroughly modernist sensibilities. For such critics the poetry of Rabindranath Tagore (1861–1941)—a serene and harmonious poetic cosmos expressed in a refined, Sanskritized diction—had set a standard against which Das's writings would inevitably be found deficient. For their part Das and other young Bengali modernists of the 1930s felt that a new poetic sensibility was needed. According to them Tagore's poetry with its classical elegance and decorum obscured the grim realities of the war-ravaged world and was out of touch with the times. But Bengali modernism was driven as much by a conscious defiance of Tagore's poetics as by internationalism. Literary modernism in the West, the young Bengali poets of the 1930s felt, had more successfully articulated the predicament of the 20th-century subject. They, like their counterparts in the West, believed that an investigation of the changed circumstances required a radical examination of a precarious and fractured subjectivity. Theirs was an exploration of interiority that paradoxically demanded that a renewed attention be paid to the essence of things.

Das took on the modernist project, reinvigorated the poetic diction, and refreshed the poetic lexicon without shunning the sexually suggestive, the mundane, or the ugly. In so doing he expanded the reach of Bengali poetry. For the first time in his work, lepers, beggars, suicides, melancholia, hydrants, vultures, frogs, and mosquitoes were allowed to cohabit in Bengali verse alongside the conventionally beautiful. At the metrical level, too, he was no less innovative. While broadly modernist, Das's oeuvre is eclectic and resists classification under any single heading or school. As the poet himself pointed out in the introduction to his *Sreshtha Kabita* (Best Poems) (1954), "Some have said that this poetry is mainly about nature, or chiefly about historical and social consciousness, others regard it as poetry of utter apathy; some deem my poetry as symbolist; solely from the unconscious, surrealist. I have come across other labels too. Almost all are correct but only in part—they are descriptive of a particular poem or a certain phase, not of the entire poetic corpus."

BIBLIOGRAPHY

Chaudhuri, Sukanta. *A Certain Sense: Poems by Jibanananda Das.* Translated by various, edited by Sukanta Chaudhuri. New Delhi: Sahitya Akademi, 1998.

Das, Jibanananda. "Bengali Poetry Today." *The Statesman,* 6 November 1949.

Das Gupta, Chidananda. *Jibanananda Das.* New Delhi: Sahitya Akademi, 1972.

Seely, Clinton B. *A Poet Apart: A Literary Biography of the Bengali Poet Jibanananda Das.* Newark: University of Delaware Press, 1990.

Debali Mookerjea-Leonard

DAS, KAMALA (1934–)   Bilingual poet from Kerala, India, Kamala Das (now known as Kamala Suraya) was born in Punnayurkulam, a village in South Malabar, India, on March 31, 1934. She is the daughter of V. M. Nair, a former managing editor of the widely circulated daily *Mathrubhumi,* and Nalappat Balamani Amma, a renowned Malayali poet. Das's great-uncle, the writer Nalapat Narayan Menon, encouraged her earliest poetic efforts, and she grew up under the influence of her mother's poems and the sacred writings of the matriarchal community of Nayars, from which she hails (Bhanot). Kamala was privately educated. At 15 she married K. Madhava Das, a banker with the Reserve Bank of India. She was only 16 when she gave birth to her first child and has commented that she "was mature enough to be a mother only when [her] third child was born" (Warrier).

Das has published in both English and Malayalam (under the pen name Madhavikutty). In December 1999 Das's conversion to Islam created a hullabaloo in the media. Less than a year later the newly minted Kamala Suraya (aka Suraya Begum) publicly announced plans to register her own political party, which she has named Lok Seva (Bhanot). She is the most senior woman writing English-language poetry in India and has never had difficulty getting successfully published there. In recent years she has prominently contested Indian national elections.

In her poem "AN INTRODUCTION," the speaker is clearly someone notably like the poet herself. She writes: "I am Indian, very brown, born in / Malabar, I speak three languages, / Write in / Two, dream in one" (Nine Indian Women Poets 10). Plagued continually by the English-versus-Malayalam tug-of-war that confronted bilingual writers in India in the 1960s and 1970s, she fiercely confronted her critics and explained her reasons for choosing to write in English. Out of these early intellectual controversies sprang the creative environment that exists in India today for the fertile production of outstanding literature in Indian English. In a sense, then, the polemics of such courageous poets as Kamala Das paved the way for the vast number of Indian writers who today write unselfconsciously in the English language and no longer see any reason to justify their choice.

Das's poetry was controversial not just for the language in which she wrote, but also for the subjects that she explored. Delving deeply into her psyche, she examined her position as a wife and mother, confined to narrow domestic roles and aching to break out of them to realize her fullest potential. This restlessness is seen in such works as "The Invitation," in which she writes: "I have a man's fist in my head today / Clenching, unclenching . . ." (Contemporary Indian Poetry 49). Unafraid to disclose the most intimate secrets of her personal life, Das wrote frankly about her dissatisfaction in sexual relationships, her lack of desire in marriage, her painful innocence, and her resultant trauma when forced to confront marital intimacy while still a teenager. This is expressed most graphically in her poem "The Maggots," which depicts figures from Hindu mythology, Krishna and Radha, making love on the riverbank: ". . .Radha felt / So dead that [Krishna] asked, What is wrong, / Do you mind my kisses, love? And she said, / No, not at all, but thought, What is / It to the corpse if the maggots nip?" (Nine Indian Women Poets 13). By humanizing Radha's sexual dissatisfaction, Das's poem legitimizes a woman's candid response to unpleasant conjugal union. The great amount of sensual imagery in her poetry embodies as well the poet's continual endeavor to satisfy her "endless female hungers."

Das's autobiography, My Story, with its titillating references and frank disclosures of sexual liaisons, became a bestseller in India. But there is little in it to fulfill the promises of the book's jacket. The prose is mediocre and contains none of the sophisticated imagery in her better poems. Das strode magisterially across the poetry horizon in India with her flamboyant public and poetic statements, but the quality of her later work is generally considered inferior, and critics have viewed her conversion to Islam and her entry into politics as publicity stunts designed to continue to keep her in the public eye when her literary reputation was flagging.

Das's English-language writing shows definite signs of "mother-tongue interference"—most notably in her frequent omission of definite articles. Whether this practice has been deliberate (to create, for instance, a distinctively Indian idiom) or merely designed to annoy the purists (as indeed it has), Das has to this day remained controversial as a writer and as a person. Indian poet and scholar Vrinda Nabar, for instance, has taken her to task for her cavalier attitude toward grammar. Nevertheless, Das has been acknowledged countrywide as a writer of national standing and was awarded the PEN Prize in 1964, the Kerala Sahitya Akademi Award for Fiction in 1969, the Chaman Lal Award for Journalism in 1971, the Asian World Prize for Literature in 1985, and the India Priyadarshini Vrikshamitra Award in 1988.

BIBLIOGRAPHY
Bhanot, Preeti. "Kamala Das." Available online. URL: www.english.emory.edu/Bahri/Das.html. Accessed on April 22, 2007.
Bhatnagar, M. K., and M. Rajeshwar. Kamala Das: A Critical Spectrum. New Delhi: Atlantic Publishers and Distributors, 2000.

De Souza, Eunice, ed. *Nine Indian Women Poets,* New Delhi: Oxford University Press, 1997.

Dwivedi, A. N. *Kamala Das and Her Poetry.* New Delhi: Atlantic Publishers and Distributors, 2000.

Haq, Kaiser. *Contemporary Indian Poetry,* Columbus: Ohio State University Press, 1990.

Kaur, Iqb l. *Perspectives on Kamala Das's Poetry.* New Delhi: Intellectual Publishing House, 1995.

Nabar, Vrinda. *The Endless Female Hungers: A Study of Kamala Das.* New Delhi: Sterling, 1994.

Mittapalli, Rajeshwar, and Pier Paolo Piciucco. *Kamala Das: A Critical Spectrum.* New Delhi: Atlantic, 2001.

Raveendran, N. V. *The Aesthetics of Sensuality: A Stylistic Study of the Poetry of Kamala Das.* New Delhi: Atlantic Publishers and Distributors, 2000.

Warrier, Shobha. Interview. Rediff on the Net. Available online. URL: http://www.rediff.com/news/1996/3107adas.htm. Accessed on April 22, 2007.

Rochelle Almeida

"DAY COOLS, THE . . ." EDITH SÖDERGRAN (1916)

This poem appeared in SÖDERGRAN's debut collection, *Dikter* (Poems), and it is perhaps the best known and most quoted of all her work. As with most of her poetry, it is written in free verse. At the time so free a prosody was highly unusual for lyrical poetry in Swedish, a language whose natural melody, tones, and cadences lend themselves to songlike verse. But Södergran found regular rhythms and end rhymes stifling. She wrote in an introductory remark to her second collection that her poems "are to be taken as careless sketches" (*Love & Solitude* xi). "The Day Cools . . ." ("*Dagen svalnar . . .*") is written as a sequence of four numbered stanzas. Each stanza serves as a separate "sketch," and the four of them together tell a story of love, lust, and loss. True to Western lyrical tradition, which dates back to the ancient Greeks, this poem features a first-person speaker, an "I" addressing a beloved, a "you." In classic lyrical poetry the "I" speaks in metaphors to describe emotions so abstract and incomprehensible that they can be communicated only via images and associations. But Södergran, whose early published work reflects the influence of French and Russian symbolist poetry, crafts her images to induce a sensual reception rather than an identifiable emotion. Unlike classical lyricists, she does not project her images onto a symbolic canvas that stands apart from the persons in the poem. For example, when the speaker of Shakespeare's famous 18th sonnet asks, "Shall I compare thee to a summer's day?" the image of the summer day takes the place of his lady love's physical form, rendering her to an abstraction so that we can perceive the speaker's idea of her. But in "The Day Cools . . . ," as in most of Södergran's poems, the speaker melds the figure of her physical body with its associated image, which results in a sensual experience as well as an emotional one. The poem begins: "The day cools toward evening . . . ," emphasizing physical sensation—a drop in temperature—rather than an image of a darkening sky. The speaker then urges her lover: "Drink the warmth from my hand, / it throbs with Spring's own blood." This image evokes both the speaker's desire to give herself physically to her lover and her close kinship—a blood relation—to the Earth. The female body's strong association with the Earth and its natural cycles is a recurring theme in Södergran's poetry. While Södergran's biographers have speculated that she wrote this poem in response to a failed love affair with a married doctor at the Davos sanatorium, feminist scholars have focused instead on the poem's unabashed presentation of a sexual, creative, and psychologically complex female speaker. The poem's stylistic innovations, arresting imagery, and distinctly female speaker have earned it an honored place in literary history. But perhaps the poem's greatest legacy is its power to reach across time and space to stir the sensual receptors of readers who have forgotten how it is to love with abandon and descend into despair.

BIBLIOGRAPHY
Södergran, Edith. *Love & Solitude: Selected Poems 1916–1923.* Translated by Stina Katchadourian. Seattle: Fjord Press, 1992.

Ursula Lindqvist

"DAYS OF 1908" CONSTANTINE P. CAVAFY (1932)

Among CONSTANTINE CAVAFY's latest compositions, "Days of 1908" ("Μερες του 1908") is one of a series of poems that name specific years in their titles and that, as such, may be called "memory poems." The tone is suggestively autobiographical, as if the vision of this poem's sublime youth is also part of the poet's own store of erotic memories. Memories are the matrix for a number of Cavafy's love poems, many of which are unabashedly and openly homoerotic. Young men—lurking anonymously in the streets of the modern metropolis (a city often taken for Alexandria, Cavafy's own birthplace and lifelong homing spot)—populate the public sphere of streets, cafés, theater, and cheap hotels in search of erotic gratification. These young men are also either socially displaced, as in "Days of 1908" (which features a working-class but "reasonably educated young man, twenty-five years old"), or entirely marginalized, as in "Days of 1896."

Cavafy's fascination with youthful male beauty is proverbial, and here, as in other poems, it initially peeps, furtively and restrained, through the seams of the poem until it sheds all veils in celebratory exhibitionism. What begins as a third-person, objective narration of a young man's toils to make ends meet by gambling and borrowing—because he "was out of work that year"—gradually slips (in the second stanza) into an indirect expression of the character's own regard for his youth and education: "He was offered a job at three pounds a month / in a small stationary store, / but he turned it down without the slightest hesitation. / It wasn't suitable. It wasn't the right pay for him." In the third stanza we are invited to sympathize with the young man's gambling exploits, as his presentation gradually acquires ominous undertones of waste and decay, subjects that are elsewhere explicitly associated with young men of his sort. Here decay is hinted at by way of metonymy; the young man's only suit, "a very faded cinnamon-brown," is in a wretched state.

Although the young man of "Days of 1908" is not explicitly in pursuit of erotic encounters, as others are, the wasting effects of his nightly pursuits are ameliorated by the cathartic effect of the concluding stanza. Its apostrophic turn ("O Summer days . . .") to summer as an omniscient voyeur brings into play the Sun's gaze upon the young man's total nakedness "at the baths and on the beach" and invokes an awareness of the young man's splendid physical beauty. That recollected moment suffuses the poem with a sense of gleaming redemption. Epiphanic in tone, the concluding stanza is a veiled affirmation of art's contention to redeem and transcend both time and place by converting memories into works of art and into celebrations of the poetic promise of immortality, just as the young man—"impeccably handsome, a miracle"—is hoisted out of the anguish of his dissolute nightlife into the sublimity of the poem's summertime light.

George Syrimis

"DEATH FUGUE" PAUL CELAN **(1947)** There is little question that "Death Fugue" ("*Todesfuge*") is PAUL CELAN's most celebrated and anthologized poem, a work that, as Sidra DeKoven Ezrahi avers, has become "as much an icon of the Holocaust as the photograph of the little boy with his hands raised in the Warsaw Ghetto." Composed during World War II and appearing in May 1947 in a Bucharest magazine (in Romanian translation) with the title "Tango of Death," it was his first published poem and the first to feature his newly crafted pen name, Celan. Today every German pupil knows the text since it is required reading in German high schools. On the 50th anniversary of Kristallnacht (November 10, 1938), the countrywide pogrom against Jews living in Germany, their homes, and their businesses, the poem was recited by Ida Ehre in the Bundestag, the lower house of the German parliament. Often quoted in art and film, it has been canonized to the extent that it is "part of the official ritual of remembrance in Germany." There is an account that Theodor Adorno, upon reading "Death Fugue," with its fusion of surreal imagery and shocking beauty, wrote his famous 1951 stricture that "to write poetry after Auschwitz is barbaric." Actually Adorno intended to translate one of Celan's volumes and, according to his editor, retracted his celebrated dictum in 1966 (in *Negative Dialectics*) after becoming better acquainted with Celan's writings. Commentators have noted that initially the poem was denounced for its aesthetic treatment of the indescribable, for being overly romantic and sublime, and for dimming the terror of the Holocaust. In the 1960s, as the poem gained monumental recognition, especially in Germany, Celan felt "Death Fugue" was being appropriated to allay national guilt. Consequently, he refused to recite the poem publicly and forbade its inclusion in anthologies.

While the poem is rich in metaphors, the particular images and occurrences it delineates are certainly based on historical fact and on accounts given by survivors. The introduction to the poem, when it was first published, made it clear that the poem's language was rooted in fact. Described by John Felstiner as "the Guernica of post-war European literature," "Death Fugue" is a meditation on the collective fate of the Jews, beginning with the recurring, haunting voice of the prisoners that opens the opus: "Black milk of daybreak we drink it at evening / we drink it at midday and morning we drink it at night / we drink it and we drink / we shovel a grave in the air." This incantatory refrain appears at the start of each of the stanzas, and is then followed by a chilling description of the inmates and the death camp commander. The sameness of the words—divested of punctuation, reformulated in different combinations and cycles—underlines the annihilation of the individual, replaced by the walking dead. At one point the "We drink it" is substituted by "We drink you," amplifying the relentless atmosphere of despair. The paradoxical and irreducible metaphor, image, and oxymoron of *black milk* combine to indicate an impossible situation. Milk—which usually provides nourishment and is a symbol of life, purity, motherhood, fertility, and innocence—is transformed into something like bile (a black, bitter liquid that devours all color and highlights the seemingly immense unspeakability of the camps). In essence the speakers are imbibing death in a warped universe that has denuded itself of the potential for growth. Also, *black milk* denotes the bitterness of confinement, which the prisoners had to bear every day. Celan specialists have observed that it is probable that inmates actually named the drink they were given "black milk."

The unidentified camp outside Germany transmits to the reader the typical monotonous drudgery of forced labor chronicled by survivors: the gangs of prisoners slaving on the brink of collapse. The usage of the first person "we" transports the reader behind the barbed wire. It is noteworthy that Celan employs the "we" (instead of "I") to refer to the victims. One could maintain that such use strives to envelope all people, not just the designated Jews of the poem, in the horror, positing that the Nazi terror could strike at all people.

Further, the unspecified, collective "we" invokes the stripping away of any trace of individuality from the internees. This use of the first-person-plural pronoun announces that Celan and the reader are inseparably bound to the events signified and to the murdered millions. The trope of the German master—who writes to his golden-haired Margarete while whistling commands to the Jews to dance as they dig their mass graves and who summarily executes his captives—encases within its signifying system manifold possible interpretations. First, the German language, as Jewish Italian Holocaust survivor Primo Levi recalls, was spoken in the camps to inmates who frequently did not understand what they were being told. Likewise, the word *master* (*Meister*) works on various levels. *Master* could refer to the mastery of the craft of industrialized extermination, as the German devolved to, or to the master of the concentration camps, or to the infamous "master race." During the poem the "master" is described addressing the Jews in the camp, ordering the victims to play music while their kin were marched into gas chambers. The tango motif alludes not only to the brisk, enchanting dance that enthralled European society during Celan's adolescence, but also to the sickening tangos the SS officers at the concentration camps near Chernivtsi, in Lemberg (now Lviv, Ukraine), and in Auschwitz would customarily order the Jewish fiddlers to play while watching their victims walk into the gas chambers or during torture and shootings. Before demolishing the camp, the entire orchestra was executed. In many cases one group of prisoners would hum nostalgic tunes while another group would dig graves. The tango theme references the European, Judeo-Christian culture of German society that had once included Jewish citizens. On still another level, the tango device is embedded within the timbre of the poem, which shimmers with a symphony of musical sounds and builds to a crescendo toward the end. The "fugue" of the title may pertain to the fugal composition in music known for its acutely structured and disciplined form, featuring an exact and monotonous conformation. At the same time the word *fugue* could denote the polyphonic, reciprocal exchange between the Nazis and their victims, present in the poem—and do so without an artful undertone of pathos, which would embellish the devastating horror of the Holocaust. The poem's metrical and lilting rhythm, especially as read by Celan, reminds us of the commandant's grotesque decree that those who dig their own graves must simultaneously dance and play. In fact, the rhythmical nature of the verse permeates the fabric.

The poem's brew of Genesis, Wagner, and the biblical Song of Songs, melded with the inferno of the camps, shatters the lyrical fabric evoked by the beautiful passages. The German woman Margarete (perhaps a lover, perhaps a spouse, to whom the SS executioner writes and of whom he dreams) embodies stereotypical Germanic traits—"Golden" blonde hair—and stands in sharp contrast to Shulamith, the winsome princess from the Song of Songs (6:13), the archetype of doomed beauty, with her ashen-colored tresses. Later in the poem Shulamith has been incinerated, reduced to ashes, evoking the dual meaning of "ashen hair." Shulamith is the all-purpose metaphor for the Jewish woman burned in the crematoria of the concentration camps. The blonde Margarete, safe in Germany, recalls the virginal and romantic beloved of Goethe's *Faust* and is the personification of German ideal womanhood. The name Margarete also calls attention to the fact that the commander of Auschwitz was reading *Faust* during his idle hours. In that regard Celan underlines the warped reality of Nazi Germany, wherein young German men, cultured enough to read fine literature and write to their girlfriends, could simultaneously shoot their compatriots (or, as the poem puts it, reaching "for the rod in his belt he swings it").

The act of "digging" appears elsewhere in the Celan canon, most obtrusively in the poem "There Was Earth in Them," which depicts Jews digging and digging, all day and all night. In that poem the Jews never praise God, do not hear anything, do not grow wise, and devise no kind of language. In "Death Fugue" the "grave in the air" points to the horrific reality that the Jews were usually not buried but cremated, their ashes rising as clouds of smoke into the sky, disappearing into air. Only in the world of the concentration camps and extermination is death conceivable as a form of release that literally allows the victims to escape the terrifying, immured oppression by entering "a grave then in the clouds there you won't lie too cramped."

The "vipers" signify evil and disease, and according to one interpretation are linked to hair. Hair—customarily the emblem of fertility, plenteousness, and sexuality—is totally obliterated here. Celan marshals prototypical elements associated with the Third Reich and its extermination machine: the hounds/dogs, the graves, the spades, the blue eyes of the commander, the autocratic ordering.

The conjoining of Margarete and Shulamith at the close of the poem, contrary to the opinion of certain readers, was not a nod by Celan to an appeasing, forgiving, placatory union between the German and the Jew, but rather a direct reflection of the abnormal state that had led to Shulamith's demise. The poem's concluding lines evince the unbridgeable gap between the Jewish tradition of the Bible and the Nazi use of Faust's Margarete. The two women, twinned at the poem's coda, remain unreconciled, as far apart as Germans and Jews were after the Third Reich sent millions of Jews to the ovens. Celan's choice—to place Shulamith in the last sentence—may reveal his desire to grant to this comely female dancer from the Song of Songs (the epitome of the Jewish beloved) the poem's last words and, thus, conclusively to deny the expurgation of Jewish identity that the Nazis so strove to accomplish.

BIBLIOGRAPHY
DeKoven Ezrahi, Sidra. *By Words Alone: The Holocaust in Literature.* Chicago: University of Chicago Press, 1980.
Felstiner, John. *Paul Celan: Poet, Survivor, Jew.* New Haven, Conn.: Yale University Press, 1995.

Dvir Abramovich

"DEDICATION" Czesław Miłosz (1945) "You whom I could not save," Czesław Miłosz implores, "Listen to me" (ll. 1–2). In classical tradition, a "dedication" is a formal act, a delineation of space in response to loss. The poet offers up Warsaw to the memory of the dead: "Here is a valley of shallow Polish rivers . . . the wind throws the screams of gulls on your grave" (ll. 10, 12). Images of this "broken city" imply severance from the larger world, as rivers are too shallow to be ferried and a bridge disappears into fog, never reaching any connecting shore. In the year before this poem was written, the Warsaw Uprising of 1943 had bathed the city in blood; when the fight ended, 85 percent of the

city had been destroyed by the Germans. Though in 1945 the larger war was ending, Miłosz uses the rhetoric of contradiction to inform the dead that their victory has been pyrrhic: "You mixed up farewell to an epoch with the beginning of a new one, / Inspiration of hatred with lyrical beauty, / Blind force with accomplished shape" (ll. 7–9).

Tradition would demand a heightened tone for ceremony, except World War II has perverted all ritual. The poet takes refuge in "simple speech" to say "I would be ashamed of another. / . . . / I speak to you with silence like a cloud or a tree" (ll. 3–5). Locating a universal language in nature is an ongoing theme of his work, yet Miłosz is also responding to the timely question, posed by philosopher Theodor Adorno, as to whether poetry could be written after the horrors of Auschwitz. Miłosz suggests that the solution to Adorno's concern lies in the "salutary" aims of poetry. In the fourth stanza the diction intensifies, as the supplicant reaffirms his identity as poet: "What is poetry which does not save / Nations or people?" (ll. 14–18). The poet's salvation is his desire for "good poetry"—poetry that has both aesthetic and moral qualities. Of this period in his life, later Miłosz would say, "I had to go back to poetry to save myself from philosophy."

But the speaker is not pure in his "dedication," either to the dead or to poetic principle. Miłosz subtly complicates the poem by resisting the siren's call to self-sacrificing devotion, which is the secondary meaning of "dedication." The speaker is haunted not by the ghosts of idealized ancestors, but instead by peers whom he knew in all their human compromises. He cannot help but remark, "What strengthened me, for you was lethal" (l. 6). The elegant closing gesture is one of appeasement, not of martyrdom: "They used to pour millet on graves or poppy seeds / To feed the dead who would come disguised as birds. / I put this book here for you, who once lived / So that you should visit us no more" (ll. 22–25). The poet knows that holocaust has, paradoxically, given life to these poems, and he feels the burden of having survived. He can only pray that the hungry dead will be content to consume the art—and not the artist.

Sandra Beasley

DEPESTRE, RENÉ (1926–   )

René Depestre—poet, novelist, essayist, and political and social activist—has been the voice of freedom for oppressed peoples of all lands, but his writings have been particularly inspirational to his fellow Haitians in their continued struggle for political and social stability. Depestre was born in 1926 in Jacmel, Haiti. He attended a Christian primary school, but when his father died in 1936, young René left his mother, two brothers, and two sisters to live with his maternal grandmother. He attended high school at the Lycée Pétion in the capital of Port-au-Prince.

In 1945 Depestre published his first collection of poetry, *Étincelles* (Sparks), at the age of 19 and was immediately noticed by high officials in the government of Haitian president Élie Lescot. Depestre and his friends Théodore Baker, Jacques-Stephen Alexis, and Gérald Bloncourt founded a weekly newspaper, *La Ruche* (The Hive), which appeared between 1945 and 1946. Both Depestre's poetry and the content of *La Ruche* were critical of the corruption of Lescot's government, and the first edition of *La Ruche* was seized, leading to a student revolt in January 1946, in which Depestre himself participated. This revolt helped topple Lescot's government, which was quickly replaced by military rule. Depestre was arrested and imprisoned but shortly thereafter received a scholarship to the Sorbonne in Paris; he was, in effect, exiled from Haiti under the guise of an academic award.

Depestre had already met Haitian writers and intellectuals in his country, such as Jean Price-Mars, Léon Laleau, and René Bélance, the latter of whom wrote a preface to Depestre's second poetry collection, *Gerbe de Sang,* in 1946. As Depestre pursued his studies in literature and political science in Paris (1946–50), he was acquainted with French surrealist poets, including ANDRÉ BRETON, as well as other writers, artists, and intellectuals from around the world. He was also involved in the bourgeoning NEGRITUDE MOVEMENT begun by poets AIMÉ CÉSAIRE (Martinique), LÉON-GONTRAN DAMAS (Guiana), LÉOPOLD SENGHOR (Senegal), and Alioune Diop (who founded the publishing house Présence Africaine). Depestre admired the movement's objective, which was to garner respect for blacks of

French colonial origin and give voice to writers of Africa and the West Indies.

Depestre participated in decolonization movements in France, which led to his expulsion from that country, and much of his life between 1950 and 1980 was spent in traveling from one country to another—sometimes by choice, more often because his political and social ideals met with disfavor by host governments. He resided in Prague until 1952, when he was expelled, and traveled to Cuba on the invitation of writer Nicolás Guillén. Ever controversial in his writings and protests, he was expelled from Cuba by Fulgencio Batista's regime. Denied asylum by France and Italy, Depestre lived in Austria, Chile, Argentina, and Brazil. After a stay in Brazil Depestre returned to Paris in 1956, where he met with other Haitian writers, such as Jacques-Stephen Alexis. He participated in the first Pan-African Congress organized by the publishing house Présence Africaine in 1956, and he contributed articles to such French magazines as *Esprit* and *Lettres françaises*. He returned to Haiti (1956–57) but refused to cooperate with the Duvalier regime and encouraged his countrymen to rebel. He was under constant surveillance during his sojourn in Haiti and eventually returned to Cuba at the invitation of world revolutionary Che Guevara. Heartened by the Cuban revolution, he involved himself in the administration of the country, serving in a variety of posts (minister of foreign relations, National Cultural Council, Radio Havana-Cuba, among others). He traveled in fulfillment of these duties (to the USSR, China, and Vietnam) and participated in the Pan-African Festival in Algiers in 1969.

Throughout his travels and his sojourn in Cuba, Depestre created a body of poetry of great renown. His best-known collection of poems (one of the few collections of his writings in English translation), *Un arc-en-ciel pour l'occident chrétien* (A Rainbow for the Christian West), was published in 1967. Its poems are a thematic blend of politics, erotica, and voodoo (the indigenous religion of Haiti)—themes common to his poetry in general. The collection expresses the poet's desire to assert his cultural and racial dignity and rid himself of the influences of European colonialism. In the opening poem, "Preface," the speaker catalogs racial prejudice and violations of black civil rights in every corner of the world—Birmingham, Alabama; Pretoria, South Africa; Europe; Africa; and the West Indies—and vows to overcome them to become "a brand new Black."

Alienated by Castro's government as of 1971, Depestre returned to Paris in 1978, where he worked as an administrator for the United Nations Educational, Scientific and Cultural Organization (UNESCO), which promotes world peace through collaboration in education and research. In 1979 he published his first novel, *Le mât de cocagne* (Festival of the Greasy Pole), and in 1980 he published the novella *Alléluia pour une femme-jardin,* which received France's highest literary honor, Le Prix Goncourt, in 1982.

Depestre left UNESCO in 1986 and devoted himself almost exclusively to writing. In 1988 he published the novel *Hadriana dans tous mes rêves* (Hadriana in All My Dreams), which evokes his youth in Haiti. The novel received lavish critical praise and numerous honors, among them the Prix du Roman (Novel Prize) from the Belgian Royal Academy of French Language and Literature. Depestre received French nationality in 1991 and continued to win honors and acclaim for his works. For his collection of poems *Anthologie personnelle* (Personal Anthology, 1993) he received the Apollinaire Prize; for the adaptation of *Festival of the Greasy Pole* for the theater, he received the Grizane Prize from Italy. In addition he received prestigious writing fellowships, such as the Guggenheim in 1995. He is the subject of a documentary film by Jean-Daniel Lafond made in Montreal, *Haïti dans tous nos rêves* (1996).

Besides his poetry and fiction Depestre has written numerous important essays on surrealism, ethnology, history, and the Negritude Movement. He lives in the village of Aude in southern France with his second wife and continues to write. His influence on world literature is immense, and his stature will likely continue to grow.

BIBLIOGRAPHY

Depestre, René. *A Rainbow for the Christian West.* Translated and introduction by Joan Dayan. Amherst: University of Massachusetts Press, 1977.

Torres-Saillant. *Caribbean Poetics: Toward an Aesthetic of West Indian Literature.* Cambridge: Cambridge University Press, 1997.

Patrick Day

"DESCRIBING A SUIT" (N.D.) (MUHAMMAD) HAFIZ IBRAHIM

One of the few poems by HAFIZ IBRAHIM available in English translation, "Describing a Suit" is an excellent illustration of Ibrahim's famed use of irony and sarcastic humor to call attention to social issues. A leader of the neoclassical movement in Arabic poetry in the early 20th century, Hafiz Ibrahim was dubbed the "Poet of the People" for championing the poor. In this poem Hafiz Ibrahim condemns social inequalities in early 20th-century Egyptian society through a comparison between his speaker's old suit and his newly purchased one. Hafiz Ibrahim begins the poem by describing his speaker's reaction to wearing his new suit: "I have a suit, blessings upon it. / I strut around in it, a superman." Unlike his old suit, in which "people I visited / Shunned me like someone quarantined by the plague," his new suit has instantly changed the public's reaction to him. Now, "[p]eople who see me think I'm grand! / My standing is that of a mayor or prince." In this materialistic society wealth equals status, and the speaker observes that "[a] gracious appearance is all [my people] love." But the poet knows that a social standing based on superficiality is precarious. Even his new suit, and for that matter, his body, will become old eventually. The poem ends with the biting statement: "A person to them is as valuable as the splendid / Rig he wears, as a brand new pair of shoes." In these concluding lines Ibrahim criticizes the nobility, who fail to see the humanity in those poorer than themselves because they value people only for the objects they can acquire. The speaker is revealed as a tragic and misguided figure in that he will never gain the respect he desires as long as respect is based on external trappings rather than internal worth. The poem's overall structure emphasizes Hafiz Ibrahim's ironic message by using an overly lofty tone and formal language to describe an ordinary commodity, thus hinting that the poem's subject is not worthy of its poetic praise.

BIBLIOGRAPHY

Allen, Roger. *An Introduction to Arabic Literature.* Cambridge: Cambridge University Press, 2000.

Badawi, M. M. *A Critical Introduction to Modern Arabic Poetry.* Cambridge: Cambridge University Press, 1975.

Hafiz Ibrahim (Muhammad). "Describing a Suit." Translated by Christopher Tingley with help from Christopher Middleton and Salma Khadra Jayyusi, in *Modern Arabic Poetry: An Anthology,* edited by Salma Khadra Jayyusi, 77–78. New York: Columbia University Press, 1987.

Emily S. Davis

"DESERT, THE: THE DIARY OF BEIRUT UNDER SIEGE, 1982" ADONIS ('ALI AHMAD SA'ID) (1985)

"The Desert" includes selections from the poetic diary of ADONIS during the Israeli invasion of Lebanon in June 1982 and the siege of Beirut. The poem is dated "June 4, 1982–Jan. 1, 1983." It is made up of 35 numbered (but not dated) stanzas in the bilingual edition *Victims of a Map.* The poetic diary also appeared in a slightly different arrangement in Adonis, *Kitab al-Hisar: Huzayran 82–Huzayran 85* (The Book of Siege: June 82–June 85), under the titles of "Sahara I" and "Sahara II." *Kitab al-Hisar* also includes prose passages about the siege, which help readers to understand the poetry with its references to shelters, power failure, and so on.

In "Desert" Adonis does not name the enemy, nor does he directly describe the carnage wrought by modern war. Instead he creates a series of snapshots of what it is like to live under such conditions. Lacking a linear narrative thread, the stanzas express—in their very structure—the fragmentation of life in violent conflicts. Adonis writes a poetic version of Pablo Picasso's *Guernica* by depicting the disjointedness of everyday life in a war zone. In a compelling image the poetic persona describes his alienation from time itself—by becoming a shadow—and says: "Daylight is a thread / Snipped by my lungs to stitch the evening." Such strange, almost surrealistic imagery matches the unspeakable horrors of war. With bombing and killing marking the cityscape, even smoke is identified with people's breath, and "Death alone has become our meeting point."

Adonis perceives the relationship between militarism and capitalism in stanza 15: "He wears Jihad uniform, struts in a mantle of ideas. / A merchant—he does not sell clothes, he sells people." This state of violent strife changes the very fabric of self and home: "The houses leave their walls / And I am / Not I." The observant eye of the poet captures beautifully and tragically how everything is touched and tarnished by war: "Only some holes known as stars / Remain in the sky."

Repetition and use of brackets mark the longer stanzas. Repetition is used for emphasis, as in stanza 29, with its incantatory "The Night descends . . ." at the beginning of each line. Yet each nocturnal descent is followed by a different bracketed scene, thus offering a variety of moments: "The night descends on the bed (the bed of the lover who never came) / . . . / The night descends (the wind whispers to the windows)."

Despite the gloomy and horrific atmosphere of this poetic diary, an inkling of hope manifests itself timidly: "The cities break up / The earth is a train of dust / Only love / knows how to marry this space." Finally, like the long night of mystics that ends in dawn, the poet wonders: "Or should I say: the road to the light begins in the forest of darkness?"

The politics of the poem—its denunciation of Israeli violence and civil war—remain a subtext. The poem itself paints the scene of physical destruction and spiritual loss that applies to all wastelands.

BIBLIOGRAPHY

Adonis. "The Desert: The Diary of Beirut Under Siege, 1982." In *Victims of a Map,* translated by Abdullah al-Udhari, 135–165. London: Al Saqi Books, 1984.
———. *Kitab al-Hisar: Huzayran 82-Huzayran 85* (The Book of Siege: June 82–June 85). Beirut: Dar al-Adab, 1985.
Khatibi, Abdelkebir. "La poésie/La guerre." *Detours d'écriture* (special issue on Adonis) 16 (1991): 235–236.
Meschonnic, Henri. "Le poéte arabe contre le chant de la langue." *Detours d'écriture* (special issue on Adonis) 16 (1991): 141–152.
Tannous, Jean. "Jadaliyyat al-nur wa'l-zil fi *Kitab al-Hisar*" (The Dialectic of Light and Shadow in the Book of Siege). *Fusul* (Special issue on Adonis) 16, no. 2 (Fall 1997): 48–55.

Ferial J. Ghazoul

DHARKER, IMTIAZ (1954–   )

Imtiaz Dharker is a poet, documentary filmmaker, and graphic artist who writes in English. Born in Lahore, Pakistan, Imtiaz arrived in Scotland as a toddler and grew up in Glasgow and the Pollokshields, a community known for its large Asian, Indian, and Pakistani community and about two miles south of the city's center. "I loved being in Scotland," she told James MacGregor. "I had a lot of very good friends at school. I found the Scots were so friendly, and I feel I am Scottish." She enrolled in Hutchesons' Girls' School and went on to earn a master's degree in English literature and philosophy from Glasgow University. While she was a university student there, she met and married her husband, Anil Dharker, and soon after they moved to his homeland, India.

Upon first arriving in Bombay, Imtiaz began developing her career as an artist and filmmaker while caring for her young family. She mounted a number of solo art exhibits of her drawings and paintings—and won, among other prizes, the Balrah Sahni Award for Art in 1992. She is the producer of over 200 documentary films, some of them for world organizations including UNICEF and CRY; she has won a number of prestigious awards for her cinematography, too, including the Silver Lotus for Best Short Film (in 1980).

Dharker's poetry revolves around the themes of borders and of movements across them. Often her poems focus on language and the problems and insights arising from its usage (especially the ramifications of a fear-fraught diction) and the search for freedom in alien places where politics and cultural conflicts mediate one's experience of others and the world.

The poems in *Purdah and Other Poems* explore selfhood as a veiled ontology (or theory of existence), suggesting, as in "PURDAH, 1," subtle and shifting psychological states of being. Arundhathi Subramaniam has commented that the poems in this collection discover "a somewhat interior politics by probing the multiple resonances of the veil" and explore "the subtle interplay of advance and retreat across 'the borderline of skin.'" The poems in *Postcards from God*—for instance, "NO-MAN'S LAND"—are much more overt, political, and angry even as they retain a spiritual core of firm, feminist self-confidence. In *I Speak for the Devil* (2001), Dharker explores human vulnerabilities through what Tishani Doshi has called the poet's process of "peeling away, coming undone, making and unmaking, putting together again. . . . Always, there's the effort to get at what's underneath; tear away the cloaks, the veils, the skin, the parts that can be stitched on, ripped off, traded, worshipped." Dharker told James MacGregor that *I Speak for the Devil* is "about growing up in Scotland, about walking out of your house into another country."

Dharker's books proffer a sequence of radii, and the poetic geography has widened with each successive work. Bruce King has called her poetry "consciously feminist, consciously political, consciously that of a multiple outsider, someone who knows her own mind, rather than someone full of doubt and liberal ironies" (quoted in Subramaniam). As Subramaniam put it, "The landscapes of the self" in *Purdah,* for example, are enlarged in Dharker's treatments of "the metro and the country" in *Postcards,* but her poems' concerns "expand to embrace the world" in *I Speak.* Darkher herself has provided another iconography—a Sufi-like metaphysics—to describe her poetic trajectory: "If the starting point of *Purdah* was life behind the veil, the starting-point of the new book [*I Speak*] is the strip-tease, about what happens when the self 'squeezes past the easy cage of bone.'"

Dharker lives and works in Bombay with her husband. They have a daughter, Ayesha Dharker, a talented, internationally known movie actress who has performed prominent roles in *Star Wars* films. Dharker continues to visit Scotland; she participated in and read her work at the Edinburgh Arts Festival in August 1999.

BIBLIOGRAPHY
Dharker, Imtiaz. *Purdah and Other Poems.* Delhi: Oxford University Press/India, 1989.
———. *Postcards from God.* Delhi: Viking/Penguin, 1994; Bloodaxe Books, 1997.
———. *I Speak for the Devil.* Bloodaxe Books, 2001; Delhi: Penguin Books/India, 2003.
Doshi, Tishani. "Squatter-speak." In *The Hindu.* Available online. URL: http://www.hindu.com/lr/2004/05/02/stories/2004050200300500.htm. Accessed on May 2, 2004.
MacGregor, James. "Jamilla Driven by Scottish Work Ethic." Online at Netribution. Available online. URL: http://www.netribution.co.uk/news/northern_exposure/68/4.html. Accessed on May 25, 2001.
Pinto, Jerry. "Imtiaz Unbound." India Poetry International Web. Available online. URL: http://india.poetryinternationalweb.org/piw_cms/cms/cms_module/index.php?cwolk_id=23257 &x=1. Accessed on April 22, 2007.
Subramaniam, Arundhathi. "Imtiaz Dharker." Poetry International Web. Available online. URL: http://india.poetryinternationalweb.org/piw_cms/cms/cms_module/index.php?obj_id=23260. Accessed on April 22, 2007.

R. Victoria Arana

DHOMHNAILL, NUALA NÍ (1952–)
Nuala Ní Dhomhnaill is the most highly acclaimed poet writing in Irish today. Her renown has spread far beyond her native shores by means of bilingual collections that have made her work accessible to a wide readership of non-Irish-language speakers. The poet can be considered as a preserver of both her near-extinct native tongue and its concomitant poetic tradition and rich cultural heritage. At the same time she is a poetic innovator in that she combines native Irish folk traditions and poetic genres with a modern awareness of social reality and contemporary life in Ireland. In her work motifs from Celtic folklore and myth are often juxtaposed or complemented with women's experiences that have been marginalized, omitted, or distorted in traditional renderings. Her œuvre thus opens up a revisionary and often iconoclastic perspective on prevalent national, mythological, and religious representations of femininity. In this respect her work, despite its rootedness in Irish, is in line with the tradition of feminist myth revision as practiced by the Japanese YOSANO AKIKO, the Persian FORUGH FARROKHZAD, and the Anglo-American poets Sylvia Plath and Adrienne Rich.

Dhomhnaill was born to Irish parents, both doctors, in Lancashire, England, in 1952. When she was five years old her family returned to Ireland, and Nuala grew up with relatives in the West Kerry Gaeltacht (Irish speaking district), one of the few remaining areas where Irish is spoken as a first language. From 1969 to 1973 she studied English and Irish at University College Cork, where she met her future husband, Dogan Leflef, a Turkish geologist. She joined the Irish-language poetry group Innti (In Her) and published her first poems in various magazines. In 1973 she left Ireland, following her husband to Holland and then to Turkey, where she lived for seven years and gave birth to two of her four children. In 1980 homesickness for the Irish language and the rural community she had experienced as a child made her return to Ireland. She was joined by her husband, and the family moved to a Dublin suburb, where they have lived since.

Dhomhnaill's first volume of poetry in Irish, *An Dealg Droighin* (The Sloe Thorn, 1981), appeared one year after her return to Ireland and was followed by three further collections in Irish, *Féar Suaithinseach* (Amazing Grass, 1984), *Feis* (Festival, 1991), and *Cead Aighnis* (Leave to Speak, 1998). Dhomhnaill has repeatedly emphasized the disillusionment and depression she suffered in the years subsequent to her return, both of which are reflected in her poetry. In an interview (1986) she talks of her sense of being invisible in her own country, claiming to suffer a "double bout of it because of being a woman and writing in Irish" (Cronin 5). Almost 20 years later, however, she has not only "become the most articulate and prominent of poets in Irish" but also "one of the most visible poets in Ireland today" (Denman 253). Her four bilingual collections to have appeared in print so far are *Selected Poems: Rogha Dánta* (Raven's Arts Press, 1986), *Pharaoh's Daughter* (Gallery, 1990), *The Astrakhan Cloak* (Gallery, 1992), and *The Water Horse* (Gallery, 1998). These collections display her impressive "range of translators that reads almost like a 'Who's Who' of contemporary Irish poetry" (Denman 253), including internationally renowned poets Michael Hartnett, Paul Muldoon, Medbh McGuckian, and Seamus Heaney. Dhomhnaill has received numerous awards—for instance, the 1988 O'Shaughnessy Award for Poetry and the 1991 American Ireland Fund Literary Award. From 2001 to 2004 she was Ireland professor of poetry.

Dhomhnaill's familiarity with Irish folklore and myth provides her with an imaginative framework within which to deal with issues as diverse as female sexuality and desire, love, motherhood, depression, death, language and culture loss, and migration (see "MARVELLOUS GRASS"). In this frame of reference, the Celtic otherworld serves as a paradigm for the unconscious as well as for all that has been marginalized or repressed in the dominant discourse, not least of all women's (internal) worlds, voices, and experiences. Accordingly, rather than simply adopting the traditional motifs and stories, she adapts, revises, and updates them in crucial and often humorous ways. By endowing her contemporary female speakers with an authority rooted in pre-Christian and prenationalist matriarchal traditions, the poet, moreover, revises the nationalist allegory of Ireland as a woman, which permeates the Irish poetic tradition and has resulted in two-dimensional and stereotypical representations of virginal maidens and sacrificial mothers. While the subtle nuances of the Irish language are at times difficult to retain in English translations, the poet's iconoclastic, at times bawdy humor, her biting irony, as well as her vitality come across, particularly in the congenial translations by Paul Muldoon (*The Astrakhan Cloak*) and Medbh McGuckian (*The Water Horse*).

BIBLIOGRAPHY

Cronin, Michael. "Making the Millennium: An Interview with Nuala Ní Dhomhnaill." *Graph* 1 (1986): 5–9.

Denman, Peter. "Rude Gestures? Contemporary Women's Poetry in Irish." *Colby Quarterly* 28, no. 4 (1992): 251–259.

Haberstroh, Patricia Boyle. *Women Creating Women: Contemporary Irish Women Poets.* Dublin: Attic Press, 1996.

O'Connor, Mary. "Lashings of the Mother Tongue: Nuala Ní Dhomhnaill's Anarchic Laughter." *The Comic Tradition in Irish Women Writers,* edited by Theresa O'Connor. Gainesville: University Press of Florida, 1992, 149–170.

Schrage-Früh, Michaela. *Emerging Identities: Myth, Nation and Gender in the Poetry of Eavan Boland, Nuala Ní Dhomhnaill and Medbh McGuckian.* Trier, Germany: WVT, 2004.

Michaela Schrage-Früh

"DIARY OF A PALESTINIAN WOUND"

MAHMUD DARWISH (1969) In the original Arabic of this poem by MAHMUD DARWISH, there are 24 numbered stanzas representing the journal of a "wound," specifically Palestinian. It is the diary of the violated and wounded, of the dispossessed and occupied. "Wound" here is a synecdoche for the wounded: The part stands for the whole. The poem is addressed to a woman, the Palestinian poet FADWA TUQAN, who had written a bittersweet poem in the aftermath of the resounding defeat of Arab armies in the 1967 Six-Day War with Israel. Ironically, the victory of Israel—and its occupation of Arab lands including the West Bank—made it possible for Palestinians to write albeit under Israeli subjugation. The English translation by

Lena Jayyusi and Christopher Middleton renders only 11 of the stanzas into English, but they preserve the tone of the original.

Despite the defeat of the regular Arab armies, and possibly because of the defeat and the occupation of the Palestinian lands invaded by Israel, a resistance movement came into being in the aftermath of that war during the late 1960s. Palestinian fighters were willing to sacrifice their lives for their homeland, and they engaged in combat. The French writer Jean Genet visited Palestinian camps about that time and wrote *Le captif amoureux* (Prisoner of Love), portraying the guerrilla warfare the Palestinians were waging to gain their national rights.

The poem is an apostrophe, a poetic address to an absent Fadwa Tuqan, whom the poet refers to as "sister." The poem promises steadfastness while admitting of the Palestinian tragedy. It uses motifs of sacrifice and redemption, of martyrdom and resurrection, echoing the best-known Palestinian who died on the cross to save the world—Jesus Christ—without naming him.

In stanza 1 the poet assures his addressee that there is no need to remember Palestine as Palestine has become one with the Palestinians: "Mount Carmel is in us / and our eyelashes the grass of Galilee." Here Darwish responds to Tuqan's poem in which she evoked the memory of beloved ones in the manner associated with classical Arabic poetry. The poet assures his interlocutor—who had addressed her poem "Lan abki" (I Shall Not Cry) to Palestinian poets of resistance—that captivity under occupation has not broken them: "Before June we were not fledgling doves / so our love did not wither in bondage." On the contrary, the poet asserts, it is precisely this captivity that brought about reversals and transformations. Martyrdom was turned into a feast and songs have became weapons: "And we came to know what makes the voice of the nightingale / a dagger shining in the face of the invaders. / We came to know what makes the silence of the graveyard / a festival . . . orchids of life."

Stanza 14 is one of the most cited verse lines of Darwish. It takes a stand against leaving one's country and treating it like a commodity that one can take with him or her. Darwish asserts the love bonds with the homeland:

Ah my intractable wound!
My country is not a suitcase
I am not a traveler
I am the lover and the land is the beloved.

The poet ends his poem by contrasting what the occupying forces strive for and what the Palestinian poet does. The enemy fabricates false archaeological claims to exclude the Palestinians from their historical land. The Palestinian poet, however, counters these claims by planting trees and singing of his love to his country. While history is falsified by myths of exclusivity, the Palestinians express their devotion to their homeland in cultivating it and singing for it.

BIBLIOGRAPHY
Abou-Bakr, Randa. "The Dialectics of Emergence and Withdrawal: Pre-Exile Phase." *The Conflict of Voices in the Poetry of Dennis Brutus and Mahmud Darwish.* Wiesbaden, Germany: Reichert Verlag, 2004, 21–54.
Darwish, Mahmud. "Yawmiyyat jurh falastini." *Diwan Mahmud Darwish.* Vol. 1. Beirut: Dar al-ʿAwda, 1979, 524–562.
———. "Diary of a Palestinian Wound." In *Modern Arabic Poetry: An Anthology,* edited by Salma K. Jayyusi, 200–202. New York: Columbia University Press, 1987.
Tuqan, Fadwa. *"Lan abki." Al-Layl wa'l-fursan.* Beirut: Dar al-Adab, 1969, 48–56.

Ferial J. Ghazoul

DIEGO, GERARDO (1896–1987)

Gerardo Diego's career can be considered one of the most heterogeneous and prolific in the history of modern Spanish literature. Born in 1896 in Santander, the young poet studied philosophy and letters at the University of Deusto, where he became close friends with author Juan Larrea. After having performed brilliantly on his examinations, first in Salamanca under Miguel de Unamuno, then in Madrid with Menéndez Pidal and Américo Castro, he published his early poetry and prose articles in some of the most significant avant-garde journals of the day: *Ultra, Cervantes, Grecia,* and *Reflector.* An important yet distant participant in the avant-garde movement *ultraísmo* between 1918 and 1919, he soon became allied with Chilean poet VICENTE HUIDOBRO's cubist-inspired *creacionismo*—in great part as a result of his correspondence with fellow poet Larrea. But even following Diego's visit to Huidobro in Paris in 1922 and his subsequent familiarity with the cubism of Juan Gris, Fernand Léger, and María Blanchard, Diego firmly maintained his independence from Huidobro and orthodox *creacionismo*—as from *ultraísmo*. In spite of his involvement with *ultraísmo* and *creacionismo,* he treats such typically 20th-century topics as cultural memory and modernization's transformation of time and space in a way radically different from that of his peers in the Spanish avant-garde. *Imagen* (Image, 1922) and *Manual de espumas* (Guide to Foam, 1924) express not only a vanguard taste for experimentalism, but also the powerful desire for existential reorientation and belonging characteristic of modernism. A lyrical tone of remembrance emanates from the exaggerated representation of sensation and perception—the very techniques that locate *Imagen* and *Manual de espumas* within the avant-garde.

Throughout his lengthy career Diego maintained a balance between avant-garde poetics and the articulation of subjectivity and human experience through the musicality of his poetry. The product of a lifelong devotion to the piano and such modern composers as Claude Debussy and Manuel de Falla, Diego's musical lyricism sets the tone for much of *Imagen,* the essential humanism of *Versos humanos* (Human Verses, 1925), and the later collections *Ofrenda a Chopin, 1918–1962* (Tribute to Chopin, 1918–62, 1969), *La fundación del querer* (The Foundation of Love, 1970), and *Cemeterio Civil* (Civil Cemetery, 1972). Just as the lyric tenor of *Imagen* and *Manual de espumas* does not negate the fundamental vanguardism of these early collections, Diego's avant-garde sensibility does not disappear with his eventual return to humanism and classical poetic forms. Even after the appearance of *Versos humanos* in 1925, for which Diego was awarded the National Literature Prize, some of his work continued to evince an avant-garde sensibility; particularly inclined toward the plastic and perceptual poetics of his earlier work are *Poemas adrede* (Deliberate Poems) and *Fábula de equis y zeda* (Fable of *X* and *Z*), both published in 1932. Diego's heterogeneous body of work includes a marked Christian strain—*Viacrucis* (Way of the Cross, 1931), *Ángeles de Compostela. Poema* (Angels of Compostela,

1940); the Spanish taste for landscape—*Soria. Galería de estampas y efusiones* (Soria, Gallery of Postcards and Effusions, 1923), *El jándalo* (Returned from Andalusia, 1964), and *Soria sucedida* (*Soria* Succeeded, 1977); and a tendency to incorporate the techniques and qualities of the popular lyric.

Apart from his lifelong devotion to poetry, Diego gave an extraordinary number of piano recitals featuring both of the lyric arts. He also wrote prolifically on a wide range of topics in Spanish culture for the press, including José Ortega y Gasset's *Revista de occidente, litoral,* his own journal *Carmen* and its supplement *Lola,* and the newspapers *ABC* and *Arriba.* He also created commentaries for the radio program *Panorama Poético Español.* Diego mixed his prodigious scholarship of classic Spanish literature together with active knowledge of the avant-garde. His role in the 1927 centenary of Luis de Góngora, in honor of which he also published his *Antología poética en honor de Góngora* (Poetic Anthology in Honor of Gongora, 1927), confirms this tendency toward cultural and literary syncretism. Apart from his output as poet and cultural critic, Diego remained a committed pedagogue and academic from the award of a doctorate 1916, after which he held professorships at secondary schools in Gijón, Soria, Santander, and Madrid; through his election to the Royal Spanish Academy in 1947; and beyond. Diego's highly influential *Antología. Poesía española 1915–1931* (1932) and its sequel, *Poesía española. Antología* (Contemporáneos, 1934), inscribed the first Spanish avant-garde of *ultraísmo* and *creacionismo* and the later "Generation of 1927" into the history of Spanish letters. Diego's several anthologies and autoanthologies carried enormous weight in Spanish educational and cultural institutions for over half a century. During the latter part of his life and after his death in 1987, Diego was the subject of notable homages and exhibitions, as well as having been the 1980 recipient of the prestigious Miguel de Cervantes Prize.

BIBLIOGRAPHY

Diego, Gerardo. *Songs and Sonnets of Love Still Innocent: A Representative Anthology of the Poetry of Gerardo Diego.* Translated by Carl W. Cobb. University of Mississippi, Oxford: Romance Monographs, 1997. (This bilingual volume focuses on the theme of love in Diego's poetry. It includes "El ciprés de silos" [The Cypress at Silos Monastery]—the best-known poem from the corpus of his work—and examples from Diego's major collections and anthologies.)

Harris, Derek, ed. *The Spanish Avant-garde.* Manchester, U.K., and New York: Manchester University Press, 1995.

Renée M. Silverman

DIOP, DAVID (1927–1960)   David Mandessi Diop occupies an important place in modern African poetry. Although his only collection is made up of 22 poems and his career as a poet was abruptly terminated in an air crash, his work enjoys a great deal of privilege because of the unique consciousness that it expresses. This originality explains why his poems are featured in most anthologies of modern African poetry. Diop is generally identified with Negritude, a cultural and political philosophy that LÉOPOLD SÉDAR SENGHOR, AIMÉ CÉSAIRE, LÉON DAMAS, and others propagated in their student days in France in the 1930s. Although Diop was not among those who originated the NEGRITUDE MOVEMENT, his own work has come to be seen as expressing this consciousness in a way that it invites comparison with Senghor's poetry. Negritude celebrates the African cultural heritage, redefines the black identity, and negates the misrepresentation of Africa, its people, and their values. It is associated with a segment of the educated elite in Francophone Africa and the West Indies. Negritude is best understood as a logical response to the French colonial policy of assimilation, a policy that disregarded every form of indigenous cultural expression among the colonized and suggested that they should rather aspire to supposedly ennobling European values. Negritude set out to inspire pride in black people about themselves, and poetry has frequently been a medium for propagating it.

It is possible to understand Diop's attitude to Negritude only in relation to his vision of Africa, which is also a product of his personal experience. Born in 1927 in Bordeaux, France, of a Senegalese father and a Cameroonian mother, he based his knowledge of Africa for a long time only on information from others. He started writing while in school, and his poems were anthologized in Senghor's *Anthologie de la poésie nègre et malgache* (1948). He read Aimé Césaire's *Cahier d'un retour au pays natal* (NOTEBOOK OF A RETURN TO THE NATIVE LAND), and his own poems also appeared in *Présence Africaine,* a periodical devoted to promoting African letters in France. Diop did not go to Africa until 1950 but had earnestly desired to visit the continent earlier. He participated in the building of modern Senegal, though he did not enjoy sound health. He died with his wife in an air crash near Dakar in 1960 at the tragically young age of 33. His only book of poems, *Coups de pillon,* preserves his poetic achievement and has since been translated and published as *Hammer Blows.*

Diop's vision of Africa permeates his work, and there is a sense in which all his poems articulate a common consciousness. He exhibits an incredible sense of attachment to Africa and rejects every outlook on the continent that accommodates any of the prejudices of Europeans about Africa and its people. This outlook probably explains why he attributes most of the woes of the continent to the colonial experience. The period before the colonial encounter consistently emerges in his poetic imagination as the glorious era in the African experience. The Africa that one encounters in his poetry is precolonial, without the artificial nations and borders imposed by the colonizing powers. The fact that Diop did not see the need to reconcile with Europe has often prompted critics to view his work as providing a contrast to the poetry of Senghor, the poet-politician whose writings advocated harmony, reconciliation, and the blending of values between Europe and Africa. On the contrary, in Diop's work anger is the enabling energy, and his poetry represents the contact with Europe as devastating. He constantly decries the violence visited on Africans through slavery and the colonial engagement, but he equally projects an optimistic vision for the continent. Decrying the polluting effects of European culture, Diop's poetry promotes African solidarity. This vision of restoration animates his poems, whose typical structure recognizes three historical epochs in the African experience—a glorious past, the dark era of colonial domination, and the future with all the promise of restoration. This strong emphasis, in a sense, makes Diop's work one that vigorously engages the European distortion of African history. But he generally appeals to his imagination to reconstruct his own rendering of historical experiences.

BIBLIOGRAPHY

Brodesky, Richard. "Poetry and History in David Diop's *Coups de Pilon.*" *South Atlantic Bulletin* 39, no. 4 (Nov. 1974), 121–125.

Diop, David. *Hammer Blows and Other Writings* (bilingual edition). Translated and edited by Simon Mpondo and Frank Jones. Bloomington: Indiana University Press, 1973.

Egudu, Romanus. *Modern African Poetry and the African Predicament.* New York: Harper and Row, 1980.

Fraser, Robert. *West African Poetry: A Critical History.* London and New York: Cambridge University Press, 1986.

Oyeniyi Okunoye

"DIS NIGERIA SEF" Kenule (Ken) Saro-Wiwa (1977)

"Dis Nigeria Sef" is the longest poem in Ken Saro-Wiwa's *Songs in a Time of War.* This poem does not belong among the war poems; the writer acknowledges in one of his memoirs that it was written in 1977, long after the cessation of hostilities. Frank and dispassionate, the poem is important because it reveals a clear assessment of the Nigerian condition. It is the passionate outburst of a patriot who at once decries the stagnation of a cherished land and inscribes positive aspects of the Nigerian identity. This speaker believes that Nigeria is a place where nothing works—and still will not give a thought to denouncing the country.

A deceptively simple poem, "Dis Nigeria Sef" runs to 276 lines. The first 178 lines graphically depict the apparent failure of Nigeria due not just to the visionlessness of its leaders, but to the collective lack of will to transform the country. The speaker blames the state of the country on the attitudes and dispositions of its people. In the remainder of the poem, the speaker admits that there are things worthy of celebration: the uniqueness of the Nigerian state and its potentials for greatness. The poem reveals the vision of transformation that the persona nurses for his land while admitting that many aspects of the Nigerian experience are disgusting and unacceptable. In sum the poem urgently advocates adopting the desirable aspects of modernity and calls for a national reorientation to transform Nigeria.

"Dis Nigeria Sef" succeeds as poetic utterance largely because its subject influences its techniques. The fact that the poet uses Pidgin English as opposed to standard English is important. Pidgin English has become a popular medium in Nigerian life and is an effective tool for the comic and satirical. The poem effectively uses pidgin expressions that many Nigerians are familiar with to evoke a familiar reality.

This rhetorical stratagem thus maximizes the poem's potential for mass appeal. The division of the poem in two parts also creates a sense of balance in the way Nigeria is represented. This sense of balance comes from the way the patriotic zeal of the persona emerges from an objective portrait of Nigeria. The fact that no fewer than 30 of the 31 rhetorical questions that occur in the poem are found in the first part intensifies the crucial sense of indignation that is predominant in it.

Oyeniyi Okunoye

DOG WOMAN Chris Abani (2004)

One of Chris Abani's several books of poetry, *Dog Woman* is a series of persona poems (poems voiced through characters other than the poet) employing the conventions of language poetry and elegy to explore the intersection of race, gender, and memory. It is not so well known as *Kalakuta Republic,* his book of prison poems, but it is his most ambitious book and among the few volumes of poetry that explore patriarchy from a male perspective.

Abani describes this volume as a "vision quest into one soul" (11), an attempt by a male poet to explore the ways in which masculinity is formed on the terrain of women. The problem he attempts to surmount is that "men have no language for it— / The suffering of others" (82). Searching for such a language, he creates a palimpsest of Igbo proverbs, Catholic liturgy, classical myths, pop culture references, Spanish phrases, and quotes from modern poets through which the ghosts of the "dark women of history" speak (17). Many of the poems are testimonials about the women's death at the hands of men, songs each woman makes to history because "someone / in some future time / will think of us" (33). At the same time the women rise through the cage of Abani's language to question his own participation in patriarchy and to evade his attempts to reviolate them by reinvoking them. "I am a ghost / made by your shame" (54), they say to him. "This is what men are like" (53), the poet agrees, and "Guilt can never be enough" (81). In this sense, he acknowledges, these poems are more about men "which we become by defining how / we are not women" (80). Their voices tangle in the poems, sometimes the poet's, sometimes the women's (often in gray type), as the women unstitch the poet's attempt to speak for them. He concludes, "This is not my story—I shouldn't tell it—these cannot be my words. / Still: . . . / This is everybody's story—we must tell it" (91).

Wendy Belcher

DOMIN, HILDE (1909–2006)

Hilde Domin did not start writing poetry until age 42. She had left Germany in 1932, emigrating first to Italy, then to England, and in 1940 to the Dominican Republic. Despite this exile, the German language remained her home and eventually suggested both a literary career and in 1954 a return to Germany. Domin's first contact with literary modernism had been through Spanish and Latin American authors. Her husband, the art historian Erwin Walter Palm, translated a substantial number of poems from Hispanic classical modernity into German (collected in *Rose Risen from Ashes [Rose aus Asche]*, 1955). Domin herself later translated poems by UNGARETTI and others. She had studied law, sociology, and philosophy and in 1935 completed a doctorate on Renaissance political thought at the University of Florence.

Exile provided Domin with a sense of the fragility of human existence, the importance of memory and vision, and the irreplaceable role of one's mother tongue. But as she reminds her readers, German is also the language of the victims and survivors of World War II, and she declared her love of the German language and of her German *Heimat* (home, sphere of authentic spiritual comfort) even at times when it was unpopular to do so. Domin is now considered the poetic voice of *Rückkehr* (Hans-Georg Gadamer), of return from exile. In the face of Auschwitz, Beirut, and Vietnam, Domin saw a growing need for a poetry that facilitates conciliatory communication. She insisted on the ability of poetry to express appropriately what needs to be said to society or to oneself. Her philosophy of *Dennoch* (and yet, however) makes a case for trust and dialogue and expresses the hope that humankind will improve. Biblical and mythological imagery,

employed with respect yet often questioned, points out possible directions along such a road.

Domin's political (public) poems are concerned with the growing indifference of modern society toward injustice, environmental degradation, and war and with the media's failure to reflect adequately the challenges of these developments. She sees a rivalry between television and poetry: Poetic language is superior because it is dialogical and sharpens readers' sensitivity toward contemporary situations that claim their attention and that can be ameliorated, yet that the media present as remote and hopeless. The language of poetry can be honest and accurate but is not precise in the scientific sense. The poem is seen as a basic commodity. It allows readers to consider their position, to see what is *"menschlich"* (human and humane), and to think of solutions to contemporary problems. The use of a rhetorical device known as *zeugma,* where the grammatical status of a phrase is left ambiguous, mirrors this on a linguistic level. Domin's poetry is addressed to individuals because they represent the future of their society. Poetry opens up a sphere of freedom of thought, perception, and action. Even when insisting on its own autonomy, it remains engaged with the public sphere as a voice that can be heard.

The language of Domin's poetry is comprehensible and invites a response or reaction. She employs closely connected concepts and images. Her lines are generally short, pointing at the unsaid, especially in her most laconic volume, *Here (Hier,* 1964). Rhythms are seldom regular but always audible, often adding to the poignancy and urgency of a poem's message, as in her paradoxically light poem "ONLY A ROSE AS SUPPORT." Devices from classical rhetoric (inversions, variations, paradox) are used frequently but unobtrusively.

Periods of intense poetic production in Domin's creative life were followed by times of reflection and poetological statements. Her anthology *Double Interpretations (Doppelinterpretationen),* combining interpretations of poems by their author and a critic, is an eloquent endorsement of both modern poetry and criticism. After 1987 Domin edited three volumes of her work—collected poems, autobiographical writing, and essays—and was ready to comment on her own work during her frequent public appearances, in interviews, and in published interpretations. She consistently took a special interest in young audiences.

Hilde Domin was awarded, among many other prizes, the Heine-Plakette (1972), the Rilke-Preis (1976), the Großes Bundesverdienstkreuz (1994), and the Konrad-Adenauer-Stiftung prize for literature (1995). She died in 2006.

BIBLIOGRAPHY

Kafatou, Sarah. "About Hilde Domin." *Harvard Review* 7 (1994): 143–146.

Stern, Dagmar C. *Hilde Domin. From Exile to Ideal.* Bern: Peter Lang, 1979.

Stern, Guy. "In Quest of a Regained Paradise. The Theme of Return in the Works of Hilde Domin." *Germanic Review* 3 (1987): 136–142.

Van D'Elden, Karl H. "Interview with Hilde Domin." *West German Poets on Society and Politics. Interviews with Karl Van D'Elden.* Detroit: Wayne State University Press, 1979, 80–91.

Christophe Fricker

"DON'T ASK ME FOR THAT LOVE AGAIN" FAIZ AHMED FAIZ (1941)

This most famous poem of FAIZ AHMED FAIZ (*Mujh Se Pheli Si Muhabbat*) appears in his collection *Naqsh-e-Faryadi* (The Picture of a Dissenter), published in 1941, the year that Faiz married Alys George, an English journalist and human rights campaigner whom he had met in the late 1930s. Alys would have fully understood the sentiments expressed in "Don't Ask Me for That Love Again," a love poem with a difference in that it celebrates the innocent nature of first love and shows how life (especially anguish caused by brutal injustice) transforms one's understanding of the meaning of that emotion. Like Faiz, Alys was a political radical. The activist daughter of a London bookseller, she joined the Communist Party when she was 16 and traveled as a journalist to India in 1938, when she was 23. Upon marrying Faiz the 26-year-old Alys converted to Islam and eventually became a Pakistani citizen. Her marriage to Faiz lasted to the end of his life. They had two daughters and many grandchildren. Because the poem is a paean to true love of various sorts, the background of Faiz's relationship to Alys is relevant here.

The poem is composed of two stanzas, the first of 10 lines, the second of 14. The first stanza begins, as the title does, with the exhortation "That which then was ours, my love, / don't ask me for that love again" (ll.1–2). "That love" is then described as wondrous, golden, "burnished with light—/ and only because of you." When he was in the flush of that miraculous rapture, the only sorrows for which he could weep were, the poet confesses, his lover's sorrows since it was impossible to believe that there could be any other sorrows in the world worth considering. The poet's life was all bliss and possibility since "A glimpse of [the lover's] face was evidence of springtime." In the throes of this obsessive passion, the poet recalls that even the sky "was nothing but [his lover's] eyes" (l. 9). The stanza ends with the poet's remembering his feelings then and his aspiration: if he might win her love, "Fate would be helpless" (l.10).

The second stanza shifts tone abruptly in its first line: "All this I'd thought, all this I'd believed" (l.11). The poet now acknowledges the existence of "other sorrows" and of "comforts other than love" (l.12). The rest of the stanza conveys sharply his realization that whole "dark centuries" can be blamed on "the rich" and their greed for material possessions, like "brocades and silks." The next seven lines develop the conceit of history as a brocade whose threads unravel symbolically when the poet sees the poverty "in alleys and in open markets" and the bloody deaths all around him, not to mention the long history of slavery, during which human beings, too, were "sold and bought, again and again." The picture of the present is not a pleasant one, and "This too deserves attention," he affirms. Returning from the alleys of current political reality, the poet almost does not know what to say to his lover—"you still are so ravishing—what should I do?" The poem ends with an echo of the sentiments that "there are other sorrows" and "other comforts" and that his lover should not ask the still-loving poet "for that [first] love again."

"Don't Ask Me for That Love Again" is one of Faiz's most celebrated and beloved poems because it combines the two talents for which he is most famous: his ability to evoke luminous, romantic emotions through intimate revelation and to proclaim precisely and sharply the need for a clear understanding of the injustices and crimes of the rich and powerful against their most vulnerable victims, the poor, injured human beings with whom they have dealt so unmercifully and unlovingly through the ages.

The poem has been translated into many languages and into English by many poets, among them Agha Shahid Ali. Faiz recorded the poem in Urdu for the Library of Congress. It can be heard at http://audiopoetry. wordpress.com/tag/poet/faiz-ahmedfaiz/. It is included in many anthologies, among them J. D. McClatchy's *The Vintage Book of Contemporary World Poetry* (1996), pages 335–336.

R. Victoria Arana

DREAM GRASS YVAN GOLL (1951) YVAN GOLL's
Dream Grass (Traumkraut) celebrates the poet's love for his wife, Claire. The emotional pitch of the collection, published a year after his death, reflects the trauma of the poet's struggle with leukemia, which took his life in 1950. Images combine a surreal exuberance with expressionistic urgency. "Dreamgrass grew / Nightshade lovepale" (*"Das Traumkraut wuchs / Nachtfarben liebesfahl"*) reads the title poem, with a hint of the mysticism sometimes found in Goll's imagery. Goll was bilingual, writing in French and German but choosing French throughout most of his career; he returned to the German of his childhood as he approached death. The poems of *Dream Grass* employ figures associated with the earliest Germanic poetry, for instance, the kenning "bonehouse" in the lines "Home to my ancestors / This tottering bonehouse / Built on sand" (*"Behausung meiner Ahnen / Dies schwanke Knochenhaus / Auf Sand gebaut"*). To Goll, the world of his dying, in "The Sacred Body" (*"Der heilige Leib"*), is nonetheless a Godless universe, the universe of expressionistic anguish over modern alienation from sacred sources of meaning. Restless to live therefore in the celebration of his love, the poet finds catharsis in the passionate expression of his feelings. His lover is both seductress and death mother in a plummeting of the mythic subconscious typical of Goll's strongest imagery: "In your eyes trout speed / And lightning bolts drown" (*"In deinen Augen schnellen Forellen / Und erlöschen die Blitze"*) (*"To Liane, Strassburg, October*

29, 1948") (*"An Liane, Strasbourg, 29 Oktober 1948"*). Even close to death, happiness lies in devotion to the one with whom one is most deeply connected. Perfection of soul lies in acts of love—for instance, in the building of a "Rain Palace" (*"Der Regenpalast"*) or a "House of Embers" (*"Die Hütte aus Asche"*), two of the most notable poems from the last pages of the collection. The latter poem closes with an image of the beloved's body, phoenixlike, transformed, "Your golden body gleaming like the nightly sun" (*"Dein goldener Leib erstrahlte als nächtliche Sonne"*).

Dream Grass and *Neila,* a posthumous companion volume of lyrics, are well represented in the English *Selected Poems.* "Neila" is an anagram for "Liane," the term by which Claire is most frequently identified in Goll's poetry. The poems of *Dream Grass* resolve many of the tensions that inflect the dialogue in poems between Yvan and Clair Goll in *Ten Thousand Dawns,* a collaborative volume that hauntingly traces their first love, separation, and reconciliation.

BIBLIOGRAPHY
Goll, Yvan. *Die Lyric in Vier Bänden.* Berlin: Argon, 1996.
———. *Ten Thousand Dawns: Love Poems of Yvan and Claire Goll.* Translated by Thomas Rain Crowe and Nan Watkins. Buffalo: White Pine, 2004.
———. *Yvan Goll: Selected Poems.* Translated by Robert Bly, George Hitchcock, Galway Kinnell, and Paul Zweig. San Francisco: Kayak, 1968.

Donald Wellman

DRUMMOND DE ANDRADE, CARLOS (1902–1987) Carlos Drummond de Andrade is
regarded by critics as the 20th century's finest and most accessible Brazilian poet. Described by friends as timid and reserved, he transformed the problematizing of his own identity into a recurrent theme of his poems, which are lyrical, self-effacing, and extremely private while revealing more general social concerns. Making recurrent use of a lyrical persona, "Carlos," in his poems, Drummond de Andrade presents himself as an outsider constantly perplexed by his lack of self-understanding and his alienation from the world around him.

Born on October 31, 1902, in Itabira do Mato Dentro, Drummond de Andrade experienced at first hand the disconcerting changes brought about by

20th-century technological progress—as well as the alienating effects of those changes. His personal trajectory (from a small mining town to Rio de Janeiro) mirrors the economic and political changes that took place in Brazil in the 1920s: the shift from an agricultural and aristocratic society to an industrial and bourgeois nation. The "I" of his poems is a man who finds himself impotent and solitary in a world whose logic and meaning elude him.

Coming from Itabira, a town deep in the interior of the landlocked state of Minas Gerais, Drummond de Andrade is responsible for making the name of his hometown (Itabira-out-in-the-wilds) well known in Brazil. As a keyword, *Itabira* stands for the tradition against which the poet affirms his own individuality. It symbolizes a past that one can neither avoid nor understand. In his poems both Itabira and the poet's ancestors are markedly thematized. Born into a privileged family, Carlos was the ninth son of a landowner. He studied at religious schools both in Minas Gerais and in Rio de Janeiro. In 1920, after his father sold the family's land and mansion in Itabira, the whole family moved to Belo Horizonte, where Carlos worked for a newspaper and met Brazilian modernist writers, including Emílio Moura, Abgar Renault, Pedro Nava, Oswald de Andrade, and Mário de Andrade. Pressured by his family to earn a college diploma, Drummond de Andrade graduated in pharmacy in 1925, but he never worked in this field. In that same year he married Dolores Dutra de Morais and returned to Itabira, where he obtained employment as a teacher of geography and Portuguese. Also in 1925 he coedited the modernist journal *A Revista* (The Journal/The Review). In 1926 he returned to Belo Horizonte and worked as a newspaper editor. In 1928 two important events took place: His daughter Maria Julieta was born, and he published his poem *"No meio do caminho"* ("In the Middle of the Road") in the influential modernist journal *Antropofagia*. The simplicity of the poem, which treats the poet's encounter with a "stone in the middle of the road," became a literary scandal. In 1929 Drummond de Andrade took a job in the Brazilian Department of Education. In 1930 he published his first book of poems, *Alguma Poesia* (Some Poetry), followed by *Brejo das Almas* (Wasteland of Souls, 1934) and *Sentimento do Mundo* (A Feeling about the World, 1940).

Drummond de Andrade was at first strongly influenced by the modernist poets Oswald de Andrade, Mário de Andrade, and Manuel Bandeira. His adherence to the radical first phase of Brazilian modernism is noticeable in the short poems and in the colloquial language of his first two books, which are marked by irony and humor, as well as by the investigation of personal and national origins (see *"Hino Nacional"* [National Anthem] in *Brejo das Almas*). His poems parallel a search for the "Brazilian" language and the history that took place in the first decades of the 20th century. Differently from the early modernists, however, Drummond de Andrade's poems recover the individuality of a skeptical and melancholic author who finds himself torn between an unfamiliar past and an uncertain future. In *Sentimento do mundo*, readers encounter an "I" who is powerless when facing the world—"I have only two hands / and a feeling about the world" (*"Sentimento do Mundo"*)—but whose "shoulders are holding up the world" (*"Os ombros suportam o mundo"* ["Your Shoulders Hold up the World"]). The self-reflexive and socially aware poetry of *Sentimento do mundo*, well summarized in *"Mãos dadas"* ("Holding Hands")—"The present is so big, let's stay together"—also characterizes the poems of *A rosa do povo* (Rose of the People, 1945). Strongly reflecting the World War II and the Estado Novo dictatorial period in Brazil (1937–45), *A rosa do povo* thematizes fear and beauty in times of war and the passage of time, as well as the relationship between the media and individuals.

In 1934 Drummond de Andrade moved to Rio de Janeiro, where he wrote for newspapers and magazines and worked in the office of his friend Gustavo Capanema, who was minister of education and public health. Drummond de Andrade left this position 11 years later, when he became editor of a communist newspaper. A few months after that, due to disagreements regarding the newspaper's political orientation, Drummond quit this job and became head of the History Section of the Diretoria do Patrimônio Histórico e Artístico Nacional (Office of the Patrimony of National History and Arts). He retired from that position in 1962.

From the 1950s until his death on August 17, 1987, Drummond de Andrade published more than a dozen books of poems and more than 20 books of prose, including collections of texts published in newspapers as well as of essays and short stories. From the 1950s on Drummond increasingly used traditional metrical schemes and poetic forms, including the sonnet. His mature works focus on questions of origin, memory, and the desire for communion and peace despite a menacing technology. Throughout his works one finds an investigation of the meanings of poetry and love—and an attempt to define their place in the world.

In *Lição de Coisas* (Lesson of Things, 1962), strongly influenced by concrete (pattern or shape) poetry, Drummond de Andrade recovers the irony and formal preoccupation of his first works, therein valuing the sonorous and visual aspects of his poems. The popularity of his poetry can be explained at least partially by his success as a columnist in important newspapers, including *Jornal do Brasil*. In *Versiprosa* (Verse Prose, 1967) one can perceive the influence of Drummond's prose texts on some of his poems, which are characterized by a journalistic tone and topics from current events regarding politics, sports, and anonymous lives. In *Corpo* (Body, 1984), the 80-year-old Drummond de Andrade, already free from the desire and obligation to innovate, offers sentimental poems that explore the body, its language, and its limitations, as well as its relationship with feelings such as love. In "Favelário Nacional" (National Slum Book), a poem in 21 parts, he questions the poet's ability and right to write about the slums, all the while examining related topics such as the rapid growth of Brazilian cities, violence, poverty, hunger, and poignant anonymity. Throughout his life Drummond de Andrade participated in many educational radio shows and inaugurated the public radio program *Cadeira de Balanço* (Rocking Chair).

A translator of Honoré de Balzac, Choderlos de Laclos, Marcel Proust, FEDERICO GARCÍA LORCA, François Mauriac, and Molière, Carlos Drummond de Andrade saw his own works translated into nine languages. The collection of poems *Travelling in the Family* (1986) is the best anthology of his works translated into English. Drummond de Andrade received numerous awards for his works, including the prize of the Brazilian Union of Writers, of the Paulista Association of Literary Critics, and of the PEN Club of Brazil (for

Lição de coisas), as well as the National Walmap Prize of Literature and the Prize Estácio de Sá for Journalism. In Portugal he received the Morgado Mateus Foundation Prize. The Mangueira samba school, famous for its community activism, paid homage to the poet in 1987 by choosing him as the theme of its carnival parade, titled "In the Kingdom of Word," which won first place. Since the poet's death eight books of poetry have been published, including *Farewell* (1996), the last book organized by Drummond, and *O amor natural* (Natural Love, 1992), a collection of erotic poems that surprised his readers. The Brazilian government recognized the importance of Carlos Drummond de Andrade on the national scene by releasing a 50-cruzeiro bill bearing his picture, a self-portrait, and verses, as well as a postal stamp. His texts have been adapted to theater, and readings of his texts have been released on CD. Since 1995 an anthology of his works translated into five languages is available online at http://www.carlosdrummond.com.br. In 1998 a museum and a memorial were built in the poet's honor in his hometown, Itabira.

For more than half a century Carlos Drummond de Andrade meticulously investigated poetry's most basic themes: the individual, home, family, friends, the social impact of change, love, poetry itself, playful exercises, and existence—as he himself pointed out when organizing an anthology of his works in 1962. Never afraid of contradicting himself, he wrote about human beings in search of self-understanding and of communion with others, some unable to break with tradition and some willing to begin anew. He defended the virtue of patience in a time of speed: "Live with your poems before you write them / If they're vague, be patient. If they offend, be calm" (*"Procura da poesia"* ["LOOKING FOR POETRY"]). As the most famous line of his poem "José" attests (one of many that have become proverbs in Brazil), Carlos Drummond de Andrade never feared to leave his questions without an answer: The line is "What now, José?"

BIBLIOGRAPHY

Drummond de Andrade, Carlos. *Looking for Poetry: Poems by Carlos Drummond de Andrade and Rafael Alberti and Songs from the Quechua.* New York: Knopf, 2002.

————. *The Minus Sign: Selected Poems.* Translated by Virgínia de Araújo. Redding Ridge, Conn.: Black Swan Books, 1980.

————. *Souvenir of the Ancient World.* Translated by Mark Strand. New York: Antaeus, 1976.

————. *Travelling in the Family: Selected Poems.* Edited by Thomas Colchie and Mark Strand, translated by Elizabeth Bishop and Gregory Rabassa. New York and Toronto: Random House of Canada, 1986.

Kinsella, John. *From Poetry to Politics and Back Again: The Brazilian Trinity of Manuel Bandeira, Carlos Drummond de Andrade, João Cabral de Melo Neto.* Bristol, U.K.: University of Bristol, 2000.

Pontiero, Giovani. *The Amorous Theme in the Poetry of Carlos Drummond de Andrade.* Naples, Italy: Instituto U.O., 1982.

Sternberg, Ricardo da Silveira Lobo. *The Unquiet Self: Self and Society in the Poetry of Carlos Drummond de Andrade.* Valencia, Spain: Albatros Ediciones, 1986.

Williams, Frederick G., and Sérgio Pachá, eds. *Carlos Drummond de Andrade and His Generation: Proceedings of the Colloquium Held at the University of California, Santa Barbara, 1981.* Santa Barbara: Jorge de Sena Center for Portuguese Studies, 1986.

Luciana Namorato

DUINO ELEGIES RAINER MARIA RILKE (1923)

Many readers consider RAINER MARIA RILKE's *Duino Elegies* (*Duineser Elegien*), which Rilke completed in 1922, not only his most accomplished poetry, but also, plausibly, the most perfect lyrical sequence of the 20th century. So well crafted are the 10 poems that constitute the *Duino Elegies* that many bilingual readers consider the German effectively untranslatable. Too much of their elegiac brilliance gets lost because a large part of their genius reposes in the German language itself, which Rilke molds and touches with pathos and fire in ways that have not been equaled, some say, ever. If the challenge of translating the *Elegies* is daunting, their inspirational value to poets is so great that dozens of translations of the whole and many more of its parts have been attempted and published. They have been called "dramatic inner monologues of pathos and gleaming imagery" (Barnstone 66); and they certainly do represent the luminous, visionary outpouring of a vibrant poetic ego seeking immortal truths.

Rilke began composing his elegies in 1911, while he was a guest of Princess Marie von Thurn und Taxis and staying at Duino Castle, her cliffside Italian retreat, but according to his letters, he did not work on the poems in earnest, or as a set, for another 10 years—not until well after the Great War. Before the war, he crisscrossed Europe, staying for spells in Capri, Rome, Florence, Leipzig, Munich, Paris, Vienna, and many other places. After the war had been in progress for some time, he volunteered for military service and served in the Austrian army for several months in 1916 (though not in combat), before he was honorably discharged for poor health. Following the war's disruptions he wanted to find someplace to settle and work. In 1921 he negotiated with prosperous friends to help him afford the rent of the run-down (but once imposing) Château de Muzot in the Swiss Alps. He settled into his picturesque stone house by the Rhône with one of the last of his romantic partners, the painter Elizabeth Dorothée Klossowska (the separated wife of art historian Erich Klossowski). Klossowska, who signed her paintings "Baladine," was "Merline" or "Mouky" to Rilke. Theirs was a passionate and profoundly harmonious relationship: Together the lovers renovated the building and furnished it, tending to its grounds and gardens and setting up the poet's work space. Although he did not know it, by then he was suffering from the leukemia that would end his life in 1926.

When Merline had to leave for the 1921 Christmas season, Rilke welcomed the solitude and began what he called "wrestling with the angels": It was his chance to return to and finish the poetic sequence begun in 1911 and destined to become the *Duino Elegies*. Left to himself after 40-some years of living the creative life, after a long and varied series of wondrous affairs of the heart, after living through the despair of the war, after having met and befriended so many of the giants of European art and literature, Rilke was not only ready to be visited by inspiration—he felt possessed. At first, some of his 55 SONNETS TO ORPHEUS began to pour out of him. He felt their arrival as "dictations" and as insights "entrusted" to him by terrifyingly beautiful, angelic powers. These "angels" were not those of Judeo-Christian lore, but presences that embody themselves, he thought, in immortal poetry. The creativity unleashed by producing the *Sonnets to Orpheus* spilled over and generated the *Duino Elegies* as well.

Overall the *Duino Elegies* appear to be freely associative (though they are carefully assembled) and teem with images and intertextual references, which makes them difficult to summarize fairly. But each one embodies a particular poetic project and entertains an aspect of the poignancy of human life that the poet hopes he can net with luxuriant allusions and figurative language. The First and Second Elegies (the only two actually begun at Duino) are impassioned meditations on the very conditions of creativity. In the First Elegy the poet exclaims that *"das Schoene ist nichts /als des Schrecklichen Anfang, den wir noch grade extragen"* (beauty's nothing / but the start of terror we can hardly bear) (Poulin 5) and adds, *"Ein jeder Engel ist schrecklich"* (Every angel's terrifying) (Poulin 5). Lines 26 through 53 of the First Elegy survey an evocative list of the daily sources of inspiration (seasons, stars, waves, playing a violin through an open window, longing, a hero, and so on) that a poet passes up, distracted by other aspects of life. The section ends with a comparison of the poet to an arrow that must be parted (freed) from the string (likened to the poet's beloved) that launches it if the arrow is to realize its truest purpose. The rest of the poem touches on voices, recollections, and legends whose subtexts all signify that it is the *eternal* spirits that invest true poetry, for even angels (the eternal spirits themselves) "often can't tell whether / they move among the living or the dead" (*Engel [sagt man] wu ten oft nicht, ob sie unter / Lebenden gehn oder Toten*) (Poulin 10–11). The Second Elegy is a paean to those eternal spirits that are the poet's truest inspiration. The poem begins by repeating the line "Every angel's terrifying." He calls these dangerous spirits *"fast tödliche Vögel der Seele"* (Almost deadly birds / of [the] soul) (Poulin 12–13), but knows he must seek and encounter them because, like the touch of a lover, they represent "a pure duration" and "the promise of eternity" (Poulin 17).

The Third Elegy considers the true source of passion and its relationship to myths and natural history, making the claim that *"uns steigt, wo wir lieben, unvordenklicher Saft in die Arme"*—"when we love, / a sap older than memory rises in our arms" (Poulin 22–23). The

Fourth Elegy delves into the connections between people, their affections and hostilities, the hopes and thwarted expectations of parents and children, the sorrow of bereavements, the winter of the spirit, the difficulties of communicating these realities honestly and truly because *"ist unbeschreiblich"* (l. 85); it is, at bottom, indescribable. The Fifth Elegy, dedicated to Frau Hertha von Koenig, was inspired by Picasso's painting *Les Saltimbanques,* which she owned; in this meditation Rilke compares Picasso's standing acrobats to lovers and wonders whether, if an audience could see the astonishing acrobatics of lovers' emotions, it would toss its coins of happiness to them. The Sixth Elegy (a complex skein of metaphors) in essence compares heroes (and, by implication, poems) to figs—and since figs come from trees and heroes have mothers, the poem compares the creation of poetry to the miraculous powers of wombs and to the transformative functions of the roots, branches, flowers, and leaves of the fig tree. The poem, like the proven hero, once having achieved its happy feat, becomes something different and quite unexpected: *"stand er am Ende der Lächeln,— anders"* (stood at the end of smiles, someone else) (Poulin 44). The Seventh Elegy invokes the terrifying angel of the first elegy and, while addressing it by name, variously announces the poem's central theme: "Love, the world exists nowhere but within. / Our life is lived in transformation. And diminishing, the outer world vanishes" (Poulin 51). The Eighth Elegy is dedicated to Rudolf Kassner, an Austrian philosopher with whom Rilke profoundly disagreed over what is the essential psychic orientation of human beings. Rilke's poem is a meditation on his own yearning for an unlimited openness toward experience, the capacity to face and move into the universe directly and frontally. The poem ends in protest against Kassner's defensive cautions—and with a question: *"Wer hat uns also umgedreht . . . ?"* (Who turned us thus?) The Ninth Elegy is a bittersweet paean to living, to being, to each individual's *once*—for, as Rilke puts it, our having been on Earth is irrevocable: *"irdisch gewesen zu sein, scheint nicht widerruf bar"* (Poulin 60). The Tenth Elegy gives form to a parabolic lesson taught by the allegorical figure whom Rilke calls Lament, who leads the poem's hero to the source of joy (*"die Quelle des Freude"*), which is flowing through a gorge far below, and about which Lament says, *"Bei den Menschen / ist sie ein tragender Strom"* (ll. 101–102) (For men it is a basic river). The poem ends epiphanically on the counterintuitive but joyful realization that, in such a place, it is lucky to fall: *"wenn ein Glückliches fällt"* (Poulin 76).

In a letter dated November 13, 1925, Rilke wrote to his Polish translator, Witold Hulewicz, intimating that the personal outpouring of the *Duino Elegies* embodied a sort of manifesto, which the *Sonnets to Orpheus* realized (Snow, *Sonnets* xvii–xviii). In form, though, nothing could be further from what we might like to think of as a manifesto. The *Duino Elegies* symbolize—using a deeply personal idiom; they do not proclaim. But Rilke's comment does indeed prod us to appreciate significant differences between the two masterpieces that Rilke produced in a paroxysm of inspiration within the single month of February 1922.

Translations of the *Duino Elegies* include those of Martyn Crucefix (Enitharmon Press, 2007), Graham Good (Ronsdale, 2005), Mirando Gray (Far Corner Books, 1982), Robert Hunter (Hulogosi Communications, 1993), G. K. Knight (Henry Regnery, 1961), J. B. Leishman and Stephen Spender (Hogarth, 1952), C. F. MacIntyre (University of California Press, 2001), Stephen Mitchell (Shambhala Press, 1996), A. Poulin, Jr. (q.v.), Edward Snow (q.v.), and David Young (W. W. Norton, 2006). Many lovers of Rilke's poetry argue vehemently about the flaws and virtues of the various translations; scholars consider Poulin's renditions the most reliable, but readers who do not know German would be well advised to compare several translations.

BIBLIOGRAPHY

Gass, William H. *Reading Rilke: Reflections on the Problems of Translation.* New York: Basic Books, 2000.
Paulin, Roger, ed. *Rainer Maria Rilke's Duino Elegies.* Riverside, California: Ariadne Press, 1996.
Rilke, Rainer Maria. *Duino Elegies and the Sonnets to Orpheus.* Bilingual edition. Translated by A. Poulin, Jr. Boston: Mariner Books, 2005.
———. *Duino Elegies.* Bilingual edition. Translated by Edward Snow. New York: North Point Press/Farrar Straus and Giroux, 2000.
———. *Sonnets to Orpheus.* Bilingual edition. Translated by Edward Snow. New York: North Point Press/Farrar Straus and Giroux, 2004.

R. Victoria Arana

DUO DUO (1951–)

Duo Duo is the pen name of Li Shizheng, who was born in Beijing in 1951. In 1965, when Chinese leader Mao Zedong inaugurated the Cultural Revolution, the 14-year-old Li Shizheng was sent to Baiyangding to work in the countryside, where he began reading and writing poetry. In young manhood he befriended a small cadre of innovative writers, including BEI DAO and GU CHENG, who later came to be known collectively as the Misty Poets. Because they wanted to counteract the standardized idiom of the Communist Party bureaucracy, the project they imagined became to reinvent the Chinese language in order to safeguard its lyrical and subtly expressive qualities for modern times. In that connection these poets were attracted to poetry from other languages and nations. Duo Duo admired especially the poems of Charles Baudelaire, Robert Desnos, FEDERICO GARCÍA LORCA, Sylvia Plath, Dylan Thomas, and MARINA TSVETAEVA.

Duo Duo's earliest poetry was brief and barbed in its expression of resistance to political despotism. In 1976 he composed his celebrated and ironic poem "Instruction," which—in such phrases as "wrongdoers of the mind"—alluded to China's lost generation, accused of having "misused parables"; they are, as he put it, "people who have missed life, stuck in a place where life is misunderstood / Everything they have gone through—is a mere tragedy of birth" (see Lee's translation in *The Boy* 29). That poem has been compared to Bei Dao's renowned poem "THE ANSWER." Later, in the 1980s, Duo Duo developed a more discursive style that suited even better his desire to express philosophical ideas sensuously, with careful attention to speech rhythms and startlingly lyrical qualities.

In 1989 Duo Duo participated in the Tiananmen Square protests against government corruption and the regime's part in precipitating rampant inflation. The morning after the Tiananmen massacre, when the government brought out tanks to crack down on the demonstrators, Duo Duo was on his way to England for a reading tour. Having eluded arrest, he sought political asylum first in England, then in Germany and the Netherlands, and he remained in exile for the next 15 years. During this period his poetic language went through another, even more radical, shift, taking up the themes of exile and deracination. Among those poems written after 1989 is his meditative "The Rivers of Amsterdam," in which he feels that the "rivers flow backwards" and experiences a brief vision of his "motherland / On Amsterdam's rivers, slowly sailing by . . ." (*The Boy* 107). Severed from his Chinese-speaking community, Duo Duo could freely experiment with the Chinese language, employing it in groundbreaking if uncanny ways. Some readers have accused his poetry of bordering on nonsense, while others consider his eccentric approach to Chinese verse definitely valuable in light of the objectives of the group to which he belonged in his youth.

In 2004 Duo Duo was allowed to return to China, where he was honored both by a younger generation of poets and by the authorities. That same year he received the official Xinhua News Agency's Poet of the Year Award.

BIBLIOGRAPHY

Duo Duo. *The Boy Who Catches Wasps: Selected Poems of Duo Duo.* Bilingual edition, translated from Chinese by Gregory B. Lee. Brookline, Mass.: Zephyr Press, 2002.
———. *Crossing the Sea: Poems in Exile / Poems in China.* Edited by Lee Robinson, translated by Ming Yu Li. Toronto: House of Anansi, 1998.
Finkel, Donald, ed. and trans. *A Splintered Mirror: Chinese Poetry from the Democracy Movement (Bei Dai, Duo Duo, Gu Cheng, Jiang He, Mang Ke, Shu Ting, and Yang Liang).* San Francisco: North Point Press, 1991.

R. Victoria Arana

DUPIN, JACQUES (1927–) Born in Privas, France, the son of a psychiatrist and director of the local mental hospital, Jacques lost his father at the age of four in 1931. In 1944 he moved to Paris to study law, history, and political science. Three years later he befriended the poet RENÉ CHAR, who helped him publish several poems in the modernist journals *Botteghe oscure* and *Cahiers d'art.* In 1949 Dupin joined the editorial staff of the literary magazine *Empédocle,* where his colleagues included Albert Camus and Char. One

year later Dupin became editor of *Cahiers d'art,* and his first book of poetry, *Cendrier du voyage* (Travel Ashtray), was published. In 1951 he married Christine Rousset and moved to Vanves. From 1955 until 1981 Dupin worked for the Maeght gallery, first as a librarian and later as editor of the affiliated publishing house, for which he edited numerous catalogs and the influential magazine *Derrière le miroir.*

Dupin's poems are sparse and dense and, at the same time, highly melodious sound sculptures. The materiality and beauty of the French language is hardly anywhere more manifest than in Dupin's work, a slow and courageously perceptive articulation of membranes of silence in the face of what idealist German philosopher Georg Wilhelm Friedrich Hegel calls the terror of emptiness. Dupin's essays and poems continue, and bleed into, each other. His work has been nourished by mutually enriching cocreative friendships not only with poets such as Pierre Reverdy, ANDRÉ DU BOUCHET, and PAUL CELAN (who translated Dupin into German), but also by a wide range of sculptors and painters, including Alberto Giacometti, Joan Miró, Pierre Tal-Coat, Antoni Tàpies, Eduardo Chillida, and Francis Bacon. These sympoetic dialogues across artistic media are manifest in numerous collaborative works, from Dupin's lyrical and precise book-length essays on (or, rather, *with* and *through*) visual artists and their creative processes, to portraits of Dupin produced by Giacometti and Bacon. In 1961 Dupin's comprehensive monograph *Joan Miró* was published (a new edition followed in 1993). One year later, in his volume *Textes pour une approche. Sur Alberto Giacometti* ("Giacometti. Three Essays," brilliantly translated by the poet John Ashbery, 2003), a series of dense and lucid exploratory essay and prose poem fragments that approach Giacometti's work-as-process, Dupin outlines a new poetics of perception. In content and style Dupin's Giacometti book is a productive continuation of the German avant-garde author and art critic Carl Einstein's *Georges Braque* (1932).

Dupin's lyrical work began with the volumes *Lichens* (1958) and *Saccades* (Fits and Starts, 1960). In 1966 he cofounded the journal *L'Éphémère,* together with du Bouchet, YVES BONNEFOY, Celan, and others. One year later his poetry volume *Proximité du murmure* (The

Encroaching Murmur, 1967) was published, followed by *Un récit* (A Narrative, 1975), *Histoire de la lumière* (The Story of Light, 1978), *Bleu et sans nom* (Blue and Nameless, 1981), and *Une apparence de soupirail* (A Basement-window Vision, translated as "Songs of Rescue," 1982). Later books of poetry include *Le Grésil* (The Hail, 1996) and *Écart* (Gap, 2000). Apart from an early unpublished Medea play, he wrote only one theater text, *L'Éboulement* (The Crumbling, 1977). In synesthetic symbiosis with his poetry output, Dupin continues to write lyrical and concise book-length essays in response to visual art, for example, on Tapiès (1994) and Claude Garache (1999), illustrated by the artists. In 1988 Dupin was awarded the French Prix National.

Olaf Berwald

E

EAGLE OR SUN? Octavio Paz (1951) The slim surrealistic volume of prose poetry *¿Águila o sol?* (1951) takes its title from a Mexican coin with an eagle and the sun on opposing sides. The phrase, equivalent to the English "heads or tails," underscores a characteristic theme for Paz: the reconciliation of opposites. The eagle on the coin was a symbol of the ancient Aztec Empire, and the sun on the coin's reverse served as the center of Aztec cosmology. While the title suggests random chance and opposition, Paz unifies the duality into a new creative experience. The typography of the prose poems breaks with the traditional line structure of lyric poetry, opening the form to all sorts of possibilities. Paz believed that poetry was not bound by form but was instead the occasion of a liberating experience mediating text and reader.

For Paz poetry had the power to resolve duality. Structure and form illustrate this power, and Paz synthesizes the genres of poetry and prose. The volume is divided into three major sections. *"Trabajos del poeta"* (Works of the Poet) is written in numbered paragraphs. In this section Paz engages in a personal battle with language. The prologue begins, "Today I fight alone with a word. That which belongs to me, to which I belong: heads or tails, eagle or sun?" The labor of finding the right word when "a simple monosyllable would be enough to make the world burst" led him to abandon many of the relationships and pleasures others seek. Yet by eliminating these purveyors of "infected language," the poet opens himself to a new language:

poetry. Nevertheless, the work of the poet is Sisyphean, since he must repeat the struggle to find the experience—with every poem. The speaker struggles with words, with language, with himself, and with history throughout the collection.

The second section, titled *"Arenas movedizas"* (Quicksand), is much like a short story about a nightmare. The speaker awakens during a night spent at an inn and walks out into the deserted landscape. There he encounters an Indian peasant who asks for the speaker's eyes for his fiancé, who "wants a little bunch of blue eyes." The Indian forces the narrator to kneel, raises his machete, and shines a light into the eyes. At that point he realizes the eyes are not blue and releases the narrator, who returns to the inn. This gruesome nightmare symbolizes the struggle within Paz between Mexican and cosmopolitan influences, including that of the surrealists. The parable raises questions about the nature of poetry and the poet. Blue eyes, the eyes of foreigners, will not be the source of true poetry; the poet must look to his roots.

Paz sees the poet's creativity as linked to the regeneration of nature. In the last section, with the same title as the volume (*"¿Aquila o sol?"*), Paz returns to Mexico's pre-Columbian past, his childhood, and the topic of poetry. Removed from his country and his language, the poet is entrapped. It is only when he is able to find a unity with his past that he has the freedom to create. In the final poem of the volume, *"Hacia el poema"* (Toward the Poem), Paz writes, "We turn and turn in the animal belly, in the mineral belly, in the belly of time. To find the way out: the poem." The typography in this section more closely resembles poetry's lineation. The one- or two-sentence strophes make suggestions as to the origin of poetry. The fourth paragraph hints that in order to create, the poet must give up his beliefs about history, language, and poetry and set free the words he holds. In the final paragraph Paz merges the two sides of the coin when the rule of the "incandescent eagles" is united with the "future noon" and "the solar song" and the poet is free to sing. To use "words, phrases, syllables, stars that turn around a fixed center . . . that meet in a word" becomes the poet's goal because, when that happens, the poem also "creates a loving order." This loving, caring, better world is not only the subject of poetry, it is also brought into being by the poem itself.

BIBLIOGRAPHY
Paz, Octavio. ¿Aquila o sol? Translated by Eliot Weinberger. New York: New Directions Books, 1976.

Jean Shepherd Hamm

ECOPOETICS   Poetry aspires to reveal the world for what it is. Ecopoetics reaffirms the world in its complexity and proposes an engagement with—or attunement to—an original world: one dynamic and rich and devised of a continuum of interrelations, an overlooked/missed world rarely registered in our everyday, natural attitude. As a discipline poetry is vigorous, imaginative, and alternative; it opens up clearings in our mental conception of the world, providing us with new paths of investigation, and it makes available other possible worlds to those commonly offered to our understanding. Ecopoetics extends this art form (poetry) with the intention of foregrounding an investigation into *ecology*: a word derived from the Greek *oikos* (home) and *logos* (word, reason, thought). As a discipline ecopoetics investigates how the human is situated within its habitat; how "home" is defined and built; where (or whether) borders exist between body and world, human and other, space and place; and how sense activities, physical presences, memory, and moments of thinking locate and assist the human desire to navigate the self in the world.

Ecopoetics thus contributes to the dissident project of resistance to dominant cultural modes of thinking. What is often written as the legacy of the Enlightenment—science, rationalism, the dominion of humans over nature—is critiqued for its pernicious cultural legacy: a body of encyclopedic "knowledge" deeply rooted in formulations of the world in terms of "classes" and "species." Moreover, ecopoetics holds this "epistemological fallacy" to account for its contribution to the current ecological crisis. To halt the unsustainable exploitation of natural resources, the reduction of the number of world species, and the destruction and pollution of vital components of the fabric of our life requires a shift in vision. According to Gregory Bateson, our ecological problems stem to a great extent from the current "mutating ideology that conceives of species against species," a scientific premise deriving from the incorrect supposition that the "unit of survival in the bio-taxonomy" is "the individual, family line" (484).

The correct unit, "organism plus environment," would readdress the epistemological error and offer a new series of units or differences: gene-in-organism, organism-in-environment, ecosystem, and so forth, and thus promote conceptions of the interaction and survival of ideas, programs, units, and the like, within circuits, or complexes of differences (Bateson 484).

Twentieth-century science pushed the focus of knowledge systems toward the level of the gene; late 20th-century and 21st-century thought is now arguing for the conception of a "unit of survival" with a larger complexity: the ecosystem unit. Ecopoetics embraces this new proposition. Moreover, the coupling of poetics to science (as suggested by the prefix *eco-*) rescues the redress from being seen as affiliated with playful theoretical discourses and nonrational modalities. In short, ecopoetics offers a way of viewing the world that embraces art *and* science, yet is radically new in its use of poetic devices and scientific underpinnings. Jonathan Bate clarifies this focal point: "Ecopoetics asks in what respects a poem may be a making . . . of the dwelling place . . . According to this definition, poetry will not necessarily be synonymous with verse: the poeming of the dwelling is not inherently dependent on metrical form. However, the rhythmic, syntactic and linguistic intensifications that are characteristic of verse-writing frequently give a peculiar force to the *poiesis*: it could be that *poiesis* in the sense of verse-making is language's most direct path of return to the *oikos,* the place of dwelling, because metre itself—a quiet but persistent music, a recurring cycle, a heart-beat—is an answering to nature's own rhythms, an echoing of the song of the earth itself" (75–76).

It would be a mistake to consider ecopoetics as merely an extension of romanticism; rather than advocating the "imaginative reunification of mind and nature" (Bate 245), ecopoetics attempts to locate the human in the world. It thus radicalizes "nature poetry" by offering far less utopian visions than the romantics did, often through the formulation of urban modalities, nonorganic metaphors, and an increased scientific inflection on the everyday objects that appear to mind. Kate Soper writes that an "uncritical ecological naturalism" is another form of "social conservatism" and that radical ecopoetics must, therefore, negotiate this obvious yet highly significant claim.

Romantic and aestheticizing approaches to nature have as readily lent themselves to the expression of reactionary sentiment as sustained the radical critique of industrialism, and this means that left-wing ecologists, however understandably eager they may be to reseize this tradition of romanticism for their own purposes, are dealing with a problematic legacy.

We have come to an understanding of ecopoetics as both a radicalized body of knowledge concerning how things appear to mind and how the human is located within this appearance; ecopoetics thus conceived can be written as a new form of phenomenology, as Alice Oswald does in her poem "River":

> put your ear to the river you hear trees
> put your ear to the trees you hear the widening
> numerical workings of the river

It is rare to find an image of a river coupled to mathematics. Rivers are one of the most remarkable features in our landscape; their continuous movement portrays the flux and instability of nature and identity. In this poem Oswald arrests the idea of the river as an organic, flowing force by positing the argument that such an energy source can be understood in terms accessible to our reductive, pattern-seeking cognitive engines (our ears and brains) by conceiving of it as "numerical." But this sort of scientific language, which resonates with ideas of a static and fixed resource, is undermined by the poem's diction. The technological idiom hints that the river is an entity vulnerable to possible methods of analysis in isolation and therefore to exploitation; however, the "workings" of the river foreground a process, the endless change and dynamism of the natural world. The "numerical workings" of the river can be calculated to a degree. If one understands the interdependency of all things in the world as suggested by the investigation that the poem proposes (into the tree, which results in finding the river, and vice versa), one can read the "workings" of the river as an element in one of the most remarkable processes on Earth, the hydrologic cycle: the continual flow of water from sea to cloud to river and into life forms along the way, providing all living organisms with two essential resources—hydrogen and oxygen.

Oswald's poem urges the addressee to enter into complicity with the environment, for her philosophy states that knowledge is embodied, not objective. This is one of the fundamental premises of ecopoetics. It derives from an ideological perspective that desires the conception of difference or alterity as nonoppositional; we are challenged to view things in relation. Such a perspective, according to Charlene Spretnak, is attuned to the "unitive dimensions of being," an ecological unconscious that sometimes appears to consciousness as the "deep interconnection with others and with all of nature."

The search for this ecological imperative within poetry is one method of discriminating the ecopoetic from the wealth of poetry that surrounds us during this 21st-century environmental renaissance. In his taxonomy of ecological imperatives Jonathan Skinner offers us further parameters for locating the ecopoetic within creative works. For Skinner the ecopoem may offer one (or more) of four models, or conceptual frameworks. These are the *topological*: a science of place and referential dimension to that which is "outside" the poem; the *tropological*: a figurative discourse that functions like ecosystems themselves; the *entropological*:

where direct materials form a method of poetry; and the *ethnological*: where wild landscapes are investigated as societies "peopled" by their components, together with their distinctive characteristics and relations to one another. Skinner's model offers the literary critic a method of bracketing the ecopoetic as an art form with unique qualities that can be appreciated methodically (and meticulously) for new modes of signification and poetic effects.

Skinner's outline suggests that one might briefly consider here historic ideas relating to quests, investigations, and representation. Before the deployment of the term *atlas* for a collection of maps, the Dutch and Spanish colonialists used to speak of the "speculum." The Latin word for *mirror* was replaced by the name of the mythical Greek Titan who supposedly supported the heavens on his shoulders. That shift was paralleled by the move from the medieval conception of a fixed, unchanging, and hierarchical vision of the planet and of a closed circle of civilization with a vertical sense of infinity to a new model offered by Renaissance thought. In 16th-century Europe, during the so-called Age of Discovery, the sea and the land dominated the European worldview as intellectuals began to abandon spiritual parameters and models of knowledge; in short, the round Earth, as an icon, became every bit as important as the Cross (as a symbol of salvation) or Heaven (as the seat of God). Since the 1960s the world's peoples have become familiar with a new icon and worldview: the blue planet viewed from space. This object is often seen as beautiful and unique—but also as limited (in terms of resources), fragile, and endangered. Our new maps, methods of orientation, and types of "navigation" seek to investigate this newly reconceptualized Earth, envisioned nowadays as a planet that is the very mirror image of ourselves. Ecopoetics embodies the scientific quest as also a spiritual quest to find the most resonant images and icons to create those moments in poetry where the constructions of verse and the reflections on nature, combined, herald a secular and ecological revelation.

This radical form of poetics as quest can be seen to have precursors within the whole tradition of literature from antiquity and the pre-Socratic poets to traditional Japanese meditative verse, from classic Indian spiritual writings on into British and American postromantic poetry. Some canonical figures worth reinvestigating in this light include Henry David Thoreau (United States), William Wordsworth (Britain), William Carlos Williams (United States), and Ted Hughes (Britain); but one should also probably revisit the *Kokinwakashu* (Japan), Matsuo Basho (Japan), Johann Wolfgang von Goethe (Germany), RABINDRANATH TAGORE (India), CZESLAW MILOSZ (Poland), JOHANNES BOBROWSKI (Germany), SAKUTARO HAGIWARA (Japan), and Kokin Wakashu or Kokinshu (Japan). It is interesting to see roots to the poetics of our ecological situatedness in Sufi poetry, Hindu poetry, Buddhist poetry, and Christian mystical poetry; however, most relevant to our current ecological crisis are the poets writing specifically in response to the most recent environmental, ecological, and political texts of the late 20th century, including Seamus Heaney (Ireland), Alice Oswald (Britain), John Burnside (Britain), Mary Oliver (United States), Allison Funk (United States), LESLIE MURRAY (Australia), NICANOR PARRA (Chile), and JAMES K. BAXTER (New Zealand). These poets have tasked themselves with the poetry of experiences engendered by the renewal of the familiar, with making our conception and enjoyment of the world fuller and thus enabling us to see the world in all its complexity and vitality.

BIBLIOGRAPHY

Bate, Jonathan. *The Song of the Earth.* London: Picador, 2000.

Bateson, Gregory. *Steps to an Ecology of Mind.* New York: Ballantine, 1972.

Burnside, John, and Maurice Riordan, eds. *Wild Reckoning—An Anthology Provoked by Rachel Carson's Silent Spring.* London: Calouste Gulbenkian Foundation, 2004.

Coupe, Laurence, ed. *The Green Studies Reader: From Romanticism to Ecocriticism.* London: Routledge, 2000.

Dobson, Andrew. *Green Political Thought.* 3rd ed. London: Routledge, 2000.

Oswald, Alice. *Woods etc.* New York: Faber and Faber, 2005.

Skinner, Jonathan. "Boundary Work in Mei-mei Berssenbrugge's 'Pollen.'" Paper presented at the CUNY Conference on Contemporary Poetry, New York, N.Y.: November 5, 2005, and at the Association for the Study of Literature and the Environment Conference, Eugene, Oregon, June 24, 2005.

Spretnak, Charlene. "Radical Nonduality in Ecofeminist Philosophy." In *Ecofeminism: Women, Culture, Nature,* edited by Karen J. Warren, 425–436. Bloomington: Indiana University Press, 1997.

Tom Bristow

ÉCRITURE   The poetic writing that is here identified as *écriture* shares a provenance with language-centered writing in the United States and Canada: the "language games" of Ludwig Wittgenstein's logical positivism and the objectivist heritage in poetry associated with Louis Zukofsky among others. Minimalist poetic processes of composition have inspired a similarly attentive practice and stance toward composition as a material process keying on the physical presence of a breathing person. "I live the text as a *body*," writes Anne-Marie Albiach (Interview). *Écriture* privileges the nominal flatness of language, the *"différance"*—as theorized by Jacques Derrida—that allows signs to defer to one another in relational chains that inscribe meaning. Similarly influential is Michel Foucault's construction of "enunciation." Social factors that constitute a regime of discourse often exist in an unresolved tension with the intentional use of language. "Such investigation strips bare an indeterminate time, / abasing the relapsed, gestures from this time forward" (Albiach from "Incantation" in *A Geometry* 16).

Attesting to both the lexical minimalism of *écriture* and its poststructuralist formalism, the poets associated with this style of writing (Emmanuel Hocquard, Claude Royet-Journoud, Jean Daive, in addition to Albiach) pursue a synchronic reading of the network of words on the page, their alignments and folds. In "Diptych" Hocquard asks, "Where is the dividing line?" and comes to associate the line with shadows and creases, "The dark / not / a limit" (*Late Additions* 51), comparing the page to a relief map. Words do not mold the edges that distinguish "outside" from "inside." "*Outside* and *inside* / are useless / when we speak / of a crater's edge" (51). The play of perception creates a drama of indeterminacy, leaving its trace as *écriture.* "The beast dies in the crease of the page," writes Claude Royet-Journoud in the poem "*i. e.*"—reducing metaphor to page layout. "We must set foot in the blank space," he continues, inscribing an orientation for the reader as subject within the space of enunciation. There is no image, "beast" or otherwise; there is text or writing. The white space in the middle of a line, the use of quotation, the refusal of metaphor are minimalist acts, holding the reader's attention: "the image / held up the loss / 'it was there' / eaten by his question" ("*The Maternal Drape*" or the *Restitution*). Albiach similarly relates the figure to page as a turning in of perception on itself, "the internal figures dissolve" ("Figures of Memory," in *A Geometry* 21).

For the poets associated with *écriture,* the image is a presence, not a trope, "involution of discourse" (Albiach, from "Winter Voyage," in *Mezza Voce* 62). Royet-Journoud registers the written name as a black body, the light framing a surface, "black body in which to lodge the name / the light is only on the table" ("The Overwhelming," from "Namework," in *The Notion of Obstacle* 44). Jacqueline Risset, in *The Translation Begins,* stages the drama of written discourse this way: "having responded already and listening in order to respond" (24). Jennifer Moxley in her translator's note writes, "whenever language is present semantics will attempt a takeover" (96), catching exactly the relationship between *language theory* and *writing practice* that animates the attention to detail that distinguishes *écriture.* This poetry is available to readers of English because of the passionate dedication of small literary publishers like those identified below. See also FIELD POETICS and POETRY BEYOND THE PAGE.

BIBLIOGRAPHY

Albiach, Anne-Marie. *A Geometry.* Translated by Keith Waldrop and Rosmarie Waldrop. Serie d'Ecriture. Providence, R.I.: Burning Deck, 1998.
———. Interview. Henri Deluy, Joseph Guglielmi, Pierre Rottenberg. *Action Poétique* 74 (1978): 14.
———. *Mezza Voce.* Translated by Joseph Simas. Sausalito, Calif.: Post-Apollo Press, 1988.
Hocquard, Emmanuel. *Late Additions.* Translated by Rosmarie Waldrop and Connell McGrath. Peterborough: Spectacular Diseases, 1988.
———. *A Test of Solitude.* Translated by Rosmarie Waldrop. Serie d'Ecriture. Providence, R.I.: Burning Deck, 2000.
Maulpoix, Jean-Michel. "La poésie française depuis 1950." *Poésie, prose, critique littéraire.* Available online. URL: http://www.maulpoix.net/Habiter1950.html. Accessed on April 22, 2007.

Risset, Jacqueline. *The Translation Begins.* Translated by Jennifer Moxley. Serie d'Ecriture. Providence, R.I.: Burning Deck, 1996.

Royet-Journoud, Claude. *i. e.* Translated by Keith Waldrop. Serie d'Ecriture. Providence, R.I.: Burning Deck, 1995.

———. *"The Maternal Drape" or the Restitution.* Translated by Charles Bernstein. Windsor, Vt.: Awede, 1985.

———. *The Notion of Obstacle.* Translated by Keith Waldrop.: Windsor, Vt.: Awede, 1985.

Donald Wellman

"ELEGY FOR SLIT-DRUM" Christopher Okigbo (1966)

Christopher Okigbo's "Elegy for Slit-Drum," a poem in the unfinished sequence *Path of Thunder: Poems Prophesying War,* is emblematic of his late work, in which the escalating political crisis in Nigeria plays a crucial role. In the mid-1960s ethnic tensions among the predominantly Muslim Hausa and Fulani peoples in the north, the Muslim and Christian Yoruba in the southwest, and the predominantly Christian Igbos in the southeast were exacerbated by widespread poverty and rumors of corruption in the national government. The poem was composed in May 1966 during the tumultuous period between the coup d'état of January 1966, led by the Igbo general Ironsi, which unseated the widely despised government of Abubakar Tafawa Balewa, and the countercoup of July 1966, led by General Yakubu Gowon. In the days following the first coup there had been a genuine feeling of elation throughout the country, because Nigerians from all ethnic groups had hoped that a change in regime would enable a more unified national government. But accusations soon spread that General Ironsi had set out to serve only the Igbos rather than to represent all Nigerians. Ethnic tensions flared up again, leading to the countercoup, to massacres of Igbos, who fled to the southeast, and eventually to the secession of the southeastern region of Nigeria as the Republic of Biafra. The ensuing struggle is known as the Nigerian civil war, or the Biafran war (1967–70).

Okigbo's poem comments on these current events, offering "condolences . . . from our swollen lips laden with / condolences" to those innocent people who were killed as part of General Ironsi's coup. The speaker tells us, "the General has carried the day," and "the elephant has fallen." As in earlier poems Okigbo uses images of the elephant and stone to symbolize forces that resist change, in this case the corrupt government brought down by Ironsi's coup. In the poem as in the rest of the poem sequence, the forces of change are represented by thunder. Throughout his career Okigbo wrote about the intertwined forces of destruction and renewal, often through the vehicle of a priestly, questing speaker who enacts a ritualized search for enlightenment over the course of a poem sequence. Here, too, Okigbo identifies himself as the "oracle" who "enlightens" readers about the forces of creation and chaos at work in these political upheavals. Speaking as an oracle, Okigbo worries that the same thunder that brought about this positive political change may also lead to more violence, warning, "Thunder that has struck the elephant can make a bruise." For this reason the poem repeats the mantra of "condolences": the dead must be mourned but not used as motivation for further killing. As the oracle says, "we should forget the names / we should bury the date," so that the country can move forward. Sadly, as Okigbo feared, the violence did escalate, and he himself was killed while serving in the Biafran army in 1967.

BIBLIOGRAPHY

Okafor, Dubem. *The Dance of Death: Nigerian History and Christopher Okigbo's Poetry.* Trenton, N.J.: Africa World Press, 1998.

Okigbo, Christopher. "Elegy for Slit-Drum." *Labyrinths with Path of Thunder.* Ibadan, Nigeria: Heinemann, 1971. Reprinted in *The Heinemann Book of African Poetry in English,* edited by Adewale Maja-Pearce. Oxford: Heinemann, 1990, 27–29.

Emily S. Davis

"ELITED PROSE" Édouard Glissant (1979)

In "Elited Prose," from his collection *Yokes* (1979), we see an example of Édouard Glissant's broader creative view. Whereas in "Gorée," his condemnation of slavery is clear and direct, Glissant does not repeat a militant *négritude* sensibility in all his poems, for his vision is more complex. "Elited Prose," as its title suggests, is a prose poem in six lines that is actually only one sentence long. It is, however, a perfect expression of Glissant's view of opportunity—of the capacity of blacks to achieve virtually anything, in spite of (or perhaps because of) racial or cultural heritage. The unnamed "He" of the poem is perhaps a poet himself, a man who "filters golden speech through the quick of his mind" and is equally adept in a rural environment, knowing how a "sheep is threaded on a spit." The man has experienced certain privileges, as have some Africans who served as "aides" to colonials, but he has also been hunted as a slave and so is like "not the Trojans but Hector whom they [the Greeks] hunt." His resiliency and adaptability allowed him to reside in "Real France," but he has suffered racial prejudice nonetheless. In spite of this, he has refused to be bitter and retained his optimism in humankind: "[He] is nigger but universal, adapts his level as he goes along, in short has faith in man." Glissant, in his personal experiences of exile, has likewise been a student of other cultures, never completely at home in any one, and yet never completely alien. History, as horrific as it seems, also informs the present and admits the possibility of hope in the future—all of which the narrator of "Elited Prose" expresses in several short lines.

BIBLIOGRAPHY

Glissant, Édouard. "Elited Prose." In *Black Salt,* translated by Betsy Wing. Ann Arbor: University of Michigan Press, 1998.

Patrick L. Day

ÉLUARD, PAUL (1895–1952)

Paul Éluard was the nom de plume of Eugène Émile Paul Grindel, an important French poet of the 20th century who was active in the dada movement and a founder of surrealism with LOUIS ARAGON and ANDRÉ BRETON, among others. Éluard became affiliated in 1926 with the French Communist Party, from which he was excluded in 1933 but rejoined in 1942. Apart from his being one of the great love poets of the 20th century, his works also reflect his political commitment during the world wars, his resistance against the Nazis, and his deep interest in philosophical questions of knowledge, time, identity, and overcoming the loneliness of human beings.

Éluard was born on December 14, 1895, in Saint-Denis, a northern industrial suburb of Paris, into a lower-middle-class family. His father was a book-keeper, and his mother added to the family income by dressmaking. In 1912 Éluard was treated for tuberculosis in the Swiss sanatorium at Davos, where he began to write his first poems, particularly inspired by American poet Walt Whitman. He fell in love with a Russian woman, Gala (Helena Dmitrovnia Diakonova), whom he married in 1917 and with whom he had a daughter, Cécile (born 1918). In December 1914 Éluard joined the French army, worked in a military hospital, served as an infantryman, and was badly injured by poison gas. Like many others he emerged from the war as a nihilist, disgusted by the hypocritical norms and morality of society.

A year after *Le Devoir et l'inquiétude* (Duty and Anxiety, 1917)—his first noteworthy volume of poetry—appeared, he was discovered by the critic Jean Paulhan, who introduced him to the dada movement. In 1920 Éluard became a coworker for the journal *Trois roses* (Three Roses) in Grenoble (together with Breton and Aragon), met TRISTAN TZARA, Benjamin Péret, Philippe Soupault, and other intellectuals, and founded the journal *Proverbe*. In 1921 he published a proclamation in verse of surrealist theories, *Les nécessités de la vie et la conséquence des rêves* (The Necessity of Life and the Consequence of Dreams), which was deeply influenced by Freudian psychoanalysis and the idea of automatic writing that Bréton had discovered in 1919. In this work Éluard defended the freedom of the subconscious and of dreams from the overwhelming power of the conscious.

On March 15, 1924, after a marital crisis, Éluard began a seven-month trip from Marseilles to Tahiti, India, Indochina, Ceylon, the Antilles, New Zealand, and Australia. Because he had not said good-bye to anyone, rumors of his death were widely circulated and finally regarded as true. His poems from this period reflected his difficulties: He suffered another bout of tuberculosis, and Gala left him for the surrealist artist Salvador Dalí. After his return he became a member of the surrealist group and was regarded as their major poet from 1924 to 1938. He worked with others on *La Révolution surréaliste* (1924–29), *Le Surréalisme au service de la révolution* (1930–33), and *Minotaure* (1933–39). His reputation as a poet was established with the publication of *Capitale de la douleur* (Capital of Pain,

1926), an attempt to come to terms with the pain of war, violence, and private loss, by turning pain into a meaningful experience. The collection includes two of his most famous love poems, "*L'Amoureuse*" (Woman in Love) and "*La Courbe de tes yeux*" (THE CURVE OF YOUR EYES). The poems of *The Capital of Pain* inspired the 1965 Jean-Luc Godard film *Alphaville, une étrange aventure de Lemmy Caution*. In 1930 Éluard and Bréton published *L'Immaculée conception* (The Immaculate Conception), a series of surrealist poems in prose in which they simulated demented states and tried to communicate with the vegetative life of the fetus in the womb. In 1929 Éluard met RENÉ CHAR and Nusch (Maria Benz), who, having worked as a model for his friends Man Ray and Pablo Picasso, was considered a mascot of the surrealist movement; he married her in 1934. His subsequent poetry, inspired by Nusch, became one of participation in life, confrontation with the real world, and universal, fraternal love.

After the fascists attempted a putsch in Paris on February 6, 1934, to topple the National Assembly, Éluard was actively involved in the antifascist vigilant committee of intellectuals, read a speech by Bréton at a congress in Vienna, and traveled together with Bréton to Prague to open the International Surrealist Exhibition. As a sign of his solidarity with all men, he renewed his affiliation with the Communist Party in 1938, which led to a break with Bréton. In the same year he abandoned surrealistic experimentation as a result of his concern over the Spanish civil war and his support for the Spanish Republic. During World War II he served in the French army and became a poet of the Resistance from 1942 onward, publishing poems under pseudonyms (i.e., Jean du Hault and Maurice Hervent) and leading the Comité National des Écrivains in the northern zone. In 1942 he published his collection *Poésie et Vérité* (Poetry and Truth), while his most famous poems of those years, "*Liberté*" and "*Au rendez-vous allemand*" (German Rendezvous), were spread throughout France by planes of the Royal Air Force in 1943. To avoid the Gestapo, Éluard and Nusch constantly changed addresses, hiding in a mental hospital in Lozère, while he continued publishing throughout the war ("Au rendezvous allemand" was published in 1944). After the liberation he was awarded a medal for his work in the Resistance but suffered a great shock in November 1946 with the premature death of Nusch from a brain hemorrhage. Under the impact of this loss he wrote *Le Temps déborde* (1947), and global peace, liberty, and independence became his new, lasting passions. Éluard became more and more active in the cultural field within the international communist movement, unable because of his idealism to see the reality of the Soviet Union and Stalin's regime. He traveled in Britain, Belgium, Czechoslovakia, Mexico, and the Soviet Union, but not the United States, where he was refused a visa. As a participant in the world peace movement, he took part with Picasso in a congress for peace in Wrocław, Poland, in 1948. In 1949 at a peace congress in Mexico he met Dominique Lemort, whom he married in 1951 and to whom he dedicated his *Le Phénix*. Again, his personal happiness enabled Éluard to reaffirm his belief in human goodness and the possibility of love and meaning; private concerns became enlarged to a concept of global fraternal love.

Éluard published over 70 books, including poetry, literary and political works, and poetic texts dedicated to such painters as Ernst and Picasso. Painting, like poetry, was a means for him to disseminate truth and to overcome the barriers between human beings. For Éluard the poet was a seer (*vates*) and a priest who could through a renewal of language effect changes in all areas of existence—political, social, and sexual. His love poetry has gained a special status as it celebrates universal solidarity, the overcoming of loneliness, and the merging of souls. Among his best-known later works are *Poésie ininterrompue* (Unbroken Poetry, 1946) and *Poèmes politiques* (Political Poems, 1948). In 1952 Éluard, already ill, spent the summer in Benac (Dordogne) and finished his *Poésie ininterrompue II*. On November 18, 1952, he died from a heart attack in Charenton-le-Pont and was buried in Père Lachaise Cemetery in Paris.

BIBLIOGRAPHY

Boulestreau, Nicole. *La Poésie de Paul Éluard: la rupture et le partage. 1913–1936*. Paris: Klincksieck, 1985.
Caws, Mary Ann. *The Poetry of Dada and Surrealism: Aragon, Bréton, Tzara, Éluard and Desnos*. Princeton, N.J.: Princeton University Press, 1970.
Éluard, Paul. *Selected Poems*. Translated by Gilbert Bowen. London: Calder, 1988.

————. *Last Love Poems of Paul Éluard.* Translated by Marilyn Kallet. Baton Rouge: Louisiana State University Press, 1980.

Gateau, Jean-Charles. *Paul Éluard et la peinture surréaliste.* Geneva: Droz, 1982.

Nugent, Robert. *Paul Éluard.* New York: Twayne, 1974.

Vanoyeke, Violaine. *Paul Éluard: Le poète de la liberté. Biographie.* Paris: Julliard, 1995.

Heike Grundmann

ELYTIS, ODYSSEUS (1911–1996)   Odysseus Elytis (born Odysseus Alepoudelis), a major poet in the Greek language, was not well known beyond his own country before he won the 1979 Nobel Prize. After he received the award his reputation spread, and now he is considered one of the most significant poets of the 20th century. Elytis merges ancient Greek literary conventions and modernist European poetics, especially surrealism, into a style respecting both traditions but imitating neither; he identifies strongly with his native land and often speaks as the voice of his country. A consistent critic of the materialism and decadence of modern life, Elytis frequently asserted that a new world of justice, harmony, and freedom was possible. Because the Sun is a recurring symbol in his works, Elytis sometimes called himself a "solar metaphysician." In addition to writing poetry, Elytis was an essayist, media director, graphic artist, critic, and translator. The list of honors he received includes the Greek National Book Award for Poetry and the National Poetry Prize (1960), the Order of the Phoenix (1965), several honorary doctorates, the Commandant de la Légion d'Honneur award (1989), and the Nobel Prize.

Born in Heraklion (Iraklion), Crete, on November 2, 1911, Odysseus was a descendant of an old family of Lesbos. As a child he spent his summers in the Aegean islands, and imagery of the Sun and sea permeates his poetry. When Odysseus was six, the Alepoudelis family, owners of a major soap manufacturing concern, moved to Athens, where Odysseus received his secondary school education and spent a short time at the law school of Athens University. When he began to write Elytis adopted a pen name to establish some distance from his famous family. Several early poems appeared in the magazine *Nea Grammata* (New Cul-

ture) and were greeted as an indication of poetic reform and innovation. Elytis's first volume of poetry, *Prosanatolizmi* (Orientations), was published in 1936. These early works introduced surrealism into Greek literature, yet Elytis had already thrust aside some surrealist techniques, such as automatic writing and a concentration on the paradoxical. Replete with optimism and images of light and clarity, *Prosanatolizmi* secured Elytis the title "sun-drinking poet." He rejected this reading of his work, claiming that poetry was neither optimistic nor pessimistic, but was a place where contradictions no longer have meaning.

In 1937 Elytis went to reserve officer's cadet school and during World War II served as a second lieutenant on the Albanian front. His *Azma iroiko ke penthimo yia ton hameno anthipologhagho tis Alvanias* (Heroic and Elegiac Song for the Lost Second Lieutenant of Albania) (1945) was based on his war experience. The poem uses the death of a young soldier and his subsequent resurrection as a symbol for the triumph of justice and freedom over oppression. The poem also establishes the theme of fusion of the physical and spiritual life, which reappears in his later works.

In 1948 Elytis moved to Paris, where he lived for five years, writing in French for *Verve* magazine and studying philosophy and literature at the Sorbonne. There he established friendships with leaders in the avant-garde, including Pablo Picasso, Henri Matisse, ANDRÉ BRETON, Marc Chagall, and Alberto Giacometti. During these years Elytis also represented Greece at world conferences such as the International Meetings of Geneva (1948) and the International Art Critics Union (1949).

For 11 years Elytis published no poetry. Then his *To Axion Esti* (It Is Worthy) (1959), which won Greece's First National Award for Poetry, was published. Often called a "spiritual autobiography," *To Axion Esti* again celebrates the Greek landscape and tradition, but now as a place where good struggles against evil, where pain exists alongside joy, but where universal values still triumph. The ability to merge past and present Greece and the poetic skill Elytis exhibited in the poem earned him great critical acclaim. The poem is structured in the pattern of Byzantine liturgy and alternates prose and verse throughout. When Mikis Theodorakis set *To Axion Esti* to music, it gained widespread popular appeal with Greeks and became a kind of anthem.

During the next decades Elytis held a variety of positions. He was a member of the National Theatre's administrative council, program director of the Greek National Radio, art and literary critic for a Greek newspaper. *Kathimerini,* president of the governing body of the Greek Ballet, and adviser to the Greek National Theatre. In addition, he traveled extensively throughout the world, visiting, among other countries, the United States in 1961 and the Soviet Union in 1963.

During these years Elytis also continued to write innovative poetry, to do translations, and to write philosophical and literary essays. His translations include works by FEDERICO GARCÍA LORCA, Arthur Rimbaud, and PAUL ÉLUARD, as well as the poems of Sappho and the Apocalyspe of St. John. *Open Papers,* a collection of essays published in 1974, traces the many poetic influences on Elytis. From the joys of the Greek landscape to reading surrealist poets, from meeting Picasso to the German occupation of his homeland, the work provides an intimate portrait of the poet's mind. In the same year Elytis published his theoretical ideas about writing in another volume of essays, *Offering My Cards to Sight* (1974).

The publication of *Maria Nefeli* in 1978 represented a departure from the youthful optimism of earlier works and did not receive immediate accolades from critics. The poem also departed from the depiction of women found in most works by Elytis. Maria is not a child of nature and the open country, but a strong, urban woman seeking recognition for who she is. As a modern woman Maria engages in a dialogue with the Responder, Antifonitis, who represents traditional values. The discussion is carried out in a variety of stanzaic forms, moods, and styles. *Maria Nefeli* illustrates the hope that amid the turmoil of modern existence, individuals possess the capacity to find peace. In addition to other topics, the speakers in the poem discuss death, something critics did not expect to find in the works of Elytis.

The long poem *O micros maftilos* (The Little Mariner, 1984) took several years to complete and underwent many revisions before it was published in its entirety. Like Elytis's two previous long poems, the structure of *O micros maftilos* is complex. Each of the poem's three main divisions uses a line of Greek verse as its title: one from the ancient poet Sappho, one from the medieval poet Romanos, and the third from the 19th-century poet Kalvos. The work also contains *eisodos* (entry) and *exodus* (exit) prose poem sections. Within each division the poem is arranged in alternating clusters of lines, with subtitles consisting of each of the Greek poets' lines and the word *Projector.* In addition, the Projector clusters provide information on Greek history, and each of the other clusters is written in a different format and deals with different topics. The Little Mariner is the poet's persona traveling through the Greek landscape, often encountering the evil of life, but always with a clear vision for a better world.

Elytis lived simply, even after winning the Nobel Prize award of $190,000. He lived the last 20 years of his life in a small apartment in Athens. Never marrying, Elytis maintained that to do so would cause his poetry to suffer. On March 18, 1996, at the age of 84, he died.

The works of Odysseus Elytis have continued to gain recognition since his death. There are now translations of some of his writings in 12 different languages, even though the complexity of language and structure makes translation difficult. Elytis believed that the poet's imagination allowed him to see the same things as others but to see them differently. The fusion of modern and traditional, of personal and political, of the real and the surreal, and the belief that poetry is life itself blend to create the unique voice of Odysseus Elytis. This voice helped to transform not only Greek literature but the literature of the world.

BIBLIOGRAPHY

Elytis, Odysseus. *O mikros naftilos* (*The Little Navigator*). Athens: Ikaros, 1985.

———. *The Little Mariner.* Translated by Olga Broumas. Port Townsend, Wash.: Copper Canyon Press, 1988.

———. *O ilios o iliatoras* (*The Sovereign Sun*). Athens: Ikaros, 1971.

———. *The Sovereign Sun: Selected Poems.* Translated by Kimon Friar. Philadelphia: Temple University Press, 1974.

———. *To axion esti* (*Worthy It Is*). Athens: Ikaros, 1959.

———. *The Axion Esti of Odysseus Elytis.* Translated by Edmund Keeley and George Savidis. Pittsburgh: University of Pittsburgh Press, 1974.

Jean Hamm

"ENCOUNTER" CZESŁAW MIŁOSZ (1936) With his lyric "Encounter," the poet CZESŁAW MIŁOSZ returns to the village of his childhood in Lithuania for a meditation on transience in the natural world. The first four lines establish a simple narrative mechanism: In a dawn so still that a bird's flutter seems like warning, a hare crosses the road and by extension, the path of man; a traveler gestures to the rabbit with his hand, choosing an act that is cognizant without being predatory. The second half of the poem reflects on the first, as the speaker observes equilibrium in that past moment—a mutual quiet—and in the more lasting silence of the present, acknowledging, "today, neither of them is alive" (l. 5).

The truths of this spare poem are interstitial, found in the spaces between words. Nonetheless, bound to his duties as speaker, Miłosz allows his rhetorical language to falter and stutter: "O my love, where are they, where are they going"—interrupted once more by the primary moment—"the flash of a hand, streak of movement, rustle of pebbles" (ll. 7–8). The poet's essential question telescopes neatly between the past, in which it could trace the red wing's and hare's literal journeys, and the present, in which it interrogates the unknowable destinations of the soul. The final line affirms his intent not to mourn, but to "wonder" and contemplate. Written in Wilno (present-day Vilnius) shortly after Miłosz's first trip abroad, this is the voice of a young poet finding his first grasp on mortality and coming to terms with what he does not know—a humility that could always be found in Miłosz's poetry, even in the dense philosophies of later work.

The presence of the red wing is notable not only for the image's beauty, but for Miłosz's strategic creation of a plural and potent animal force. Otherwise the poem might be reduced to the dynamic of hunted-hare and hunter-man. Instead, it is clear that the men are only one part of a much larger equation—while humans merely ride along, birds are able to rise in darkness. The poet was a great naturalist, particularly attentive to the names of creatures and vegetation native to his birthplace. In interviews he elaborated on his "amazement for the innumerable and boundless substance of this earth . . . everything is intelligent and probably eternal."

Sandra Beasley

"ENGOMI" GEORGE SEFERIS (1955) First published in the slim volume . . . *Cyprus, Where It Was Ordained for Me . . . ,* "Engomi" is considered one of GEORGE SEFERIS's most characteristic poems. It is a free-verse ode in five uneven-length stanzas, the last one of which contains two lines deeply indented to suggest sharp mood breaks that coincide with shifts in spirit, or psyche.

The poem is named after the archeological site of Engomi, in the Bay of Famagusta, Cyprus. Seferis and Maro, his wife, visited Cyprus for a month in 1953. Their sojourn proved to be one of the most joyful periods of Seferis's emotional and sexual life. But the visit could well have turned out differently. In the aftermath of World War II, Cyprus was still—as it had been since 1914—a British Crown colony. Some 80 percent of the population were Greek-speaking Orthodox Christians; 20 percent were Turkish-speaking Muslims, many of whom harbored nostalgia for the days when Cyprus had been part of the Ottoman Empire. Seferis was highly conscious of the diplomatic ramifications of any words he would speak on the subject of Cypriot independence: Greece had suffered through World War II and a civil war after that, and it could ill afford to turn against its allies to support the aspirations of Cyprus for self-determination. At the same time, Cyprus represented for Seferis what was Greek about his own heritage, without the overlay of modern Greek government. Cyprus was also the place most sacred to the Greek goddess of love, Aphrodite. Seferis's visit to Engomi, to its ruins on a sparse plain, provided him with revelations about the spaciousness of the Hellenic legacy and with a memorable visionary experience: that "love transcendent had a sharply sensual edge" (Beaton 308). Filled with new inspiration, Seferis wrote to his sister that he had "fallen in love with this place. Maybe because I've found there things still living, that have been lost in that other Greece . . . perhaps because I feel that this people has need of all our love and all our support" (Beaton 310).

The poem begins with a stanza of description of Engomi as seen from a distance under curvy clouds and as the Sun was setting on "arms in motion as they dug." The second stanza reveals how the operations of the archaeologists resembled those of surgeons opening a body—"the curtains of pain spread wide open / to reveal, naked and indifferent, the tomb." In the next stanza the speaker focuses on "those at work" and their "taut shoulders, the arms that struck / this dead silence with a rhythm heavy and swift / as though the wheel of fate were passing through the ruins." At this point the speaker is struck by the sudden sensation of time's having stopped, and he experiences an image of awe-inspiring love: "an Assumption" of the Virgin Mary melded with Aphrodite. The rest of the poem—which owes much of its rhetorical power to an allusion to the book of James (or Protevangelium), XVIII.2, of The Apocryphal New Testament (Collected Poems 286)—relates the speaker's vision of suspended time in all its concrete detail: "girls kneaded, but they didn't touch the dough / women spun, but the spindles didn't turn / lambs were drinking, but their tongues hung still / above green waters," and so on. After the body of the Virgin / Aphrodite had finally risen into the heavens, all the suspended animations resumed, and "The world / became again as it had been, ours: / the world of time and earth." In sum, the poem blends ancient ritual with modern perspectives, the sacred and the sensual, the scientific and the aesthetic—to celebrate a place where the continuous legacy of Hellenic civilization has reached unbroken into the present.

BIBLIOGRAPHY
Seferis, George. "Engomi." From Logbook III, in Collected Poems. Revised ed. Translated, edited, and introduced by Edmund Keeley and Philip Sherrard. Princeton, N.J.: Princeton University Press, 1995.

R. Victoria Arana

"ENOUGH FOR ME" FADWA TUQAN (1969)

FADWA TUQAN's short poem "Enough for Me" articulates in a mere 10 lines the demand (in this case, of the Palestinians) for a homeland in a personal and unpretentious mood. Tuqan's earlier poems, such as "SONG OF BECOMING" and "I Shall Not Weep," had already established her as an important Palestinian poet committed to the national cause. In those poems Tuqan assumes the role of a national bard by expressing and mobilizing the collective claims. "Enough for Me," however, has a relatively different tone in that it communicates what the love for one's own country means to the poet herself.

The poet demands the gift of dying on her country's soil. She longs for that spiritual moment in which she vanishes into the beloved soil that enables her to take root in its embrace and "then sprout forth as a flower." The poet's plea is not an empty death wish, but a devotion to future generations that will live in an independent country. The implication of the poem is, therefore, that bare existence under dispossession is nothing but to be doomed to oblivion and to be eradicated from historical memory. Death in one's own country, on the other hand, is a solemn way of securing an afterlife and resurrection, a fate very different from being disposed of as a wasted corpse.

The brevity of "Enough for Me" reinforces, rather than weakens, its rhetorical power. By means of the conceit of burial and germination, the poem recapitulates the urgency of a homeland and the need for national self-determination. In so doing "Enough for Me" does not employ a zealous and hyperbolic language; rather, it affirms itself in a modest and self-effacing tone, assuring that the poet does not call for the obliteration of the enemy, but for a piece of land with which she can identify her soul. What is important for the poet is the metaphysical security that the soil of her country offers her.

BIBLIOGRAPHY
Tuqan, Fadwa. A Mountainous Journey: An Autobiography. Translated by Olive Kenny and Naomi Shihab Nye, foreword by Salma Khadra Jayyusi. Saint Paul, Minn.: Graywolf Press, 1990.

Firat Oruc

"EXILE" TASLIMA NASRIN (2005)

The poem "Exile" appears in the Love Poems of Taslima Nasreen. It expresses the emotional pain of this exiled writer and her yearning for her homeland. Exposing her innermost vulnerability and loneliness, the poet addresses her country as would a pining woman in a letter to her beloved in a distant land. NASRIN's pain and anguish as an exile are expressed through the idiom of unrequited love in a style that does not fail to evoke the humility of one totally surrendered to the fire of longing.

Simple yet eloquent and tender in tone, the poem comprises three stanzas. The function of the first stanza is more than just phatic, as the poet initiates a direct inquiry and interrogates the homeland to find out about its well-being. Each verse poses a question; rather, each verse rephrases the same question: "Are you keeping well, my country?" The repetition of "my country" in each line suggests a sentiment of closeness and belonging that the poet feels toward her country and indicates a bond that has obviously not been severed or weakened by events, distance, and time. The homeland comes across as an idée fixe that the poet cannot shake off. In the second stanza the poet informs the homeland that her heart yearns for it and asks whether this yearning is mutual. The message carries a sense of urgency, with the poet informing the homeland that her life is running out in the process of thinking and dreaming about the homeland. Once again the poet does not relinquish her gentle but persistent questioning and invites a response from the homeland, her blank understated queries opening a space of ambiguity, hinting at a tacit sense of betrayal: "My life is running out thinking of you / and yours? / I die dreaming of you? / And you?" The third stanza develops a negative romantic tonality that deploys the imagery of shattered and silenced womanhood. The poet communicates to the homeland the devastated state to which she has been reduced in the language of a discarded (female) lover and describes the symptoms of her inner wounds and psychological damage: "I hide my wounds in secret / my sorrows / my tears / hold back in secret / my unruly hair / flowers, sighs." The final verses evoke the magnanimity of the female in the role of unconditional lover and eternal well-wisher when the poet concludes by blessing her country despite her own misery: "I am not well / you keep well, my beloved country."

Though the poem is an expression of the personal anguish of the poet as an exile, it may also be read as a muted and symbolic testimony to the violence and abuses against women that are the explicit subject of so many of her other poems. From a feminist perspective the symbolic power of this poem is better appreciated when read in conjunction with poems such as "Happy Marriage," "Noorjahan," "The Game in Reverse," "Garment Girls," "At the Back of Progress," and *Edul Wara*

("Official Home Page"), which most readers are likely to find shocking and disturbing for their depiction of forms of unmitigated female victimization involving acts of oppression, violence, and terror. For a reading concerned more with issues of uprootedness, "Exile" may be read in conjunction with "The Exile's Poem" (*Love Poems*), in which the poet elaborates a discourse on food, grief, and nostalgia and attempts (seated in her "air-conditioned room in Scandinavia") to recuperate her native land through a primordial act of eating rice and fish curry by hand.

BIBLIOGRAPHY
Nasrin, Taslima. *Love Poems of Taslima Nasreen.* Translated by Ashim Chowdhury. New Delhi: Rupa, 2005.
———. Nasrin / Nasreen, Taslima. Official Home Page. Available online. URL: http://taslimanasrin.com/index2.html. Downloaded on August 28, 2005.

Shonu Nangia

"EXPERIENCE" JOHANNES BOBROWSKI (1962)
One week before its first publication in Germany's leading weekly newspaper, *Die Zeit,* in November 1962, JOHANNES BOBROWSKI recited *"Erfahrung"* at a literary meeting of the legendary Gruppe 47, an informal alliance of German postwar authors that included the novelists and Nobel Prize recipients Heinrich Böll and Günter Grass. He immediately won this group's prestigious literary award.

While the short poem's title suggests a concrete and tangible singular event, the dense text exposes the reader to a precarious montage of contrastive juxtapositions and conflicting mythological layers reminiscent of superimposed film cuts. Consisting of only three lines, the first stanza echoes the beginning of Friedrich Hölderlin's fragment "Mnemosyne," where the "one sign" that "we are" laments the absence of, as well as inescapable submission to, interpretive pain. Composed in an anonymous passive voice, Bobrowski's "sign(s)"—"cross and fish"—have been "written" on a "cave's" wall. It remains open to interpretation whether the "cave" is a Christian catacomb, the locus of Plato's famous myth of liberation, or a prehistoric site. Bobrowski's opening simultaneously connotes Christian and Platonic materialities and refers to Georges

Bataille's and Carl Einstein's juxtapositions of prehistoric cultures and high modernism.

Written in the present tense, the second stanza offers a geological and historical report on opposite movements, immersions, and emergences. In the dreamlike narrative of this stanza, nature and history are presented as inextricably interwoven. Emerging as an indirect object, a lyrical "I" is first made explicit in the third stanza. In danger of drying up, it is the river (*der Strom*) that addresses the anonymous poem's "I" in the final, unpunctuated stanza. The stream here symbolizes both geological matter and a psychological as well as poetological suggestion (the stream of consciousness), but its "voice" consists of "sand." This fragmentary concluding apostrophe can, however, also be read as originating in the nameless "I" and addressing the river. Narrative membranes between subject and object become permeable in the arrest of mourning ("open yourself / I cannot get through / your dead / are adrift inside me"). The trauma of the Shoah and of World War II—or, as Bobrowski's colleague Peter Weiss wrote, "all the dead ones who inhabit us"—makes the writing process for German postwar writers both unbearable and indispensable. The text of Bobrowski's "Experience" is not told by an active subject. The self only temporarily surfaces as a location, a reflexive object, or a possessive pronoun. Prepositions assume the role of protagonists in Bobrowski's dreamscape. Bobrowski's poem presents the building up of terror and its pressing need to be translated into perceptive heterotopia. At once enabling and demanding a slow reading, "Erfahrung" asks to be granted transitory passage through opening horizons of readers in the 21st century. The best and most widely available translation in English, by Ruth and Matthew Mead, unfortunately suffers from several imprecise (even wrong) verb choices.

BIBLIOGRAPHY

Bobrowski, Johannes. "Experience." In *From the Rivers,* translated by Ruth and Matthew Mead. London: Anvil Press, 1975, 52. Reprinted in Johannes Bobrowski, *Shadow Lands. Selected Poems.* New York: New Directions, 1994, 154.

Olaf Berwald

EZEKIEL, NISSIM (1924–2004)   Perhaps the best-known Indian poet writing in English, Nissim Ezekiel was born in Bombay (now Mumbai) on December 24, 1924, into a Bene Israeli Jewish family. His father was a botanist, his mother, the principal of a Marathi school that she had founded. At 23 Ezekiel obtained a master's degree in English from Wilson College, University of Bombay, and sailed the following year to London to study philosophy at Birkbeck College.

Upon his return to India three years later, he began a lifelong commitment to literature as a poet, essayist, playwright, literary critic, editor, publisher, and professor. In 1952 Ezekiel married Daisy Jacob, an Englishwoman. They had two children, a son, Elkana, and a daughter, Kavita. His sister, Asha Bhende, was a well-known stage actor and theater personality. From 1961 to 1972 Ezekiel headed the English department of Mithibai College, Bombay. During this period he had short tenures as visiting professor at the University of Leeds (1964) and the University of Chicago (1967). In the 1970s he served as reader in the English department at the University of Bombay, from which he retired in the 1990s. After a prolonged battle with Alzheimer's disease, Nissim Ezekiel died in Bombay on January 9, 2004, at age 79 (Thayil).

Ezekiel, one of the most decorated and publicly recognized of poets writing in the English language in India, received the country's highest literary honors, among them the Sahitya Akademi cultural award in 1983 and the Padma Shri in 1988. He greatly influenced the current generation of Indian poets writing in English. Not only did they take their inspiration from him, but he was a mentor to many of them, including the late Dom Moraes, ADIL JUSSAWALLA, and Gieve Patel (Joffe).

Ezekiel's checkered educational and professional career in England and in India fueled his poetic works, which ranged in subject from his personal life, his status as a member of a religious minority in India, his deep attachment to and love for the city of Bombay, to his struggle with sexuality and the rigors of marriage. Criticized for writing the kind of Englishman's English that was deemed a slavish imitation of Western forms of poetic diction, Ezekiel experimented with language, producing a series of "Very Indian Poems in Indian

English" that caricatured the typical idiom of Indian speakers of English. These appeared in *Latter-Day Psalms* (1982).

He has been described as "the Yudhishtra of the Mahabharata of post-Independence Indian-English poetry" by G. J. V. Prasad ("Indian Men Poets," in *South Asian Literature in English: An Encyclopedia* 151) in that he blazed a trail along which many contemporary Indian poets followed, constructing through his poetry a modern urban India in which English poetry could develop a strong voice, identity, and readership. This he achieved through the editing of the *P.E.N. Quarterly*, through publishing the work of fledgling poets, through regular poetry readings, and by traveling overseas to introduce foreign readers to his work. Drawing on his bilingual background, he experimented with the translation of Marathi poetry, an attempt at responding to critics who for decades had labeled Indians writing in English as elitist, removed from reality, and confined to the privileged.

Bent on creating an idiom that was a decided departure from the rhythmic conventions of late 19th-century English poetry in India, Ezekiel used free verse. The tone of his poems is conversational but always deeply introspective. His first collection of poetry, *A Time to Change* (1952), explores subjects that assaulted his senses daily on the streets of Bombay ("The Old Woman," "On Meeting a Pedant," "Morning Prayer," "The Prophet"). While there are some deeply personal poems in this collection ("An Affair," "To a Certain Lady," "Failure"), the overall tenor is one of attempting to find his voice through a medium that was still unfamiliar to most Indians and that could scarcely find a publisher or readers at that time.

With the publication of *Sixty Poems* (1953) Ezekiel's voice became far more confident. The self-confessional tone of the early poems gave way to a far more detached method of observation of his place in his marriage and in life. The love poems in this collection are remarkably more explicit in their sexual exploration of images. A wealth of erotic images inhabits these poems, but also a gentleness that one associates, for instance, with the quietness of mature love rather than with the passion of first romantic stirrings described, for instance, in "Nakedness I" and "Nakedness II." By this stage in

his writing career Ezekiel's indebtedness to the Bible, Jewish scripture, the intonation of the chants of Hindu mystics, and the Dhamnapada of the Buddha became obvious, as in "Prayer I" and "Prayer II." This spiritual journeying was perhaps inevitable in someone whose own cultural heritage was Jewish, especially at a time when the community in India was dwindling and when people were being drawn into the practices of other, more dominant religions on the subcontinent.

In *The Third* (1958), which contains poems written between January 1954 and December 1958, Ezekiel turned to a variety of themes, some of which he had entertained earlier (his relationship with women, for instance) and some new. His work became more descriptive of place (for instance, "Letter from Rangoon," where the color and variety of cultural images provide a smooth canvas on which his feelings for the city are given free rein). Of Rangoon he writes: "The Buddhist city smells / Of God and the Beast" (*Collected Poems, 1952–1988,* 109), and in "The Cur" he describes a mangy street dog as "Gangrenous in a vital limb / And drawn by some disorder of the brain / To foul decaying stuff" (95).

In *The Unfinished Man* (1960) Ezekiel's twin strengths—his eye for the visual and his ability to evoke sentiment through the erotic image—came into their own. This collection was followed by *The Exact Name* (1965), which contains what is perhaps his best-known and much-anthologized work, "NIGHT OF THE SCORPION." In this poem Ezekiel's indebtedness to the customs and traditions of India is evident in the rhythms he chose to match the cadence of the chants of the Hindu mystic whose powers the poet describes. In like manner the infinite variety of India is evoked in "In India," a poem in which the country's ethnic multiplicity is underlined by the idiosyncrasies of its distinct cultural communities: "The Roman Catholic-Goan boys, / The whitewashed Anglo-Indian boys, / The musclebound Islamic boys . . . never missed their prayers" (*Collected Poems, 1952–1988,* 132). "Poet, Lover, Birdwatcher" is a somewhat autobiographical poem in which he comments on the similarities between the skills required to write poems, attract women, and study birds. He writes: "To force the pace and never to be still / Is not the way of those who study birds / Or women" (*Collected Poems, 1952–1988*, 135). The tone is clever, of course, but never smug, which is why his lines are always endearing, always amusing.

Hymns in Darkness (1976) presents perhaps the most candidly autobiographical of his later poems. He describes himself, for instance, in "Background, Casually," as "A mugging Jew among the wolves / They told me I had killed the Christ, / That year I won the scripture prize" (*Collected Poems, 1952–1988*, 179). In this poem Ezekiel's painfully traumatic experiences as a Jew in a Roman Catholic school in Bombay are the clearest indication we have of the cultural and religious alienation he experienced growing up as a member of a maligned minority in India. Yet this did not create in him a desire to emigrate to foreign shores, as so many creative writers of his generation had done. By the end of the poem he admits his indebtedness to the land of his birth when he writes: "I have made my commitments now. / This is one: to stay where I am, / As others choose to give themselves / In some remote and backward place. / My backward place is where I am" (*Collected Poems, 1952–1988*, 181). Ezekiel referred to India in general and to Bombay in particular as a "backward place," but he had once taken umbrage at the derogatory comments made about India by none other than future Nobel laureate V. S. Naipaul, who had visited India as an adult and in *An Area of Darkness* (1964) had denigrated the country of his ancestors as a place of "death, negation, distortion, degradation" (Gieve Patel xxi). Ezekiel's fierce defense of the land of his birth was played out artistically and creatively in the number of poems he wrote in which the sights, sounds, smells, and feel of India are repeatedly evoked. Despite the "squalid pavement," "the naked child," and the "indifferent man" who make up the callous scenario described in "Woman and Child" (*Collected Poems 1952–1988*, 265), Ezekiel could not bear to be separated long from the city he loved. In the set of poems that make up "Edinburgh Interlude" (entitled "Mangoes"), he writes: "Perhaps it is not the mangoes / that my eyes and tongue long for, / but Bombay as the fruit / on which I've lived, / winning and losing / my little life" (*Collected Poems 1952–1988*, 293).

Alzheimer's disease left Nissim Ezekiel in a zone that detached him from reality for years before he finally succumbed. He was perhaps ready for death long before it came to relieve him of the complex relationships associated with a deeply adventurous personal and creative life. In his poem entitled "At 62" he had written, "Death / in the distance / and near, is my only halo" (*Collected Poems 1952–1988*, 273).

BIBLIOGRAPHY

Anonymous. "Nissim Ezekiel." Available online. URL: http://en.wikipedia.org/wiki/Nissim_Ezekiel. Accessed on April 22, 2007.

Das, Bijay Kumar. *The Horizon of Nissim Ezekiel's Poetry*. New Delhi: B.R. Publishing Corporation, 1995.

Joffe, Lawrence. Obituary. Nissim Ezekiel, Gifted Poet Nurturing English-Language Verse in India." *The Guardian*, (9 March 2004). Available online. URL: http://books.guardian.co.uk/obituaries/story/0,11617,1165441,00.html. Accessed on April 22, 2007.

Mishra, Sanjit. *The Poetic Art of Nissim Ezekiel*. New Delhi: Atlantic, 2001.

Mohanty, Niranjan. "Irony in the Poetry of Nissim Ezekiel." *World Literature Today* 69, 1 (1 January 1995): 51–55.

Patel, Gieve. Introduction to Nissim Ezekiel's *Collected Poems, 1952–1988*. New Delhi: Oxford University Press, 1989, xv–xxvii.

Prasad, G. J. V. "Indian Men Poets." In *South Asian Literature in English: An Encyclopedia*, edited by Jaina Sanga, 150–155. Westport, Conn.: Greenwood Press, 2004.

Raghu, A. *The Poetry of Nissim Ezekiel*. New Delhi: Atlantic Publishers and Distributors, 2002.

Thayil, Jeet. "14 Attempts at a Tribute: Nissim Ezekiel." *The Rediff Special*. Available online. URL: http://www.rediff.com/news/2004/jan/12spec.htm. Accessed on January 12, 2004.

Rochelle Almeida

F

"FAITHLESS WIFE, THE" FEDERICO GARCÍA LORCA (1921–1927) "The Faithless Wife" ("*La casada infiel*") is part of *Gypsy Ballads* (*Romancero gitano*), FEDERICO GARCÍA LORCA's most famous poetry cycle (1921–27), which pays tribute to the verve of Spain's legendary outsiders whose freedom-loving spirit, wild passions, and uncompromising ways had always fascinated the poet. In this ballad a Gypsy narrator tells the story of his love affair with a married woman who had deceived him by claiming she was a maiden, a fact the speaker discloses in the very beginning: "*Y que yo me la llevé al río / creyendo que era mozuela, / pero tenía marido*" (So I took her to the river / believing she was a maiden, / but she already had a husband). What follows is the Gypsy's memory of the lovers' first night (the trip to the riverbank, the undressing, and his taking the mistress back home)—their passionate first and last tryst. Having uncovered his mistress's deceit, the narrator, following a Gypsy tradition, presented the woman with a sewing basket, but decided not to fall in love "because having a husband / she told me she was a maiden / when I was taking her to the river" ("*porque teniendo marido / me dijo que era mozuela / cuando la llevaba al río*.).

In one of his lectures dedicated to the Flamenco art of the "deep song" (*cante hondo*), García Lorca remarked that "it is admirable how through lyric designs, a feeling slowly attains form and how it finally attains the precision of something almost material" (*Es admirable cómo a través de los diseños líricos, un sentimiento va tomando forma y cómo llega a concrecionarse en una cosa casi material*). "The Faithless Wife" is another example of the poet's fascination with the different ways in which the tension between the infinite and the finite manifests itself in life and art. Driven by pride, the Gypsy narrator chose to tame his feelings, but his understated "I decided not to fall in love" stands in sharp contrast with "that night I ran / on the best of roads" (*aquella noche corrí / el mejor de los caminos*), an image that, regardless, betrays the intensity of his passion. The tension between the suggested expanse of this passion and the restrained words that cannot do it full justice gives dramatic energy to his story and also to García Lorca's poem. The ballad reenacts the Gypsy drama and provides a key to the poet's own creative drama: his constant effort to compress the immeasurable emotion in the minimalist lyric space.

BIBLIOGRAPHY

"The Faithless Wife." In *The Selected Poems of Federico García Lorca*. Edited by Francisco García Lorca and Donald M. Allen, translated by Stephen Spender and J. L. Gili. New York: New Directions, 2005.

García Lorca, Federico. "Arquitectura del cante-jondo." In *Poetas del 27: la generación y su entorno. Antología comentada*. Introduction by Víctor García de la Concha. Madrid: Colección Austral, 1998, 73.

Alina Sokol

FAIZ AHMED FAIZ (1911–1984)

Faiz Ahmed Faiz is considered one of the best-loved poets of the

Urdu language, along with MUHAMMAD IQBĀL. Faiz was born in Sialkot, preindependence British India, the talented and handsome son of Sultan Mohammed Khan, a wealthy and leading Punjabi lawyer who had risen from humble agrarian roots. Faiz's early education was traditional and included Koranic studies as well as Arabic and Persian. As a youth he was a student at the Scotch Mission High School in Sialkot, where he learned English from missionaries and from which he graduated in 1927. He then studied philosophy and English at Punjab University's Murray College in Lahore, earning a B.A. in 1931 and a master's degree in English literature in 1933. During this time he was also enrolled in the university's Oriental College to study Persian and Arabic literature and was awarded an M.A. in Arabic literature in the same year. In 1935 he was appointed lecturer at M.A.O. College in Amritsar, where he worked for some years before taking another academic position and returning to Lahore in 1940. He was at this point a member of the Progressive Writers' Movement, a London-based organization of intellectuals committed to fighting totalitarianism, and he was openly sympathetic to socialist ideals, although he said he never joined the Indian Communist Party.

Faiz published his first volume of poetry, *The Picture of a Dissenter* (*Naqsh-e-Faryadi*), in 1941 and married Alys George, an Englishwoman, in the same year. That collection contains his famous poem "DON'T ASK ME FOR THAT LOVE AGAIN." When Nazi Germany invaded the USSR in 1941, Faiz joined the British Indian Army as a captain, rising to the rank of lieutenant colonel in the following two years. After World War II he became the editor of the *Pakistan Times*, gaining a distinguished reputation in journalism. In 1951 he was charged as an accomplice in the Rawalpindi Conspiracy Case, the failed coup attempt against the Liaquat government, pronounced guilty, and imprisoned for the next four years. The harsh jail term at least afforded him privacy, which he used to create more of his impassioned lyrical poetry, many in the form of *ghazals*, a traditional Arab verse form. Two of his best-loved books, *Dast-e-Saba* (Hand of the Breeze, 1953) and *Zindan-Nama* (1956), were composed in prison. The beautiful, firm poems in these volumes—as in his numerous later collections—combine a conversational voice, elegant diction, and a deep concern for the griefs and loves of humanity with a socialist alignment toward contemporary history. In 1962, while living in England, he was awarded the Lenin Award for Peace (the USSR's equivalent of the Nobel Prize). He returned to Pakistan in 1964. In 1971 he was named cultural adviser to the government of Pakistan and in 1972 was appointed chairman of the Pakistan National Council of Arts. In 1976 he was awarded the Lotus Prize of the Afro-Asian Writers Association. He traveled to Beirut, Lebanon, and while there (1978–82) edited the Afro-Asian Writers Association's quarterly *Lotus*.

Faiz published his poetry in Urdu in a series of distinct and distinguished collections (in 1965, 1971, 1978, 1981, 1982, and 1984). These volumes include stirring anthems, poignant love lyrics, *ghazals*, and poems occasioned by his thoughts and feelings about the plight of ordinary people in a world of political opportunism. In addition to the poetry, he published three volumes of essays on literature and culture. His best poems have been translated into numerous languages, including Arabic, English, French, Hindi, Hungarian, Japanese, Persian, Russian, and Spanish. Faiz returned to Lahore in November 1983 and died on November 20, 1984.

R. Victoria Arana

"FANTASIA TO LIFE, A" GU CHENG (1971)

This 10-stanza poem was written in 1971 when GU CHENG was only 15; it is a poem from among the ones he "wrote on the riverbank with twigs" (Gu xii). However, its publication and warm acceptance by the public in 1979 proves that what is expressed in this poem found a ready echo in Chinese readers; even today some of its lines are frequently quoted and recognized as a register of his stylistic innovation. In this poem Gu Cheng relies heavily on imagination, but his novel images are clearly related to natural objects. The poet's clear sense of optimism, "the resonance between Nature and me" (Gu xiii), and the poet's rendition of the poet's true function surface when the poet, touched by nature, expresses his ambition to make his lines known to the world and to share his happiness with (and in) nature. Considered in view of what later happened to him, the poem appears prophetic.

The poet begins by imagining that he embarks on a voyage, his hopes and dreams packed with him. The images of shell, sail, cicada's chirr, with pictorial vividness and sound, create a beautiful picture of harmony. The second stanza mirrors the poet's carefree, sun-tanned personality and a life characterized by freedom. The lines "let the sunlight cascade / dye my skin black" are frequently quoted because they express an eagerness to be immersed in close contact with nature. The image of the Sun is personified as the boat tracker in the third stanza. Combined with the previous stanza, the fourth stanza represents the lapse of time, from day to night. The night scene in the next stanza attracts the poet with its charms and the twinkling stars. Gu Cheng's romantic inspiration is fully exemplified in the following line: "I drop the new moon—golden anchor." The next stanza focuses on the overcast day when it is shrouded with gloom. The poet is in awe of the boundlessness of the universe. He imagines that his poems are transmitted to the world in a timeless sense. Here the impressive images are "the golden sheaves of wheat" that form a cradle that harbors "my heart and muse." The following stanza romanticizes the acceptance of poems when the poet brings them to greet the world. What is most meaningful are the lines "With my eyes closed / the world and I have no more in common." The poet says that he strives to make his poems known to different lands in spite of difficulties. In the next stanza the poet keeps on walking in the scorching sunlight, and his footprints are like seals marking his travel. The last stanza makes clear the poet's ambition: to create a poem that will echo in the years to come.

Understood in connection with the title, this poem is a romantic rendering of life, of a poet's life, of a poet's ambition. He hopes that his poems will be appreciated by people in different lands. The poet's assertive voice reinforces his ambition. It sounds idyllic and unrealistic, but it fully mirrors Gu Cheng's strong interest in nature and the natural milieu, which is his realm of inspiration.

BIBLIOGRAPHY
Gu, Cheng. Preface. In *Selected Poems of Gu Cheng*. Translated by Eva Hung. Hong Kong: Chinese University of Hong Kong (Rendition Paperbacks), 1990.

Shan Xuemei

"FARMERS' DANCE" Shin Kyong-nim (1973)

"Farmers' Dance" is the title poem of Shin Kyong-nim's first collection of poetry, *Farmers' Dance,* and an example of his *minjung* (folksong) poetry. In this collection Shin presents us with a heart-felt vision of displaced farmers in South Korea who faced the industrialization and urbanization of President Chung Hee Park's administration during the 1960s and 1970s and have either stayed in hopeless rural towns or moved to city slums. Most of them are helpless and desperate, watching their families break up, losing what little land they had, and wondering "what's the use of struggling in this small rural town." Without hope for the future some of them choose to commit family suicide by ingesting herbicide or eating poisonous fish.

Shin's depiction of an empty, desolate rural town in "Farmers' Dance" is particularly poignant because here he portrays a deteriorated version of a traditional farmers' dance. Traditionally, a farmers' dance was performed to inspire excitement for a rural festival or to celebrate the planting or the harvest of a year's rice crop. Thus the dance was always associated with joy, laughter, and communal unity and was closely related to the natural rhythms of an age-old agricultural lifestyle. But the farmer-musicians presented in this poem are different from the traditional ones. They perform on "a temporary stage" set up in an "empty school yard" only for a handful of spectators in the evening; their dance and music are not for celebrating the village spirit, but for earning a few coins with their "faces . . . smudged with make-up." After their performance they do not feel a sense of harmony or unity shared with the audience. Feeling alienated and abandoned, they drink up hard liquor (*soju*) and try to forget about their hard lives. The remote rural town looks so forlorn and hopeless at night that they even make a joke of inviting legendary robber-rebels Kok-jung and Suh-rim to visit. Returning home, they dance for themselves, letting the blaring sounds of *kkwaengggwari* (pipes) and *jing* (a gong) fill the night sky. The contrast between the traditional setting in which a farmers' dance used to be performed and the makeshift stage for this night's performance before the now-departed spectators is so dramatic that it suggests both the inner and the outer breakdown of displaced people. Even so,

Shin can express his deep anger and frustration at Park's dictatorial regime only figuratively, by letting the farmers mention legendary robber-rebels. In the context of widespread urbanization and industrialized progress in Korea, the farmers' final dance gestures—in the absence of the old-time, agrarian, and communitarian excitement—look all the more desperate, forced, heavy, and agonizing.

Han Ji-hee

FARROKHZAD, FORUGH (1935–1967)

Forugh Farrokhzad remains one of the most acclaimed—and condemned—poets in Persian literature. The honesty and passion of her poetry and her authentic portrayal of female experience in mid-20th-century Iran challenged her social world and its literary stereotypes and, more remarkably, defied one thousand years of patriarchy. Farrokhzad's life spanned a transitional time in Iranian history, which saw a drive for constitutional representation, modernization, and change when the restricted roles and rights of Iranian women were, at least superficially, being addressed. In 1936 the Pahlavi government abolished the chador (veil), established coeducational schools, and officially encouraged women to participate in civic life. Farrokhzad would nevertheless challenge convention at every stage of her brief life.

Farrokhzad was born the third of seven children on January 5, 1935, in Tehran. Her father was a career military officer, and the family was comfortably middle class. She attended government schools through ninth grade, then transferred to Kamalolmolk Technical School to study sewing and painting. At 16 Farrokhzad fell in love with and married a relative, Parviz Shapur, 15 years her senior. One year later, in 1952, she gave birth to a son, Kamyar. Within two years Farrohkhzad and her husband had separated, and, as is standard in patriarchal societies, with the divorce she lost custody of her child. Farrokhzad's first poetry collection, *Asir* (The Captive), was published in the summer of 1955. By fall she was hospitalized after an emotional breakdown, the consequence of disappointment and loss. Farrokhzad's next two collections appeared in rapid succession: *Divar* (The Wall) in 1956 and *Esian* (Rebel-

lion) in 1958. Farrokhzad then began an important romantic and artistic alliance with writer and cinematographer Ebrahim Golestan. Under his influence she explored filmmaking, acting, and producing. In 1962 she produced her most noteworthy documentary, *The House Is Black,* depicting a leper colony. The film won international acclaim and several awards. After a lapse of six years Farrokhzad's fourth volume, *Tavallodi Digar* (Another Birth), was published in 1964. On February 14, 1967, Farrokhzad died at age 32 in a car crash. A posthumous volume of verse, *Iman Biavarim be Aghaz-e Fasl-e Sard* (Let Us Believe in the Dawning of a Cold Season) was published in 1974.

Farrokhzad's corpus presents a profound evolution of language, voice, and thematic preoccupation. Her early work is best characterized as introspective and confessional in tone, formatted in traditional lyric style, and concerned with love—self, sexual, and romantic. *Asir* has autobiographical roots in Farrokhzad's confinement within marriage. There is struggle between the speaker's desire for freedom and her internalization of society's value system, chiefly its conventional morality. The poems remain emotionally reactive and not analytic of what is felt to be an unsatisfactory situation. Farrokhzad's next two volumes are charged with the spirit of revolt and further develop a voice of feminist protest. *Divar* depicts the resistance she meets living as a woman outside a marital identity. Farrokhzad reacts bitterly to society's unequal treatment of women. In these poems she moves beyond personal confinement to express a range of social frustrations. In *Esian* Farrokhzad progresses to metaphysical rejection of traditional Koranic teachings on the nature of good and evil. By exorcizing her rage in *Divar* and *Esian* Farrokhzad releases herself from repression and achieves a more balanced perspective. Throughout the 1950s she composed in traditional verse forms, even though the modernist movement had gained prominence in Iran. Of the 86 poems in her first three books, only 12 do not resort to rhyming couplets. Thus Farrokhzad's earlier works are distinguished mainly by novelty of subject matter. In *Tavallodi Digar* (Another Birth), Farrokhzad overcomes victimization and anger to search for a social identity for women. What was initially personal is now universalized, rendered collective. Moreover, she makes radical formal modifications. Line-length regularity and stanzaic organization are abandoned to free-flowing structure. Words and images are chosen for their familiarity and street-fidelity. Across the decade her principal literary influences included Persian modernist NIMA YUSHIJ and Argentinean poet ALFONSINA STORNI, whom Farrokhzad read in translation. Her posthumously published *Let Us Believe in the Dawning of a Cold Season* (1974) offers a darker vision and somber mood. She expresses loneliness, grief, and betrayal of her earlier belief in enduring love: "the lamp of connection is dark." Her continuing preoccupation with death eerily foreshadows her own impending fatal accident.

Farrokhzad's work is becoming more and more available in English, and many translations by different hands appear online. The best hard-copy translations are those of Hasan Javadi and Susan Sallee in *Another Birth* (Emoryville, Calif.: Albany Press, 1981) and those of Jascha Kessler (with Amin Banani) in *Bride of Acacias* (Tehran, Iran: Caravan, 1982).

BIBLIOGRAPHY

Hillmann, Michael. *A Lonely Woman: Forugh Farrokhzad and Her Poetry*. Washington, D.C.: Three Continents Press, 1987.

Milani, Farzaneh. *Veils and Words: Emerging Voices of Iranian Women Writers*. Syracuse, N.Y.: Syracuse University Press, 1992.

Talattof, Kamran. *The Politics of Writing in Iran*. Syracuse, N.Y.: Syracuse University Press, 2000.

Anett Jessop

FIELD POETICS

Field poetics may be defined by a systematic integrity that overrides individual authorial intention. The system in play is usually a form of language, purely acoustic, or purely visual, often scored speech or another verbal matrix. Among the most uncompromising works with this characteristic are the mesostics and chance-based compositions of John Cage and works associated with Oulipo: Ouvroir de Littérature Potentielle (Workshop of Potential Literature): Raymond Queneau, François Le Lionnais, Claude Berge, Georges Perec, and Italo Calvino. Typical of Oulipo poetics is the "S + 7" method, by which each noun is systematically replaced by the noun to be found seven places away in a chosen dictionary. The method frees text production from personal agency, yielding fascinating results that speak to the essential arbitrariness of all linguistic conventions. The productions of the Noigandres Group in Brazil and of the Vienna Group, both highly abstract in their methodologies, speak to a similar ethos of composition and to the international scope of different forms of field poetics. Abstract and experimental processes of text production like those cited here reflect a widely held belief that alternative models of language hold the potential for renovating current usage, restoring human and spiritual universals that have become obscured by social alienation and contemporary consumerist values. In 1919, speaking for the Dadaist Revolutionary Central Council, Richard Huelsenbeck and Raul Hausmann demanded, among other items, "The immediate expropriation of property (socialization) and / the communal feeding of all; further, the erection of cities of light, and gardens which will belong to society as a whole and prepare man for a state of freedom." This manifesto reflects a desire characteristic of field poetics: to renew through radical change.

Precursors of contemporary field poetics include the symbolist stage of Stéphane Mallarmé, futurism (both Italian and Russian), the imagism and vorticism of Ezra Pound, and the antipoetics associated with dada. An important distinction must be made between the use of white space as a weighted silence in Mallarmé's "Un coup de dés" (A Throw of the Dice) and the imagist impulse as shaped by Pound. Pictorial function is secondary, distinguishing these poems from emblems or word-pictures, for instance, the calligrammes in Apollinaire's collection of that title. In his "Vorticism" essay of 1914, Pound defined the image as "the word beyond formulated language" (88). "The image is not an idea," Pound continued; "it is radiant node or cluster . . . a vortex, from which and through which, and into which, ideas are constantly rushing" (92). A similar use of the image of the vortex was integral to Italian futurist poetics—for instance, Carlo Carra's *Interventionist Demonstration* (1914), associated with F. W. Marinetti's "*Paroles en liberta*," a spinning wheel of words, reflecting machine speed; however, Pound's evocative theorization of systems of self-sustaining form, correlated to the flow of an energy like an electrical current, remains deeply influential for most poetries associated with field poetics to this day. The Noigandres Group of Brazil specifically acknowledged this indebtedness to Pound's poetics, as did far-flung avant-gardes such as the VOU Club of Japan (Kitasono Katue) and the objectivists associated with Louis Zukofsky in the United States. Pound's poetics greatly influenced the Beat, black mountain, and language poetries of North America.

VOU Club poetics, like works produced in Germany and associated with the Bauhaus or the Merz poetics of Kurt Schwitters as well as works produced in Russia under a suprematist or cubo-futurist impulse, implement a concrete and abstract formalism that might seem to belie the acoustic function of these texts as scored speech. Notable examples here are the *zaum* texts of Velimir Khlebnikov, Kurt Schwitters's *Ursonate,* and the sound poetry of Bernard Heidsick and Henri Chopin. The evolution of different forms of scored speech clearly originates with Italian futurism, then morphs both in German through dada and in Russian through suprematism into an abstract and highly formal or constructivist poetics. Continuing examples of this practice may be found in works by Gerhard Rühm, Ernst Jandl, Friederike Mayröcker, and other members of the Vienna Group. Readers of English are indebted to Rosmarie Waldrop for her translations of these texts and to Rosmarie and Keith Waldrop for their publication of them through Burning Deck's Série d'Écriture (see bibliography at end of article).

Italian futurism itself generally prized explosive violence and machine aesthetics over individual expression. Many readers are distraught over this celebration of violence and the eventual association of futurism with fascism. Referring to the Italian campaign in Ethiopia (1935–1941), Marinetti wrote, "For twenty-seven years we Futurists have rebelled against the branding of war as anti-aesthetic. . . . Accordingly we state: . . . War is beautiful because it establishes man's dominion over the subjugated machinery by means of gas masks, terrifying megaphones, flame throwers, and small tanks. War is beautiful because it initiates the dreamt-of metalization of the human body." In Marinetti's visual texts sonic structures replace the usual human markings of verbal expressions.

The lettrism of Isadore Isou, very different in its political impulse, leading to the politics of the Situationist International, also undertakes to embrace a universal sense of human integrity, located in experiences of sound prior to conscious individualism. Lettrism derives from the performance art of the dadaists, such as Hugo Ball and Marcel Janco. These artists explored the interface of antipoetic systems and acoustic experiment, verging on babbling. Tristan Tzara and Francis Picabia pushed the relation between free form verbalism and machine aesthetics toward the mapping of individual psychic apparatuses.

The exploration of interiority is a continuing function of field poetics insofar as a search for spiritual integrity motivates the practice. Whether interior space seems best adumbrated by the Buddha or Carl Jung, field poetics obviates the subjectively compromised spaces of the Freudian imagination. For instance, the sources of poetics as different as Cage's chance operations and Jack Kerouac's "spontaneous bop prosody" are Buddhist. Wilson Harris's "cross cultural imagination" evokes spiritual resonances with the collective psychic processes described by Jung, as does the poetry of Charles Olson. Clausfriedrich Claus, working with small transparencies, creates overlays of Jungian and mystical texts where desiring machines, resembling large insects, crawl over the landscapes of layered texts.

The spiritual inflection is present in many practices associated with field poetics. Pound's composite or ideogrammic images inscribe readings of a divine imprint or coherence. Spiritually based readings associated with acrostics, riddles, and palimpsests are central to the alphabetic mysticisms of the Gnostics and Jewish interpreters of Kabbalah. Concrete poetry shares some aspects of this history, having an affinity with mystical functions of the emblem or icon. Field poetics, in its scoring of the visual and acoustic properties of language, operates as a distinctly empowering decoding or reading practice, taking the form of annotations, secret keys, and glosses of a source text. One of the most striking examples of this latter process is the work of the contemporary poet Susan Howe. Religious traditions of visual poetry are also associated with trance states, producing glossolalia (or speaking in tongues), predecessors of the dada performance pieces and also of the mystically inspired *Gematria* of Jerome Rothenberg and Harris Lenowitz, and the ethnopoetic experiments undertaken by Rothenberg in association with tribal informants (for instance, the *Horse Songs* of Frank Mitchell).

The discovery of a divine or spiritual imprint within the textures of language reflects for some the ancient religious yearnings of human beings. In this context poetry of pared-down concretions, like PAUL CELAN's final works in *Threadsuns,* provides examples of processes associated with field poetics. For instance, in the lines cited here images of holocaust and of feverish reading of sacred texts collide:

Jetzt, da die betshemmel brennen,
eß ich das Buch
mit allen
Insignien
(Now, as the prayerstools burn,
I eat the book
with all the
insiginia)

Seemingly unrelated to Celan's impulse, recent poetries such as those associated with Fluxus (Dick Higgins, George Brecht, Toshi Ichiyanagi, and Yoko Ono, among many other practitioners) or the work of Canada's Four Horsemen (bp Nichol, Raphael Barreto-Rivera, Steve McCaffery, and Paul Dutton) share the desire to articulate a divine or spiritual presence. This vector has consistently identified field poetics in the English language practice. Charles Olson in his essay "The Human Universe" articulated the best-known and most comprehensively constructed model of field poetics, citing the quantum mechanical realities described by Werner Heisenberg and Riemann calculus, as well as his own fieldwork in the Yucatán. Olson's theorizations, especially his "Projective Verse" (1950), influenced both Fluxus poetics and the spontaneous bop prosody of Allen Ginsberg and Jack Kerouac. The sound poetry of Canada's Four Horsemen, also influenced by the range of Olson's practice, has been described as rhizomatic, "tunneling invisibly below the surface to appear in unexpected places." In many ways the philosophy of desiring machines mapped by Giles Deleuze and Felix

Guattari is descriptive of the underlying push of all varieties of field poetics, understood as a vector or line of flight leading away from individual egotism toward an embrace of systems that either purify or renovate human affective potential, placing perception and process ahead of conceptualization, and thereby warping the theory-practice loop that underlies Western pragmatism, print culture, and the accountant's grid.

The conceptual integrity of field poetics with respect to layered processes of composition was established early in the modern period. Like Pound, Marcel Duchamp considered the linear nature of standard syntax to be counterproductive to a grasp of the field of available meaning in any one instance. Duchamp, anticipating Wittgenstein, employed language games that derive from the machine aesthetics of futurism, the antipoetics of dada, and the intellectual intensity that arises from ironic operations on language at the simple level of the phoneme. For instance, the title for his painting *Le passage de la vierge à la mariée* enacts a small warp in its verbal field, highlighting a complex punning association between *"vierge"* (virgin) and *"verge"* (the common French word for penis). The play of significance lies in the difference created by the presence (or lack) of a single letter, the "i" of "vierge," teasingly representative of an individual ego, among other possible meanings. Today's language-centered poetries in the United States (by Charles Bernstein, for instance) embody a continuation of a similarly trenchant punning sensibility. Contemporary French poets identified with the practice of *écriture* (Anne-Marie Albiach, Claude Royet-Journoud, and Emmanuel Hocquard) explore the difference between subjective positions and author functions, modifying common senses of both "literal meaning" and "lyricism."

An antihumanistic aspect is common to different practices of field poetics. For some, like Duchamp, this impulse originates in a critique of the often selfish individualism associated with the family drama, hence the turn toward the purity of manufactured items or toward found objects lacking personal history; for others, the wor[l]d system based on Western philosophical thought and its humanistic citation of the rights of man has been a mask for ruthless exploitation, including slavery and environmental destruction. This later critique is the source for Charles Olson's poetics and important to other poets—including Wilson Harris and AIMÉ CÉSAIRE—associated with emerging identities in formerly colonized regions of the world.

Readers of English are fortunate in that many of the works cited in this essay can be found in *Poems for the Millennium,* edited by Jerome Rothenberg and Pierre Joris. Ubuweb (www.ubu.com) is a particularly rich online resource for many of the topics relating to field poetics.

BIBLIOGRAPHY

Albiach, Anne-Marie. *A Geometry.* Translated by Keith Waldrop and Rosmarie Waldrop. Série d'écriture. Providence, R.I.: Burning Deck, 1998.

Celan, Paul. *Light Duress.* Translated by Pierre Joris. Los Angeles: Green Integer, 2005.

Hausmann, Raoul, and Richard Huelsenbeck. "What Is Dadaism and What Does It Want in Germany (1919)." In *En Avant Dada: A History of Dadaism. The Dada Painters and Poets: An Anthology,* edited by Robert Motherwell. Reprint, Cambridge: Belknap, 1989, 21–48.

Hocquard, Emmanuel. *A Test of Solitude: Sonnets.* Translated by Rosmarie Waldrop. Série d'écriture. Providence, R.I.: Burning Deck, 2000.

Jandl, Ernst. *Reft and Light: Poems by Ernst Jandl with Multiple Versions by American Poets.* Providence, R.I.: Burning Deck, 2000.

"Mallarmé, Stéphane. *Collected Poems.* Translated by Henry Weinfield. Berkeley: University of California Press, 1994.

Mayröcker, Friederike. *Heiligenanstalt.* Translated by Rosmarie Waldrop. Providence, R.I.: Burning Deck, 1994.

McCaffery, Steve. "Sound Poetry—A Survey." Excerpted from *Sound Poetry: A Catalogue,* edited by Steve McCaffery and bp Nichol. Toronto: Underwich Editions, 1978. Available online. URL: http://www.ubu.com/papers/mccaffery.html. Accessed on April 22, 2007.

Motte, Warren F, ed. *Oulipo: A Primer of Potential Literature.* French Literature Series. Chicago: Dalkey Archive Press, 1998.

Olson, Charles. "Human Universe." In *Selected Writings,* edited by Robert Creeley. New York: New Directions Press, 1971.

Pound, Ezra. "Vorticism." In *Gaudier-Brzeska: A Memoir.* New York: New Directions Press, 1970, 81–94.

Rothenberg, Jerome, and Pierre Joris, eds. *Poems for the Millennium: A Global Anthology of Modern & Postmodern Poetry.* Vol. 1, *From Fin-de-Siècle to Négritude*; Vol. II, *From Postwar to Millennium.* Berkeley: University of California Press, 1995, 1998.

Royet-Journoud, Claude. *i. e.* Translated by Keith Waldrop. Série d'écriture. Providence, R.I.: Burning Deck, 1995.

Rühm, Gerhard. *I My Feet: Poems and Constellation.* Translated by Rosmarie Waldrop. Providence, R.I.: Burning Deck, 2004.

Donald Wellman

"FIERY SHE-WOLF, THE" VASKO POPA (1975)

On the surface Vasko Popa's fifth poetry collection, *Wolf Salt* (1975), appears to be one of his most hermetic works since it revolves around a wolf motif without many points of reference outside of the apparent symbolic. But once the reader breaks the "code" by understanding how Popa incorporated Serbian folklore into his poetry, the poems come to life: The lame wolf represents the pagan past of Serbia; the she-wolf is the Serbian land; the wolf shepherd is St. Sava, the Serbian saint who brought Christianity to the Serbs; further, if wolves represent the Serbs, then the wolf bastard is the modern Serbian man. The strength of this collection resides in how Popa utilizes the cycle form as a way of approaching his subject matter: the regenerative power of the Serbian people despite centuries of oppression. A manageable way of seeing how well the poet pulls this off is by taking a close look at one of the cycles "The Fiery She-wolf."

"The Fiery She-wolf" is a cycle in five sections, each documenting an aspect of the she-wolf's journey toward overcoming her tormentors. The first section is a description of the she-wolf. The imagery here sets the tone. She resides "In heaven's foothills" and is therefore a sacred animal (l. 2): "Her body is a live coal"; her offspring "Wolves play over her back / And live in her crystal womb" (ll. 3, 14–15). The second section is a hellish world in which her tormentors "force-feed her with burning coals" and give her "boiling quicksilver milk" to drink (ll. 6–8). Despite her torture, she still manages to snatch a star in her jaws to return "to heaven's foothills" (ll. 12–14). After she is caught "in steel traps / Stretched from horizon to horizon" (in the third section), her persecutors "hack her to pieces / And leave her / To the vulture's talons" (ll. 2–3, 9–11). Still, with the "stump of her tongue" the she-wolf drinks

"Living water" from the sky and heals herself (ll. 12–14). Through her regenerative powers she overcomes her oppressors. In the fourth section, being able to clean the "dog-ash off her body," she takes on attributes of Perun, the pagan thunder god of the Slavs: "Lightning spawns / In her gaping jaws"; and "In the chasms / Below the forests of her eyebrows / Thunderbolts are ready for anything" (ll. 2, 5–6, 12–14). Finally, in the fifth section the she-wolf has once more returned to "heaven's foothills" (l. 2). The difference here, however, is that her progeny have "Turned to stone in her womb" (l. 4). The she-wolf, though surviving her torture, now carries the dead within her. She then transforms again: from Perun in the previous section to Dabog, a Slavic god of the underworld. Despite her Hades-esque persona in the concluding section, the she-wolf "rises dead with thirst / Towards . . . the top of heaven / . . . the watering place of the long-tailed stars" (ll. 13–15). In each section Popa reveals how the she-wolf is able to exist and persevere because of her divine connection as represented in images of stars, holy hills, clouds, and thunder.

As "The Fiery She-wolf" demonstrates, Popa uses the cycle to reinforce folkloric elements within his work through repetition and rephrasing to work up a rich metaphoric froth that transcends the locality of one's history to tap into a more universal statement about the human condition. In the case of this poem cycle and *Wolf Salt* as a whole, the perseverance of a people is showcased. They are shown capable of throwing off their oppressors to maintain their cultural integrity.

BIBLIOGRAPHY

Alexander, Ronelle. *The Structure of Vasko Popa's Poetry.* Columbus, Ohio: Slavica, 1985.
Lekić, Anita. *The Quest for Roots: The Poetry of Vasko Popa.* New York: Peter Lang, 1993.
Popa, Vasko. "The Fiery She-Wolf." *Collected Poems.* Translated by Anne Pennington and Francis R. Jones. London: Anvil Press Poetry, 1997, 225–229.

Steven Teref

FIVE GREAT ODES PAUL CLAUDEL (1910)

Five Great Odes (*Cinq Grandes Odes*) comprises five confessional poems composed by French poet, dramatist, and diplomat PAUL CLAUDEL between 1901 and 1908. They were collected and published in book form in 1910. The first poem, "The Muses" ("*Les Muses*"), was written in the tumultuous time between Claudel's consideration of monastic life and his encounter with Rosalie Vetch, a married Polish woman of whom he became deeply enamored. The four subsequent poems—"Spirit and Water" ("*L'Esprit et l'eau*") (1906), "Magnificat" (1907), "The Muse Who Is Grace" ("*La Muse qui est la Grâce,*" 1907), and "The Closed House" ("*La Maison fermée,*" 1908)— were produced after his return from a diplomatic mission to China and his subsequent marriage to Reine Sainte-Marie Perrin. The *Odes* exhibit many of the central themes of Claudel's verse (biographical allusions, biblical motifs, and so on) and often express a penitential tone, perhaps tied to his deep Roman Catholic faith, perhaps a result of his illicit relationship with Vetch.

In "The Muses" the poet is inspired by a classical frieze in the Louvre museum and comments on the way in which God preserves the poet's beloved, who is protected, at least in part, from the ravages of time. The poet's present is connected to the ancient, pagan past through the poetic inspiration of the Muses, the nine goddesses of the arts of ancient Greece. The other poems in the collection focus on the quest of the poet to achieve absolution from his sins, which culminates with his return to Catholicism (in "Magnificat") and his opportunity to pass along his faith to his daughter, Marie. The final poem of the collection, "The Closed House," rejects the paganism of the first poem, "The Muses," by celebrating four theological virtues: prudence, strength, temperance, and justice. The poem also honors the triumph of wholesome conjugal love within a church-sanctioned marriage and condemns the poet's earlier, illicit erotic love, found in "The Muses."

Structurally, *Five Great Odes* follows a musical evolution—moving from the erotic, uninhibited Bacchanalian attitude of "The Muses" toward the devotional tone that the Muse Grace adopts in glorifying God. Overall the poems sustain a powerful personal lyricism that conveys the power of love—whether adulterous or married—while favoring the religious culmination embodied in the emotive musicality of the Catholic Mass, which Claudel attended almost daily throughout his life.

Joseph E. Becker

FLOWERS FROM HELL Nguyễn Chí Thiên **(1954–1979; pub. 1984)**   Most if not all of Nguyễn Chí Thiên's poems in the 1984 bilingual edition *Flowers from Hell* were composed in his head while Thiên was a political prisoner in a North Vietnamese concentration camps between 1958 and 1976. Because he was not allowed to have paper and pencils, Thiên had to memorize his poems. Those published in English translation in 1984 were set down in writing between his release in 1976 and before 1979. The manuscript was dramatically delivered in person to the British diplomatic delegation when the poet, risking arrest, broke through Vietnamese guards at the British embassy in Hanoi on July 16, 1979, and appealed straightforwardly to the diplomats to publish his work in the West. Thiên was immediately rearrested upon leaving the British embassy and spent the following 16 years in prison, sometimes in total darkness and solitary confinement. He continued to compose poetry mentally as a means of survival, memorizing hundreds of poems. Because he was so closely watched, he was able to write them down only once he was permitted to leave Vietnam in 1995. A complete version of *Flowers from Hell,* which includes hundreds of poems from the second set of prison poems, was published in Vietnamese in 1996.

In the original the poems are versified in strict meters and strong rhyme schemes. Most of the poems are fairly short, seldom running to more than half a page. And most of them are harshly critical, bitterly resistant expressions of dissidence from communism. Their themes are resistance, dreams of freedom, bitterness about the passage of time, life in the prison camps, excoriations of the degradations 'brought upon Vietnam by the communist system, memories of past pleasures and the careless days of youth, his mother's love, his impossible love for a special woman, his betrothal to poetry, hard labor, clouds, trees, birds, recollections of nature, hunger, and the behavior of prisoners and prison keepers. Some are letters to imaginary persons, some to real people such as Bertrand Russell, who is invited to visit Vietnam and castigated for expressing support for the Vietcong: "the Party's gagged our mouths all these long years. / After your visit you'll hate them, / you'll want to drag them out and chop them up. / Almost a hundred years of age, / you're less

expert than any famished child / in Communism, my dear sir" (53). The moods swing from deepest despair to hatred, then back to optimism about the human spirit and the joys of remembered freedoms, love, and companionship under clear skies. The poems cry out the poet's sense that "All pathways to life's gate are blocked" (63) and "Oh, how it hurts, the century's big mistake!" (65). Interspersed among the bitter laments and the revivifying recollections are the poems of staunch resistance, like "The Party Banished Me to the Wilds." Its last stanza describes the way the party buries political prisoners, "wishing I'd turn to mud down there. / A miner I've become— / I'll dig up precious ore, and tons of it, / not gold nor diamond for a woman's toys: / uranium ore for atom bombs" (71). These collected poems are Thiên's bombs: explosive and moving verbalizations of the indomitable and free-thinking human spirit.

R. Victoria Arana

FRENCH RAP   In the 20th century, French-language poetry was often influenced by American music. Guillaume Apollinaire, Léopold Sédar Senghor, and Boris Vian innovatively mined jazz and blues music for their own modern poetry. In much the same way French rap musicians have carved out a poetic tradition of their own based on American rap.

Rap first reached French shores in 1982, thanks to the efforts of two Frenchmen living in New York. Bernard Zekri and Jean Karakos recorded the first rap song in French, titled *"Change de Beat"* ("Change of Beat"), and organized the New York City Rap Tour in Europe. The daily newspaper *Libération* further legitimized rap's presence in France when it printed a series of articles about New York rap in 1982 (Cannon 152).

In the early years rap found an eager audience in young immigrants from the Caribbean living in Paris. The first DJ to learn the spinning techniques of Jamaican and U.S. disc jockeys was Dee Nasty, who broadcast rap each Sunday on the Radio Nova channel. In response to his rejection by major labels, he began to produce and sell rap records independently in the streets in 1984 (Cannon 157).

Political changes in France helped to popularize rap. When François Mitterrand became president of France in 1981, he legalized "free radio" stations on the FM band for the first time. A station named Carbone 14 began to play rap day and night. Jack Lang's appointment to the Ministry of Culture in 1982 further legitimized rap, along with the street arts of *le tag* (graffiti) and *le smurf* (break dancing). Lang sponsored music festivals and invited rappers to perform at official functions, such as the garden party for the National Assembly (Gross et al. 15). Matthieu Kassovitz's film *La Haine* (*Hate,* 1985) further awakened the mainstream to rap's powerful urban protest. Featuring the ideological rap of IAM and NTM, *La Haine* was the first film to depict life in the Parisian *banlieues* (the suburbs where many immigrant communities are located).

In the 1990s rap became increasingly diverse and popular. The anthology *Rappattitudes* (1991) introduced a wide variety of styles and groups, including MC Solaar, IAM, and the female rapper Saliha. In 1991 MC Solaar produced his first 12-inch 45-rpm record, *Bouge de là* (Get Outta Here), followed by the album *Qui sème le vent récolte le tempo* (He Who Sows the Wind Shall Reap the Beat, 1992). Subsequent albums featured Solaar's poetry rap style, discussed below.

Regional rap also emerged in the 1990s. While rappers from Toulouse and Lyon were popular, Marseilles became the main stage for the emergence of rap in southern France, due to the success of groups like Massilia Sound System, Fonky Family, and IAM. With the albums *De la planète Mars* (From the Planet Mars, 1991) and *Ombre est lumière* (Shadow Is Light, 1993), the Marseilles group IAM embraced the city, elevating it in their lyrics to the mythical status of ancient Egypt. Today IAM's members are still involved in the rap industry; former lead singer Akhenaton, or Philippe Fragione, launched a successful solo career in 1995 and created his own record label, Côté Obscur, to help young recording artists (Radio France Internationale).

French rap has also become the favorite genre of the Francophone, or French-speaking, worlds of Africa and the Caribbean. In the former French colony of Senegal, for example, at least 6,000 rap groups exist today. The best-known of these groups, Daara J, is from Senegal. Daara J's style of Sene rap (rap from Senegal) incorporates Cuban rumba, soul, and ragamuffin music into its unique style (Cornwell).

It may well be French rap's *banlieue* ideology, or belief system, that sets it apart from American rap. French youths have adapted urban, American hip-hop culture—rap, graffiti, and break dancing—to voice their frustration with the unjust treatment of immigrants and minorities in the *cités* (projects). French rap thus has become one tool in resisting racism, oppression, and alienation in France's *banlieues.* These themes are epitomized in the music of Suprême NTM, whose members were imprisoned in 1996 for police defamation. Even though French rappers are inspired by the black power discourse in U.S. rap, they are also well known for promoting positive ways of transcending their social circumstances through self-awareness, affirmation, and education.

Unlike American rappers, French rap artists come from diverse ethnic origins, and primarily from former French colonies in Africa and the Caribbean. While groups like Suprême NTM are white and Caribbean, Saliha is Arab and Italian, and Dee Nasty is a white artist from the Parisian *banlieues.* In spite of their distinct origins, these poet-singers share a search for an ethnic voice apart from the French majority and outside the French republican model of integration (Cannon 162). Perhaps for this reason rap has replaced traditional music in much of the North African community in France, allowing immigrant youths to stay connected with Arab heritage as well as the hip counterculture (Gross et al. 14).

In France rap is often called "the true poetry of the people" and commonly considered part of a classical poetry lineage (Caffari and Villette 96). It relies heavily on rhetorical devices such as onomatopoeia, acronym, aphorism, assonance, neologism, alliteration, and rhyme. Repetition and fluidity are created through tightly interwoven sound and meaning (Caffari and Villette 101–102). Solaar illustrates how poetry and *banlieue* ideology can work in harmony, making fun of people who call him a "capitalist" by breaking down the French word *capitaliste* into separate French syllables, then repeating them to create a kind of baby talk: *"Ce monde est caca, pipi, cacapipi-taliste"* (What is this world? This capisstalist shitstem) (Cannon 163). MC Solaar, like most French rappers, carries the heavy burden of showing both continuity with and rupture from linguistic norms and poetic conventions.

The French rapper also follows the American rap tradition of cutting up and reassembling music of all genres or dialogue into fragments through mixing, scratching, and sampling. The rapper employs a variety of techniques, including versatile syntax, wordplay, and borrowing from multiple registers such as vernacular, street slang, and literary diction. Often the slang is a product of *verlan,* which involves cutting the original word in two or three parts and putting the last syllable first and first syllable last. Other rap lyrics are imported from the Arabic or African speech patterns of artists' immigrant families. Rap's jazz and blues dialogue also recalls the traditions of the African *griot* (oral historian from a family of musicians), as well as the French *paroleur* (storyteller).

The rap style of MC Solaar, born Claude M'Barali in Senegal in 1969, is poetic and popular. His fans appreciated the intelligent humor and lyrical poetry of his first album, *Bouge de là* (Get Out of My Way, 1991) and *Prose Combat* (1994), which features the hit "Nouveau Western." This rewrite of French singer Serge Gainsbourg's classic "Bonnie and Clyde" cleverly bridges canonical and popular lyric traditions. Solaar's songs generally abound in reference to literary figures like Umberto Eco and Raymond Queneau, as well as Western films and urban culture (Caffari and Villette 102). While some rap fans believe that Solaar belongs to and enriches the French poetic tradition, he is accused by some of betraying rap's basic ideology in the name of fame. Solaar has said that in spite of his membership on the Cannes Festival jury in 1998, he is committed to helping his community and erasing stereotypes. In 1995 he founded his own label, Sentinel Nord, to encourage and finance the work of young rap artists. In the same year he held three writing workshops for aspiring young rap artists in the city of Marseilles alone (Sberna 186).

BIBLIOGRAPHY

Caffari, Marie, and Agnès Villette. "Le rap français: évaluation de textes contemporains." In *Black, Blanc, Beur: Youth Language and Identity in France,* edited by Farid Aitsiselmi, 95–112. Bradford, West Yorkshire, U.K.: Department of Modern Languages, University of Bradford, 2000.

Cannon, Steve. "Paname City Rapping: B-boys in the *banlieues* and beyond." In *Post-Colonial Cultures in France,* edited by Alec G. Hargreaves and Mark McKinney, 150–166. London: Routledge, 1997.

Cornwell, Jane. "Rap around the World." *The Weekend Australian,* February 5, 2005. p. B18.

Durand, Alain-Philippe, ed. *Black, Blanc, Beur: Rap Music and Hip-hop Culture in the Francophone World.* Oxford: Scarecrow, 2002.

Gross, Jean, David McMurray, and Ted Swedenburg. "Rai, Rap and Ramadan Nights: Franco-Maghribi Cultural Identities." *Middle East Report* 178 (Sept.–Oct. 1992): 11–24.

Hughes, Alex, and Keith Reader, eds. *Encyclopedia of Contemporary French Culture.* London: Routledge, 2001.

Radio France Internationale. Available online. URL: http://www.rfimusique.com. Accessed on July 20, 2005.

Sberna, Béatrice. *Une Sociologie du rap à Marseille: Identité marginale et immigrée.* Paris: L'Harmattan, 2001.

DISCOGRAPHY
Compilations

Rapattitude, 1990. Virgin; 1995, Delabel. *La haine: musiques inspirées du film.*

IAM, 1991. *De la planète mars,* Delabel.

——— (1993) *Ombre est lumière,* Delabel.

MC Solaar (1991) *Qui sème le vent récolte le tempo,* Polydor.

——— (1994) *Prose combat,* Polydor.

Suprême NTM (1991) *Authentik,* Epik/Sony.

Heather Brady

G

GARCÍA LORCA, FEDERICO (1898–1936)

The poet and playwright Federico García Lorca is the most universally loved 20th-century Spanish author, known for his musical writing style and also for his tragic, untimely death during the first days of the Spanish civil war (1936–39). He is the most famous member of the Generation of '27, a group of avant-garde poets who rejuvenated the Spanish poetic tradition for the first time since its creative outburst during the Renaissance. Brutally assassinated at the age of 37 by General Francisco Franco supporters, and thus a casualty of a military regime, García Lorca remains a powerful symbol of the creative genius whose aesthetic legacy political repression was unable to destroy.

García Lorca was born in 1898 in Fuente Vaqueros, a small village near the Moorish city of Granada, into a wealthy family of a prosperous farmer and a schoolteacher. Music and literature were important parts of his childhood. Later he studied law at the University of Granada and then moved to Madrid, where he continued his education at the University of Madrid and lived in the Residencia de Estudiantes (Student Residence), a vibrant center of Spain's contemporary intellectual life. There García Lorca met the filmmaker Luis Buñuel and the artist Salvador Dalí, whose personalities and interest in surrealist aesthetics influenced his own work. He also met other poets (including Emilio Prados, RAFAEL ALBERTI, and JUAN RAMON JIMÉNEZ) who attempted to give voice to the new sensibility that emerged in the first decades of the 20th century. Much like their counterparts across Europe, these poets explored the potential of modernist aesthetics and also searched for inspiration in Spain's eclectic folklore. García Lorca became the leader of the group. His first book of poetry, *Book of Poems* (*Libro de poemas*), was published in 1921; although he earned a law degree in 1923, he immediately gave up a legal career in favor of his true calling, literature.

In poetry García Lorca sought to reconcile surrealist imagery with the elements of Spain's folk tradition, in particular those of the deep song (*cante hondo* or *cante jondo*), a musical style of García Lorca's native southern Spain and one that forms the core of Flamenco art. In the characteristic tension in this art between the extreme emotion and terse, minimalist form, García Lorca perceived the essence of the Spanish spirit with which he also personally identified. He paid tribute to the deep song in the *Poem of the Deep Song,* (*Poema del Cante Jondo,* 1921) and later in the *The Gypsy Ballads* (*Romancero Gitano,* 1927), a series of lyrical ballads about Gypsy life that idealizes the figure of an outsider whose love for freedom may be his tragedy. Passion, death, personal honor, and love of freedom—the central themes of the deep song—acquired new life in García Lorca's poetry (see "The FAITHLESS WIFE") and also became the focus of his dramatic work. The historical drama *Mariana Pineda* (1928), for example, romanticizes a young 19th-century revolutionary accused and summarily executed on charges of conspiracy against the government.

In 1929–30 García Lorca traveled to New York City, where he enrolled in courses at Columbia University. This experience marked a turning point in his life. The alienating atmosphere of a giant modern metropolis came as a shock to the Andalusian poet, who did not speak English. *The Poet in New York* (*Poeta en Nueva York*), García Lorca's most pessimistic but also most personal collection of poems published posthumously in 1940, fully chronicles these impressions. García Lorca hails American poetic voices represented by Walt Whitman (see "ODE TO WALT WHITMAN") but condemns the terror-inducing cold city that he eventually fled for Havana. In Cuba he delivered his famous lecture "The Play and Theory of Duende" (*"Juego y teoría del duende"*), in which he develops the idea of *duende,* a demonlike figure of Spanish folklore, as a key concept in the discussion of Spanish aesthetics.

In the following years García Lorca traveled to Latin America, delivering public lectures on art in Argentina and Uruguay. He wrote less, but his poetic style became more polished and refined, achieving supreme mastery in his "LAMENT FOR IGNACIO SÁNCHEZ MEJÍAS" (*"Llanto por Ignacio Sánchez Mejías,"* 1935), a poem in four parts written after the famous bullfighter and García Lorca's close friend was killed in the rink. He also continued to write for the theater, finishing his dramatic trilogy about passions that permeate life in rural Spain. The first part of this trilogy, *Blood Wedding* (*Bodas de sangre,* 1933), centers on a love triangle; in *Yerma* (1934), a woman murders her husband, who does not share her desire to have children; *The House of Bernarda Alba* (*La casa de Bernarda Alba*), published in 1945, depicts a rigid mother whose tyrannical ways destroy the lives of her daughters.

Demons that García Lorca sang in his poetry came to haunt him in real life. A homosexual artist fascinated by the dark side of the Spanish soul, García Lorca was an enigmatic figure whose very being represented a threat to the conservative military regime that eventually triumphed in Spain. The poet was among the first targets of Generalissimo Francisco Franco's forces, who found and shot the poet. García Lorca's death deeply affected the intellectual community across the world. Trying to make sense of the tragedy, ANTONIO MACHADO, Spain's other great poet, pointed out that *"el crimen fue en Granada, su Granada"* (the crime was in Granada, his Granada). Spain destroyed the very artist who had devoted his entire life to understanding and giving form to its complex spirit.

BIBLIOGRAPHY

Gibson, Ian. *Federico García Lorca: A Life.* London and Boston: Faber and Faber, 1989.

García Lorca, Federico. *The Selected Poems of Federico García Lorca.* Edited by Donald M. Allen, introduction by W. S. Merwin. New York: New Directions, 2005.

———. *The Collected Poems: A Bilingual Edition (Revised).* Edited by Christopher Mauer. New York: Farrar, Straus and Giroux, 2002.

———. *Three Plays: Blood Wedding, Yerma, the House of Bernarda Alba.* Edited and translated by Carmen Zapata and Christopher Maurer. New York: Farrar, Strauss and Giroux, 1993.

Alina Sokol

GEORGE, STEFAN (1868–1933)

Stefan George was the only German ever admitted to the circle around French symbolist poet Stéphane Mallarmé. George was born in Bingen on the Rhine. In his youth he traveled not only to Paris to meet the symbolists, to read and translate their poetry, but also to other European destinations in search of innovative writing. George contemplated writing in French, published his *Algabal* (1892) in Paris, and even invented a private language based on Romance roots before returning to German and Germany. Here he set out to renew and restore poetry through translation (of Baudelaire, Dante, Shakespeare's sonnets, contemporary poets), establishing models (via anthologies of 18th- and 19th-century German poets), and cultivation of young talents. Through his thorough understanding and charisma, George created and inspired a productive and devoted circle of friends. The coherence and ambition of his circle were sustained by George's poetic work. Often his poems were read aloud by those attending formal gatherings of the circle or on more intimate occasions. George never received a university degree and never had a home of his own but moved about, staying with friends in Berlin, Munich, Heidelberg, and elsewhere.

At the center of George's attempt to renew German poetry stand his own poetic achievements. Most scholars distinguish an earlier and a later period (before and after *The Seventh Ring [Der Siebente Ring]* 1907); many argue that at the later stage George's concern was less with form and language and more with influencing society. This critical position implies that the poet transformed himself into a publicist or even a guru and reduced his creative output to a vehicle for ideas. Such a view underestimates, among other things, the significance of George's poetic discovery of Friedrich Hölderlin's late hymns, in which poetic language itself is the key to understanding and hence a prediction of historical processes.

George was never a politician, nor were his friends. The circle's attitude toward politics can be described in the phrase from Ernst Jünger's late diaries: "This is not a time for action but a time for something to happen." George himself claimed an ability to foresee and to interpret future events until in the 1920s this capacity was increasingly called into doubt by the poet himself. The ambition to create and control poetic counterworlds had by then given way in his worldview to a recognition of the openness, presence, and power of surprising events.

Greek antiquity, the Middle Ages, and the Levant provide the setting and imagery for George's evocation of ways of living that are radically and provocatively different from industrialized, formalized, and disintegrated modern Germany. Examples of individuals featured in his poetry are as wide-ranging as Pope Leo XIII, Goethe, Nietzsche, empress Elizabeth ("Sissi") of Austria (1837–1898), a male prostitute from Roman times, and many of George's friends. By evoking distance, both in space and in time, George enables his poetry to question the attitudes of his contemporaries and to demonstrate that supposedly incomprehensible or unprecedented events often do form part of a tradition and can be appreciated more readily in different societies. George's opposition to modernity and his quest for ideals of friendship and unity are best illustrated by his image of the order of the Templars. Friendship, for George, was both a challenge and an inspiration, and his volume *The Star of the Covenant* (*Der Stern des Bundes,* 1914) in particular develops ways of establishing and enriching friendship.

The turning point in the poet's life was the chance encounter in Munich with the teenage poet Maximilian Kronberger, who died at the age of 16 and was later hailed by George as the embodiment of a divine power: "I see in you the god," he wrote. Inspired by this experience, George reintroduced into German poetry religious attitudes and forms (humility, devotion, ritual) and their idioms.

George's language can be extremely difficult. His vocabulary, syntax, and imagery are extraordinarily hermetic. He frequently used paradox to make the reader reconsider ways of thinking (as in the phrase "I am one and I am both," which draws on mystical traditions). His consistently high register, carefully structured cycles, regular rhythms, and, up to about 1907, prevalent use of rhyme—all indicate both the significance of form and an intention to create and communicate meaning. But George could also write more simply, and some of his poems that revive the forms, language, and themes of popular poetry could well pass for folk songs.

Between 1892 and 1919 George supervised the editing of the *Journal for Art* (*Blätter für die Kunst*). To a lesser but still considerable extent he influenced the *Yearbook for the Spiritual Movement* (*Jahrbuch für die geistige Bewegung,* 1910–12) and numerous works of scholarship, among them Friedrich Gundolf's best-selling *Goethe* (1916) and Ernst Kantorowicz's monumental *Frederick the Second, 1194–1250* (*Kaiser Friedrich der Zweite,* 1927). An "official" history of the George circle was written by the poet and historian Friedrich Wolters: *Stefan George and the Journal for Art* (*Stefan George und die Blätter für die Kunst,* 1930). George took an interest not only in the content of these volumes but also in their outward appearance. Together with the artist Melchior Lechter, he had a pivotal influence on modern typography and book design.

George's ideas were remote from day-to-day political concerns and emphasized singularity rather than individuality; they do not constitute a program and always require interpretation. After George's death some of his friends saw the National Socialist movement as the political manifestation of the poet's predictions, whereas a majority, notably the many Jewish members of the circle, went underground or emigrated. George's opposition to the tyranny of systems was most impressively translated into action by his followers, the brothers

Stauffenberg, who played a key role in the attempt to assassinate Hitler on July 20, 1944.

BIBLIOGRAPHY

Goldsmith, Ulrich K. *Stefan George: A Study of His Early Work.* Boulder: University of Colorado Press, 1959.

Metzger, Michael M., and Erika A. *Stefan George.* New York: Twayne, 1972.

Norton, Robert E. *Secret Germany: Stefan George and his Circle.* Ithaca, N.Y.: Cornell University Press, 2002.

Rieckmann, Jens, ed. *A Companion to the Works of Stefan George.* Rochester, N.Y.: Camden House, 2005.

Strathausen, Carsten. "Of Circles and Riddles: Stefan George and the 'Language Crisis' around 1900." *German Quarterly* 76, no. 4 (2003): 411–425.

Christophe Fricker

"GERMANY" BERTOLT BRECHT (1933) BERTOLT

BRECHT wrote a number of poems and songs that lamented the disastrous state of Nazi Germany. "Germany," dating from 1933, is the most famous. Hitler's Nazis began their totalitarian control of Germany during February 1933. Like many other communists, Brecht responded by fleeing the country. One of Brecht's long-term artistic and political collaborators, the musician and composer Hanns Eisler (1898–1962), also fled from certain arrest in Berlin. Brecht responded to their exile by writing lyrics and poems that denounce Nazism, and Eisler wrote music for many of these works. Their collaborative works of this period of crisis were published as a small volume in early 1934 by a press set up in Paris by German exiles to produce anti-Nazi propaganda. There was, of course, no possibility of the work being published in Nazi Germany. In the book *Lieder, Gedichte, Chöre* (Songs, Poems, Choruses), "Germany" is a key poem from this collection and an important example of the sort of direct attack on Hitler that Brecht produced in response to the Nazis' increasingly violent subjugation of German society.

The poem is an urgent lamentation on the disastrous direction in which Germany was headed. The speaker addresses Germany directly—the county is personified as a "pale mother." The first of seven stanzas accuses Germany of being "soiled" and willfully shamed and stained within the milieu of disapproving European peoples. The second and third stanzas condemn the

effects of the German rulers' oppression of Germany's most vulnerable "sons." Censorship within Hitler's Germany is attacked in the fourth stanza: "Lies are roared aloud" in the "house" of Germany, but "the truth"—as spoken by Brecht and other vituperative opponents of fascism—is repressed, concealed. The fifth, sixth, and final stanzas lament the combined fear and mockery that this personified Germany faces from all surrounding states: People laugh at the dilapidated, diminished condition of Germany, but they also reach for weapons when this aggressive entity approaches. Germany, then, is both laughable and dangerous, foolish and lethal.

There are two important English translations of the poem. Students of Brecht should engage with the versions in *Selected Poems* and in *Poems, 1913–56.* In the former, other countries, personified as nervous people, will reach for their knives, "As at the approach of a robber." In the latter, however, the personified country approached by Germany "grips his knife / As on seeing a murderess." This second version makes the state of affairs appear even more dramatic and urgent and closer to the original, in which the fear caused by Germany's descent into fascist virulence causes others to be *already* holding their weapons and prepared to respond to Germany as a "murderess"—not just a "robber."

BIBLIOGRAPHY

Betz, Albrecht. *Hanns Eisler: Political Musician.* Cambridge: Cambridge University Press, 1982, 121–123, 314.

Brecht, Bertolt. *Poems, 1913–56.* Edited by John Willett and Ralph Manheim. London: Eyre Methuen, 1976, 218–220.

———. *Selected Poems: Translation and Introduction by H. R. Hays.* New York: Reynal and Hitchcock, 1947, 112–115.

Cook, Bruce. *Brecht in Exile.* New York: Holt, Rinehart, and Winston, 1982, 21.

Esslin, Martin. *Brecht: A Choice of Evils.* London: Eyre Methuen, 1980, 52.

Kowalke, Kim H. "Brecht and Music: Theory and Practice." In *The Cambridge Companion to Brecht,* edited by Peter Thomson and Glendyr Sacks, 218–234, especially 222–224. Cambridge: Cambridge University Press, 1994.

McCullough, Derek. "Hanns Eisler." In *Encyclopedia of Contemporary German Culture,* edited by John Sandford, 179–180. London: Routledge, 1999.

Kevin De Ornellas

GIBRAN KHALIL GIBRAN (KAHLIL GIBRAN) (1883–1931)

Lebanese author and artist Gibran Khalil Gibran is one of the world's best-known writers, his works having been translated into more than 20 languages. His 1923 volume *The PROPHET* remains the best-selling volume ever issued by Alfred A. Knopf. Gibran drew on both Eastern and Western traditions to write about what it means to be both a physical and a spiritual being in the modern world. Especially during the 1960s, Gibran's philosophical works found favor with widespread audiences. In his first inaugural address President John F. Kennedy quoted Gibran ("Letter to Syrian Youth") when he said, "Ask not what your country can do for you; ask what you can do for your country."

Gibran was born to a Maronite Christian family in Bechari, Lebanon, in 1883. His family's economic situation was unstable, making it difficult for Gibran to obtain a formal education. He did, however, receive instruction in languages and religion from a local priest. At the age of 12 Gibran immigrated with his mother and siblings to the United States, settling in Boston, near relatives. Two years later Gibran returned to Lebanon to complete his secondary education. Having displayed artistic talent, he was accepted at the prestigious École des Beaux Arts in Paris. The famed sculptor Auguste Rodin was among his instructors. Although Gibran is best known as an author, he continued to work as a sculptor and artist throughout his life and illustrated several of his own books.

At the age of 21 Gibran returned to Boston and lived in Chinatown for the next several years. Gibran's melancholy was exacerbated by the deaths from tuberculosis of his half-brother and sister and the death of his mother from cancer. After these events, he moved to New York, where he lived for most of his life. He died from a liver ailment on April 10, 1931.

Gibran's earliest writings were in Arabic, including his 1910 collection of short stories '*Ar'is al-Muruj* (Nymphs of the Valley) and his 1914 volume of poetry and prose *Dam 'ah wabtisamah* (Tears and Laughter). By the time he moved to New York works in his native language had made him a celebrity in the Middle East.

Gibran's work is characterized by a longing for connection and unity. His feelings of alienation from the two cultures in which he lived as an outsider were increased by the horrors of World War I. In spite of his critical and financial success, Gibran was deeply troubled by the deplorable economic conditions in Lebanon, where, by the beginning of the war, large numbers of citizens were starving. Searching for deeper spirituality and understanding, Gibran turned away from organized religion. At the same time, his work was becoming increasingly more mystical and philosophical. Strong biblical influences are apparent in the rich images and style of his work, as are lyrical influences of his Arabic literary background. Much of his writing tries to answer the important questions of human existence while Gibran struggles with these questions himself, creating a sense of unresolved internal turmoil in his work.

In 1918 Gibran published his first work in English: *The Madman: His Parables and Poems*. The title character feels he possesses a deeper understanding of life than the masses, who consider him a madman, a theme Gibran treats in other works. Five years later Gibran published the first volume of a planned trilogy consisting of *The Prophet, The Garden of the Prophet,* and *The Death of the Prophet.* This first book became Gibran's most critically acclaimed and most widely read work. The sequels, two separate volumes, were published after his death.

Gibran stipulated in his will that all subsequent royalties from his writing be given to the Lebanese village of his birth.

BIBLIOGRAPHY

Gibran, Khalil. '*Ara'is al-Muruj,* 1910. Translated by H. M. Nahmad. Published as *Nymphs of the Valley.* New York: Knopf, 1948.

———. *Dam 'ah wabtisamah,* 1914. Translated by Anthony Rizcallah Ferris. Published as *Tears and Laughter,* edited by Martin L. Wolf. New York: Philosophical Library, 1949. Also published as *A Tear and a Smile.* Translated by Nahmad with an introduction by Robert Hillyer. New York: Knopf, 1950.

———. *The Madman: His Parables and Poems.* New York: Knopf, 1918.

———. *The Forerunner: His Parables and Poems.* New York: Knopf, 1920.

———. *The Prophet.* New York: Knopf, 1923.

———. *Jesus the Son of Man: His Words and His Deeds as Told and Recorded by Those Who Knew Him.* New York: Knopf, 1928.

———. *The Garden of the Prophet.* New York: Knopf, 1933.

Jean Hamm

GIULIANI, ALFREDO (1924–)

Alfredo Giuliani is one of the most important theoreticians and poets of the *neoavanguardia* (neo-avant-garde movement) in Italy. He was born in the town of Monbaroccio (near Pesaro) in 1924 and has lived most of his life in Rome, where he graduated from university with a degree in philosophy in 1949. He has published five books of poetry: *Il cuore zoppo* (The Crippled Heart, 1955), *Povera Juliet e altre poesie* (Poor Juliet and Other Poems, 1965), *Il Tautofono* (The Tautophonous, 1969), *Chi l'avrebbe detto* (Who Would Have Said It, 1973), and *Versi e nonversi* (Verses and Non-Verses, 1986). In addition, he published a novel, *Max* (1972), produced three books of criticism (1965, 1977, 1984), translated poems and prose from English and French, edited the most famous anthology of Italian poetry of the neo-avant-garde: *I novissimi: poesie per gli anni 60* (The Newest: Poetry for the Sixties), which was published in Italy in 1961, and authored two volumes of neo-avant-garde prose. He also served as a poetry editor of influential *neoavanguardia* magazines.

The neo-avant-garde was a loose group of poets and writers—many of whom called themselves Group 63 after the 1963 conference in which they participated in Palermo—who reacted strongly against aulic (i.e., courtly) and elevated language (such as GABRIELE D'ANNUNZIO's poetry) and crepuscular, confessional poetry. They sought to break away from the Italian lyric tradition—in some sense, following in the footsteps of the futurists, without an emphasis, however, on destruction and a cult of violence. Rather, they emphasized violence to language, using nonsense and other tortuous manipulations of the word and were influenced by Freud and Marx. They reacted forcefully against the capitalistic environment in which they found themselves, a society on the cusp of vast economic changes that were already overwhelming Italian society. Giuliani explains that their poetry imitates the "universal schizophrenia" afflicting the contemporary world; their vision is "schizomorphic" and tries to replicate the discontinuity and fracture of society. For this reason the vast majority of these poems are not rhymed or in a particular poetic meter, but trace the birth and death of specific thoughts or obsessions in free verse.

His first poetic sequence, *Corpus. Frammenti di autobiografia* (Corpus. Fragments of Autobiography, 1950), is not well known, yet it is anything but insignificant. The poem begins rather playfully, "The old Corpus who generated my father was noble and practical / and he liked to live with fantasy and ease," but shifts in tone when describing Giuliani's adolescence, his relation to his mother, his own emerging sexuality, his evasion of a priest who tries to molest him, and the day he discovered love and realized that "To lose love is nothing, to find it again / is a million of things, and one thing, terrible and long." About old age and decay he says, "One day I discovered that I smelled like my grandmother." Above all he learns about the impossible struggle to convey with words the extreme edge of perceptions, whether "coitus death or grief." He ends the poetic sequence asking truth, the "word of iron rust," to show him his "spectre," his double, as the French poet Charles Baudelaire would say.

In *Povera Juliet e altre poesie* Giuliani writes in a masterfully quiet voice: "It was in the calm resurrection after the rain . . . the centuries have not unmade us." Here also is his poem "Compleanno" (BIRTHDAY). He included in this volume *"poesia di teatro"* (poetry of theater), several brief plays in the style of the theater of the absurd, one of which appropriately begins: "What do you think of death?" Another piece, called "A Lecture by Jorge Luis Borges," shifts between the mimicked noise of speakers ("uuuuuKROOKRAKKUAK.bok.bok") and BORGES's phrases and words like *pampa* or *agonizar* (left untranslated just like the speaker noise). In another section of *Povera Juliet* Giuliani writes, "the feet of the dead man become slender in my music" (*i piedi del morto si assottigliano nella mia musica*), insisting on the necessity of the dead and death in his poetry. In other poems of the same volume Giuliani speaks of "the meticulous mimicking of linguistic signs that cover the earth, human and others, / and the sky that burns them in the sun of here." And yet in other poems, Giuliani writes in a polymorphous and indecipherable language, as though to point to the ultimate lack of absolute relation between word and object, between poet and world.

Giuliani's *Il Tautofono* is perhaps the least successful book, in which the poet seems to be almost bored with what he writes. Few of these poems, if any, are memorable.

Casuali (Casual Things), the last section of his *Versi e nonversi,* contains some of the simplest poems he has written, as when he says: "I like to make myself melancholy on the mattress of rain" or in which he unusually returns to rhythmic forms, like the "Little Song" ("Canzonetta"). There he addresses his beloved as "dear little onion of my eyes," states that "I'll let the poor god enrich himself" (an acidic reference to religion), and plays on words rather untranslatably: "the bushes bush me / the roads enroad me / the clouds cloud me." In another poem, "Augustine's Poetics," referring to the Christian philosopher, he writes, "A man can hear an entire poem," from beginning to end, "but not the order of centuries"; that is, "We have been made a part of the centuries because of damnation." Yet as Augustine says, we have not been "forbidden" poetry. But what can we hope from poetry in such "damned times" as we are living in? Explaining his change toward more understandable poetry in this last volume, he writes in "Getting Old": "I didn't understand / time; I used to say: it's ridiculous" and "now that I grow old, I adore simple explanations." And as if in contradiction, the final poem of Giuliani's *Versi e nonversi*—"Chomsky Poem"—is a riff on American grammarian Noam Chomsky's definition of grammatical nonsense and contains lines (for instance, "[the] world is masturbation of a god furiously") in which syntax completely breaks down. As Giuliani wrote in his preface to *I novissimi:* "Certainly the senselessness is a mere 'content' of our world"; yet for him and others, "it will be the only possible and painful stylistic solution." Nonsense for Giuliani has become rather iconic, "like the madonnas and angels of ancient Annunciations."

BIBLIOGRAPHY

Eco, Umberto. *Open Work.* Translated by Anna Cancogni. Cambridge, Mass.: Harvard University Press, 1989.

Giuliani, Alfredo. *I Novissimi: Poetry for the Sixties.* Translated by David Jacobson, Luigi Ballerini, Bradley Dick, Michael Moore, Stephen Sartarelli, and Paul Vangelisti. Los Angeles: Sun and Moon Press, 1995.

———. "Introduction" (my translation) to *I novissimi: Poesie per gli anni '60.* 2d ed. Turin: Einaudi, 2003.

Wagstaff, C. "The Neo-avantgarde." In M. Caesar and P. Hainsworth, eds., *Writers and Society in Contemporary Italy.* London: Palgrave, 1984.

Jacob Blakesley

GLISSANT, ÉDOUARD (1928–   ) Édouard

Glissant—poet, novelist, essayist, educator, and social activist—is one of the most important writers to emerge in the wake of *négritude,* a literary school founded in the 1930s by AIMÉ CÉSAIRE (Martinique), LÉON-GONTRAN DAMAS (Guiana), and LÉOPOLD SENGHOR (Senegal), whose aim was to restore dignity to blacks under colonial rule and gain respect for their artistic achievements.

Glissant was born in 1928 in the village of Sainte-Marie, Martinique. Shortly after his birth Glissant's mother moved with her five children to Lamentin, an industrial region. Glissant's father, a plantation manager, stayed in Sainte-Marie, but Édouard visited him frequently, and the two traveled throughout Martinique to agricultural sites. Glissant attended primary school in Lamentin and high school at the prestigious Lycée Schoelcher in the capital, Fort-de-France, which fellow writers Césaire and Damas had attended before him. Although he received a sound education, Glissant was disillusioned early by the system's Eurocentric curriculum and its inattention to Martinican history and culture. Students were not allowed to speak their native Creole language in class and instead were forced to conform linguistically to continental French standards. His early educational experiences would inform his poetry and his concept of cultural relativism, in which no one culture is considered superior to another and in which shared cultural experiences are desirable.

Glissant studied philosophy at the Sorbonne and ethnology at the Musée de l'Homme in Paris while establishing himself as a poet. His early poems "*Un champ d'îles,*" "*La Terre inquiète,*" and "*Les Indes*" were included in *Anthologie de la poésie nouvelle* (Anthology of New Poetry), edited by Jean Paris, and Glissant played an important role in the Congrès des Écrivains et Artistes Noirs (Congress of Black Writers and Artists) in Paris in 1956. In the 1950s he contributed to the literary review *Les lettres nouvelles* and published his first novel, *La Lézarde* (The Ripening), which was awarded the Prix Renaudot in 1958, securing him a prominent place in the world of letters.

In 1959 Glissant became an activist, cofounding with Paul Niger the Front Antillo-guyannais (Antillean-Guyanean Front) and becoming acquainted with other black writers and intellectuals. The group demanded the decolonization of France's Caribbean departments and the restoration of indigenous identity (Martinique is still officially a *département d'outre mer* of France—an overseas department similar to a commonwealth). President Charles de Gaulle disbanded the group in 1961 and forbade Glissant to leave France, believing it necessary to keep a close watch on his revolutionary activities. During this time Glissant published a play, *Monsieur Toussaint* (1961), and a second novel, *Le quatrième siècle* (The Fourth Century, 1964), to much critical acclaim. Although acquainted with writers of the Négritude Movement and a participant in some of their enterprises, such as Présence Africaine (a group of writers promoting black literature and culture), Glissant did not wish to identify himself solely as a black writer in opposition to a white European tradition, and thus he did not engage in much of the militancy of the Negritude Movement. Considering himself a world exile not fully at home in any country, Glissant developed a global perspective of literature in which all countries and cultures could harmoniously coexist and complement one another. The *Créolization* that Glissant writes of in his essays is the foundation of this literary philosophy. Because his native Martinique is a mix of cultures—Caribbean, African, European—the entire world may be viewed as a hybrid in which no cultural or nationalistic hierarchy exists. Glissant's point of view is often that of the "other"—an outsider looking in and remarking on the range of differences between cultures, which are seen as beneficial to one's human development. In his collection *Sel noir* (Black Salt), whose poems span the years 1947–79, one sees the variety of themes he treats—not only the ravages of European slavery and colonialism experienced by blacks (in the poem "GORÉE"), but also a celebration of the creative potential experienced by embracing these differences and adapting to them (in the poem "ELITED PROSE").

Glissant returned to Martinique in 1965, founded L'Institut martiniquais d'Études (Martinican Studies Institute)—a center for research and teaching—and started a humanities journal, *Acoma,* the same year. He remained a prolific writer in the 1970s, 1980s, and 1990s, publishing a series of novels—*Malemort* (1975), *La Case du commandeur* (1981), and *Mahogony* (1987)—as well as several collections of poetry—*Boises* (Yokes, 1979), *Pays rêvé, pays réel* (1985), and *Fastes* (1991). He also published three seminal essays on poetic form and function—*L'Intention poétique* (1969), *Le Discours antillais* (Caribbean Discourse, 1981), and *Poétique de la relation* (Poetics of Relation, 1990).

From 1982 to 1988 Glissant edited *Le Courier de l'UNESCO,* the magazine of the United Nations Educational, Scientific and Cultural Organization, which promotes world peace through sharing knowledge. In 1989 he was named distinguished professor at Louisiana State University, where he directed the Center of French and Francophone Studies. Since 1995 he has been distinguished professor of French of the Graduate Center of the City University of New York (CUNY). Glissant has received numerous awards and distinctions, and many colloquia have been held in honor of his life and work, including those in Guadeloupe, Martinique, Paris, Louvain (Belgium), CUNY, the University of Porto (Portugal), and the University of Oklahoma (Norman).

BIBLIOGRAPHY

Amoia, Alba, and Bettina L. Knapp, eds. *Multicultural Writers since 1945: An A-to-Z Guide.* Westport, Conn.: Greenwood Press, 2004.

Dash, Michael J. *Edouard Glissant.* Cambridge: Cambridge University Press, 1995.

Glissant, Édouard. *Black Salt.* Translated by Betsy Wing. Ann Arbor: University of Michigan Press, 1998.

Patrick L. Day

"GOD HAS PITY ON KINDERGARTEN CHILDREN" YEHUDA AMICHAI (1955)
"God Has Pity on Kindergarten Children" has become one of YEHUDA AMICHAI's most quoted and anthologized

poems. Appearing in his first volume of verse, *Achshav u-beyamim acherim* (Now and in Other Days, 1955), it operates on multiple levels, but given its historical proximity to Israel's war of independence of 1948, one is hard pressed not to view its surface theme as that of the savagery of war and the sacrifice of young soldiers. The poem also typifies Amichai's inclination, especially in his early poetry, to challenge and to transform in an acutely ironic fashion the traditional perception of God as merciful. Amichai had a complex relationship with Orthodox Judaism and conducted a grand theological argument with the Almighty, rejecting any submissive reverence and the certainties of an exclusive faith. For example, the companion piece to "God Has Pity on Kindergarten Children"—"A God Full of Mercy" (El male rachamim, 1960)—limns similar terrain, featuring a speaker who relates a life redolent of pain and misery, angry at a God who keeps all lenity, all compassion strictly to himself, which is why he is so "full of mercy."

The title "God Has Pity on Kindergarten Children" positions the reader to expect a poem praising God's benevolence, but it quickly develops into a searing tract about a universe devoid of higher kindliness. The first two lines foreground the poem's central theme, that childhood and youth provide a type of protection and shelter denied to adults: *"Elohim merachem al yaldey hagan, pachot mize al yaldey beit hasefer"* (God has pity on kindergarten children. He has less pity on school children). At first we are told that God does show mercy, but it is dispensed in a discriminatory manner, only to those who are regarded as totally pure—kindergarten children and, to a lesser extent, schoolchildren. In a sense it is not just God who offers his concern and protection to the innocent and powerless, but also the institutions of home, kindergarten, and school that proffer a shield. On the other hand, God denies the vulnerable grownups (embodied here as soldiers) of his sanctuary, even though soldiers are customarily in more peril than small children. Amichai marshals the image of soldiers crawling on all fours in the hot sands toward the first aid station, bloodied and wounded, to underline the idea that combatants (in this instance, during the war of independence) were not the objects of God's watchfulness. This particular image struck a chord with

Israelis, who were all too well acquainted with the high cost of successive wars. In this poem the soldiers, left entirely alone, have reverted to their infant state, dragging themselves as children do to be tended to. More broadly, this "last station" could symbolize the final destination for all of us.

The following stanzas convey the message that omnipotence does not have a duty to provide protection against danger or death. In the end, only love acts as a buffer for suffering adults. The second stanza suggests that "true lovers" *may well* be deserving of God's love: *"ulay al ha-oavim be-emet yiten rachamim veyachus veyatzel kehilu al hayashen ba-safasl she-bash-dera ha-tziburit"* (But perhaps He will watch over true lovers and have mercy on them and shelter them like a tree over the old man sleeping on a public bench). Still, the tree that shelters the young lovers can provide only a limited degree of safety. It cannot insulate the lovers from rain, cold, or physical injury. From the second word of the second stanza (*perhaps*), it is evident that God's sanctuary is contingent on something else. Those who love truly (as the poem largely implies) can be likened to children in their naïveté and righteousness, and they are thus more worthy of protection, albeit only a fractional sort. The idea developed in this poem—that only love can afford redemption, that only love will drive away pain and cruelty—is a recurring theme in the Amichai poetic corpus.

The last section of the poem suggests that generosity and empathy handed down in the form of "coins of compassion" by a mother (or mother figure) may generate happiness for the adults shunned by a discriminating God. Acts of (metaphorically) maternal charity, Amichai says, will lead in turn to our protection. The referencing of "the mother" evokes the association of "motherly love" with its accompanying warmth and affection, remembered from childhood. This trope is not surprising. Time and again reminiscences from childhood (nostalgic glimpses into a world of peace and innocence) dapple Amichai's poetic canvas. One critic appositely noted that "a whole coin" often emblematizes completeness in Amichai's poetry, observing that the soldiers, hurt and incomplete, can also parabolically signify people stuck in the mechanical drudgery of urban life, with its attendant isolation, estrangement, and disjunction. Ultimately, it is God who is cast as the designer of such afflictions. The poem avers that human beings should not rely on God for refuge or mercy, but must be responsible for their own safe conduct. Amichai is asserting, contra Jewish religious dogma, that human goodness, kindness, and love are far superior shields and can function as a worthy substitute for God's uncertain protection. Compassion is to be reclaimed here on Earth, rather than from the heavens, so evidently impoverished of kindness. The poem can be classified as a modern opus, an existential meditation on the relationship between us and our creator. It confirms God's presence in human affairs, but demonstrates humankind's loss of faith and profound disappointment in what can only be seen as divine indifference to the uncertain lives of human beings.

Dvir Abramovich

GOD'S SHADOW REZA BARAHENI (1976)

God's Shadow: Prison Poems is REZA BARAHENI's powerful narrative, 99 pages long, of the excruciating physical and mental torture he suffered in 1973 at the hands of SAVAK, the Iranian secret police. The account is told through a vivid prose memoir and a collection of poems—two of them ("The Doves" and "The Light of Home") composed while Baraheni was in prison. In his acknowledgments Baraheni says of those two poems: "I wrote on prison walls with my fingernails, memorizing each stanza, erasing it so that I wouldn't get caught, and scratching the following stanzas in the same fashion until the whole poem was completed" (9). The rest of the collection was written during his visit to the United States in 1974. Baraheni wrote all the poems originally in Persian and translated them himself into English. In the acknowledgments he names several friends who read the English versions and helped him to polish them: David St. John, Burt Blume, Michael Henderson, and Denise Levertov.

The introduction is a 26-page narrative that, like a crime thriller, begins dramatically with the abduction of the author by "a tall, bearded young man" who, at a stoplight, steps up to Baraheni's car and coolly threatens to shoot him if he makes a false move. The man is an undercover SAVAK policeman, it turns out, who gets in the car, thrusts the gun into Baraheni's ribs, and begins the drama that the rest of the book describes in harrowing detail. Baraheni's introduction reads like fiction, but it is supported with factual details, national statistics, and notes on the real names and identities of his torturers. The abduction, search, and seizure of his papers, bloody interrogation procedures, instruments of torture and torture chambers, cells for solitary confinement, cries of fellow prisoners being burned, whipped, and jabbed with heated or hot-wired iron prods, being strung up upside-down, being raped; Baraheni's experience of unbearable pain and of passing out only to wake up to increased torture—are all described in unflinching detail in the prose memoir.

The poems are no less graphic. Some of them ("Ahmad Agha's Prison Dream") are surreal renditions of what happens to a prisoner physically; some of them ("Nostalgia" and "Ass Poem"), of what happens mentally and morally. Each poem unfolds a different nightmarish account of the tormented existence of political prisoners in Iranian jails. In "Torture Chambers," for example, the poet compares the rooms in which torture is administered to the shops and offices of commodity brokers. The effect of interlarding the physical description of the trappings of torture with the topics of political discourse carried out by the hideous "toads" and "apes" who administer pain in that setting is shocking and bizarre: "whips of woven wire dangle," "the electric baton is the stiff prick of a stallion," a "Dr. Shadi . . . pulls the nails in the cool manner of a manicurist," and so forth, "and all this happens when the Persian / press vomit White Revolution day and night / every month they torture 2000 people"; "in Iran the bowels / of the earth await your pleasure and the / gates of hell open their mouths wide as the oil / pipelines the lines lead to those / brokers' chambers . . ." (54–56, spaces in original). "Barbecue" graphically describes the humiliation of a prisoner whose entire buttocks and anus have been burned raw so that he cannot sit on a toilet or contain his fecal matter (57–58). "The Prisoner's Biography by His Wife" (from the perspective of the one person who was once the prisoner's most intimate companion) describes a husband's nightmares, hallucinations, and waking traumas years after he has been released and the couple is attempting to live a normal life in places far from the bloodied whipping rooms where he was beaten by the "six men" he cannot get out of his damaged mind (76–80). "What Is Poetry" is composed of 15 short stanzas, each beginning with the words "poetry / is . . ." (73–74), but this is no predictable catalog of characteristics. Instead the metaphors are meant to define *poetry* in a completely new way: for instance, as "a shark's fin cutting a prisoner's throat / delicately and precisely"; as "a cliff where executioners hurl poets into canyons below"; as "the needle used to sew up Farrokhi's lips," and so on. The point of this litany appears to be that an exact and graphic idiom is required to express the inhumanity perpetrated in some prison systems; that to prettify the language is to deprive human beings of the dignity that their suffering entitles them to; and that only by means of poetry (incisively conceived and forceful) can one hope to muster the linguistic wherewithal to speak these outrageous truths candidly.

Like Baraheni's "Exile Poem of the Gallery," published a quarter of a century later, the poems of *God's Shadow* provide readers with a rich, vicarious sense of how certain worldly realities—including the art and the poetry of others—will appear to a poet who has survived having "a dagger thrust in his throat" (*Making Meaning* 13).

BIBLIOGRAPHY
Baraheni, Reza. "Exile Poem of the Gallery." In *Making Meaning*. Toronto: Art Gallery of Ontario, 2000.
———. *God's Shadow: Prison Poems*. Bloomington: Indiana University Press, 1976.

R. Victoria Arana

"GOLDEN BOAT, THE" RABINDRANATH TAGORE (1894)

"The Golden Boat," one of RABINDRANATH TAGORE's most famous and most enigmatic poems, is the title piece of a poetry collection of the same name. It captures the blend of earthy awareness and cosmic mysticism that—as a hallmark of Tagore's poetry and philosophy—made him a towering figure of 20th-century Bengali literature. The poem's imagery is enchanting but elusive; consequently, the work is open to many interpretations—as it has been from its first publication.

The poem begins with images of unrest—roiling clouds, threat of rain—which are observed by a first-person narrator sitting on a riverbank "sad and alone." The monsoon rains are beginning just after the rice has been harvested, and the river swells from the influx of water. In the second stanza the speaker describes the flood waters swirling into the rice paddy and its environs, but no one is present to observe the scene except the solitary speaker. The third stanza features an approaching boat guided by someone who may be singing and whom the speaker seems to know. The boat's full sails carry it downriver, and the person guiding it looks ahead without regard to the waves breaking harmlessly on the boat's sides. In the next stanza the speaker wonders where the person is going—to some foreign land, perhaps—and asks the individual in the boat to stay for a time. The narrator seems to reassure the sailor that he may proceed where he wishes because the narrator wants him only to "come to the bank a moment" and smile. The speaker offers the sailor his entire rice paddy, perhaps in recompense. In the fifth stanza the speaker tells the boatman to take as much as he can carry—to take everything and, in the end, to take the speaker himself. But in the final stanza the speaker discovers that the boat is too small, loaded as it is with the rice paddy, and he resumes his position on the empty riverbank watching the tumultuous clouds as he realizes he has lost everything to the golden boat.

The poem most closely resembles the *bhakti* devotional poems of the 13th–17th centuries. *Bhakti* (devotion) is a yogic path in Hinduism that emphasizes the absolute devotion of individuals to a deity to whom they pledge their entire existence. Thus the narrator could be interpreted as experiencing a confused period in life (symbolized by the storm clouds and torrential rains). He has possessions, but their stability is not assured—the flood waters threaten them all the time; and in the broader spiritual sense, he realizes he has become too attached to temporary things that any mishap could take away. When the boatman appears, symbolizing the deity (the speaker repeatedly points out that he seems to recognize the boatman), sailing unhindered through the chaotic floodwaters (symbolizing the uncertainties of life, perhaps), the narrator offers him all his material wealth (the rice paddy) and finally his own being. After giving the boatman his rice paddy, however, he realizes there is no room for him. This portion of the poem may well indicate that the speaker went through all the external motions of devotion (giving up his material possessions), but did not experience a true inner conversion to absolute devotion (there is no room for him). Thus he is left watching the storm clouds, alone and desolate on the riverbank. The poem may be read as an admonitory tale cautioning readers to be prepared to give themselves truly and entirely to their spiritual endeavors or face the consequences of losing what they most value without gaining inner peace in return. The poem is found in one of the best English collections of Tagore's verse, edited by Krishna Dutta and Andrew Robinson: *Rabindranath Tagore: An Anthology* (New York: MacMillian, 1997).

Joseph E. Becker

GOLL, YVAN (1891–1950)

Born Isaac Lang on March 29, 1891, in Saint-Dié in the province of Lorraine, France, Ivan Goll—poet, editor, and translator—contributed in many ways to the major developments of modernism in the arts. Notably, his experiences of childhood and exile were multicultural (German-Jewish and French), and his work reflects his personal struggles and passions, expressing a cultural hybridity inflected by alienation, anguish, and the need for personal acknowledgment. His collaborators included Herman Hesse, Hans Arp, Hans Richter, Marc Chagall, Pablo Picasso, and James Joyce. His early poetry, marked by German expressionism, sounded the themes of pacifism and universal brotherhood. Upon his arrival in Paris after World War I, his direct contact with cubist poets in the tradition of GUILLAUME APOLLINAIRE and BLAISE CENDRARS transformed his style into one of lucid fragments, collagelike in its construction. In 1922 in a collection he edited for the review *Les Cinque continents* (The Five Continents), he gathered (under the heading "surréalisme") a group of poets largely influenced by Apollinaire. In October 1924 Goll published the groundbreaking journal *Surréalisme*. His conception of surrealism emphasized verbal constructions, relying on disparate phrases, and avoided the Freudian play between language and the

unconscious aspects of mental life. ANDRÉ BRETON, vying for poetic ascendancy, attacked Goll's surrealism in his first surrealist manifesto (1924).

In 1921 Goll married Claire Studer, a young journalist and his most important collaborator. Theirs was a stormy and passionate relation, for Studer was the lover of RAINER MARIA RILKE during the first years of courtship with Goll (1917–19), and for eight years Goll engaged in a deeply therapeutic extramarital affair with the poet Paula Ludwig (1931–39). Love and heartbreak and reunion are the subjects of *Ten Thousand Dawns,* a text important to understanding the themes of *Jean sans Terre* (LANDLESS JOHN) and *Traumkraut* (DREAM GRASS), Goll's most significant publications. *Traumkraut* is a work of paranoid surreality, according to Francis J. Carmody. Goll's work resolutely opposes any form of transcendentalism. His *Jean sans Terre,* translated into English by Kenneth Rexroth, Galway Kinnell, and William Carlos Williams, among others, is typical of his anguished exploration of the emotions of dispossession.

Displaced by the rise of Nazism, like many intellectuals of Jewish origin, Goll and Claire spent the war years in New York City. There he was briefly reunited with Breton, whose work Goll featured in his journal *Hemispheres,* only to fall out with Breton again in disputes over rights to published material. During this period Goll was one of the first to recognize seminal Caribbean authors, including NICOLAS GUILLÉN and AIMÉ CÉSAIRE, whose work he was the first to translate into English. He also began an investigation of Kabbalah and other aspects of Jewish mysticism that serve in his poetry as geometric tropes in an abstract address to language. After returning to France in 1947, Goll resumed writing in German.

Goll's most important collaborator during the most productive years of his life was his wife. Unfortunately for his reputation and for hers, Claire accused PAUL CELAN of plagiarizing from her husband's last works. Celan, who was among the poets who had donated blood to Goll when he was in the hospital, never recovered from the shock of this slur. Goll died of leukemia on February 27, 1950.

Today there is a consensus among scholars that Goll's work needs to be reexamined in the light of its multiple merits, not the least of which are its depiction of alienation in modern society, its documentation of the experiences of exile and human anguish, and its use of language that is notably constructivist and imagistic, reflecting the multiple cultures and languages that shaped the poet's life. Goll's poetry, according to Jules Romaine, serves as an epigraph (Carmody 15), summarizing the alienation of much of modern experience in those years between the two world wars and immediately following World War II.

BIBLIOGRAPHY
Carmody, Francis J. *The Poetry of Yvan Goll.* Paris: Caractères, 1956.
Goll, Yvan. *Die Lyric in vier Bänden.* Berlin: Argon, 1996.
———. *Jean sans Terre.* Preface by W. H. Auden, translated by Lionel Abel, Louise Bogan, William Carlos Williams, et al. New York: Thomas Yoseloff, 1958.
———. *Ten Thousand Dawns: Love Poems of Yvan and Claire Goll.* Translated by Thomas Rain Crowe and Nan Watkins. Buffalo, N.Y.: White Pine, 2004.
———. *Yvan Goll: Selected Poems.* Translated by Robert Bly, George Hitchcock, Galway Kinnell, and Paul Zweig. San Francisco: Kayak, 1968.
Yvan Goll. Special Issue. *Europe* 899 (March 2004).

Donald Wellman

GONZÁLEZ MARTÍNEZ, ENRIQUE
(1871–1952) Enrique González Martínez is commonly acknowledged as the last modernist, a designation accorded him based on his most frequently cited poem, the sonnet *"Tuércele el cuello al cisne"* (WRING THE SWAN'S NECK). In the often misinterpreted lines of this sonnet, the poet denounces the excessess and artificiality of modernism. His repudiation of the frivolity and conceptual emptiness of modernists paved the way for a reorientation and renovation in Latin American poetics. It is also a point of departure, along with the poet's personal, professional, and literary experiences and their political context, for understanding the work of one of the most representative figures of Mexican sensibility and spirituality.

Born in Guadalajara, capital of the state of Jalisco, in l871, González Martínez became a physician shortly before he was 22. He practiced medicine in various states of Mexico for 17 years, writing poetry in his spare time. Upon moving to Mexico City in 1911, he engaged actively in literary, academic, and other professional endeavors. Among these were teaching French and Mexican literature, establishing and editing the literary magazines *Argos* and *Pegaso,* and serving as president of the Ateneo de Juventud (Athenaeum of Youth), an association of young writers. Like many other Latin American authors, he became a diplomat representing his country in Chile, Argentina, and Spain.

From his initial recognized works published at the beginning of the 20th century—*Los senderos ocultos* (Hidden Paths) and *La muerte del cisne* (The Death of the Swan)—to his last work, *El nuevo Narciso* (The New Narcissus), published in 1952, certain aspects stand out and are recurrent in his work: an intimate, serious, and serene tone as he addresses the business of being human, articulating the concerns of humankind from a perspective enhanced by the range and diversity of his experiences, a certain pantheism that may be attributed to his medical studies and practice, a philosophical depth as he looks for answers to the enigmas of human existence, a grave expression of emotions devoid of romantic sentimentalism, and a metaphysical anxiety when faced with the indecipherable and the unknowable.

While daring to question the symbolist notion of beauty and distancing himself from the rhetoric and objectivity of the 19th-century French Parnassians, González Martínez did accept the stylistic perfection, the artistic excellence emphasized by the modernists. At the same time, his poetry unrelentingly probes the nature of human existence, demonstrating González Martínez's consciousness of our physical surroundings and our perspective of life as a spiritual journey. In the trajectory of Latin American poetics, considering the spectrum of his work (he collected and edited his poetry in three volumes of *Poesías* [1938–40]), the poetry of González Martínez must be acknowledged and appreciated for the liberating role it played in the transition from the modernist to the *vanguardista* movement in Mexican national literature. Samuel Beckett's translations of González Martínez's poems in *Anthology of Mexican Poetry,* among the most favorably regarded poems of the "last modernist," are skillfully and insightfully done.

BIBLIOGRAPHY
Brushwood, John S. *Enrique González Martínez*. New York: Twayne, 1969.
González Martínez, Enrique. In *Anthology of Mexican Poetry*, edited by Octavio Paz, Poems translated by Samuel Beckett. Bloomington: Indiana University Press, 1958.
Paz, Octavio, ed. *Anthology of Mexican Poetry*. Bloomington: Indiana University Press, 1958.

Effie Boldridge

GOODISON, LORNA (1947–)

Born in Kingston, Jamaica, Lorna Goodison is one of the best-known contemporary poets of the Anglophone Caribbean. Her work has been internationally acclaimed, widely anthologized, and translated into several languages. The eighth of nine children, Goodison grew up in colonial Jamaica, and, despite the economic hardships her family faced, she received a good education, studying at the Jamaica School of Art then at the Art Students League in New York City. Before achieving celebrity as a poet, she worked in advertising and public relations. In 1972 she married but divorced six years later, a painful experience recorded in her first poetry collection, *Tamarind Season,* published in 1980. International recognition of her work came with the publication of her second collection, *I Am Becoming My Mother,* awarded the Commonwealth Poetry Prize for North and South America in 1986. In this volume Goodison celebrates motherhood and the life cycle as well as giving voice to known and unknown black women struggling for freedom, as in, for instance, "WE ARE THE WOMEN" and "MY LAST POEM." Several other collections have followed, in which the poet has shown a refined poetic craft, using the healing and incantatory power of language to approach concrete topics related to racial identity and the condition of women, as well as more universal concerns such as the relation of human beings with nature and spirituality; namely, *Heartease* (1988), *To Us, All Flowers Are Roses* (1995), *Turn Thanks* (1999), and *Travelling Mercies* (2001). Goodison has also published short stories (*The Baby Mother and the King of Swords,* 1990) and has taught creative writing. As a painter she has exhibited her artworks in different countries. She has lived in both Jamaica and the United States and has traveled widely to perform her poetry.

Goodison has a deep love for green things (as soon as she could, she left Kingston to live in the countryside), and her work has a particular feeling for natural elements. In her poems both the Caribbean landscape and the city of Kingston appear as settings, but, while the latter is often associated with unhappiness, dispossession, dirt, and disease, the former is a site of inspiration, peace, and communion. An important natural element in her poetry is water, which acquires a sacred meaning, appearing as rain, with regenerative powers; as a large and deep body where death becomes something sweet, a passage into a new form of existence; and as the primal source of life, the maternal waters breaking to give birth to a new creature. But the Caribbean landscape is not the only one appearing in Goodison's poems, as the setting of many poems is Africa, especially Egypt, a country with which the poet likes to identify her roots. All these landscapes appear always surrounded by light; even at night a big moon shines on them. In the world of the poet the idea of light is joined with the idea of truth. For Goodison "poets are the ones who should write about truth and light" (1990 293). A personal truth becomes, through poetry, universal, and the experience of the poet is seen as a mystical descent into the deepest meanings of life. Goodison finds in poetry the most authentic religious dimension, where one can be "rebound to the source" (Goodison 1990: 292). Hers is a poetry of celebration. Even when it denounces a dreadful event or when it expresses a sad feeling, there is, despite an elegiac note, a continual thanksgiving to life, and the poems always end with a high momentum in which the poet exults and exhorts her readers to hope and to rejoice in the triumph of the spirit. Goodison draws inspiration from both her African and her European heritages to explore with a critical eye the black experience in the Americas. A strong social engagement and a feminist outlook characterize her many poems portraying strong, ordinary women carrying on their everyday struggle for survival (for example, the poem "For My Mother") and brave black women fighting for the emancipation of their people ("Bedspread," for Winnie Mandela; "Nanny," about the legendary Maroon chieftain; and "For Rosa Parks," among others). Firmly rooted in Jamaica, Goodison's poetry reaches out to the world in a lyrical plea for justice.

BIBLIOGRAPHY

Baugh, Edward. "Goodison's Rituals of Redemption." *Sargasso* (2001): 21–30.

Binder, Wolfgang. "An Interview with Lorna Goodison." *Commonwealth* 13, no. 2 (Spring 1991): 49–59.

Narain, Denise deCaires. "Lorna Goodison." *Writing Across Worlds: Contemporary Writers Talk*. Edited by Susheila Nasta. London: Routledge, 2004, 45–57.

Narain, Denise deCaires. "More Body Talk: Righting or Writing the Body?" The Work of Lorna Goodison, Mahadai Das, Grace Nichols and Marlene Nourbese Philip." *Contemporary Caribbean Women's Poetry: Making Style*. London: Routledge, 2002, 148–212.

Goodison, Lorna. "How I Became a Writer." *Caribbean Women Writers: Essays From the First International Conference*, edited by Selwyn Cudjoe, 290–293. Wellesley, Massachusetts: Calaloux, 1990.

Goodison, Lorna. "Not Exile, But Making a Life." *Defining Ourselves: Black Writers in the 90's*. Edited by Elizebeth Nunez and Brenda M. Green. New York: Peter Lang, 1999.

Kuwabong, Dannabang. "The Mother as Archetype of Self: A Poetics of Matrilineage in the Poetry of Claire Harris and Lorna Goodison." *Ariel* 30, no. 1 (Jan. 1999): 105–129.

Sabrina Brancato

"GORÉE" ÉDOUARD GLISSANT (1979)

"Gorée" initially appeared in ÉDOUARD GLISSANT's collection *Yokes* (1979) but is also included in the collection *Black Salt* (1998), an anthology in English translation of three separate collections of Glissant's poetry—*Le sel noir* (Black Salt), *Le sang rivé* (Riveted Blood), and *Boises* (Yokes)—all published between 1947 and 1979. Like most of the other poems in these collections, "Gorée" is very short (only three sentences) and is actually a poem in powerful prose rhythms. The subject, an enslaved African, is first seen awaiting transport by sea from Gorée, an island off the coast of Senegal, to the Americas, where he will work the plantations. To describe the African, who will be uprooted from his home, Glissant uses the metaphor of a tree: "He inhabited his cry treefull: his roots spilled into ravines / shouting out." The captive's facial expression as he looks upon the slave ships is severe, as is the contempt he feels for his captors, but the power of his gaze, which "stayed many a wind-bare sail," is ultimately powerless, and he is transported nonetheless, "steered between coast and bluff shore." As his ship approaches the foreign islands of the Caribbean, the man realizes that his future is futile, as hopeless as when "yesterday's dreams garrotte dreams of tomorrow to their death."

BIBLIOGRAPHY

Glissant, Édouard. "Gorée." In *Black Salt*. Translated by Betsy Wing. Ann Arbor: University of Michigan Press, 1998.

Patrick L. Day

"GRASS, THE" KIM SU-YOUNG (1968)

"The Grass" is the last poem KIM SU-YOUNG wrote before he met his death in 1968. It is included in the posthumous collection of poetry *The Great Root*, published in 1974. As one of his famous political engagement poems, it reveals Kim's groundbreaking poetic vision of *minjung*, which empowers ordinary working-class people. Most people view wild grass as ugly and worthless and feel no guilt in removing it from their property. But Kim notices that grass is so persistent that it not only sustains its life by growing even in rocky soil but also generates and spreads its life even after efforts are made to uproot it and cast it out. Thus he presents the grass as a perfect symbol of the true resistant spirit of ordinary working-class people who are seemingly powerless and ignorant but always carry on their strong will to live. In this poem Kim suggests his main theme by remarking that the grass "stays low" in the strong wind instead of being pushed down. In other words, the grass is always taking initiative in the struggle with the wind: It lowers itself when the wind blows; it straightens up fast when the wind loses its power; it even laughs when the wind weeps. The constant confrontation between the grass and the wind, then, becomes a symbol of the historical struggles between the powerful "haves" and the seemingly powerless "have-nots." On the surface the former seem to have controlled the latter with their political and economic supremacy. But their wealth and power would not have been possible without those working-class people who have always formed the great root of society. Kim thus praises the persistent spirit of grasslike people who have spread their roots despite the hardship and endured the oppression of dictatorial regimes. Kim applauds their courage and willpower to go on with their lives and at the same time empowers them by announcing that they have always been the true owners of Korea.

Han Ji-hee

"GRAVE FOR NEW YORK, A" ADONIS (ALI AHMAD SA'ID) (1971)

Written in spring 1971, this poem depicts the desolation of New York City as emblematic of empire. ADONIS wrote the poem after a visit to the United States, during which he participated in an International Poetry Forum. Unlike his poem "The DESERT," where Adonis presented the pains of war and siege without naming and anchoring the context, in this poem he refers explicitly to a multitude of historical figures and geographical locations. He pits poets against politicians, the righteous against the exploitative. The English translation of this long poem from Arabic skips some short passages of the original (indicated by ellipses), but the overall effect remains intact. The poem is made up of 10 sections, each denouncing New York City in a different way. It opens by presenting the beastly nature of the city and by satirizing the Statue of Liberty:

> A civilization with four legs; in each direction
> murder and
> a road leading to murder
> and in each distance the moaning of the
> drowned.
> NEW YORK,
> A woman—the statue of a woman
> lifting in one hand a rag called liberty by
> a document called history, and with the other
> hand suffocating a child called Earth

In this poem, the layout and the different fonts create visual effects—all the more necessary as prosodic music is absent. Adonis invokes Walt Whitman, his poetry and poetics, but in vain can he find his traces. Adonis recalls Whitman's "Crossing Brooklyn Ferry" and *Leaves of Grass* as foils to present-day American cities: "And I said *Brooklyn Bridge!* But that is the bridge which connects *Whitman* with *Wall Street,* which connects the green leaves with the greenbacks. . . ." One of the compelling images in this poem—Dantesque in its infernal gore—is that of decapitated John the Baptist, who becomes Everyman: "And I say: Since John the Baptist each one of us carries his severed head on a plate and waits for the second coming."

"A Grave for New York" is crowded with allusions: Abraham Lincoln and Walt Whitman on one hand, and Lt. William L. Calley and Robert McNamara on the other, so the United States is shown in its egalitarian face as well as in its imperial face. As Abraham Lincoln sought racial equality, Adonis links him to Harlem: "And while I look at you among marble stones of Washington, and discover your likeness in Harlem, I think: When will your next revolution come? And my voice rises: Set *Lincoln* free from the whiteness of marble, from *Nixon,* from the guard dogs and the hunting dogs." Here we encounter the radical Adonis, who calls things by their own names, pitting the democratic father of the American nation against the Vietnam War generals and the oppressors of African Americans. In invoking known revolutionaries such as Karl Marx, Lenin, Mao Zedong, and Ho Chi Minh, Adonis also links them to revolutionaries and unorthodox thinkers in Arab history. He refers to Ali ibn Muhammad, the black leader of *thawrat al-zanj* (revolt of the blacks) in ninth-century Iraq, and al-Niffari, the 10th-century mystic who rebelled against traditional cultural norms. Adonis also refers to the vagabond poet and a pre-Islamic outlaw Urwa ibn al-Ward—as if to suggest that revolutionaries of different epochs and cultures present a continuum.

In the same vein, to indicate a global geography and the need to flow into each other, Adonis uses rivers: Hudson, Tigris, Nile, Al-'Asi (Orontes), Tiber, and Hwang Ho. The finale of the poem contrasts dehumanizing New York to Beirut—the city that Adonis chose to make his own: "But, / Peace be to the rose of darkness and sands, / Peace be to Beirut."

This rich poem, like T. S. Eliot's *The Waste Land,* needs to be read with annotations for readers to grasp all the references and allusions. Some have read the work as prophetic: "The age of cats and dogs is the twenty-first century, and human beings will suffer extermination: This is the American Age!" Others have read the foretelling of the catastrophe of the Twin Towers on 9/11 in the poem's imagery: "The wind suddenly blows again from the East, uprooting the tents and the skyscrapers." The political and cultural context of the early 1970s in the United States and the rest of the world is necessary as a framework that allows readers to decipher the significance of names and events.

BIBLIOGRAPHY

Adonis. *Al-A'mal al-Kamila* (complete works). Vol. 2. Beirut: Dar al-'Awda, 1971, 645–673.

———. "A Grave for New York." Translated by Lena Jayyusi and Alan Brownjohn. In *Modern Arabic Poetry: An Antholoogy,* edited by Salma Khadra Jayyusi, 140–151. New York: Columbia University Press, 1987.

Al-Maqaleh, Abdel-Aziz, "Tombeau pour New York. Tombeau pour la domination et le racisme." In *Adonis: Un poète dans le monde d'aujourd'hui 1950–2000,* edited by Nasser El Ansary et al., 60–65. Paris: Institut du Monde Arabe, 2000.

Elfadel, Ibrahim. "L'Équation comme 'Tombeau pour New York.'" In *Adonis: Un poète dans le monde d'aujourd'hui 1950–2000,* edited by Nasser El Ansary et al. 300. Paris: Institut du Monde Arabe, 2000.

Hartman, Michele. "Writing Arabs and Africa(ns) in America: Adonis and 'Ashour from Harlem to Lady Liberty," IJMES 37, no. 3 (August 2005): 397–420.

Ferial J. Ghazoul

"GRAVEYARD BY THE SEA, THE" PAUL VALÉRY (1922)

"The Graveyard by the Sea" is a meditative poem by French poet PAUL VALÉRY. The poem was inspired by the cemetery in his birthplace, Sète, where his parents were buried. Valéry considered the poem one of his finest meldings of lyric beauty with philosophical observation. While the poem indicates that there is a profound sense of order in the universe, the order is not solely based on the mind's logical apprehension of it. Thematically, the work is the poet's reflection on the human condition—particularly mortality. The speaker is wandering among the tombstones in the cemetery while looking out over the ocean beside which the graveyard is located. One of the strongest images in the poem is of the undulations of the sea that are offset by the stillness of the cemetery, in which the lifeless remains of once active human

beings rest. The speaker philosophizes that the dead also remind the living of the permanence of certain things in the world—like the Sun and the sky—that continue regardless of the relative shortness of human existence. This realization gives the speaker renewed hope that even if an individual life is but a temporary occurrence in the greater scheme of the universe, human beings have the ability to view existence objectively and can take some consolation from their part in the overall cycle of existence. From a psychological perspective the vicissitudes of instinct are offset by the conscious personality that tends by virtue of memory to remain stable even though the conditions within which an individual finds him- or herself are subject to constant change. The poet conveys this sense of permanence by emphasizing the various cycles of the world: day and night, the ebb and flow of the tides, and the process of birth and death. Even if an individual seems insignificant in the grander scheme of things, each life is an important contribution to the continuity of the human life cycle.

Joseph E. Becker

GU CHENG (1956–1993)

Gu Cheng was born in 1956 in Beijing, China, and committed suicide after he killed his wife in New Zealand in 1993. In his 37 years he saw the miseries brought about by the Chinese Cultural Revolution (1966–76), the emergence of the Democracy Movement, the surge of emigration, and the wide acclaim he received for being a renowned representative of the Misty Poets.

Gu Cheng was the son of Gu Gong, a poet. Regarded as a genius at an early age, Gu Cheng is said to have written poems when he was still a child. His poems "The Cause of Stars and Moon" and "Chimney" were written when he was only 12. In 1969 the Gu family was sent to the countryside for reeducation and remained there for five years, during which Gu Cheng helped his father with farm tasks and enjoyed close contact with nature. In 1974 Gu Cheng's family returned to Beijing, and the young man took on different temporary jobs—as painter, carpenter, shop assistant, and so on. In 1976 he took an active part in the Democracy Movement.

The year 1979 was a meaningful one in Gu Cheng's life: His poem "A Fantasia to Life" was published in a district newspaper, and more than 10,000 copies were sold in a short time; he made his first public appearance when attending the first national poetry conference; he joined the literary journal *Today*'s literary community and became a representative figure, together with BEI DAO, SHU TING, and other Misty Poets; "A Generation," one of his most celebrated poems, greeted its readers; and he met his future wife, Xie Ye, and they fell in love. The year 1983 saw the couple happily married. Gu Cheng's first collection of poetry, *Eyes of Darkness,* came out in 1986. Gu Cheng and Xie Ye attended the International Poetry Festival in 1987 and visited and lectured in many countries, including Austria, Holland, Switzerland, Denmark, Great Britain, and France. He traveled to America in 1988, where he gave poetry readings, then went to New Zealand and later immigrated there. Li Ying (Ying'er) came to live with Gu Cheng and Xie Ye in 1989 and got involved in the couple's personal life. Gu Cheng went to Berlin in 1992 on a Deutscher Akademischer Austausch Dienst (DAAD, German Academic Exchange Service) cultural exchange grant, during which time he visited and lectured in Holland, Spain, and Romania—staying in Beijing with his wife for only one week in 1993. He suffered from a breakdown after learning of Li Ying's disappearance and began writing his autobiographical novel *Ying'er* in Berlin, which he completed in July 1993. In September 1993 he returned to New Zealand. The tragic ending happened on October 8, 1993, when the couple left behind Mu'er, their son.

The world Gu Cheng tried to create in his poetry is characterized by innocence, purity, beauty, and idealism, but it is shaped by unbearable realities, a strong sense of loss, and the poet's self-exile. The "obstinate child"—who "want[s] to draw / windows all over the earth / to let the eyes accustomed to darkness / to learn the habit of light" (Gu, xvii)—was worn and torn between the harsh realities of a foreign land and his ideal dream.

Gu Cheng is nicknamed by some a "fairytale poet." The images in his poetry are natural, direct, fresh, and novel but also tackle death, which becomes inseparable from life in his later poems. If idyllic lyricism characterizes his early poems, his poems after the mid-1980s—long sequences such as "The Bulin File,"

"A Eulogy World," and "Quicksilver"—are rich in experimental elements. According to his translator Eliot Weinberger, Gu Cheng's early and later poems suggest different features: "From the Imagism and Symbolism of the early lyrics, he moved on to Dadaism or one of the Futurisms. He ultimately landed in a completely idiosyncratic corner of Surrealism." Gu Cheng was the winner of the Thumb Poetry Award of Hong Kong (1984) and a DAAD grant (1992); English translations of Gu Cheng's works include *Nameless Flowers: Selected Poems of Gu Cheng* (2005), *Sea of Dreams: The Selected Writings of Gu Cheng* (2005), *Ying'er, The Kingdom of Daughters* (with Lei Mi, 1995), and *Rendition Paperbacks Selected Poems of Gu Cheng* (1990).

BIBLIOGRAPHY

Barnstone, Tony, ed. *Out of the Howling Storm.* Hanover, N.H.: Wesleyan University Press, 1993.

Brady, Anne-Maria. "Dead in Exile: The Life and Death of Gu Cheng and Xie Ye." *China Information* 11, 4 (Spring 1997): 126–148. PDF form available online.

Gu Cheng. "Preface." *Rendition Paperbacks Selected Poems of Gu Cheng.* Edited by Eva Hung. Hong Kong: Chinese University of Hong Kong, 1990

Li Xia, ed. *Essays, Interviews, Recollections and Unpublished Material of Gu Cheng, Twentieth Century Chinese Poet: The Poetics of Death.* New York: Mellen Press, 1999.

Weinberger, Eliot. "Next Stop, Forbidden City." *London Review of Books* 27, 12, 23 June 2005. Available online. URL: http://www.lrb.co.uk/v27/n12/wein01_.html. Accessed on April 22, 2007.

Shan Xuemei

GUILLÉN, JORGE (1893–1984)

Classical and traditional Spanish poetry, especially that of the 16th and 17th centuries (the "Golden Age" of Spanish literature), and the poetic trends in Europe at the beginning of the 20th century are the primary inspirations for Jorge Guillén's poems. He is one of the writers grouped under the name Generation of '27, a group of poets credited with bringing Spanish poetry to a level of quality not reached since the Golden Age. For them poetry is not a frivolous exercise but an attempt to capture the essential meaning of life and its fundamental components. Guillén is considered the most intellectual and the most elegant among these poets—and his poems the most difficult to interpret.

Pedro Jorge Guillén Álvarez, the son of Julio Guillén and Esperanza Álvarez, was born in Valladolid, Spain, to a comfortably well-off merchant family of liberal inclination. He was educated in both Spain and Switzerland. Later, from 1917 to 1923, he taught at the Sorbonne in Paris. There he met and, in 1921, married Germaine Cahen. He received a Ph.D. in Spanish literature and taught at two Spanish universities and at Oxford. He left Spain for political reasons in 1938, during the civil war, and moved to the United States to teach at several universities there and in Latin America. In Bogotá, Colombia, in 1961 (14 years after the death in 1947 of his first wife), he married Irene Mochi. When the Spanish dictator Francisco Franco died in 1975, Guillén returned to Spain.

Guillén received many honors during his lifetime, from Spain and other countries, among them the Premio Cervantes in 1976. In 1978 Guillén was elected an honorary member of the Real Academia Española, an organization whose members are the literary elite of the country.

Guillén's poetry was published in four collections, most of which were revised several times with a considerable number of new poems added to each new edition. His works were published as *Cántico* (Canticle, 1928, 1936, as *Cántico: Fe de vida* [Testimony of Life] 1945, 1950); *Clamor: Tiempo de historia* (Clamor: Time of History) and *Maremágnum* (Sea of Confusion, 1957); *Que van a dar en la mar* (They Will End at the Sea, 1960); *A la altura de las circunstancias* (To Rise to the Occasion, 1963); *Homenaje: Reunión de vidas* (Homage: A Gathering of Lives, 1967); *Aire nuestro* (Our Air, 1968); *Final* (1987); and *Y otros poemas* (And Other Poems, 1973). The 1987 edition of *Aire nuestro* includes all his poems published up to that date. Guillén also wrote a number of critical essays on literary subjects.

Guillén's poetry has been called *"poesía pura"* (pure poetry). Reality is reflected not in its prosaic entirety, but through its fundamental, essential qualities: ordinary subjects, ideas, and emotions attain universal meaning through his vision, his poetic intuition, and his masterful, selective use of figurative language. His special use of tropes is apparent especially in the four editions of *Cántico,* the best known and the most critically acclaimed of his collections. The significance of this collection lies in

Guillén's ability to create poems full of vitality and sensory impact despite his highly structured poetic style. In many of the poems in *Cántico* Guillén effectively communicates a concept, an abstraction, or a philosophical thought by grounding it in a concrete experience, in everyday reality, eliciting from the reader an insight into something universal through a specific sensory perception. To attain this effect he frequently uses personification, images of nature, and representations of the relationship between humans and the natural world. The poem *"Las doce en el reloj"* ("TWELVE O'CLOCK, NOON"), which captures the feeling of unity between poet and nature, is a good example of his technique.

Love, both as a concept and as a primary human emotion, is at the center of the poetry in *Cántico. Clamor,* however, is more socially engaged, its themes more specific to contemporary times and more reflective of the negative aspects of modern society; thus its language is more familiar. "Potencia de Pérez" ("THE POWER OF PÉREZ") is a denunciation of Franco's dictatorship. The poem appeared in *Maremágnum,* which was banned in Spain by government censors. In *Homenaje* Guillén transcends some of the anguish of *Clamor*; here, as in *Cántico* and *Y otros poemas,* Guillén writes primarily about love and the essence of poetry. Overall, however, his works reflect a variety of themes regarding human experience and meditate on the universality of this experience.

In 1987 Jorge Guillén published all his poems in a single volume, *Aire nuestro. Final.* Guillén's poetic production constitutes an organic, cohesive, if progressive, lifelong reflection on a number of main themes expressed in an idiosyncratic poetic style. Since distinct personal, social, and political circumstances are reflected in each collection, each one constitutes an entity unto itself but at the same time is an essential part of a coherent and developing whole.

BIBLIOGRAPHY

Guillén, Jorge. *Our Air.* 2 vols. Translated by Carl W. Cobb. Lewiston, N.Y.: Edwin Mellen, 1997.
MacCurday, G. Grant. *Jorge Guillén.* Boston: Twayne, 1982.

Mercedes Tibbits

GUILLÉN, NICOLÁS (1902–1989) Nicolás Guillén was the most influential Caribbean Spanish-language poet of the 20th century. A leading figure of

the NÉGRITUDE MOVEMENT in the 1930s and 1940s, Guillén emerged as the poet laureate of the Cuban revolution in the 1960s and remains the island's most beloved writer since José Martí.

Nicolás Cristóbal Guillén Batista was born in Camagüey, Cuba, in 1902 to parents of Afro-Hispanic descent. The young Nicolás was greatly influenced by the social and political liberalism of his journalist father, Nicolás Guillén Urra, who was murdered by soldiers in 1917. Despite tremendous economic hardship, the boy's mother, Argelia Battista Arrieta, ensured that her son completed his secondary education. During this period Guillén published his first poems, compositions reflecting the modernist aesthetic of RUBÉN DARÍO. Although he enrolled in the College of Law at the University of Havana in 1922, the young poet soon lost interest in pursuing a legal career and went home to assume an editorial post at the journal El Camagüeyano. In 1926 Guillén returned to Havana, where he obtained a civil service position that afforded him a comfortable existence while allowing him to expand his cultural horizons. Life in the Cuban capital put Guillén in contact with the latest literary currents, as well as with other poets, including FEDERICO GARCÍA LORCA and American poet Langston Hughes. It was also during this period that he developed the aesthetic that would first distinguish him as a major literary innovator. Drawing on the African-based popular dance known as son, Guillén combined rhythmic form with the speech and folklore of the island's black population to create the collection Motivos de son (Motifs of Son, 1930). He further articulated his Afrocentric vision of Cuba with the more polemical Sóngoro consongo: poemas mulatos (1931), where the much anthologized poem "Pequeña oda a un negro boxeador cubano" (SMALL ODE TO A BLACK CUBAN BOXER) first appeared. Following Fulgencio Batista's coup and the subsequent U.S. military intervention, Guillén raised the banner of anti-imperialism and pan-Caribbean nationalism in West Indies, Inc. (1934) and Cantos para soldados y sones para turistas (Songs for Soldiers and Sones for Tourists, 1937). By then a significant figure in the leftist intelligentsia, Guillén spent much of 1937 attending revolutionary congresses in Spain and Mexico. Contact with such preeminent figures as ANTONIO MACHADO, PABLO NERUDA, RAFAEL ALBERTI, and TRISTÁN TZARA in Spain and Diego Rivera and Alfaro Siquieros in Mexico brought Guillén to the Communist Party. The poet's sympathy for the ill-fated Spanish Rebublic led to his short collection España: poema en cuatro angustias y una esperanza (Spain: Poem in Four Fears and One Hope, 1937). Over the next two decades Guillén devoted himself almost entirely to politics. In addition to running an unsuccessful campaign for mayor of his native Camagüey in 1940, Guillén served as editor of the newspaper Hoy from 1941 to 1945. It was also during this period that Guillén traveled to Haiti to meet Jacques Roumain, one of the seminal figures of Francophone négritude. With the end of World War II and the onset of the cold war, Guillén's political affiliations forced him into self-imposed exile. Traveling throughout South America, he championed the cause of Latin American solidarity in El son entero (The Complete Son, 1947). A subsequent voyage to the Soviet Union, Eastern Europe, and China deepened his commitment to socialism and resulted in the polemical collection La paloma de vuelo popular (The Dove of Popular Flight, 1958). Notable from this period of strongly ideological poetry is "Elegía a Jesús Menéndez" (1951), a powerful tribute to the writer's slain friend and fellow revolutionary. While Guillén was awarded the Lenin Peace Prize in 1954 by the Soviet Union, his status as one of communism's preeminent voices received its ultimate consecration after the triumph of the Cuban revolution in 1958. In 1961 Guillén's colleagues elected him president of the Union of Cuban Artists and Writers, a position he held until his death. His later collections, Tengo (I Have, 1964), Cuatro canciones para el Che (Four Songs for Che, 1969), and La rueda dentada (The Toothed Wheel, 1972), echoed his commitment to restoring Cuba's African identity while celebrating the virtues of the revolution. The most complete bilingual anthology of Guillén's poetry is Roberto Márquez and David Arthur McMurray's Man-Making Words (University of Massachussets Press, 1972). A good critical introduction is Ian Isidore Smart's Nicolás Guillén: Popular Poet of the Caribbean (Columbia: University of Missouri Press, 1990).

Eric L. Reinholtz

"GUNIB" TITSIAN TABIDZE (1927) "Gunib," composed in 1927, belongs to TITSIAN TABIDZE's second creative period, after he left behind his early affection for European-inspired symbolism and before he began penning overtly socialist-realist poems on Soviet themes. "Gunib" is perhaps the most profound meditation in the corpus of Georgian literature on Georgia's relationship to its north Caucasus neighbors. Set during the aftermath of the Caucasian War, which terminated in Russia's victory and the surrender in 1859 of Imam Shamil, the leader of the pan-Caucasian resistance to the Russian conquest, the poem is also a lyrical self-interrogation in which the poet seeks to redeem what he calls the "treachery" of his people by means of the cathartic truth of poetry.

In "Gunib" the poet imagines himself as a warrior on the north Caucasian side. His lyric persona returns to Gunib, a village high in the mountains of Dagestan, a republic of the present-day Russian Federation that borders on Georgia. In Gunib in 1859 Imam Shamil surrendered to the Russians. The poet meditates in his poem over the Georgian complicity in Imam Shamil's defeat, for many of the leading officers in the czarist Russian army of the time were of ethnic Georgian origin. Titsian (as the poet is generally referred to in Georgia) ponders the irony that his fellow countrymen "sold themselves into slavery" when, under the illusion that they were achieving a military victory for themselves, they collaborated with an enemy power.

"Gunib" is not merely a political poem, nor was Titsian Tabidze a political poet. Part of its magic is the muted nature of its indictment, mediated by a layer of complex historical allusions. While the poem's allusive nature can be accounted for in part by the demands of Soviet censorship, such an explanation tells only half the story and obscures the nature of Titsian's genius, which is most comfortable making bold statements through indirect, erudite suggestion.

Nor is "Gunib" merely one poet's indictment of his nation; most fundamentally it is a poet's dialogue with himself that reveals the poet at the height of his lyric genius. The speaker of the poem is simultaneously a traitor and a hero; he applies to himself both the terms *murid*, which evokes the tradition of Islamic freedom fighters of the north Caucasus, and *giaour*, the Islamic term for infidel.

The last lines are devoted to a celebration of the incantatory power of poetry and the poet's unique ability to redeem through language the treachery of a faithless world: "I never donned the fighter's armor," Titsian writes, "But this battle"—by which he means the art of poetry itself— "moves even me to ecstasy. / I don't want to be a poet drunk on blood. / Let this day be my penitence. / Let my poems wash away your treachery." Notably, unlike the majority of Titsian's poetry, "Gunib," one of his most significant works, was never translated into Russian. The poem appears in English in the literary journal *Two Lines: Journal of Translation* (San Francisco, 2006).

Rebecca Gould

GUO MORUO (1892–1978)

Guo Moruo played a variety of roles including poet, critic, writer, dramatist, historian, archaeologist, activist, diplomat, and government official. He witnessed the turbulence of recent Chinese history both before and after the founding of the People's Republic of China in 1949. Guo Moruo is acclaimed as a monumental figure who is as important as Lu Xun to 20th-century Chinese thinking.

Originally named Guo Kaizhen, Guo Moruo was born in 1892 in Lushan, Sichuan Province. With the help of his elder brother, he studied medicine in Japan in 1914. As early as 1919 Guo Moruo started to write, translate, and publish his poems. He devoted himself to literature instead of medicine after he earned a bachelor's degree in medicine in 1923. In his view the establishment of a new literature would exert a greater influence on people than medicine could. He was drawn to Marxism in 1924 and joined the army to fight against Chinese military dictator Yuan Shikai. He was wanted by Jiang Kaishi (Jiang Jieshi, or Chiang Kaishek, leader of the anticommunist Kuomintang and later president of the Republic of China in Taiwan) in 1927 because of his critical article "Look at Today's Jiang Kaishi," and he became a member of the Communist Party the same year. To avoid being caught and prosecuted, Guo Moruo went to Japan in 1928 and worked on ancient Chinese literature, but he returned to China after the Japanese invasion of China. During that period he wrote a number of political articles and also worked on literature and research.

After the founding of the People's Republic, Guo Moruo was assigned different official posts, including president of the Chinese Academy of Social Sciences, president of the University of Science and Technology of China, and a number of other high literary positions. Actively involved in diplomatic efforts toward world peace, he helped to promote Sino-American and Sino-Japanese relations and was awarded the Lenin Peace Prize by the USSR in 1951. Cultural authorities agree that "his personalities were flawed" during the Chinese Cultural Revolution. He died in 1978.

Guo Moruo had varied interests. From the early 1920s to mid-1930s he focused on the creation of new poetry, while translating theoretical books and progressive literature from Russian, English, and German into Chinese. From the late-1920s to mid-1930s he did intensive research on ancient Chinese societies. From the late-1930s to mid-1940s he surveyed the thoughts of the ancient masters and wrote several historical plays. He focused in the 1950s on the periodization of ancient times and collected ancient literature. In the 1960s his influence on the social sciences and art was felt through his research on historical figures and historical plays. His interest in ancient characters and artifacts were continuous.

Guo Moruo was a prolific writer. His writings are a cultural documentary of the specific period in which he lived. The *Collected Works of Guo Moruo* includes 20 volumes of literature, eight volumes of history, and 10 volumes on archaeology. His writings have been translated into Japanese, Russian, English, and other foreign languages.

As for his contribution to literature, Guo Moruo published his first anthology of poetry, *The Goddesses,* in 1921. That volume marked a new high in Chinese romanticism. He cofounded the Creation Society in Shanghai, which promoted modern and vernacular literature. He wrote several historical plays, including *Qu Yuan, Cai Wenji,* and *Wang Zhaojun.*

As a critic Guo Moruo dedicated his writing to upholding Chinese vernacular literature while absorbing some of the highlights of Western thought and literature. From 1919 to 1978 he unwaveringly promoted the idea that Western thought should be appreciated against a local backdrop; that the task of intellectuals is to awaken people's awareness of the national cultural heritage while applying the advances of Western science. He argued that it was important to popularize science in China and that one way to accomplish that was through literature.

It is generally recognized that Guo Moruo's intellectual growth was closely connected with the important events in Chinese history, and his achievements in such fields as literature, history, and sociology have in turn influenced the development of those and related fields in China. Guo Moruo contributed enormously to modern Chinese thinking, and his accomplishments call for continued intensive research.

BIBLIOGRAPHY

Chen Xiaoming. *From the May Fourth Movement to Communist Revolution: Guo Moruo and the Chinese Path to Communism.* Albany: State University of New York Press, 2007.
Guo Moruo. *Selected Poems from The Goddesses.* Beijing: Foreign Languages Press, 1958; reprint, 1984.

Shan Xuemei

GUSTAFSSON, LARS (1936–)

Lars Gustafsson is one of Europe's leading contemporary poets and public intellectuals. As a writer, adjunct professor of Germanic studies and philosophy at the University of Texas at Austin, and cultural critic for leading Swedish newspapers and journals, Gustafsson has contributed to cultural debates on two continents over the past five decades. He has degrees in philosophy from Uppsala University in Sweden and Oxford University in the United Kingdom. Since his literary debut in 1957, Gustafsson has published 76 volumes of poetry, prose, plays, and essays. His latest—and 19th—poetry collection, *Den amerikanska flickans söndagar* (The American Girl's Sundays), came out in 2006 to positive critical reviews. A total of 18 volumes of his work have been published in English and 11 remain in print, including three volumes of poetry: *Elegies and Other Poems* (2000), *The Stillness of the World before Bach: New Selected Poems* (1998), and *Warm Rooms and Cold* (1975). William Jay Smith and Leif Sjöberg have also published an anthology, *The Forest of Childhood: Poems from Sweden* (1996), with new English translations of six of his poems. Gustafsson has won many Swedish and European literary prizes, the first in 1960 and most recently in 2006. He is an influential cultural figure in Germany, where much of his work has appeared in translation, as well as in Sweden. Gustafsson has long been known for taking controversial positions in contemporary cultural debates as an editor of and critic for various Swedish publications. He regards creative writing as a vital instrument of the philosopher's craft. As he states on his faculty Web site at the University of Texas–Austin: "I tend to regard myself as a philosopher who has turned literature into one of his tools."

Gustafsson was born in Västerås, the capital of Västmanland Province in east-central Sweden. He studied philosophy at Uppsala University just north of Stockholm, one of Sweden's two oldest and most prestigious academic institutions. He earned a Fil. lic. (Ph.D.) degree there in 1961 and a Fil. Dr. (considered a higher degree than the American Ph.D.) in 1979, both in philosophy. His decision to settle in Austin, Texas, in 1982, writing in exile during the academic year and spending summers at his cottage in Sweden, has distinguished him from his Swedish peers and afforded him a certain outsider status in his home country. Some of his literary works are set in Texas, others in Sweden, others in both places and points in between. "I move between these two worlds with a certain ease," Gustafsson said in an interview with the *Austin Chronicle*. "If I had stayed in Sweden all my life, I would have become a less interesting writer."

Gustafsson has recounted that he received a call to poetry at age 14, when he was vacationing with his parents on a peninsula extending into a lake in north Västmanland. "A dipper hung over the water out there, the evening breeze came in a rush, the dark stream kept flowing in its quiet inexorable rhythm." From that moment he knew that poetry, "that language, which in some mysterious way was identical with the wordless authority of the scenery," would be his language (Sjöberg 172). Gustafsson's early poetry of the 1960s consisted primarily of long poems akin to those written by the English poet T. S. Eliot, exploring various aspects of the human condition. His well-known *Kärleksförklaring*

till en sefardisk dam (Declaration of Love to a Sephardic Lady, 1970), translated into English by Robin Fulton and published in excerpt in *Contemporary Jewish Writing in Sweden: An Anthology* (2004), is a good example of his earlier writing. In the 1970s he began writing more ballads, sonnets, and didactic poems, and in recent years he has experimented with visual montage in shorter, lyrical poems that engage imminent and universal existential questions through figurative language. His well-known poem "*Världens tystnad före Bach*" (THE STILLNESS OF THE WORLD BEFORE BACH, 1982), published in English in a collection of the same name in 1998, provides an excellent instance of that style.

Gustafsson's poetry has been characterized as intellectually sophisticated, technically accomplished, unromantic, and just plain strange; for example, his poetry collection *Artesiska brunnar cartesianska drömmar* (Artesian Wells Cartesian Dreams, 1980) engages Descartes's statement that "waking life and dream never can be kept apart by reliable criteria" (Sjöberg 172). Gustafsson's status as a renegade outsider in Swedish society was reinforced by his conversion to Judaism in 1981, a year before he moved to Austin. This was considered a radical act for a prominent cultural figure in a rational and secular society with an unsavory history of discrimination against Jews. His poetry—as radical as its creator—merits study for its technical sophistication, preoccupation with existential and epistemological questions, and intricate geographies of place and mind.

BIBLIOGRAPHY

Gathman, Roger. "Lone Star Sweden: Lars Gustafsson." *The Austin Chronicle* books section, 25 February 2000. Available online. URL: http://www.austinchronicle.com/gyrobase/Issue/print?oid=oid%3A75963. Accessed on April 23, 2007.

"Gustafsson Face Page." Available online. URL: http://www.utexas.edu/depts/german/faculty/gustafsson.html. Accessed on July 23, 2006.

Gustafsson, Lars. *Elegies and Other Poems.* Edited by Christopher Middleton. New York: New Directions, 2000.

———. *The Stillness of the World before Bach: New Selected Poems.* Edited by Christopher Middleton, translated by Christopher Middleton, Yvonne L. Sandström, and Harriet Watts. New York: New Directions, 1998.

———. *Warm Rooms and Cold.* Translated by Yvonne L. Sandström. Providence, R.I.: Copper Beech Press, 1975.

———. *Lars Gustafsson: Selected Poems.* Translated by Robin Fulton. New York: New Rivers Press, 1972.

"Lars Gustafsson." *Contemporary Jewish Writing in Sweden: An Anthology,* edited by Peter Stenberg. Lincoln: University of Nebraska Press, 2004.

Sandström, Yvonne. "The Machine Theme in Some Poems by Lars Gustafsson." *Scandinavian Studies* 44, no. 2 (1972).

Sjöberg, Leif, and William Jay Smith, eds. and trans. *The Forest of Childhood: Poems from Sweden.* Minneapolis: New Rivers Press, 1996.

Ursula A. L. Lindqvist

H

HAAVIKKO, PAAVO (1931–) Paavo Haavikko is considered one of the leading Finnish writers of the postwar period. He is especially known as a pioneer of the new modernist poetry in the 1950s but has been prolific and influential in many other genres as well, including novels, essays, aphorisms, and dramas. Haavikko was born in 1931 in Helsinki, Finland, where he grew up in a working-class neighborhood. He was greatly influenced, he has said, by his reading of T. S. Eliot's *Four Quartets* at age 18; in general, his early work shows a familiarity with both classical texts and modern European trends. He published his first collection of poetry, *Tiet etäisyyksiin* (Roads to Far Away), in 1951, although his earliest poems, included in a later volume, date from 1949. He published four more collections in the 1950s, culminating in the masterful *Talvipalatsi* (WINTER PALACE) in 1959. His poetry from that decade broke with Finnish literary tradition by expanding beyond traditional poetic forms, using language and rhythm in new ways, and building meaning primarily through series of juxtaposed images.

Haavikko's poetry was at first considered strange and difficult, but has now achieved classic status in the Finnish canon. Much of his early poetry deals with metaphysical questions: the relationship between literary tradition and the new poetry, the process of creation, and language itself. With his first novel, *Yksityisia asioita* (Private Concerns, 1960), he turned his attention to social and political critique, taking a stance against both totalitarian ideologies and weak liberal compromises. His only poetry collection from the 1960s, *Puut, kaikki heidän vihreytensä* (The Trees, in All Their Verdancy, 1966), is a critical examination of Finland's recent history. From the 1970s on he has published in a variety of genres, continuing to write poetry but also prose fiction and nonfiction. Throughout his career one of the main subjects of his poetry and other writing has been history. He often uses historical events or characters to reflect on the present. This is particularly evident in his dramas, for example, *Kuningas lähtee Ranskaan* (The King Goes Forth to France, 1974); but reexamining history takes a prominent place in his poetry as well. *Synnyinmaa* (Homeland, 1955) takes a critical look at Finland's history; in *Lehdet lehtiä* (Pages as Leaves, 1958), a series of poems follows the progress of Finland's Winter War against the USSR via the memoirs of its defense minister. Some of Haavikko's best-known works reinterpret Finnish folklore and the national epic, *Kalevala,* especially the epic poem *Kaksikymmenta ja yksi* (Twenty-one, 1974), the television drama *Rauta-Aika* (Iron Age, 1982), which used the *Kalevala*'s characters, and *Kullervon Tarina* (1982), which portrayed the tragic hero Kullervo. In these as well as in his poetry collection set in medieval times, *Neljätoista hallitsijaa* (Fourteen Rulers, 1970), his focus is on the use and abuse of power.

Since the 1980s Haavikko has continued writing poetry alongside his many other literary productions, especially aphorisms and dramas. In all of these genres, he comments on an ever-wider range of topics, including history, literature, politics, and economics, among others. He has also worked as a columnist at the weekly magazine *Suomen Kuvalehti* and other papers, where he has written about politics and contemporary issues. He is known for his skeptical, realistic, and often pessimistic view of the world; his broad range of works and ideas; and his originality. Alongside his writing career, he also worked at the major Finnish publishing house, Otava, for about two decades before becoming the managing director of his own firm, Art House, in 1989, a small press specializing in nonfiction and scientific books.

Haavikko received the Neustadt International Prize for Literature in 1984, the Nordic Prize of the Swedish Academy in 1993, and the Nordic Council Drama Competition's prize in 1996. His poetry collections have been published in 12 languages. In English the translations of Anselm Hollo are notable, including a 1999 edition of his selected poems from 1949–88.

BIBLIOGRAPHY
Haavikko, Paavo. *Selected Poems*. Edited and translated by Anselm Hollo. Chicago: Carcanet Press, 1999.
Laitinen, Kai. "How Things Are: Paavo Haavikko and His Poetry." In *Books Abroad: An International Quarterly of Comment on Foreign Books* 43 (1969): 41–46.
Schoolfield, George, ed. *A History of Finland's Literature*. Lincoln and London: University of Nebraska Press, 1998.

Sonia Wichmann

HAN YONGUN (1879–1944)

Han Yongun is revered as a Buddhist, philosopher, activist, and poet who left a large imprint on Korean history. Some even say he is greater than RABINDRANATH TAGORE, the Nobel laureate poet and philosopher, and Mahatma Gandhi, the political and spiritual leader of the Indian independence movement, for Han was a resistance leader, which Tagore was not, and a great poet, having achieved a poetic stature that Gandhi never reached.

Born in a small town, Hongsung, in western Korea in 1879, Han was smart enough at the age of six to start learning old Korean literature written in Chinese characters. At the age of 17, in 1896, he participated in the Donghak Civil Disobedience Movement, led by intellectuals, farmers, and the poor protesting against heavy taxation imposed by the regional administrator. The movement was put down by the national guards, and many protesters, including most of the leaders, were killed. Witnessing the people's dream for a righteous world cut down so ruthlessly, Han turned to the precepts of Buddhism at the age of 28 and became a Buddhist monk. While devoting himself to Buddhist religious practices, however, he realized that Korean Buddhism—which emphasized staying in a deep, remote mountain temple and pursuing profound awakening and ultimate spiritual liberation—was indifferent to social and political concerns. Thus believing that civic engagement in real life is a true application of Buddha's teaching, Han carried out his words in a series of crucial historical events. After the Eulsa treaty was drawn up between Korean minister Lee Wan-yong and Japanese field marshal Count Terauchi Masatake in 1905, Han traveled to Japan as one of the 52 delegates representing Buddhist monks in Korea to see how much technological development Japan had made. When Korea lost its sovereignty to Japan in 1910, Han went to the Manchurian province of China and to Russian Siberia and spent three years encouraging resistance leaders. When he came back to Korea at the age of 35, he published his *Great Tripitaka of Buddhism*, a concise version of *The Korean Tripitaka*. In it he systemized his Buddhist philosophy into the Huayan Doctrine, which views everything in terms of a cosmic alteration of reality and appearance and of being and nonbeing. In 1919, as a representative of the Korean Buddhist National Association, Han signed the Declaration of Independence in joint agreement with 32 intellectual leaders representing every social sector. With them he announced the justness of Korean independence, then joined thousands of protesters shouting, "Viva Independence!" For this incident he was arrested and imprisoned. Yet even in prison his spirit was not bent: He kept his resistance by writing a manifesto urging Korean independence. After his release he embodied his dream of Korean independence, based on his Huayan Doctrine, in the collection of poetry *Nim ui Ch'immuk* (The Silence of Love, 1926). Feeling the energy of *Nim* (motherland) in its material absence, he envisioned the ultimate fading of Japanese power and an independent Korea. His poem instantly grabbed the attention of millions of Koreans who had been longing for their country's independence. And he became the most famous resistance poet of the Japanese occupation. Unfortunately, he died of Alzheimer's disease at the age of 65, just before Japan announced its surrender to the Allies in 1945 at the end of World War II. It is generally agreed that Han made a huge contribution to Korea, not only by modernizing Mahayana Buddhism with his Huayan Doctrine, but also by practicing his Buddhist religion in his everyday life through the independence movement, and in his renowned resistance poetry. Just as he envisioned the presence of *Nim* in its absence, many Koreans feel his spirit's presence even after his death. His most famous poem, "THE SILENCE OF LOVE," is known and recited by almost all South Koreans, and his name will be forever attached to the Korean independence movement. In 1962 his patriotism received nationwide recognition, and he was honored with the presidential medal. In commemoration of his poetic achievement, the Man-hae (his name as a Buddhist monk) Literary Award was established in 1973 and is given every year to a writer whose works have inspired nationalist causes.

BIBLIOGRAPHY
McCann, David R. *The Columbia Anthology of Modern Korean Poetry.* New York: Columbia University Press, 2004.

Han Ji-hee

"HAPPY YOUTH" GOTTFRIED BENN (1912)

Published in his first collection *Morgue and Other Poems,* "Happy Youth" (*"Schöne Jugend,"* also translated as "Beautiful Youth") lyrically captures the world of disease and death that the young Doctor Benn confronted daily while treating the poor and suffering in Berlin's city hospitals. Considered an exemplary expressionist poem, "Happy Youth" co-opts a literary form traditionally invested in describing the beautiful to render the ugliness and ephemeral quality of life. Its matter-of-fact tone and clinical language belie the author's deep cynicism about the prospects for humanity while offering to poetry a radically new conception of the poet's task.

A brilliant image begins this poem: "The mouth of a girl who had lain a long time in / the rushes looked so nibbled away." A body part once active is now, ironically, passive and being consumed, a victim of its former purpose, subject to the creatures that sustain their own lives by this mouth's death. As the next stanzas reveal, the poetic subject's position with respect to this corpse is not that of an unsuspecting person, having chanced upon a corpse outdoors. "The breasts broken open, the feed-pipe so full of / holes." Instead, the subject is a part of the action, hunting through the victim's chest, noting internal organs by name. As the circumstances become clearer, the poem begins to read like a doctor's notations—brief, detached, detailed, and without embellishment. Moreover, in an uncanny way, the doctor's task becomes one with that of the critic: He dissects the body as the reader deconstructs the text.

After the discovery of the rats' nest below the victim's diaphragm, one would expect the poem's second half to suggest the circularity of life presaged in the first verse, underscoring the natural process of death and regeneration. Yet the first rat—notably a young female, too—is also found dead. Her remaining siblings, feeding off of flesh and blood as if enjoying a Eucharistic feast, are as good as dead as well. Notably, it is in reaction to these creatures—and not to the girl—that the poem's speaker indulges in a momentary speculation: They "spent a happy youth here. / And short and sweet their death was too." And yet any suggestion of sentimentality is erased by the callous gesture of the rats' drowning and the gruesomely festive depiction of the suffering beasts, who will no doubt meet the same fate as their host.

Though offering a shocking irreverence reminiscent of French poet Charles Baudelaire's "Carrion," Benn conveys little of the latter's eroticism in rendering the young woman's corpse. Rather than emphasizing the seductive beauty found in even the most ravaged of bodies, Benn rejects this redeeming position. Instead he shows youth and beauty to be quickly expendable in the natural order of things.

BIBLIOGRAPHY
Benn, Gottfried. "Happy Youth." In *Modern German Authors,* Vol. 6, *Gottfried Benn: The Unreconstructed Expressionist,* text and translation by J. M. Ritchie, 106. London: Wolff, 1972.

Michele Ricci

HERBERT, ZBIGNIEW (1924–1998)

Zbigniew Herbert's wry language and incisive wit have gained him some of the highest praise given to European poets of the post–World War II period. Not only a poet, Herbert was also an essayist, dramatist, and teacher. His famous poetic persona, Mr. Cogito, enabled him to attain an ironic distance from his personal experiences of the frightening suppression of human rights and the absurdities of daily life, especially in war-torn Poland, Herbert's birthplace and homeland.

Zbigneiw Herbert was born on October 29, 1924, in Lwów (present-day L'viv), in the easternmost part of the country. The region suffered atrocities from both the Soviet and the German armies during World War II, each of which took brutal possession of the city. Herbert's uncle was executed by the Soviets in 1940. When Herbert was still a teenager, he joined the Polish underground's fighting forces. During that same period (1942–44), he studied Polish literature at the Jan Kazimierz University, which operated clandestinely during the war. In 1944 he enrolled in the Fine Arts Academy in Kraków. He earned an M.A. in economics from the University of Kraków in 1947, an M.A. in law from the Nicholas Copernicus University of Torun in 1948, and an M.A. in philosophy from the University of Warsaw in 1950. In Warsaw he supported himself by working in a series of low-profile jobs—as a shop clerk, bank teller, accountant—while writing columns and essays for a popular cultural periodical, *Tygodnik Powszechny,* a Catholic magazine to which many distinguished writers, including Czesław Miłosz, contributed in those days under pseudonyms. Stalinist censorship extended to Soviet satellite countries and prevented many writers from publishing dissident material under their own names; Herbert's response was to resign from the Polish Writers' Union and "write for the drawer," as he put it. Nevertheless, he did publish his first volume of verse, *Chord of Light* (1956), under his own name. As a result he became almost immediately a cultural hero, celebrated as an antitotalitarian poet who had crafted an idiom suited to a realistic rendition of contemporary conditions of life and thought. His humanistic poems contained clear, objective references to classical literature and daily life, but

gone from his innovative poetic idiom was any hint of the hackneyed tenor of defiance and clichéd protest of earlier poets. Instead Herbert developed a way of expressing quotidian truths by indirection or allusion and, thereby, creating the savvy voice of a sort of poetic antihero for the times.

Between 1957 and 1968 Herbert published his collections of poems *Hermes, the Dog and the Star* (1957) and *Study of the Object* (1961), his acclaimed volume of essays *The Barbarian in the Garden* (1962), and *Selected Poems* (1968), Milosz's superb translation into English of Herbert's best-loved poems. Between 1968 and 1981 Herbert traveled out of the country to read his works and was invited to teach (as writer in residence) in various countries, including Germany and the United States (at the University of California, Los Angeles). The publication of *Mr. Cogito* in 1974 received the highest critical accolades. Herbert returned to Poland in 1981, once the Solidarity movement had effected positive change in civic life, but he was prevented from leaving the country, once again, when martial law was imposed later that same year. The enforced captivity did not hinder Herbert's output. Among the many publications that followed, a sequel to *Mr. Cogito* appeared: Herbert's *Report from the Besieged City* (1984). From 1986 to 1992 Herbert was allowed to live in Paris, where he stayed until communism collapsed in Poland. He then returned to Warsaw, where he remained until his death on July 28, 1998, from emphysema.

For his achievements Herbert was awarded numerous prizes including the prestigious Herder Prize for Poetry in 1973, the Petrarch Prize (Verona, Italy) in 1979, and the Jerusalem Prize in 1991. As Stanisław Baranczak observed in *A Fugitive from Utopia* (1987), "Polish readers have always revered poets who succeed in defining the nation's spiritual dilemma; what is exceptional in Herbert is that his popularity at home is matched by a wide acclaim abroad."

See also "Pebble."

BIBLIOGRAPHY
Baranczak, Stanislaw. *A Fugitive from Utopia: The Poetry of Zbigniew Herbert.* Cambridge, Mass.: Harvard University Press, 1987.

Gutman, Huck. Full texts and audio lecture on "Pebble," "Why the Classics," and "The Envoy of Mr. Cogito. Available online. URL: http://www.uvm.edu/~sgutman/ Herbert.html. Downloaded on April 23, 2007.

Herbert, Zbigniew. *The Collected Poems: 1956–1998*. New York: Ecco Press, 2007.

R. Victoria Arana

"HE WAS ASKING ABOUT THE QUALITY—" CONSTANTINE CAVAFY (1930)

The charms of shopping have never been more celebrated than in this most delicate and intriguing poem about mutual and tacit recognition. "He Was Asking about the Quality—"("Ρώτουσε για την ποιότητα—") elaborates on a moment of successful intersubjective gaze by projecting ironically libidinal, epistemological, and ontological questions in its title. Walking idly about the streets a young man—"Beautiful / and interesting—so that he appeared to have reached / his fullest sensual yield" (l. 7–9)—sees in a little shop a figure that attracts him. He enters pretending to ask about the quality of the handkerchiefs. The matter at hand, however, is quite a different one.

The veiled acquiescence of the third stanza answers successfully the latent question at hand: What kind of man are you? Here language functions surreptitiously, *handkerchiefs* allegorically signifying something else. Disguised and subdued, language almost seems redundant or incidental; but its failure or weakness to express the unspeakable turns into the crucial communicative gestures ("choked voice . . . faded" and "distracted . . . low voice") that let each other know that they stand on common ground. Once the quality of "the handkerchiefs" has been established—the critical ontological question of the poem—the two men, the clerk and the customer, achieve "their only aim: the touching of their hands / over the handkerchiefs, the coming closer of their faces, of their lips / as if by chance, a momentary contact of the limbs."

Such successful recognition scenes are a further elaboration of the discourse of secrecy and concealment that we find in CAVAFY in many guises. Our ability to recognize this discourse inevitably involves a subjective engagement and a willingness to see beyond and below the obvious and the literal; the recognition of such a discourse, in other words, calls for suspicious readings. But the poem is not a simple paean to the efficacy of gay cruising practices. It is also a poem about urban alienation and freedom, of cautious transgression, and ever-present surveillance as is evident from the last two lines.

George Syrimis

"HEY, PEOPLE" NIMA YUSHIJ (1941)

NIMA YUSHIJ's poem "Hey, People" ("*Ay Adamha*") has been much anthologized in the years following its 1941 publication, often in support of leftist ideologies. The poem was written during the productive period when Nima (the name commonly used) worked for the innovative *Musiqui* magazine, and its publication coincided with the deposition of Reza Shah and widespread participation of intellectuals in public life in Iran. As Kamran Talattof observes, many critics have read the poem as a call for revolution (84).

The poem begins with an urgent address: "Hey, you over there," directed toward a festive crowd on a seaside shore. The message relates that someone is drowning—struggling against the waves of an "angry, heavy, dark, familiar sea." The voice of alarm turns to accusation: against the crowd's "old world" affluence, selfish concerns, and apathy before the suffering and sacrifice of the castaway, now fatigued, face disfigured with fear (vainly heroic). Emblematically, even the waves meet resistance against the "silent shore." In the end the wind carries the faint cry of alarm away, but, elsewhere, the shout persists—the call for awareness and action.

"Hey, People" is an example of Persian modernist New Poetry, wherein formalism and metric regularity are replaced by social conscience and organic, "natural" structure. The poem bears the stamp of the French symbolists, whose work Nima Yushij was examining in his manifesto *The Value of Feelings*. At this point in his career he had traveled through the romanticism of "Legend," the realism of "The Soldier's Family," to the symbolic. Yushij offers a recurring vocabulary of images: The inclusive and collective "you," of the "People," morphs to a conflict of perspectives—the complacent versus the voices of reform and transformation (in art as well as politics). He emphasizes other binaries for comparative effect: sea/shore, day/night, old/new. An always appreciative observer of the environment, he imbues natural settings with poetic mood, as in the despair and urgency of "Hey, People."

Yushij's contribution is enormous: Persian poetry entered the 20th century, with few exceptions, in fossilized imitation of the great medieval poets of the classical period. These giants—Ferdowsi, Khayyam, Sa'di, Rumi, Hafez—had pioneered a distinguished poetic tradition. In the 500 years since, however, their descendants had been content merely to imitate the conventions, motifs, and rules. Iranian society and Persian poetry were not modernized in the same graduated evolution as seen in the literatures of the West. Persian poetry made the leap from a medieval idiom to the modern in the space of one generation. Imagine, as Ahmad Karimi-Hakkak suggests, a comparable jump in Western literature from Alexander Pope to e.e. cummings—in 50 years' time (5). In Iran the voices for change were many, but the task of articulating a modern aesthetic fell to one man, Nima Yushij.

BIBLIOGRAPHY
Alishan, Leonardo P. "Ten Poems by Nima Yushij." *Literature East & West* 20, nos. 1–4 (1976): 21–31.
Karimi-Hakkak, Ahmad. *An Anthology of Modern Persian Poetry.* Boulder, Colo.: Westview Press, 1978.
Talattof, Kamran. *The Politics of Writing in Iran.* Syracuse, N.Y.: Syracuse University Press, 2000.

Anett Jessop

"HICCUP" LÉON DAMAS (1937)

"Hiccup" ("Hoquet") like "BARGAIN" is from Damas's first collection, *Pigments* (1937). It reveals the inferiority complex felt by blacks of Africa and the Caribbean because of centuries of abuse and exploitation by white European colonials. The solution to this problem lies neither in assimilating white European values nor in denying the difference of one's color or cultural heritage, for such attitudes lead to a catastrophic loss of identity, and thus the peoples of these countries must celebrate their *négritude*—their "blackness"—and their unique cultural identity.

In "Hiccup" the central metaphor of the title signifies the speaker's attempt to repress the traumatic memories of his childhood. Swallowing water at intervals as a remedy is futile, for the images always resurface, like hiccups: "back comes my childhood / in a hiccup that jolts / my instinct / like the cop shaking the tramp."

One sees in Damas's style the influence of French surrealism—the strange quality of the central metaphor, the absence of punctuation and formal meter and rhyme. The lines are short—some containing just one word—like the be-bop style of American jazz, revealing Damas's admiration for artists of the Harlem Renaissance in the United States.

Throughout "Hiccup" is the refrain, "Disaster / tell me about the disaster / tell me about it." The speaker defies readers to pity themselves, when his own life has been more disastrous than readers can imagine. This "disaster" lies in his mother's insistence that he imitate every aspect of white bourgeois culture, such as refined table manners, Catholic worship, and European education: to wit, "My mother hoping for a syllabus son / Unless you learn your history lesson / you shall not go to mass on Sunday / in all your Sunday best." Most important, the child must use the French language perfectly: ". . . you must speak French / the French of France / the Frenchman's French / French French." Thus Damas reveals how oppression is achieved by French colonials, directly and indirectly, through linguistic dominance.

Revealing how deeply the child has been shamed by the color of his skin (the "pigment" of the collection's title), his mother forbids him to play the banjo or the guitar—instruments of "blacks." She explains that the superior "mulattos"—those with at least some white racial heritage—play only the violin.

Patrick Day

HIKMET, NAZIM (1902–1963)

Turkey's most esteemed 20th-century poet, Hikmet (or Nazim, as he is most often called in Turkey) developed a compelling poetic voice derived from a distinctive combination of personal and political themes, a sharp focus on the actual historical world, and an innovative free-verse style. Seen by many readers worldwide as a major writer of overtly political poems, he is also a significant and original contributor to the traditions of love poetry, verse portraits of historical and contemporary characters, and verse narrative.

Born in Salonica (now Thessaloníki, Greece), then part of the declining Ottoman Empire, Hikmet grew up in Istanbul, Turkey. His 1961 poem "Autobiography" accurately and openly observes that at age 19, he was "a student at the Communist University in Moscow," where he became a lifelong communist. In the words of Soviet dictator Stalin's daughter, however, he was a "romantic communist," a label adopted by his biographers to indicate his commitment both to Marxism and to a personal and broadly humane vision of life.

His early poetry articulates themes that recur throughout his life. His comparison of a woman to "a soft / white worm" in his body suggests his frequently troubled relationships with women. His 1929 long poem *The Diary of Gioconda* blends love and politics as it whimsically represents Da Vinci's *Mona Lisa* as speaking and falling in love with a Chinese man (an actual comrade of Hikmet) finally beheaded for his opposition to the government of Chiang Kai-shek. Hikmet's commitment to historical fact in light of social justice is evident in *The Epic of Sheikh Bedreddin,* a dream vision narrative of the uprising led by a 14th-century mystic socialist against Sultan Mehmet I, seen in terms of "the eternal opposition" of "oppressor and oppressed."

Extreme anticommunism in Turkey, especially in the military, led to Hikmet's repeated arrests, abuse, and imprisonment from 1938 to 1950. He was convicted of inciting members of the army to revolt when actually he had merely shared his poetry with some soldiers. By then his realism, plain speech, and distinctive free verse had already transformed Turkish poetry, and during his imprisonment his innovations continued. His *9–10 P.M. POEMS* to his wife, Piraye, movingly combine personal and political themes. The major portions of *HUMAN LANDSCAPES FROM MY COUNTRY* represent human character immersed in social context through multiple voices and narrative shifts influenced by modern cinema. His direct and indirect references in many poems to his imprisonment contribute to a distinctive lyrical persona, at once suffering and hopeful, who declares, "we must live as though / we will never die."

Released from prison after extraordinary efforts by his advocates in Turkey and internationally, Hikmet was drafted into the army despite ill health. He fled Turkey by boat and was eventually welcomed in the Soviet Union. His later poems often reflect his exile, including his longing for his homeland. He imagines himself, for instance, "a walnut tree in Gülhane Park in Istanbul" ("The Walnut Tree") and elsewhere says, "bury me in a village graveyard in Anatolia" ("Testament"). His travels on behalf of world peace, and his antinuclear protest are reflected in several poems, including "The Japanese Fisherman," spoken in the voice of the victim of atomic testing and radioactive fallout. The love poems continue, including those in the voice of his fourth wife, Münnever. Other late poems are infused with an awareness of pending death, as in "The Last Bus," where "The great darkness is closing." Yet as is typical of Hikmet, the poem concludes affirmatively: "I love guests even more. / Heat is more golden than ever before, / snow more pure." Here, as throughout his career, lyric themes alternate with political ones. Within a three-week period in 1958, for example, he wrote an entirely personal lyric using the image of bees to suggest the "forgotten youth" he still longs for ("Bees") and an entirely political poem, "Great Humanity," lamenting the conditions of poverty and hunger of the vast majority of people.

Some readers will object to a too blatantly doctrinaire quality in some of Hikmet's poems or to emotionalism or lack of discipline in others. But his best poems originally and effectively unite broad social themes with individual concerns in a direct and honest voice. His imaginative scope is evident in the poem "Uluda ," the mountain visible to him from Bursa prison. Beginning as a meditation on his relationship with the mountain, personified as being able "to laugh and be angry" and stir "a little in sleep" in response to winter snows, the poem veers into fantasy: "the Monk who lives up there at the summit . . . comes down to the plain shouting and yelling before the wind." After shifting to a satiric vein—"women skiers drinking cognac" in the mountain's hotel—the poem suddenly concludes with the arrival in the prison of "one of the dark-browed men from the mountains"—a convicted murderer. The imagined natural and social worlds outside the prison surprisingly yet authentically connect to the speaker inside the prison, as the frightening representative from outside becomes an inmate.

Although Hikmet's work was banned in Turkey throughout most of his life and at the time of his death, it was always available in translation in several languages. His work is now readily available in Turkey. English translations of selected poems, including useful introductions and modest annotation, are done by Ruth Christie, Richard McKane, Talât Sait Halman, Randy Blasing, and Mutlu Konuk. Saime Göksu and Edward Timms have written an essential biography of the poet.

BIBLIOGRAPHY

Göksu, Saime, and Edward Timms. *Romantic Communist: The Life and Work of Nazim Hikmet.* New York: St. Martin's Press, 1999.

Hikmet, Nazim. *Nâzim Hikmet, Beyond the Walls: Selected Poems.* Translated by Ruth Christie, Richard McKane, and Talât Sait Halman. London: Anvil Press, 2002.

———. *Poems of Nazim Hikmet.* Translated by Randy Blasing and Mutlu Konuk. Revised and expanded edition. New York: Persea Books, 2002.

Paul Munn

"HILSA" BUDDHADEVA BOSE (1943)

BUDDHADEVA BOSE's poetry is characterized by pointed images and a visibly meticulous arrangement of words and lines. What shines through most of Bose's poems is not spontaneity or even literary pleasure, but the workings of a critical mind. The pleasure of reading Bose's poetry is also largely intellectual. "Hilsa," one of Bose's most memorable shorter poems, is an outstanding example of his economy of words, his creative synthesis of rural and urban scenarios, and his detached cynicism. The poem, which first appeared in *Damayanti,* is about the mass of Hilsa fish—a Bengali delicacy—harvested during the night in the river Padma (now in Bangladesh) and transported overnight by train to Calcutta, India, where it is distributed to be sold in the local markets. The first line is beautiful and terse as it establishes the natural premises of the poem: "Asharh's in the heavens, and Bengal's monsoon-drunk." (Asharh is the first month of the rainy season in the Bengali calendar.) Against a background of "rows of coconuts on cloud-colored" riverbanks and a century-old palace, Bose introduces "half-naked" fishermen in "little darting boats" as they "furiously cast the nets, haul the ropes." The fishermen are creatures of need and habit, and in the poet's view are "famished themselves, but are food's pipeline for others." The night ends with the "blind black wagons" being filled up with "heaps of hilsa corpses, the water's lucent harvest, / hillocks of death for the river's deepest delight." It is impossible not to compare Baudelaire's "Albatross" and its "drunken sailors" to the "hilsa" and the "naked fishermen." The scene of the poem shifts at the end of the poem to Calcutta, "in a bleary morning, leached of color and light." The air is fragrant with "the rising smell of frying hilsa," and "the clerk's wife's kitchen" is "tangy with mustard." The last line of the poem is characterized by a terrible beauty that is both a mark of Baudelaire's influence and of Bose's creative genius: "The monsoon's here, and with it the hilsa-fest." The monsoon, or the rainy season, has been the subject of sublime art, literature, and music in most Indian languages and traditions. The way Bose has managed in "Hilsa" to juxtapose that classical-romantic connotation of the monsoon with the sordid banality of seasonal commerce is quite remarkable.

BIBLIOGRAPHY

Bose, Buddhadeva. *Selected Poems of Buddhadeva Bose.* Translated by Ketaki Kusari Dyson. New Delhi: Oxford University Press, 2003, 38.

Rini Bhattacharya Mehta

HOLUB, MIROSLAV (1923–1998)

Miroslav Holub, who famously asserted, "I prefer to write for people untouched by poetry," is a major literary figure of the postwar period and the Czech poet who has perhaps been most widely translated into English. He also achieved significant acclaim in the field of immunology. As many critics have pointed out, Holub's marriage of science and poetry resulted in a unique style of poetic expression. Unlike his contemporaries, Holub resisted lyricism, sentimentality, and the first-person singular in his poetry, which has been dubbed intellectual, commonsensical, and precise—adjectives many critics readily use when faced with a poet/scientist, even before considering the poetry itself. But to a more involved reader, it is clear that the world of science functions in Holub's poetry as a metaphor for larger, even global humanistic issues. In Holub's poems one can discern a nearly programmatic avoidance of the personal sphere; but rather than view this trait simply as the approach of a rational scientist, it is more useful to consider, alongside his scientific background, Holub's penetrating knowledge of history and myth and his amazing use of metaphor.

Holub was born in Plzeň in western Bohemia. His father was a lawyer and his mother a language teacher. He attended high school in Plzeň, then was conscripted to work on a railroad after graduating in 1942, instead of immediately starting his university studies; Czech universities were closed during the German occupation. After the war he worked as a research assistant in the Faculty of Natural Sciences at Charles University in Prague. At approximately the same time, he started his studies at the Faculty of Medicine. After graduating he worked as a researcher at the Microbiology Institute of the Czechoslovak Academy of Sciences. At this time Holub began writing and publishing poetry in literary journals, even as he continued to work and conduct a rigorous program of scientific research. But his literary career did not truly start until the late 1950s, when he published his first collection of poems, *Denní služba* (Day Duty, 1958). In the 1960s Holub conducted research at distinguished scientific institutes abroad, spending time in Germany and the United States, among other places. His literary output during this period included seven published collections of poetry, among them *Achilees a želva* (Achilles and the Turtle, 1961), *Jdi a otev i dve e* (Go and Open the Door, 1962), and *A koli* (Although, 1969). These collections showcase Holub's already mature poetic style characterized by the use of litany, incisive wit, and irony, a style that would not undergo significant changes until the 1980s. Holub brought new themes to Czech poetry, focusing on ordinary, nonheroic characters working in research laboratories and in hospitals. These characters are frequently transformed in the course of a poem into larger metaphors for theater, science, and human history. Holub approaches his themes with a noticeably impersonal voice and in an intellectual rather than a sentimental manner. But this impersonal and distant approach manages to convey firmly grounded humanistic values—a certain celebration of humanness—which Holub applies universally. Critics who note the apparent unfeeling rationality of Holub's poetry do not take into account the process by which his intellectual poem becomes a human avowal.

An approach Holub often takes is to comment on nature as something imperfect, something that human beings need to correct. Such a perspective might seem on the surface to be rationalist, but Holub usually offers a counterexample that demonstrates the importance of being modest and listening to nature, or he undermines his "scientific" statement by the use of irony. In the latter case his celebration of the human sounds simultaneously serious and overstated. This sort of playfulness and dry wit convert his words into complex works, poems that are much more than purely rational constructs. His poem "Wings" from this period is representative of Holub's scientific/human approach and his skillful use of irony. The poem begins with a list of human achievements in the field of science, the typical "science-overcoming-nature" paradigm: "[w]e have / a map of the universe / for microbes" (*Intensive Care* 14). However, the following three lines quickly overturn the solemnity of the initial statement as the speaker continues playfully: "we have / a map of a microbe / for the universe" (14). After the brief list of scientific achievements is exhausted, Holub arrives at the conclusion that what "gives us wings" is not the serious and the solemn, but rather that which makes us most human, such as "the ability to seek the right screw / under the sofa / for hours" (14).

After the productive 1960s, Holub was forced by an oppressive government to fall into poetic silence during the 1970s. To secure his prestige as a scientist, Holub publicly renounced the liberal political views he had expressed during the Prague Spring of 1968. He found a position at the Prague Institute of Clinical and Experimental Medicine, where he focused on immunological research until 1994. Although he was allowed to continue his scientific research, Holub's renouncing of the radical politics of the 1960s was not enough to gain him the government's approval. One of the main reasons for his continued disfavor was his poem "The Prague of Jan Palach," in which he mentions the self-immolation of the student Jan Palach in January 1969 at Wenceslas Square in Prague in protest against the entry of Warsaw Pact tanks into Czechoslovakia in 1968. Like other artists and members of the intelligentsia who were politically active in the late 1960s, Holub was punished as part of the crackdown that followed the Soviet-led intervention. He was not allowed to publish poetry for 12 years during the "normalization" of the 1970s. His collection of poems *Naopak* (On the Contrary) was not published until 1982.

Holub's work from the late 1980s and 1990s includes not only poetry but also brilliant essays, for instance, *K principu rolni ky* (The Jingle Bell Principle, 1987), in which he makes use of his broad scientific knowledge as well as his penchant for drawing associations between different realms of human experience. One of the collections from this period that shows how Holub's treatment of his lifelong thematic preoccupations began to change is *Interferon, ili O divadle* (Interferon, or On Theater, 1986). It uses as a thematic basis the world of anatomy, from which Holub makes fascinating analogies with theater. The poems are dense and pose formally as brief scripts rather than poems. The most significant change in style is the introduction of a lyrical subject with personal experience; the lyrical subject retains much of Holub's earlier ironic and witty turns, but this work is decidedly personal, unlike Holub's collections from the 1960s.

The 1990s, marked by the liberation of Czechoslovakia from the communist regime, put new demands on the artist's role in society. Holub, who was not well received by the Czech public before the fall of communism because of his somewhat severe-sounding poetry, was in an even more difficult position now. Many condemned him for his public renunciation of his political views and viewed with suspicion his travels to the West before 1989. Despite these troubles at home, Holub's literary as well as scientific work was well received abroad. His rather unmelodious poetic style, so difficult for Czech ears, combined with his focus on concepts, rather than on the musical subtleties of language, turned out to be very suitable for translation into English. Numerous translations of Holub's poetry include *Interferon, or On Theater, Intensive Care,* and *Rampage.*

BIBLIOGRAPHY

Holub, Miroslav. *Intensive Care: Selected and New Poems.* Various translators. Oberlin, Ohio: Oberlin College Press, 1996.
———. *Interferon, or On Theater.* Oberlin, Ohio: Oberlin College Press, 1982.
———. *The Rampage.* Translated by David Young and Dana Habova. New York: Faber and Faber, 1997.
———. *Vanishing Lung Syndrome.* Translated by David Young and Dana Habova. Oberlin, Ohio: Oberlin College Press, 1990.

Daniela Kukrechtová

"HOOKS OF THE IDYLL" Jacques Dupin **(1967)** Published first in 1967 in Jacques Dupin's poetry volume *Proximité du murmure* (The Encroaching Murmur), *"Agrafes de l'idylle"* is constituted of slow, breathless, fragmentary sentences. Its title in the original French sounds a radical negation of writing: a cognate of *graphein,* the Greek for *to write,* is preceded by *a-,* the Greek prefix of contradiction. Approaching the unconscious and inhabiting the very boundaries of writing, the 14 short lines of the poem announce themselves as a disintegrating, lethal idyll. Dupin's posthuman sonnet performs acts of unwriting and continues what the German post-Kantian writer Novalis declared to be the only remaining task of poetry, "to represent the impossibility of representation" (*Undarstellbarkeit darstellen*).

A series of past participles (*exténuée, anéantie*) indicates not only passivity and an irreversible loss of spontaneity, but exhaustion, obliteration, and annihilation, laconically tempered by the hope of a nomadic "almost" (*presque*). Far from being autonomous, selfhood is staged as mournful spectatorship and autopsy; and the lyrical "I" is immersed in, or rather has irreversibly become, a retrospective and self-consuming "theater." Consisting of multiple layers of lucid dream segments, Dupin's poem sketches the continued supply of replaceable dead bodies. "Memory" appears as a series of desperate and impossible attempts at return and recovery, a heterotopian movement that still remains encapsulated in—and as—transitory visual effects.

An unassuming sculpture of sounds and images and one of the most haunting and beautiful poems available in the French language, *"Agrafes de l'idylle"* offers and embodies a poetics that overcomes ossified notions of supposedly irreconcilable commitments to art and to politics. Dupin's poem provides soundings of the remains of writing as vulnerable acts and breathing intervals between, and within, modernity's anonymous, self-replicating murders.

A careful English translation is available in Paul Auster's excellent bilingual edition (Jacques Dupin, *Selected Poems.* Winston-Salem, N.C.: Wake Forest University Press, 1992, 63).

Olaf Berwald

HOVE, CHENJERAI (1956–)

Chenjerai Hove has emerged as one of the most important voices in postindependence Zimbabwean letters, his name often appearing in any major discussions that also acknowledge the contributions of writers like MUSAEMURA ZIMUNYA (b. 1949), DAMBUDZO MARECHERA (b. 1952), or even the much younger feminist writer Yvonne Vera (1964–2005). The son of a local chief, Hove was born in the village of Mazvihwa near the mining town of Zvishavane in southern Zimbabwe in 1956. His early education was at the Catholic Marist Brothers schools at Kutama and Dete. He later became a teacher, after studying in Gweru, and finally took degrees at the Universities of South Africa (UNISA) and Zimbabwe. He writes both in English and in his native Shona. Hove's experience as a young man is not entirely different from that of many other writers across the continent, especially those writers whose fathers' privileged positions enabled their children to acquire Western educations.

Chenjerai showed promise at an early age, and by the time he was a teenager, he had read the works of a number of African writers, especially the novels and essays of CHINUA ACHEBE, WOLE SOYINKA, Ayi Kwei Armah, and others. The influence of a writer like Achebe is, however, far more visible in his writing than we are likely to find of those of other writers. That influence is particularly evident in the simple but profound prose style that defines his essays, short stories, and, sometimes, his poetry. His career as a writer has taken him to many African countries and beyond. He was writer-in-residence at the Universities of Zimbabwe, Leeds, Lewis and Clark (the last in Oregon, United States), as well as in Leiden University in the Netherlands. Hove's essays are often politically profound. He cherishes interrogating the mischief implicit in the balkanization of African people, but also highlights the implications of such divide-and-rule tactics on the sociocultural life of Africans.

Hove seems to suggest that African people are essentially the same: The cultural life of his Shona people of Zimbabwe is not fundamentally different from that of the Igbo of southeastern Nigeria. This is so in spite of the artificial boundaries erected by the colonial powers. In one particularly interesting essay, "Shades of Power: Colonial and Postcolonial Experiences of a Writer," Hove condemns the politics of cultural balkanization as a fraud. Using his personal experience while growing up as illustration, he shows how the dispositions of his father seem to have been defined by Okonkwo—that archetypal character in Achebe's *Things Fall Apart,* just as his father's progressive vision and love for education is equally delineated in the admirable figure of Ezeulu—also the prime persona in Achebe's *Arrow of God.* More significantly, however, Hove asks the question: "Is the colonial or post-colonial a historical or psychological space?" (*Palaver Finish* 57). All a writer can do, he says, is to write, create, and pour out the images and metaphors given to him by a combination of history, feeling, and imagination (57). What emerges as his aesthetic, therefore, does not depart fundamentally from the views of writers across the continent who insist on the recognition of the historical, even as the emotive and the aesthetic must be brought into practice in the process of artistic composition. Here, we find echoes of Achebe, Es'kia Mphahlele, and Mbulelo Mzamane, among others, who have since argued along similar lines. Hove adds: "a historian is one who thinks and analyses history, and a writer or artist is one who feels history, be it colonial or postcolonial. . . . I always tell people that if they want to know about the history of a country, do not go to the history books, go to the fiction. Fiction is not fiction. It is the substance and heartbeat of a people's life, here, now, and in the past" (57).

Chenjerai Hove, like Achebe, has the facility with his medium for the precise use of the English language across age groups, enabling him to write for young people as well as for adults. He also writes in the typical, domesticated English form often referred to—in places like Nigeria, western Cameroon, and Sierra Leone—as local pidgin, or Creolized English. This tactic is evident in his "Palaver Finish," the lead essay in his book of essays by the same title (25–28).

As a poet Hove is as fascinated by the past as he is by the present. While he takes time out to write for children (as, for instance, in the poem "Nursery Rhyme After a War"), some of his more accomplished poems are devoted to interrogating the lunacies of political leadership in Africa generally and in his country, Zimbabwe, in particular. The despondent citizenry—following the loss of vision by the political elite in postindependence Zimbabwe—is as resonant in his weekly newspaper column as it is in his poetics and adult poetry. In "To the Wielders of Flags," for instance, he appeals to the emergent political leaders of postindependence Zimbabwe—those "young men" and "maidens smelling of history's latest perfumes"—to "hear the call of those under the rocks" (*Sister Sing Again Someday* 48–49). Whereas the quest for self-determination had inspired many young Zimbabweans to fight against settler-colonialism and inhumanity for a number of decades in the 20th century, political liberation did not bring the anticipated social fulfilment among the populace. The new leaders soon became worse than the white settlers, with the devastating consequence that a people long given to individual and collective sacrifice toward the attainment of national aspirations soon capitulated to despair. The politicians, he appeals, should reexamine the earlier dreams of providing a better future and economic well-being for ordinary citizens and redress the alienation of the mass of the people: "To you / leaning / leaning on the rock of state / contain the whirlwind / burn the flame of poverty / burn the flame of poverty on infants' faces" (*Sister Sing Again Someday* 49). Images of home, village life, city life, migrations and exile, politics, poverty, and nature resonate in many of his poems—be they his adult poetry or poems for children. Poems like "Red Hills of Home," "You Will Forget," "Lost Bird," "Migratory Bird 1," "Child's Parliament," "The Other Syllabus," and "Country Life" attest to his fascination with life as a total experience (Maja-Pearce 203–214).

Among his numerous publications are *Masimba Fanhu* (1986), *Nduri Dzorudo* (1978), and *Matenda Mashava* (1980). Others written in English, or a kind of English, are *Bones* (1988), *Shadows* (1991), *Ancestors* (1994), *Up in Arms* (1982), *Swimming in Floods of Tears* (coauthored with Lyamba wa Kabika, 1983), *Red Hills of Home* (1985), *Sister Sing Again Someday* (1989), *Rainbows in the Dust* (1997), and *Guardians of the Soil* (with Iliya Trojanow, 1997). He has also published two collections of his essays, *Shebeen Tales* (essays, 1994) and *Palaver Finish* (2002).

BIBLIOGRAPHY

Hove, Chenjerai. *Palaver Finish*. Harare, Zimbabwe: Weaver Press, 2002.

Maja-Pearce, Adewale. *The Heinemann Book of African Poetry in English*. London: Heinemann, 1990, 203–214.

Zimunya, Musaemura, Peter Porter, and Kofi Anyidoho, eds. *The Fate of Vultures: New Poetry of Africa*. London: Heinemann, 1989, 47–49.

Osita Ezeliora

HUIDOBRO, VICENTE (1893–1948)

One of the most influential and controversial Chilean writers of his era, Vicente Huidobro, born on January 10, 1893, in his early years rebelled against the stifling restrictions of his wealthy, aristocratic family. Yet Huidobro's affluent origins also furnished him with the connections and opportunities that enriched his later writing. Not merely a bilingual poet who composed his masterwork, ALTAZOR, in both French and Spanish versions, Huidobro also actively participated in the French cultural and literary developments of his day, including the French avant-garde movement. Huidobro brought the avant-garde movement to the Spanish-speaking world, and his work has had lasting implications for Spanish literature. The innovations and novelties that characterize his poetry transformed the idea and expectations of Chilean poetry for generations.

Huidobro began writing at a young age and published his first work at 17. Soon after, he began experimenting with literary magazines and achieved success with his participation in the magazine *Nord-Sud*. In 1913 he published two books, *Canciones en la noche* (Songs in the Night) and *La gruta del silencio* (The Grotto of Silence), which illustrate the first state in his own literary development: modernism. But these early volumes also suggest Huidobro's constant desire for the new, for an unconventional approach to writing, one free from the trammels of rhyme and regular meters. In 1916 Huidobro departed for Europe, and in Paris he found ample support for his innovative tendencies. Although he spent some time in Buenos Aires and Madrid before arriving in Paris, Paris so inspired him that he remained there for 10 years. He met expatriate American writer Gertrude Stein and GUILLAUME APOLLINAIRE. The magazine *Nord-Sud,* begun in 1917, gives ample evidence of Huidobro's bilingualism; it also reflects his growing sense of the poetic. Some of his poems from this period, including "Arte poética" ("ARS POETICA"), were later collected in the volume *El espejo de agua* (The Mirror of Water).

"Arte poética" gives a clear sign of Huidobro's already evolving concept of the poet. Famously denoting the poet a *"pequeño dios,"* or little god, Huidobro posits his idea of the poet as master and creator of a new world, a world at once evoked and described within his poetry. This concept evolved into Huidobro's own literary movement, *creacionismo,* or creationism. Creationism owed much to the already extant cubism, but it was an ultimately fleeting, one-man movement that revolved entirely around Huidobro's own literary production. Poetry, according to creationism, springs from the emotions and intelligent will of the poet and must be a means of reorganizing the reader's perception of the world—the poetic images proceeding nonlinearly to avoid seeming to narrate or describe the topic. Poets, he argued, should strive to capture "the [essentially] inexpressible." Huidobro's first collection of manifesto-like articles, published in 1914, at once incited an angry critical response; the long remainder of Huidobro's career followed that early pattern. Although he was unsuccessful at promoting creationism, his efforts did give rise to Spanish ultraism.

In 1921 the exhibition of illustrated poems *Salle XIV* also evoked severe reactions from the public, and the book published the following year, *Finis Britannia: Une redoutable société secrète s'est dressée contre l'impérialisme anglais* (The End of Britain: A Fearful Secret Society Has Been Established to Oppose English Imperialism) was equally controversial.

In 1925 Huidobro returned to Chile and began increasingly to devote his time to the political sphere.

There he chafed against his marriage and around this time became infatuated with a young student, Ximena Amunategui. Although the scandal his public passion created forced him to leave the country, he returned in 1928 and abducted—or rescued—Ximena from her high school. Despite the celebrity (and perhaps because of the notoriety) of their relationship, their union, like Huidobro's first, eventually failed.

During these years Huidobro published excerpts in both French and Spanish from his long and greatest poem, ALTAZOR, but not until 1931 was the completed volume published. During that year Huidobro also released *Temblor de cielo* (Tremors of Heaven). Today *Altazor* is frequently cited as the work Huidobro produced at the height of his poetic powers, although both it and *Temblor de cielo* were virtually ignored by critics when they first appeared. In *Altazor* over the course of seven cantos, Huidobro explores the possibilities and limitations of poetic language; the protagonist, Altazor, narrows his fall throughout the seven cantos of the poem, and his language is increasingly incapable of describing his experiences, until it finally deteriorates into an incoherent yowl.

Like *Altazor, Temblor de cielo* is constructed around seven cantos, but it deals with the famous love affair of Tristan and Isolde. *Temblor de cielo,* however, also deconstructs the world, ending with the death of both the speaker and heaven itself. Huidobro later transformed *Temblor de cielo* into a play, suggesting the facility with which he moved between genres.

In the next five years Huidobro published a variety of works, from poetry and plays to novels and political articles, and in 1937 he became involved in the Spanish civil war (1936–39), ardently supporting the Republican cause. His involvement presages his later, ultimately fatal, involvement in: World War II. Huidobro's passion for causes in both situations, however, bears out his lifelong involvement in and concern for political and social issues.

Published in 1941, Huidobro's last books, *Ver y palpar* (Seeing and Touching) and *El ciudadano del olvido* (The Citizen of Oblivion), reflect his most mature literary development. Like earlier texts, including *Altazor,* these two volumes experiment with words and with the poetic form. A few years later Huidobro separated from Ximena, then became involved in the Allied armies' advance into Nazi Germany. Despite two wounds, Huidobro remained active, participating in radio broadcasts and lectures. During this period he met Raquel Señoret, and the two soon married. In 1945 Huidobro suffered a stroke, and on January 2, 1948, shortly before his 55th birthday, he died of complications.

Huidobro left behind an immense collection of work, ranging from newspaper articles, to plays, to speeches, to his better-known poetry. A participant in several significant literary movements, including his own creationism, Huidobro influenced 20th-century Latin American literature significantly. Many Latin American poets—including NICANOR PARRA, the proponent of antipoetry, Gonzalo Rojas, and OCTAVIO PAZ—owe much to this predecessor of poetic invention and ingenuity.

BIBLIOGRAPHY

Huidobro, Vicente. *Altazor, or, A Voyage in a Parachute: Poem in VII Cantos (1919).* Translated by Eliot Weinberger. Middletown, Conn.: Wesleyan University Press, 2003.
———. *The Selected Poetry of Vicente Huidobro.* Translated by Stephen Fredman and David M. Guss. New York: New Directions, 1981.
Quiroga, José. "Vicente Huidobro: The Poetics of the Invisible Texts." *Hispania* 75, no. 3 (1992): 516–526.
Wood, Cecil G. *The "Creacionismo" of Vicente Huidobro.* Fredericton, N.B.: York Press, 1978.

Winter Elliott

HUMAN LANDSCAPES FROM MY COUNTRY NAZIM HIKMET (1938–1950)

Nazim Hikmet's five-book "epic novel in verse"—some 17,000 lines long—is a major work by Turkey's most accomplished 20th-century poet. *Memleketimden İnsan Manzaralari* made a significant contribution to the traditions of the long poem and to the genre of verse committed to social and political themes. Composed during Hikmet's imprisonment from 1938 to 1950, the poem depicts several characters based closely on his fellow prisoners, including Halil (like Hikmet, a communist), an imprisoned intellectual who declares his "love of those who don't live off others' labor, / the love of working people."

Human Landscapes mixes genres, blending techniques of epic narrative, lyric poetry, the screenplay (Hikmet participated in filmmaking), and the novel (he translated Tolstoy's *War and Peace* while writing the book). Several features of the work make it, above all, a powerful poem. The highly variable free-verse lines—many just one word long, many indented in various ways—effectively emphasize key words and images. Sometimes the free verse combines with simile to intensify character portraits. Describing "a leading intellectual," the narrator emphasizes his slow movement:

No matter where he was,
he always appeared to be underwater—
languid, limp,
barely stirring,
like a lazy sea-creature.

The images, heightened by the lineation, contribute to a devastating satire on a passionless thinker—the opposite of Hikmet.

The authorial narrative voice sometimes sounds like that of a lyrical poem, shifting from reporting to expressing feeling, as when the speaker in the first-person directly addresses the character Tanya, an 18-year-old Soviet partisan tortured and hanged by the Nazis during World War II: "Tanya, / your picture's here in front of me in Bursa Prison. . . . They hanged you for loving your country, / I'm in prison for loving mine." The tone of admiration and the emotion of kinship are clear—and clearly Hikmet's.

The narrative frequently dwells on depraved characters, yet several figures—including Halil and his wife, the heroic Soviet soldiers fighting the invading Germans, Tanya the partisan, and the young steelworker Kerim—suggest no small measure of hope for humanity. Periodically Hikmet perceives in the natural world an emblem of the potential in the human world for renewal. Like Hikmet's lyric poems taken as a whole, this epic is fundamentally optimistic, even though the formidable obstacles to human progress—greed, political corruption, selfishness, and superstition—are not slighted.

In their comprehensive *Romantic Communist: The Life and Work of Nazim Hikmet,* Saime Göksu and Edward Timms detail the complex history of the poem's creation. Originally conceived as an "Encyclopedia of Famous People," it evolved into a portrayal of "representative types" of people, few of them famous, the full range of society. A four-book plan gave way to five books, and the chronological scheme expanded to include contemporary history: the siege of Moscow by Germany in World War II (in the conclusion of book 4). The work appeared in Turkish only after Hikmet's death, published by his son in 1966.

BIBLIOGRAPHY

Hikmet, Nazim. *Human Landscapes from My Country: An Epic Novel in Verse.* Translated by Randy Blasing and Mutlu Konuk. New York: Persea Books, 2002.

Gōksu, Saime, and Edward Timms. *Romantic Communist: The Life and Work of Nazim Hikmet.* New York: St. Martin's Press, 1999.

Paul Munn

I

"I AM GOYA" Andrey Voznesensky **(1960)** "I Am Goya" ("Я - Гойя!"), composed in 1957, first appeared in Andrey Voznesensky's debut collection, *Mozaika* (Mosaics), which was published in Vladimir, USSR, in 1960, when the poet was 27 years old. It is reputedly "one of the poet's favorites, and he always recites it at his public readings" (Blake and Hayward 111). Many readers familiar with the original version in Russian particularly appreciate its verse form and sound qualities, especially its use of alliteration and assonance.

The poem's inspiration has its origin in the poet's childhood. In the middle of World War II, the poet's father took a leave of absence from his post in Leningrad (present-day St. Petersburg) to visit his family, ensconced for their safety in the mountain town of Kurgan, near the Soviet republic of Khazakhstan, to which Andrey and his mother had moved from Vladimir. Andrey was only a child, probably not yet 10 years old, when the momentous visit occurred. His father had packed very lightly and had brought with him only some food and a slim volume of the etchings of the famous Spanish painter and printmaker Francisco Goya, most likely *Los desastres de la guerra* (The Disasters of War, 1863). The book fascinated the child with its dark vision of the horrors of war and its depiction of inhumanity and atrocity.

The poem is not a description of Goya's work as such, but an instance of identification with its signify-

ing power. The poem's imagery—like Goya's—relates to the violence and injustice of warfare and emphasizes war's effects on both victims and perpetrators. The poem begins with the words "I am Goya!" followed by an image of the speaker, a blinded victim on a barren field, his eyes gouged out by the enemy. The speaker next becomes an emblem of despair, saying, "I am grief" ("Я - Горе.") and calls himself the voice of war and the charred remains the filth of Soviet cities in the snows of 1941. Next the speaker says, "I am hunger"—adding, "I am the throat of a hanged woman naked clanging like a bell over the empty square." ("Я – горло / Повешенной бабы, чье тело, как колокол, / било над площадью голой...") Twice more the speaker exclaims, "I am Goya!" and between those exclamations boasts, "I have flung back the ashes of uninvited guests from the west and driven stars into the commemorative sky, like nails."

As commentators have pointed out, in Russian the words for *Goya, grief, throat, voice, hunger,* and *naked* alliterate on their initial syllable (gó-) so that the guttural opening sound of all of these words—followed by an accented throaty *o* and sometimes a velar *l* as well—emphasizes (by constricting the throat) a strong sensation of choking or sobbing.

Inspired by Goya, this poem—in many ways the consummate elegiac expression of the desolation, anguish, and wretchedness of war—has in turn inspired other artists, including the English composer Nigel Osborne, who wrote, produced, and recorded a symphonic piece, also titled "I Am Goya," conducted by Richard Hickox and featuring the baritone Stephen Varcoe (1977).

BIBLIOGRAPHY

Blake, Patricia, and Max Hayward, eds. Introduction to Andrei Voznesensky's *Antiworlds*. New York: Basic Books, 1966. Available online as "Andrei Voznesensky." URL: http://www.penrussia.org/n-z/an_voz.htm#i. Accessed on April 23, 2007.

Voznesensky, Andrei. *Antiworlds*. New York: Basic Books, 1966.

R. Victoria Arana

IBARBOUROU, JUANA DE (1895–1979)

Juana de Ibarbourou was a superstar in her time. The bold love poetry in her first two collections, *Las lenguas de diamante* (Diamond Tongues, 1919) and *Raíz salvaje* (Wild Root, 1922), brought her instant fame in Uruguay and recognition as a major poet throughout the Americas. Beautiful, happily married, and financially secure, she published a third collection, *La rosa de los vientos* (Compass Rose), in 1930, then for 20 years authored stories, religious prose, children's plays, and textbooks, before bringing out four new collections in the 1950s—*Perdida* (Lost, 1950), *Azor* (Falcon, 1953), *Romances del destino* (Ballads of Destiny, 1955), and *Oro y tormenta* (Gold and Storm, 1956)—in addition to several later volumes. She received literary awards at home and abroad, and her embrace by the Latin American intelligentsia was confirmed in 1929 when a group of diplomats and writers officially declared that she belonged to the hemisphere: She was not simply *"Juana de Ibarbourou"*—"Juana of [her husband] Ibarbourou"—but *"Juana de América"*—"Juana of America." Schools, libraries, streets, and parks are named after her, as is an international literary prize and the Lions Club chapter in Uruguay's capital, Montevideo. Her poems are set to music and sung at ceremonies, in concert halls, and by schoolchildren. She was the first woman admitted to the Uruguayan Academy of Letters (1947), the first president of the new Uruguayan Writers Association (1950), and the first recipient of Uruguay's National Prize for Literature (1959). She served her country as cultural attaché in Colombia and the Dominican Republic.

Juana de Ibarbourou has been termed one of the Southern Cone's trailblazing "four women in search of freedom" of the early 20th century (Jehenson), yet her life and work differed significantly from that of others. Like Nobel laureate GABRIELA MISTRAL (Chile), Ibarbourou grounded her poetry in the natural elements of her native land, at a time when the prevailing literary models came from Europe and the United States, and she began to move away from the Latin American modernist movement's cult of exotic oriental palaces and princesses. But unlike Mistral, Ibarbourou depicts sensual woman as a beautiful element of nature who begs her lover: "I grow for you, take me, gather me as you would a flower. I flow for you, drink me as you would a spring . . ." (paraphrase of "The Strong Bond" in *Las lenguas de diamante*). Unlike ALFONSINA STORNI (Argentina), Ibarbourou was a woman of means, not struggle (her first paying job was at age 60-something, when she became a diplomat), and her poetry admits no bitterness. Unlike compatriot Delmira Agustini, whose poetry was similar in theme, her life was not cut short by murder at the hand of a crazed husband. Today Ibarbourou is celebrated for opening doors for later women writers, as well as for her life, honors, work with children, and love poetry. Among youthful Spanish readers today, perhaps only *Twenty Love Poems and a Desperate Song* (1924) by PABLO NERUDA (Chile) is more popular.

Born Juana Fernández in rural Uruguay in 1892 or 1895 (both are officially recorded), she published poems in local media at a young age, married a military man of French Basque descent, Lucas Ibarbourou, moved with him to his various posts around the country, and settled in Montevideo in 1918, where she later had a son. Within a year she had published *Las lenguas de diamante,* immediately hailed for its expression of "loving and being loved with a freshness and vigor unknown in Spanish letters" (Weiser 44). It was cited for its sensual imagery and distinctive voice: "In an era when few women published poetry, she dared to describe sexual passion from a woman's point of view" (Sullivan 172). *Raíz salvaje* continued the erotic connection between a woman's soul, her body, and elements of benign nature drawn from the country flora that she had loved as a child: "this traveling wave that is my sister" (Poetserv). The immortality of her body (not her soul) was guaranteed in its recycling as food for plants; she might return to Earth in a lovely plant to watch over her loved one ("Immortal Flesh" in *Raíz salvaje*; "LIFE-HOOK" in *Las lenguas de diamante*). *La rosa de los vientos* marked a new path for Ibarbourou, as her poetry became less emotional, and more thoughtful, revisioning death not as the opportunity to create an impassioned scene during the crossing, as in "Rebelde" (Rebel) from *Las lenguas de diamante,* but as the possibility for rest and escape from this world. Whereas her early verses were clear, simple, and musical, with readily accessible images and clichés derived from the romantic and Latin American modernist traditions, the later collections reflect the poet's exploration of surrealistic and avant-garde imagery, the incorporation of religious themes in resigned, subdued tones, and disillusionment with the passage of time. Although she is best remembered for her love poetry, her variation in themes is signified by the inclusion of her poems in anthologies of love, erotica, and the macabre.

Is Ibarbourou's star fading? Some literary critics grumbled from the beginning that her poetry was too narcissistic, too facile, too pagan, too earthbound and nonmetaphysical, dismissible as mere joyous, frivolous, self-indulgent self-contemplation by a desirable woman who understands the evanescence of her beauty: "She fears aging more than dying" (Anderson Imbert and Florit 241). Some contemporary revisers of the literary canon appear to be edging her off the stage: A 2005 U.S. college reader omits her poems and relegates her to almost footnote status, albeit recognizing the legacy to future women writers of her daring erotic images and effective use of the female body as rebellion against a patriarchal society that had excluded intellectual women (Chang-Rodríguez and Filer 283). Of the early "pre-feminist four," Ibarbourou is the only one excluded entirely from Marjorie Agosín's influential *A Dream of Light and Shadow: Portraits of Latin American Women Writers*. Nevertheless, Ibarbourou's poems continue to appear in new Spanish anthologies and in translation around the world; a 1991 international literature conference at San Diego State University paid homage to her among the four founding mothers; a new collection of her work marked the 100th anniversary of her 1895 birth year; Uruguay's largest peso bill bears her likeness; and Uruguayan poet Héctor Rosales dubbed her "one of this century's most outstanding figures in Latin American poetry" when a major Madrid publisher reissued her first two collections in 1999. Unfortunately, English translations of Ibarbourou's poems are dispersed in general anthologies and not easily located (see Irving, Weiser, and Sonntag Blay for sources).

BIBLIOGRAPHY
Agosín, Marjorie, ed. *A Dream of Light and Shadow: Portraits of Latin American Women Writers*. Albuquerque: University of New Mexico Press, 1995.

Anderson Imbert, Enrique, and Eugenio Florit, eds. *Literatura hispanoamericana: Antología e introducción histórica*. Vol. 2. Rev. ed. New York: Holt, 1970.

Chang-Rodríguez, Raquel, and Malva Filer, eds. *Voces de Hispanoamérica: Antología literaria*. 3rd ed. Boston: Heinle, 2004.

Irving, Evelyn Uhrhan. "Juana de Ibarbourou." In *Spanish American Women Writers: A Bio-Bibliographical Source Book,* edited by Diane E. Marting, 261–71. New York: Greenwood, 1990.

Jehenson, Myriam Ivonne. "Four Women in Search of Freedom." *Revista/Review Interamericana* 12, no. 1 (1982): 87–99.

Poetserv. "Juana de Ibarbourou. 'Running Water.'" Translated by Carlos Reyes. Available online. URL: http://www.poetserv.org/SRR22/ibarbourou.html. Downloaded on Aug. 12, 2005.

Rosales, Héctor. "Juana, retorno de la extranjera." *Letralia* 68 (Apr. 19, 1999). Available online. URL: http://www.letralia.com/68/en03-068.htm. Downloaded on Aug. 1, 2005.

Sonntag Blay, Iliana L. *Twentieth-Century Poetry from Spanish America: An Index to Spanish Language and Bilingual Anthologies*. Lanham, Md.: Scarecrow, 1998.

Sullivan, Clare E. "Juana de Ibarbourou." In *Modern Spanish American Poets*. Second Series, edited by María A. Salgado, 171–176. *Dictionary of Literary Biography* 290. Detroit: Gale, 2004.

Wieser, Nora Jacquez, ed. *Open to the Sun: A Bilingual Anthology of Latin-American Women Poets*. Van Nuys, Calif.: Perivale, 1979.

María Roof

IBRAHIM, MUHAMMED (MOHAMED) HAFIZ (1871–1932)   Popularly known as Hafiz (or Hafez), Ibrahim is one of the most famous Egyptian

poets of the early 20th century. Hafiz Ibrahim embraced the neoclassical movement initiated by late 19th-century poets, including Mahmud Sami al-Barudi (1839–1904), his idol and the father of modern Arabic poetry. Responding in part to the sudden availability of texts by ancient Arabic poets made possible by the printing press, Ibrahim and his rival and friend the Egyptian poet laureate Ahmad Shawqi (1868–1932) modeled their poetry on earlier forms such as the elegy and the panegyric, a departure from the late medieval styles that had dominated Arabic poetry for the past several hundred years. Though less respected for his poetry during his lifetime than Shawqi, Ibrahim was dubbed "Poet of the Nile" and "Poet of the People" for his political commitment to the poor. His most important poetic innovation was to take up the concerns of the majority of Egyptians by writing, for instance, on the British Empire, women's rights, poverty, and education.

Ibrahim himself struggled financially throughout life. Born in Dayrut to an Egyptian engineer father and a Turkish mother, he was sent to live with his uncle in Cairo at the age of four after his father's death and received only intermittent schooling. Like his idol Barudi, Ibrahim entered a military academy, graduating in 1891 as an officer. In 1896 he was sent to the Sudan, and the letters and poetry he sent to friends and family during this time describe his misery and his homesickness for Cairo. Accused of participating in a failed army revolt, he was court-martialed and dismissed from the British-controlled military in 1900. After writing a poem in praise of the religious reformer Muhammad Abdu, he found himself under Abdu's patronage. As a member of Abdu's intellectual circle, Ibrahim came into contact with the major political players of his day. In 1907 he completed a long prose work, *Layali Satih* (The Nights of Satih). During this period he also studied French and produced a loose translation of Victor Hugo's *Les Misérables*. In 1911 he took a post at the National Library (Dar al-Kutub), which finally brought him some degree of financial stability but necessarily curbed his political expression. He remained in the employ of the National Library until his death in 1932.

The bulk of Hafiz Ibrahim's poetry consists of elegies to fallen Egyptian heroes, for example, Abdu,

Mustafa Kamil, and Sa'd Zaghlul, as well as occasional poetry, the most famous of which is his scathing poem on the occasion of the Dinshaway incident in 1906, when British soldiers shot several villagers and sparked a national outcry for the end of British occupation. Ibrahim's poetry is difficult to find in English for two reasons. First, some of his most strident political poetry was apparently recited for friends but never written down. In addition, his success stemmed as much from his oratory skills and charisma as from the poems themselves, which makes them difficult to capture in translation. He was famous for his wit and use of irony, which can be seen in one of his popular poems: "Describing a Suit," available in English translation in Jayyusi's *Modern Arabic Poetry*. The generation of romantic poets that succeeded him in the 1930s, including the poet and critic Taha Husain (Husayn), was scornful of Ibrahim's reliance on conventional forms and advocated a simpler, less artificial poetic style. However, the Poet of the Nile remains a beloved figure in Egypt and an icon of its struggle for independence from Britain in the early 20th century.

BIBLIOGRAPHY
Ahmed, Jamal Mohammed. *The Intellectual Origins of Egyptian Nationalism.* London: Oxford University Press, 1960.
Badawi, M. M. *A Critical Introduction to Modern Arabic Poetry.* Cambridge: Cambridge University Press, 1975.
Husain (Husayn), Taha. *Hafiz wa Shawqi* (Hafiz and Shawqi). 1933. Reprint, Cairo: Maktabat Nahdat Misr, 1955.
Jayyusi, Salma Khadra. *Modern Arabic Poetry: An Anthology.* New York: Columbia University Press, 1987.
Khouri, Mounah A. *Poetry and the Making of Modern Egypt (1882–1922).* Leiden, Netherlands: E. J. Brill, 1971.
Rizk, Yunan Labib. "The Summer the Poets Departed." *Al-Ahram* 652, nos. 21–27 (August 2003).

Emily S. Davis

"I DO NOT CRUSH THE WORLD'S COROLLA OF WONDERS" Lucian Blaga (1919)

As a poet holding the sovereign power of creation—and both identifying and distinguishing himself from his fraternity of versifiers—Lucian Blaga begins his poem "I Do Not Crush the World's Corolla of Wonders" as a retort, a vindication of his poetic philosophy to those who consider poetry to be a literal and one-dimensional revelation of the inherent mysteries of life and death in idiomatic language created with the conventional resources of a poet's oeuvre. The poem, with its predominant metaphor of efflorescence (and its antithesis), seems to be part of an ongoing dialogue with surrounding urbanity in denying the inadvertent violence attributed to the presumption of poetic creation when a poem is seen as a destroyer rather than an enhancer of "the world's corolla of wonders." The first few lines express a mode of violence—"crush," "kill," "strangle"—that poets ironically manifest in their works. It is a trait Blaga disowns without ceremony. His own poetic power in no way subverts nature's.

He conceives his own role as augmenting the mysteries of the universe embodied in the phenomenal world, spanning life and death. He criticizes all poetic order that paradoxically executes a vision at the expense of empirical truth ("the light of others / strangles the spell of the hidden"). He is different in that, as a poet, he enhances rather than dilutes the "secret of the world," just as the moonlight invests the night with deeper mystery. His way of doing so suggests an unfathomable sensuality leading to a consummation of the transcendent kind: "I do myself enrich the dark horizon / with shivers, great shivers of sainted secret." And as a poet he endorses the "incomprehensible" aspect of such an experience, not for the orgasmic epiphany, but because he loves the totality and paradox of creation in all its diversity and color—"flowers and eyes and lips and tombs." In this yearning for an absolute state of primal being, we see Blaga's affiliation with his predecessor Mihai Eminescu. Blaga goes beyond the domain of scientific enquiry in the cause of understanding the world, a task made possible only through love. It is a love that a poet can execute without the presumption of creation.

BIBLIOGRAPHY

Blaga, Lucian. *Poems of Light*. Translated and introduced by Don Eulert, preface by Constantin Ciopraga. Bucharest: Minerva, 1975.

Rupendra Guha Majumdar

"IN PRAISE OF SELF-DEPRECATION"

Wisława Szymborska (1976)   First published in *A Large Number* (*Wielka liczba*) in 1976, Wisława Szymborska's "In Praise of Self-Deprecation" has been translated by many poets and has even been given slightly different titles, including "In Praise of Feeling Bad about Yourself." It is a short poem about the difference between human beings and our fellow creatures on "the third planet" from the Sun. While the translations of this poem referenced below vary substantially in wording and lineation, they both preserve the concept and the "kick" of the poem in its original Polish.

The poem begins with the images of a buzzard, a panther, piranhas, and snakes who live without "scruples," innocently, never questioning their actions. In the second stanza, Szymborska invokes animals of all types, sizes, and reputations who live their lives uncritically and "are glad of it" (Krynski and Maguire translation, 21). In stanza three we are told that no matter how much the hearts of killer whales might weigh, they are "light."

The final lines of the poem have been variously translated. Kryski and Maguire, for instance, render them this way: "There is nothing more animal-like / than a clear conscience / on the third planet of the Sun" (21). Baranczak and Cavanagh translate them a little more euphonically: "On this third planet of the Sun / among the signs of bestiality / a clear conscience is Number One" (168). The point is that human beings can feel responsibility for their actions, possess scruples, and often experience pangs of guilt. The poem wryly suggests that self-consciousness and free will may not be aspects of human life exclusively, but our feeling remorse for having committed certain actions may well be what distinguishes human beings from other living creatures. The poem's kick comes retroactively when a reader realizes that human beings do indeed behave—sometimes, at least—like buzzards, snakes, piranhas, and so forth.

BIBLIOGRAPHY

Szymborska, Wisława. "In Praise of Self-Deprecation." Translated by Magnus J. Krynski and Robert A. Maguire. In *A Book of Luminous Things*, edited by Czeslaw Milosz, 21. San Diego: Harcourt Brace/Harvest Books, 1996.

————. "In Praise of Feeling Bad about Yourself." Translated by Stanislaw Baranczak and Clare Cavanagh. In *Poems New and Collected,* 168. New York: Harcourt/ Harvest Books, 2000.

R. Victoria Arana

"INSTINCT" EDITH SÖDERGRAN (1920) This poem first appeared in SÖDERGRAN's fourth volume, *Framtidens skugga* (The Shadow of the Future), the last collection of her poems published before her death. It expresses a culminating spiritual experience. Starting with her second volume and continuing into this one, Södergran moves away from the symbolist influences that characterize her earlier work and engages more fully with German expressionism and Russian futurism. She also deepens her poetic engagement with Nietzschean philosophy, recuperating the figure of the modern individual from an outlook of despair over a senseless world to a position of hope in the individual's inner creative power. External chaos is not what defines and delimits a person's creative potential, Södergran determined; inner self-doubts do. A person's primal instinct, located in the body and connected to the Earth's origins, is where the power to overcome these limitations lies (Hackman 157). "I let my instincts build while my intellect watches," Södergran writes in an introductory remark to her second collection. "My self-confidence comes from the fact that I have discovered my dimensions. It does not behoove me to make myself smaller than I am" (*Love & Solitude* xi). This strong confidence drives Södergran's poem "Instinct," a 13-line, unrhymed, lyrical poem that features a speaker who declares her power to save the world even as the poet herself lies dying of tuberculosis. As in "THE DAY COOLS . . . ," the female body dominates the poem's imagery. Here, however, it is in physical decay: "When I lie exhausted on my bed / I know: in this weakened hand lies the fate of the earth." The speaker's hand is a metaphor for her ability to write poetry, which Södergran believed was the antidote to modern humanity's spiritual desolation. The speaker's physical weakness, ironically, increases her creative power; she is able to reconnect with her primal instinct through the bodily experience of acute and prolonged pain. "My body is a mystery," the poem begins. "As long as this brittle thing is alive / you will feel its power." While the poem's English translation makes it appear to retain the classic lyrical "I-You" form of address, in the language of the Swedish original, the pronouns are not personal but universal. The poem's "I" represents all individuals who use their intellect to serve their creative instincts, and in the Swedish new critical tradition the term for a poem's speaker is actually "the poem's I" (*diktens jag*). The "I," then, is the figure of the poet. The poem's "you," however, is plural, a detail often lost in translation. (English, for example, uses the same pronoun for both the second-person singular and the second-person plural, while in Swedish and many other languages there are two distinct sets of pronouns.) Thus the poem's "you" whom the speaker will save are the human masses who lack the poet's creative power. As in most of Södergran's work, the speaker is female, reflecting Södergran's consistent ideological and figurative conflation of the reproductive capacity of the female sex and the creative power of the female poet. The poem concludes: "It is the power that trembles in my shoe, / it is the power that moves in the folds of my dress, / and it is the power, fearing no abyss, that stands before you." Thus while the speaker's body lies weakly on the bed, her instincts stand erect and fearless, creating a powerful poem.

BIBLIOGRAPHY
Hackman, Boel. *Jag kan sjunga hur jag vill. Tankevärld och konstsyn i Edith Södergran's diktning.* Stockholm: Söderströms, 2000.
Södergran, Edith. *Love & Solitude: Selected Poems 1916–1923.* Translated by Stina Katchadourian. Seattle: Fjord Press, 1992.

Ursula Lindqvist

IN THE FORTIETH YEAR (V SOROKO-VOM GODU) ANNA AKHMATOVA (1946) This 1940 cycle of five poems is included in *Poems and Long Poems (Stikhotvoreniya i poemy)* published in1979. The poem's first appearance in the journal *Leningrad* (1946) was suppressed swiftly, and the publication led to the poem's condemnation when Andrei Zhdanov, Joseph Stalin's cultural watchdog, moved to have AKHMATOVA expelled from the Union of Soviet Writers that same year. The poem is "one of her most famous cycles" (Reeder 30).

The opening poem suggests that the events of 1940 have sealed the fate of the century, now that it has seen Paris overrun and a stunned silence hangs over the city, where Akhmatova honeymooned in 1910. The second poem is addressed "To the Londoners" and calls up Shakespeare to suggest that World War II is providing the material for him to write another play of similar stature to *"Hamlet, Caesar* or *Lear."* The implication is that events such as these require the master's hand. To underscore the devastation of the London blitz, Akhmatova declares that "bearing the dove Juliet to her grave" would be preferable to events beginning in September 1940. Certainly the news of Juliet's death would be easier to read, and yet time seems not to care what kind of history it writes.

In the third poem Akhmatova narrows the focus from a concern for history to her concrete memory of a postrevolution émigré living in London. The epigram is taken from a poem that OSIP MANDELSTAM wrote for this mutual friend. After the overwhelming news of the bombing has been absorbed, Akhmatova's thoughts turn to Salomeya Andronikova, "a Petersburg beauty" (Reeder 813). This friend personifies the untroubled loveliness of the "thirteenth year" with its "lilacs" and is therefore a striking contrast to the 40th and its thorns. Her "Daryal eyes" invoke the natural splendor of the Daryal Pass in the central Caucasus. In the end, however, she is a "Shade," a ghost of memory.

The fourth poem in the cycle turns to look north in response to the German invasion of Denmark and the Soviet invasion of Finland—Normandy prudently being substituted to preempt the censor (814). Here again, Akhmatova conflates personal history with contemporary events and alludes to the power and responsibility of writing. She envisions now "deserted houses" she once visited and knows that "Someone's recent coziness" is disrupted, that the war is "reprinting" the stories of familiar places.

Akhmatova's memory is so troubled by the losses she has faced because of ideological conflicts both domestic and foreign that she closes the cycle by "giving you notice / That I am living for the last time." Using a variety of similes drawn from nature, she has written lyrically of her ghosts, haunted by the comfortless cries of those lost ones who survive in her memory. At the end of the poem, she promises not to survive her death, not to intrude on the peace of those she leaves behind.

BIBLIOGRAPHY
Akhmatova, Anna. *The Complete Poems of Anna Akhmatova.* Expanded edition. Edited with an introduction by Roberta Reeder, translated by Judith Hemschemeyer. Boston: Zephyr Press, 1997.
Berlin, Isaiah. "Anna Akhmatova: A Memoir." In *The Complete Poems of Anna Akhmatova.* Expanded edition, edited with an introduction by Roberta Reeder, translated by Judith Hemschemeyer, 35–55. Boston: Zephyr Press, 1997.
Nayman, Anatoly. *Remembering Anna Akhmatova.* Translated by Wendy Rosslyn. New York: Henry Holt, 1991.

A. Mary Murphy

"IN THE MONTH OF ATHYR" CONSTANTINE P. CAVAFY (1917)

Late antiquity and the Hellenistic era were two of CONSTANTINE CAVAFY's favorite historical periods, and he set a considerable number of his poems in them. Situated sometime during the first three centuries of Christianity, "In the Month of Athyr" ("Εν τω μηνί Αθύρ") complements other poems about young male believers in the new and growing faith. It is also one of a series of epitaphic poems commemorating the premature death of young men—in this case of Lefkios, about whom so little is known since all that is left as evidence of his existence is a worn headstone. As in other historical poems on this theme, Cavafy is fascinated by past—real or imagined—subjectivities, and in this poem he attempts to rescue Lefkios's identity from the oblivion by resorting to a reconstruction of the minute traces still legible on the stone and their half-erased indications that a life (cut short in the prime of young, "Alexandrian" manhood) was mourned with Christian "tea[r]s" by loving "[f]riends."

But the reading of history, or of other subjectivities for that matter, is neither an easy nor a straightforward affair for Cavafy. It often requires focused attention and, more often than not, imaginative engagement and reconstruction. At times it calls for direct empathy. The challenge here is a fragmentary text; a body of gaps and breaks, fissures and fissions, parts and members; a text devoid of the rules of the page, lacking the comforting predictability of syntax, of verb, conjugation, and copula. As a textual body it cannot hold together; it can neither conjugate nor copulate. In short, it is a glimpse of a lost totality, of the absence of Lefkios.

Athyr (or Hathor) is the name of an Egyptian goddess for whom a month was named that corresponds to September or October of our calendar—and, for the Mediterranean annual cycle, to the beginning of autumn. The word literally means "house of Horus," the domain where the Sun rises and sets. Athyr is the goddess of tombs and of mortuary rituals, as well as the supreme goddess of sexual love. She is also the protector of the body from harm and is connected with healing and childbirth. Although the month's name in the poem's title may be perceived initially as a convention of temporal specificity, so common in Cavafy, Athyr personifies some of the most significant themes of the poem, which include death, decay, love, circularity, and revitalization, or rather resuscitation (through poetry and in particular through the act of reading). As the goddess of love and death, healing, and solar rejuvenation, Athyr foreshadows not only Lefkios's death and decay but also his redemption and purification. His name is after all *Lefkios*—"white" and by extension "pure." The circularity that Athyr symbolizes is paralleled by the reconstruction of the inscription's fragmented second line at the end of the poem, signifying Lefkios's death in flesh and his rebirth into language: "In the month of Athyr Lefkios went to sleep." The circularity is reinforced by the inscription's reference to yet another, later religious system of eschatological salvation, manifested in the resurrected body of Jesus Christ (mentioned in line 2), the *logos* par excellence.

The poem achieves the restitution of Lefkios's memory by intervening in the process of gradual erasure, the perishable materiality of the gravestone, a materiality just as vulnerable to decay as Lefkios's body. Lefkios's redemption is admittedly as tenuous as it is virtual—virtual to the extent that it lasts as long as the reading event itself. What ensures his immortality is the tenacity of readers. The assurance is that as long as the poem (or its antecedent stone) is read, and read aloud, Lefkios will be remembered; his memory will resound in the last two lines where language once again becomes articulate, fluent, and lucid.

George Syrimis

"INTRODUCTION, AN" KAMALA DAS (1965)

Easily the most candid of her self-confessional poems, "An Introduction" by KAMALA DAS, while seemingly simplistic, is an attempt to review her life in verse. This poem might well be said to have started a trend among Indian women poets in English to reveal little-known aspects of their lives in tones that are bold, courageous, and almost defiant. Breaking away from the Indian trend toward keeping oneself anonymous, even hidden, in one's creative work, Das's reputation as a firebrand feminist rests at least in part on this poem, in which she speaks frankly about her early marriage, her unsatisfactory sexual relationships, her lack of joy in becoming a mother until her third child was born, and her defiance of a traditional Indian mindset that wished to impose customary roles upon her.

The poem starts with an apparent self-portrait ("I am Indian, very brown"), followed by an attempt to localize herself in her regional and multilingual space (". . . born in Malabar, / I speak three languages , / Write in / Two, dream in one"). The reference to her writing in two languages alludes to her facility in both English and Malayalam, her mother tongue and the regional language of Kerala. Critics have noted the decided influence of her mother tongue on her English poetry, seen particularly in what some consider her rather disingenuous use of nonstandard grammar and broken sentence structure.

As the poem continues, however, the scenario depicted becomes far more vivid, the tone one of confiding in the reader about the most secret, even shameful, aspects of the speaker's love life. There are references, for instance, to the heartlessness with which her partner took his pleasure while oblivious to her feelings. There are also references to strange sexual liaisons in which her partner indulges (some of which are hinted as homosexual) and which she is expected to both tolerate and accept. Her partner is portrayed as a callous, insensitive person unable to satisfy her own "endless female hungers." Das portrays her speaker as naive and innocent, as someone who was forced to take up feminist cudgels as a result of the gender injustices to which she was subjected as a wife and mother. To characterize this self-reflexive speaker as someone preyed upon by those closest to her and by the strictures of her society, Das depicts the speaker's partner as not caring that she "shrank pitifully" from his embraces and from the roles he forced her to assume. To defy these societal norms and conventions, Das's speaker "wore a shirt and my / Brother's trousers, cut my hair short and ignored / My womanliness" (*Nine Indian Women Poets* 10). Still, it seems this woman did not find the self-fulfillment she so desperately sought.

It is possible to see in this poem not just the anguished cry of a female child forced to grow up in a hurry, squeezed into positions from which there was no easy way out, and aching for the enlightenment that would enable her to find her path to self-possession, but also the cries of a generation of Indian women who, despite their education and the comforts of upper-middle-class life, were unable to find the strength to rebel against rules imposed by their oppressive patriarchal environment. In that sense, "An Introduction" speaks for a vast number of earlier Indian women who struggled toward the assumption of choices of which the modern Indian sorority can currently boast.

BIBLIOGRAPHY

Das, Kamala. "An Introduction." In *Summer in Calcutta: Fifty Poems*. New Delhi: R. Paul, 1965. Reprint, Kerala: D.C. Books, 2004.

Rochelle Almeida

IQBĀL, MUHAMMAD (1877–1938) Muhammad Iqbāl is the greatest early 20th-century Muslim poet and philosopher of the Indian subcontinent. Born on November 9, 1877, in Sialkot (present-day Pakistan), Iqbāl was the first great Indian poet to create a distinct style of poetry that draws on both Eastern and Western intellectual traditions. His poetry, however, is not necessarily a fusion of the two traditions, but rather an informed creative effort to define a future for Muslims. His works retrieve the traditional Muslim past while simultaneously infusing modern knowledge of the West, without replacing the sociocultural spirit of Islamic society. He is, therefore, quite different from other Muslim intellectuals of his time, who could only imagine progress through pure mimicry of Western aesthetics.

Iqbāl's mother, Imam Bibi, was a housewife, and his father, Shaikh Noor Muhammad, was a tailor. Iqbāl received his early education at the high school division of the Scotch Mission College (now Murray College) in Sialkot. On May 5, 1893, he enrolled in college-level classes of the same institution. During this time, as in his earlier years, his main influence was Maulvi Mir Hassan, a renowned scholar of classical Persian and Arabic literature. It was also Mir Hassan who, though not a poet himself, gave Iqbāl his first lessons in the conventions of Urdu and Persian poetry. Iqbāl also sent some of his poems to the greatest Delhi poet of his time, Nawab Mirza Khan Dagh (1831–1905), who soon informed him that his poetry did not need much instruction, but Iqbāl always remembered Dagh as his *ustad* (teacher). During the same period, in 1892 Iqbāl entered into an arranged marriage with Karim Bibi, which caused him great anguish. The couple had three children, but they eventually separated in 1916; all the same, Iqbāl supported his wife until his death.

Iqbāl moved to Lahore in 1895 to study at Government College, where he earned a bachelor's degree in philosophy, Arabic, and English literature. There the orientalist Sir Thomas Arnold greatly influenced his work. Hence, Iqbāl, who would later have a distinctive worldview—informed by Eastern and Western traditions—acknowledged for the rest of his life the influence of his two teachers, Mir Hassan and Arnold. During his stay at Lahore, Iqbāl began frequenting the local poetry scene, where he read some of his early poems to great popular acclaim; he was the featured poet of Anjuman Himayet-e-Islam's annual poetry conventions for five years consecutively. Hence, Iqbāl, though highly philosophical in all his works, also started out as a popular voice in Indian Urdu poetry. Most of his early poems were compiled in 1924 in his Urdu collection *Bang-e-Dara*.

In 1905 Iqbāl went to England for further education and earned a law degree from Lincoln's Inn, a bachelor of arts from Cambridge University, and a Ph.D. in phi-

losophy from Munich University. His doctoral dissertation, "The Development of Metaphysics in Persia,"
was published in 1908. While in Europe Iqbāl observed
the house of his colonial masters, which added philosophical depth to his later works and also caused him
to be more reflexive about the questions of selfhood,
the plight of Indian Muslims, and the past and future
of Islamic *ummah* (community). His three-years stay in
Europe affected Iqbāl greatly, as may be expected of a
colonial subject, and his poetry after that became more
comparative, introspective, and critical of both East
and West. His European sojourn also caused him to
choose Persian for his more philosophical works. His
European stay resulted in the publication in 1915 of
Asrar-e-Khudi (translated as *Secrets of the Self* by Reyn-
old A. Nicholson), in which Iqbāl expounds his philosophy of selfhood and for which he was knighted.
His shift to Persian in the view of many scholars won
him a worldwide Muslim audience, whereas his works
in Urdu were limited to an Indian audience. *Asrar-e-
Khudi* marks the beginning of a trend in his works,
where he offers philosophical solutions to the existential human problems informed by an original Islamic
view of life.

Iqbāl became actively involved in the activities of
the All India Muslim League while in Europe. Upon his
return from Europe in 1908, he began practicing law
full time, and he also accepted a teaching position at
Government College in Lahore. Teaching did not agree
with him, and he soon ended that employment. His
law career also suffered because he refused to accept
any cases that came after the 10th of each month, for
this time he devoted to his poetry and the sociopolitical renewal of Indian Muslims. He also participated
actively in politics and in 1926 won a parliament seat
from the Muslim constituency of Lahore.

In 1928 Iqbāl gave a series of six lectures on Islam,
published as *The Reconstruction of Religious Thought in
Islam,* which constitute the most important modern
imagination of Islam and the importance of *tajdid*
(reform) over *taqlid* (tradition). This is probably Iqbāl's
most important philosophical work, as well as his most
neglected. If it were reintroduced into the Muslim
political imaginary, it could provide a foundation for
the literal reconstruction of the Islamic way of life in
the modern world. It was also his public articulation of
the two-nation theory in his annual address to the All
India Muslim League at Allahabad in 1930 that eventually became a political reality in league politics and
resulted in the creation of Pakistan. It must be understood, however, that Iqbāl was opposed to an overly
Western idea of a nation-state, and that for him the
Muslim nation-state was a necessary step toward
achieving global solidarity with the Muslim *ummah.*
But regardless of the deeper aspects of Iqbāl's views on
the nation, he is fittingly valorized as the national poet
of Pakistan.

In 1933 Iqbāl visited Europe once again to attend
the Round Table Conference arranged between the
British government and Indian leaders. During this
time he also traveled to continental Europe to
exchange views with such scholars and intellectuals
as Henri Bergson, the influential theorist on aesthetics, and the French scholar of Islam and the Arab
world Louis Massignon. On his return in 1933, Iqbāl,
along with other Muslim scholars, was invited to visit
Kabul by Muhammad Zahir Shah, the king of Afghanistan, who sought advice to start a new university in
Afghanistan.

The last phase of Iqbāl's poetry focused mostly on
the state of the Muslim *ummah:* its relation to the Muslim past, its colonized present, and possibilities for the
future. His later works, mostly in Persian, include
Payam-e-mashriq (Message of the East), *Javed Nama,* an
Eastern response to Dante's *Divine Comedy,* and *Mas-
navi Pas Che Baid Kard O Aqwam-e-mashriq* (What
Should Be Done O People of the East). Iqbāl's last
work, *Armaghan-e-Hijaz,* was published in 1938. He
died on April 21, 1938, after a prolonged illness, and
was buried by the main gate of the famous Badshahi
Mosque of Lahore.

Allama Sir Muhammad Iqbāl greatly influenced the
literature, culture, and politics of the subcontinent.
Throughout his career his poetical themes progressed
from personal treatments of life and faith to universal
aspects of what it means to be human and participate
in creating a better world. Iqbāl lived the life he wrote
about, and he is remembered as the "Poet of the East"
and the "Philosopher of the Muslim Ummah," as well
as the national poet of Pakistan.

BIBLIOGRAPHY

Iqbāl, Muhammad. *Poems from Iqbāl: Renderings in English Verse with Comparative Urdu Text.* Rev. ed. Oxford: Oxford University Press, 2004.

Singh, Iqbāl. *The Ardent Pilgrim: An Introduction to the Life and Work of Muhammad Iqbāl.* Rev. ed. Oxford: Oxford University Press, 1997.

Masood A. Raja

"I SING OF CHANGE" Niyi Osundare (1981)

"I Sing of Change"—a short, hopeful expression of utopian desire in seven irregular stanzas—is the first poem of Niyi Osundare's *I Sing of Change.* It begins with a three-line epigram from W. B. Yeats in which awakened poets are exhorted to sing out so that "the whole earth change its tune." From the poem's first stanza, in which the poet praises "the beauty of Athens / without its slaves," readers quickly learn to appreciate Osundare's perspective on the past and the present. The poet evokes "a world free / of kings and queens / and other remnants" of history. He brings to mind a world without iron curtains and calls for "the end / of warlords and armouries / and prisons." The changes the poet envisions are more than merely political, though. He imagines a planet where from the deserts fruit trees spring "after the quickening rains" and both the Sun and the stars dissipate ignorance. The poem ends with a one-line stanza: "I sing of a world reshaped." Overall the tone of the poem is insistent, and the message is elegant and straightforward: The world is not a particularly good place (yet); and though it has hosted splendid nations that have produced beautiful art and worthy civilizations, none has been wholly admirable, nor wholly free.

BIBLIOGRAPHY

Osundare, Niyi. *I Sing of Change.* Ibadan: privately printed, 1981. The poem is widely reprinted and is included in *The Penguin Book of Modern African Poetry,* 4th ed., edited by Gerald Moore and Ulli Beier. London: Penguin, 1998, 283.

R. Victoria Arana

"ITHAKA" Constantine P. Cavafy (1911)

"Ithaka" is Constantine Cavafy's best-known poem, having won him his first international acclaim when T. S. Eliot published a translation of it in *The Criterion* in 1924. One of the few "second-person" poems Cavafy wrote (along with "The City" in 1894 and "God Abandons Anthony" in 1911), "Ithaka" not only returns to the *Odyssey* to reconfigure both its framework and its purpose, but also diverges from Dante's and Tennyson's poetic engagements with the Odyssean theme.

"Ithaka" takes the form of a didactic monologue addressing Odysseus, in advance of his return from Troy, regarding his journey's actual purpose and the best way to approach and to understand it. Where the Homeric epic described a grueling voyage back to a beloved home, a journey prolonged by the punishing god Poseidon, and where Dante and Tennyson had depicted Odysseus as bored with his island and eager to depart once again to foreign lands for excitement, Cavafy's "Ithaka" guards the value of home but transforms it into a destiny rather than an origin, whose value is found in the journey of discovery it inspires. Thus the poem begins with a seemingly counterintuitive wish for Odysseus's pending journey to be a long one, explaining the joys to be met in its unfolding—of "coming into harbors seen for the first time," of buying precious jewels and perfumes "at Phoenician trading stations," of gathering knowledge from the scholars he will come across in "many Egyptian cities." The speaker explains that the obstacles and hard times to be encountered on the journey are products of a fearful soul and not of an angry god ("Laistrygonians and Cyclops, / wild Poseidon—you won't encounter them / unless you bring them along inside your soul, / unless your soul sets them up in front of you"). The speaker concludes by addressing the insignificance of the actual Ithaka and the real meaning of the journey: "If you find her poor, Ithaka won't have fooled you. / Wise as you will have become, so full of experience, / you will have understood by then what these Ithakas mean."

By turning the single, literal Ithaka into a plural symbol of destinations that inspire adventurous, homeward-bound journeys, Cavafy transforms the heroism of the Odyssean myth into a romantic disposition toward the sensual expression of life and the development of the individual soul. Through the lenses of this romantic disposition, one could well perceive Cavafy's

Ithaka as symbolizing a further destination: death, not so much as a terrifying prospect, but as an inspiration to live every day to the fullest.

BIBLIOGRAPHY

Cavafy, C. P. *Collected Poems.* Translated by Edmund Keeley and Phillip Sheppard, edited by George Savidis. Princeton, N.J.: Princeton University Press, 1975; London: Hogarth Press, 1975.

Jusdanis, Gregory. *The Poetics of Cavafy: Textuality, Eroticism, History.* Princeton, N.J.: Princeton University Press, 1987.

Keeley, Edmund. *Cavafy's Alexandria: A Study of a Myth in Progress.* Princeton, N.J.: Princeton University Press, 1976.

Yianna Liatsos

"I THANK GOD" BERNARD BINLIN DADIÉ (1956) This 13-line free-verse poem starts with gratitude, "I thank you, my God, / for having created me black," and establishes a mood of celebration. The next line, a continuation of the initial thought, creates a startling counterpoint: "for making me the mixture of all sufferings." The initial mood of rejoicing is negated, leaving a feeling of tremendous weight and shared pain. This impression is reinforced when the narrator asserts that white is a color of special status, "the color of occasions," while black is drab and heavy, "the color of every day." The feeling of burden is strengthened when the poet, now a metonym for Africa, states, "I have been carrying the world / since the beginning of time," a reference to every form of exploitation and abuse that black peoples everywhere have endured. In this poem, DADIÉ, spokesperson for the "dark" continent, both cries and decries the suffering of his people.

When the poet writes, "We are the night / we are the mystery," he evokes the historical European view of Africa as a dark and mysterious continent, faintly implying the traditional European conceit that whites brought enlightenment to black Africa. Yet the last two lines of the poem—"And with us, and for us, / there are the stars."—restore the positive mood suggested by the opening. The stars, compasses in the sky, beacons of light and hope, shine for Dadié and his people. In closing his poem thus, the writer summons a shining road ahead for Africa and its peoples.

One last and intriguing aspect of the poem must be explored, the lines that read "and my smile on the world / created the day in the night." Surely there is an allusion here to Africa as the cradle of life, the origin of humankind. This thought connects with the preceding lines: "I have been carrying the world / since the beginning of time." Africa has borne not only the burden of the world's suffering and pain; she has also carried the world in her womb. When Africa smiled, she gave life—and martyrs—to the world.

BIBLIOGRAPHY

Dadié, Bernard Binlin. *"Je remercie Dieu"* (I Thank God). In *La Ronde des jours,* translated by Debra Popkin. In *Encyclopedia of World Literature in the 20th Century,* edited by Leonard S. Klein. New York: Frederick Unger, 1981.

Annette Olsen-Fazi

"IT IS AFTER THE MOMENTS . . ." ANNA DE NOAILLES (1921) This poem by ANNA DE NOAILLES, from *Les Forces éternelles* (1921), explores themes of betrayal, isolation, and renewal. Its persona, or narrative voice, expresses frustration at finding oneself, after an implied moment of intimacy, alone beside a now somnolent lover. Many of Noailles's male contemporaries dismissed her work as "feminine," but this persona is conspicuously androgynous, both lover caressed by hope and "warrior madness" cleaving a passage through a maze of paths. The voice is tempered by stanzas in traditional French meter and *rimes croisées* (alternating rhyme, abab). The first five stanzas are quatrains, with three alexandrines (12-syllable lines), followed by an eight-syllable line. The sixth and final stanza expands (appositely) to five lines: four alexandrines and an octosyllabic line.

In the opening stanza the persona identifies the lyric present as *"après les moments"* of lovemaking. Caesura, an internal pause within a line that comes at the midpoint in the traditional alexandrine, separates the present from recent ecstasy:

C'est après les moments | les plus bouleversés
(It is after moments | the most convulsive)
De l'étroite union | acharnée et barbare,
(Of intimate union | keen and savage) . . .
    (literal translation)

The "keenness" of that unbridled passion is implied by enjambment, the syntax of the second half of the first line running on, without grammatical break, to the close of the second.

In the second stanza the speaker acknowledges a silence within which the miracle of "union," with Noailles's possible allusion to Genesis 2:24, comes apart. The course of this dissolution is mapped out by the sequence of pronouns: *"nous"* (we) becomes, in line three, *"chacun de nous"* (each of us); and, in line four, *"soi-même"* (a self).

In the third stanza the speaker addresses her silent partner *"près de moi"* (beside me) as *"vous,"* the pronoun reserved for formal address; and this emotional distance is reinforced by an apt use of synecdoche, as she reduces her lover to vacant eyes that moments earlier "seemed to burn [her] beneath [her] eyelids." This lover is then diminished to "a puny animal gorged on its meal" and, finally, regarded as "a dead man sculpted on his stone." In either instance there is no fulfillment. The puny animal has overindulged, and the dead man hardly "possesses" the stone that captures his likeness. Thus the speaker acknowledges, in stanza four, that she cannot penetrate her satiated lover's "vision," even as she feels an inexpressible hope "wafting its young palms" over her.

In the final stanza the speaker likens her unquenchable desire to a "warrior madness" that even at rest wishes to "cleave itself a passage along a thousand winding paths!" Lying beside a "contented" lover within whom she detects no evidence of the silent confusion "in which [her] ecstatic sadness struggles," she asks: "What can there be, O my love, in common between you and me!"

BIBLIOGRAPHY

Noailles, Anna de, "It is after. . . ." In *French Poetry: 1820–1950*. Translated by William Rees. New York: Penguin Books, 1990, 434–436.

Philip H. Christensen

"IT IS THE COURAGE OF MEN WHICH IS DISLOCATED" AIMÉ CÉSAIRE (1960) In

this unrhymed prose poem CÉSAIRE develops the central image of torrential rain and its effects—both destructive and cathartic—on island cultures: "The rain, it's the testy way here and now to strike out everything that exists, everything / that's been created, cried out, said, lied about, soiled." The rain is of biblical proportions and intent; it is at once a punishment for the abuses and "lies" of colonialism, and at the same time a means by which this ignoble past is erased so that oppressed peoples may rebuild their cultures from scratch.

In the poem's second paragraph the rain's relentlessness is contrasted to human courage, which is never fully sustained. Playing on the two meanings of "fall" (the fall of rain and the fall of man), the poet contrasts the rain's purposefulness with the fickle nature of humankind: "Where on earth did you hear that rain falls? / It is the courage of men which is dislocated. Rain is always wholehearted." Rain is merciless in its assault, and it spares no creature. The poet seems to chide his people for their lack of courage and purpose, both of which he sees in the personification of the rain: "Rain exults. It is a / levy en masse of inspiration, a jolt of tropical sleep; a tumultuous assault against everything that burrows in warrens; the thrust counter-current / to gravity of a thousand crazed rounds of ammunition. . . ." The word *ammunition* lends a military quality to the rain, but unlike the rain, the poet's own people have been unwilling to engage in violent revolution to achieve freedom.

The storm reaches a crescendo as lightning strikes, evaporating everything. But in the lightning's destructive wake, there is peace: "Finally! The tree bursts with grenade. The rock explodes. Tenderness: now and then this great / repose. Tenderness: now and then this orchestra playing and intertwining steps like plaited wicker." And yet revolution and its resultant peace do not come without a price; bloodshed and the devastation of the natural world are necessary sacrifices, or to reverse a metaphor, there must be a storm before the calm: "Tenderness, but that of adorable tortures: the setting in motion of a fire of bit-braces which drill / and force the void to scream star. It is blood." But the sacrifice is worth the toll of lives, as the poet makes clear when he triumphantly proclaims, "No more monarchy."

The poem closes with the evocation of the *assegai* dance, a ritual of African peoples in which the *assegai*—a spear—is brandished. The poet foresees the triumph of oppressed peoples, who will dance the victory dance of their African roots. In a final metaphor that echoes the title of John Steinbeck's novel *The Grapes of Wrath*, the poet explains that the violence sown in revolution will result in a palliative "alcohol" of peace and renewal: "The vineyard of wrath has peddled to the very sky the alcohol of its repose and its salvation."

BIBLIOGRAPHY

Césaire, Aimé. *The Collected Poetry of Aimé Césaire.* Translated and edited by Clayton Eshleman and Annette Smith. Berkeley and Los Angeles: University of California Press, 1983.

Patrick L. Day

"I WANT TO MEET . . ." KARIN BOYE (1927)

This poem ("*Jag vill möta . . .*") appeared in Swedish poet KARIN BOYE's third collection, *Härdarna* (The Hearths, 1927), and represents her earlier, conventional, and more popular poetry, before a radical formal shift occurred eight years later. It employs regular meter, perfect rhyme, and a five-quatrain stanzaic structure. Yet the poem's formal simplicity belies a lofty and complex philosophical agenda that pervades all of her poetry. Boye believed lyrical poetry to be a more direct, intimate, and transformative communicative art than prose, though she also was an award-winning writer of novels, short fiction, and polemical essays. In her critical essay "Daydreaming as a Philosophy of Life" (1931), first published in the avant-garde cultural journal *Spektrum*, Boye argues that poetry is the most brutally honest of the written arts, holding poet and reader accountable to their ideals as well as to imminent material and cultural conditions. Boye believed poetry could reconnect individuals to a central source of creative power, thereby reconnecting them spiritually to one another, in the way that a prism gathers and redistributes light (thus her choice of the journal's title, *Spektrum*). In the essay Boye writes, "So concentrated becomes our interest in that focal point—people's lives—that we have nothing left for isolated worlds of beauty, culture for culture's sake. So forceful [is our interest] that it does not stop at the finished piece of art but bores down to the fragment of life that the artist lays bare. It is there we seek guidance for our common journey." This ideal is embodied in the poem "I Want to Meet . . .," which contrasts an artificial, fearful, and chilling power—one that employs weapons and armor—with a natural, liberated, and warming power present at life's creative source: "More powerful than iron / is life in nascence, / driven out of the earth's heart / without defense." Tellingly, the speaker concludes not by casting off the trappings of false power, but by expressing a strong desire to do so: "Spring dawns in winter's regions, / where I froze. / I want to meet life's powers / weaponless." The power of this poem, then, lies in its lyrical expression, which seeks to implant a common desire to disarm and reconnect. The contrast between artificial and constructed power, on the one hand, and natural and raw reproductive power, on the other, illustrates a cornerstone of Boye's philosophy of language. In another critical essay, "Language Beyond Logic" ("*Språket bortom logiken,*" 1933), Boye argues that poetry empowers its practioners to reach beyond the artificial limitations of cognitive language to a central source of creative expression. For Boye this applies to readers and reciters of poetry as well as to its writers; these acts of communication are interdependent. Given that "I Want to Meet . . ." imparts a powerful, immediate, and suprarational effect on audiences still today, it would seem Boye's faith in the communicative power of lyrical poetry is well placed.

BIBLIOGRAPHY

Boye, Karin. "Dagdrömmeriet som livsåskådning" (Daydreaming as a Philosophy of Life) and "Språket bortom logiken" (Language Beyond Logic). In *Det hungriga ögat* (The Hungry Eye): *Journalistik 1930–36 Recensioner och essäer* (Journalism 1930–36 Reviews and essays), edited by Gunnar Ståhl. Stockholm: Legus, 1992.

Ursula Lindqvist

J

JACOBSEN, ROLF (1907–1994) One of Norway's greatest modern poets, Rolf Jacobsen has been credited with breathing new life into Norwegian poetry in the 1930s by introducing a style known as New Simplicity. In an interview he once described this new poetry as "free verses without structured meter—rhythm, but without meter. I wondered for a long time if this couldn't also be a new poetic form for our time" (Grinde 7). Such free verse departed substantially from the rhymed and metered lyrical verse of the romantic period, which reached a nationalist zenith in 1905 when Norway declared its independence from Sweden. Norway's most famous romantic poet, Bjørnstjerne Bjørnson, who wrote the poem that became the national anthem, had become a cultural icon by the early 20th century. Yet Jacobsen found the inspiration for a new, simple, free, and modern style of Norwegian poetry by reading verse that was even older and more canonical—the Icelandic sagas and old skaldic poetry, written in Old Norse during Iceland's famous Age of Writing, A.D. 1100–1350 (Revisiting the sagas and skaldic poetry, as well as Norse myth and legends, was a popular activity for Nordic modernist writers, starting with the publication of Swedish poet Vilhelm Ekelund's *Melodier i skymningen* [Twilight Melodies] in 1902.) Jacobsen's other motivation for trying to revive Norwegian poetry was the arrival of the technological age in Norway. Unlike TARJEI VESAAS, who lived most of his life in the Norwegian countryside, Jacobsen was born in the capital city, Oslo, and lived in or near that city for most of his life, although from the age of six to 13 he lived in villages along the river Glomma in southeastern Norway. Accordingly, Jacobsen's poetry examines the relationships between country and city, the natural and the technological, the old and the new. As scholar Harald Naess wrote in 1974: "Formally speaking, modern Norwegian poetry began with him forty years ago, and one of his major concerns, which is to show the dangers of 20th-century technical civilization, is finally receiving full attention today" (Naess 265).

Jacobsen published 12 volumes of poetry during his lifetime, and four collections of his poetry in English translation remain in print: *Breathing Exercise* (1986), *Night Open* (1993), *The Roads Have Come to Their End Now* (2001), and *North in World: Selected Poems of Rolf Jacobsen, A Bilingual Edition* (2002). This last collection, for which translator and poet Roger Greenwald worked closely with Jacobsen on his translations, won the American Translators Association's Lewis Galantière Award in 2004.

Jacobsen earned a reputation early on for championing the newness and the technological life of cities in his poetry. His first volume, *Jord og jern* (Earth and Iron, 1933), contained poems such as "Metaphysics of the City" that seemed to celebrate city life: "But up in the day you, of course, are dancing over the asphalt / with the soles of your feet on fire." This same collection contains poems titled "Rain," "Marshes," and "The Clouds," in which Jacobsen weaves together technological and natural lexicons to describe the motion of natural phenomena, as in "The day travels in a tunnel" (from "The Clouds"). But he believed it was essential to maintain a kinetic relationship between the natural and the technological worlds, both of which modern humans inhabit. "I've always had one leg in the green, one in the grey, one in nature and one in technological reality," Jacobsen once said. "I found my own niche in the technological where no poet had been before. At least not in our country" (Grinde 9). Following the publication of his second book, in 1935, and the onset of World War II, during which the Germans occupied Norway, Jacobsen stopped publishing poems for 16 years. With the exception of his marriage to Petra Tendø in 1940 (the couple had two sons), this was a dark period in Jacobsen's life. During the occupation he signed editorials in support of the German occupiers and belonged to the Norwegian National Socialist Party, although he is not believed to have supported the Holocaust or accepted the cult of Hitler. Following the war and the liberation of Norway, Jacobsen was convicted of treason and sentenced to three and a half years of hard labor. (One of his famous writer colleagues, Nobel Prize winner Knut Hamsun, also was convicted of treason but was sentenced to an asylum and house arrest because of his age.) Following this rough time, Jacobsen moved his family to a town 65 miles north of Oslo and worked as a journalist and newspaper editor. "After the war . . . I had to find myself again. Rediscover a world turned totally upside down," he said later (Grinde 9).

The poems in his first volume after the long silence, *Fjerntog* (Express Train, 1951), continue Jacobsen's interweaving of the natural and the technological, but with a much darker tone. In "Gaslight," for example, Jacobsen describes "unending boulevards . . . where no bells ring and no trains run / —in those green cities, cellars dark with food." His latest poems, in the collection *Nattåpent* (translated as Night Watch or Night Open, 1985), have a deeply reflective quality to them. Poems such as "Trees in Autumn" and "SUDDENLY. IN DECEMBER" use the seasons to depict monumental events in human life. His tender love poems in this final collection to his departed wife especially endeared him to readers.

Throughout Jacobsen's work remains his commitment to powerful expression through simple language and form, a style that has made him revered in Norway and well respected internationally. His work has been translated into 20 languages and has often been compared to that of his Swedish contemporary TOMAS TRANSTRÖMER and to the Scandinavian-American poet Carl Sandburg of the Chicago School. Jacobsen won many major Nordic literary prizes, including the Swedish Academy's Grand Nordic Prize, called the "little Nobel," in 1989. He also served for years on the Norwegian Academy for Language and Literature. He once said that while the new media of the technological age had lessened poetry's public profile to some extent, he believed there were still many readers of all social classes who need poetry. (This need is supported materially in Norway by the government's Cultural Fund, which provides generous subsidies to writers and purchases 1,000 copies of each new title.) "When I've been asked who I write for I say I write for the half tired," Jacobsen said in 1983. "This is an age of tiredness. . . . Most of us don't have the time to acquaint ourselves with the problems of the day. They throw themselves in an armchair and switch on the television. Those are the dead-tired, and they exist in all social classes. I write for the half-tired, those who still possess some curiosity, and still have the ability to wonder, wrestle with a question" (Grinde 11). Thanks to the work of translators Olav Grinde, Robert Bly, and Roger Greenwald, English readers of all social classes also have the opportunity to reach, half-tired, for a book of Jacobsen's poetry, and wonder.

BIBLIOGRAPHY

Grinde, Olav. "Interview with Rolf Jacobsen." *South Dakota Review* 21, no. 1 (1983): 7–13.

Jacobsen, Rolf. *Breathing Exercise: Poems of Rolf Jacobsen.* Translated by Olav Grinde. Buffalo, N.Y.: White Pine Press, 1986.

———. *Night Open.* Translated by Olav Grinde. Buffalo, N.Y.: White Pine Press, 1993.

———. *North in the World: Selected Poems of Rolf Jacobsen, A Bilingual Edition.* Edited and translated by Roger Greenwald. University of Chicago Press, 2002.

———. *The Roads Have Come to an End Now: Selected and Last Poems.* Translated by Robert Bly, Roger Greenwald, and Robert Hedin. Port Townsend, Wash.: Copper Canyon Press, 2001.

Naess, Harald. "The Poetry of Rolf Jacobsen." *American Scandinavian Review* 62 (1974): 265–269.

Ursula A. L. Lindqvist

JAMAICA Andrew Salkey (1973)

Andrew Salkey's long poem *Jamaica* bears the subtitle *An Epic Poem, Exploring the Historical Foundations of Jamaican Society*. Published in 1973, after more than two decades of work, *Jamaica* sprawls across centuries of Jamaican history and includes a wide range of events and themes. Framed by a prologue, "I into history, now," and an epilogue, "Is the lan' I want," the poem consists of four major sections. The first section, "Caribbea," addresses the land and sea in direct empathy: "Caribbea, / knowledgeable, / patient, / raise your emancipated breasts, / maternal, / absolute, / elegant, / malachite eyes" (106). The second section, "Slavery to Liberation," focuses on five significant years in Jamaican history. The third section, "Mento Time," depicts everyday urban life in 20th-century Kingston in the rhythm of Mento music, a precursor of ska, rock steady, and reggae genres. The fourth section, "Caribbean Petchary," focuses on three historical events and closes with an ode to the petchary bird (the gray kingbird known for its loud "Pittire" song): "you and Caribbea are one in us; / you are Caribbea!" (93).

Many of the poem's various subsections turn upon the events of key years in Jamaican history: 1692, in which the city of Port Royal suffered a massive earthquake; 1796, the year of a major rebellion, the Maroon War; 1833, in which slaves were emancipated by the British Parliament; 1865, the year of the Morant Bay Uprising; 1907, in which an earthquake devastated Kingston; 1938, the year of labor riots, the consolidation of the worker's movement, and the founding of the People's National Party; 1944, in which the first elections were held; and 1951, in which Hurricane Charlie wreaked considerable damage to the island and left thousands homeless.

The language of *Jamaica*, like much of Salkey's work, attempts to render Jamaican speech—its articulations, elisions, and cadences—on the printed page. Salkey's foregrounding of Jamaican speech as a poetic medium harmonizes with the poem's overarching theme of harnessing the island's history, and the experience of its people, to articulate Jamaican identity and culture. "Culture," goes one of the poem's several refrains, "come when you buck up / on you'self. / It start when you' body make shadow / on the lan'" (107). Salkey's approach to Jamaican history through epic poetry at once stylizes the experiences of the colonized and demonstrates the potential of doing so. Rejecting both willful ignorance and mimicry of the colonizer, Salkey's poem both performs and argues for an expansive and adaptive approach to Jamaican poetry: "I into history, now. / Is not'ing but song I singin' / an' name I callin' / an' blood I boilin' / an' self I raisin', / in a correc' Anancy form, / a t'ing I borrow / an' makin' me own, wit'out pretty please / or pardon" (12). For Salkey, Anancy, the wily spider-man of Ashanti mythology, emblematizes the adaptive culture of the African diaspora and the grafted African roots of Caribbean literature. Like the figure of Anancy, the poem embodies and argues for fashioning art out of both evolving diasporic traditions and ambivalent legacies of European colonialism—such as the English language—which the Caribbean artist may borrow, adapt, infuse, and inflect with local geography, imagery, experience, and voice.

BIBLIOGRAPHY

Salkey, Andrew. *Jamaica: An Epic Poem, Exploring the Historical Foundations of Jamaican Society*. London: Bogle L'Ouverture Press, 1983.

Alex Feerst

JIMÉNEZ, JUAN RAMÓN (1881–1958)

Nobel Prize laureate Juan Ramón Jiménez was one of the leading figures in Spain's modernist movement. Born in the Andalusian town of Moguer, at age 16 Jiménez moved to Seville to begin his university studies in law. Exposed to contemporary poetic currents, Jiménez soon lost interest in legal studies. Within a year he published his first poems in a Madrid literary review, attracting the attention of modernist luminaries Rubén Darío and Francisco Villaespea. In April 1900 the two writers invited Jiménez to Madrid and introduced him to the capital's literary elite. Although the brief visit resulted in the publication of the two short impressionistic collections *Almas de violeta* (Violet Souls, 1900) and *Ninfeas* (Water Lilies, 1900), the young poet disliked the urban environment and returned to Moguer. A month later the unexpected death of Juan Ramón's father, Victor Jiménez, drove the poet into a severe emotional crisis requiring hospitalization at mental institutions in Madrid and Bordeaux, France. While recovering from depression Jiménez continued to expand his poetic horizons. Over the next decade he produced a number of collections, including *Arias tristes* (Sad Arias, 1903), *Elejías* (Elegies, 1908), *Poemas mágicos y dolientes* (Poems of Magic and Pain, 1909), and *Poemas agrestes* (Country Poems, 1911). Strongly influenced by French symbolism, Jiménez's poetry from this period is marked by classical versification, abundant sensorial imagery, and a preponderant theme of solitude. The year 1913 was decisive for Jiménez. He completed the work for which he is still best known, the children's story *El Platero y yo* (*Platero and I,* 1914). Resuming his studies in Madrid, he met his great love, the Spanish-Indian translator Zenobia Camprubí. In 1916 the couple married during a visit to New York. The result of this journey was the poet's most important work, *Diario de un poeta recién casado* (Diary of a Newlywed Poet, 1916), which includes an especially moving "NOCTURNE" (he produced several). Introduced by Zenobia to Anglophone poets such as Walt Whitman and W. B. Yeats, Jiménez developed a new creative sensibility. Discarding traditional forms for rhythmic free verse and elaborate imagery for simpler language, Jiménez also shed the melancholy of his earlier work for a more contemplative transcendentalism. The collection established Jiménez, along with ANTONIO MACHADO, as one of Spain's most influential poets. He continued to mine this vein of "naked poetry" in *Eternidades* (Eternities, 1918) and *Piedra y cielo* (Stone and Sky, 1919) while encouraging young poets through his active involvement in numerous literary journals. This influence began to decline in the late 1920s after the poet repudiated the new aesthetic of younger poets such as FEDERICO GARCÍA LORCA, Luis Cernuda, RAFAEL ALBERTI, and VICENTE ALEIXANDRE. Rejecting both their interest in surrealism and their revival of baroque formalism, Jiménez withdrew to Andalusia to edit his writings until the outbreak of the Spanish civil war in 1936. With the fall of the republic, Jiménez and his wife went into exile, living in the United States, Cuba, and, Puerto Rico. The poetry from this period—which includes the collections *Romances de Coral Gables* (Coral Gables Ballads, 1948), *Animal de fondo* (Animal of the Depths, or Essential Animal, 1949), and *Dios deseado y deseante* (God Desired and Desiring, 1957)—is marked by an almost pantheistic spirituality and awareness of mortality. In 1951 Zenobia was diagnosed with cancer. In 1956, three days before her death, Jiménez was awarded the Nobel Prize. Inconsolable, he went into complete seclusion and died in May 1958. Today, Juan Ramón Jiménez is remembered as one of the seminal figures in Spain's poetic revival. Although his literary status has not endured to the same degree as that of Machado or García Lorca, many of his poems are still cherished for their stylistic simplicity and deep spirituality. Among the few available English translations of Jiménez, the most accessible are by Robert Bly in *Lorca and Jiménez: Selected Poems.* The best general criticism available in English on Jiménez's poetry is perhaps that of William Kluback.

BIBLIOGRAPHY

Jiménez, Juan Ramón. *El Platero y yo / Platero and I: A Dual-LanguageBook.* Translated by Stanley Applebaum. New York: Dover, 2004.
———. *Diary of a Newly Wed Poet: A Bilingual Edition of* Diario de un poeta recién casado. Introduction by Michael P. Predmore, translated by Hugh A. Harter. Selinsgrove: Susquehanna University Press, 2004.
———. *Lorca and Jiménez: Selected Poems.* A dual-language anthology. Translated by Robert Bly. Boston: Beacon Press, 1997.
———. *Selected Writings of Juan Ramón Jiménez.* Translated by H. R. Hays. New York: Farrar, Straus and Giroux, 1999.
Kluback, William. *Encounters with Juan Ramón Jiménez.* Bern, Switzerland, and New York: Peter Lang, 1995.

Eric Reinholtz

JOURNEY TAKAMURA KŌTARŌ (1914) TAKAMURA KŌTARŌ's 1914 book *Dōtei* (Journey) may be the single most important poetry collection to the development of 20th-century Japanese poetry. In *Dōtei* Takamura showed himself to be the first Japanese poet to break effectively with traditional poetic convention.

Influenced by Western art and literature of the time, as well as by the poetry of Walt Whitman and others, Takamura employed a free verse and colloquial language that sharply diverged from the literary language and fixed forms in which poetry had traditionally been written in Japan. Other similarly successful volumes of poetry, such as SAKUTARŌ HAGIWARA's 1917 *Tsuki ni Hoeru* (HOWLING AT THE MOON), appeared around this time, but *Dōtei* broke the mold, much as Whitman had in the West during the previous century. *Dōtei* is a collection of 107 poems from which Takamura would later incorporate 11 into his enormously successful 1941 *Chieko Shō* (THE CHIEKO COLLECTION). *Dōtei*, as its title poem "Journey" forecasts, conveys a journey—Takamura's journey into a new life. Having rejected the life planned for him as his family's eldest son and having recently left his life of decadence with Pan no Kai (The Pan Society), Takamura enters a new life with Chieko Naganuma, whom he would marry shortly after the publication of *Dōtei*, as the couple begins a new life together in conscious harmony with the wonders of nature. The poems in this volume encompass Takamura's dissatisfaction with what he saw as a staid and stagnant tradition-bound existence in Japan at the time (such as in "Father's Face" and "The Land of Netsuke"), as well as his rootless and decadent time with Pan no Kai, and finally his finding his way with nature as his guide. Particularly in the poems about his relationship with Chieko, such as "Fear" and "Family of Owls," Takamura demonstrates the uniqueness of their journey into life, as they eschewed traditional marital and social roles, seemingly to the consternation of society. Even more important, though, was their journey into life guided by nature, as evidenced in such poems as "Two of Us" and "One Evening." *Dōtei* is ultimately about nature's ability to direct one's life properly and about the necessity of living in harmony with nature and in harmony with one's own soul.

John G. Peters

K

KALIA, MAMTA (1940–) Mamta Kalia, known for her short stories as well as her poems, writes in both Hindi and English of her disaffection with traditional roles for women and the exaltation of males in Indian societies. She has been credited with initiating a wave of women's vernacular poetry with its "stripped-down style, street language, and forcefulness" and exploring the "themes, attitudes, voices and registers of [modern Indian] women" (King 155). Her distinct poetic voice sounds out a hard-edged critique of patriarchy, as in her lines from *Tribute to Papa*: "I am seriously thinking of disowning you, papa, / you and your sacredness." In "Against Robert Frost" the speaker admits that she "can't bear to read Robert Frost. / Why should he talk of apple-picking / When most of us can't afford to eat one?" and adds: "I haven't even seen an apple for many months— / Whatever we save we keep for beer / And contraceptives." In other poems she critiques traditional female roles—as, for example, she does in "Anonymous," where she gives voice to the world's generic housewife, whose life is reduced to a stark litany: "I cook, I wash, / I bear, I rear, / I nag, I wag, / I sulk, I sag."

Kalia started writing at the age of nine. She grew up in a middle-class family but felt hemmed in by its concern with respectability (its "clean thoughts, clean words, clean teeth"). She studied English literature and did postgraduate study in English at Delhi University. Following that she served as principal of a high school in Allahabad for 28 years. During her career as an educator she has distinguished herself as a prolific writer and has published more than 25 books, including four novels and 10 collections of short stories. Her novel *Beghar* was a major success and ran to five editions. She has written a collection of one-act plays, edited several books, and been a regular contributor to leading magazines. Her two collections of verse in English—*Tribute to Papa and other poems* and *Poems 78*—have been particularly well received by critics both in India and abroad. Her antipatriarchal poetry has been compared to that of Sylvia Plath and deemed stronger.

Mamta Kalia has been honoured with the Sahitya Bhushan Samman (2004), the Mahadevi Verma Memorial Award (1998), and the Yashpal Samman (1985). She is director of the Bhartiya Bhasha Parishad in Kolkata, in connection with which she has hosted symposia on the contemporary sociocultural ethos.

BIBLIOGRAPHY
De Souza, Eunice. *Conversations with Indian Poets.* Oxford: Oxford University Press, 2001.
Kalia, Mamta. *Tribute to Papa.* Calcutta: Writers Workshop, 1970.
———. *Poems 78.* Calcutta: Writers Workshop, 1979.
King, Bruce. *Modern Indian Poetry in English.* Delhi: Oxford University Press, 1987.
Nare, Veena. "A Comparative Study of Mamta Kalia's 'A Tribute to Papa' and Sylvia Plath's 'Daddy.'" In *Studies in Comparative Literature,* edited by Mohit K. Ray. New Delhi, Atlantic, 2002.

R. Victoria Arana

KEANE, JAYNE FENTON (1971–)   An Australian citizen, Jayne Fenton Keane is an experimental poet, playwright, and composer celebrated for her multimedia and electronic innovations for the elaboration, preservation, and performance of poetry. Her poems avail themselves of new technologies to create overlays of sound and suggestive echoes and reverberations that emphasize their lexical and denotative meanings. Thematically, they vary enormously, but Keane is perhaps most renowned for her poems exploring identity in cutting-edge ways and critiquing current trendy ideologies. Many of her poems appear to be staged in the mind, where (as one critic put it) "dogma, fear, attraction, and all corners of the psyche are equally immediate" (http://voices.e-poets.net/KeaneJF/).

Jayne Fenton Keane was born in the United Kingdom. Her parents, Leslie and Linda Fenton, migrated to Australia when she was 18 months old. Jayne grew up and attended schools in Adelaide, South Australia. She completed her first degree (in biological science and physical education) at Flinders University. She then worked as an environmental education manager for a community organization, which allowed her to pursue her passion for conservation and ecology. She held her first collaborative art-poetry exhibition in Adelaide in 1991, just before moving to Queensland. She pursued her interest in social justice by working as a training and development officer for welfare service providers in central Queensland. While shaping her multidisciplinary poetics, she has engaged in human rights work, written medical training programs, and lectured and done research.

Keane first read her poetry to a public audience in Rockhampton, Queensland, Australia, in 1993, after several years of publishing in journals. Around that time she began developing an interest in practicing and critiquing *embodiment* as a method for performing poetry (see POETRY BEYOND THE PAGE). In 1994 she hooked up to the Internet for the first time and began experimenting with computer software. Also in 1994 she imagined her first collection of multimedia poems and began to develop an aesthetic, a methodology, and a theory about them. But at that time, she did not have the electronic tools to realize this vision. In 1996 she and her husband moved to Australia's Gold Coast in Queensland, where they have lived ever since.

When she discovered the Adobe Flash™ program in 1997, she began producing and manifesting the collection of poems that she had imagined before the tools were available. In 1998 she finished these experiments, and they were eventually published on her first Web site, a project accomplished in collaboration with David Keane. That trend-setting, experimental collection represented the largest single-authored compilation of Flash™ poetry on the Internet at the time—and remained so for a few years. In 1999 Keane competed in the National Poetry Slam finals in the United States and did so again the following year. An instant celebrity as a result, she has since been invited all around the world to perform her avant-garde work at literature, music, and arts festivals. In 2000 her first collection of poems (*Torn*) was published by the now-defunct Plateau Press. In 2000 Keane was invited to do a postgraduate honors degree in arts by Griffith University (Australia).

In 2002 her collection *Poems in a Flash* won the Mayne Multimedia Award at the Adelaide Festival of Arts Literary Awards. That same year her second collection, *Ophelia's Codpiece,* was published by Post Pressed. In addition she launched a second Web site (also done in collaboration with David Keane), graduated with a B.A., and was granted a scholarship to embark on graduate work toward a Ph.D. in three-dimensional poetic natures. This was also the year that Keane founded Australia's National Poetry Week in a bid to get poetry into public spaces and therefore to expand public consciousness of poetry. She has been the director of this festival ever since.

In 2003 Keane launched the international festival "Notes to a Stranger," which invited poets all over the world to leave personal notes in their poetry books and to deposit them at designated places and times in public spaces. Poetry books were left on trains, cosmetic counters, and under the windshield wipers of police cars. Keane ran that festival for two years. She served (for those same two years) as codirector of the Queensland Poetry Festival.

Her third book, *The Transparent Lung* (Post Pressed), appeared in 2004. That year she worked on her second Flash™ poetry collection (*Scenes from a Backward Glance*) with support from Arts Queensland, and she was offered a residency as research fellow and poet in residence at Cornell University's Ornithology Lab. She was the lab's first poet in residence. During that residency she wrote and composed a collection of audio works, a spatially interactive installation, and a radio play. That year, too, she participated virtually in a liquid sound concert, which broadcast her sound poems underwater at three world-renowned spa venues in Germany. Some of that work was also published on a CD released by Important Records in the United States, and she was invited to join the Belly of the Whale group of international composers to write music for an expo in Japan.

In 2006 she participated in an Asialink Literature Residency, holding the inaugural post of poet in residence at the National Science and Technology Museum in Taiwan. During that residency she traveled to India as well, where she was inspired to write a book on traditional Ayurveda cooking that included photography, poetry, and dialogues with space (published in India by CGH Earth). Keane was granted funding by Arts Queensland to work on her third Web site, scheduled for release by the end of 2007.

Many of her creative works can be experienced online by accessing her continually updated Web sites and those of groups with which she is affiliated—for example, her Web page at e-poets.net: http://voices.e-poets.net/KeaneJF/, her principal Web site at www.poetinresidence.com, and http://www.poetrypoetry.com/TheVault.html (the Poetry Poetry online archives), to name just a few links. She is gaining renown as well for her inspirational work in poetry dissemination and curatorship in the age of electronic media.

R. Victoria Arana

KIM CHI-HA (KIM YONG-IL) (1941–)

Kim Chi-ha is regarded as a cultural icon representing Korean history of the 1970s in terms of both literature and politics. With his famous long poem "Five Robbers," which was published in the literary magazine *Sah-sahn-gkye* (World of Ideas) in 1970, Kim was catapulted to the front line of political activism against the military dictatorship and entered into a cat-and-mouse relationship with President Park Jung-hee for a decade until Park was felled by gunshots.

Kim Chi-ha was not, however, a reckless greenhorn when he submitted his manuscript of resistance poetry for publication. He anticipated the impact that his poems might have, for he was a natural leader who had inherited the spirit of protest against despotism from his father and grandfather. He was born in Mokpo, southern Korea, in 1941 to a family who had a staunch belief in democratic ideals. His grandfather was a farmer-activist who had participated in the historical Donghak Civil Disobedience Movement. His father, who was an electronic technician, put his considerable energies into communist activism and was, as a consequence, tortured so brutally that he became paralyzed on one side. Growing up with his grandfather and father, Kim gravitated almost naturally to participating in the April 19 student protest of 1960 when he was a sophomore and to playing a leading role (as a student representative of South Korea) in the National Student Association for the Unification of South and North Koreas. After the May 16 coup d'état in 1961, he became one of the principal targets of Park's military regime and had to lead the life of a renegade for two years, as a dock worker, miner, or menial laborer. In 1963 he ended his fugitive life and reenrolled at Seoul National University, and in 1964 he participated once again in the student protests calling for the cancellation of the unequal treaty between Korea and Japan. Even during this unstable life, he published five poems in 1969 in the literary magazine *The Poet* and began the career of an activist poet.

Given Kim's background in political activism, the impact of "Five Robbers" seems thoroughly calculated. In it Kim satirizes business magnates, congressmen, high-level government officials, military leaders, and cabinet members who are obsequious to Park's dictatorial regime and insensitive to the suffering of the poor, in the poetic form of what he calls *"dahm-shi,"* a modernized version of a traditional folk art genre of satire against authority (*pansori*). With the publication of this long poem, Kim broke new ground in the production of engagement poetry. Unlike other modernists who had a tendency to imitate difficult intellectual poetry of Western modernist poets, Kim reinterprets the traditional oral-narrative pulse of *pansori* through a modern-day sensibility and invites readers to experience the excitement of gripping folk images, satiric humor, and stirring cadences. However, by pointing out pro-Park supporters as enemies blocking the coming of democracy, Kim antagonized Park's regime and was imprisoned on charges of violating anticommunist acts. President Park wanted to warn intellectuals by showing that even literary works would not be exempt from legal prosecution under the criminal category of spreading dangerous ideas.

After the publication of this poem, Kim was repeatedly imprisoned on various charges and in 1974 was sentenced to death on the charge of rousing insurrection. Many domestic and international intellectuals and activist leaders, including Jean-Paul Sartre, Simone de Beauvoir, Noam Chomsky, and Howard Zinn petitioned the Park regime to spare Kim Chi-ha's life. In February 1975 he was released. Nevertheless, he was almost immediately imprisoned again on another charge and was condemned to solitary confinement until December 1980. Kim's political activism and consequent ordeal paralleled Park's rise (1963) and fall (1979).

Although he spent many of his most productive years in prison, he kept writing engagement poetry, hoping to see a democratic nation come into being during his lifetime. He wrote "WITH A BURNING THIRST" in 1982, after his release from prison.

He was awarded the prestigious Lotus Prize by the Association of Asian and African Writers in 1975. An international panel of judges paid respect to Kim Chi-ha's commitment to democracy by presenting him in 1981 with the Bruno Kreisky Award for achievements in the field of human rights and the title of "great poet." He received recognition for his outstanding literary achievements from Poetry International in 1981, the Yee-Sang Literature Prize in 1993, and both the Ji-yong Literary Award Prize and the Man-hae Literary Award in 2002. Since his release from prison, Kim has worked on an alternative philosophy of life based on traditional Korean values, and in 1998 he founded Yul-Ryo, a way of life dedicated to the promotion of those ideals. In 2003 he published a collection of prose, *The Road to Life and Peace,* in which he suggests the possibility of new, dynamic life based on the unification of the two Koreas. Some critics fault his raw emotion and claim he has not achieved a highly artistic and philosophical

vision. His ambitious *dahm-shi* form is for that reason not enthusiastically adopted by younger poets. Yet many of his *dahm-shi* are adapted to oral performance, and in most protest meetings his poetry has been sung to rouse up resistance to oppression. For many Koreans Kim Chi-ha's name is an icon of democracy in the history of Korea, as President Park's name is an icon of ruthless dictatorship.

BIBLIOGRAPHY
Kim, Chi-ha. *Heart's Agony: Selected Poems of Chiha Kim.* Edited and translated by Kim Won-jung and James Han. Buffalo, N.Y.: Whitepine Press, 2002.
McCann, David R., ed. and trans. *The Middle Hour: Selected Poems of Kim Chi Ha.* New York: Human Rights Publishing Group, 1980.

Han Ji-hee

KIM SU-YOUNG (1921–1968)

Kim Su-young is a representative modernist poet of Korea. Armored with a modernist sensibility, he urged intellectuals to take ethical responsibility for sociopolitical issues and plant their knowledge in the fertile soil of real-life action. He himself poured his commitment to political activism into his poetry and in doing so reshaped Western modernism into a Korean poetic style.

Kim was born in Seoul in 1921. Since he was the eldest son born after two deceased sons, his grandfather and father endeared him to themselves. He loved reading and writing from an early age, and with the support of a relatively affluent family, he entered Zohuku Prep School in Tokyo in 1941 after graduating from Sunryn Commerce High School in Seoul. In 1943 he returned home to avoid being drafted by the Japanese army and joined a theater company. In 1945 he published "A Song for Myojung" and began the career of a professional poet. In 1949, enjoying friendship with Kim Kyong-rin and Park In-hwan, he published a joint collection of poetry and prose titled *A New City and a Chorus of Citizens* that drew literary attention to their new modernist poetry. In this collection Kim criticized blind worship and purposeless imitation of Western modernity and urban lifestyle. It is not surprising that his new poetic sensibility made a revolutionary impact on Korean writers and that he instantly came to be considered at the core of Korean modernist poets of the 1950s. The period of the Korean War and its aftermath was an era of chaos. The war turned Korean society upside down, and Kim's life was no exception. When the North Korean army seized Seoul, he was forced to join a communist literary association and support the communist cause. But when the South Korean army, with the support of UN forces, restored Seoul, he was arrested on the charge of being a communist helper and sent to the POW camp on Guhjeh Island. There he was subjected to torture and other dehumanizing treatment. After being reclassified as a "gray" (neither communist nor right-wing conservative), he was released in 1952. His war experience and consequent psychological trauma seems to have branded in his mind the helplessness of an individual in the face of the cruelty and arbitrariness of ideology. Surviving the postwar period, he published a collection of poetry, *Play of the Moon,* in 1959. This collection portrayed the anguish and sorrow of innocent, ordinary people as well as the confusion and disillusion of intellectuals who witnessed the horrors of war while surviving in the wreckage. The drastic change in Kim's perception of poetry and society, however, was made while he was participating in the April 19 civil revolution. President Seung-man Lee and his Liberation Party committed election fraud to prolong their antidemocratic regime. When the opposition party made it a political issue and the media reported it, Lee's cabinet began to control the media, oppress intellectuals and activists, and ban "socially dangerous" meetings. Kim, witnessing another variety of absurdity in the arbitrariness of the powerful, shifted his main poetic concern from modernism to engagement. He overcame his sense of personal helplessness as a mere poet and restored the radical role of poetry in society: He stood up for those who were living at the mercy of the whims of power and spoke for them in a voice of society's conscience. Writing many poems, critical pieces, essays, and journal articles, he kept talking about the dream of democracy and freedom and suggested civil disobedience as a means to pursue those ideals. After witnessing the May 16 coup d'état led by General Park Jung-hee, Kim made his sarcasm more pungent and his spirit of resistance fiercer. Until his premature death in a traffic accident at the age of 47, he tried to keep his conscience and artistic freedom intact. Even now, his poetry and democratic vision continue to be appreciated and honored. He is remembered as a true intellectual who faced political oppression with courage, passion, and an intense sense of commitment, sentiments reflected in his poem "THE GRASS." He inspired many political activists, intellectuals, and student activists during the 1970s, 1980s, and 1990s to keep up their fighting spirit and pursue democratic ideals. Furthermore, by empowering the common people as the root of society, he is revered as a groundbreaking poet of the *minjung* (poor working class), cultivating a popular poetic genre that came to full bloom in the 1980s. Kim's name is linked with the country's civil disobedience movements, and he is honored for his famous catchphrase, "Poetry, spit at all oppressive things!"

BIBLIOGRAPHY

Brother Anthony of Taize (An Sonjae). *Variations: Three Korean Poets.* (Kim Su-Young, Shin Kyong-Nim, and Lee Si-Young.) Ithaca, N.Y.: Cornell University Press, 2001.

McCann, David R., ed. *The Columbia Anthology of Modern Korean Poetry.* New York: Columbia University Press, 2004.

Han Ji-hee

KLING, THOMAS (1957–2005)

Kling, a self-declared "historian" of languages and literary and cultural traditions was the most innovative *poeta doctus* (learned poet) in Germany at the end of the 20th century. A distinctly urban poet, Kling elaborated inventive textual juxtapositions of works from earlier epochs and the hyperreflective self-awareness of high modernism. Born in Bingen, STEFAN GEORGE's hometown, Kling grew up in Düsseldorf. After his literary studies at the Universities of Cologne, Düsseldorf, and Vienna, he spent several years in Finland. For the last 10 years of his life, he lived at a dismantled former NATO nuclear missile site in Hombroich, near Cologne, together with his partner, the painter and photographer Ute Langanky, a colleague and collaborator at one time of the most successful contemporary German painter, Gerhard Richter.

Kling's poetry performances—or what he called "speech installations," sometimes accompanied by the jazz drummer Frank Köllges—changed the reception dynamics of poetry in Germany from 1983 onward. Many of Kling's poems are organized around visual stimuli such as paintings and photographs. One can read his whole work as an experimental textual anatomy of visual violence. He collaborated on juxtapositions of text and image with Langanky, for example, in the volume *Gelände* (Terrain, 1997). His first volume of poetry was published in 1986. Among his most important contributions to 20th-century poetry are his books *morsch* (friable, 1996) and, especially, *Fernhandel* (Foreign Trade, 1999). The latter volume offers Kling's most sustained project of seismographic cultural archaeology translated into lyrical praxis, a cycle of long poems entitled and rearticulating *"Der Erste Weltkrieg"* (The First World War). The violence of the war in the trenches is evoked and complemented by ironic reflections on the media's marketing techniques of warfare. Kling's repeated, seemingly anachronistic announcement "CNN Verdun" alerts the reader that every act of writing and perception can degenerate into an opportunistic mode of embedded reporting. *Fernhandel* also contains Kling's most important exploration of Greek and Roman mythology, his *Acteon* cycle, a postmodern reconfiguration of the hunter who observes a goddess bathing and is punished by being turned by her into a stag and being devoured by his own dogs. These poems operate on highly intertextual ground, from the explicitly mentioned predecessors Ovid and Pound to the painter and writer Pierre Klossowski's series of inventive essays on Actaeon, *Le Bain de Diane* (The Bath of Diane, 1956).

Kling outlined his aesthetic program in a series of entertaining and polemical, immensely learned, yet tangible and straightforward essays, collected in his prose volumes *Itinerar* (1997) and *Botenstoffe* (Transmitters, 2001). In 1997 Kling's German translation of the Roman poet Catullus was published. His editorial merits include a volume of texts by the Austrian poet Friederike Mayröcker, published in 1998, and an anthology of German poetry since the Middle Ages, aptly entitled *Sprachspeicher* (Speech Storage, 2001).

Kling's two final poetry volumes are *Sondagen* (Soundings, 2002) and the posthumous *Auswertung der Flugdaten* (Decoding the Flight Data, 2005), a prosimetrical volume that alternates between lyrical texts and lucid, vivid, and exhilarating essays, including "Die Ausstreuung der Glieder bei Ovid" (The Distribution of Body Parts in Ovid's Work). His elegiac poem on September 11, 2001 ("MANHATTAN MOUTHSPACE TWO") first appeared in *Sondagen*.

While Kling—a recipient of numerous literary awards, including the ELSE LASKER-SCHÜLER Prize (1997) and the Peter Huchel Award (2001), and member of the prestigious German Academy for Language and Poetry—often launched polemical attacks on Germany's contemporary literary scene, he supported several younger poets, including ANJA UTLER, whom he helped to gain recognition. In his mid-forties, Kling contracted lung cancer and died in Dormagen in 2005.

Olaf Berwald

KOLATKAR, ARUN BALKRISHNA (1932–2004)

Arun Kolatkar is considered one of the most influential writers of India's postindependence period. A bilingual poet who wrote in English and Marathi, he is most famous for his two early volumes of poetry: *Jejuri* (1976) in English and *Arun Kolatkarchya Kavita* (1976) in Marathi. *Jejuri* won the Commonwealth Poetry Prize in 1977. It was so popular that three editions were quickly published to keep up with demand. Kolatkar's poetry is acclaimed for its nitty-gritty honesty, dramatic originality, and formal properties. A maverick of sorts, Kolatkar preferred to publish his works in little magazines and local periodicals of various sorts, beginning as early as 1955. Late in life, however, he published several more volumes of poetry in Marathi as well as English and gained widespread, enduring fame as one of India's most important poets.

Kolatkar was born in Kolhapur, Maharashtra, on November 1, 1932. He attended schools there and graduated from the Rajaram High School in Kolhapur. Interested in graphic arts from an early age, he enrolled in art schools in Kolhapur and Pune and earned a diploma in painting in 1957 from the J. J. School of Art in Bombay (now Mumbai), at which he had enrolled in

1949. He subsequently earned his livelihood in advertising, working for such prestigious advertising agencies as Lintas—first as graphic designer, then as art director. Kolatkar lived in Mumbai, where he was famously inaccessible and averse to publicity and self-promotion, but known to his close circle of friends as an amateur musician and darkly witty.

His early Marathi poetry was decidedly avant-garde: difficult sometimes to decipher because partly in underclass argot, modernist in its sensibility, and surreal in expressive strategy. It has been associated critically with India's Little Magazine Movement of the 1950s and 1960s. Like the poetry of America's Beat generation, Kolatkar's early Marathi poetry seems humorous while disturbing, sinister, and mischievous all at once. According to Amit Chaudhuri, it was written in what was for him "a time of reappraisal and ferment" when Kolatkar was interested in conveying "the extremities of urban and psychological experience" and the way the world looks to "a social outcast who had been dabbling in mind-altering drugs while reading up on Surrealism, William Burroughs, Dashiell Hammett, Indian mythology and Marathi devotional poets like [17th-century] Tukaram" (Chaudhuri). During this period Kolatkar translated and reworked Tukaram's "rather belligerent hymns to God" into English. Kolatkar was interested in historical versions of machismo as a way of communicating the "proximity between the disreputable, the culpable, and the religious—a living strand in Indian devotional culture and an everyday reality in places like Banaras and Jejuri" (Chaudhuri). The net result was a seamless, crossbred aesthetic. *Jejuri* and the later volume in English, *Kala Ghoda Poems* (2004), possess some of these traits and take for subject matter the working-class Kala Ghoda neighborhood of Mumbai but in general are not so daringly noir as the poems Kolatkar composed in Marathi, where he played dangerously fast and loose with the traditional properties of poetic idiom without losing expressive power. In his later Marathi works—*Chirimiri, Bhijki Vahi,* and *Droan* (all published in 2004)—where Kolatkar's poetic voice is less solipsistic and terrifying, the poems are more obviously satirical, and the social realities of Mumbai's underworld are referenced with something more like sympathy.

Sarpa Satra (2004), composed in English, is similar to *Bhijki Vahi* (2004), which, like Kolatkar's long narrative poem *Droan,* combines the representation of contemporary life in urban India with traditional myths and allegorical storytelling stratagems and offers a contemporary commentary on the ambiguities, complexities, and contradictions of life in a great Indian metropolis—a poetic commentary not so much social or cultural as, perhaps, philosophical and pragmatic. There is no hint of the ideological rhetoric associated with the political Left.

For many readers *Jejuri* represented an in-your-face version of the period's anxiety-ridden search for identity in the postcolonial era. It is a poem about the 1960s experience of an agnostic, cosmopolitan young Marathi man who visits a dilapidated temple complex at Jejuri in the company of a busload of (perhaps sincere) pilgrims. He takes note of the place as a physical reality, one—for him, at least—seemingly devoid of any consequential spirituality or current relevance. The poem conveys the modernist sense of dislocation from cultural roots of the modern metropolitan and his emphatic recognition of the shabbiness of city life wherever he happens to go for respite or illumination. In contrast, readers of the *Kala Ghoda Poems* consider this later work a milestone of a different sort for Indian poetry in English, remarkable for conveying a mature poetic vision of urban India with its "pockets of daydreaming, idling, and loitering, its loucheness," an India that contrasts in remarkable ways with that represented in the acclaimed novels of Salman Rushdie and that heads up another genealogy of literary and cinematic influence just as important as Rushdie's (Chaudhuri).

Kolatkar received the Kusumagraj Puraskar awarded by the Marathwada Shitya Parishad in 1991 and the Bahinabai Puraskar in 1995. He was six times awarded the prestigious CAG Award in the field of advertising and elected to the CAG Hall of Fame during his lifetime. He was posthumously awarded honors for *Bhijaki Vahi* by the Sahitya Akademi.

BIBLIOGRAPHY
Chaudhuri, Amit. Introduction to *Jejuri.* New York: New York Review of Books, 2006.
Islam, Khademul. "Arun Kolatkar (1932–2004): Of Coups, Quest and the Letter." *The Daily Star* 5, no. 128 (October 2, 2004).

Kolatkar, Arun. *Jejuri*. New York: New York Review of Books, 2006.

Ramnayaran, Gowri. "No Easy Answers." In *The Hindu* (September 5, 2004). Available Online. URL: http://www.thehindu.com. Accessed on April 23, 2007. Contains full text of the extraordinary "An Old Woman" from *Jejuri*.

R. Victoria Arana

KUNENE, MAZISI (1930–2006)

Mazisi Kunene is one of the most important 20th-century poets to draw inspiration exclusively from African oral traditions, in this case the Zulu language, culture, and religion. Born in Durban, South Africa, Kunene began writing poetry at a young age and had published in small local journals by the time he was 10 or 11. In 1956 he won an award for a collection of poems titled *Idlozi Elingenantethelelo* (The Unforgiving Ancestors) in the Bantu Literary Competition. After completing an M.A. in Zulu poetry at Natal University (now the University of KwaZulu-Natal) in Durban, Kunene moved to England to continue his study of Zulu poetry at the School of Oriental and African Studies in London. He put aside his academic plans while in England, however, to become involved in the movement against apartheid, the white-controlled government's policy of racial segregation and oppression of the black population in South Africa. Kunene worked with organizations such as the African National Congress (ANC), serving at different times as its UN representative and finance minister. Exiled for 34 years by the South African government for his political activism, Kunene taught at various universities, including University College of Roma in Lesotho, Stanford University, the University of Iowa, and the University of California at Los Angeles, before finally returning to South Africa in 1994, after the fall of apartheid, to teach African literature at the University of KwaZulu-Natal.

While in exile Kunene wrote in Zulu and translated his works into English, rather than composing in English, arguing that African artists creating in English found themselves drawing from European and American history and culture rather than from their own. Among Kunene's major influences are the Zulu poets Magolwane, the legendary ruler Shaka's court poet, and the 20th-century poet and critic B. W. Vilakazi.

As Ursula Barnett notes, for Kunene "the African poet's main role . . . is to express the consciousness of his people and to preserve their history and communal identity" (Barnett 106). For this spirit of commitment to the continuity of African artistic traditions Kunene was named the poet laureate of Africa by UNESCO.

Unfortunately, many of the Zulu-language versions of Kunene's early collections have remained unpublished, and thus up until recently his poetry was available primarily through his English translations. A collection entitled *Zulu Poems,* a translation of his early poetry into English, was published in 1970, followed by the epic poems *Shaka the Great: A Zulu Epic* (1979), a chronicle of the rise of the Zulu Empire in the 19th century under Shaka, and ANTHEM OF THE DECADES: A ZULU EPIC DEDICATED TO THE WOMEN OF AFRICA (1981), a philosophical exploration of the origins of human life and the symbiotic relationship between forces of creation and destruction. A collection of later short poems, *The Ancestors and the Sacred Mountain,* was published in 1982. Along with other South African writers who spoke out against the South African government, such as the poet DENNIS BRUTUS, Kunene's books were banned in his home country until the end of apartheid. After his return to South Africa, Kunene published his more recent work in Zulu, including *Isibusiso sikamhawu* (Mhawu's Benediction, 1994), *Indida yamancasakazi* (The Mystery of Women, 1995), *Amalokotho kanomkhubulwane* (Nomkhubulwane's Good Intentions/Wishes, 1996), *Umzwilili wama-Afrika* (The Canary of the Africans, 1996), and *Igudu likaSomcabeko* (Somcabeko's Horn Pipe for Dagga Smoking, 1997).

BIBLIOGRAPHY

Barnett, Ursula. *A Vision of Order: A Study of Black South African Literature in English (1914–1980).* London: Sinclair Browne, 1983.

Goodwin, Ken. *Understanding African Poetry: A Study of Ten Poets.* London: Heinemann, 1982.

Maduka, Chidi. "Poetry, Humanism, and Apartheid: A Study of Mazisi Kunene's Zulu Poems." *The Griot* 14, nos. 1 and 2 (1985): 57–72.

Ndebele, Njabulo S. *South African Literature and Culture: Rediscovery of the Ordinary.* Manchester, U.K.: Manchester University Press, 1994.

Reddy, Vasu. "The Writer as Philosopher: Interview with Mazisi Kunene." *South African Journal of African Languages* 16, no. 4 (1996): 141–144.

Emily S. Davis

KURGHINIAN, SHUSHANIK (1876–1927)

Armenia's pioneer feminist poet, Shushanik Kurghinian, was born on August 18, 1876, in Alexandrapol, Armenia, into the poor family of Harout Popolji. She wrote in her autobiography, "Sometimes father would bring his shoe-repair 'workstation' home, in order to save money, and I would work for him—demanding my wages, every single kopek. Mother, being raised in a traditional household, would reprove of my 'ill behavior toward my parent,' blaming those harmful books for corrupting me." At 17 the outspoken young woman organized the first women's faction of the Armenian Social-Democratic Hnchakian Party. Her first poem, "At Night in the Valley," appeared in 1898; the following publications raised great hostility against her. Listed as a person to be arrested for her activities against the Russian czar, hardly finishing her studies at the Olginsky Progymnasium in Alexandrapol, Kurghinian escaped to Rostov-on-Don in Russia. Her husband, Arshak Kurghinian, stayed behind and traveled occasionally to see her while she lived in exile with her children. Experiencing utmost hardship and poverty, Kurghinian nevertheless immersed herself in the revolutionary underground and wrote some of her best poems during the 1907–08 period.

In 1907 Kurghinian secretly published her first small compilation of poetry under the title *Ringing of the Dawn*. A second volume was forthcoming, but it was rejected for political reasons and never released. Her poetry gave voice to the most silenced groups and raised important social issues, such as the unjust conditions that forced poor women to lives of prostitution and penury and to die destitute. From the start of her poetic career Kurghinian used poetry to promote feminist ideals from the working class woman's perspective, envisioning a social revolution through women's struggle for equal rights and emancipation. In numerous poems—including "The Seamstress," "Sold," and "Let Us Unite"—Kurghinian addressed her sisters of burden, calling them to solidarity and urging them to break away from the chains of patriarchy. In doing so Kurghinian did not extol women as objects of beauty or motherhood, but presented them as the battered, voiceless sex—sold and appropriated into marriage.

In 1921, after long journeys in Russia, Kurghinian returned to a newly established Soviet Armenia. She actively took part in rebuilding the country and wholeheartedly believed in Russia as the powerful ally for her star-crossed homeland. Bedridden for the last years of her life, Kurghinian stayed at various hospitals for treatment of goiter. She died on November 24, 1927.

During the Soviet era, Kurghinian's poems were used only for socialist propaganda, thus undermining the artistic merit of this visionary writer and activist. As Victoria Rowe wrote, "Soviet literary criticism ignored the gender specific aspects of Kurghinian's works because they posited that socialist society would eliminate women's problems, and any specific addressing of women's issues was condemned as 'bourgeois'" (Rowe 183). In this context, cast solely as those of a proletarian poet, Kurghinian's feminist works were marginalized and remained unknown. Singling out Kurghinian from her feminist contemporaries, Rowe notes how Kurghinian's poetry added new elements to Armenian women's writing, shifting away from the elitist texts of Srpuhi Dussap, Sibyl, and Mariam Khatisian and toward the peasantry and the urban proletariat (Rowe 195). Shushanik Kurghinian remains one of the most catalytic figures of Armenian literature, a poet who dedicated her life to improving the social condition of working-class women and other outcast members of society.

BIBLIOGRAPHY

Ghazarian, Hovhannes. *Shushanik Kurghinian.* Yerevan, Armenia: National Academy of Sciences, 1955.

Ishkhanian, Bakhshi. *The Concept of Work and the Worker in the Poetry of Ada Negri, Hakob Hakobian and Shushanik Kurghinian.* Nor Nakhijevan, Armenia: 1909.

Kurghinian, Shushanik. *Literary Heritage: Poetry, Prose, Plays, Letters.* Edited by J. Mirzabekian. Yerevan, Armenia: National Academy of Sciences, 1981.

———. *I Want to Live: Poems of Shushanik Kurghinian.* Translated by Shushan Avagyan. Watertown, Mass.: AIWA Press, 2005.

———. "Let Us Unite." *The Other Voice: Armenian Women's Poetry Through the Ages.* Translated by Diana Der-Hovanessian. Watertown, Mass.: AIWA Press, 2005, p. 25.

———. *Ringing of the Dawn.* Nor Nakhijevan, Armenia: 1907.

Rowe, Victoria. *A History of Armenian Women's Writing: 1880–1922.* London: Cambridge University Press, 2003.

Shushan Avagyan

LALIĆ, IVAN (1931–1996)

The late Ivan Lalić was a Yugoslav in the truest sense of the word. Born in Belgrade and educated in Zagreb, the capitals of the former Yugoslavia's republics of Serbia and Croatia, respectively, Lalić divided most of his life between those two places.

Lalić began his publishing career in 1955 and published a total of 14 poetry collections. He made his living as senior editor of the prestigious publisher Nolit in Belgrade. In addition to his highly esteemed poetry, Lalić made a name for himself as a translator and literary critic. He translated the works of T. S. Eliot, Walt Whitman, and Friedrich Hölderlin, among others, including a modern French poetry anthology and an American poetry anthology, into Serbian (Lalić's wife, Branka Lalić, collaborated with him on the latter). Lalić's poetry has received numerous national and international awards and been widely translated. In English the American poet Charles Simic has published two collections of Lalić's work: *Fire Gardens* (1970) in collaboration with Bill Truesdale and *Roll Call of Mirrors* (1989). Francis R. Jones, Lalić's greatest champion in English, has published five collections of translations: *The Works of Love* (1981), *The Last Quarter* (1987), *The Passionate Measure* (1989), which won the 1991 European Poetry Translation Prize, *A Rusty Needle* (1996), and *Fading Contact* (1997).

Lalić's poetry reflects the interculturality of his life. Lalić was a Yugoslav poet who honored all the cultural legacies of the former Yugoslavia. In his *Dubrovnik* cycle, for instance, he explores Croatia's heritage, while his cycle on *Byzantium* gives voice to Serbia's. As Jones has noted on many occasions in his essays on the poet, Lalić's view of himself as less of a Yugoslav and more of a Mediterranean poet largely accounts for this all-inclusive and unbiased attitude.

Lalić's larger concern lies with the province of memory among the ruins in time's wake. His verse is layered with evocative imagery, the remnants of culture. Despite the elegies to culture and people throughout his work, Lalić lauds the power of memory to give wings to hope (see "MNEMOSYNE"). This perseverance of memory provides "spaces of hope," as the poem by the same name calls it, allowing life to continue by "destroying the void around it" (ll. 1, 15). His poems provide a "moderate mercy" where "light grows" (ll. 2, 17). That is perhaps Lalić's greatest triumph and most memorable accomplishment.

BIBLIOGRAPHY

Jones, Francis R. Introduction to *Fading Contact*. London: Anvil Press Poetry, 1997, 9–17.

———. Introduction to *The Passionate Measure*. London: Anvil Press Poetry, 1989, 7–12.

———. Introduction to *A Rusty Needle*. London: Anvil Press Poetry, 1996, 13–26.

Lalić, Ivan V. "The Spaces of Hope." In *The Passionate Measure,* translated by Francis R. Jones. London: Anvil Press Poetry, 1989.

Steven Teref

"LAMENT FOR IGNACIO SÁNCHEZ MEJÍAS" FEDERICO GARCÍA LORCA (1935)

"Llanto por Ignacio Sánchez Mejías," considered FEDERICO GARCÍA LORCA's masterpiece, describes the tragic death of Ignacio Sánchez Mejías, a famous bullfighter and García Lorca's close friend. A professional *torero* who loved literature and music and wrote poetry, Sánchez Mejías retired from bullfighting in 1927. Considering a comeback, he accepted an injured friend's request to replace him on August 11, 1934, in the scheduled *corrida* (bullfights) of Manzanares (Ciudad Real). Before the event many things went wrong, and the bullfighter confessed to his friends a feeling that this fight would be his last. The premonition turned to prophecy, and García Lorca, who could not be in town during the fight, arrived too late to witness it. The tragedy deeply impressed the poet, who saw in Ignacio's end a reenactment of the eternal drama: a poet meeting his fate. García Lorca had explored this theme in his earlier works; but in the "Lament," written at the height of his poetic career, the idea receives García Lorca's most personal and fullest expression.

The poem consists of four separately subtitled sections that, by revisiting the details of the fatal bullfight and paying tribute to the killed *torero*, trace the complex process of coming to terms with death. The first part, The Goring and the Death (*La cogida y la muerte*), balances terse, mesmerizing images—the bells of arsenic, a coffin with wheels, death laying eggs in the wound—against the drummed, one-verse refrain *"a las cinco de la tarde"* (at five in the afternoon). Constantly repeated, this allusion to the standard time at which bullfights begin becomes an eerie harbinger of the inevitable, a bell tolling for the dead and building up to the climax of open terror: *"¡Ay, qué terribles cinco de la tarde!"* (How horrifying, these five[s of] the afternoon!). The emotion bursts open in The Spilled Blood (*La sangre derramada*), where the poet shifts from the detached third-person to the more personal "I" that refuses to accept Ignacio's end. An emphatic leitmotif—*"¡Que no quiero verla!"* (I don't want to see it!), referring to Ignacio's blood—grows stronger throughout the poem; and its final resolute rendition *"No. / ¡¡Yo no quiero verla!!"* (No. I won't look at it, ever!) is an act of rebellion against death. In the two parts

that follow—Presence of the Body (*Cuerpo presente*) and Absence of the Soul (*Alma ausente*)—the rebellious tone gives way to confused awareness and eventual acceptance of the irreversible. But the challenge to death grows stronger when, in a tone of resigned calmness, García Lorca affirms poetry as the force to resist oblivion: *"No te conoce nadie. No. Pero yo te canto. / Yo canto para luego tu perfil y tu gracia."* (No one knows you. No one. But I sing you— / sing your profile and grace, for later on.)

In this poem García Lorca, with sublime harmony, reconciled the influences that had inspired him throughout his life. Gypsy lament, medieval ballad, and surrealist imagery—all come together to transform one bullfighter's accidental death into an expression of the universal drama of humankind. More important, the poem achieves a buildup of strength to face that drama with dignity.

BIBLIOGRAPHY
García Lorca, Federico. "Lament for Ignacio Sanchez Mejias." Translated by Alan Truebood. In *The Poetical Works of Federico García Lorca*. Vol. 2, *Collected Poems,* Christopher Maurer. New York: Farrar, Strauss and Giroux, 1991.

Alina Sokol

LANDLESS JOHN YVAN GOLL (1936–1941)

Yvan Goll's *Jean Sans Terre* is a collection of five books of interrelated poems written over eight years (from 1936 to1944). Goll maps the anguish of dispossession, the suffering and distress of the alienated human individual suffering the worst depredations of mechanization and urbanization. This aspect, especially marked in the first three volumes, is to be identified with Goll's expressionistic poetics and his vision of possible healing for human suffering in brotherhood and mutual support against oppression. The language is symbolically rich rather than forcefully immediate, *"Des moulins de fièvre / Tournent doucement / Pour moudre le rêve / Des derniers amants"* (Fevered mills / Turn sweetly / To grind the dream / Of the final lovers) (70). The figure of Jean, or Landless John as he is called in some translations of individual poems, can be identified with wanderers: sailors, vagabonds, or pilgrims; with exiles from economic and political persecution: the Diaspora of ancient Jews (he encounters Ahaseurus), and the flight from pogroms and extermination under fascist regimes. An allegorical figure, Jean represents the countless forms of homelessness. He is a modern man without faith, man alone *"Sans passeport / Sans père sans frère"* (Without passport / Without father or brother) (14), who hopes to recover some feeling for the healing power of religion, a very secular Jew who interrogates those whom he meets as well as enacts the roles of the many wandering figures the poem evokes. In becoming Jean, Yvan finds his personal freedom, discovering an inner world where there is scope for divinity, *"Et je me libère / Et je deviens Jean / Tout-à-fait sans Terre / Ange du dedans"* (And free myself / And become Jean / Even without a land / Angel of within) (114). Goll's angel is not a figure of doubt and denial, but a personification of interiority.

The sum of different representations of the human condition, Jean is Don Juan, the lover (42); he is Joan of Arc (92, 94), the figure most identified with France; but also perversely because he is Jean, a hermaphrodite, testifying to the range of brotherly identifications to which Goll opened himself in the writing of this poem. At different stages in its evolution, *Jean Sans Terre* represents a reflection of Goll's personal experience. This feature of the composition is especially true of the fourth book of the collection, written in 1944 in New York City. The fifth book contains uncollected poems and variants. These pages employ images drawn from the uncertainties of forced exile: a harbor without boats or a lighthouse without pity (in "Jean Sans Terre Reaches the Last Port") (194). Goll's language expresses unblinking realism; face to face with the polluting alienation of the industrialized New World, he compares the mouth of the Hudson to pestilent green and black fluids (in "Jean Sans Terre Salutes the Harlem River") (276). "Goll's imagery lies somewhere between cubist and surrealist techniques" (Carmody 97). The poet's insistence is on graphic specificities combined with psychological overtones: *"Si tu te dénudes / Jusqu'en ton esprit / Toute solitude / Soudain se guérit"* (If you strip bare / To your spirit / All solitude / Of a sudden cures itself) (103).

The six- and eight-syllable lines of the first three parts of *Jean Sans Terre*, rhythmically similar to the "green grow the rushes o" of English ballads, echo the measures of France's ancient *lais* of *geste* and romance; they pose an almost impossible hurdle for the translator into English. Referencing similar meters, Chaucer's host complained of the jog trot doggerel used for "The Tale of Sir Thopas." Still no English verse can equal the tightly patterned puns and rhymes of *"Femme sois ma mère / Femme sois ma mer / En qui Jean sans Père / S'oublie et se perdj* (Woman be my mother / Woman be the sea / Where fatherless Jean / Forgets himself, loses his way) (104). The most widely available English edition of *Jean Sans Terre* was published in New York City in 1958, with some guidance by Claire Goll. In 1944 four books of *Jean Sans Terre* appeared in a deluxe edition from the Grabhorn Press in San Francisco. W. H. Auden, Louise Bogan, and Allen Tate among others wrote introductory notes. Translators included many of the most notable figures in American poetry of the 1940s: Paul Goodman, Galway Kinnell, W. S. Merwin, Clark Mills, and William Carlos Williams. The order of the poems varies widely from the order in which they were composed, and the quality of the translations is uneven; nonetheless, *Jean Sans Terre* is notable testimony to 20th-century social alienation and remarkable poetry in both its imagery and its meters. (Translations are Donald Wellman's; citations, to the Glauert-Hesse edition.)

BIBLIOGRAPHY

Carmody, Francis J. *The Poetry of Yvan Goll.* Paris: Caractères, 1956.

Goll, Yvan. *Die Lyric in Vier Bänden.* Vol. 3, *Jeans Sans Terre / Johann Ohneland.* Edited by Barbara Glauert-Hesse. Berlin: Argon, 1996.

———. *Jean sans Terre.* Preface by W. H. Auden, translated by Lionel Abel, Louise Bogan, William Carlos Williams, et al. New York: Thomas Yoseloff, 1958.

Donald Wellman

"LANDSCAPES" Andrée Chedid (1949)

The poem "Landscapes" has been taken from *Selected Poems of Andrée Chedid.* The piece was originally published in *Textes pour une figure* (Texts for a Figure), Chedid's first book of French poetry, which dates back to 1949. It also reappears in the well-known *Textes pour un poème* (Texts for a Poem, 1987), a compiled volume containing poetry produced by the author between the years 1949 and 1970. "Landscapes," one of Chedid's earliest poems, is comparatively long, comprising 56 lines. It is also one of her richest in terms of the density of the archetypal images and metaphors it deploys, despite its apparent surface-level opacity. The poem illustrates the convergence of the inner and the outer worlds that is the hallmark of Chedid's entire poetic project wherein one encounters a deconstructive re-creation of a universal "primordial spiritual reality underlying physical experience" (Cochran iii).

"Landscapes" opens with an indication on the part of the poet of a reality beyond the apparent, a message that is symbolically postulated in advance through the overall opaque texture of the poem itself. The poet makes it known that obscured by physical reality and the word itself, this mysterious and silent dimension of reality remains invisible and hidden to conscious memory (*Derrière le visage et le geste / les êtres taisent leur réponse / et la parole dite alourdie / de celles qu'on ignore ou qu'on tait / devient trahison;* [Behind faces and gestures / we remain mute / and spoken words heavy / with what we ignore or keep silent / betray us]). Evoking the impossibility of "knowing" this primal source of existence ("I dare not speak for mankind / I know so little of myself"), the poet prepares the ground for the poem's second movement. Uniting two levels of experience, the poet thus proceeds, in the next stanza, to project a psychic "elsewhere" onto the body of the Earth in an attempt to "decipher and recreate the archetypal images of the subconscious" and convey complete reality (Cochran ix). The poet turns to the landscape and contemplates it as a reflection that affords her a deferred revelation, mediated through the verb, of the primal psychic impulses of the poet's individual self and of humankind, too. The projection allows the poet to return to the "deepest depths within herself where all experience is universal" (Cochran xvi).

Reconciling the temporal with the eternal, death with life, the remainder of the poem develops a sequential contemplation of varied landscapes. The poet hints at a dialectical coexistence of death and life using topographic imagery evocative of her native Mediterranean Middle East. Symbols such as "desert," "bird," "oasis," "water," "tree," "sea," and words with connotative power such as *open valleys, captive summits, untamed evergreens,* and *errant pathways* are deployed. The landscape and the natural elements that shape it—associated with the harshness of existence, worldly suffering, and death—are equally a metaphor for beauty, vibrancy, freedom, and peace. The Earth's body, endowed with primeval spiritual significance, serves as a surface reflecting the unnamable, timeless, hidden principle underlying the ebb and flow of the apparent. The outer landscape depicted also comes across as a landscape reflecting the (hostile) elements of both the inner and the outer worlds that the poet must traverse before self-realization can happen.

Chedid's poem "In the Flesh" (Prendre corps), originally published in 1979 in *Cavernes et soleils* (Caverns and Suns), is an enriching counterpoint to "Landscapes" because it may be viewed as an extension of the Chedidian concept of landscape. Here, using a less arcane code, the poet turns the flesh and body of the human into an organic and visceral landscape that is the site of the play and display of spirit.

BIBLIOGRAPHY
Chedid, Andrée. *Cavernes et soleils.* Paris: Flammarion, 1979.
———. *Textes pour une figure.* Paris: Pré-aux-Clercs, 1949.
———. *Textes pour un poème.* Paris: Flammarion, 1987.
Cochran, Judy, trans. *Selected Poems of Andrée Chedid.* New York: Edwin Mellen Press, 1995.

Shonu Nangia

LASKER-SCHÜLER, ELSE (1869–1945)

Known for her vivid wordplay and emotionally charged verse, Else Lasker-Schüler is among the most significant German poets of the early 20th century. Her identities as woman, Jew, and exiled artist each find voice in her poetry, which blends an intense subjectivity with the ever-present specter of the historical and cultural contexts in which it was created. Born in Wuppertal-Eberfeld, Germany, into an assimilated Jewish bourgeois family, Else Schüler enjoyed a happy childhood. Her intense love for her family, particularly for her mother and brother Paul, would become a recurring theme in her poetry. Having displayed talents for drawing and writing verse at an early age, Lasker-

Schüler could not suppress her imaginative, spontaneous nature as a young artist and woman. Her marriage in 1894 to the physician Berthold Lasker was accompanied by a conventional life that her adventurous nature soon found too confining. Significantly, however, Dr. Lasker brought Else to Berlin, where she established contacts with authors and writers, including Peter Hille and GOTTFRIED BENN, receiving the inspiration and means to embark on her artistic career. In 1899 Lasker-Schüler gave birth to a son, Paul, who is presumed not to be the son of Dr. Lasker, and whose ambiguous origin testifies to Else's own affinity for fantastic speculation and mystery.

In 1902 Lasker-Schüler published her first poetry volume, Styx, followed in 1905 by the more innovative Der siebente Tag (The Seventh Day), thus establishing herself as a poet of love—both erotic and spiritual—and of self-actualization. Using free verse and unusually evocative metaphors, Lasker-Schüler expressed a range of emotions, from ecstatic and adoring to despondent and searching. As her reputation grew, Lasker-Schüler adopted a bohemian lifestyle, spending much of her days in Berlin's cafés, where she conversed, wrote, and drew. Her divorce from Lasker in 1903 left her strapped economically, a situation that would become progressively worse throughout her life and lead her to seek financial help from prominent friends such as critic Karl Kraus. Though stormy and brief, her subsequent marriage to Herwarth Walden, composer and founder of the expressionist literary journal Der Sturm (The Storm), provided Lasker-Schüler with a publishing venue, further promoting her literary reputation. While writing works in other genres such as drama, prose, and the epistolary novel, Lasker-Schüler published Meine Wunder (My Miracles) in 1911. In that volume of poetry, she integrated symbols that would become recurring motifs—such as stars, hearts, and angels—as she pursued with renewed vigor the themes of love and loss. In particular, she employed intense color and fanciful imagery that find parallels in the work of expressionist painters, including her close friend Franz Marc, to whom she paid homage in her verse. Soon after appeared Lasker-Schüler's Hebräische Balladen (Hebrew Ballads, 1913), in which she lyrically rendered biblical episodes and themes, marking the poet's increasing engagement with her Jewish origins.

Lasker-Schüler's eccentric lifestyle became by this point an inextricable part of her aura: She often referred to herself as the "Prince of Thebes" and walked through Berlin's streets dressed in costume. Her refusal to conform to conventional feminine modes of behavior manifested itself in her verse, enriching and complicating her approach to questions of sexuality and identity. Her son Paul died in 1927—a tragedy from which she never fully recovered. In 1932 Lasker-Schüler was awarded the prestigious Kleist-Prize for Literature, only to be faced a few years later with exile. Lasker-Schüler's flight from Nazi Germany took her via Switzerland ultimately to Palestine, where she settled, almost penniless. Her last volume of poetry, Mein blaues Klavier (MY BLUE PIANO, 1943), eloquently and poignantly explores the themes of exile and loss. Lasker-Schüler died in Jerusalem of angina pectoris in January 1945.

BIBLIOGRAPHY

Cohn, Hans. Else Lasker-Schüler, The Broken World. London: Cambridge University Press, 1974.

Falkenberg, Betty. Else Lasker-Schüler: A Life. Jefferson, N.C.: McFarland, 2003.

Jones, Calvin N. The Literary Reputation of Else Lasker-Schüler: Criticism 1901–1993. Columbia, S.C.: Camden House, 1994.

Lasker-Schüler, Else. Concert. Translated by Jean M. Snook. Lincoln: University of Nebraska Press, 1994.

———. Hebrew Ballads and Other Poems. Translated and edited by Audri Durchslag and Jeanette Litman-Demeestère. Philadelphia: Jewish Publication Society of America, 1980.

———. Star in My Forehead: Selected Poems. Translated by Janine Canan. Duluth, Minn.: Holy Cow! Press, 2000.

———. Your Diamond Dreams Cut Open My Arteries: Poems by Else Lasker-Schüler. Translated by Robert Newton. Chapel Hill: University of North Carolina Press, 1982.

Schwertfeger, Ruth. Else Lasker-Schüler: Inside this Deathly Solitude. New York and Oxford: Berg, 1991.

Michele Ricci

"LAST WALK: HOMAGE TO PASCOLI"

EDOARDO SANGUINETI (1982)   This poem by EDOARDO SANGUINETI was originally published as part of the proceedings of a conference in 1982 devoted to the

Italian poet Giovanni Pascoli, one of the founders of modern Italian poetry, known for his innovative and musical verses rich in assonance, consonance, onomatopoeia, and linguistic and metrical virtuosity. His homage to another writer, not unusual for Sanguineti, indicates how much he honors much of the poetic tradition, despite his belonging to the *neo-Avantguardia.* Sanguineti has written poems of homage to Catullus, Goethe, and Shakespeare and has translated and adapted many poems and plays, from the classical Greeks and Dante to BERTOLT BRECHT. The dedication of "Last Walk" to Sanguineti's wife and his reference to their children signal a contrast to Pascoli, who never married nor had children and was instead a father-husband figure to his younger sisters, whom he wanted to keep together in his house, his nest (*nido*).

Sanguineti's poem is structured in seven sections and composed in free verse of long lines tied together loosely by interlinear rhymes, assonance, and consonance, as the first line makes clear: *"ti esploro, mia carne, mio oro, corpo mio, che ti spio, mia cruda carta nuda"* (I explore you, my flesh, my gold, my body, that I spy on, my crude nude paper). Sanguineti's linguistic wordplay draws attention to itself in a way Pascoli's did not, and his sense of humor far exceeds the latter's perpetual poetic sobriety. For example, the fifth section begins: *"io ti farò cucù e curuccuccù, ragazza lavandarina"* (i will coo for you and cuckoo for you, small laundry girl). What comes across most clearly is the joy with which Sanguineti weaves words to celebrate his wife, *"quella reginella ridarella, . . . quella raganella griderella, la bella sopranella / in sottanella, . . . quella stella bianca, stella nana, unica mia sovrana disumana . . ."* (that little laughing queen, . . . that yelling little frog, the beautiful little soprano / in petticoats, that white star, dwarf star, my only inhuman sovereign).

BIBLIOGRAPHY

Ballerini, L., B. Cavatorta, E. Coda, and P. Vangelisti, eds. *The Promised Land: Italian Poetry after 1975.* Los Angeles: Sun and Moon Press, 2000.

Sanguineti, Edoardo. *Libretto.* Translated by Padraig J. Daly. Dublin: Daedalus, 1999.

———. *Natural Stories #1.* Translated by Jana O'Keefe Bazzioni. Toronto: Guernica, 1998.

Jacob Blakesley

"LEDA" RAINER MARIA RILKE (1907) In this sonnet German poet RAINER MARIA RILKE does not follow the conventional Greek myth of Leda's encounter with the divine Zeus, who took the form of a swan to seduce her. Instead of a noble god descending in disguise to Earth, Rilke's Zeus is a pathetic figure, so anxious for an encounter with his chosen woman that he effectively bungles his sought-after liaison. He is even overwhelmed by the swan's beauty, and Leda—no passive recipient of the god's unwanted advance—becomes the director of the encounter: It is she who permits Zeus to advance and tames the king of the gods, who becomes "truly a swan in her lap" (l. 14). Ironically, Zeus, well known in ancient myth for his prowess and profligacy, is easily managed by Leda, so that he becomes the ravished one—by the beauty of his chosen form (a majestic swan) as well as by Leda's enthralling embrace. Readers can readily perceive Freudian tones in the depiction of Zeus falling prey to Leda's wiles, and he is clearly controlled by his desire for the feminine, while the feminine is clearly in control of the situation as Rilke presents it in this humorous version of the Greek myth.

Joseph E. Becker

LÉGER, ALEXIS   See PERSE, SAINT-JOHN.

"LESSON FROM THE *KAMA SUTRA*" MAHMUD DARWISH (2000) MAHMUD DARWISH's poetry partakes of different cultural and mythological traditions. We find in his poems allusions to seminal texts from ancient Greece, Mesopotamia, pre-Islamic Arabia, Persia, and India. In this poem the title is taken from an Indian classic on eroticism, *The Kama Sutra,* written about 2,000 years ago by Vatsyayana. *The Kama Sutra* is commonly known as a manual of physical pleasures with a description of the different positions of coitus. But Darwish's poem, while it manifestly deals with an erotic encounter, turns what is physical into a delicate portrait of passion. The sensuality is there, but also the aesthetics and poetics of lovemaking. The poem is unambiguously sensual and builds up to an orgasmic finale, yet it can be read as the consummation of any desire or longing. The beloved in the poem may be a desired woman, or a homeland to regain, or a dreamt-of Utopia.

The delicate poem uses repetition effectively. The locution "Wait for her" becomes a leitmotif. In the Arabic version, practically every other line of the poem is the imperative "Wait for her!" In the English rendition by Sinan Antoon, about half the 20-some lines open with "Wait for her . . ." This repetition gives the poem an incantatory character, as if it were a prayer in some ancient temple or a spell. The erotic content of the poem works beautifully with the form, as if the repetitive phrase is a prayer to the beloved and is simultaneously a lover's sexual thrusts into the body of the beloved. In the *ghazal* tradition of lyrics, erotic love and devotional mysticism intersect. The great Sufi poems use physical imagery to express divine longing. Thus the poem points to the flesh and the spirit, the erotic and the patriotic—all at the same time.

The poetic diction used by Darwish evokes imagery of Indian miniatures, the exquisite gardens of a Taj Mahal, and the epic passions encountered in South Asian myths and legends. The language is refined and courtly—waiting with "an azure cup," "among perfumed roses." Masculinity is implied in identifying patience as princely and knightly: "Wait for her with the patience of a horse trained for mountains, / Wait for her with the distinctive, aesthetic taste of a prince." Having created an erotic subtext, Darwish moves to underline the masculine-feminine encounter by identifying the incense as "womanly" and the sandlewood scent as "manly." When the poet writes, "Wait for her and do not rush. / If she arrives late, wait for her. / If she arrives early, wait for her," the wording suggests a manual of lovemaking with instructions to the male.

The poem is composed in the form of an apostrophe, where the poet addresses someone and tells him over and over to "wait." However, this addressee is none other than the poetic persona, the speaker himself; thus the poem is an interior monologue in which the speaking person in the poem is addressing himself. This reflexivity makes the imperative more moving, as if the speaker is telling himself not to rush and to discipline his passion so that he might achieve a sublime finale with his partner. The reader undergoes the same

subtle and disciplined excitement until reaching the blissful ending.

This type of repetition in lyrics is called "anaphora"; it indicates an imitation of thought or action. Shakespeare used it in *Richard II* (4.1: 220–224) to indicate nostalgia with its obsessive recall of the past. Darwish uses it to create a slow movement as if in a musical composition: "Wait for her to sit in the garden . . . / Wait for her so that she may breathe the air . . . / Wait for her to lift the garment. . . ." Tenderness overcomes the wild desire in offering her "water before wine," not glancing at her breasts, "the twin partridges sleeping on her chest," "touching her hand," and speaking to her "as a flute would to a frightened violin string." The final note comes at the end of the poem when the two achieve the blissful moment rendered as "the death you so desire." Here, as in Renaissance literature, *desired death* is a metaphor for orgasm and sexual fulfillment.

BIBLIOGRAPHY
Darwish, Mahmud. "Dars min Kama Sutra," *Sarir al-Ghariba* [The Stranger's Bed]. Beirut: Dar Riyad al-Rayis, 2000, 125–128.
———. "Lesson from the Kama Sutra." In *Unfortunately, It Was Paradise,* edited and translated by Munir Akash and Carolyn Forché, with Sinan Antoon and Amira El-Zein, 115–116. Berkeley: University of California Press, 2003.

Ferial J. Ghazoul

LETTERS TO A YOUNG POET RAINER MARIA RILKE (1903–1908)

Many readers have called RAINER MARIA RILKE's *Letters to a Young Poet* life altering, and many writers of all ages have felt as moved as the original recipient must have been by reading these letters. The 10 letters have been called timeless. Their message, sage advice to creative writers, is still current. Their genre appears to be prose, but they are poetry in prose.

Instead of giving pointers about writing as such to Franz Xaver Kappus, the young poet who was a student of one of Rilke's own former teachers, Rilke gives the young poet guidance on living. Rilke tells Kappus to listen to the voice within. He counsels him on the process of going inward and looking outward. All things, Rilke remarks, will influence one's writing. Inspiration comes from living—if the work is really meant to be. If the young man is to be a poet, the words, Rilke says, will come. There will be no escaping the inner need to write. He must write for himself, first and foremost—not for others.

In these letters Rilke advocates writing about what one knows, and he advocates knowing as much as is possible, starting with nature. He advocates waiting to write about love until one has experienced it well enough to describe it so perfectly to another that the poet brings this love alive to his reader. Most important, Rilke advocates patience in all things. He says with patience and learning, the time will come when words are ripe for the writer's picking, and the writer may harvest a garden worthy of a long winter. Patience is a great passion. Patience is the passion of a life lived largely alone, even in the company of others. This is something Rilke knew well at an early age. Readers of *Letters to a Young Poet* may be surprised to discover that Rilke was only 28 when he first responded to Franz Xaver Kappus.

There are several good versions of this text in English. One of the most respected is the translation of Stephen Mitchell (1984), but also of great significance is the version translated by M. D. Herter Norton (1934) and its revised edition (1954, reprinted 1962).

BIBLIOGRAPHY

The Academy of American Poets: Rainer Maria Rilke. Available online. URL: http://www.poets.org/poet.php/prmPID/295. Accessed on April 23, 2007.

Gass, William H. *Reading Rilke: Reflections on the Problems of Translation.* New York: Knopf, 1999; reprinted by Basic Books, 2000.

The Rainer Maria Rilke Archive. Available online. URL: http://us.geocities.com/renate_h/index.html. Accessed on April 23, 2007.

Rilke, Rainer Maria. *Letters to a Young Poet,* translated and introduction by Stephen Mitchell. New York: Random House, 1984.

Rilke, Rainer Maria. *Letters to a Young Poet.* Translated by M. D. Herter Norton. 1934. Rev. ed. 1954. Reprint, New York: Norton, 1962.

Geraldine Cannon Becker

"LETTER TO A POET" LÉOPOLD SÉDAR SENGHOR (1945)

Published in his first collection of poetry, *Chants d'ombre* (*Songs of Darkness* or *Shadow Songs*), "Letter to a Poet" is a short praise poem by LÉOPOLD SÉDAR SENGHOR to Martinican poet and statesman AIMÉ CÉSAIRE, to whom the piece is dedicated and directly addressed and with whom Senghor (along with LÉON DAMAS) founded the NEGRITUDE MOVEMENT. While the poem celebrates the insight of Césaire and the friendship of the two authors, it simultaneously celebrates facets of Negritude thought that they shared and, like other poems in *Chants,* transcends its specific subject through its depiction of Césaire within its discourse on Negritude.

"Letter to a Poet" is divided into three stanzas. In the first Senghor uses "Black sea gulls" (Stanza 1, l. 2) as his primary metaphor and uses imagery that both conveys a transatlantic linkage across the black diaspora and applauds the revolutionary ideology of Césaire, who had been elected to office in Martinique in 1944. The black gulls have brought the speaker "tidings" from Césaire, "mixed with spices . . . of the Islands" (3–4). This special species of gulls—which are generally not black (though some species do have black wings or wing tips)—travels across oceans. Here the unusual imagery implies a broader racial community. The gulls show Césaire's "influence" and "distinguished brow" (1. 4) and are now his "disciples . . . proud as peacocks" (1. 5), suggesting the global significance of both Césaire's political thought and the Negritude Movement itself, as well as the realization of the black pride it sought to inspire. Césaire "keep[s] their . . . zeal / From fading" through, the poem suggests, his "wake of light" (1. 8), or enlightenment.

The second stanza contrasts images of nobility and the working class and compares the persona's memory of his friend with racial memory of ancestors. Césaire is seen to have "praised the Ancestors and the legitimate princes" (2.15), to have his own "nobility" even while he, in the speaker's memory, "recline[s] royally . . . on a cushion of clear hillside" (2.11), a reference to the imagery used by the speaker in Césaire's NOTEBOOK OF A RETURN TO THE NATIVE LAND (1939). Such intertextual references indicate that the homage being paid to Césaire is simultaneously a celebration of Negritude thought. In addition, however, the praise of (black) ancestry celebrated in the Negritude Movement is here both practiced by the poem and identified as a strength of the person being praised: For his "rhyme and counterpoint" (2.16), he received the wages of poor men and the "amber hearts and soul-wrenching dance" of women. Imagery in the second stanza—much of which alludes to *Notebook of a Return* and to homage paid with a sacrifice of food or libation—thus champions Negritude thought even as it honors Césaire as its proponent. In the short third stanza, the speaker longs for his friend's return, predicts it, and uses a "mahogany tree"—and the implication that it be carved, for example, as a mask—to conclude his celebration of Césaire.

While "Letter to a Poet" may be criticized for traces of male-centered language—e.g., "bluntly fraternal greetings!" (1. 1), the spreading of Negritude thought through male "gulls like . . . boatmen" (1. 2), and the praise of Césaire through "the many plum-skin women in the harem of [his] mind" (1. 9)—such a critique does not diminish the Negritude ideals expressed by the poem.

BIBLIOGRAPHY
Senghor, Léopold Sédar. *The Collected Poetry*. Translated by Melvin Dixon. Charlottesville: University Press of Virginia, 1991.

Yasmin Y. DeGout

"LET US UNITE" SHUSHANIK KURGHINIAN (1907)

One of KURGHINIAN's famous poems calling women to solidarity in their struggle against oppression, "Let Us Unite" was first published in the volume *Ringing of the Dawn*. In this poem Kurghinian tries to raise women's self-consciousness to defy the patriarchal system that has kept them within the confines of the home, preventing them from entering the public sphere: "Enough of old wooden rules and laws / sacrificing our youthful days, / keeping us behind four walls." The fifth stanza emphasizes women's role and participation in the struggle for social justice, and their equal place by their comrades' side: "Our lucky men, the cocky boys / should not be proud, should not boast. / They could not have reached anywhere / without our help, without our care." The poet's voice, unlike the elegiac and lyric tones of her contemporaries, is brusque, demanding, and assertive. This self-righteous stance was a radical move away from

women's "angelic" poetry and the lyric style that dominated the Armenian literary salons of her contemporaries. Her language is simple but effective for the time. Like her other poems, "Let Us Unite" incorporates many dialectical terms close to the speech patterns of the working class and peasantry to whom her poetry was directed. Kurghinian "sang songs" of rebellion, scrupulously working on perfecting her rhymes and rhythms, usually iambic tetrameter, so that her stanzas could be easily remembered and learned by heart.

BIBLIOGRAPHY
Ghazarian, Hovhannes. *Shushanik Kurghinian*. Yerevan, Armenia: National Academy of Sciences, 1955.
Ishkhanian, Bakhshi. *The Concept of Work and the Worker in the Poetry of Ada Negri, Hakob Hakobian and Shushanik Kurghinian*. Nor Nakhijevan, Armenia: 1909.
Kurghinian, Shushanik. In *Literary Heritage: Poetry, Prose, Plays, Letters*, edited by J. Mirzabekian. Yerevan, Armenia: National Academy of Sciences, 1981.
———. *I Want to Live: Poems of Shushanik Kurghinian*. Translated by Shushan Avagyan. Watertown, Mass.: AIWA Press, 2005.
———. "Let Us Unite." *The Other Voice: Armenian Women's Poetry Through the Ages*, translated by Diana Der-Hovanessian. Watertown, Mass.: AIWA Press, 2005, 25.
———. *Ringing of the Dawn*. Nor Nakhijevan, Armenia: 1907.
Rowe, Victoria. *A History of Armenian Women's Writing: 1880–1922*. London: Cambridge University Press, 2003.

Shushan Avagyan

"LIFE-HOOK" JUANA DE IBARBOUROU (1919)

"Life-Hook" (*Vida-garfio*), called "Clinging to Life" in another translation, from JUANA DE IBARBOUROU's first poetry collection, *Las lenguas de diamante* (1919), shows themes and modes of expression that recur in her popular early work. The playful, almost flirtatious attitude of many of her poems here treats the usually somber notion of death as life-giving renewal, transformation, and rebirth, the continuation of life in another form. Ibarbourou's images denote a sense of physicality rather than metaphysics, no "dark night of the soul," in fact, no soul at all! Although the body will decompose and revert to atoms after death, its senses will remain intact, so that she can *hear* the laughter of birds and the charming chatter of a fountain, *feel* the sun warm her bones and the breeze cool her flesh, *see* the fierce red sunsets, *touch* the soil with hands eager to tunnel and scratch back to the surface. Her body should not be buried deep because it will struggle to make a quick transition back to life and, by implication, should be allowed to. She must not be buried among the dead but among the living, so that her body can become the physical medium in which seeds send out roots, the roots become a plant, and the plant becomes her instrument to return to Earth and continue the connection with her beloved, in one great chain of eternal evolving and being.

One can understand why Ibarbourou's portrayal of death—which ignores and thereby negates the concepts of purgatory, heaven, and hell—was considered irreligious and pagan, against which she felt forced to march out her Roman Catholic practices and later wrote two volumes of religious prose. The poem reflects no fear of death but, rather, joyous acceptance of it as a continuation of life as we know it. Love conquers all, even death.

Although this poem reflects none of Latin American modernist tropes of exotic palaces and princesses, it subtly reflects a more profound sense of the Orient in its embrace of the concept of reincarnation. In several of her writings Ibarbourou played with the idea that she might have been a shrub in a previous life. Ibarbourou's images in this poem differ from others in her works by alluding not to nature in the wild but to human-influenced nature, for example, in her references not to a flock of birds but to a birdhouse or aviary; not to a mountain stream, but to a fountain; not to seeds dispersed by the wind, but to those sown on purpose by her loved one. The original Spanish version has five stanzas of four (mostly 14-syllable) lines each, of varying rhythm, with rhyming second and fourth lines.

BIBLIOGRAPHY

Ibarbourou, Juana de. "Vida-garfio"/ "Life Hook," translated by Sophie Cabot Black and Maria Negroni. In *Twentieth-Century Latin American Poetry: A Bilingual Edition,* edited by Stephen Tapscott, 123–127. Austin: University of Texas Press, 1996.

María Roof

LIHN, ENRIQUE (1929–1988)

Known as one of the most influential Chilean poets of the 20th century, Enrique Lihn is also one of the most distinctive and independent. As a child Lihn aspired to be an artist, but he concluded that he was destined for literary, not visual, expression, although much of his poetry retains an extensive degree of sensory detail. He was influenced by his meeting with NICANOR PARRA in 1947, and his early ventures with poetic expression quickly gained force. Yet, despite his admiration for and association with Parra, Lihn was not a follower of his or of any of the other, earlier Latin American poetic movements. Later, for example, he rejected outright the "creacionismo," or creationism, of VICENTE HUIDOBRO.

Lihn's early poetry shares some similarities with PABLO NERUDA's established structures, and he was variously drawn to both Gonzalo Rojas and Nicanor Parra. Although Lihn approved of Parra's concept of the antipoem, he did not consider himself an antipoet and often returned to many of the same poetic forms rejected by Parra. Lihn's interest in antipoetry, however, suggests a recurring preoccupation throughout his own poetry. Concerned with its ability to connect with and depict reality, Lihn frequently questions the usefulness of poetry.

In 1949 Lihn published his first book of poetry, *Nada se oscurre* (Nothing Slips Away). His third book, *Poemas de este tiempo y de otro, 1949–1954* (Poems of Our Time and Another, 1949–54), published in 1955, is a turning point in his career. Lihn regarded his first two books as relatively inconsequential, though selections from them continue to be included in anthologies. In 1963, however, *La pieza oscura y otros poemas* (The Dark Room and Other Poems) confirmed Lihn's reputation as an important and influential poet. The book also establishes Lihn's interest in language and in the effects and meanings of words. Its title poem, "THE DARK ROOM" ("*La pieza oscura*"), reflects the book's interest in childhood and the evolution of the self. It also reveals Lihn's tendency to re-create or reuse previous poetic traditions, instilling in them a degree of self-criticism and mockery. An often uncomfortable and sometimes violent undertone runs through the text. Love and violence, life and death become confused and conflated with each other; his poetry suggests that their difference is merely one of interpretation, not reality.

In 1965 Lihn received a UNESCO fellowship and began his travels through Europe. Much of his subsequent poetry focused on that and subsequent explorations, including the 1966 volume *Poesia de paso* (Poetry in Passing). With his travel poetry Lihn preserves unexceptional places in poetry, emphasizing poetry's connectivity to the culture from which it springs. The 1969 volume *La musiquilla de las pobres esferas* (The Little Music of the Poor Spheres) continues to question the nature of poetry—a volume of poetry that, in effect, deconstructs poetry and language. Lihn continued to travel during the next few years, landing in Paris and Cuba before eventually returning to Chile. There he directed a poetry workshop for three years and attained the position of professor of literature at the Universidad de Chile. Both pursuits suggest another of Lihn's lasting legacies; a significant poet in his own right, he also influenced the younger generation of writers.

Lihn was already known to the English-speaking audience through the publication in 1969 of *This Endless Malice: Twenty-five Poems of Enrique Lihn*. As his popularity grew in the United States, Lihn visited New York for the first time in the early 1970s. There he gave readings and signed a contract for an English edition of *The Dark Room and Other Poems*, which was published by New Directions in 1978. In 1977, following a stint as visiting professor at the University of California, Lihn received a Guggenheim grant allowing him to continue his world travels. The poet published a number of collections reflecting those travels, including *Escrito en Cuba* (Written in Cuba, 1969) and *Pena de extrañamiento* (Sentence of Exile, 1986). In keeping with his interest in politics and culture, he often incorporated politically charged commentary into his depictions of countries and situations.

Although best known as a poet, Lihn was also productive in other genres as well. Always self-critical, Lihn destroyed plays, novels, and other writings that did not meet his expectations. His novels include *Batman en Chile* (Batman in Chile, 1972), *La orquesta de cristal* (The Crystal Orchestra, 1976), and *El arte de la palabra* (The Art of Speaking, 1980). Like his poetry, they interrogate and sometimes demolish the idea of narrative.

Chronologically Lihn succeeds both Neruda and Parra, but he retained his individual style and interests, both sometimes described as eccentric, until his death in July 1988. While fighting a battle with cancer, Lihn still managed to compose his last work, appropriately and ironically concerned with death. *Diario de muerte* (Journal of Dying, 1989), described by the critic Luis Correa-Díaz as his masterpiece, does exactly what its title suggests: It chronicles the experience of dying. This last work, then, concludes Lihn's lifelong attempt to situate poetry within a realistic context. With his last poetic words, this posthumously published work unites the real-life situation of Lihn's death with the power of his poetry.

BIBLIOGRAPHY
Correa-Díaz, Luis. "Enrique Lihn." *Dictionary of Literary Biography*. Vol. 283, *Modern Spanish American Poets, First Series*. Edited by María A. Salgado. Detroit: Gale Group, 2003, 185–190.

———. *Lengua muerta: Poesia, post-literature and erotismo en Enrique Lihn*. Rhode Island: Ediciones INTI, 1996.

Flores, Angel, ed. *Spanish American Authors: The Twentieth Century*. New York: Wilson, 1992.

Lihn, Enrique. *The Dark Room and Other Poems*. Edited by Patricio Unger, translated by Jonathan Cohen, John Felsteiner, and David Unger. New York: New Directions, 1978.

———. *This Endless Malice: Twenty-five Poems*. Translated by William Witherup and Serge Echeverria. Northwood Narros, N.H.: Lillabulero, 1969.

———. *Figures of Speech*. Translated by Dave Oliphant. Austin, Tex.: Host, 1999.

———. *If Poetry Is to Be Written Right*. Translated by Dave Oliphant. Texas City: Texas Portfolio Press, 1977.

Travis, Christopher. "Beyond the *Vanguardia*: The Dialectical Voice of Enrique Lihn." *Romance Quarterly* 49, no. 1 (2002): 61–74.

Yúdice, George. "The Poetics of Breakdown." *Review-Latin American Literature & Arts* 23 (1978): 20–24.

Winter Elliott

"LILACS AND THE ROSES, THE" LOUIS ARAGON (1940)

LOUIS ARAGON's collection *Le crève-coeur* (Heartbreak, 1941) contains 22 poems written between October 1939 and October 1940, the last nine of which express the heartbreak caused by the calamity of the German invasion of France and the subsequent occupation. The best known of them, *"Les lilas et les roses,"* first published in *Le Figaro*, owes its title to the two flowers that symbolize the two stages of the May–June 1940 war, the German invasion of the Low Countries on May 10, 1940, and of France in June. On June 14 the German army entered Paris, which surrendered without a fight; French soldiers and civilians fled toward the south of France, and an armistice was signed by Marshal Petain that marked the beginning of collaboration between the Vichy regime and Nazi Germany.

The poem consists of three eight-line stanzas framed by a single four-line stanza at the beginning and the end; it is written in the traditional French alexandrine (12-syllable) verse with different alternating rhymes (abab) in each four-line section. Aragon omits all punctuation, thereby creating an incessant flow of memories, a "whirl" (tourbillon) of seemingly loosely juxtaposed images. Syntactically, nearly all the images are the direct object of the constantly reiterated *"je n'oublierai pas"* (I shall not forget), which in large part constitutes the only principal clause. This technique of an accumulation of images without explicit interpretative connection may in Aragon's case be partly due to surrealist ideas about the operation of the unconscious, but here also creates the impression of the writer's being haunted by an uncontrollable surge of memory.

The poem begins with an evocation of the violent change brought about by the German invasion: *"Ô mois des floraisons mois des metamorphoses / Mai qui fut sans nuage et Juin poignardé"* (O months of flowering months of changes / May that was cloudless and June that was stabbed in the back). The "cloudlessness" of May expresses in a figurative and a literal sense the passivity of the French army in the first month of the "pseudo-war" (*"drôle de guerre,"* as it has been called) that was ended by the treason ("stabbing in the back") of those who did not defend France but began to collaborate with the invaders.

The second stanza recalls the "tragic illusion" (*"l'illusion tragique"*) of the Belgians, who prematurely expected an easy victory of the French and British troops over the German invaders in May 1940: *"Le triomphe imprudent qui prime la querelle"* (The unwise triumph that prevailed over the quarrel). May is the month of the lilac, which blooms only briefly; in its transience it betokens the enthusiastic greeting of the French troops in Belgium, whom the "elated populace" smothered with flowers in their "intoxicated" hope of victory: *"Entourés de lilas par un peuple grisé"* (Surrounded by lilacs by an elated populace). Again images of beauty and death are sharply juxtaposed: *"Le sang que préfigure en carmin le baiser"* (The blood that the carmine kiss foreshadows).

In the third stanza Aragon turns in a wistful and nostalgic tone to France itself as it once was: *"Je n'oublierai jamais les jardins de la France"* (I shall never forget the gardens of France). The rose as the symbol of love and beauty, standing for all that is precious in the French name and history, is shamefully repudiated by the headlong flight of French troops and civilians down rose-bordered roads: *"Le démenti des fleurs au vent de la panique / Aux soldats qui passaient sur l'aile de la peur"* (The denial of the flowers by the panicked wind / By the soldiers who passed by on the wing of fear). The personification of bicycles as "delirious" and of cannons as "ironic" and the characterization of campers as "false" have an almost dadaistic playfulness about them, expressing the pseudo-character of the *"drôle de guerre"* that was not really fought.

The "whirl of images" gains a new focal point in the next stanza. The speaker's memory recalls seemingly disconnected elements such as the village of Sainte-Marthe, a general, black foliage, and a Norman villa. They are related in Aragon's mind by the fateful news of the surrender of Paris in June 1940, which he received at Sainte-Marthe in Normandy: *"On nous a dit ce soir que Paris s'est rendu"* (They said to us that evening that Paris has surrendered). The unconnected phrase *"un général"* could be a reference to the fact that in June 1940 Charles de Gaulle fled France for England, fearing that the new collaborationist government would arrest him.

What cannot be expunged from memory is depicted in the last stanza in the image of lilacs tinged by the shadow of death: *"Douceur de l'ombre dont la mort farde les joues"* (Sweetness of the shadow by which death colors cheeks). The expression *"lilas des Flandres"* (lilacs of Flanders) alludes to the dead of another world war (the poppies of Flanders) and turns the lilacs into flowers of death. Roses, the oldest symbol of love and beauty, evoke here both the burning red of distant conflagration ("*l'incendie au loin*") and the "roses of Anjou" symbolizing the glorious French past. Through the whirl of syntactically disconnected images clustered around the symbols of the lilac and the rose, the poem transforms the traumatic events of May–June 1940 into a painful soul-searching of the French nation.

BIBLIOGRAPHY

Adereth, M. *Aragon. The Resistance Poems.* London: Grant & Cutler, 1985.

Aragon, Louis. *L'OEuvre poétique.* 2d ed., Vol. 3, Book 9. Paris: Messidor/Livre Club Diderot, 1989, 1,069–1,139.

Aragon, Louis. *Le Crève-coeur—Le Nouveau Crève-coeur.* Paris: Gallimard, 1980.

Becker, Lucille Frackman. *Louis Aragon.* New York: Twayne, 1971. Available online. URL: http://www.adpf.asso.fr/adpf-publi/folio/aragon/aragon10.html. Accessed on April 23, 2007.

Heike Grundemann

LIMA, JORGE DE (1893–1953)

Professor, doctor, poet, novelist, and essayist, Jorge de Lima distinguished himself as a multitalented and avid social commentator. Born in União dos Palmares, in the state of Alagoas, Brazil, he received his secondary schooling in Maceió (Alagoas). One of the most prolific poets of the 20th century, Jorge de Lima when only 14 composed and published his first poem, "*O acendedor de lampiões*" ("Lamplighter," 1907). In addition to sustaining his successful writing career, de Lima was also an astute physician. After studying medicine for a time in Bahia and receiving a medical degree in Rio de Janeiro, he returned to his native Alagoas (Maceió) to practice medicine. He later became director of education and health in that state.

De Lima relocated permanently in 1930 to Rio de Janeiro, where he taught Brazilian literature at the University of Brazil and took advantage of the many literary activities of that city. The poet's extensive academic pursuits, coupled with his extensive travels in his native country, provided him with experiences that led to a greater sensitivity to the social, political, and economic issues confronting Brazil. While de Lima gained fame as a poet, he also published novels and essays.

The evolution of de Lima's poetry depicts the flexibility of his writing. Scholars suggest that his poetry encompassed three phases: the Parnassian phase (characterized by his competent verse, written without inspiration), the Northeastern phase (referring to poetry inspired by the region of Brazil inhabited by significant populations of Indian- and African-ancestored people), and the religious phase. These phases represented de Lima's sensitivity to the progression and transitions of Brazilian culture. In his poetry, especially during his second phase, de Lima captured the realities of an emerging culture. Among de Lima's principal and most famous literary works are *XIV alexandrinos* (Fourteen Alexandrines, 1914); *Novos poemas* (New Poems, 1929); *A túnica inconsútil* (The Seamless Coat, 1938); *Tempo e eternidade* (Time and Eternity, 1935); *Poemas negros* (Black Poems, 1947), and *Invençao de Orfeu* (Invention of Orpheus, 1952). During de Lima's second phase he gained greatest recognition as a poet and social commentator. Although he was not the first Brazilian poet to focus on African-Brazilian themes, his "*Essa Nega Fulô*" (THAT BLACK GIRL FULÔ, 1928), later published in his *Black Poems,* stands as an example of his concerns for highlighting the importance of African influences on Brazilian cultural history. "*Essa Nega Fulô*" is de Lima's most frequently cited and anthologized poem. An excellent translation of that poem and other popular poems by this poet are found in editor Stephen Tapscott's *Twentieth-Century Latin American Poetry: A Bilingual Anthology* (University of Texas Press, 1996).

James J. Davis

"LINEAR EQUATION WITH THIS SINGLE UNKNOWN QUANTITY, A" JOSÉ EMILIO PACHECO (1978–1983)

This poem from JOSÉ EMILIO PACHECO's volume *Los trabajos del mar* (The Labors of the Sea, 1978–83) describes urban pollution. Mexico City has only one river that has not been turned into a sewer and covered by concrete. That river, however, is heavily polluted, and the sighting of a fish in it, even a half-dead one, defies expectation and leads Pacheco to reflect on ecology, life, and poetry. The first four and a half lines of "A Linear Equation with This Single Unknown Quantity" introduce elements of surprise in the sudden incongruity, and even more powerfully, the hallucinatory visual illusion, or error, of seeing a fish alive in the fetid water. The adjectives describing the water (*obscene*) and the air (*lethal*) signal a sense of moral outrage and despair. Traditional considerations of nature's elements as life-giving undergo an inversion when water and air cause poisoning and death. The end of this first sentence in the middle of line five, a caesura, creates a strong poetic pause, the equivalent of an exclamation point.

In contrast, the second half of line five and the next six lines start with an exclamatory word (literally, "What sick frenzy . . .!), use shorter phrases with no verbs (in the original Spanish), and foreground a new sense of urgency and anxiety. The observation of frenzied movement in the fish's lips repeats the disturbing image of its gasping mouth and anticipates the mobility of the round shape ("the zero of its mouth"). At this point the poem shifts meaning to another level, since the gasping mouth is perceived as a nullity, with all of *zero's* symbolic meaning, spelled out as perhaps a mouth of no significance or (for even greater despair) as a trope for no potential communication, for a message that cannot be expressed. This nothingness (or unutterable word) is ironically the ultimate (which can also mean the last) voice of nature in the Central Valley of Mexico. Who can hear that voice?

The situation of the fish is hopeless, but the poem is not just about the fish, which is anthropomorphized as having a choice, implying free will, but really referring only to the inevitable consequence of selecting one of two ghastly options, both leading to death: stay in the water and die, or breathe the air and die. Both the land and the aquatic worlds are trapped in a single environment of pollution. The poet is disquieted by the double "agony" (which also means death throes) of the water and of its living being. The poem suggests that the river, as giver of life to the fish, tragically suffers not only from its own noxious state, but also from contemplating its creation, its child fish forced to come to the surface to escape its dying life matrix and find only another form of death.

From line 14 on, the poet's denotative, detached description is abandoned, for the experience has evolved into the subjective and personal. The observer becomes the observed, as the sighting of the fish by the poet is returned to him in the fish's staring back. The inexpressible word suspected in the moving O of the fish's mouth now has become a plea from nature, its will as a living being to be heard: to have its irrevocable sentence heard, or to have its irreversible (death) sentence understood.

The poet appears to admit failure in line 19, in not knowing what the fish wished to say, but, of course, the voiceless has been given a voice, for the poet understood the inexpressible word uttered in the "omnipotent" and irrevocable "tongue of our mother death." For readers of the poem in Spanish, the "voiceless fish," *"el pez sin voz,"* replicates a conventional phrase about a man with no voice or vote, *"el hombre sin voz ni voto,"* meaning an individual who, having no voice and no vote, is ignored during governmental decision-making processes. Political connotations are suggested in the poem's metaphoric distortion. The last three lines, comprising a single sentence, generate a paradox: "I shall never know what it wished to tell, / that voiceless fish, speaking only / with the omnipotent tongue of our mother death." Since *death* appears here as the final word in the sequence of negative signifiers (*never, voiceless, only, death*), it is obvious that death itself is impregnated with the connotations of the sequence. Death (the commonality we share with the fish), therefore, is determined as a lack of recurrence (never), as a sociopolitically powerless status (voiceless fish), and as a handicap or limitation (a fish *only* capable of speaking the language of death). Death, not nature, is defined as our mother. Therefore, our common nature (death) is social as well as spiritual; it defines us as lacking power and also makes us incapable of reaching out to other creatures to understand them.

Pacheco has taken an ecological issue to an existential level, since he recognizes the incompetence of death as latent in all that exists, or at least in all that exists now in our endangered or already destroyed ecologies and societies. Another message of the poem is that humankind's destructiveness affects us at the spiritual level and impedes us from reaching out to or communicating with what is different, yet shares our basic conditions of life and mortality. The tragedy presented to the reader is complete, for the poet can describe the devastation caused by human actions, but he feels he cannot interpret nature.

Hispanic poets of Pacheco's generation frequently express the notion that poetry has abandoned the romantic idea of the visionary or prophetic poetic voice. The claim that the poet is an ordinary citizen, who shares with the rest of us the common and unremarkable experience of living in pragmatic and technically oriented societies, was established in the Hispanic world during the 1960s. Pacheco's nostalgia for the poetry of romanticism has to do not with the authority the poet enjoyed as a prophet, but with the loss of some presumed qualities, such as, in this case, the ability to understand nature. Contemporary Hispanic poets have lost metaphysical empathy with nature, and Pacheco perceives this loss as a handicap produced by so much destruction in our world; for poets are also human and connected to their own human environment. Just as human beings lose compassion or are trapped by indifference in relation to their surroundings, so poets become impoverished, their interpretive and communicative faculties diminished.

In its formal aspect the final tercet integrates the suffering and shortcomings of our present condition into a uniform verse form and a graceful, clear, and simple sentence. The line pauses also coincide with the logical grammatical pauses and deliver meaning in a straightforward manner. Therefore, the form of the tercet builds a semiotic value, that of harmony, in opposition to the semantic content, with is disconnection and destruction. The tension between form and content was clearly explored in 16th- and 17th-century Spanish baroque poetry and in modernism at the turn of the 20th century in Hispanic America. But Pacheco adds a dramatic contrast between the final three lines and the more contemporary irregular expression in lines 6–11. By doing this the poet seems to imply that poetry is a complex instance, capable of absorbing and integrating extreme forms of communication and representation; perhaps he is telling us that at least through poetry, we can reinvent or "recycle," and therefore save a world that is in the past. Unlike the politics of ecology, poetry is capable of such miracles.

BIBLIOGRAPHY

Pacheco, José Emilio. *Selected Poems.* Edited by George McWirter, translated by Thomas Hoeksema, George McWhirter, Alastar Reid, et al. New York: New Directions, 1987. Poem "A Linear Equation" translated by George McWirter, 168.

Emilia Mondragón

"LOOKING FOR POETRY" CARLOS DRUMMOND DE ANDRADE (1945)   In "Looking for Poetry," from *A rosa do povo* (Rose of the People, 1945), CARLOS DRUMMOND DE ANDRADE investigates the writing process through a succession of negations. As the title suggests, patience and the ability to respect poetry's caprices are essential qualities of a poet. In the first stanza daily events and personal feelings are deemed useless for poetry, for poetry remains impassible before life's complications and human suffering ("Next to it [poetry], life is a static sun / without warmth or light"). In the second stanza the speaker touches upon remembrance, a recurrent theme in Drummond de Andrade's works, only to deny its crucial significance to poetry. The "secret of houses"—family life—and the "movement of machines" (which refers to society's recent changes) are described as unacceptable subject matters since poetry "leaves out subject and object." Riches, history, tradition, pain, and love are all proven ephemeral, and therefore worthless, by the destructive action of time, whose selective ability becomes an ally to poetry ("What faded was not poetry. / What broke was not crystal"). As the fifth stanza states, neither the mirror (the poet's present image) nor memory (the account of the poet's past) can be considered the keys to writing poetry. In the poem's first five stanzas (which include 13 imperative forms in the original) events, feelings, memory, and history are eliminated as possible key elements, or themes. It may seem at this point that readers are left with nothing, and one could ask, What is left for its author, Carlos Drummond de Andrade, whose works ("Caso do vestido" [Story of the Dress] in *A rosa do povo* and "Viagem na família" [Traveling in the Family] in *José,* for example) so often explore the themes that are discarded here?

The last four stanzas resolve readers' apprehensions by presenting the "kingdom of words," a place where poems find themselves "in dictionary condition," dormant and waiting to be written. Extreme care is an important quality for those responsible for the poems' awakening. True poets must live with each emergent poem and understand its needs and demands, "its command of words / and its command of silence." According to "Looking for Poetry," poets are responsible for arranging words in a way that some of their manifold latent meanings can become available to readers. Without poets the words would "hide in the night" and be forgotten. Toward the end of the poem it becomes clear that Drummond de Andrade does not intend to restrict the scope of certain poetic themes by describing them as "unacceptable." As his own works prove, any event can become the theme of a poem. In "Looking for Poetry," its speaker points to the useless-ness, nonetheless, of good ideas and true feelings in the absence of a close relationship between poet and words. As this poem suggests, the writer's ability to invite readers to explore hidden facets of words is the most challenging aspect of being a poet.

BIBLIOGRAPHY
Drummond de Andrade, Carlos. *Travelling in the Family: Selected Poems.* Edited by Thomas Colchie and Mark Strand, translated by Elizabeth Bishop and Gregory Rabassa. New York and Toronto: Random House of Canada, 1986, 50–51.

Luciana Namorato

MA ANANDAMAYEE, SHREE SHREE

(1896–1982) Shree Shree (or Sri) Ma Anandamayee was born on April 30, 1896, in the village of Kheora in the Brahmanbari District of East Bengal (now Bangladesh) to Shri Bipin Behari Bhattacharya and Mokshada Sundari Devi. Her parents gave her the name Nirmala Sundari. From childhood she was exceptional in many respects, especially in her tendency to go into trances (*sadhana*) while listening to *kirtanas* (devotional music). These trances anticipated her *mahabhava* (supreme divine state). She also was in the poetical habit—like the mystics of ancient times—of talking to objects of nature, like trees and wind, and also to her own shimmering reflection in the water. She would also ask questions of her parents and elders that were often of a metaphysical or universal nature—about the image of God, the name of God, the essence of *kirtanas,* and the multiplicity of life forms.

According to the child-marriage custom of that time in Bengal, Nirmala Sundari was married at the age of 12 years and ten months, on February 7, 1909, to Sri Ramani Mohan Chakroborty (also known as Bholanath Pitaji) of the Atpara village of Bikrampur in Dhaka. They did not live in a *sangsaric,* or conjugal, manner till she was an adult. Subsequently, in December 1922 Bholanath received *diksha* (initiation) from Ma herself and thus became her worthy disciple. Two others of Ma's devoted disciples were Gurupriyadevi and Bhaji. It was the latter who started addressing her as "Ma Anandamayee" (Bliss-Bestowing Mother) after witness-

ing a moment of radiant joy on her face in the Siddheswari Kali temple in Dhaka. Gurupriyadevi, the daughter of a civil surgeon and Ma's closest female devotee, later took charge of the administration of the various ashrams of Ma across northern and eastern India. She also kept the invaluable records of Ma's *Lila* (the divine "play" of her last 20 years)—accounts of her sayings (known as *Matri Vani*) that have been published in 17 volumes in Bengali, Hindi, and English.

Ma had disciples from many religions and from various parts of India and the world. Prime Minister Jawaharlal Nehru and, later, his daughter Prime Minister Indira Gandhi, were both closely associated with her. To all she extended her unbounded love and radiant knowledge: "The light of the world comes and goes, it is unstable. The Light (i.e., the eternal) can never be extinguished. By this light you behold the outer light and everything in the universe: it is only because it shines ever within you that you can perceive the outer light. Whatever appears to you in the universe is due solely to that great Light within you, and only because the Supreme Knowledge of the essence of things lies hidden in the depths of your being is it possible for you to assume knowledge of any kind" (*Matri Vani*).

Swami Sivananda Sarswati Majaraj, founder of the Divine Life Society, was a great admirer of Ma Anandamayee and often eulogized her contribution to the being and becoming of modern India: "Shree Anandamayee is one of the finest flowers of the Indian mystical life; she is the best image to contemporary consciousness of the silent and radiant greatness of a God-intoxicated individual. In her we find the brooding East brought into a dynamic realization, in everyday life, of the transcendental states of spiritual awareness and being. She is one of the most shining diamonds in the luminous crown of contemporary Indian spiritual life." Ma herself never set down her thoughts in writing, but her disciples collected and published them, deeming them as the purest and holiest of poetic language.

Rupendra Guha Majumdar

MACHADO, ANTONIO (1875–1939) Antonio Machado is regarded in Spain as the greatest Spanish-language poet of the 20th century—some even say since the 1600s. But he did not enjoy this reputation during his lifetime. He was born in Seville in July 1875, the son of a lawyer from a long line of free-thinking intellectuals. He was sent by his cosmopolitan parents to one of Madrid's most innovative independent schools, where he received a progressive education in humane letters, languages, and literature. The Spanish-American War of 1898 and his trip to Paris in 1899 profoundly affected his artistic development and inspired his first collection of poems, *Soledades* (Solitude, 1903), as well as its second, greatly expanded edition, *Soledades. Galerías. Otros poemas* (1907), a brilliant gathering of distinctly postsymbolist temper. By teaching—at first the French language, then Spanish literature—in the town of Soria, in Castile, Machado earned enough to marry his 15-year-old child bride, Leonor, in 1909; when she died two years later, he fell into a nearly suicidal depression, from which he was lifted somewhat by the success of his second volume of verse, *Campos de Castilla,* published that same year. During an earlier brief visit to Paris, he had attended lectures by the French philosopher Henri Bergson, an association that deepened Machado's aesthetic appreciation of the value of temporal rhythms in art as in life, a major feature of his art. After Leonor's death Machado requested to be transferred to Baeza, in Andalusia, where he began his serious study of philosophy with, among others, José Ortega y Gasset. After his move to Segovia in 1919, Machado's poetry, having

by then matured somewhat, began to reflect his intellectual involvement in the liberal republican political movements of that city. In 1928 he met the poet Pilar de Valderrama, the addressee of his famous "Guiomar" love poems. She was a married woman, and their affair, never apparently consummated, ended with the onset of the Spanish civil war (1936–39). The poems that emerged from Machado's impassioned defense of Spanish liberalism, which he signed "Juan de Mairena" and which were published all together in 1937, branded him a troublemaker, and he was forced to flee from Spain in January 1939. He died a month later in southern France. From 1939 until the late 1960s, Machado's poetry was officially silenced in Spain by the Franco government. Today critics laud his windswept poetry for its strength and vitality. Machado had an exquisite appreciation for the clarity and nuances of the Spanish language: His poetry—metrically disciplined, musical, and sonorous—works in ways that no English translation can quite imitate. Alan S. Trueblood's translations in the bilingual, wide-ranging scholarly edition of Machado's *Selected Poems* (Harvard University Press, 1982) are the best.

R. Victoria Arana

MAHAPATRA, JAYANTA (1928–) Jayanta Mahapatra is a well-known Indian poet who has created a distinctive voice as an Indian writing in English, marked by a sensuous and meditative rendering of his native Indian milieu, with particular reference to his origins in the eastern Indian state of Orissa. Born to middle-class parents in Cuttack in 1928 and educated in the local missionary Stewart School and Ravenshaw College and, later, in Science College, Patna, Mahapatra earned a master's degree in physics and began teaching at his alma mater in 1949. He continued teaching physics until 1986. Mahapatra started writing stories and poems in English in his early forties, gradually concentrating on poetry and working determinedly to hone a style all his own. Simultaneously, he brought out a literary journal, *Chandrabhaga* (1979–85), a platform for new Indian writing in English. Within a decade Mahapatra found his poetic voice. He fleshed out reminiscence in an emotive language of longing

and loss, which somehow transcended the immediate moment conjured in the poem, to suggest to the reader broader vistas of meaning and experience. Mahapatra's impressive output includes, among other publications, *A Rain of Rites* (Athens: University of Georgia Press, 1976), *Relationship* (New York: Greenfield Review Press, 1980), *Life Signs* (New Delhi: Oxford University Press, 1983), *Temple* (Sydney: Dangaroo Press, 1989), and *A Whiteness of Bones* (New Delhi: Viking Penguin, 1992). Mahapatra won the prestigious Jacob Gladstein Memorial Award (Chicago) in 1975. At the national level he was the first poet writing in English to win the National Academy of Letters (Sahitya Akademi) Award in 1981 for RELATIONSHIP. In 1995 he was honored with the Gangadhar Meher National Award for Poetry. Among contemporary Indian poets writing in English, Mahapatra has established himself as a poet of singular vision and power.

Mahapatra's poetry draws its inspiration from its Oriya roots and sensibility. He has also translated Oriya stories and poems. His attempts at writing poetry in Oriya, published in two collections, do not match his level of achievement in English. But he likes to style himself as an Oriya poet who accidentally writes in English. All the same, Mahapatra's poetic output can be linked to two different traditions—the Western modernist tradition of Ezra Pound, T. S. Eliot, and PABLO NERUDA on the one hand, and the oral traditions of Indian poetry and the metaphysical concerns of important 17th-century Oriya religious poets, such as Salabega, on the other. In his stark precision Mahapatra displays the virtuosity of early Eliot; but in his desire to touch the unknown and mysterious bases of human existence (as in his ability to nudge everyday reality to reveal unperceived webs of association), he expresses the cosmic consciousness of classical Indian poetry. The opening lines of "Dawn at Puri" from *A Rain of Rites* (1976) illustrates this effort: "Endless crow noises./ A skull on the holy sands / tilts its empty country towards hunger." The lines also convey Mahapatra's characteristic attachment to Orissa's landscape and people. While most Western commentators are drawn toward memory's work in his poetry—Bruce King calls it a "poetry of inner spaces" (King 195)—emphasizing subjective feelings and private associations, Mahapatra

himself has sought to move in a direction that connects his work to the shared history and experiences of his native culture. In a piece he wrote for a national newspaper a few years ago, Mahapatra says: ". . . much of Indian poetry in English appears lifeless, stuck in the mire of trifling intimacies, without the arms of history and tradition." In his more ambitious, longer works, such as *Relationship* and *Temple,* he tries to represent broad swathes of social life, loss, and suffering interfused with a poet's special vision of recuperative beauty. Although not explicitly political, many of his later poems address problems of hate and hunger in a strife-torn world.

BIBLIOGRAPHY
King, Bruce. *Modern Indian Poetry in English.* Delhi: Oxford University Press, 1987.
Mahapatra, Jayanta. *Selected Poems.* Delhi: Oxford University Press, 1987.
Mahapatra, Jayanta. "Hedging the Heart." *The Hindu.* Available online. URL: http://www.hinduonnet.com/thehindu/2001/03/18/stories/1318067e.htm. Accessed on March 18, 2001.
Shankar, R. *Jayanta Mahapatra the Poet: Quest for Identity.* New Delhi: Prestige, 2003.

R. S. Nanda

MANDELSTAM, OSIP YEMILYEVICH (MANDELSHTAM AND MANDEL'SHTAM) (1891–1938)

Considered one of the four most important Russian poets of the 20th century, along with ANNA AKHMATOVA, BORIS PASTERNAK, and MARINA TSVETAEVA, Mandelstam became part of the Poet's Guild with Nikolay Gumilyov (who was executed in 1921) and Sergei Gorodetsky in 1911. Two years later he published his first collection of poems, *The Stone (Kamyen),* and wrote the Acmeist manifesto, *The Morning of Acmeism (Utro akmeizma,* 1919). Acmeism, like other early 20th-century literary movements, was a rejection of obscure symbolism in favor of clear and precise presentation and meaning. The acmeists infused the sharp imagistic clarity of their poetry with the modernistic depth and breadth of their sophisticated education in classics, history, and art. Mandelstam is considered by many the most important Russian poet since Pushkin.

Osip Mandelstam was born in Warsaw into a family of middle-class Jewish intellectuals, raised in St. Petersburg, and educated at an elite boys' school. After graduation in 1907, he traveled and studied in Paris, Heidelberg, and again in St. Petersburg, after his 1911 conversion to Christianity, but never completed a degree. His poems first appeared in journals in 1910, but after his marriage and the publication of his second collection, *Tristia* (which means "Sorrows"), both in 1922, his poetic output began to slow and stopped completely in 1925. He turned his attentions to prose, writing memoir, fiction, and criticism. His critical work was collected in *On Poetry* (*O poezii,* 1928) and subsequently has had a significant impact on Russian scholarship. To earn a living Mandelstam worked as a translator of literary works into Russian. His commissioned trip to Armenia (resulting from the patronage of Bolshevik revolutionary and intellectual Nikolay Bukharin) to report on the Soviet Five-year Plan there resulted in his travel memoir *Journey to Armenia* (*Puteshestvie v Armeniiu,* 1933) and in his return to poetry. His poems present significant challenges for translators, in addition to those normally encountered in such a process, in that the formal complexity of meter and rhyme are not readily translatable from Russian, yet are essential to his poems' content. After 1933, when his acclaimed *Conversation about Dante* (*Razgovor, o Dante*) also appeared, he was neither published again during his lifetime nor for a long period following his death. Nevertheless, he wrote presciently in one short poem that although he sees himself among myriad victims, he will be resurrected and speak. Not until after Stalin's death in 1953 did Mandelstam's work and reputation begin their long rehabilitation.

His opposition to Stalinist repression, coupled with his conviction that it is the responsibility of the poet to write the truth, led him to compose one of the best-known poems of the period: "THE STALIN EPIGRAM." The lyric is a scathing condemnation of the totalitarian leader and his regime. This dangerous poem and many others survive because they were committed to memory, particularly by his wife, Nadezhda, his "beggar-woman for companion" during the "dreadful joy, lovely poverty," as he described his Voronezh exile in an untitled poem (translated by James Greene, 1978)

from the collected works (*Sobraniye sochineniy,* 1967). Denounced in 1934 by one of his friends, Mandelstam suffered interrogation and exile, but his life was spared. He suffered sufficient mental distress that he attempted suicide during a hospital confinement and then spent the remainder of his three-year sentence living in Voronezh, where he wrote the poems collected in *Voronezh Notebooks* (*Voronezhkskiye tetradi,* 1980). Only one year later he was denounced for the second time for anti-Soviet activity and sentenced to five years of labor. He died at a transit camp near Vladivostok in December 1938 and was buried in a common grave, "the emblematic martyr of poetry under Communism" (Kirsch). His wife's memoirs are important for the story they tell about the way she saved his poems for posterity.

BIBLIOGRAPHY

Cavanagh, Clare. Osip *Mandelstam and the Modernist Creation of Tradition.* Princeton, N.J.: Princeton University Press, 1995.

Doherty, Justin. The *Acmeist Movement in Russian Poetry: Culture and the Word.* Oxford: Clarendon Press, 1995.

Freidin, Gregory. A *Coat of Many Colors: Osip Mandelstam and His Mythologies of Self-Presentation.* Berkeley: University of California Press, 1987.

———. "Mandelshtam, Osip Emilyevich." Gregory Freidin's Selected Publications. Available online. URL: http://www.stanford.edu/~gfreidin/Publications/mandelstam/mandelshtam_web02.pdf. Downloaded on June 22, 2005.

Harris, Jane Gary. *Osip Mandelstam.* Boston: Twayne, 1988.

Kirsch, Adam. "Poetic Injustice." Nextbook. Available online. URL: http://nextbook.org/cultural/feature.html?id=38. Accessed on July 29, 2004.

Mandelstam, Nadezhda. *Hope Abandoned.* Translated by Max Hayward. New York: Atheneum, 1974.

———. *Hope Against Hope: A Memoir.* Translated by Max Hayward, introduction by Clarence Brown. New York: Atheneum, 1970; reissued New York: Modern Library, 1999.

A. Mary Murphy

"MANHATTAN MOUTHSPACE TWO"
THOMAS KLING (2001) During an unpublished conversation in Cologne, Germany, in 2003, two years before his premature death, THOMAS KLING, who had visited New York City briefly a decade before and who

planned to visit the United States for a series of poetry readings in the near future, emphasized that New York was the most central city in his imagination, a polysemic myth and inexhaustible intercultural network of voices. A few days after the September 11 attacks on the World Trade Center, Kling wrote "Manhattan Mouthspace Two" as a literary monument to the victims who died in the Twin Towers, an elegy whose textual disintegration traces their dying. Kling's text, which consists of 21 numbered segments, was first published in the influential literary magazine *manuskripte* in 2001. One year later it became the opening part of his poetry volume *Sondagen* (Soundings).

Together with W. S. Merwin's moving apostrophic poem "To the Words" (2001), *"manhattan mundraum 2"* (Manhattan Mouthspace Two) remains the most complex lyrical articulation of mourning in the context of the killings. While Merwin's elegy (a grieving, gentle apostrophe to language itself) refrains from rearticulating the grim details of the deaths, Kling forces the reader to reconstitute the presence of suffering. The poem is a spontaneous sequel to an earlier *"manhattan mundraum"* by Kling, which is organized along ludic correlations with FEDERICO GARCÍA LORCA's poetry cycle *Poeta en Nueva York* (written 1929–30), incorporates images of the Museum of Natural History, and fuses an urban landscape with an x-rayed anatomy of Manhattan as a mouth whose teeth are the towering buildings.

Biblical rhetorical elements, variations of a psalm and gospel song, alternate with explicit insertions of Islamic terms and are contrasted with fragmented quotations from the trapped victims' final cell-phone calls while the ceilings are coming down. Kling creates a moving approximate mimesis through rhythm. Ashes, *"todtnmehl"* (flour of death/of the dead), permeate the poem. As Kling highlighted during a private dialogue, the text's graphic design not only thematizes but also performs a self-implosion and becomes visibly fragmented.

As in many of his poems that perform the process of mourning, *"manhattan mundraum 2"* simultaneously reflects on the installation of the dead as part of an exhibition (for example, in his elegy "Retina Scans," first published in 2000, where a recently exhumed prehistoric young female body is mourned and at the same time displayed as being displayed). Kling's lyrical reporters are at the same time emotionally involved and capable of assessing the costs of visual representation. The specular "I" conducts a self-as-media-critique. Far from being mutually exclusive, emotional immediacy and a sustained awareness of visual arrangements of victimhood support and amplify each other in Kling's poem, as they do in his challenging and indispensable entire work.

The poet Michael Hofmann's concise translation was published in Thomas Wohlfahrt and Tobias Lehmkuhl's groundbreaking bilingual anthology of works by young German poets.

BIBLIOGRAPHY

Kling, Thomas. "Manhattan Mouthspace Two." Translated by Michael Hofmann. In *Mouth to Mouth: Contemporary German Poetry in Translation,* edited by Thomas Wohlfahrt and Tobias Lehmkuhl, 18–13. Newcastle, Australia: Giramondo, 2004.

Olaf Berwald

MANSOUR, JOYCE (1928–1986)

Joyce Mansour wrote 16 volumes in French of radical, female-centered surrealist poetry as well as a number of prose and dramatic works. With her first collection of poems, *Cris* (SCREAMS, 1953), she quickly acquired international celebrity as an uninhibited and explosive talent, a poet whose works bristled with erotic, orgiastic, and captivating imagery. Conservative readers, however, were appalled to find instance after instance of taboo words— *labia, penis, pubis, testicles, sperm,* and so on—liberally scattered through her poems. Mansour's poetry was celebrated and embraced by some, deplored and denounced by others—but all agreed that it was deliberately perverse and often very violent. Mansour's poetry was avant-garde not merely in its exploitation of sexual references (e.g., "Break everything,/ Smash the image of the paternal penis"); it was revolutionary especially because it was feminist and focused—from a libertine female persona's perspective—on many other matters long considered too indelicate or in-your-face for lyrical poetry. Mansour's most fundamental concern was Eros: "love and its multiform manifestations (filial, paternal, maternal, sadistic, incestuous, hermaphroditic, lesbian, 'natural,' demonic, intellectual, etc.)." (Denariez Pohlmann 10). Just like the surrealist male, Mansour communicated ideas about life in the 20th century: its crucial challenges to individual freedoms, the arts, sanity, desire, and culture. Her treatments of these topics were complex but transparently clear at the same time. Her poem "I Want to Sleep with You" ("*Je veux dormir avec toi*"), from *Déchirures* (TORN APART, 1955), appears on numerous Internet sites and exemplifies her style.

A major characteristic of Mansour's work is its oneiric mutability: Her poems capture the poet's changing moods, her quicksilver shifts from nihilistic to pantheistic points of view, from visionary to furious ways of thinking, from sadism to bitter or droll humor. Mansour's dislocations of expectations and her startling juxtapositions of images, together with her incantatory phrasing, create a hallucinatory effect: "to crystallize chaos" and "to intensify existence rather than diffuse it" (Denariez Pohlmann 13). Because of its vertiginous and ecstatic emotional dynamics, Mansour's poetry lends itself readily to oral, or dramatic, performance; not surprisingly, many of her lyrics have been set to music and performed (in the original French) by well-known singers, including Ouroboros. Today her lyrics are famous, especially in France, and available on music CDs there and in Francophone regions around the world.

The daughter of Jewish-Egyptian parents, Joyce Patricia Adès was born in Bowden, England, because, it is said, her mother wanted her to have an English passport. When the baby was just a month old, her parents returned with her to Cairo, where the poet grew up, attended school, and excelled at running, high jumping, and dressage. Her mother died when Joyce was 15 years old. Various artists have commented on Mansour's works, but little is known about her personal life. Once, when Mansour was asked for an autobiographical piece, she responded with six words: "Autocratical, Autocritical, Autodidactical, Automasticator, Autochewer, Autoerotical" (TORN APART, front matter). She was admired for her physical beauty and potent personality. She married young. Her (first) husband, however, disappeared just six months after their wedding. That did not slow her down. In young womanhood she read between 250 and 300 books a year (Gavronsky 5). While still in Egypt, she met the Egyptian surrealist poet George Henein (1914–73) and made many other literary contacts. She had a voracious interest in life and literature.

Her second husband, Samir Mansour, an "Egyptian playboy," encouraged his wife's artistic interests. In the spirit of adventure Samir and Joyce Mansour took up residence in Paris in 1953, acquiring and furnishing a "sumptuous art-filled apartment in the sixteenth arrondissement" (Gavronsky 6). There they consorted with and entertained poets, socialites, and affluent expatriates from around the world, including, for instance, Jean Claude Abreu, the Paris-born scion of the wealthy Cuban Abreu family. Almost immediately Joyce Mansour drew into her circle of friends and acquaintances some of the most renowned surrealists, among them LOUIS ARAGON, ANDRÉ BRETON, RENÉ CHAR, and PAUL ÉLUARD. She collaborated with many of them in impromptu ways, and several of her published works were generously illustrated by well-known surrealist painters and draughtsmen.

Mansour died of cancer in 1986 at the age of 58. Her husband participated actively in the collection and publication of her complete works.

BIBLIOGRAPHY

Denariez Pohlmann, Karin. *Surrealism: Joyce Mansour's All That.* Paris: La Pensée Universelle, 1995.

Gavronsky, Serge. "Joyce Mansour (1928–1986): Eater of Man-Words." Introduction to Mansour's *Screams.* Translated and with an introduction by Serge Gavronsky. Sausalito, Calif. Post-Apollo Press, 1995.

Mansour, Joyce. *Prose et poésie, oeuvre complète (1953–1986).* Arles, France: Actes Sud, 1991.

———. *Screams.* Translated and with an introduction by Serge Gavronsky. Sausalito, Calif.: Post-Apollo Press, 1995.

———. *Torn Apart / Déchirures.* Translated and with an introduction by Serge Gavronsky. Fayetteville, Ark., New York: Bitter Oleander Press, 1999.

Marks, Elaine. "Women and Literature in France (Review essay)." *Signs* 3, no. 4 (Summer 1978): 832–842.

Matthews, J. H. *Joyce Mansour.* Amsterdam: Editions Rodipi, 1985. In French.

DISCOGRAPHY

Ouroboros. (Singer). *Poètes et Chansons: Joyce Mansour.* Paris: Epm Musique (Buda Records/CD Audio release), 2004.

Voice with instrumental accompaniment: guitars, accordion, alto sax, trumpet, cello, double bass, percussion.

R. Victoria Arana

"MAN WALKS BY WITH A LOAF OF BREAD ON HIS SHOULDER, A" CÉSAR VALLEJO (1927–1939)

At a time when the arts in European capitals tended toward "art for art's sake," not realism or social concern, CÉSAR VALLEJO delineated the paradox of conscientious intellectuals whose life of the mind involves metaphysical concerns, while their daily lives evolve in a deficient physical world. This poem—which catalogs the deprivation of the poor and the spiritual bankruptcy of many others—is one of his clearest expressions of this lived duality, for how can writers be concerned with abstractions (including those of the social sciences, philosophy, and aesthetics) when marginalized people live in horrid conditions? The social concern that was evident in Vallejo's first poetry collection in 1918 continued into later works such as this one.

This poem sets up paired contrasts between concrete realities (cracking lice, spitting blood, digging for food in trash bins, and so on) and the topics discussed by psychologists, philosophers, and artists of its time. The use of "I" indicates the poet's disconformity with this apparent divorce between the concerns of artists and intellectuals and those of the common people, and the juxtaposition signals the lack of relevance of one to the other. Poverty, infirmity, lack of sanitation, death, exploitation, violence, and ignorance neither inform "high culture" nor affect it, and vice versa. But the poetic "I" acts as a bridge to break the separation, to name what is on the streets. Vallejo was vociferous in his criticism of "ivory tower" intellectuals who remained aloof from real conditions and complained that art had become too narrowly defined as an entity and end unto itself.

The poem is dated November 5, 1937, and was first published in 1939. With access to Vallejo's letters, however, critic Jason Wilson backdates the composition of this poem to 1927, noting that it reflects the either/or debate in Paris between social activism (led by the French Communist Party) and the surrealists, who struggled to find a place within Marxist historical materialism for poetry and the imagination. The poem tries "to hold the irreconcilable world of proletarian suffering and intellectual debates together in alternative lines" (211). Since Vallejo stopped writing poetry at this time, Wilson concludes that he identified with the have-nots, which was consistent with his marginal status as a Latin American in Paris and with his "understanding that only suffering leads to real knowledge, not books or cerebral debates about ideas" (211).

BIBLIOGRAPHY

Vallejo, César. "A man walks by with a loaf of bread on his shoulder." Translated by Clayton Eshleman. In *Twentieth-Century Latin American Poetry: A Bilingual Anthology,* edited by Stephen Tapscott, 103–104. Austin: University of Texas Press, 1996.

———. *César Vallejo: The Complete Posthumous Poetry.* Edited and translated by Clayton Eshleman and José Rubia Barcia. Berkeley: University of California Press, 1978.

Wilson, Jason. "César Vallejo and 'El bruto libre': Notes on the Burden of European Culture." *Romance Quarterly* 49, no. 3 (Summer 2002): 206–214.

María Roof

MARECHERA, DAMBUDZO (1952–1987)

With barely three and a half decades on Earth, novelist and poet Dambudzo Marechera left so much of his presence that it is possible to think of him (as some Africans do) as a "still-birth" genius. His literary accomplishments easily evoke memories of admirable writers within the British and African literary traditions who also spent a short period on Earth. Names as evocative as John Keats, P. B. Shelley, George Gordon (Lord) Byron, Wilfred Owen—all British—also remind us in Africa of poets as diverse as CHRISTOPHER OKIGBO, Esiri Dafiewheri, Sesan Ajayi, Pol Ndu, and Birago Diop, among others. Marechera becomes particularly relevant because of his idiosyncratic lifestyle, which was at once humane but terrifyingly rambunctious. Like Ogun, the Yoruba god of iron made famous by WOLE SOYINKA, Marechera was, until his death in 1987, "a recluse, and a gregarious imbiber."

Dambudzo Marechera was born on June 4, 1952, in Rusape, in the Vengere Township ghetto of Zimbabwe. His early education was at the St. Augustine's Mission,

Penhalonga, from which he proceeded to the University of Rhodesia and New College at Oxford. At each of these institutions, Marechera had one unpleasant experience after another from his mentors—and created even more problems for them.

Marechera grew up in a minority-white-racist society, where the dominant population suffered racial discrimination. Like many of his contemporaries, he was quite aware of his humanity as a black person, but also observed a black humanity that was not totally humanizing. In one instance he records having (at age seven) witnessed a man beat up and rape his wife in public in Vigere Township. Marechera grew visibly "troubled," developing a temper that finally pushed him from one social difficulty to another. In 1973 he was expelled from the (then) Rhodesian University along with several other students for rioting against white racism. His escape to the United Kingdom did not avail him the rosy life he anticipated. Instead he was constantly in trouble, in and out of jail sometimes for offences as demeaning as petty theft. But as a writer, Marechera demonstrated vibrant energy, giving rise to the publication of a number of brilliant literary works that include his acclaimed novel, *House of Hunger,* and the posthumously published collection of his poems, *Cemetery of Mind,* among others.

One interesting manifestation in his poetry is the resonance of the exilic consciousness. This is especially prevalent in *The Black Insider,* to the extent that Flora Veit-Wild felt compelled to describe the book as "an important and unique literary contribution to the question of what exile has meant for a whole generation of Zimbabweans" (*The Black Insider* 17). In an interview Marechera proclaimed: "If one is living in an abnormal society, then only abnormal expression can express that society" (*The Black Insider* 211). Marechera was also fascinated by a peculiar kind of Euro-modernism that allowed him to explore what he called "the private voice," even while addressing themes of public interest. This aesthetic is what he refers to as "my own idiosyncratic, irrelevant perhaps anarchistic vision" (*Insider* 211). On the question of the English language as a creative medium, he wrote: "I find the only way I can express myself is by abusing the English language in such a way that it says what I want to say" (*Insider* 213). To this end, he follows Chinua Achebe's earlier insistence that for the African writer, the English language must be domesticated to carry the sensibilities of the African peoples.

Marechera was a strong advocate of interracial relationships. The so-called crisis of miscegenation becomes totally nonsensical in a discussion of Marechera because, as he insisted, "for me personally, it is not a problem. It is just another human relationship you can write about. I actually find love of people of the same race very much as an incest" (*Insider* 215).

Marechera made important statements on the African experience and the discourse of history. One fundamental lesson from this writer is the appeal that humankind must strive for a future devoid of bitterness. The bitterness and pain inflicted on African peoples and on the rest of the so-called Third World through slavery and colonialism should be read, he affirmed, as a reminder of an unholy past that must not necessarily dictate the direction of our common humanity. For him, then, forgiveness should be central to our conduct, rather than revenge—especially vengeance informed by racial constructs of the colonial supremacists. As he eloquently asserted: "it was simply an illusion that one can revenge oneself on history" (*Insider* 215).

The intensity of the spiritual conflict that defines Marechera becomes evident in the aesthetic and moral ambiguities that we find in a number of his poems. In the Amelia poems, for instance, he admits: "In one poem I treat her (Amelia) as if she is dead, in another as if she is a ghost, in another as if she were merely a sort of spiritual voice beyond the flowering jacaranda trees at Cecil Square, sometimes as a prostitute, especially a ghost-prostitute, and sometimes as the one person in the world I can shout at" (*Insider* 217).

There is evidence that Marechera was fascinated by highly cerebral poetry. The title of his posthumously published collection, *Cemetery of Mind*—a title selected from one of his poems—attests to his love for the intellectually stimulating kind of poem. Poetry, for him, transcends mere assemblage of words. Poetry involves feelings, but feelings cannot truly be expressed. The planet of artistic creativity, the human brain, is functional only in its most sober moment. *Cemetery of Mind* captures this mental construct, one that is better understood as an alienated and conflicted territory of the human body. The pains and joys of living, the frustrations that confront him within the confines of the racist Britons of the 1970s as "a black insider" who is vulnerable to constant arrests, ridicule, dehumanization, and imprisonment—all combine to add to his frustration in colonial Zimbabwe (then known as Rhodesia), still under minority white control. The experience of racism in its rawest form, as well as the impressive black resistance that took place in Britain at the time, inspired Marechera to invoke his sense of history and of black oppression across historical epochs. The result is the strong rendition of colonial violence and the inhumanity of the racist white supremacists in a poem he curiously calls "I Am the Rape."

In that singular echo of Marecheran ingenuity, the violations he suffered define his humanity as a black man. The abstract and the concrete cohere in the metaphoric, and what emerges is the voice of a poet whose sense of history and geography interrogate the colonial location of his humanity as "savage," the unsung slave ("labourer") eternally condemned to providing service and thereby satisfying the gluttonous colonialists. If "goodness" and "evil" are choices available to a humanity whose innate wisdom allows it to go for comfort and happiness, he seems to be asking, then, why must the white world hold his blackness against him? Why should a humankind so privileged with the wisdom of distinguishing between the compassionate and the odious suddenly feign ignorance of centuries of inhumanity against the black world? Marechera's revulsion could be pinned down to what he sees as white hypocrisy. But the victimized blacks should not be complacent or resign themselves to a morbid fate. He suggests, therefore, that the oppressed "Smash, Grab, [and] Run." The revolt by black immigrants in Britain in the 1970s is aesthetically preserved here for posterity. Where liberal Britain and the powerful north could hypocritically boast of exporting democratic ideals to the rest of the world, the politics of eugenics that manifests itself in actual daily experiences tells otherwise.

The Britain of the 1970s, to which Marechera ran to escape from the repressive white Rhodesian government, was not the Eden he imagined. Instead he encountered a Britain where "Barbed wire is the ivy on my walls / . . . / the striking truncheon outpaces thought / [and] the burgeoning Molotov cancels discussion." Given the violence and ruthlessness of the white supremacists, especially among the state's security operatives, the revolts that followed were phenomenal, to the extent that he would admit: "And for just this once in my black British life / Exploded the atoms in me into atoms of power" (*Cemetery* 31). Where vengeance is not necessary as a way of correcting the injustices of history, then the injustices of the present must be addressed as they come, especially since complacency is tantamount to self-annihilation. Marechera died on August 18, 1987, of an AIDS-related illness.

BIBLIOGRAPHY
Habila, Helon. "On Dambudzo Marechera: The Life and Times of an African Writer." *Virginia Quarterly Review* (Winter 2006): 251–260. Available online. URL: http://www.vqronline.org/articles/2006/winter/habila-on-dambudzo-marechera/. Downloaded on April 23, 2007.
Marechera, Dambudzo. *Cemetery of Mind: Collected Poems.* Compiled by Flora Veit-Wild. Harare, Zimbabwe: Baobab Books, 1992.
———. *The Black Insider.* Edited by Flora Veit-Wild. Harare, Zimbabwe: Baobab Books, 1990.
———. *Cemetery of Mind: Collected Poems.* Compiled by Flora Veit-Wild. Harare, Zimbabwe: Baobab Books, 1992.
Pattison, David. *No Room for Cowardice: A View of the Life and Times of Dambudzo Marechera.* Trenton, N.J.: Africa World Press, 2001.

Osita Ezeliora

"MARSYAS, ENCIRCLED" Anja Utler (2004)

The long poem *"marsyas, umkreist"* ("Marsyas, encircled") from Anja Utler's volume *münden—entzüngeln* (merging—untonguing, 2004) evokes and reinvents a mythological protagonist's execution by gradual skinning. According to classical Greek mythology the satyr and flute player Marsyas challenges the god Apollo to a musical competition. They agree that the winner will have full control over his antagonist's life. Changing the rules to his advantage, Apollo wins and punishes Marsyas's hubris by having him flayed alive. In a notebook entry from 1911, Franz Kafka, who published some of his early texts in the literary magazine *Marsyas,* laconically alludes to Raphael's fresco *Apollo and Marsyas* (1509–11). While Raphael's fresco presents a triumphant Apollo mocking his immobilized victim Marsyas before the torture begins, Titian's oil painting *The Flaying of Marsyas* (1575–76) shows the cruelty of the slow murder and the enthusiasm of its spectators and bystanders. Utler's Marsyas poem, a radical rehearsal of the spoken word as a form of perceptive survival, not only forms fruitful tensions with pictorial traditions and literary predecessors from Alcaios to ZBIGNIEW HERBERT's Marsyas poem (1957), but also suggests intermedial correlations with musical Marsyas adaptations, including Patrick Bebelaar and Frank Kroll's jazz composition *Apollo & Marsyas* (1997).

The poem is divided into seven parts. Five of these begin with different programmatic subtitles whose verbal tensions announce a struggle for physical and emotional survival, for example, *"beschattet—umklammern"* (shaded—clasping), *"durchtasten—erinnert"* (groping—remembered). Referring to the poem's epigraph, a quotation from a linguistics handbook, occasional phonological abbreviations for inverse sounds are inserted into the text, indicating painful breathing. Utler's text explores the permeable boundaries between nonverbal sounds of pain and fragile attempts at speech during dying. Throughout the poem, violence is conveyed phonetically through dense reiterations of consonants and prefixes.

In the penultimate stanza the mouth is defined as an inhabitable zone of obliteration, where intimacy, vulnerability, articulation, and silence are inextricably interwoven: *"diese stürzende wunde / der mund"* (this falling wound / the mouth). In this poem Utler juxtaposes poetological reflections on the writing process with botanical, anatomical, or rather forensic, descriptions. The process of dismemberment and dissolution is mostly rendered in the present tense. Rhythm and metrical design evoke various temporal suspensions, ruptures, and accelerations.

While for the most part rendering the text in a careful manner, Tony Frazer's translation occasionally reduces a verse's artful ambiguity to a one-dimensional logic. For instance, *"vom entsetzen entbunden,"* which can be simultaneously read as "released/unbound/delivered by" and "released/abdicated/delivered from horror," loses its fertile semantic tension of birth as trauma, liberation, and exposure in Frazer's verse, "delivered from horror." Another example of a reductive translation can be found in Frazer's decision to use "in silence" for the German *"im stillen,"* which thus loses its indispensable alternate meaning, "while breastfeeding."

As Utler emphasized at a public reading in Bremen in May 2005, during which she delivered a precise and moving performance of *"marsyas, umkreist,"* Marsyas's death can be read as a mode of metamorphotic survival. Marsyas is transformed into a river that originates (Utler uses *"entspringt"*—an echo of, and homage to, RAINER MARIA RILKE's *Duino Elegies*) and "springs forth" from his own blood. Having become an ear and eyewitness to an execution, the reader gradually encounters what the French language aptly calls a *"nature morte,"* a still life void of dissenting voices, a posthuman pastoral whose dissolvent utopian potential needs to be explored further.

BIBLIOGRAPHY

Utler, Anja. "marsyas, encircled." Translated by Tony Frazer. In *From Mouth to Mouth: Contemporary German Poetry in Translation,* edited by Thomas Wohlfarth and Tobias Lehmkuhl, 252–265. Newcastle, Australia: Giramondo, 2004.

Olaf Berwald

MARTINSON, HARRY (1904–1978)

Harry Martinson is known not only for infusing 20th-century Swedish nature poetry with a new lyricism, but also for being the most celebrated poet to rise up from Sweden's working class and join the literary elite. Martinson was the first autodidact ever to serve on the prestigious Swedish Academy, which awards the international Nobel Prize in literature. Martinson himself shared this prize (with Swedish prose writer Eyvind Johnson) late in life, after he had left the academy, in 1974, for his epic science fiction poem ANIARA: A REVUE OF MAN IN TIME AND SPACE (*Aniara: En revy av människan i tid och rum*), first published in 1956 and consisting of 103 cantos. This book-length poetic work, which tells the story of a ship of human emigrants lost in space following a nuclear apocalypse on Earth, has joined the modern classics of world literature and is available in an excellent English cotranslation by Stephen Klass and Leif Sjöberg (Story Line Press, 1999). Martinson also won every other major Swedish literary prize. While known primarily as a poet, Martinson was a prolific and versatile writer who transgressed the boundaries of literary genres. He became a popular writer, in addition to a respected poet, by writing best-selling "travelogues" about life on the high seas. In these works Martinson mixed poetry and philosophy with exotic descriptions of the many places he had visited while stoking coal fires on ships as a youth. Martinson saw travel as a grand metaphor for self-discovery, a theme that recurs throughout his work. He also wrote a two-part autobiography, several collections of nature stories and essays, a novel on Finland's Winter War of 1939 with the USSR (in which he fought as a volunteer for the Finnish army against the Soviets), and a "hitchhiker novel," *Vägen till Klockrike* (The Road, 1948), as well as a radio play about the Portuguese explorer Ferdinand Magellan. But Martinson's most celebrated work is unquestionably his lyrical poetry, of which he published 11 volumes during his lifetime in addition to his master epic, *Aniara*. (Four additional collections of his poetry and prose were published following his death.) Nature provides the theme and structure for all of Martinson's poetry, as well as the worldview reflected in it. As he writes in the poem *"Den stora sorgen,"* (The Great Sorrow, 1971), "The laws of Nature are well on the way / To bringing us all into account" (Hallberg 63).

Martinson was born into poverty in southern rural Sweden, and his father died when he was six years old. One year later his mother abandoned him and his siblings to immigrate to California, leaving the children to be raised on public welfare (several decades before the formation of the now-famous Swedish social welfare state). Martinson despised growing up in an orphanage, and at the age of 14 he ran away, soon taking to the seas as a crewman on various merchant ships. He traveled to the major ports in Europe, India, and the Americas before the tuberculosis he contracted while stoking the coal fires onboard forced him to return home. During his many hours at sea Martinson read works of Eastern philosophy, particularly Taoism, as well as works by English, American, and continental

European romantic poets. The range of philosophical and literary works Martinson explored as a self-educated nomad was far more diverse than what he likely would have been exposed to as a university student. These influences helped shape his belief that revering nature was the key to sustaining humankind. In an essay titled *"Den godartade möjligheten"* (The Benign Possibility, 1948) Martinson venerates the Taoists' call for maintaining nature's balance and harmony: "Taoism is a faith for artists and peasants and for all men who think and feel under the open sky" (Hallberg 69). For Martinson nature and humanity have intrinsic worth, and the modernizing view that nature should serve humankind in utilitarian ways was not only alienating people from nature, but also from themselves. Martinson sought to regenerate this vital link in his poetry. His debut collection, *Spökskepp* (Ghost Ship, 1929), reflects the influence of Rudyard Kipling and the Swedish romanticists Gustaf Fröding and Dan Andersson (Sjöberg 403). In 1930 he and four other 20-something poets published a joint collection titled *5 Unga* (Five Young Ones), which subsequently was hailed as an important event in the development of literary modernism in Sweden. Through the influence of one of the other four "young ones," poet and critic Artur Lundkvist, Martinson began studying the work of Walt Whitman, Carl Sandburg, and Edgar Lee Masters, and their influence is strongly reflected in his subsequent volumes of poetry in the 1930s (Sjöberg 403).

Another major influence in Martinson's life and work was his marriage in 1929 to proletarian and feminist writer Moa Schwartz, who was 14 years older than he. (She took his surname, published under the name Moa Martinson, and is a celebrated writer of prose fiction in her own right.) Not only did she nurse him when he still was sick with tuberculosis and support him in the crucial early stages of his writing career, but their home became a gathering place for other writers and intellectuals engaged in feminist, socialist, and Marxist critical thought. Important intellectual differences and opposing worldviews, however, drove the couple apart. For example, Moa Martinson, who was making her reputation as a proletarian writer of feminist novels in the 1930s, lauded the Soviet experiment with social realism and its call for producing novels with proletarian hero-protagonists. Harry Martinson, however, attended the writer's congress in Moscow as a guest of the Soviet government in 1934 and was deeply troubled by its motto, taken from Lenin, that "The poet is the engineer of the human soul." Martinson considered "the feeble-mindedly materialistic title 'engineer'" despicably utilitarian and characteristic of all that was wrong with modern civilization. When the Soviet Union invaded Finland in 1939 in a conflict known as the Winter War, Harry Martinson fought as a volunteer with the Finnish army, perceiving the conflict in ideological terms as a decadent modern civilization—i.e., the Soviet Union—seeking to crush a smaller, vulnerable, and more agrarian nation, Finland. The following year Martinson wrote in a novel, *Verklighet till döds* (Reality Unto Death), set during the Winter War: "There unyielding Finns from the woods [*skogsfinnar*] were fighting for paradoxical but true things, for feelings and sentiments, for everything that makes the materialist spout his bile as soon as he catches a glimpse of the vague and obscure words" (Hallberg 68). The year after that, in 1941, Harry and Moa divorced. In 1942 Martinson married Ingrid Lindcrantz; the union would last for the remainder of his life and produce two daughters.

Among Martinson's admirers are the American poets Robert Bly and David Ignatow, who have written about the way in which Martinson employs natural metaphors to convey emotion and spiritual connection. Bly has additionally translated some of Martinson's poetry into English in *Friends, You Drank Some Darkness: Three Swedish Poets* (1975). In addition to Bly's work and Sjöberg's and Klass's excellent translation of *Aniara*, two other Martinson texts remain in print in English: *Views from a Tuft of Grass*, a translation of *Utsikt från en grästuva* (1963), a collection of nature stories and essays; and *Wild Bouquet: Nature Poems* (1985), an anthology of Martinson's nature poems translated elegantly into English by William J. Smith and Leif Sjöberg. Ignatow wrote in 1986, "In the long history of American nature poetry, with Emily Dickinson as its most brilliant exponent, there is nothing quite so open and penetrating in expressing our identity with oneness, with the living processes of being as we find in *Wild Bouquet*" (Sjöberg 404). Martinson's particular

poetic kinship with America's beloved nature poets, including Dickinson and Whitman, make his work a must-read for any American student exploring world poetry.

BIBLIOGRAPHY

Bly, Robert. *Friends, You Drank Some Darkness: Three Swedish Poets, Harry Martinson, Gunnar Ekelöf, and Tomas Tranströmer.* Translated by Robert Bly. Boston: Beacon Press, 1975.

Hallberg, Peter. "Earthworm and Cosmos: Harry Martinson's Vision of Man and Nature." *The Feeling for Nature and the Landscape of Man: Proceedings of the 45th Nobel Symposium held September 10–12, 1978.* Gothenburg, Sweden: Kungliga Vetenskaps-och Vitterhets-Samhället i Göteborg, 1980, 63–76.

Martinson, Harry. *Views from a Tuft of Grass.* Translated by Lars Nordström and Erland Andersson. Los Angeles: Green Integer, 2004.

———. *Wild Bouquet: Nature Poems.* Translated by William J. Smith and Leif Sjöberg. Kansas City, Mo.:BMK Press of the University of Missouri–Kansas City, 1985.

———. *Aniara: An Epic Science Fiction Poem.* Translated by Stephen Klass and Leif Sjöberg. Brownsville, Oreg.: Story Line Press, 1999.

Sjöberg, Leif. "Martinson, Harry." In *Dictionary of Scandinavian Literature,* edited by Virpi Zuck, 403–406. Westport, Conn.: Greenwood Press, 1990.

Ursula A. L. Lindqvist

"MARVELLOUS GRASS" Nuala Ní Dhomhnaill (1986)

"*Féir Suaithinseach*" exemplifies Nuala Ní Dhomhnaill's method of addressing issues of women's and cultural identity by rewriting folklore and myth from a female perspective. Taking its cue from an Irish folk story titled "The Boy Who Became Pope," the poem—consisting of six sections of from four to seven irregular lines each (occasionally end-rhymed in the Irish original)—gives a voice to a marginal female character, endowing her with allegorical significance. The poem's speaker addresses a priest who, years ago, caused her mysterious illness by dropping the "blessed host" during her Holy Communion. Since then the girl's lips have been "locked," suggesting her refusal to eat or speak. Apparently, she has been suffering from anorexia, a disorder that expresses her shame at having occasioned the dropping of the host: "I—I said nothing. / I was ashamed." The priest's confusion when seeing her face hints at sexual attraction while the image of a "mud-thorn" penetrating the girl's "insides" suggests physical penetration, even rape. Accordingly, by refusing to eat the girl attempts to arrest her sexual development, which she blames for her failed communion. She can be cured only if the local men find the host, hidden under "a patch of marvellous grass," so that the priest may resume the interrupted ritual. On a metaphorical level the image suggests that the status of women needs to be restored by those who diminished it in the first place: the representatives of patriarchy (the men) and Catholicism (the priest). Another noteworthy aspect is the metaphorical connection between the girl and the land. The speaker's hope to "sit up in the bed / as healthy as [she] was when young" evokes the nationalist myth of Cathleen Ní Houlihan, the old woman symbolic of Ireland who regains her youth when young men sacrifice their lives for her. This myth was employed most famously in William Butler Yeats's play *Cathleen Ní Houlihan* (1902) and has been deeply influential in 20th-century Irish literature. References to "the rank growth, the dust, the misery / that grows on my tragic grassland" imply that anorexia has infected not only the girl but Ireland itself, since a culture denying women's sexuality withers just like a girl denying her bodily needs. In a country deprived of the earth mother's gifts of prosperity, all that is left to grow on the "tragic grassland" are "misery" and "useless plants." Thus instead of sending men out to die, the girl instructs them to retrieve the "marvellous grass" symbolic of fertility and life. In this respect she is reminiscent of the Celtic fertility goddesses whom Ní Dhomhnaill revives in many of her poems. The poet thus effectively blends her revision of folklore and myth with her exploration of the metaphorical and sociopsychological implications of the modern disease anorexia, relating both to contemporary issues of female and cultural identity.

BIBLIOGRAPHY
Bourke, Angela. "Fairies and Anorexia: Nuala Ní Dhomhnaill's 'Amazing Grass.'" *Proceedings of the Harvard Celtic Colloquium XIII*. Cambridge, Mass: Harvard Celtic Colloquium, 1995, 25–38.
Ní Dhomhnaill, Nuala. "Marvellous Grass." In *Selected Poems: Rogha Dánta*. 1986. Translated by Michael Hartnett. Dublin: Raven Arts, 1993, 75.

Michaela Schrage-Früh

MAYAKOVSKY, VLADIMIR (1893–1930)

One of the most distinctive and influential of 20th-century Russian poets, Vladimir Mayakovsky was also a dramatist, essayist, and visual artist. Of Russian and Ukrainian descent, he was born in Bagdadi, Georgia, where his father, a government employee, was a forester. The family was a close-knit and happy group. After the death of the elder Mayakovsky from septicemia in 1906, the poet's mother moved her three children to Moscow. At 12 Vladimir began his career as a revolutionary; at 16 he was arrested and released into his mother's custody. After his third arrest in the same year, he was sent to prison, where he was far from a model prisoner. During his three months in solitary confinement, he began to write poetry, but his early work so discouraged him that he decided to study the visual arts. He enrolled in 1911 at the Moscow Institute of Painting, Sculpture, and Architecture, where he met David Burliuk, who introduced him to modernist poetry. Two of Mayakovsky's poems appeared in the 1912 avant-garde collection *A Slap in the Face of Public Taste*.

In spite of Mayakovsky's revolutionary views both as a person and as an artist, he wanted to serve Russia during World War I. His arrests disqualified him from military service, and he worked from 1915 to 1917 as a draftsman at the Petrograd Military Auto School. In 1915 he met the critic Osip Brik and his wife, Lily. The two had decided early in their marriage that they were not going to be a bourgeois couple; Mayakovsky fell in love with Lily, to whom he wrote many of his love poems and with whom he had a 10-year affair. The year 1915 also saw the publication of *A Cloud in Trousers* and THE BACKBONE FLUTE, two of his most influential works.

The former is part of a trilogy that includes the poems "Man" (1917) and "About That" (1923). The triparite composition has trinitarian implications and suggests that Mayakovsky, like Joyce, hated religion but had absorbed its imagery. The voice in the first poem is clearly that of the poet himself, but the title hints at an ethereal figure who is male, like God the Father. Significantly, the two women in the poem are named Maria, as if to suggest the Virgin Mary and Mary Magdalene; the poem's theme is love. "Man" presents the artist as a Christ-like figure who suffers for humankind, an image that may show the influence of the Russian novelist Fyodor Dostoyevsky. Mayakovsky had already explored this theme in *Vladimir Mayakovsky: A Tragedy* (1913). The Holy Spirit is associated with deep understanding, and "About That" explains the lot of humankind. The first section takes its title from Oscar Wilde's "The Ballad of Reading Gaol," and the second takes its title from a short story by the 19th-century Russian author Nikolay Gogol about Christmas Eve. Both suggest the image of a doomed man. Eastern Orthodox theology links Christ's birth with his death: He entered time in order to die, and he was born and buried in a cave. The themes of Mayakovsky's trilogy are human love as a creative force and human suffering as humankind's condition, a joining of modernist and Christian concerns.

After the 1917 Russian Revolution, Mayakovsky drew posters and wrote poetic slogans for the Russian Telegraph Agency (ROSTA). As a futurist/symbolist poet he saw a poem as a device, and unlike his contemporaries Boris Pasternak, Anna Akhmatova, and Sergei Yesenin, he saw no contradiction in using his poetry as a propaganda tool. Nor did he seem to see a contradiction between his own voice and the collective values espoused by the Soviet socialist realist aesthetic. Western critics tend to dismiss Mayakovsky's overtly Soviet works as inferior poetry, although his eulogy "Vladimir Illych Lenin" (1924) is well regarded. All his poetry is well crafted, metered skillfully, and linguistically adept.

Joseph Stalin admired Mayakovsky, but Vladimir Lenin was not impressed with him. Nonetheless, Mayakovsky was among a group of Soviet artists allowed to travel abroad. In 1922 he journeyed to Paris, where he met Pablo Picasso and Jean Cocteau; in 1925 he sailed to North America. In Mexico he met Mexican painter Diego Rivera; in the United States he read his poetry in several major cities. His "Brooklyn Bridge" (1925) praises the structure as a technological marvel that will inspire awe eternally but ends with the image of a victim of capitalism throwing himself into the East River. During his 1928 trip to Paris, Mayakovsky met and fell in love with Tatiana Alekseevna Yakovleva, an émigrée who seems to have been his equal in height and intellect. He tried unsuccessfully to persuade her to return to the Soviet Union, and in 1929 he was denied permission to travel to France. Her marriage that December to a French diplomat may have triggered the poet's final depression.

Some critics believe, however, that Mayakovsky's ardor for both Lily Brik and Tatiana Yakovleva was shaped by the conventions of love poetry. In letters and in poems to each, he speaks as if he were always the scorned admirer.

In 1925 Yesenin committed suicide, and Mayakovsky's "To Sergei Yesenin" (1926) criticizes his fellow artist for his overdramatic reaction to the plight of the lyric poet in the Soviet Union. The poem further seeks to counteract any sense that this romantic gesture is worth imitating. Mayakovsky may have been admonishing himself, since images of suicide can be found throughout his oeuvre and he suffered periodic depression. In spite of his harsh judgment of Yesenin, Mayakovsky shot himself five years later, in April 1930. His suicide note is surprisingly calm, as if it had been carefully composed and was one final expression of his poetic genius.

BIBLIOGRAPHY
Brown, Edward J. *Mayakovsky: A Poet in the Revolution.* Princeton, N.J.: Princeton University Press, 1973.
Marshall, Herbert, trans. and ed. *Mayakovsky.* New York: Hill and Wang, 1965.
Railing, Patricia, ed. *Voices of Revolution: Collected Essays.* Vol. 3. Cambridge, Mass.: MIT Press, 2000.
Terras, Victor. *Vladimir Mayakovsky.* Boston: Twayne, 1983.
Woroszylski, Wiktor. *The Life of Mayakovsky.* Translated by Boleslaw Taborski. New York: Orion Press, 1970.

Karen Rae Keck

MEIRELES, CECÍLIA (1901–1964)   Cecília Meireles has often been called the best female poet of the Portuguese language. She is considered the first great female Brazilian writer and the first female voice to be heard during the Brazilian modernist movement

in 1922. She was born in 1901 in Rio de Janeiro, the same city where she died and was laid to rest on November 9, 1964. Her father died three months before her birth, and her mother, an elementary school teacher, died when Cecília was only three years old. Raised in Rio by her grandmother, a native of the Portuguese Azores islands, the young Cecília developed a deep interest in Brazilian culture and other world cultures through her grandmother's stories of her birthplace and origins. Meireles began to write poems at age nine.

A prolific and dexterous writer, today Meireles is popularly perceived as a flexible, independent, and critical thinker who carefully incorporated the issues of the time in her poetry. She published her first volume of poetry, *Espectros* (Ghosts, 1919) at age 18. She would later publish more than a dozen volumes of poetry. Several volumes of her complete works have appeared posthumously. While Meireles devoted most of her adult life to writing poetry, she dedicated much of her time to her other vocation and passion: early childhood education. She was an elementary school teacher who also founded and directed a children's library in Rio de Janeiro and authored several children books. Later she taught Brazilian literature and culture at the university level, with appointments at the University of Texas (United States) and the Federal University of Rio de Janeiro. In addition to teaching Meireles was an active journalist. She reported frequently on educational issues in the Rio de Janeiro daily *Carioca* and served as the education editor of *Diário de Notícias*. Interested in world literatures, Meireles studied and spoke several languages. An avid traveler and international lecturer, she completed many translations into Portuguese of the works of major international writers, and she lectured extensively outside Brazil.

Distinguished as one of Brazil's ingenuous and skillful female writers, carefully selecting the appropriate word to capture her intended motive, Meireles produced pensive and philosophical poetry in which the following themes dominate: the transitions of life, the brevity of life, love, the infinite, nature, and artistic creation. Her poems mirror the uncertainty and dubiousness of life's fleeting trajectory. This is evidenced in her prize-winning signature poem *"Viagem"* (Voyage, 1939) in which she questions categorically—"Where am I going?" Although she was a devout Catholic, she did not express herself through religious imagery. The poem is an expression of her spiritual journey. The final verse is simply: *"Por onde é que eu vou?"* (Where shall I go?). Implicit in this question is a sense of the futility in human existence. The early deaths of her parents left strong emotional scars in her. Also, before the publication of *"Viagem,"* her first husband, Fernando Correia Dias, a painter, had committed suicide (in 1936) and left her with their three daughters. These personal experiences appear in an indirect way in her poetry. Happier times came in 1942, when she married Heitor Grillo, who helped to raise her daughters and provided emotional stability in her life. Meireles expressed her love for Grillo in a poem entitled *"Cantar de Vero Amar"* (Song of True Love, 1964), written shortly before her death from cancer. Some of the best translations of Meireles's poetry are in found in Henry Keith and Raymond Sayer's *Cecília Meireles: Poems in Translation* (Washington, D.C.: Brazilian American Cultural Institute, 1977). Although she won many literary awards and honors during her lifetime, Keith and Sayers suggest in their introduction (not paginated) that "if she had not been a woman, she would have surely been granted immortality by election to one of the forty places in the Brazilian Academy of Letters."

James J. Davis

"MEMORIES OF YOUTH" NICANOR PARRA (1954)
Although NICANOR PARRA characterizes his later works as "ecopoetry" (see ECOPOETICS), his first volumes belong to an earlier movement, which he termed "antipoetry." While the title of Parra's second volume (*Poemas y antipoemas*) announced Parra's new concept of the antipoem to the literary world, he merely allowed his works to denote the term's significance and never offered a concrete definition of an antipoem. He has, however, suggested what antipoetry is *not*: It is not poetry typical of Parra's literary predecessors, nor is it lyric, nor, particularly, is it figurative poetry. As its name implies, Parra's antipoetry is a reaction to poetic conventions that he perceived were

fraudulent and estranged readers from what is real. Thus in *Poemas y antipoemas* Parra roots his poetry in a sensory realism defined by pragmatic and sometimes gross detail. Among the poems of that early volume, *"Recuerdos de juventud"* (Memories of Youth) exemplifies both Parra's characteristic poetic style and his concept of the antipoem.

The speaker of *"Recuerdos de juventud"* is stalled in his own reality, caught in the quicksand of his life. His attempts at forward movement are thwarted. The first line of the poem, describing his movement as *"yo iba de un lado a otro"* (I kept going back and forth), establishes its tone as one of frustration and subtle resentment. The poem's description of movement, however, does not simply suggest the passage of time, which might be implied by the title, or any other sort of material advancement. Instead, *"Recuerdos de juventud"* takes as its subject a poet's early attempts at communication and finds both his vocabulary and his connection to other people fragmented. He is provoked to *"una tempestad de frases incoherentes"* (a storm of incoherent sentences) as well as *"unos movimientos agotadores de caderas"* (certain exhausting pelvic motions)—the latter suggestive of the graphic, physical detail typical of Parra's imagery.

Though the speaker has retired to cemeteries to write, he continues to chase the same idea, back and forth, repeating again the image of a kind of circular movement with no forward development or true progress. Ultimately, despite the speaker's attempts at contact and communication, his spectators, oblivious to his presence, *"leían el periódico / O desaparecían detrás de un taxi"* (went on reading the paper / Or disappeared behind a taxi). The speaker is left with nowhere to go and nothing to do. In a bizarre conjoining of images (of a concrete image with one less tangible), the speaker thinks of the *"trozo de cebolla visto durante la cena"* (the slice of onion I'd seen during dinner), then immediately thinks of *"el abismo que nos separa de los otros abismos"* (the abyss that separates us from the other abysses). Ultimately, the poet is unable to bridge the gulf between himself and his audience with his poetry—but his image of the real, mundane object, the onion, comes across clearly.

BIBLIOGRAPHY

Parra, Nicanor. *Poems and Antipoems.* Edited by Miller Williams, translated by Fernando Alegría et al. New York: New Directions, 1967.

Winter Elliott

MENESES, VIDALUZ (1944–   )

One of the most acclaimed poets writing in Central America and a public figure of distinction in Nicaragua, Vidaluz Meneses held leadership positions in the new Ministry of Culture established by the Sandinista National Liberation Front (FSLN) after it overthrew the Somoza dictatorship in 1979. She later became a university dean, ecumenical center director, and codirector of a national coalition of 300 nongovernmental organizations.

Meneses enjoyed a comfortable early life as the daughter of a military officer. Like compatriot poets DAISY ZAMORA, Michèle Najlis, and GIOCONDA BELLI, her growing conviction during the 1960s and 1970s of the need for radical political change led to her transformation from a traditional young woman into a covert participant in the revolutionary process. She and others defined themselves as faith-based revolutionaries, like poet Father ERNESTO CARDENAL, and challenged the values of their own class. When the Sandinistas lost the 1990 elections, the decade of changes came to an abrupt halt, and Meneses embarked on a difficult search to reconcile historical sacrifices, recast her social role, and find ways to build a new society outside the paradigm of revolution.

Meneses's poems reflect her experiences as a person whose marriage and family were split by political events. A frequently anthologized work from her first collection, *Llama guardada* (Guarded Flame, 1975), "When I Married," suggests an ironic contrast between the biblical models for women and their reality. Meneses was optimistic the Sandinista government would create the conditions for the emergence of a "new woman," as in "Compañera" from her second collection, *El aire que me llama* (Air That Calls Me, 1982): "Make your name yours / and plant it like a flag / in conquered territory. Now nothing can stop you." Her "Last Postcard to My Father, General Meneses," from her third and most political collection, *Llama en el aire* (Flame in the Wind, 1990), acknowledges her ideological distance from her father, assassinated in Guatemala in 1978 while Nicaragua's ambassador there: ". . . history prevented you / from witnessing this great moment, / still less from understanding it. / . . . / [We are] Each one ranged on their own side / like two ancient and noble knights, / embracing before the final duel." Meneses interpreted the 1990 electoral loss as a betrayal of those who had died in the struggle: "I will not stifle their voices crying for the kingdom / we have not been able to build, / I will not ignore the blood on the ground" ("Wailing Wall").

Meneses's title for her fourth collection, *Todo es igual y distinto* (All Is the Same and Different, 2002), indicates much of its content—the lamentable return to old social and economic inequities after 1990, though the poems also sing of chancing new love and the indebtedness of women poets to their foremothers who succumbed to suicide (Virginia Woolf, Sylvia Plath, ALFONSINA STORNI).

Meneses's poems appear in anthologies published around the world, but the total number available in English is under 20, and few critical treatments have appeared in the United States. (Translator María Roof is preparing *Flame in the Air: Poetry by Vidaluz Meneses, Bilingual Edition,* which includes all her published poems and extensive interviews with the author on her life and works.)

BIBLIOGRAPHY

Meneses, Vidaluz. "Compañera." In *Nicaragua in Reconstruction & at War: The People Speak,* edited and translated by Marc Zimmerman, 278. Minneapolis: MEP, 1985.

———. "Last Postcard to My Father, General Meneses" In *Lovers and Comrades: Women's Resistance Poetry from Central America,* edited by Amanda Hopkinson, 56. London: Women's Press, 1989.

———. "Wailing Wall." In *Poets of the Nicaraguan Revolution: An Anthology,* compiled and translated by Dinah Livingstone, 231. London: Katabasis, 1993.

———. "When I Married." Translated by Nora Jacquez Wieser. In *Open to the Sun: A Bilingual Anthology of Latin-American Women Poets,* edited by Nora Jacquez Wieser, 117. Van Nuys, Calif.: Perivale, 1979.

María Roof

"METEOR OF AUGUST 13TH, THE" RENÉ CHAR (1947)

In several respects "Le Météore du 13 août" is typical of CHAR's work, particularly of the collection *Furor and Mystery,* in which it appeared in 1947. In general terms the poem is a series of images that must be understood on their own terms—within the context of the poem at hand. At first opaque, the individual images come into focus one by one and steadily reveal the poem as a whole.

A first glance reveals a series of oppositions: light and dark, night and day, sky and earth. With these contrasts in mind, the first line becomes more tractable: A meteor is a piece of the heavens fallen to Earth. Meteors are visible only in the dark of night, yet the meteor lights up the sky and represents "my poem's noon." This connection between the poem (and poetry) is appropriate because of the brief brilliance of a single poem, but is also important because it establishes the poem as a vehicle for overcoming night and darkness.

The second section of the poem, "Novae," presents a nocturnal world similarly lit by temporary, if brighter, sources of light. The night is distant but still present: "Death avoided us." The danger of darkness is still there, as is a certain anxiety. Everything anticipates the dawn, the true end of the night, literally and figuratively: The poetic speaker jumps out of bed and speaks with children, both images of new beginning and possibilities.

After the novae fade, there comes the third section of the poem, "The Moon Changes Gardens," where the brief flashes—"Demented lights, obedient to the night"—have finished and the tainted world searches for true light. Also characteristic of Char is the affinity with nature. The speaker's bed is bordered by hawthorn, there is saxifrage outside the window, and the seeming wild men of the 14th line are "in phase with the meteor."

But the question remains: Where is the day? This is where the central image of the poem returns as a conceit: The speaker, whom we know to be a poet, or rather his presence, must "be a meteor in your soul." The poet is the source of enlightenment, and the poem ends as a birdsong—an age-old metaphor for poetry—ushers in the break of day.

Tom Dolack

MIŁOSZ, CZESŁAW (1911–2004)

Czesław Miłosz was one of many who survived World War II only to endure additional years of political oppression. Many Eastern European poets share the themes of violence and exile; still, even within this movement of witness, Miłosz was marked by isolation. He resided in America for over 40 years and was fluent in English, yet he elected to compose exclusively in Polish—even during those decades when Polish officials banned his work. When accepting the Nobel Prize in literature in 1980, Miłosz described the importance of writing in Polish as his "native tongue." Even that sentiment displaces him: On June 30, 1911, his mother, Weronika, gave birth not in Poland but in Szetejnie, a small Lithuanian village that was part of the Russian Empire. Polish was only one of the writer's childhood languages, the tongue of the gentry, along with peasant Lithuanian and the Russian of his playmates.

In his early years Miłosz and his family moved around Russia as dictated by the work assignments of his father, Aleksandr, a civil engineer for the czar's army. Miłosz was given a strict Roman Catholic education, including classical Latin. His schoolboy attempts to translate Ovid's tales would mature into accomplished translations from Greek, French, and English; he would later introduce T. S. Eliot's *The Waste Land* into Polish. After World War I ended in 1918, the family settled in Poland and Miłosz studied in the city of Wilno (present-day Vilnius, now in Lithuania).

Although his writing had blossomed—in 1933 he published his first book, *Poemat o czasie zastyglym* (A Poem on Frozen Time)—Miłosz rejected the literature department in favor of receiving a master of law degree in 1934. He then spent a year in Paris, befriending French poet and distant cousin Oscar Miłosz and beginning *Trzy zimy* (Three Winters). Poems such as "Song" and "Slow River" contain early hallmarks of his poetry: sensuous detail, polyphonic structure, and political unrest as channeled through nature. This second book came out in 1936, as he took a job at a Polish radio station in Wilno. A year later he was fired for voicing leftist beliefs.

Miłosz moved to Warsaw and found his home in the underground press. He cofounded the literary movement Zagary (Catastrophists). These artists foresaw that international political struggle would yield violence of apocalyptic proportions. In 1942, after the outbreak of World War II, Miłosz edited the seminal but clandestine anthology *Pie niepodległa* (Invincible Song: Polish Wartime Poetry). As the Germans increased their stranglehold of Warsaw, Miłosz witnessed the systematic relocation of Jews to the ghetto, as well as the deadly uprising. Amid those horrors Miłosz found a small measure of happiness by marrying Janina Dłuska in 1944; she would later bear him two sons.

Miłosz's most significant work up to that point, *Ocalenie* (Rescue), was published in 1945 and included the important poems "ENCOUNTER," "Campo dei Fiori," and "DEDICATION." He was acclaimed for his harsh yet elegant lyrics, which despaired of navigating the atrocity of war. In recognition of the young poet's stature, the communist government made Miłosz a diplomat. Ironically, his posts on behalf of the Polish People's Republic in Paris and Washington, D.C., only confirmed Miłosz's dissatisfaction with homeland politics. In 1951 he broke with the regime and sought political asylum in France. This defection created a lasting schism with intellectuals who once embraced him, most notably the Stalinist Chilean PABLO NERUDA. Miłosz had translated Neruda's work into Polish; now the Chilean vilified Miłosz in a newspaper article called "The Man Who Ran Away."

Branded a traitor, Miłosz fought to reunite his family in France. They settled, and 1953 proved an *annus mirabilis* for the poet, who broadened his genres. He continued to write in verse, and *Swiatlo dzienne* (Daylight) is notable for the poem "CHILD OF EUROPE." But it was his philosophical text from that same year, *Zniewolony umysl* (The Captive Mind), that won praise for its penetrating examination of how oppressive regimes compromise intellectual culture. Miłosz received his first major award, the Prix Littéraire Européen, and published the memoir *Zdobycie wladzy* (The Seizure of Power) about life in Warsaw. More prose followed: *Dolina Issy* (The Issa Valley), a novelization of his Lithuanian childhood, and *Radzinna Europa* (Native Realm).

Yet, poetry still beckoned—and so did America. In 1957 he turned his critical eye toward craft in *Traktat poetycki* (A Treatise on Poetry), arguing that poetry is fundamental to human community. In 1960 Miłosz accepted an invitation from the University of California, and he was soon appointed a professor of Slavic languages and literatures at Berkeley. There he met Robert Hass, a poet on the English faculty who would become Miłosz's lifelong friend and translator. Hass praised the poet for his discerning eye, which always sought a higher order amid carnage, and noted that "working with Czesław is like reliving the whole of the 20th century through this prism of great specificity."

In the wake of these new beginnings, Miłosz made a major decision. As a teenager he rejected his religious upbringing, claiming that "in a Roman Catholic country intellectual freedom always goes hand in hand with atheism." Now he embraced the Catholicism of his youth. He began studying Hebrew to render the Old Testament in Polish.

For nearly 20 years Miłosz was content to toil in relative obscurity, exploring the willful dissonance between his native landscape and his California surroundings. He commented, "I have two points of reference. One, a village in which I was born and always the world was north, south, east or west of that village. And another where I live in Berkeley. . . . My imagination works on two points of reference and how to combine them—a whole poetry can be built around them." He prided himself for resisting "disintegration," crediting Oscar Miłosz for "inoculat[ing] me against both France and America." Even the decidedly stateside perspective of his 1969 book *Widzenia nad zatoką San Francisco* (A View from San Francisco Bay) was drafted first in Polish, then translated by the author.

Miłosz became a U.S. citizen in 1970. By then he had retired, but students still sought the poet-cum-professor lectures on Russian novelist Fyodor Dostoyevsky. Any burgeoning sense of community was punctured by his longing for Wilno/Vilna/Vilnius, as evidenced in the 1969 publications *Miasto bez imienia* (City Without a Name) and *The History of Polish Literature*. His Western following was ardent and growing, and awards accumulated: a Guggenheim Fellowship in 1976; an honorary doctor of letters from the University of Michigan, Ann Arbor, in 1977; the Neustadt International Prize for Literature in 1978.

In 1980 Miłosz won the Nobel Prize in literature. This award followed the appointment of a Polish pope, John Paul II, and coincided with news coverage of the Workers' Accord between Solidarity (the Polish federation of trade unions) and the government, which permitted independent trade unions in Poland. The press seized on Miłosz's win as a political statement from the Nobel committee—to the consternation of those in Stockholm and Berkeley.

In his acceptance speech a poet known for his oblique philosophies shed light onto his private muses. He acknowledged influences such as scientist Emanuel Swedenborg and French philosopher Simone Weil, quoted by Miłosz for her assertion that "Distance is the soul of beauty." Yet the ever-contrary poet spoke of how the tangible present foiled distance, admitting that "I must speak of poetry in its encounter with peculiar circumstances of time and place." He challenged Poland to seek morality and transparency: "Anthologies of Polish poetry publish poems of my late friends— Wladyslaw Sebyla and Lech Piwowar, and give the date of their deaths: 1940. It is absurd not to be able to write how they perished, though everybody in Poland knows the truth: they shared the fate of several thousand Polish officers disarmed and interned by the then accomplices of Hitler, and they repose in a mass grave." He implored us to "forgive my laying bare a memory like a wound" even as he drew blood.

Ecco Press reissued Miłosz's *Selected Poems*, first published in 1973, to an American audience hungry to learn about the Nobel winner in their midst. He accepted this fame graciously if begrudgingly, giving readings and expressing admiration for American poets, particularly Walt Whitman. In the next decade he wrote several new books with English translations; he received the National Medal for the Arts and an honorary doctorate from Harvard University in 1989 and joined the American Academy of Arts and Sciences.

The fall of the Iron Curtain at the end of the 1980s allowed Miłosz to return to Poland, whose government could no longer ignore its famed exile. He set up residencies in California and Kraków. His first wife, Janina, had died in 1986 after a 10-year battle with Alzheimer's disease, and Miłosz was accompanied by his second wife, the American historian Carol Thigpen, whom he married in 1992. Together they and the poet's countrymen of Poland celebrated Miłosz's 90th birthday in

2001. This brief moment of unity in Miłosz's life would not last. Although almost 30 years younger than her husband, Carol died within the year from cancer.

In his Nobel speech Miłosz asked, "What is this enigmatic impulse that does not allow one to settle down in the achieved, the finished? I think it is a quest for reality." In one of his last interviews, Robert Faggen quoted Miłosz's definition of poetry as "the passionate pursuit of the real." Unflinchingly, the master of suffering in lyric denied that his writings had ever attained this goal. "The real, by which I mean God, continues to remain unfathomable." Restored to his beloved country but alone in his Kraków apartment, Miłosz died of natural causes on August 14, 2004.

BIBLIOGRAPHY

Faggen, Robert, ed. *Striving Towards Being: The Letters of Thomas Merton and Czesław Miłosz.* New York: Farrar, Straus and Giroux, 1996.

Fiut, Alexander. *The Eternal Moment: The Poetry of Czesław Miłosz.* Translated by Theodosia S. Robertson. Los Angeles: University of California Press, 1990.

Haven, Cynthia L., ed. *Czesław Miłosz: Conversations.* Jackson: University Press of Mississippi, 2006.

Miłosz, Czesław. *New and Collected Poems: 1931–2001.* Multiple translators. New York: HarperCollins, 2001.

———. *Selected Poems: 1931–2004.* Multiple translators. Edited by Robert Hass. New York: HarperCollins, 2006.

Mozejko, Edward, ed. *Between Anxiety and Hope: The Poetry and Writing of Czesław Miłosz.* Alberta, Canada: University of Alberta Press, 1988.

Nathan, Leonard, and Arthur Quinn. *The Poet's Work: An Introduction to Czesław Miłosz.* Cambridge, Mass.: Harvard University Press, 1991.

Sandra Beasley

"MIRROR TO KHALIDA, A" ADONIS (ALI AHMAD SA'ID) (1968)

This poem is made up of five movements, each with a subtitle. It was published in 1968 in the collection *Al-Masrah wa'l-Maraya* (Theater and Mirrors), in which the poet attempts polyphonic lyricism. ADONIS has always been preoccupied with the relationship of the individual to the group, of individualism in relation to the collectivity. Lyricism, on the whole, represents a single voice, but in this collection the dramatic and reflective dimensions add nuances to the single voice; and in some of his poems in this collection, there are different voices and a chorus.

In "A Mirror to Khalida" Adonis opts for a musical structure—one in which there is development but also point and counterpoint. "Mirror" in the title draws the reader's attention to reflection and mimesis, thus evoking indirectly issues of representation that have preoccupied generations of philosophers and critics from Plato to Erich Auerbach. Khalida is the name of the poet's wife and companion since the mid-1950s. Their relationship goes beyond the conjugal bond to cover intellectual and aesthetic correspondence. Khalida Said (born in 1932), whom Adonis met when he was studying at the University of Damascus, has written extensively and persuasively on the Adonisian poetics. Her name means "eternal" (the feminine form of the adjective). Especially in this poem the female figure takes on a semimythical presence, combining the absolute and eternal with fertility.

In part 1, entitled "The Wave," the poet characterizes Khalida's fluidity, movement, and paradoxical nature. Her sorrow is mixed with hope, "sadness around which / the branches burgeon." This part touches on the Sufi and surrealistic inclinations of Adonis, where opposites meet and where the multiple is the expression of one. The lesson Khalida (as a person and as the eternal feminine) taught the poet is condensed in the following lines: ". . . the light / of the stars, / the face of the clouds, / the moaning of dust / are but one blossom."

Part 2, "Under the Water," is a prelude to the union of the lovers. Having characterized Khalida as a wave, "Water" seems both appropriate and suggestive. The imagery of nocturnal sleep, the dissolution of the night, and the singing of the blood evoke eroticism. What is implicit here becomes explicit in part 3, "Lost," where the erotic encounter enlists the language of conquest: The lips are a "fortress," the hands "herald of an army," and yet the conquered and the conqueror enter together the "forest of fire." Both the rhythm and the alliteration employed in the Jayyusi translation evoke the poetics of the original with its musical rhyme scheme.

Part 4, "Weariness," and part 5, "Death," are counterpointed as a finale, following a climactic moment. Exhaustion proliferates and then disappears. In part 2 as well as in part 4, the pronoun used is *we,* while in part 3, the *I* is both contrasted and integrated with the *you* in a dramatic war dance. As if to block the spectators from viewing the action that moments before was on stage, part 5 draws the curtain across the scene of pleasure. Everything in part 5 grows old, including the bed and the pillow. The fire itself is extinguished.

While the finale picks up the imagery of part 2, it also goes beyond the erotic sense of dying and touches on the interplay between the temporal and the eternal. One is pitted against the other—the tension between the beauty of the moment, which culminates in an unspeakable bliss verging on the absolute, and the eventual erosion of such moments. This love poem thus has a philosophical lining where the eternal and the absolute are juxtaposed to the temporal and the ephemeral. Using Khalida as the main figure, Adonis succeeds in invoking the real and what is beyond. The name is both a person and a symbol.

BIBLIOGRAPHY

Adonis. "Miratun li-Khalida." In *Al-Masrah wa'l-Maraya.* Beirut: Dar al-Adab, 1968, 224–227.

Adunis ('Ali Ahmad Sa'id). "A Mirror to Khalida." Translated by Lena Jayyusi and John Heath-Stubbs. In *Modern Arabic Poetry,* edited by Salma Khadra Jayyusi, New York: Columbia University Press, 1987.

Ferial J. Ghazoul

MISTRAL, GABRIELA (1889–1957)

The poet and teacher Lucila Godoy y Alcayaga, who later used the pseudonym Gabriela Mistral, experienced a life of contradictions. Though she was to write passionate poetry focused on diverse manifestations of love—amorous, maternal, divine—recurring tragedies destroyed many of her relationships. Her response to those tragedies—a movement from bitter, painful despair toward comfort in religion and nature—underlies her poetry. At the same time, Mistral was to be known as a teacher and an emissary, both official and unofficial, of her native country, Chile, and of all Latin America. Interested in women's issues including maternity, throughout her life Mistral combined an almost mystical sensibility with her appreciation for female feelings and rights, as in the short poem *"Una Mujer"* (A Woman). Her understanding of the common condition of humanity imbued her prose and poetry with compassion and fervor and allowed her to stand as an advocate for the voiceless and powerless.

Born on April 7, 1889, of Spanish, Basque, and Indian heritage, Gabriela Mistral—as she was widely known during her life and is still recognized today—spent her youth in Vicuña, a town in the Elqui valley of Chile. Many of Mistral's later works focus on childhood, and her own childhood was perhaps the happiest time of her life. She regarded her first home as perfection, and she never attained a permanent home again through an adulthood marked by frequent travel and an almost nomadic lifestyle. Mistral's first home, set in the mountains, also contributed to her love of nature.

Though her father was only a brief presence in her life (he left his family when Mistral was three years old), he did have an impact on his daughter's future, for he was also a poet, though certainly less accomplished and talented than his daughter. Mistral was reared by her mother and an older half-sister. Her paternal grandmother also played an important role in the formation of the future writer, teacher, and diplomat. Though not always a devotee of Catholicism, Mistral remained throughout life a spiritual person, and her grandmother's early biblical teachings provided a foundation for that religious devotion.

Mistral's youth was not one of unblemished happiness. It contained moments suggestive of the pain and suffering that followed the poet throughout life. She was accused of having stolen school materials, a formative moment that prefigures later injustices against the writer. Several years later she was denied admission to the Normal School in La Serena based on her writings and political leanings. Despite this setback Mistral studied independently and soon became eligible to teach in the school system, embarking on an illustrious career that lasted until the Chilean government awarded her a pension in 1925. Success characterized her teaching career; her teaching and her writings both evidenced a deep concern for the children under her care.

In 1909 Mistral's beloved Romelio Ureta, a railroad employee and an embezzler of company funds, unable to replace the stolen money, committed suicide. This was not the only suicide to afflict Mistral's life; many years later both her adopted son and a married couple, her good friends, committed suicide. Many critics associate the death of Ureta with the work that earned Mistral her first important public recognition. *Los sonetos de la muerte* (The Sonnets of Death) won the first prize (a gold coin) in a poetry contest in Santiago in 1914. Scholars tend to interpret *Los sonetos* as reflecting an actual event in Mistral's life, as they do with her later work, which has also been largely understood as autobiographical.

Around this time Lucila Godoy Alcayaga began to use her now well-known pseudonym. Although modest (she did not accept her first award in person), she adopted her pen name to distinguish between her two careers, as writer and educator. Her choice of a pseudonym has been understood as symbolic. The less accepted interpretation relates "Gabriela" to the Italian poet GABRIELLE D'ANNUNZIO and "Mistral" to the French poet Frédéric Mistral. More commonly, however, her name has been explained as a reference to the archangel Gabriel and to the fierce wind, the "mistral" of Provence, thus combining both spiritual and worldly elements.

Despite her increasing fame in her native country, Mistral's first collection of poetry, *Desolación* (Desolation), was first published in Spanish in the United States. The book does not have a unifying theme but is instead a compilation of individual works previously and separately published. Despite its disparate nature, *Desolación* is sometimes considered her best achievement and suggests many of the themes that preoccupied Mistral throughout her life and appeared in various forms in many of her publications: motherhood, spirituality, teaching, death, love.

In 1924 *Ternura* (Tenderness) appeared. This collection of children's poetry (sometimes referred to as cradle songs) elevates poetry on such everyday subjects as motherhood and children to a highly artistic level. *Ternura* also reflects Mistral's identity as a teacher in that she intended the volume for schoolchildren. Although *Ternura* contains poems for children previously published in *Desolación, Ternura* contrasts sharply, on the whole, with that earlier volume. Imbued with religious overtones, *Ternura* is more optimistic and sentimental. *Ternura* moved beyond the bitterness and despair that colored *Desolación.*

Though Mistral had temporarily embraced Buddhism, she returned to Catholicism around 1925, when she returned to Chile after a period abroad. Mistral focused on St. Francis of Assisi, becoming a laical member of his order. But she soon left for Europe. In France she was approached by her half-brother, who left in her care his young son Juan Miguel Godoy, called "Yin Yin." Mistral cared for the boy until his suicide in 1943 at the age of 17. For the next several years Mistral was a cultural nomad, frequently assuming consular positions in foreign countries only to leave— or be forced to leave—for one reason or another. In 1936, for example, she was ordered to leave Spain because of her critical comments about the country. Soon afterward, in 1938, her third book of poetry, *Tala* (Felling, 1938), was published in Buenos Aires, Argentina. Ever politically active and concerned with the welfare of the young, Mistral donated the proceeds to children orphaned during the Spanish civil war (1936–39). *Tala* is a much more mature volume than *Desolación,* expressing acceptance of death and approbation of the Latin-American identity.

In 1942 and 1943 Mistral experienced two of her greatest sorrows when her Jewish friends Stefan Zweig and his wife, Charlotte Altmann, committed suicide in Brazil in despair over the Nazi advances in Europe and her nephew, on August 14, 1943, also took his own life. The Nobel Prize, awarded to her in 1945, provided little comfort. Mistral continued to revise her previous volumes, collecting her children's poetry from all earlier books within a new edition of *Ternura.*

During the remainder of her life, Mistral wandered from the United States to Mexico to Italy. She was drawn, however, to the United States and returned there time and again. In 1953 she settled in New York City, where she spent most of her remaining years. Although she continued to write until her death, her final volume of poetry was published in 1954. *Lagar* (Wine Press) addresses in new ways those same topics that attracted the poet from her earliest days of writing: religion, nature, and death. The volume contains poems dealing with World War II. *Lagar* also cements Mistral's vision of religious faith, her understanding of both this world and divinity being implicit in the volume's poems. *Lagar* also contains a section of poems on *"locas mujeres"* (crazy women)—among them the famous "Una Mujer" (A Woman)—and examines the problems that marginalized women face. Sickness and poor health prevented Mistral from returning to her native country until 1954 (she received the Chilean National Prize in absentia three years earlier), and her 1954 visit was brief.

Mistral's *Poema de Chile* (Poem of Chile), which she was working on to the very end, remained unfinished upon her death from cancer on January 10, 1957, on Long Island, New York. As a poet and pacifist, Mistral's influence on her countrymen and future writers has been massive, yet relatively little of her work has been translated into English. Ironically, though *Desolación* was first published in the United States (in Spanish), only selections of her works have been published in English. Nevertheless, among her English-language translators and editors are such well-known writers as Langston Hughes and Marjorie Agosín.

Gabriela Mistral remains a source of critical fascination and discovery. She has most recently been viewed as transgressive. Although she was always recognized as a proponent of human rights and women's issues, both her sexuality and her activism have come under question. Her letters to Victoria Ocampo and her poetic emphasis on the female form have produced homoerotic readings of her writings, and Licia Fiol-Matta, in her *Queer Mother for the Nation,* has studied Mistral's use of secular authority to fashion her own identity. Much work, however, remains to be done on this impressive and enormously influential Latin American poet.

BIBLIOGRAPHY

de Vazquez, Margot Arce. *Gabriela Mistral: The Poet and Her Work.* Translated by Helene Masslo Anderson. New York: New York University Press, 1964.

Fiol-Matta, Licia. *A Queer Mother for the Nation: The State and Gabriela Mistral.* Minneapolis: University of Minnesota Press, 2002.

Mistral, Gabriela. *Selected Poems of Gabriela Mistral.* Translated by Langston Hughes. Bloomington and London: Indiana University Press, 1957.

———. *Selected Poems of Gabriela Mistral.* Translated by Doris Dana. Baltimore: Johns Hopkins University Press, 1971.

———. *A Gabriela Mistral Reader.* Translated by Maria Giachetti, edited by Marjorie Agosín. Fredonia, N.Y.: White Pines, 1993.

Tapscott, Stephen, ed. *Twentieth-Century Latin American Poetry: A Bilingual Anthology.* Austin: University of Texas Press, 1996.

Rosenbaum, Sidonia Carmen. *Modern Women Poets of Spanish America: The Precursors, Delmira Agustini, Gabriela Mistral, Alfonsina Storni, Juana de Ibarbourou.* New York: Hispanic Institute in the United States, 1945.

Taylor, Martín C. *Gabriela Mistral's Religious Sensibility.* Berkeley: University of California Press, 1968.

Winter Elliott

MIYAZAWA KENJI (1896–1933)

Miyazawa Kenji was virtually unknown in Japan during his lifetime, but after his death his fame grew rapidly. He is now considered one of Japan's greatest modern poets and writers of juvenile fiction. His exuberant, dynamic style, generated by a combination of ancient Japanese and modern Western sensibilities, attracts poets and scholars both within and outside Japan. The eldest of six siblings, Miyazawa was born into a wealthy merchant family in Hanamaki, a small town in Iwate prefecture in the northeast of the main island of Japan. The Iwate region, often called the Tibet of Japan, has a harsh climate and unaccommodating soil, and thus Miyazawa saw how the peasants in the area suffered greatly from frequent poor harvests. Consequently, most of his relatively short life was dedicated to improving the lives of those peasants through his knowledge of agricultural science and his art. At the same time, his parents' devout Buddhism greatly influenced his life and art. Miyazawa was a follower of the bodhisattva ideal of Mahayana Buddhism, the ideal by which bodhisattvas (beings who have found the source of *nirvāna* [salvation]) forego their own *nirvāna* to help all the other sentient and nonsentient beings that are suffering in *samsāra* (this world) to attain *nirvāna*. Thus, in this ideal bodhisattvas constantly and endlessly repeat their round trips between *nirvāna* and *samsāra;* by extension, all the beings in this world are potentially both a bodhisattva and a fallen one.

Around age 13 Miyazawa started to write *tanka* (a short poem), traditional poems consisting of five lines

(5-7-5-7-7 syllables). However, the imagery of Miyazawa's *tanka* largely differs from that of traditional *tanka*. Whereas previous *tanka* lyrically express human emotion through natural images charged with traditional implications such as snow, Moon, and flowers, Miyazawa's contain such un-*tanka*-like phrases as "roughfaced quartzite, like a sea slug, crawling along the water's bed." Also when he was in his mid-teens Miyazawa's lifelong love of nature began. He had an animistic and shamanistic affinity with and reverence toward nature that often verged on religious asceticism. In his communion with nature he jotted down in his notebook the poems and stories that welled up in his mind. Many of his poems, especially his later free verse, were created in this kind of improvisational, jazz-type manner, and there are aural jazz elements such as syncopation in his style, as well as direct references to jazz in his poems, such as "*Iwate keiben tetsudō shichigatsu (jazu)*" (Iwate Light Railway: July [Jazz]; 1925).

Between 1915 and 1920, while he was studying at a local agricultural college, Miyazawa began writing children's stories full of animistic and shamanistic fantasies about nature. After graduating he taught at an agricultural high school in his hometown, Hanamaki (1921–26), began to write free verse, and published at his own cost two books: one a collection of free verse, *Haru to shura* (Spring and Asura, 1924), and the other children's tales, *Chūmon no ōi ryōriten* (The Restaurant of Many Orders, 1924). They drew little critical attention, with the notable exception of the poet Kusano Shimpei (1903–88) and the dadaist Tsuji Jun (1884–1944). Besides these collections and a few tales and poems sporadically published in local newspapers and magazines, Miyazawa never again published in his lifetime.

After resigning from teaching Miyazwa lived alone in the suburbs of Hanamaki, tilling the fields during the day and writing poems and tales at night, giving record concerts for the young farmers nearby, many of whom were his former students, and reading aloud tales written both by himself and by others such as Hans Christian Andersen and the Brothers Grimm. Due to his severely ascetic lifestyle and overwork, helping and advising local peasants and farmers, he collapsed with pneumonia and was subsequently too weak to leave his bed for a few years. But during his recuperation he revised his tales and poems and also rewrote his free verse as classical, non-*tanka* poems. Barely after recovering he took up work as an engineer-salesman for a local rock-crushing company on the verge of bankruptcy. Sadly, here, too, he overworked and soon collapsed, never to recover again. He died in fall 1933, immediately after the three-day local Shinto festival celebrating that year's bumper harvest.

Miyazawa's life and art were an ardent pursuit and expression of innocence, which derives from both his bodhisattva ideal and his ultramodern, ultra-ancient cosmic vision. He is ultramodern in that—along with sensitivity to animism, shamanism, and Buddhist doctrines of the transience and relativity of the world—his work shows that he firmly embraces modern Western sensibilities and scientific findings, including astronomy, geology, and Einstein's relativity theory. Yet Miyazawa is also ultraprimitive in that (through this knowledge of modern sciences) his understanding of such ancient sensibilities as animism, shamanism, and Buddhism extends beyond the order of mere thousands or ten thousands of years, back into an astronomical scale of billions of years. Miyazawa expresses such a cosmic vision in, for instance, his "Proem," an introductory poem for his first volume of *Spring and Asura,* a symbolic title whose suggestion of duality prepares the reader for his two worlds of thought. An *Asura* (Sanskrit) is a Hindu-Buddhist deity driven by arrogance, jealousy, and contention. The poem opens with "The phenomenon called 'I' / is a blue illumination / of the hypothesized, organic alternating current lamp" and combines Buddhist concepts of karma, transience, and relativity with Einstein's fourth-dimensional relativity theory, mythological terms, and geological concepts ("*Asura*'s billion years" and "the Cenozoic era and alluvial epoch"). This kind of cosmic perspective gives Miyazawa's work dynamism, both centripetal and centrifugal: Sometimes his writing captures the life of an ant traveling among pebbles under a flower; at other times it rides the wind to tour the galaxies. Regardless of the poet's subject matter, his cosmo-mystic vision endows the universe with a vital spirit, making innocence and salvation a matter concerning every entity: not merely human beings but all sentient beings and nonsentient things. Thus Miyazawa's *"Nōmin geijutsu gairon kōyō"* (Notes for the Outline of Agrarian Art, 1926) asserts that in the new age the whole will become "one consciousness, one creature" (my translation). He argues that agrarian art is "a concrete expression of Cosmic Consciousness through the earth, man and personality" (my translation). To practice this kind of agrarian art, which he calls "the fourth dimensional art," one must "first of all become, together with others, the shining modica of the universe and be scattered throughout the limitless sky" (my translation). This encompassing vision infuses Miyazawa's fantasies for children, whom he considered to be particularly close to nature and essential innocence, and by extension, to the "ultra-primordial" state. It also explains why his style abounds in scientific terms and images, incantatory Buddhist sutra passages, and Iwate dialects: These "marked" elements help create "fissures" or "cracks" in the "wall" of the world through which the reader is transported into the "other world," the realm of "innocence." What is notable in Miyazawa's poems and tales is that before the reader is aware that it has happened, this world (experience) turns into, or rather overlaps with, the "other world" (innocence), and vice versa, just as a person contemplating "this side" and "the other side" of a Möbius band finds that the two surfaces become indistinguishable from each other. In other words, Miyazawa's style often involves a palimpsest-like superimposition of two worlds, as suggested, for instance, by the title *Spring and Asura,* by that volume's "Proem," and by the way in which, through the Mahayana bodhisattva ideal, the sordid reality of Iwate is transposed into *Ihatove,* a utopian vision of "innocence restored."

Thus in relation not only to Japanese but to world literature, Miyazawa's cosmic utopian vision of innocence renders his work exuberant and colorful. Ironically, precisely this informing view was responsible both for Miyazawa's initial neglect and his current fame, inside and outside Japan. The Miyazawa Kenji Memorial Museum, opened in 1982 in Hanamaki, has become not only a national tourist spot but also the center for Miyazawa studies, attracting scholars from Japan and overseas. Hiroaki Sato's translations in *A Future of Ice:*

Poems and Stories of a Japanese Buddhist (San Francisco: North Point Press, 1989), Gary Snyder's in *The Back Country* (New York: New Directions, 1968), and John Bester's in *The Winds from Afar* (Tokyo and Palo Alto, Calif.: Kodansha International, 1972) are good English translations of Miyazawa's poems and tales.

Hagiwara Takao

"MNEMOSYNE: AN ODE TO MEMORY"
IVAN LALIĆ (1975)   The consequence of history—erasure—is a common theme in IVAN LALIĆ's oeuvre. But instead of wallowing in what is lost, he focuses on the remains, which most often take the form of memory. As such, it is fitting that of all the Greek muses Lalić evokes in his poetry, it is to Mnemosyne, the muse of memory, that he dedicates a whole poem.

The poem opens with the speaker driving in the rain through the ruins of the ancient Roman city of Aquileia and the tourist town that has grown out of its excavation. For Lalić this resurfaced city is a "healed scar," a "silence / On which history floats like oil on water" (ll. 16, 17–18). This first section sets the scene where the ruins of the once wealthy Aquileia serve as a trigger for meditating on the nature of memory. In the second section the image of water gives way to that of earth and its "stubborn wrath / Eating the letters from the stone" (ll. 12–13). Lalić questions the origins and purpose of this "feud" (l. 17). All that remains is the gathering of its "consequences," the shards of what survives (l. 18). The third section revisits the ruins "peeled like a scab" (l. 4). Lalić draws constant connections throughout the poem linking ruins, healing, and memory. These ideas dance around each other provocatively, even as they break down for the poet, as they do here in the poem's most moving moment:

> Is there a choice, is there an order
> In the long migration of landscape into landscape,
>   wall
> Into emptiness, emptiness into tree, into shadow,
> Shadow into hope; hope into wall? (ll. 15–18)

It is an appeal for rebuilding, for a saving, of sense against the entropy of nature and time. Again for Lalić "There's no clean future: space stays infected / With the fever of signs, the germ of remembering" (ll. 19–20). What one carries around is what survives, and out of this we build meaning.

In the poem's concluding section, even though it is "terrible . . . to recognize love / In the waning / our task / Is to remember, to deliver blows" (ll. 10–11, 18–19). What makes this chronicling bearable is that nature, or the world, renews itself. As Lalić aptly puts it, "The task of the peach is to blossom" (l. 20). This is arguably what makes the restoration of Aquileia—and the remembering of what is left of it—worthwhile.

BIBLIOGRAPHY
Lalić, Ivan V. "Mnemosyne." In *Fading Contact*. Translated by Francis R. Jones. London: Anvil Press Poetry, 1997, 75–78.
———. "Mnemosina." In *Smetnje na vezama*. Belgrade: Srpska književna zadruga, 1975.

Steven Teref

MODERNISM, POETRY AND The term *modernism,* with or without capitalization, has inspired a vast literature of definition, commentary, and contentious discussion. Nuanced, scholarly distinctions dividing proto- or early modernism from high modernism and from spin-offs like Anglo-American modernism fill library bookshelves. But as Peter Nicholls explains in his study *Modernisms: A Literary Guide,* no persuasive definition of *modernism* (as a monolithic term) has yet been elaborated because no coherent movement by that name ever came to pass. Instead numerous intersecting theories and practices donned the sobriquet, and many strands of literary fashion calling themselves modernist sprang up in the 20th century from literary circles all over the world. "Modernism was not an organic phenomenon whose characteristics can be catalogued according to some ideal taxonomy, but a series of anguished questions about identity, desire, memory, culture, and the nature of modernity itself," as Lawrence Rainey explained in his review of Nicholls's book.

Rainey himself produced a thick volume, *Modernism: An Anthology,* the purpose of which is to lay out key texts from a number of literary avant-garde movements whose modernist experiments with language have been variously subclassified—as cubist, dadaist, expressionist, futurist, modernist, surrealist, and vorticist. But even this volume of over 1,200 pages does not venture beyond the European scene. To that rich tradition other literatures have added their own versions of a modernist poetics and an associated literary history. From Brazil emerged what Louis Madureira has labeled "Cannibal Modernities" (see RAUL BOPP and CARLOS DRUMMOND DE ANDRADE), literary circles that appropriated, consumed, metabolized, and expelled European influences while producing a new indigenous literature, saturated in the imagery and reality of the Brazilian landscape and indigenous ways. A hispanophone *modernismo*—which privileged intuition, symbolism adapted from the occult sciences, and an antibourgeois attitude—materialized from Central America with the poetry of RUBÉN DARÍO (Nicaragua, 1867–1916) at about the same time that AIMÉ CÉSAIRE (Martinique, b. 1913) and LÉOPOLD SÉDAR SENGHOR (Senegal, b. 1906) were elaborating a modernism they called NEGRITUDE. The American *modernismo* was cosmopolitan in outlook and Francophile in literary taste and personal style, while the Negritude Movement looked to Africa and its epic history for aesthetic inspiration. A collection of essays edited by art scholar and critic Kobena Mercer, *Cosmopolitan Modernities,* explores some of the intersections between modernist artistic innovations and the historical crises of COLONIALISM in different nations and cultures. The cosmopolitan ethos of modernist poetics emerged in the East as well as in the West, and poets like China's DUO DUO and GU CHENG and Japan's YOSANO AKIKO invented ways in their languages of renewing perceptions, creating evocative discontinuities, and merging tradition with contemporary diction to break through conventional associations and stale habits of thought. The modernist poets published in little magazines and founded a great many, including—to mention only those in English—*The (New) Adelphi* (1923–55), *Art and Letters* (1917–20), *BLAST* (1914–15), *Blue Review* (1913), *The Chapbook* (1919–25), *Close-up* (1927–33), *Contact* (1920–23), *Coterie* (1919–20), *The Criterion* (1922–39), *The Egoist* (1914–19), *The Enemy* (1927–29), *(New) English Review* (1908–37), *Experiment* (1928–31), *The London Aphrodite* (1928–29), *The London Mercury* (1919–39), *The New Coterie* (1925–27), *Open Window* (1910–11), *The*

Owl (1919–23), *(New) Oxford Outlook* (1919–32), *Oxford Broom* (1923), *The Palatine Review* (1916–17), *The Poetry Review* (1912–present), *Purpose* (1929–40), *Rhythm* (1911–12), *Transatlantic Review* (1924–25), *transition* (1927–38, published in France and Holland), *The Tyro* (1921–22), *Voices* (1919–21), *Wheels: An Anthology of Verse* (1916–21), and *The Window* (1930).

Modernist poems make it fairly obvious that many if not most modernist poets were fascinated by dreams, archetypes, and the subconscious; alluded to local folk legends and world mythology; deployed multiple and simultaneous perspectives; and were inspired by cubist art, "primitivisms," and the theory of relativity from physics. They deplored the stodginess of Victorian-era realism, the maudlin exhaustions of the romantics, and the prolix and bankrupt sentimentalities of the philistine bourgeoisie. Their rebelliousness took the form of uninhibited interest in taboo, fringe politics, erotics and erotica, and avant-garde lifestyles. Yet what makes modernist poetry interesting is not its general message, but the keen particularities of its individual and widely divergent phenomenologies and poetic experimentation.

The critically acknowledged giants of modernist poetry, worldwide, are ANNA AKHMATOVA, GUILLAUME APOLLINAIRE, LOUIS ARAGON, GOTFRIED BENN, ANDRÉ BRETON, PAUL CELAN, RENÉ CHAR, RUBÉN DARÍO, T. S. ELIOT, GU CHENG, HAGIWARA SAKUTARO, NAZIM HIKMET, JUANA DE IBARBOUROU, JUAN RAMÓN JIMÉNEZ, IVAN LALIĆ, ELSE LASKER-SCHÜLER, FEDERICO GARCÍA LORCA, OSIP MANDELSTAM, JOYCE MANSOUR, VLADIMIR MAYAKOVSKY, EUGENIO MONTALE, FERNANDO PESSOA, EZRA POUND, RAINER MARIA RILKE, GEORGE SEFERIS, EDITH SÖDERGRAN, GEORGE TRAKL, MARINA TSVETAEVA, TRISTAN TZARA, and YOSANO AKIKO.

Among the many learned journals featuring contemporary scholarship on modernism are *Modernism/ Modernity,* published by Johns Hopkins University Press; *Journal of Modern Literature,* published by Indiana University Press, and *Twentieth-Century Literature,* published by Hofstra University. One of the best comprehensive online biographies on literary modernism can be accessed at http://personal.rhul.ac.uk/uhle/012/ModsRg.html. John Cook's *Poetry in Theory* is the best collection of world modernist poetry available to date. Cook provides, alongside the poetry, important tracts on aesthetics, culture, the modern imagination, and

modernist theories about language written by critics as well as the poets themselves. Organized chronologically, the book includes texts translated from French, German, Italian, Spanish, and Russian as well as writing from Africa, Britain, the Caribbean, Ireland, India, and the United States. To date no anthology has been published of world modernist poetry that includes writing from the Middle East and the Far East. In view of that lack, this volume provides useful bibliographies in the entries on individual modernist poets listed above and on other poets and poems generously cross-referenced throughout.

BIBLIOGRAPHY

Aching, Gerard. *The Politics of Spanish American Modernismo: By Exquisite Design.* New York: Cambridge University Press, 1997.

Cook, John. *Poetry in Theory: An Anthology, 1900–2000.* London: Blackwell, 2004.

Davies, Alastair. *An Annotated Critical Bibliography of Modernism.* Totowa, N.J.: Barnes and Noble, 1982.

Edwards, Steve, and Paul Wood. *Art of the Avant-Gardes (Art of the Twentieth Century).* New Haven, Conn.: Yale University Press, 2004.

Frank, Joseph. "Spatial Form in Modern Literature." In *The Widening Gyre: Crisis and Mastery in Modern Literature.* New Brunswick, N.J.: Rutgers University Press, 1963, 3–63.

Keene, Donald. *Dawn to the West: Japanese Literature of the Modern Era.* Woodacre, Calif.: Owl Press, 1992.

Madureira, Luis. *Cannibal Modernities: Postcoloniality and the Avant-garde in Caribbean and Brazilian Literature.* Charlottesville: University of Virginia Press, 2005.

Mainardi, Patricia. "The Political Origins of Modernism." *Art Journal* 45 (1985): 11–17.

McCabe, Susan. *Cinematic Modernism: Modernist Poetry and Film.* Cambridge: Cambridge University Press, 2005.

Nicholls, Peter. *Modernisms: A Literary Guide.* Berkeley and Los Angeles: University of California Press, 1995.

Rainey, Lawrence. *Modernism: An Anthology.* Malden, Mass.: Blackwell, 2005.

Wood, Paul. *Varieties of Modernism.* New Haven, Conn.: Yale University Press, 2004.

R. Victoria Arana

MONTALE, EUGENIO (1896–1981) Prolific and challenging, Eugenio Montale—a contemporary of UMBERTO SABA, SALVATORE QUASIMODO, and GIUSEPPE UNGARETTI—was perhaps the most widely

influential Italian modernist writer of the group—especially during the period immediately following World War I. Montale's lofty achievements as a poet, translator of poetry, editor, essayist, and literary critic were internationally recognized and rewarded in 1975, when he received the Nobel Prize in literature.

Born in Genoa, Italy, Montale was the youngest child of Domenico and Guiseppina (*née* Ricci) Montale, well-off owners of an import business. They summered at their villa on the Ligurian rivera until World War I broke out. The child grew up in an atmosphere of respect for literature and the arts and read widely in Italian and French classics. He was also interested in music at an early age and, because he aspired to become an opera singer, received voice lessons through adolescence and young manhood—both before and after his service as an officer in the Italian infantry on the Austrian front. When his voice teacher died in 1923, Montale reconsidered his career aspirations and, taking up writing, changed direction. His first volume of poems, *Ossi de sepia* (Bones of the Cuttlefish), was published in 1925. It was more or less a reflective commemoration of the landscape and life forms of the Liguria coast where he grew up and represented, according to Sven Birkerts, "a quiet revolt against the pomp and high-flown rhetoric of D'Annunzio and his followers" (Paine et al 271). See "ON THE THRESHOLD."

Montale moved to Florence in 1927 to take an entry-level position in publishing. The following year he was appointed director of the prestigious research library in the Palazzo Strozzi in that city, the Gabinetto Viesseux, through which he met many important literary figures of the day, including James Joyce, Italo Svevo, and Ezra Pound, whom he admired as a poet despite his fascist inclinations. With time Montale's poetry became increasingly coded, evocative, and vaguely symbolic, but it was never political. Nevertheless, in 1938 he was summarily fired from his government-paid job for refusing to join the Fascist Party, then in power in Italy. By that time he had met the American scholar Irma Brandeis, who was doing research in Florence on Dante's poetry. His next volume of verse, *Occasioni* (The Occasions, 1939), contains poems that refer to her as Clizia and treat their relationship in ways that recall Dante's poems to Beatrice.

In the years following that publication Montale dedicated his energies to translation, principally of English and American writers, including Shakespeare, Emily Dickinson, T. S. Eliot, Herman Melville, and Eugene O'Neill, and he continued publishing many volumes of verse—among them *Finisterre* (Land's End) in 1943. In 1948 he became a correspondent for the popular Italian newspaper *Corriere della sera* and moved to Milan, distinguishing himself there as a prolific author of essays on widely diverse topics, ranging from politics to the arts. He published a collection of new poems reflecting a renascence of the spirit after the war, *La bufera e altro* (The Storm and Other Poems), in 1956. In 1958 he married Drusilla Tanzi (after a friendship of many years). In 1962 he published his highly experimental volume *Satura,* whose poems resemble many nonpoetic forms of writing—pessimistic notes, dry commentary, dramatic dialogues, short and memorable sayings, and prose—but possess, nevertheless, the force of poetry. His collections *Accordi e pastelli* (Harmony and Pastels, 1962) and *Xenia* (1966) memorialize his love for Drusilla and their marriage. Drusilla died in 1963. In 1967 he was made life-member of the Italian Senate. *Mottetti* (Motets, 1973) and *Quaderno di quattro anni* (Notebook of Four Years, 1977) contain crisp poems comparable to those of the English and American imagists—spare and concrete and reliant on objective correlatives for the expression of deep emotion and sadness about the transience of life and beauty. Significant translations of Montale's poetry into English began to appear in the 1970s, culminating in the critically acclaimed *Collected Poems, 1920–1954: Bilingual Edition,* translated and edited by Jonathan Galassi, and the hundred poems of Montale translated by Harry Thomas. His lyrical sketches in prose are available in English as *The Butterfly of Dinard,* and a selection of his essays has been published in *The Second Life of Art.*

Montale died in Milan on September 12, 1981. He has since been recognized as one of the greatest poets of his age: a sovereign voice reminding his listeners—with concise and startling aptness of diction—that humble contemplation and deep appreciation of the world's flora and fauna, of topography and of the paraphernalia of human life are essential elements of civilized human existence.

BIBLIOGRAPHY
Montale, Eugenio. *Mottetti*. Translated and introduced by Dana Gioia. New York: Graywolf Press, 1990.
———. *Collected Poems, 1920–1954: Bilingual Edition*. Translated and edited by Jonathan Galassi. New York: Farrar Straus and Giroux, 2000.
———. *Montale in English*. Translated and introduced by Harry Thomas. New York: Handsel Books, 2005.
Paine, Jeffrey, et al. *The Poetry of Our World: An International Anthology of Contemporary Poetry*. New York: HarperCollins, 2000.
Pell, Gregory Michael. *Memorial Space, Poetic Time: The Triumph of Memory in Eugenio Montale*. Leicester, U.K.: Troubador, 2005.

R. Victoria Arana

MOREJÓN, NANCY (1944–)

African-Cuban writer Nancy Morejón is the preeminent poet of post-revolutionary Cuba. A spokesperson for the poor, for ordinary life in Cuba, for women, and for African and Spanish tradition, she has gained a wide following and significant critical recognition. Morejón has also worked as a translator, teacher, and journalist, but most of all she is a poet of the people. She received the Premio del la critica (Critic's Prize) in 1982, 1986, 1997, and 2000. She was inducted into the Royal Academy of Cuban Language in 1999. Then in 2001 she was awarded Cuba's National Prize for Literature, the first time a black woman achieved the honor.

Born in 1944, Nancy Morejón grew up in an old section of Havana. Her parents were a dock worker and a seamstress, both active in political movements. Morejón was a superb student and only 15 when she earned her credentials to teach English. After studying French literature she graduated (the first Afro-Cuban to do so) with honors from the Universidad de la Habana and speaks English, Spanish, and French fluently. She has worked as a translator in the Cuban Ministry of the Interior, as a professor, and as an editor of Cuba's leading literary magazine, *Unión de Escritores y Artistas de Cuba*. She has also translated a number of works, written critical studies, and penned dramas. Currently Morejón is director of the Caribbean Studies Center in Havana. All this makes her one of Cuba's most important modern writers and an influential force in Caribbean literature.

Morejón's first book of poems, *Mustimos* (1962), was published when she was only 18. The work reveals a poet with great sensitivity and demonstrates her ability to blend her Spanish and African background into a Cuban culture, a common thread in her later works. Her first major English translation, *Granada Notebook,* did not appear until 1984. Since that time a number of works have been translated into English, as well as several other languages. In recent years Morejón has traveled the world, presenting readings of her work and lecturing.

Morejón's poetry ranges from the personal to the political. She often writes of the black experience but does not identify herself solely as a black writer. She believes she has many identities—African, Spanish, Cuban, woman, daughter, writer—and celebrates them all. Her poetry is at once surrealistic and simple, metaphysical and social. She blends a strong veneration for the folk traditions of her ancestors in poems that sometimes echo the rhythms of drums and chants, with contemplation about the questions of life. Her political poems often depict the suffering of the enslaved or oppressed. Morejón strongly supports the national ideological foundation of Cuba and feels the world has a flawed impression of the island country. Combining her love for Cuban culture and her strong political commitment, Nancy Morejón creates original and authentic national poetry, giving voice to the ordinary citizen of modern Cuba.

BIBLIOGRAPHY
Morejón, Nancy. *Black Woman and Other Poems/Mujer negra y otros poemas*. Translated by Jean Andrews. Bilingual edition. London: Mango, 2004.
———. *Grenada Notebook/Cuaderno de Granada*. Translated by Lisa Davis. New York: Círculo de Cultura Cubana, 1984
———. *Looking Within: Selected Poems, 1954–2000*. Translated by Gabriel Abudu, edited by Juanamaría Cordones-Cook. Detroit: Wayne State University Press, 2003.
———. *Ours the Earth*. Translated by J. R. Pereira. Mona. Jamaica: Institute of Caribbean Studies, 1990.
———. *Where the Island Sleeps Like a Wing*. Translated by Kathleen Weaver. San Francisco: Black Scholar Press, 1995.

———. *With Eyes and Soul: Images of Cuba.* With Milton Rogovin and David Frye. Buffalo, N.Y.: White Pine Press, 2004.

Jean Hamm

"MOURNING ON THE WASHING-LINE IN JANUARY" Rolf Dieter Brinkmann (1975)

This poem from his best-known collection, written shortly before his death in 1975, depicts "a / freshly washed pair of / black tights" hanging on a wire "between two / bare trees." The poem exemplifies many of Rolf Dieter Brinkmann's convictions about the nature and process of poetry writing. Brinkmann's expressed goal of overcoming the artificial boundaries between "high poetry" and "poetic writing" is reflected in this poem on two levels. First, rather than focusing on what he regarded as "serious subject matter," he makes an unremarkable, everyday event the theme of the poem: wet laundry hanging from a clothesline. However, this poem also presents an attack on traditional hermetic poems—poetry that, through symbols, deliberately buries meaning that the implied reader is forced to decipher. Brinkmann's poem resists all efforts of nonliteral interpretation. How does the author's impulse, which he describes as "mourning," relate to the hanging of the tangled, long-legged tights on a metal wire? The poem mentions the feeling in the title but does not refine or illustrate it. By seducing the reader to imbue the stockings or the clothesline with symbolic value, Brinkmann forces the reader to realize that the author simply sticks to a spontaneous description of what is there. The black tights (whatever they may allude to) do not drip teardrops. Any interpretation of the poem along those lines would sound overblown compared with the austerity of Brinkmann's language. What the poem says is only this: "from the tangled / long legs water / drips in the bright / early light onto the stones." The conventional tools of interpretation (often aimed at uncovering didactic messages) prove to be inadequate for dealing with such a spontaneous poem. This poem illustrates Brinkmann's search for an "authentic effect" in poetry. By stripping his poetic discourse of all artificiality and literary embellishment, he removes himself as the author from the text, allowing the implied reader unmediated access to the scene that inspired the poem. "Mourning on the Washing-Line in January" is, nevertheless, a poignant example of Brinkmann's attempt to subvert existing literary norms and notions of a "bourgeois high culture" through his writing, as well as his search for an aesthetic that makes poetry accessible to a wider spectrum of people by advocating vibrancy, topicality, and immediacy in literary writing.

BIBLIOGRAPHY
Brinkmann, Rolf Dieter. "Trauer auf dem Wäschedraht im Januar." In *Westwärts 1 & 2.* Reinbek bei Hamburg, Germany: Rowolth, 1975.

Terrill, Mark, trans. and ed. "Mourning on the Washing-Line in January." In *Like a Pilot: Rolf Dieter Brinkmann, Selected Poems 1963–1970.* Austin, Tex.: Sulphur River Literary Review Press, 2001.

Woolley, Jonathan. "Beyond the Beats: An Ethics of Spontaneity in the Poetry of Rolf Dieter Brinkmann." *College Literature* 30, no. 4 (2003): 1–31.

Peter C. Weise

MUGO, MICERE M. GITHAE (1942–)

Micere Mugo was born in Baricho on the slopes of Mount Kenya in the Kirinyaga District of Kenya. Exiled from Kenya for her political activities, Mugo is currently a Zimbabwean citizen, though she describes herself as a Pan-Africanist and an internationalist. In addition to being an internationally acclaimed poet, Mugo is an accomplished playwright and since 1993 has taught in the Department of African American Studies at Syracuse University in New York State.

In 1961 Mugo, whose parents were both committed social activists, became the first African child in Kenya to gain admittance to the "white only" Limuru Girls School. Her admission was part of a broader campaign for civil rights and racial integration in the larger context of demands for Kenyan independence. The experiences of this campaign, in addition to her progressive upbringing, encouraged Mugo's early political development as a Marxist and feminist.

Upon graduating from Limuru with a high school diploma in 1962, Mugo turned down an offer from Oxford University and attended Makerere University (1963–66). Following graduate studies at Nairobi University in 1967, she began her career as a high school teacher. After two years of teaching, during which time she was promoted to full head mistress at Kabare Girl's High School, Mugo won a prestigious Commonwealth Scholarship for further graduate studies. She moved to Fredericton, Canada, and completed her master's and doctoral degrees in literature at the University of New Brunswick, graduating in 1973. While in New Brunswick Mugo worked as a black power activist and student leader, organizing for the release of U.S. political prisoners, including Angela Davis and George Jackson.

Mugo's poems express her concerns for the experiences of working-class and poor women. Her poem "WIFE OF THE HUSBAND" conveys with her signature light touch the oppression of women in patriarchal villages. Rooted in activism and struggles for progressive social change, Mugo's poetry is deeply informed by her twin political influences, Marxism and socialist feminism. As with the best of political poetry, Mugo's works do not sacrifice artistry in the presentation of political commitment.

Recently Mugo has turned toward theoretical and poetic investigations of connections between African orature, compositions communicating through verbal art and articulated in performance, and human rights. This work has included an analysis of the relationship between art and human rights through an examination of the narrative arts of the Ndia people in the Kirinyaga region of her birthplace. In the collection *My Mother's Poem* Mugo offers an exploration in English of what she sees as the "righting" impulse in orature.

Since September 11, 2001, Mugo has spoken and written against the abuses of civil liberties carried out under the administration of U.S. president George W. Bush. Immediately following September 11, she helped to organize teach-ins on the context and aftermath of the events of that day. Following assaults by mainstream media Mugo prepared alternative texts to address the post 9-11 culture in the United States. She also developed course syllabi that would allow for a transformation of the classroom space in order to foster critical learning about the relationship of the United States to the rest of the world.

BIBLIOGRAPHY

Mugo, Micere Githae. *Daughter of my people, sing!* Nairobi, Kenya: EALB, 1976.
———. *The Long Illness of Ex-Chief Kiti.* Nairobi, Kenya: EALB, 1976.
———. *My Mother's Poem and Other Songs: Songs and Poems.* Nairobi, Kenya: East Africa Educational Publishers, 1994.
———. *Orature and Human Rights.* Rome: Institute of S.A. Dev. Studies, NUL, Lesotho, 1990.
Mugo, Micere Githae, and Ngugi wa Thiong'o. *The Trial of Dedan Kimathi.* London: Heinemann, 1976.

J. Shantz

MURRAY, LESLIE ALLAN (1938–)

An only child born to a nurse, Miriam, and farmer, Cecil, in the village of Nabiac on the remote north coast of New South Wales, Australia, on October 17, 1938, Les Murray grew up at a dairy farm in nearby Bunyah, the grandson of Presbyterian immigrant crofters from the Scottish Borders who emigrated to escape poverty. Murray lost his mother when he was 12 and lived alone with his father until winning a Commonwealth Scholarship to read modern languages at Sydney University. There he coedited *Arna and Hermes,* was literary editor of *Honi Soit,* met his future wife, Valerie Morelli, an immigrant with two children from Budapest, Hungary, and left without taking a degree. Marriage in 1962 after Murray's military service in the Royal Australian Naval Reserve (1960–61) was followed by his holding the position of translator of scientific and technical material at the Australian National University. Numerous writer-in-residence posts (including Sydney, New South Wales, Copenhagen, and Stirling) led to his success as a poet, enabling Murray to purchase in 1974 land that his father had lost over family conflicts following the death of his grandfather. He coedited *Poetry Australia* (1973–80), was poetry editor at the publisher Angus and Robertson (1976–91), and since 1990 has been the literary editor of *Quadrant.* In 1986 Murray left Sydney and returned to the family farm in Bunyah. Ten years later the poet had a near fatal liver abscess but recovered to continue publishing. In 1996 he won the much acclaimed T. S. Eliot Prize. In 1998, nominated by English Poet Laureate Ted Hughes, he received the Queen's Gold Medal for Poetry. Today Murray holds a vast array of national poetry awards. Those of his collections held in highest critical regard include *The Daylight Moon* (1987) and *Dog Fox Field*

(1990). *Selected Poems: The Vernacular Republic* offers the best sampling of Murray's work.

Murray has made his mark with a free-flowing vernacular, at times public and declamatory, at other times meditative and intimate. His signature is a response crafted of concern for family folklore, landscape, and history, charged by a simultaneous respect for bushland, Aborigines, and Aboriginal culture and a regard for the European pioneers and 19th-century settlers. As in his poems "New Heiroglyphics" and "Toward the Imminent Days," a tension exists in the majority of his verse caused by a primitive inhuman silence set in opposition to an irrefutable modern presence. Murray's voice is often in contradistinction to a metropolitan outlook. In 1979 Murray published his most ambitious work, *The Boys Who Stole the Funeral,* where 140 14-line units provide a prolonged and sustained narrative with resonating lyrical and meditative verse throughout. Technically expert and adroit poetry followed, but not until *The Daylight Moon* (1987) was Murray's temperament extended from the reimagination of the world in his early verse to a comprehensive poetry of experience. Leading from this collection and *Dog Fox Field* (1980), Murray's *Translations from the Natural World* (1992) ushered in a new level of poetic achievement. His attention to the natural world here crystallized his past preoccupation with the environment into poetry celebrating nature as an almost forgotten temple of a complex religion. The volume seeks to represent traces of the vast poetry of thousands of years in hundreds of original languages that have been lost in Australia. Murray's thinking reconnects to and eulogizes such markings. In short, his career is a poetic tribute to the land's original inhabitants and its originating song. Later, in the collections *Conscious and Verbal* (1999) and *Poems the Size of Photographs* (2002), we find a mature poet whose earlier jocularity has been transformed into an untempered seriousness. The latter collection continues Murray's midphase theme of the relationships among world, language, and art, but concerns itself—albeit on a subtle level—with the pronounced remove (or worrying translation and transformation) from "thing" into "thought" or experience into idea, in dense, short lyrics, at times more difficult than ever before.

BIBLIOGRAPHY

Alexander, Peter. *Les Murray: A Life in Progress.* Oxford and Melbourne: Oxford University Press, 2000.

Bourke, Lawrence. *Vivid Steady State: Les Murray and Australian Poetry.* Kensington: New South Wales University Press and New Endeavour Press, 1992.

Gaffrey, Carmel, ed. *Counterbalancing Light: Essays on the Poetry of Les Murray.* Armidale: Kardoorair Press, 1997.

Hergenhan, Laurie, and Bruce Clunies Ross, eds. *Poetry of Les Murray: Critical Essays.* Brisbane: University of Queensland Press, 2002.

Matthews, Steven. *Les Murray.* Manchester, U.K.: Manchester University Press, 2001.

Smith, Angela, ed. *Les Murray and Australian Poetry.* London: Menzies Centre for Australian Studies, 2002.

Tom Bristow

"MY BLUE PIANO" Else Lasker-Schüler (1943)

"My Blue Piano," the title poem of Lasker-Schüler's last volume, touchingly articulates the pains of exile and loss while retaining the lyrical elements that have come to be synonymous with the author's style. Though scholars believe that Lasker-Schüler had already begun work on this poem in 1936 in Switzerland, "My Blue Piano" stands as a testimony of the poet's heightened sense of alienation and artistic paralysis in the final years of her life. Likewise, it captures the feeling of *Weltschmerz* (world's pain) that plagued war-torn Europe, and particularly the brutal conditions in Nazi Germany that drove innumerable artists and intellectuals into exile. Lasker-Schüler dedicated *My Blue Piano,* "'To my unforgettable friends, men and women in the cities of Germany and to those, who like myself were expelled and now are scattered across the world'" (Schwertfeger 103).

The poem's title calls to mind the incongruously evocative imagery that permeates Lasker-Schüler's verse. In the first verse she again invokes the color "blue"—ubiquitous in her works—to create a mood of sadness and inner peace, intoning, "I have at my house still a blue piano / And yet cannot play a note." In attributing that mood to a musical instrument, she emphasizes poetry's melodious quality. The verses that follow bear out this message: The poetic subject still possesses the means to create beautiful lyrics but is unable to do so. Notably, assigning the color blue to the instrument rather than the poetic subject does more than create an exceptional image; it suggests that so pervasive is the pain that plagues the poet that it has seeped into and indelibly marked the creative instrument itself. From the world of silent darkness, the third stanza takes the reader "there"—to a nightmarish scene where quiet is suddenly broken by the cacophony and chaos of a bizarre performance: "Star-hands four are playing there / —The moon-woman sang in the boat—." Foreboding and jarring, this third verse suggests that the one place where music is still played and enjoyed is also a place of imminent doom; that is, as in the next verse, rats dance on a sinking ship, just as Nazi supporters frantically celebrate before the apocalypse to come. The final stanza retains this mood of spiritual despair, "Ah, open to me, angels fair / . . . / To me, still living, heaven's door—," prayerfully beseeching the angels to grant deliverance from suffering.

As if to provide proof of poetry's musical potential already implied by the title, Lasker-Schüler uncharacteristically employs a rigid rhyming structure, preserved fairly well in the translation, within which she restricts herself to only three final sound patterns. In the German version one of these patterns is not merely a rhymed sound but a thrice-repeated word: *door*. From the cellar door to heaven's door, what first appears to be a moment of creative weakness soon is justified by its effect in relating these figures. Moreover, by reiterating the image of the door, Lasker-Schüler underscores the transitory essence of the exile experience.

BIBLIOGRAPHY

Lasker-Schüler, Else. *Your Diamond Dreams Cut Open My Arteries: Poems by Else Lasker-Schüler.* Translated by Robert P. Newton. Chapel Hill: University of North Carolina Press, 1982, 279.

Michele Ricci

"MY LAST POEM" LORNA GOODISON (1986)

This is the first of LORNA GOODISON's poems on her relation with poetry, and it is also the first of her second collection, *I Am Becoming My Mother* (London: New Beacon Books, 1986). The contradiction between the poem's title and its actual position in the text makes clear that this is the last "something" before something

new begins, which is particularly significant because the collection considered as a whole expresses a philosophy of life in which the idea of "becoming" and the figure of the "mother" are essential elements. The word *becoming* suggests the possibility of regeneration and rebirth, the eternal flow of the life cycle, while the word *mother* has to be understood in a much broader sense than we may be used to—as the root not merely of our individual lives (one's personal mother), but also of the whole history that preceded us (a precedent matrix, or universal mother). *I Am Becoming My Mother* expresses the discovery of being part of a whole, celebrates the poet's deep understanding of primal life, and gives voice to other women. "My Last Poem" opens with a description of the process of writing poetry, where poems spontaneously come to the surface, delivering themselves to the poet, who takes pride in "making them shine." But this one is somewhat different, because the poet needs it to feed her child during a cold winter marking her father's slow death. Here poetry replaces food and becomes the means through which the mother fulfills her nurturing function. Since mothering is seen as the ultimate function of a woman, this is the poet's "last" poem because she has lived several lives, as a "daughter, sister, mistress, friend, warrior / wife," and this last poem should be "a high holy ending for the blessed / one / me as mother to a man." But later the poet admits that this one may not in fact be her last poem and that she will "keep the word love" to write other poems. The "last poem" stands, therefore, for the last life, the life as a mother, but it communicates also the beginning of something that has love at its center: the experience of motherhood in the broader sense discussed above. In this way the poem acts as an overture for the collection, anticipating the process of all the other poems to come.

Sabrina Brancato

"MYRES, ALEXANDRIA, A.D. 340" CONSTANTINE P. CAVAFY (1929)

"Myres, Alexandria, A.D. 340" is one of CONSTANTINE CAVAFY's longest and most dramatic poems, centered around the elusive character of Myres, whose appropriation by different systems of signification—the pagan-cultivated, homosexual hedonism of Alexandria and the emerging, puritanical austerity of Christianity—is central to the poem's narrative and climactic ending.

Cavafy had admitted to a predilection for the "ancient pleasures" of the Hellenistic and late antiquity periods and for the freedom they afforded to his poetic adventures. The reference to Alexandria is also by no means coincidental. It is Cavafy's privileged historical site and the home of many of his young eroticized poetic figures, all eponymous, as opposed to the anonymity of his modern subjects (see "DAYS OF 1908," for instance). So the mention of Myres's origin is both a reference to the multicultural splendor of the Greek metropolis and especially to its cultivated and cosmopolitan eroticism, which seems to have fascinated Cavafy as well as a number of poetic figures featured in some of his other eponymous poems, including "Ianthes," "Iases," and "Lanes."

The poem is a tightly structured and eloquently paced study of the disjunctions between appearance and essence, knowledge and being. The first three stanzas introduce a reluctant observer entering an alien space. Curious and intrigued, but at the same time also reserved and measured, this pagan's account of Myres's funeral is almost folkloric; so this is the way Christians bury their dead! The next stanza, however, turns back in time to recount Myres's affiliation with another social system, for despite the intimacy the narrator assumes he had with Myres, their relationship, whatever its nature may have been, was forged within the domain of a group of young Greek, or at least Hellenized, gay revelers. And from here on, the transitions from the past to the present are initiated by a series of contrasting couplets, separated and distanced by the strophic convention: from the sad memory of the happy, young beloved (l. 22) we turn to the lamenting old Christian women (l. 23); the narrator's ignorance of Christianity (l. 30) leads on to the narrator's admission of knowledge about Myres's religious faith (l. 31); and as if to highlight the rising power of the new religion, Myres's timid whispers at the pagan temple (l. 52) are juxtaposed to and drowned out by the chanting of the Christian priests at his funeral (l. 54).

There is something ominous and disturbing about the narrator's disintegration at the end of the poem. It is not only the loss of the memory of Myres, as such, that is at stake, but also the entire Hellenic tradition of homoeroticism as "those dark-clad people, chattering about morals" (the Christians, in Cavafy's "Theater of Sidon, A.D. 400") march on to imperial recognition and eventually to official status. But the poem "Myres" is also about Cavafy's other favorite themes: times of decline and change, critical moments of opportunity and loss, when communal and personal identities are put to the test and grand historical shifts penetrate and intrude into the most intimate corners of the psyche of individuals.

BIBLIOGRAPHY

Cavafy, Constantine. The *Complete Poems of Cavafy*. New York: Harcourt Brace, 1976.

George Syrimis

MY SISTER, LIFE (SUMMER, 1917) BORIS PASTERNAK (1922)

PASTERNAK said that the 50 poems that *My Sister, Life* comprises should be read and understood as a whole. The book describes a time both in the life of the poetic speaker and in the life of his country. The speaker is pursuing a woman with whom he is in love, and he has many hopes and fears about the resolution of his feelings. He is parted from his beloved, and he seeks in verse to amuse her, to keep her mindful of him, to woo her as he travels to meet her. She rejects him, and he struggles with the loss. In "To Elena" the speaker names his beloved, who is also Helen of Troy, matchless and unattainable. The country also has recently undergone a revolution that promised but did not bring a new order. The poems about his trip hint at the aftermath of the revolution and convey the hope it engendered. In the narrative the speaker, humankind, nature, and nation are one in a rare ecstatic moment. The poems initially invoke the ghost of Russian romantic writer and poet Mikhail Lermontov, who for Pasternak embodies a free, Russian poetic spirit; later poems evoke the energy of 19th-century Russian poet Alexander Pushkin, who for him embodies a cultured, cosmopolitan spirit. For Pasternak these two impulses coexist in the intensity of the poetry and of the era. "In Memory of the Demon," the first poem in the book, explicitly alludes to Lermontov and his work, while the four poems that set the tone for the chapter "Lessons in Philosophy" implicitly bring forth the intellectual world Pasternak sees as Pushkin's. These four poems seek to define entities like *soul* and *creativity* and so are like academic philosophy, but many of the other poems are philosophical *in tone* since they are reflections of and on reality. In "The Mirror" the surface of the mirror reflects the cup immediately in front of it, while at the same time seeming to reach out to take in the rest of the room and the garden outside. These also appear to rush to meet the mirror, which contains them all. The poems in this volume, like a mirror, reflect reality and, like "The Mirror," invite thought.

BIBLIOGRAPHY
Gifford, Henry. *Pasternak: A Critical Study.* Cambridge: Cambridge University Press, 1977.
O'Connor, Katherine Tiernan. *Boris Pasternak's My Sister—Life: The Illusion of Narrative.* Ann Arbor, Mich.: Ardis, 1988.
Pasternak, Boris. *My Sister—Life.* Translated by Mark Rudman and Bohdan Boychuk. Evanston, Ill.: Northwestern University Press, 2001.
Rudova, Larissa. *Understanding Boris Pasternak.* Columbia: University of South Carolina Press, 1997.

Karen Rae Keck

NASRIN, TASLIMA (1962–) Internationally renowned Bangladeshi poet Taslima Nasrin is one of the best known writers of contemporary Bengali language literature and poetry. No other Bengali literary personality other than TAGORE (India) perhaps has ever been as extensively translated as Nasrin. The urgency of her themes, the evocative power of her language and imagery, the originality of her feminist poetics, the courage with which she denounces human rights abuses and all forms of barbarity in the name of religion, the ferocity with which she has been persecuted for her writing, and her uniqueness as a fugitive female writer with a *fatwa* on her head distinguish her as an author-poet whose impact on the literary history of humanity will be abiding.

Taslima Nasrin was born in Mymensingh, a small town in northern Bangladesh (former East Pakistan), to a Muslim family. She received a liberal education, studied medicine, and became a gynecologist. In the rural areas of her country she became aware of the brutality and widespread physical, emotional, and sexual violence against women. She thus began publishing articles critical of the Islamic code. Her attacks on political and social Islam earned her the enmity of fundamentalists. By the time her most celebrated novel, *Shame* (*Lajja*), depicting the nightmarish fate of the country's religious minorities was published (1993), her persecution had reached a state of frenzy. Islamic political parties organized demonstrations of hundreds of thousands demanding her life. Her books banned,

an official arrest warrant and a *fatwa* on her head, Nasrin went into hiding, then fled the country. She found asylum in Sweden (1994), but her "exile" continues, which is the theme of "EXILE." Her works remain proscribed in her native country, notable among which is the internationally acclaimed *Amar Meyebela* (My Bengali Girlhood), part of a series of autobiographical novels. Although she has indicated that she would prefer to reside in the Indian state of West Bengal in order to maintain her links to the Bengali language, in 2005 the Indian government denied her request for Indian citizenship for political reasons.

Nasrin has received several prestigious awards for literary excellence as well as for her humanist engagement. These include the European Parliament's Sakharov Prize for Freedom of Thought (1994), Le Prix de L'Édit de Nantes (1994), the World Economic Forum's Global Leader for Tomorrow Award (2000), the Ananda Award (1993, 2002), the UNESCO Prize for the Promotion of Tolerance and Non-Violence (2004), and the Grand Prix Condorcet-Aron (2005). The year 2005 also saw her nominated for the Nobel Peace Prize.

Religion and its perversities, the degradation of the feminine, and sexuality—woven together, these topics form the thematic core of Nasrin's discourse. Some of her poems, like the ones available in translation in the collection *Love Poems of Taslima Nasreen,* are in a more lyrical vein and articulate the poet's existential musings on love, longing, desire, despair, and intimacy.

BIBLIOGRAPHY

Priskil, Peter. Taslima Nasrin: *The Death Order and its Background*. Freiburg, Germany: Ahriman International, 1997.

Nasrin, Taslima. *Lajja*. New Delhi: Penguin India, 1994.

———. *Love Poems of Taslima Nasreen*. Translated by Ashim Chowdhury. New Delhi: Rupa, 2005.

———. *My Bengali Girlhood: A Memoir of Growing Up Female in a Muslim World*. South Royalton, Vt.: Steerforth Press, 2002.

Shonu Nangia

NEGRITUDE MOVEMENT Emerging in France in the 1930s and 1940s, the Negritude Movement comprised French-speaking Caribbean and African writers who sought to challenge European dominance and create black consciousness. Its principal founders include AIMÉ CÉSAIRE of Martinique, who coined the term *négritude* in *Notebook of a Return to the Native Land* (1939); LÉOPOLD SÉDAR SENGHOR of Senegal, whose essay "Negritude: A Humanism of the 20th Century" (1970) remains a definitive expression of Negritude ideology; and LÉON DAMAS of French Guiana, whose *Pigments* (1937) became one of the earliest poetic expressions of Negritude thought. The Negritude Movement would evolve during the 1950s and 1960s, growing to include more than two dozen writers and to influence countless others.

Negritude poets were heavily influenced by Harlem Renaissance writers; by anticolonial antecedents; by the student group led by Etienne Léro, which published *Légitime Défense* (1931), a scathing rejection of French cultural assimilation (Kennedy 40); and often by Marxism or communism. Early Negritude writing was published in *L'Etudiant noir* (The Black Student), founded in 1934 by Césaire, Senghor, and Damas while students in Paris; in *Présence Africaine,* founded in 1948 by Alioune Diop; in Césaire's *Poètes d'expression française d'outremer* (1947) and Senghor's *Anthologie de la nouvelle poésie nègre et malgache* (1948), which included Jean-Paul Sartre's preface *"Orphée noir"*; and in various individuals' collections of poetry.

The Negritude Movement aimed to create black pride, to initiate political transformation, to challenge stereotypes of blacks, and to celebrate African and diasporan culture. Negritude thinkers asserted that Africa

and the Black diaspora are rooted in a valid cultural matrix that differs from the European cultural tradition. This matrix, "the sum of the cultural values of the Black world" (Senghor, "Negritude" 28), has its own conceptions of spirituality and art; it is characterized by harmony and rhythm (Senghor 31–34) and by "integration and wholeness" (Ashcroft, Griffiths, and Tiffin 21), rather than European dualism and dichotomy, logic, and reason.

Negritude writers simultaneously rejected Eurocentric values, especially those denigrating blackness and allowing European colonization, this being a "bridgehead in the campaign to civilize barbarism" (Césaire, *Discourse* 176), destroying "societies that were not only ante-capitalist . . . but also anti-capitalist," democratic, and cooperative (178). Negritude thought thus preceded the various independence movements of the 1950s and 1960s in which many Negritude poets would serve as activists.

In addition to its founders (as recognized by Ellen Conroy Kennedy), Negritude writers came from across the French-speaking Caribbean and Africa and included René Maran (Martinique/French Guiana); Léon Laleau, Jacques Roumain, and Charles Pressoir (Haiti); Guy Tirolien and Paul Niger (Guadeloupe); Fily-Dabo Sissoko (Mali); Antoine-Roger Bolamba, Tchicaya U'Tam'si, and Martial Sinda (Belgian Congo, now Democratic Republic of the Congo); DAVID DIOP (Senegal); Jacques Rabémananjara and Flavien Ramaivo (Madagascar); as well as those immediately influenced by their ideas, such as EDOUARD GLISSANT (Martinique), RENÉ DEPESTRE (Haiti), Elolongue Epanya Yondo (Cameroon), and Edouard J. Maunick (Mauritius).

Its underlying premises are expressed throughout the poetry of the Negritude Movement. For example, Césaire's NOTEBOOK OF A RETURN TO THE NATIVE LAND overtly challenges European hegemony and Eurocentric notions of logic and reason; its persona asserts that "we hate you / and your reason" (49), arguing that "[n]o race has a monopoly on beauty, on intelligence, on strength" (77). Black pride is seen when the persona proclaims, "I accept . . . my race" (73), and announces a wish to "bind my black vibration" in "brotherhood" (85). Analogously, the speaker in Laleau's "Betrayal" (*Black Music*, 1931) describes having a "haunted heart . . . from Senegal" that "chafes within the grip of / Borrowed feelings, European ways" (15), thereby identifying an underlying African identity across the diaspora and also the devastation wrought by colonization.

Such sentiments are echoed in Damas's *Pigments* (1937), especially in the lead poem, "BARGAIN." The persona of "Sell Out" also angrily proclaims, "I feel ridiculous / in their drawing rooms . . . my hands hideously red / with the blood of their / ci-vi-li-za-tion" (51); and the speaker of "Blues" angrily rejects "their laws" (52): "Give my black dolls back to me / So that I can . . . become myself once more" (52). Similarly, Roumain's "Dirty Niggers" (*Ebony Wood*, 1945) proclaims, "we're simply / done . . . with being / your negroes / your niggers / your dirty niggers" (23), challenging Eurocentric stereotypes and oppression leveled against blacks. Likewise, the persona of Tirolien's "A Little Black Boy's Prayer" laments, "I'd rather listen to . . . some old man / telling about Zamba and Br'er Rabbit / and lots of other things that aren't in books" (34). His "Ghetto" notes European artists influenced by African art and asserts that "all men . . . are made in my image" (36). In such poems from *Golden Bullets* (1961), Tirolien celebrates African culture, thereby calling for black pride.

Analogously, Senghor's "Return of the Prodigal Son" (*Songs of Darkness*, 1945) celebrates indigenous African culture through a persona who is "[h]omesick for the Black land" (135). Likewise, in "Prayer for Peace" (*Black Host*, 1948), Senghor's persona expresses rage against European colonization: "Oh, I know she too is Europe, she too . . . / raped my children to fatten cane and cotton fields" (137). This rage is also expressed in Rabémananjara's chant for freedom from false imprisonment by French colonial rule in *Song* (1947). Diop's "The Time of Martyrdom" (*Pounding*, 1956) expresses a similar rage—"The white man killed my father / For my father was proud. The White man raped my mother / For my mother was beautiful" (182)—and a similar indictment of European colonization—"The white man turned to me, / His hands red with black blood, . . . / And with the voice of a master called: 'Hey, boy! . . .'" (182). Likewise, his "Africa" solicits black pride for an "Africa of proud warriors in ancestral savannas" (186).

While little has been written on women in the Negritude Movement, T. Denean Sharpley-Whiting's *Negritude Women* (2002) points to the activities and writing of Jane, Andrée, and Paulette Nardal (sisters whose salon instigated publication of *La revue du monde noir,* 1931–32) and of Suzanne Césaire, as well as others.

The Negritude Movement also had its critics and shortcomings. In celebrating black culture, Negritude thinkers at times replicated the very stereotypes they sought to destroy, and in their attempt to define an African cultural matrix they replicated the dualistic (either-or) thinking of Europe: "The danger was that . . . it functioned only as the antithesis of the thesis of white supremacy . . ." (Ashcroft, Griffiths, and Tiffin 21). Martinique-born revolutionary writer Frantz Fanon suggests that Negritude thought accepts European fictions of race that inaccurately define all blacks within a single, monolithic rubric (127, 136), that it sentimentalizes and inaccurately renders African history (130–131), and that it manifests that same neurotic urge to prove equality to a "white world" that is characteristic of colonized peoples (18, 139). Writers such as Ralph Ellison and James Baldwin challenged the idea of a single black culture, as did WOLE SOYINKA, who mockingly coined the notion of "tigritude" (Kennedy xxiii–xxv).

Notwithstanding such criticisms, the Negritude Movement, though similar in tone and rhetoric to the Black Arts Movement in the United States, significantly preceded its American counterpart and has achieved a continuing influence on African and diasporan writers.

BIBLIOGRAPHY

Ashcroft, Bill, Gareth Griffiths, and Helen Tiffin. *The Empire Writes Back: Theory and Practice in Post-Colonial Literatures.* New York: Routledge, 1989.

Césaire, Aimé. *Notebook of a Return to the Native Land.* Full-length edition. 1947. In *Aimé Césaire: The Collected Poetry,* translated by Clayton Eshleman and Annette Smith. Berkeley: University of California Press, 1983, 35–85.

———. *Discourse on Colonialism.* New York: Monthly Review Press, 1972, 9–25. Reprinted in *Colonial Discourse and Post-Colonial Theory: A Reader,* edited by Patrick Williams and Laura Chrisman. New York: Columbia University Press, 1994, 172–180.

Fanon, Frantz. *Black Skin, White Masks.* 1952. Translated by Charles Lam Markmann. New York: Grove Weidenfeld, 1967.

Jack, Belinda Elizabeth. *Negritude and Literary Criticism: The History of "Negro-African" Literature in French.* Westport, Conn.: Greenwood, 1996.

Kennedy, Ellen Conroy, ed. *The Negritude Poets: An Anthology of Translations from the French.* New York: Thunder's Mouth Press, 1975.

Kestelloot, Lilyan. *Black Writers in French: A Literary History of Negritude.* Translated by Ellen Conroy Kennedy. Philadelphia: Temple University Press, 1974. Reprint. Washington, D.C.: Howard University Press, 1991.

Leiner, Jacqueline. "Africa and the West Indies: Two Negritudes." *European-Language Writing in Sub-Saharan Africa.* Albert S. Gérard, editor. Budapest: Akad Kiadó, 1986, 135–1152.

Moore, Gerald. "The Politics of Negritude: Frantz Fanon, Leopold Senghor, Leon Damas, Aime Césaire, David Diop, and Tchicaya U'Tamsi." In *Protest and Conflict in African Literature,* edited by Cosmo Pieterse and Donald Munro. New York: Heinemann, 1969, 26–42.

Rodriguez-Luis, Julio, et al., eds. *A History of Literature in the Caribbean.* Vol. 1, *Hispanic and Francophone Regions.* Amsterdam: Banjamins, 1994.

Senghor, Léopold Sédar. "Negritude: A Humanism of the 20th Century." In *The Africa Reader: Independent Africa.* London: Vintage, 1970, 179–192. Reprinted in *Colonial Discourse and Post-Colonial Theory: A Reader,* edited by Patrick Williams and Laura Chrisman. New York: Columbia University Press, 1994, 27–35.

Shapiro, Norman R. *Negritude: Black Poetry from Africa and the Caribbean.* New York: October House, 1970.

Sharpley-Whiting, T. Denean. *Negritude Women.* Minneapolis: Minnesota University Press, 2002.

Yasmin DeGout

NERUDA, PABLO (1904–1973)

Pablo Neruda loved the rural, claiming that his poetry "gathers up earth and rain and fruit." Yet he also loved the energy of cities, the music of busy marketplaces. He was loyal to his people of Chile even as their government persecuted him. Like his hero Walt Whitman, Neruda embraced contradictions. His rich life yielded not only volumes of poetry but also news articles, speeches, a novel, a play, and memoir. Neruda's translations range from poetry of RAINER MARIA RILKE to Shakespeare's *Romeo and Juliet.* His always-open house welcomed many artists of the 20th century, including OCTAVIO PAZ, FEDERICO GARCÍA LORCA, NAZIM HIKMET, Mexican painter Diego Rivera, and Spanish painter Pablo Picasso. He was a poet adored by thousands of students, miners, lovers, farmers—even soldiers and police officers.

Although he eschewed academic theory, Neruda viewed his direct language as an evolution beyond the "pure poetry" of his youth. He relished the "impurity" in poetry of everyday life, "worn away as if by acid by the labor of hands, impregnated with sweat and smoke, smelling of lilies and urine, splashed by the variety of what we do, legally or illegally." Neruda drafted his poems in green ink—the color, he noted, of hope.

Pablo Neruda was born Ricardo Eliecer Neftalí Reyes Basoalto on July 12, 1904, in Parral, Chile. His mother, Rosa Neftalí Basoalto de Reyes, died within weeks. His father, José de Carmen Reyes Morales, moved them to Temuco to marry Trinidad Candia, who would nurture the sickly "Neftalí," as he was called, and to whom Neruda would dedicate his earliest poems. With his half-siblings Rodolfo and beloved "Laurita," Neftalí grew up in the extreme but beautiful landscape of coastal mountains. Class stratifications of the region made an impression; his father, a freight conductor for the railway, did not approve of Neftalí's hope to join the precarious ranks of artists.

Though geographically isolated, Neftalí found refuge in the library and became a voracious reader of Victor Hugo, Charles Baudelaire, Walt Whitman, and other seminal influences. The teenage Neftalí contributed articles to local newspapers. As he began publishing poems, he adopted the name "Pablo Neruda," asserting independence from his father. Most believe the poet created the name from "Paolo," popular in Italian poetry, and the surname of Jan Neruda, a Czech author he admired.

Neruda moved to Chile's capital, Santiago, for university study. He joined the bohemians with his distinctive costume of black cape and wide-brimmed hat. At only 23 Neruda sold his possessions to fund publication of *Crepusculario* (The Book of Twilight), which incorporated the aesthetics of French poet Charles Baudelaire and other symbolists. This first book received a surprising degree of attention but generated little income. After several years of struggling to earn a living tutoring French, Neruda parlayed his reputation as a poet into an appointment as consul *ad honorem* to

Rangoon, Burma (Myanmar), the first of many homes abroad.

In 1924 Neruda's second book was published, *Veinte poemas de amor y una canción desperada* (Twenty Love Poems and a Song of Despair), from which he gained a large and fervent audience. Poems such as "I Like for You to Be Still" and "TONIGHT I CAN WRITE" fixed Neruda's place in the hearts of young lovers and scholarly critics, who admired his tonal balance between that of mournful adult and enthralled child. The women of his poems bridge the void between an ascetic male speaker and the delights of the natural universe: Pressed to identify his muses, Neruda demurred: "Marisol and Marisombra: Sea and Sun, Sea and Shadow. Marisol is love in the enchanted countryside . . . dark eyes like the wet sky of Temuco . . . Marisombra is the student in the city. Gray beret, very gentle eyes. . . ." These dichotic figures had real-life counterparts, pursued by the poet in what would be a pattern of simultaneous love affairs.

While traveling as consul to Ceylon (Sri Lanka), Java (in Indonesia), and Singapore, Neruda wrote the first poems for *Residencia en la tierra* (Residence on Earth). According to the poet the title refers to his residence in language, using his native tongue as if to taste the soil of Chile. Surrounded by English-speaking colonists, burdened with paperwork, the poet felt disconnected. *Residencia's* three volumes span 1925 to 1947 and hold some of his darkest and most surreal work, including "WALKING AROUND," "ARS POETICA," "ODE WITH A LAMENT," "SEXUAL WATER" and "Ode to Federico García Lorca." In 1933 Neruda met and bonded with Lorca, whose later assassination by Franco supporters during the Spanish civil war (1936–39) would harden the devastated Neruda's communist stance. Later poems in *Residencia,* such as "Song to Stalingrad" and "Tina Modotti Is Dead," reflect the poet's increasing awareness of political unrest.

In 1939 Neruda's consulship moved to Paris. He pulled off a diplomatic feat, securing ocean passage to Chile for 2,000 Spanish refugees, mostly Republicans fleeing Franco. The poet began work on his most ambitious book, *Canto General,* which includes paeans to land such as "AMOR AMERICA (1400)" and the sequence "The Heights of Macchu Picchu," inspired by a 1943 visit to these Inca ruins in Peru. In 1945 Neruda won the National Prize for Literature in Chile and was elected to the senate, representing constituents from mining regions. He soon came in conflict with President Gabriel González Videla, who used force to break up striking workers. Neruda's *Canto* radiates anger in texts such as "Standard Oil Co.," "UNITED FRUIT CO.," and the incendiary 1948 speech to the Chilean senate, "I Accuse," in which he named 628 people being detained in Pisagua concentration camp without formal charges. After this speech Videla revoked Neruda's office and ordered his arrest. Communists and other supporters smuggled the poet into Argentina. Years of travel to Europe, China, and the USSR followed. By 1950, when the epic *Canto General* was published, Neruda had become a poet of worldwide fame, a political exile, and an enthusiastic Stalinist.

In 1952 limited editions of *Los versos del capitan* (The Captain's Verses) circulated. The author was anonymous; but Delia del Carril, Neruda's second wife and editor of many years, recognized his style. Neruda had begun an affair with Matilde Urrutia, who inspired the verses and would become his third wife; he openly declared his love in 1959 with the publication of *Cien sonetos de amor* (One Hundred Love Sonnets). Neruda's romances were turbulent, sometimes tragic. Years earlier, his first wife, María Antonieta Hagenaar Vogelzang, gave birth to Neruda's daughter, Malva Marina. Neftalí's childhood sickliness paled in comparison to that of Malva Marina, who was diagnosed with hydroencephalitis. Her parents separated (Neruda was already involved with del Carril), and the poet's only child died at age eight in German-occupied Holland.

Amid such sadness Neruda found comfort in nature and the simplicity of objects. He was a renowned collector of stones, seashells, flotsam, and wooden ship prows, which he displayed in his treasured houses. While escaping Chile one of his disguises was as an ornithologist; he was an expert on native birds. In 1954 Neruda published *Odas elementales* (Elemental Odes) as a celebration of ordinary things, using the language of ordinary people. The warmth and humor of "Ode to a Fallen Chestnut" and "Ode to Laziness" further endeared him to readers, while the politically charged "Ode to the Atom" and

"Ode to Copper" confirmed his continuing activism. His intriguing 1958 book *Estravagario* attempts to reconcile the poet's dual identities as rebel exile and icon of the literary establishment.

Neruda was often rumored as a contender for the Nobel Prize, but his enemies were as dedicated as his fans. Some complaints strained credulity, such as the accusation that Neruda knowingly granted a Chilean visa to one of Bolshevik revolutionary Leon Trotsky's attempted assassins. Other criticisms had heft: Neruda campaigned for artistic freedom but refused to speak against Stalinist leaders for repressing Soviet writers—even when the Kremlin banned the work of 1958 Nobel Prize winner Boris Pasternak. Still Neruda received many awards, including the first International Peace Prize. In 1965 he received an honorary doctorate from Oxford University, the first granted to a Latin American. A year later Fidel Castro ordered 100 of Cuba's intellectuals to sign "Carta de los Cubanos," an open letter condemning Neruda for betraying his communist ideals with appearances in the United States and Peru. Neruda was deeply wounded and never returned to Cuba, which had once greeted him warmly.

Chile's government, on the other hand, formed an unofficial détente with the poet: Officials disliked his politics, but he was too famous to keep out of the country. By the 1960s Neruda's health was failing; he complained of gout and phlebitis, but doctors confided to his wife a diagnosis of prostate cancer. Neruda devoted his attention to arranging his houses: La Chascona in Santiago, La Sebastiana in Valparaiso, and particularly the ocean views of Isla Negra. Visitors flowed in, and though Matilde did not permit the parties of Neruda's glory days, she managed his households admirably.

In October 1971 Neruda received the Nobel Prize in literature. Over a congratulatory handshake with the king of Sweden, he discovered their mutual passion for minerals and chatted about Easter Island, subject of "Rapa Nui" in *Canto General*. Neruda's eloquent acceptance speech included harrowing tales of escaping Chile on horseback over the Andes. Those travails taught him that "the best poet is he who prepares our daily bread: the nearest baker who does not imagine himself to be a god." He made a veiled apology for sup-porting Soviet dictator Stalin, whose crimes had since been exposed by Soviet premier Nikita Khrushchev.

Neruda's final years were productive despite his spreading cancer and his fear that Chile verged on civil war. Some of his work would not be published until after his death, including *El mar y las campanas* (The Sea and the Bells) and his memoir *Confieso que he vivido*. He endorsed his friend Salvador Allende's repeated bids for the presidency. Allende eventually won, but on September 11, 1973, the Popular Unity government was overthrown in a coup led by General Augusto Pinochet. President Allende was killed in his office. An army raid came to Isla Negra, and a mourning Neruda greeted them with disdain, saying "Look around—there's only one thing of danger for you here: poetry."

On September 23 Neruda died of complications from cancer at a hospital in Santiago. La Chascona had been ransacked by the military; his wife insisted they hold Neruda's wake in the house's ruins, confronting dignitaries and the press with Pinochet's destruction. As the poet's casket made the journey to the cemetery, people flowed into the streets. Public demonstrations had been forbidden. Soldiers trained guns on the crowd, but they did not disperse. Their call and response placed Neruda among victims of the revolution: "Comrade Pablo Neruda—" "Present!"; "Comrade Victor Jara—" "Present!"; "Comrade Salvador Allende—" "Present!" Neruda would have cherished this defiant close to the life of a poet who, first and foremost, placed himself among his people.

BIBLIOGRAPHY

Bloom, Harold, ed. *Modern Critical Views: Pablo Neruda.* New York: Chelsea House, 1988.

de Costa, René. *The Poetry of Pablo Neruda.* Cambridge, Mass.: Harvard University Press, 1979.

Feinstein, Adam. *Pablo Neruda: A Passion for Life.* New York: Bloomsbury, 2004.

Felstiner, John. *Translating Neruda: The Way to Macchu Picchu.* Stanford, Calif.: Stanford University Press, 1980.

Neruda, Pablo. *Memoirs (Confieso que he vivido).* Translated by Hardie St. Martin. New York: Farrar, Straus and Giroux, 1997.

———. *Pablo Neruda; Selected Poems.* Translated by Anthony Kerrigan, W. S. Merwin, Alastair Reed, and Nathaniel Tarn, edited by Nathaniel Tarn. Boston: Houghton Mifflin, 1970.

———. *The Poetry of Pablo Neruda*. Multiple translators, edited by Ilan Stavans. New York: Farrar, Straus and Giroux, 2003.

Poirot, Luis. *Pablo Neruda: Absence and Presence*. Translated by Alastair Reid. New York: W.W. Norton, 1990.

Urrutia, Matilde. *My Life with Pablo Neruda*. Translated by Alexandria Giardino. Stanford, Calif.: Stanford University Press, 2004.

Sandra Beasley

NERVO, AMADO (1870–1919)

Amado Nervo is a central figure in Hispanic-American modernism and the author of a vast production of poetry and prose in the form of short stories, novels, literary criticism, chronicles, literary journalism, and articles on Mexican and European customs, fin de siècle fashion, technological advances, and so forth. Amado Nervo was a pen name.

Juan Crisóstomo Ruiz de Nervo was born in Tepic, Nayarit, Mexico, on August 27, 1870. After secondary schooling he studied for the priesthood but left the seminary to pursue a career as a writer. When Nervo moved from Tepic to Mexico City in 1894, he had already written many poems immersed in the modernist aesthetic. Some of these were later published in his first book, *Perlas negras* (Black Pearls, 1898), and others were included in his much later collection, *La mañana del poeta* (Morning of the Poet, 1938). Since Nervo was also an experienced literary journalist, he was immediately accepted as a collaborator in the Mexican capital's modernist literary magazine, *Revista azul*. A year later, in 1895, Nervo published a short novel, *El bachiller* (The Graduate), whose controversial moral content launched his literary career and opened the doors of the most important national newspapers. In 1898 Nervo published two books of poems: his *Perlas negras* and *Místicas* (Mystics), a work that explored the intensity and contradictions of his religious beliefs.

In 1900 Nervo traveled to Paris as a newspaper correspondent to report on the Universal Exposition there. He remained in Paris and for the next four years worked in journalism and translation, establishing a lasting relationship with RUBÉN DARÍO, the leading figure of modernism, and meeting French literary figures. Ana Cecilia Luisa Dailliez, a young Frenchwoman, soon became his companion and a fundamental figure in the poetry he wrote after her premature death in 1912.

Nervo published a number of volumes of verse during his stay in Paris—*Poemas* (Poems, 1901); *El éxodo y las flores del camino* (Exodus and the Path's Flowers, 1902), a book of poems and poetic prose, *Lira heroica* (Heroic Lyre, 1902), and *Cantos escolares* (Schoolchildren's Poems). In 1905, after a short period in Mexico, where he published one of his best books of poetry, *Los jardines interiores* (The Inner Gardens) and became director of the *Revista moderna* (Modern Review), Nervo was sent to Madrid, Spain, as secretary of the Mexican embassy.

He stayed in Spain for more than a decade and wrote *En voz baja* (In a Low Voice, 1909) and a work of literary criticism devoted to the 17th-century nun Sor Juana Inés de la Cruz, *Juana de Asbaje* (1910), the first modern appreciation of this great Hispanic-American poet. Some of Nervo's best chronicles and literary criticism belong to this period. A corpus of writings collected under the title *La lengua y la literatura* (Language and Literature, 1907) is invaluable for understanding the ideas of the time regarding English, French, and, especially, Spanish as languages and the need to simplify some of their features to transform them into more functional systems. No less important are Nervo's firsthand commentaries on the literary polemics in Madrid in the early 1900s.

After Ana Cecilia's death in 1912, Nervo suffered a grave emotional crisis. His poetry became more intimate, almost confessional in tone, and showed a deep concern with death. Nervo returned to his Catholic roots, as he had before, but now imbued with Buddhist and Theosophic ideas. His poetry loses the "modernist fever"—the need to create imaginary and sometimes extravagant scenarios, difficult rhymes, verse experimentation, and sophisticated language. With this new approach to poetry Nervo produced his last books of poems, some of which were published posthumously: *La amada inmóvil* (The Still Beloved, 1920, written in 1912), *Serenidad* (Serenity, 1914), *Elevación* (Elevation, 1917), *El estanque de los lotos* (Pool of Lotuses, 1920), *El arquero divino* (Divine Archer, 1920), and *La última luna* (Last Moon, 1938).

In 1914 the new Mexican revolutionary government removed Nervo from his diplomatic post in Madrid, but four years later he was named ambassador to Uruguay. He spent the last six months of his life in Montevideo, one Uruguayan capital.

At the time of his death Nervo's celebrity had extended throughout the Hispanic world. For decades afterward some of his most famous poems would be recited from memory by common people and his verses included in popular songs. The Uruguayan government sent Nervo's remains to Mexico in a frigate escorted by two ships, one Cuban and another Argentine. As the ships headed north, other boats joined them from Brazil, Venezuela, and elsewhere. The floating funeral caravan was forced to stop at several ports so that other countries could render honors to this extraordinary poet.

Despite his popularity, Nervo's fame declined in intellectual circles after his death, particularly among the Mexican avant-garde known as "Los Contemporáneos." Post–avant-garde writers ignored Nervo. Both generations considered his work, especially his poetry written after 1912, as "corny," filled with clichés and easy rhyme. Not until the mid-1950s did Nervo's image begin to recover. Today he is considered a master in many genres. In his relatively transparent Spanish, devoid of rhetorical phrases, Nervo also wrote chronicles and articles that are an extraordinary source for understanding the literary sensibilities of his time, as well as the effervescent spirit at the end of 19th-century Europe and the major cities of Hispanic America. His short stories employ the same flexible, direct prose, which showed that the Spanish language was capable of joining the new "sleek and efficient" century.

Nervo's conceptualization of the short story deserves more study. His subtle sense of humor and playful plots produce a relativistic perception of characters and events. This perception, unrecognized in Nervo's fiction by the next generations of Hispanic-American writers, has influenced contemporary Latin American fiction writers. One of his short stories is perhaps the first piece of science fiction produced by a Mexican, *La última guerra* (The Last War).

In poetry Nervo experimented with different verse forms, creating a luxurious musicality through difficult enjambments and phrase repetition. However, his contemporaneity probably resides in his perception of poetry. As José Emilio Pacheco observed in his *Antología del Modernismo* (Anthology of the Modernista Movement, 1969), Nervo wanted to translate all his experiences into language. Nothing was too trivial to be rejected by poetry, which was, after all, a way of living and exploring the world.

BIBLIOGRAPHY
Nervo, Amado. *The Soul-giver* (El donador de almas). Translated by Michael F. Capobianco and Gloria Schaffer. Lewinston, N.Y.: E. Mellen Press, 1999.
———. *Confessions of a Modern Poet: Amado Nervo, 1870–1919.* Boston: B. Humphries, c. 1935.

Amelia Mondragón

NETO, ANTÓNIO AGOSTINHO (1922–1979)

António Agostinho Neto was born in the Icolo i Bengo region of Angola in 1922. Agostinho Neto became one of those rare figures who emerged as a respected artist as well as a political leader of international importance.

As the child of schoolteachers Neto had a middle-class upbringing. He worked in the colonial health services between 1944 and 1947 before going to Portugal to study medicine at the Universities of Coimbra and Lisbon. While there he came to know other future independence leaders from the Portuguese colonies, including Amilcar Cabral of Portuguese Guinea and Eduardo Mundlane of Mozambique.

Neto, along with other intellectuals from the Portuguese colonies, was initially influenced by the NEGRITUDE MOVEMENT of LÉOPOLD SENGHOR and AIMÉ CÉSAIRE. Between 1951 and 1952 he was part of the group of Angolans living in Lisbon who published the journal *Mensagem* under the nationalist banner "Let's Discover Angola." Coming to view Negritude as an elite movement, culturally distant from the lives of poor and working-class Angolans, Neto shifted his energies toward participation in political organizations connected with the Portuguese Communist Party, with which he had been associated since the 1940s.

Neto soon became involved in nascent groups organizing for Angola's independence from Portugal. He was arrested in 1951 and again in 1952 for his involvement in the Portuguese Movement for Democratic Youth Unity. Following his arrest in 1955, Neto was imprisoned by colonial authorities until 1957. In the face of a great public outcry, along with an international campaign involving figures such as Jean-Paul Sartre, LOUIS ARAGON, and Diego Rivera, the colonial authorities were forced to release him to continue his medical studies.

Neto returned to Angola in 1959 to practice medicine and in 1962 became the leader of the underground national liberation organization, the Popular Movement for the Liberation of Angola (MPLA). Upon his arrest in 1960 Neto was transferred to prisons in the Cape Verde Islands and Portugal. Following his escape from a Portuguese prison in 1962, he returned to Angola to take up the armed struggle against the colonial forces.

Neto's poetry and his life's struggle for national liberation and socialism are intertwined. While he used his poetry to condemn colonialism and to persuade the poor of the need for revolution, his works never sacrifice artistic quality for political expedience. Neto's poetry transcends divisions between art and activism and community and campus. His poems inspired contract workers, who collected his works as quickly as they could be printed during the Angolan independence struggles, and they influenced fellow poets and literary commentators.

In poems informed by a close familiarity with diverse streams of modern poetry, Neto expresses a deep concern for the people and land of Angola. His works, especially the poems presented in the important collection *Sacred Hope* (1974), confront and oppose oppression and the unnamed apartheid practiced by Angola's Portuguese colonizers. Neto's poems tear down the façade of civility and enlightenment to attack the violence and poverty underpinning Western civilization and its colonial projects. At the same time, Neto counters the alienation and exploitation experienced by the poor Angolans with the call to take action against colonial oppression. Neto's ringing call for revolution presents socialism as the alternative to colonialism and suggests that only direct action will convince the colonialists to give up control of Angola. His long poem "SATURDAY IN THE SAND-SLUMS," for instance, details the physical and psychological conditions of life for the oppressed of Africa.

After 15 years of guerrilla struggle, in which he was a committed participant, Neto lived to see Portugal's withdrawal from Angola. With Angola's independence on November 11, 1975, Neto became the first president of the new republic. He held the position until his death in 1979 in Moscow.

BIBLIOGRAPHY

Appiah, Anthony Kwame. "Antonio Agostinho Neto (1922–1979)." In *The Poetry of Our World: An International Anthology of Contemporary Poetry,* edited by Jeffery Paine, 341–353. N.Y.: HarperCollins, 2001.

Khazanov, A. M. *Agostinho Neto.* Moscow: Progress Publishers, 1986.

Neto, Agostinho. *Sacred Hope: Poems.* Translated by Walter Bgoya (1974). Reissued by Newbury, Mass.: Journeyman Press and UNESCO, 1988.

J. Shantz

"NEW HIEROGLYPHICS" LES MURRAY (1992)

"New Hieroglyphics" is representative of LES MURRAY's later creative works. In the preface to *The Paperbark Tree* (1992), in which this poem first appears, Murray writes: "Poetry is the principle that controls reality." The pronouncement is significant in suggesting the poet's later aesthetic preoccupation: to reflect explicitly on the process of making poems. It is what in another later-period poem, "Fastness" (*The Daylight Moon,* 1987), Murray says his poetry is working toward: "beyond the exact words, I need / the gestures with which they were said, / the horizons and hill air that shaped them" (249). "New Hieroglyphics" anticipates the recent poetry of *Poems the Size of Photographs* (2002), in which Murray employs short lyrics dominated by the image in an attempt to find those poetically significant "gestures."

In the poem "New Hieroglyphics," an inspired series of ingenious word-pictures—symbolic pictographs in airport-sign style—are evoked in an attempt to cognate the world outside of verbal (logocentric) language:

Most emotions are mini-faces, and the speech balloon is ubiquitous. A bull inside one is dialect for placards inside one. Sun and moon together inside one is *poetry.* (509)

The bull's "dialect" does not correspond to our language world, yet the poem's images slowly unfold into word-pictures that deliver the poetic hinterland without pressure or haste. There is a grace in this collection as if a certain spiritual existence depended on the treatment of landscape, culture, and word, none necessarily reduced to an instant meaning or purpose. Murray's terseness thrusts toward reflection and, as with the following example, brings mediation into sharp relief: "A figure riding a skyhook / bearing food in one hand is the pictograph for *grace*." We find that the imaginary device for attaching to the heavens provides a different idea of "giving" or "embellishment" than we are habituated to; it is, however, a difficult translation of "benediction" when read in unison with the incredible images that follow: "two animals in a book read *Nature*, two books / inside an animal, *instinct*" (508). The first image comments on the textuality of the world, the animals *inside* the book giving us an *idea* of "nature" that remains abstract and almost useless. When the books are displaced and seen inside the animals, we experience something visceral, "instinct," a quality of perception and living that needs no glossing. Murray is arguing that words should *not* create reality but, when subordinated to the task of imagining the living on their own terms, can convey meanings, something for which we must give thanks. As hieroglyphics are figures standing for words, Murray's "new hieroglyphics" represent an inversion of the archetypal poem, the net result being that the reader's imagination is released into the sense outside the logos and upon the universal world beyond the human, which, once lost, is retrieved and radicalized by the power of poetry.

BIBLIOGRAPHY
Murray, Les. *New Collected Poems*. Manchester, U.K.: Carcanet, 2003.

Tom Bristow

"NIGHT OF THE SCORPION" Nissim Ezekiel (1965)

Perhaps the most frequently anthologized of Nissim Ezekiel's vast oeuvre of poetic works in English, "Night of the Scorpion" is also most evocative of the cultural traditions of India, the country of his birth. The poem presents a scary scenario in which a scorpion has bitten the speaker's mother on a rainy night. Attempting to save her life, "the peasants came like swarms of flies" (*Collected Poems, 1952–1988*, 130). Ezekiel describes the eerie scene in which traditional chants and incantations were used to rid the poison of its sting. It is clear that the narrator, perhaps the poet himself, is skeptical of the peasants' ability to save the mother merely through the power of words. Nevertheless, the peasants are permitted to work their verbal magic on the inert patient.

The strength and distinctiveness of this poem lies in the mantra-like chants evoked by the rhythmic repetition of prayerful lines and phrases, each of which ends with the words "they said." As the multitude chants its prayers in unison, Ezekiel's diction conveys both the urgency of the peasants' utterances and the enchanted powers contained within them. Evident here are the polarities between the suave, intelligent, skeptical, educated narrator and the earthy, emotional, naive chanters, whose faith contrasts with the narrator's seeming lack of religious belief. This opposition between traditionalism and modernity manifests the contrast that characterizes India's teeming millions as a whole.

Strong visual images associated with prayer and ritual dominate this poem: candles, lanterns, paraffin, and matches. Like the narrator, his father, who was also present and is described as a "sceptic, rationalist," refused to believe the powers of mystic chants and tried "every curse and blessing, / powder, mixture, herb and hybrid" (*Collected Poems, 1952–1988*, 131). His father's efforts, however, were futile, and the narrator knew that only the powers of "the holy man" could effect a cure.

Twenty-four hours later the poison lost its sting, and his mother, upon waking, said only, "Thank God the scorpion picked on me / and spared my children" (*Collected Poems, 1952–1988*, 131). This utterance not only suggests the typical selflessness of the Indian mother, long evoked in traditional Indian epics and Hindu Vedic literature, but also brings to the seriousness of the larger and implicit contemporary situation a matter-of-fact tone that dispels the poem's earlier gravity and creates an anticlimactic, albeit symbolic, conclusion that completely disarms the reader.

Rochelle Almeida

"NIGHT RAIN" J. P. CLARK-BEKEDEREMO (1962)

This is one of the earliest poems of JOHN PEPPER CLARK-BEKEDEREMO and has been widely anthologized. One of the most successful of his poems, it was first published in *Poems* (1962) and reprinted in *A Reed in the Tide* (1965). Set in the Niger delta region of Nigeria, it describes the ordeal of a poor family when the small shed they live in—the type fishermen in most fishing communities erect along riverbanks in West Africa—is ravaged by a rainstorm. In the assault on the household rain gains entrance "through sheaves slit open / To lightning and rafters." To make matters worse, it is dark and the speaking child cannot even see the mother. The poem starts with the persona situating the incident in time. He admits that he does not know what time of night it is. Theirs is the traditional world in which only cock crows give an idea of time. But he has been forced to awaken because the house is flooded. That water has gained entrance into the house through "sheaves slit open" indicates that the family is poor. The mother is busy moving "wooden bowls and earthenware," her precious possessions, out of the way in their "roomlet." The boy enjoys the thought of his brothers, who are still asleep "on loosening mats" and rolling to the rhythm of the flood. He knows that the entire community is experiencing the flood and suggests that they make the best of the situation "under [the rain's] ample soothing hand."

This poem dramatizes a conflict between human beings and nature in which humans are often obviously victims. But the poem does not eliminate the possibility of taming nature if all the resources available to humanity are mobilized. The material constraints of the family that we encounter become a limiting factor. This situation underscores the plight of humankind when the possibilities of dominating the environment are not realized so as to be explored. In this seemingly primitive state people become helpless and hopeless when incapable of taming natural forces. The poem makes a significant statement from a seemingly ordinary incident, principally because it is the child who renders the entire experience.

This poem is important not just for what it says but also for how it is executed. There is a deliberate effort to capture the rhythm that the flood produces through appropriate onomatopoeic words (*drops, dribbling, drumming*). Run-on lines also reinforce this sense of movement and the persistence of the flood. The poem depicts the poverty of the household with the use of suggestive words and expressions ("roomlet," "loosening mats," "her bins, bags, and vats." Harmony is also created from the way the poet adopts imagery from the immediate locale. For instance, "Great water drops" are said to be "Falling like orange or mango / Fruits showered forth in the wind." The use of *deploying* to capture the action of the helpless mother also confirms that the situation is in some way akin to a war. Even though a certain innocence underlies the rendering of the experience due to the perspective of the child, innocence does not undermine the significance of the issues the poem raises. That the persona renders the incident in the present-continuous and future tenses makes it particularly arresting.

BIBLIOGRAPHY

Clark, John Pepper. *A Reed in the Tide.* London: Longman, 1965.

———. "Night Rain." In *Penguin Book of Modern African Poetry.* 4th ed. London: Longman, 1998, 257–258.

———. *Poems.* Ibadan, Nigeria: Mbari, 1962.

Oyeniyi Okunoye

9–10 P.M. POEMS NAZIM HIKMET (1945)

NAZIM HIKMET's series of 32 free-verse poems addressed to his wife, Piraye, from Bursa Prison in Turkey in 1945 constitutes a significant contribution to the tradition of the love lyric as it powerfully synthesizes authentic expressions of love, longing, and desire with references to the actual circumstances of Hikmet's prison life. The poems make important connections between Hikmet's personal situation and historical realities. They fulfill the promise of the poet to think only of his wife between the hours of nine and ten at night (lights-out time in the prison) and, with the exception of the first poem, are titled only by a date, beginning on September 20, 1945, and concluding on December 14, 1945.

The language of the Piraye sequence is direct, unadorned, and strikingly concrete. The form is open, a free verse of mainly short lines with varying margins for emphasis and expressive force, a form Hikmet established early in his career and used throughout his life. The opening poem establishes a pattern for several other poems in the sequence, linking autobiographical detail and personal emotion to the context of World War II, the "news":

How beautiful to think of you:
amid news of death and victory,
in prison,
when I'm past forty . . .

Recalling images of Piraye—"your hand resting on blue cloth, / your hair grave and soft / like my beloved Istanbul"—the poem builds to anguished action:

And jumping
right up
and grabbing the iron bars at my window,
I must shout out the things I write for you
to the milk-white blue of freedom . . .

These poems are mainly intimate and personal, but several observe an equivalence between the conditions of the poet and the world outside prison. In "21 September 1945," for example, the poet sees an analogy between the condition of his family and the rest of humanity, now suffering but surely bound to prosper in the future: "our fate is like the world's. . . ." Some poems make directly political statements, as when the poet imagines a future in which his Marxist ideals are fulfilled. The personification of freedom humorously suggests the poet's optimism:

And yes, my love,
freedom will walk around swinging its arms
in its Sunday best—workers' overalls!—
yes, freedom in this beautiful country. . . .
("6 December 1945")

Hikmet wrote other poems to Piraye besides those in this sequence, as well as poems based on her letters to him. Her letters also serve as the source for the verse letters from Halil's wife, Aysha, in *Human Landscapes from My Country,* composed at the same time as the Piraye sequence. Saime Göksu and Edward Timms's

Romantic Communist: The Life and Work of Nazim Hikmet insightfully discusses Hikmet's poems in their biographical context.

BIBLIOGRAPHY
Hikmet, Nazim. *Poems of Nazim Hikmet.* Translated by Randy Blasing and Mutlu Konuk, 1994. Revised and expanded edition. New York: Persea Books, 2002.
Göksu, Saime, and Edward Timms. *Romantic Communist: The Life and Work of Nazim Hikmet.* New York: St. Martin's Press, 1999.

Paul Munn

NOAILLES, ANNA DE (1876–1933)

Anna de Noailles, née Anna-Elisabeth de Brancovan to her Romanian father and Greek mother, was raised along with her younger sister and older brother in Paris, where she was educated at home in languages, the arts, and music. She spent summers at the family's estate on Lake Geneva, and the images of Noailles's poetry draw on this landscape as well as on the Île de France and the romantic panoramas of Lamartine, Vigny, and Hugo. The death of Noailles's father when she was only nine profoundly influenced her, and the precariousness of the individual soul is an overarching theme throughout her writings. In counterpoint to this theme, Noailles celebrates, with particular indebtedness to 19th-century German philosophers Arthur Schopenhauer and Friedrich Nietzsche, the Will that strives despite the inevitability of its dissolution.

In 1897 Anna-Elisabeth de Brancovan married Count Mathieu de Noailles and became a member of one of France's oldest families. A salon hostess, admired for her charm, beauty, and facility with her adopted language, French, Noailles was Marcel Proust's model for Comtesse Gaspard de Réveillon in his early novel *Jean Santeuil*: "Her deep serious eyes, her graceful fragile body seemed to be the outward and visible signs of that profound inner self for which they had been created" (469). Noailles's salon attracted illustrious writers and artists in the last years of la belle époque, including Colette, Sarah Bernhardt, Jean Cocteau, PAUL VALÉRY, and Proust.

In her first volume of poetry, *Le Coeur innombrable* (1901), "the innumerable heart" is Noailles's metaphor for the unquenchable desire to embrace the whole of life. This collection enjoyed enormous popularity and received the Archon Despérouses Prize from the French Academy. Noailles was named to the Légion d'Honneur and was the first woman elected to the Académie Royale de Langue et de Littérature Française de Belgique. Within 10 years and following publication of several more volumes, Noailles was recognized throughout Europe as one of France's greatest poets.

Along with Valéry and five others, Noailles joined La Nouvelle Pléiade, a circle of poets rejecting the obscurity and free verse of the symbolists in favor of a classical style setting off romantic, often pagan, themes. While her poetry reflects a sensual devotion to nature and the French landscape, Noialles's later work explores terror at the prospect of personal annihilation, the poet rejecting any notion of life beyond the natural world. Her poem "IT IS AFTER THE MOMENTS . . ." ("C'est après les moments . . .") embodies these ideas.

As Noailles's popularity increased, her health began to fail, and she suffered a breakdown following the birth of her son. Eventually bedridden, she did much of her entertaining and writing from bed. (This bed is on exhibition at the Musée Carnavalet in Paris.) At her death in 1933, Noailles was given a state funeral at the the Church of La Madeleine, with over 10,000 mourners in attendance.

In the latter half of the 20th century, the few who wrote about Noailles tended to marginalize her as a "poetess" of "feminine" themes. Among recent reappraisals, Engelking writes: "[Noailles] broke new ground for women writers through the example of her success, and, by defying poetic convention, produced some startlingly fresh images . . ." (343). Perry comments that "a new interpretive community" will enable Noailles's voice to "emerge from its involuntary silence and make itself heard once again," something "like Persephone who periodically returns from Hades" (30).

A recent biography in French is Claude Mignot-Ogliastri's Anna de Noailles (1986). In English Engelking provides an excellent introduction, and Perry has written the first book-length study, with prose translations of selected poems. For English prose translations of two poems, see William Rees, French Poetry: 1820–1950.

BIBLIOGRAPHY

Engelking, Tama Lea. "Anna de Noailles, 1876–1933." In French Women Writers: a Bio-Bibliographical Source Book, edited by Eva Martin Sartori and Dorothy Wynne Zimmerman, 335–345. New York: Greenwood Press, 1991.

Perry, Catherine. "Anna de Noailles." In Modern French Poets. Vol. 258, Dictionary of Literary Biography. Edited by Jean-François Leroux. Detroit: Gale Group, 2002.

———. Persephone Unbound: Dionysian Aesthetics in the Works of Anna de Noailles. Lewisburg, Pa.: Bucknell University Press, 2003.

Proust, Marcel. Jean Santeuil. Translated by Gerard Hopkins. New York: Simon & Schuster, 1956.

Rees, William, comp. and trans. French Poetry: 1820–1950. New York: Penguin Books, 1990.

Philip H. Christensen

"NOCTURNE" JUAN RAMÓN JIMÉNEZ (1916)

"Nocturno" (Nocturne), from the collection Diario de un poeta recién casado (Diary of a Newlywed Poet), is an excellent example of JIMÉNEZ's "naked poetry." Employing simple language and rhythmic free verse, "Nocturno" is a meditation on the traveler's longing for his homeland. The musical title evokes at once the poem's temporal setting, its nostalgic content, and the melodic quality of its structure. Substituting the harmonious flow of the ocean for the play of musicians, Jiménez's nocturne transports a shipboard speaker back to his homeland. The image of night trains crossing the countryside parallels the passenger's voyage on the waves of a sea "sin 'estaciones' de parada" (with no station stops), uniting past with present, land with water. The elliptical phrase, ". . . Me acuerdo de la tierra" (I remember the land), repeated later in the poem to re-create the movement of the ocean, introduces the object of the speaker's yearning: "Madre lejana, / tierra dormida" (remote mother, sleeping earth). Literally and figuratively adrift on a dark sea, he pines for the "brazos firmes y constantes" (strong and faithful arms) and the "regazo quieto" (peaceful lap) of the "tierra madre" (mother earth) who awaits "el mirar triste / de los errantes ojos" (the sad gaze of the wanderer's eyes). The poem's last stanza makes plain its underlying transcendentalism. Light triumphs over darkness in "la madrugada . . . / blanca, rosada, o amarilla" (the dawn . . . white, pink, or yellow). With the concluding verse again echoing the sea, the solitary traveler feels reunited with every human in history through this unconditional love of the earth: *"los que, sin ser suyos ni sus dueños / la amaron y la amaron . . ."* (those who, neither its slaves nor its masters, loved it and loved it). The mother earth conceit unifies the poem's tenor.

BIBLIOGRAPHY
Jiménez, Juan Ramón. "Nocturno." In *Canción*. 1936. Barcelona: Seix-Barral, 1993.

Eric Reinholtz

NOCTURNES Léopold Sédar Senghor (1961)

The fifth independent collection of poetry by Léopold Sédar Senghor, *Nocturnes* was published in 1961, the year after Senghor became president of Senegal, and it was awarded the International Grand Prize for Poetry from the Poets and Artists of France. The collection is divided into two sections.

The first and longer section, *"Chants pour Signare"* (Songs for Signare), is a group of love lyrics originally published in 1949 as *"Chants pour Naëtt"* (Songs for Naett), written for Senghor's first wife, Ginette Eboué, before being "tactfully reworked out of deference to his [second] wife, Colette Hubert [a French woman]" (Vaillant 302). "[U]se of the historically specific term *signare*," says Melvin Dixon, "suggests a merger of the two actual women, for a *signare* was an aristocratic mulatto woman of the 18th and 19th centuries who was usually kept as a mistress by French military personnel, much like the quadroon or octoroon who appeared in Louisiana . . ." (xxxiv).

The 24 poems in "Songs for Signare" are untitled (except one), and each indicates accompanying instrument(s) ranging from *gorong* (drum) or *khalam* (stringed instrument) to jazz orchestra. Highly imagistic, these poems express love through densely metaphorical language often used to depict simple scenarios. For example, the poet knows his love's "music" with his eyes covered ("I was sitting . . .") or recollects their return home through "mangrove swamps" ("Your face beauty . . ."); his love is depicted waiting at the port for the boat bringing mail ("To forget all the lies . . .") or running her hands through the poet's hair when he is tired ("The head of mine . . ."). His love's beauty is conveyed through the image of a "smile that sets [the poet] a riddle" ("You have stripped . . ." 1.6). The way he adores her is imaged through the poet's taking "long parched draughts" of her face ("Was it a Mograbin night . . ." 3.1). Pursuing and winning her is conveyed through the metaphor of "Dyogoye the famished Lion" (2.1) bringing "to bay" an antelope that has "soft panting . . . flanks" (1.4) and that undergoes a "jubilant death rattle" ("She flies she flies . . ." 1.6). Missing his love is depicted as "hat[ing] the Orient face of the blue Beloved" (1.3) ocean as it carries him away ("A long journey . . .").

Like others of Senghor's poems, *Nocturnes* celebrates black womanhood using imagery of woman as land, homeland, and Africa—e.g., "When shall I see again, my country, the pure horizon of your face? / When shall I sit down once more at the dark table of your breast?" ("Long, love have you held . . ." 1.4–5). Black women are celebrated as the poet "dream[s] of the girls at home, like dreaming of pure flowers" ("To forget . . ." 2.2) or as "Ebony flute[s]" ("Song of the Initiate" 1.1). According to Janice Spleth, "the woman in the poems becomes a personification of the poet's African ideal and . . . is described physically in terms of the African terrain and especially the childhood paradise" (91). Yet *Nocturnes* also utilizes imagery that can apply to any woman—e.g., "your smile like the sun on . . . my Congo" ("A hand of light . . ." 1.2)—or to white or mixed women—seen in the image of Singare, who has "the blues eyes of a fair negress" and "skin with bronze" ("Relentlessly she drives . . ." 2.3,6), or in metaphors such as "black patina, ivory patiently ripened in the black mud" ("Song of the Initiate" 2.2).

"Songs" also continues the celebration of African culture of the Negritude Movement, which Senghor helped to found, as seen in the call that they "shall be steeped . . . in the presence of Africa" ("And we shall . . ." 1.1), or the honoring of African folk wisdom via the "Benin wizards" and "the High Priests of Poéré" ("You have stripped . . ." 2.3–4). Part of this celebration is conveyed through links between "Eden-Childhood-Africa" (Vaillant 302) and through "an idyllic pastoral Africa" that is "contrasted with the harsh realities of civilised Europe" (Reed and Wake ix): "For a long time I shall sleep in the peace of Joal / Till the

Angel of Dawn gives me up to your light / O Civilisation, to your harsh and cruel reality" ("Roads of insomnia . . ." 3.2–4). Alternate to the theme of the "manna" of childhood ("A long journey . . ." 2.1) the theme of aging, as found in "It is surprising. . . ."

The second section of *Nocturnes*, "*Élégies*" (Elegies), contains five slightly longer poems, two of which were previously published in *Présence Africaine* and all of which are traditional elegies in the 17th-century use of the term: "reflective poems that lament the loss of something or someone (or loss or death more generally)" (*Bedford Glossary* 130). "Elegy of Midnight" depicts a persona suffering from insomnia, surrounded by the unbearable light of books, whose anguish is "momentarily alleviated by a . . . fantasy of making love" (Kennedy 192) and who prays for "the Kingdom of [his African] Childhood" (4.3). Here woman is depicted as "deep earth laid open to the black Sower" (3.2), and the tortured insomniac will "sleep at dawn, [his] pink doll in his arms / [His] doll with green eyes and golden, and so wonderful a tongue / Being the tongue of the poem" (4.12–14). The poem thus continues the themes and imagery found in "Songs." "Elegy of the Circumcised" likewise expands on the themes of childhood innocence and aging found in "Songs." Depicting the rite of circumcision as a necessary passage from the "friendly Nights . . . of Childhood" (3.7) into "the noontime of . . . age" (3.9), led by the "Master of the Initiates," whose "wisdom" is needed "to break the cipher of things" (4.3) and undertake adult male duties, the poem depicts the loss of childhood as a rebirth through song and poem: "The Phoenix rises . . . over the carnage of words" (4.8).

In "Elegy of the Saudades" (nostalgia) the poet depicts learning the Portuguese origin of his name— "*Senhor* the name a captain once gave his faithful laptot [a soldier of the Senegalese light infantry]" (1.4)—and imagines the colonial history that led to or came from this colonial encounter. "Elegy of the Waters" calls for "Rain on New York . . . Moscow . . . China" (3.7–9) to put out the "Fire! Burning walls of Chicago . . . / Fire on Moscow" (9–10) and renew life. The final poem, "Elegy for Aynina Fall," is "a dramatic poem in praise of Aynina Fall, who led striking workers to protest the harsh conditions of labor in the construction of a railroad" (Dixon xxxiv).

BIBLIOGRAPHY
Kennedy, Ellen Conroy, ed. *The Negritude Poets: An Anthology of Translations from the French*. New York: Thunder's Mouth Press, 1975.
Murfin, Ross, and Supryia M. Ray. "Elegy." In *The Bedford Glossary of Critical and Literary Terms*. 2d ed. New York: Bedford/St. Martin's, 2003.
Senghor, Léopold Sédar. *The Collected Poetry*. Translated and introduced by Melvin Dixon. Charlottesville: University Press of Virginia, 1991.
———. *Nocturnes*. 1961. Translated and introduced by John Reed and Clive Wake. African Writers Series. London: Heinemann Educational Books, 1969.
Spleth, Janice. *Léopold Sédar Senghor*. Twayne's World Author Series, French Literature, edited by David O'Connell. Boston: Twayne, 1985.
Vaillant, Janet G. *Black, French, and African: A Life of Léopold Sédar Senghor*. Cambridge, Mass.: Harvard University Press, 1990.

Yasmin Y. DeGout

"NO-MAN'S LAND" IMTIAZ DHARKER (1994)

IMTIAZ DHARKER calls herself a Scottish Muslim Calvinist and writes in English. Her "No-Man's Land" first appeared in her second volume of poetry, *Postcards from God*. This poem begins with a stark visual image and a hair-raising auditory one: "A bleak view. A stretch of empty beach" and the screech of seagulls. The place thus evoked is preserved in memory because of what was said and not said between two unidentified interlocutors sitting on the beach who at some earlier point had reached an impasse in their relationship. The speaker—recalling that the other person had asked, "Is there no way back[?]"—heard "the words for what they [were]: / a half meant signal sent / from no-man's land . . ." (stanza 2). The speaker remembers feeling that the two of them were (metaphorically) "countries out of reach."

Here the memory ends, and an associative thought occurs about "Places washed by the sea; / places that men may trample, / stamp across with heavy feet, / batter with their bombs / and bullets, shatter / in staccato sound." These places, the poet defiantly asserts, "still go free." In the final stanza the speaker explains that the trampled and battered places are cleansed eventually by "a rhythm that [men] cannot change," those natural processes "soothing away [the] furrows / from the forehead of the earth / with a mother's light relentless hand."

The poem's evocation of conflict (and its association with "bleak" environments) and the speaker's comfort in realizing that time and nature are cleansing and restorative are both buttressed by the poem's versification. The stanzas are ragged, and lines are unmetered and often end on jarring words (*trample, heavy feet, bombs, shatter*), but the light-handed rhyming of first lines with final lines in each stanza (*beach/screech, sand/ land, reach, sea/free, sand/hand*) produces a soft repetition of *and*-sounds at the end that bolster the concluding idea of a "soothing" feminine energy tirelessly at work on the planet. The poem's conceit becomes clear, almost physical: Parts of the Earth have been made into no-man's lands, but the Earth is no man's land.

R. Victoria Arana

NORDBRANDT, HENRIK (1945–) Henrik Nordbrandt is unique among Denmark's major contemporary poets in that his poetry, of which he has published 25 volumes to date, evokes distinctly non-Danish settings. He published his first volume of poetry, *Digte* (Poems) in 1966, the same year he made his first trip to Greece. Since then he has spent more time living in Turkey, Greece, Spain, and Italy than in Denmark. This influence is clearly visible in his poem titles, among them "Baklava," "China Observed through Greek Rain in Turkish Coffee," and "On the Way to Ithaca." Nordbrandt is like many Scandinavians of his generation who, weary of the long months of darkness that characterize Nordic winters, seek out warmer climates. Such seasonal migration has become relatively common for contemporary middle-class Scandinavians, made possible by an economic boom since World War II and the coinciding five weeks of annual vacation guaranteed by the Scandinavian social welfare model. Nordbrandt, however, has chosen to live most of his life in these warmer regions—an unusual act for a state-supported artist—and turn his appreciation for them into an essential ingredient of his poetry, summoning not only contemporary Mediterranean landscapes but also the rich cultural and literary heritage of the ancient Greeks. In an essay published in the weekly

Danish newspaper *Information* in 1995, which he wrote in Turkey, Nordbrandt explained that the light that drew him to the Mediterranean had to do with the worldview it represented as much as the climate: "Herodotus was born not far from here. A little more than three hundred kilometers away Socrates modeled an outlook which basically reflects this very landscape: light here, shadow there, and no twilight in between, no breeding ground for the demons of irrationality" (Bredsdorff 313).

Such appreciation of the clear delineation between light and shadow points to what Danish scholar Thomas Bredsdorff calls a major tendency in Nordbrandt's poetry: the interplay of presence and absence. What makes Nordbrandt a modern, even postmodern, poet, according to Bredsdorff, is that "absence is no tragedy; on the contrary, absence is what makes poetry possible" (Bredsdorff 315). A generic Nordic melancholy, accordingly, does not manifest itself in Nordbrandt's poetry; in place of this is a distinctly Danish sense of irony that Nordbrandt renders poetic. "Nordbrandt has created a new metaphysics of the void," wrote Gerard Rasch on the occasion of Nordbrandt's participation in the Poetry International Festival Rotterdam in 2000. "In unusual metaphors, in decadent, even 'gothic,' images, in endlessly meandering sentences, he conjures up a world where loss and fulfillment occur simultaneously." This tendency manifests itself strongly in poems such as "THE CATAMARAN" ("Katamaran," 1995) and "The Screw" (*"Skruen,"* 1987). "The Screw," for example, begins with the speaker claiming: "In my dream I found the screw / that held everything together." In the poem the speaker busies himself with figuring out how to assemble the gadget that the screw holds together, and once he completes the task he discovers that "my wife had left me / and my children were grown up." At the conclusion acts of construction and deconstruction coalesce: "So I smashed everything and started all over again." The futility of love is another theme in Nordbrandt's poetry. In real life Nordbrandt married twice and divorced both times, and at age 46 he lost the woman with whom he planned to spend the rest of his life when she died suddenly of thrombosis at age 28. Bredsdorff characterizes Nordbrandt's poetry collection *The Worms at the*

Gate of Heaven (*Ormene ved himlens port,* 1995) as "a mental journey from loss to recovery" in the aftermath of this personal loss.

Nordbrandt was born in Fredericksburg on the outskirts of the capital city of Copenhagen. As a child he suffered from chronic ear, nose, and throat infections, which accounts in part for his attraction to Mediterranean climates. He entered the University of Copenhagen for the first time in 1967 but dropped out the following year to return to Greece, where he married his first wife, Martha Birgitta Keiding. The union lasted three years. Nordbrandt returned to his studies in Copenhagen at different points through 1975, learning Chinese, Arabic, and Turkish, but he never completed a degree and showed no interest in academic life. He was more drawn to the life of a bohemian intellectual who travels, revels in new experiences, and writes about them. Nonetheless, in 1977 he married again, and his marriage to Anneli Fuchs lasted until 1983. In addition to his poetic works, he also dabbled in fiction, publishing two volumes of essays, a political thriller, two children's books, and a Turkish cookbook (Bredsdorff 312). Over the years Nordbrandt has received many Nordic literary prizes, including the Danish Academy Major Prize (1980), the Swedish Academy Nordic Prize (1990), the Danish Booksellers' Golden Laurels (1995), and the Nordic Council Prize for Literature (2000). His poetic influences include the contemporary Danish poet INGER CHRISTENSEN, who was his teacher at the University of Copenhagen's Writer's Workshop; the modern American poet Wallace Stevens; the modern English poet T. S. Eliot, the modern Swedish poet Gunnar Ekelöf, and the medieval Turkish poet Yunus Emre. Three volumes of Nordbrandt's poetry have been translated into English, with his assistance, and remain in print: *God's House* (1979), *Selected Poems* (1982), and *The Hangman's Lament: Poems, A Bilingual Edition* (2003). This last edition won translator Thom Satterlee the American-Scandinavian Foundation Translation Prize while it was still in manuscript in 1998. A dominant literary force in Scandinavia since the 1970s despite his living abroad most of this time, Nordbrandt demonstrates through his life as well as his work that presence and absence are inextricably linked.

BIBLIOGRAPHY

Bredsdorff, Thomas. "Henrik Nordbrandt." In *Twentieth-Century Danish Writers,* edited by Marianne Stecher-Hansen, 311–316. Detroit: Gale Group, 1999.

Nordbrandt, Henrik. *God's House.* Translated by Alexander Taylor. Williamantic, Conn.: Augustinus/Curbstone, 1979.

———. *The Hangman's Lament: Poems, A Bilingual Edition.* Translated by Thom Satterlee. Los Angeles: Green Integer 95, 2003.

———. *Selected Poems.* Translated by Alexander Taylor. Williamantic, Conn.: Augustinus/Curbstone, 1982.

Rasch, Gerard. "Henrik Nordbrandt." Translated by Ko Kooman. *Poetry International Web.* Available online. URL: http://international.poetryinternationalweb.org/piw_cms/cms/cms_module/index.php?obj_id= 432. Accessed on April 23, 2007.

Ursula A. L. Lindqvist

NOTEBOOK OF A RETURN TO THE NATIVE LAND AIMÉ CÉSAIRE (1939)

The poem—divided into stanzas of varying length and written in unrhymed free verse—begins with the refrain, repeated throughout, "At the end of the wee hours . . . ," as the speaker wakes from a troubled sleep to survey the degradation of life in his small Martinican town. The dawn presages no hope: The speaker curses the "venereal sun" and the forces of civic order and religion, which he likens to an evil curse, or "grigri": "Beat it . . . , you cop, you lousy pig, beat it, I detest the flunkies of order and the / cockchafers of hope. Beat it, evil grigri, you bedbug of a petty monk." John Milton is evoked in the first stanza, the Antilles representing "paradises lost" in the wake of French colonialism.

Surrealism's influence is evident throughout the poem. The narrator spews a stream of dark images of an Antilles devastated by colonialism. Following surrealism's reliance on the subconscious and automatic writing, AIMÉ CÉSAIRE creates a feeling of spontaneous poetic consciousness. The natural beauty of the islands belies an endemic illness that persists from decades of European exploitation: "At the end of the wee hours bourgeoning with frail coves, the hungry Antilles, the Antilles pitted / with smallpox, the Antilles dynamited by alcohol" is "bursting with tepid / pustules, the awful futility of our raison d'être." One cannot help noticing in these lines an echo of the French poet Charles Baudelaire, whose contradictory image of *"fleurs du mal"* (flowers of evil) becomes in Césaire's poem "flowers of blood."

The Antilleans are divorced from any sense of identity, having been stripped of it by European colonials. Antilleans, not given the opportunity to participate in white society, are in limbo, their own roots having been destroyed and their dream of material well-being thwarted by white supremacy and French empire, evoked here by the narrator's allusion to "Josephine, Empress of the French, dreaming way up there above the nigger scum." Césaire uses the pejorative *nigger* to reflect white racism.

Efforts to "civilize" Antilleans—through the French-based school system or through the Catholic religion—are futile because poverty and hunger are more pressing concerns: ". . . neither the teacher in his classroom, nor the priest at catechism will be able to get a word / out of this sleepy little nigger, no matter how energetically they drum on his shorn skull, for / starvation has quicksanded his voice into the swamp of hunger." Furthermore, the history of the French aristocracy and Catholic dogma are ridiculously misplaced and alien to island culture.

The speaker passes from his memories of boyhood poverty and starvation to adulthood, and the reader is shown that conditions have not changed, as the speaker describes his present poverty and his house—a wooden shanty with a roof of corrugated iron, described as a rotting "carcass," sparsely furnished, containing "spectral straw chairs, the grey lamp light, the glossy flash of cockroaches in a maddening buzz."

The passing of the seasons is marked by the metamorphosis of nature—mango trees burgeoning in late summer, the cyclones and maturation of sugarcane in the fall, and the processing of sugar as winter approaches. But even Christmas, generally a time of celebration, brings little hope to Antilleans, who worry about not having enough to eat. It is as if this Christian feast—once foreign to precolonial Antilleans—remains a celebration in which they cannot fully indulge. Yet they attend church, and there is temporary joy in community, in singing, in sharing food and drink, and in worship. But as this joy climaxes, there is a foreboding that after this day life will return to its burdens of poverty and despair: "At the peak of its ascent, joy bursts like a cloud. The songs don't stop, but now anxious and / heavy roll through the valleys of fear, the tunnels of anguish and the fires of hell."

Once again, the refrain "At the end of the wee hours . . ." reveals the stark reality of the new day with its "aborted dreams" like a terminated fetus. The speaker flashes back to memories of childhood, his father a man—like Césaire's own, striving to make a better life for Aimé and his six siblings—who could be driven to "towering flames of anger" from the pain of struggle. The speaker's mother works as a seamstress in a sweatshop, and the speaker is "awakened at night / by these tireless legs which pedal the night . . . a Singer / that my mother pedals, pedals for our hunger and day and night." Even the speaker's grandmother is forced to beg for money, and over her bed, reflected by the feeble flame of an oil lamp, is a jar on which the word *Merci* is written in gold letters, Césaire here playing on the two meanings of the word: one denoting thanks (money given by passersby), the other a plea for "mercy."

In spite of these travails, the speaker will not abandon hope but instead takes courage by reclaiming the dignity and pride of his "Negritude"—his "Blackness": "my negritude . . . takes root in the red flesh of the soil / it takes root in the ardent flesh of the sky." Thus after the ravages of slavery and French colonization, the speaker dreams of a better future that will be achieved through pride in his color, his culture, and his creation.

BIBLIOGRAPHY

Césaire, Aimé. *The Collected Poetry of Aimé Césaire.* Translated and edited by Clayton Eshleman and Annette Smith. Berkeley and Los Angeles: University of California Press, 1983.

Davis, Gregson. *Aimé Césaire.* Cambridge: Cambridge University Press, 1997.

Patrick L. Day

"OCTOPUS THAT DOES NOT DIE, THE"

SAKUTARŌ HAGIWARA (1917)   Composed as a prose poem and narrated from an omniscient point of view, this piece by SAKUTARŌ gives an account of the sad life of an octopus neglected for a long time in "a certain aquarium" (281). The poet delicately describes the "dim rock shadows" and "pale crystal ceiling rays of light" that drift across the forgotten octopus, left for dead in stagnant brine behind the dirty glass of his tank. The reader shares in the narrator's omniscience and perceives a process that must be understood, finally, as symbolic of the physical and metaphysical effects of isolation and confinement.

The octopus ate everything he could in the tank, slept for a while, then woke, but only to starve day after day. Finally, desperate, he "tore off his legs and ate them. First, one leg. Then, another"—until they were all consumed. Then he "turned his body inside out" and finally after a time "finished eating all of his body." The octopus had cannibalized itself methodically: "Epidermis, brains, stomach. Every part, leaving nothing at all. Completely." The octopus vanished but "did not die" and "was eternally alive *there*. . . . Eternally—most likely through many centuries—an animal with a certain horrible deficiency and dissatisfaction was alive, invisible to the human eye." So ends the piece.

Some of the narrator's earlier bizarre declarations, unintrusive on the first go-around, remain for the reader to conjure on second thought. Somehow, "willowy seaweed" eventually grows back in the tank and is ignored by the invisible octopus. The poet may be implying that once the octopus is utterly involuted, real foodstuffs are no longer of any interest to this sort of creature, a living thing that has turned on itself and consumed every part of itself except for its "horrible" vitality. Furthermore, the speaker of this report turns out to be *not* a logical or reliable storyteller (even if we *do* swallow the tall tale he tells). While a reader can certainly entertain the notion of spiritual immortality (even the undying effects of such "deficiency and dissatisfaction" as the poem evokes), how is one to interpret an eternity that lasts only "centuries"? One response might be to take this sort of expression in the language of the poem as colloquial, representative of the way ordinary people exaggerate, mix metaphors, and sound sometimes entirely irrational when they attempt to verbalize essentially ineffable emotional states or disturbing thoughts. In sum, "The Octopus That Does Not Die" presents a multilayered conundrum to anyone who attempts a close reading. What remains clear, however, is that prolonged solitary confinement must be "terrible" indeed.

BIBLIOGRAPHY

Hagiwara Sakutarō. *Howling at the Moon: Poems and Prose of Hagiwara Sakutarō.* Translated and introduced by Hiroaki Sato. Copenhagen and Los Angeles: Green Integer (#57), 2002.

R. Victoria Arana

"ODE TO GOSSIPS" ANDREY VOZNESENSKY (1960)

ANDREY VOZNESENSKY first published "Ode to Gossips" in his second collection of verse, *Parabola*, published in Moscow (1960); he then slightly altered the poem when he republished it in *Antimiry* (Antiworlds, 1964). Stanley Moss's excellent translation preserves the work's eclectic diction and saucy tongue-in-cheek tone. The poem's speaker blusters at first, opening the eight-stanza poem by announcing, "I praise the keyhole, / Long live slanderers, may all / Reputations fall / Into a creaking bed" (*Antiworlds* 81). The ears of gossips are "like toilet bowls," and their stories "gurgle and echo / Down the sewerage of years. . . ." In the central part of the poem, the speaker relates that while he "was living in Siberia, messages / . . . / Came in like machine-gun bullets, flashes / Of gossip mowed me down." The gossipers relished relaying—via letters and long-distance telephone calls—a barrage of lascivious details about the infidelity of the speaker's woman. In the final five stanzas the speaker returns to Moscow to find his "Darling Natasha" smelling not of sin but of "snow and spring." He deduces that the slander "came to prove" her "longing" and her "love" for him. In an ironic twist of logic, he sees that malice powers gossip, not truth. Still, the speaker's question ("But why this deathly silence?") reveals his foreboding when, back in Moscow, he notes at the end of the poem that his "phone has stopped ringing."

If this poem, like so many others by Voznesensky, is a parable of sorts, it is not simply about spiteful gossips, but also about the constant state of dread and paranoia that a person feels, no matter what, when he or she is kept under constant KGB-type surveillance (whether by nosy, chitchatting characters or the silent, lethal types). "Ode to Gossips" was reissued in 1964, after Soviet premier Nikita Khrushchev's informants and sycophants "called for an end to the [dissident writers'] editions of 100,000 copies, the favorable reviews, and the trips abroad for writers who, they claimed, flout party opinion and play the game of Western bourgeois ideologists" and after Khrushchev himself hurled his menacing personal tirade in 1963 against Voznesensky and his fellow poet YEVGENY YEVTUSHENKO and their "'rotten, overpraised, unrealistic, smelly writings'" (Blake and Hayward xiii). "Ode to Gossips" was the poet's sardonically defiant gesture against his enemies. Voznesensky was cleverly likening himself not only to the poem's first victim of gossip (its tortured speaker), but also to the other innocent and slandered injured party (Natasha), the beloved who came out smelling clean as "snow" and sweet as "spring" in the end.

BIBLIOGRAPHY

Blake, Patricia, and Max Hayward, eds. Introduction to Andrei Voznesensky's *Antiworlds*. New York: Basic Books, 1966. Available online as "Andrei Voznesensky." URL: http://www.penrussia.org/n-z/an_voz.htm#i. Accessed on April 23, 2007.

Voznesensky, Andrey. "Ode to Gossips." Translated by Stanley Moss. In *Antiworlds*. New York: Basic Books, 1966.

R. Victoria Arana

"ODE TO WALT WHITMAN" FEDERICO GARCÍA LORCA (1929–1930)

The central poem of the *Poet in New York* (*Poeta en Nueva York*) cycle, "Ode to Walt Whitman" is one of FEDERICO GARCÍA LORCA's lyric landmarks in which the poet uses avant-garde form (including free verse and surrealist imagery) to express his views on the relationship between an artist and his audience. As its title suggests, the poem pays homage to Walt Whitman, one of the founders of contemporary American verse, who strove to achieve in his poetry qualities found in the natural world and whose work was sometimes banned in his native United States for its explicit references to the male body. This tension between an innovative artist and the reception of his work by the general public is one of the central themes and also an organizing principle of this poem. Already in the opening García Lorca's portrayal of Whitman—a near mythical figure of natural nobility, beauty, and wisdom—contrasts with the image of New York miners, an anonymous mass engaged in the monotonous labor in a city of *"alambre y muerte"* (wire and death). Throughout the poem García Lorca matches in Spanish both Whitman's vigorous and fluid poetic style and his imagery to denounce the crowd that misconstrues a poet's aspiration for an ideal purity found in nature in terms of base desires.

Like in the rest of the *Poet in New York*, desperation and frustration with the country of "machinery and lament" (*"máquinas y llanto"*) are dominant moods in the "Ode." Nonetheless, the poem marks the turning point within the context of García Lorca's oeuvre at large. "Ode to Walt Whitman" is one of the first works in which the poet openly discusses homosexuality, the subject he had been unable to address in conservative Spain. Through his homage to Whitman, the poet finds ways to connect this idea of forbidden love with the idea of nature and also of art. Addressing intermittently Whitman and the crowd, García Lorca distinguishes between a natural longing for love in its many manifestations ("the little boy who writes the name of a girl on his pillow," "the boy who dresses as a bride in the darkness of his wardrobe," "the solitary men in casinos who drink prostitution's water with revulsion,") and the sexual urges of *"maricas"* (faggots), an ignorant mass eager to destroy what lies beyond their understanding: "Mothers of mud. Harpies. / Sleepless enemies of the love that bestows crowns of joy." The speaker's indignation with this mass escalates throughout the poem, reaching the tone of a manifesto in which Whitman's particular story is an allegory for the universal situation of an artist and in which Whitman's love of nature is a symbol of pure love that in itself is a form of art.

Much like the reception of Whitman's own work, the reception of García Lorca's poem was controversial. Only 50 copies were published in Mexico in 1934, and despite its innovative nature, the poem was not published in Spain during García Lorca's lifetime.

BIBLIOGRAPHY

"Ode to Walt Whitman." Translated by Greg Simon and Steven F. White. In *The Poetical Works of Federico García Lorca. Volume II. Collected Poems,* edited by Christopher Maurer. New York: Farrar, Straus and Giroux, 1991.

Alina Sokol

"ODE WITH A LAMENT" Pablo Neruda (1935)

A speaker praises his loved one, yet finds he is unable to satisfy her: This is not an unfamiliar trope in Neruda's work. But in "Ode with a Lament," from the second volume of Neruda's somber *Residencia en la Tierra* (Residence on Earth), the loved one's demands are even higher—her soul "a bottle filled with thirsty salt" (l. 3). Her skin is compared unerotically to "a bell filled with grapes" (l. 4), an image of illness that forces the reader to readjust any presumption of the relationship at hand. In return the poet's offerings become more surreal and violent: "I have only fingernails to give you, / or eyelashes, or melted pianos, / or dreams that come spurting from my heart" (ll. 5–7).

In a world of "submerged hearts / and pale lists of unburied children / There is much death" (ll. 17–19), and the speaker laments his shame at being safe while his love is sacrificed. He sags under the weight of "an interminable / wet-winged shadow that protects my bones" and is haunted "while I dress, while / interminably I look at myself in mirrors and windowpanes, / I hear someone who follows me, sobbing to me / with a sad voice rotted by time" (ll. 25–30). The closing invocation is to the love's funeral self: "Come to my heart dressed in white, with a bouquet / of bloody roses and goblets of ashes. . . ." (ll. 38–39).

The unusual images in this bleak poem may spring from Neruda's most personal, internalized griefs. His mother, Rosa, died within weeks of his birth, and Neruda often linked the appearance of roses with intimations of mortality. In this case the "girl among the roses" (l. 1) may well be Neruda's own daughter, Malva Marina, born the year before the poem's publication. Neruda's only child was plagued from birth with brain hemorrhaging and excess fluids in her oversized head, a volatile state that may inspire some of the poem's most raw, disturbing visions: "You stand upon the earth, filled / with teeth and lightning . . . You are like a blue and green sword / and you ripple, when I touch you, like a river" (ll. 31–32, 36–37). Despite the frantic efforts of the poet's family and friends to "cure" Malva Marina with kind attention and the best doctors, she was diagnosed with hydrocephaly and did not live past her eighth year.

Neruda prized the form of the ode, which directly addresses an admired object and originates in song. Much of his later collection *Odas elementales* follows the classical Pindaric structure of strophe, then antistrophe, culminating in epode. In "Ode with a Lament," however, the abject mourning of stanza four interrupts this formal rhythm. The poem becomes not so much ode as hymn: an appeal to what is loved but inaccessible, held apart—as in death—by the hand of the divine.

Sandra Beasley

"ODYSSEUS TO TELEMACHUS" JOSEPH BRODSKY (1972)

Like many of JOSEPH BRODSKY's poems, "Odysseus to Telemachus" examines the corruptive effects of empire on the individual. In "Torso" (1977), the subject is the Roman Empire, described as "the end of things," a place where a person finds the grass turned into stone. In "Odysseus to Telemachus," however, the treatment of political power is less obvious. Often developing a tension between Homer's cunning Odysseus and Brodsky's own vision of the man as quietly introspective, the poem never addresses government directly. Instead, by humanizing Odysseus and his poignant separation from his son, Telemachus, the poem treats exile as a devastating consequence of power.

With a dropped line of direct address, this ode acts as both a persona poem and an epistle to Telemachus, for Odysseus is still not home. The poem employs irony, reiteration, and allusion to treat the theme of exile, all characteristic of Brodsky's work. In the first stanza irony is used to distance Odysseus from his status as a Trojan War hero. Brodsky's Odysseus cannot "recall who won" the war, though he deduces that the Greeks did as "only they would leave / so many dead so far from their own homeland." Here readers familiar with *The Odyssey* know that the Greeks not only won the war, but that Odysseus was largely responsible for their victory by designing the infamous Trojan horse. What follows is ambiguous: Perhaps Odysseus literally does not remember the war; perhaps he does not want to remember. In either case he is *othering* his own side by referring to the Greeks as an autonomous "they" while the outcome of the war becomes nebulous compared with the death it incurs. In the world Brodsky creates for Odysseus, even the politically charged divinities of the Greek pantheon hold little meaning compared with the loss of family. In the second stanza Odysseus's reference to "some filthy island, / with bushes, buildings, and great grunting pigs" (where he feels utterly disoriented) alludes to the island of Circe where Odysseus's men were changed into swine. Here Odysseus describes the enchantress Circe—later his lover for a year, and in many myths the mother of his son Telegonus—as "some queen or other," at once rendering her anonymous and inconsequential. Instead,

he emphasizes again to his son what his memories do not hold: "I can't remember how the war came out; / even how old you are, I can't remember." Ultimately, in the third and final stanza, Odysseus begins to doubt his role as a father. Such doubts, however, are in the end what attest to his humanity, making the ramifications of his 20-year absence all the more moving. "Away from me," he tells his son, "you are quite safe from all Oedipal passions. / And your dreams, my Telemachus, are blameless."

BIBLIOGRAPHY

Bethea, David M. *Joseph Brodsky and the Creation of Exile.* Princeton, N.J.: Princeton University Press, 1994.
Brodsky, Joseph. "Odysseus to Telemachus." In *A Part of Speech,* poem translated from Russian by George L. Kline. New York: Farrar, Straus and Giroux, 1981.
Polukhina, Valentina. *Joseph Brodsky: A Poet for Our Time.* New York: Cambridge University Press, 1989.
Rigsbee, David. *Styles of Ruin: Joseph Brodsky and the Postmodernist Elegy.* Westport, Conn: Greenwood Press, 1999.

Stacy Kidd

OJAIDE, TANURE (1948–)

Tanure Ojaide is one of the most prolific poets to have emerged from Nigeria in the last three decades of the 20th century. Even though he is best known as a poet, he has also published a collection of short stories, a memoir, a novel, three books of literary criticism, and a book on creative writing. His work operates within the tradition of the socially sensitive poetry that has come to be identified with the second generation of Nigerian poets, a generation that became prominent after the Nigerian civil war (1967–70). In addition to being a major promoter of the antidictatorial poetry that flowered in Nigeria due to the sustained exposure of the country to military rule, he has also come to be identified (through poems like "WHEN GREEN WAS THE LINGUA FRANCA") with the protest poetry that the crisis of marginalization and neglect in the oil-rich Niger delta region inspires.

Ojaide's work has largely been fed by childhood experiences in his birthplace, and he has also drawn on *udje,* the satirical tradition of the Urhobo, his cultural group. Like some other poets from the Niger delta region of Nigeria, Ojaide articulates a profound consciousness of the natural environment and decries all man-made efforts at severing the bond between the people of the region and their land. The poet in Ojaide constantly identifies with the yearnings and legitimate desires of the helpless masses in Africa while being critical of visionless and irresponsible politicians and military rulers.

Ojaide was born in 1948 in Igherhe of parents from Ibada village in the delta region of Nigeria. He was exposed to formal education early due to the value his father placed on schooling. His close association with his maternal grandmother also saw to his immersion in the oral practices of the Urhobo, a tradition that was later to be an object of his scholarly enquiry. He was raised in an agrarian environment long before the disruptive intrusion of the delta region by multinational oil companies that visited violence on the environment in the name of prospecting and exploring for oil. He witnessed their destruction of the agrarian economy, which impoverished his people and their land, and his concern continues to provoke something like nostalgic reflection in his work. But Ojaide's indignation is not restricted to the plight of his immediate physical and cultural environment; he gives expression to the failure of the Nigerian ruling elite and creates a space for celebrating other aspects of human experience that he finds remarkable in his land and elsewhere.

Even though Ojaide is heir to the Urhobo culture of poetry performance, his own training and exposure have uniquely shaped his poetic craft. Although his secondary education was disrupted by the Nigerian crisis of the late 1960s and the civil war, he attended the University of Ibadan, where he mingled with other budding poets and wrote the poems that eventually appeared in his first collection, *Children of Iroko*. He taught briefly at secondary and postsecondary institutions before starting his teaching career at the University of Maiduguri, where he met SYL CHENEY-COKER, who introduced him to the work of Latin American poets. His acquaintance with the work of older Nigerian poets including WOLE SOYINKA, JOHN PEPPER CLARK, and CHRISTOPHER OKIGBO equally challenged him to write more accessible poetry. He proceeded to Syracuse University in the United States in 1978, where he earned an M.A. in creative writing and a Ph.D. in English. On returning to Maiduguri in 1981, he devoted himself to creative writing and started winning prizes. Among these are the Association of Nigerian Authors' Prize, Commonwealth Poetry Prize for the Africa Region, the BBC Arts and Africa Poetry Prize, and the All-Africa Okigbo Prize for Poetry. He moved to the United States in 1989 and has been a professor of African-American and African studies at the University of North Carolina at Charlotte. Among his published collections of poetry are *I Want to Dance and Other Poems* (2003), *In the Kingdom of Songs: Poems 1995–2000*, *Invoking the Warrior Spirit: New and Selected Poems* (1999), *When It No Longer Matters Where You Live* (1999), *Invoking the Warrior Spirit* (1998), *Delta Blues and Homesongs* (1997), *The Daydream of Ants* (1997), *The Blood of Peace* (1991), *The Fate of Vultures and & Other Poems* (1990), *The Endless Song* (1989), *Poems* (1988), *The Eagle's Vision* (1987), *Labyrinths of the Delta* (1986), and *Children of Iroko* (1973). Ojaide's work enjoys critical attention and has been performed in various parts of the world.

BIBLIOGRAPHY

Ojaide, Tanure. *Poetry Performance and Art: Udje Songs of the Urhobo.* Durham, N.C.: Carolina Academic Press, 2003.

———. *Poetic Imagination in Black Africa: Essays on African Poetry.* Durham, N.C.: Carolina Academic Press, 1996.

Okome, Onookome. *Writing the Homeland: The Poetry and Politics of Tanure Ojaide.* Bayreuth, Germany: Eckhard Breitinger, 2002.

Olafioye, Tayo. *The Poetry of Tanure Ojaide: A Critical Appraisal.* Lagos, Nigeria and Oxford: Malthouse, 2002.

Oyeniyi Okinoye

OKARA, GABRIEL (1921–)

Gabriel Okara belongs to a generation of Anglophone African poets that emerged after the pioneer poets of West Africa: politicians and nationalists who found the medium of poetry useful for propagating their visions and political manifestos and who, because they had not set out to become poets, paid little or no attention to injecting any form of artistic discipline into their work. In contrast, Okara is one of those in the region who truly pioneered serious poetry in the medium of English. In both thematic interests and artistic refinements, his poetry is significant. His poems are among the most frequently anthologized in Anglophone Africa and reflect the concerns and realities that preoccupied the emergent educated elite of his time: the clash of cultures and the pain of being alienated from one's ancestral roots due to the alienating influence of Westernization.

Born Gabriel Imomotime Gbaingbain Okara in Bomoundi in 1921 in what is now Bayelsa State of Nigeria, Okara received his early education in his immediate community and in Port Harcourt. He then attended the famous Government College, Umuahia. He also attended Yaba College in Lagos, where he studied for his senior Cambridge exams. He later trained as a book binder and artist and worked with the Information Service of the old Eastern Government of Nigeria. He was in the service of Biafra during the Nigerian civil war, serving as the director of the Biafran Cultural Affairs Department. Following that, he was appointed director of the Rivers State Arts Council and also held the chairmanship of *The Tide,* a newspaper. He was a commissioner in Rivers State until the late 1980s.

Though much better known as a poet, Okara is also a novelist. His one published novel to date, *The Voice,* has been acclaimed as an experimental work, especially because of its attempt at imposing Ijaw linguistic principles on English.

Okara developed an interest in English poetry early and claims that his reading of William Wordsworth's "Sping" in particular inspired him to compose poetry. His early poems were published in such journals as *Black Orpheus, Nigeria Magazine, Presence Africaine,* and *Transition* before they were brought together in *The Fisherman's Invocation* in 1978. His second book of poems, *The Dreamer, His Vision,* was joint winner of the Nigerian Literature Prize for 2005.

Okara's poems in *The Fisherman's Invocation* reveal him as a poet with deep communal consciousness: The persona of his poems almost always represents his community. He shows an enduring interest in the crisis of self-definition that the colonial engagement has created for the colonized (see "PIANO AND DRUMS"). He is acutely conscious of his physical environment and constantly hints at the transience of human existence. He exhibits at the same time great skill at capturing the essence of his Ijaw culture and nostalgically re-creating childhood experiences in and around his birthplace. His poems that focus on the Nigerian civil war demonstrate sensitivity to detail and a graphic awareness of the confused state of things that the events of that war precipitated. His work evinces immense spirituality as well, a debt he owes to his Ijaw cultural background, which has also been the source of the homely symbols and memorable imagery in his work.

It is not difficult to appreciate Okara's poems relating to his experience of the Nigerian civil war as he was never far from the theater of combat. Another major influence on Okara's poetry is his wide reading, which accounts for his literary debts to Dylan Thomas, W. B. Yeats, and G. M. Hopkins. An important development in his recent poetry is its widening political consciousness.

BIBLIOGRAPHY
Egudu, Romanus. *Modern African Poetry and the African Predicament.* London and Basingbroke: Macmillan, 1978.
Fraser, Robert. *West African Poetry: A Critical History.* Cambridge: Cambridge University Press, 1986.
Okara, Gabriel. *The Fisherman's Invocation.* London: Heinemann Educational Books, 1978.

Oyeniyi Okunoye

OKIGBO, CHRISTOPHER (1932–1967)
Though his career was cut short by his untimely death at 35, Christopher Okigbo is one of the most important Nigerian poets of the late colonial and early postcolonial period. Along with contemporaries such as WOLE SOYINKA and J. P. CLARK, Okigbo is known for his innovative interweaving of African oral tradition and musical sources with European modernism. Okigbo was born in Ojoto, Nigeria, the son of an Igbo schoolteacher and his wife. Though his parents were both devout Catholics, they also maintained their own shrine to the ancestral gods Ikenga and Udo. Okigbo was believed to be the reincarnation of his maternal grandfather, who had been the priest at the local shrine to the river goddess Odoto, and he described his decision in 1958 to turn his attention full time to poetry as his way of taking up the priestly duties that were supposedly his birthright. While studying classics at University College, Ibadan, Okigbo developed literary friendships with Soyinka, Clark, and CHINUA ACHEBE. After graduating Okigbo held a series of jobs, working briefly at the Nigerian Tobacco Company, the United Africa Company, the federal Ministry of Information in

Lagos, the Fiditi Grammar School near Ibadan (as a teacher), and the University of Nigeria at Nsukka (as a librarian). From 1962 to 1966 Okigbo served as a West African representative for Cambridge University Press. In 1967 he and Achebe started a publishing company with the goal of producing literature for young people, but the venture was halted by the Nigerian civil war, in which the primarily Igbo region of eastern Nigeria seceded and declared itself the independent state of Biafra. Okigbo was killed in battle in August 1967 near Nsukka only a month after joining the Biafran army.

Okigbo wrote poetry for approximately 10 years before his death. His earliest poems were published in the University of Ibadan's student journal the *Horn*. Four of these were republished as *Poems: Four Canzones* in the literary journal *Black Orpheus* in 1962. The work *Heavensgate*, published by Mbari, came out the same year. Okigbo's collection *Limits* was also published in 1962 in the journal *Transition*, though it did not appear as a book (again published by Mbari) until 1964. Parts of the poem cycles *Silences* and *Distances* were also published in *Transition* and *Black Orpheus* between 1963 and 1965. Okigbo compiled his collected works in *Labyrinths*, published posthumously with the unfinished poem sequence *Path of Thunder* as *Labyrinths with Path of Thunder* in 1971. Heinemann published its own compilation of Okigbo's verse entitled *Christopher Okigbo: Collected Poems* in 1986, which included works that Okigbo had excluded from his own compilation. Okigbo constantly revised his poetry, and most of the poems from earlier collections that he included in the volume *Labyrinths* were completely reworked. This ongoing process of rewriting and revision, along with the recurrent theme of the individual's ritualistic quest for spiritual and artistic fulfillment and the use of repeating motifs—such as the elephant, the bird, the talking drum, and the priest—have led critics to claim that Okigbo's work can be viewed as one long, unfinished poem.

Okigbo's poetry is difficult to interpret, in part due to its sometimes inscrutable symbolism and to its structural use of series of impressionistic images or vignettes rather than an overarching narrative line. A voracious reader, his work draws from varied sources, including Yoruba and Igbo praise songs, modernist poets (e.g., T. S. Eliot, Ezra Pound, and W. B. Yeats), and ancient Greek and Latin works. Music was also a key influence on Okigbo. Before turning to poetry in 1958, he had devoted much of his time to playing jazz clarinet and piano and had composed several works. Okigbo once claimed that he was more influenced by composers than by other poets, citing European impressionist composers such as Claude Debussy and Maurice Ravel as inspirations for *Heavensgate*. Likely because of his interest in music, critics have commented that Okigbo ultimately seems more concerned in his poetry with the combination of sounds he is creating than with the meaning produced. When asked in an interview about the intellectual difficulty of his poetry, Okigbo explained, "I think it is possible to arrive at a response without passing through the process of intellectual analysis, and I think that if a poem can elicit a response, either in physical or emotional terms from an audience, the poem has succeeded. Personally, I don't think that I have ever set out to communicate a meaning" (Serumaga 47).

Okigbo has been criticized for the difficulty of his poetry and for his focus on the mental state of the individual over the social situation of the Nigerian people, which prominent African intellectuals such as Chinweizu and Kofi Awoonor perceived as evidence of the negative influence of Western artists on African poets. These critics viewed later poems such as "Elegy for Slit-Drum," from *Path of Thunder*, as more socially conscious and artistically mature than his earlier work, because it dealt more explicitly with the degenerating political situation in Nigeria. But Okigbo himself, as well as colleagues such as Soyinka and Achebe, rejected what they viewed as a false separation of the private and the public, arguing that art concerned with the development of the individual was a necessary element of a struggle to liberate the people of Africa. Okigbo refused a first-prize award for *Silences* at the 1966 Dakar Negro Arts Festival because he believed judging artistic merit based on racial categories was misguided. To commemorate the 10-year anniversary of Okigbo's death, Achebe and Okigbo's nephew, Dubem Okafor, edited *Don't Let Him Die: An Anthology of Memorial Poems for Christopher Okigbo,* which included poetic tributes by a wide range of authors.

BIBLIOGRAPHY

Anozie, Sunday O. *Christopher Okigbo: Creative Rhetoric.* New York: Africana Publishing Group, 1972.

Awoonor, Kofi. *The Breast of the Earth: A Survey of the History, Culture, and Literature of Africa South of the Sahara.* New York and Enugu, Nigeria: Nok Publishers International, 1975.

Chinweizu, Onwuchekwa Jemie, and Ihechukwu Madubuike. *Toward the Decolonization of African Literature.* Washington, D.C.: Howard University Press, 1983.

Goodwin, Ken. *Understanding African Poetry: A Study of Ten Poets.* London: Heinemann, 1982.

Nwoga, Donatus Ibe, ed. *Critical Perspectives on Christopher Okigbo.* Washington, D.C.: Three Continents Press, 1984.

Okigbo, Christopher. "Interview with Robert Serumaga." Reprinted in *Critical Essays on Christopher Okigbo,* edited by Uzoma Esonwanne. New York: G. K. Hall, 2000.

Emily S. Davis

OMEROS DEREK WALCOTT (1990)

Omeros is DEREK WALCOTT's longest and most ambitious poem, evoking the tradition of epic poetry through its stylistic features. The title is a variation on the modern Greek pronunciation of "Homer." Various characters have Homeric names: Helen, Achille, and Hector. The poem is composed in hexameter lines, which follows the meter of both *The Iliad* and *The Odyssey,* and the rhyme scheme is a loose terza rima (aba bcb etc.) that is reminiscent of Dante's *The Divine Comedy.*

The narrative of *Omeros* centers on the tourist and fishing village of Gros Ilet on the island of St. Lucia, in the Caribbean Sea, and develops four main subplots. One is a love triangle involving two local fishermen, Achille and Hector, and Helen, a woman of stunning beauty. Helen was formerly the servant of Dennis and Maud Plunkett, two British expatriates whose marriage forms a second subplot. The third concerns another fisherman, Philocete, who suffers from an open sore on his shin that is finally cured by Ma Kilman, a practitioner of *obeah* (a Caribbean form of magic). The final storyline follows the narrator, a representation of Walcott, as he tries to construct a poem comparing Helen to Helen of Troy while wandering across Europe and America reflecting on the history of colonialism.

Throughout the different narrative strands of the poem, Walcott continually meditates on the nature of language and art in the Caribbean world. He explores different metaphors of wounding since, for Walcott, the legacy of colonialism scars all inhabitants of the Caribbean. Walcott represents the theme of affliction both literally and symbolically in the figure of Philocete, whose sore represents the communal pain that African descendants in the Caribbean experience with the loss of their language and history. Philocete's cure requires that he perceive his world not only with metaphors of wounding, but also with metaphors of renewal. The narrator compares Philocete to Adam at the moment of his cure, declaring, "And the yard was Eden. And it's light the first day's."

Walcott's allusion to the Bible fits with his recurrent pattern of linking praise of the natural world to praise of God. Throughout the poem Walcott depicts the natural world as a necessary component to overcoming the pain inherent in the legacy of colonialism. Philocete's cure enables him to recognize divinity in nature. The narrator experiences a parallel form of healing when the ghost of Homer (Omeros) challenges him to see the island of St. Lucia without artistic vanity and celebrate the everyday beauty of the island. This meeting enables him to recognize that he can desist from using allusions to Homer and write about Helen and St. Lucia "with no Homeric shadow." The natural world of the Caribbean, particularly the sea, becomes the source of inspiration for both art and everyday life.

BIBLIOGRAPHY

Farrell, Joseph. "Walcott's *Omeros*: The Classical Epic in a Postmodern World." In *Epic Traditions in the Contemporary World: The Poetics of Community,* edited by Margaret Beissinger, Jane Tylus, and Susanne Wofford, 270–296. Berkeley: University of California Press,1999.

Ramazani, Jahan. *The Hybrid Muse: Postcolonial Poetry in English.* Chicago: University of Chicago Press, 2001.

Eugene Johnson

"ON A RED STEED" MARINA TSVETAEVA (1921)

"On a Red Steed," *"Na krasnom kone,"* first appeared in TSVETAEVA's *Remeslo* (Craft) in 1923. In this poem the female speaker traces the development of a woman poet, explores her source of inspiration, and identifies the sacrifices she has to make for the sake of her calling. The poem is a subversion of traditional poetic and sexual images. It starts with the words "No Muse, no Muse." For the woman poet the traditional image of a beautiful female source of inspiration is inaccessible. Rather than reject the sexually charged concept of personal inspiration, Tsvetaeva makes it her own by replacing the gentle muse with an imperious knight on a red stallion who demands that she renounce all she has and become his.

"On a Red Steed" is an example of Tsvetaeva's mature style. She combines stanzas of different lengths and various meters as well as ellipses and dashes to render palpable the raw energy of the events, such as the poet's struggle with the elements and her ride with the knight. The poem epitomizes Tsvetaeva's poetic self-image, identifying the poet as someone who must leave worldly attachments behind. It is possible, roughly, to identify a prologue, a bipartite epilogue, and three episodes in between in which the budding poet rids herself of three elements of everyday life that stand between her and poetry: love, religion, and her own pride. In the first episode a house is on fire. Something is collapsing, but it is not the pillars of the house that cave in: What makes a cracking noise is the girl's doll, symbolizing love and domesticity. Suddenly the knight appears, rescuing the doll from the flames only to demand that the girl smash it to pieces herself. To her own surprise the girl finds the experience not devastating, but liberating. The second episode begins with a blizzard and ends by destroying a part of the girl's old world. This time the target is religion. Again it is the knight who comes to the girl's aid, crashing into the altar of a church and revealing the void behind it. The third and hardest struggle the girl faces is the one against her own pride. Heaven, the unearthly place from which the knight comes, is obtainable to her only "through the law of the grain—into the earth" and requires the aspiring poet to die to the world. Having secured victory, the bruised woman is discovered by the knight. He signals his appreciation of her sacrifice with the words "this is how I wanted you," and the young poet pledges to be his forever, thus accepting the fate of an artist who is no longer at home on Earth. The reward for her sacrifice is two large wings and the "terrible" company of the knight, whose identity is revealed in the last stanza as "My Genius." The last

words of the poem are thus an answer to the first line, "No Muse, no Muse."

BIBLIOGRAPHY
Tsvetaeva, Marina. *Poem of the End: Selected Narrative and Lyrical Poetry with Facing Russian Text.* Translated by Nina Kossman with Andrew Newcomb. Dana Point, Calif.: Ardis, 1998.

Josephine von Zitzewitz

"ON BEING A POET IN SIERRA LEONE" SYL CHENEY-COKER (1980)

First published in *The Graveyard Also Has Teeth,* "On Being a Poet in Sierra Leone" is an example of SYL CHENEY-COKER's self-referential—one might almost say *egocentric*—style. This 34-line free-verse poem—which contains minimal punctuation (only two exclamation points and six commas)—is deceptively casual looking and sounding. Only upon closer inspection do the poetic devices emerge, and these are insistent and mostly aural: assonances and consonances that punctuate the lexical meanings by emphasizing certain words, as in the lines "I am seeking the verisimilitudes in life / the fire of metaphors the venom of verse" (ll. 2–3). The emphatic alliterations of *verisimilitudes, venom,* and *verse* and the long *i*-sounds of *I, life, fire*—not to mention the mirrored sound effects of *life* and *fire*—all contribute to the poem's striking sonority, a quality long associated with lyrical poetry and sermonic discourse. The poem is a convoluted apostrophe to "my country," felt as an embodiment of the speaker's driving force ("you are my heart"), but a heart "living like a devastated landscape" (l. 4). The poet confesses to having alternately "condemned and sold" and "loved and hated" his fatherland, but to have felt all the while "the poetry of being you / a colossus strangled by fratricidal parasites"—a country "betrayed" by his very own "hermetic poetry" and by his estranged language, considered "too 'intellectual'" (ll. 12–13) for ordinary communication with his people (Sierra Leone's students, farmers, fishermen). The speaker says that he wants "to be the breakfast of the peasants who read / to help the fishermen bring in their catch / I want to be your national symbol of life" (ll. 21–23). But these desires, however "simple," are not easy to fulfill in Sierra Leone, a "disastrous gloating python / in whose belly all my anger dies" (ll. 29–30). The poem ends, nevertheless, with an expression of positive will: "I am going to be happy to stop carrying my pain / like a grenade in my heart, I want to be simple / if possible to live with you, and then one day die leaving / my poetry, an imperfect metaphor of life!" (ll. 31–34). It is significant that in this poem Cheney-Coker calls his poetry, his entire oeuvre, "an imperfect metaphor of life," thus asking readers and listeners to bear in mind that this poem is not an aesthetic manifesto or a patriotic ode (its title notwithstanding), but a sincere effort to speak to Sierra Leone directly and to capture in words the emotionally rocking realities of his homeland and the baffling torments of even the simplest existence there.

R. Victoria Arana

"ONLY A ROSE FOR SUPPORT" HILDE DOMIN (1957)

This poem, *"Nur eine Rose als Stütze,"* appeared in 1959 in a revised version as the title poem of HILDE DOMIN's first collection. The poem consists of four stanzas of five lines each. The first two stanzas speak of the poet moving into her new room in the sky. She finds a comfortable home in a playful and poetic environment where the bed linen is provided by sheep that resemble clouds. This reversal of the usual metaphor is aptly situated in a context of uncertainty about what is inside and what is outside (reminiscent of Italian *metafisica* painting), what is permanent and what is transient.

The atmosphere of security seems to permit the speaker to close her eyes. Her commitment to feeling and listening to her surroundings takes the place of visual perception. The first three stanzas all begin with "I," whereas the fourth is introduced by a sudden "But." The speaker finds herself unable to sleep and becomes aware of the insufficiency of her own willpower. The concluding paradox finds that only a rose, supposedly the most fragile of flowers, is her support.

The rose has been seen as a symbol of the German language. Upon her return to her native country after 22 years of exile, Hilde Domin found herself struggling to come to terms with a society and a state that had changed dramatically. Only the German language could provide certainty and orientation. The poet has welcomed this interpretation of one of her best-known poems.

Relatively long lines follow the semantic and grammatical structure of the poem. A style rich in adjectives and *"wie"*-comparisons sets itself apart from the rules established by GOTTFRIED BENN in his influential essay "Problems of Lyric Poetry." The frequent use of three consecutive unstressed syllables supports the impression of an airy, light, and at the same time vulnerable condition. Domin, with an almost stereotypically lyrical vocabulary (using *rose, air,* and *clouds* as central images), revived and reinterpreted poetic possibility.

BIBLIOGRAPHY

Domin, Hilde. "Only a Rose for Support." In *Contemporary German poetry. An Anthology,* translated and edited by Gertrude Clorius Schwebell, with an introduction by Victor Lange, 61. New York: New Directions, 1964.

Christophe Fricker

"ON THE SLAUGHTER" AND "IN THE CITY OF SLAUGHTER" HAYYIM N. BIALIK (1903 and 1904)

At the same time that Zionism was crystallizing as a political movement, HAYYIM BIALIK's poetic output was coming into the limelight. Many of his readers believe that Bialik reached his artistic apex with his *Poems of Wrath* series, a shockingly powerful bracket of pieces. The first poem, *"Al ha-Shehitah"* (On the Slaughter, 1903), was composed before the artist's visit to Chișinău in the aftermath of the pogroms that raged in that city. Dispatched by the Jewish Historical Commission of Odessa to interview survivors and compile firsthand reports of the massacre, the 35-year-old poet took some 60 photographs of the atrocities. The poem's title betrays a sense of subversive anger and irony, since the term *Al ha-Shehitah* is borrowed from the penultimate passage of the blessing pronounced by the ritual slaughterer before slitting an animal's throat. Bialik may have been suggesting that the Jews, the emasculated victims, are the ones who had brought this calamity on themselves, or that the pogrom was not only evidence of God's nonintervention, but—worse— a display of ritual martyrdom commanded by God. The speaker is wrapped in complete desperation, shattered by the lack of divine intercession.

As the poem begins the narrator, in a thunderous outburst, turns to the heavens and solicits immediate justice and retribution for the victims, although he is uncertain that God is still there and whether, sitting upon his throne, he will listen to the supplicant's angry demands: *"shamaim bakshu rachamim alay! Im yesh bacehm el velael bachem native— veani lo metzahativ-hit-palelu atem alay! Ani—libi met vehein od tfila bisfatay"* (Heavenly spheres, beg mercy for me! If truly God dwells in your orbit and round, And in your space his His pathway that I have not found—Then you pray for me! For my own heart is dead; no prayer on my tongue). In essence when the poet states that his "heart is dead," he bespeaks a loss of faith in God, yoked with a feeling of extreme disappointment, *"ad matay-an ana-ad matay?"* (O until when? For how much more? How long?). Conversely, the poet could be pointing to his own inadequacy since he cannot pray, cannot find the right registers that would open the gates of heaven and lead him to God. In different ways this passage under-lines the Jew's renouncing of his own personal capacity to connect with his creator. Thus he pleads with the heavens to pray for him. Moreover, the pity he appeals for is not sought for him but for the Jewish people as a whole and underlines the deeply veined sense of dejection embodied in the words "hope has passed." The stormy and prophetic tone of the poem is striking for its depiction of the gentiles' savage brutality: *"hatalyan eh tzavar—kom she-khat! Arfeni ka-kelev lecha zeroha im kardom, vekol ha'haretz li gardom—vehanchnu-anachnu hamehat! Dami mutar hach kodkod"* (Ho, heads-man, bared the neck—come, cleave it through! Nape me this cur's nape! Yours is the axe unbaffled! The whole wide world-my scaffold! And rest you easy: we are weak and few. My blood is outlaw. Strike then, the skull dissever). And yet alongside his indictment of the mobs, Bialik expresses overwhelming disgust with the helplessness and impotence of the Jews.

The poem's tone and title imply that the murdered are akin to acquiescent animals whose necks are pre-sented to the slaughterer's knife. At one point the poet offers himself to the killers: *"hatalyan eh tzavar—kom she-khat"* (Ho, headsman, bared the neck—come, cleave it through). By directly addressing the hangman, who represents the criminals who butchered the Jews, the speaker identifies with the victims and concur-rently states that the whole land has become a killing field and, by extension, intimates that killers rule the

Earth rather than God. Instead of God's mighty hand, the ax and scaffold rule his domain. Power now resides with the wicked. At the same time the speaker depicts the helplessness of the victims, whose blood runs freely, and reminds us that the rioters murdered young children and the elderly, and as such their blood will forever stain the clothes of the executioners like the mark of Cain: *"dam yonek vesav al kutnatcha velo yimach lanetzach"* (Let blood of babe and greybeard stain your garb—stain to endure forever).

Imbued with fury, the poet demands that justice appear at once. He warns that if it appears only after the destruction of the Jews, only after he is killed, then let the throne of God be smashed, dooming the perpe-trators to live in a world of hellish violence. The poem concludes with the speaker cursing those who seek vengeance for the crimes perpetrated because even Satan has not conceived of a revenge for the death of a young boy. Yet immediately afterward he promises that the blood of the victims will seep through the darkest recesses of the Earth and corrode its depths until it rots and reverts to the chaotic state before cre-ation. The evildoers will be plagued for eternity by the memory of the dead; their punishment will be to be consumed by guilt for their deeds. There is no passage toward redemption or forgiveness for the gentiles. The buried message of the poem is that if mercy, compas-sion, justice, and a path to God do not emerge in the backwash of the pogroms, anarchy will reign as retri-bution for the innocent blood of the Jews that was spilled.

It is noteworthy that the narrator assumes different personas throughout the opus. At the beginning he adopts the witnessing posture, then embraces the first-person stance, reverts to the eyewitness position, and at the end takes on the role of the prophet of wrath. Although the poem is clearly a charge sheet of the hor-rific acts committed against the Jews, it also embodies a new perception of a reality denuded of a God that will protect his people.

"On the Slaughter" was followed by the epic master-piece *"Be'ir Haharegah"* (In the City of Slaughter, 1904), the longer of the two lamentations; it again foregrounds the bloodbath by the perpetrators. Bialik was so upset by the massacre that he wrote the poem without delay so as to stir Russian Jewry out of its submissiveness. Thematically it is structured as a searing address to God by the prophet, who surprisingly scolds the survivors for their meek capitulation and denounces their lack of resistance to the attacks. One might venture the observation that Bialik, in castigating the chosen people for their supposed cowardice and meekness, overlooks the few acts of resistance by the Jews during the assault. In a similar vein the poet laments the absence of justice, portraying the God of the Jews as an impotent entity, unmoved by his people's suffering and unable to quell the violent storms of an indifferent, uncivilized world. The penetrating eye of the poet, overflowing with tears of shame, takes the reader on a visceral survey of the physical and spiritual devastation. The explicit account reports on the cemetery where the ground is soaked with the blood of the martyrs. From there the prophet-speaker moves to the synagogue, disgusted with the mourners' slavishness and loss of pride and dignity. One of the cardinal leitmotifs of the poem is the self-flagellation of a people who have reached the nadir of humiliation and are unable to rise against their enemies. All in all the two poems had a practical effect of goading the Jews to establish Jewish self-defense squads composed of youths who resisted further desecration of life and fought back.

Dvir Abramovich

"ON THE STATE OF THE UNION" AIMÉ CÉSAIRE (1960)

"On the State of the Union" is indicative of how AIMÉ CÉSAIRE's vision of NÉGRITUDE had evolved from the concerns of being a Martinican struggling for racial equality with white Europeans into a universal view of civil rights for blacks.

In the first stanza the poet imagines an address to the U.S. Congress in which the state of the union is described as "tragic." In a series of metaphors the poet compares the United States to a "mine without ore, / cavern in which nothing prowls, / of blood not a drop left."

The second stanza evokes the memory of Emmet Till, a young Chicago black who was brutally murdered in Mississippi in 1955 for allegedly whistling suggestively at a white woman. The case became an impetus for the nascent Civil Rights movement of the 1950s and 1960s in the United States. The description of Till's vibrancy is in direct contrast to the bloodless Earth of the first stanza: "EMMET TILL / your eyes were a sea conch in which the heady battle / of your fifteen-year-old blood sparkled. / Even young they never had any age, / or rather more than all the skyscrapers." But Till's youth was no match for the centuries of persecution of the weak by the strong, the influence of the past that drove whites to lynch Till, and the poet alludes to the Salem witch trials, and even further back to the beginning of biblical time, when Cain slew Abel: "five centuries of torturers / of witch burners weighed on them, / five centuries of cheap gin of big cigars / of fat bellies filled with slices of rancid bibles / a five century mouth bitter with dowager sins, / they were five centuries old EMMET TILL, / five centuries is the ageless age of Cain's stake."

In the third and final stanza the poet vows to remember Till and his blood that was shed, "may it mix with my bread." He then addresses Till directly, asking the rhetorical question, "Hey Chicago Boy / is it still true that you're worth / as much as a white man?" He knows that Till's life was never worth that of a white man's, which is why Till was murdered in cold blood. Still, the poet imagines the hope that Till must have felt, seeing the Mississippi River in the springtime before his death: "Spring, he believed in you. / Even at the edge of night, at the edge of the MISSISSIPPI rolling its / bars, its barriers, its tomb-like avalanches between the high banks of racial hatred . . . loosener of fear clots, dissolver of the clots of hatred swollen with age and in the flow of blood- / streams. . . ." But in the end the white murderers, mounted on "bizarre immemorial billygoats," perhaps a pejorative image of their backwardness, attacked and killed Till, with their disdainful appellation for him as "Chicago Boy."

BIBLIOGRAPHY
Césaire, Aimé. *The Collected Poetry of Aimé Césaire.* Translated and edited by Clayton Eshleman and Annette Smith. Berkeley and Los Angeles: University of California Press, 1983.

Patrick L. Day

"ON THE THRESHOLD" EUGENIO MONTALE (1925)

"On the Threshold" (*"In Limine"*) was originally published in EUGENIO MONTALE's first volume of verse, *Cuttlefish Bones* (*Ossi di sepia*, 1925). It is a short poem in four stanzas: The first and third stanzas have five lines each; the second and fourth are quatrains. In Italian the poem has a subtle rhyme scheme that enhances the meanings conveyed by the words. The poem describes thoughts inspired by a walled fruit orchard close to a turbulent sea. But the sequence of ideas expressed is metaphysical, not physical, and the poem poses difficulties of interpretation by shifting metaphors forcefully in mid-conceit. "On the Threshold" could well be compared to the metaphysical poetry of John Donne as profitably as it can be compared to the poems of other early 20th-century European modernists.

In the first stanza, for instance, only the first and fifth lines rhyme (a,x,x^1,a), so that the words thus emphasized are orchard (*pomario*) and reliquary (*reliquiario*). The rhyme equates these two words, reinforcing the stanza's proposition that the orchard is a sort of shrine where certain relics are kept or hidden. This first stanza is an apostrophe to an unnamed auditor urging the listener to "be happy if the wind inside the orchard" draws back "the tidal surge of life" and makes the orchard seem not a garden (*orto*) "but a reliquary" of memories. In short, the stanza suggests that the "dead web / of memories" (*un morto / Viluppo di memorie*) is under the surface, drawn down the way that waves draw items strewn on a beach and perhaps bury them in the pebbles or sand. The second stanza, which rhymes b,c,c,b (*volo, grembo, lembo, crogiuolo*), picks up and extends the imagery relating to the wind mentioned in the first line of the poem. The circularity of the rhyme scheme also draws attention to this stanza's topic: the "whir" (*Il frullo*) of "the eternal womb" (*eterno grembo*), which transforms the orchard into a "crucible" (*crogiuolo*). The third stanza, which rhymes d,e,x^2,e,d, describes the turbulence on the other side of the orchard wall—a turbulence that has made and will continue to make history—and suggests that beyond the wall one could come suddenly and unexpectedly upon a ghost or phantom of personal redemption (this idea is proposed in the disorientingly *unrhymed* line). The words for "wall" and "future" (*muro, futuro*), at the ends of the first and last lines, do rhyme, however, thereby reinforcing the poem's suggestion that within the orchard one is somehow in a

fertile place, sheltered from the forces of history. The final stanza issues another command: to search for a gap or tear in the netting of memories that binds one to this place and to escape through it to freedom. This stanza, rhymed f, x^3, f, x,[4] (*rete, fuggi, sete, ruggine*), ends with suggestive consonance (in the *uggi-*) but avoids a conclusive rhyme; the speaker finally breaks free from each of the expected sound patterns that the rhymes have established earlier. In the end the speaker, it seems, has been addressing himself all along. "On the Threshold" is thus self-reflexive, exhortative, and future-oriented. The poem ends with references to quenchable thirst and the dissipation of bitter rancor—outcomes possible once the poet is able to leave the reliquary of memory, the place of gestation, the shelter of rooted ways.

As G. Singh points out in the introduction to his translation of Montale's *Quaderno di Quattro Anni,* a much later volume, Montale explored certain key concepts in countless poems all through his poetic career: the present's incontrovertible link to the past, the legacy of the past as a burden from which one must attempt a break, the dead hand of history versus new promises of fertility, and the self-conscious formation of an ever-new identity (see Singh viii–xi). These core ideas all appear in "On the Theshold," an early poem by one of Italy's greatest modernist poets (see MODERNISM).

BIBLIOGRAPHY

Montale, Eugenio. "On the Threshold." Translated by Jonathan Galassi. In *Montale in English,* edited by Harry Thomas, 4–5. London: Penguin, 2005.
Singh, G. "Introduction" to Eugenio Montale, *It Depends: A Poet's Notebook/Quaderno di Quattro Anni.* New York: New Directions, 1980.

R. Victoria Arana

ON THE WAVES OF THE WIRELESS JAROSLAV SEIFERT (1925)

On the Waves of the Wireless can be called JAROSLAV SEIFERT's first mature collection of poetry, although he was only 24 when it was published and although, as he recollects in his memoir *All the Beauties of the World,* it was composed on a lark and as a jeux d'esprit. As first published the book's design was an explosion of typographical exuberance and sight gags. Seifert recounts how he and his graphic designer friend Karel Teige raided the typefaces of their Prague printer to produce a collection unlike anything seen before in Czech. A love poem, for example, was offset by the brand name of a condom manufacturer on the facing page. Despite the jokes and playfulness, the work is a masterpiece of poetic vision in keeping with Seifert's avant-garde manifesto of poetism, which "rather than inventing new worlds, reinvents the world as it is to become one vast poem." This can most clearly be seen in the 1938 revision *Svatební cesta* (Honeymoon), which removed typographical idiosyncracies to let the poetry speak for itself.

The book's epigraph is an inversion of lines from the romantic poet Karel Hynek Mácha, known to every Czech reader: "On the face a faint grief / and deep in the heart a smile." Seifert proclaims that although the world as we see it seems sometimes intolerably sad, there is always a cause for hope and rejoicing. *Na vlnách TSF* may thus be seen as a programmatic, book-length expansion of the "Monologue of the handless soldier" from his first collection, *Méesto v slzách* (City in Tears, 1921), in which a war veteran who has every reason to be bitter and resentful refuses self-pity and instead praises the world in which he and his able-bodied fellows live. Where *Miesto* adopted the voices of anonymous Prague citizens and the proletariat, *Na vlnách TSF* is unabashedly high-brow, invoking APOLLINAIRE, BLAISE CENDRARS, and MAYAKOVSKY. The poems grew out of a trip to Paris with Teige in 1924 but equally out of the enthusiasm for French modernism, which was a feature of Czech literary life in those years. Even the title plays on this enthusiasm; at the time there was no Czech term for the wireless radio, and the French term *télégraphe sans fils* was used instead.

The most accomplished celebration of modernism and technology, however, is not one of the Paris poems, but rather the piece that Seifert chose as the title poem of the 1938 revision, "*Svatební cesta*" (Honeymoon), where the ecstatic description of a train journey through the Alps mimics the rhythm of the railway carriage itself, and French words are expertly, even impertinently, caught up in the Czech rhyme scheme. There is also a healthy, thrilling dose of sexual joy in the poem. Throughout his life Seifert loved women and loved to celebrate their charms.

Dana Loewy includes the collection as *Svatební cesta* among his translations, published as *The Early Poetry of Jaroslav Seifert* (Northwestern University Press, 1997).

Samuel Willcocks

OSUNDARE, NIYI (1947–   )

Born Oluwaniyi Isaac Osundare to a peasant farmer and a weaver in Ikere-Ekiti in southwestern Nigeria, Osundare is the most significant poet to emerge in Nigeria after the Nigerian civil war (1967–1970). He is the leading promoter of a form of poetry that is both socially responsive and performance-oriented, and he has performed his poetry around the world. He accords great importance to an accessible poetic medium and the urgency of social transformation. He demonstrated this by contributing poems to *Sunday Tribune,* an Ibadan-based weekly from 1985 to 1990. Those poems eventually formed his seventh collection, *Songs of the Season.* He is, moreover, a distinguished scholar, social critic, newspaper columnist, and playwright.

Osundare was educated on three continents—Africa, Europe, and North America. He graduated with a bachelor of arts degree in English from the University of Ibadan in 1972, earned an M.A. in modern English from the University of Leeds in the United Kingdom, and was awarded a Ph.D. from York University in Toronto, Canada, in 1979 for his study of bilingualism and biculturalism in African writing. He taught English at the University of Ibadan for about three decades before moving to the United States, where he has been a professor of English. A much decorated poet, Osundare has received many national and international awards, including the Association of Nigerian Authors' Poetry Prize, the Noma Prize for the Best Published Book in Africa, the Commonwealth Poetry Prize, the Fonlon Prize for Literature with concern for human rights, and honorary doctorates from universities in France and the United States. His poems have been translated into French, Italian, Russian, and Korean.

An egalitarian outlook that derives inspiration from Marxism generally permeates his early work, and he consistently expresses a desire to see Africa overcome such recurrent problems as injustice, poverty, despotism, and visionless leadership. But he does not subordinate artistic discipline to his political concerns. An infectious sense of optimism also colors his vision. While much of his early poetry—represented by *Songs of the Marketplace, Village Voices,* and *A Nib in the Pond*—thrives on topicality and defines his poetic commitment, his later work (*Moonsongs, The Eye of the Earth, Waiting Laughter, Midlife, Horses of Memory,* and *The Word Is an Egg*) exhibits a greater sense of artistic control as shown in the way he adopts either a unifying idiom or a major concern as an organizing device for each collection. This stratagem makes it possible to characterize much of his later work. For instance, most of *Moonsongs* (1988) was written in the late 1980s while Osundare was in the hospital recovering from an attack on him. *The Eye of the Earth* (1986), joint winner of the Commonwealth Poetry Prize, is a celebration of the Earth as both environment and source of sustenance. *Waiting Laughter* (1990) envisions collective renewal for Africa; the autobiographical *Midlife* (1993) offers the poet an opportunity for self-reflection on attaining the age of 40. *Horses of Memory* (1998) celebrates the memory of Osundare's father, while *The World Is an Egg* (2000) is concerned with the pleasure and process of creating poetry.

In the context of modern Nigerian poetry in English, Osundare's work has come to be seen as inaugurating a generational shift in terms of poetic concern and method. Osundare sees much of the work of earlier Nigerian poets like WOLE SOYINKA and CHRISTOPHER OKIGBO as both obscure and insensitive to experience in the immediate social world due to its excessive preoccupation with personal experiences. He therefore makes a case in his poetry and essays for a new kind of poetry that devotes more attention to problems shared by the society, especially those that concern the common people. Consequently, his poetry promotes the dreams and desires of marginalized social formations, ridicules the failure of the indigenous African political elite, anticipates the possibilities of radical social transformation, and celebrates desirable aspects of African life. There is also a delight in nature in much of his work, especially in *The Eye of the Earth,* which fuses a nostalgic recollection of his agrarian roots with a larger concern for the environment. Much of his recent work benefits immensely from his interaction with other cultures and situations, and he has demonstrated his ability to engage issues that are not necessarily political in *The Word Is an Egg.* In most of Osundare's poems, especially those that engage the political and related issues, the poet-persona passionately identifies with the populace, who are consistently represented as violated, while demonizing the politician. Osundare's work shares this concern with the poetry of other Nigerian poets such as Femi Fatoba, TANURE OJAIDE, and Odia Ofeimun.

Niyi Osundare is a culturally rooted artist also aware of developments in many traditions. He acknowledges influences from a variety of sources, ranging from the African to the Western, the oral to the written. He particularly admits his debt to the Chilean PABLO NERUDA, as well as to the Angolan poet-statesman AGOSTINHO NETO. While his extensive reading and innovative engagement of English injects dynamism into his poetry, the poetic traditions and the rich linguistic strategies of the Yoruba provide the basic resources with which he works. Osundare's use of the poetic practices of the Yoruba people of southwestern Nigeria has given his work a distinctive identity. His poetry owes much to the traditions of praise poetry (*oriki*) and poetry of abuse. The song of abuse, whose practitioners traditionally enjoy immunity in Yoruba society, is an instrument for regulating social behavior through indicting wrongdoers and exposing their lapses to social ridicule. Rather than serve the traditional function of chronicling genealogies and celebrating related values, *oriki* also becomes a means of acknowledging exemplary acts and ideals, especially those that promote the common good. The poet also utilizes rhetorical strategies from the Yoruba tradition of performance, such as the call/response pattern, tonal variation, repetition, and the refrain, most of which anticipate ultimate delivery as oral performance (through which, in this context, poetry is believed to be fully realized). The tendency to grant oral artists immunity in the process of discharging their responsibility in the traditional Yoruba society may have empowered Osunadare's bold engagement of the ills of the larger Nigerian society, as the poet does in "SIREN."

Osundare survived Hurricane Katrina, which ravaged New Orleans in 2005, just a few weeks after he had delivered a valedictory lecture marking his formal disengagement from the University of Ibadan, but he lost manuscripts and all his personal effects to the hurricane and subsequent floods.

BIBLIOGRAPHY

Aiyejina, Funsho. "Recent Nigerian Poetry in English: An Alternative Tradition." In *Perspectives on Nigerian Literature, 1700 to the Present.* Vol. 1. Edited by Yemi Ogunbiyi. Lagos, Nigeria: Guardian Books, 1988, 112–128.

Bamikunle, Aderemi. "Niyi Osundare's Poetry and the Yoruba Oral Artistic Tradition." *African Literature Today* 18 (1992): 49–61.

———. "The Development of Niyi Osundare's Poetry: A Survey of Themes and Technique." In *Research in African Literatures* 24, no. 4 (Winter 1995): 121–137.

Osundare, Niyi. *Thread in the Loom: Essays on African Literature and Culture.* Trenton, N.J.: Africa World Press, 2002.

———. "Yoruba Thought, English Words: A Poet's Journey Through the Tunnel of Two Tongues." In *Kiss and Quarrel: Yoruba/English, Strategies of Mediation.* Edited by Stewart Brown. Birmingham, U.K.: Centre of West African Studies, University of Birmingham Press, 2000, 15–31.

Na-Allah, AdulRasheed, ed. *The Poeple's Poet: Emerging Perspectives on Niyi Osundare.* Trenton, N.J.: Africa World Press, 2002.

Oyeniyi Okunoye

"O THE CHIMNEYS" NELLY SACHS (1947)

In her study *Keepers of the Motherland: German Texts by Jewish Women Writers,* Dagmar C. G. Lorenz comments that NELLY SACHS wrote *In den Wohnungen des Todes* (In the Dwellings of Death), the collection of which "O the Chimneys" is a part, after Sachs had fled to Sweden from Nazi Germany in 1940, had begun to study the Hebrew Kabbalah, and had shed her earlier faith that assimilation into European civilization was possible for Jews.

"O the Chimneys" ("*O die Schornsteine*") is a short, unrhymed poem in four irregular stanzas. Each stanza represents a cry of grief and indirectly conveys the speaker's distress and bewilderment regarding the heartlessness of the designers of the Nazi crematoria in the concentration and extermination camps. The poem is composed of exclamations and questions. It combines bitter descriptions of those "houses of death" with references to the Torah. The first, second, and fourth stanzas begin with the exclamation "O the chimneys"; the third stanza begins with "*O die Wohnungen des Todes*" (O the dwellings of death). In each stanza the poet uses a different euphemism for the crematoria, calling them "*sinnreich erdachten*" (cleverly devised) dwellings in the first stanza; in the second they are "*Freiheitswege*" (freedomways, freeways) for the dust of Jeremiah and Job; in the third they are houses "*Einladend hergerichtet*" (invitingly readied) / "*Für den Wirt des Hauses. der sonst Gast war*" (for the landlord, who used to be a guest), houses whose chimneys are like fingers that define the difference between life and death; in the fourth they are only chimneys, those fingers pointing to "*Israels Leib im Rauch durch die Luft!*" (Israel's body in smoke through the air).

In the first stanza the image is introduced of Israel's body drifting (*zog aufgelöst*) as smoke through the air, blackening a star (the Sun). The second stanza asks, "*Wer erdachte euch und baute Stein auf Stein / Den Weg für Flüchtlinge aus Rauch?*" (Who designed you and built you stone by stone / the path for refugees of smoke?). The third stanza, in its biting, ironic reference to a landlord who was once a guest, concisely represents the historical reality of tables turned on European Jews, who had once (before Hitler's time) lavishly regaled their gentile friends.

The poem's images are restrained, and the poem's tone is a lament, not simply for the fate of Jewry in Europe, but also—as indicated in the third stanza—for what had become of the rest of the European population.

BIBLIOGRAPHY

Lorenz, Dagmar C. G. *Keepers of the Motherland: German Texts by Jewish Women Writers.* Lincoln: University of Nebraska Press, 1997.

———. *O the Chimneys: Selected Poems, Including the Verse Play* Eli. New York: Farrar, Straus and Giroux, 1967.

R. Victoria Arana

OVER THE ROOFS OF THE WORLD OLIVE SENIOR (2005)

Over the Roofs of the World (2005) is Jamaican poet OLIVE SENIOR's third collection of poetry. In her second collection, *Gardening in the Tropics,* a cycle of poems is connected by themes of cultivation and a repeated opening line. In similar fashion this collection is organized mostly around various birds—their characteristics, names, and the associative lore surrounding them. Though Senior hews to speech rhythms and moves gracefully between disparate levels of tone, her poems use conventional English orthography, and her spacing and punctuation, even at moments of great emotional intensity or when shaping lines for visual or aural effects, are spare and minimalist.

The collection begins with the image of Columbus (Colón), lost en route to the New World, choosing a course to follow a flock of birds passing overhead. Senior's opening conceit of navigation and progress deftly places the seasonally migrating birds at the decisive moment of colonial history, making their fortuitous flight the force that impelled Columbus's course. Many of Senior's bird poems are framed by borrowed texts and contexts drawn from poetic and historical archives, such as "Owl," which cites a line from *Hamlet*, "Woodpecker," which proceeds from an Amerindian myth, and "Parakeet," which flows from a Jamaican revival hymn. "Thirteen Ways of Looking at Blackbird" responds to Wallace Stevens's seminal poem of virtually the same title. "The Secret of Crusoe's Parrot" retells Daniel Defoe's *Robinson Crusoe* from the perspective of the parrot, who learns language and contempt for the "senseless cries" of "uncivilized birds" from Crusoe (19). "Magpie," for example, is a tour de force of wordplay, weaving puns such as "Pied Piper" and "easy as pie" with the Magpie's metaphorical and linguistic travels, its eating disorder "pica," and virtuoso descriptive sequences—for example, an apostrophe to the Magpie as "celebrant of the variegated, the parti-coloured / mixture of paint, pigment, picture of pied beauty" (32).

In addition to the cycle of bird poems, the collection includes "Ode to Pablo Neruda," a mediation on the poet's self-discovery in the form of a dialogue with Chilean poet PABLO NERUDA, in which Senior's reflections are woven together with quotations from Neruda. Among the images Senior adopts for her role is that of "Spider's apprentice. To master language. As / Trickster, to spin and weave tales"—in which she alludes to Anancy, the Ashanti-derived spider-trickster figure of Caribbean folklore (94). "Rejected Text for Tourist Brochure" is perhaps the collection's most directly political statement, a wistful and sardonic rhapsody to the beauty of Jamaica that is being rapidly despoiled by economic development and the whims of the tourist industry, as noted in the poem's cutting refrain, "Come see my land / and know / that she was fair" (53).

BIBLIOGRAPHY
Senior, Olive. *Over the Roofs of the World*. Toronto: Insomnia Press, 2005.

Alan Feerst

P

PACHECO, JOSÉ EMILIO (1939–   ) José Emilio Pacheco, born in Mexico City in 1939, is regarded as one of the most versatile writers of the 20th century in the Spanish-speaking world. Besides writing poetry and fiction, he is also known as a scholar, journalist, and scriptwriter.

Although Pacheco has produced great works in all these literary genres, outside of Mexico he is best known for his fiction and poetry, genres that he has enriched with technically remarkable works. Pacheco enjoys the favor of widely differing readerships. Readers of his fiction are often unaware of his contributions to poetry. Alternately, lovers of his poetry may know little of his fiction. His three collections of short stories—*La sangre de Medusa* (The Blood of Medusa, 1958), *El principio del placer* (The Beginning [or Principle] of Pleasure, 1962), and *El viento distante* (The Distant Wind, 1963)—are mainly explorations of childhood and adolescence as painful passages into manhood. Pacheco's ventures in short fiction would later culminate in the novel *Las batallas en el desierto,* where the process is restated with an extraordinary sense of humor. His novels *Moriras lejos* (You Will Die in a Distant Land, 1967) and *Las batallas en el desierto* (Battles in the Desert and Other Stories, 1980) are pioneering works of postmodern Latin American narrative, especially because of their themes and the realistic yet subjective forms of representation.

Pacheco's poetry also occupies a central position in contemporary Spanish-language poetry. His work proves that it is still possible to write exceptional poetry in Spanish in the wake of the brilliant era of the modernists, the Vanguard, and Post-Vanguard Hispanic-American poets, as well as the great postwar Spanish writers. Poetry critics and readers alike have enjoyed Pacheco's work since 1963, when *Los elementos de la noche* (The Elements of Night) first appeared. It revealed an impeccable lyric meditation on time and its devastating effects. This is a fundamental theme of Pacheco's poetic work. And through 12 books of poetry over four decades, he has combined this theme with many of the issues of contemporary society—environmental concerns, the animal kingdom, personal alienation, genocide, and the perception of the history of humankind as an irrational spiral toward misery and destruction.

After his first book of poems Pacheco wrote *El reposo del fuego* (The Repose of Fire, 1966), *No me preguntes cómo pasa el tiempo* (Don't Ask Me How the Time Goes By: Poems 1964–1968, trans. 1978), *Irás y no volverás* (You Will Go and Not Return, 1973), *Islas a la deriva* (1976), *Desde entonces* (Since Then, 1980), *Los trabajos del mar* (The Labors of the Sea, 1983), in which appears the poem "A LINEAR EQUATION WITH THIS SINGLE UNKNOWN QUANTITY," *Miro la tierra* (I Look at Earth, 1986), *Ciudad de la memoria* (City of Memory and other poems, 1989), *El silencio de la luna* (The Silence of the Moon, 1996), *La arena errante* (Errant Sand, 1999), and *Siglo pasado (Desenlace)* (2000). Critics feel that *No me preguntes cómo pasa el tiempo* (Don't Ask Me How the Time Goes By: Poems 1964–1968) initiated a more direct poetic language. Departing from his earlier works, his rhymes are less formal, and his verse runs more freely. Although these poetic aspects are quite common in contemporary poetry, in Pacheco's case they stirred up a polemic among critics, since his first two books were viewed as distinct from the drastic experiments of the Hispanic-American avant-garde and post-avant-garde productions of the time. A fresh look at the first two books of poems, however, reveals that all the contemporary poetic devices were present, occupying the background of the poems, creating a texture and depth that adds vitality and contemporaneity to the classic meters and poetic forms that were not used often in Latin American poetry during the 1960s.

Pacheco's poetic style cannot be easily summarized, since he uses a multitude of linguistic registers and discourses (e.g., conversational, lyrical, philosophical, and scientific). Gradually he transmutes from one to another, developing layers of meaning in his images and metaphors by creating alternative and simultaneous perceptions. This protean quality represents one of Pacheco's greatest achievements, for he is capable of touching a vast array of readers.

Besides the volumes already indicated as available in translation, there are two anthologies of his poetry in English translation: *Signals from the Flames: Selected Poetry of José Emilio Pacheco,* translated by Thomas Hoeksema (Pittsburgh: Latin American Literary Review Press, 1980) and *Selected Poems,* edited by George McWhirter, translated by Thomas Hoeksema, George McWhirter, Alastair Reid, and Linda Scheer (Pittsburgh: Latin American Press, 1987).

BIBLIOGRAPHY
Friis, Ronald J. *José Emilio Pacheco and the Poets of the Shadows.* Lewisburg, Pa.: Bucknell University Press, 2001.

Amelia Mondragón, with Jerrold M. Davis

PAINTING ANDRÉ DU BOUCHET (1983) One of DU BOUCHET's most challenging palimpsests of synesthetic theory and praxis, his book-length poem *Peinture* (1983) at once discusses and inhabits creative processes of unwriting and unpainting. Examining fluid thresholds between "painting," disappearance, and the open, the text performs collusions of rhythm,

the visual, and the tactile. Gradual and rapturous modes of immobilization and disappearance are approached through experimental gestures of what du Bouchet calls "decentering." Far from merely celebrating the transitory and contingent, the poem insists on locating irreversible loss and identifying "the place of disappearance." "Painting" emerges as the locus of sudden blindness (*peinture – où je cesse de voir*), and writing takes on the task of searching for prereflexive immediacy and inventing a not-yet-represented "face before painting" (*antérieure de la peinture*), a face that needs to be restored or reproduced for, and as, a sustained look (*Restitué au regard*).

Du Bouchet's poem exemplifies what it writes into being: a scattered, sparse landscape of clearings (*clairsemé*). Productive spontaneity and tradition are presented as the labor of renewal in the guise of a drawing that perpetually reconstitutes itself (*à nouveau, se dessinera*). Evoking uncannily embedded exposures "beneath the eyes," and operating with laconic paradoxes such as "transparent blocks of stone," du Bouchet's ethics and poetics of survival culminate in the surprising assertion that a tangible opening for genuine dialogue is at hand, despite the apparent destruction of language—"the destroyed word is intact" (*la parole détruite est intacte*).

Paul Auster provides a careful translation in his du Bouchet anthology, *The Uninhabited* (New York: Living Hand, 1976).

Olaf Berwald

PARRA, NICANOR (1914–) A professor of theoretical physics at the University of Chile, Nicanor Parra is also one of Chile's most influential modern poets. Often compared to American poets from Walt Whitman to Allen Ginsberg, Parra is regarded as equal in significance to his greatest compatriot poets: GABRIELA MISTRAL, VICENTE HUIDOBRO, and PABLO NERUDA (who was his contemporary). Parra is considered the founder of the "antipoem," and his poetry reflects his scientific interests as well as his emphasis on the realities of ordinary life.

Born on September 5, 1914, into a middle-class family, Parra grew up with eight brothers and sisters, one of whom, Violeta, became a celebrated artist in her own right. Nicanor began to write poetry while still young, and his pursuit of science did not undermine, but rather complemented, his interest in poetry. At only 23 he received an award for his first book of poems, *Cancionero sin nombre* (Untitled Songbook), and at the same time graduated with a degree in mathematics from the University of Chile in Santiago. Parra had begun to compose poetry much earlier, beginning an ambitious project when he was only 11: an epic tracing the history of his homeland's Araucano Indians, Spaniards, and Chileans. As Edith Grossman observes, these early compositions, while relatively insignificant, lent Parra his future identity as both a poet and a scientist.

Parra has acknowledged the importance of other poets to his writing. FEDERICO GARCÍA LORCA's *Romancero gitano* (The Gypsy Ballads), for example, had a significant influence on Parra's *Cancionero sin nombre*. But even when the influences of other writers are not direct, as they were in the case of *Cancionero,* they are important. Parra's conceptualization of antipoetry is in part reactionary. As a member of the Generation of 1938, Parra emphasized reality in his poetry and abandoned previous traditions dependent on surrealist creative processes and far-fetched metaphors.

Although Parra's first published work was awarded a municipal prize in 1937, he did not truly come into his own as a poet nor fully develop his distinctive poetic ideology until the publication of *Poemas y antipoemas* (Poems and Antipoems), which appeared in 1954 and was subsequently published in English translation in 1967. Parra did not write *Poemas y antipoemas* from a foundation of clearly defined theory. The book's title derived, he wrote, from his casual notice of a French book by Henri Pichette titled *Apoèmes,* and from there Parra divined his own title. Although Parra famously developed the term, he did not coin the word *antipoem*; unbeknown to him, Vicente Huidobro had used the word previously in a somewhat different sense. Parra's idea of the antipoem, then, is difficult to characterize in brief because Parra never defined the term, and his own remarks only declare what it is *not.* From his statements and from his own works, readers may deduce that antipoetry, as Parra conceived of it, is verse written against and in defiance of those previous, highly stylized poetic conventions still being followed in his own day.

With *Poemas y antipoemas* Parra announced a new emphasis for Chilean poetry and for all poetry in Spanish. No longer was poetry to be a rarified genre, dependent on convention and tradition, but a genre reactive to the real world and to the common people. Real-world events, real people, and real problems all feature in Parra's poetry, and poems such as "Recuerdos de juventud" ("MEMORIES OF YOUTH") suggest the poet's preoccupation with the aesthetics of accessible poetry and the common language. With his antipoems Parra emphasizes direct contact with the reader and deft replication of both linguistic and social realities.

Despite its novel theme, however, *Poemas y antipoemas* was not received with universal acclaim; instead, many critics were outwardly appalled by its use of sometimes gross or shocking details in pursuit of veracity and authenticity. Other critics overemphasized Parra's debt to English-language poets, including Walt Whitman. Regardless of the unenthusiastic responses, *Poemas y antipoemas* was widely acknowledged as a turning point for Latin American verse, winning two literary prizes (in 1954 and 1955).

Although 17 years divided Parra's first book from his second, he did not wait nearly so long to publish a third work, *La cueca larga* (The Long Dance), which appeared in 1958. Parra continued his experimentation with vernacular language and common expressions in the new poems appearing in this volume. Despite its apparent resemblance to *Cancionero sin nombre*—both books emphasize ballads—*La cueca larga* is a more mature work, showcasing the development of Parra's sometimes quixotic phrasing and sense of humor.

Parra's next volume, *Versos de salón* (Salon Verses), appeared in 1962. It is one of his most significant works, for here his conception of antipoetry appears in its most polished form. Like *Poemas y antipoemas, Versos de salón* was not universally well received. His caustic humor, unusual imagery, and direct cautionary addresses to the reader sometimes provoked the vituperative responses Parra seemed to anticipate in earlier poems like "Advertencia al lector" (Warning to the Reader) in *Poemas y antipoemas* and "Cambios de nombre" (Name Changes) in *Versos de salón*. Despite the controversial nature of his work, Parra continued to be well received in avant-garde circles and in 1962 coauthored with Neruda *Pablo Neruda y Nicanor Parra,* translated, at last, in 1997 as *Pablo Neruda and Nicanor Parra Face to Face.*

In 1969 Parra produced a collection of selected works, *Obra gruesa* (Thick Work). Other poems and collections followed, including *Sermones y prédicas del Cristo de Elqui* (Sermons and Homilies of the Christ of Elqui) in 1977 and *Hojas de Parra* (Leaves of Parra) in 1985, but he was slowly shifting his focus away from antipoetry to something he designated as "ecopoetry" (see ECOPOETICS). The same political consciousness and awareness of the real world that Parra instilled in his antipoetry characterized his ecopoetry. Concerned with the state of the environment and with the future of the world, Parra has, as he put it, "evolved toward a poetry of global commitment." To this day, all the same, Parra strongly disapproves of exotic language, exotic subjects, and metaphor.

BIBLIOGRAPHY

Agosín, Margorie. "Contemporary Poetry of Chile." *Concerning Poetry* 17 (1984): 43–53.

———. "Pablo Neruda and Nicanor Parra: A Study of Similarities." *Poesis: A Journal of Criticism* 6–7 (1984–1987): 51–60.

Grossman, Edith. *The Antipoetry of Nicanor Parra.* New York: New York University Press, 1975.

Parra, Nicanor. "A Talk with Nicanor Parra." Interview with Miller Williams. *Shenandoah* 18, no. 1 (1966): 71–78.

———. Interview with Marie-Lise Gazarian Gautier. *Interviews with Latin American Writers.* Elmwood Park, Ill.: Dalkey Archive Press, 1989.

———. *Antipoems: New and Selected.* Edited by David Unger. New York: New Directions, 1985.

———. *Sermons and Homilies of the Christ of Elqui.* Translated by Sandra Reyes. Columbia: University of Missouri Press, 1984.

———. *Poems and Antipoems.* Edited by Miller Williams, translated by William Carlos Williams et al. New York: New Directions, 1967.

Winter Elliott

PASOLINI, PIER PAOLO (1922–1975) Pier

Paolo Pasolini has been called one of the most enigmatic figures of the European intelligentsia of the second half of the 20th century. His sympathies were with the poor and oppressed inhabitants of city slums and projects during an era of totalitarian fascist regimes. In his "stark but compassionate, emotional, but never sentimental" works (Smith 65), he explored classic themes: human sensuality, sexuality, religious beliefs, power relations, fate, and death. His neorealist treatments of these themes, especially following World War II, combined a disheartened sense of general devastation with intelligence and a cautious optimism for the world's downtrodden. In his native Italy he achieved distinction at an early age as an intellectual, poet, painter, playwright, novelist, screenwriter, and journalist. Then from the late 1950s, he became a world-renowned film director. Pasolini was an influential creative force, especially during the 1960s, when many of his provocative films and avant-garde publications made cultural news worldwide. Blending gritty realism, biblical and classical references, and nostalgia for the revelry and expressive freedoms of Boccacio, Chaucer, and others, Pasolini's art represents a critique of bourgeois conformity and of decaying human values.

Pier Paolo Pasolini was born in Bologna on March 2, 1922. During his boyhood he lived in or near that city, speaking the old language of Friulan, learned from his mother, which was spoken mainly by country folk of the vicinity. He composed many poems in this tongue, but most of his greatest works are in a contemporary version of the classical Italian lyrical style derived, as Alberto Moravia has noted, from Dante and Petrarch, "who also spoke of the misfortunes of Italy" (Moravia 2). Pasolini became interested in poetry at an early age, inventing his first verses, it is said, at the age of seven. He began publishing his poems in various periodicals at the age of 19. By the time he was 32 he had published several novels, a large number of essays, and two acclaimed collections in Friulan, *Poesie a Casarsa* (1942) and *La meglio gioventù* (1954). These were soon followed by *Le ceneri di Gramsci* (Gramsci's Ashes, 1957), *L'usignolo della chiesa cattolica* (The Catholic Church's Nightingale, 1958), and *La religione del mio tempo* (The Religion of My Age, 1961). In 1962 he was arrested on charges of pornography, but he was given a suspended sentence. The arrest did not affect his outlook or productivity, which continued with *Poesia in forma di rosa* (Poetry in the Shape of a Rose, 1964), *Trasumanar e organizzar* (*trasumanar* was Dante's neologism to signify "to transhumanize, to pass beyond the human," 1971), and *La nuova gioventù* (The New Youth, 1975).

Pasolini directed over 25 films, including *The Gospel According to Matthew* (1965), *The Hawks and the Sparrows* (1966), *Oedipus Rex* (1967), *The Decameron* (1971), *The Canterbury Tales* (1972), *A Thousand and One Nights / Arabian Nights* (1974), *Notes Towards an African Orestes* (1975), and *The 120 Days of Sodom* (1976).

He was murdered—it is still disputed by whom and why—in November 1975 at Ostia, near Rome. Some theorize that his razor-sharp social criticism was cutting too close for comfort and that his assassination was ordered by enraged politicians, but the courts determined at the time that he was killed when his relations with underworld homosexuals had spun out of his control. The case was reopened in 2005 when new evidence came to light.

BIBLIOGRAPHY

Moravia, Alberto. "Pier Paolo Pasolini." Introduction in *Pasolini: Roman Poems* (q.v.), 2–5.

Pasolini, Pier Paolo. *Pasolini: Roman Poems*. Translated by Lawrence Ferlinghetti and Francesca Valente. San Francisco: City Lights Books (Pocket Poets Series No. 41), 1986.

———. *Poems*. Edited by Norman MacAfee, translated by Luciano Martinengo, introduced by Enzo Siciliano. New York: Farrar Straus and Giroux, 1996.

———. *Stories from the City of God: Sketches and Chronicles of Rome 1950–1966*. Edited by Walter Siti, translated by Marina Harss. New York: Other Press, 2003.

Smith, Lawrence R., ed. *The New Italian Poetry, 1945 to the Present: A Bilingual Anthology*. Berkeley and Los Angeles: University of California Press, 1981, 65–111.

R. Victoria Arana

PASTERNAK, BORIS L. (1890–1960) One

of Russia's finest avant-garde poets, Boris Leonidovich Pasternak was born in 1890 to an ethnically Sephardic Jewish family with roots in Odessa. His father, who gave up a law career to paint, was a successful illustrator and portraitist, and his mother, who was offered a position at the Odessa Music School, was an accomplished pianist. Their circle of friends included novelist Lev Tolstoy, composer Aleksandr Scriabin, and German poet RAINER MARIA RILKE. Pasternak was a good student, although he found the structure of school confining. In spite of that, he studied law at Moscow University and philosophy at Marburg. He drew, and he composed music in addition to playing the piano. Around 1910, when he discovered he lacked perfect pitch, he abandoned music for literature.

Pasternak's early poetry, which he later repudiated or rewrote, concerns changes in the seasons; people are notably absent. Nature imagery would remain a prominent feature of his total oeuvre. The symbolists were an early influence on his writing as was the aesthetics of German-Jewish neo-Kantian philosopher Hermann Cohen. For them art gives objective expression to an artist's subjectivity and enters thereby into the cultural milieu. Art then outlasts the consciousness of the artist and becomes a part of the world's cultural endowment. The artist as an individual has a priestlike function because he or she can access both the personal and the infinite. Although Pasternak associated with poets in the avant-garde movements in Russia, his verse, often written in metered quatrains, does not fit tidily into any one school.

Woman as a source of creativity is a theme in much of Pasternak's verse. He had complicated relationships with women. In the summer of 1917, infatuated with Elena Vinograd, a social worker whom he had met in 1909, Pasternak produced his first significant collection of poetry, MY SISTER, LIFE (1922). Vinograd rejected his courtship and married according to her family's wishes. He then married the painter Evgenia Lurye in 1922, and tensions arising from juggling two artistic careers in a small apartment may have contributed to their eventual estrangement. His intense correspondence (1926–41) with fellow poet MARIA TSVETAYEVA aroused jealousy, and his first marriage ended in 1931. Even before the official dissolution of his marriage to Evgenia, Pasternak had begun an affair with Zinaida Neigauz, who at the time was married to one of Pasternak's friends. Pasternak married Neigauz in 1934, and they remained together until his death in 1960. But he continued to have affairs—most notably with Olga Ivinskaya, whom he met in 1946 and who, besides being the inspiration for his heroine Lara in *Doctor Zhivago,* became his mistress and the heiress to the money his works earned in the West.

, Pasternak also had complicated and multifaceted relationships with the cultures in which he lived. He found Jewish culture too exclusionary, and he eventually converted to Eastern Orthodox Christianity. He loved Russia but felt a part of the broader European culture in which he had been reared. His parents and sisters were in Berlin at the time of the 1905 revolution and lived there most of the rest of their lives, but he and his brother, Aleksandr, remained in Russia. Due to a leg injury Pasternak was unable to fight in either World War I or World War II, but served as a clerk in the Urals during the first war and as a firewatcher in Moscow during the second. He feared exile from the Soviet Union so greatly that he declined the Nobel Prize in literature in 1958, lest the Soviet government not allow him to return from Sweden.

His relationship with the Soviet authorities was often tense. To earn a living he produced translations since his poetry, which was at odds with the socialist realist ideal of art celebrating the achievements of the Soviet state, gained him no money. In 1926 he published a long narrative poem, *The Year 1905,* a series of vignettes expressing the hope that attended the revolution that year. The poem seems to have satisfied the requirements of the government in spite of its personal tone. He had mixed feelings, nevertheless, about Soviet leader Stalin, whom he admired for a time as a man of action but eventually condemned as a barbarous leader.

In the 1930s Pasternak was on the edge of acceptability: His poetry was suspect because of its focus on the personal, but his translations of Georgian poetry, which he admired, won favor, as did *Second Birth* (1932), which joins the themes of personal and national rebirth. He became secretary of the Writers' Union in 1934. Two years later he attacked the mechanistic qualities of Soviet art, whereupon he was officially denounced. Publishers subsequently rejected his work. The government, always highly suspicious of him, imprisoned Ivinskaya twice, once for four years in the early 1950s and once after his death.

In the thaw that followed Stalin's death in 1953, Soviet journals published some of Pasternak's autobio-graphical poems, and he was at last able to read in public. But no publisher inside the Soviet Union would accept his religious poems, which appeared only in the émigré press. Nor would any Soviet press publish his enormously successful novel, *Dr. Zhivago,* which (published in Italy) received international accolades and became a best seller in Western Europe and the United States. (See THE POEMS OF DR. ZHIVAGO, published as a kind of appendix to the novel). Although he was well regarded as a poet, the novel appears to have been the primary reason he was awarded the Nobel Prize. When the Writers' Union expelled him, his fame seems to have kept him from prison. In the end, neither the party's displeasure nor poverty kept him from writing, and even disease did not stop him. He lived out what he wrote in his poem "English Lessons" and faced his own death singing. His last collection, the volume WHEN THE WEATHER CLEARS, was published posthumously.

BIBLIOGRAPHY

Barnes, Christopher J. *Boris Pasternak: A Literary Biography.* 2 vols. Cambridge and New York: Cambridge University Press, 1989–1998.

Hingley, Ronald. *Pasternak: A Biography.* New York: Knopf, 1983.

Pasternak, Boris. *Safe Conduct: An Early Autobiography and Other Works.* Translated by Alec Brown and Lydia Pasternak-Slater. New York: New Directions, 1958.

Pasternak, Boris, Marina Tsvetaeva, and Rainer Maria Rilke. *Letters: Summer 1926.* Translated by Margaret Wettlin, Walter Arndt, and Jamey Gambrell. New York: New York Review of Books, 2001.

Zaltsberg, Ernst. "Boris Pasternak: Composer and Poet." *Clavier* 36 (1997): 24–27.

Karen Rae Keck

PAVESE, CESARE (1908–1950)

While more often remembered as a writer of fiction, Italian author Cesare Pavese nevertheless composed a sizable body of poetry. The sole collection of his poems to be published during his lifetime, *Lavorare stanca* (Work's Tiring, 1936, expanded edition, 1943), has in recent years been cited as a significant, even groundbreaking, book—both within Italian literature and internationally. Born September 9, 1908, into a northern Italian family of lower-middle-class background, Pavese grew up in Turin and as a youth spent considerable time on his parents' farm in the Langhe hills just outside that city. Years later Pavese's poetry would explore human experience in both those environments. Pavese's poetry was ignored in Italy initially because in the 1930s and early 1940s his literary stance was out of step with the nation's prevailing literary fashions. Most other Italian poets of the era composed poetry faithful to the ideology of fascism or to the tenets of the neotraditionalist and formalist literary movement in Italy known as hermeticism. Pavese rejected both those aesthetics in favor of a poetry more atuned to the high modernism then prevalent in the United States and elsewhere in Europe.

After graduating from the University of Turin in 1930, having written his thesis on Walt Whitman's poetry, Pavese joined the Fascist Party in 1932, though he soon disassociated himself from it because of its cultural and social repression. A decade later he joined the Italian Communist Party and in due course underwent a similar sense of disillusionment. For income during those years Pavese translated numerous English-language literary works into Italian for the publisher Giulio Einaudi. Pavese's own poetry—strongly influenced by American authors whom he read during this period—possessed a high degree of thematic and stylistic distinctiveness within Italian literature. A characteristic Pavese poem from this period (see "SOUTH SEAS") incorporated narrative to explore events from the lives of a range of lower-class characters in rural or urban Italy. Pavese generally portrayed these various personae from the point of view of a tragic or ironic sensibility, rather than from a propagandistic, didactic, profascist perspective. Pavese expressed such narratives through long, strongly rhythmic lines, often utilizing unconventional anapestic meter with a set number of beats—usually four or five per line. He also infused his poems with textured symbolism that underscored the diametrically opposed forces he endured during his formative years as an intellectual and creative artist in fascist Italy. In 1935, viewed as subversive by the Italian political authorities, Pavese was imprisoned in southern Italy for several months. After the publication of *Lavorare stanca* and frustrated by the lack of critical appreciation for his poetry, Pavese turned to fiction, producing nine novels, the best-

known of which were *Tra donne sole* (Among Women Only, 1948) and *La luna e i falò* (The Moon and the Bonfire, 1950). Another important book by Pavese was the 1947 prose work *Dialoghi con Leuco* (Dialogues with Leuco), a reinterpretation of Greek mythology. On August 27, 1950, shortly after receiving Italy's highest literary award, the Premio Strega, given in recognition primarily for his fiction, Pavese—allegedly because of frustrations with love and politics—committed suicide by taking an overdose of barbiturates.

Pavese's poems have been translated into English for two major collections: the acclaimed translation of *Lavorare stanca* by William Arrowsmith, titled *Hard Labor*; and a more comprehensive collection of Pavese's poetry, *Disaffections: Complete Poems 1930–1950*, translated by Geoffrey Brock—the latter featuring all of *Lavorare stanca* (as Work's Tiring) as well as translations of some of his previously uncollected early poems and his increasingly recognized later poetry, such as the posthumously published sequence that Brock translated as "Death Will Come and Will Have Your Eyes."

BIBLIOGRAPHY

Lajolo, Davide. *An Absurd Vice: A Biography of Cesare Pavese.* New York: New Directions, 1983.

Pavese, Cesare. *Disaffections: Complete Poems 1930–1950.* Translated by Geoffrey Brock. Port Townsend, Wash.: Copper Canyon Press, 2002

———. *Hard Labor.* Translated by William Arrowsmith. Baltimore: Johns Hopkins University Press, 1979.

Ted Olson

PAZ, OCTAVIO (1914–1998)

Nobel laureate Octavio Paz was a spokesperson for 20th-century Mexico, a poet whose work today transcends his native land to connect with the world. Influenced by surrealism, Paz wrote of contradictions; but in his work opposites are blended and seen as part of the whole. Paz always used his art to establish relationships among cultures, people, and time. Primarily a leftist, Paz was not an extremist, so he sometimes angered both ends of the political spectrum. He remained active in politics, however, and served in the Mexican diplomatic corps in the United States, India, France, and Japan. In addition to a large body of poetry, Paz wrote essays and literary criticism, translated major literary works, and was an editor. Not only was Paz a Nobel Prize winner (1990), he also received numerous other honors, including a Guggenheim Fellowship, the Belgian Grand Prix International de Poésie, the Jerusalem Prize, the Spanish Critics Prize, the Mexican National Prize for Letters, and the T. S. Eliot Award for Creative Writing. Paz also received appointments as visiting professor at several universities, including Harvard and Cambridge.

When Octavio Paz was born in Mexico City in 1914, his father, a journalist and lawyer, was serving as assistant to Emiliano Zapata, a leader of the 1911 revolution. Paz's mother was from a prominent family of Spanish descent. During the revolutionary turmoil of the decade of Octavio's birth, the Paz family and many others were forced to flee the country. After living in Los Angeles for a few years, Paz's family returned to Mexico City but was now unable to afford a large house in the city. They moved to Mixcoac, a town near enough to allow the father to continue his political work. Although the family was now poor, Paz had access in the Mixcoac house to an expansive library and was taught by Marist brothers. He reported that he first learned the craft of writing by immersing himself in the classics of Spanish literature and the great writers of Latin America. Paz attended the National University of Mexico but left without obtaining a degree to concentrate on writing.

Paz was already published when he began his university studies. Several poems and stories had been printed in small regional publications. He also began publishing his own literary magazine, *Barandal*, at 17. Later he helped launch several other magazines, including *Vuelta*, one of Mexico's most influential publications. *Luna Silvestre* (Forest Moon), Paz's first book of poetry, was published when he was 19.

At the encouragement of Chilean poet PABLO NERUDA, Paz travelled to Spain to attend a meeting in 1937 of leftist writers. While there Paz became so involved in the Spanish civil war (1936–39) that for a period he joined a unit fighting against Francisco Franco. In 1944 Paz received a Guggenheim Fellowship that allowed him to study in the United States. There he continued his education in poetry, reading the works of Walt Whitman, T. S. Eliot, Ezra Pound, and William Carlos Williams.

After World War II Paz accepted his first diplomatic post in France. This position allowed him to read extensively, and he concentrated on French authors, several of whom he translated and wrote about. In each of his diplomatic posts Paz tried to absorb the culture around him. He was particularly influenced by his study of Eastern literature and philosophy while he was in India. In spite of his fascination with India, Paz resigned his post in 1968 in protest against his own government's suppression of neo-Zapatista demonstrations against one-party rule in Mexico that ended in the deaths in Mexico City of 300 students.

In 1950 Paz published one of his most influential works: a philosophical essay about the nature of the Mexican character. *El laberinto de la soledad* (The Labyrinth of Solitude) is part autobiography, part Mexican history, and part philosophy, all played out against the background of the dual cultural heritage of Mexico.

When Paz was in France he became acquainted with a number of surrealist writers, including ANDRÉ BRETON. Many of Paz's works show surrealist influences, especially EAGLE OR SUN (*Águila o sol?*, 1951), which unites dissimilar images and blurs their distinctions. The volume outlines Mexico's history, present, and future through a series of poems. The title is derived from the two sides of a Mexican coin, is equivalent to the expression "heads or tails," and represents two sides of a single entity. Paz's style is often experimental at the same time that it draws on tradition. The 1953 volume *Piedra de sol* (Sun Stone) is a lyrical poem following the circular structure of the ancient Aztec calendar. Written in one sentence of 584 lines, the poem explores love, myth, the art of writing, and time.

Paz combines the contradictory in other ways as well. Critics often note the poetic nature of his prose and the elements of prose that are found in his poetry. For example, *El mono gramático* (The Monkey Grammarian, 1974), an examination of India, is variously called a narrative, an essay, and a poem. Paz looks for other ways to unify opposites and obscure dissimilarity. In 1972 he collaborated with three other poets to compose *Renga*, a collection of poems in Spanish, English, French, and Italian. Another work, *Air Born/Hijos del aire* (1979), contains sonnets written in Spanish and English. Critics feel that Paz's most significant theme throughout his career was the power of language to synthesize the dualities of existence.

Octavio Paz was a modern poet of the highest caliber. When he was awarded the Nobel Prize in 1990, he was praised for his "fruitful union of cultures," his superb love poetry, and his gift of seeing both light and shadows. Paz died of cancer of the spine in 1998. He had become so much of a national figure that the public announcement of his death was made by the president of Mexico, Ernesto Zedillo.

BIBLIOGRAPHY

Paz, Octavio. *Águila o sol?* Mexico City: Tezontle, 1951.

———. *Águila o sol?/Eagle or Sun?* Translated by Eliot Weinberger. New York: October House, 1970.

———. *El arco y la lira: El poema; La revelación poética; Poesía e historia.* Mexico City: Fondo de Cultura Economica, 1956.

———. *The Bow and the Lyre: The Poem, the Poetic Revelation, Poetry and History.* Translated by Ruth L. C. Simms, Austin: University of Texas Press, 1973.

———. *Blanco.* 2d ed. Mexico City: J. Mortiz, 1972.

———. *Blanco.* Translated by Eliot Weinberger. New York: The Press, 1974.

———. *Selected Poems of Octavio Paz.* Translated by Muriel Rukeyser. Bloomington: Indiana University Press, 1963.

Paz, Octavio, and Tomlinson, Charles. *Air Born/Hijos del aire.* Mexico City: Pescador, 1979.

Jean Hamm

P'BITEK, OKOT (1931–1982)

Okot p'Bitek was born in Gulu, northern Uganda, the son of Opii Jebedyo and Lacwaa Cerina. Okot's father, Opii, a gifted storyteller, was attracted to the African Church Missionary Society in his youth and became for some time a school teacher. Okot's mother, Lacwaa Cerina, was interested in Acoli folk song and taught her son many of the songs that found their way indirectly into his poetry. As a young man p'Bitek received a prestigious education, attending Gulu High School and King's College in Budo. After graduating he worked as a teacher at Sir Samuel Baker's School near Gulu, married his first wife, Anek, and in 1953 published his first novel, *Lak Tar* (White Teeth), which was written in Acoli. He also played soccer for Uganda, traveling to Britain to compete internationally. From 1958 until 1963 he remained in Britain to pursue further studies. He earned an education diploma at Bristol, a law degree at Aberystwyth, and a B.Litt. from Oxford in social anthropology. His thesis there was titled "Oral Literature and Its Social Background Among the Acoli and Lang'o'." According to one p'Bitek scholar p'Bitek's research for his thesis renewed and strengthened his love for Ugandan orature (Heron 3), an interest that permeated all his creative writing.

When he returned to Uganda in 1964, he organized the Gulu Festival of Acoli Culture and worked for some time at Makerere College. He married Auma Kalina Kireng, his second wife, and translated his poem *"Wer pa Lawino"* ("SONG FOR LAWINO") into English. When he had first presented *"Wer pa Lawino"* in the Lwo language to publishers in 1956, it was rejected, but the poem (slightly adapted) was published in his own English translation in 1966 and has been considered one of the most important poetic works to have emerged from Africa at mid-century (the Lwo version was finally published in 1971). He accepted a year's fellowship at the University of Iowa's International Writing Program, 1969–70. *Song for Lawino: An African Lament* was soon followed by *Song of Ocol* (1970), *Song of Prisoner* (1971), and *Song of Malaya* (1971; *malaya* means *prostitute*). According to Heron, p'Bitek was strongly influenced by his mother's knowledge of music and her grounding in orature: "Despite his travels, her influence continued to be important and he discussed with her everything he did until her death in 1971" (Heron 2).

Like Ngugi wa Thiong'o, p'Bitek strongly espoused African languages for creative writing and produced his own translations into English as afterthoughts or addenda to his primary literary work. Besides his own poetry p'Bitek collected and translated Acoli folk songs and folktales in his anthologies *Horn of My Love* (1974) and *Hare and Hornbill* (1978). Also in the 1970s p'Bitek wrote *Religion of the Central Luo* (1971), *African Religions in Western Scholarship* (1971), and *Africa's Cultural Revolution* (1973).

Okot p'Bitek will be long remembered for his presentation of contrasting lifestyles among colonial Africans and for his criticism of those who would disregard African customs and traditions in the face of Westernizing forces. His satirical characterizations of self-styled modern African businessmen and politicians offended the Ugandan government, and p'Bitek was forced to emigrate. He taught at the University of Nairobi, Kenya, for almost a decade (1970–80) and held brief writer-in-residence appointments at the University of Texas at Austin and the University of Ife in Nigeria. After military dictator Idi Amin's regime was toppled, p'Bitek returned to Uganda and taught at Makerere University until his death in 1982.

BIBLIOGRAPHY
Heron, George A. *The Poetry of Okot p'Bitek*. London: Heinemann Educational Books, 1976.

p'Bitek, Okot. *Song of Lawino: An African Lament*. New York: Meridian Books, 1969.

———. *Song of Ocol*. Nairobi, Kenya: East Africa Publishing House, 1972.

———. *Two Songs* (includes *Song of Malaya* and *Song of Prisoner*). Nairobi, Kenya: East Africa Publishing House, 1971.

R. Victoria Arana

"PEBBLE" ZBIGNIEW HERBERT (1956) "Pebble" ("Kamyk"), first published in *Struna swiatła* (A Chord of Light, 1956), is a poem that many readers consider a quintessential example of ZBIGNIEW HERBERT'S MODERN-ISM. It is concrete while also allusive; it is clear and simple on the surface, but thickly implicative, like a parable. It purports to make evident statements about a small round stone but also seems to allude to human qualities of modesty, nobility, staunch resistance, and survival. What readers admire in this poem is its capacity to mean all these things without pretentiousness, obscurity, or indirection. In his commentary on the poem Sven Birkerts wrote: "it is a very Polish poem, considering that nation's recent—more exactly, modern—history. And it is a very modern poem. . . . The only way to survive, to endure [history's] almost geological pressure, is to acquire the features of a pebble, including [the poem implies] the false warmth once you find yourself in somebody's hands" (Paine 253).

The poem is composed of short lines in free verse. It begins with five couplets followed by a quatrain and a final triplet. The first four couplets, though not punctuated, constitute a single sentence whose core is expressed in the poem's first four words, *"Kamyk jest stworzeniem / doskonałym"* (The pebble / is a perfect creature—as translated by Miłosz and Scott, in Paine). The second through fourth stanzas extend that state-

ment with adjectival modifiers, but paradoxically these modifiers only further assert the unmodifiable solidity of the pebble: "equal to itself / mindful of its limits" (ll. 2–3). The third couplet modulates into subtle humor with a modifier that plainly does not modify: *"wypełniony dokładnie / kamiennym sensem"* (filled exactly / with pebbly meaning). In the next stanza the poet mentions the pebble's odorless scent—unevocative, unfrightening, and unarousing. The fifth couplet, an independent clause, sums up the pebble's essential quality in direct and physical terms: "its ardor and coldness / are just and full of dignity." It is a statement about the pebble's replication of the temperature of its surroundings: A pebble is not unruly or contrary, not cold when it is subjected to heat, or vice versa. From this summary of the qualities of a pebble, the poet segues to his own emotional response to the small stone. He admits to feeling "a heavy remorse" upon holding it in his hand, because "its noble body / is permeated by false warmth" (*i ciało jego szlachetne / przenika fałszywe ciepło*, ll. 13–14). Ironically, the only dishonesty in this poem is the warmth conveyed by the human hand. The poem's final triplet, following a dash and indented, takes on a different spirit and expresses a sentiment from a social perspective that is all too human: "—Pebbles cannot be tamed" (*—Kamyki nnie dają się oswoić*). The final lines reverse that projection, stating that the pebble regards human beings "to the end . . . with a calm and very clear eye" (*do końca będą na nas patrzeć / okiem spokojnym bardzo jasnym*).

In his comment on the poem Birkerts said that "Herbert belong[ed] to the generation of Europeans that saw the native realm reduced to rubble," but, unlike so many others of his generation, he adopted a resistant modernism "without experimental hoopla" to express his conviction that civilization is undone by "the vulgarity of the human heart, which always produces a simplified version of human reality" (Paine 254). "Pebble" is not a simplified vision of geology or humanity, but a parable about the difference between human beings and stones.

BIBLIOGRAPHY
Herbert, Zbigniew. "Kamyk." Original, full text in Polish. Available online. URL: http://www.literatura.zapis.net. pl/okresy/wspolczesnosc/herbert/kamyk.htm. Accessed on April 27, 2007.

————. "Pebble." Translated by Czesław Miłosz and Peter Dale Scott and accompanied by Sven Birkerts's commentary. In *The Poetry of Our World: An International Anthology of Contemporary Poetry,* edited by Jeffrey Paine et al. New York: HarperCollins, 2000, 253–269.

R. Victoria Arana

PERSE, SAINT-JOHN (ALEXIS LÉGER) (1887–1975)

Saint-John Perse is the penname of Alexis Léger, diplomat and poet. Léger's political convictions led him into exile from France during World War II, and his talent earned him the Nobel Prize in literature in 1960. Perse was born Marie-René Alexis Saint-Léger Léger on the island of Guadeloupe in the French Antilles, where he spent his first 10 years. His father was a lawyer, and his family owned coffee and sugar plantations. In 1899 the Légers returned to France, where the boy completed his primary and secondary education. Alexis studied law before beginning his diplomatic career.

Alexis Léger served as a foreign service officer in China from 1916 to 1921. At a conference on disarmament in Washington, D.C., he met French statesman Aristide Briand (11 times premier of France and Nobel Peace Prize laureate) and became his assistant, serving as *chef de cabinet* for Briand from 1925 until 1932. He then served as secretary-general of the French Foreign Ministry from 1933 until 1940. In 1940, opposing his government's foreign policy of appeasing Nazi Germany, Léger began a prolonged voluntary exile in the United States after a brief stay in England. He was consequently removed from the French Legion of Honor and deprived of his citizenship and possessions by the Vichy government, which collaborated with the Germans before and after their occupation of France.

The diplomat's cultural circles included PAUL CLAUDEL, the painter Odilon Redon, and the composers Igor Stravinsky and Nadia Boulanger; his literary circles included the novelist André Gide and the poet PAUL VALÉRY, yet much of Perse's poetry was written while he lived in the United States, where he refused a post at Harvard University and took a position at the Library of Congress to concentrate on writing. He did not end his exile until 1957, when he moved to a villa in Provence. In 1958 he married Dorothy Milburn Russell, an American, in Washington, D.C. After that he divided his time between Aix-en-Provence, France, and the United States until his death in France at the age of 88.

Léger's first publication was a translation of *Robinson Crusoe,* and he also translated Pindar. But his international reputation is based primarily on his own poems, collected in volumes after initial publication in journals. His collection *Éloges* (Elogies and Other Poems)—which included the poem "Écrit sur la porte" (Written on the Door), the series *Images à Crusoé* (Pictures for Crusoe, 1909), and *Pour fêter une enfance* (To Celebrate a Childhood), plus the 18 lyric poems of the *Éloges* series—was published in 1911, four years after the sudden death of his father and the same year that he completed his final degree. Then came *La gloire des rois* (The Glory of Kings), which contained "Amitié du prince" (Friendship of the Prince, 1924). Léger used the pen name Saint-John Perse for the first time in 1924 for *Anabase* (Anabasis), a collection written in China (later translated by T. S. Eliot). Perse then published *Éxil* (Exile) in 1942; a later edition was expanded to include "Poéme à l'étrangère" (Poem to a Foreign Lady, 1943), "Pluies" (Rains, 1943), and "Neiges" (Snows, 1944)—all of which appeared together as a tetrology entitled *Éxil* (EXILE, AND OTHER POEMS) in 1944. This was followed by publication of *Vents* (Winds, 1946), *Amers* (Seamarks, 1957), *Chronique* (Chronicle, 1959), and *Oiseaux* (Birds, 1962). *Œuvres complètes* (The Complete Works)—which includes poetry, prose, and correspondence—was published in the Bibliothèque de la Pléiade series in 1972. It was followed by *Chanté par celle qui fut là* (Sung by One Who Was There, 1970) and *Chant pour un équinoxe* (Song for an Equinox, 1975).

Perse composed poems "for himself and almost in spite of himself; and the thought of a literary career was repugnant to him," wrote Arthur J. Knodel (xi). The poems of *Éloges* celebrate Perse's youth and island childhood using imagery of the islands. In "Written on the Door," for example, the persona, whose skin is "the colour of mules or of red tobacco" (1.1), whose cheek is "rough" when he "comes[s] home covered in mud" (1.5), finds joy in his daughter, who is "very beautiful when she gives orders to the black women" (1.3) and who has "a very white arm among her black hens" (1.4). Similarly, in "To Celebrate a Childhood" the persona mourns that he "shall not know again any place of mills and sugar-cane" (3.8) where "a cloud . . . called-by-their-name, out of their cabins, / the servant women!" (3.13, 16). He also recalls that his "nurse was a mestizo and smelled of the castor-bean" (4.11). Likewise, in the eighth canto of *Éloges,* the speaker remembers being taught the names of fish (2.3). Such images are also seen in "Pictures for Crusoe," in which the city is "like an abscess" ("The City," 2.4), in contrast to the "faultless vase of the sea" and the pleasing imagery often used to depict the island. Imagery in such poems conveys both Perse's nostalgic longing for Guadeloupe and his identification with the colonial class of his childhood and its aesthetic values.

La gloire des rois includes five poems that sing the praises of a fictional royal family. The poems convey the values of the kingdom. The prince in particular has been read as a depiction of Perse's vision of "an ideal leader of men," evidencing such traits as acuity (Ostrovsky 57). *Anabase*—the title coming from the Greek *anabainein,* an expedition or ascent into another country (Winspur 26)—is a long poem of 10 cantos framed by two three-stanza songs; it uses epic features and a variety of voices to recount the expeditions of a conqueror and his retinue. According to Steven Winspur it conveys an "imaginary expedition into another land that characterized . . . the ideal act for the reader . . . of poetry" (27). It embodies also a desire to "follow nature's own onward march" (33) and the "goal of expressing culture's transhistorical spirit" (47). In Perse's words, it is about *"la solitude dans l'action"* (the solitude of action, Winspur 35). In contrast, *Vents,* written in four long sections, "stress[es] . . . a return to European civilization" (Hackett 272). The poems up to and including *Vents* convey "a rebellion against human contracts and restraints; a desire for adventure as well as for solitude and self-sufficiency; an absorption in nature in both its spacious and minute aspects" (Hackett 270–271).

Amers, Perse's longest poem, uses the sea as its central metaphor. Combining characteristics of a variety of poetic and performance genres—epic, tragedy, choral lyric, ritualistic stage (Winspur 91)—it offers an invocation, cantos from the vantage of a series of personas (the port officers, the master of navigation, the prophet, etc.), before it turns to the "Chorus" and the final "Dedication." *Chronique* (also told in a series of cantos, but not through a panorama of personae) begins by establishing "the freedom, vitality" of a great age; then "[t]he Poet's voice . . . evokes the wanderings still to be undertaken, the roads without limit to be explored—roads that go beyond Death itself" (Ostovsky 197). In contrast, *Oiseaux* is the only work in Perse's canon published with art that is integral to its creative production. It was first published with 12 colored lithographs of birds done by Georges Braque that are referenced throughout its 13 cantos, and it has been said "to examine *human* excellence in light of the bird's excellence" (Winspur 154), while the birds described throughout the poem (and the paintings of them) are seen to symbolize "the liberation of the soul" (Jennings 147) and may even be seen to represent the inner strength of humankind (Jennings 147).

Chanté par celle qui fut là, written in 1968, the year that Perse lost two close friends, is "a grave and yearning poem, full of tenderness and sorrow," told through "the voice of a woman, forshadowing her bereavement" with a song "of love, of pain, and of memory" (Ostrovsky 206). *Chant pour un équinoxe,* Perse's last collection of poems, includes the title poem, in which "the dying poet sees his art invested, incarnated, and reincarnated in a new life" (Ostrovsky 210); "Nocturne," "a brief, sharp outcry" that is said to be "the sole utterance of despair ever to pass the lips of this poet (210); and "Sécheresse," his last poem and one that moves from an initial invocation of sterility and destruction (212) to imagery of "the great surge of life arising anew" (213). Winspur argues that "it is not so much God who is being denounced in the final line of 'Sécheresse' but a form of language that produces the sort of transport of which religion is merely one version" (159).

Perse's poetry generally lacks direct reference to the politics of his day (though it spans centuries in its historical references) and relies on metaphors and other internal tropes (Winspur 34). Perse's early poetry is "closely related to the rhythms of ordinary speech (Hackett 271). Jennings notes that Perse's "use of alliteration is so skillful as scarcely to be noticed" (139). Perse used unrhymed, prose-style stanzas throughout his writing career. Roger Little notes his inclusion of "rhythmic echoes of phrase, of word, of individual sound" and "interwoven patterns of imagery and narrative" (17), his use of recurrent phrases (17), "repetitions and substitutions at the level of individual words," and lines that are created in "phonic, rhythmic and semantic parallelism" (19).

Perse's essays on literature treat authors ranging from Dante and Valéry to Gide and RABINDRANATH TAGORE; others focus on poetry itself or French literature in general. Roger Little's work on the author includes *Word Index of the Complete Poetry and Prose of Saint-John Perse* (1967), *Saint-John Perse: A Bibliography for Students of His Poetry* (1971), a biography, and an annotated edition of *Éxil* (1973). Among the best available anthologies in English is Perse's *Collected Poems,* a bilingual edition by many contributors published by Princeton University Press in 1971.

BIBLIOGRAPHY

Hackett, C. A., ed. *Anthology of Modern French Poetry: From Baudelaire to the Present Day.* New York: Macmillan, 1952.

Jennings, Elizabeth. *Seven Men of Vision: An Appreciation.* New York: Barnes and Noble, 1976.

Knodel, Arthur. *Saint-John Perse: A Study of His Poetry.* Language and Literature 14. Edinburgh: Edinburgh University Press, 1966.

Ostrovsky, Erika. *Under the Sign of Ambiguity: Saint-John Perse/Alexis Léger.* New York: New York University Press, 1985.

Perse, Saint-John. *Élogies, and Other Poems.* Translated by Louise Varèse. Bollingen Series 55. New York: Pantheon, 1956.

———. *Éxil.* Roger Little. Edited by London: Athlone Press, 1973.

———. *Letters.* Bollingen Series 87.2. Translated and edited by Arthur J. Knodel. Princeton, N.J.: Princeton University Press, 1979.

———. *Œuvres complètes.* Paris: Éditions Gallimard, 1972.

Winspur, Steven. *Saint-John Perse and the Imaginary Reader.* Histoire des idées et critique littéraire 261. Geneva: Librairie Droz S. A., 1988.

Yasmin Y. DeGout

"PERSONAL CREED" ("*CREDO PERSONAL*") CLARIBEL ALEGRÍA (1987) Beliefs

expressed in "Personal Creed" shaped CLARIBEL ALEGRÍA's writings after the 1959 triumph of the Cuban revolution and forced her admitted "awakening" to the world around her. A second major jolt was the 1980 assassination of Archbishop Oscar Romero, just after he had invoked the name of God to order the Salvadoran National Guard, military, and police to obey a higher commandment and end their repression of the people. Patterned on the Apostles' Creed, the poem redirects the focus from Christianity's promised afterlife to this world's reality, depicts disappeared and murdered victims as Christ-like in their sacrifice, and suggests a nonindividualized, collective identity among believers.

An important context for "Personal Creed" is Liberation Theology's impact throughout Latin America and the contention that Roman Catholicism entailed more than its customary message to the downtrodden that suffering on Earth be humbly accepted as God's will. The church hierarchy in Latin America historically had aligned itself with the richest social sectors and the military, and in some countries these groups operated in tandem to oppress and exploit the populace. Liberation Theology proposed a reading of the Bible that justified daily struggle for better conditions here and now, and Alegría's poem reflects this reorientation.

"Personal Creed" wholly rewrites the Apostles' Creed (an import via Europe) using American historical realities, starting with Spain's conquest of the New World by "sword and cross," which established a pattern of pillage and exploitation abetted by the church. But like the ancient Roman governor ignorant of the power of martyrdom who attempted to subdue subversion by crucifying Christ, American government leaders unwittingly fan the flames of insurgency by condoning official or renegade violence and casting a blind eye on indiscriminate detentions, disappearances, and murders by military or paramilitary death squads. As the poem suggests, historical accounts portray the 1979–92 civil war in El Salvador as a living hell for the defenseless—75,000 dead; hundreds of thousands displaced, tortured, raped; one-third of the population missing family members.

In Claribel Alegría's New World "Personal Creed," death is not final, and hope is renewed by reinventing the Bible's greater lesson: the crucified descended into the hell of detention centers like the "Media Luna" and rose again, not to ascend into heaven but to return to the struggle, and not as individuals but as members of a collective force called "the people," united against their oppressors—as a force that will eventually triumph and demand the final judgment, on Earth, of their assassins. The suggestion is that peace and justice will come to the land only after that "force" (like the truth and reconciliation commissions in countries recovering from civil strife) addresses the multitude of crimes committed against the people of El Salvador.

In its "bare bones" poetic expression devoid of rhetorical devices, "Personal Creed" valorizes righteous struggle against oppression but also beauty and art in the broadest sense—Marc Chagall's invention of blue cows, Julio Cortázar's playful "cronopios," that might decorate airmail packages with feathers (random acts of beauty). More significant than a communion of saints and life everlasting are unity and a communion of all who embrace the ethos of hope derived from death portrayed in this, actually, not-at-all-personal creed.

BIBLIOGRAPHY

Alegría, Claribel. "Personal Creed." In Luisa in Realityland. Translated by Darwin J. Flakoll. Willimantic, Conn.: Curbstone, 1987, 135.

Maria Roof

PESSOA, FERNANDO (RICARDO REIS, [ALBERTO] CAEIRO, ÁLVARO DE CAMPOS, AND BERNARDO SOARES) (1888– 1935)

Scholars consider Fernando Pessoa one of the 20th century's greatest poets: a giant like James Joyce, ANNA AKHMATOVA, and William Butler Yeats. His reputation has grown posthumously—in part because he published only a fraction of his complete works in three slim volumes during his lifetime. To compound the problems of celebrity, many of his poems were published in magazines and journals under one of his several poetic pseudonyms, four of them representing entirely fictional personae that Pessoa invented "for the progress of civilization" (quoted in Honig and Brown ix) and in whose distinctly separate voices he created separate, whole corpora of poetry. The names under which he composed poems were thus much more than mere pen names; they stood for diverse cultural forces that Pessoa designed to mock the pretensions of the cultural and intellectual circles of his day and to shock Europe into "broadening" its "consciousness of humanity" (x).

Born in Lisbon, Portugal, Pessoa was the offspring of a prosperous and cultured family. His father, a music critic, died when the boy was only five. His mother then married a diplomat and moved with her son to South Africa, where Pessoa grew up multilingual. He could write in English, Portuguese, Spanish, and German. At the age of 17 Pessoa returned to his birthplace to attend university, but he soon abandoned academia and became a translator. In 1914, when he was 26, Pessoa invented the character Alberto Caeiro, whose The Keeper of Sheep embodied a pagan sensationalist poetic idiom. In poem IX ("I am a keeper of sheep"), the poet, for instance, writes, ". . . my thoughts are all sensations. / I think with my eyes and ears / And with my hands and feet / And with my nose and mouth" (Honig and Brown 17). Pessoa's Caeiro suffers no "dissociation of sense and sensibility," as T. S. Eliot described the modern malaise, for as he puts it: "To think a flower is to see it and smell it / And to eat a fruit is to taste its meaning" (17). The poems of Pessoa's Álvaro de Campos, in contrast, are those of "a masked buffoon, jokester, and trickster" (Honig and Brown ix) who wishes to "fall into [his] grave with a bang!" and so end the "farce in [his] soul!" (42). Álvaro de Campos is an over-the-top Whitmanesque figure expressing himself in bursts and fragments of thoughts, a sailor who wishes to "feel" adventure on the seas as "one great passive orgasm! . . . / Dead drunk on everything having to do with the sea"—including sailors and faraway coasts, and who desires a "voluptuous" demise, sucked to death by "strange green absurd sea leeches!" (59). Still different is Pessoa's Ricardo Reis, an exiled monarchist and a doctor whose poems are traditional compositions in classical forms on the roses "in the gardens of Adonis" (127), chess players in Persia calmly moving their pieces "In the shade of a spacious tree" while "invaders were burning down the City" (129), and the effects of memory, which does not "distinguish / What I saw from what I was" (136). Reis's poems are clean, crisp odes more like those of Greek antiquity (or of A. E. Housman) than anything composed by 19th-century romantics and Victorians. The poems that Pessoa signed "by Fernando Pessoa" are thus also products of a specific personality, "the lost identity-seeker in the haunted drama of selfhood" (Honig and Brown xii). Though individually they may convey glimpses of modernist solipsism and a fractured perspective on life, collectively they allude to poems from across the ages and all over the world, thus creating a collage of obscure allusions and attitudes toward universal conditions of human existence. Some, for example, resemble Japanese *tanka* (such as "We Took the Town After a Heavy Bombing" and "Lightly, listlessly, my thoughts"), while others are spare in a manner reminiscent of Emily Dickinson. Some, like "THIS," are complex poems meriting close reading. To the variegated oeuvre of the heteronymic poems in Portuguese, one must add those that he wrote in other languages, including English (his *Sonnets* and *Inscriptions*). Reading through a collection of translations such as the one published by Edwin Honig and Susan Brown, one might be struck by the comedic effect of such a deliberate distillation and juxtaposition of 20th-century voices. While one may be able to sympathize momentarily with one or another poetic expression, the realization must soon dawn that we have been "had" (so to speak) by a poet wearing carnivalesque masks that mirror archetypal sentiments and the typical neuroses of his (and our) day.

BIBLIOGRAPHY

Pessoa, Fernando. *Poems of Fernando Pessoa.* Translated and edited by Edwin Honig and Susan M. Brown. New York: Ecco Press, 1986. Reprint, San Francisco: City Lights Books, 1998.

R. Victoria Arana

PETERS, LENRIE (1932–   )

Born in Bathurst (now Banjul), the Gambia, in 1932, Lenrie Peters trained as a physician and emerged in the 1960s as one of the rare breed of early West African writers who combined medical practice with creative writing. His early education was in the Gambia. He later attended Prince of Wales School in Sierra Leone before moving to England, where he studied medicine at Trinity College, Cambridge.

Like many of his contemporaries from West Africa, Peters demonstrates—through his poetry, fiction, and plays—that it is possible to define one's identity as totally different from one's training as a scientist. A mention of the name Lenrie Peters evokes memories, in a way, of other African writers—including CHINUA ACHEBE, who originally enrolled to study medicine; Cyprian Ekwensi, who trained as a pharmacist; T. M. Aluko, who studied engineering; and Elechi Amadi, who read physics and mathematics. While writing his novel, plays, and several collections of poems, Peters was involved in students' unionism at Trinity College and was elected president of the African Students Union. His profession as physician took him to many parts of the world. He worked in a number of hospitals in the Gambia, Northampton, and Guildford (England). He was later to become the first Gambian to preside over the affairs of the massive examinations body the West African Examinations Council.

Peters's poetry draws on his global travels and medical training to craft emotionally charged poetic forms that both celebrate and lament the human experience of love, nostalgia, humor, and the promise of hope. But the sense of nostalgia that one feels in his poetry is not necessarily a call to embrace the kind of romantic and naive nativism found in a number of poems by some of his contemporaries, which gained immense popularity through their devotion to Africa's historical past.

Peters is never fascinated by poetry that assails political leadership in his country. There is a continentalist dimension to his poetry that easily marks him as one of the rare Pan-Africanist writers. Peters has been largely acknowledged as a highly talented writer as well as a poet with a "catholic mind," even though his diction is often marked by deployment of "anatomical and physiological imagery" (Senanu and Vincent 109). His first poems appeared in 1964 under the Mbari Series in Ibadan, Nigeria. In 1965 his novel *The Second Round* appeared under the Heinemann African Writers Series imprint; in 1967 *Satellites* was published; *Katchikali* appeared in 1971, while *New Poems* was published in 1981. Apart from being featured in literary magazines in many parts of Africa and Europe, his poems are among the most anthologized, appearing in Donatus Nwoga's *The West African Verse* (Longman, 1967) and in the highly influential *A Selection of African Poetry,* introduced and annotated by K. E. Senanu and Theo Vincent.

While Romanus Egudu has described Peters as perhaps the only African poet who is seemingly unconcerned about his home country, there is evidence in Peters's poetry that he is not only invested with an admirable sense of Africanity, but also involved in exploring the themes of "home" and "return"—indications that his absence from "home" began to have a nostalgic impact on him. Like most students studying abroad who eagerly anticipate returning to their country upon completion of their degrees, Peters (as his poems indicate) felt a sense of loss, yearning especially for his familiar Africa of tropical scenery. That topography, now gradually giving way to a lone European territory, compelled him to compose, for instance, "Autumn" and "Parachute Men." Such evidence of Africa as "home" and of a desired "return" to it can also be found in other poems—e.g., "Wings my ancestors used," "We have come home," "Time Was," "Homecoming," "The rhythm of the past (on History)", and "I shall return."

In "Homecoming," for instance, Peters explores his preoccupation with home by subjecting nature to philosophical scrutiny. "Home" in this sense transcends the perceptual place of abode, becoming a spiritual territory to which humankind ultimately returns, especially "After we have paced the world / And longed for returning" (*Satellite* 13). Life in this context is presented in its most transient character. What we remember is sometimes not as much as what is forgotten. In this instance the relics of our memories are only as strong as the "new skeletons" now inhabiting the place we used to live in. But the theme of return so prevalent in his earlier poetry is not limited to the experience of students returning home after acquiring a Western education; it is also not supplied in his examination of life as a tragic journey.

Life, Peters always seems to be suggesting, must be celebrated and enjoyed to its logical conclusion. A celebration of life implies a celebration of love in its purest sense. What seems like a spiritual engagement with his mental landscape thus enjoys a sociality of experience to such a level that humankind should eschew pessimism in every respect while embracing the best that life offers. Our sense of achievement ("I shall return / With unslippered feet / When I have done with spear and shield / And a lion's tongue / To show I have destroyed the beast") and our fear of dying ("Before I knock on the locked / Gates of hell") should, therefore, not becloud our humanity and sense of love, for the prime objective should be, as he put it (using quasi-medical diction), "To be perfused into / The noble greatness of life / To release my inner power / Against false barriers and strife / Then to unite the energies / Of the sexual bower" (*Satellites* 102–103).

BIBLIOGRAPHY

Egudu, Romanus N. *Four West African Poets.* New York: Nok, 1977.

Nwoga, Donatus. *West African Verse.* London: Longman, 1967.

Peters, Lenrie. *Katchikali.* London: Heinemann, 1971.

———. *Satellites.* London: Heinemann, 1967.

———. *Selected Poetry.* London: Heinemann, 1981.

———. *The Second Round.* London: Heinemann, 1965.

Senanu, K. E., and T. Vincent. *A Selection of African Poetry.* 1976. Reprint, London: Longman, 2003.

Osita Ezeliora

"PIANO AND DRUMS" GABRIEL OKARA **(1978)** This work, first published in *The Fisherman's Invocation* (1978) but written much earlier, is the best-known and the most anthologized of GABRIEL OKARA's poems. It is also representative of his poetry because it engages the conflict of cultures, a major concern of Okara's poetry. It dramatizes the conflict that the African lives with who has been exposed to Western values. The poem, set in the riverine area of the Niger delta, presents the persona's experience as a metaphor for the experience of the entire society.

The poem relates an occurrence at the center of which stands the persona, who talks about hearing familiar sounds ("jungle drums telegraphing / the mystic rhythm,") that he immediately associates with his own culture. While still thinking about this (and "the simple paths" that he associates with those rhythms), he hears another sound, produced by the piano, which ("speaking of complex ways") strikes him as strange. He then goes on to reflect ("in the morning mist") on the significance of each of the two for him. He is left "lost," "wandering," and confused as to whether he should relate more to the drumming he first heard or to the piano, which came much later.

The poem dramatizes the conflict of Westernized Africans: whether to identify with African values of "green leaves and wild flowers" or with the Western values as a result of their education ("new horizons with / coaxing diminuendo, counterpoint"). There is also a sense in which the experience of the persona can be taken as representing the situation of African peoples in general: Colonialism introduced a new way of life that has made the African identity a hybrid consciousness.

"Piano and Drums" harmonizes theme and technique. The poem relies basically on symbols in realizing its theme. Drums represent African ways and traditions that the persona inherited, while the piano symbolizes foreign cultural practices and assumptions that the colonial encounter has bestowed on Africa. The poem suggests that the attempt at reconciling these conflicting cultural orientations normally leaves the persona perplexed. The word choice reinforces the thematic interest of the poem. For instance, the "jungle drums" produce a "mystic rhythm," while the piano produces a "tear-furrowed concerto." That such musical terms as *diminuendo, counterpoint,* and *crescendo* are applied to Western culture suggests that its "complex ways" are out of the ordinary and mystifying to the African. It is also significant that the third stanza, where the persona shifts his focus to the encounter with the West, starts with *Then.* The abrupt transition that this word introduces seems to suggest that the African experience can be divided into two periods, with the intrusion of the West being a major event having enduring cultural and historical consequences.

Oyeniyi Okunoye

"PICASSO" Rafael Alberti (1967) This poem is a homage to the work of Rafael Alberti's friend the famous painter and fellow Spaniard Pablo Picasso (1881–1973). Alberti met the artist in 1933; in the following decades they collaborated on various projects and remained close until Picasso's death. The poem forms part of *To Painting* (*A la pintura*), dedicated to Picasso, in which Alberti pays tribute to the

form of expression that he had once pursued and that he never ceased to love. *To Painting* is the culmination of Alberti's lifelong effort to *"pintar la Poesía / con el pincel de la pintura"* (paint Poetry with the paintbrush of painting). The last poem of the collection, "Picasso" brings this project to a magnificent closure. Drawing his inspiration from Picasso's oeuvre, Alberti weaves together many themes that he had explored throughout his earlier work: the relationship between poetry and painting, the place of the artist in history, the ties between art and politics, and the potential of poetic language as a form of creative expression.

The poem unfolds into a panoramic retrospective of Picasso's paintings, tracing the trajectory of his art from early works, through the blue, rose, and cubist periods, building up to and ending abruptly with *Guernica,* Picasso's monumental black-and-white masterpiece dedicated to a Basque town that a German aerial attack eradicated on April 26, 1937. Alberti masterfully guides his verse to mimic the intensely expressive style of Picasso's paintings. The endless cascades of rhymes (*araña, / braña, entraña, cucaña, / saña, pipirigaña . . . se laña y se deslaña, / se estaña y desestaña*) re-create the dazzling web of Picasso's artistic world while at the same time sweep the reader into the often mischievous world of Alberti's poetry.

These worlds do not exist in a vacuum. For Alberti both painting and poetry draw their vigor from the lives of real people whose collective destiny art is charged to represent. Through verbally re-created sketches of Picasso's protagonists (naked boys running along the beach, a woman ironing, a pregnant girl) a grave face of the country emerges at the onset of historical darkness. By its side is the bull, the symbol of Spain and also of death, the omnipotent force that has always fascinated Spanish artists. *Guernica* is another instance of an artist confronting this force, this time particularly terrifying because it originated in the people themselves. The painting (and the poem) is also a warning: *"el juego del arte comienza a ser un juego explosivo"* (the game of art becomes an explosive game). A diversion after all, art may not triumph over death, but true art waits only to reveal its explosive power.

BIBLIOGRAPHY
Alberti, Rafael. *To Painting: Poems.* Translated and intro-
duced by Carolyn L. Tipton. Evanston, Ill.: Northwestern
University Press, 1997.

Alina Sokol

PIGNOTTI, LAMBERTO (1926–) Lam-
berto Pignotti was born in 1926 in Florence, Italy. He
lived and studied in the Tuscan city for over 40 years,
then transferred his studio to Rome in 1968. He continued even then to maintain connections with the
Renaissance city through his professorship in the
department of architecture at the University of Florence. Pignotti has also taught in the Department of Literature for Discipline Delle Arti, Della Musica e Dello
Spettacolo at the University of Bologna. There he
mounted a wide range of courses dealing with the relationship between the avant-garde arts and both mass
and news media.

Pignotti is known for theorizing the first forms of
technological and visual poetry. His interests lie in the
endless combinations between written language and
visual media; this concatenation of word and image is
fundamental to Pignotti's work. During the 1960s he
collaborated with many other Italian poets, including
Eugenio Miccini and Giuseppe Chiari. He has since
mounted numerous exhibits and graphic-multimedia
installations (his favored form of publication) in Italy
and the rest of Europe; these displays demonstrate his
exploration of the intersections between verbal and
pictorial language systems. His work has been linked
critically and aesthetically to a range of theoretical formulations by such intellectuals as the Russian formalist
Viktor Sklovskij, the Canadian sociologist Marshall
McLuhan, the German philosopher Herbert Marcuse,
and the art historian Ernst H. Gombrich.

Pignotti is considered a *visual* poet who prefers the
artistic stratagem of collage. He is noted for conveying
poetic insights by using the language of mass communication. He insists that culture does not pertain exclusively to the elite but defies social and economic levels
and involves all classes of society. Pignotti believes that
pictures are deceiving; and he enjoys distorting meaning (through creative strategies of deconstruction and
decomposition) to demonstrate how meaning is "made."

He has published numerous books on poetry and
visual poesis throughout his professional life. His creative works have been placed in public buildings and
in prestigious private collections.

BIBLIOGRAPHY
"Lamberto Pignotti Biography." Artist's profile, criticism,
and gallery. Available online. URL: http://www.artantide.
com/artisti/BiografiaArtista.php?lng=2&idArtista=34.
Accessed on September 24, 2005.

Chris Picicci

"PLAGUE COLUMN, THE" Jaroslav Seifert
(1969)   The title poem in Seifert's collection *Morový
sloup* (1977, Cologne; 1981, Prague), composed as a
free-verse narrative, uses a 300-year-old Prague monument as a symbol for Czech fate and history. Plague
columns were erected in nearly every town throughout
Europe in the 15th through 17th centuries as remind-
ers of big plague epidemics. Like many Seifert poems
from the 1960s, "The Plague Column" shows the poet's
personal view and interpretation of history, culture,
and human experience. It is notable for its balanced
tone, mature poetic style and form, musical language,
and presentation of an emotional and spiritual challenge to the reader. Throughout the collection the poet
attempts to understand history as well as aging and
death by eroticizing his relationship to his native land
and stressing the importance of love. Love in Seifert's
treatment is always both physical and spiritual and,
in this collection in particular, connected to time. In
Morový sloup love functions as the only shield for protecting oneself from the passing of time, historical
injustice, and death. Its title poem crystallizes Seifert's
lifetime preoccupation with love, beauty, and the
feminine.

The poem begins with a description of the plague
column, with its four frowning statues that dominate
the column, making the "four corners of the earth"
subject to their penetrating gaze. The speaker then
meditates on the nature of time, signified by the
shadow of the column. Seifert masterfully arranges the
levels of the present and the past so that the reader is
not able to tell one from the other easily. The visible
present manifests itself in the column's presence in the

speaker's description, while the present "plagued" by the limits on people's freedom is implied: The present-day plague is invisible and silent. The past emerges from the interweaving of the history of the plague, the speaker's personal history, and more recent tragedies of public history, such as the fascist and communist oppression experienced by Czechs throughout Seifert's lifetime: "Our lives run / like fingers over sandpaper, / days, weeks, years, centuries. / . . . I still walk around the column / where so often I waited, / . . . always astonished at the water's flirtatiousness / as it splintered on the basin's surface / until the Column's shadow fell across your face." Seifert quickly introduces the eternal motif of erotic love, which has resisted death since ancient times. After describing the plague chapel of Saint Roch and the thousands of bodies that were laid around the chapel in the time of plague, the speaker says: "For a long time I would visit / these mournful places, / but did not forsake the sweetness of life." The sweetness of life manifests itself for the speaker in "the perfume of women's hair" or, taking a walk near the chapel, in the image of "girls / undressing at night." In contrast to a plague column, a monument erected to memorialize bad times and tragic death, Seifert's poem attempts to erect an everlasting monument to love, perhaps an ordinary experience, but nevertheless life-giving and protecting against ancient as well as more recent "plagues."

Daniela Kukrechtová

POEMS OF DR. ZHIVAGO, THE BORIS PAS-TERNAK (1957)
Published as if an appendix to PAS-TERNAK's novel, Dr. Zhivago, these poems highlight the novel's theme of suffering and may serve as the key to understanding the work as a whole. Several poems contain explicitly Christian images: even "Hamlet," the first one, shows the speaker suffering as Christ did when he faced crucifixion. The speaker could be Hamlet himself about to move from the comfort of his own thoughts into public view, where he continues his charade of ignorance about his uncle's crime and of madness. On the other hand, the speaker could be the actor playing Hamlet waiting to reenter the play and act his part. Some suggest the speaker is the figure of the Poet,

an embodiment of VLADIMIR MAYAKOVSKY, who saw the poet on center stage in life, or an image of ALEKSANDR BLOK, whom Pasternak admired as a force of nature channeling energy into verse. Although each poem can be read separately, each has a meaningful place in the collection. The cycle of the poems as a whole begins with "Hamlet" and ends with "The Garden of Gesthemane." The former alludes to Christ's prayer and trial, while the latter is a reflection on Christ in prayer before the Passion. Both poems hint that the speaker's suffering is both inevitable and chosen. The overtly religious poems have a cyclical structure that parallels their placement in the calendar year but also suggests the festal cycle of the liturgical year, which is measured from Easter to Easter. The birth of Christ and the events of the Passion are inseparable from the resurrection, the source of hope. Similarly, the raising of Lazarus and the triumph of Palm Sunday are connected integrally to the humiliation and humility of the trial and Passion of Jesus. The verses as a whole also follow a seasonal cycle from spring to spring, traditionally a time of hope. "March," the second poem in the collection, celebrates the awakening of life and hope in the spring, while "August," the 14th, accepts the loss of beauty as well as the departure of the speaker's lover. The allusion to the Transfiguration as a prefiguring of the Passion further reinforces the theme of inevitable suffering. The seasonal cycle underscores the nature imagery abundant in Pasternak's work.

BIBLIOGRAPHY
Gifford, Henry. Pasternak: A Critical Study. Cambridge: Cambridge University Press, 1977.
Moreau, Jean-Luc. "The Passion According to Zhivago." Translated by Constance Wagner. Books Abroad 44 (1970): 237–242.
Pasternak, Boris. The Poems of Dr. Zhivago. Translated by Donald Davie. Manchester, U.K.: Manchester University Press, 1965.
Rudova, Larissa. Understanding Boris Pasternak. Columbia: University of South Carolina Press, 1997.

Karen Rae Keck

POEM WITHOUT A HERO ANNA AKHMATOVA (1968)
Scholars consider this complex autobiographical triptych an exceptional achievement. In it

ANNA AKHMATOVA revisits pre–World War I St. Petersburg with the hindsight of several decades and from the perspective of Tashkent and Moscow. The cycle, "the work that would crown her last years" (Reeder 30), was composed between 1940 and 1962 and is "the fulfillment of the Symbolists' dream" (Zhirmumsky quoted in Hemschemeyer 8). *Poem without a Hero* is dense with Russian literary and cultural allusions that make the work obscure to the average reader.

It opens with "In Place of a Forward," in which Akhmatova writes, during her World War II evacuation from then Leningrad to Tashkent, that the poem came to her unbidden and that it is a memorial act for those whose voices she continues to hear. The opening epigrams are taken from a coat of arms and from 19th-century Russian poet Alexandr Pushkin. The addendum, added four years later, cites Pilate: "What I have written—I have written." It was Akhmatova's response to "various false and absurd interpretations" (544), giving rise to the suggestion that she should revise and explain her text. She then places three dedications, the first two for the central characters of the cycle's plot contained in part two. These dedicatees are an officer and the actress who rejected his passionate love.

The remaining structure of the work proceeds thus: Part one consists of chapter one, "Across the Landing: Interlude," chapters two, three, and four and Epilogue; part two contains "The Other Side of the Coin: Intermezzo"; and part three, Epilogue. Among the quotations in part one is OSIP MANDELSTAM's "clear voice: 'I am ready to die'" (554). The 24 stanzas of part two include two-and-a-half stanzas of ellipses, a strategy of poets in Russian and Soviet shifting politics. Under the constant danger of censorship and retribution, the silences are allowed to do their work by implication. *Poem without a Hero* is "the weaving together of the lyrical principle and the historico-philosophical principle" (Vilenkin 253). BORIS PASTERNAK observed of the poem that "The words seethe as in a cauldron" (Vilenkin 251).

It is a companion piece to *REQUIEM,* another of her great cycles dedicated to Russian historical reality, but far less accessible because of the private world she recalls. She declined to annotate the work because it had been written for those who knew the world about which she spoke. She intended for the poem to "be buried with her and her century; it was not written for eternity, nor even for posterity" (Berlin 51). In the part three Epilogue she addresses her city and her past to declare, "We are inseparable, / My shadow is on your walls" (575).

BIBLIOGRAPHY

Akhmatova, Anna. *The Complete Poems of Anna Akhmatova.* Expanded edition. Edited and introduced by Roberta Reeder, translated by Judith Hemschemeyer. Boston: Zephyr Press, 1997.

Berlin, Isaiah. "Anna Akhmatova: A Memoir." In *The Complete Poems of Anna Akhmatova,* edited and introduced by Roberta Reeder, translated by Judith Hemschemeyer, 35–55. Boston: Zephyr Press, 1997.

Vilenkin, Vitalii. "On *A Poem Without a Hero.*" In *Anna Akhmatova 1889–1989,* edited by Sonia I. Ketchian, 249–265. Oakland, Calif.: Berkeley Slavic Specialties, 1993.

A. Mary Murphy

POETRY BEYOND THE PAGE Poetry beyond the page, or performance poetry as it is commonly called, refers to poetry that is performed, recorded, spoken, or published in multimedia formats. It involves the creation, activation, enactment, or engineering of a poem in a space outside of a traditionally printed page. Poetry readings are examples of poetry taking place beyond the page. In the last 100 years poetry readings have segued through various formats: salon, cabaret, theater, open mic, festival, feature, audio, film, hypertext, hypermedia, machine generation, and an infinite variety of expressions of these within numerous aesthetic demarcations and ideologies. Poetry readings bring poets into contact with the public and with each other. Poetry beyond the page is an ideal way to converse and experiment with conceptual, linguistic, and technological developments in the 20th and 21st centuries. It has become an alternative place of communal gathering for the sharing of poetry.

The terms *performance poetry, sound poetry,* and *multimedia,* or *new media, poetry* are most commonly used to describe different types of poetry beyond the page. Performance poetry can be divided into several genres—spoken word, oral narrative or ballad, theatrical, slam, hip-hop, embodied, signed, sound or enacted poetry—and may involve a fusion with other media such as music, video, dance, or technology (see FRENCH RAP; ARAB RAP AND HIP HOP CULTURE; *ÉCRITURE*). The label *performance poetry* is often used to indicate that poetry is being acted out in some way: through voice, dramatic styles (e.g., comedy, cabaret), or a familiarized text (i.e., one that may or may not be memorized but with which the poet is familiar enough to engage the audience). Performance poetry is culturally defined and is expressed differently in different cultures. In general, performance is not something bestowed on poetry to create the phenomenon known as a performance poem but instead is intrinsic to the creation of the work, even if the performance comes later.

When writing a poem for publication outside of a book, poets consider medium, space, language, and audience. For example, a poem written for a Flash™ animation would be different from one performed on a stage at a festival. The form of a poem beyond the page has few traditions outside of the various ballad forms of history.

Performance poets are part of an alternative canon to traditional published poetry. This canon includes ancient Greek epics, the opera tradition of the Southern Song dynasty (1179–1276) in China, and the griot (or storytelling) traditions of Africa. The ancient Indian civilization produced the Mahabharata, one of the largest oral narratives ever composed and recorded. The potential for orality to engage with language, the sonic imperatives contained within the utterance, and the textual features of form, rhythm, image, tone, and rhyme—all combine to make performance poetry an alternative site for experimentation within poetry today. The performance of poetry on the Internet has helped create another expression of poetry beyond the page. Performance poetry is an integrated, unique medium that clearly demonstrates a capacity to reinvigorate contemporary poetry.

One style of performance poetry that is growing increasingly popular is slam poetry. Poetry slams are competitive performance poetry events that follow a particular format started in Chicago in 1986. The idea for slam emerged from the "Poetry Bouts" in Chicago and New York in the early 1980s, in which poets dressed up as boxers and "fought" with poems until a winner was declared. This format still exists today and is sometimes called the Taos poetry bout. Slam poetry in the United States has largely followed the same set of rules since 1986. A slam poetry evening in the United States, and increasingly other parts of the world, involves poets signing up for a three-round poetry "bout" where poets are given up to three minutes to recite a poem and the most successful poets in each round progress to the final round, when a winner is chosen. Before the competition starts the emcee chooses three judges randomly from the audience, and after poets have recited their poems, the judges give them a score (out of a maximum 10 points) for their performance and the quality of the poem. The overall winner is then eligible for a spot on a registered venue's team to compete in the National Poetry Slam Competition. During the year various heats are held at a venue, which culminate in a night's competition where finalists vie for spots on a team. The top four slammers from a venue form the official team. At the national finals teams compete against each other by accruing individual scores to make up a team score. The same process of judging is used nationally, culminating in the selection of an overall winning team and top individual poet.

Oral poetry competitions can be traced at least as far back as 390 B.C., when Plato was writing about verse contests in Ion, where Socrates discusses Ion's performance in a contest of the Rhapsodes held during the festival of Asclepius. The idea of competitive performance poetry traverses many cultures and time periods. Between Plato and slam lie the early troubadours and jongleurs of medieval and early-Renaissance Europe who competed for court favors and reputation. One of the longest-running traditions of oral poetry competitions can be found in Welsh and Celtic culture, where bardic competitions have run for at least 2,000 years. In medieval and Renaissance Scotland a form of verse quarreling known as "flyting" was popular, as poets won competitions by delivering the cleverest, most abusive poem in the most complex verse forms. Latino Décima poets practicing in the mid-16th century (with their medieval Spanish and Moorish roots) were judged on their improvisational skills, the accuracy of their compositions, and their ability to outwit their opponents.

African griots sing ritual songs and summon spirits as part of a tradition that supports wandering storytellers who are expected to know their particular village's life and history in intimate detail. They seek the favors of kings and businesspeople to fund their craft, though most of them have ordinary jobs when they are not being griots. This tradition continues in Africa today and has been in existence for hundreds of years. In Australia there has been a competitive performance poetry cup run in Tasmania since 1984.

Poetry beyond the page is not necessarily contingent on orality, however, as it may be expressed through the sign language of deaf poets, dance, music, or new media. At the same time that slam poetry was being developed in the mid-1980s, the increasing accessibility of the Internet and CD-ROM publishing created spaces for authors to begin experimenting with different types of poetry. The most popular of these early electronic forms was developed using hypertext and hypermedia. According to the *Oxford English Dictionary* (Additions Series), hypertext is a text "which does not form a single sequence and which may be read in various orders; specially text and graphics . . . which are interconnected in such a way that a reader of the material (as displayed at a computer terminal, etc.) can discontinue reading one document at certain points in order to consult other related matter." Hypermedia, on the other hand, extend the text through other media, such as graphics, sound, or animation. Of the hypermedia forms, poetry written in Shockwave® and AdobeFlash® programs are emerging as the most popular forms on the Internet. Although hypertext has been around since 1968, it did not become a significant literary tool until the mid-1980s.

Sound poetry, or text-sound as it is sometimes called, is poetry that uses verbalization of sound as poetic content that may or may not be based on words. This kind of poetry has a heritage that stems back to ancient chants but has become increasingly focused on the nonlingual elements of text in the 20th century. Repetition, fast-talking, nonsense, nonmelodic choral voice work, partial words, percussive expulsions, imitation, and interpretation of social noise—all feature extensively in the work of sound poets. The tradition of contemporary text sounding is

said to stem from Arnold Schoenberg's *Sprechgesang*. Sound poetry is sometimes scored in a tradition that blends elements of concrete poetry, musical composition, and visual art, informed particularly by the dadaists, e.g., TRISTAN TZARA, ANDRÉ BRETON, and LOUIS ARAGON.

Audio poetry is distinct from sound poetry and spoken word because it positions itself in relation to music. Poets compose music (or sound) and text to create poetry. Music may be used as subtext, as a way to convey other meanings, or as a soundtrack to provide a musical score to a poem in the same way that music scores a film. Other practitioners of audio poetry believe that meaning is conveyed in both sound and language and that, used together, they can create a different kind of aurally fused poetry.

Poetry beyond the page takes many forms and is a growing area of practice for an increasing number of contemporary poets. The diversity of poetry's expression demonstrates that it is a flexible and dynamic art that will continue to evolve and expand. Links are provided below to enable further research.

ONLINE RESOURCES

Competitive performance poetry:
http://www.poetryslam.com/
http://www.poetinresidence.com
http://www.spokenwordberlin.net/
http://www.poetrycircus.org/overallCircus.htm
http://www.wordolympics.com/
http://www.4luvofpoetry.com/ambolten.html
http://www.wordforward.org/

**New media poetry
(hypertext, hypermedia, flash, video):**
http://www.e-poets.net/
http://www.csd.uwo.ca/%7ejamie/hypertext-faq.html
http://trace.ntu.ac.uk/
http://no-content.net/#
http://www.subtle.net/
http://vispo.com/uribe/index.html
http://www.incident.net/
http://cmart.design.ru/
http://epc.buffalo.edu/
http://vispo.com/misc/BrazilianDigitalPoetry.htm
http://www.poemsthatgo.com/
www.poetinresidence.com/scenes

Concrete and visual poetry:

http://concretismo.zip.net/
http://www.thewordproject.com/
http://www.epm.net.co/VIIfestivalpoesia/html/visual.html
http://www.sinologic.com/webart/

Sound poetry:

http://www.jaapblonk.com/
http://www.ubu.com/sound/

Performance poetry:

http://www.suite101.com/welcome.cfm/performance_poetry

Jayne Fenton Keane

POPA, VASKO (1922–1991)

Vasko Popa stands as the most renowned and influential poet of post–World War II Yugoslavia. No poet before or after has displayed the craft found within his cyclical verse. What is perhaps even more extraordinary is that—as the poet and translator Charles Simic has noted on numerous occasions—most if not all of Popa's books were planned and mapped out years in advance of his elaboration of them.

Born in 1922 in Grebenac, the Kingdom of Serbs, Croats, and Slovenes (later, Yugoslavia, and now Serbia), Popa discovered Marxism while in high school and became a lifelong Marxist. During World War II and shortly thereafter, Popa traveled to Bucharest (Romania), Vienna (Austria), and Belgrade (Yugoslavia) to study, among other things, French and German literatures. While traveling through Serbia, a part of then Yugoslavia, en route to Vienna in 1943, he was briefly interned in a concentration camp in Bečkerek by the Germans. After World War II he returned to Belgrade, where he joined the Communist Party and made a living as an editor for the Nolit publishing house from 1954 until retirement. In the early 1950s he was secretary-general of the Society for Yugoslav-French Cultural Cooperation just after being a journalist for Radio Belgrade and the *Literary Newspaper*.

In 1953 Popa published *Bark,* his first book of poems, to much controversy. The surreal-influenced poems rankled the party bureaucrats who dominated Yugoslavia's literary world. Despite this shaky beginning, he eventually won over resistance as his work matured. Popa reached a high level of poetic creativity with *Earth Erect* (1972) and *Wolf Salt* (1975) by richly reimagining Serbian culture—intertwining Slavic pre-Christian symbols and mythology with Serbian history and its Christian Orthodox heritage. Popa published eight collections of poetry. His ninth, *Iron Garden,* was left largely unfinished aside from one cycle, *The Little Box.* This final cycle has proven to be one of his most enduring works.

What makes Popa's work so exceptional is the seamless blending of folkloric, classical, and surrealistic elements. His subjects carefully unfold with mathematical precision in a series of cycles, and many of his books are constructed as cycles within cycles.

Popa's poetry has been translated many times and published in various collections. The most notable are the revised and expanded version of *Homage to the Lame Wolf* (1987), translated by Charles Simic (the original 1979 version won the PEN Translation Prize) and *Collected Poems* (1977), translated by Anne Pennington. The latter was later revised and expanded by Francis R. Jones (1997) after Pennington's death in 1981.

In addition to his poetry, Popa compiled *The Golden Apple* (1958), a collection of Serbian folk poems (translated by Anne Pennington and Andrew Harvey in 1980). Other anthologies Popa assembled were *Tumultuous Hilarity* (1960) on poetic humor and *Midnight Sun* (1962) on poetic dreams.

Despite initial resistance to his poetry, Popa became a much lauded poet at home as well as abroad. His first book won the Branko Radičević Award for Poetic Achievement, and his second collection, *Unrest Field* (1956), was granted the Jovan Jovanović-Zmaj Award. Austria bestowed its Austrian State Award for European Literature upon him in 1968. He was the recipient of the Seventh of July Award in conjunction with the critical success of *Earth Erect* (1972) and later of the AVNOJ Award and the Skender Kulenović Award, in 1978 and 1983, respectively.

In addition to being a member of the Vojvodina Academy of Arts and Sciences in Yugoslavia, Popa was invited to other prestigious organizations. In 1972 he was elected to the Serbian Academy of Arts and in 1977 to the Parisian Academie Mallarmé.

BIBLIOGRAPHY

Alexander, Ronelle. *The Structure of Vasko Popa's Poetry.* Columbus, Ohio: Slavica Publishers, 1985.

Lekić, Anita. *The Quest for Roots: The Poetry of Vasko Popa.* Balkan Studies, Vol. 2. New York and Bern: Peter Lang, 1993.

Popa, Vasko. *Collected Poems.* Translated by Anne Pennington and Francis R. Jones. London: Anvil Press Poetry, 1997.

———. *Homage to the Lame Wolf.* Translated by Charles Simic. Field Translation Series. Oberlin, Ohio: Oberlin College Press, 1987.

Simic, Charles. "The Metaphysician of the Little Box." In *The Metaphysician in the Dark.* Anne Arbor: University of Michigan Press, 2003, 171–182.

Steven Teref

"POWER OF PÉREZ, THE" Jorge Guillén (1957)

"*Potencia de Pérez*" (The Power of Pérez) was published in *Maremágnum* (1957), a collection of poems that is part of *Clamor.* Jorge Guillén's attitude toward the world is less positive in *Clamor* than in *Cántico.* The recurring topic is contemporary life with its confusion and lack of humanity; its tone, however, is not moralizing or arid because Guillén expresses this theme through a plethora of perspectives and images based on his personal and poetic experience, which infuse the collection with a rich and nuanced vision. "*Potencia de Pérez*" is a satirical take on Spanish leader Francisco Franco's dictatorship. Pérez, like Franco, assumes power after winning a civil war, is ruthless, and considers his mandate to govern as coming directly from God, an assumption that Guillén uses to great ironic effect. Pérez/Franco has "*Destino tan insigne / Que excluye a muchedumbres de adversarios / Presos o bajo tierra: / No votan, no perturban. !Patria unánime!*" (Such a glorious destiny / that it excludes the multitudes of adversaries / who are imprisoned or beneath the soil. / They do not vote, they cause no disturbance. Unanimous homeland!). It is a long poem with numerous characters: the dictator himself and the bureaucracy that he has created (which includes the police, the clergy, and civil servants, people and organizations that agree with his reactionary views and objectives and implement his mandates). Guillén ridicules them, often making them speak using rhymes, rhythms, words, and expressions that highlight their corruption and the absurdity of their ideas, as exemplified in the following stanza (in lines of six syllables rhyming abab, which create a dreary, singsong effect, reflecting the mediocrity of the characters) from the "Police Chorus": "*Correctos, brutales, / Sutiles, entramos / Salimos, rivales / De lobos y gamos*" (Proper, brutal, / subtle, we come, / we go, the rivals / of wolves and bucks). Throughout the poem rhymes and rhythms change frequently to mimic the various personalities of Pérez and his henchmen. Although Pérez/Franco has established his residence in a royal palace and attends magnificent parades in his honor, at the end he is nothing but what his name, Pérez, indicates, a common and undistinguished man.

BIBLIOGRAPHY
Guillén, Jorge. *Our Air.* 2 vols. Translated by Carl W. Cobb. Lewiston, N.Y.: Edwin Mellen, 1997.

MacCurday, G. Grant. *Jorge Guillén.* Boston: Twayne, 1982.

Mercedes Tibbits

"PRAYER TO THE SUN" Karin Boye (1935)

This poem, "*Bön till solen,*" appeared in Karin Boye's fourth and final collection of poetry, *För tradets skull* (For the Tree's Sake, 1935). (A fifth collection, *De sjudödssynderna* [The Seven Deadly Sins], was published posthumously in 1941.) This poem is representative of Boye's high modernist work, departing dramatically from her earlier poetry in both its formal experimentation and its explicit conflation of religious incantations and sexual imagery. Tropes of pain as repressed pleasure and hermaphroditic sex abound in this poem, as do Christian liturgical invocations (Göransson and Mesterton 1990). Boye appropriates these stock religious phrases, which parishioners recite in unison to invoke the divine during a worship service, summoning a "merciless" and violent god. The Gloria Patri (expressed in English as "Glory to God"), which is used to summon the spirit of God, becomes in Boye's poem "Merciless One with eyes that have never seen the darkness!" and "Liberator who with golden hammers breaks forth frozen waters!" The speaker thus desires a violent and brutal god rather than the gracious and beneficent divinity of Christian tradition. The other invocation is the Kyrie Eleison (expressed in English as "Lord, have mercy"), which Boye renders simply as "Save me" in the poem's third line (and repeats as the poem progresses). Boye preserves the lyrical convention of the "I—You" address to forge a lover's intimacy between the speaker and her god. Yet the collective practice of the liturgical tradition, in which parishioners recite the invocations in first person but do it in unison, posits the poem's speaker as both individual and collective. This desire for unity is also manifest in Boye's sexual imagery, which is androgynous. "Straight as thin lines the flowers' stalks are sucked into the heights" is a phallic image, while "their perianths want to tremble closer to you" is a yonic one. The speaker experiences this intensely painful sexual longing vicariously, through the primal intercourse between the flowers and trees rooted in the earth and the distant yet imminent Sun whose light is their life source. In the final line of the second stanza, the fusion between the human and her divine life force is complete: "Yours are stalk and stem. Yours is my backbone." This fused being, the united humanity, is what the speaker calls on her god to save: "Save it. / Not my life. Not my skin. / Gods do not rule over surface things." The speaker does not desire individual salvation, which is meaningless, but a preservation of the unity she experienced at the moment of climax—a sense of spiritual community with all living things. By the conclusion the speaker's initial cry to her "merciless god" becomes a more subdued and desperate plea: "Save, save, seeing god, what you gave." Boye shows us here that the god who "sees"—connoting here not so much physical sight as insight—is the god who creates (gives) those rare and fleeting moments of ecstasy, when the ego barriers that divide humans and nations crash down and forge a perfect unity of individuals.

BIBLIOGRAPHY

Göransson, Sverker, and Erik Mesteron. *"Karin Boyes modernism: en läsning av "Bön till solen"* (Karin Boye's Modernism: A Reading of "Prayer to the Sun")." In *Den orörliga lågan: Analyser av femton 1900-talsdikter* (The Unquenchable Fire: Close Readings of 15 20th-Century Poems), edited by Sverker Göransson and Erik Mesterton, 27–31. 1990. Reprint, Göteborg, Sweden: Daidalos, 1998.

Lindqvist, Ursula. "The Politics of Form: Imagination and Ideology in 1930s Transnational Exhibitions and Socially Engaged Poetry." Ph.d. diss., University of Oregon, 2005.

Ursula Lindqvist

"PRELUDE" RENÉ DEPESTRE (1967) "Prelude" (*Prélude*) is the first poem in RENÉ DEPESTRE's best-known collection, *A Rainbow for the Christian West* (*Un arc-en-ciel pour l'occident chrétien,* 1967). It is written in unrhymed free verse and divided into four parts, the last of which is "prose poetry," narrating a dream. Written in a stream-of-consciousness style typical of surrealist poets, the poem evokes strange, uncommon images.

From the beginning the speaker shocks us into the realization that he is black: "Yes, I am a tempest-nigger / A nigger rooted in the rainbow." Much of Depestre's intent is apparent here: the tempests—both natural and political—of his native Haiti; his unmuzzled rebellion against racism (and the racist epithet "nigger"); the panoply of races in the world (the "rainbow" made up of colors, including the speaker's own). The speaker is a black "everyman" who criticizes white customs and religion: "I have come to stuff your ferocious laws . . . / Your tricks your taboos your white man's lies!"

Having escaped the oppression of his native land, the speaker finds the same racism everywhere in the world and vows to expose it: "I devote myself to the stamp collecting of your cowardly acts / Here I am a brand new Black / I finally feel that I am myself / In my new solar geography / Me in the great joy of saying good-bye / To your ten commandments of God / To your hypocrisies to your bloody rites." One feels a sense of freedom as the speaker now refers to himself as "Black" (not pejoratively as "nigger"); and just as the Sun is the center of the universe, so too does the new consciousness of blacks assume a central place, represented by the speaker's "new solar geography." Paramount to this rebirth of consciousness is the speaker's return to his roots—the "savage stride" of his NEGRITUDE—his blackness. He will return to his indigenous voodoo spirituality—heretofore forbidden by colonizers as heretical.

At the end the speaker recounts a surrealistic dream in which he confronts a prominent white family in antebellum Alabama. The family represents the white middle-class ideal. All of them fear the potential threat of the black intruder, but they attempt to appear worthy of his respect, despite wishing to annihilate him: "A beautiful family standing up in its scum! / A noble family who knows how to act like a family! / For the sake of impressing the nigger enemy of the family." The intruder, conjuring against the family its own Judeo-Christian traditions, assumes the figure of Abraham, making ready to kill them all: "His [Abraham's] woodcutter-axe is my black-man-arm! / Tremble in your fruits and in your branches / White family of Alabama!" The poem ends with these lines, leaving unstated whether the intruder will spare the family as Abraham spares Isaac in the Bible.

Patrick Day

"PRE-MORNING" YEVGENY YEVTUSHENKO (1995) "Pre-Morning" ("Predutro") is the title poem of YEVGENY YEVTUSHENKO's first book of poetry published after his *Collected Poems* in 1991. The 11 quatrains that make up the poem are set in a liminal time, when the day is coming into being but has not yet come to be. The persona of the poem expresses delight in the openness that characterizes this special time; he loves this period of possibility, which touches the past but is not entirely shaped by it. The nature imagery and the few religious allusions add to the tone of reverence that is consonant with the solemn joy of this special time. Pre-morning is a space of glorious solitude when the speaker is free from social constraint. He can be happy in a way impossible when he wears a face that meets other faces and when the day is taking its ultimate shape. In spite of the wonders of this freedom, the persona also has the assurance from the past that the future holds good for him. The work's confiding speaker is less oratorical than the typical persona in Yevtushenko's verse; he asserts calmly that he loves the way his life has come to be and the knowledge that he has a future through his children. He has friends and family, whose images remain with him even as he jogs in this indeterminate stage of the day. His referring to them as icons suggests that each is as mysteriously a creation of God as the time of day is. He reflects also on love for Russia, to which he is inextricably attached. This love, however, is paradoxical in bringing pain as well as felicity. He loves the Earth, nature, humankind—all moving together in this life. He feels all the same the pain that comes from life in this world, as well as the joy that comes from the potential of the day and of the other self or child whom he addresses in

stanza 10. Even as he confesses that he remains imperfect, he wonders at the beauty of the place and time in which he meditates, and he expresses a thankful paean for love that creates and re-creates.

BIBLIOGRAPHY
Pursglove, Michael. "Yevgeny Yevtushenko." In *The Literary Encyclopedia,* edited by Robert Clark, Emory Elliott, and Janet Todd. London: Literary Dictionary Company. Available online. URL: http://www.litencyc.com/php/speople.php?rec=true&UID=5904. Accessed on April 27, 2007.
Yevtushenko, Yevgeny. *Pre-Morning: A New Book of Poetry in English and Russian.* Edited by Albert C. Todd. Baltimore: Vestnik Information Agency, 1995.

Karen Rae Keck

PRÉVERT, JACQUES (1900–1977) One of the most popular and successful 20th-century French poets, screenwriters, and *paroliers* (writers of song lyrics), Jacques Prévert lives on today in the hearts of his countrymen. His work is studied at every level of the French educational system, and factory workers to presidents know his poems by heart. A deliberate man of the people, Prévert was an artistic pioneer, a sometime member of the French bohemian elite, and a lifelong champion of ground-breaking creativity.

Born to a devoutly Catholic family in the fashionable Paris suburb of Neuilly-sur-Seine, Jacques was the oldest of three children. All his life he mocked the conventions and obsessions of his petite bourgeoisie background while praising the fortitude and sincerity of the ordinary citizen. As a child he was attracted by the vibrant Parisian world of song, art, and literature. His father knew many in the entertainment industry and took the boy behind the scenes to meet actors, artists, directors, and singers.

Young Prévert never liked school and was often in trouble with his teachers. Several of his works, such as "Le Chancre" (The Lazy Student), are gently ironic memories of those years. Prévert left school at 15, did odd jobs, and was drafted into the army at 20. He made friends with Yves Tanguy, the future surrealist painter. The two separated temporarily in 1920 when Tanguy was sent to Tunisia and Prévert traveled to Istanbul. There he met Marcel Duhamel, surrealist writer and future founder of Gallimard's *Série noire* (a line of hard-boiled detective fiction).

Returning to Paris in 1922, Prévert moved into 54, rue du Château, which became the unofficial headquarters of the nascent French surrealist movement. Members included poet Robert Desnos; painter and violinist Georges Malkine; surrealist writer LOUIS ARAGON; poet, art critic, and essayist Michel Liéris; and poet, actor, essayist, and director ANTONIN ARTAUD. Leading them all was the father and genius of French surrealism, ANDRÉ BRETON.

A believer in the French republican ideals of "Liberté, Egalité, Fraternité," Prévert flirted with the Communist Party but never became a member. He eventually broke with Breton and the artistic and political debates of Parisian intellectual circles, devoting himself to his own poetry, plays, and songs. With the publication of *Paroles* (Spoken Words) in 1945, Prévert became a household name in France.

Prévert's verse deliberately imitates speech, often using the vernacular of the French working class. It is rich in wordplay and humor and amazingly clever in its multiplicity of possible meanings. This, among other factors, explains Prévert's popularity among a people that loves to experiment with the variations and complexities of language.

Among Prévert's most important works of poetry are *Grand bal du printemps* (Gala Springtime Ball, 1951), *Lumières d'homme* (Lights of Man, 1955), *La pluie et le beau temps* (Rain and Sunshine, 1955), *Poèmes* (1961); and *Choses et autres* (Some Things and Others, 1972).

Many of Prévert's poems and songs have been performed in cabarets and on stage by stars of *"la chanson française,"* a distinctive style of French singing originating in the streets of Montmartre, a Parisian neighborhood home to artists. Yves Montand, Juliette Gréco, and Edith Piaf all gave voice to the poet's work. Prévert was passionate about film and, together with his brother Pierre, wrote many immortal screenplays like those for Marcel Carné's *Le Jour se lève* (Day Breaks) and *Les Enfants du paradis* (Children of Paradise).

When Prévert declared that he loved his fellow man, children played a great part in that affection. The poem included in *Paroles*, "TO PAINT THE PORTRAIT OF A BIRD" (*"Pour faire le portrait d'un oiseau"*) from *Paroles*, is one of Prévert's best-known children's poems. An attentive reading of the work, however, shows it to be much more than verse only for youngsters.

BIBLIOGRAPHY
Prévert, Jacques. *Selected Poems.* Translated by Sarah Lawson. London: Hearing Eye, 2002.
———. *Paroles: Selected Poems.* Translated by Lawrence Ferlinghetti. San Francisco: City Lights Books, 1958.
———. *Blood and Feathers: Selected Poems of Jacques Prévert.* Edited and translated by Harriet Zinnes. Reprint, Kingston, R.I.: Moyer Bell, 1991.

Annette Olsen-Fazi

"PROEM: THE HARD *KEYURA* JEWELS . . ." MIYAZAWA KENJI (1922)

MIYAZAWA wrote his "Proem" poem "The Hard *Keyura* Jewels . . ." (1922) as a supplement to his first collection, *Spring and Asura* (1924). While the first two lines or so of the manuscript seem to be missing, the poem clearly expresses the central philosophy of Miyazawa's life and art: the bodhisattva ideal. The *keyura* jewels (*yoraku*, in Japanese) of this poem stand for bodhisattvas, who are often depicted as wearing them. In the first stanza the clause "[t]he hard *keyura* jewels hang straight down" suggests not only the fall of innocent creatures (an animistic metaphor for the hard jewels in the poem) but also the noble, unbending determination of the bodhisattvas who, like those who jump into the water to save the drowning, forsake their heavenly existence to save the sentient beings who are drowning and suffering in the lake, a metaphor for our worldly experience (or *Asura* status as unsaved beings).

The phrase "angels' cries" in the second stanza might appear to carry Judeo-Christian implications, but the original word, *ten'nin* (heavenly beings), together with *"keyura* jewels" indicates Miyazawa's primarily animistic/shamanistic and Buddhist sensibilities. In this and the third stanza the speaker, who opens the poem in the objective third person, further distances the reader from those who fall and drown by asking if the reader has heard their cries and by saying that the reader will merely pity them. However, the fourth stanza, because it starts with the word *but,* suddenly and forcibly turns around this indifferent bystander's viewpoint into that of the very sufferers drowning in the icy lakes, "biting" the bitter salt water. The agony of the drowning is skillfully intensified by paradoxical expressions such as "the water is so cold that it tastes hot" and "so bitter it seems tasteless." The fifth, penultimate stanza, rather than depicting the physical sensations of the drowning, moves into the minds of the fallen: "did I fall in this lake? / Is it possible that I should have fallen?" The last stanza sums up the point of the poem by revealing that those who have fallen are none other than ourselves and that some of us willingly fall (i.e., forgo our own salvation), following the bodhisattva ideal. In fact, the speaker explains, "I have told you this / not to prevent you from falling, / but so [that you will fall, and that] you'll swim across it [the lake] when you fall"— which suggests that we are all potentially bodhisattvas as well as "fallen angels" or, according to the Buddhist term, *Asura*. The poem's last two sentences ("and the strongest fall by their wish / and then soar with others") take us back, through a Möbius band–like twist, to the opening lines, thereby exemplifying the Mahayana bodhisattva ideal, by which bodhisattvas constantly and endlessly go between *nirvana* (salvation, innocence) and *samsara* (fallenness, experience) like the blue illumination of "the karmic alternating current lamp" that "flickers busily, busily / with landscapes, with everyone / yet remains lit with such assuredness" ("Proem" to *Spring and Asura*).

Hagiwara Takao

"PROFESSOR DERRIDA ESHU" CHINWEIZU (1986)

As a student of American literature and culture at the State University of New York (Buffalo) during the mid- and late 1970s, CHINWEIZU encountered the writings of Jacques Derrida, the father of deconstructionist literary criticism, because Derrida was making a big impression in American academic circles during that period, and SUNY-Buffalo was, along with Yale University, one of the avant-garde places to study poststructuralist literary theory. In 1975–76, the year that Chinweizu was writing his dissertation at SUNY-Buffalo, the literature faculty sponsored a course administered through SUNY-Buffalo's Paris program, and Derrida was the featured professor. Chinweizu's poem "Professor Derrida Eshu" sends a salvo of critical bullets into the world of fashionable academic discourse that Derrida inspired.

By titling his brilliant dramatic monologue as he does, Chinweizu complicates his lampoon and its ultimate message, making it possible for the poet, writing a decade later, to hit at least two clear targets: Nigerian teachers infected by deconstructionist theory, and those solemn, unoriginal scholars anywhere who do not realize to what an extent Derrida was himself a trickster. A close reading of the text reveals how Chinweizu also ridicules the obscurities of his fellow contemporary poets, seduced by foreign critics into writing stale, impenetrable, and tasteless verse.

On the one hand, the persona of "Professor Derrida Eshu" can be read as a playful contemporary mask for Eshu. The professor's name is structured so that the word that counts the most is *Eshu* (the Yoruba appellation for the youthful trickster god of boundary crossing, rule breaking, sexuality, opportunity, and communication). In this construction the title (Professor) and forename (Derrida) relate to the word *Eshu* as modifiers. Given this appreciation of the speaker's surname and identity and the fact that the entire poem represents a 20-line speech made by Eshu, the work expresses (playfully and satirically) that all of deconstructionist literary theory is nothing but an invention of this powerful and joyfully disruptive deity.

The speech contains condescending nouns of address such as might be used by stuffy (British) tutors—and imitated by copycat (African) academics. The poem begins with the line "It [poetry] is not a thing for enjoyment, my dear boy," and near the end the speaker asserts (about literary criticism), "That's how it is done, my boy." The speaker's description of good poetry as "complex, uncommon *stuff*" (emphasis added) is another hint that he has appropriated the pretentious idiom of Anglo-American academics, for whom the casual word *stuff* (for *material* or *language*) often suggests an approach of nonchalance or superciliousness toward a topic. These mind-set markers connote what Chinweizu has elsewhere labeled "blancophilia" and "negrophobia" ("On Negrophobia"), contagious cultural diseases that must be cured if Africans are to survive the postcolonial era and promote a healthy society for the future.

The killjoy academic is more particularly satirized throughout the major part of the poem by the diction attributed to him. Early in the poem the speaker creates a mock-funereal atmosphere: Poetry, he says, "isn't like tasty food or excellent wine; / It isn't like oven-fresh bread or succulent pear" (ll. 2–3). Instead, he says, it must "be probed / With seismoscopes and divining rods" and "packed in heavy water, / Placed in a vacuum chamber cased in lead, / And cracked by an atom-smasher" (ll. 4–8). Banks of computers are necessary, he adds, to process and to decode the poem's "indeterminacy wave forms" (ll. 9–11). The "printouts of eigen-values" can only be properly "interpreted by holy mouths, / Each well anointed and perfumed" (ll. 12–14). The poem ends with a dismissive and conclusive insult: "If you, or just anybody can understand it, / It isn't a poem at all— declared the Great / Professor Derrida Eshu" (ll. 18–20).

In his essay "On Negrophobia: Psychoneurotic Obstacles to Black Autonomy," Chinweizu explains fully his criticism of diseased, mimetic behaviors among postcolonial Africans and diasporan people of African descent. Against the background of Chinweizu's radical ideology, "Professor Derrida Eshu" encapsulates reasons—given more fully in *Toward the Decolonization of African Literature* (1980) and in his interview with Akubuiro—for his cold-shouldering of so much of what African poets produced in the 20th century. Chinweizu composed a serious version of this poem's fundamental message in his longer, prophetic poem "ADMONITION TO THE BLACK WORLD."

BIBLIOGRAPHY

Akubuiro, Henry. "Chinweizu Hits Soyinka and Clark Again: I don't read them. . . ." *The Sun News* (Nigeria), 27 August 2006. Available online. URL: http://www.sunnewsonline.com/webpages/features/literari/2006/aug/27/literari-27-08-2006-0 01.htm. Accessed on April 27, 2007.

Chinweizu. *Invocations and Admonitions: 49 Poems and a Triptych of Parables.* Lagos, Nigeria: Pero Press, 1986.

———. "On Negrophobia: Psychoneurotic Obstacles to Black Autonomy: Or Why I Love Michael Jackson." Available Online. URL: http://www.africawithin.com/chinweizu/on_negrophobia.htm. Accessed on April 27, 2007.

R. Victoria Arana

"PROPHECY" AIMÉ CÉSAIRE (1946)

Like much of AIMÉ CÉSAIRE's poetry, "Prophecy" possesses a stream-of-consciousness style in unrhymed, free verse with lines of varying length. The poet reminisces about Caribbean islands before European colonization, the fecundity of their vegetation, and the wonders of the animal world: "there where the vigorous night bleeds a speed of pure vegetation / where the bees of the stars string the sky with a hive more ardent than the night." This edenic world eventually becomes menacing, as colonizers (in this case, the British) arrive and disrupt the Caribbean paradise.

The poet identifies as his task the marshaling of oppressed peoples through his own poetry, "where the rainbow of my speech is charged to unite tomorrow with home." This dream of unification, the commingling of races into a peaceful "rainbow," is what the poet prophesizes as a response to the division of "isles" into "islets" by colonial powers, the poet watching the Caribbean islands ". . . dissolve little by little into British isles into islets into jagged rocks in the limpid sea of air." Yet finally, this image of dissolution is not permanent, for the poet remains undaunted, and he boldly claims that in this "limpid sea" of divided territories, ". . . my mug / my revolt / my name / prophetically bathe."

BIBLIOGRAPHY

Césaire, Aimé. *The Collected Poetry of Aimé Césaire.* Translated and edited by Clayton Eshleman and Annette Smith. Berkeley and Los Angeles: University of California Press, 1983.

Patrick L. Day

PROPHET, THE GIBRAN KHALIL GIBRAN (1923)

The Prophet, a book of 26 poetic essays, has been translated into over 20 languages, has had 45 editions in America alone, and is GIBRAN KHALIL GIBRAN's best-known work. In spite of its popular success, the book has received little critical attention.

The prophet of the title, Almustafa, is preparing to sail home from a 12-year sojourn in foreign countries. He is approached by the Orphalese, the people of the area from which he is sailing, with questions about the mysteries of life. The Orphalese are abstractions (ploughman, rich man, woman, merchant, etc.) who request that Almustafa speak to them about subjects such as work, religion, and joy.

Almustafa's sermons are delivered through a series of aphorisms, parables, and observations revealing the prophet's philosophy. Almustafa—and, it is presumed, Gibran since there are a number of similarities—believes that the individual is a spiritual entity exiled to the material world. Unable to find peace in this existence, we are continually dragged down by the body and long to be free from the burden. Searching for fame and fortune is futile and destructive to the soul, yet work is essential to a meaningful life.

> And in keeping yourself with labour you are in
>   truth loving life,
> And to love life through labour is to be intimate
>   with life's inmost secret. (Ch. 7)

Glimpses of the divine are perceived in acts of love and pity, yet to understand the good, one must know the evil; to appreciate the beautiful, be conscious of the ugly; to feel peace, experience turmoil.

> The deeper that sorrow carves into your being,
>   the more joy you can contain. (Ch. 8)

A diverse range of readers regards the paradoxes and proverbs that fill the pages as spiritual truths that speak directly to them. While multitudes have read The Prophet with delight in the beauty of its language and its mystical view of life, literary critics have more often denigrated the work as transparent, trite, naive, or vague, with little literary significance. In the end, the reader must decide the work's merits.

BIBLIOGRAPHY

Gibran, Kahlil. The Prophet. New York: Knopf, 1923.

Jean Hamm

PROSE OF THE TRANS-SIBERIAN AND THE LITTLE JOAN OF FRANCE, THE
BLAISE CENDRARS (1913) BLAISE CENDRARS's La Prose du Transsibérien et de la Petite Jehanne de France (The Prose of the Trans-Siberian and the Little Joan of France), published in Paris in September 1913, is in many respects a foundational text for modernism in literature and the arts. Cendrars's best-known work, the original edition, a projected 150 copies, accompanied or "illuminated" by the colorful, mostly abstract, graphics of Sonia Delaunay, folded in an accordion style that, when unfolded, measured two meters. The sum total (the length of all the "books" in the original edition, taken together) would equal the height of the Eiffel Tower. Each copy, as it came through the silkscreen process, is a unique work of art, with slight variations in hue and intensity of color, sometimes retouched by the hand of the artist. Her contribution forms one of the first significant abstract expressions in the history of modern art.

The poem is frequently cited as either cubist or futurist because of the modernity of its theme of global transportation in a shrinking and violent world. In defiance of any labels such as "futurism," publicity for the poem made much of its innovative nature as the first simultaneous composition. The phrase "simultaneity" is meant to characterize the collaborative and visual nature of the published work. Both Delaunay's designs on the left side and the eccentrically jammed and violent typography of the text on the right allow the viewer to engage the composition with a single sweep of the eye. The text reflects Cendrars's interest in speed, both in the jump cuts between segments of the poem and in the disjointed nature of the phrasing. Cendrars like Arthur Rimbaud is a poet of endlessly varied series. This is true of his prose, like Moravagine, as well as of the poetry of La Prose du Transsibérien et de la Petite Jehanne de France. Chefdor compares La Prose to Rimbaud's "Drunken Boat" fusing "immediacy of perception" and "the recollection of experience, passing from a present tense to the litany-like" effect (44). The rhythms are controlled by syntax, not meter, erasing a cardinal distinction between prose and poetry. That erasure is one reason that the poem is identified as a "prose."

Cendrars, in a letter published in Herwath Walden's Der Sturm in 1913, described the poem as an illuminated billboard reflecting the fevered pace of modern life (quoted in Perloff 10). The composition emphasizes this modernity of conception, in the process collapsing the distinction between high and low culture, an erasure distinctive of all Cendrars's literary productions. For this same reason the poem is called a "prose" in the sense of the Latin *dictu,* which Cendrars understood as common speech (Miriam Cendrars 30, 43–44). RAINER MARIA RILKE, in conversation with Frank Budgen, identified the poem as an instance of "street corner balladry" (quoted in Bochner 103). Ironically at several points in *La Prose* Cendrars identifies himself as a bad poet who has no sense of how to set himself the task of composing a work like that in hand.

> *Et j'étais déjà si fort mauvais poète.*
> *Je ne savais pas aller jusqu'au bout.*
>   (Cendrars, *Oeuvres Complètes,* I:16)
>   (And I was already such a bad poet
>   That I didn't know how to go about it.)
>   (Translated by Wellman)

In this respect *La Prose,* in addition to its many other qualities, is a highly self-reflexive work, its autobiographical flatness of ordinary detail being another hallmark of the poem's innovative style. The poem, in its use of the rail journey motif as a figure for both speed and a revolution in consciousness, is based on Cendrars's experiences as an apprentice to a jewelry salesman in St. Petersburg, Russia. At 16 Cendrars took the train as far as the Russian border with Manchuria at Harbin. This trip, through a devastated landscape undergoing the stress of both the Russian revolution of 1905 and Russia's loss that same year to Japan in the Russo-Japanese War, provides the main structure of the poem.

> *J'ai déchiffré tous les textes confus des roues et*
>   *j'ai rassemblé les éléments épars d'une*
>   *violente beauté*
> *Que je possède*
> *Et qui me force (Oeuvres Complètes,* I:31)
>   (I deciphered all the scrambled texts of the
>   wheels and rearranged the scattered elements
>   into a violent beauty
>   That I master
>   And that drives me)
>   (translated by Wellman)

Accompanying the poet is the figure of Little Joan of France, clearly an association with Joan of Arc and French national identity. First the poet presents her as a child prostitute, a pathetic product of the homelessness and alienation of modern life; sometimes he castigates her maliciously; finally, he treasures, soothes, and protects her weary form. The account of the trip is supplemented by a coda that apostrophizes Paris. Marjorie Perloff concludes her examination of the significance of *The Prose* by writing, "the poet's hallucinatory vision remains rooted in the most ordinary reality . . . a mordant ecstasy of 'profound *aujourd'hui*'" (42–43). This ecstasy or rebirth through immersion in daily life is the stance to be most deeply treasured throughout Cendrars's oeuvre.

BIBLIOGRAPHY

Bochner, Jay. *Blaise Cendrars, Discovery and Re-creation.* Toronto: University of Toronto Press, 1978.

Cendrars, Blaise. *Blaise Cendrars: Complete Poems.* Translated by Ron Padgett, introduction by Jay Bochner. Berkeley: University of California Press, 1992. Appendix with *Poesies complètes.*

———. *La prose du Transsibérien et de la Petite Jehanne de France.* Translated by Donald Wellman. Available online. URL: http://faculty.dwc.edu/wellman/CENDRARS.html. Accessed on April 27, 2007.

———. *Œuvres complètes.* 16 vols. Edited by Raymond Dumay and Nino Frank. Paris: Le Club Français du Livre, 1968–1971.

———. *Poésies complètes avec 41 poèmes inédits.* Paris: Denoël, 2001.

Cendrars, Miriam. *Blaise Cendrars: L'or d'un poète.* Paris: Gallimard, 1996.

Chefdor, Monique. *Blaise Cendrars.* Boston: Twayne, 1980.

Perloff, Marjorie. *The Futurist Moment.* Chicago: University of Chicago Press, 1986.

Donald Wellman

"PURDAH, 1" IMTIAZ DHARKER **(1992)** "Purdah, 1" is the lead poem in IMTIAZ DHARKER's collection by the same name. Its seven irregular stanzas in free verse imply something like a spiritual biography by virtue of the sequence of moments each stanza captures. The first stanza is only three lines long and marks the moment that elders decide a girl must wear the veil: "One day they said / she was old enough to learn some shame. / She found it came quite naturally." The second stanza seems to shift the focalization to that of the girl, who finds "a kind of safety" and "a place to hide" behind the cloth she is compelled to wear, but also compares this attire to "the earth that falls / on coffins. . . ." The second and third stanzas testify—in the third person—about the different ways that people look to her and that she feels about her body, now that she wears the veil, and this estranging outlook intimates the initial stages of a dissociated sensibility. The fourth stanza (which begins "We sit still, letting the cloth grow / a little closer to our skin.") ends with the evocative lines "Voices speak inside us, / echoing in the spaces we have just left." The first-person-plural voice that we hear in this stanza is paradoxically that of suppressed, *unvoiced* thoughts, but thoughts shared, even so, by the women in purdah. The final two stanzas are voiced, once again, in the third person—but now they reveal the beginning of the girl's mental breakdown or revolt ("She stands outside herself, / sometimes in all four corners of a room"), followed by a consciousness of her spirit spiraling ever "inward and again / inward." The back-and-forth motion between points of view that characterizes this poem blurs the border between the social self and the private self and emphasizes the dislocation of spirit that comes from seeing the image of one's veiled self all around oneself, so that "Wherever she goes, she is always / inching past herself" (stanza 6). The poem's ambiguities and paradoxical images of light and burial tease us serially into identification, sympathy, horror, and a kaleidoscope of related thoughts on the similarities between purdah and other forms of uniform socialization.

R. Victoria Arana

QUASIMODO, SALVATORE (1901–1968)

Italian poet, critic, translator, and Nobel Prize winner in literature in 1959, Quasimodo was born on August 20, 1901, at the dawn of the 20th century in the town of Modica, just outside of Ragusa, Sicily. As a child he read translations of Greek lyric poetry, though he did not seriously study Greek and Latin until adulthood (under the direction of Mariano Rampolla). He attended technical schools in Messina and Palermo and moved to Rome in 1920 to enroll as an engineering student at the Polytecnico. In 1926 he abandoned his studies for economic reasons and was eventually granted a position in the civil engineering department of the Italian government, allowing him to travel throughout the country. He became familiar with Reggio di Calabria, Imperia, Cagliari, and Milan, where he settled in 1934.

Quasimodo's brother-in-law, Italian novelist Elio Vittorini, introduced him to the literary circles with which he soon became actively involved. His oeuvre can be situated within two periods divided by World War II. His poems before the war contain metaphysical and highly complex imagery. His first collection, published in 1930 in Florence, is entitled *Acque e terre* (Waters and Lands). Between 1930 and 1938 Quasimodo acted as head of the "Hermetic" school of poetry, whose verse was marked by verbal uncertainty, intended to elicit an emotional response from the reader. Its static, fragmentary style is characterized by the use of symbolism, analogies, and metaphors. In 1932 Quasimodo released *Òboe sommerso* (Sunken Oboe), in which his theory of the "poetics of the word" can be detected. Four years later he published *Eràto e Apollion* (Erato and Apollyon). In 1938 Quasimodo became editor of the weekly magazine *Tempo,* and during the war he was granted a professorship in 1941 in Italian literature at the Giuseppe Verdi Conservatory of Milan. In 1940 his translations of *Lirici greci* (Greek Lyrics) appeared in editions of *Corrente,* an antifascist magazine published by young intellectuals in Milan. In his *Nuove Poesie* (New Poems) of 1942, Quasimodo reveals his reliance on classical stylistics and an acute understanding of life. Within these poems breathes a heightened interest in Earth and nature.

During World War II dictator Benito Mussolini imprisoned the poet for antifascist activities. After the war Quasimodo became more committed to his writing, often commenting in it on the social conditions of postwar Europe. He believed poets had a responsibility to represent the society in which they wrote. He joined the Italian Communist Party in the late 1940s but resigned in protest over the party's insistence that he write political poems in support of party causes.

His poetry produced after World War II has a distinct change in both theme and style. In *Giorno dopo giorno* (Day after Day, 1947) he depicts Italy's hardships and its role in the war. In *La vita non è sogno* (Life Is Not a Dream, 1949) he becomes more preoccupied with society as a whole. Finally, during this period he published *Il falso e vero verde* (The False and True Green, 1956). His later works continue to show a transformation from individualism toward a more civil poetry, *"poesia civile."* In *La terra impareggiabile* (The Incomparable Earth, 1958) Quasimodo eloquently attempts to fuse varying poetic forms. His final collection of verse, *Dare e avere* (To Give and to Have, 1966), contains poems with a more down-to-earth, rational, honest, and convincing tone.

Quasimodo married twice, Bice Donetti and Maria Cumani, and had a daughter, Orietta, in 1935 by Amelia Specialetti. Besides the Nobel Prize the poet received other literary prizes, including the Antico Fattore, awarded in Florence in 1932, and the Etna-Taormina International Prize in Poetry, conferred in 1953. Quasimodo died suddenly in Naples on June 14, 1968, after suffering a cerebral hemorrhage.

BIBLIOGRAPHY

Quasimodo, Salvatore. *Quasimodo.* Translated and introduced by Jack Bevan. Middlesex, U.K.: Penguin Books, 1965.

———. *Salvatore Quasimodo Complete Poems.* Translated and introduced by Jack Bevan. London: Anvil Press Poetry, 1983.

———. *To Give and to Have and Other Poems.* Translated and introduced by Edith Farnsworth. Chicago: Henry Regnery, 1969.

Chris Picicci

R

"RAIN IN THE PINEWOOD, THE" GABRIELE D'ANNUNZIO (1903)

This is probably the most widely known of D'ANNUNZIO's poems and the one that is usually taken as most emblematic of his "panism," the ability to experience the vibrant life of nature in one's own body and soul. The poem is included in *Alcyone* (Halcyon), where the best moments of D'Annunzio's poetic craft and poetic sensibility are to be found. There summer is protagonist, representing the full power of life, and the poet is wholly immersed in this life, merging with the natural elements and becoming all senses. "*La pioggia nel pineto*," comprising four long stanzas of 32 verses, describes a walk in the pinewood of Viareggio, in Tuscany, where the poet used to spend summers. He and his companion, Ermione, are surprised by rain as they walk through the woods. When the first drops fall the poet strains to listen and urges the woman to do the same. They hear no other sound than the rain, falling rhythmically, thin and slow at the beginning then thick and heavy, tapping on the foliage in a variety of tones: "And the pine / has a sound of its own, / and myrtle and juniper / others again. . . ." Then, accompanying the rain, other sounds produced by nature envelop the two lovers: first, the sound of the cicadas growing softer as the rain gets more intense; then the sound of the frog in the distance. And they become one with the wood, no longer human creatures, but finally part of the "rough green vigour" entangling them. The formal features of the poem beautifully serve the thematic purposes. The celebration of nature is rendered in a mimetic way by use of repetitions, onomatopoeic words, and a lexical choice based on phonic criteria, all of which make the poem highly musical. The magical tone that attends the metamorphosis of the lovers merging with the landscape is conveyed through similes and simultaneity of sensations. Beautiful images—for instance, "the heart in the breast like a peach / unspoilt by touch" and "the teeth in their gums / white as almonds before they are ripe"—render the transformation of the woman into an arboreous creature. A poem of immense evocative power, this is probably the most refined example of early 20th-century Italian decadence.

BIBLIOGRAPHY

D'Annunzio, Gabriele. *Halcyon*. Translated with an introduction by J. G. Nichols. New York: Routledge, 2003.

Sabrina Brancato

RAMANUJAN, ATTIPAT KRISHNASWAMI (A. K. RAMANUJAN) (1929–1993)

Attipat Krishnaswami Ramanujuan—Raman to his friends—was born on March 16, 1929, into a Tamil family in Karnataka, in southwestern India. His professional life was mainly identified as a professor of linguistics with the Department of South Asian Studies, University of Chicago, where he taught from 1961 to 1993. As an academic he acquired a multifaceted eminence as a linguist, folklorist, translator of classical

Tamil and Kannada poetry, and leading light in the field of Indo-English poetry.

After graduating with a degree in English literature from Mysore University in 1949, Ramanujan took a job teaching English in Kerala and later in Dharwar and Poona. He nurtured a love of Shakespeare all his life. In 1955 he visited Indiana University to study linguistics on a Fulbright Fellowship and received a Ph.D. degree (on the generative grammar of Kannada) from there in 1963.

Ramanujan's first work of translation was *The Interior Landscape: Love Poems from a Classical Tamil Anthology* (1967). This was followed by *Speaking of Siva* (1973) and *Hymns for the Drowning* (1987). His own poetry in English progressed alongside his endeavors of translation of Tamil and Kannada texts. His first volume of original poetry was *The Striders* (1966), followed by *Relations* (1971), *Second Sight* (1986), and the posthumous *The Black Hen* (1995). In between he wrote a large number of scholarly essays on a wide range of subjects—Indian literature, classical literature ("Three Hundred *Ramayanas*"), literatures of the *bhakti* movement and the modern period, and Indian folklore (*Folktales from India,* 1992). Ramanujan was influenced by both Indian and Western thinking: on the one hand, by Tamil, Kannada, Sanskrit classical, and contemporary modern Indian literature; on the other, by Swiss linguist Ferdinand de Saussure (1857–1913), French anthropologist Claude Lévi-Strauss, Sigmund Freud, Carl Jung, Noam Chomsky, and Jacques Derrida. Ramanujan is said to have noticed a parallel between the Bhagavad Gita and Walt Whitman's *Song of Myself* in their conception of a "double self," as actor-subject and as object.

In poems like "One More on a Deathless Theme," "Towards Simplicity," "Death and the Good Citizen," and "Love Poem for a Wife and Her Trees," we observe Ramanujan's concerns with visions of marriage and family life and the equations of nature and the human body. In his well-known seminal poem "The Striders," the self is more of an absence than a presence. His long poem *Elements of Composition* (1986), later dismantled in its linear form, constitutes a meditation on the self and poetry, punctuated by epiphanic moments from his own life. His subjects range from the reading of

Homer in Chicago to an epitaph for a street dog. In his poem "Self-Portrait" he marks his ongoing, existential dilemma: "I resemble everyone / But myself. . . ."

Ramanujan's idea of human integrity and social or natural equations is often an ironic one, tending to recast conventional modes of perception. As Vinay Dhardwadkar observes, "Ramanujan's refusal to accept merely conventional measures of coherence was a part of his search for a different kind of integrity. In poetry this integrity injects a unique urgency into his negotiations between body and mind, nature and culture, and history and contemporaneity" (*Collected Poems*). Perhaps this was why Ramanujan returned again and again to the domains of *bhakti* poetry or the classical poetry of saints like Nammavar. According to Ramanujan the four genres of classical Tamil poetry—*akam, peruntinai, kaikkilai,* and *puram*—"cover and formalize the main possibilities of lyric poetry" ("Form in Classical Tamil Poetry"). At his death in 1993 he was working on a definitive edition, in translation, of classical Tamil poetry.

Among Ramanujan's many honors were the Padma Shri from India and his election to the American Academy of Arts and Sciences. He was often nostalgic for his Indian peer group, writers like U. R. Anantha Murthy and Girish Karnad, who had chosen to remain in India. Ramanujan lived between these two worlds of consciousness and synthesized them brilliantly as Indo-Anglian poet and Indologist par excellence at the University of Chicago. In his self-effacing, witty manner he saw himself as the hyphen in the Indo-American equation, accountable to an age of plurality.

A. K. Ramanujan died peacefully at the age of 64 on July 13, 1993.

BIBLIOGRAPHY
Ramanujan, A. K. *Collected Poems*. Edited and with an introduction by Vinay Dhardwadkar. Oxford: Oxford University Press, 1995.

Rupendra Guha Majumdar

"RED LOCUST, THE" NOVICA TADIĆ (1981)
NOVICA TADIĆ's "The Red Locust" is a key representative poem from this Montenegran (Yugoslavian) poet's seminal 1981 collection *Ždrelo* (Maw). This poem has

a majority of the hallmarks found in the poet's oeuvre. The poem, much like the collection from which it comes, transcends the dark, surrealistic leanings of his earlier poetry to mine a richer mythology and metaphoric base.

The poem belongs to a small cycle (Shelters) in which the poems are thematically unified by an illusion of safety provided by various types of shelter. However, the title of the sequence transcends its obvious irony to reveal the insecurity and danger the poet feels about his total environment and expresses as a pervading sense of isolation and exploited vulnerability.

In the strange and disturbing opening image ("My doorbell / filled today / with bloody cotton."), the poem sets a tone of uneasiness, evoking dread over what is to follow. Not only is the image simply horrific, but the presented world is unable to function normally, for the cotton would prevent the door buzzer from working. It is a muffled, muted world in the face of horror. The strangeness within Tadić's verse helps set the stage for his unfolding hellish dramas.

When the woman on the couch in the second stanza is described as being "sprawled, stunned, thunderstruck," the reader fears the worst, even though her exact fate is unknown. By excising the site of horror, Tadić masterfully preys on the reader's imagination to heighten tension. The speaker is an inexplicable presence appearing almost to revel in the woman's misfortune. He even mocks her, it is suggested in the final stanza, by reading to her from "her favorite volume," although she appears beyond being capable of listening. There is a running motif throughout much of Tadić's work of a tortured figure, often female, suffering at the hands of a sadistic (or indifferent) speaker. According to literary critic Bojana Stojanović-Pantović, the cruelty displayed by the speaker is a mask (another common motif in Tadić's poetry), for the speaker is more often the victim of countless demons and nightmarish creatures. It is a way for the speaker to hide his suffering and project it onto someone else. The victim, when not the speaker, is a sacrificial figure, like the woman in "The Red Locust."

The central figure, however, is the menacing and "enormous" red locust that "across the city roofs springs" and "will nip off all her hair / like the last grass

on earth." According to Tadić, this locust has broken off from the biblical swarm that once plagued Egypt and now assails Belgrade, the capital of former Yugoslavia. The grotesque insect represents, at its most fundamental level, the tyranny of religion. But the color of the locust infuses the poem with a political subtext. Although red is associated with blood and would seem to lock the poem into a gothic reading, red also has another meaning, no doubt intended by the poet, the color closely associated with communism, the ruling ideology of former Yugoslavia.

Invoking religious imagery was a way for Tadić to comment in relative safety about the communist government of Yugoslavia. Under the protection of metaphor, he could address the injustices in a country whose leader—Tito (Josip Broz)—possessed an almost absolute power. By developing a metaphoric strategy, Tadić found a way to convey sentiments when it was not always safe to do so. The by-products of his style were, first, that he found an engaging way of writing political poetry and, second, that he created haunting works of art that linger in the reader's mind long after the political shelf-life of the poem has expired, thus preventing his poems from becoming mere political artifacts of a time gone by.

BIBLIOGRAPHY
Tadić, Novica. *Night Mail: Selected Poems*. Edited and translated by Charles Simic. Oberlin, Ohio: Oberlin College Press, 1992.
———. "The Red Locust." Translated by Steven and Maja Teref. *New American Writing 23*. (2005): 243.
Stojanović-Pantović, Bojana. "Neimenovano *to*" ("The Unnamed *It*"). In *Ždrelo*. Translated (unpublished) by Maja Teref, 133–139. Banja Luka, Bosnia: Zadužbina Petar Kočić, 2002.

Steven Teref

RELATIONSHIP JAYANTA MAHAPATRA (1980)
Originally published in New York by the Greenfield Review Press in 1980, *Relationship* is a visionary poem of 673 lines divided into 12 sections incorporating MAHAPATRA's ambitious attempt to inscribe his Oriya roots and ancestry in a song that weaves dreamlike moments of doubt, despair, and illumination into a complex whole. For its "awareness of Indian heritage,

evocative description, significant reflection, and linking of personal reminiscence with race memory" (unpublished citation), it won Mahapatra the Sahitya Akademi award in 1981.

Central to the poem are the historical ruins of the temple at Konarka, dedicated to the Sun God and shaped like a monumental chariot, a witness to the maritime and architectural glories of the Indian state Orissa. The setting allows the poet to immortalize facets of Orissa's troubled history by staging a personal quest "at the altar of [his] origins" (section four). The evocation of origins is mythic and primeval, partaking in the eternal mysteries of a shared past. Mahapatra's marshaling of images for this purpose is strikingly disturbing and original, inviting the reader to take a leap into the unknown. Elemental images of earth and sky, sun and wind, stone and ash are combined with evocative feelings of apprehension and amnesia, alternating with climactic moments of self-fulfillment, affirming love, and renewal. The poem is in the form of prayer that redoubles as sleep and song enclosing snatches of the cultural past and ending in a release from fear and uncertainty. The poet-speaker says candidly in the opening lines of section eight: "It is my own life / that has cornered me beneath the stones / of this temple in ruins, in a blaze of sun." The "solitary traveler" of the opening section—with his intended "initiation into the mystery of peace"—discovers his moment of recognition: love irradiating "other people's lives." In the end the poet lays claim to his "mysterious inheritance": ". . . I put my hand toward a dream the sun / has kept awake through the years" (section eleven). In effect the poem enacts a process of poetic affiliation with a reclaimed destiny.

BIBLIOGRAPHY

Mishra, S. K. "The Largest Circle: A Reading of Jayanta Mahapatra's *Relationship*." *Journal of Literary Studies* 8, nos. 1 and 2 (June–Dec. 1985): 37–56.

Rayan, Krishna. "The Tendril and the Root: A Study of Jayanta Mahapatra's *Relationship*." *Literary Criterion* 26, no. 1 (1991): 61–70.

R. S. Nanda

REQUIEM ANNA AKHMATOVA **(1963)** ANNA AKHMATOVA's stunning song for the dead was written in stages, most of it between 1935 and 1940, with the epigram and opening movement added two decades later. As with her other poems that could invoke the wrath of the authorities, *Requiem* was committed to memory by the poet's friends. Originally appearing in Munich, Germany, in 1963, it was not published in the Soviet Union until 1987. The 15-part poem stands where the intimate and the universal meet, borrowing something of its structure from Christianity's Way of the Cross, from condemnation through crucifixion.

From the start Akhmatova makes clear that she remained in the USSR as witness, true to her concept of the moral responsibility of the poet, rather than enter voluntary exile. The "I" of the poem is both Akhmatova and a composite suffering woman. The impetus for the poem comes during the purges carried out by Stalin's head of the NKVD (precursor to the KGB), Nikolay Yezhov, when a freezing, faceless woman who recognizes the poet asks in a whisper whether Akhmatova can describe their collective ordeal. It becomes a national duty as well as a private lament. Hence, the cycle is specific in its details but also shows that identical circumstances are the shared reality of thousands of other women.

The dawn arrest refers to Akhmatova's son, Lev Gumilyov, and her lover, Nikolay Punin, who were apprehended in 1935. The speaker identifies with "the wives of the Streltsy," a group of soldiers defeated and either executed or banished by Peter the Great. The weight of Russian history thus is brought to bear on Akhmatova's historical moment, so that centuries of wailing women form the backdrop of her story. Her ex-husband and fellow acmeist poet Nikolay Gumilyov had been shot by the Bolsheviks in 1921, and now their son has been carried off in a Black Maria (a type of police van). She finds it difficult to reconcile her earlier, frivolous life with the life spent standing in line, literally at the foot of the cross, outside the cruciform-shaped Kresty prison in Leningrad (St. Petersburg). It is here where she would have any memorial statue set, not in the pretty places of her youth.

The motif of sacrifice continues with the crying of Mary Magdalene and the silence of the Mother. So many are taken that she cannot name them all, but she prepares a burial shroud for them from their "overheard words," an allusion to dissidents like her fellow poet and friend OSIP MANDELSTAM, who had also been condemned. She offers up her "exhausted mouth / Through which a hundred million scream" as an assurance that the silenced have a voice in her. The poem promises memory of the horrors taking place even as the stars continue to shine and the rivers Neva, Don, and Yenisey swirl and flow.

BIBLIOGRAPHY

Akhmatova, Anna. *The Complete Poems of Anna Akhmatova.* Expanded edition. Edited and introduced by Roberta Reeder, translated by Judith Hemschemeyer. Boston: Zephyr Press, 1997.

Ljundgren, Anna. "Anna Akhmatova's *Requiem*: A Retrospective of the Love Lyric and Epos." In *Anna Akhmatova 1889–1989,* edited by Sonia I. Ketchian. Oakland, Calif.: Berkeley Slavic Specialties, 1993.

A. Mary Murphy

RESEARCH INTO FEAR TAMURA RYŪICHI (1963)

During the 1960s TAMURA RYŪICHI published two poems as separate, exceptionally slim volumes. One was *Research into Fear* (or *A Study of Fear,* 1963); the other was *Decaying Matter* (or *A Perishable Substance,* 1966). One of Tamura's translators commented: "In these two long poems Tamura surveys art, history, society and mankind, and touches on those aspects of thought and experience which create anguish in human beings" (Grolmes x). The two "aspects of thought and experience" (the topics of these poems) are, respectively, fear and mortality. Each poem advances its treatment of the topic by means of fragmentary images, broken sequences of uncanny apparitions, laconic first-person observations, and urgent commands. These are difficult poems, more evocative than constative. Tamura's poems cast an oracular spell.

In *Research into Fear* the images collide into each other. Because the imagery comes in snippets and scraps, the poem seems to represent a consciousness taking random impressions of a reality too inchoate (fear) to relate in a fashion any more coherent than this poem can manage to do; still, a surreal sequence takes shape and makes sense. Phrases resemble speech shorn of all excess, made spare to convey something essential. What matters—the speaker seems to imply—is simply the posited experience; only stark, unsentimen-

tal language is bearable where this topic is concerned. No wonder Nobel Prize laureate Kenzaburo Oe felt that Tamura Ryūichi was a writer whose "strong, sad, and compassionate voice" evoked nothing less than awe (Grolmes xviii). To enter the spiral of this poem is to participate imaginatively in someone else's nightmare or daylight terror. The poem induces dread, then horror, followed by apprehension, numbness, feelings of insignificance, and finally fear's dissipation. *Research into Fear* is composed of 10 numbered sections. The sections are numbered, ominously, in reverse order, suggesting a countdown to an explosion or some other fearful ending. By poem's end, however, the reader has raw poetic data from which to arrive at more than one conclusion regarding the emotion in question.

The first part ("10.") begins by evoking apprehension: "An evening / you can hear a needle / hit the floor / the whiskey glass on the table cracks" (ll. 1–4). (We do not know what causes the silence, nor the glass to shatter; this is how it starts; this is what happens.) Next "unfamiliar cards" appear with inscriptions the speaker cannot read, X-ray negatives that picture blood vessels as "orchid veins" and "ashy streams." Here "skin and subcutaneous fat embrace / regions of darkness / . . . they might as well / be touched by rubber gloves / . . . scalpels and tweezers." In a captious allusion to the Christian view of salvation (via Holy Communion), the speaker commands: "ask a poet you like / what bread he can imagine / ask a painter you like / what wine she can see / in a stream of milky blood— / modern cities cremated / at the slightest incursion of meaning / the negative world caving in." There is reverberation. A "pin lifts from the floor / a milky stream turns the color of blood / beneath smooth skin." "10." ends as bafflingly as it began: "a door bangs / someone goes out / or / someone comes in." "9." embodies the fear of losing one's mind when it is surrounded by emptiness. The poet fears not being able to revive the ability to think once that ability dies. The speaker recalls past artists and wonders how Brueghel would have painted the emptiness he now perceives, or how Mozart would have expressed it, what *he* would have needed to convey it, "perhaps . . . a flute." Other artists come to the speaker's mind: Spanish surrealist painter Joan Miró; then French postimpressionist painter Henri Rousseau;

then "the metaphors" of Saint John the Evangelist, 17th-century English metaphysical poet John Donne, and French 19th-century poets Charles Baudelaire and Stéphane Mallarmé. Meanwhile, the speaker says, "and in my mind / four thousand days and nights / are at war." "8." begins with a one-word line ("There") that refers to the speaker's mind, where "days and nights divide" and "keep harmony and order" or "wage war" while "the tip of a needle" glints objectively and surreally with the light from an "unnamed star." In "7." the speaker drums an appalling list of vicious, marauding actions taking place at tower, castle, and estate, while an unnamed but menacing "they . . . express in every art form / white-hot rhythms" and "dangerous similes / self-exposing manifestos / ultrahypocritical art movements that suppress hypocrisy." Part "6." speaks in alarming mystical riddles: "Gouge your eyes out if you want to see / cut off your ears if you want to hear." In this section the speaker contrasts the terrifying language of kings, angels, and slaves and pronounces on the depraved joys of slaves and the despotic powers of kings. He ends with the perturbing prediction "if you can see your own angel" you will see "its ears are in its wings." Part "5." dwells on the apparition of "trembling wings / trembling tongue . . . piercing . . . flicking . . . beautiful tongues" that the speaker saw in the mouth of "a pure green snake" in one temple he visited and around a bodhisattva he met in the "autumn wind." Part "4." contrasts the clear (if short-lived) objective light that spills from a falling needle to the frightening darkness "in a dove's voice / in a snake's design / in the arms of Sakuraiwa Kannon" (a goddess of mercy). Part "3." evokes, in its incantatory 11 lines, the evolution through history of sounding instruments ("Animal horn / becoming metal horn / recorder / becoming flute") and implies that—their egos aside—artists are merely instruments, too ("Mozart becoming Debussy"). Part "2." employs the similes of "a hunter stalk[ing] game" and of "hunger stalk[ing] wild animals" to explain how darkness (dread) closes in "on mind." In part "1." the dire images of needle, angel, tongue, tower, castle, and "animal horn / becoming metal horn / recorder / becoming flute" all reappear, in the midst of which the speaker notes the absurdity of life ("our lives are too long to commit crimes" and "too short to pay for our crimes") and observes cryptically that "soul is form." Part "0." is empty.

Whether the title *Research into Fear* or *A Study of Fear* seems more appropriate to this countdown poem, the work's overall structure suggests that fear is experienced in phases, the first being the most alarming and irrational. As one nears the zero hour or the final second of fear, one's thoughts swirl to comforting mantras and irresolvable paradoxes. The final state is either annihilation or freedom. No language can express the end of fear.

BIBLIOGRAPHY

Tamura, Ryūichi. *Research Into Fear.* In *Dead Languages: Selected Poems 1946–1984,* translated by Christopher Drake, 34–40. Rochester, Michigan: Katydid Books (Oakland University), 1984.

———. *Poetry of Ryūichi Tamura.* Translated by Samuel Grolmes and Yumiko Tsumura. Palo Alto, Calif.: CCC Books, 1998.

R. Victoria Arana

RILKE, RAINER MARIA (1875–1926)   Popularly known as the greatest 20th-century poet writing in the German language, Rainer Maria Rilke also mastered an elegant lyrical prose and was even adept at composing graceful poems in French. He wrote more than 400 poems in French dedicated to the canton of Valais in Switzerland. Though he is probably best known for his SONNETS TO ORPHEUS and the DUINO ELEGIES, Rilke never limited himself to strict poetic conventions and traditional verse forms, but instead brought images to life in various sorts of versification, transforming his material through close attention to detail and skillful use of archetypes. Some of the more intensely delicate and joyfully energetic of his French lyrics are in *The Roses & the Windows.* Among his most famous individual poems are "AUTUMN DAY," "ARCHAIC TORSO OF APOLLO," "BUDDHA IN THE GLORY," and "LEDA."

Rilke is most often considered a modernist poet. His penetrating attention to religious problems—the lack of faith and deep anxiety of the times—and his desire for solitude even in the presence of others guarantee him a space of his own in the realm of poetry, a space he mapped for himself. His famous advice to would-be poets in the renowned LETTERS TO A YOUNG POET is "Go into yourself. Search for the reason that bids you to write; find out whether you would have to die if it were denied you to write." Another of his celebrated prose works is his semiautobiographical *Notebooks of Malte Laurids Brigge.*

René Karl Wilhelm Johann Joseph Maria Rilke was born in Prague, the son of Josef Rilke, a railway official (after a failed military career), and Sophie Entz (known as "Phia"), the daughter of a bank official with the title of imperial counsellor and relatives among the Entz-Kinzelbergers, a well-to-do manufacturing family. Rilke did not have a happy childhood. He was torn between his parents, both of whom he tried to please to no avail. His mother, never happy with her fallen hopes for higher social standing, had suffered the loss of a baby daughter just before Rilke's birth. Phia dressed her son as a girl until he was five years old, putting him in trousers only on his first day of school. She gave him dolls to play with, and he would comb their hair for hours. Mother and son would play games together, where she would encourage him to call himself "Sophie" when he was being a "good girl."

His father, having failed at a military career, however, gave Rilke toy soldiers and dumbbells. Later Rilke glossed over his father's failures and blamed his mother entirely for the traumas of his youth, saying she treated him like a little doll. Yet she is the one who first instilled in Rilke the love of language and encouraged him to read and write poetry, nurturing his talents. Even as a young child he could copy out from memory many of 18th-century German poet Friedrich Schiller's ballads. Rilke's father did not like the way the boy was encouraged by his mother; he believed his son needed a more masculine occupation.

Young Rilke wrote poems with military themes and drew pictures of soldiers, trying to make both parents happy with his artistic inclinations. The poetically ambitious youth took on topics of military significance to impress his father but also wrote poems celebrating events like his parents' wedding anniversary. Rilke's parents separated when he was nine, and Rilke was enrolled until 1891 in military school at St. Pölten and Mahrisch-Weisskirchenn—altogether a very unhappy time for him. He then entered business school in Linz, Austria, after preparatory studies and also worked in his uncle's law firm. Thanks to his uncle's assistance, Rilke continued his studies at the Universities of Prague,

Munich, and Berlin. On the advice of a close acquaintance, Lou Andreas-Salomé, Rilke changed his first name from the feminine René to the more masculine Rainer after he left Prague.

Salomé had been a friend and lover of German philosopher Friedrich Nietzsche before she met Rilke, and she had studied psychoanalysis for a year with Sigmund Freud. The two captivated each other's attention, probing the depths of each other's being. Of first meeting her Rilke writes: "I felt at first so confused that I could scarcely separate my impressions, and thought I was drowning in the breaking waves of some foreign splendor." The relationship was not sustainable at that pitch, but the two remained confidants for the rest of their lives.

After Rilke joined an artists' colony at Worpswede in Lower Saxony, Germany, he wrote *Letters to a Young Poet,* but it was a requirement for his writing that he be alone, even among a crowd. In spring 1901 (on April 28), Rilke married the young sculptress Clara Westhoff, and she bore him a daughter, Ruth, by December of that year. In their middle-class family atmosphere he felt stifled and had to break away. Rilke could never settle down comfortably with Clara, but these two also continued their long-distance relationship for the rest of their lives. Even though Rilke has been quoted as saying, "A *togetherness* between two people is an impossibility," he had many lovers, both male and female. All the while Rilke loved and preserved his necessary solitude—for only in the midst of it could he feel his true being and exercise his creativity.

After Rilke left Westhoff he returned to Paris and associated closely with the sculptor Auguste Rodin, who had been Clara's teacher. Rilke worked as Rodin's secretary and planned to write a book about him. Rilke also admired the work of French artist Paul Cezanne, but it was with Rodin that he learned the importance of making his observations as objective as possible to bring a work more fully into being for the majority of people. This led to Rilke's famous involvement with "thing poems," of which one outstanding example is the most definite "art thing" poem: "Archaic Torso of Apollo" (published in his 1908 collection, *New Poems*). Rilke's writing style continued to evolve. As he was breaking away from Rodin, another impressive work marked the start of a new period. During this time Rilke wrote a psychologically unhinged, eternally alive lyrical poem, THE PANTHER.

His days in Paris, though exciting, were also difficult for a person of Rilke's sensibilities. There were many things to fear, and Rilke honed in on these as he wrote the semiautobiographical novel *The Notebooks of Malte Laurids Brigge,* one of his most important prose works, a story in the form of the confessions of a Danish expatriate living in Paris. After laboring over it for six years, he published it in 1910. Aside from the strange terrors and fears expressed in *New Poems* and *The Notebooks,* the retiring Rilke felt there were also many positively stimulating encounters to be had with the modernists.

For about 12 years Rilke had what has been called a "creativity crisis," brought on in part by the outbreak of World War I and by a stormy love affair with painter Lou Albert-Lasard. Rilke was called up and endured basic training in Vienna at the beginning of 1916. He was transferred to the War Records Office, thanks to the intercession of influential friends, and he was discharged from the military in June 1916. This brief stint of military service was a traumatic reminder of the early horrors of the military academy and threw him into the crisis that almost smothered his creativity. Having started the *Duino Elegies* in 1912, he named this series of poems after a stay (between October 1911 and May 1912) at Castle Duino, near Trieste, home of Princess Marie von Thurn und Taxis. After his discharge from service, he sought a realm of his own and the solitude to "go within" and return to his writing. He found this in the Chateau de Muzot, close to Sierre, in Swiss Valais; in 1922 Rilke's patron, Werner Reinhart, purchased the building so that Rilke could live there rent-free. There Rilke completed the *Duino Elegies* and his *Sonnets to Orpheus,* which he wrote in a burst of creative energy just before and after the completion of the elegies. Both sets of poems have been called "among the high points" of his work.

Rilke had suffered from undiagnosed illnesses all his life, but he began to suffer even more, requiring longer and longer stays at a sanatorium in Territet, near Montreux, on Lake Geneva. He continued to write poems in these years, writing over 400 of the poems in French, among which are "The Roses" and "The Windows" (published in 1927). Roses and windows appear throughout his poems as a recurring motif for his outlook on the world. Rainer Maria Rilke was diagnosed with leukemia shortly before his death on December 29, 1926, and he died in the Valmont Sanatorium in Switzerland. The story he would have readers believe is that his leukemia was discovered when an infection developed from a wound that refused to heal, where he had been pricked by the thorn from a rose he had picked for a beautiful woman. He had penned his own epitaph for the headstone in Raron cemetery, to the west of Visp, where he was laid to rest on January 2, 1927: "Rose, oh pure contradiction, joy / of being No-one's sleep, under so / many lids."

BIBLIOGRAPHY

The Academy of American Poets: *Rainer Maria Rilke.* Available online. URL: http://www.poets.org/poet.php/prmPID/295. Accessed on April 27, 2007.

Casey, Timothy J. *A Reader's Guide to Rilke's Sonnets to Orpheus.* Dublin: Arlen House, 2001.

Freedman, Ralph. *Life of a Poet: Ranier Maria Rilke.* New York: Farrar, Straus and Giroux, 1996.

Gass, William H. *Reading Rilke: Reflections on the Problems of Translation,* New York: Knopf, 1999.

Metzger, Erika, and Michael Metzger, eds. *A Companion to the Works of Rainer Maria Rilke.* Rochester, N.Y.: Camden House, 2001.

The Rainer Maria Rilke Archive. Available online. URL: http://us.geocities.com/renate_h/index.html. Accessed on April 27, 2007.

Geraldine Cannon Becker

RITSOS, YANNIS (1909–1990)

Considered one of the three greatest Greek poets of the last century (the other two are ODYSSEUS ELYTIS and GEORGE SEFERIS), Yannis Ritsos professed for most of his life a nonaligned sort of communism and stalwartly opposed the various oppressive regimes that overtook Greece and Europe during his lifetime. He was imprisoned several times for participating in civil uprisings and for his socialist writings and speeches—most conspicuously when he was confined for five years to Greek concentration camps (from 1947 to 1952) in the period following World War II during Greece's civil war. Ritsos was again arrested immediately after the April 1967 coup d'état by a right-wing military junta, deported to the island of Samos, and forbidden to publish. He was, nevertheless, enormously and continuously popular among the Greek common people—and prolific, with well over 100 volumes of verse, essays, and plays published while he was alive. He was nominated nine times for the Nobel Prize in literature but was never awarded it. Instead, he received the USSR's Lenin Peace Prize in 1977, which he said he valued more highly anyway. His popularity was amplified by his impassioned public readings of his poems, events that became symbols of Greek resistance not only to invading powers, but also to the right-wing regime that ruled Greece from 1967 to 1974.

Yannis Ritsos was born in Monemvasia, in the Peloponnese (southern Greece), on May 1, 1909. In his troubled youth his father died insane, and his mother and elder brother died of tuberculosis, which he himself contracted. He entered law school in 1925 but abandoned his studies when he suffered an attack of consumption and was obliged to spend five of the next six years in a sanatorium. In 1934 he joined the Greek Communist Party and published his first volume of verse (*Trakter*). It was followed by *Epitaphios* in 1936. Both of those collections displayed revolutionary zeal, and *Epitaphios* (Funeral Procession), a tribute to a young worker who had died during a political demonstration, caused the authorities so much consternation that its author was arrested and the few unsold copies of the book were burned on the Acropolis as a state warning to dissidents. At the end of the German occupation of Greece in October 1944, Ritsos joined the Communist guerrilla forces fighting the country's right-wing dictatorship in the civil war of 1944–49, a conflict that pitted factions supported by the Soviet Union on the one side and Britain and the United States on the other and cost tens of thousands of lives. About that period Ritsos wrote *Romiosini* (Greekness, 1947), which fused the heroism of his day with that of legendary and historical Greek freedom fighters and set their actions against a perpetual background of limestone hills, olive groves, and rocky coastlines. In 1954 he married Falitsa Georgiadis, a medical doctor who lived on Samos. Their daughter, Eleftheria, was born in 1955. Not until 1972 were Ritsos's writings once again allowed to be published. Shortly thereafter scores of works that he had written and secreted away in the censored years saw the light of day. From 1974 onward he received numerous literary awards and honorary doctorates.

In 1991 Edmund Keeley published *Yannis Ritsos: Repetitions, Testimonies, Parentheses,* a hefty selection of poems translated from a series of Ritsos's works from 1963 through 1975. This collection includes an introduction to the poet and a comprehensive chronology of his life and works. Though not the only such collection, it is a good starting point for a fuller appreciation of the output of this prolific poet, dramatist, graphic artist, and orator. More of his works are being translated each year into the world's languages. His *Monochords,* a series of hundreds of one-line poems, translated by Arthur Spyrou, is a collection of koanlike thoughts crafted to evoke spiritual and intellectual epiphanies of all sorts.

Ritsos died in his sleep on November 14, 1990, at the age of 81. He was buried with full state honors. His works have since been translated into over 40 languages.

BIBLIOGRAPHY

Ritsos, Yannis. *Late into the Night: Last Poems of Yannis Ritsos.* Translated by Martin McKinsey. Oberlin, Ohio: Oberlin College Press, 1995.

———. *Monochords.* Translated by Arthur Spyrou. Brooklyn, Australia: Paper Bark Press, 1996.

———. *The Fourth Dimension.* Translated by Peter Green and Beverly Bardsley. Princeton, N.J.: Princeton University Press, 1993.

———. *Yannis Ritsos: A Voice of Resilience and Hope in a World of Turmoil and Suffering: Selected Poems (1935–1989).* Bilingual edition. Translated, introduced, and annotated by George Pilitsis. Brookline, Mass.: Hellenic College Press, 2001.

———. *Yannis Ritsos: Repetitions, Testimonies, Parentheses.* Translated and introduced by Edmund Keeley. Princeton, N.J.: Princeton University Press, 1991.

R. Victoria Arana

"ROBBEN ISLAND SEQUENCE" Dennis Brutus (1978)

One of many poems by Dennis Brutus reflecting on the prison experience, "Robben

Island Sequence" is fairly typical of the poet's later work, in which Brutus sought to eliminate the tight verse structure and ornate diction of his earlier work to achieve greater clarity and reach a wider audience. Whereas Brutus had originally been influenced by the 17th-century English metaphysical poets, he draws more directly on the American free-verse tradition of Walt Whitman and Langston Hughes in this poem to describe from memory in straightforward language some of the hardships that he faced on Robben Island, the notorious prison facility off the coast of South Africa. Comprising nearly 70 lines of varying length, "Robben Island Sequence" is divided unequally into three sections. The first and longest focuses on one of the meaningless jobs that convicts were forced to perform, collecting stones and seaweed from the sea. It begins somewhat impressionistically by recording the different shades of red discernible in the blood spilled by barefoot prisoners, who were assaulted by "the bright blade-edges of the rocks" (l. 14) on the beach. It ends with an image of man's injustice to man as the speaker recalls the warden "Kleynhans laughing" (l. 36) and holding a convict's head under the water. An aubade of sorts in that it alludes ironically to songs of lovers parting at dawn, the second section of the poem explains what it was like "to be a prisoner, a political victim" (l. 51) faced with the prospect of a new day on Robben Island and the need to endure. Here again the threat of violence is all too real, as the criminal prisoners, in search of their next sexual conquest, survey the young political prisoners. The effects of such violence are addressed in the third and final section of the poem, which details the various injuries of those waiting in line at the prison infirmary, where most things are treated with castor oil. "Robben Island Sequence" ends on a quasi-nostalgic note, as the speaker observes, "what a bruised and broken motley lot we were!" (l. 69). Thus Brutus proudly identifies with the political prisoners who remain on Robben Island, although he is permanently removed from the struggle against oppression in South Africa as an exile. Since "Robben Island Sequence" was first published in *Stubborn Hope* (1978), it has been anthologized several times, most recently in *The Vintage Book of Contemporary World Poetry* (1996).

BIBLIOGRAPHY
Brutus, Dennis. *Stubborn Hope*. London: Heinemann, 1978.
McClatchy, J. D., ed. *The Vintage Book of Contemporary World Poetry*. New York: Vintage, 1996.

Alexander B. McKee

"ROMANCE TO NIGHT, A" GEORG TRAKL (1912)

"A Romance to Night" ("*Romanze zur Nacht*") is a perfect example of TRAKL's preoccupation with the horrors of modernity in rural settings and its effects on the individual's physical and unconscious existence. It showcases Trakl's most characteristic poetic technique of creating impressionistic collages of images and moods to mimic the fragmentation of the self in relation to external reality, with all its different facets and remnants of underlying truths.

In a disconnected series of simple images, the poem's five stanzas describe several inhabitants of a town who seem disconnected from life, faith, and other individuals—for example, their own children, their neighbors, even their own lives—and how such disengagement leads inevitably to death and the collapse of meaning. The first image is of a man walking through a deserted town at midnight and a young boy, perhaps his son, who wakes from a nightmare only to disappear slowly within the moon, for his father has left his side and cannot comfort him. We also receive images of a mad woman crying in front of barred windows, a murderer, the afflicted facing imminent death, a naked injured nun who seeks to recapture her faith, and finally "The dead," who "paint silence on the walls / With their white hands" while the "The one sleeping continues to whisper." The speaker has led us from the basic rupture between a son and his father to the ultimate rupture between a sleeping God and his creation. The reader, however, is never completely certain whether these impressions are based on a nightmare or represent waking reality, whether these visions are caused by the unconscious or by actual phenomena. But in modernity the boundaries have been blurred, and the poem can be seen as a metaphor for modern/industrialized society and the dreamlike existence some people seem to endure, witnessing life via fragmentary impressions. Yet throughout the poem we still encounter beauty—lovers floating on a pond, a mother singing, and laughter—which lend hope that reality could only be a nightmare and we are merely waiting to wake up, or for God to awaken.

As with most of Trakl's poems, it is extremely difficult to extract unambiguous meaning. But that is precisely what Trakl attempts to achieve: to portray the confrontation of an individual with a reality that has lost all apparent meaning and, as a result, has broken into mere impressions. Discovery of underlying truths, if these exist, depends solely on the reader's sensibility or perception.

BIBLIOGRAPHY
Trakl, Georg. "A Romance to Night." In *Autumn Sonata: Selected Poems of Georg Trakl,* translated by Daniel Simko, 16–7. Mt. Kisco, N.Y.: Moyer Bell, 1989.

Daniel Pantano

S

SABA, UMBERTO (1883–1957) Umberto Poli was born on March 9, 1883, in Trieste, which at the time was part of the Austro-Hungarian Empire. His father, Ugo Poli, an Italian Christian, abandoned the child's Jewish mother, Rachele Coen, even before she had given birth. Umberto later chose the name Saba ("bread," in Hebrew) to honor his mother's heritage. Saba became an important 20th-century poet and novelist whose works expressed the difficulties of childhood and the hurt of abandonment by his father, whom he met for the first time at the age of 20. His mother was a stern and dedicated woman who hired a Slovenian nanny, Peppa Sabaz, to help raise her son during his early childhood. His most important work is his *Canzoniere* (Songbook), which he originally wanted to call *Chiarezza* (Clearness). The title he ultimately gave the volume was borrowed from Francesco Petrarca's famous *Rerum vulgarium fragmenta,* or *Canzoniere.*

Saba had an unorthodox academic career and was, as he complained, unfairly treated by his Latin and Greek teacher in high school. He soon abandoned formal classical studies, enrolled in the Imperial Regia Accademia of commerce and nautical science, and eventually worked as a cabin boy. He attended the University of Pisa for one year (1903–04). In 1907–08 he served in the military in the southern Italian city of Salerno, an experience that he later said helped him to find himself among his fellow soldiers. He returned to Trieste in 1908 and the following year married Carolina Wölfler. They had a daughter, Lina, shortly thereafter. In 1911 the family moved to Florence and later lived in Bologna. Saba served in the army from 1915 to 1918 but never fought at the front. A year after World War I he returned to Trieste and took proprietorship of an antiquarian bookstore. During Italy's fascist period and as a result of the government's racial laws of 1938, Saba was forced to sell his bookstore and leave the city. He fled Trieste with his family and lived in various Italian cities, trying to escape deportation to a German concentration camp.

Saba published numerous works, including *Military Verses* (1908), *House and Land* (1909–10), *Trieste and a Woman* (1910–12), *Quiet Desperation* (1913–15), *Light, Drifting Things* (1920), *The Love Thorn* (1920), the *Songbook* (first edition, 1921, second edition, 1945), *Prelude and Songs* (1922–1923), *Autobiography* (1924), *The Captives* (1924), *Girls* (1925), *Figures and Songs* (1926), *Prelude and Flight* (1928–29), *A Dying Heart* (1925–30), *Little Berto* (1929–31), *Words* (1933–34), *Last Things* (1935–43), and *Mediterranean* (1947). In 1953 he began a short autobiographical novel, *Ernesto,* which was published posthumously in 1975. Saba considered himself faithful to poetic tradition, with a straightforward style that was different from the popular hermetic poetry of his time. He used poetry to cope with his frustrations and to reveal candidly his innermost feelings, as, for instance, in his early poem "To My Wife."

In 1946 Saba received his first great critical acclaim, the Viareggio Prize. His celebrity grew after that: He received an award from the Lincean Academy in 1951 and in 1953 an honorary degree from the University of Rome. In his acceptance speech Saba forgave the injustice done to him early in his academic career and said that the honor bestowed on him was a vindication for his maltreatment in high school. Throughout his life Saba suffered from mental illness and depression; his mental state declined precipitously from 1950 onward. He died at the age of 74 on August 25, 1957, in Gorizia, a year after the death of his wife.

BIBLIOGRAPHY

Saba, Umberto. *The Dark of the Sun: Selected Poems of Umberto Saba.* Translated by Christopher Millis. Lanham, Md.: University Press of America, 1994.

———. *An Anthology of His Poetry and Criticism.* Translated by Robert Harrison. Troy, Mich.: International Book Publishers, 1986.

———. *Songbook: Selected Poems from the Canzoniere of Umberto Saba.* Bilingual edition. Translated by Stephen Sartarelli. New York: Sheep Meadow Press, 1998.

Chris Picicci

SACHS, [LEONIE] NELLY (1891–1970)

Nelly Sachs was awarded the 1966 Nobel Prize in literature, along with S. Y. Agnon, for lifelong achievements in poetry. Her experience of World War II—according to the Nobel Foundation—"transformed her from a dilettante into a poignant spokesperson for the grief and yearnings of her fellow Jews." In her Nobel speech she commented that Agnon represented Israel but her poetry "represent[ed] the tragedy of the Jewish people."

Born in Berlin on December 10, 1891, Leonie Nelly Sachs was the only daughter of Margarete (née Karger) and William Sachs, a wealthy manufacturer. The family lived in the fashionable Tiergarten section of the city, During her early years Leonie was schooled at home by her parents and private tutors and in 1903 was enrolled in the Aubert Academy. But her family's extensive library was her first source of knowledge. Through her school years Leonie often expressed the desire to become a dancer. That passion did not interfere, however, with her pursuit of literary knowledge. When she was 15 years old, for example, she began an extensive correspondence with the Swedish writer Selma Lagerlöf, whose *Wonderful Adventures of Nils Holgersson* had just been published (a second part came out a year later, in 1907). Sachs completed her schooling in 1908. She lived at home, was unrequited by her only serious love, and never married. To the end she proved a devoted daughter to doting parents. She kept up her interests in music, dancing, and literature and continued her childhood practice of writing poetry.

Sachs's first book, *Legenden und Erzählungen* (Legends and Narrations, 1921), was written in a style similar to Lagerlöf's. It was followed by publication in various newspapers of some of her early poems, mostly written in a light romantic style. But Sachs's writing career did not begin in earnest until, with the help of friends Gudrun Harlan, Selma Lagerlöf, and the Swedish royal family, Nelly and her mother emigrated from Germany to Sweden in 1940 to escape Nazi persecution (her father had died in 1930 after a long illness). Sachs had just received orders to report to a Nazi work camp when her visa arrived, and she caught one of the last flights to Sweden before a clampdown on emigration, arriving on May 16, 1940. Once settled in Stockholm, she set about improving her Swedish language skills, made translations into German from Swedish (including the poetry of Gunnar Ekelöf, Johannes Edfelt, and Karl Vennberg), and continued writing. She became friends with HILDE DOMIN, INGEBORG BACHMANN, and PAUL CELAN, and in 1952 she became a Swedish citizen.

Sachs was 56 years old when her first major collection of poems was published in 1947: *In den Wohnungen des Todes* (In the Dwellings of Death), which included one of her most venerated poems, "O THE CHIMNEYS" ("*O die Schornsteine*"). As the Nobel Prize Committee put it, that book provided, "a cosmic frame for the suffering of her time, particularly that of the Jews." The Nobel Committee also observed, "Although her poems are written in a keenly modern style, with an abundance of lucid metaphors, they also intone the prophetic language of the Old Testament."

Most recent scholars of Sachs's poetry consider that she meant to transcend the Judaic tradition and emphasize her own, much broader version of human suffering and dislocation—and that she succeeded. In subsequent publications—*Sternverdunkelung* (Eclipse of Stars,

1949), *Und niemand weiß weiter* (And No One Knows Where to Go, *or* And No One Knows How to Go On, 1957), *Flucht und Verwandlung* (Flight and Metamorphosis, 1959), her collected poems titled *Fahrt ins Staublose* (Journey into Dustlessness, 1961), and her posthumous *Suche nach Lebenden* (Search for Living Persons, 1971)—Sachs's poetry becomes more personal, mystical, and visionary. "Writing was my mute outcry," she wrote; "I only wrote because I had to free myself" (*Contemporary Authors*). Her broad themes engage the human condition, anguish, metamorphosis, exile, and hope of redemption.

Sachs also wrote verse dramas, including *Zeichen im Sand* (Signs in the Sand, 1962), and her highly acclaimed miracle play in verse, *Eli,* first broadcast in West Germany over the radio. She received numerous prizes besides the Nobel, among them one from the Swedish Poets Association (1958), the Droste-Hülshoff Prize (1960), and the Friedenspreis des deutschen Buchhandels (Peace Prize of the German Book Trade, 1965). In her acceptance speech for the latter, she surprised the audience by saying, "In spite of all the horrors of the past, I believe in you." In 1967 an English-language version of selected poems and her play *Eli* (translated by various individuals) appeared under the title *O the Chimneys,* with an introduction by Sachs's friend Hans Magnus Enzensberger.

Nelly Sachs died of cancer on May 12, 1970, shortly after hearing of Paul Celan's suicide. Much of her correspondence and many of her papers, clippings, translations, and photographs are reposited at the Leo Baeck Institute and Center for Jewish History in New York City.

BIBLIOGRAPHY

Bower, Kathrin. *Ethics and Remembrance in the Poetry of Nelly Sachs and Rose Ausländer.* Studies in German Literature, Linguistics and Culture. Ontario: Camden House, 2000.

Rudnick, Ursula. *Post-Shoa Religious Metaphors: The Image of God in the Poetry of Nelly Sachs.* Bern, Switzerland: Peter Lang, 1995.

Sachs, Nelly. *Collected Poems I: 1944–1949.* Translated by Michael Hamburger, Ruth Mead, Matthew Mead, and Michael Roloff. Los Angeles: Green Integer, 2006.

———. *Collected Poems II: 1950–1969.* Translated by Michael Hamburger, Ruth Mead, Matthew Mead, and Michael Roloff. Los Angeles: Green Integer, 2004.

———. *O the Chimneys: Selected Poems, Including the Verse Play* Eli. New York: Farrar, Straus and Giroux, 1967.

———. *The Seeker, and Other Poems.* Bilingual edition. New York: Farrar, Straus and Giroux, 1970.

Turnheim, Ilse. "Guide to the Papers of Nelly Sachs (1891–1979)—1891–1992." Leo Baeck Institute and Center for Jewish History, New York City. Available online. URL: http://www.cjh.org/nhprc/NellySachs.html#a0. Accessed on April 27, 2007.

R. Victoria Arana

SAKUTARŌ HAGIWARA (1886–1942)

Sakutarō Hagiwara was born in Maebashi, Japan, in 1886, a year marked by popular unrest against the emperor Meiji's government, riots organized by the People's Rights Movement, efforts to liberalize the treatment of women, and reform movements in literature and the arts. The firstborn son of an affluent doctor of medicine, the boy grew up aware of his wider cultural surroundings but pampered by his wealthy parents and spoiled by his mother, Kei. He was allegedly so indulged that his domestic entourage gratified his every whim. Although he was still a schoolboy when YOSANO AKIKO's sensational *Midaregami* (TANGLED HAIR) was published in 1901, Sakutarō later credited that poem with inspiring him to be a poet. Just one year after Yosano's publication, Sakutarō's poetry was featured for the first time in his school magazine: five poems in the traditional 5-7-5-7-7-syllable *tanka* form. He continued producing *tanka* prolifically for another 10 years, then took up differing forms, pushing into new prosodic territories and inventing some of the stylistic features of *Shintai shi* (new-form poetry) and *Jiyu shi* (free-style poetry), becoming thereby, according to some, the inventor of modern Japanese poetry (*Kindai shi*).

In Tokyo, after repeatedly (and paradoxically) failing Japanese-language courses, he lived on his father's financial resources; attended plays, concerts, and other musical events; and took mandolin and guitar lessons. In 1913 five of his *shi* inspired by the poetry of Muro'o Saisei (1889–1962) appeared to high acclaim in *Zamuboa,* a prestigious Tokyo literary magazine. Following that he met TAKAMURA KŌTARŌ (1883–1956) and many other poets and intellectuals and in 1914 inaugurated Ningyo Shisha (Mermaid Poetry Society) to discuss music, literature, and culture. Sakutarō read Japanese poetry as well as European poetry and philosophy in translation, later citing 19th-century philosophers Arthur Schopenhauer and Friedrich Nietzsche, in particular, in his own critical writings. The years 1913–15 were his most productive and inspired, but they coincided with a period of self-diagnosed "nervous disease," which, he confessed, caused him great pain and produced nightmarish visions and hallucinations. For a time he quit poetry but returned to the limelight once again in 1917 with his first volume of poems, *Tsuki ni Hoeru* (Howling at the Moon). It was straightaway granted critical acclaim whether or not the Ministry of the Interior had censored and removed two poems for "disturbing social customs" (*Howling* 2002, 33). The remaining poems were still disturbing, only for a different reason. Sakutarō's imagery here is harrowingly bizarre, marked by memorable (because often quite deranged) juxtapositions of everyday things and natural processes. His poems—whether one line long, whether in verse or near-prose—seem not to be about their topical subject matter but instead about something else that the concrete images merely suggest through a private erotic symbolism, the meaning of which is ultimately impossible to pin down. His poetry has been compared to that of Charles Baudelaire, (*Howling* 2002, 33), but it is deeply Japanese, infused by a mood of *mononoaware* (wistful melancholy) over the tenacity yet transcience of all sorts of living things and the aesthetics of *yugen* (mystery, gloom, elegance, truth beyond human grasp). These qualities are evident in "SPRING NIGHT" and "THE OCTOPUS THAT DOES NOT DIE," which provides a telling example of Sakutarō's *Jiyu shi* prose-poetry.

Sakutarō's most famous poems are available in Hiroaki Sato's excellent English translations, reissued in 2002 as an affordable paperback along with Hiroaki's first-rate introduction to the poet's life and complete works.

BIBLIOGRAPHY

Sakutarō, Hagiwara. *Howling at the Moon: Poems of Hagiwara Sakutarō.* Translated and introduced by Hiroaki Sato. Tokyo: University of Tokyo Press, 1978.
———. *Shin Bungei Tokuhon: Hagiwara Sakutarō.* Introduction in Japanese by Hiroaki Sato. Tokyo: Kawade Shobō Shinsha, 1991.
———. *Howling at the Moon: Poems and Prose of Hagiwara Sakutarō.* Translated and introduced by Hiroaki Sato. Copenhagen and Los Angeles: Green Integer (#57), 2002.

R. Victoria Arana

SALKEY, ANDREW (1928–1995)

Felix Andrew Alexander Salkey was born in Colón, Panama, to Jamaican parents, raised in Jamaica from the age of two, and educated in Kingston. After emigrating to England in 1952, he worked for the BBC, appeared on the influential BBC radio program *Caribbean Voices,* earned a B.A. from the University of London in 1955, and taught Latin and English literature. In 1966, with John La Rose and EDWARD KAMAU BRATHWAITE, Salkey helped found the Caribbean Arts Movement and was instrumental in establishing and editing its journal, *Savacou.* From 1976 he taught at Hampshire College in Massachusetts, where he worked until his death in 1995.

Salkey's wide-ranging work includes short stories, poetry, novels, children's books, travel journals, and radio plays. Among his most famous poems are the epic JAMAICA, the collection *Away* (1980), and annual poems about Chile that Salkey wrote to memorialize that nation's 1973 coup d'état and subsequent existence under a fascist regime. He wrote several volumes of dialect stories featuring the Ashanti-derived spiderman Anancy, including *Anancy's Score* (1973), *Anancy, Traveller* (1992), and *Brother Anansi and Other Stories* (1993). His children's books include *Hurricane* (1960), *Jonah Simpson* (1969), *Joey Tyson* (1974–76?), *Earthquake* (1979), *The River That Disappeared* (1980), *Danny Jones* (1980), and *Riot* (1980). *Havana Journal* (1971) and *Georgetown Journal* represent his travel writing. His novels include *A Quality of Violence* (1959), *Escape to an Autumn Pavement* (1960), *The Late Emancipation of Jerry Stover* (1968, 1969), *Adventures of Catullus Kelly* (1969), and *Come Home, Malcolm Heartland* (1976). Salkey's many awards include the Thomas Holmes Poetry Prize in 1955 for the epic poem *Jamaica Symphony* (later published as *Jamaica*), the 1979 Casa de las Américas Poetry Prize for *In the Hills Where Her Dreams Live: Poems for Chile, 1973–1980,* and a Guggenheim Fellowship for his novel *A Quality of Violence* (1959). A collection of stories, *In the Border Country* (1998), was published posthumously.

Salkey supported and publicized the work of many West Indian writers and contributed numerous introductory essays for books and anthologies; in addition, he edited several collections of West Indian writing including *West Indian Stories* (1960), *Stories from the Caribbean* (1965), *Island Voices* (1970), *Breaklight* (1971), and *Caribbean Essays* (1973).

BIBLIOGRAPHY

Dance, Daryl Cumber. "Andrew Salkey." In *Fifty Caribbean Writers: A Bio-Bibliographical and Critical Sourcebook,* edited by Daryl Cumber Dance, 418–427. Westport, Conn.: Greenwood Press, 1986.

Morris, Mervyn. "Anancy and Andrew Salkey." *Jamaica Journal* 19, no. 4 (Nov. 1986/Jan. 1987): 39–42.

Walmsley, Anne. *The Caribbean Artists Movement, 1966–1972—A Literary and Cultural History*. London: New Beacon Books, 1992.

Alex Feerst

SALLAH, TIJAN M. (1958–)

Tijan Sallah—poet, essayist, biographer, anthologist, professor, and economist—represents a "third generation" of postcolonial African poets (Ojaide and Sallah 1–7) who "tap . . . their people's oral traditions and techniques" to generate poetic innovations. He also belongs to a generation of expatriate poets born on the African continent, educated in Africa and the United States, and successfully employed in careers outside of the academy. Sallah, a senior economist with the World Bank in Washington, D.C., pursues his creative writing in Potomac, Maryland. His professional expertise is in macro- and microeconomics—in particular, the rural development of water and other environmental resources for the Middle East and North African region. His dedication to literature, however, has been of much longer standing than his vocation as an economist. He began composing poetry while he was in secondary school in the Gambia, and he has since published in a broad spectrum of literary and associated genres: poetry, short stories, cultural monographs, as well as biographical and critical essays. While working at the World Bank, he put his spare time to the service of literature and collaborated with TANURE OJAIDE to produce *The New African Poetry: An Anthology* (1999) and with Ngozi Okonjo-Iweala to write a full-length study of CHINUA ACHEBE's life and development into a great moral leader: *Chinua Achebe, Teacher of Light: A Biography* (2003). Sallah's own poetry is noteworthy for its neomillennial combination of attributes: its chic cosmopolitan tone, its wide range of topics and responses to contemporary life, and its deep cultural and aesthetic roots in the Gambia.

Tijan Sallah was born in 1958 in Serekunda, his country's largest city, to a Wolof / Muslim family. As a child he received instruction in the Qur'an and attended Western elementary schools. His parents enrolled him in St. Augustine's High School (in Banjul, the capital city), an all-male Catholic missionary school run by Irish priests of the Holy Ghost Order. The curriculum was British, and students read the plays of Shakespeare, key works by canonic poets (e.g., the romantics and William Butler Yeats), classic novels (e.g., Robert Louis Stevenson and George Orwell), and the writings of James Joyce. It was just as compulsory to memorize literary texts as to memorize the facts of biology, chemistry, physics, and mathematics, but the young Sallah was undaunted: He was a brilliant student. When one of his favorite English teachers, the Reverend John Gough, praised his writing and encouraged him to "try [his] hand at poetry," the young man composed his first poem, "The African Redeemer," a tribute to Kwame Nkrumah, the first leader of independent Ghana.

In 1977 while still a teenager, Sallah traveled to Georgia in the United States to attend Rabun Gap Nacoochee High School for a year before enrolling at Berea College in Kentucky. Both the high school and the college are well known for their emphasis on agriculture and environmental policy. While an undergraduate at Berea, Sallah published his first collection of poems, *When Africa Was a Young Woman* (1980), an internationally acclaimed book.

After graduating with two bachelor's degrees from Berea, Sallah enrolled at Virginia Polytechnic Institute in Blacksburg, from which he earned an M.A. and a Ph.D. in economics (1987). In 1989 he joined the World Bank through its Young Professionals Program. All the while he wrote stories and poems, soon publishing a series of books in quick succession. His first collection of short stories, *Before the New Earth,* came out in 1988; a second volume of verse, *Kora Land,* appeared in 1989; a third collection, *Dreams of Dusty Roads: New Poems,* was published in 1993.

In his review of *Kora Land* for *World Literature Today,* David Dorsey noted the poet's "unaffected grace of feeling and expression" and the "quiet and clear [poetic] force" of his treatments of a broad spectrum of topics and images, including traditional customs, domestic and community roles, the Senegambian landscape, ancient African history, contemporary urban types—and even "rakes, brooms, refrigerators, head ties, World Bank statistics, Texaco gas stations, mango boughs, and sweaty armpits" (Winter 1990).

In his article "My Approach and Relation to Language," which appeared in *the Washington Review* (August–September 1993), Sallah defends his production and publication of poetry in English: "I, of course, would have liked to write in my own mother-tongue. Who would not? But the fact is that Wolof is not a written language"; nevertheless, "poetry is alive and well among the Wolof" bards and minstrels, who have inspired "the aesthetic and thought-patterns of such great African poets as Birago Diop and Léopold Senghor of Senegal." He adds that it is not necessarily a betrayal of one's mother-tongue to write in "an alien language—a colonial language"; any language "can be domesticated to serve one's own culture-specific" uses, or as he put it metaphorically: "English becomes my horse-of-speech. I ride it to my African destination."

In *Dreams of Dusty Roads,* for instance, a collection of contemporary poetry, his incantatory "Prayer for Roots" incorporates Gambian rhythms and parabolic wisdom steeped in African imagery, and his poem "Woman (for F. Haidara)" pays tribute to "a tall beauty of giraffe-grace" who is "Timbuktu" and whose head is anchored "on the rock of tradition." In these poems with crystalline language and sophisticated themes, Sallah does not hesitate to employ Wolof diction (e.g., *terranga* for Senegambian "hospitality"; *Kora jalos* for Mandinka "griots"). He also uses simple imagery, as in "Death of Roaches," to satirize greedy chiefs and those who steal and profit by association with them; nor does he refrain from the fun of mocking "Americans / And their self-congratulatory" behaviors, doing so by wittily imitating the rhythms and refrains of "Old MacDonald Had a Farm" ("Meditation on America").

Sallah's idea of a good poem is one that harnesses the "magical . . . sacred power" of words so intimately that they "speak to you as if the words run close to your heart" (Grayson 4). The four poets he considers "must reads" for young poets—regardless of who they are or where they live—are T. S. Eliot, WOLE SOYINKA, William Shakespeare, and CHRISTOPHER OKIGBO. Like them, Tijan Sallah is a poet attuned to the grip and subtleties of human interactions and to the rolling consequences of misapplied powers.

BIBLIOGRAPHY

Grayson, Sandra M. "An Interview with Tijan M. Sallah, Poet." *Network 2000: In the Spirit of the Harlem Renaissance* 4, 4 (Fall 1997): 1–4.

Ojaide, Tanure, and Tijan M. Sallah. *The New African Poetry: An Anthology.* Boulder, Colo., and London: Lynne Rienner, 1999.

Parekh, Pushpa Naidu, and Siga Fatima Jagne, eds. *Postcolonial African Writers: A Bio-Bibliographical Critical Sourcebook.* Westport, Conn.: Greenwood Press, 1998.

Sallah, Tijan. *Before the New Earth.* Calcutta, India: Writers Workshop, 1988.

———. *Dreams of Dusty Roads: New Poems.* Washington, D.C.: Three Continents Press, 1993.

———. *Kora Land.* Washington, D.C.: Three Continents Press, 1989.

———, ed. *New Poets of West Africa.* Lagos, Nigeria: Malthouse Press, 1995.

———. *When Africa Was a Young Woman.* Calcutta, India: Writers Workshop, 1980.

———. *Wolof: The Heritage Library of African Peoples.* New York: Rosen Publishing Group, 1996.

Sallah, Tijan, and Ngozi Okonjo-Iweala. *Chinua Achebe, Teacher of Light: A Biography.* Trenton, N.J.: Africa World Press, 2003.

R. Victoria Arana

SANGUINETI, EDOARDO (1930–) Edoardo Sanguineti was born in Genoa, Italy, in 1930. As a child he was misdiagnosed with a fatal heart disease, which prevented him from physical activity for many years. He received a degree in Italian literature at the University of Turin in 1956, with a thesis on Dante. For many years he was a professor of modern Italian literature (in Turin, Salerno, and Genoa).

Sanguineti has published widely and profusely in various genres: poetry, literary criticism (dealing with both medieval and modern Italian literature), novels, plays, and newspaper articles. He has also produced free translations and adaptations of Greek and Roman playwrights and of Dante, Ariosto, Goethe, and others, and he has edited important anthologies of poetry, especially one of 20th-century Italian poetry, *Poesia italiana del Novecento,* which features annotations from an avant-garde point of view. He has also participated in politics—both as a member of Genoa's city council and as a federal representative, as a member of the Communist Party. Communism and politics as a whole have greatly influenced Sanguineti and his idea of poetry for most of his long career. One of his heroes, as he explains in an interview, is Karl Marx (in addition to Charles Darwin and Sigmund Freud, who have significantly influenced him as well).

In 1956 Sanguineti's *Laborintus* was published and immediately made a great impression because of its rich, allusive, and difficult style. It is a long poem whose Jungian and dreamlike imagery dissolves in a linguistic magma of disconnected words and syntax, a polylinguistic (including Greek, Latin, French, and English) deconstructive jumble. The main character of the poem, Palus Putredinis, is a symbol of man in modern society, and the almost incomprehensible style reflects the poet's belief that no communication is possible in modern capitalistic society: Language has irrevocably degenerated.

In 1961 the influential anthology *I novissimi* (The Newest), edited by ALFREDO GIULIANI, made its decisive mark on postwar Italian poetry. This is the founding text of the neo-avant-garde, otherwise known as Gruppo 63 (Group 63), which viewed language as ideology (Sanguineti's motto is "language and ideology"). *I novissimi* breaks with much of the poetic tradition of the past (whether hermetic, crepuscular, or neorealist verse). Some of Sanguineti's *Laborintus* and other poems are included in this anthology.

In 1964 Sanguineti published *Triperuno,* a collection that contains a section of 17 poems titled *Purgatorio de l'inferno* (obviously influenced by Dante). This work signals a relative shift in Sanguineti's poetics. From now on he increasingly incorporates his own life in confessional poems that are, however, highly stylized by his ingenious use of language and languages. Here, by using his famous parentheses, which are ironic in function and conflate the seriousness of what follows, he manages to avoid sentimentality and frigidity when he writes, for example: "(and i wanted to say, but tears almost suffocated / me, really; i wanted to say: with a love like ours, we): / one day (we);" . . . "(we) must die."

In *Reisebilder* (Travel Notebooks, 1971) Sanguineti's poetry once again takes an autobiographical turn in which he says to his wife, "(but tonight, before we discuss whether or not to have a fourth child, / I'll explain to you two passages from the [Communist] *Manifesto*)." He tells her that he is now "that obscene middle-aged faun" and imagines himself a "double of a mediocre English comic." Much of the poetry alludes to daily events and conversations, and in Sanguineti's poetic shorthand it is often difficult to understand exactly what he is referring to.

In *Postkarten* (Postcards, 1978) Sanguineti pretends to give us his poetics for the first time. A poet, he says, writes poetry so that another after his death can continue the project, because "we [poets] try to write the complete works of the human race, all together." This is similar to Shelley's idea that all writers write together one great poem. Yet in another poem Sanguineti distances himself from such an exalted conception and speaks of writing a "very quotidian" poetry. His style is "to have none." Today poetry is "still practicable, probably," even though we live in times of "distracted perception." In another of these "postcards" he says that he will leave five words: *Non ho creduto im niente* ("I haven't believed in anything").

By the time he published *Stracciafoglio* (1980), it is clear that Sanguineti believes "a poem is corrected by another poem, a corollary with a codicil." He defines himself as an "aspiring historical materialist." He was born with an instinct for cataloging the "polymorphous" universe, because the world is a "permanent exhibition." For this reason, to preserve and to catalog, he lives in the "perpetual, minute recuperation of little pieces lost to life, lost from sight" (*perpetuo, minuzioso recupero di minuzie perdute di vita [e di vista]*). This indeed is the raison d'être of his poetry: a Proustian preservation of memory against time.

In *Scartabello* (Notebook) and *Cataletto* (Coffin), both published in 1981, Sanguineti again addresses his wife, his children, and also the reader, writing about his travels, politics, family, and daily life. Half tongue-in-cheek, he says that letters (epistolary texts) are the real literature. "I am my letters, in essence . . . / I am the surrogate of myself." Many of his poems read like snippets from letters, diary entries, and so forth. In another poem he makes fun of the assumption that changing spectacles will change one's view of the world. He may have hoped "to be able to give myself, at a cheap price, another life and another visual perspective," but "nothing has become better for me . . . / and I am always myself." Moreover, he cannot even reread his work, his "hemorrhage of words," for fear of intoxicating himself (and he warns his readers thus to beware). And yet Sanguineti was becoming slowly reconciled to the world, despite his "native deep horror" of what exists.

In 1987 Sanguineti published *Bisbidis,* which contains *"Codicillo"* ("Codicil"), *"Rebus,"* *"L'ultima passeggiata"* ("The Last Walk"), and *"L'alfabeto apocalittico"* ("Apocalyptic Alphabet"). He begins by stating that he is writing (and living) "for future memory." He becomes a grandfather and appropriately writes a poem about the experience of seeing his grandson; he calms him with similar sounds as he did his own child, a time that seems to him "a century ago." Now he follows only this *"basso bisbis di un bisbidis, che mi ronza qui dentro, debolmente, senza neanche più, diventarmi parola, frase, verso"* (low murmur of a whisper, which buzzes here inside of me, weakly, without any longer becoming for me a word, phrase, verse). *"L'alfabeto apocalittico"* is a genial riff on language and utter playfulness at work, as in C : *"celibe è il cosmo, in chiara crisi cronica, / cubo cilindro & circumsfera conica"* (celibate is the cosmos, in clear chronic crisis, / cylindric cube & conic circumsphere). *L'ultima passeggiata,* an operetta, is an homage to the Italian poet Giovanni Pascoli.

In *Senzatitolo* (Without Title), which appeared in 1992 and includes *"Glosse"* (Glosses), *"Novissimum testamentum"* (Newest Testament), and *"Omaggio a Catullo"* (Homage to Catullus), Sanguineti's poetic gift finally reaches its apex in a serious (and tragic) poem, *"Novissimum testamentum,"* in which he says: "publicly I declare and certify / that for ever I renounce the universe." He has no fear of his fears, because the fact that "nothing is born again gives me courage." To his wife he leaves "words of love," so that when he has "a tongue of ashes and dust, / with four vocal cords of worms," it will provide her some comfort. *"Glosse,"* meanwhile, continues the line of diaristic poetry in which Sanguineti analyzes and decomposes language. In his poem about *"noi"* (we), he shows how this little pronoun is, for his wife and himself, "our anagram and drama." In *"Omaggio a Catullo,"* which contains some lovely translations from the Latin poet, Sanguineti interpolates himself into the poetry.

In 1996 Sanguineti published *Corollario* (Corollary), in which he entreats his readers to incise the following on his grave: *"Me la sono goduta, io, la mia vita"* (I've enjoyed my life fully). In another poem he speaks of going to a temple of Aphrodite: ". . . I greedily plunged my hand, trembling and nude . . . / underneath a rare altar, inside the tiny frozen abyss of that vulva of truth." The communist themes have disappeared, and Sanguineti portrays himself and his family. In *Cose* (2001), Sanguineti speaks of himself and his wife (his "paradise of paradises") as "hourglasses, with all the sand in the bottom." Yet he desires so much to live now, having understood that "it is an epic drama, to be sure, to succeed in taking leave, decorously, from this now planetary museum." The imperative is "eat, drink, and above all, fuck." He tells his wife, his *"diletissima complice"* (most delightful accomplice): "I am a wolf-like cat, ugly, and joyful" (*sono un gatto lupesco, e laido, e lieto*). His latest poems pay homage to Johann Wolfgang von Goethe and William Shakespeare. It remains to be seen whether he, like his poetic predecessors Giorgio Caproni or Franco Fortini, will write those icily essential poems of old age. In any case, for this poet whose greatest sorrow would be to "die without a brief period of consciousness," he will not leave the stage in any sort of pathetic or bathetic way.

BIBLIOGRAPHY

Ballerini, L., B. Cavatorta, E. Coda, and P. Vangelisti, eds. *The Promised Land: Italian Poetry after 1975.* Los Angeles: Sun and Moon Press, 2000.

Sanguineti, Edoardo. *Libretto.* Translated by Padraig J. Daly. Dublin: Daedalus, 1999.

———. *Natural Stories #1.* Translated by Jana O'Keefe Bazzioni. Toronto: Guernica, 1998.

Jacob Blakesley

SARO-WIWA, KENULE (KEN) BEESON

(1941–1995) Ken Saro-Wiwa was a controversial individual who actively propagated any cause he identified with. Even though Saro-Wiwa came to be known in various parts of the world only as a result of the global protests that trailed his kangaroo trial and his eventual execution by hanging in 1995, he is one of the most controversial and versatile writers to have come out of Nigeria. His execution (brought about by the Sani Abacha-led junta) was widely condemned for its lack of transparency and fairness, and it terminated an eventful and promising career.

A poet, novelist, dramatist, humorist, television producer, businessman, publisher, politician, scholar, and ethnic rights activist, Saro-Wiwa gave expression to his conviction and died in the process of promoting the cause of the Ogoni, his ethnic group. He had condemned the government's neglect of his people's economic plight in oil-producing areas of Nigeria and its indifference to the ecological disasters that further impoverished them.

Born Kenule Beeson Tsaro-Wiwa on October 10, 1941, in Bori, he grew up on Ogoni land. He studied English at the University of Ibadan and was later appointed assistant lecturer there. When the Nigerian civil war broke out in 1966, he relocated to the east and accepted a faculty appointment at the University of Nigeria, Nsukka. He could not cope with the hostility of his colleagues, who were mainly Igbo nationalists, and had to leave Nsukka when the Republic of Biafra was declared in 1967. He returned to his Ogoni homeland, where he was a secondary school teacher and also started a transport business. He then accepted an appointment as a teaching assistant at the University of Lagos. At age 26 in 1976, he was appointed administrator of Bonny Island during the civil war when he identified with the federal side against the Biafran secessionists. He later was a commissioner in his home state and served in various ministries until 1973, when he was relieved of his duties due to his disagreement with the military administrator.

Following that Saro-Wiwa founded various businesses. He set up Saros International Publishers, which issued most of his own titles. His popular comedy television series *Basi and Company,* broadcast on the network service of the Nigerian Television Authority, was watched by an estimated 30 million viewers. He also served as president of the Association of Nigerian Authors. Saro-Wiwa spent the last years of his life in organizing the Ogoni to agitate for self-determination in the face of injustice and neglect. He was responsible for the formation of the pan-Ogoni organization Movement for the Survival of Ogoni People. He mobilized international support for agitations and confrontations with law enforcement agencies and incited the anger of General Sani Abacha, the military dictator who presided over his trial by a special tribunal and ordered his hanging.

Saro-Wiwa was better known as a fiction writer and a dramatist than poet. His only published book of poetry is a slim collection of just 20 poems. His work gives expression to his convictions, especially to his perception of Nigeria. His best-known work is probably *Sozaboy,* a novel "written in rotten English" that is critical of the various clandestine motives behind the Nigerian civil war. His collection of short stories, *A Forest of Flowers,* is also remarkable: Here he presents the war from the perspective of females of the minority groups and shows it to be from their perspective a needless and unreasonable project.

His only collection of poems, *Songs in a Time of War,* includes poems about the Nigerian civil war. The collection explores various experiences related to the war, but, surprisingly, the poet-persona betrays no serious emotion about it. His concern, as stated in the first poem of the collection, is to sing of his love for Maria, his wife. Many of the poems paint familiar scenes of war and of losses associated with war and its perpetrators—destruction and unimaginable pain and denial—but the poems affirm that those far from the theater of war can still enjoy the pleasures of life, love, and longings. While most of the poems are written in standard English, "DIS NIGERIA SEF," the longest and last poem in the collection, is written in Nigerian pidgin.

BIBLIOGRAPHY

McLuckie, Craig W., and Aubrey McPhail, eds. *Ken Saro-Wiwa: Writer and Political Activist.* Boulder, Colo., London: Lynne Rienne, 2000.

Na' Allah, Abdul-Rasheed, ed. *Ogoni's Agonies: Ken Saro-Wiwa and the Crisis in Nigeria.* Trenton, N.J.: Africa World Press, 1998.

Ojo-Ade, Femi. *Ken Saro-Wiwa: A Bio-critical Study.* New York and Lagos, Nigeria: Africana Legacy, 1999.

Saro-Wiwa, Ken. *Songs in a Time of War.* Port Harcourt, Nigeria: Saros International, 1985.

Oyeniyi Okunoye

SATIN SLIPPER, THE PAUL CLAUDEL (1925)

The Satin Slipper (*Le Soulier de satin*), subtitled "The Worst is Not the Surest," is an epic verse drama by French poet, dramatist, and diplomat PAUL CLAUDEL. He began writing the play after a diplomatic assignment in Brazil in 1918 and completed the work in 1925 (despite losing the manuscript of act 3 during an earthquake in Japan in 1923). The full play runs some 11 hours and has rarely been performed in unabridged form (although the complete work was staged, most recently, in Edinburgh, Scotland, in August 2004). As in his other dramas and much of his poetry, Claudel focuses on illicit love, religious faith, and the interaction of the transcendent spiritual world with that of the flawed and limited human sphere.

The drama is set in late 15th-century Spain, where the protagonist, Rodrigue, falls madly in love with a married woman, Prouhèze, who is in an arranged marriage with Don Pélage—a husband whom she admires but does not love. After discovering his wife's love for Don Rodrigue, Pélage takes his wife on a military mission to North Africa to quell a rebellion. Before they leave, she offers her satin slipper to the Virgin Mary with the hope that the Virgin will protect her from committing sin. Throughout the play the forces of history, as Catholic Spain expands its empire abroad, conspire to keep the two lovers forever separated and their love unconsummated. Though the work is ostensibly about divine grace and the triumph of religious faith, it also contains Eurocentric elements and racist overtones, which modern audiences may find disturbing.

The diversity of places, the lyrical beauty (influenced by the biblical psalms and Catholic liturgy), the large cast, and complex action—despite the heavy theological flavor of the work—draw the audience into the play and unfold a vast religious-historical panorama of the late 15th century. *The Satin Slipper* also marks Claudel's apotheosis in dealing creatively with the trauma of his youthful love affair with the married Polish woman Rosalie Vetch. He seems with this play to have taken the emotional distresses he suffered during and after that affair and related them to the sufferings of Christ, whose divine love expanded throughout the world. The lovers Rodrigue and Prouhèze represent the ideal renunciation of earthly love and desire for the higher forms, the love of God and of religious faith.

Joseph E. Becker

"SATURDAY IN THE SAND-SLUMS" AGOSTINHO NETO (1974?)

This poignant and painful poem, one of AGOSTINHO NETO 's longest, documents in stark detail the conditions of life for poor Africans in the shantytowns surrounding Angola's capital city, Luanda. The poem "*Sabado nos musseques,*" expresses the anxieties experienced by the poor. The word *anxiety* occurs throughout, appearing as an angry shout as the poet articulates the numerous manifestations of alienation, fear, and deprivation—emotional and psychological as well as material—afflicting the poor residents of the slums. These anxieties, rooted in poverty, exclusion, and colonial oppression, are embodied in almost every aspect of life, in both the surrounding social environment as well as specific activities undertaken as people try to escape the circumstances of daily life in the shantytown.

Anxiety is stirred by material deprivations such as the lack of running water and electricity or the lack of proper building materials for housing: "Anxiety / in the skeleton of stick and mud / bent threateningly / as it bears the weight of the zinc roof // and in the backyards / sown with excrement and foul smells / in the grease-stained sticks of furniture / in the streets full of holes / and in beds without matresses." Poverty is part of the general state of anxiety expressed in the presence of police and soldiers assailing the populace ("Anxiety / in the lowly child / who flees in fear from the policeman / on duty"), by adults molesting children, in partners fighting over old debts, and in domestic disputes over household finances. This anxiety comes to encompass the very being of all who experience it: "Anxiety / in those who laugh and in those who cry / in those who have insight / and in those who have breath but no understanding."

The poem is an indictment of the exploitation suffered by Angolans under the apartheid of Portuguese colonialism. At the same time it sounds a note of hopefulness in the sense of purpose growing within the shantytown: "Saturday jumbled night / in the townships / with mystical anxiety / and implacably / marches on unfurling heroic banners / in the enslaved souls." The poem gives life to Neto's belief that in resistance people might turn despair into defiance and deliverance: "In men / burns the desire to make the supreme effort / so that Man / shall be reborn in every man / and hope / shall turn no longer / into the lamentation of the crowd." This rebirth is for Neto the promise of liberation and socialism.

BIBLIOGRAPHY

Appiah, Anthony Kwame. "Antonio Agostinho Neto (1922–1979)." In *The Poetry of Our World: An International Anthology of Contemporary Poetry,* edited by Jeffery Paine, 341–353. New York: HarperCollins, 2001.

Neto, Antonio Agostinho. "Saturday in the Sand-Slums." Translated by Michael Wolfers. In *The Poetry of Our World: An International Anthology of Contemporary Poetry,* edited by Jeffery Paine, 345–352. New York: HarperCollins, 2001.

J. Shantz

"SAY IT SOFTLY—" ELSE LASKER-SCHÜLER (1911)

Published in her volume *My Miracles*, "Leise Sagen" ("Say It Softly—") embodies LASKER-SCHÜLER's greatest expressionist achievements. She combines extraordinary, unconventional imagery with simplicity of form to render love as both spirited frisson and melancholic surrender. The title, along with its distinguishable poetic subject and addressee, posits a conception of the poem as intimate space, casting the reader at once as welcomed listener and awkward interloper.

"You took for yourself all the stars / Above my heart." In the first couplet of this love poem, Lasker-Schüler already makes use of stars and hearts—symbols that recur throughout her lyrical work. These symbols, far from giving shape to an intimate setting of union, however, signal an act of violation, while at the same time evoking an intense visual shift from light to darkness. This image prefigures Lasker-Schüler's perception of the twin dimensions of love—at once joyful, impul-sive, and frenetic, while also demanding and depleting. The following couplet, with its astonishingly evocative verse "My thoughts are curling" conveys playful glee, only to be followed by verses that reveal a countervailing force that renders desire exhausting and almost unmanageable. The expressiveness of the usual noun-verb pairings is exemplified once more with the image of the archangel's eyes that, once stolen, serve not as something with which to see, nor to be looked into, but as objects for consumption: "I nibble on the honey / Of their blueness." More precisely, their blueness is enjoyed with the sense of taste.

The relationship established in the poem's beginning couplets sustains a sense of the lover as both frenetic and submissive; that is, the first five verses sit as if temporally or causally independent of one another, unconnected by conjunctions, adverbs, or punctuation, almost as if interchangeable. Love appears at first to be less of a process and more a group of events unbounded by causality. Just as the poem effects a subtle loosening of the chronology of erotic unfolding, it also appears to set into question the integrity of the poetic subject. Distinguished as the central couplet in the poem's economy, the often-quoted verse "No more do I find my image / In the mirror of the streams" invites the reader to understand that along with this process of surrender in eroticism belongs the loss of self or, more accurately, the subject's own failure to perceive self. In a provocative twist the poem's two final couplets both reinforce and undermine the poetic subject's sense of disintegrated self in love by attributing "substance" to the subject, while at the same time bearing witness to the subject's deconstruction at the very moment of contact.

"*Leise sagen*—" became the center of a legal controversy when the newspaper *Hamburger Blatt* accompanied a printing of the poem with the disparaging characterization of Lasker-Schüler's lyrical style: "a complete softening of the brain." In defense of his wife, Herwarth Walden brought legal action against the newspaper and published a scathing piece in the July 1912 issue of his magazine *Sturm* (Storm), culminating with the declaration: "After all, art requires love" ("Deutsche Dichter und Deutsche Richter." *Der Sturm* 3 (July 1912): 102–104).

BIBLIOGRAPHY

Lasker-Schüler, Else. *Your Diamond Dreams Cut Open My Arteries: Poems by Else Lasker-Schüler.* Translated by Robert P. Newton. Chapel Hill: University of North Carolina Press, 1982, 135.

Michele Ricci

"SCHOONER *FLIGHT,* THE" DEREK WALCOTT (1979)

This quest poem fuses DEREK WALCOTT's highly metaphoric style with distinctly Caribbean Creole speech patterns. The narrator, a poet/sailor named Shabine, speaks English Creole, declaring, "Well, when I write / this poem, each phrase go be soaked in salt." This use of English Creole marks a shift in Walcott's poetic practice. In his early poetry Walcott's poetics echoed the modernist style of W. B. Yeats, T. S. Eliot, and W. H. Auden and stood in contrast to that of EDWARD KAMAU BRATHWAITE, among others, who sought to create a poetics based on the Caribbean folk tradition. With "The Schooner *Flight,*" however, Walcott combines traditional English versification, such as iambic pentameter, with a distinctly Caribbean voice.

Shabine, like Walcott, has mixed racial ancestry and consequently feels alienated in Trinidad following the failed black power revolution of 1970: "I have Dutch, nigger, and English in me / and either I'm nobody or I'm a nation." The poem begins with Shabine taking work on the schooner *Flight* to escape his self-destructive relationship with his mistress, Maria Concepcion, and the government officials for whom he has been smuggling liquor. Walcott echoes the opening of the medieval religious allegory *Piers Plowman,* "In summer season, when soft was the sun," with the first line, "In idle August, while the sea soft." This allusion signals that Shabine's journey has spiritual as well as physical dimensions. His experience is simultaneously an individual quest for identity and peace and the collective project of founding a Caribbean culture not deformed by corrupt government practices or the legacy of colonialism.

In the 11 parts of the poem Shabine witnesses both the beauty and the pain intrinsic to Caribbean life. He sees fishermen living in harmony with nature as they pull their nets from the sea at sunset. He also meets his white grandfather, who refuses to acknowledge him. Along with this personal slight connected to colonial racism, Shabine experiences the communal pain inflicted by colonial history. While sailing through fog, Shabine sees the ghosts of the Middle Passage, and off the coast of Dominica he witnesses the extermination of the Carib Indians in a visionary dream. Finally, he faces death when a storm threatens to drown the schooner. This crisis of the natural world enables him to acknowledge his faith in God and the healing power of the Caribbean natural world: After the storm the sea is compared to paradise. Shabine finds peace in achieving the artistic representation of Caribbean culture: "I am satisfied / if my hand gave voice to one people's grief." "The Schooner *Flight*" ends with the image of spiritual renewal found in the beauty of nature, which Walcott's poetry suggests is available to all who live in the Caribbean.

BIBLIOGRAPHY

Breslin, Paul. *Nobody's Nation: Reading Derek Walcott.* Chicago: University of Chicago Press, 2001.
Hamner, Robert D., ed. *Critical Perspectives on Derek Walcott.* Washington, D.C.: Three Continents Press, 1993.
Walcott, Derek. "The Schooner *Flight.*" In *Collected Poems 1948–84.* New York: Farrar, Straus and Giroux, 1986.

Eugene Johnson

"SCHUBERTIANA" TOMAS TRANSTRÖMER (1978)

Published in 1978, "Schubertiana," a poem from TOMAS TRANSTRÖMER's eighth volume of poems, *Sanningsbarriären* (Truth Barriers), explores the ways in which music functions as an antidote to the fragmentation that often defines contemporary life. As typically happens in Tranströmer's work, the poem's five sections treat a wide range of disparate images but cohere by touching at least briefly on a central theme, in this case the music of Austrian composer Franz Schubert. The poem describes a modern world in which people are isolated and fragmented, appearing either as disembodied hands or as bodies made anonymous by urban sprawl. In their isolation they encounter threats to their physical and emotional well-being, ranging from car accidents to duplicitous individuals to anonymous murderers. Tranströmer suggests that like the signal that enables the migrating swallow to home in a specific location across thousands of miles, the music of

Schubert provides an almost intuitive means of orienting oneself in an alien and alienating environment. For Tranströmer aesthetic experience in general and music in particular is a liberating force because its evocative power calls people out of the mental space in which they feel they must defend themselves against external threats and leads them into a space in which they may connect to and experience a communion with something outside of themselves. The poem concludes with an extended image that captures all of these forces: Two people sit at a piano playing Schubert together, and while the mechanics of their playing may be awkward, through their playing they achieve a state in which "happiness and suffering weigh just the same." Furthermore, Tranströmer notes that while the two feel that the music acts as a kind of mirror for them, a source of confirmation sorely lacking in the world he describes, such is not the case for those associated with the divisiveness he outlines elsewhere in the poem. These people, who "believe that everybody can be bought," fail to draw sustenance from Schubert: "they don't recognize themselves here," he writes, because "it's not their music."

BIBLIOGRAPHY

Tranströmer, Tomas. "Schubertiana." Translated by Samuel Charters, in *Tomas Tranströmer: Selected Poems 1954–1986,* edited by Robert Hass. Hopewell, N.J.: Ecco Press, 1987, 143–144.

Sean McDonnell

SCREAMS Joyce Mansour (1953)   Joyce Mansour's first volume of verse, *Cris* (inarticulate expressions of pain, rage, or surprise; but also, *cris de bataille,* battle cries), brought her to the immediate attention of France's literati—in particular to the attention of male surrealists who found in her poetry a stunning instance of what André Breton identified as the primary objective of art: to present revolutionary, liberating truths as experienced in the unconscious. Mansour's debut collection dealt the patriarchal, bourgeois culture of the 1950s a swift kick in the pants by flouting all sorts of conventions established by polite society to restrain female expression and govern female behavior. As the expression of radical feminist thought at mid-century,

Mansour's poetry—in its alternately confrontational, subversive, and swaggering postures—went miles beyond Simone de Beauvoir's groundbreaking *The Second Sex* (1947). At the same time, this collection of Mansour's poems is not merely bellicose; it is also a rare example of feminist existentialist philosophy rendered as a profusion of lyrical cries (not really plaintive) meant to command serious attention to the true existence (the genuine emotional lives and physical desires) of women.

Mansour's poetry is "brazen" (as Gavronsky avers) and committed to overturning even the most admirable liberating efforts of the surrealists, primarily because, in her view, the most revolutionary artists of her day (Breton, Paul Éluard, René Char, and Louis Aragon) were constitutionally unable to recognize that their sexist upbringings and patriarchal culture were blinding them to a vast multitude of humanity: the personal (especially erotic) world of women. The male surrealists' depictions of the erotic lives of women were always tasteful, allusive, mythological: "a highly literary enterprise . . . audacious . . . but [ultimately] writerly" (Gavronsky, *Torn Apart,* 1). It was Mansour's project to map what Gavronsky calls "the iconic topos of sex, in all its *jouissance* [juicy joyfulness] and grandeur" (*Torn Apart,* 1). Mansour would avail herself of poetic devices of all sorts but resort to no indirection, no euphemism.

Cris, in Gavronsky's translation, is composed of 50 pages of short units, two to a page, and most of them only seven or eight lines long. Each of these units, or stanzas, is an exclamation or expostulation. Many of them rely on images that seem at first innocuous but that on closer inspection divulge a nightmarish subtext. In one of them, for example, the first four lines say: "Seashell drags across a deserted beach / Caressed by a finger distracted by the sea / Leaving behind a mucous trail / Attracting the enemy despite itself." The image of the moving shell and shoreline setting (evoked by the words *seashell* and *deserted beach*) establishes an odd context for the distracted, caressing finger in the second line. The third line, with its reference to "mucous trail," suggestively blurs the signifying properties of the erotic words in the preceding lines (*caressed, attracting*). The assertion that the "mucous trail" attracts the mollusc's enemy seems factual enough, whether or not it is biologically accurate. The fifth through final lines, however, abruptly shift the topos: "He comes closer immobilizing her with a sneaky hand / He takes her soul from its tender bed / And inhales her agony" (48). Seagulls do not have "sneaky" hands. Moreover, by aggressively gendering and animating the mollusk ("her soul" . . . "her agony") as well as the raptor (whoever "He" is), Mansour has dramatized (in phantasmagorical terms) a male's soul-destroying seduction and consumption of a female too young or innocent (tender) to realize what was happening to her.

Mansour closes *Cris* with the following polysemic declaration: "Men's vices / are my domain / Their wounds my sweet desserts / I love to chew on their vile thoughts / For their ugliness makes my beauty" (50). In just five lines the concluding unit of *Cris* emphasizes what the oneiric imagery in the body of the work connotes.

BIBLIOGRAPHY

Mansour, Joyce. *Screams*. Translated and with an introduction by Serge Gavronsky. Sausalito, Calif.: Post-Apollo Press, 1995.

———. *Torn Apart / Déchirures*. Bilingual edition. Translated and with an introduction by Serge Gavronsky. Fayetteville, Ark., and New York: Bitter Oleander Press, 1999.

R. Victoria Arana

"SCYTHIANS, THE" ALEKSANDR BLOK (1918)

"The Scythians" is ALEKSANDR BLOK's last significant poem, composed from and for a particular moment in history. It forms part of the "January Trilogy" of 1918, together with "The Twelve" and the essay "The Intelligentsia and the Revolution."

Revolutionary Russia had been trying to withdraw from World War I. "The Scythians" was published on the day the government accepted the German terms for a separate peace. Hopes were running high in Russia, although it was forced to cede large areas to Germany. Many were convinced that the revolution would spread, first to Germany and then to the rest of Europe and possibly the world. Blok's poem reflects a utopian hope that the world revolution was imminent and that Russia was going to take the lead, putting an end to warfare and the suffering of the oppressed: "Come . . . / into our peaceful arms! . . . / Comrades! We shall be brothers!"

Blok combines this messianic role ascribed to Russia with the idea of an impending Asian invasion of Europe that would sweep away the spiritually degraded old civilization. This idea, as well as the perception of Russia as a shield between Europe and the East, is based on ideas developed by Vladimir Solovyov in the 1890s. Russia, he affirms, is both European and Asian, and while Europe has for centuries been looking "derisively" at backward Russia, "Russia is a Sphinx." In "The Scythians" Mother Russia is prepared to give up her mediating role and turn against the West. The poet delivers a stark warning to Europe to play fair, promising that those who are with Russia will eventually share her peace. But those who try to destroy the revolution are calling her wrath upon themselves, and like a changeling Russia will "turn an Asiatic mask to you" and open wide the floodgates to the East. Blok's East/West opposition is spiritual rather than geographical. He glorifies revolutionary violence, symbolized by the Scythians' "impulsive ardour" and cannibalism, as the birth pangs of the victory of the generous Russian spirit that encompasses everything (including "the Frenchman's shaft / of wit, the German's genius . . .").

Like "The Twelve" before it, "The Scythians" is an attempt at capturing and communicating the hidden harmony, which the poet has "heard" in the chaotic events of the revolution. But its musicality is fundamentally different from that of "The Twelve." "The Scythians" consists of 19 quatrains, nine of which end in an exclamation point. While "The Twelve" is essentially narrative and comprises different moods and melodies, "The Scythians" is a sustained admonition listing the "Asiatic" elements of the Russian character and ending in an open threat. Rhyme scheme (abab) and meter stay the same throughout the poem. The title and the poem can be read as a metaphor for Russia and its fate, reminiscent of the prophecy in the 1910 cycle "On Kulikovo Field." However, the Blok of "The Scythians" is no remote prophet but the voice of Russia itself (or so he thinks), and this voice is collective: "Yes, we are Scythians!"

BIBLIOGRAPHY

Blok, Aleksandr. *Selected Poems*. Translated by John Stallworthy and Peter France. Manchester, U.K.: Carcanet, 2000.

Josephine von Zitzewitz

"SECRET GERMANY" STEFAN GEORGE (1928)

This poem forms the central piece of GEORGE's last volume, *Das neue Reich* (The Kingdom Come, 1928), and combines the poet's central themes: autobiographical recollection, a fierce critique of modern society, the invocation of poetic ancestors and heroes, allusions to World War I, and commonalities between Germany's potential and ancient Greece. The poem also brings together the forms to which George was most dedicated: hymns, dramatic voices, and epigrammatic lines addressed to friends (so-called *Sprüche*).

The initial invocation is addressed not to the Muses but to the abyss. Confronting the most extreme form of negation permits the poet to see how modern man is trapped in a greedy and shameless lifestyle, oblivious to any determining force in his life. This confrontation opens up a "new sphere" granted by the gods as an alternative to a world of systems and norms, of speed and distraction. The poet, upon his return home from the Mediterranean coast, finds this sphere embodied in seven figures who represent experiences or encounters that transcend everyday routine. Six of the seven figures can be identified as friends or former friends of George. Each of the six friends was in a certain way an outsider, and so was the seventh (who appears first), the archaeologist Hans von Prott, who in 1903 committed suicide in Greece. The hymn concludes with the warning that what society at present values most will vanish, and any hope for imminent renewal is shown to be in vain.

"*Geheimes Deutschland*" reflects George's (and modernity's) discovery of German lyric poet Friedrich Hölderlin's late hymns. Hölderlin's influence on George is fundamental but deliberately obscured. George's lines about the disappearance of gods and their possible return, however cautiously framed, were considered dangerously ambivalent in the 1920s. Its trocheo-dactylic meter places the poem neatly within the classical tradition. The language is deliberately difficult (with its elision of prefixes, sometimes ambiguous grammatical structures, rare diction, and absolute metaphors), but its difficulty emphasizes the poem's distance from everyday life and is designed to make the reader reflect on his or her own life. The title has been taken to be synonymous with the circle of George's friends, but there are crucial differences, such as the fact that George's circle was never kept secret.

BIBLIOGRAPHY

George, Stefan. *The Works of Stefan George. Rendered into English by Olga Marx and Ernst Morwitz*. 2d rev. and enlarged ed. Chapel Hill: University of North Carolina Press, 1974, 371–374.

Christophe Fricker

SEFERIS, GEORGE (GIORGIOS SEFERIADIS) (1900–1971)

George Seferis is the pen name of one of Greece's most famous 20th-century poets. Well known as a diplomat, statesman, lawyer, and political figure in the international arena, Seferis was also a highly respected novelist and poet outside of his country, and his poetry was translated into many languages. He is recognized by students of Greek literary history for the stylistic purity of his poems, but his poetry is not easily accessible and—with its riddlelike simplicity—resembles the challenging, oblique discourse of the French symbolists. Even his sparse (and often very short) poetry is densely erudite, forged out of allusions to Greek history and legend and incorporating hints of his modern vision for the Greek nation. The linguistic simplicity is deceptive, especially in English translation, which has no clear way of conveying the differing registers of Greek speech. Despite these difficulties Seferis's poetry is alluring. Reading it one feels in the presence of a sophisticated intelligence with high aesthetic standards. Seferis was awarded the Nobel Prize in literature in 1963.

Giorgios Seferiadis was born to Stelios and Despo Seferiadis in Smyrna (now Izmir, Turkey) on February 29, 1900. At 14 he moved with his family to Athens and enrolled in secondary school. From 1918 to 1924 he studied in Paris, where he earned a law degree. He was 24 when he visited England for the first time and only 26 when he began his career in the Greek Ministry of Foreign Affairs. In 1941 he married Maria Zannou. When the Communist Party of Greece took control, he accompanied the Greek government-in-exile to Crete, Egypt, and South Africa, where he served in the Greek embassy in Pretoria. He was press officer to the Greek government in Cairo, Egypt, from 1942 to 1944 and accompanied the Greek government-in-exile to Italy in 1944. During World War II he held the position of director of the political bureau of the regent Archbishop Damaskinos. After the war he resumed his diplomatic career and was appointed to a new series of ambassadorships. His diplomatic assignments took him to many posts worldwide, including England, Albania, Italy, Egypt, Turkey, Lebanon, Syria, Jordan, Iraq, Cyprus, the United States, Great Britain, and the United Nations.

Among his most famous book-length works are *Mythistorima* (1935), *Book of Exercises* (1940), *Logbook I, II,* and *III* (1940, 1944, 1955), *Book of Exercises II* (1962), *Three Secret Poems* (1966); to these must be added the poem "ENGOMI," which was first published in his slim volume of verse . . . *Cyprus, Where It Was Ordained for Me* . . . (1955). While some of his poems are metrical and rhymed or versified in otherwise strict rhythms (like his haiku), many of his best poems are in free verse, in which form, critics agree, he excelled.

Seferis was awarded the Nobel Prize in 1963. In the presentation speech Nobel Prize Committee chairman Anders Österling remarked that Seferis's poetry enunciates an "eloquent joy inspired in him by his country's mountainous islands with their whitewashed houses rising in terraces above an azure sea, a harmony of colours that we find again in the Greek flag"; he added that the judges recognized the brilliance of Seferis's "lyrical writing, inspired by a deep feeling for the Hellenic world of culture." In the following years Seferis was awarded honorary doctorates from several universities, including Oxford and Princeton. He was appointed an honorary fellow of the Modern Language Association in 1966 and was a fellow at the Institute for Advanced Study in Princeton in 1968. In 1969 he issued a statement condemning the dictatorship of Giorgios Papadopoulos, who led the military coup d'état in 1967 and ruled Greece from 1967 to 1974. Seferis died in September 1971. His funeral in Athens, which was attended by an immense number of fellow citizens, reignited a protest movement against the Greek regime that he had so eloquently appraised and condemned during his lifetime.

BIBLIOGRAPHY

Beaton, Roderick. *George Seferis: Waiting for the Angel, A Biography.* New Haven, Conn.: Yale University Press, 2003.

Seferis, George. *Collected Poems.* Revised ed. Translated, edited, and introduced by Edmund Keeley and Philip Sherrard. Princeton, N.J.: Princeton University Press, 1995.

R. Victoria Arana

"SEGREGATION" CARLOS GERMÁN BELLI (1958)

An early poem, "Segregation" represents Peruvian CARLOS GERMÁN BELLI's role as a nexus among the Latin American avant-gardes, the poetry of social concerns, and his own later, formally complex neoclassical verse. Belli uses short *arte menor* verses (fewer than eight syllables) with sparse and irregular rhyme to create an oral, conversational tone. We see an abject, childish, narrative position, close to that of CÉSAR VALLEJO's THE BLACK HERALDS, whereby the boy narrator focuses on the existential and material suffering of *"Yo, mi mamá, mis dos hermanos / y muchos peruanitos"* (My mother, my brother, myself / and many little Peruvians). Belli's adoption of a simple—perhaps deceptively simple—lexis, including terms such as *"árbol . . . frutos . . . techo"* (trees, fruits, roof) to describe social injustice, *"porque arriba todo tiene dueño"* (because above everything's owned), signals his links to social and politically committed poets, including Chile's GABRIELA MISTRAL, and their use of verse as denunciation. The poem operates through binaries of weakness/strength, dispossession/possession, up/down, and beauty/shame, dividing the little Peruvians and the bosses. The distinction drawn between the values of high culture and the lives of the *"Peruanitos"* and their naive and secretive lives is reminiscent of the position of Diogenes the Cynic and his questioning of the values in contemporary classical Greek society. Furthermore, Belli undercuts social divisions to display the power that poetry, and particularly socially themed and formally innovative poetry, holds as a weapon of the weak. Structured repetition within and across lines reveals Belli's thematic complexity, as in the recurring need to escape from hierarchy, *"lejos, muy lejos de los jefes . . . / . . . lejos, muy lejos de los dueños"* (far, very far from the bosses . . . / . . . far, far away from the owners), and reinforces both social striation and the desperate need to escape it by withdrawal. The deceptive faux-naïf indicated in the subtitle, *"a modo de un pintor primitivo culto*" (in the style of an educated-primitive painter), adds a satirical, almost mocking tone. Thus the values of *"buen decir"* (well-spoken language), the correctness and beauty represented by accepted cultural production, are shown as complicit in the organization of society along unjust lines; meanwhile, the narrator-as-victim displays the importance of poetry as a tool for recording injustice and for satirical diatribes against the social order.

BIBLIOGRAPHY

Aherne, Maureen, and David Tripton, eds. *Peru: The New Poetry*. London: London Magazine Editions, 1970.

Borgeson, Paul W., Jr. *Los Talleres del Tiempo. Versos escogidos de Carlos Germán Belli*. Madrid: Visor, 1992.

Ben Bollig

SEIFERT, JAROSLAV (1901–1986)

Jaroslav Seifert, who in 1984 became the first Czech to win the Nobel Prize in literature, is the most widely read and beloved poet of the Czech Republic. Over 20 years after his death, he still speaks to all generations of Czechs. Adults know his love for the native land and its people expressed in his outspoken poems and speeches against the German occupation. Later, during the communist regime teenagers avidly read his poems about love, and children recite his playful and melodious rhymes. He is famous for having written, "If an ordinary person is silent, it may be a tactical maneuver. If a writer is silent, he is lying." Seifert earned his reputation early in his career—both as a poet of beautiful verse and as a spokesman for the oppressed. These two only apparently irreconcilable elements can be found throughout his work.

Seifert was born in 1901 to a poor family in Žižkov, a working-class neighborhood of Prague. His father was a locksmith and manager of a small general store. Although Seifert's parents were poor, they could afford to send him to a local high school. He attended six grades of high school, did not complete his studies, and began to work as a journalist. Admiring the Russian Revolution of 1917, Seifert soon started working for the official Communist Party newspaper *Rudé Právo* (The Red Right). In the 1920s he was a notable contributor to left-wing and communist journals and newspapers, including *Červen* (June), *Proletkult* (Proletarian Culture), and *Rovnost* (Equality). The poetry Seifert wrote in this period is often highly didactic and shows strong sympathy for the proletariat and anarchism. Seifert's early proletarian poetry reflects his thorough knowledge of his own working-class background, shown, for instance, in *"Město v slzách"* (City in Tears, 1921) and *"Samá láska"* (Nothing but Love, 1923). Even in these early revolutionary poems, however, it is apparent that Seifert sees the cure to the world's ills in poetry rather than politics. Apart from the thematic focus on love and beauty superseding all revolutions, the formal features show a promising poetic development, unlike the stale communist verses of some of his contemporaries. The main feature of these early poems is hyperbole, which blunts the directness of the naive and overblown gestures then typical of Czech proletarian verse.

Seifert further developed hyperbole and other linguistic and formal poetic devices in the 1920s when he became the leading representative of the avant-garde and one of the founders of a modernist group of artists and writers called Devětsil (Nine Forces). The artists around Devětsil articulated the aspirations of an ambitious movement called poetism. Poetism regarded life itself as an art form, and its utopian aim was to fuse life with the arts, so that in the remote future art would become life and life art. The movement sought to loosen connections; its leading artists were innovative, radical, and provocative. Poetry played a significant role in the movement. Seifert's verse in this period abounded with syntactical and semantic playfulness. His poems were based on puns and biblical and literary allusions. He played with typography and used lyrical anecdote. The characteristic collection from this period is *Na vlnách TSF* (Over the Waves, 1925). In this period he also translated international avant-garde poetry (e.g., GUILLAUME APOLLINAIRE and ALEKSANDR BLOK).

The playfulness in his verse disappeared, however, as the threat of war emerged again in the 1930s. Not only did Seifert's tone become much more serious and bitter, but his formal poetics became more subjective and independent of the contemporary literary movements. His verse displayed rhythmical regularity and rhyming patterns, which were based on the musicality of the Czech language. He employed these formal devices in the collections *Jablko z klína* (An Apple from Your Lap, 1933) and *Ruce Venušiny* (The Hands of Venus, 1936) to express more personal themes such as the memory of childhood. The poet's childhood recollections were often melancholy, especially when the social and economic situation worsened in the late 1930s as a result of political strife between ethnic groups. Later Seifert used the same Czech formal features to attempt to strengthen national conscience and to enliven national traditions. These prosodic features also served as a source of certainty and comfort in the tragic period after March 1939 when Hitler sat in Prague and announced "Czechoslovakia has ceased to exist" and when Seifert published *Světlem oděná* (Robed in Light, 1940) and *Přilba hlíny* (A Helmetful of Earth, 1945). Seifert exploited the regular and melodic form until after the war—in, for instance, *Maminka* (Mother, 1954). But the 1960s brought a change in his poetics that had a key impact on the intensity of poetic production in Czechoslovakia.

His collection *Koncert na ostrově* (Concert on the Island, 1965) marked both formal and thematic transformations of Seifert's poetry that would mature until his death. As before, the motif of time occupies the key position in the thematic development. But Seifert traded the sadness and melancholy of memory for an intensive experience of one's own finite existence. Formally the new features of Seifert's poetry include a narrative style, spoken colloquial language, and the melody of a spoken phrase to replace the melody of a song. Seifert grows more comfortable using free verse instead of regular rhyme. Among the major collections from this period still published in the Czech Republic are *Halleyova kometa* (Halley's Comet, 1967) and *Odlévání zvonů* (The Casting of the Bells, 1967). Because of his support for dissident writers and his criticism of the Soviet occupation, which began in 1968, Seifert was not allowed to publish poetry in Czechoslovakia in the period 1968–78. His collection *Morový sloup* (The Plague Column), written during that period and published in Cologne, Germany, in 1977, did not come out in Czechoslovakia until 1981. Seifert's fresh entrance in the poetry of the 1960s stirred both the older and the younger generations of poets. With poems like "THE PLAGUE COLUMN," he again powerfully revealed the depths of Czech national life and pointed out the role of an individual in historic times. Emphasizing concrete time, Seifert did not rely on concepts such as the "happy future." He put forward the continuity of human and cultural values. Seifert continued to use this poetic method in the 1970s and 1980s in his last two collections, *Deštník z Piccadilly* (An Umbrella from Piccadilly, 1979; released in samizdat [the secret publication and distribution of government-banned literature in the former Soviet Union] in 1978) and *Býti básníkem* (To Be a Poet, 1983).

Even though Seifert gained national and international acclaim, the communist establishment continued to make things difficult for him. Only after he won the Nobel Prize in 1984 did the Czechoslovak leaders start celebrating his achievements, especially his early poetry. But they disparaged Seifert's later works and proffered him to the nation as an unsubtle rhymer. Despite this damage many Czechs appreciate Seifert's poetry for its linguistic, formal, and thematic complexity. Translators of Czech poetry are aware of the nearly impossible linguistic and poetic challenges. The natural musicality of Seifert's verse, his linguistic playfulness, and the folklore elements make the task even harder. The most significant translations include Ewald Osers's *The Poetry of Jaroslav Seifert* and Dana Loewy's *The Early Poetry of Jaroslav Seifert*.

BIBLIOGRAPHY

Menclová, Věra, Bohumil Svozil, and Václav Vaněk, eds. *Slovník českých spisovatelů.* Prague, Czech Republic: Libri, 2000.

Seifert, Jaroslav. *The Poetry of Jaroslav Seifert.* Translated by Ewald Osers. North Haven, Conn.: Catbird Press, 1998.

———. *The Early Poetry of Jaroslav Seifert.* Translated by Dana Loewy. Evanston, Ill.: Northwestern University Press, 1997.

Daniela Kukrechtová

"SELF-PORTRAIT" YUN DONG-JU "Self-Portrait" is a poem published in YUN DONG-JU's only collection of poetry, *The Sky, the Wind, the Stars and Poetry.* This collection, published after his death in 1948, includes 12 poems found posthumously as well as 19 poems he had initially included in the handmade collection he

gave to his friend Jung Byong-wuk. Later, a second edition (1955) came out with 62 more poems; the third, expanded edition came out in 1976 with 85 more poems. The latest edition, *The Anthology of Yun Dong-ju's Handwritten Poetry* (1999), includes 125 poems. As many scholars have pointed out, Yun's poetics can be characterized as the "poetics of shame." Having lived during the Japanese occupation, Yun seems to have felt constantly ashamed of himself for lacking the courage to engage in resistance activities and choosing instead to study and seek transcendental beauty in nature, taking little notice of his countrymen's suffering. This taint of shame is not unique to him, however, but can be applied to almost all Korean intellectuals who studied in Japan then. It is not difficult to imagine how they might have felt about studying in the country that had occupied their motherland and victimized their people. Thus Yun's "Self-Portrait" is a representative portrayal of Korean intellectuals who endured a similar psychological cycle of shame, helplessness, hatred, sorrow, and resignation.

The recurrent poetic motifs in Yun's poetry are the night sky, moon, wind, and stars. Traditionally these are symbols of sacred gods that guide and protect people. Since Yun's youth was an era when many weak-minded scholars and writers, for fear of their lives, took Japanese names and wrote articles, novels, and songs encouraging young Korean men to support Japan, it is easy to imagine how desperately Yun wanted to keep his conscience and literary integrity intact. Just as (in his poem "Suh-Shi" [Foreword]) Yun calls on the moon, the sky, the wind, and the stars to protect him, the speaker in "Self-Portrait" looks at the moon, clouds, sky, and wind as the sources of his inspiration. But this time the poet sees them only as reflections inside a remote, deserted well, which symbolizes his inner self; despite his innocent resolution to commit himself to the pursuit of transcendental beauty, he does not feel he has earned the seal of approval he desperately wanted from the cosmic animus he honors. Instead, what he receives is only a fragmented sense of his inner self: The more he looks at the man in the well—actually the image of himself mirrored there—the more shame and hatred he feels toward him. But while oscillating wildly between hatred and self-pity, Yun tries to reconcile his split selves, pondering his feelings with stoic resignation. In the end he suggests that even if he is not courageous enough to be what he would like to be (a freedom fighter), he nevertheless finds solace in his determination to keep his conscience and integrity intact. He hopes his anxiety and shame will pass and belong someday only to memory, just as he holds his hand out to his split self in "A Poem Too Easily Written." Even though Yun may have felt extreme personal anguish and shame, it is due to the intensity of his inner struggle. He glows more brightly today than those other poets who more easily compromised with their times.

BIBLIOGRAPHY
Yun Dong-ju. "Self Portrait." Translated by Peter Lee. In *The Silence of Love: Twentieth-Century Korean Poetry,* edited by Sammy E. Solberg, 81. Honolulu: University of Hawaii Press, 1990.

Han Ji-hee

SENGHOR, LÉOPOLD SÉDAR (1906–2001)

Léopold Sédar Senghor was both a statesman and a poet. From 1960 to 1980 he served as the first president of Senegal, following its independence from France. Almost 30 years earlier, along with AIMÉ CÉSAIRE and LÉON DAMAS, he founded the NEGRITUDE MOVEMENT in French-speaking Caribbean and African letters. He published dozens of essays on topics ranging from Negritude thought and black literature to African socialism, as well as eight individual volumes of poetry and five collections of previously published works.

Born to a large, prosperous family of the Serer people in Senegal, his home life was rooted in African culture, while in school he received a classical French education, advancing to university study in Paris. French poets (including Arthur Rimbaud, Charles Baudelaire, PAUL CLAUDEL, and SAINT-JOHN PERSE), French anthropologists (including Leo Frobenius), and French novelists (including Stéphane Mallarmé) influenced his writing and his revaluing of Africa (Westley 98).

In Paris Senghor met Césaire and Damas, and the three founded the Negritude Movement and began publishing *L'etudiant noir* (The Black Student) in 1934, the same year in which Senghor earned the *agrégé d'université degree* (comparable to the Ph.D.). After teaching Latin, Greek, and French in Senegal for several years, Senghor joined the French army to fight against the Germans, spending two years as a prisoner of war before returning to Paris and becoming "the first African . . . professor at the National Training College for administrators." (Kennedy 123).

In 1945 Senghor was elected as deputy to the French National Assembly, subsequently serving in a variety of other government posts leading to the presidency of Senegal. He assisted ALIOUNE DIOP in founding the influential international magazine *Présence africaine* in 1948, the same year he published *Anthologie de la nouvelle poésie nègre et malgache,* which included Jean-Paul Sartre's preface "Orphée noir." He would also cofound the journal *Ethiopiques* and publish the Senegalese newspaper *La condition humaine.* Senghor continued his writing and activism, organizing the 1956 Congress of Black Writers and Artists in Paris and sponsoring the 1966 World Festival of Black Arts in Senegal.

As prose writer and proponent of Negritude thought, Senghor's essay "Negritude: A Humanism of the 20th Century" (1970) remains a definitive expression of Negritude ideology, defining Negritude as "the sum of the cultural values of the black world" (28) and "as an instrument of liberation" (27). African culture, he asserts, "is diametrically opposed to the traditional philosophy of Europe," which is "static, objective, dichotomic" (30). African culture seeks "synthesis" (30), is "fundamentally ethical" (31), contains "balance and harmony" (32), and creates art that is "rhythmical," for rhythm is "the main virtue, in fact, of negritude" (34). Senghor thus advances Negritude as a celebration of African culture and a challenge to European dominance.

Senghor's early essays on Negritude were collected into *Liberté I—négritude et humanisme,* published in Paris in 1964. Among the dozens of later pieces, available translations include "Negritude and the Concept of Universal Civilization" (1963), pieces in *Prose and Poetry* (1965), and "Negritude and the Civilization of the Universal" (1995) (see David M. Westley's "A Select Bibliography of the Works of Léopold Sédar Senghor" for a fuller listing of Senghor's prose, poetry, interviews, and translations).

Senghor's volumes of verse include *Chants d'ombre* (Songs of Darkness, 1945), *Hosties noirs* (Black Host or Black Victims, 1948), *Chants pour Naëtt* (*Songs for Naëtt,* 1949), *Ethiopiques* (*Ethiopics,* 1956), NOCTURNES, (1961), which won the International Grand Prize for Poetry from the Poets and Artists of France, and others. Translations include selections in *Prose and Poetry* (1965) and in Ellen Conroy Kennedy's *The Negritude Poets* (1975), *Selected Poems of Léopold Sédar Senghor* (1977), *The Collected Poetry* (1991), and *Poems of Léopold Sédar Senghor* (1996).

While some view his poetry as "personal and contemplative rather than ideological" (Kennedy 121), Negritude thought is found throughout Senghor's works. "French Garden" (1934) refers to "the tom-tom's call / bounding / over continents" and causing the persona's heart to leap (130). This imagery conveys the collective African identity posited by Negritude thought, also seen in *Songs of Darkness.* "Night of Sine" bids us to "listen to our dark blood beat / . . . the deep pulse of Africa in the midst of lost villages" (130). Similarly, in "Prayer to the Masks" the persona prays to the "lion-headed Ancestor" (132) to "[f]ix your immutable eyes on your subjugated children" (133), both paying homage to the African cultural past and critiquing European colonization. Likewise, in "Ode for Three Kôras and Balaphong" the speaker celebrates "African night, . . . mystical and bright black and brilliant / . . . Night dissolving all my contradictions . . . in the primal unity of your negritude" (134–135).

In poems from *Black Host,* Senghor clearly critiques European dominance. "Prayer for Peace" speaks of "Africa crucified" and of "Haiti . . . , which dared proclaim its Manhood to the Tyrant's face" (136). It requests forgiveness for "those who hunted my children like wild elephants / Who trained them to the whip and made them the black hands of those whose hands were white" (137), those making Africa "a vast cemetery beneath the white sun" (138). Conversely, the persona also expresses fondness for France and asks the Lord to bless all people. To Senghor himself this "split . . . between the call of the Ancestors and the call of Europe" is "the very crux" of his poetry (Kennedy 129). Similarly, poems in *Nocturnes,* like many preceding and following this collection, celebrate the beauty of African culture, just as pieces throughout Senghor's canon render images from his childhood, celebrating Serer culture specifically and African culture more generally.

The honors and awards received by Senghor—among them his induction into the French Academy of Moral and Political Sciences in 1969 and a three-day UNESCO colloquium held in honor of his 90th birthday—do not convey the wealth of his contribution to world culture. It is a contribution broadly made through his participation in the development of the Negritude philosophy, his political and governmental leadership, his prose and poetry, and his cultural activism in the advancement of political and artistic enterprises.

See also "BLACK WOMAN," "LETTTER TO A POET," and "TO NEW YORK."

BIBLIOGRAPHY

Ba, Sylvia W. The Concept of Negritude in the Poetry of Léopold Sédar Senghor. Princeton, N.J.: Princeton University Press, 1973.

Guillaume, Alfred J. "Negritude and Humanism: Senghor's Vision of a Universalist Civilization." In The Harlem Renaissance: Revaluations, edited by Stanley Brodwin, William S. Shiver, and Amritjit Singh, 271–280. New York: Garland, 1989.

Ikiddeh, Ime. "Negritude and the Poetry of Léopold Sédar Senghor: A Historical Reassessment." Calabar Studies in Modern Languages 2, no. 2 (1977): 1–19.

Kennedy, Ellen Conroy, ed. The Negritude Poets: An Anthology of Translations from the French. New York: Thunder's Mouth Press, 1975.

Kluback, William. Léopold Sédar Senghor: From Politics to Poetry. New York: Peter Lang, 1997.

Senghor, Léopold Sédar. "Negritude: A Humanism of the 20th Century." In The Africa Reader: Independent Africa. London: Vintage, 1970, 179–192. Reprinted as Colonial Discourse and Post-Colonial Theory: A Reader, edited by Patrick Williams and Laura Chrisman. New York: Columbia University Press, 1994, 27–35.

Vaillant, Janet G. "Perspectives on Léopold Senghor and the Changing Face of Negritude." ASA Review of Books 2 (1976): 154–162.

Westley, David M. "A Select Bibliography of the Works of Léopold Sédar Senghor." Research in African Literatures 33, no. 4 (2002): 88–100.

Yasmin DeGout

SENIOR, OLIVE (1941–   )

Olive Senior was born in Trelawny, Jamaica, the seventh of 10 children. From the age of four she lived with her great uncle and aunt in Westmoreland. She attended high school in Montego Bay and published her first piece in the Jamaican newspaper The Gleaner when she was a high school student. She began reporting part time for the paper through its western Jamaica office and after finishing high school moved to the paper's Kingston office.

While studying journalism in Cardiff, Wales, Senior received a scholarship to Carlton University in Ottawa, Canada, from which she graduated in 1967 with a degree in journalism. She then worked in a variety of publishing and editing positions at the Jamaica Information Services, the Jamaica Chamber of Commerce, and the Institute of Social and Economic Research at the University of the West Indies, where she edited Social and Economic Studies. During that time she also wrote The Message Is Change, an account of the 1972 elections in Jamaica. In the early 1980s Senior worked at the Institute of Jamaica, where she edited the Jamaica Journal and served as managing director of the Institute of Jamaica Publications. Since devoting herself full time to writing, Senior has traveled widely and lived in various places abroad, including Portugal, England, and Canada. She has taught at a range of universities in the Caribbean, England, Canada, and the United States, including Barnard College in New York City and the Humber School for Writers in Toronto, Canada. She currently divides her time between Jamaica and Toronto.

Senior's published work includes three collections of poetry, Talking of Trees (1986), Gardening in the Tropics (1994), and OVER THE ROOFS OF THE WORLD (2005); three collections of short stories: Summer Lightning (1986), which received the 1987 Commonwealth Writers Prize in 1987; Arrival of the Snake-Woman (1989); and Discerner of Hearts (1995); as well as several scholarly books including the A-Z of Jamaican Heritage (1984), Working Miracles: Women's Lives in the English-Speaking Caribbean (1991), and the Encyclopedia of Jamaican Heritage (2003).

BIBLIOGRAPHY

Allen-Agostini, Lisa. "Olive Senior: An Embodiment of Conflict." Sunday Guardian, 12 March 2000, 19.

Dawes, Kwame, and Neville Senu, eds. *Talk Yuh Talk: Interviews with Anglophone Caribbean Poets.* Charlottesville: University of Virginia Press, 2001.

Flemming, Carrol. "Olive Senior, 'Discerner of Hearts.'" *Caribbean Writer* 11 (2002).

Pollard, Velma. "Olive Senior: Journalist, Researcher, Poet, Fiction Writer." *Callaloo* 36 (Summer 1988): 478–479.

Rowell, Charles H. "An Interview with Olive Senior." *Callaloo* 36 (Summer 1988): 480–490.

Serafin, Steven. R., ed. "Olive Senior." *Modern Black Writers.* Supplemental Vol. 2. New York: Continuum, 1995.

Tanna, Laura. "One-on-One with Olive Senior." Parts 1, 2, 3. *Jamaica Gleaner* (October 17, 2004; October 31, 2004; November 7, 2004).

Alan Feerst

SEROTE, MONGANE WALLY (1944–)

One of the foremost South African poets to emerge during the black literary renaissance of the late 1960s and early 1970s, Serote began writing to document the hopes and fears of people suffering under apartheid. Unlike many of his predecessors in the protest tradition who were forced to seek an audience abroad, he reached many people within his own country because his poetry was never censored there. Born in Sophiatown, Serote grew up in Alexandra, a black township outside Johannesberg, where he was exposed early to the political activism of his grandfather and others in the community. Upon leaving school Serote joined the South African Students' Organization (SASO), which initiated the Black Consciousness movement. His participation in this group led to his detention, under the Terrorism Act, for nine months in 1969. But it also helped him develop his voice as a poet, as he worked in the Publications Unit of SASO. In fairly rapid succession Serote produced two volumes of short poems, *Yakhal'inkomo* (1972) and *Tsetlo* (1974). Like much of his poetry, this work bears the influence of Walt Whitman and Langston Hughes in its free-verse structure, but it also draws upon the African tradition of *izibongo*, or praise poetry (see, for example, "CITY JOHANNESBURG"). Constrained by the lyric form, Serote went on to write two long autobiographical poems, *No Baby Must Weep* (1975) and *Behold Mama, Flowers* (1978), which explore the personal struggle to overcome social restrictions and achieve an experience of community.

In 1974 the poet moved to the United States to pursue a master's degree in creative writing at Columbia University in New York City. Upon his return to southern Africa in 1979, he became an active member of the exile community in Gaborone, Botswana. In 1986 he moved to London, where he served as head of the African National Congress (ANC) Department of Arts and Culture. Collected in *The Night Keeps Winking* (1982) and *A Tough Tale* (1987), the poems that Serote wrote at that time are frequently characterized by a militant tone. The poet returned to South Africa after 16 years of exile when the ban on the liberation movements was lifted in 1990. Following the historic elections of 1994, he became an ANC member of parliament and now chairs the parliamentary committee on arts, culture, science, and technology. Despite his role in the new government, Serote refuses to abandon his career as a poet. In long poems like *Third World Express* (1992), *Come and Hope with Me* (1994), and *Freedom Lament and Song* (1997), he continues to explore the many challenges that South Africa faces as a new nation. Mongane Serote remains strongly committed to realizing human potentialities through his writing in the postapartheid era.

BIBLIOGRAPHY

Barboure, Dorian. "Mongane Serote: Humanist and Revolutionary." In *Momentum: On Recent South African Writing,* edited by M. J. Daymond, J. U. Jacobs, and Margaret Lenta, 171–181. Pietermaritzburg, South Africa: University of Natal Press, 1984.

Solberg, Rolf. "Interview." In *Writing South Africa: Literature, Apartheid, and Democracy, 1970–1995,* edited by Derek Attridge and Rosemary Jolly, 180–186. Cambridge: Cambridge University Press, 1998.

Watts, Jane. "The Poetry of Mongane Serote." In *Black Writers from South Africa.* New York: St. Martin's Press, 1989.

Alexander B. McKee

"SEXUAL WATER" PABLO NERUDA (1935)

Among many cultures, the powers of seduction and destruction are sides of the same coin. In "Sexual Water," from the second volume of *Residencia en la Tierra* (Residence on Earth), PABLO NERUDA imbues the force of water with an erotic, corporeal energy, noting that with "drops like teeth . . . it falls biting . . . only a breath, moister than weeping" (ll. 2, 8, 11). The land that awaits rainfall is parched with a drought, "a death rattle coming from a granary, / stores, locusts" (ll. 19–20). These natural plagues seem to be an objective signifier for social unrest, as next we are shown "girls / sleeping with their hands upon their hearts, / dreaming of bandits, of fires" (ll. 22–24). People are mired in sex and commerce, a collage of "blood, daggers, women's stockings . . . corridors where a virgin screams . . . blankets and organs and hotels" (ll. 28–31), as if it were Sodom, poised for the strike of God.

By the third stanza the speaker has asserted himself, adopting a tone of involuntary witness—the anaphora of "I see" begins line after line, and "like an eyelid atrociously and forcibly uplifted / I am looking" (ll. 35–36). Just as heavy rain after a long dry spell brings flash floods rather than relief, the speaker sees cultural upheaval bringing violence upon the very people who longed for it: "a red noise of bones, / a clashing of flesh, / and yellow legs like merging spikes of grain . . . I listen, shaken between gasps and sobs" (ll. 38–42). The speaker qualifies his role as observer by recognizing his own deep division of self: "with half my soul upon the sea and half my soul upon the land, / and with the two halves of my soul I look at the world" (ll. 44–45). He knows both sides of the coin, seductive and destructive.

In the end the speaker realizes that the siren song of water cannot be resisted, even as the cost of change cannot be denied. He conflates transformative desire with the needs of the body: "though I close my eyes and cover my heart entirely, / I see a muffled waterfall . . . like a waterfall of sperm and jellyfish" (ll. 46–50). The final haunting image fuses a moment of birth and of death: "I see a turbid rainbow form. / I see its waters pass across the bones" (ll. 51–52). For something to be created, something must be destroyed. Neruda is a master at finding the personal in the political, the human dynamic in the natural world. Here he deftly manipulates the matter of rainfall into the crisis of revolution.

Sandra Beasley

"SHEPHERDS OF ABRUZZO, THE" GABRIELE D'ANNUNZIO (1903)   This is the first of seven poems grouped under the heading "Sogni di terre lon-

tane" (Dreams of Distant Places), which are part of D'ANNUNZIO's poetic masterpiece Alcyone (Halcyon). If the entire work is a passionate celebration of the summer and of the communion of the human soul with nature, the seven poems of this series represent a moment of melancholy when the summer is close to an end, its light and colors are diluted, and the poet abandons himself to a nostalgic feeling in the remembrance of past days and faraway places.

As well as a common theme, the poems also share elaborate formal characteristics, with hendecasyllabic (11-syllable) stanzas, a similar rhyme scheme, a preference for parataxis (series without conjunctions), and realistic descriptions. "I pastori" is constituted of four stanzas of five hendecasyllables: In each stanza two lines rhyme with each other, two are free, and one rhymes with the first line of the following stanza, while the stanza's closing line rhymes with the last line of the last stanza.

In "I pastori" D'Annunzio evokes the atmosphere of his native land, Italy's Abbruzzi, in September, when the shepherds migrate with their flocks from the Appenines to the plains of the Adriatic coast. With vibrant emotion the poet re-creates the transhumance and describes the figures of the shepherds, embodying an old and simple world and the poet's nostalgia for his roots. When autumn approaches it is time to abandon the mountain folds and highland pastures and to winter on the green plains near the Adriatic. Before leaving, the shepherds drink long from the alpine springs "so that the taste of native water may / remain in exiled hearts and offer comfort." Then with their hazel staffs they walk along the paths that have been used for centuries by their forefathers. The image of the "silent grassy river" conveys the gentle movement of men and flocks toward the sea. But then the silence is broken by the joyous voice of the first shepherd who catches sight of the coast. Finally, we see the shepherds walking on the shore, and we witness with the poet the atmosphere of immense peace, with the sun shining on the sheeps' coats and making them as light as the sand, with the sweet sounds of the water. A solitary verse closing the poem expresses the longing of the exiled poet for his native land: "And why, I ask, am I not with my shepherds?"

BIBLIOGRAPHY

D'Annunzio, Gabriele. *Halcyon*. Translated with an introduction by J. G. Nichols. New York: Routledge, 2003.

Sabrina Brancato

SHIN KYONG-NIM (1935–   )

Shin Kyong-nim is one of the most beloved contemporary Korean poets. He is honored as a *minjung* poet for his love of the working-class. Born in 1935 to relatively rich parents in Chungju, in south-central Korea, he recalls in his essays that his house was always filled with farmers, laborers, miners, and peddlers who worked for his father or just stopped by to sell things. Talking with them, he learned various dialects; hearing stories and news about the capital, Seoul, he imagined the big city he had never visited; laughing with the powerless and the have-nots, he developed a good rapport with them at an early age. His rapport with the *minjung* grew even deeper when later he lived from hand to mouth as one of them.

After he published his critically acclaimed poem *"Gaeldae"* (Reed) in 1956, he disappeared from the mainstream literary scene for 10 years, wandering from one rural place to another while making a living as a farmer, miner, or peddler. This experience is at the heart of his first collection of poems, *Farmers' Dance* (1973), in which he presents the lives of *mot-nan-nom-dul* (the poor and powerless). Critics loved this collection and praised him highly not only for presenting poor people "like a realist novelist's short stories," but also for modernizing the "familiar melody of *Minyo*," a popular folk song genre (Paik "Foreword," 250). Instantly Shin became one of the representative *minjung* writers to succeed KIM SU-YOUNG and his vision of empowering ordinary citizens through a populist national poetry. The following year he was granted the Man-hae Literary Award, which honors the poetic legacy of HAN YOUNG-UN. Even after achieving such huge literary successes, Shin did not forget his people. In his second and third collections of poetry—*Sae-jae* (1979) and *Dallumseh* (1985)—he shows deep understanding and unusual compassion toward both rural and urban working-class people. In *Namhan River* (1987) he changed poetic forms, dropping the short poem with *minyo* (folk song) prosody and adopting an extensive

format to feature his latest, epic vision of Korean history. His efforts were not accorded critical appreciation, and he confessed that he himself was not satisfied with his experiment. He returned to the short poem form, and his next collection of poetry, *Love Song for the Poor Folks* (1988), brought him enormous success once more. In this collection, unlike earlier ones, Shin depicts the inner landscape of the poor and puts a human face on the collective masses of ignored losers living on the margins of capitalist society: Though poor and uneducated, an electronic worker takes pride in his skills and hopes for a better future; a young man represses his passion for his lover because of his financial situation; and a newly wed wife living in a mountaintop slum laughs and cries with peddlers sharing stories of hard life. For this collection he was once again honored critically, and he was presented in 1990 with the Yee-sang Literary Award. He has produced since then numerous collections of poetry and today plays a significant role as a leading poet in Korea. In 1998, for instance, he was honored with the Dae-san Literary Award for *The Silhouette of My Mother and Grandmother*.

Shin teaches at Dongkuk University in Seoul, South Korea, as an honorary professor, spending considerable time giving domestic and international lectures and interviews, actively participating in the country's Nationalist Literary Writers Association, and sharing literary visions with international writers at home and abroad. Shin Kyong-nim is as significant as Kim Su-young in the history of Korean poetry because he awakens readers to the beauty of folk songs and celebrates the resilient spirit of ordinary people surviving hard lives with laughter and hope (see "FARMERS' DANCE"). If Kim Su-young set the first stepping stones toward the genre of *minjung* poetry, Shin can be said to have built a *minjung* house and peopled it with unforgettable individuals.

BIBLIOGRAPHY

Paik Nak-chung. "Foreword to *Farmer's Dance*." In *National Literature and World Literature* [in Korean]. Seoul: Changbi, 1978.

Paik Nak-chung, and Yeom Mu-ung, eds. *The Literary World of Shin Kyeong-nim* [in Korean]. Seoul: Changbi, 1995.

Shin Kyong-nim. *Essays*. Seoul: Munhaksekyesa, 1988.

Han Ji-hee

"SHOUT NO MORE" Giuseppe Ungaretti (1947)

Published in 1947 in his postwar volume *Il dolore* (Affliction)—a book that not only articulates experiences of World War II but also works through the poet's loss of his young son—Guiseppe Ungaretti's short poem *"Non gridate più"* invites the reader to rethink the value of an unassuming yet active and creative silence as opposed to an orchestrated and pompous manner of mourning. Invocations of selfless patience and the ability to listen are contrasted with an industrious discharge of political, militaristic, religious, and scholarly clamor.

The poem consists of two stanzas of four verses each. The first stanza chastises a nameless group for desecrating "the dead ones" (who also remain anonymous) by shouting. The second stanza suggests that the deceased still produce living sounds, even though they cannot be clearly understood anymore. Like grass while growing, the fragile voices of the dead are afraid of being killed (again) by the boots of "man." Altogether the eight short melodious verses that constitute *"Non gridate più"* (even occasional rhymes are interwoven in the text) encapsulate a programmatic criticism of pseudo-omniscient abuses of history and attempts at commodifying its victims, be it in the form of praises or officially staged grief. Whether this poem can itself remain immune to its own attacks on the brutality of discursive disfiguration, including "normalization," remains an open question. While highly readable, Andrew Frisardi's English version of the poem in Ungaretti's *Selected Poems* (Manchester: Carcanet, 2003) is as good a translation as one can probably find, though it does level off several vital nuances of the second stanza.

Olaf Berwald

SHU TING (1952–)

Shu Ting is the pen name of Gong Peiyu, who is regarded as one of the most important poets of contemporary China. She made a name for herself in the 1980s when she was acclaimed, together with Bei Dao and Gu Cheng, as one of the most important representatives of the Misty Poets. She was the only female in the group and the first to be recognized by the public, who engaged in heated discussions of the images and style of her poetry. With the publication of her masterpiece, "To an Oak," about the equality in love between a man and a woman, she was thought to have inaugurated a pioneering feminist voice. According to scholar, translator, and poet Tony Barnstone, Shu Ting "has opened the field in modern Chinese poetry to include romance, emotion, and love when these subjects were strictly taboo in the national and literary media" (Barnstone 23), a unique contribution in contemporary times of the Misty Group, whose writing has been closely linked with "literary Modernism in China" (Barnstone 4).

Shu Ting was born in Shima Town, Fujian Province, in 1952. Her parents were middle-class intellectuals who separated and left their daughter to live with her maternal grandmother. Gong Peiyu's childhood and girlhood witnessed major political and cultural changes in China, including the cataclysmic Cultural Revolution (1966–76). She was sent to be reeducated in the countryside in 1969, together with other so-called intellectual youths of her time, before she completed middle school. She returned to the city in 1972 and held a series of temporary jobs, namely at construction sites, a steel factory, and a textile mill. Her personal situation at the time and her infatuation with words aroused the young woman's interest in writing poems as early as 1969, when she was 17. Chinese interested in literature are known to have become familiar with her poems even before the poems were in print. Without her knowledge, "To an Oak" first appeared on the Democracy Wall in Beijing in 1978, a popular location for dissident activists to post news items and large posters. Later, in 1979, her poems were seen in the literary magazine *Today,* edited by Bei Dao and Meng Ke, and in *Shikan,* the official poetic journal of China at the time. In 1980 Shu Ting was admitted to the Fujian Federation of Literary and Art Circles, after which she focused on professional creative writing. Some of her other well-known poems are "Motherland, Dear Motherland" (winner of Best Poem Award from 1976–79), "A Boat with Two Masts," and "The Wall." In 1982 Shu Ting married Chen Zhongyi, a literary critic, and soon after that her creative writing slowed due to her pregnancy. In 1984, however, she produced a new series of poems, *Your Names,* written as an answer to readers concerned about her and her writing.

Shu Ting's poetry collections are *A Boat with Two Masts* (1980), *Selected Lyrical Poems of Shu Ting & Gu Cheng* (1981), *The Singing Iris* (1986), and *The Archaeopteryx* (1992). Since 1984, during which time she visited many foreign countries, including the United States, Germany, Great Britain, France, Italy, Holland, and India as a lecturer and writer, she has written volumes of prose as well as poems. Her prose works are *Mist of My Heart* (1988), *Berlin, a Feather That Does Not Shine* (1999), and *This Evening with A Good Mood* (2002).

Shu Ting's more than 100 poems have been characterized as having a "sure sense of atmosphere, lyrical precision, and . . . parallelisms" (Barnstone 24)—attributes that mirror the influence of classical Chinese *lu shi* poetry. According to Cheng Zhongyi, Shu Ting is an introverted poet who "becomes engulfed by the world of ordinary onlookers and, as an ordinary woman with ordinary vision and feelings, dissolves herself in life, becoming a mere bubble in its stream, a bit of straw, a fallen leaf" (Chen Zhongyi 131). Love, human relations, and nature are the focus of Shu Ting's poetry, and she herself once said that every one of her poems was written to a particular person (132). But the themes and concerns of the poems go beyond the individual. Her ideals of "trust, reconciliation, respect and compassion" (133) in her writing have become a source of inspiration to many.

In 1981 and again in 1983 Shu Ting won the National Poetry Award; and in 1985 and 1996 she figured among the Ten National Best Poets. In the age of spiritual aridity, Shu Ting was looked upon as a spiritual godmother. She is still regarded as a unique figure in modern Chinese poetry, although in recent years interest in her work has slightly waned (Hong Zicheng).

BIBLIOGRAPHY

Barnstone, Tony, ed. *Out of the Howling Storm: The New Chinese Poetry.* Hanover, N.H.: Wesleyan University Press, 1993.

Hung, Eva, ed. *Renditions Paperbacks Selected Poems by Shu Ting.* Hong Kong: Research Center for Translation & The Chinese University of Hong Kong, 1994.

Chen Zhongyi. "Afterword: Some Thoughts on Shu Ting's Poetry." In *Renditions Paperbacks, Selected Poems by Shu Ting,* edited by Eva Hung. Hong Kong: Research Center for Translation and The Chinese University of Hong Kong, 1994.

Osing, Gordon T. *Mist of My Heart: Selected Poems of Shu Ting.* Beijing: Chinese Literature/Panda Books, 1995.

Hong Zicheng. "Editor's Foreword on The New Selection of Menglongshi." Chinese version. Available online. URL: http://www.eduww.com/lilc/go.asp?id=2934. Accessed on March 5, 2004.

Xuemei Shan

"SILENCE OF LOVE, THE" HAN YONGUN (1926)

"The Silence of Love" is one of the poems published in HAN YOUNGUN's first volume of poetry, *Nim ui Ch'immuk* (The Silence of Love, 1926). This collection contains 88 poems invoking *"Nim."* Nim literally means "a beloved one," and for that reason Han's poetry can be read on the surface as romantic. Considering the period when Han's poetry was written, however, *Nim* may also have another layer of meaning: the motherland or freedom itself. When read this way Han's poetry comes to wear a shade of resistance. Given that Han was a Buddhist monk, *Nim* can also refer to the monk's beloved Buddha, or to the "Buddhist Sutras," which in turn would situate this volume in the category of religious poetry. Then again, according to his note for *The Silence of Love, Nim* can virtually mean every animate and inanimate thing: He says, "Nim is not only a beloved one but also everything brought forth in the world. If common people are Nim for Buddha, philosophy is Nim for Kant. If spring rain is Nim for a rose, Italy is Nim for Mazzini." Han's poetry requires a breadth of knowledge and an understanding of poetry's way of developing multiple layers of coherent meaning. There is one basic premise, however, that links all the meanings of *Nim* in Han's poetry, which is his Buddhist philosophical vision of the Huayan Doctrine. Imported from India, the Huayan Doctrine has been creatively interpreted by many distinguished Buddhist monks throughout the history of Korean Buddhism. Han also approached the Huayan Doctrine in his own creative way (see YIM SUNG-JEH).

According to Han, countless individual existences are closely intertwined with one another and manifest themselves differently each time. Han sees that it is impossible for one entity to have an absolute form of existence in a given time and space: Everything in the world is constantly dissolving itself and transforming into another form. Likewise, he presents *Nim* in this poem not as fixed but as changing from "love" to "old vow" to "flower of golden metal." Thus when in the opening line he says, "You have gone. Ah, my love, you have gone," that remark does not necessarily set the tone of dejection and sadness caused by a lover's absence. Rather, it leads the reader to learn the speaker's negative capability in actively embracing the disappointment and helplessness caused by the lover's absence. Just as the speaker in the last line does "not let go of" *Nim* and expects the beloved to reappear in a different form, he suggests that the reader should not be disappointed, but instead wait for the day of reunion (whether when the lover returns, the country is at last liberated, or the subjects and objects of *Nim* are tenderly reconciled). Clearly, the title poem in *The Silence of Love* is an excellent example of the core dynamic of Han's poetry, which is to embody the constant alteration between reality and appearance based on the Huayan Doctrine. It leads readers to achieve a revolutionary perspective on contradictions in life, showing the various ways everything looks through enlightened eyes.

BIBLIOGRAPHY

Kim Jaihiun, ed. and trans. *The Silence of Love: Poems by Yong-un Han.* Charleston, Ill.: Prairie Poet Books, 1985.

Solberg, Sammy E., et al., eds. *The Silence of Love: Twentieth-Century Korean Poetry.* Honolulu: University of Hawaii Press, 1990.

Song Wuk. *Anthology of Yong-un Han's Poetry and Prose.* Vol. I. Seoul: Shinkumunhwasa, 1973.

Yim Sung-jeh. "A Study of Yong-un Han's Zen," Ph.D. diss. Seoul: Yonsei University, 1995.

Han Ji-hee

"SIREN" Niyi Osundare (1983)

"Siren," from *Songs of the Marketplace,* Niyi Osundare's first collection, has eight stanzas. It describes the visit of typical Nigerian politicians to rural dwellers. The poem takes its title from the police car siren whose blaring traditionally announces the presence of major political officeholders in the country. It evokes the pomp and commotion that mark such an event: People dance and pretend to be happy to receive their leaders, while outriders and security escorts in their convoy visit violence

on the same people in the name of clearing the way. The politicians arrive in imported air-conditioned cars, while the poor dutifully line the roads and endure the scorching tropical sun. All that the people get for their patience and endurance is empty promises. The visit ends without a sincere plan to provide such basic amenities as motorable roads or to address problems caused by erosion and drought. Ironically, the people themselves pretend to be satisfied with their leaders, and they dare not show ingratitude by raising questions. But the eighth stanza hints that innocent children who watch these senseless scenes will eventually raise questions about them.

The poem decries the alienation of Nigerian leaders from their people, ridicules the hypocrisy of their interaction with the electorate, and satirizes the poverty of the masses, which sharply contrasts with the opulence of their leaders. In this sense the satirical intent of the poem is double-edged. While the politicians are presented as corrupt, arrogant, and insensitive to the needs of the people, the masses are equally indicted for being hypocritical. The poem, however, envisions an end to this cycle of mutual deceit.

The strength of "Siren" resides in its use of evocative images and suggestive expressions. The description of "kwashiokored children" lining the streets and waving "tattered flags" comments succinctly on their health status and the poverty of their parents and sharply depicts the contrast between the malnourished rural dwellers and their flamboyant leaders, who shamelessly ride in the most expensive cars made.

Structurally the poem may be divided into two parts: The first seven stanzas depict the atmosphere that marks the civic receptions for politicians, while the last and shortest stanza states the vision of the poet about the necessity for change. A cynical tone runs through the poem. By repeating the word *siren* three times at the beginning of the first seven lines of the poem, the poet reemphasizes that the coming of the politicians is a rude intrusion into the serene life of the countryside. The allusion to Thomas Hardy's *Far from the Madding Crowd* further underlines that political power in this environment accelerates economic mobility, which inevitably estranges the beneficiaries of wealth and power from the rest of the country. The success of the poem also depends on the poet's use of hyperbole, coinages, and the rhetorical question in the first stanza.

BIBLIOGRAPHY

Osundare, Niyi. "Siren." In *Songs of the Marketplace*. Ibadan, Nigeria: New Horn Press, 1983.

Oyeniyi Okunoye

SLAVE SONG DAVID DABYDEEN (1978) DAVID

DABYDEEN wrote the 14 poems that *Slave Song* comprises while an undergraduate at Cambridge University. The set of poems won Cambridge University's Quiller-Couch Prize and the Commonwealth Poetry Prize in 1978. Several individual poems were published before their collective publication in 1984. Throughout the volume Dabydeen renders the sound of the spoken Guyanese language, using characteristic slang like "Juk" for *poke* and alternate spellings for Guyanese vowels, yielding such lines as "Tie me haan up . . . Haal me teet out . . . Set yu daag fo gyaad / Maan till nite" from the collection's title poem (28). In the introduction Dabydeen details the logic underlying his dialect technique, tracing it to the raw and "brutal" conditions of plantation labor and colonial life. Dabydeen appends—in a semi-tongue-in-cheek imitation of T. S. Eliot's didactic footnotes in *The Waste Land*— "translations" of each poem into standard English and annotations that offer cultural translations and scholarly elaborations on the poems' implicit social dynamics and literary precursors. The annotation to "The Servants' Song," for example, explicates the poem as "an example of Guyanese peasant humour, simple and bawdy in a Chaucerian way but more crude" (50).

Dabydeen has called empire, in addition to its social, economic, and political aspects, a "pornographic" project; the erotic dimension of colonial power differentials is a significant and overarching theme of the collection (Dawes 213). "Love Song" grows from a cane cutter's fantasy about a white woman; "Nightmare" portrays a white woman's rape fantasy from the cane cutter's perspective; by contrast, "Brown Skin Girl" addresses the modern phenomenon of Guyanese women who offer themselves as prostitutes or mistresses to foreigners in hope of escape. Though all speak in the Guyanese vernacular, each poem comes from a different perspective, constituting in Mark McWatt's analysis "a carefully constructed mask by means of which the poetic persona inhabits the men and women" (16). The personae include a chorus of laboring women, male cane cutters, servants, and an old man. In channeling these disparate voices of Guyanese experience, Dabydeen writes, "The English fails where the Creole succeeds" (14).

BIBLIOGRAPHY

Dawes, Kwame, and Neville Senu, eds. *Talk Yuh Talk: Interviews with Anglophone Caribbean Poets*. Charlottesville: University of Virginia Press, 2001, 196–214.

Grant, Kevin, ed. *The Art of David Dabydeen*. Leeds, U.K.: Peepal Press, 1997.

Alex Feerst

"SMALL ODE TO A BLACK CUBAN BOXER" NICOLÁS GUILLÉN (1931) This poem

from the collection *Sóngoro consongo* (1931) is an outstanding example of NICOLÁS GUILLÉN's poetry, reflecting both his Afrocentrism and his nationalist response to U.S. imperialism. The poem was inspired by and written for featherweight champion Eligio Sardiñas Montalvo. Fighting under the name Kid Chocolate, Sardiñas Montalvo became a favorite at New York's Madison Square Garden in the late 1920s and something of a Cuban national hero. In "*Pequeña oda a un negro boxeador cubano*," Guillén transforms the boxer into an archetypical Afro-Hispanic hero. The diminutive boxer with his "*cuerpo de ardilla*" (squirrel's body) and confident "*punch de tu sonrisa*" (punch of your smile) is pitted against the monstrous "*Norte . . . fiero y rudo*" (hard and cruel North). The short meter and freeverse composition with its rapid sequence of boxing images captures the essence of the sport while alluding to the impending battle between tiny Cuba and the beastlike Broadway, a metonym for the United States, "*que estira su hocico . . . / para lamer glotonamente / toda la sangre de nuestro cañaveral*" (that stretches out its snout to lick gluttonously all the blood of our canefields). The repeated interjection of boxing-world Anglicisms ("ring," "clinch," "training," "jab," "punching bag," "shadow boxing," "black jack") literally exemplifies Anglo-Saxon hegemony in Latin America. Although the protagonist, like his homeland, may seem at a disadvantage, he will ultimately rise to the challenge—*"pulido, fino, fuerte"* (polished, fine, strong). The poem's final stanza foretells the victory of both the hero and his people. Just as *"Europa se desnuda para tostar su carne"* (Europe strips itself to brown its skin) to the music of "jazz" and "son," so the poet exhorts his countryman, *"frente a la envidia de los blancos"* (before the envy of the whites), "to shine as a black man while the boulevards applaud" (*lucirse negro mientras aplaude el bulevar*), and to speak as a true black man (*hablar en negro de verdad*).

BIBLIOGRAPHY
Guillén, Nicolás. "Pequeña oda a un negro boxeador cubano." In *Obra Poetica,* 1922–1958. Havana, Cuba: Letras Cubanas, 1985.

Eric Reinholtz

"SNOW AND SPRUCE FOREST" TARJEI VESAAS (1946)

"Snø og granskog" appeared in TARJEI VESAAS's first poetry collection, *Kjeldene,* which can be translated into English as *From the Sources,* connecting the idea of a physical underground water source to the idea of an even deeper, metaphysical source, such as life, creativity, or spirituality. The poem is a good example of three common features in Vesaas's poetry: a spiritual searching, a natural landscape that at times is rendered unnatural or mystical, and phrasing that produces sounds that exemplify the poetic experience being described. The spiritual searching in this case is for the elusive idea of home, which in the predominately rural Nordic region always involves a natural environment in addition to, or in communion with, a building or familial bonds. The poem begins, "Talk about what home is— / snow and spruce forest / is home." The speaker uses the first-person plural *we* throughout, suggesting not only a kinship between humans and nature but also among humans who share this home. The boundaries of this home are not clearly delineated, however; the snow and the forest are "wherever we are," so much a part of us that they are "mixed into our own breath." In the line following "breath," Vesaas uses the aural properties of his native Norwegian to produce the sound of human breath

huffing in the cold air: *Heile heile tida* (The whole, whole time). In reading the poem aloud, then, the reader becomes one of the "we" who are present in the snow and spruce forest, one of the "we" who are "coming home" (Greenwald xvi). The strangeness of this natural setting is precisely the speaker's claim that it is the forest and the snow, not a cabin into which we retreat to escape them, that are home. In the process Vesaas suggests that we carry our idea of "home" in our hearts and minds rather than simply occupy it in body, although it is our bodily experience of this "home" that forges the link: "—and feeling so it flares in you / what it is to be where you belong." In his classic architectural work *Nightlands: Nordic Building,* Christian Norberg-Schultz describes the Norwegian valleys of Telemark, where Vesaas lived most of his life: "Here, people are at home, and animals are safe. Here, place is an understood world, even in threatening weather" (Norberg-Schultz 32). While Vesaas's poem draws from a particularly rural Nordic landscape to affirm this affiliation, the powerful simplicity of its language and the inclusiveness of its we-speaker seduces all who are engaged in our all-too-modern quest to recognize "home" in our lived-in natural environments.

BIBLIOGRAPHY
Norberg-Schultz, Christian. *Nightlands: Nordic Building.* Translated by Thomas McQuillan. Cambridge, Mass.: M.I.T. Press, 1996.
Vesaas, Tarjei. *Through Naked Branches: Selected Poems of Tarjei Vesaas.* Edited and translated by Roger Greenwald. Princeton, N.J.: Princeton University Press, 2000.

Ursula A. L. Lindqvist

SÖDERGRAN, EDITH (1892–1923)

Although she lived in Finland and Russia for most of her life, Edith Södergran was a pioneer of modern Swedish poetry. She is best known for revitalizing Swedish lyrical poetry in the early 20th century by crafting simple, haunting poems with great philosophical depth and for being among the first Swedish-language poets to write entirely in free verse. Her work has had a lasting impact on subsequent world-class poets in Sweden as well as her native Finland, including KARIN BOYE, HARRY MARTINSON, and TOMAS TRANSTRÖMER. But Södergran's celebrated status today contrasts sharply with the poverty, illness, war, and isolation that ended her life at the age of 31.

Södergran was born in St. Petersburg, Russia, in 1892, the only child of Finnish-Swedish immigrants. Her mother was a well-educated second-generation immigrant from the Finland-Swedish community living in St. Petersburg, and her father, who was from a peasant family in western Finland, had come to Russia to work as an engineer. (Finland is officially bilingual, with both Swedish and Finnish required in schools and government. In 1900 13 percent of Finland's population spoke Swedish as a native language, and the remaining 87 percent spoke Finnish. Today Swedish-speaking Finns comprise about 6 percent of the population.) Shortly after Södergran was born, the family moved to Raivola, a village on the Karelian isthmus that at that time connected Finland and Russia. A great larch forest that Peter the Great had planted surrounded the village, and these woods provide a setting for many of Södergran's imagistic poems (Schoolfield, "Edith Södergran," 565). Södergran spoke Swedish at home and attended a German girls' school in St. Petersburg, where she mastered German and Russian. Her early poetry, from her school years, is entirely in German and follows conventional forms of rhythm, rhyme, and meter. These early poems, about 200 in all, were published as a posthumous collection under the title *Vaxdukshäftet*, "The Wax-covered Notebook." In 1907, when Södergran was 15, her idyllic childhood evaporated. Her father died of tuberculosis, and soon Södergran was diagnosed with the disease. For a time she and her mother lived on a family inheritance. They were able to pay for extended treatments at sanatoriums in Nummela, Finland, and in Davos, Switzerland. In the Davos sanatorium's well-stocked library, during her convalescence Södergran eagerly read the work of many world poets and philosophers: William Shakespeare, Walt Whitman, A. C. Swinburne, Friedrich Nietzsche, Arthur Schopenhauer, and Rudolph Steiner, among others. Södergran's poetry began to evolve and to mature. She switched from writing in German, which she called her "best" language and the language of her intellect, to writing in Swedish, which she called the language of her soul. In 1916 she and her mother

returned to Raivola, and that year Södergran sent her first collection, *Dikter* (Poems), to a publisher in Helsinki. In 1917 czarist Russia collapsed in the Russian Revolution. When Finland, a culturally autonomous state that had been a grand duchy under the Russian czar, declared independence, civil war broke out between rival factions in the fledgling republic. In an isolated village wedged between two war-torn nations, Södergran and her mother eked out a meager existence, cut off from most sources of income. The themes of death, isolation, and heightened sensual awareness pervade Södergran's poetry from that period. Illness and starvation ended Södergran's short life in 1923.

Those hardships did not, however, prevent her from leaving behind an impressive body of work: *September-lyran* (September Lyre, 1918), *Rosenaltaret* (The Rose Altar, 1919), *Brokiga iakttageleser* (Motley Observations, a collection of aphorisms, 1919), *Framtidens skugga* (The Shadow of the Future, 1920), and *Landet som icke är* (The Land That Is Not, 1925, published posthumously). At the time Södergran made her debut, poets in other European cultural centers, such as St. Petersburg and Berlin, had been experimenting with so-called modern forms and concepts for about a decade. That artistic experimentation, which swept Europe and the United States in the early 20th century, is known today as modernism because artists, including poets, sought to reject their society's centuries-old traditions and embrace fresh approaches to art. But the experimental spirit was slow in reaching geographically isolated Scandinavia, which, with the exception of Copenhagen, Denmark, lacked cosmopolitan cultural centers at the turn of the 20th century. Södergran, however, was born and educated in St. Petersburg, a thriving cultural mecca for avant-garde writers. Thus during her school years she was exposed to radical trends in continental European literature and philosophy. Södergran was particularly influenced by the work of German expressionists, Russian futurists, and Anglo-American imagists. Nietzsche's philosophical prose work *Also sprache Zarathustra* (*Thus Spoke Zarathustra*) had a lasting impact on her. In particular, she embraced Nietzsche's concept of the *Übermensch* (denoting "ultra human being"), which for Södergran represented the rise of a new, future-oriented, creative individual. In 1919, when *Septemberlyran* first appeared, she wrote an open letter to the leading Swedish daily newspaper in Helsinki that issued a call to such individuals to build a future through art: "My book will not have failed in its goal if a single individual envisions the immensity in this art . . . I hope that I will not be alone with the greatness I have to bring" (Olsson 15–17). It turns out she was not alone. Södergran's work inspired other young Finnish-Swedish poets, including Hagar Olsson and Elmer Diktonius, to perpetuate her modernist legacy and extend this new lyrical vein to Sweden and the rest of Scandinavia. Södergran's work resonates today not only with literary scholars, who have declared her the mother of Swedish modernism, but also with the general public. Södergran's *Samlade dikter* (Collected Poems) is still in print, and her work is read today throughout Scandinavia. Her output—including such poems as "INSTINCT" and "THE DAY COOLS"—have been translated into many languages, with Stina Katchadourian's work (Fjord Press, 1992) featuring the most elegant English translations available.

BIBLIOGRAPHY

Jones, W. Glyn, and M. A. Branch, eds. *Edith Södergran: Nine Essays on Her Life and Work.* New York: Dorset Press, 1992.

Schoolfield, George. "Edith Södergran." In *Dictionary of Scandinavian Literature,* edited by Virpi Zuck. Westport, Conn.: Greenwood Press, 1990.

———. *Edith Södergran: Modernist Poet in Finland.* Westport, Conn.: Greenwood Press, 1984.

Södergran, Edith. *Love & Solitude: Selected Poems 1916–1923.* Translated by Stina Katchadourian. Seattle, Wash.: Fjord Press, 1992.

Södergran, Edith, Hagar Olsson, and Silvester Mazzarella. *The Poet Who Created Herself: The Complete Letters of Edith Södergran to Hagar Olsson with Hagar Olsson's Commentary and the Complete Letters of Edith Södergran to Elmer Diktonius.* Norwich, England: Norvik Press, 2001.

Ursula Lindqvist

"SOLDIER DREAMS OF WHITE TULIPS, A" MAHMUD DARWISH (1967)

This popular poem by MAHMUD DARWISH has had more than one translation in English (see the Akash and Forché renderings in my citations). It is a striking poem and rare in its subject matter. It humanizes the enemy and, more specifically, the soldier enemy who invades one's country. In political and military conflicts the Other is often demonized or at best turned into an icon of brutality and aggression. Darwish in this poem writes almost tenderly of an anonymous Israeli soldier whose dreams attest to his nonviolent nature. His dream of an "olive branch" in a poem written in 1967 foreshadows the speech of the late Yāsir 'Arāfat, chairman of the Palestine Liberation Organization, who addressed the UN General Assembly in November 1974 calling for a peaceful settlement of the Palestine question: "Today I have come bearing an olive branch and a freedom fighter's gun. Do not let the olive branch fall from my hand."

The poem revolves around a conversation between an unnamed Israeli soldier and the named poetic persona (Mahmud) in a bar or café. One infers the setting from casual indications; for instance, "When I filled his fourth glass" and when the soldier addresses the speaker as "Mahmud, my friend." The dialogue is presented in the English translation in italics (in contrast to the regular font of the lyrical narrative): "He drew on his cigarette. He said, as if fleeing from a swamp of blood. / I dreamt of white tulips, an olive branch, a bird embracing the dawn on a lemon branch."

This dream of peace opens and ends the poem and is recalled in the midst of it, thus constituting its poetic backbone. The point of the poem is that soldiers are pushed into war by propaganda or go unreflectively. They are made to think this is the way to be patriotic. Their authentic feelings of wanting to live peacefully are smothered by a mobilizing discourse. The dream stands for the soldier"s repressed wish not to die or kill.

The poetic dialogue shows how such a peace-loving soldier ends up murdering others who cannot defend themselves: "I saw what I did: / a blood-red boxthorn / . . . / Like a tent he collapsed and died, his arms stretched out like dry creek-beds. / When I searched his pockets for a name, I found two photographs, one of his wife, the other of his daughter." The dead ones were peasants and workers, not well-trained fighters, yet the soldier says that he did not feel sad for them since "sadness is a white bird that does not come near a battlefield / . . . / I was there like a machine spitting hellfire and death, / turning space into a black bird."

Antiwar poems proliferate in our conflict-ridden world. While a poet like Wilfred Owen wrote magnificent personal poems about his experience in World War I, Darwish writes imaginatively and empathetically of a young Israeli soldier who would rather not be engaged in combat but instead relax at home, drinking his mother's coffee.

BIBLIOGRAPHY

Darwish, Mahmud. "Jundi yahlam bi'l-zanabiq al-bayda'." In *Diwan Mahmud Darwish.* Vol. 1. Beirut: Dar al-'Awda, 1979, 311–322.

———. "The Soldier Dreams of White Tulips." In *Unfortunately, It Was Paradise,* edited and translated by Munir Akash and Carolyn Forché. Berkeley: University of California Press, 2003, 165–168.

———. *The Soldier who Dreamt of White Lilies.* Bilingual edition. Translated by H. Martens, A. Bushnaq, and A. R. Yaghi. Amman: n.p. [University of Jordan?], 1969.

Ferial J. Ghazoul

"SOLDIER OF URBINA, A" JORGE LUIS BORGES (1946)

"A Soldier of Urbina," from *El otro, el mismo* (The Self and the Other, 1946), is typical of BORGES's mature poetry. Classical in structure and containing both historical and literary allusions, it is also an outstanding example of Borgesian metaphysics. An Italianate sonnet written in hendecasyllables, the poem's form—typical of the Castilian Renaissance—alludes to its content: the improbable fate of a 16th-century Spanish soldier. The central conceit, an obscure reference in the title made clear only in the last line, is that this weary veteran of the regiment of Diego of Urbina is Miguel de Cervantes. As is often the case in Borges's conjectural treatments of history, the future author of *Don Quixote* is portrayed at the furthest point from his ultimate destiny: *"Sospechándose indigno de otra hazaña /. . . A sórdidos oficios resignado"* (Beginning to fear his own unworthiness /. . . resigning himself to minor duty). Another common Borgesian motif is the mirror relationship between reality and art. Like the protagonist of his unwritten masterpiece, the unnamed Cervantes retreats from *"la saña de lo real"* (the cruel weight of reality) into a *"mágico pasado"* (magical past). Borges, however, rewrites literary history by replacing the worn-out chivalric romances that actually inspired

Cervantes's parody with more consecrated ballads: *The Song of Roland* and the Arthurian legends. This curious substitution recalls Borges's own fascination with the medieval epic and in doing so creates a typically Borgesian labyrinth entwining more than 1,000 years of the European canon. Yet another instance of literary reflexivity is the dream metaphor. A prominent metaphysical motif in Borges's own writing, the paradoxical relationship between dream and reality also evokes the baroque poetry of Cervantes's contemporaries, Francisco de Quevedo, Luis de Góngora, and Pedro Calderón de la Barca. It also recalls Borges's almost mystical conception of artistic creation. The final tercet thus reveals both the identity of the melancholy soldier and the divine madness that is the secret of artistic creation: *"Atravesando el fondo de algún sueño. / Por él ya andaban don Quijote y Sancho"* (Suddenly plunging deep in a dream of his own, / he came on Sancho and Don Quixote, riding).

BIBLIOGRAPHY

Borges, Jorge Luis. "A Soldier of Urbina" In *Personal Anthology,* translated by Alastair Reid, 111. New York: Grove Press, 1967.

Eric L. Reinholtz

"SONG OF BECOMING" FADWA TUQAN (1967)

FADWA TUQAN wrote "Song of Becoming" in the aftermath of the 1967 Arab-Israeli War that resulted in the defeat of the tripartite Arab coalition (Egypt, Syria, and Jordan) by Israel. The defeat also meant that the Palestinian struggle against dispossession, which had been going on since 1948 (the year the United Nations recognized Israel), was still unresolved and that the creation of a Palestinian nation-state was not going to happen soon. "Song of Becoming" takes a defiant stance against this despair and calls for continued resistance to occupation. The means for what Tuqan calls "plain rejection" would no longer be the armies of other Arab nations, but the Palestinian youth who had gained an irrevocable level of national consciousness and were beginning to assume "the roles of great heroes in history."

"Song of Becoming" is therefore a celebration of this new generation that came into being in the first 20 years of the Palestinian dispossession. It invokes national sentiments and views the post-1967 momentum not as a loss but rather as an opportunity for the Palestinians to "build [themselves] anew" in the face of destruction. In that respect "Song of Becoming" has an epic tone by virtue of its desire to reread all the previous moments in the nation's history as steps toward its coming into existence. From that perspective in "Song of Becoming" the nation is represented mythopoetically as the Phoenix, the bird that rose renewed from its ashes after having been consumed by fire for many years. Another aspect of the poem's epic quality lies in Tuqan's deliberate attempt to force the physical limits of time and space to account for the heroic potentials of the new generation she praises. Those legendary "boys" have "grown suddenly . . . more than the years of a lifetime." "Soaring high towards the sun," they personify "the voice" and "the anger" of rejection to the extent that even the poet who recites their "song of becoming" is compelled to recognize that they surpass her poetry—"all poetry."

"Song of Becoming" remains one of the landmark poems in Fadwa Tuqan's literary career as well as of modern Palestinian literature. It has been a source of inspiration for many Palestinians in search of a national consciousness.

BIBLIOGRAPHY

DeYoung, Terri. "Love, Death, and the Ghost of Al-Khansa." In *Tradition, Modernity, and Postmodernity in Arabic Literature,* edited by Kamal Abdel-Malek and Wael Hallaq. Leiden, Netherlands, and Boston: Brill Publications, 2000.

Tuqan, Fadwa. *A Mountainous Journey: An Autobiography.* Translated by Olive Kenny and Naomi Shihab Nye, foreword by Salma Khadra Jayyusi. Saint Paul, Minn.: Graywolf Press, 1990.

———. "Song of Becoming." Translated by Naomi Shihab Nye with Salma Khadra Jayyusi. In *Anthology of Modern Palestinian Literature,* edited by Salma Khadra Jayyusi. New York: Columbia University Press, 1992, 316.

Firat Oruc

SONG OF LAWINO: AN AFRICAN LAMENT Okot p'Bitek (1966)

First composed in 1956 in Acoli, a Ugandan language, Okop p'Bitek converted this book-length poem into English, and it was published a decade later. The author's note informs readers that the English-language version "clipped a bit of the eagle's wings and rendered the sharp edges of the warrior's sword rusty and blunt, and has also murdered rhythm and rhyme" (4), but the work still soars and is pointed enough to be considered "a biting yet compassionate satire on virtually every aspect of modern African life: love, sex, fear, hate, politics, and the relationship between black and white, African and European" (back cover).

The work comprises 13 sections, each titled provocatively to hint at its content and composed in irregular, free-verse stanzas: (1) My Husband's Tongue is Bitter, (2) The Woman with Whom I Share My Husband, (3) I Do Not Know the Dances of White People, (4) My Name Blew Like a Horn among the Payira, (5) The Graceful Giraffe Cannot Become a Monkey, (6) The Mother Stone Has a Hollow Stomach, (7) There Is No Fixed Time for Breast Feeding, (8) I Am Ignorant of the Good Word in the Clean Book, (9) From the Mouth of Which River? (10) The Last Safari to Pagak, (11) The Buffalos of Poverty Knock the People Down, (12) My Husband's House Is a Dark Forest of Books, and (13) Let Them Prepare the Malakwang Dish. The poem's speaker is Lawino, a spirited Acoli woman and a chieftain's daughter, a leader among the young women with whom she grew up. She deplores her husband's turn to newfangled fashions and his predictable, postcolonial adherence to Western manners, ideologies, and mores. She denigrates the false values of copy-cat behaviors and rails literally and symbolically against those who would "uproot the pumpkin in the old homestead" (9), the reliable and traditional source of community sustenance.

Throughout the work Lawino most often directly addresses Ocol, her husband—only now and again turning her words to other listeners, who are appealed to for support in turning Ocol around and away from what Lawino considers mentally and socially unhealthy behaviors. In the first section Lawino complains of the way her husband insults and berates her for her traditional ways: His tongue "is fierce like the arrow of the scorpion, / It is ferocious / Like the poison of a barren woman / And corrosive like the juice of the gourd" (16). She objects when Ocol "pours scorn / On Black People" (16) and accuses her of "blocking his progress"

(17) because he suddenly considers her "primitive" and "ignorant, poor and diseased!" (17). In the next section Lawino describes the absurdity of "the modern girl" whom Ocol has chosen as his second wife and laughs at Clementine's efforts to look European by powdering her face and wearing blood-red lipstick: "She looks as if she has been struck / By lightning; / Or burnt like the knogoni / In a fire hunt" (24). Lawino describes the absurdity of pointy Western brassieres on flat-chested, barren African women, and she summarizes the traditional idea of a good wife; she expresses no jealousy, instead imploring Ocol "to refrain from heaping abuses" on her head, "stop being half-crazy," and recognize that "the ways of [their] ancestors / Are good" (29).

The third section contrasts the behaviors of the Acoli with those of whites—their dances, attire, gatherings, games. In section 4 Lawino proudly touts her family's prestige and history and describes Ocol's sincerity when he was courting her, in contrast to his present demeanor, behind dark glasses, "the scabies on [his] buttocks" covered by hot, inappropriate European clothing (49). Section 5 is a praise song to her own beauty, and Section 6 a celebration of the traditional home and hearth. In Section 7 Lawino defends her Acoli sense of time, which is natural, not regimented by clocks and calendars that have no awareness of real-life processes and their irregular durations.

Sections 8 and 9 contrast the religious practices of Africa with those of white people; and in Section 10—in which she shows how white practices seem to her like superstition and witchcraft—Lawino carefully describes Acoli hygiene, medicine, and psychology and Acoli attitudes toward death. Section 11 pokes fun at the Western- style political campaigns in which Ocol participates, frenzied contests between "brothers" that bring forth no benefits to the people. Here Lawino reveals a sophisticated understanding of postcolonial political practices and of the sorts of power maneuvers that brought Ugandan dictator Idi Amin to power. In Section 12 Lawino describes the effects of Western-style higher education: "Ocol has lost his head / In the forest of books" (199). Lawino grumbles that the manhood of young males "was finished / In the classrooms, /Their testicles / Were smashed / With large books!" (208).

Section 13, the work's exhortation, appeals to Ocol to submit to an Acoli cleansing ritual that can cure him of his deadly infatuation with white ways. The ritual is described in picturesque detail, each part of it involving physical actions and psychological effects. Lawino tells Ocol that once he is cured, he needs to pray to the ancestors, "Ask them to forgive / Your past stupidity . . . / For when you insulted me, / . . . / You were insulting your grandfathers / And grandmothers, your father and mother!" (213). The work ends with a declaration of love for Ocol and with an expression of hope for the future, so long as "no one uproot the Pumpkin" (216).

BIBLIOGRAPHY

p'Bitek, Okol. *Song of Lawino: An African Lament.* New York: Meridian Books, 1969.

R. Victoria Arana

"SONNET 41" TANIKAWA SHUNTARO (1953)

While Tanikawa is not the first Japanese poet to use the sonnet form, he has made unique contributions to the sonnet genre through his *62 Sonnets* (*62 no sonetto*), in which the poet seems to have used the form of the Sicilian *strambotto,* comprising two quatrains and two tercets. But due to fundamental differences between Japanese and Western languages, Japanese sonnets, including Tanikawa's, lack the metrical and rhyming patterns of Western sonnets, depending instead for their rhythm on syllable patterns within their lines, just as in their different ways *tanka* (5, 7, 5, 7, 7 syllables per line) or *haiku* (5, 7, 5) do. "Sonnet 41," with its nostalgic opening line about looking up at the azure of the sky, is one of the most famous and best-loved poems not only of this sonnet sequence but of Tanikawa's entire output. More than a love poem, the sonnet expresses pantheistic rather than monotheistic feelings about the fallen state of humanity (e.g., "But the brightness that has come down through the clouds / Will never go back to the sky"). The combination in this sonnet of pantheism—a traditional Japanese sensibility—and Judeo-Christian religiosity in response to humanity's fall seems to appeal greatly to modern Japanese readers, whose psyches subsume the two different sensibilities. Throughout the poem the fallen state of humankind is suggested through contrasting images of the primary innocence (or divinity) of the universe/nature and the greed of human beings: the sun "everlastingly lavishly expends itself" in contrast to people busily picking up even after dark, or humans who "are basely born / and don't know how to rest well, like the trees." The image of cutting and hurting ("The window cuts off what is overflowing") in the penultimate tercet is completed in the metaphysical conclusion of the last tercet: "To be is to injure space and time, / and the pain reproaches me. / When I'm gone my health will return." This tercet's startling self-referential equation/union of "I" (the human speaker) and the universe recapitulates and intensifies the speaker's statement of cosmic and pantheistic loneliness and nostalgia expressed in the sonnet's opening quatrain, a human longing for that lost, original innocence when there was no painful rift between human speech and nature's "speech," or between culture and nature. Hence the poet's paradoxical, animistic, and pantheistic statement: "When I'm gone" (i.e., when base human speech ceases) "my health will return" (i.e., nature's divine "speech" will resume). Thus Tanikawa's "Sonnet 41," and by extension *62 no sonetto*, together with his *Nijūokukōnen no kodoku* (Solitude of Two Billion Light-Years, 1952), communicate a cosmic loneliness and yearning for union with nature through pantheistic and Judeo-Christian sensibilities, expressing the essential tone of his entire creative career and thereby attracting not only Japanese but also international audiences to his work.

BIBLIOGRAPHY

Tanikawa Shuntaro. *62 Sonnets and Definitions*. Translated by William I. Elliott and Kazuo Kawamura. Santa Fe, N.M.: Katydid Books, 1992.

Hagiwara Takao

SONNETS TO ORPHEUS RAINER MARIA RILKE (1923)   RAINER MARIA RILKE's *Sonnets to Orpheus* (*Die Sonnette an Orpheus*) comprises 55 sonnets in two series. The first series (*Erster Teil*) contains 26 poems; the second (*Zweiter Teil*), 29. Poet and translator Willis Barnstone provides a breezy but comprehensive 97-page narrative introduction to this celebrated work of high MODERNISM and shows how Rilke's sonnet sequence weaves together numerous strands of Rilke's turbulent life, poetic aspirations, and aesthetics.

Many readers agree that *Sonnets to Orpheus* embodies Rilke's visionary power at its peak and represents the zenith of his technical skill as a versifier. Critics have admired the sonnets' various ways of resonating with and departing from conventions established by earlier modernist sonneteers, including Charles Baudelaire and PAUL VALÉRY (whose "GRAVEYARD BY THE SEA" Rilke intensely admired). Formally, their variety is noteworthy, especially to readers of German who can appreciate the stunning ways that Rilke's metrical and musical patterns complement the ideas expressed by the words.

The work takes up Roman poet Ovid's story of the love of Orpheus for Eurydice (in *Metamorphoses*, 8 A.D.) and endows it with new significance, emphasizing the durable relevance of their momentous destinies. The two sequences together are dedicated "as a monument for Vera Ouckama Knoop," who is the Eurydice to Rilke's Orpheus. Vera, a childhood friend of Rilke's daughter, Ruth, grew to be a talented dancer, musician, and fine arts draughtsman, whose death in young womanhood so startled and troubled Rilke's feelings about the transience of human life and the transcendence of spirit that, as he later put it in a letter to his Polish translator (Witold Hulewicz), his agonized creative response felt to him as though terrifying angels were "dictating" these poems to him (see *DUINO ELEGIES*). Between February 2 and 5, 1922, "he had completed, in order, without altering a line, all but one of the twenty-six poems that would form the First Part" (Snow, *Sonnets*, x). Between the 5th and the 11th of the month, unblocked by the gift of the sonnets, Rilke completed the *Duino Elegies*; and between February 11 and 23, "he had produced twenty-nine more sonnets, which he arranged (moving the last poem written to the beginning of the sequence) to form a matching group" to the first series (Snow xi).

Several influences found their way into Rilke's creative crucible for *Sonnets to Orpheus*. As early as 1920, Rilke's close friend Elizabeth "Merline" Klossowska had given him a translation of Ovid's *Metamorphoses*; and upon departing from Rilke's château for the 1921 Christmas season, she had pinned above his desk a postcard of Giovanni Battista Cima da Conegliano's painting of Orpheus making music under a tree. On

January 1, 1922, Vera Knoop's mother wrote to Rilke, recounting Vera's death from leukemia and enclosing a 16-page diary that Vera had written during her last days (Barnstone 68). Rilke had just finished translating some of Michelangelo's exuberant erotic sonnets. But the main source of the *Sonnets* was Rilke's capacity to render clearly—and to his satisfaction, at last—his latest revelations and his oldest convictions about the relationship of life to art.

What Rilke achieved in *Sonnets to Orpheus* cannot be described; it must be experienced. Barnstone, all the same, has this to say in the introduction to his translation: Rilke "makes the disappeared dancer more than a paradigm. . . . She is his and *our* intimate cosmos, in and around us. And he draws on the two existences of Eurydice, the early talented dream child and the young dancer . . . who is snatched away by mindless, eroding time" (76). Rilke's mystical, pantheistic poetry—here especially—sings with joy to Eurydice and to Orpheus, to the timeless accomplishment of lives lived joyously and creatively, and to the everlasting quality of true music, once it has been heard. The sequence's final poem (II:XXIX) ends with an affirmation of *being in eternity*: "*Und wenn dich das Irdische vergass, / zu der stillen Erde sag: Ich rinne. / Zu dem raschen Wasser sprich: Ich bin*"—which Poulin renders as "And if the earthly has forgotten / you, say to the still earth: I flow. / To the rushing water speak: I am" (Poulin 194–195).

BIBLIOGRAPHY

Rilke, Rainer Maria. *Duino Elegies and the Sonnets to Orpheus.* Bilingual edition. Translated by A. Poulin Jr. Boston: Mariner Books, 2005.

———. *Sonnets to Orpheus.* Bilingual edition. Translated by Willis Barnstone. Boston: Shambhala, 2004.

———. *Sonnets to Orpheus.* Bilingual edition. Translated by Edward Snow. New York: North Point Press/Farrar, Straus and Giroux, 2004.

R. Victoria Arana

"SOUTH SEAS" Cesare Pavese (1930)

This was Pavese's first successful poetic composition. In "South Seas" ("*I mari del Sud*") are three qualities evident in many of his later poems: Pavese's effort to create a "poem-story" (*poesia-racconto*); the poet's choice of conventionally "unpoetic" subject matter (lower-class characters—many of whom are social outcasts—in rural and urban settings); and the poet's approach to poetic language and meter. Pavese crafted poems that possessed colloquial, often dialectical Italian phrasing built on a subtle, seemingly prosaic, meter but versified in accentual-syllabic meters and frequently employing anapestic rhythms. After writing a variety of formative poems, Pavese (in September 1930) composed "South Seas," in which the narrator recounts a walk in the Langhe hills with his older cousin, whose stories from world travel intrigue the poet. The storytelling aspect of "South Seas"—representing Pavese's attempt to construct a short story in verse form—is realized through the juxtaposition of dialogue from various characters portrayed in the poem, with contextualizing commentary from the poem's central consciousness (which is ostensibly Pavese's own). The poem refers to the cousin's former employment on whaling ships (in part also an allusion to Pavese's interest in American literature; notably, he translated Herman Melville's novel of the whaling trade, *Moby-Dick,* into Italian). Nevertheless, "South Seas" exhibits more of the influence of Homer than of Melville, according to William Arrowsmith, in that Pavese's poem offers a straightforward, unembellished depiction of the aforementioned walk in the hills, with the narrative's action beginning in media res. The one section of the poem to employ a distinctly modernist sensibility is the last stanza, which succinctly underscores the irony between the poet's innocence—his naive interpretation of the meaning of the cousin's adventurous life at sea—and the cousin's realistic, even cynical perspective on the significance of his own experience. "South Seas" is arguably the finest example of Pavese's direct narrative style. Later he perfected two other types of poetry: poems constructed more upon images than upon narratives and poems that are overtly erotic. A quality distinguishing Pavese's poetry from his Italian literary predecessors—a quality possibly developed from his extensive reading of American literature—is his celebration of things seen as significant in and of themselves, not solely for their possible allegorical references. "South Seas" represents the first flowering of Pavese's innovative poetic vision. Pavese recognized that it was his breakthrough work and positioned "South Seas" as the initial poem in

Lavorare stanca (1936), the first and only volume of his poetry published during his lifetime.

BIBLIOGRAPHY

Pavese, Cesare. *Hard Labor* Translated by William Arrowsmith. Baltimore: Johns Hopkins University Press, 1979.

Ted Olson

SOYINKA, WOLE (1934–   )

Born Oluwole Akinwande Soyinka on July 13, 1934, near Ibadan in western Nigeria, Wole Soyinka is one of the most important literary figures in sub-Saharan Africa and the first African to win the Nobel Prize in literature (1986). He was awarded the Agip Prize for Literature in 1986 and named commander of the Nigerian Federal Republic the same year. He has honorary doctorates from the University of Leeds and Harvard University and was named a fellow of the Society for the Humanities at Cornell University. He has taught, among other places, at the Universities of Ife, Lagos, and Ibadan; Churchill College, Cambridge; University of Sheffield; University of Ghana; and Emory University in Atlanta. Today he lives near Los Angeles.

Eclectic and versatile, Soyinka is a poet, playwright, novelist, essayist, literary critic, and social commentator who has authored in excess of 40 works. Known principally for his plays set in Africa—of which the most famous are *The Lion and the Jewel* (1964), *Death and the King's Horsemen* (1975), and *The Beatification of Area Boy* (1996)—he draws consciously on his people's mythology and ceremonies. In non-African situations, as in his important poem "TELEPHONE CONVERSATION," the narrator's ethnicity often forms an ironic counterpoint to the mores and biases of white Europe. Yet one of Soyinka's greatest strengths is that he never idealizes traditional Africa or condemns all that comes from the West.

Soyinka reached artistic maturity during the 1950s and 1960s when many African and Caribbean writers, especially from former French colonies, broke with the heritage of Europe, attempting to identify an artistic, intellectual, and cultural voice unique to peoples of African heritage. That was dubbed the NEGRITUDE MOVEMENT. Though he believes in the unique character of African creativity, Soyinka never subscribed to Negritude. In 1962 he responded to founders of the movement such as Senegal's LÉOPOLD SÉDAR SENGHOR and Martinique's AIMÉ CÉSAIRE by quoting a Yoruba proverb that says "a tiger does not have to proclaim its tigritude." *Idanre and Other Poems* (1967), his first collection, celebrates its Yoruba heritage.

Like many contemporary African intellectuals, artists, and writers, Soyinka has long been concerned with the consequences of colonialism on his continent, including those postcolonial cultural conditions that have led to the entrenchment of corrupt political regimes. Soyinka's first public dissention occurred during the Biafran war (1967–70) when he called for a cease-fire over national radio. Seen as a traitor, he was jailed for 22 months by the military government of Nigeria. The war and its causes are explored in *Season of Anomy*. His imprisonment is described in *The Man Died: Prison Notes* and in the collection of poems *A Shuttle in the Crypt* (1971). His subsequent volumes of verse—the epic poem *Ogun Abibiman* (God of the Black Man's Land), *Mandela's Earth and Other Poems* (1988), *Outsiders* (1999), and *Samarkand and Other Markets I Have Known* (2002)—continue his exploration of contemporary culture and political events in an ever more cosmopolitan manner.

Soyinka's forthrightness has often caused him trouble. Nigeria's succession of military dictatorships has been hostile to the country's outspoken artistic and intellectual community for which Soyinka was often the spokesperson. In danger of imprisonment, Soyinka fled Nigeria on motorcycle after the authorities seized his passport in November 1994. *The Open Sore of a Continent* (1996) describes the political conditions leading to his forced exile. The government's hostility toward dissident poets culminated in the execution of writer Ken Saro-Wiwa in 1995, after which it pronounced a death sentence in absentia on Soyinka himself in 1997. The sentence was subsequently revoked by a later government.

Today Soyinka criticizes religious excess, condemning the recent stoning of adulterous and sexually active unwed women in western Nigeria. He continues to draw on Yoruba myth for his work and hopes some day to return permanently to his beloved Africa.

BIBLIOGRAPHY

Gibbs, James, and Bernth Lindfors. *Research on Wole Soyinka.* Trenton, N.J.: Africa World Press, 1993.

Jones, Eldred. *The Writing of Wole Soyinka.* 3rd ed. London: James Curry, 1988.

Soyinka, Wole. *Art, Dialogue, and Outrage: Essays on Literature and Culture.* Ibadan, Nigeria: New Horn Press, 1988.

Wright, Derek. *Wole Soyinka Revisited.* New York: Twayne, 1993.

Annette Olsen-Fazi

"SPRING NIGHT" HAGIWARA SAKUTARŌ (1917)

Although it is not one of SAKUTARŌ's more harrowing compositions and does not contain the nightmarish imagery of so much of his poetry, "Spring Night" nevertheless creates a hauntingly melancholic mood by employing visual imagery to evoke the mystery of things not seen and a sort of godlike compassion for them. The poem alludes to the grand scheme of things in an unembellished way characteristic of what is best in Sakutarō's poetry. The poem begins by calling attention immediately to concrete imagery: "Things like littlenecks, / things like quahogs, / things like water-fleas, / these organisms, bodies buried in sand" (101). The setting is a beach, but by the fourth line the images summoned to the mind's eye by the words *littlenecks, quahogs,* and *water-fleas* are revised by the appositive "bodies buried in sand." The reader is thus given to understand that the real subject of this poem is not the aquatic life (those specific "things") invoked by gross comparisons ("like . . . like . . . like"), but an immense and various world of "organisms" entirely out of sight. Out of sight, too, "hands like silk threads innumerably grow," and these "move as the waves do." The poem's speaker feels "pity" for the organisms over which "the brine flows" and conveys compassion (by means of synecdoche) for other unseen lives: "even the tongues of clams, flickering" are "looking sad" on this spring night. Then the speaker sees something on the beach in the distance that strikes him: "a row of invalids, bodies below their waists missing, is walking, / walking unsteadily." The shiver of recognition that the invalids and the unseen organisms are equally frail and equally alive is expressed succinctly by an expletive and the observation that follows: "Ah, over the hair of those human beings as well, / passes the spring night haze, all over, deeply, / rolling, rolling in."

The poem works by juxtaposing two initially contrasting sets of signifiers: The first evokes the vast world of hidden and invisible life forms; the second carefully describes a single file of frail human beings. The juxtaposition calls attention to the circumstance that the people are also only faintly seen, also partly submerged in the sand and surf through which they walk in the dark of night. "Spring Night" closes with the ambiguous line "this white row of waves is ripples." The image in that line seems to refer at once to the receding foam of breakers on the beach, to the people "walking unsteadily" in the surf, and—by the extension implied in the poem's initial similes—to all of the inconspicuous generations ("ripples") of life moving about in the planet's biosphere virtually unnoticed (see ECOPOETICS), but moving nevertheless—moving back and forth "as the waves do."

BIBLIOGRAPHY

Sakutarō, Hagiwara. *Howling at the Moon: Poems and Prose of Hagiwara Sakutarō.* Translated and introduced by Hiroaki Sato. Copenhagen and Los Angeles: Green Integer (#57), 2002.

R. Victoria Arana

"STALIN EPIGRAM, THE" OSIP MANDELSTAM (1970)

This precisely executed image of Stalin and his reign of terror led to OSIP MANDELSTAM's arrest and exile and ultimately to his death in the gulag. After sharing this poem (*"My zhivem, pod soboiu ne chuia strany"*) with a small group of friends, Mandelstam was denounced in 1934 by an acquaintance and consequently was banished from all major urban centers; subsequent arrests and sentences resulted in his death in transit to a labor camp. "The Stalin Epigram" is a 16-line lyric in the tradition of Russian acmeism (akin to American imagism) in its clarity and articulates Mandelstam's repulsion over the horrors he observed. It is exemplary of the sense of responsibility among many Russian poets to record what they had seen.

The poem opens with remarks on the effects of the oppression experienced by political dissidents and displaced peasants. Mandelstam writes that people speak in muted tones because of their constant fear of the state, in conversations that cannot be overheard even by those nearby. He then paradoxically and at great risk reveals what those whispered conversations entail and that Stalin is their subject. Readers understand that Stalin is a constant concern for the dissidents. One of Mandelstam's tactics is to underscore Stalin's origins and lack of refinement, which are in contrast to Mandelstam's middle-class intellectual background. Stalin, born in the mountains of Georgia, is depicted with the hands of a laborer and wearing work boots; his edicts are the work of a blacksmith, hammered out on an anvil instead of eloquently composed at a desk.

Mandelstam also includes in his picture a glimpse of the groveling minions who attach themselves to anyone in a position of power, dehumanizing the wheedling parasites through his visual and aural images. Stalin plays with the obsequious behavior of these sycophants. Stalin and Mandelstam both know that total power resides in Stalin's whim, needing only his gesture to determine anyone's fate. Along with the filth Mandelstam skillfully associates with Stalin in his descriptions of Stalin's hands and moustache, the most chilling effect is saved for the poem's conclusion.

The final two lines of the portrait reveal Stalin's sensual pleasure in exercising his power, savoring the sweetness of each death as though it were summer fruit, rich with flavor and juice. These deaths are of Stalin's intimates, his long-time compatriots, and he metaphorically embraces each one. The poem's last lines nearly eroticize Stalin's relationship with death and in so doing expose him as an extraordinarily sinister figure.

BIBLIOGRAPHY

Cavanagh, Clare. *Osip Mandelstam and the Modernist Creation of Tradition.* Princeton, N.J.: Princeton University Press, 1995.

Doherty, Justin. *The Acmeist Movement in Russian Poetry: Culture and the Word.* Oxford: Clarendon Press, 1995.

Mandelstam, Osip. *Osip Mandelstam: 50 Poems.* Translated by Bernard Meares, introduced by Joseph Brodsky. New York: Persea Books, 2000.

———. *Selected Poems of Osip Mandelstam.* Translated by W. S. Merwin and Clarence Brown. New York: Atheneum, 1974; reissued New York: New York Review of Books Classics, 2004.

A. Mary Murphy

"STILLNESS OF THE WORLD BEFORE BACH, THE" LARS GUSTAFSSON (1982) This poem (*"Världens tystnad före Bach"*) appeared in Swedish in LARS GUSTAFSSON's poetry collection of the same title in 1982, at the mid-point of the poet's literary career to date. Over the past 50 years Gustafsson has experimented with many poetic styles, from longer, epic-style poems to ballads to didactic verse, and he perceives all of his poetry as creative manifestations of his intellectual work as a philosopher. This poem is characteristic of Gustafsson's shorter, didactic poems that employ sensual imagery to raise existential questions. For Gustafsson "poetry is not feelings; rather, it is the intellectual's visual work and a trying on of masks," literary critic Mikael van Reis wrote recently in the newspaper *Göteborgs-Posten*. "Like a master graphic artist, Gustafsson forces stillness and the metaphysical feeling up to their maximum. . . . In *The Stillness of the World before Bach* this plays out in a kind of phenomenological study where his landscape images can float in a translucent state of balance and vacancy, but where in the tranquility there is simultaneously a deep, sometimes cavernous, ambivalence."

Gustafsson begins his poem with a deceptively simple question: "what kind of world" existed prior to Johann Sebastian Bach's music, composed in the 17th and early 18th centuries. He then imagines that such a world—"world" here perceived as only Europe, a geographically and intellectually delineated world—must have been characterized by a stillness that we who live in a post-Bach, and more demonstratively complex and truly global world, can scarcely fathom. Gustafsson's poem cites some of Bach's groundbreaking works, Trio Sonata in D, A-minor Partita, *Musical Offering,* and *Well-tempered Clavier,* as testaments not only to the ways in which Bach reinvented Europeans' relationship to music, but also to the ways in which his music has fundamentally altered our experience of the world. The poem then evokes a deceptively nostalgic pre-Bach world through a sequence of sounds and images that suggest through contradiction both vacancy and presence. The absence of Bach is depicted in "Isolated churches / where the soprano line of the *Passion* / never in helpless love twined round / the gentler movements of the flute." The presence of a stiller, pre-Bach world is imagined in "broad soft landscapes / where nothing breaks the stillness / but old woodcutters' axes." This is followed by other vignettes of a tranquil, pre-Bach world: dogs barking, ice skates cutting into ice, "swallows whirring," and the sound of the sea in a shell held to a child's ear. But Gustafsson stops short of sentimentality in evoking these images of a stiller, simpler world; rather, he makes it clear that something vital is missing: "and nowhere Bach nowhere Bach / the world in a skater's stillness before Bach." In the end Gustafsson suggests that it is impossible for a postmodern human to imagine how it was to live in an early-modern world. He also implies that it is meaningless to evoke nostalgia for a simpler, more peaceful time and place, when we can understand such "stillness" only in relationship to the "loudness" of our contemporary world.

BIBLIOGRAPHY
Gustafsson, Lars. "The Stillness of the World Before Bach." Translated by Philip Martin. In *The Stillness of the World Before Bach: New Selected Poems.* Edited by Christopher Middleton, 95. New York: New Directions, 1998.
Van Reis, Mikael. "Lätt förklädd äldre herre" [Easily Disguised Elderly Gentleman]. *Göteborgs-Posten,* 17 May 2006.

Ursula A. L. Lindqvist

STORNI, ALFONSINA (1892–1938)

Alfonsina Storni is a controversial figure in Latin American letters, variously deemed a pioneer of early 20th-century feminist poetics whose eroticism, reclaiming of the female body, and challenges to male privilege projected a female voice that could never again be silenced (Fishburn, et al.); or, in contrast, nothing but a minor poet whose works pale alongside those of her contemporary Hispanic male writers, as well as alongside those of truly great women poets across the ages (Phillips). Nevertheless, her poetic statements are still compared to those of the 17th-century Mexican poet Sor Juana Inés de la Cruz, and this indicates the high regard in which many readers hold her immensely popular poems. No history or anthology of modern poetry in Spanish can omit her work.

Born during her parents' visit to their native Switzerland in 1892, Storni lived in rural Argentine cities from age four, where she ranged relatively free from parental discipline. During her preteen years, when her father's businesses failed, she had to work to pro-vide for the family and began to write poems on pilfered telegraph forms. Storni is best known as a poet, but she was also an accomplished playwright who showed her early interest in theater as an actress traveling with a troupe for a year. She earned a teaching degree in 1910 at the Normal School in Coronda, Argentina. As a rural schoolteacher, her romantic involvement with a prominent journalist and (married) political figure led her to flee provincial narrow-mindedness and move to the capital, Buenos Aires, in 1912, where at age 20 she gave birth to a son and struggled to survive financially. She had a radical mastectomy for breast cancer in 1935, and three years later, at age 46, in pain and despondent because of the cancer's suspected spread, mailed a newly composed sonnet, "I'm Going to Sleep," to a newspaper and threw herself into the Mar de la Plata, "to unite herself with the symbol of the sea which reappears continually throughout her works" (Talamantes 5).

Storni's seven volumes of poetry can be grouped by themes and style. Her first four books take passionate love as their overt theme and record its three progressive stages as experienced by a female persona (Jones 64ff): (1) hopeful passion seeking mutual consummation, with its exaltation and concomitant pain in *La inquietud del rosal* (Anxiety of the Rosebush, 1916), which may have triggered her dismissal from a desk job at an exporting firm because "it was considered scandalous for a woman with an illegitimate child to write so openly about love and relationships with men" (Talamantes 11); (2) disillusionment with love in *El dulce daño* (Sweet Pain, 1918) and *Irremediablemente* (Irremediably, 1919), in which the sweet torture of love irrevocably links life to sorrow; and (3) renunciation of the quest for passionate love in *Languidez* (Languor, 1920). During her 20s, these publications—and poems like "ANCESTRAL WEIGHT" (*"Peso ancestral"*)—won prizes and widespread recognition for their promise.

Problematic for some of the influential members of the mostly male literary establishment was the social dimension of Storni's works, which echoed parallel challenges to political repression and systems of male privilege and machismo in industrialized cities of Latin America, the United States, and Europe. Storni questioned male authority and brandished eroticism as liberation. Women would no longer serve as mere muses for male poets, as blank body objects to be inscribed and used by men for their purposes, but rather were, in her view, meant to be the agents/writers/creators of their own destinies. Storni consciously assumed her role as woman-warrior: "I am a like a she-wolf / I broke from the flock" (*La inquietud del rosal*).

Early critics trivialized these first collections and their portrayals of gender inequalities as "unaesthetic, unrefined emotions"—the embittered expressions of unrequited love by a woman scorned. However, contemporary feminist critics have recast much of this poetry as the poet's postmodern ironic use of tropes from the Latin American modernist literary tradition in order to subvert thematic norms, deconstruct limiting social stereotypes that "encage" rather than "engage" men and women, rewrite gender relations, turn restrictive Judeo-Christian myths on their head, and empower the female reader. Likewise, in her frequent prose publications Storni grounded women's rights in economic independence, and "thousands of women readers saw her as a model of what they or their friends or daughters could hope to achieve some day" (Jones 132).

In often-anthologized poems Storni lamented men's inferiority to women—"Little tiny man, little tiny man / release your canary that wants to fly" (*Irremediablemente*)—but also recognized women's need for men. She refused the passive "womanly" role: "You would have me be white . . . , foam . . . , pearl . . . lily chaste" (*El dulce daño*). Women's undeserved suffering under patriarchal conditions has a historical dimension in the poem "Peso ancestral" (Ancestral Weight) from *Irremediablemente* and is boldly shouted by the pregnant woman who prays, "Oh, Lord, may my child not be born a woman!" (*Languidez*). Storni railed against materialistic values wrought by industrialization's homogenization, dehumanization, and assembly-line relations that, surprisingly, had contaminated even her: "Houses in a row . . . People now have square souls . . . Yesterday I myself cried a tear / Oh, my God, it was square!" (*El dulce daño*). Storni "reveals an aspect until then little known in feminine poetry: a forceful and poignant interpretation of modern city life, with its piercing loneliness, its chilling indifference, its soulless uniformity and maddening monotony, its spiritual vacuity,

its unending vulgarity . . . which rots and perplexes the soul" (Rosenbaum 206).

Storni's last three collections reflect acceptance of the impossibility of ideal love and of passion as poetic material. She pens less subjective, more abstract, cerebral and analytical poetry and in *Ocre* (Ocher, 1925) reveals a new sense of humor in warning the legendary "love-'em-and-leave-'em" Spanish Don Juan to keep away from this century because now women are educated and sophisticated and can act just as he did! Minute analysis of the objective world distant from her personal feelings in *Mundo de siete pozos* (World of Seven Wells, 1934)—in which she was not writing to move hearts, but to startle minds with unusual images (Jones 77)—was unpopular with her readers, as she foresaw. Her final collection, *Mascarilla y trébol* (Mask and Clover, 1938), published in the year of her death, expressed, she believed, her postcancer psychological changes and a new lyrical direction in its hermetic poems of disillusionment, with experimental versifications typical of the Vanguard movement, including her unrhymed "anti-sonnets" and other poems considered by critics "obscure" or "entirely incomprehensible" (Talamantes 13). Like other Vanguard poets, including Chilean VICENTE HUIDOBRO, Storni here used the building blocks of poetry, words, to create a poetic reality independent of empirical reality, often through trance-like, surrealistic "automatic writing" that flowed directly from the subconscious unfiltered by the constraints of reason. As she herself recognized in the preface, this collection rejected the consumption of poetry by passive readers and required instead the active and creative collaboration of readers to generate meanings.

Alfonsina Storni—along with her well-known Southern Cone contemporaries, 1945 Nobel laureate GABRIEL MISTRAL (Chile), Delmira Agustini, and JUANA DE IBARBOUROU (Uruguay)—today is considered a vanguard creator of poetry in Spanish as a space of affirmation for women. Although her complete works are not yet translated into English, excellent renditions of many of her poems are widely available.

BIBLIOGRAPHY
Fishburn, Evelyn. "A Feminist Re-reading of Alfonsina Storni's Poetry." In *Feminist Readings on Spanish and Latin*

American Literature, edited by Lisa P. Conde and Stephen M. Hart, 121–136. Lewiston, N.Y.: Mellen Press, 1991.

Jehenson, Myriam Ivonne. "Four Women in Search of Freedom." *Revista/Review Interamericana* 12, no. 1 (1982): 87–99.

Jones, Sonia. *Alfonsina Storni.* Boston: Twayne, 1979.

Kirkpatrick, Gwen. "The Creation of Alfonsina Storni." In *A Dream of Light and Shadow: Portraits of Latin American Women Writers,* edited by Marjorie Agosín. Albuquerque: University of New Mexico Press, 1995, 95–117.

Kunheim, Jill. *Gender, Politics and Poetry in Twentieth-Century Argentina.* Gainesville: University Press of Florida, 1996.

Phillips, Rachel. *Alfonsina Storni: From Poetess to Poet.* London: Tamesis, 1975.

PoemHunter.com. Links to biography and books. Available online. URL: http://www.poemhunter.com/alfonsinastorni/poet-35931/. Downloaded on May 15, 2005.

Rosenbaum, Carmen Sidonie. *Modern Women Poets of Spanish America.* New York: Hispanic Institute, 1945.

Storni. Alfonsina. *Alfonsina Storni: Selected Poems.* Edited by Marion Freeman. Fredonia, N.Y.: White Pine, 1987.

Talamantes, Florence Williams, ed. *Argentian's Feminist Poet: The Poetry in Spanish with English Translations.* Los Cerillos, N.Mex.: San Marcos Press, 1975.

Wieser, Nora Jacquez, ed. *Open to the Sun: A Bilingual Anthology of Latin-American Women Poets.* Van Nuys, Calif.: Perivale, 1979.

María Roof

"STRUGGLE FOR THE TAAL, THE" BREYTEN BREYTENBACH (1976)

Written in prison, this poem ("*Taalstryd*") fits squarely into the Afrikaner tradition of dissident writing associated with the Sestigers. At the same time, however, it marks a certain departure for the poet, as it directly challenges Afrikaans as the language of the oppressor in apartheid-era South Africa. Hoping to redeem his mother tongue (*taal* is Afrikaans for "language"), Breytenbach makes subversive use of it here to expose the white government's policy of linguistic imperialism. "The Struggle for the Taal" comprises 55 unrhymed lines of varying length divided into 10 stanzas. Written in the first-person plural, the poem addresses the rebellious black youth of South Africa on behalf of all Afrikaners. The first stanza begins on an elegiac note, as the speaker acknowl-

edges, "We ourselves are aged" (l. 1) and appeals to his listeners "to commemorate our death" (l. 10). But the tone turns vengeful in the second stanza, which accuses "you bastards" (l. 14) of being ungrateful for the "schools, clinics, post-offices, police-stations" (l. 15) put in place by the government. Like an angry schoolmaster, the speaker browbeats his listeners for the next three stanzas, insisting more than once that they learn to speak Afrikaans with humility. He goes on to argue for the justness of the Afrikaner cause in the sixth stanza by describing his own people as "missionaries of Civilization" (l. 38). The next two stanzas underscore the ironies implicit in the speaker's position, as they endorse the violent imposition of language on others as part of the civilizing project. This is most obvious in the climactic eighth stanza of the poem, which surreally imagines bullet wounds as "red mouths" (l. 46). In the last two stanzas the speaker once again adopts the plaintive tone of the first stanza. Despite the obvious threat of violence underlying the poem, he insists by way of conclusion that "we are down already" (l. 52). In this way Breytenbach speaks to the fears of many Afrikaners, who believed that their culture was somehow under siege. His poem proved remarkably prophetic when the white government's efforts to impose Afrikaans as the official language of instruction resulted in the Soweto student uprising of 1976. Denis Hirson's translation of "*Taalstryd*" into English was originally published as part of *In Africa Even the Flies Are Happy* (1978). A slightly different version of "The Struggle for the Taal" can also be found in *The True Confessions of an Albino Terrorist* (1985), Breytenbach's account of his own ordeal as a political prisoner in South Africa.

BIBLIOGRAPHY
Breytenbach, Breyten. *In Africa Even the Flies are Happy: Selected Poems 1964–1977.* Translated by Denis Hirson. London: John Calder, 1978.

———. *The True Confessions of an Albino Terrorist.* New York: Farrar, Straus and Giroux, 1985.

Alexander B. McKee

"SUDDENLY. IN DECEMBER" ROLF JACOBSEN (1985)

This poem appeared in ROLF JACOBSEN's final poetry collection, *Nattåpent* (translated as Night

Open, or Night Watch). Jacobsen was by this time 78 years old, a canonical poet, one of Norway's most important cultural figures—and a grieving widower. This collection contains many poems that conjure moments he shared with his wife, Petra, and the emotions brought by her passing. "Suddenly. In December" ("*Plutselig. I December*") is a five-stanza poem set during the Christmas season, when Scandinavians traditionally spend time with family. Throughout Scandinavia the Christmas holiday is three days long, from December 24 to 26, with national holidays observed on all three days, in part to allow for families and extended families to spend time together. (Jacobsen, who converted to Catholicism, going against the grain in the predominantly Lutheran nation in which society was mostly secular, also considered Christmas a religious holiday.) A holiday season such as Christmas is a time of year when loved ones who have passed away are often the most keenly missed and their absence most strongly felt. This is what Jacobsen expresses in this bittersweet poem.

In the poem's opening line a sudden and overwhelming sense of loss hits the speaker: "Suddenly. In December" as he stands "knee-deep in snow." The next line begins: "Talk to you and get no answer. You're keeping quiet." The ample periods punctuate the suddenness of this feeling as well as its finality. By the end of the first stanza we realize that the reason the speaker gets no answer from his love is that he stands, knee-deep in snow, by the grave of his beloved, where she is buried "—under the snow. Under the wreath of cedar." All five stanzas, then, are words that the speaker is saying to the departed who he knows cannot hear him, yet to whom he continues speaking. He recalls details of their long life together: "your sewing machine / and the long nights of work" and "your new dress, my face and our old stairs." He mourns her: "Dear friend, where is our happiness now, / your good hands, your young smile." Finally, he longs to be reunited with her: "Companion beyond death. Take me down with you." Each mournful stanza ends with the repeated line, "—under the snow. Under the wreath of cedar." The repetition underscores the finality of the speaker's loss—each set of ruminations ends in death—yet the repetition also communicates the speaker's resistance to this fact. The wreath of cedar, a traditional symbol of Christmas, also ironically marks December as a season of death, as evergreens are the only things that grow during the darkest, coldest month of the year in Norway, and therefore the only tribute that can be freshly picked from the outdoors and placed on a snowy grave. In the poem's next-to-last line, the speaker calls to his beloved: "Dearest, you who are sleeping. Eurydice." The speaker here imagines himself as Apollo's son Orpheus from Greek mythology, who, mourning the death of his wife, Eurydice, composed music so beautiful and sorrowful that, when played, touched even the heart of Hades, lord of the underworld. Composing this poem in his simple and sweet style was Jacobsen's way of playing "music" that mourns a lost love so deeply and beautifully that anyone hearing it must pause, suddenly, and be moved.

BIBLIOGRAPHY

Jacobsen, Rolf. *North in the World: Selected Poems of Rolf Jacobsen, a Bilingual Edition.* 2nd. Edited and translated by Roger Greenwald. Chicago: University of Chicago Press, 2002.

Ursula A. L. Lindqvist

SUH JUNG-JU (1915–2000)

Suh Jung-ju holds a controversial position in Korean literary history, just as Ezra Pound does in American literary history. Suh is probably one of the most beloved poets for his philosophical vision and impeccable poetic images and language. Yet he is regarded as one of the most notorious intellectuals for aligning himself with antidemocratic regimes, such as the Japanese puppet government during the Japanese occupation, the right-wing conservative regime of Lee Seung-man in the 1950s, and the military dictatorships of Park Jung-hee and Chun Doo-hwan in the 1970s and 1980s. Even after death his choices continue to haunt his literary fame, and recently his poetic vision has been criticized and demystified by some critics as that of "a slave in a silk vest" (Kim Myung-in). Although many critics and readers still defend him and recite his poems by heart, Suh's literary genius has lost much of the aura that once charmed the Korean people. Now his greatness is measured only in terms of artistic craftsmanship.

Born in 1915 in the town of Jilma-jae in southern Korea, he was taught Confucian philosophy from an early age at a *suhdang* (a small, exclusive private school). His learning was interrupted in junior high school, however, when he was pointed at as one of the four leaders who celebrated the first anniversary of Kwangju Students' Resistance against the Japanese occupation. He was expelled in 1930 and forced the following year to leave the school to which he had transferred. Yet he managed to graduate from Central Buddhist College in 1935, where he steered his interests into reading. He read mostly Western philosophers and writers translated into Japanese, among whom Lev Tolstoy and Friedrich Nietzsche had a profound influence on his view of life and Charles Baudelaire on his artistic vision. In 1936 he started a promising poetic career with the publication of "Wall" but had to struggle to support his wife and son. Later, he recalled that he endured this period by relying on his instinct for survival and developing a mindset of resignation and adaptability (Jang Suk-ju).

His first volume of poetry, *Hwa-Sa-Jip* (Flower and Snake Collection, 1941), reflects perhaps Suh's effort to appease his spiritual thirst to live in a world of beauty without minding real-life burdens. Critics appreciate his experiment with Baudelaire's aesthetics and praise his "art for art's sake" vision, elaborated by morbid images and symbols. This collection granted him a special badge—founding a "Life" school of poetry among many other Koreans.

As he entered an economically stable period, he distanced himself from Western influences and began searching for Eastern philosophy and Korean sensibility. His second collection of poetry, *Gui-Chok-Do,* reflects his spiritual quest to find an ultimate home for the soul. Its theme of achieving spiritual rebirth through deep meditation and peaceful reconciliation with oneself becomes a major feature of his poetics and continues to be explored in the following collections. In *Shilla-Cho* (1960), his fourth collection of poetry, his intellectual appreciation of Eastern philosophy, particularly of Buddhism, deepens and is artistically manifested in terms of the new Shilla kingdom. Originally Shilla was one of the three ancient kingdoms of Korea whose national religion was Buddhism. Reimagining

Shilla's way of life as an ideal for modern day Koreans, he tried to suggest a road to salvation based on Zen sensibility. In his fifth and sixth collections, *Dong-Chon* (1968) and *Myth of Jillma-jae* (1975), his spiritual quest becomes mystical and shamanistic. Particularly in his *Myth of Jillma-jae,* in which his earlier myth of the kingdom of Shilla (with its brilliant Buddhist civilization) turns into an ordinary narrative about a rural hamlet with narrow-minded, poverty-stricken people, Suh's philosophical insights into the human condition and his artistry in narrating them are perfect, and critics acclaim his having become a maestro. Today, despite his political faux pas, Suh is regarded as one of the most important among Korean poets, whose technical influence on Korean poetry has been great. He pioneered a path of "art for art's sake" poetry in Korea and awakened a host of succeeding poets to the beauty of a Korean sensibility based on Zen Buddhism and folk dialect. His understanding of the human condition and his vital poetic imagery are matched only by the world's rarest talents.

BIBLIOGRAPHY

McCann, David R. *The Columbia Anthology of Modern Korean Poetry.* New York: Columbia University Press, 2004, 96–109.

Han Ji-hee

SZYMBORSKA, WISŁAWA (1923–) Wisława Szymborska is considered one of the most important 20th-century European poets and essayists. Robert Hass, for instance, has called her "unquestionably one of the great living European poets," and Charles Simic considers her "one of the finest poets living today." She was awarded the Nobel Prize in literature in 1996.

Szymborska was born in Kornik, western Poland, on July 2, 1923, and has lived in Kraków since she was eight years old. She made her literary début at age 21, in March 1945, with the poem "*Szukam slowa*" (I Seek the Word), which was published in the newspaper *Dziennik Polski* (Polish Daily). After World War II, in September 1945, she enrolled at the Jagiellonian University in Kraków to study Polish literature and sociology. For most of her career (1953–81), she worked as poetry editor and columnist at the Kraków literary weekly *Zycie Literackie* (Literary Life), where the well-known series of her essays *"Lektury nadobowiazkowe"* first appeared. The collection of them in *Lektury nadobowiazkowe* (Nonrequired Reading) has been translated into many languages.

With print runs comparable to those of popular novels, a number of Szymborska's books have been best sellers. She has published profusely and regularly, and the list of her major works is long: *Dlatego żyjemy* (That's Why We Are Alive, 1952), *Pytania zadawane sobie* (Questioning Yourself, 1954), *Wołanie do Yeti* (Calling Out to Yeti, 1957), *Sól* (Salt, 1962), *101 wierszy* (101 Poems, 1966), *Sto pociech* (No End of Fun, 1967), *Poezje wybrane* (Selected Poetry, 1967), *Wszelki wypadek* (Could Have, 1972), *Wielka liczba* (A Large Number, 1976), *Ludzie na mo cie* (People on the Bridge, 1986), *Poezje: Poems* (bilingual Polish-English edition, 1989), *Lektury nadobowi zkowe* (Nonrequired Reading, 1992), *Koniec i pocz tek* (The End and the Beginning, 1993), *Widok z ziarnkiem piasku* (View with a Grain of Sand, 1996), *Sto wierszy—sto pociech* (100 Poems—100 Happinesses, 1997), *Chwila* (Moment, 2002), and *Rymowanki dla dużych dzieci* (Rhymes for Big Kids, 2003). Translated collections of her poetry have been published in Arabic, Bulgarian, Chinese, Czech, Danish, English, German, Hebrew, Hungarian, Italian, Japanese, Romanian, Serbo-Croatian, Slovak, Swedish, and others. They have also been widely published in anthologies of world poetry. She has also published translations from French poetry, especially baroque lyrics. Her own poems belong to the long humanist tradition and go counter to some contemporary movements. They contain witty intellectual observations, poetic paradoxes, and social satire expressed as a sort of tender irony.

In her Nobel Prize acceptance speech Szymborska confessed to writing poetry goaded by her own ignorance. She said that poetry wrestles with a question something like, What do I know about this? Each poem "marks an effort" to come to grips with uncertainties, so that "as soon as the final period hits the page, the poet begins to hesitate, starts to realize that this particular answer was pure makeshift, absolutely inadequate." The quest for language in which to wrap one's experience of reality is, for Szymborska, the project of poetry. In that speech she self-deprecatingly compared the photogenic creative processes of painters and sculptors with those of poets, who, when they are working, appear to be only staring endlessly into space, although they are struggling, sometimes mightily, against the limits of language to compose something valuable in their heads. Representative of her aesthetic, "IN PRAISE OF SELF-DEPRECATION" and "VIEW WITH A GRAIN OF SAND" are only two of her enormous output of simply expressed but ethically challenging poems. Another work highly recommended for its wry humor is her 27-line "Under a Certain Little Star," in which she apologizes profusely to necessity, happiness, the dead, time, old loves, "far-off wars," "open wounds," "cut-down trees," and a dozen other important (and some unimportant) entities for not being able to "be everywhere" and for not being able ultimately to justify herself; the poem concludes with a self-reflexive apology to "speech, that I borrow weighty words, / and later try hard to make them seem light" (Paine 304–305). It is a poem that recognizes the situation of human beings in the worlds of history, nature, and culture and also recognizes the very real limitations under which human beings manage their lives from moment to moment.

Besides the Nobel Prize, Szymborska was awarded the City of Kraków Prize for Literature (1954), the Polish Ministry of Culture Prize (1963), the Goethe Prize (1991), the Herder Prize (1995), an honorary doctor of letters degree from Poznań University (1995), the Polish PEN Club prize, and others.

BIBLIOGRAPHY

Szymborska, Wisława. *Poems New and Collected.* Translated by Stanislaw Baranczak and Clare Cavanagh, New York: Harcourt/Harvest Books, 2000.

———. "Under a Certain Little Star." Translated by Magnus J. Krynski and Robert A. Maguire. In *Poetry of Our World: An International Anthology of Contemporary Poetry,* edited by Jeffery Paine. New York: HarperCollins, 2000.

R. Victoria Arana

T

TABIDZE, TITSIAN (1893–1937) Titsian Tab-idze is regarded as one of the most important Georgian poets of the 20th century, second in influence and talent only to his poet-cousin Galaktion Tabidze. Born in 1893 (some sources cite 1895) in Shuamta, western Georgia, Titsian received a first-rate education in the gymnasium of the nearby city of Kutaisi, where his schoolmates included the famous Georgian-turned-Russian poet VLADIMIR MAYAKOVSKY. The most significant influence on Titsian's intellectual growth was exercised, however, by those of his peers who stayed in Georgia: Paolo Iashvili, with whom he was to form a friendship that ultimately cost him his life, and Valerian Gaprindashvili. Together these poets created the first modernist literary movement in Georgia, the "Blue Horns" (Tsisperqantselebi in Georgian); "blue" signified the symbolist poets' celebration of beauty, while "horns" in the Georgian context referred to the Georgian tradition of drinking wine from the horns of large deer. The name "Blue Horns" thus reinforced the national content of this literary movement alongside its commitment to the symbolist ideal of celebrating the transitoriness of life. Heavily influenced by the French poets Charles Baudelaire and Isidore Ducasse Lautré-amont, the Blue Horns were nevertheless an entirely Georgian phenomenon. Tabidze was one of the main ideologues of the movement, the other being Grigol Robakidze, and he was distinguished among his contemporaries for the influence exerted on his poetry by Russian as well as French literature. Russian literature became particularly influential on his work during his years at Moscow University (1913–17).

As was typical of the times, Tabidze's poems were published during his lifetime in leading avant-garde literary journals such as *Barikada, Lomisi,* and *Rubikoni,* rather than as separate books. This was because of the limited audience for Georgian literature and the lack of funding for book publishing. Tabidze had several highly significant relationships with major Russian poets including BORIS PASTERNAK (Tabidze's primary translator into Russian), Andrey Bely, and Sergey Esenin. Tabidze also translated Tolstoy's *Haji Murat* for the first time and many masterpieces of Armenian poetry into Georgian.

In 1937 his best friend, Paolo Iashvili, was taken away by the NKVD (secret police) for questioning; Iashvili was groundlessly accused of being a spy. Tabidze was arrested a week later. His interrogators tried to persuade him to sign a document denouncing Iashvili as a spy, but Tabidze refused. Tabidze was executed soon after by his interrogators, and his works were banned until 1957, four years after Soviet leader Stalin's death. Tabidze was survived by his wife, Nina Tabidze, who wrote a book chronicling her husband's friendships, and by his daughter Nitka. His grave has never been discovered, but he is remembered and honored in the Tbilisi Museum in Tbilisi, Georgia, which opened in 1985. Tabidze was not the only great Georgian poet to die during the 1937 purge of the Georgian intelligentsia, yet he is perhaps the most prominent one.

The most reliable critical edition of Tabidze's poetry was published in 1963 by the publishing house Literature and Art. The most important scholarly account of his life and the literary culture of early 20th-century Georgia is Soso Sigua's *Georgian Modernism* (Tbilisi: Didostati, 2002). Three of Tabidze's poems can be found in English translation in Venera Urushadze's *Anthology of Georgian Poetry* (Soviet Georgia, 1958).

Rebecca Gould

TADIĆ, NOVICA (1949–)

Novica Tadić was born in a Montenegrin village and grew up in communist Yugoslavia, where he came into his own as a poet. He survived Slobodan Milošević's dismantling of Yugoslavia and, as of this writing, lives in Belgrade, the capital of Serbia and Montenegro, where he is the editor in chief of the literary publisher RAD.

Tadić's place within Serbian poetry is rather distinctive—however, not entirely outside established traditions. Most notably, Tadić follows in the footsteps of Serbia's most famous poet, VASKO POPA. Where Popa was a lyric poet known for fortifying the myths of Serbian history and its heroes, reconciling Slavic pagan imagery with an Eastern Orthodox heritage as his template to showcase the strength of the human spirit, Tadić, on the other hand, dismantled myth and undermined it by creating a kind of antimyth that exhibits human weakness, cruelty, and suffering—as he does, for example, in "THE RED LOCUST." Of all the books of poetry Tadić has published since his first collection in 1974, he is most noted for his trilogy *Ždrelo* (*Maw,* 1981), *Ognjena Kokoš* (*Fiery Hen,* 1982), and *Kobac* (*Sparrow Hawk,* 1990). In these books Tadić took the dark surrealism of his earlier work and infused it with ideas and images from Bogomilism, a medieval Balkan Christian heresy that held to the belief that Satan created the material world. Tadić used this belief system initially to protest against the communist government of Yugoslavia and, later, NATO, when NATO forces bombed Yugoslavia in 1999 during the Kosovo conflict. Serbian critic Bojana Stojanović-Pantović appropriates the image from Edvard Munch's *The Scream* to describe entering Tadić's world. Immersing oneself in the "infernal limbos" of Tadić's poetry is much like set-ting foot into the "horrifyingly disfigured mouth that represents the point of entry into a dark cave of the human maw" (Stojanović-Panković 135).

Despite the iconoclastic nature of Tadić's poetry, it has received time and again Serbia's top literary awards, including the highly esteemed Vasko Popa award. Having suffered at the hands of the Yugoslav military both as a youth and an adult, Tadić has been outspoken against any representation of the tyranny of the state. In 2005 he refused the prestigious Desanka Maksimović Award in part because Maksimović was a poet who always supported the communist regime.

In addition to his 14 collections of poetry, Tadić's work has also been represented in many anthologies of Serbian poetry. His poetry has been translated into French and many other languages including English. A collection of his works, *Night Mail: Selected Poems,* was edited and translated by the American poet Charles Simic.

BIBLIOGRAPHY

Tadić, Novica. *Night Mail: Selected Poems.* Edited and translated by Charles Simic. Oberlin, Ohio: Oberlin College Press, 1992.

Stojanović-Pantović, Bojana. "Neimenovano *to*" ("The Unnamed *It*"). *Ždrelo.* Banja Luka, Yugoslavia: Zadužbina Petar Kočić, 2002, 133–139. Translation (unpublished), Maja Teref.

Steven Teref

TAGORE, RABINDRANATH (1861–1941)

Born in Calcutta, India, Rabindranath Tagore was a Bengali poet and the first Asian to win the Nobel Prize in literature, in 1913. While Tagore is best remembered for his poetry, he also made significant contributions to philosophy, art, drama, music, and fiction. His work inspired a variety of personages, including the physicist Albert Einstein, fellow Nobel laureate William Butler Yeats, and the Indian independence leader Mohandas Gandhi. Tagore's work continues to inspire Bengali writers.

Tagore's father, Debendranath Tagore, was a religious reformer who advocated a monistic faith and opposed much of the Hindu belief system, particularly the practice of *sati,* the ritual immolation of widows. His father encouraged the intermingling of Western ideas with traditional Indian culture, and Tagore grew up in a well-educated, literary household that included a brother who became a philosopher and poet. Educated at home, Rabindranath learned Bengali and English simultaneously and began writing poems by the time he turned eight. He published his first book of poems at 17.

Tagore traveled to England in the late 1870s, where his father wanted him to pursue law, but after a year of studies at University College, London, the young man's homesickness grew unbearable, and he returned to India. In 1883 he entered an arranged marriage with a young woman chosen by his family, Mrinalini Devi Raichaudhuri, who bore him four children. In 1890 he moved to East Bengal (now Bangladesh), where he started collecting folklore and producing poems—all together some seven volumes of poetry, including the highly esteemed "Śonār Tarī" (see "THE GOLDEN BOAT")—through the latter part of the decade. In addition he composed 44 short stories, including the famous "Punishment," which depicts the plight of villagers in rural Bengali culture. Despite his increasing popularity and his prolific output, a number of critics derided his use of the common language of Bengalis.

In the early 1900s Tagore turned to longer works of prose fiction and produced several novels with a psychological flavor. He also founded a school, Visva-Bharati, which became a university in 1921. His successes were tempered by personal tragedy: His wife died in 1902, a daughter the following year, and his younger son in 1907. Nevertheless, he continued writing and soon gained an international following—notably the Irish poet William Butler Yeats and the American Ezra Pound. They lauded his work and helped establish Tagore's popularity in Great Britain and the United States, respectively. Tagore's literary endeavor culminated in the 1913 Nobel Prize in literature. The Nobel Committee cited "his profoundly sensitive, fresh and beautiful verse, by which, with consummate skill, he has made his poetic thought, expressed in his own English words, a part of the literature of the West."

During the 1910s Tagore began producing plays and continued doing so for over a decade and a half. He also wrote travelogues, dance dramas, musicals, and essays. In his later years he took up art. Along with

his literary and artistic endeavors, he supported a number of Indian causes, particularly those of Gandhi; but he constantly warned against the dangers of polarization and nationalistic fervor. During the last decade and a half of his life, Tagore became reclusive, though he did travel extensively. His passing came peacefully in August 1941, a few hours after he dictated his final poem. His influence on Bengali culture is immense, and his contributions to human understanding range across diverse fields. Though less widely read in recent years, Tagore's poetry continues to inspire Indians, and his philosophy (stressing the need for a new world order based on transnational values and ideas) continues to encourage international cooperation and consensus building.

One of the best biographies of Tagore is Krishna Dutta and Andrew Robinson's *Rabindranath Tagore: The Myriad-Minded Man* (New York: St. Martin's Press, 1995). Other biographies of note are Krishna Kripalani's *Rabindranath Tagore: A Biography,* 2d rev. ed. (Calcutta, India: Visva-Bharati, 1980) and *Rabindranath Tagore: A Biography* by Uma Das Gupta (New Delhi: Oxford University Press, 2004). Critical examinations of Tagore's work include *Rabindranath Tagore: Universality and Tradition,* edited by Patrick Colm Hogan and Lalita Pandit (Madison, N.J.: Fairleigh Dickinson University Press, 2003) and *Rabindranath Tagore* by Mary M. Lago (Boston: Twayne, 1976).

Joseph E. Becker

TAKAMURA KŌTARŌ (1883–1956) Takamura Kōtarō is known as one of the founders of modern Japanese poetry. One of the first to break with traditional poetic form and language, Takamura influenced much of the poetry that would follow him. He is also known for his touching tribute to his wife, Chieko, chronicled in his collection *Chieko Shō* (THE CHIEKO COLLECTION). Takamura was born in Tokyo on March 13, 1883. His father, Takamura Kōun (1852–1934), was a famous sculptor who won a grand prize for sculpture at the 1893 Chicago World's Fair. At five years Takamura began learning to sculpt, an activity he continued for the rest of his life, and he considered himself more a sculptor than a poet. In 1897 he began

studying sculpture formally at the Tokyo School of Fine Arts. In 1906 he went abroad to study it, first to New York City, later London, and finally Paris. He returned to Japan in 1909 greatly altered intellectually. Influenced by Western art, literature, and culture, Takamura found Japan to be uninspiring. Soon thereafter he joined Pan no Kai (The Pan Society), a society of young artists and writers who lived a life of decadence. Takamura would later regret this time of his life. In 1911 he met Chieko Naganuma (1886–1938), a progressive-thinking woman who had graduated from Japan Women's University and was an aspiring painter and a member of the feminist society Seitōsha (Blue Stocking Society). Takamura and Chieko had much in common regarding their ideas about art and the roles of men and women. They married in 1914. Shortly before that Takamura, who for some time had been writing poetry as well as sculpting, published his first collection of poetry, *Dōtei* (JOURNEY). From the start Takamura and Chieko's relationship was unusual for its time. In an era of arranged as well as strongly patriarchal marriages, Takamura and Chieko's marriage was the exception. The couple shared the housework and had separate art studios. They spent the next 18 years poor but evidently happy. In 1932, however, Chieko became depressed and tried to commit suicide. Soon after she was diagnosed with schizophrenia. For the next several years Takamura tried to care for her, but the undertaking eventually become too much for him, and he committed her in 1935. She died of tuberculosis in 1938. In 1941 Takamura published his best-known collection of poetry, *Chieko Shō,* chronicling his relationship with Chieko from the time of their courtship until just after her, death. Over time Takamura came to reject much of the Western thought that had so influenced him. This change in thinking coincided in part with the outbreak of World War II, during which Takamura produced three books of patriotic poetry in quick succession: *Ōinaru Hi ni* (On That Great Day), *Ojisan no Shi* (Uncle's Poems), and *Kiroku* (Record). Unlike Takamura's previous poetry, most of the poems in these volumes are jingoistic verse of little literary merit. During the war Takamura was also appointed the head of the Poet's Division of the Japanese Literature Patriotism Society. After the war he was much criticized for his wartime activities, and he soon came to regret his conduct and retired to live a self-imposed exile in a hut in the mountains of Iwate, in northern Japan. During this time he wrote a brief poetry sequence, *Angu Shōden* (A Brief Account of Weak Mindedness) in 1947, a collection that saw a return of his poetic powers in which he rejects his wartime activities and recaptures his earlier poetic abilities. He published two more collections in 1950: *Tenkei* (Type) and *Chieko Shō Sono Go* (After the Chieko Collection). In 1952 Takamura returned to Tokyo, having been commissioned to create a sculpture. He remained in Tokyo until his death from tuberculosis on April 2, 1956. He is known today primarily for his influential collection *Dōtei*, which broke with poetic tradition and pointed the way toward a new way of writing poetry, and for his portrait of his relationship with Chieko recorded in *Chieko Shō,* an account that transcends temporal and cultural boundaries. Because of Takamura's use of free verse and colloquial language as well as his emphasis on universal ideas, his poetry translates well into English. Three translations of his poetry and prose have been published to date: Soichi Furuta's *Chieko's Sky* (Kodansha International, 1978), Hiroaki Sato's *A Brief History of Imbecility* (University of Hawaii Press, 1992), and John G. Peters's dual-language *The Chieko Poems* (Green Integer Books, 2005).

BIBLIOGRAPHY

Keene, Donald. *Dawn to the West: Japanese Literature of the Modern Era.* Holt, Rinehart, and Winston, 1984, 293–308.

Peters, John G. "Kōtarō Takamura." In *Great World Writers: Twentieth Century.* Vol. 11. Tarrytown, N.Y.: Marshall Cavendish, 2004. 1501–1510.

Ueda Makoto. *Modern Japanese Poets and the Nature of Literature.* Palo Alto, Calif.: Stanford University Press, 1983, 232–283.

John G. Peters

TAMURA RYŪICHI (1923–1998) Tamura

Ryūichi and his poetry are considered national treasures in Japan today. He was one of the giants of Japanese poetry to have emerged from the catastrophe of World War II and its aftermath. His own generation of wartime survivors regarded Tamura's past-conscious but avant-garde aesthetics as a major healing force that showed a spiritual way forward for modern Japan. After the 1960s Tamura enjoyed an international reputation, and much of his poetry has since then been translated into other languages.

Tamura was born on March 18, 1923, in Ōtsuka, a suburb of Tokyo. He was not six months old when the Kantō earthquake struck Japan, devastating the entire area around Tokyo and Yokohama. Many historians consider that the destruction caused by that earthquake inspired Japanese elites to turn imperialistic and antidemocratic as a way of rebuilding the nation's economy. The militarization of Japan was in full swing throughout Tamura's childhood and adolescence. Tamura scholar and translator Christopher Drake reminds us that the poet was eight years old when Japan invaded China in 1931 and 18 when Japan attacked Pearl Harbor. In that interval the youth lived in the backrooms of a restaurant that specialized in chicken dishes, owned by his grandfather and run by his parents. The family grew prosperous on the expanding trade that resulted from an influx of exurbanites leaving the earthquake-shattered big cities and seeking new lives elsewhere. Among those fleeing the ruins were "more than six hundred geishas and a large number of other entertainers and performing artists" who "played shamisen [a three-stringed lyre], danced, and sang traditional songs night after night"—many of whom at one time or another worked in the Tamura restaurant or in nearby teahouses and geisha establishments (Drake xiv). Tamura's grandfather, locally known as an old-style raconteur and lavish party-giver, was the boy's most influential teacher. Tamura's grandfather took him frequently to Kabuki plays and to "hot springs and entertainment spots all over the country" (Drake xiv). In an autobiographical piece he produced much later, Tamura described the atmosphere he grew up in as "a self-enclosed world all to itself where you're constantly running into people you've never seen before, where morning and evening are reversed, and where people use secret languages and metaphors" (Drake v). He was to learn in middle school that his schoolmates, children of less marginal professionals, felt disgust or embarrassment when they discovered the sort of background Tamura came from and would

flash him, as Tamura put it, "exactly the same expression people get when they open the door of a stall in a public lavatory and find somebody squatting inside" (Drake v).

Poetry and current history played increasingly key roles in Tamura's spiritual development during his teenage years. His first exposure to Japanese poetry (*tanka* and *Nō* theater) was in 1936 at the Tokyo Third Commercial High School, where he also studied English, business, and the Chinese classics. When he was 14 Japan sent a major military force against China and began a period of intense nationalistic propaganda, but the young man seemed immune to its seductions and was more interested in Western cinema and creative writing. When Tamura was 16 some of his young literary friends (later to become major poets of the post–World War II era) introduced him to MODERNISM through a number of small magazines. One especially influential publication was *Shin-ryōdo* (New Territory), inspired by the English anthology *New Country* (1933); *Shin-ryōdo* was Tamura's introduction to the early works of W. H. Auden, Stephen Spender, Cecil Day Lewis, and others. Ayukawa Nobuo, one of Tamura's circle, translated T. S. Eliot's *The Waste Land* in 1940. In spring 1941 Tamura enrolled at Meiji University, where he read European novels and studied Kabuki plays. After December 8, 1941, when many of the more established poets whom he had respected for their independent spirit began to turn out chauvinist verse, Tamura stated ironically that "the greatest modern poem was the Japanese high command's announcement of war" (Drake xvii). In 1943 he was drafted, joined the Imperial Navy, failed the naval pilot's exam (he was too tall), and was detailed as an artillery soldier to Wakasa Bay, where he was quartered in a Zen temple. He took with him tales by Nagai Kafū and the writings of Stendhal and Arthur Rimbaud. Over the next two years he saw death and destruction all around but survived the war that killed over two and a half million Japanese, wounded even greater numbers, and left many more psychologically disoriented if not lastingly damaged emotionally.

After the war Tamura drifted for several months, finding his Ōtsuka home destroyed and Tokyo again in ruins. He took a job in May 1946 editing children's books. Soon he was organizing the Arechi (Wasteland) group of writers. They revived *Arechi* (Wasteland), their bimonthly literary magazine, published their collection *Wasteland Poems 1951,* and followed that with a number of group anthologies in subsequent years. Tamura's first solo volume of poetry, *Yonsen no Hi to Yoru* (Four Thousand Days and Nights), was not published until 1956. His objective, he said, was to allow his poems "to catch sight of the invisible spiritual waste as well as the obvious material destruction" (Drake xix). He had by then developed a poetic strategy that employed the first person, but it was not confessional or linked to his own ego. It gave him the poetic wherewithal to represent Japanese subjectivity in folk rhythms, self-parody, elegiac songs, and meditations on the worlds of human beings, other living creatures, and geological phenomena. Those characteristics are evident in his renowned collection *Kotoba no nai Sekai* (*The World Without Words,* 1962) and his subsequent works, *Midori no Shiso* (A Green Thought, 1967) and *New Year's Letter* (1973).

In their massive work of translation, *Poetry of Ryuichi Tamura,* which includes English versions of all the poems from the four volumes of Tamura's poetry mentioned above, Samuel Grolmes and Yumiko Tsumura assert that "the recurring images and thematic development [of each volume] . . . expand the significance of the poems far beyond the effect of any single poem" (ix). Grolmes's introduction contextualizes Tamura's work and explains the provenance of Tamura's titles, three of which connect to works by English poets (Eliot, Andrew Marvell, Auden). This volume includes Tamura's remarkable long poem *A Study of Fear* (RESEARCH INTO FEAR in Drake's translation), which Tamura published by itself in 1963.

Tamura published 28 volumes of poetry and received many honors and awards. During the 1967–68 academic year he flew to the United States to fill the position of distinguished writer in residence at the University of Iowa, where he participated in its International Writing Program. Following that he traveled to England, India, and Scotland. For *The World Without Words* he was awarded the prestigious Kōtarō Takamura Poetry Prize. In 1998, the year of his death, Tamura received Japan's highest literary honor, the Japan Academy of Arts Award for Poetry.

BIBLIOGRAPHY

Tamura, Ryuichi. *The Poetry of Ryuichi Tamura.* Translated by Samuel Grolmes and Yumiko Tsumura. Palo Alto, Calif.: CCC Books, 1998.

———. *Dead Languages: Selected Poems 1946–1984.* Bilingual edition. Translated with an introduction, notes, and commentary by Christopher Drake. Rochester, Mich.: Katydid Books (Oakland University), 1984.

R. Victoria Arana

TANGLED HAIR YOSANO AKIKO (1901)

Tangled Hair (sometimes translated as *Untangled Hair*), YOSANO AKIKO's first substantial publication, made its appearance on the Japanese literary scene on August 15, 1901, and inaugurated the feminist voice in what was just then emerging as "the new style poetry." The volume made its 23-year-old author immediately famous. It was unusual, if not unheard of, for the Tokyo New Poetry Society to publish the works of women, much less a whole book by one. As Yosano scholar Janine Beichman put it, "it may be hard to imagine how daring it was [then] . . . to publish an entire volume by a woman poet, especially one who wrote so frankly about sexual desire." Almost immediately *Tangled Hair* was hailed as a fresh work renewing and energizing the Japanese romantic tradition, a work exemplary of the best uses to which the *tanka* form could be put in modern times.

The best recent analysis of *Tangled Hair,* its inspiration, and its formal characteristics can be found in Beichman's magisterial study of Yosano's earliest creative period, *Embracing the Firebird: Yosano Akiko and the Birth of the Female Voice in Modern Japanese Poetry.* Beichman contextualizes the stylistic features of *Tangled Hair* in the reading of Japanese poetry that Yosano did as a child and young person, and she deciphers some of the allusions in the work's sequence of *tanka,* relating them to the experiences that Yosano was having around the time of the work's composition. The series of *tanka* loosely describes the experience of falling in love and of sharing one's lover; the poems express, perhaps, some of the states of mind that Yosano may have passed through during the earliest days of her passionate relationship with the man who would eventually become her husband and lifelong companion, Yosano Tekkan. Tekkan was officially a monogamist but managed to keep many young women at one time as his lovers and sexual partners. *Tangled Hair* intimates an acceptance of free love, of the fact that one's lover may have other lovers at any one time, and it subtly conveys the idea that sexual desire permeates one's experience of nature and of passing strangers. Nevertheless, as Beichman takes pains to demonstrate, *Tangled Hair* is not a simple work: It embodies a complex principle of organization and situates itself in a literary genealogy, owing a great deal to classic *haikai renga* and *renga* methods of connecting poetic segments of a larger implicit story (that is, employing sequences of different voices). In addition, Beichman has demonstrated connections between Western paintings, in particular those of Titian, and the works of Yosano Akiko—allusions that create additional layers of meaning and further emphasize the hybrid quality of Yosano's erotics and aesthetics.

BIBLIOGRAPHY

Beichman, Janine. *Embracing the Firebird: Yosano Akiko and the Birth of the Female Voice in Modern Japanese Poetry.* Honolulu: University of Hawaii Press, 2002.
Yosano, Akiko. *Tangled Hair: Selected Tanka from Midare-gami.* Bilingual edition. Translated by Sanford Goldstein and Seishi Shinoda. Boston: Cheng & Tsui, 2002.

R. Victoria Arana

TANIKAWA SHUNTARO (1931–)

Tanikawa Shuntaro is one of the most prolific contemporary Japanese poets, notable not only for the quantity of his work but also for the range of styles he has explored, including sonnets, *renshi* (the modern version of classical *renga,* or linked poetry), nursery rhymes, satiric verses, and nonsense poems. Unlike the poems in *Arechi* (Wasteland, 1946–48)—a poetry journal founded by Ayukawa Nobuo (1920–86) and others whose works strongly reflect their World War II experiences—Tanikawa's poems express the poet's feeling, through the "here and now" of nature, of a pantheistic sense of communion with the universe. For his particular vision he and his poetry are deemed unique in and outside of Japan. Tanikawa was also able to make a living as a poet in Japan. Since 1962 he has received

many prestigious prizes and awards, including the Saida Takashi Drama Prize, the Asahi Cultural Prize, and the HAGIWARA SAKUTARŌ and Noma Awards.

Tanikawa was born in Tokyo in 1931, the only son of Tanikawa Tetsuzō (1895–1989) and his wife, Takiko (1897–1984). Tetsuzō was a famous philosopher who, together with a few others, first introduced the posthumous works of the then-unknown poet MIYAZAWA KENJI (1896–1933). One may be able to see in the cosmic pantheism of Tanikawa's poems some influence of Miyazawa. On the other hand, his close relationship with his mother, Takiko, also seems to have formed the positive pantheism his poems reflect.

Tanikawa started to write poetry when he was about 18 years old. By that time he had become disillusioned with his school and teachers. Trying to persuade his father not to insist that he go to university, Tanikawa showed him his manuscripts of poems; immediately recognizing his son's poetic talent, Tetsuzō showed this work to his friend the poet Miyoshi Tatsuji (1900–64). Miyoshi helped him publish five of his poems in *Bungakukai* (Literary World) in 1950. In 1952 Tanikawa published his first collection of poems, *Nijūokukōnen no kodoku* (Solitude of Two Billion Light-Years), in which he explored the cosmic loneliness of humanity. "SONNET 41" from *62 no sonetto* (62 Sonnets, 1953) and *Aini tsuite* (On Love, 1955), which followed *Nijūokukōnen,* further develop this theme. These publications established Tanikawa's fame as a new kind of poet whose mingling of traditional Japanese lyricism with Western modernist sensibilities offered a refreshing alternative to the socially oriented, war-conscious poems published, for instance, in *Arechi* (Wasteland). While Tanikawa's marriage, divorce, and remarriage (in 1954, 1955, and 1957, respectively) seem to have added some social consciousness to his poems as seen, for instance, in *"21"* (1962) and *Rakushu 99* (99 Satires, 1964), his poetic sensibilities have remained essentially unchanged throughout his career.

Since around 1950 Tanikawa has also boldly expressed himself through various media other than poetry, including essays, radio dramas, children's songs, picture- and storybooks, film scenarios, Japanese translations of *Mother Goose* and Charles Schulz's *Peanuts,* and public readings. His deceptively simple style seems to arise from two interrelated factors: his view of poems primarily as "tasty food," rather than ideological and/or philosophical inquiry, and his professional commercialism. Especially for the latter reason, he has been concerned in his work with encouraging his readers and audiences to feel refreshed and positive about life, rather than depressed and discouraged. Thus his poems are not morbid, abstruse, or cynical. While his motifs are mostly mundane and often explore the minutiae of everyday life, many of his poems impart some sense of cosmic pantheism and are tinged with nostalgia, humor, and pathos.

During his first visit to the United States in 1966, Tanikawa was inspired by American poets reading their poems in public, and he has since often read in public, both in Japan and abroad.

In 1989 he again divorced, and in 1990 he married Sano Yōko, whom he later divorced in 1996. From the late 1990s Tanikawa began giving public readings accompanied by DiVa, his son Kensaku's jazz band, which broke up in 2002. Since his debut with *Nijōokukōnen,* Tankikawa has published nearly 30 volumes of his poems, including his latest, *Shagaru to konoha* (Chagall and a Leaf, 2005).

Despite Tanikawa's creativity in poetry and other genres, as the poet Ōoka Makoto (b. 1931) points out, there seems to be a strong predilection for silence in Tanikawa's poems. As Tanikawa himself wrote in "At Midnight in the Kitchen I Just Wanted to Talk to You" (*"Yonaka ni boku wa kimi ni hanashikaketakatta"*): "When you have nothing to say, it's because your body is satisfied." In this sense Tanikawa's poems parallel Bashō's *haiku,* which often express cosmic paradoxes through the shortest of poetic forms, a mere 17 syllables, which verges on silence. Throughout his varied and abundant work, Tanikawa maintains his distinctive poetic sensibility.

William I. Elliott and Kawamura Kazuo's translation of *62 Sonnets and Definitions: Poems and Prose Poems* (Santa Fe, N. Mex.: Katydid Books, and Honolulu: University of Hawaii Press, 1992), their translation of *Floating the River in Melancholy* (Portland, Oreg.: Prescott Street Press, and Tokyo: Shichōsha, 1988), and Harald Wright's translation of *Map of Days* (Santa Fe, N.M.: Katydid Books, and Honolulu: University of Hawaii Press, 1996) represent good English versions of Tanikawa's poems.

Hagiwara Takao

TCHERNIHOVSKY, SHAUL (1875–1943)

One of the giants of contemporary Hebrew poetry, Shaul Tchernihovsky was Hebrew's most productive and original sonneteer, creating a new linguistic canvas that reflected and spotlighted new dimensions of Jewish spiritualism and chronicled the pioneering era in Palestine early in the 20th century. He departed from his peers in both substance and form, avoiding the preachy style common to Hebrew poetry of the time and replacing biblical rhetoric (though not necessarily biblical poetic lexicon) with thematic and structural innovations. At heart Tchernihovsky's writing, while textually underwritten by the scriptures, draws on those tales to configure a new creative reality that in key ways is unlike the Bible's world. By avoiding the archaic scriptural vocabulary of his contemporaries and employing the style of the romantic and Greek poets, he liberated Hebrew from its rigid grammatical rules and earned the title of first modern Hebrew poet. His revolutionary works set new trends and anchored a radical aesthetics that has influenced later generations of Israeli poets. Critics lauded his exquisite depiction of character and honest writing, which focused in part on daily life, celebrating the simple existence of individuals. Propelled by a modernist yearning to reassess traditional mores, Tchernihovsky revivified literary myth in accordance with pantheistic values and infused Hebrew poetry with its currents, imbuing his poetry with overtones sharply extraneous to the literary realm within which he was working. Free of the weight of exile and orthodoxy, as one critic put it, Tchernihovsky "stands at the beginning of an era and he is its inaugurator."

In addition to poetry, Tchernihovsky wrote plays, medical essays, children's poems, stories, feuilletons, journalistic entries, and humoristic pieces. An admirer of Greek culture and classics, especially their pantheistic traditions, he used Greek poetic techniques and added, through his sonnets, idylls (his preferred metric) and copious translations, adding elements new to

Hebrew poetry. In his youth he was given the nick-name "the sharp-witted Greek" for his affection for Greek mythology, and critics tagged him "The Greek." Radiating with joy and energy, Tchernihovsky's verse was modeled on Greek prosody. He continuously underlined the pantheistic idea that God is identical with the universe. He penned spiritual poems that tackled the subject matter of paganism and Hellenism, but he never found a way to reconcile Hebrew experience with the alien culture and religion. "Before the Statue of Apollo" (*"Lenochach pesel apolo"*, 1899), for example, concerns the sculptor of a statue of Zeus who is unmoved by his masterpiece during its dedication, but instead is awe-struck by the Hebrew concept of an abstract, unreachable God—while a group of liturgical sonnets titled "To the Sun" ("Lashemesh," 1919), in contrast, expresses a pagan appreciation of nature. In this spirit Tchernihovsky enriched Hebrew literature, drawing on the endless fount of Greek variety and resources. For his longer poems and for almost all of his idylls, he utilized dactylic hexameter, a mode typical of the Greek epic. He penned 470 poems, more than 30 stories, and many translations.

Shaul Tchernihovsky was born in 1875 in the village of Mikhailovka, bordering the Ukraine and the Crimea, and grew up in a modern religious home in which the ideas of the Enlightenment and Zionism were openly discussed. His father, Tuvia Guttman, a storekeeper, and his mother, Bila Karp, imbued the young boy with a love for Jewish law and ensured that he was taught the Hebrew language and its literature. From a young age Tchernihovsky was exposed to Talmudic texts, Hebrew poems, which led him to compose at age 12 a poem about the biblical Uriah the Hittite. After attending Russian school he was sent in 1890 to Odessa to conclude his studies at a private high school. There he learned German, Latin, and English and composed his earliest Hebrew poems. His first poem, "In My Dream" (*"Bachalomi"*) published in December 1892, marked the beginning of his nationalist stage, evincing an attraction to the Land of Israel and to the ideas of political Zionism. In other early poems such as "My Ideal" (*"Masat Nafshi,"* 1893) and "I Believe" (*"Ani Ma-a-min,"* 1894), Tchernihovsky revealed his ideological manifesto, articulating the yearnings of

generations of Jews to return to the land of their ancestors. Tchernihovsky later served as the honorary secretary of the Zionist organisation Nes-Tziyona (Miracle of Zion).

While in Odessa he met his mentor, the scholar Yosef Klausner, who encouraged him to concentrate on writing and sent his early poems to various journals. In the years 1899–1906 Tchernihovsky studied medicine at the University of Heidelberg but graduated from the University of Lausanne in Switzerland. During that period he met his future wife, Melanie Karlovna van Gozias, an ultra-orthodox Christian from a noble Russian family. The poet's time in Heidelberg and Lausanne was one of enormous artistic development during which he authored many of his most distinguished works. When he returned to Russia he tried to secure a permanent position, failing due to anti-Semitism. After three years he left Russia, sojourning briefly in Constantinople, Turkey, hoping for a position as a doctor in Palestine. When it did not materialize he settled in Berlin. He traveled to Melitopol and later worked as a doctor in the villages around the Kharkov area in the Ukraine. Accused of affiliating with revolutionaries, Tchernihovsky was jailed by the czarist authorities in 1907. When his medical qualifications were recognized in 1910 he made his abode in St Petersburg.

Chezyonot and U-manginot A (Visions and Melodies Aleph) was Tchernihovsky's first collection, published in Warsaw in 1898. It included not only 46 original poems of love and nature, but also translated works. This collection proved to be one of his most popular, with its romantic descriptions. But the poems also expressed sorrow, anger, and desperation at the struggles of the Jew within a hostile world, and several of the works celebrated the empowerment of the pioneering Jew in Palestine. In 1901 Tchernihovsky published *Chezyonot and U-manginot Bet* (Visions and Melodies B). Another cardinal literary preoccupation for Tchernihovsky was the life of King Saul, an interest stemming from the poet's attraction to marginal, downtrodden figures rather than the pious. Tchernihovsky's early ballad *"Ein Dor"* (In Ein Dor, 1893) narrates events from Samuel I, most prominently the encounter at Ein Dor between the king and the witch, and moves toward

Saul's rueful end in a manner reminiscent of *Macbeth*. Tchernihovsky wrote five meditative pieces about Saul, one at each juncture of his creative life. His 1937 ballad "*Anshey Chayil Chebel*" (A Band of Valiant Men), based on Samuel I and recording Saul's tragic end, has been lauded as one of the most splendid dirges in modern Hebrew literature. Elsewhere Tchernihovsky claimed through his art that his generation was stagnant and retrograde because it held on to old values and resisted change.

The idyll emerged as Tchernihovsky's signature medium, a form into which he poured his ideological tendencies. Critics promptly acknowledged him as the father of the Hebrew idyll. Even though some of his idylls dealt with harsh and explosive subjects, serving as all-purpose charge sheets against the authorities and their behavior toward their subjects (and sometimes against civilizations), on the whole the idylls radiated good-natured, enviable tranquility. "*Hakaf hashvura*" (The Wooden Spoon, 1907), about prison life, demonstrates Tchernihovsky's ability to marry social indictment and melancholic equanimity. Another example is "*Levivot*" ("Boiled Dumplings," 1902), a brilliant account of a summer morning in the Ukraine in which an elderly villager prepares dumplings while thinking about her granddaughter, who has been imprisoned for her dissent against the czar. "Boiled Dumplings" vividly illustrates Tchernihovsky's bittersweet humor, sophisticated construction, and feeling for folklore.

Tchernihovsky's epic and passionate *Baruch mimagenza* (Baruch of Maynce, 1901) recounts Jewish history and its pogroms and persecution during the Crusades. Driven mad by the murder of his wife and by being forced to convert, Baruch kills his two daughters to spare them similar abasement. Time and again Tchernihovsky revisited the theme of Christian treatment of Jews, displaying astonishment at the barbarism committed against the Jewish people.

Hand in hand with his artistic elaborations Tchernihovsky contributed medical essays to the Russian *Jewish Encyclopaedia* and was commissioned to edit the *Book of Medicinal and Natural Science Terminology*. He served as physician in the Russian army during World War I. While working as a doctor amid the turbulent days of the Russian Revolution, he continued to write poems, composing another piece about King Saul and translating poems by Anacreon and Horace, Plato and Homer. In 1923 he published *Hechalil* (The Flute), a book of poems for children revolving around Jewish daily life and tradition and informed by a sense of childishness.

Between 1924 and 1928 he lived in Hungary (where he was called "The King of Hebrew poets" by the Hungarian minister of education), spent a year in Poland at the invitation of a friend, and afterward visited the United States. He finally immigrated to Palestine in 1931, first settling in Jerusalem, then moving to Tel Aviv, where he worked for many years as a doctor for municipal schools. In 1935 he was awarded an honorary title by the Finnish government, and his work by then had gained worldwide recognition. In 1936, after obtaining a contract with Schocken House Publishers, he moved to Jerusalem, where he lived for the rest of his life. Tchernihovsky's prose works are gathered in *Shloshim ushlosha sipurim* (Thirty-one Stories), first published in 1941.

Afflicted with chest pains for many years, near the end of his life Tchernihovsky suffered also from leukaemia. He passed away in his home in Jerusalem on October 14, 1943, and was buried in the old cemetery in Tel Aviv. The last poem he composed, "*Kochvei shamayim rechokim*" (Distant Stars in the Sky), published posthumously, once again echoed the King Saul narrative in the way that its lonely hero reflects on life and reminisces about his youth—just as Saul did in "*Ein Dor.*"

In honor of his contribution to Jewish culture, Beit Hasofer, an archival literary center, was renamed after him. Tchernihovsky was instrumental in bringing Hebrew poetry closer to European literature in introducing major genres and thematic changes and in bringing to the fore innovations that have since characterized the contemporary canon. His ballads are still regarded as perhaps the finest and most inventive written by a Hebrew poet. His poetry has been translated into many languages, including English, French, Russian, Spanish, and Yiddish.

Dvir Abramovich

"TELEPHONE CONVERSATION" Wole Soyinka (1960)

Paradoxically apologetic and bitingly sarcastic, Soyinka's "Telephone Conversation" is a 35-line poem dealing with bigotry and the absurdity of racist hierarchies. Written in free verse, the poem portrays an African's attempt to rent an apartment in London. Describing a conversation with a prospective landlady conducted from a public phone, the poem's speaker recounts the experience of negotiating suitable lodgings. "The price seemed reasonable, location / Indifferent. The landlady swore she lived / Off premises." Before making an appointment to view the flat, the apartment seeker nevertheless feels compelled to reveal his ethnicity: "Nothing remained / But self-confession. 'Madam,' I warned / I hate a wasted journey—I am African.'" The word *confession* wryly implies culpability, and the speaker's suggestion of self-incrimination is reinforced by the landlady's stony silence and underlined by the narrator's rueful "Caught I was, foully." The narrator is trapped indeed, "Shamed / By ill-mannered silence" broken only by sudden explosions of authoritative anxiety: "HOW DARK?" and again, "ARE YOU LIGHT / OR VERY DARK?" The capital letters suggest not so much the volume of the woman's voice as the insult of her questions.

For a few lines the speaker disconnects from the conversation and focuses on his surroundings, perhaps to detach himself from the woman's racism. In so doing, however, he perceives his backdrop and situates the story in London, describing the "Red booth. Red pillar box. Red double-tiered / Omnibus squelching tar." He suggests through the repeated use of *red* both an allusion to the color of the British Empire on its maps and his own indignation at being so interrogated. Moreover, the red bus seems to be an uncanny (if psychologically significant) metaphor for England itself, "squelching" the "tar"-hued subjects of its former colonies.

As a retort, to answer the woman's questions, the narrator states that he is "West African sepia," dryly referring to the British colonial system's practice of officially classifying subjects according to skin tone. The next passage marks a distinct shift in tone. Astounded by the indignity to which he is being subjected, the narrator embarks on a monologue at once witty and sarcastic. Describing his various bodily parts, he claims to be "DARK" ("brunette") only on his face and explains that "the rest" (palms and soles) are light, "peroxide blond," an oblique reference to how he pic-

tures the woman at the other end of the line and a sassy and contemptuous way of describing the lighter skin on those parts of his own body. In a final protest the speaker mentions his "bottom," saying that friction, caused "Foolishly, Madam—by sitting down, has turned" it "raven black." He tries to keep the woman from hanging up by challenging her, "Madam . . . wouldn't you rather / See for yourself?" Several levels of meaning enter into play in these final lines of Soyinka's picture of the banality of evil. While some of him may be viewed as "peroxide blond," colored by contact with the racist British colonial system, he is obviously black, if not "raven black," and an African to the bottom of his heart, identity, and soul. The phrase "Foolishly . . . sitting down" refers to a former taboo in West Africa against allowing the "natives" to sit in the presence of European colonials. The phrase suggests—with ironic subtlety— that the speaker frequently has dared, by sitting, to proclaim his black identity and his fundamental rights. In cheekily asking, "wouldn't you rather / See [my bottom] for yourself?" the speaker tempts the woman to subject herself to another international sign of insolence.

Annette Olsen-Fazi

"TEMPEST, A" AIMÉ CÉSAIRE (1968)

In 1968 AIMÉ CÉSAIRE overtly confronted the problem of colonialism for the last time. True to his philosophy of a new world culture that would embrace non-Western traditions and blend them with the finest of Western culture, he adapted Shakespeare's play *The Tempest* to the Caribbean. Although retaining aspects of Shakespeare's original, Césaire's *Tempest* provides an ideal template for a portrayal of the ills of colonialism. The setting and situations themselves—Europeans shipwrecked on an island—provide a trenchant metaphor for colonial rule, for although ostensibly in power, the colonizer (here personified as Prospero) is also "enslaved" on the island as long as he retains his power over its indigenous people. The play explores the relationship between Prospero the colonizer and his colonial subjects, Caliban and Ariel (characters reinvented by Césaire). These two represent the possible reactions to colonialism—rebellion or passivity. Caliban rebels unreservedly; Ariel accepts his fate while appealing to

Prospero's conscience. Ultimately, Caliban is destroyed in his attempt at revolution, but not before discovering that Prospero's claim to rule is illegitimate. Ariel, on the other hand, remains alone with Prospero at the end, presumably to suffer for the rest of his days. One is thus left with the conclusion: To rebel, even if it results in ultimate defeat, is preferable to assimilation and the acceptance of abuse. Caliban's final speech represents Césaire's views on colonial power—views shared by many of the brightest black leaders of the period:

> Prospero, you are the master of illusion.
> Lying is your trademark.
> And you have lied so much to me
> (lied about the world, lied about me)
> that you have ended by imposing on me
> an image of myself.
> Underdeveloped, you brand me, inferior,
> that's the way you have forced me to see myself.
> I detest that image! What's more, it's a lie!
> But now I know you, you old cancer,
> and I know myself as well.

BIBLIOGRAPHY
Césaire, Aimé. *A Tempest*. Translated by Richard Miller. Paris: Editions du Seuil, 1969.

Patrick L. Day

"THAT BLACK GIRL FULÔ" JORGE DE LIMA (1928)

One of the major aspirations of Brazilian modernist and regionalistic writers during the 1920s was to affirm Brazilian identity through focusing on the Brazilian northeast and its culture and history. Jorge de Lima was one of the main exponents of the regionalist poets who focused on Afrocentric themes in Brazilian poetry, although he did not consider himself of African descent. *Essa Negra Fulô* (That Black Girl Fulô, 1928) is de Lima's signature poem on the African presence in Brazilian history. It describes vividly the situation of a young female who arrives "(a long time ago)" at the speaker's grandfather's hacienda and there works as a house slave. She is subjected to the harsh realities of slavery. Fulô is required to attend to her masters' personal needs, despite the humiliating nature of the tasks. She must demonstrate subservience and fidelity to survive the ordeal, as observed in the second stanza: "Hey Fulô! Come, Fulô / (the voice of the Mistress) /—come make up my bed, / come brush my hair, / come help me lay out / my wardrobe, Oh Fulô!"

Described by the poet as *"uma negra bonitinha / chamada negra Fulô"* (a pretty little black girl / by the name of Fulô), the central character symbolizes, on the one hand, admiration for the physical beauty and endurance of the female slave; on the other hand, she embodies the horrendous experience of the transatlantic slave trade. De Lima recounts a historical fact in Brazil's trajectory to independence. The poet's consistent repetition of the refrain "That Black Girl Fulô" after each stanza reveals his increasing emphasis, on the depravity of the slave trade in Brazil. Additionally, de Lima displays the psychological and emotional impact of the slavery system on Brazilians of African descent. The poem of 25 stanzas underscores the hostile treatment by slave masters/mistresses of their slaves, who were relegated to performing dehumanizing tasks. The poet takes care to give examples of this treatment. One example is the description of a beating that Fulô endures after being accused of stealing: "The Master goes to see / the black girl whipped. / The black girl stripped. / The Master said: Fulô! / (His vision had turned / as dark as Fulô.)" The striking simile in the last line conjures up the animalistic and inhuman treatment meted out to slaves by masters.

Skillfully employing dialogue, de Lima authentically portrays the transatlantic slave trade. Through captivating imagery the poet reveals the life of the black female in Brazil. This poem might have been dedicated to the black population who suffered the traumas of the most destabilizing effort ever inflicted on the continent. Afro-Brazilians were later to perceive the poem as a negative reminder of their past.

BIBLIOGRAPHY
de Lima, Jorge. "That Black Girl Fulô." In *Twentieth-Century Latin American Poetry: A Bilingual Anthology,* edited by Stephen Tapscott, 128–130. Austin: University of Texas Press, 1996.

James J. Davis

THIÊN, NGUYÊN CHÍ (1939–)

Nguyên Chí Thiên—one of Vietnam's most honored poets—

was born in Hanoi in 1939 and lived there with his parents until 1954. At 17 he was diagnosed with tuberculosis, and the family moved to Haiphong to care for him better. In 1958 Thiên attempted with friends to publish the maverick periodical *Vì Dân* (For the People), inspired by the Nhân-Vän-Giai-Phâm, the group that started the Let-a-Hundred-Flowers-Bloom movement in North Vietnam. To publish *Vì Dân,* Thiên had to elude government censorship. Soon he and two of his collaborators were arrested for dissident activities and condemned to two years of hard labor and torture in the Yên-bái prison camp. Thiên was released in 1960, the only one of the three to have survived. In 1961 in defiance of the "reeducation" that he had received at Yên-bái, Thiên joined Union and Solidarity, an anticommunist front, and was almost immediately arrested and again condemned for two years of prison and reeducation. Because of his stubbornness he was not freed at the end of his initial term but shuttled from one detention camp to another, doing extended time in at least six prison compounds.

In July 1978, 17 years later, he was "pardoned" and released—a six-foot-tall man who weighed only 80 pounds. Returning to Haiphong, he found that his parents had both died during his internment. Nor were his problems over. Ostracized for his ideological stance, he soon discovered that the communist regime refused to allow him legal employment. He was forced to run errands, buy and sell small amounts of contraband rice liquor, and rent out his room to prostitutes. But during this period he wrote scores of poems he had composed and memorized during his years in prison. In 1979 he traveled with a friend to Hanoi to investigate covertly ways of getting his writings to Western diplomats for publication outside Vietnam. On July 16, 1979, Thiên breached Vietnamese security at the British embassy, and he handed a letter written in French and a gathering of 191 of his poems, titled FLOWERS FROM HELL (*Hoa Đia-Nguc*), to three British diplomats who promised to see that his work got published. His letter included the sentences "I think it's up to us, the victims, rather than anyone else, to show to the world the incredible sufferings of our people, oppressed and tortured at pleasure. Of my broken life there is left one dream: to see the largest possible number of men wake up to the fact

that Communism is a great scourge for mankind" (Thiên xxi–xxii). When he left the embassy by the back door, Thiên was immediately arrested and imprisoned. The diplomats, however, kept their word, and his poetry began to appear in the West, both in Vietnamese and in dozens of other languages. In 1982 the BBC aired some of his poems. Poets (among them LÉOPOLD SENGHOR), statesmen (including France's François Mitterrand, England's John Major, and King Hussein of Jordan), and nongovernmental organizations (Amnesty International, Human Rights Watch, and so on) joined together to demand his release. In 1985 Thiên, still in prison, was made an honorary member by PEN International. In 1989 he received the PEN/Barbara Goldsmith Freedom to Write Award and in 1989 the Amsterdam Poetry Prize. All this time he continued composing poems and memorizing them—to be set down in writing later. Not until October 1991 was he once again released from prison, although he was kept under house arrest. Four years later—and after a strong public campaign supported by the U.S. government—Thiên was allowed to leave Vietnam and make his way to the Washington, D.C., area, where he joined his brother's family and later testified before Congress about his life and views. His 1996 edition of poems (in Vietnamese) contains hundreds more than the 88 poems and 70 poetic notes available in English in the Yale Center's 1984 edition of *Flowers from Hell.* Thiên's poetry continues to be translated into many languages, and his poetic voice for freedom is considered one of the 20th century's most esteemed.

In 1998–2000 he received a PEN International Award to continue to write. Today, after over 27 years of imprisonment for writing dissident poetry, Thiên is a U.S. citizen (since October 2004) and lives in California. He is frequently invited worldwide to speak and read from his works.

BIBLIOGRAPHY

Campbell, Colin. "Verses Carry 'Sound of Sobbing' from Vietnam." *New York Times,* 12 June 1985.

Thiên, Nguyên Chí. Autobiography (helped with English by Jean Libby). Available online. URL: http://www.vietnamlit.org/nguyenchithien/autobiography.html. Accessed on April 28, 2007.

————. *Flowers from Hell: A Bilingual Edition of Poems.* Selected and translated by Huỳnh Sanh Thông. New Haven, Conn.: Yale Southeast Asia Studies, 1984.

R. Victoria Arana

"THIS" FERNANDO PESSOA (1931) Published in the modernist literary magazine *Presença* in 1933, this poem points to FERNANDO PESSOA's obsession with the contrast between feelings and thoughts. It illustrates the main theme of the poetry signed with his own name (which Pessoa himself called his "orthonymous" poetry, in opposition to his "heteronymous" poetry, those poems written under one of his heteronyms, such as Alberto Caeiro, Ricardo Reis, and Álvaro de Campos). At the same time this poem clarifies the genesis of his heteronyms.

The opening lines ("They say I fake or lie / In everything I write")—directly followed by the speaker's answer "No"—affirm an author's right to a multiplicity of identities. In the first stanza the heart is deemed useless for writing poetry. Imagination, which for Pessoa is synonymous with intellect, is presented as the source of all feelings.

The second stanza presents readers with the image of a terrace, which offers the poet a view of "something else." This image points to the impossibility of accessing reality directly, a fact that is described as a "lovely thing." Dreams and daily events do not offer the poet access to feelings. The intellect has a destructive quality since the very act of thinking about such feelings already distances the thinking "I" from the "I" that feels. For this reason every emotional account is a "false" expression, because emotions do not occur at the intellectual level. This (productive) distinction between experience and writing explains the poet's inability to be honest. As one reads in the poem *"Autopsicografia"* (Autopsychography, 1932), the poet has no other alternative and must even fake that "he's suffering the pain he's really feeling."

In the last stanza of "This," the writing process is described as taking place far from its object, or thematic motivation. The poet is "free of emotions." He is "serious about what isn't," about what does *not* exist in reality (or in the realm of emotions), but exists only in the realms of reason and the mind (or reflection).

The poem's argument in favor of thought over sensibility should not be taken for a denial of poetry's affective potential. "This" ends with an affirmation of the readers' privileged access to feelings that are not transferred from poet to readers, but rather built in—and through—the poem. The last verse (in the original) breaks from the preceding verses, both formally, through an interruption of the rhyme scheme, and thematically. Instead of the explanatory tone of the previous verses, this last verse consists of a question ("Feelings?") followed by an exclamatory answer ("That's the readers' / Lot!") emphatically directed to readers. Poet and readers are on opposite sides. While on the one hand readers can access feelings through poetry, the poet—or anyone who reflects about his or her own experience—is condemned to face constantly an unabridged distance between sentiments and reasoning. A similar idea is explored by Pessoa in the poems *"Tenho tanto sentimento"* (I'm So Full of Feelings, 1933) and *"Gato que brincas na rua"* (Cat, You Tumble Down the Street, 1931). In the latter the cat, like those unconcerned with such notional problems, is presented as more likely to find happiness than the poet.

BIBLIOGRAPHY

Pessoa, Fernando. *Fernando Pessoa & Co.: Selected Poems.* Edited and translated by Richard Zenith. New York: Grove Press, 1998.

Luciana Namorato

"TO AN OAK" SHU TING (1977) SHU TING's poetry features descriptive, eye-catching, and symbolic images and the portrayal of moments of emotional surge. "To an Oak," her masterpiece, can be understood as her romanticization of love, which functions as a necessary link, showing Shu Ting's feminine consciousness together with "Huian Woman" and "Peak Shennu" (Goddess). Shu Ting projects a pair of novel artistic images—the kapok tree and the oak, two tall trees—to symbolize woman and man, respectively, then elaborates her view of love from the perspective of the woman.

The one-stanza poem can be divided into two parts. Opening with two *if*s, the poem's speaker is critical of two selfless symptoms of women in love and asserts that hers is different from the blind admiration of "the trumpet creeper" and the dependence of "the lovesick bird." Then in a succession of similes involving a "brook," a "peak," "sunlight," and "spring rain," she emphasizes more clearly that to love does not mean simply to devote. In this way she has summarized what she thinks are incorrect and inappropriate understandings of love. The second part of the poem establishes what she thinks is proper and true. The image of the kapok with the "huge, red flowers" is introduced to stand as an equal to the oak, with "trunk of steel and iron branches" when they salute and communicate, each with its own individuality and uniqueness. Focusing on the idea of sharing whatever comes up, be it "burdens of cold, storms, lightning" or "joys of mists, vapors, rainbows," the poem's speaker points out that this is the "great love," when love is complete with physical and spiritual integrity.

"To an Oak" has been regarded as an early cry of feminism in contemporary Chinese poetry. Equality in love between men and women has often been interpreted as the theme of the poem. When it first appeared (in the late 1970s as China saw the end of the 10-year-long Cultural Revolution and when people were still bound by traditional attitudes toward love), the poem caused heated discussion. In an interview on April 23, 2000, in Chongqing, China, Shu Ting explained that the poem was triggered by a male poet's doubt of the coexistence of talent and beauty in women. This anecdote adds to the feminist implication of the poem. For many young people, especially women, "To an Oak" has since served as a guide for their spiritual journeys and self-actualization.

BIBLIOGRAPHY
Hung, Eva, ed. *Selected Poems by Shu Ting.* Hong Kong: Research Center for Translation and Chinese University of Hong Kong (Renditions Paperbacks), 1994, 24–25.

Shan Xuemei

"TO MY WIFE" UMBERTO SABA (1909?) "To My Wife," composed between 1909 and 1910 and first published in *Casa e campagna* (House and Land), is among the most famous of UMBERTO SABA's poetic compositions. It is one of five poems in the series and, according to some, certainly the most scandalous. In this poem the newlywed Saba compares his wife to various animals and insects (hen, heifer, dog, rabbit, swallow, ant, and bee) associating her with a shy, spirited, and self-renewing nature and its creatures. Saba intended this to be a religious poem. It is written like a prayer, but this mattered little to his wife, who initially took offense at its frankness.

Saba represents his wife as having the core qualities of various animals that they both knew well and saw every day while living in the countryside. There are several obvious connections between biblical passages and Saba's encomium of various animals. Each stanza shares the same beginning, with the anaphora "You're like . . ." (*Tu sei come . . .*); this repetition reinforces the idea of incantation that is often one of the hallmarks of prayer and meditation. The elementary and direct lexicon can be understood by a child, but the tone is elevated by its syntax and other rhetorical figures.

The poem is made up of six stanzas of varying lengths, for a total of 87 lines in Italian, and features occasional strong rhyming lines with no apparent order. Through his wife, Carolina, Saba finds virtue in the various animals, and the poet's recurrent use of simile makes this point obvious. Saba includes a first-person point of view twice in the poem when he writes, "I give you gifts when you're sad" and, in the last stanza: "And so I see you in the bee / and in all females / of all the untroubled creatures / who come close to God / and in no other woman." The poet's intimate idiom for his idiosyncratic vision reinforces the poem's expression of the strictly personal relationship of the poet with this poem, with God's creatures, and with his wife, a sacred connection that his observations of both tamed and untamed fauna help him express.

BIBLIOGRAPHY
Saba, Umberto. *The Dark of the Sun: Selected Poems of Umberto Saba.* Translated by Christopher Millis. Lanham, Md.: University Press of America, 1994, 11–15.
———. *An Anthology of His Poetry and Criticism.* Translated by Robert Harrison. Troy, Mich.: International Book Publishers, 1986.
———. *Songbook: Selected Poems from the Canzoniere of Umberto Saba.* Bilingual edition. Translated by Stephen Sartarelli. New York: Sheep Meadow Press, 1998.

Chris Picicci

"TO NEW YORK" (ALSO "NEW YORK")

LÉOPOLD SÉDAR SENGHOR (1956)   Published in his fourth collection of poetry, *Éthiopiques* (Ethiopics), "To New York" is a short poem in three single-stanza sections by LÉOPOLD SÉDAR SENGHOR. Dedicated to "jazz orchestra and trumpet solo," it asserts that positive black cultural values "can contribute to the automated, industrialized but dehumanized West" (Kennedy 127).

In Section I the persona explains why he was "[a]t first . . . bewildered by [New York's] beauty" (Section 1, l.1). Senghor here renders New York as both awe-inspiring and emotionally bankrupt. Personified, the city has "blue metallic eyes and icy smile" (1.3), and skyscrapers both "strike lightning into the sky" (1.7) and wear "weathered skin" (1.9). The visitor has had to live "without well water or pasture" (1.13), without a "laugh from a growing child" (1.15); and the city's dehumanization is further rendered through its lack of "smell or sweat" (1.17), its "artificial hearts paid for in cold cash / And not one book offering wisdom" (1.18–19), and its "murky streams" that "carry away hygienic loving / Like rivers . . . with the corpses of babies" (1.23–24). While such imagery clearly condemns an overindustrialized urban space—one that imagery codes as a site of "white power"—it also implies a distinction between this culture and black culture, which is, in contrast and through imagery, emotionalized and sexualized, if also human and loving. This contrast and its implications, which are found in Senghor's prose on Negritude and for which the NEGRITUDE MOVEMENT was critiqued, are continued in the evolving racial discourse of the poem.

In Section II, a praise song to Harlem, Senghor offers a remedy to the emotional bankruptcy of the city and calls for political redress for the black underclass: New York must "listen to . . . the tom-tom's rhythm and blood" (2.24, 28), to "God's trombones" (2.3)—to Harlem. With intertextual references throughout the stanza—e.g., to work by Harlem Renaissance-era poets James Weldon Johnson ("God's Trombones"), Countee Cullen, Claude McKay, and Langston Hughes—Senghor highlights the historical link between the Harlem Renaissance and the Negritude Movement, while depicting Harlem as the site of regenerative culture. Harlem has "outrageous smells" (2.5–6); it is a "festival of Night . . . more truthful than the day" (2.8–9), with "[b]allets of water lilies and fabulous masks / And mangoes of love" (2.17) and a black "nocturnal heart" (2.27). Yet in addition to having the answer to the staleness of New York—black culture, Negritude—Harlem also requires redress. It is a time for "reckoning" (2.1), and "the muted anguish of [New York's] tears" (2.25) are falling. The black community, if also oppressed and depicted in subtly stereotyped images, is passionate, rhythmical, and cultured.

Section III of "To New York" admonishes the city to "let black blood flow into [its] blood" (3.1). Emphatically conveying Negritude thought, it suggests that this "black blood" can "wash the rust" (3.2) away and that the city should open its ears "to God," who has "saxophone laughter" (3.11) and who "slept a Negro sleep" (3.13). Senghor thus suggests that especially black music carries the culture that can cure the city.

BIBLIOGRAPHY
Kennedy, Ellen Conroy, ed. *The Negritude Poets: An Anthology of Translations from the French.* New York: Thunder's Mouth Press, 1975.
Senghor, Léopold Sédar. *The Collected Poetry.* Translated by Melvin Dixon. Charlottesville: University Press of Virginia, 1991.

Yasmin Y. DeGout

"TONIGHT I CAN WRITE" PABLO NERUDA (1924)   "Tonight I can write the saddest lines," PABLO NERUDA declares in the opening, and the reader believes him. In simple incantatory language the poet's longing for a lost love suffuses his perceptions of the natural world: "To hear the immense night, still more immense without her. / And the verse falls to the soul like dew to the pasture" (ll. 13–14). The speaker repeatedly invokes the infinite, *estrellada* (starry) sky that sheltered many of their most intimate moments, and "Because through nights like this one I held her in my arms / my soul is not satisfied that it has lost her" (ll. 29–30). Somewhere she still lives under the same sky, and this illusion of proximity torments rather than comforts him: "In the distance someone is singing. In the distance. . . Another's. She will be another's" (ll. 17, 25).

Neruda's couplets capture conflicting impulses: the adolescent surrendering to passionate grief, versus the poet harnessing that energy, declaring *escribir* (writing) as a mechanism of control. This tension yields a delightfully unreliable narrator: "I loved her, and sometimes she loved me too . . . She loved me, sometimes I loved her too . . . I no longer love her, that's certain, but maybe I love her" (ll. 6, 9, 27). Neruda places "Tonight I Can Write" as the close of the series— "Though this be the last pain she makes me suffer / and these the last verses that I write for her" (ll. 31–32). The reader must decide whether this is a poet's final authority, or whether it will prove to be one more in a series of self-contradictions.

In 1924 the publication of *Veinte poemas de amor y una canción desperada* (Twenty Love Poems and a Song of Despair) sealed the perception of early Neruda as an emotionally direct speaker, a poet of love and loss. He had an ambivalent relationship with this reputation for lyric poetry—and particularly with the popularity of "Tonight I Can Write," which he would often withhold at readings until the last moment. Yet sometimes Neruda delighted in his role as "matchmaker-poet," patron saint of lovers in all languages. His friend Jorge Edwards, a fellow author, observed, "He thought of love as natural expansion, like breathing."

Sandra Beasley

"TO PAINT THE PORTRAIT OF A BIRD" JACQUES PRÉVERT (1945)

JACQUES PRÉVERT's "To Paint the Portrait of a Bird" is a free-verse poem in three movements involving, first, the painting of a birdcage, then the wait for a bird, and finally the deliberate erasing of the bars, allowing the bird to stay or fly away. French schoolchildren learn that the poem is about the importance of patience and the wisdom of allowing liberty to those we love.

The beginning of the poem suggests the yearning of everyone to catch the object of his or her desire—and how one might begin: "First paint a cage / with an open door." The reader is advised to "paint / something pretty / . . . something useful" to make the birdcage as attractive as possible so that "she" (the seduced bird, a metaphor for a lover) will want to stay. Patience, the poet counsels, is often necessary, for "it could also take long years / before she makes up her mind" to come into the painter's carefully created space.

Once the bird/beloved has entered the relationship, "she" must not feel jailed. The speaker exhorts: "when she is in / with the brush gently close the door / then / erase every single bar one by one / being careful not to touch any of the bird's feathers." If love reigns, the bird will stay, and the relationship can be trusted. "If she sings it is a good sign / a sign that you can sign."

For adults the same poem may well be a metaphor for the artistic process. As the lover must be patient, gentle, and creative, so the artist/poet must await the inspiration of the muse. Art should not be imprisoned in schools or genres, which would be the death of creativity. Instead, erasing the prisons of convention, the artist must cast away the strictures of established forms and expectations, allowing inspiration to arrive, then to soar free.

BIBLIOGRAPHY

Prévert, Jacques. Translation of "Pour faire le portrait d'un oiseau" by Monique Pasternak. Available online. URL: http://www.kannibaal.nl/prevert.htm. Downloaded on April 27, 2007.

Annette Olsen-Fazi

TORN APART JOYCE MANSOUR (1955)

Torn Apart (*Déchirures*), JOYCE MANSOUR's second volume of poetry, is a collection of 117 numbered poems that together appear to undertake an exploration of what the poet sees beyond the fabric of religious belief when that fabric is subjected to tears (slits, slashes, or rips) through which she can glimpse a truer worldly reality. (*Déchirures* means "tears" in that sense; Gavronsky's title for his translation of the book into English is evidently an evasive tactic, to avert confusion with *tears,* the secretions from the eye.) The images and experiences conveyed in *Déchirures* do not construct a counternarrative to any religion's grand narrative, nor do they entail a coherent personal vision of religious experience; all the same, they undeniably refer to God (who is addressed repeatedly) and to the poet's reflections on the relationship of her contemporaries to religious faith, or its annulment.

Early in the sequence (in Poem 2) the speaker affirms that "there's a god inside the church / Singing out of boredom" (9). However we read the lines, it is a wry comment. The speaker is indicating here not the capitalized God invoked in other parts of the book, but an erotic object observed with clairvoyant insight, a divine being exposed as uninterested in the edifice of God. The word *singing* (*chantant*) could refer instead— or as well—to the congregation, equally bored and unaware of the divine creature in their midst. In Poem 9 the speaker envisions a false messiah, a golden idol born as a living creature: "the Golden Calf shall emerge from thighs in labor / It shall come out spotless from those contracted innards / Ready to be God for us, people of little love. / Moses get ready" (15). Poem 11 centers on those "who worship" the eagle (a transcultural symbol of empire) instead of God. In Poem 15 the speaker suggests that God, like scavenger birds, loves responsive female flesh: "My breasts smile when the sun shines / Despite my dress despite my husband / For vultures love me / And God does, too" (19). After a string of angry poems that show the ugliness and bleakness of existence—e.g., violence in a graveyard (Poem 17), roomers "in a rat trap" feeding on "embryos in the shape of salamis" (Poem 22)—the poet evokes a number of the world's religions by referencing the death of "a" deity: "Have pity on us, God of our fathers . . . / . . . A God who has nothing left to do / But die" (Poem 29). Poem 58 announces: "I've had it with rats" and nasty fish bones, dirty beggars, sordid crimes, and visions of the tomb "waiting for me in tomorrow's shadow"; "I've had it with everything / And my disgust is dying of boredom" (Poem 58). In the next poem a telephone call from the speaker's lover causes the speaker to quiver (*frémir*) and her hard-boiled heart to overheat (Poem 59). The erotic and other torments of existence cause human beings unbearable suffering— which Mansour evokes with a biblical image of masses of supplicants: "We beg, arms raised / We wait, arms raised / For your mercy" (Poem 69). The religious iconography possesses archetypal traits, and the poems capture dreamlike or nightmarish scenes; for instance, "Goats galloped in salty meadows / Followed by the devil dressed in satin" (Poem 79), while bombs, hospitals, and destruction occupy Poem 84, and a "lynched Negro" appears in Poem 85. More than midway through the book, the poet, referring to the strenuousness of her efforts (which she calls the "leaves of [her]

delirium"), cries out, "Weep my soul for the earth is naked . . . / My sex is drying out / And the golden leaves of delirium / Fall down" (Poem 92). In the final poem, Poem 117, the speaker addresses God (a god reduced to ineffectual gestures in her preceding discourse): "Listen to me / . . . / Don't hunch your shoulders / . . . / I've paid my tithe / And my prayers are as good as my neighbor's" (95).

What is striking about *Déchirures* is its sustained representation of sexuality and other physical desires breaking through from the margins of propriety to declare themselves to be deep-seated (if suppressed or despised) aspects of human life that new forms of spirituality must strive to embrace. The volume is a sustained and exasperated effort to draw attention to an obverse side of religions developed by men—an effort *perverse* in the purest etymological sense of that word, an effort to overturn.

BIBLIOGRAPHY
Mansour, Joyce. *Torn Apart / Déchirures.* Translated from French and introduced by Serge Gavronsky. Fayetteville, Ark., and New York: Bitter Oleander Press, 1999.

R. Victoria Arana

"TO ROOSEVELT" RUBÉN DARÍO **(1904)** This poem by DARÍO explores the many facets of the struggles facing Spanish America, particularly after the Spanish-American War of 1898. The signing of the Treaty of Paris that ended the war between Spain and the United States culminated in the ceding of Puerto Rico, Cuba, the Philippines, and Guam to the North American nation. Many Spanish Americans started to see the threat inherent in the "magnanimous giant" to the north—a threat that began to plague scholars and literary artists, among them Rubén Darío.

In 1904 Darío addressed issues raised by the Uruguayan José Enrique Rodó in his essay *Ariel* (1900), a response to the motives behind the U.S. interference in Spanish-American affairs. As Rodó had expressed his fear of an imperialist influence in Spanish America, Darío also portrayed that very concern since the United States had previously been involved in the shaping of various Spanish-American nations. While Rodó's essay hoped to foster an understanding of the role of the

Spanish-American intellectual in contrast to the United States and its "authority" in the region, others, like Darío, voiced their strong opposition to the overwhelming presence felt because of the evident U.S. expansionist ideology. Darío reflects this idea in "To Roosevelt."

Darío's poem marked another response to the U.S. threat. According to Keith Ellis, this poem was a "literary manifestation of a great socio-political problem that was rooted in the relations between the United States and Spanish America" (1974, 96). Darío's goal was to address the imperialist motives of the United States and make it clear that the U.S. desire to "colonize" the region would not be as simple as creating a corollary to the already established Monroe Doctrine. Here the modernist poet addresses President Theodore Roosevelt, whom he considers a hunter, a direct threat to Spanish-American autonomy: "You're the United States, / you're the future invader / of the guileless America of indigenous blood / that still prays to Jesus Christ and still speaks in Spanish" (Acereda and Derecha 2001, 167–169). While the United States possessed qualities that various Spanish-American nations admired, Darío, as well as others like Rodó and the Cuban poet José Martí, recognized that their neighbor threatened their nations' ideals and aspirations. Darío attributes certain positive qualities to the United States by referring to "something of Washington" in the North American region and in Roosevelt in particular. The American Revolution inspired the Spanish colonies in the New World to fight for their independence from Spain. According to John T. Reid, "Some of the more enthusiastic Spanish American patriots held the United States as a perfect example to imitate, first as a people who had broken away from European domination, and later as a political model to follow as closely as possible" (1977, 18). However, the visionary poet now applies the qualities of the hunter and tyrannical Nimrod to that predatory nation. In this poem the Spanish-American nations are those that represent the America that has remained loyal to its faith and emancipatory language, while the very revolutionary characteristics at first admired to the north are now being threatened by the primitive/modern, simple/complicated hunter, the United States.

While the last two verses of the first stanza describe characteristics attributed to Spanish America, the second stanza details further North American qualities: "You're a strong and splendid specimen of your kind; / you're cultured, you're skillful; you're the opposite of Tolstoy. / And breaking horses or slaying tigers, you're an Alexander-Nebuchadnezzar" (Acereda and Derucha 169). Whereas Spanish America is "naïve," the United States appears as strong and able—fostering the belief that it is invincible, that it reserves the right to interfere in the affairs of others when it so desires. Ellis states, "By rejecting Tolstoy [, Roosevelt] reveals his opposition to what is simple and peaceful" (97). Roosevelt saw the United States as the protector of the nations in its backyard, reflected in the third stanza: "You think that life is a conflagration, / that progress is an eruption, / that where you put your bullet / you set the future" (169). The importance of this stanza is directly connected to Darío's response that the United States has been wrong in depending on its "prowess" and influence: "The United States is powerful and big. / When it shudders, a deep earthquake / runs down the enormous vertebrae of the Andes. / If you cry out, it's heard like the roaring of a lion" (169). The poet, however, recognizes, as did José Enrique Rodó, the power this young nation possesses—a power that threatens the Spanish-American republics since, as he states, when crisis arises in the north, it is felt everywhere. Three characteristics attributed to the United States in the poem characterize it in the eyes of Spanish Americans: physical prowess, greed, and "cynical propaganda." These combined characteristics reflect the hostility of the North toward the South.

The remaining stanzas emphasize the cultural and ideological differences between the United States and Spanish America. The poem draws particular attention to the fact that the Spanish-American region predates North American power, and it focuses on the south's venerable knowledge of the world (and the universe) long before the young nation (the United States) was founded. Rubén Darío then abandons previously deployed characteristics of the modernist literary movement (e.g., his elaborate use of symbol and imagery) to embrace other perspectives that contradict his earlier, fastidious aesthetic. The religious influence that permeates all Spanish-American culture closes the circle created by Darío in this poem. Through an expression of strong religious belief, Darío warns Roosevelt (and the country he represents) that God protects his "nations" and is the only power that could capture and colonize the Spanish-American republics.

BIBLIOGRAPHY

Acereda, Alberto and Will Derusha. *Selected Poems of Rubén Darío: A Bilingual Anthology.* Lewisburg, Pa.: Bucknell University Press, 2001.

Ellis, Keith. *Critical Approaches to Rubén Darío.* Toronto: University of Toronto Press, 1974.

Reid, John T. *Spanish American Images of the United States, 1790–1960.* Gainesville: University Presses of Florida, 1977.

Enrique Morales-Díaz

"TO SERGEI YESENIN" VLADIMIR MAYAKOVSKY (1926)

MAYAKOVSKY explains in "How to Make Verse" that he wrote this poem, which was published in a volume commemorating Yesenin, to counteract the negative effect of his rival poet's suicide on artists and on Soviet society. Critics reading this poem and considering Mayakovsky's own suicide have speculated that in this poem he abjures himself and expresses his own artistic struggles. Although Mayakovsky was initially grieved to learn of Yesenin's death, he came to see this self-destructive act not as a heroic, creative response to an untenable life as a Communist Party hack, but as a meaningless act of cowardice born of alcoholism. Far better to die of world weariness than to be a slave to drink or to cut one's wrists when one has run out of ink. The poem, in spite of its jibes, acknowledges that the dead poet had a rare gift: His skillfully arranged words had an impact on others. But he betrayed his talent. He can no longer disclose the greatness of his soul through artistic expression; dead, he cannot justify or clarify either his life or his death. Consequently, lesser writers and critics will talk of his death as if the noose and the knife alone communicated the meaning of his suicide and its comment on his experiences as a living man. His life and work are now in their hands, and he has lost his true strength. The power of Yesenin's work could have increased joy, a rare feeling in the world, but he chose instead to model despair, to inspire others to kill themselves. The poem jeers at Yesenin, whose drinking isolated him from his peers and transformed him from a person in a class by himself to a low-class man, as the puns on *classless* suggest. Echoing the final lines of Yesenin's suicide poem, the end of Mayakovsky's poem asserts that living is far more challenging than dying is.

BIBLIOGRAPHY

Brown, Edward J. *Mayakovsky: A Poet in the Revolution.* Princeton, N.J.: Princeton University Press, 1973.

Liukkonen, Petri. "Sergei Esenin." Pegasos. 1999. Available online. URL: http://www.kirjasto.sci.fi/esenin.htm. Accessed on April 29, 2007.

Liukkonen, Petri. "Vladimir Mayakovsky." Pegasos. 1999. Available online. URL: http://www.kirjasto.sci.fi/majakovs.htm. Accessed on April 29, 2007.

Marshall, Herbert, trans. and ed. *Mayakovsky.* New York: Hill and Wang, 1965.

Terras, Victor. *Vladimir Mayakovsky.* Boston: Twayne, 1983.

Karen Rae Keck

"TOWARD THE IMMINENT DAYS" LES MURRAY (1972)

In this poem, an epithalamium 183 lines long, LES MURRAY urges what can only be called "fullness of being" by tapping into the energetic contours of the Australian theme of "country as mind." Murray has identified the distinguishing motif of Australian poetry as an "endless detailed rehearsal of . . . Australian peculiarities" (Murray in Imlah 373). It is from this peculiar attention to the fabric and makeup of local life that the poet's observation spins into meditation. "Toward the Imminent Days" (*Poems Against Economics,* 1972) encapsulates much of the quality in Murray's early poetic voice. As with the third section of "Walking to the Cattle Place" (in *Poems Against Economics,* 1972), where Murray writes: "it is like watching / an emergence," "Toward the Imminent Days" presents the "emergence" of an awareness and reimagines an alternative position to our paltry existence as isolated humans on the planet's surface. Moreover, it reconfigures encounter and exchange—opposed relations of the human and nonhuman, what is known as negative dualism—as *integrated* elements within the patterns of change and consistency.

Singing, All living are wild in the imminent days,
I walk into the furrows end-on and they rise
    through my flesh
burying worlds of me.

Out walking in farmland, the protagonist's biological self is trespassed by an energy that moves through the body, reaches the mind, and transforms his cultured ego—a conscious thinking subject, determined by sociological imperatives—into a being that is "wild," elated, but also giddy: "It is the clumsiest dancing, / this walking skewways over worm-ocean . . . / but it marches with seed and steadiness, knowing the land." The phrase *worm ocean* brings the most particular, small-scale item of our everyday world out of our collective blind spot into our attention. One cannot ignore that Murray is shifting his subject into the light of Darwinian knowledge. Darwin helped us understand the processes that make and remake this Earth and that last millions of years; and the worms remind the poem's speaker of the "dead men in the fathoms of fields" on which he is standing. They momentarily highlight the poem's background theme of human temporality. *Fathom* is an intriguing word choice, too, laden with the notions of embracing, bringing things together, and breadth of comprehension. Murray's poetic diction attempts to awaken the human to a new measure of things. More than merely complementing the oceanic metaphor, the word *fathom*, here, is one of Murray's best signifiers of an understated ecological principle of continuum. (See ECOPOETICS.)

BIBLIOGRAPHY

Imlah, Mick. Les Murray overview in *The Oxford Companion to Twentieth-Century Poetry in English*. Edited by Ian Hamilton. Oxford: Oxford University Press, 1996.

Murray, Les. *Poems Against Economics*. Sydney: Angus and Robertson, 1972.

Tom Bristow

TRAKL, GEORG (1887–1914)

Georg Trakl, who was strongly influenced by French impressionist poetry, is commonly seen as one of the leading figures of the Austro-German expressionist movement in literature during the early part of the 20th century. The fourth of six children, Trakl was born on February 3, 1887, in Salzburg, Austria, to Tobias Trakl, a Protestant hardware businessman, and Maria Halik, a Catholic housewife. Tobias Trakl's fortunate business enterprises enabled the family to reside in one of the most affluent neighborhoods of Mozart's birth city. The children enjoyed the care of a governess, Marie Boring, who taught them French and the piano and introduced them to many cultural necessities. Behind this perfect family façade, however, a different reality resided: a father's lack of interest in family life and an unnurturing mother who was manic-depressive and addicted to opium.

Trakl attended a Catholic elementary school and in the fall of 1897 entered the Salzburg Staatsgymnasium, a humanistic high school. In 1905, after having failed twice to be promoted, he dropped out of school and began an apprenticeship at the Weisser Engel (White Angel) pharmacy in Salzburg. During this time he first experimented not only with poetic expression but with alcohol, drugs (mostly opium and cocaine), prostitutes, and attempts at suicide. He also began an incestuous relationship with his younger sister Margarete, who, born in 1891, eventually, after becoming an accomplished pianist, committed suicide in Berlin in 1917.

Trakl moved to Vienna in 1908 to further his pharmacy studies and received a degree in 1910 from the University of Vienna, only a short time after his father's death. In Vienna he became a member of a bohemian literary group whose members introduced him to the works of Charles Baudelaire, Paul Verlaine, Arthur Rimbaud, STEFAN GEORGE, Friedrich Nietzsche, Fyodor Dostoyevsky, and Hugo von Hofmannsthal. After a mandatory year of military service, unable to bear the civilian life, Trakl reenlisted as a pharmacist for the military hospital in Innsbruck, where he met Ludwig von Ficker, the editor and publisher of the Christian existentialist journal *Der Brenner*, who became Trakl's strongest supporter and benefactor for the remainder of his short life. In addition to securing funds donated by Austrian philosopher Ludwig Wittgenstein for emerging poets, von Ficker was instrumental in convincing the editors of the leading publisher of literary expressionism at the time (Kurt Wolff-Verlag in Leipzig, Germany) to publish Trakl's first and only full-length collection of poems: *Gedichte* (Poems, 1913). His ironically titled "A ROMANCE TO NIGHT" is from this period.

At the outbreak of World War I in August 1914, Trakl's medical unit was ordered to Galicia, Poland, and entered the battle of Grodek, where Austrian and Russian soldiers faced each other. At one point Trakl was forced to oversee and care for well over 90 severely wounded soldiers. This extreme suffering affected him severely, and he attempted to shoot himself when driven to the breaking point. His unit members, however, prevented Trakl's suicide and committed him to a mental institution in Kraków, Poland, where he shared a cell with a soldier who was suffering from delirium tremens. There Trakl died on November 4, 1914, from an apparent overdose of cocaine.

Trakl's poetry is marked by nightmarish visions of disintegration, death, and murder, as well as of natural decay. His poems bear haunting witness to a world devoid of faith, meaning, and hope. In the majority of his poems Trakl creates a series of unconnected metaphors of disordered images and disorienting impressions to denote the fragmentation and meaninglessness of modern existence. Truth is what Trakl attempts to detect through his poetry—more specifically, that one's unconscious horror mirrors the horror we experience in reality as we cope with our human condition. Nevertheless, we sense that Trakl still captures glimpses of beauty in this wasteland that he usually equates with erotic or familial relationships, a beauty that in his view can be seen only in contrast with death and horror. Although Trakl is considered an expressionist, he employs rural imagery rather than the industrialized cityscape used by most expressionist artists and writers. The conclusions, however, remain the same: Humankind has reached a point at which we are unable to return to a natural life of faith and purpose, to a life free of artificiality and the distresses of godlessness.

BIBLIOGRAPHY

Detsch, Richard. *Georg Trakl's Poetry: Toward a Union of Opposites.* University Park: Pennsylvania State University Press, 1983.

Simko, Daniel, trans. *Autumn Sonata: Selected Poems of Georg Trakl.* Mt. Kisco, N.Y.: Moyer Bell, 1989.

Stillmark, Alexander, trans. *Poems and Prose: A Bilingual Edition.* Evanston, Ill.: Northwestern University Press, 2005.

Williams, Eric D., ed. *The Dark Flutes of Fall: Critical Essays on Georg Trakl.* New York: Camden House, 1991.

———. *The Mirror and the Word: Modernism, Literary Theory, and Georg Trakl.* Lincoln: University of Nebraska Press, 1993.

Daniel Pantano

TRANSTRÖMER, TOMAS (1931–)

Tomas Tranströmer is arguably the most important poet writing in Swedish after World War II. His work, which has been translated into more than 30 languages, has been recognized with many international awards, including the Övralids Prize, the Neustadt International Prize for Literature, and the Bonnier Award for Poetry. Born in 1931 in Stockholm, Tranströmer lived a largely solitary childhood. While Sweden remained officially neutral during World War II, the threat of invasion by Nazi Germany lingered as a real possibility that colored Tranströmer's early memories. His parents were divorced, and he was raised by his mother, spending much time in libraries and museums or exploring the natural world. These pursuits later were the source of much of the imagery in his poetry. As an adult, in addition to writing poetry, Tranströmer worked as a psychologist in a center for delinquent adolescents.

When his first volume, *17 Poems* (*17 dikter*), was published in 1954, the hallmarks of his style were already apparent. Tranströmer is best known for his striking, spare, eerie images and metaphors that invoke a sense of psychological depth without reciting the discrete particulars of an individual personality. He cites the works of T. S. Eliot and the French surrealists as primary influences, and the images in his poems often yoke together disparate areas of experience, treating simultaneously the realms of the natural and industrial, the personal and societal, and the interior and exterior. Despite their widely varied forms, Tranströmer's poems frequently return to a set of central themes. He is often concerned with the effect of the depersonalized, bureaucratic state on the inner life of the individual, and his poems often find in the rhythms of nature a source of spiritual substance otherwise obscured by industrial society. Aesthetic experience, and music in particular, also serve for Tranströmer as a primary means of achieving a sense of well-being, of not being dulled by an unsupportive society. Critics often cite his third volume, *The Half-Finished Heaven* (*Den halvfärgida himlen*), published in 1962, as the beginning of his mature career. In 1974 he published what may be his masterwork, *Baltics* (*Östersjöar*), a book-length poem in six sections that form an extended meditation on his family history, the political climate of postwar Europe, and the landscape of the islands of the Baltic Sea. His poem *"SCHUBERTIANA"* (1978) comes from this fertile period. He has continued to publish poems, though his output slowed considerably after he suffered a stroke in 1991. Since the 1970s Tranströmer was widely translated into English by a number of sympathetic translators, including Robert Bly, Samuel Charters, Robin Fulton, and May Swenson. Fulton's *New Collected Poems* (Bloodaxe, 1998) and *Selected Poems, 1954–1986* (Ecco, 1994), edited by the poet Robert Hass, are among the best selections available in English.

BIBLIOGRAPHY

Bankier, Joanna. "Breaking the Spell: Subversion in the Poetry of Tomas Tranströmer." *World Literature Today* 64, 4 (1990): 591–595.

Hass, Robert. "Tranströmer's Baltics: Making a Form of Time." In *Poets Teaching Poets: Self and the World,* edited by Gregory Orr, 9–22. Ann Arbor: University of Michigan Press, 1996.

Sellin, Eric. "Musical Tranströmer." *World Literature Today* 64, 4 (1990): 598–600.

Sean McDonnell

TSVETAEVA, MARINA (1892–1941)

Marina Ivanovna Tsvetaeva is one of the most original poetic voices of 20th-century Russia. Her large oeuvre comprises lyric and narrative poetry, autobiographical prose, literary essays, and a wide correspondence. She was born in 1892 into an affluent Moscow family. Accompanying their consumptive mother, a pianist, to various European spas, the young Tsvetaeva and her sister attended schools in Switzerland, Germany, and France. Like many of her fellow poets, such as ANNA AKHMATOVA and BORIS PASTERNAK, Tsvetaeva made her first literary steps during the "Silver Age" around the turn of the century. In 1910 she published her first collection, *Vechernyi al'bom* (Evening Album), at her own expense.

It was reviewed by such illustrious poets as Maximilian Voloshin, Nikolay Gumilev, Valeriy Bryusov, and Marietta Shaginian. Tsvetaeva was never associated with any prevailing school of poetry. Although an ingenious innovator of the poetic idiom, she was not beset by the iconoclastic fervor of the futurists, who aimed at destroying the 19th-century poetic tradition. Her poetry, though profound and highly complex, lacked the philosophical rigor that characterized acmeism and symbolism. Tsvetaeva's next collection, *Vol'shebnyi Fonar'* (The Magic Lantern, 1912), resembled the preceding one in both style and subject matter. In 1912 Tsvetaeva married Sergey Efron, with whom she was to have two daughters and one son. The chaotic aftermath of the Russian Revolution of 1917, during which one of her daughters starved to death, saw Tsvetaeva trapped in Moscow. During that time she published her first mature collection, *Versty* (Mileposts, 1921), followed by *Versty, Vypusk I* (Mileposts, Book, 1922), both drawing inspiration from folk songs and fairy tales. *Lebedinnyi Stan* (The Demesne of Swans)—written at the same time as *Versty, Vypusk I* and treating current events such as the civil war of the early 1920s—was published posthumously in 1957. In 1922 Tsvetaeva left Russia to join her husband in Berlin. From August 1922 she lived in Prague before settling in Paris in 1925. During much of her émigré period Tsvetaeva eked out a meagre living by holding various odd jobs. The early years of her emigration were her most productive. She published the collections *Razluka* (Separation) in 1922, *Remeslo* (Craft) in 1923, and *Posle Rossii* (After Russia) in 1928, and she composed several longer narrative poems and verse plays. But her increasingly complex poetry was often deemed inaccessible by the Russian émigré press.

The collection *Remeslo* draws heavily on European literary heritage. Tsvetaeva's sources include the Bible, which inspired the cycles *Doch Iaira* (Jairus's Daughter), *Blagaia Vest'* (The Good News), and *Vifleem* (Bethlehem), and Greek mythology, which inspired the cycle *Khvala Afrodite* (Praise of Aphrodite) and the poem *"Orfei"* (Orpheus). About half of these source-based poems are radical transformations of the source material. In *Doch Iaira* the dead girl is portrayed as happy in her death and unwilling to be resurrected.

The title of the collection is a stark contrast to Tsvetaeva's frequent allusions to poetry as a form of incantation or magic, for example, in the cycles *Uchenik* (The Pupil) and *Vyacheslavu Ivanovu* (To Vyacheslav Ivanov). It is in *Remeslo* (Craft) that her poem about her vocation as a poet, "ON A RED STEED," first appeared.

In *Posle Rossii* Tsvetaeva completely abandons Russian folk tradition as a source of inspiration in favor of classical Western literature. Many critics regard *Posle Rossii,* comprising the poems written between 1922 and 1925 in Berlin and Prague, as Tsvetaeva's most important and mature collection. It exhibits a synthesis of various previous styles. In her reworkings of literary sources Tsvetaeva, who denied the existence of a gender divide in art, subverted traditional sexual roles by rewriting male sources. An especially telling example are the three poems in which she "corrects" Shakespeare's version of Hamlet. At the same time Tsvetaeva began to focus more and more on longer narrative poems and literary essays. After her move to Paris in 1925 she produced no further collections of lyric poetry. The decline in output and quality coincided with an attempt to simplify her work, supposedly to make it more accessible.

In 1937 Tsvetaeva said in a letter to the critic Ivask: "I can be led only by contrast, that is, on the all-presence of everything." The presence of opposites indeed runs as a red thread through all her life and work. The incorporation of literary material into her poetry emphasizes, according to Michael Makin, its contradictory tendency to accept and transgress inherited conventions. The lonely figure of the poet, a recurring theme in Tsvetaeva's work, is portrayed as a rebel opposing *byt,* nitty-gritty everyday life, in favor of *bytie,* the spiritual aspects of existence. Her art takes the poet to a plane between this world and another, alienating her from her surroundings without allowing full access to the next world. Opposites also prevailed in Tsvetaeva's love life: Though she was a wife and mother, she had various heterosexual and homosexual affairs, including those with Konstantin Rodzevich and Sofia Parnok. Her friends and lovers provided crucial inspiration. Tsvetaeva dedicated cycles and individual poems to mentors and friends such as ALEXANDR BLOK, Akhmatova, VLADIMIR MAYAKOVSKY, Pasternak, Anna Teskova, Sergey Efron, Sofia Parnok, and RAINER MARIA RILKE and produced a large number of poems that bore direct reference to events in her life. The end of her love affair with Rodsevich inspired *Poema Gory* (Poem of the Mountain) and *Poema Kontsa* (Poem of the End). The poetic result of the foiled meeting with Rilke was *Popytka Komnaty* (Attempt at a Room), the failure to meet Pasternak in Berlin prompted the cycle *Provoda* (Wires), and Rilke's death led to the composition of *Novogodnee* (New Year's Letter). Her epistolary friendships with Rilke in 1926 and with Boris Pasternak deserve special attention, for Tsvetaeva's letters are literary works in their own right.

From the 1930s onward Tsvetaeva's work was no longer published in the Soviet Union. Her poetry was incommensurable with the compulsory doctrine of socialist realism. Besides, she was known to have been a staunch supporter of the White cause during the civil war. In 1938, however, Tsvetaeva returned to the Soviet Union, where her husband and son were already living. In 1939 Sergey Efron was executed and her daughter sent to a labor camp. Tsvetaeva was officially ostracized and became destitute. In 1941, following the outbreak of the German invasion of the Soviet Union, she was evacuated to the provincial town of Elabuga, where she hanged herself 10 days later, having failed to secure a job. The tentative "rehabilitation" of Tsvetaeva began in 1956, when the editors of the liberal almanac *Literary Moscow* decided to include some of her verse. Her works are attracting greater general interest and critical attention as a result of recent scholarly works on her epistolary romance with Pasternak and the poems they addressed to each other.

BIBLIOGRAPHY

Karlinsky, Simon. *Marina Tsvetaeva: The Woman, Her World and Her Poetry.* Cambridge: Cambridge University Press, 1985.

Makin, Michael. *Marina Tsvetaeva: Poetics of Appropriation.* Oxford: Clarendon Press, 1993.

Peters Hasty, Olga. *Tsvetaeva's Orphic Journeys in the Worlds of the Word.* Evanston, Ill.: Northwestern University Press, 1996.

Josephine von Zitzewitz

TUQAN, FADWA (1917–2003)

One of the most important female voices in modern Arab poetry, Fadwa Tuqan belongs to the post–World War II generation of Arab writers who sought political and economic independence for their nation as well as a break with traditional forms of Arabic literature. Nevertheless, Fadwa Tuqan's case had its own peculiarities simply because her nation (Palestine) has had no state to claim and because the literary tradition she inherited was thoroughly male dominated.

The seventh of 10 children, Fadwa Tuqan was born on March 1, 1917 (the year of the Balfour Declaration, Britain's first explicit endorsement of a Jewish homeland in Palestine), in Nablus, a town known for its strict adherence to conservative values. Her well-to-do family belonged to the landed Palestinian gentry of the region, both after the collapse of Ottoman rule (in 1918) and during the British mandate that followed. She was, nevertheless, brought up in strictly old-fashioned ways. Her parents, like many other Arab families, believed that preventing their daughter access to formal education was the safest way to protect her from the nontraditional values and liberal norms that flourished under British rule. Tuqan's father was active in the Palestinian resistance and was twice imprisoned for anti-British activities. As a result of the family's resentment of the colonial educational system, Tuqan had to end her formal education after graduation from secondary school. Yet her brother, the poet Ibrahim Tuqan, was not prevented from attending the American University of Beirut.

Ibrahim played a crucial role in Tuqan's exposure to literature. He acted as her mentor and introduced her to classical Arab literature. He was also hailed as the poet of Palestinian struggle for independence. Despite her acknowledgment of the intellectual debt to her brother, Tuqan did not feel comfortable with the artistic and political orientation she was expected to follow. In her autobiography she described her teenage life as "living like animals behind iron bars."

Not until 1948 did Tuqan, in her own words, "emerge from the harem" to which she had been confined. That year marked not only the dispossession of the Palestinians due to the creation of Israel but also the emergence of a progressive Palestinian nationalism that was critical both of corrupt Arab monarchies and the traditionalism of Arab societies. During this period Tuqan began to experiment with free verse, which signaled a break with the rigid metrical system of classical Arab literature and a call for literary modernity in Arab poetry. Between 1948 and 1967 Tuqan published three volumes of poetry that articulated such classical themes as love and emotional freedom, but with a modernist sensibility. The earliest volume, *Alone with the Day,* appeared in 1952, followed by *I Found It* (1958) and *Give Us Love* (1960). The tone of the poems in these collections is personal and elegiac.

Tuqan emerged as an influential, politically committed Palestinian poet after the 1967 Arab-Israeli War. The Israeli occupation of the West Bank (including her hometown, Nablus) and her firsthand witness to the ordeal of many refugees forced to leave subjugated Palestinian cities led her to focus on the collective destiny of her nation, rather than on the introverted themes of her earlier poems. Her collections of poetry during this period—*Before the Locked Gate* (1967), *Horsemen of the Night* (1969), and *Alone on the Summit of the World* (1973)—were monumental projects of poeticizing the Palestinian cause. In this new stage Tuqan defiantly extolled the Palestinian freedom fighters and described the sorrows of being uprooted from one's own country. Her poems proved to be very influential. "Song of Becoming" and "Enough for Me," along with other poems, inspired the new Palestinian generation in their resistance to occupation. The diction of her nationalist poems articulated the obligation of individual sacrifice and the necessity of holding on to one's roots.

Tuqan published her autobiography, *A Mountainous Journey,* in 1985. It is a document in which the tragic narrative of the Palestinian nation and the personal story of the hardships of being a woman in a male-dominated society are intertwined. In general Tuqan's work can be read as a record of 20th-century Palestinian women who have suffered at once from the loss of their homeland and from repressive patriarchy.

Fadwa Tuqan received numerous awards for her literary accomplishment, among which are the International Poetry Award in Palermo, Italy, and the Jerusalem Award for Culture and Arts. She was also the subject of a documentary film directed by Liaha Bonder in 1999.

She died on December 13, 2003, in her hometown, Nablus.

BIBLIOGRAPHY

Attar, Samar. "A Discovery of Self and Other: Fadwa Tuqan's Sojourn in England in the Early Sixties" *Arab Studies Quarterly* 25, no. 3 (2003): 176–184.

Golley, Nawar Al-Hassan. *Reading Arab Women's Autobiographies: Shahrazad Tells Her Story.* Austin: University of Texas Press, 2003.

Nowaihi, Magda M. al-. "Resisting Silence in Arab Women's Autobiographies." *International Journal of Middle East Studies* 33, no. 4 (2001): 477–502.

Tuqan, Fadwa. *A Mountainous Journey: An Autobiography.* Translated by Olive Kenny and Naomi Shihab Nye, foreword by Salma Khadra Jayyusi. Saint Paul, Minn.: Graywolf Press, 1990.

Firat Oruc

TURNER DAVID DABYDEEN (1993) DAVID DABYDEEN's long poem *Turner,* first published in 1993, is told from the perspective of a submerged black figure in J. M. W. Turner's renowned 1840 painting *Slavers Throwing Overboard the Dead & Dying.* By writing from the perspective of this figure who is visually central to the work but has long been marginal to Euro-American history and submerged in critical discussion of the work, Dabydeen resuscitates a perspective on the Middle Passage and reinjects it into the artistic record of the Atlantic.

After his death the drowned man, his "mind a garment of invention," creates an imaginary home and populates it with creatures, family, and personal memories. He names the ship's captain Turner, after the scenario's creator, and gives the same name to a stillborn baby he rescues ("What was deemed mere food for sharks will become / My fable"), thus creating a resonant circuit of reference in the poem between Turner the artist and his progeny (9).

Dabydeen has called the poem "a great howl of pessimism about the inability to recover anything meaningful from the past. But it's a kind of howl that is also a release into the future" (Dawes 197–198). Critics have also taken a more optimistic view of the poem, as a demonstration not only of forward movement in time, but of the world-making powers of the diasporic

imagination, able to infuse flotsam and jetsam with cultural significance for lives set permanently adrift (Pillai).

BIBLIOGRAPHY

Dawes, Kwame, and Neville Senu, eds. *Talk Yuh Talk: Interviews with Anglophone Caribbean Poets.* Charlottesville: University of Virginia Press, 2001, 196–214.

Doring, Tobias. "Turning the Colonial Gaze: Re-visions of Terror in Dabydeen's *Turner.*" *Third World Perspectives on Contemporary Art and Culture* 38 (1997): 3–14.

Grant, Kevin, ed. *The Art of David Dabydeen.* Leeds, U.K.: Peepal Press, 1997.

Pillai, Shanthini. "Beadless in a Foreign Land, or a Jouti of a New Kind: David Dabydeen's *Turner.*" In *Postcolonial Cultures and Literatures: Modernity and the (Un)Commonwealth,* edited by Andrew Benjamin, Tony Davies, and Robbie B. H. Goh. New York: Peter Lang, 2002, 291–299.

Williams, Emily A. *Poetic Negotiation of Identity in the Works of Brathwaite, Harris, Senior and Dabydeen: Tropical Paradise Lost and Regained.* Lewiston, N.Y.: Edwin Mellen Press, 1999.

Alex Feerst

"TWELVE O'CLOCK, NOON" JORGE GUILLÉN (1928) JORGE GUILLÉN's "*Las doce en el reloj*" appeared in his first collection of poems, *Cántico* (1928). Its theme is the completeness reached at a moment in time—noon, the present—by a man, the poet, immersed in a place, the world, which is perfect. The clause "All is complete," the poem's central idea, both opens and closes the poem. "*Las doce en el reloj*" exemplifies the serenity and contentment of young Guillén when writing the poems included in this collection. Like many of these poems, this one uses specific images of reality as universal symbols, and it exhibits some of the fundamental characteristics of Guillén's style. The world is presented in relation to a perfect geometric form: the circle, noon. Man, the poet, "god" (not capitalized), is at the center of creation, one with nature, and a witness. And nature is described through images that do not reflect a particular place or landscape but symbolize its essence: a poplar tree, a bird, the wind, a flower, stalks of grain. Surrounding them is the Sun, representing love, another of Guillén's recurring themes—and one that unites all these elements to each other and to the poet. *"Era yo, / Centro en aquel instante / De tanto alrededor, / Quien lo veía todo / Completo para un dios."* (I was the center / of the surroundings, / and saw that it was all / complete for a god.) The symbolic quality of the images does not detract from the vitality and sensory impact of the poem, expressed through specific colors (silver, green, and gray) and implied color (in the Sun, the bird, the flower, and the grain) and through the movement of "stirred," and "rustling" in the wind, as well as the emotion of the "adoration" in the bird's song and of the flower feeling "its praises sung." The regularity of the rhythm and of the rhyme scheme (the lines are all of seven syllables with the even-numbered ones ending in assonant *–o*) parallels the symmetry of the poet's experience. In *"Las doce en el reloj,"* the sentiment of perfection that fills the poet is transmitted undiminished to the reader.

BIBLIOGRAPHY

Guillén, Jorge. *Our Air.* 2 vols. Translated by Carl W. Cobb. Lewiston, N.Y.: Edwin Mellen, 1997.
MacCurday, G. Grant. *Jorge Guillén.* Boston: Twayne, 1982.

Mercedes Tibbits

TZARA, TRISTAN (1896–1963)

The poet Tristan Tzara embodies the transnational character of 20th-century artistic avant-garde movements. Born Sami Rosenstock in Moineşti, Bacau, Romania, he published his early poetry in the Romanian journal *Simbolul* (Symbol) alongside that of his mentors, Romanian poets Ion Minulescu and George Bacovia. This early poetry reflects a symbolist preoccupation with an aesthetics of suggestion that preempts the logic of conventional lyrical form (Maruta 122). In 1916 he fled to Zurich, Switzerland, at age 20, with fellow artist Marcel Janco, to avoid conscription into the Romanian armed forces in World War I. The rest, as they say, is history. In Zurich the poet renamed himself Tristan Tzara, began publishing poems and manifestos in French, and, along with his pacifist artist companions, founded dadaism, an influential early 20th-century avant-garde movement. Radical artists in many European and American cities during the 1910s and 1920s were publishing such manifestos, which amounted to declarations of new sets of rules or principles to guide new forms of art for a new age. Among these Tzara's Dada Manifesto of 1918 quickly spread among Europe's avant-garde and aroused the interest of artist-intellectuals in Paris and New York in particular. In 1919 ANDRÉ BRETON, editor of the radical journal *Littérature* in Paris, wrote to Tzara in Zurich: "Your manifesto fired me with enthusiasm; I no longer knew from whom I could expect the courage which you demonstrate. All my attention is turned toward you today. . . . Aren't we going to see you in Paris soon?" (Peterson 5). In 1920 Tzara moved to Paris to continue his writing and artistic radicalism. He remained in Paris for the remainder of his life, publishing 30 volumes of poetry in French, serving in the French resistance against the Germans during World War II, and becoming a French citizen after the war. Yet he remained outside the literary and intellectual establishment. In 1924, following a dispute with Breton, the latter declared the dada movement dead and Tzara's contributions no longer relevant. (Breton welcomed Tzara back into the fold under the umbrella of a new movement, French surrealism, in 1929.) Yet despite the tendency of many literary historians to discount Tzara's post-dada literary and critical contributions, Tzara published his most significant work, both qualitatively and quantitatively, after 1924. After dada he published nearly 50 book-length works of poetry, prose, critical essays, and plays that have had a significant impact on generations of French and European artists and intellectuals. His masterpiece, the anti-epic, book-length poetic work APPROXIMATE MAN (*L'Homme Approximatif,* 1931), was first translated into English by Mary Ann Caws in 1973 and reissued by Black Widow Press in 2006. The same press also reissued Lee Harwood's English translations of Tzara's *Chanson Dada: Tristan Tzara Selected Poems* in 2006, and translations of Tzara's dada manifestos remain in print in English and Spanish for the U.S. market.

Despite his myriad contributions to French letters over five decades, Tzara is best known as the founder of dadaism, a nihilistic, anti-art movement he founded as an exiled intellectual waiting out the war in neutral Zurich. There Tzara and Janco came together with the Alsatian painter and poet Hans Arp, the German poet Hugo Ball, and his wife, the German playwright Emmy

Hennings, to found the Cabaret Voltaire in Zurich in 1916, considered the official birthplace of the dada movement. The cabaret's members ridiculed the bourgeois clichés that they believed had caused the war. One of its members, Hans Richter, later recounted: "We insulted, we despised—and we laughed. . . . We took our laughter seriously; laughter was the only guarantee of the seriousness with which, on our voyages of self-discovery, we practiced anti-art" (Simpson 389). Such "anti-art" took outrageous forms: Poetry was reduced to babble, and paintings and sculptures featured violently dismembered and reconstituted elements. The movement's name emerged when Tzara, Arp, and Richard Huselbeck pushed a paper knife into a French dictionary—symbolically dismembering the celebrated imperial language of Enlightenment art and culture. Tzara quickly became the group's chief proponent, and his "anti-manifestos," published in avant-garde journals in France and Italy, reflect a deep suspicion of all arbiters of art and culture and their infantilizing systems of thought. In his Dada Manifesto of 1918, Tzara writes: "I am writing a manifesto and there's nothing I want, and yet I'm saying certain things, and in principle I am against manifestos, as I am against principles . . . DADA was born out of a need for independence, out of mistrust for the community. People who join us keep their freedom. We don't accept any theories." The real purpose of the manifestos, then, was not to publish the movement's position paper, but rather to whip up publicity for the outrageous soirées organized by the Cabaret Voltaire. These evenings were designed as anti-events; they repudiated the possibility of a new art that could give meaning, expression, and material existence to a new and better world. Between 1915 and 1923 the dada movement spread to New York, Barcelona, Berlin, Hanover, and Cologne, in addition to Zurich and Paris. In 1925 Tzara married the Swedish painter Greta Knutson, and she joined their artist colony in Paris. Two New York–based dadaists who later joined the dada colony in Paris, Man Ray and Marcel Duchamp, sought "authorization" from Tzara to use the word *dada* in the title of their New York–based journal, *Dada Bulletin,* which appeared in 1921. Tzara famously replied: "You ask for authorization to name your periodical Dada. But Dada belongs to everybody."

When dada moved to Paris, however, Parisians—accustomed to serving as arbiters of culture and taste—had no patience with the dadaists' outrageous public performances and nonsensical poetry. Following a public argument with Tzara, Breton declared dadaism officially finished in 1924 and announced the birth of a successor movement: surrealism. Surrealism built on the dadaists' rejection of reason and rationality as a basis for art. They embraced psychoanalyst Sigmund Freud's teachings about the unconscious and the interpretation of dreams, believing that surrealist poetry had the potential to unite the conscious and subconscious worlds. In poetry this came out in startling image-associations that had no rational connection, much like the images in dreams. Tzara, while appreciating the artistic innovation of irrational association in poetry, totally rejected Freudian teachings as a poetic method, reiterating his suspicion of all artistic theories. Thus, all Tzara's poetry, including *Approximate Man,* resists linguistic systems and ideational systems alike, relying on random associations of image, sound, and sense to propel the poem's action. Tzara's particular blend of nonaffiliated Marxism, polemical humanism, and radical stylistic innovation has made him a pariah among the Parisian literati, but an inspiration for artistic radicals, particularly refugees from Eastern Europe. Tzara died of cancer in 1963.

Astrid Vicas documents Tzara's impact on the post–World War II lettrist movement founded in Paris by Romanian political refugee Isidore Isou, who was among many who attended Tzara's funeral in 1963. Another of the lettrist movement's original members, Guy Debord, founded the Situationist International in 1957. By remaining outside the Parisian literary establishment, Tzara had produced a body of radical artistic work that had a lasting impact on future generations of European and American radical artists and intellectuals.

BIBLIOGRAPHY
Hoffman, Irene. "Documents of Dada and Surrealism: Dada and Surrealist Journals in the Mary Reynolds Collection." Chicago: The Art Institute, 2001. Available online at the Art Institute of Chicago website. URL: http://www.artic.edu/reynolds/essays/hofmann.php. Accessed on June 27, 2005.

Maruta, Vasile. "'L'ésprit de révolte' dans l'art à Paris et à Bucarest" ["The spirit of revolt" in art in Paris and Bucharest]. *Forum for Modern Language Studies* 36, no. 2 (2000).

Peterson, Elmer. *Tristan Tzara: Dada and Surrational Theorist.* New Brunswick, N.J.: Rutgers University Press, 1971.

Richter, Hans. *Dada: Art and Anti-Art.* Translated by David Britt. London: Thames and Hudson, 1965.

Simpson, Louis. "Dadaists and Surrealists." *Modern Poets of France: A Bilingual Anthology.* Ashland, Ore: Story Line Press, 1997.

Tzara, Tristan. *Approximate Man and Other Writings.* Translated by Mary Ann Caws and Peter Caws. Boston: Black Widow Press, 2006.

———. *Chanson Dada: Tristan Tzara Selected Poems.* Translated by Lee Harwood. Boston: Black Widow Press, 2006.

———. *Seven Dada Manifestos and Lampisteries.* Translated by Barbara Wright. Edison, N.J.: Riverrun Press, 2003.

Vicas, Astrid. "Reusing Culture: The Import of Détournement." *Yale Journal of Criticism* 11, no. 2 (1998): 381–406.

Ursula A. L. Lindqvist

UNGARETTI, GIUSEPPE (1888–1970)

Giuseppe Ungaretti, the most influential 20th-century Italian poet, whose condensed style embodies at once sensual tangibility and inexhaustable interpretive openness, spent his first 24 years in Alexandria, Egypt, where his parents, Italian immigrants from the Lucca region, owned a bakery. When he was two years old Ungaretti lost his father. When he was 24 he moved to Paris, where he attended Henri Bergson's philosophy lectures and met avant-garde painters and poets including Georges Braque, Pablo Picasso, Amedeo Modigliani, and GUILLAUME APOLLINAIRE. In 1913 Ungaretti's close friend Mohammed Sceab, who had moved to Paris with him, committed suicide. At the outbreak of World War I, Ungaretti returned to Italy. Drafted into military service, he served on various fronts in Austria and France between 1915 and 1918. His first book of poetry, *Il Porto sepolto* (The Buried Harbor), was published in 1916. After the war he moved back to Paris, where he worked as foreign correspondent for *Il Popolo d'Italia* (The People of Italy), a newspaper founded by Benito Mussolini. In 1919 Ungaretti married Jeanne Dupoix. He served for a time as a press officer of the Italian embassy in Paris. In 1921 he moved to Rome, where he worked as an editor for the Italian foreign ministry. In 1931 his poetry volume *L'allegria* (Joy), appeared. In the same year he began to write travel essays about Egypt and various parts of Europe for an Italian newspaper. In the years that followed he lectured at universities in Spain, France, Belgium, the Netherlands, Czechoslovakia, and Switzerland. He moved to Brazil in 1936, where he took a position as professor of literature in São Paolo. In the same year *Sentimento del tempo* (A Sense of Time) was published. In 1939 Ungaretti's nine-year-old son, Antonietto, died, a loss that permeates his later work. In 1942 Ungaretti was named professor of contemporary Italian literature at the University of Rome. Subsequent poetry volumes include *Il dolore* (Affliction), which includes "SHOUT NO MORE" (1947), *La terra promessa* (The Promised Land, 1950), *Un grido e paesaggi* (An Outcry and Landscapes, with illustrations by Morandi, 1952), *Il tacuino del vecchio* (The Old Man's Notebook, 1969), *Dialogo* (1968), and *Nuove* (New Things, 1970).

Ungaretti's substantial and multifaceted translations include works by the Spanish Golden Age poet Luis de Góngora and the 20th-century Russian poet Sergey Yesenin (1936), Shakespeare's sonnets (1944 and 1946), and selected poems of Stéphane Mallarmé (1948), William Blake (1936 and 1965), and Jean Racine (1950).

Ungaretti's numerous awards include the Premio del Gondoliere (1932), Premio Roma (1949), Knokke-le-Zoute International Poetry Award (1956), and Premio Montefeltro (1960). In 1962 he was unanimously elected president of the European Writers' Organization. In 1964 he delivered lectures at Columbia University in New York City. Honorary degrees in Brazil and Peru (1968), lectures in Sweden, Germany, and the United States, and the dedication with which some of the most eminent poets have translated Ungaretti into their languages (see, for example, PAUL CELAN's and INGEBORG BACHMANN's German versions) attest to his international impact on attempts to reimagine a sustained dialogue between ethics and aesthetics.

Olaf Berwald

"UNITED FRUIT COMPANY, THE" PABLO NERUDA (1950)

"The United Fruit Company" is part of section five of *Canto General,* "The Sand Betrayed," and was inspired by PABLO NERUDA's visit to Colombia in September 1943. At the time the Colombian government was embroiled in debate over efforts to expel U.S. commercial involvement in the country. The influence of American firms that exported Central America's products had grown to the point where representatives of the United States had come to operate much of the public utilities in Colombia and, in many cases, to dominate local politics. Neruda was particularly sympathetic to Colombia's plight because his own country, Chile, faced the same battle over its copper and mineral resources.

In this poem Neruda wields a broadsword of satire, aiming a deathblow at the idea of Westernized firms serving a constructive role in Latin America. The poem starts as religious parody, comparing the divvying up of natural resources to the division of kingdoms: "When the trumpet blared everything / on earth was prepared / and Jehovah distributed the world / to Coca-Cola Inc., Anaconda, / Ford Motors" (ll. 1–5). The poet's sarcastic assignation of divine rights is further perverted as the United Fruit Company claims its share, with all the enthusiasm of a colonist molesting a native woman, "reserv[ing] for itself the juiciest, / the central seaboard of my land, America's sweet waist" (ll. 6–8). The speaker aligns firmly with "my land," and there is no pretense of neutrality.

The merchant invaders, oblivious to the country's rich history, set up shop "upon the slumbering corpses, / upon the restless heroes" (ll. 12–13) and rule via a parasitic "dictatorship of flies" (l. 20). Again Neruda does not hesitate to name names: "Trujillo flies, Tacho flies, / Carías flies, Martínez flies . . ." (ll. 21–22). This is the voice of a defiant poet in exile. Neruda alludes to Dominican Rafael Trujillo (dictator 1930–61), Nicara-

guan Anastasio "Tacho" Somoza García (1936–56), Honduran Tiburcio Carías Andino (1933–48), and Salvadoran Maximiliano Martínez (1931–44). A few years earlier Neruda had been driven from Chile after a senate speech in which he identified imprisoned dissidents by name, a heroic but politically unwise gesture. Now the movement of export becomes a gesture of draining enslavement, disguised as polite servitude: "ravaging coffee and fruits / for its ships that spirit away / over submerged lands' treasures / like serving trays" (ll. 31–34). What remains is ruin, native "Indians collapsed, buried / in the morning mist" (ll. 37–38). Neruda ends the poem with an indelible metaphor, recognizing this waste of vitality in the way much of a crop is wasted by the bruising of mechanized harvest, "a bunch of lifeless fruit / dumped in the rubbish heap" (ll. 41–42).

Sandra Beasley

UTLER, ANJA (1973–)

Anja Utler, born in 1973 in Schwandorf, West Germany, now lives in Vienna. She studied Russian literature, English literature, and speech therapy in Regensburg, West Germany; Norwich, England; and St. Petersburg, USSR; and completed a dissertation on 20th-century Russian women poets. In 1999 Utler's first poetry volume, *aufsagen* (reciting) was published, and in 2002 she co-edited a popular anthology of erotic poems from the Middle Ages to the 20th century. Her celebrated poetry volume *münden—entzüngeln* (merging—untonguing) was published in 2004. In 2001 Utler received the Poetry Prize of the Akademie Graz (Austria) and a literature fellowship of the Insel Hombroich Foundation, a former U.S. nuclear weapons site in Germany that has been dismantled and transformed into a community of artists and writers. At Hombroich Utler met the poet THOMAS KLING, who praised her poems not only for what he calls their lucid and compassionate precision, but also for their embodiment of an unusually intimate closeness with language. Shortly before his early death in 2005, Kling dedicated a poem to her. In 2003 Utler was awarded the Leonce-und-Lena Prize, Germany's most prestigious award for emerging poets.

Like her 20th-century predecessors RAINER MARIA RILKE, JOHANNES BOBROWSKI, and PAUL CELAN, with whose works her texts share many intertextual threads, Utler often superimposes various layers of meaning and makes creative use of the fact that the German language is full of words that touch on different semantic fields. Her poems often work with words that simultaneously suggest geological, botanical, and anatomical meanings. Recurring evocations of traumatic events surrounding sexuality, violence, and loss reveal acts and processes of speaking and listening as both symptoms of violence and attempts to overcome it. Refusing to write *about* a theme and refraining from a pseudo-confessional mode that permeates most contemporary poetry, Utler precludes omniscient and complacent distance. The reader is immediately drawn into the scenarios. Her poems create voices that cling to the spoken word to survive torture and persecution with resilience and lucidity.

Continuing the rich European literary tradition of exploring classical mythological characters and constellations, a tradition that in German literature has been most vigorously practiced by the poet Friedrich Hölderlin (1770–1843) and in late 20th-century novels by Christa Wolf (*Kassandra*; 1983; *Medea,* 1996) and Peter Weiss (*The Aesthetics of Resistance,* 1975–81), Utler presents and reinterprets conflicts, persecutions, and transformations from Greek and Roman mythology, whose most influential literary source remains Ovid's epic poem *Metamorphoses.* Roughly half of Utler's lyrical texts from her collection *münden—entzüngeln* (2004) form a cyclical series of mythological poems. They include "*marsyas, umkreist*" ("MARSYAS, ENCIRCLED") and "*für daphne, geklagt*" (for daphne, mourning), where the reader encounters Daphne's voice trying to speak to her father, Apollo, while she is being raped by him and shortly before she is transmuted into a laurel tree. Another mythological poem from the same volume is entitled "k_chronos" and juxtaposes the castration of Kronos and an exploration of *chronos,* the Greek word for "time."

Since the baroque poet Quirinus Kuhlmann in the 17th century, no German poet has explored the materiality and physical presence of the German language, particularly of its sound system, as radically as Anja Utler. A precise reader and charismatic performer of her works, Utler has participated in several international poetry festivals, including "Poetry on the Road" (Bremen and Münster, 2005). Utler's poetry, including her poem "marsyas, umkreist," is available in English translation in the anthology *From Mouth to Mouth: Contemporary German Poetry in Translation* and accessible at the important website www.poetryinternational.org.

BIBLIOGRAPHY

Wohlfarth, Thomas, and Tobias Lehmkuhl, eds. *From Mouth to Mouth: Contemporary German Poetry in Translation.* Newcastle, Australia: Giramondo, 2004.

Olaf Berwald

V

VALÉRY, PAUL (1871–1945) French poet Paul Valéry was born in the seaside village of Sète in 1871 to Barthélémy Valéry, a customs clerk, and his wife, Fanny. The sea always played an important role in Valéry's imagery, and the poet attributed his own meter and characteristic rhythms to the hypnotic flux and flow of the tides and waves. At 13 he began composing poetry and published a few poems while still in his teens. But his artistic endeavors did not impress his teachers, who faulted the young man for daydreaming and inattentiveness. Nonetheless, the youthful Valéry formed a group of like-minded friends who discussed poetry and other writers—particularly the influence of Edgar Allen Poe, Stéphane Mallarmé, and the symbolist school in general. As his schooling progressed Valéry become increasingly intrigued by mathematics and science because he sensed in these fields elements of the orderly, rhythmic nature of the sea that had fascinated him as a child.

An unsuccessful attempt to attend law school was followed by a year's compulsory military service, where he met Pierre Louÿs, who introduced him to several eminent literary figures including André Gide and Mallarmé, who praised and encouraged Valéry's poetic endeavors. Valéry started contributing poems to symbolist journals, but even as his poetic works received favorable reviews, he began to think they were merely a distraction from his broad interests in scientific matters. In 1892 a failed love affair seems to have sparked him to renounce poetry and focus on scientific mat-

ters. After that crisis he would not attempt to write poetry for almost two decades. He spent the period publishing scientific articles and working as a civil servant of the French government. In 1900 he married Jeannie Gobillard, a friend of Mallarmé's family. He also began meditating and recording his observations in a series of notebooks. Though he maintained his literary connections, Valéry still refused to write and contented himself with his observations and with rearing his three children.

In 1912 Gide finally coaxed Valéry to revise and consider publishing his earlier works. As he followed Gide's advice, Valéry regained his love of poetic composition but decided that his youthful works were immature. Instead he began drafting a new poem that he worked on over the next five years, publishing it as THE YOUNG FATE (1917). He spent three more years revising what he considered his worthiest poems from his youth and published them in 1920. Three years later he published another collection of verse, *Charmes* (*Charms*). With this collection Valéry's reputation was established, and he quickly rose to national prominence in French literary circles. He also became acquainted with many of the major philosophical and scientific figures of his era, including Henri Bergson and Albert Einstein. During the early-to-mid-1920s Valéry also began publishing some of his notebook observations, which became famous for their pithy flavor.

In 1925 Valéry was elected to the prestigious French Academy, and he was soon invited to give lectures and speeches throughout Europe. In 1932 he published his famous "THE GRAVEYARD BY THE SEA" (*"Le Cimetière marin"*), which has been translated by many prominent poets worldwide. In 1933 he became the chief administrator of the Centre Universitaire Méditerranéen at Nice. He became professor of poetry at the Collège de France in 1937—a position created for him. Though his international stature protected him from the Germans during the occupation of France, his health steadily declined during the 1940s, and he died of heart failure in July 1945, just a few weeks after the Allies liberated France.

BIBLIOGRAPHY

Kluback, William. *Paul Valéry: Illusions of Civilization*. New York: Lang, 1996.

Putnam, Walter. *Paul Valéry Revisited*. New York: Twayne, 1995.

Valéry, Paul. *An Anthology*. Edited by James R. Lawler. Princeton, N.J.: Bollingen, 1977.

Joseph E. Becker

VALLEJO, CÉSAR (1892–1938)

César Vallejo is one of the most important Latin American poets of his generation, along with NICOLÁS GUILLÉN (Cuba) and PABLO NERUDA (Chile). Born in the isolated northern town of Santiago de Chuco in Peru, his grandmothers were both Indians and his grandfathers Spanish Catholic priests, and he was dubbed *"el cholo Vallejo,"* a term ridiculing his racial heritage but also suggesting an ethnic origin for his fatalism. Lacking money, he occasionally interrupted university studies to work, and his firsthand knowledge of the exploitative conditions of laborers at a sugar estate where he worked marked his philosophy, writings, and politics.

Vallejo's first poetry collection, *Los heraldos negros* (The Black Heralds, 1918), follows the modernist aesthetic defined by RUBÉN DARÍO (Nicaragua). Like Darío, Vallejo eschewed apolitical cosmopolitanism in favor of a focus on the nation and region. He projected his early existential and physical angst, disillusion, and bitterness as collective orphanhood in the title poem "THE BLACK HERALDS": "There are blows in life so powerful . . . I don't know! / Blows as from the hatred of God. . . ." Even before Vallejo and other intellectuals interpreted Peruvian history via Marxist principles, he expressed solidarity, like José Martí in Cuba, with the downtrodden, especially the indigenous Peruvians.

Unjustly imprisoned for four months in 1920, Vallejo published his second collection, *Trilce* (1922), which constituted a rebellion parallel in poetry to disruptions of realist painting by cubism, surrealism, and dadaism. Free verse predominates; disrupted syntax defies logic and contributes to a sense of absurdity; neologisms and nonstandard spellings abound. Vallejo rejects philosophical idealism's suppositions about a knowable, reason-based, harmonic universe, and his rupture with discursive coherence proposes other ways of understanding reality. Abstract principles for understanding are false constructs, and reality must be experienced directly, in all its disorder, and not necessarily through known words; for example, the second line of *Trilce* XXXII reads: "Rumbbb . . . Trraprrr rrach . . . chaz." For Vallejo poetry speaks of the impossibility of conceptual comprehension, compensated, nonetheless, by multiple, complex, endless expressivity. In this sense he revolutionized poetry in Spanish.

Vallejo left Peru in 1923, never to return, and lived thereafter in France and Spain. His financial situation was often precarious; he became politically militant and made trips to the USSR. He was considered an extremist and was exiled from France, moved to Spain, then returned to Paris, where he died almost as he had predicted in his oft-quoted lines: "I shall die in Paris, in a rainstorm / On a day I already remember" (Black Stone Lying on A White Stone).

In Europe Vallejo wrote more prose than poetry, including propagandistic anti-imperialist texts, and questioned the role of intellectuals in a world of deplorable living conditions, as in "A MAN WALKS BY WITH A LOAF OF BREAD ON HIS SHOULDER." *Poemas en prosa* (Prose Poems), written between 1923 and 1937 and published posthumously as part of *Poemas humanos* (Human Poems, 1939), continue *Trilce*'s themes, including the conviction that life and death are inexorably entwined. Although major themes of his work include suffering and the irrevocable force of destiny, some of his most moving poems belong to another section of the posthumous collection, where his constant sympathy for the poor visualizes hope in collective struggle, especially in *"España, aparta de mí este caliz"* (Spain, Take This Cup from Me), written in 1937 during the Spanish civil war (1936–39). Victimhood is here converted into antifascist mass action to construct a more egalitarian society.

Translations of Vallejo's poems are readily available in English. Clayton Eshleman and José Rubia Barcia translated *César Vallejo: The Complete Posthumous Poetry,* which won the 1979 National Book Award. Eshleman edited and translated the new *César Vallejo: The Complete Poetry: A Bilingual Edition.* Efraín Kristal selected 14 poems for the *American Poetry Review* May/June 2005 Vallejo supplement, including *"Epexegesis"* ("I was born on a day / when God was sick"). Stephen M. Hart edited two issues of *Romance Quarterly* on Vallejo in 2002 with nine analytical articles and noted that "Vallejo as Icon," James Higgins's essay, "shows how deeply Vallejo has managed to embed himself in the Peruvian national psyche; the poet operates on the one hand as an official symbol of Peru, when he appears on banknotes, and also functions as a complex symbol pointing the way forward for Peru in advocating a dynamic mix of Andean and Western cultural values" (82). Higgins wrote: Vallejo "produced poems on the human condition that were taken seriously enough for him to rank alongside Eliot as one of the major poets of the 20th century" (120).

BIBLIOGRAPHY

Eshleman, Clayton, ed. and trans. *César Vallejo: The Complete Poetry: A Bilingual Edition.* Berkeley: University of California Press, 2007.

Eshleman, Clayton, and José Rubia Barcia, eds. and trans. *César Vallejo: The Complete Posthumous Poetry.* Berkeley: University of California Press, 1978.

Hart, Stephen H. *César Vallejo: A Critical Bibliography of Research.* London: Tamesis, 2002.

———. "César Vallejo in the New Millennium: Foreword." *Romance Quarterly* 49, no. 2 (Spring 2002): 82–83.

Hart, Stephen M., ed. *Romance Quarterly.* Issues on César Vallejo: 49, no. 2 and 49, no. 3 (Spring and Summer 2002).

Higgins, James. "Vallejo as Icon." *Romance Quarterly* 49, no. 2 (Spring 2002): 119–125.

Kristal, Efraín, ed. Clayton Eshleman, trans. "César Vallejo: Fourteen Poems: A Special Supplement." *American Poetry Review* 34, no. 4 (May–June 2005): 25–28.

Sharman, Adam, ed. *The Poetry and Poetics of César Vallejo: The Fourth Angle of the Circle.* Lewiston, N.Y.: Edwin Mellen Press, 1997.

María Roof

VESAAS, TARJEI (1897–1970) Norwegian Tarjei Vesaas was a well-established writer of prose fiction by the time he began writing poetry in the 1940s; yet the six volumes of poetry he published following World War II earned him distinction as one of Norway's major modern poets. His poetry is distinctive for its focus on sound rather than image, its use of rural Norwegian dialect (known as *nynorsk*) and oral folk tradition, and its complex formulations of relationship between humans and the natural environment. During a time when continental European literary critics were still conflating the "modern" with the "urban" and assuming that "rural" poetry was by nature nostalgic and romantic, Vesaas emerged as a paradox. His poetry is anchored in the rural Norwegian landscape, where he spent most of his life, and it is also undeniably modern in its stark language and its themes of alienation, anxiety, and search for meaning and self-definition. While many Norwegians consider Vesaas's poetry to be quintessentially Norwegian in its language and themes, his poetry also has had considerable appeal internationally, with two collections of his poetry in English translation remaining in print. The more recent of these, *Through Naked Branches: Selected Poems of Tarjei Vesaas* (2000), won its editor and translator, Roger Greenwald, the American Scandinavian Foundation's translation prize.

Vesaas's life can in many ways be considered as paradoxical as his poetry. He was born in Vinje in the province of Telemark in southeastern Norway, a region known for its landscape of mountains, valleys, lakes, and forests. He was born on a farm that his family had tended for nine generations, and tradition dictated that as the oldest son, Vesaas would take over for his father (Greenwald xi). But Vesaas left home to attend a folk high school in western Norway from 1917 to 1918. Such folk high schools were a product of late 19th-century democratic and nationalist movements in Scandinavia whose instruction emphasized national language, literature, and culture. By 1923 Vesaas had published his first novel, followed by two more novels over the next two years, staking out his profession in writing rather than farming. During the 1920s he received a number of grants that enabled him to leave Norway and travel extensively throughout Scandinavia and continental Europe, where he was exposed to modern literature and contemporary intellectual thought (Roger Greenwald, introduction xi). Accordingly, his intellectual heritage stems from an awareness of both Norwegian folk tradition and international modernist developments. While in Switzerland he met the poet Halldis Moren, and they married in 1934 and settled on a farm in Telemark not far from the Vesaas family farm, where they raised two children and remained for the rest of Vesaas's life. The landscape of Telemark province figures prominently in many of Vesaas's best-known poems, including "SNOW AND SPRUCE FOREST" ("Snø og granskog") and "The Loons Head North" ("Lomen går mot nord").

Moren has been credited with helping Vesaas work through a depression so deep that it brought him to the brink of suicide during the interwar 1930s. Yet during this time he continued to produce masterful prose fiction. He stopped publishing during the German occupation of Norway during World War II, but he did not stop writing. Once the occupation ended, Vesaas began publishing collections of poetry that condensed the language and themes of his fiction into powerful verse. His first collection, Kildane (The Springs), came out in 1946, followed by Leiken og lynet (The Game and the Lightning, 1947), Lykka for ferdesmenn (The Happiness of Travelers, 1949), Løynde elders land (Land of Hidden Fires, 1953), and Ver ny, vår draum (May Our Dream Stay New, 1956). All of his poetry is written in nynorsk, a written form of a spoken rural Norwegian dialect that many Norwegians consider "the people's language," as Norway still today is predominantly rural. (The "official" Norwegian, known as bokmål, which is still the language of government and industry, is closely related to written Danish, as Norway was under the dominion of the Kingdom of Denmark for many centuries.) Vesaas's allegiance to the Norwegian oral tradition accounts in part for his close attention to sound in his poetry, using language to create silences, assonances, murmurs, and pregnant pauses. As Roger Greenwald writes, "Vesaas's primary allegiance to the oral/aural rather than the visual puts his work outside, and in some ways at odds with, the visually oriented movement dominant in modern poetry" (xv). This attention to the aural makes Vesaas's poetry particularly difficult to render with similar effect in English, as the sounds and senses are not the same between the two languages. But Greenwald has paid careful attention to this task in his translations of 46 of Vesaas's poems in his award-winning anthology. This bilingual collection makes it possible for readers with some knowledge of Norwegian to sound out the poems in the original while reading the translations. (Greenwald, a poet in his own right, also consulted with Vesaas's widow, herself a poet, in translating the poems.) A reissued collection of Vesaas's poems translated by Anthony Barnett remains in print, although Greenwald's collection is well worth exploring as much for his detailed critical introduction to Vesaas's work as for his elegant and careful translations.

BIBLIOGRAPHY

Hermundsgard, Frode. Child of the Earth, Vol. 29: Tarjei Vesaas and Scandinavian Primitivism. Westport, Conn.: Greenwood Press, 1989.

Vesaas, Tarjei. Beyond the Moment: One Hundred and One Selected Poems. 2d. ed. Translated by Anthony Barnett. Lewes, England: Allardyce, Barnett, 2001.

Vesaas, Tarjei. Through Naked Branches: Selected Poems of Tarjei Vesaas. Translated and edited by Roger Greenwald. Princeton, N.J.: Princeton University Press, 2000.

Ursula A. L. Lindqvist

"VIEW ON THE PARALLEL YEAR" PAOLO VOLPONI (1986)

It is appropriate that this poem ends PAOLO VOLPONI's 1986 collection Con testo a fronte (With Parallel Text), a title that signifies that it complements some other text (testo). "Vista sull'anno parallelo" is thus a fitting conclusion because the "parallel year" of which this poem speaks (i.e., the industrial, urban, mechanized year) runs parallel to—and always distant from—the time frames of nature and the natural world. As a manager in major Italian corporations (Olivetti and Fiat), Volponi had a long and varied experience of the industrial world. This poem originates in part from those memories.

The poem is an example of Volponi's later *poemetti* (long poems). It is rhymed, and, like Dante, whom he cites, Volponi uses harsh rhyme endings (like *-arco*), which explain in part his eccentric and inventive diction (*"plutarco"* Plutarch, *"stearco"* stearic). Many words are chosen for their free association with others, like *"vello"* and *"Arco"* ("fleece" and "Argus"). Other words are archaic or industrial terms or neologisms. There is an overwhelming abundance of nouns, of objects, a teeming of substantives. That conjunctions are missing and verbs are few renders the poem ponderous and rather static, rumbling and sonorous but going nowhere.

The poem's opening lines begin to explain the title: "the parallel year does not lead or select, it dispenses." It is not human, divine, or intelligent. It appears in "soot" and "burning milk." The parallel is not the unconscious, but "blacker and less alive." It is that which "is impregnated with the odor and stain of presidential brilliantine," that which is part of "capitalistic occidental civilization." The parallel year is the year of the factory, industry, politics, and angst. Anxiety reveals the parallel. Volponi believes in recuperating the lost relationship, in the modern world, between humanity and nature as well as the relationships still possible among humans. Both of these fundamental sorts of associations appear irreparably harmed and fatally wounded by the course of modern society. Even the Moon here is a mere "machine." In some ways this poem participates in a type of FIELD POETICS.

In *"Vista sull'anno parallelo"* Volponi has become gloomy and almost entirely withdrawn. But how else to represent such a nonrelational subject—other than through the lack of vital discourse? This poem signals the end of a long stage in Volponi's poetics. His poems in the following six years before his death are more contained, generally shorter, less knotty, and more communicative.

BIBLIOGRAPHY

Ballerini, L., B. E. Coda Cavatorta, and P. Vangelisti, eds. *The Promised Land: Italian Poetry after 1975*. Los Angeles: Sun and Moon Press, 2000.

Jacob Blakesley

"VIEW WITH A GRAIN OF SAND"

WISŁAWA SZYMBORSKA (1986) First published in *The People on the Bridge* (*Ludzie na moście,* 1986), WISŁAWA SZYMBORSKA's "View with a Grain of Sand" is a landscape word painting with a twist. Instead of presenting readers with a scene featuring a beach or a lake, Szymborska engages in a metaphysical exploration of physical identity and its relationship to language. We are shown (close-up) a grain of sand falling on a windowsill with a view of a lake beyond, but there is more to the poem's subtext.

The first stanza introduces the abstract concept of naming—by beginning with "We call it a grain of sand / but it calls itself neither grain nor sand" (185). The speaker says that what we call sand "does just fine" unburdened by linguistic tags whatever their character, "general, particular, / . . . / incorrect or apt." The second stanza notes, "Our glance, our touch mean nothing to it"; it is the viewer who sees the grain fall "on the windowsill." Being unsentient matter, the grain of sand neither feels its environment nor knows it in any human sense. As the third stanza puts it, even "a wonderful view of a lake" has no self-consciousness. The view, like the grain of sand, "exists in this world / colorless, shapeless, / soundless, odorless, and painless." The senses are what endow human views of the universe with phenomenal qualities (relating to seeing, touching, hearing, smelling, and tasting), and all human languages are born of human experience and perspectives. Matter in itself obviously exists, but not in any indispensable contact with language: The lake's water "feels itself neither wet nor dry," and its waves "splash deaf to their own noise."

The poem ends with two stanzas on the topic of time. Three seconds are said to have passed, but only the poet and her "audience" have measured and counted them. Humans invent similes (the poem's speaker says) comparing the universe to themselves and wrap their own terms around things, likening, for instance, the passage of time to the actions of certain "characters": e.g., "Time has passed like a courier with urgent news." But the identities we confer on inhuman matter, space, and time—like the "courier" the poet has invented to talk about an occasion—are all "make-believe."

By sanitizing the relationship of language to things in this way, Szymborska makes the point that all efforts to get at and to pin down identity (essence) or history (existence in time) are projections from particular (and human) points of view: They are just as ridiculous as our efforts to communicate through mere words a true sense of self or of reality. The poem is self-reflexive and ironic in deprecating itself as well as the activity of writers more generally, but, at the same time, it manages to say something important about the ineffability of identity and about the touching human need for communication, achieving itself in a detached and dryly humorous sort of way.

BIBLIOGRAPHY
Szymborska, Wisława. *Poems New and Collected.* Translated by Stanisław Barańczak and Clare Cavanagh. New York: Harcourt/Harvest Books, 2000, 185–186.

R. Victoria Arana

"VIGILANCE" André Breton (1932)

André Breton published "Vigilance" in 1932 in the collection *Le Revolver à cheveux blancs* (The Revolver with White Hair), which consists of texts written between 1915 and 1932. "Vigilance" is to be found in the third part, containing poems written after 1923. It is one of the last poems written by Breton where he followed the principle of *écriture automatique,* and although the difficult and confusing elements of automatic writing are still present, they are combined here with a conscious arrangement.

In its contrast between a seemingly coherent narrative frame and the irrational, surreal imagery within it, which is not structured by any punctuation, the text plays out the clash of the desire for certainty of meaning with the denial of meaning. The speaker is clearly situated in place and time and is directed toward a goal that seems to be gained with the final achievement of knowledge, the vision of clear insight into *"le coeur des choses"* (the heart of things). The first two lines evoke the similarity of the tower of Saint-Jacques in Paris with a sunflower. *"À Paris la tour Saint-Jacques chancelante / Pareille à un tournesol."* In *L'Amour fou* (1937) Breton would explain the leaning (*chancelante*) of the tower of Saint-Jacques as his own emotional vacillation. Tower and sunflower have in common their vertical structure, and the bending of the sunflower toward the Earth could be associated with the shadow of the tower "hanging" toward the River Seine (although the real tower of Saint-Jacques is separated from the river by other buildings).

The surrealist image is not based on a comparison (as in traditional poetry), but on the *"rapprochement de deux réalités plus ou moins éloignées"* (Manifestes du surréalisme, 34), the approximation of two realities that are more or less disparate. This is the starting point of the poem, which extends the process of the destruction of seemingly stable reality to the room in which the speaker is sleeping and then even to his own body. In a kind of surreal dream-reality, he imagines himself setting fire (*"j'y mets le feu"*) to the bedroom in which he is still lying (*"la chambre où je suis étendu"*). In the following cluster of images man-made objects are metamorphosed into natural being, furniture into animals of similar shape, chairs into lions by whose fiery manes they are consumed, bed sheets into the underbellies of sharks. By this transformation the dreaming poet sees himself liberated from the bonds of convention. He focuses on his own body and confronts himself as a doppelgänger: *"Je me vois brûler à mon tour je vois cette cachette"* (I see myself burn in turn I see this shell). The body as a mere empty shell and a prison is replaced by a fiery, animate presence, an *"ibis du feu."* The self is the origin of the destructive fire but will also be consumed by it; it is a victim, but also a spectator, and will be renewed by the fire like a phoenix rising from the ashes. Thus freed from corporeality—and therefore invisible—it enters the ark, a world of primary unity: *"Lorsque tout est fini j'entre invisible dans l'arche"* (After it was all over I enter the ark invisibly).

A new stage is reached and a new chain of associations is begun, centering on weaving and cloth, then on beautiful structures in art and nature. In the "ark" the covering raiment of humanity is rent by the conniving alternation of absence and presence to reveal a more fundamental reality in which with the weaver's loom all manufacture gives way to a perfection that seems to be not art, but nature: The negation of normal reality is replaced here by positive images of conscious creation transformed into beautiful, sensual forms of nature that have survived the destruction of the loom: *"Une coquille de dentelle qui a la forme parfaite d'un sein"* (A shell of lace that has the perfect shape of a breast).

Thus the destruction of things leads back to the human; the isolation and alienation of the speaker who pays no attention to the passers-by of life (*"Sans prendre garde aux passants de la vie"*) seems to open up here via an erotic image for an I-thou relationship. The final line, *"Je ne touche plus que le coeur des choses je tiens le fil"* (I now only touch the heart of things I hold the thread), turns the speaker into a Theseus who has killed the wild beast, the Minotaur, and is now trying to find his way out of the labyrinth of images by following Ariadne's thread. This line summarizes the theme of the poem, the dissolution of conventional forms and the ensuing emergence of a new kind of reality, and its technique, the seemingly free association of images that nonetheless are connected by a continuous red thread. The poetological program of the poem therefore seems to be equivalent to a surrealist manifesto: The violent dissolution of all material forms by the poet leads into an original unity by liberating the underlying coherence of all things in the natural beauty of the artifact that is the poem itself. Such a moment of insight, though, can be attained only in a borderline situation between sleeping, dreaming, and waking (a vigilance) in an "hour of love" (*"À l'heure de l'amour"*), when subject and object merge.

BIBLIOGRAPHY

Balakian, Anna. *André Breton: Magus of Surrealism.* New York: Oxford University Press, 1971.

Breton, André. *Oeuvres complètes.* Vol. 2. Edited by Marguerite Bonnet et al. Paris: Gallimard, 1992.

———. *Manifestes du surréalisme.* Paris: Gallimard, 1962.

Caws, Mary Ann. *The Poetry of Dada and Surrealism: Aragon, Breton, Tzara, Éluard and Desnos.* Princeton, N.J.: Princeton University Press, 1970.

———, ed. *The Yale Anthology of Twentieth-Century French Poetry.* New Haven, Conn.: Yale University Press, 2004.

Stillers, Rainer. "André Breton: 'Vigilance'." In *Französische Gedichte des 19. und 20. Jahrhunderts,* edited by Hartmut Köhler, 252–264. Stuttgart: Reclam, 2001.

Heike Grundmann

VOLPONI, PAOLO (1924–1994)

Paolo Volponi, novelist and poet, was born in Urbino, Italy, in 1924. His education was conventional, and at the age of 23 he graduated with a law degree in 1947. He worked for many years in the social services division of the electronics company Olivetti, and later at Fiat. He was one of the cofounders of the New Communist Party (Rifondazione Comunista) in 1991. He held elective offices in Italy as both a representative and a senator.

He is known above all for being a left-wing novelist of considerable renown whose works address alienation in modern industrialized society—a fundamental theme in his verse as well. Yet he published poetry—three collections: *Il ramarro* (The Lizard), *L'antica moneta* (The Ancient Coin), *Le porte dell'Appennino* (The Doors of the Apennines)—before he published his first novel, *Memoriale* (Memoir, 1962). His last book published—*Nel silenzio campale* (In the Silence of the Field)—was, again, verse. Thus he significantly began and ended his literary career with poetry. Volponi himself wrote that his original motivation for writing came from fear.

In *Il ramarro* (1948) his style is hermetic, following his masters—EUGENIO MONTALE, GIUSEPPE UNGARETTI, and SALVATORE QUASIMODO. But he adds something new: an almost visionary relationship with nature. He is often desolate, finding himself more useless "than a dry wing / of a cicada." He cannot bear the vastness of day and night. Nonetheless, there are women—whose bodies "have dissolved in my mouth." Most important, however, he hears the dialogue of the dead in the discourse of woodworms and also "the noise of the skeleton of things" (*il rumore della ossatura delle cose*), the same noise he hears in his own body, threatening to overwhelm him.

In 1955 *L'antica moneta* was published, which, along with a book by PIER PAOLO PASOLINI, won the Carducci Prize. With this volume the urban city enters Volponi's poetry, even though the landscape (seemingly eternal) acquires more and more potent force. Volponi is invaded by nostalgia "of being in everyone simultaneously" and fears that the dead will return in the "yellow coats of insects." He does not know how much of himself derives from "a delicate insect," "the sea," or "the river." In this volume begin his longer narrative and autobiographical poems, in which he writes of his "splendid fear" of his father and nevertheless (or because of this) traces his origins back to the animal world: "My sister is the innocent turtledove . . . ," "My mother is also the snake. . . ." At times his poetry is reminiscent of CESARE PAVESE's.

In *Le porte dell'Appennino* (1960), which won the prestigious Viareggio Prize, Volponi writes autobiographical, narrative poems (structurally influenced by Pasolini and others at the Italian magazine *Officina*), distancing himself by using the third person (Paolo). He juxtaposes his birth with a stillborn child's—a relative of his—who is now "outside every beginning and history." In other poems Volponi seems to enact a mysterious communion with nature: *"Prodigo è il mio amore / legato ad ogni luogo"* (Prodigious is my love / tied to every place). Volponi also addresses his beloved in a "Ballad of snow," in which he says that only her glance keeps sparrows alive, "or their own fear / of dying very soon." One of the longest, substantial poems is "Fear," which Volponi describes masterfully. The poem is above all about the fear of "loving," the "terror of causing sadness," and that which "brings words to sorrow." The last poem concluding this collection is appropriately titled "Youth Dies," which in its elegiac tone recalls the poetry of Attilio Bertolucci.

Other volumes followed. *Foglia mortale* (Mortal Leaf, 1974) is a small collection of seven long poems. Volponi is always anxious, "like a mortal leaf" (*una foglia mortale*), always used to "sucking on the same illness." Everything "is in order," except that he himself is "destroyed." *Testo a fronte* (With Parallel Text, 1986) is a heterogenous collection of poems, long and short, one of which is "VIEW ON THE PARALLEL YEAR." The natural world is corrupted by modern society; the Moon itself is an "impossible color". Water is "chemically mutated." Night "is more than death: / it is the dream that the abyss does not fill." The enumeration, accumulation, and accretion of words in this collection reflect the cancer that threatens the world. In *Nel silenzio campale* (In the Silence of the Field, 1990), the last book he published, Volponi explained that he meant the title to signify "after the battle," a sort of funeral lament. He wished to write epic poetry, which includes the voices of others, not merely to denounce something, but to build in common. Volponi recognized that only a "shard" of himself survived his fear; and this shard—his poetry—"belongs entirely to others." In this last volume he imagines himself like the "mad horse" of a Greek sculpture, whose riders (children) grasp his mane, helplessly, hopelessly. He is carrying them to their perdition; he is lost to himself. Yet his last words (in "Memento") strike a note of defiance rather than resignation: "Far better to contemplate death" than "vomit all residue of vice" closing "the doors to truth."

BIBLIOGRAPHY
L. Ballerini, L. B. Cavatorta, E. Coda, and P. Vangelisti, eds. *The Promised Land: Italian Poetry after 1975.* Los Angeles: Sun and Moon Press, 2000.
Volponi, Paolo. *My Troubles Began.* Translation of *Memoriale* by Belén Severeid. New York: Grossman, 1964.

Jacob Blakesley

"VORONEZH" ANNA AKHMATOVA (1940) During OSIP MANDELSTAM's internal exile in the Soviet city Voronezh, ANNA AKHMATOVA visited her acmeist colleague, whose 1934 arrest she had witnessed, and wrote this poem in March 1936. The poem first appeared in the journal *Leningrad,* with the last four lines deleted.

The town of Voronezh is located 850 kilometers south of Moscow in the extreme west of Russia, near the confluence of the Voronezh and Don Rivers not far from Ukraine. At the time of Mandelstam's sojourn there, the population was approximately 325,000. Mandelstam's specific "crime" had been writing the dangerous lyric "THE STALIN EPIGRAM," so to counterbalance the experience of Stalinist repression, Akhmatova invokes the mighty moments of Russian history.

The first of these allusions, "the Peter of Voronezh," is a reference to a statue of Peter the Great, the reformer czar, who had revolutionized Russian political structures and commanded his courtiers and officers to emulate European customs. His presence in the poem not only casts light on the contrasting (isolationist) practices of Soviet politics and economics, but also carries the promise or hope of renewed reform. Second, Akhmatova reminds her readers of "the battle of Kulikovo," which occurred about halfway between Moscow and Voronezh on the banks of the Don, when a unified Russia defeated the Mongol Golden Horde in 1380, putting in motion the end of the "Tatar Yoke" that had already lasted a century and a half. Russia had to be patient for yet another century after Kulikovo Field, and so the hope of reform and freedom made implicit by these references is not untempered by long suffering. In Mandelstam's case the wind that "blows from the slopes" will not bring change soon enough.

Mandelstam told Akhmatova during their visit that "Poetry is power" (Mandelstam 170). And both of them believed in the power and their responsibility to record the truth of their circumstances. When Akhmatova arrived it was winter, the town was frozen, and the wind was a cold one, literally and metaphorically, in spite of the whisper of triumph that it brought. The poem begins in the middle of a sentence, as if this exile were an interruption and not an end. It was a dangerous time, and she had to tread carefully, "timidly." In the concluding four lines omitted from the original publication, Mandelstam is "the poet in disgrace," and so their great pleasure in the visit is presided over by both fear and the poetic muse. It is a time of metaphorical night without any sign of morning. The poets are not so naive as to think sunrise will come suddenly. They know their history.

BIBLIOGRAPHY

Akhmatova, Anna. *The Complete Poems of Anna Akhmatova.* Expanded edition. Edited and introduced by Roberta Reeder, translated by Judith Hemschemeyer. Boston: Zephyr Press, 1997.

Mandelstam, Nadezhda. *Hope Against Hope: A Memoir.* New York: Atheneum, 1970.

A. Mary Murphy

VOYAGE CECÍLIA MEIRELES (1939) *Viagem* (Voyage) is the title of the major collection of poetic works by CECÍLIA BENAVIDES DE CARVALHO MEIRELES up to 1939, which includes a poem by the same name. The volume won an award from the Brazilian Academy of Letters in the year it was published. The title of the book (as of the poem) refers in a general way to the poet's spiritual journey and to her view of that point when life and poetry come together as one. In Meireles's view, that is the moment when a poet realizes that all human emotions can be expressed through poetry. While Meireles was a devout Catholic, *Viagem* is an expression of the poet's existence as a human being and does not openly express her religious or social beliefs. She simply questions the human voyage through life. *"Por onde é que vou?"* (Where I am going?), Meireles asks at the beginning and end of the poem. While this is a personal question for Meireles, it becomes a universal question with regard to the sometimes pointlessness of life and the lack of direction that many face in their journey through life. When she penned the poem, she had suffered the deaths of her parents and the tragic death of her first husband by suicide. The poem opens with an unmistakable reference to that suffering: "In the perfume of my fingers / There is the taste of suffering."

Viagem is an excellent example of the highly pensive, personal, pain-filled, and philosophical poetry produced by one of Brazil's most adept poets. Here we observe many of the major themes prevalent throughout Meireles's work: the transitions of life, the brevity of life, love, the infinite, the influences of nature, and the significance of artistic creation. Her poems mirror the uncertainty and dubiousness of life's fleeting nature. Critics agree universally that *Viagem* marked Meireles's poetic maturity.

BIBLIOGRAPHY

Keith, Henry, and Raymond Sayers. *Cecília Meireles: poemas em tradução/Poems in Translation.* Washington, D.C.: Brazilian-American Cultural Institute, 1977.

James J. Davis

VOZNESENSKY, ANDREY (1933–) Poet and mixed-media artist Andrey Voznesensky was born in Moscow on May 12, 1933, the same year that YEVGENY YEVTUSHENKO was born. The two are generally considered the giants of contemporary Russian poetry. Like Yevtushenko's parents, Voznesensky's were interested in literature, science, and the arts, and the young Andrey grew up surrounded by his mother's books, especially the works of ALEXANDER BLOK, Fyodor Dostoyevsky, BORIS PASTERNAK, and Igor Severyanin (an ego-futurist poet). His father was a professor of engineering. The family lived for years about 100 miles east of Moscow in Vladimir, the ancient capital city of Rus, founded during the tenth century on the banks of the

Klyazma River. During World War II, while his father was stationed in Leningrad during the blockade, Voznesensky stayed with his mother in Kurgan, a town in the Ural Mountains just north of Khazakhstan. When Voznesensky's father visited them on leave from the battlefront, he brought with him only "a small rucksack containing some food and a little book of reproductions of etchings by Goya" (Blake and Hayward ix). Voznesensky never forgot the powerful impression that Goya's terrifying vision of war made on him as a boy; he later transformed the traumatic experience of that period of his life into one of his most famous poems, "I AM GOYA."

As a youth Vozensensky painted while, as he put it, "poetry was flowing in me like a river under the ice" (Blake and Hayward ix). Like many thoughtful Russians the teenaged Voznesensky idolized Pasternak for resisting the totalitarian language of the state and insisting instead on the inviolability of personhood and on the rights of human beings to emotional and intellectual space to themselves. Pasternak, upon receiving poems from the 14-year-old Voznesensky, telephoned and, later, mentored the younger poet. Voznesensky's early poems, unsurprisingly, were inspired by Pasternak's "moral intelligence," which proved an antidote to the falsehoods prevalent in Soviet life and literature under Stalin (Blake and Hayward x). Among those poems resembling Pasternak's in topic and tone are "Autumn," "Autumn in Sigulda," "Dead Still," and "First Frost."

When he was 19 Voznesensky enrolled at the Moscow Architectural Institute. He completed the five-year course of studies but abandoned his fledgling career as an architect when a fire at the institute in 1957 consumed the year's work of the school's entire senior class just before final examinations and graduation exercises. The young architect embraced fate, shifted his creative energies to poetry, and wrote a poem about the incident ("Fire in the Architectural Institute" *Antiworlds* 57–58). Many of Voznesensky's poems—written in different periods of his life—have been inspired by architectural topics, as critics have noted; but most are incandescent, if oblique, self-commentaries: e.g., "Master Craftsmen" (on Ivan the Terrible's blinding of the architect of St. Basil's Cathedral to ensure that

nothing so beautiful could be designed again, 53–54), a surreal meditation in "Italian Garage" (74), a tyro's confession in "The Torches of Florence" (55), and a metaphysical self-portrait in "New York Airport at Night" (63).

By the late 1950s Voznesensky, though still an admirer of Pasternak, had found his own poetic style (and a louder and more boisterous voice), surprising in its mixed diction, its juxtapositions of historical and trendy images, and its current cosmopolitan references to cultural life in many world settings. These traits, along with the poet's exuberant public recitals throughout the Soviet Union, made him immensely popular, drawing throngs by the thousands to each of his performances and making his collections of verse huge best sellers. During the 1960s Voznesensky would "recite from memory for an hour or two, with hardly a pause, in a powerful, cultivated voice. . . . Most [in the audience] brought copies of his books" and followed the artist using their books "like music scores" (Blake and Hayward ix).

Many of Voznesensky's poems resemble parables—a form of particular usefulness to dissident artists. Ostensibly about a neutral topic, "Hunting a Hare," for example, subtextually points to another reality altogether: the societal harnessing of bloodlust. John Bayley (Oxford University) rebuffed those critics of Voznesensky who distrusted the honesty of his poetry by defending Voznesensky's indirections as reasonable ways of criticizing the Soviet regime. Voznesensky often couches his social criticism in stark poetic anecdotes—as in "Foggy Street" (a cloak-and-dagger poem about "Home-bred Iagos") or his "ODE TO GOSSIPS." In another register he has produced poems about the power of art; one of the most moving is "WAR BALLAD" (sometimes titled "Ballad of 1941").

Voznesensky is the author of more than 40 volumes of poetry in Russian, two novels, a number of plays, and at least two operas. He was one of the central figures of the "above-ground" Soviet literary world during the Soviet era, but his path as a poet was often rocky. He published his first two collections *Mozaika* (Mozaics) and *Parabola* in 1960. In 1963 the Soviet government's antimodernist campaign blacklisted his writing and curtailed its publication. That year he was also officially prohibited from giving public performances of his poetry (Johnson). His best-known volume, *Antimiry* (Antiworlds), however, appeared in 1964. In 1966 he was nominated for the Lenin Prize (Literature) for *Antimiry*. While more of his poetry gradually reappeared, nearly all of his drama was censored in 1970, and he was officially put under close surveillance in 1971. By 1979 he had developed a more obscure style, and the difficult poems of *Soblazn* (Temptation) were published in that year. The rock musical *Juno and Avos,* based on his dramatic poem *Story under Full Sail* about the life of explorer/sailor Nikolay Rezanov, was produced in Moscow in 1981. His *Epitaph for Vysotsky* (1990) is a tribute to Russia's most beloved songwriter and singer, whose early death at 42 was mourned by millions across the Soviet Union. Random House published Voznesensky's *Selected Poems* in 2000 in a popular paperback edition.

His creative accomplishments have been recognized around the world. In 1978 Voznesensky was awarded the International Poetry Forum's International Award for distinguished achievement in poetry. He was subsequently elected to numerous honorary societies, including the American Academy of Arts and Letters, the Bavarian Academy of Fine Arts, and the French Académie Mérimée. He has served as vice president of the Russian PEN Center. His critical reputation, however, is still somewhat controversial. He was accused by Soviet officials of being a spy for the CIA, and academics of differing ideological persuasions consider much of his poetry simplistic, uncommitted, and merely clever. His standing remains secure, nevertheless, among great numbers of Russian citizens who are lovers of poetry and appreciate the poet's passion, verve, connection to the grand Old Russian poetic tradition, and brilliant handling of the sounds of their language. Voznesensky explained that the "drawn-out music in Russian speech . . . comes from the great distances of the Russian steppes" and added, "This cello-like note resounds in the lengths of our names—in our surnames and patronymics. Language is the music of thought; it is what our ancestors called the soul" (Bayley). British-American poet W. H. Auden admired Voznesensky as a fellow poet and noted appreciatively "the variety of tones, elegiac, comic, grotesque, quiet, rebellious" that he commanded and "the wide range of subject matter" that inspired his poetry (Foreword to *Antiworlds* vi). Voznesenzky's poems have been translated by Auden, Robert Bly, Lawrence Ferlinghetti, Jean Garrigue, Allen Ginsberg, Max Hayward, Stanley Kunitz, Stanley Moss, Louis Simpson, William J. Smith, and Richard Wilbur, among others.

BIBLIOGRAPHY

Bayley, John. *Review of An Arrow in the Wall,* Andrei Voznesensky. *New York Times,* 29 March 1987, Sec. 7. Available online. URL: http://www.nytimes.com/books/98/12/06/specials/voznesensky-arr ow.html. Accessed on April 29, 2007.

Blake, Patricia, and Max Hayward, eds. Introduction to Andrei Voznesensky's *Antiworlds.* New York: Basic Books, 1966. Also available online as "Andrei Voznesensky." URL: http://www.penrussia.org/n-z/an_voz.htm#i. Accessed on April 29, 2007.

Johnson, Emily. "Nikita Khrushchev, Andrei Voznesensky, and the Cold Spring of 1963." *World Literature Today* 75, no. 1 (January 2001): 31 ff.

Voznesensky, Andrey. *An Arrow in the Wall: Selected Poetry and Prose.* Edited by William Jay Smith and F. D. Reeve. New York: Henry Holt, 1987.

———. *Antiworlds.* New York: Basic Books, 1966.

———. *Story under Full Sail.* Garden City, N.Y.: Doubleday, 1974.

R. Victoria Arana

"WAITING FOR THE BARBARIANS"

CONSTANTINE P. CAVAFY (1898) One of CAVAFY's earlier poems, "Waiting for the Barbarians" is also one of his best known internationally, second perhaps only to "ITHAKA." With its diachronic subject of how a society relates to those it designates as the barbaric others, the poem has been interpreted as having specific geographic and historical referents (as several critics have suggested, who read the poem as a comment on the Roman and the Byzantine Empires or on sociopolitical upheavals taking place in different polities across the eastern Mediterranean during Cavafy's time). But the poem can be read as an equally complex and provocative composition without having to make specific connections to history.

"Waiting for the Barbarians" takes the form of an impassive dialogue between two anonymous subjects of an anonymous emperor who are observing and commenting on their city's preparations for the arrival of barbarians. Unlike Cavafy's "allegorical" or "suggestive" verse, this poem relies on the two figures' depersonalized questions and answers to offer an objective rendering of the scene and its meaning, thus dramatizing the ennui of the decadent empire and its longing for submission to the barbarian incursion without overt didacticism. As the poem unfolds the reader discovers that the empire has come to a standstill, not in fear of being overrun by the barbarians, but in hopeful anticipation of their arrival: The senators willingly give up legislating as they expect the barbarians to begin legislating once they arrive in the city; the emperor eagerly pre-

pares to flatter the barbarians and to offer them titles and honors; the emperor's subjects dress up and wear their most dazzling jewelry, while the rhetoricians keep a low profile because they know that barbarians are impressed by a show of wealth and beauty but dislike oratory. The empire's puzzling desire to welcome the barbarians to its city center is clarified only in the last line of the poem, after it becomes evident that the barbarians will not be arriving after all (". . . some who have just returned from the border say / there are no barbarians any longer"): "And now, what's going to happen to us without Barbarians? / They were, those people, a kind of solution."

The poem's intriguing reversal of the barbarians from "threat" to "solution" casts into relief the dead end of a decadent society, whose overrefinement and progress have brought about more despair and futility than fulfillment. Written in 1898, the poem appears to belong to a European modernist tradition that critically reflected on the promises of progress associated with the philosophy of enlightenment. Founded on the idea of reason and civilized humanism, this philosophy both exalted its own cultural inheritance while simultaneously idealizing the vitality of the nonreflective noble savage. In Cavafy's poem this tension is dramatized without resolution.

BIBLIOGRAPHY

Keeley, Edmund. *Cavafy's Alexandria: A Study of a Myth in Progress.* Princeton, N.J.: Princeton University Press, 1976.

Liddell, Robert. *Cavafy: A Biography*. New York: Schocken Books, 1976.

Cavafy, C. P. *Collected Poems*. Translated by Edmund Keeley and Phillip Sheppard, edited by George Savidis. Princeton, N.J.: Princeton University Press, 1975; London: Hogarth Press, 1975.

Yianna Liatsos

WALCOTT, DEREK (1930–)

Derek Walcott is generally regarded as the preeminent Caribbean poet and one of the greatest poets writing in English today. He has also achieved international recognition as a playwright. Walcott was born in Castries, St. Lucia, one of the Windward Islands in the Caribbean. For much of his childhood, Walcott remained an outsider. He was of mixed race on an island whose population was predominantly black. His family was English-speaking, middle-class, and Protestant, while most residents of St. Lucia were poor, French Creole–speaking, and Catholic. Walcott started his literary career at an early age. When he was 18, he borrowed money from his mother to publish privately a pamphlet of 25 poems. The following year, his play *Henri Cristophe* was produced in St. Lucia. Walcott studied at the University of the West Indies, Kingston, Jamaica, where he received a B.A. in 1953. After working briefly as a journalist, he moved to Trinidad, where he founded the Trinidad Theatre Workshop and began to establish himself as a dramatist. Not long after, he married Margaret Maillard, who helped him run the theater company.

During his time in Trinidad, Walcott began to garner international recognition as a poet. *In a Green Night* (1962) was published in Britain to critical acclaim. His reputation as a major poet was cemented with his book-length autobiographical poem, *Another Life* (1973), which represents his development from childhood to aspiring artist in a manner reminiscent of Wordsworth's *The Prelude*. In 1976, Walcott's career underwent major changes as a result of a personal crisis. His affair with a dancer in his theater company broke up his marriage and led to his resignation from the workshop. He began traveling to the United States, where he taught poetry courses at several universities. During the late 1970s, Walcott also met and befriended the poets JOSEPH BROD-SKY and Seamus Heaney, who shared his interests in the tensions between a cosmopolitan and nationalist identity. Walcott's poetry from this period—*The Star-Apple Kingdom* (1979) and *The Fortunate Traveller* (1981)—reflects his experiences as a nomadic, cosmopolitan figure. In 1981, Walcott received a MacArthur Fellowship for Poetry, and in 1982 he was appointed professor of poetry at Boston University. With the publication of *The Arkansas Testament* (1987), Walcott's poetry began to focus more on his home island of St. Lucia, although he was still spending much of his time in the United States. St. Lucia is the setting of Walcott's most ambitious poem, OMEROS (1990), which combines forms and themes from epic literature with a narrative of life in Gros Îlet, a tourist and fishing village. Walcott received the Nobel Prize in literature in 1992. His subsequent work includes *The Bounty* (1997) and two book-length poems, *Tiepolo's Hound* (2000) and *The Prodigal* (2004).

Walcott's poetry has always been characterized by a dense, metaphoric style that frequently echoes modernist poetry. For example, in *Omeros*, Walcott writes, "The wind changed gear like a transport with the throttle / of the racing sea." These lines combine two similes: the wind is like a transport and the transport is like the sea. The combination is particularly appropriate because one of the characters in *Omeros* exchanges his fishing boat for a taxi van, and his reckless driving seems motivated by guilt for having betrayed nature.

Walcott's early poetry reflects his position as outsider, both as a person of mixed-race ancestry in a predominantly black population and as a member of the colonial world looking to metropolitan centers. "A Far Cry from Africa" (1956) articulates both these positions. Walcott asks how as a colonial witness to the bloody Mau Mau rebellion in Kenya can he choose between his English and African ancestry, noting, in response to the violence of both groups in Kenya, that he is "poisoned with the blood of both." Walcott projects a similar ambivalence to colonial history in "Ruins of a Great House" (1956). Here he attacks the legacy of colonialism in the Caribbean but acknowledges that Britain was once a colony and admits that he is inspired by the literary works of colonizers like Walter Raleigh. For Walcott, the guilt of colonial oppression becomes part of the universal sins of humanity.

This seeming ambivalence to colonialism on Walcott's part led some artists in the Caribbean to critique his poetry as encouraging Eurocentric attitudes toward art. Walcott's poetry of the 1960s and 1970s makes clear, however, that he is less concerned with celebrating European literary history than with finding a poetic style independent of nostalgia for African culture. In part because of his mixed-race ancestry, Walcott was skeptical and sometimes hostile toward various manifestations of the Black Power movement in Trinidad. This skepticism led Walcott to reject the attempts of other writers to incorporate African art forms, syntax, and vocabulary into Caribbean poetry. For Walcott, African-based identity is a form of debilitating nostalgia. Provocatively, Walcott's two primary motifs for Caribbean poetry are Robinson Crusoe and Adam. Crusoe embodies the castaway who has left behind the Old World and must start to build his home from the materials he gathers from the natural world. Adam is without history; the world of Eden is an entirely new experience, and he has the prerogative to give names to all living things. Both examples provide Walcott with a mode of shaping art independently of the colonial history of the Caribbean. Walcott often uses the metaphor of amnesia to suggest that the contemporary artist must let go of quarrels with history in order to create a poetics based on lived experience. In response to V. S. Naipaul's declaration that nothing will ever be created in the West Indies, Walcott declares, "Nothing will always be created in the West Indies for quite a long time, because whatever will come out of there is like nothing that one has ever seen before" (*Voice of St. Lucia*). In the poem "Air" (1969), Walcott plays with this idea of nothing, ending his evocation of the Caribbean landscape as a brooding implacable force with the observation, "there is too much nothing here."

Since the 1970s, Walcott has been an international figure, and his continual movement between the Caribbean, the United States, and Europe has led to the predominance of travel metaphors in his poetry. Starting with "THE SCHOONER *FLIGHT*" (1979), Walcott connects travel to the adventures of Odysseus in Homer's *The Odyssey*. For Walcott, Homer created the icon of the quest figure, noting, "What we have because of Homer . . . is the moving sail, alone on the ocean, not a ship but something small on a large expanse of water, trying to get somewhere—the image of the wanderer" ("Reflections on *Omeros*" 235). Walcott ties this motif of the sea-quest to the spiritual quest for identity; for the artist in the postcolonial milieu, the dividing loyalties of race, nation, and intellectual lineage demand actively searching to find one's place. This exploration, according to Walcott's poetry, is never finished because our understanding of our place in the world is continually changing. Walcott's fascination with the story of Odysseus culminated in his epic poem *Omeros*, in which the narrator uses images and themes from *The Iliad* and *The Odyssey* to represent both his own quest to create poetry appropriate to the Caribbean experience and the quests of various characters to overcome the pain inflicted by the legacy of colonialism in St. Lucia.

Walcott's images of travel in *Omeros* suggest a return to origins. This return involves the literal return to the starting point of a journey and the imaginative return to the historical aspects that shape contemporary culture and individual identity. For Walcott and his characters, travel changes their understanding of the places where the journey started. This theme of return to origins figures prominently as well in Walcott's most recent works, *Tiepolo's Hound* and *The Prodigal*. Both meditate on what it means to leave the Caribbean and to return to it. This recent phase of Walcott's poetry echoes T.S. Eliot's comment in *Four Quartets* that the end of personal exploration "Will be to arrive where we started / And know the place for the first time." In Walcott's case, however, to arrive where we started is not to end a journey but to begin a new one.

BIBLIOGRAPHY

Hamner, Robert D., ed. *Critical Perspectives on Derek Walcott.* Washington, D.C.: Three Continents Press, 1993.
King, Bruce. *Derek Walcott: A Caribbean Life.* Oxford: Oxford University Press, 2000.
Okpewho, Isidore. "Walcott, Homer, and the Black Atlantic." *Research in African Literatures* 33 (2002): 27–44.
Walcott, Derek. "Reflections on *Omeros*." Edited by Gregson Davis. *South Atlantic Quarterly* 96 (1997): 229–246.

Eugene Johnson

"WALKING AROUND" PABLO NERUDA (1935)

In "Walking Around" NERUDA crafts an internal monologue correlating with a speaker's travels around town. Although in many of Neruda's poems "the speaker" and "the poet" are congruent, here the reader may wrestle to reconcile the speaker's disdain for everything the poet celebrated: busy markets, common people, sovereign bodies. The speaker is tortured by the stench of business everywhere he goes, as "A whiff from the barber shops sends me wailing . . . all I want is to see neither buildings nor gardens, / no shopping centers" (ll. 5–8). His unspecified job is steeped in isolation and inability to help those "dying in distress," comparable to serving "as root and tomb, / a solitary subterranean" (ll. 25, 23–24). Each work week begins with an assault: "Monday day burns like petroleum / when it sees me coming with my prison face" (ll. 26–27).

Life is dire, and the speaker ponders various escapes, dreaming of incarceration with his surly claim that "it would be delightful [to] slay a nun with a blow to the ear" (ll. 12–14). He finds no refuge in his body, which also falls into the traps of commerce. Eyes demand bifocals, feet lure him into "certain show stores reeking of vinegar," and hospitals bill a man just to watch "bones sail out the window" (ll. 31–32). The specter of bellybuttons ranks with umbrellas and poison on the speaker's list of threats to his sanity—a sanity that, by this penultimate stanza, the reader already may have begun to doubt.

Neruda leaves this poem suspended in a lyric moment rather than with a rhetorical or narrative conclusion. The speaker has walked around and continues to walk around, filled "with calm" and yet "with fury" (ll. 4 0–41). He is resigned to using his eyes to see, his shoes to walk, his bones to carry him, despite their purported betrayals. He exits from the poem passing by clothes "hanging from a wire: / underwear, towels, and shirts that weep / slow, dirty tears" (ll. 43–45). Perhaps the speaker's malaise infects even mute objects around him, or perhaps he perceives a genuine sadness in his world that no one else can see; either way, his sense of isolation is absolute.

Any first line that asserts "I happen to be tired of being a man" requires extraordinary pessimism to sustain what follows. Neruda seems to relish the task, though this same poet would later write "Ode to Joy." One understanding of this poem might focus on Neru-

da's job concurrent to its drafting: His draining consulship in Argentina required daily wrangling with politics and forms. Neruda hints at another possibility in his memoirs, where he denotes 1933 as a period of "discovering Dublin by way of the streets in Joyce." He was enthralled by the personae of James Joyce's *Ulysses* and undertook a translation of *Chamber Music*. Some critics see "Walking Around," which has always been titled in English, as Neruda's homage—replete with "sulfur-colored birds and horrific intestines" (l. 34)—to Ireland's dirty, dyspeptic streets.

Sandra Beasley

"WAR BALLAD" ANDREY VOZNESENSKY (1960)
"War Ballad" (alternatively titled "Ballad of 1941") was first published in ANDREY VOZNESENSKY's debut collection, *Mozaika* (Mozaics) (Vladimir 1960), along with "I AM GOYA." In that book the poem was "dedicated to the partisans of Kerch, a peninsula in the Crimea, where a group of partisans hid underground in old stone quarries during World War II" (*Antiworlds* 115). The poem's original and important seventh stanza was omitted from the version published in *Parabola* (Moscow 1960) and from the translation published in the Norton *World Poetry* anthology edited by Katharine Washburn and John S. Major (1997). Stanley Moss did both that translation and the one included in *Antiworlds* (which restores the seventh stanza), but the two versions differ slightly in other ways as well.

The poem's first of seven quatrains begins with an image of a piano having "crawled underground. Hauled / In for firewood" and "waiting for the axe" (*Antiworlds* 51). In the second stanza the legless piano is likened to a lizard lying "on its belly" in the mine shaft where the partisans are holed up. One of the partisans "goes down" to reach the keys with his frozen seven remaining fingers and begins to play, and the speaker feels he is witnessing "the great Northern lights" and that all "the reflections of flaming chandeliers" and the "white columns and grand tiers" of concert halls are nothing but "a great lie," for "the steel of the piano howls" in him, and he identifies with it. At this point the two translations depart radically from each other and from the original. In the Norton the poem ends with an epiphany the speaker experiences in identifying with the piano's reply to the pianist's touch: "I'll be a song for Russia. I'll be / an étude, warmth and bread for everybody" (969). In the *Antiworlds* version the poem ends with "And for my crowning crescendo / I wait for the lick of the axe" (51). The original poem, the one dedicated to the partisans who were freezing in the mineshaft, ends with "Я отражаю штолен сажу. / Фигуры. Голод. Блеск костра. / И как коронного пассажа, / Я жду удара топора!" (I reflect the gallery's soot. / Figures. Hunger. Luster of bonfire. / And as a crowning touch, / I await the impact of the axe!) Although Voznesensky was careful originally to title the poem "Ballad of the Year '41" ("Баллада 41го Года"), the poet's symbolic identification in 1960 with the doomed concert grand, reduced to firewood by the exigencies of continuing war and beleaguered communalism, is clearest in the Russian-language original.

BIBLIOGRAPHY

Blake, Patricia, and Max Hayward, eds. Introduction to Andrei Voznesensky's *Antiworlds*. New York: Basic Books, 1966. Also available online as "Andrei Voznesensky." URL: http://www.penrussia.org/n-z/an_voz.htm#i. Accessed on April 29, 2007.
Voznesensky, Andrei. *Antiworlds*. New York: Basic Books, 1966.

R. Victoria Arana

"WATER, RUSHES AND THE MOON" THORKILD BJØRNVIG (1993)

"Water, Rushes and the Moon" ("*Siv, vand og måne*") perfectly illustrates the major themes of BJØRNVIG's mature work: his love and respect for pristine nature, his abhorrence for what he called "the filth in the landscape," and his belief that art and spirituality allow one to transcend mortality.

A quietly lyrical description of nature illustrated by the moonlit scene in the first stanza sets a mood of serenely philosophical harmony. The poet, contemplating an ancient Chinese painting, is swept into a state of spiritual exaltation where he becomes one with both nature and art: "The wind in the rushes calls forth dreams / they sprout on the bottom, grow up through the water." Like the rushes that pierce the water and blossom to the moonlight, the poet also opens to the mystical beauty of the scene, and glorifies in the moonlight, dewdrops quenching his thirst for beauty.

In the second stanza the poet focuses on a fisherman asleep in his boat. In harmony with his surroundings, the fisherman, "his face resting on folded arms, half out of / the rush-plaited tent," belongs to the scene as much as the heavens, the water, and the rushes. The spirituality infusing the poem is therefore not of any specific faith; instead, it springs from the certitude that every human, every animal, every blade of grass is a necessary cell in a larger cosmic order: "In front, and above the boat— rushes / and all the rushes with their delicate wisp-like flowers / stretch past the sleeper up toward the moon."

The poet queries his reader and himself about reality in the final stanza. Dropping the dreamy distance of the first parts of the poem, he challenges all to ponder the fate of our world: "Is this the Earth? Am I seeing the dreamer in a dream?" The poet provides an answer when he prays that the Earth is "not a screeching gull-invaded refuse dump or smoking volcano" and that he is not merely dreaming when he dreams of "water, rushes and the moon."

An interesting and pertinent area of further reading could be about the world tree of Norse mythology, since it inspired the title of the collection that includes "Water, Rushes and the Moon." In Norse myth the world tree, the source of all life, is the Yggdrasil. Its destruction heralds Ragnarok, or the end of the Earth. Inasmuch as Thorkild Bjørnvig was 75 years old when he authored *The World Tree,* the poet's ruminations on the possible end of serene nature certainly mirrors his awareness of his own mortality.

Annette Olsen-Fazi

"WE ARE THE WOMEN" LORNA GOODISON (1986)

This poem, which is part of LORNA GOODISON's collection *I Am Becoming My Mother*, is representative both of the poet's particular focus on the experience of women and their strength and of her interest in Caribbean history and the heritage of slavery. It retraces the sufferings of black women throughout the long history of enslavement and exploitation in the Americas, a painful memory they keep inside them in "thread bags / anchored deep in our bosoms." Here the history of the oppression of black people (the "blood agreements" of the slave trade) is opposed to the history of black resistance, evoked through the image of "an apocrypha of Nanny's secrets." Nanny—the African freedom fighter who defeated the British during slavery times and established the free community of the Maroons on the mountains of Jamaica, a recurrent figure in Goodison's work and in the work of several other women writers from the anglophone Caribbean—embodies the resistance of black women and their determination to struggle for survival. The poem is structured in six stanzas of varied length. The longer stanzas have the slow rhythm of a prayer, while the shorter ones incisively convey resistance: "We've made peace / with want / if it doesn't kill us / we'll live with it." The repetition of the pronoun *we* at the beginning of each stanza and occasionally also at the end, together with the employment of the present tense, expresses a sense of shared experience while placing the emphasis on the connection between the past and the present. In the fourth stanza, where the poet evokes the deprivation and humiliation of black women at the hands of white people, the slow rhythm and the repetition of the word *waiting* suggest the long suffering that black women have experienced—and their incredible capacity for endurance. Here, as in many of her poems, Goodison offers strong portrayals of black women and conveys a sense of sisterhood built on heritage and memory. The last lines open up to relief and hope and celebrate rebirth: "we are rooting at / the burying spot / we are uncovering / our hope."

BIBLIOGRAPHY
Goodison, Lorna. *I Am Becoming My Mother.* London: New Beacon Books, 1986.

Sabrina Brancato

"WEAVER BIRD, THE" KOFI AWOONOR (1964)

"The Weaver Bird" is perhaps KOFI AWOONOR's most famous poem. An early work, it initially appeared in Awoonor's first volume of verse, *Rediscovery* (1964). What seems on the surface to be a simple complaint about a nest-building bird resonates with bitter colonial and postcolonial themes. Weaverbirds, a flocking species of finch (*Ploceidae*) widespread in

Africa and Asia, are well known for their communally woven nests. In fact, the weaverbird is an infamous invader who destroys its host trees. To be fully understood, Awoonor's poem must be read in this ecological light as a conceit on the destructive history and legacy of Western colonialism and imperialism in Africa.

Only 16 lines long, the poem is unrhymed—its line-end discords in due course reflective of the poem's final, unsettling tone. The speaker begins conversationally, casually telling how the weaverbird is watched with curiosity as it appropriates a family's "only tree." The speaker reports, "We did not want to send it away. / We watched the building of the nest / And supervised the egg-laying." Then disaster occurs. The following season the speaker reports: "The weaver returned in the guise of the owner / Preaching salvation to us that owned the house." The word *preaching* refers onomatopoetically to the sounds these birds make. Finches are garrulous, chatty birds; however, their flocks—like the conquerors they correspond to in this poem—are often followed in the natural world by symbiotic armies of stinging ants that build their own societies in the ground at the base of the trees that the weaverbirds occupy, thus effectively protecting the bird colonies from predators. The poem's speaker describes the dislocation caused by the assault: "We look for new homes every day"; and because the bird's droppings defile the sacred spaces and villages, the speaker grumbles: "we strive to re-build / The old shrines defiled from the weaver's excrement." In retrospect a reader recognizes that the poet is also censuring the indigenous Africans for passively indulging the invaders, those obnoxious and destructive creatures, in the first place.

R. Victoria Arana

"WHEN GREEN WAS THE LINGUA FRANCA" TANURE OJAIDE (1997)

This poem is from TANURE OJAIDE's *Delta Blues and Homesongs*, a collection of poems inspired by the plight of the people of the oil-rich Niger Delta of Nigeria. The crisis in the region came to the attention of the world community after the killing of the writer-activist KEN SARO-WIWA and other minority rights activists in November 1995. Since 1955, when oil was first discovered in Oloibiri, the environment of this area has suffered from oil spillages, gas flaring, and the indiscriminate felling of trees, resulting in the destruction of farmlands and aquatic resources. All these problems continue to threaten human survival. In *Delta Blues* Ojaide passionately articulates his concern with the injustices that the Nigerian state and the multinational oil companies operating in the region have perpetrated on the people of his region. Other poems in the collection go so far as to challenge the idea of a Nigerian nation.

"When green was the lingua franca" laments the tragic destruction of agrarian life in the Niger Delta region and the specific ways the degradation of the land has impoverished the people. The poet-persona chronicles the experience by appealing to his childhood memories of the near Edenic serenity and prosperity of the region before the invasion of the oil industry. The intruders broke the harmony between the people and their land, turning the mineral wealth of their land into a curse rather than a blessing. Two major periods are referenced in the poem. The first is the period before the coming of the oil companies (which also coincides with the poet-persona's childhood). That period was the age of innocence for both the poet and the land. But this innocence has since been lost, and the loss is what provokes the lamentation in the poem.

The success of the poem depends not just on the topical nature of its concern but also on the effective way it deploys appropriate strategies. It is at once the story of an individual and his community. The story it tells becomes credible as it comes as an eyewitness account. The temporal shift in the poem, which coincides with the end of an old order, comes at the beginning of stanza four, where the Anglo-Dutch giant Shell Oil is accused of breaking "the bond / with quakes and a hell / of flares" (13). The poet creates contrasts between the once rich and picturesque landscape of the past and the afflicted environment that is gradually suffering desertification. The tone constantly shifts from the nostalgic to the critical because the poet-persona at once underscores what he has lost and equally indicts those he feels should take responsibility for the condition of his land and its inhabitants.

BIBLIOGRAPHY

Ojaide, Tanure. *Delta Blues and Homesongs.* Ibadan, Nigeria: Kraft, 1997.

Oyeniyi Okunoye

WHEN THE WEATHER CLEARS (WHEN THE SKIES CLEAR) Boris Pasternak (1956–1959)

The poems in this volume, Pasternak's posthumously published last collection, were written shortly after those published as THE POEMS OF DR. ZHIVAGO, and the two books are similar in tone: meditative and devotional. A mood and a premise, rather than a story or cycle, structure this final grouping. The 41 poems express many of Pasternak's characteristic themes: explorations of the sources of creativity and the role of the poet and his work in society, and they explore the relationship between God and humankind. Although the late poems are like the early poems in presenting nature imagery, this final book differs in the near absence of passionate love poems. The passion of these poems is instead a hunger for personal and artistic genuineness. "Fame," for example, rejects renown as a suitable artistic goal, and "In All My Ways" proclaims authentic life to be the end of the artist. "Wind: Four Fragments on Blok" celebrates the power of Aleksandr Blok, who is as much a force of nature as the wind from which the poem takes its title, for social and academic acclaim, according to Pasternak, did not generate Blok's greatness. Several poems are based on the poet's life, as "Wind" is. "In Hospital" describes the sensations of an old man in a medical ward and draws on incidents from Pasternak's heart attack in 1952. The speaker tells what he sees as he is taken into a crowded hospital and left alone; this agony, the man comes to understand, is a part of God's love and wisdom. Another loosely autobiographical composition, "Bacchanalia," meditates on authentic experience, as does "In All My Ways." This vaguely narrative work begins with its speaker passing a church in a snowstorm so heavy that it keeps people from seeing one another. His destination is the theater, where *Maria Stuart,* a play Pasternak translated, is being staged. The Scots queen, like the people at church, knows that loss is the measure of life. At the party that follows the performance, the speaker meets a young dancer with whom he enjoys a brief and intense connection. This momentary and authentic union binds them as if they were blood relatives, even though the activities of the morning remove the traces of the night before. "Bacchanalia" is diverse in its images but unified in its quiet reflective tone, just as the book as a whole is diverse yet unified. This last group of Pasternak's poems serves both as his aesthetic manifesto and his artistic testimony.

BIBLIOGRAPHY

Dyck, J. W. *Boris Pasternak.* New York: Twayne, 1972.

Gifford, Henry. *Pasternak: A Critical Study.* Cambridge: Cambridge University Press, 1977.

Pasternak, Boris. *In the Interlude: Poems 1945–1960.* Translated by Henry Kamen. London and Oxford: Oxford University Press, 1962.

Rudova, Larissa. *Understanding Boris Pasternak.* Columbia: University of South Carolina Press, 1997.

Karen Rae Keck

"WIFE OF THE HUSBAND" MICERE GITHAE MUGO

A short poem of only 21 lines, MICERE MUGO's "Wife of the Husband" is a subtle lament about the hard labor and long hours that a woman must spend doing the work necessary to stay in her husband's and her village's good graces. The poem lists the work that a woman does: She must care for her children, clean her home, care for the animals and keep them safe, cook, keep the household fires burning, and safeguard the embers. But the only job the speaker credits her husband with is humorously expressed in the first two lines: "His snores / protect the sleeping hut." Meanwhile, "the stooping mother" continues her labors at night as the rest of her family sleeps. The poem's last stanza emphasizes the complaint by repeating the poems first two words twice: "His snores / welcome her to bed / four hours to sunrise" and "His snores rouse her from bed / six sharp. . . ."

Although the poem is deceptively simple, a good deal is conveyed through understatement. Her husband expresses no gratitude for her exertions, and the only kindness alluded to is the one conveyed by the word *welcome* in the last stanza, used ironically to express the husband's unconsciousness, snoring at the moment the wife finally gets to go to bed. The husband's snores are not useless, however, for they do the work of waking her up to another day's round of chores. Mugo's speaker preserves a wry sense of humor about her husband despite her travails. The feminism and Marxism that Mugo has elsewhere embraced more overtly is here evident, but the message (an advocacy for women's liberation through incitement to revolution) is couched in a subtle double entendre, as the last two lines can be read two ways—literally and figuratively: "Arise / O, wife of the husband!"

BIBLIOGRAPHY

Mugo, Micere Githae. "Wife of the Husband." In *The Penguin Book of Modern African Poetry.* 4th ed., edited by Gerald Moore and Ulli Beier, 153–154. London: Penguin Books, 1998.

R. Victoria Arana

"WIND AT TÌNDARI" SALVATORE QUASIMODO (1930)

This poem was first published in the collection of poems *Acque e terre* (Waters and Lands) in June 1930. *"Vento a Tindari"* is composed in unrhymed verse, with each line containing a varying number of syllables. In Italian the rhythm has a strong sense of musicality, and its content is representative of the obscurity and mystery associated with the hermetic style. QUASIMODO wrote the poem early in his literary career while working in Reggio di Calabria as a surveyor in the Ministry of Public Works. The setting is the seaside resort of Tìndari near Messina, Sicily. Here, as in much of Quasimodo's oeuvre, the theme of exile is strongly pronounced (l. 23). His use of enjambment (run-on line) allows one line to sweep into the next, creating a mellifluous continuity of sounds.

The poem begins with an evocation of Tìndari. The first stanza describes the geographical attributes of Tìndari's landscape, and the poet (the poem's speaker) mentions the Aeolian Islands and the god of the winds, Eolo. The second stanza recounts an excursion that the poet takes with friends, describing Tìndari's surrounding areas. The poet uses informal Italian to address Tìndari, and for the rest of the second and the following two stanzas (l. 11–30) he articulates how the seaside resort mentally assails him. He further laments that his residency on the Italian peninsula remains unknown to the Sicilian town. The poet feels like a fugitive, estranged not only from Tindari but from Sicily itself. The reference to "bitter bread" (l. 30) demonstrates that this staple always tastes different when consumed away from one's homeland. In the last stanza, after the poet's melancholic reflection, Tindari becomes tranquil, and the poet is suddenly awakened by one of his friends who jokingly pretends to push him from a cliff—a hermetic allusion to a Tindari legend about the salvation of a child who fell from a great height there and was saved by the Black Madonna, who caused the waters to create a soft bed of sand on which the child safely landed despite her own mother's lack of faith in the miraculous Madonna. Though the poet pretends to be afraid of the cliff, he is actually more concerned about the internal dilemma he has just experienced. After the internal struggle and conflict that the poetic persona has undergone, he concludes by once again evoking the place's name.

BIBLIOGRAPHY

Quasimodo, Salvatore. *Salvatore Quasimodo Complete Poems.* Translated and introduced by Jack Bevan. London: Anvil Press Poetry, 1983, 30–31.

Chris Picicci

WINTER PALACE, THE PAAVO HAAVIKKO (1959)

PAAVO HAAVIKKO's *Talvipalatsi* (*The Winter Palace*) represented the culmination of a decade of innovative work that helped introduce modernism to Finnish-language poetry in the 1950s. A series of nine long poems, it should be seen as one unified text in which each poem uses recurring images to build new layers of meaning—a technique that Haavikko describes in the opening lines of the "First Poem": "Chased into silver, / Side by side: / The images. / To have them tell you. . . ." He uses a recurring set of images—a house, a journey, a forest, the Winter Palace, a bird, a poet— which are realigned and take on new meanings throughout the cycle.

A kind of metapoem, the work deals chiefly with the act of writing, the creative process, and the place of the new poetry. Using a mixture of everyday and poetic language, Haavikko calls attention to language and to the poet himself. For example, in the "Fourth Poem"

he writes, "This is a journey through familiar speech / Towards the region that is no place," while in the "Third Poem" he comments: "Tourist, listen, perhaps you don't even know / I hardly get my expenses back, writing these poems, on my way / To the region that is no place." The poet's journey to "the region that is no place" takes him from the forest, "through the Winter Palace, / Built in 1754–1762," and back again to the forest, encompassing both nature and culture, Finland and abroad, present time and historical time. But above all the journey takes place in the poet's mind, "Under the roof / Thatched by my hair," as he writes in the "First Poem."

In the "Second Poem" he describes an encounter with an "exalted being" in a bottle, who fails to help him; later he remarks, "I let the exalted being out of the bottle and she / Was finished! emptied! aborted!" In the "Fifth Poem," echoing a theme of Finnish folk poetry, he has a dialogue with an all-knowing child who turns out to be "full of contraries, / . . . boy and a girl, / one and two". The child advises him, "Why are you praising the language that rules? / . . . why shouldn't you try to be free?" The idea of freedom is repeated and emphasized at the end of the cycle in the "Ninth Poem," which ends with a vision of the poet "at the bottom of the sky, / When the sky is thin, . . . / And the soul / is set free."

BIBLIOGRAPHY

Haavikko, Paavo. *The Winter Palace.* In *Selected Poems by Paavo Haavikko.* Translated by Anselm Hollo. London: Cape Goliard, 1968.

Sonia Wichmann

"WITH A BURNING THIRST" KIM CHI-HA (1982)

"With a Burning Thirst" is the title poem of KIM CHI-HA's second collection of poetry. This collection was published in 1982, after he was released from prison. This volume presents Kim's criticism of President Park Chung Hee's and his successor President Chun Du Hwan's military dictatorships and cries out for democracy. Like his predecessor Park, President Chun acquired power through a coup d'état and ruled with a firm hand. Many intellectuals who had been hoping for a democratic government after the death of

President Park were stunned by Chun's suppression of the Kwangju Students' protest demonstration in 1980. Many students and citizens were killed by national guardsmen, and the expected dawn of democracy seemed shrouded again by the black cloud of iron dictatorship. Kim, who had already made an announcement regarding his conscience, saying, "What I ask and fight for is absolute democracy, complete freedom of speech—nothing less, nothing more," is crying out here for democracy after witnessing yet another dictator take power. As an intellectual who had been fighting for democracy, Kim testifies to the stifling political reality in which people have to write the word *democracy* surreptitiously on a wooden picket in an alley. Kim also expresses grief at the situation in which fighters are arrested and beaten by policemen and national guardsmen while many citizens watch helplessly as the bleeding bodies are dragged past and notice the phrase "Viva Democracy!" written on a picket deserted on the road. Kim calls for freedom "with a burning thirst" and shouts "Viva Democracy!"

This poem surely reveals Kim's constant determination not to be weakened after excruciating pain and torture, and at the same time it expresses his zeal to inspire millions of Korean citizens to hold on to their hopes for democracy and ultimate freedom despite the bludgeons of tyrants.

Han Ji-hee

"WOMAN, A" GABRIELA MISTRAL (1954)

Found in the last of GABRIELA MISTRAL's published books of poetry, "Una mujer" (A Woman) reflects the maturity and skill of its author. *Lagar* (Wine Press) is the product of an experienced poet, although the volume reflects the issues that interested Mistral throughout her life. Known as a teacher, diplomat, and poet, Mistral was also interested in women and women's issues; much of her poetry, including "Una mujer," demonstrates that concern. Although she dabbled in Buddhism, Mistral was primarily a Christian poet, though never doctrinaire. Instead her poetry was often imbued with a quiet sense of divinity inherent in the Creation.

"Una mujer," from the section entitled "*Locas mujeres*" (Crazy women) in *Lagar,* may be interpreted on a number of levels, from the purely autobiographical to the spiritual. Like the woman in the poem, Mistral lost a child—her adopted son, Yin Yin. And like the woman in the poem, Mistral gained comfort in envisioning a future in which they might again meet. But Mistral's own past does not necessarily yield the most fruitful analysis of the poem. Instead, "Una mujer" should be regarded as a consummate blend of Mistral's feminist leanings and her religious devotion.

An excellent example of Mistral's lyric poetry, the poem examines the fate of an unnamed woman who apparently has lost all: Her house has burned, she is isolated, her son is dead. The woman may be cautiously associated with the Virgin Mary of Christian tradition, although no explicit identification is made. The poet speaks of the pine of Aleppo, a tree said to have originated in Aleppo (a region of northern Syria linked to early Christianity) and whose wood has been connected with the original Cross. More telling is the speaker's identification of the Aleppo pine with her child and her description of his death. Because these allusions are subtle, the woman may more truly represent any mother, including Mistral herself.

Despite the permanence of death, the woman in the poem is not without hope, and the poem is not pessimistic. In parentheses the poem observes that "*El día vive por su noche / y la noche por su milagro*" (The day lives for its night, the night for its miracle), suggesting that the irreversible sadness of the woman is but half of the reality. The woman also envisions her son in every tree, seeing his presence still around her, and "*en el fuego de su pecho / lo calienta, lo enrolla, lo estrecha*" (She warms and wraps and holds him close / to the fire of her breast). Despite his physical death, her love has not ended, and their separation is not eternal. Though her loss has been devastating, the woman is not destroyed; her own emotions save both her and her memory of her child. In her namelessness she is universal; she is truly "*una mujer,*" a woman, any woman.

BIBLIOGRAPHY
Mistral, Gabriela. *Selected Poems of Gabriela Mistral.* Translated by Doris Dana. Baltimore: Johns Hopkins University Press, 1971.

Winter Elliott

"WOMEN—PORTRAIT I" ZEHRA ÇIRAK
(1994) Published in ZEHRA ÇIRAK's third book of poetry, *Fremde Flügel auf eigener Schulter* (Alien Wings on Your Own Shoulder, 1994), *"Frauen—Porträt I"* is part of a versatile ekphrastic cycle in which a series of photographs or paintings (or ironically framed perceptions) is inventively described. Elizabeth Ann Oehlkers has produced an exceptionally precise and beautiful translation of this poem.

An anonymous woman whose ethnic background is not defined (it would therefore be precipitate to read this poem as a contribution to multiethnic conversations) is described as using her hair as a protective "screen" or "wall of shame." The German neologism that Çirak invents here, *Schamwand* (literally "shame wall"), reminds the reader of the German language's intrinsic sexist vocabulary especially for the female anatomy (for example, the German word for "labia" is *Schamlippen,* "shame lips," which led the feminist linguist Luise Pusch to suggest *Schamstange,* "shame stick," as an equivalent new word for the male genital). The lyrical observer interprets the nameless woman's gestures as symptoms of fearful helplessness. For a moment a glimpse of her possible autonomy is reported as being caught, but it remains an instant of hyperreflexive speculation.

While at first glance this poem might be read as a testament to feminist solidarity and a gentle call for self-liberation, the seemingly sympathetically observed woman remains an object of distanced spectatorship throughout the text. Exposed to an inquisitive yet ultimately nondialogic and omniscient gaze, the anonymous woman, whose physical and psychological contours seem to be sympathetically judged, becomes an object of compassionate voyeurism. The poem's fruitful, disquieting lack of dialogic exchange alerts the reader to the possibility that even (or especially) what presents itself as straightforward benevolence can be a subtle form of erotic subjection or epistemic appropriation, a mere exhibition of self-interested violence.

BIBLIOGRAPHY
Oehlkers, Elizabeth Ann. "Where Germany Begins: Translations from the German of the poetry and prose of Zehra Çirak, Zafer Senocak, and Yoko Tawada." MFA thesis, University of Arkansas, 1996, 64–65.

Olaf Berwald

WRIGHT, JUDITH (1915–2000) Judith Wright
is recognized as one of Australia's most important poets of the 20th century. Born on May 31, 1915, in Armidale, New South Wales, Wright published more than 50 books during her lifetime. At the University of Sydney she studied philosophy, history, psychology, and English, though she did not finish her degree. Later she was employed in various clerical, research, secretarial, and statistical positions. Her volumes of poetry include *The Moving Image* (1946), *The Gateway* (1953), *City Sunrise* (1964), *Collected Poems 1942–1970* (1971), and *Phantom Dwelling* (1985). Wright also published children's books, biographies, a novel, a collection of short stories, and a critical work on Australian poetry. In the mid-1950s after establishing herself in literary journals and with several publications behind her, Wright began a new period in which she said, "the love of the land itself and the deep unease over the fate of its original people were beginning to twine together, and the rest of my life would be influenced by that connection." Relationships among land, people, and language became increasingly important to Wright, who believed that "the true function of art and culture is to interpret us to ourselves, and to relate us to the country and the society in which we live." A committed and outspoken activist for environmental protection and Aboriginal land rights, Wright was a cultural as well as literary pioneer whose writing expressed a deep love for the Australian landscape and people.

Part of her connection to the land stemmed from being the daughter of a wealthy pastoralist family who owned a sheep station in New South Wales. Wright is said to have begun writing poetry at the age of six when her mother was ill. In keeping with the tradition of Australian pastoralist families at the time, Wright was sent to the New England Girls School when she was 14. While she was attending this school she made the decision to become a poet. As a young woman Wright moved to Brisbane, Queensland, where she wrote some of her most famous works, including "Bullocky," "Woman to Man," and "The Moving Image." It was also during this period that she grew progressively deaf and, after returning from a brief European tour, fell in love with and in time married philosopher Jack McKinney. He died 20 years later. Wright became the first woman to be appointed to the council of Australian National University as the governor-general's nominee in 1975. She founded and later became president of the Wildlife Preservation Society of Queensland and helped Nugget Coombs form the Aboriginal Treaty Committee in 1979, after moving to Braidwood in NSW. She was appointed a foundation fellow of the Australian Academy of the Humanities and became emeritus professor of the Literature Board of the Arts Council of Australia. Toward the end of her life Wright became a patron of several charitable organizations. Awarded many prizes and fellowships for her work, she became the first Australian to receive, in 1992, the Queen's gold medal for poetry. True to her tenacious spirit, Wright took part in the Aboriginal Reconciliation March in Canberra a week before her death at the age of 85 in June 2000.

BIBLIOGRAPHY

For a list of further readings the Web page *Judith Wright (1915–2000)* is available online at URL: http://www. kirjasto.sci.fi/jwright.htm). Accessed on April 29, 2007.

Jayne Fenton Keane

"WRING THE SWAN'S NECK" Enrique González Martínez (1911)

A sonnet published early in Enrique González Martínez's fertile poetic output, which appears in both *Los senderos ocultos* (Hidden Paths, 1911) and in *La muerte del cisne* (The Death of the Swan, 1915), *"Tuércele el cuello al cisne"* is one of the most frequently referenced and anthologized poems in Latin American literary studies. It is also one of the most misunderstood and restrictively interpreted. In his exhortation to "wring the swan's neck," González Martínez advocates an abandonment of the falsity of modernism, a putting aside its *"engañoso plumaje"* (deceiving plumage), and a turning away from its aesthetic frivolity. He suggests that the swan,

symbol of elegance and the external, abstract beauty of the symbolists, be replaced by the owl, an allegorical representation of wisdom and knowledge. He also asserts that the detached Parnassian eloquence and metrical formality, which ignore and are discordant with the rhythm of the universe, be discarded. *"Huye de toda forma y de todo lenguaje / que no vayan acordes con el ritmo latente / de la vida profunda . . .* (Every form eschew and every language / whose processes with deep life's inner rhythm / are out of harmony . . .). The poetics he sets forth reflect a sensibility to the complex nature of life and respect for the physical world. He also points out that elucidating the cosmic enigmas is a significant undertaking as the *"inquieta pupila (del buho) . . . interpreta / el misterioso libro del silencio nocturno"* (the owl's unquiet pupil . . . interprets the secret book of the nocturnal stillness). The publication of the sonnet in 1911, a year after the beginning of the Mexican Revolution, has led to its also being viewed as a component of a new literary pattern of consciousness (awareness of the concerns of the people), issues ignored completely by modernists. Regardless of the varied interpretations of the sonnet, *"Tuércele el cuello al cisne"* positioned the poet in Latin American literary history as the first Spanish-American poet to break with the modernist movement. Certainly González Martínez rejected the flashiness, excess, and unessential emphasized and manifest in the poetry of the modernists who imitated Rubén Darío. Likewise, Rubén Darío in *Cantos de vida y esperanza* (Songs of Life and Hope, 1905) came to terms with what was regarded as synthetic modernism. Ultimately, what is seen as overt hostility to modernism in *"Tuércele el cuello al cisne"* is a qualified criticism of the movement specifically for its lack of gravity and its superfluous elements.

BIBLIOGRAPHY

González Martínez, Enrique. "Tuércele el cuello al cisne." In *Anthology of Mexican Poetry*, translated by Samuel Beckett. Bloomington: Indiana University Press, 1958.

Effie Boldridge

Y

YEVTUSHENKO, YEVGENY (1933–) The son of a geologist-singer and a geologist-poet, Yevgeny Yevtushenko follows his family's traditions. Praised for his distinctive voice and elocutionary style, he recites his work with enthusiastic vigor; critics see his early verse as an expression and symbol of the hope that came with the thaw (1956–64) following the death of Soviet leader Stalin in 1953, the period in which he came into prominence with the publication of ZIMA STATION (1956). Commentators found in his later work, published under the Soviet regime, the "voice of Soviet life"; although he has continued to publish poetry, his novels have received more critical attention since the dissolution of the Soviet Union in the early 1990s.

Yevtushenko was born in Zima Station, a Siberian village to which his paternal great-grandfather, a Ukrainian, was sent after setting fire to a landowner's house in the late 19th century. Both of Yevtushenko's grandfathers were sent to prison during Stalin's reign. His maternal grandfather, a mathematician, died in the labor camps, and his paternal grandfather, a former Red Army commander, died in 1948, shortly after his release. Like many Soviet artists during the communist period, Yevtushenko strove to work within the system while remaining true to his personal and poetic convictions.

As a result of this balancing act, Western commentators often saw him as a Soviet dissident, while the more outspokenly dissident artists often considered him a tool of the state. As in his mentor BORIS PASTERNAK'S case, Yevtushenko's fame in the West offered him a sort of protection. The 1963 publication in English of his *Precocious Autobiography* caused the revoking of his travel privileges, and he spoke out against the Soviet-led invasion of Czechoslovakia in 1968 and the expulsion of Aleksandr Solzhenitsyn in 1974. Yevtushenko stood up to Premier Nikita Khrushchev in support of the sculptor Ernst Neizvestni. In an interview during perestroika (the "restructuring" of the 1980s under Mikhail Gorbachev), Yevtushenko compared the Soviet artist's position to that of a bullfighter who with great skill avoids being gored; the audience, however, wants to see blood. Since the end of the Soviet era some writers and critics in the West have come to share the dissidents' view of Yevtushenko and to characterize his bold declamatory style as bombastic. Others, however, still admire the vibrant confessional qualities of his verse, as well as his range of forms and styles, and credit him with the recovery of the Russian tradition of sonorous poetry.

Yevtushenko's parents introduced him to European and American writers, in addition to Russian novelist Lev Tolstoy. He considers Ernest Hemingway, VLADIMIR MAYAKOVSKY, and Boris Pasternak to be his masters. The poet's childhood, however, was not stable. His parents separated when he was quite young, and he lived with his mother in Moscow until 1941, when the German invasion during World War II caused the evacuation of children from the city to the country. He was taken to Zima Station; his parents divorced in

1944. After his return to Moscow, he attended school but was expelled at 15 after having been accused of theft. Once again in his native village, he accompanied his father, who is sometimes called the Kipling of Siberia, on two geological expeditions. After returning to Moscow, he attended the Gorky Literature Institute and was expelled in 1957, the official reason being that he attended lectures irregularly; some, however, believe his favorable remarks about Vladimir Dudintsev's *Not by Bread Alone* were the cause. Yevtushenko's early poems appeared in sports magazines, and he published two books of verse before receiving acclaim for *Zima Station.*

In spite of the poem's literary reception, Soviet leaders barred the poet from membership in Komonsol (the Communist Party's youth group). On the strength of other poems, Yevtushenko was allowed to travel to Western Europe and the United States in the early 1960s. "BABI YAR," his powerful poem about the Nazi German massacre of Jews outside the Ukrainian capital, Kiev, was known in Russia and was translated in the West but not published in the USSR until 1984. Ostensibly a denunciation of German anti-Semitism, the poem attacks Russian anti-Jewish feeling as well. "The Heirs of Stalin" (1962) warns that the cult of personality that characterized Stalin's rule might arise again. The boldness of Yevtushenko's early works was tempered in *Bratsk Station* (1965), the title poem of which extols a hydroelectric dam. Some consider it among his finest work, while others see it as merely conformist and conventional. His 1981 collection *Invisible Threads* was inspired by American photographer Edward Steichen's "Family of Man" exhibit and expresses the author's belief in the brotherhood of humankind; it also addresses his concerns about nuclear weapons. His post-Soviet work, of which PRE-MORNING (1995) is a notable example, has received little scholarly attention.

A versatile artist, Yevtushenko is also a playwright and novelist. His play *Under the Skin of the Statue of Liberty* (1972) includes Fyodor Dostoyevsky's Raskolnikov as a character and attacks U.S. foreign policy. His novella in verse, *A Dove in Santiago* (1982), comments on attitudes toward Chilean president Salvador Allende. His 1981 prose thriller, *Wild Berries,* was a finalist for the Hemingway Ritz Prize, and *Don't Die before You're Dead* (1995) is a fictionalized version of the Soviet August 1991 coup to depose Mikhail Gorbachev. He has also written screenplays and acted in films.

During the Gorbachev years (1985–91) Yevtushenko was a spokesperson for glasnost (Russian for "openness" or "candor"), a policy influenced, he said, by his writings and those of his contemporaries. He was elected to the Congress of People's Deputies in 1989. In 1996 he joined the faculty of Queens College in New York; his 1998 autobiography, *Volchii Pasport* (Wolf Passport), remains untranslated.

BIBLIOGRAPHY

Sidorov, Yevgeni. "Yevgeni Yevtushenko's Solo: On His Fiftieth Birthday." *Soviet Literature* 7 (1983): 130–140.

Urschel, D. "A Touch of the Poet: Yevgeny Yevtushenko Seizes the Stage." *Library of Congress Information Bulletin* 63 (2004): 95–97.

Yevtushenko, Yevgeny. *A Precocious Autobiography.* Translated by Andrew R. MacDonald. New York: E. P. Dutton, 1963.

"Yevgeny Yevtushenko." In *Current Biography.* New York: H. W. Wilson, 1994, 630–635.

Karen Rae Keck

YOSANO AKIKO (1878–1942)

Yosano Akiko is generally credited with introducing a feminist voice into modern Japanese literature. She was associated early with the "new style poetry," which she helped to promote and popularize. Yosano grew up as Ho Sho (or Shiyo), the daughter of a rich merchant and confectioner in Sakai, Osaka. She was born on December 7, 1878, and was immediately banished to be reared by an aunt because her father despised the baby at birth, wished she were male, and was grieving the loss of a young son just two months before the girl baby was born. Not until a younger brother was born did Ho allow his daughter back into the household. When he saw how bright she was, he provided her with the best education available. She grew up surrounded by literature, both Japanese and Chinese, since her father appreciated the arts and her great-grandfather had been a renowned scholar of Chinese literature and an accomplished composer of haiku. As a high school student Akiko subscribed to the poetry magazine *Myōjō*

(Bright Star), read Sei Shonagon's *Pillow Book,* as well as the early Japanese classic anthology of poetry *Man'yōshū* (The Ten Thousand Leaves), and delved into the 11th-century *Tale of Genji.* Within three years of graduating, Akiko was contributing to *Myōjō* and making a solid reputation for herself in Osaka and Kyoto. *Myōjō*'s editor, Yosano Tekkan, became interested in her poetry, visited her in Sakai, and began to introduce her works to members of his literary circle in Tokyo. They maintained the relationship, and Akiko eventually joined Tekkan in Tokyo to help edit and publish his literary magazine.

Their relationship blossomed into something more than collegiality, but Tekkan was married. Yamakawa Tomiko—a friend of Akiko who had met Tekkan at the same time as Akiko had—also fell in love with Tekkan; and they, too, had an extramarital affair. In 1901 Akiko published her most famous book of verse, *Midaregami* (TANGLED HAIR). That same year Tekkan divorced his wife and married Akiko. All the same, Tekkan continued his affair with Tomiko, began an affair with another friend of Akiko (Masuda Masako), and continued intimate relations with this former wife. During this period Akiko, Masako, and Tomiko collaborated on a volume of erotic poetry titled *Lovers' Clothes* that scandalized their social and academic circles and caused Masako and Tomiko to be expelled from the college at which they were students at the time. None of this free love seemed to faze any of them—unless it was Tekkan, who later went into a creative slump and suffered from anxiety about his waning reputation while his wife's name and reputation as an author were on the ascendant.

In 1911 Tekkan traveled to France. Six months later Akiko met him there and stayed for half a year. In Europe Akiko encountered other free-thinking women engaged in a women's rights struggle against patriarchal domination. Upon her return to Japan (via Germany, Holland, England, and Manchuria), Akiko spoke out in 1912 against the empire's execution of political prisoners. Tekkan remained in France for another two years, however, after his wife's departure. In 1916 Akiko began her affiliation with *Blue Stocking,* a new and formidable Japanese feminist magazine. She embarked on her prodigious career as a scholar, editor,

freelance writer, and poet—publishing some 75 books, 20 of which were volumes of her own poetry and 50 of which formed her series of newly edited classics of Japanese literature. Her scholarship was highly respected, and her modernized version of *Genji* is still considered one of the best available. She also produced a new edition of the *Man'yōshū.* In her manifesto-like critical pieces, which preceded the Imagist Manifesto of Ezra Pound by some years, she praised the accuracy of observation and the sparkling expression of the *tanka* in *Man'yōshū* and advocated a crisp lyricism founded on direct experience to replace the tired conventions into which Japanese poetry had been slipping for some time.

While she was revolutionizing the literary world of Japan, Yosano Akiko was also—with her beloved Tekkan—reintroducing it to its classic works of literature and to its authentic cultural past, not to mention raising a large and interesting family. Eleven of her 13 children reached adulthood. Among her grandchildren are a number of Japan's most prominent political figures today, including cabinet minister for economic policy and leader of the Liberal Democratic Party Yosano Kaoru.

BIBLIOGRAPHY
Beichman, Janine. *Embracing the Firebird: Yosano Akiko and the Birth of the Female Voice in Modern Japanese Poetry.* Honolulu: University of Hawaii Press, 2002.
Yosano, Akiko. River *of Stars: Selected Poems of Yosano Akiko.* Translated by Sam Hamill and Keiko Matsui Gibson. Boston and London: Shambhala, 1996.
———. *Tangled Hair: Selected Tanka from Midaregami.* Bilingual edition. Translated by Sanford Goldstein and Seishi Shinoda. Boston: Cheng and Tsui, 2002.

R. Victoria Arana

YOUNG FATE, THE PAUL VALÉRY (1917)

"The Young Fate" is a long and obscure but highly evocative poem of over 500 lines in alexandrine verse by French poet PAUL VALÉRY. This poem, frequently cited by critics as his masterpiece, presents the thoughts of a young woman sitting on a riverbank, torn between her desire for pleasure and her wish to maintain her innocence, which it seems only death can preserve. The poem's broader theme touches on the interaction of conscious and unconscious desire—a theme that from a psychological perspective fascinated Valéry. The young woman's thoughts represent the tensions produced by conscious intelligence in conflict with instinctual nature, but the theme is principally conveyed through the poem's philosophical tone. Valéry's habit of copying down thoughts and observations into his notebooks after his morning meditations helped him capture that intensity of the dynamic interchange between the conscious, controlled mind and the uninhibited instincts that threaten to overwhelm it.

The use of the classical reference to Fate—personified in the poem as the young woman—connects the poem's modern psychological themes to an emblem of the ancient world. The powerlessness of the speaker to control her desires also coincides with and underscores the existential predicament that many 20th-century philosophers have described as an inescapable aspect of human existence—including Valéry, who well remembered his 1892 renunciation of poetry and human passion that kept him from writing poems for 20 years. The poem indicates that human passion is unavoidable, as Valéry realized, and may even be foreordained. The poem's power is further supported by the rich musicality that Valéry captured in his versification. As with many of his works, the poem's rhythm and timbre are said to echo the sounds of the sea that had inspired Valéry as a youth.

Joseph E. Becker

YOUSSEF, SAADI (1934–   )   The poet Saadi Youssef was born in the vicinity of Basra, Iraq, in 1934. In 1948, the year in which the state of Israel was founded, young intellectuals broke with classical Arabic literary tradition and introduced free verse into Arabic poetry. This new style spread, unstoppable as the desert winds, and influenced the ensuing generation of writers, which included Youssef.

Youssef studied Arabic literature in Baghdad. He later had to leave the country repeatedly, due to his political involvement—a fate he shared with the majority of Iraq's progressive intellectuals. In the late 1970s, when Saddam Hussein came to power, Saadi Youssef left Baghdad for good. Today, after years of exile in various countries, he lives in London.

Youssef was influenced by the most important poets of the free-verse movement, the Iraqis Badr Shakir as-Sayyab and Abdalwahab al-Bayati, who wanted to give poetry a strong position at the phalanx of the progressive, revolutionary powers. In the 1950s and 1960s Youssef wrote political poetry and, like MAHMUD DARWISH and Amal Dunqul, could claim to be a people's poet. He sympathized with the anti-imperialist movement, which at the time allied itself with socialist and communist groups.

In the second half of the 1970s he stopped writing political verse, and his poems became increasingly evocative, like Zen koans: full of secrets yet simple. As in the children's game "I spy with my little eye. . . ," he speaks about things of an apparently everyday nature and in doing so gets at the essence of those things.

Youssef's language, characterized by lyrical realism, is authentic and direct. As a translator into Arabic of works by Oktay Rifat, Melih Cevdet Anday, FEDERICO GARCIA LORCA, JANNIS RITSOS, Walt Whitman and, above all, CONSTANTINE CAVAFY, he feels a close connection to these poets of world literature. He has published 30 collections of poetry.

Youssef is an artist who—given no choice—has taken to the seas and since the 1970s not once cast anchor again in his native country. Perpetual longing accompanies him on his travels, and the topics of exile and migration are omnipresent: "The pole lost its guiding star—but my distant home still awaits me."

Today, following the Iraq War of 2003, Saadi Youssef speaks forthrightly about the future: "We must still, it seems to me, brace ourselves for a possible series of shock waves in the aftermath of the recent seismic upheavals in Iraq." What makes his poetry so fascinating is that despite the oppressive political reality with which it engages, it is surprisingly light. As Ferial Ghazoul has described it, "Saadi's poetry avoids declamation and resounding statements. It is as if the poet is engaged in an intimate conversation and we—as readers—overhear him. Even his political poems have a subdued tone. They do not lend themselves to recital on a platform, nor can his verse be borrowed for a slogan." In 2003 Youssef was honored by the Internationales Literaturfestival—Berlin.

BIBLIOGRAPHY

Ghazoul, Ferial J. "Spiral of Iraqi Memory." In *Al-Ahram Weekly* 17–23 April, 2003. Available online. URL: http://weekly.ahram.org.eg/2003/634/bsc17.htm. Accessed on April 29, 2007.

Wolpé, Sholeh. "New Translations Do Justice to a Poet 'of the Human Universe.'" Review of Saadi Youssef's *Without an Alphabet, Without a Face: Selected Poems.* In *The Daily Star,* 6 July 2005. Available online. URL: http://www.dailystar.com.lb/article.asp?edition_id=10&categ_id=4&article_id=16501. Accessed on April 29, 2007.

Youssef, Saadi. *Without an Alphabet, Without a Face—Selected Poems.* Translated and introduced by Khaled Mattawa. St. Paul, Minn.: Greywolf Press, 2002.

Friederike Pannewick

YUN DONG-JU (1917–1945)

Yun Dong-ju is engraved in the minds of the Korean people as an unfortunate young poet who faced untimely death before his poetic genius could blossom. At the age of 27, just six months before his country, Korea, was restored its sovereignty, his life was cut short by biochemical experiments on his body performed by Japanese army scientists. His short life—filled with anxiety and agony, yet spiritually hopeful for the motherland's liberation—is emblematic of the collective lives of Koreans surviving the gloomy period of Japanese occupation.

Born in 1917 in Myongdong-chon in the Manchurian province of China, Yun began the first phase of his tragic life by being born in a foreign country. His grandfather had first moved in 1900 to one of many Korean settlements in China to escape Japanese imperialism. Joining relatives already living there who tilled the land, his family set up educational and religious institutions there and supported many resistance leaders and activists. Growing up in a relatively affluent household, Yun showed his literary talents at an early age. As his sister Yun Hyeh-won remembers, he liked reading and writing so much that his fingers were always stained with ink, and he published a school literary magazine, *New Myongdong,* at age 12. That early happiness did not last long. Yun left his family and friends to enter a junior high school in Pyongyang, located in the northern region of Japanese-occupied Korea. When he was ordered to change his Korean name to a Japanese one, he chose instead to be expelled and returned home. After finishing high school in his hometown, he left his family once more. His father, who had majored in English, wanted Dong-ju to enter Yonhui College of Medicine (now Yonsei University) in Seoul, the capital of Korea, to become a medical doctor. Dong-ju resisted his father and in protest engaged in a fast. His father relented, and Yun entered Yonhui College of Humanities in 1938 and began his study of English literature. During this period he studied all kinds of literature, music, and art, and among his favorite writers were Søren Kierkegaard, Fyodor Dostoyevsky, PAUL VALÉRY, André Gide, Charles Baudelaire, RAINER MARIA RILKE, and Jean Cocteau. He also loved playing soccer and basketball and made his own set of skis by splitting a bamboo bough in half. By 1939 he had begun to publish poems in literary magazines, most famously "Shooting the Moon" in *Chosun Ilbo* and "Mountain Echo" in *Soh-nyon* (Young Man). When he was about to graduate from college, he wanted to publish a collection of his poetry (*The Sky, the Wind, the Stars and Poetry*) as a commemorative event before leaving for Japan for further study; but his supervisor dissuaded him. He gave two hand-stitched copies of his manuscript to his supervisor and close friend and left Korea in 1942—not imagining that the volume would be published after his death and become a memento mori for all Koreans. After six months at Ritkyo University, he transferred to Doshisha University, unaware of how close he was stepping toward his final destiny. In 1943, when he was eligible for the draft by the Japanese army, he decided to return home. But he was arrested on charges of spreading dangerous ideas, sentenced to two years of imprisonment, and sent to Fukuoka Prison in Kyushu. The last two years of his life in prison were probably gruesome. According to the testimony of survivors, prisoners were treated as guinea pigs for biochemical experiments, were administered injections of unknown liquids, and suffered from horrible pains and anxiety daily. Yun endured daily torture. Soon he lost his hair, then lost so much weight that his face became deathly pale and unrecognizable. Yun seems to have met a painful death on February 16, 1945, given the testimony of one survivor who heard him crying out. When Yun was dead his family received a letter to come get the body. His body was buried in a churchyard at Dongsan, in Manchuria.

Yun spent only about five years in Korea, and for the rest of his life he wandered back and forth between China and Japan. He is still buried in Chinese territory. His poetry has cast its anchor deep in the minds of the Korean people: It has been transmitting the ring of a soul who sang that he wanted to live without a tint of shame, to love everything mortal with a heart singing to the stars, and to walk on the path allowed to him (paraphrased from his "Foreword" to *The Sky, the Wind, the Stars and Poetry*).

The Sky, the Wind, the Stars and Poetry was published in 1948, and in 1968 Yun was finally proffered the honorary title "Poet" by Yonsei University, a hollow gesture since he had already been as true a poet as any Korean poet can be. A monument to his poetry and a poetry prize bearing his name have since been set up at Yonsei University. In 2005 celebrations of the 60th anniversary of his death were held in Seoul, Japan, and China. Since his death his spirited resistance (which led him to compose poems in his native language of Hangul in spite of the Japanese order to write only in Japanese), his lyricism to pursue unison with nature, and his awe before all forms of life based on a fusion of Christian beliefs and Confucian humanism have been appreciated as main features of his poetry. Yun is an exceptional poet among world poets—due to his tragic life, posthumous official designation as poet, and brilliant but single volume of verse. Koreans feel that his poetry illuminates what is most noble about Korean life. His poem "SELF-PORTRAIT" gives readers a glimpse into his own view of an intellectual's life.

BIBLIOGRAPHY
McCann, David R., ed. and trans. *Black Crane: An Anthology of Korean Literature*. Ithaca, N.Y.: Cornell University Press, 1980.
———, ed. *The Columbia Anthology of Modern Korean Poetry*. New York: Columbia University Press, 2004.

Han Ji-hee

YUSHIJ, NIMA (1895–1960)
Theoretician and author of 20th-century Persian modernist poetry, Nima Yushij founded the New Poetry movement, forcefully articulated its vanguard aesthetic, and strongly influenced the generation of poets to follow. Nima Yushij

was born Ali Esfandiyari in 1895 in the village of Yush, Caspian province of Mazandaran, Iran. His father was a landed farmer and his mother a literate woman who recited classical poems to her four children. Nima spent his childhood wandering among the nomadic herders when their migrations brought them through his rural community. This environment would return in the imagery of his poems, and its attributes would characterize his aesthetic. At age 12 Nima was taken to the capital city, Tehran, to be educated at a French Catholic school, where he studied French language and Western literature. While not a distinguished student, he was encouraged to write poetry by one of his teachers, also a poet and follower of the French romantics.

At 25 Yushij published his first collection of poetry, *Qissih-i Rang-i Paridih* (A Pale Story), an autobiography in traditional metric forms. Soon after, he dubbed himself Nima Yushij: "Nima" after the legendary warrior-heroes of Mazandaran and "Yushij" (meaning "from Yush") to refer to the village of his birth. Fittingly, the appellation suggests an epic crusader who draws his identity and power from the locale of his origins. His new name coincided with the completion of his second collection, *Afsaneh* (Legend), in 1921, which is also the date many historians assign to the beginning of Persian literary modernism. The influence of European romanticism is evident in Nima's lyric treatment of the natural world and the plight of the lovers in his title poem. He employs the narrative romance genre, composed in a relaxed version of classical meter, and models dialogue in contrasting lines, a structure he termed "dramatic." The work earned him a small following of intellectuals. When Nima published *Khanevade-ye Sarbaz* (The Soldier's Family) in 1925–26, he demonstrated growing social awareness in his description of the costs of poverty and war. He included a preface that announced the advent of "New Poetry" (*she'r-e now*).

During Reza Shah's autocratic reign (1925–41) Nima was highly productive but published little. In 1926 he married Aliyeh Jahangir. She was well educated and the principal income earner during their lives together. Her teaching and administrative jobs required that they move several times to different towns around the Caspian before settling in Tehran in

1933. Nima called Tehran "the city of the dead." He would regularly return to his native Yush in summer. In 1934 their only child, a son, Sheragim, was born.

In 1938 Nima joined the editorial staff of *Majalle-ye Musiqui* (Music Magazine), affiliated with the Ministry of Culture. At *Majalle-ye Musiqui* he published poems and literary criticism. Most significant was the publication of a critical tract that articulated his literary testament: *Arzesh-e Ehsasat dar Zendegi-ye Honarpishegan* (The Value of Feelings in the Lives of Artists), first issued serially in 1939 and later released as a book. In the essays Nima discusses his aesthetics and the advent of modernism in art and literature, surveying developments in Europe, the Middle East, India, and Russia. Nima championed modernism as an inevitable historical and cultural progression. His foundational referents are nature (*tabi'at*) and the natural, balanced with craft (*san'at*). Naturalness comprised more rhythmic versions of verse forms and more commonplace language, embracing the cadences of speech and dialect regionalisms. To be natural is to be in consonance with one's cultural time and place; therefore to create antiquated poetry in the 20th century, Nima argued, was unnatural. He dismisses the romantic notion of the artist as extraordinary sensibility; individuals are inextricably the products of their environments, and the artist's work is a composite of her or his historical and material conditions. Therefore, the value of artists' feelings is in proportion to their register of the changes in the social structure. His poem "HEY, PEOPLE" exemplifies this aesthetic. Nima's manifestos offended traditionalists who rallied round a stale concept of cultural purity invested in the classical tradition. Progressives heard the call and proclaimed Nima the founder of the New Poetry.

During the later 1940s, following the abdication of Reza Shah and the end of World War II, Iranians experienced a relaxation of repressive social controls and widespread public involvement in politics. Nima published in the Iranian Communist (Tudeh) Party journal *Mardom* (The People). Following the fall from power of nationalist prime minister Mohammad Mossadeq in 1953 and the reinstatement of Mohammad Reza Pahlavi, many reformist writers were jailed, including Nima.

Nima enjoyed renown in his later years. The New Poetry movement gained wider recognition in the mid-1950s, as evidenced in the works and acknowledgments of the next generation's prominent poets: Ahmad Shamlu, Mehdi Akhavan-e Saless, and FORUGH FARROKHZAD. Nima died in 1960, survived by his wife and son.

Translated collections of Nima Yushij's work are not yet available in English. Examples of his poems can be found in anthologies of contemporary Persian poetry and in critical histories.

BIBLIOGRAPHY
Karimi-Hakkak, Ahmad. *Recasting Persian Poetry*. Salt Lake City: University of Utah Press, 1995.
Naficy, Majid. *Modernism and Ideology in Persian Literature: A Return to Nature in the Poetry of Nima Yushij*. Lanham, Md.: University Press of America, 1997.
Talattof, Kamran. *The Politics of Writing in Iran*. Syracuse, N.Y.: Syracuse University Press, 2000.

Anett Jessop

Z

ZAMORA, DAISY (1950–) Honored as 2006 Woman Writer of the Year by the National Congress and the National Association of Artists in Nicaragua, Daisy Zamora is one of the most prominent figures in contemporary Central American poetry. Her work is known for its uncompromising voice and broad-ranging subject matter that includes details of daily life while encompassing human rights, politics, revolution, feminist issues, art, history, and culture. During Nicaragua's Sandinista revolution she was a combatant for the National Sandinista Liberation Front (FSLN), the voice and program director for clandestine Radio Sandino during the final 1979 offensive, then vice minister of culture (1979–82) for the new government, working with minister (and poet) ERNESTO CARDENAL. Together they were responsible for a revitalization of local and international interest in Nicaraguan literature and art and supported a successful literacy campaign. She has also been a leading member of Nicaragua's National Coalition of Women.

A political activist and advocate for women's rights throughout her life, for the last several years she has taught poetry workshops at a number of universities and colleges. In 2007 she was a visiting writer at Goddard College's Residency Program in Port Townsend, Washington. She visits Nicaragua frequently, but her primary residence is now in San Francisco, California.

In 1977 Zamora was awarded the prestigious Mariano Fiallos Gil National Poetry Prize. Because her writing career was interrupted by involvement in the revolution, her first book of poetry, *La violenta espuma* (The Violent Foam), was not published until 1981, but it included work from 1968 to 1978. Her next collection was *En limpio se escribe la vida* (published as *Riverbed of Memory,* 1988), followed by *A cada quien la vida* (Life for Each, 1994) and *Fiel al corazón* (Faithful to the Heart, 2005). *The Violent Foam: New & Selected Poems* (2002) gathers works from several collections. In 1982 she edited an anthology on concepts of culture, *Hacia una política cultural de la Revolución Popular Sandinista* (Toward a Cultural Policy of the Popular Sandinista Revolution) and in 1992 the first major anthology of Nicaraguan women poets.

Zamora was a featured poet in Bill Moyer's popular PBS series *The Language of Life.* In 2002 she was awarded a California Arts Council Fellowship for poetry and also that year received an award from the Nicaraguan Writers Center in Managua for valuable contributions to Nicaraguan literature. Her poems have been included in more than 40 anthologies in Spanish, English, German, Swedish, Italian, Bulgarian, Russian, Vietnamese, Chinese, Dutch, Flemish, Slovak, and Czech.

Zamora became immersed in revolutionary activities during the 1970s when the decades-long struggle against the Somoza dictatorship in Nicaragua erupted. During the revolution she experienced exile in Honduras, Panama, and Costa Rica. Zamora has written poems on her combat experience, such as "Radio Sandino": "—THIS IS Radio Sandino / Voice of Nicaragua's liberation / Official voice of the FSLN"; and "A Scattered Squad": "I remember it like a slow motion film: / the sloping terrain, slippery, hot, / hand gripping a gun, / the smell of burning. / Helicopter sound, / sporadic machine gun fire." Her more intimate work includes poems on giving birth, the loss of a baby, divorce, and her feelings as a mother for her children and as a child toward her mother. Well known are her poems defining her effort to break with the traditional roles assigned to women, for example, as she says to her children: "No doubt you would have liked / one of those pretty mothers in the TV ads / . . . / But since you were born from me, I have to tell you: / Ever since I was a child like you / I wanted to be myself—and for a woman that's difficult—" ("Mother's Day"). She has lamented the silence in her own family about her foremothers ("Lineage") and has poems on working women ("Emilia, the Nurse," "Otilia, Ironing Woman," and "Waitress 1–3").

BIBLIOGRAPHY

Moyers, Bill. *The Language of Life: A Festival of Poets.* New York: Broadway Books, 1995.

Zamora, Daisy. *Clean Slate: New and Selected Poems.* Bilingual edition. Translated by Margaret Randall and Elinor Randall. Willimantic, Conn.: Curbstone, 1993.

———. *Life for Each.* Bilingual edition. Translated by Dinah Livingstone. London: Katabasis, 1994.

———. *Riverbed of Memory.* Bilingual edition. Translated by Barbara Paschke. San Francisco: City Lights, 1992.

———. *The Violent Foam: New and Selected Poems.* Translated by George Evans. Willimantic, Conn.: Curbstone, 2002.

María Roof

"ZERO HOUR" ERNESTO CARDENAL (1957; 1960)

"Zero Hour" is the best-known example of ERNESTO CARDENAL's "documentary" poetry and provides a fine example of the *exteriorista* poetry with which he is identified. The poem was originally conceived of as a longer epic poem about Central America similar to PABLO NERUDA's more geographically expansive *Canto general.* "Zero Hour" is one of a series of poems in which Cardenal documents the long history of oppression and international intervention in Central America and in his native Nicaragua. Originally published in 1957 in the *Revista mexicana de literatura,* the authorized edition came out in 1960. Although the poet and this particular poem are often identified with the fight to overthrow the Somoza dynasty, "Zero Hour" was written more than two decades before the Sandinista revolution. Because the poem celebrates the historical figure from whom the Sandinistas took their name (Augusto César Sandino), the poem is often associated with the decades-long struggle of the Sandinistas against the Somoza dictatorship, culminating in its defeat in 1979.

"Zero Hour" consists of an introduction and three parts. The introduction establishes the environment of Central America under dictatorship: "Tropical nights in Central America, / with moonlit lagoons and volcanoes / and lights from presidential palaces, / barracks and sad curfew warnings." The introit found in this introductory part, "Watchman! What hour is it of the night? / Watchman! What hour is it of the night?" was taken from the Bible (Isaiah 21:11) and was added to the poem in 1956 after the poet's religious conversion. It is the first example of Cardenal's use of biblical quotations in his poems. The first section following the introduction explains the economic factors behind the politics of the "banana republics." The second section depicts the struggle of Sandino, a member of the Nicaraguan aristocracy who led and fought alongside his countrymen against the U.S. Marines in the 1920s and 1930s. This section ends with the clandestine execution of Sandino on the orders of Nicaraguan dictator Anastacio "Tacho" Somoza. The final section recalls the 1954 "April Rebellion"—a failed attempt to oust Somoza in which Cardenal took part. This section also graphically documents examples of torture under Somoza.

The epic, encyclopedic, and historical character of "Zero Hour" evidences the influence of Pablo Neruda's *Canto general* (1950) and of Ezra Pound. The poem is also an excellent example of Cardenal's *exteriorista* (objective as opposed to subjective) poetry and of one of its most noteworthy features, intertextuality—the borrowing and incorporating of disparate sources into the poem. Cardenal's use of quotes—from telegrams to speeches made by the president of the United States, even to the inclusion of the song *"Adelita"*—creates an oral and multidiscursive actuality within the poem. The poet's belief that "everything fits in poetry" is evident in his lists of international companies exploiting Central America. Similar to Pound's collage techniques, Cardenal's juxtaposition of facts, quotes, and lists is intended to evoke greater meanings, requiring the reader to piece together various discursive components of the text.

Analisa E. De Grave

ZIMA STATION (AKA ZIMA JUNCTION OR WINTER STATION) YEVGENY YEVTUSHENKO (1956)

An autobiographical poem that reflects on the past while looking toward the future, *Zima Station (Stantsiya Zima)* is a narrative of encounter and discovery told in a strong voice. Inspired by a 1953 visit to YEVTUSHENKO's family in Siberia, the poem was first published in *Octobr* in 1956. Although it earned praise and drew attention to Yevtushenko's distinctive voice and gifts, it was published again only in collections of his verse.

The contemplative tale opens with the speaker asserting that although he is young, he has learned lessons from life; the poem closes with the most important lesson he has learned from his hometown: to love and to go out into the world with the memory of the town and its love. Michael Pursglove divides the poem into 12 unequal sections. The introductory section, which ends at line 62, presents the little that is known about and asks questions regarding the poet's Ukrainian great-grandfather, who was exiled to this foreign place, which became home. The second and third sections concern the speaker's family, and the third part includes a discussion between Childhood and Youth, whom he meets as he walks in the forests where he used to play. Next he meets an uncle and aunt who dwell on his life in Moscow, which they imagine as better than it is. The fifth part describes picking berries with the women of the town. One of the peasants dances in the rain with the abandon of Natasha dancing to the balalaika in *War and Peace*; her unself-consciousness expresses her Russianness and heightens the persona's sense of self-consciousness. After a conversation with the wheat, the speaker talks of the *kolkhoz* (collective farm) president, Pancratov. (His name brings to mind one of the Eastern Orthodox names for Christ, the Pantocrator, the All-Powerful, and the man's name seems to be ironic.) The next short section concerns a trip by truck. The poet next considers the poet's uncles, one of whom is an excellent carpenter but also a drunkard. At a tea shop the speaker meets a journalist from Moscow, a stranger whose life had not turned out as he had wished. Sections nine and 10 put forth the poet's meditations on love. As he prepares to leave, he walks through the town, which talks to him in the final section about life and advises him to leave since departure is not final. The speaker moves on and carries the promise with him. In telling his story he shares the wisdom of Zima Station with the world.

BIBLIOGRAPHY

Moser, Charles A., ed. *The Cambridge History of Russian Literature.* Cambridge and New York: Cambridge University Press, 1989.

Pursglove, Michael. "Yevtushenko's *Stantsiya Zima*: A Reassessment." *New Zealand Slavonic Journal* 2 (1988): 113–127.

Yevtushenko, Yevgeny. "Zima Junction." In *Selected Poems.* Translated by Robin Milner-Gulland and Peter Levi, 19–51. Baltimore: Penguin Books, 1962.

Karen Rae Keck

ZIMUNYA, MUSAEMURA BONAS (1949–)

Born in 1949 in Mutare, Zimbabwe, Musaemura Bonas Zimunya is one of the many voices that have finally registered Zimbabwe in the discourse of the postcolonial literatures of sub-Saharan Africa. Like a number of his contemporaries, as well as younger artists from Zimbabwe who came after him such as CHENJERAI HOVE, or even the late DAMBUDZO MARECHERA and Yvonne Vera, Zimunya's contribution to the development of postindependence Zimbabwean letters is remarkable. His creative efforts span poetry, fiction, and critical scholarship. Growing up during the 1950s and 1960s in Rhodesia (now Zimbabwe) was not an attractive experience, given the humiliation to which the indigenous population was subjected under the minority white regime. Yet it was not an entirely fruitless experience, and in his poetry we find evidence of his love for his country, especially a poetic resonance with the ecological and cultural idioms of his Shona people of the Zimbabwean eastern highlands, where he showed early promise as a child.

In this rural countryside communal experiences and identification with nature are often taken for granted; everyone is simply at home with such an environment. Yet the beauty that often emerges from this type of bucolic space can shape the imagination of a precocious child who looks forward to articulating the cultural sensibilities of his people as an aesthetic and moral imperative. Such is particularly the case for children born during periods of nationalist movements where literary engagements are often deployed in the projection of communal, national, and sometimes continent-wide humanisms. The poet articulates this responsibility in many ways. For Zimunya "good poetry must address itself to the entire range of the human emotion and experience: nothing more nor less" (*The Fate of Vultures* 1). Zimunya's attitude to the natural is implicit not only in his numerous poems addressing the subject, but also in what might be conceived as his poetics: Nature is all-providing and all-defining. As he writes, the natural environment affects humankind in many ways because "we live in it, live on it, and live by it" (*The Fate of Vultures* 3).

In some of his finest poems readers can feel a sense of Africanity through his imagistic evocations of color and incident in a manner reminiscent of the fantastical, the metaphysical, and the quotidian realities of many African communities, especially of his Shona community in Zimbabwe. The poems assembled in his highly lyrical selection *Country Dawns and City Lights* are particularly relevant in that they juxtapose two modernities—African communal experiences now echoed in print form and a Western modernity poised to obliterate what remains of traditional Africa. In these poems Zimunya provides readers with several dimensions of these two spaces. The message conveyed is that the beauty Africans have recklessly abandoned humbles any identification with the imagined easiness of Western modernity, just as a pretentious recourse to Westernisms gradually reveals an unavoidable sense of alienation.

In the poems "Country Dawns" and "When the Mamba Strikes," for instance, the echo of traditional Africa is presented in a candid evocation of imagery, and the pains associated with death or mortality are portrayed in a complex tapestry of flora and fauna idioms where death—in whatever shape it comes—is simply equated with the attack of the venomous snake, the mamba. In "Country Dawns," in particular, the oral-narrative mode finds condensation in Zimunya's careful selection and deployment of traditional narrative and anecdotal forms. Joy and sorrow get defined through our dialogue with plants and animals. What emerges is akin to communal rituals in which love for nature is seen to be not too distant from sexual love. Every child—male or female—experiences this transition to adulthood, and for those who eventually are privileged to compare "country dawns" with "city lights," there will always be echoes of the past, a sense of nostalgia that will constantly awaken in the artist the mnemonic implications of abandoning a vicinity best noted for its innocence and of embracing a modernity that presents fresh challenges as odious as the abandonment of fetuses in dustbins.

While the poems of *Country Dawns and City Lights* present aspects of the Zimbabwean fantastical and metaphysical, Zimunya is equally fascinated with the quotidian. In particular he evokes pity for postindependence Zimbabwe, which becomes for him a manifestation of "leadership anaemia" since the aspirations of the nationalists are sabotaged by an apparent unpreparedness and lack of vision among those politicians who finally take up the baton to direct affairs of state. The new leadership finally creates a sense of despondency among the citizenry, and even those who were exiled during the struggle find no succor on their return. In the poem "Arrivants" this image of gloom and lack of vision leads to a new wave of violence and frustration. Such consequences inspire the poet to suggest that the new citizenry in the "new" Zimbabwe are, indeed, "new arrivants with blister-feet and broken bones / that will learn the end of one journey / begins another" (*Birthright* 160–161). It is partly on such grounds that Zimunya has been celebrated at "home" as a poet whose uniqueness lies in his "uncanny ability to take the familiar and invest [it] with a menacing resonance" (Zhuwarara 1985).

Some of Zimunya's numerous publications include *Thought Tracks* (1982), *Kingfisher, Jikinya and Other Poems* (1982), *Country Dawns and City Lights* (1985), *Perfect Poise* (1993), and *Selected Poems* (1995). Others are his short story collection, *Nightshift* (1993), and a book of literary scholarship, *Those Years of Drought and Hunger: The Birth of African Fiction in English in Zimbabwe* (1992). He has also coedited a number of poetry selections, including *Birthright: Selection of Poems from Southern Africa, And Now the Poets Speak* (with Mudereri Khadani, 1981), and *The Fate of Vultures: New Poetry of Africa* (with Kofi Anyidoho and Peter Porter, 1989).

BIBLIOGRAPHY

Zhuwarara, R. "Introduction." In Musaemura, Zimunya, *Country Dawns and City Lights.* Harare, Zimbabwe: Longman, 1985.

Zimunya, Musaemura B. "Introduction." In *Birthright: A Selection of Poems from Southern Africa.* Harare, Zimbabwe: Longman, 1990.

Osita Ezeliora

APPENDIX I

SELECTED BIBLIOGRAPHY

Abdullah, Abdul-Samad. "Arabic Poetry in West Africa: An Assessment of the Panegyric and Elegy Genres in Arabic Poetry of the 19th and 20th Centuries in Senegal and Nigeria." *Journal of Arabic Literature* 35, no. 3 (2004): 368–390.

Abu-Lughod, Lila. *Veiled Sentiments: Honor and Poetry in a Bedouin Society.* Berkeley: University of California Press, 1986.

Adunis [Ali Ahmad Sa'id]. *An Introduction to Arab Poetics.* Translated from Arabic by Catherine Cobham. London: Saqi, 1990.

Agee, Chris, ed. *Scar on the Stone: Contemporary Poetry from Bosnia.* Newcastle upon Tyne, U.K.: Bloodaxe Books, 1998.

Anyidoho, Kofi, Abena Busia, and Anne V. Adams, eds. *Beyond Survival: African Literature and the Search for New Life.* Lawrenceville, N.J.: Africa World Press, 1998.

Atwan, Robert, George Dardess, and Peggy Rosenthal, eds. *Divine Inspiration: The Life of Jesus in World Poetry.* New York: Oxford University Press, 1997.

Baddawi, M. M., ed. *Modern Arabic Literature.* Cambridge: Cambridge University Press, 1992.

Baranczak, Stanslaw, and Clare Cavanagh, eds and trans. *Polish Poetry of the Last Two Decades of Communist Rule: Spoiling Cannibals' Fun.* Evanston, Ill.: Northwestern University Press, 1991.

Barbieri, Maureen E. "A Way to Love This World: Poetry for Everyone." *English Journal* 91, no. 3 (Jan. 2002): 32–37.

Barnstone, Tony, ed. *Out of the Howling Storm: The New Chinese Poetry.* Hanover, N.H., and London: Wesleyan University Press and University Press of New England, 1993.

Barnstone, Tony, and Chou Ping, eds. *The Anchor Book of Chinese Poetry: From Ancient to Contemporary, the Full 3000-Year Tradition.* New York: Random House, 2004.

Bawden, C. R., ed. *An Anthology of Mongolian Literature.* London and New York: Kegan Paul, 2003.

Benjamin, Joel, Lakshmi Kallicharan, Lloyd Seawar, and Ian McDonald, eds. *They Came in Ships: An Anthology of Indo-Caribbean Poetry and Prose.* Leeds, U.K.: Peepal Tree Press, 1998.

Bernstein, Charles. *A Poetics.* Cambridge, Mass.: Harvard University Press, 1992.

Bialostosky, Don. "Symposium: What Should College English Be? Should College English Be Close Reading?" *College English* 69, no. 2 (Nov. 2006): 111–116.

Bien, Peter, ed., with Edmund Keeley, Karen Van Dyck, and Peter Constantine. *A Century of Greek Poetry 1900–2000: Bilingual Edition.* Brooklyn: Cosmos, 2004.

Bishop, Elizabeth, and Emanuel Brasil, eds. *An Anthology of Twentieth-Century Brazilian Poetry.* Bilingual Edition. Hanover, N.H.: Wesleyan University Press, 1997.

Boullata, Issa. *Critical Perspectives on Modern Arabic Literature.* Washington, D.C.: Three Continents Press, 1980.

Brown, Lloyd W. *Women Writers in Black Africa.* Westport, Conn.: Greenwood Press, 1981.

Brown, Stewart, et al., eds. *Voiceprint: An Anthology of Oral and Related Poetry from the Caribbean.* Essex, U.K.: Longman Group, 1989.

Brown, Stewart, and Mark McWatt, eds. *The Oxford Book of Caribbean Verse.* Oxford: Oxford University Press, 2005.

Burness, Donald. *Fire: Six Writers from Angola, Mozambique and Cape Verde.* Washington, D.C.: Three Continent Press, 1977.

Caws, Mary Ann, ed. *The Yale Anthology of Twentieth-Century French Poetry.* Bilingual Edition. New Haven, Conn.: Yale University Press, 2004.

Chang Li, and Lu Shouroung, eds. *China's New Poetry (Zhongguo xinshi):* Shanghai: Shanghai People's Arts Press, 2003.

Chevalier, Tracy, ed. *Contemporary World Writers.* 2d ed. Detroit: St. James Press, 1993.

Chung, Chong-wha, ed. *Modern Korean Literature, An Anthology, 1908–1965.* New York: Kegan Paul International, 1995.

Connor, Steven, ed. *The Cambridge Companion to Postmodernism.* Cambridge: Cambridge University Press, 2004.

Copeland, Rebecca L. *Lost Leaves: Women Writers of Meiji Japan.* Honolulu: University of Hawaii Press, 2000.

Cox, Brian, ed. *African Writers.* New York: Scribner, 1997.

Crawford, Robert. *Identifying Poets: Self and Territory in Twentieth-Century Poetry.* Edinburgh: Edinburgh University Press, 1994.

Damrosch, David, et al., eds. *The Longman Anthology of World Literature, Volume F: 20th Century.* New York: Longman, 2003.

Dance, Darly C., ed. *Fifty Caribbean Writers: A Bio-Bibliographical Critical Sourcebook.* Westport, Conn.: Greenwood Press, 1986.

Davies, Carole B., and Elaine Savory Fido, eds. *Out of the Kumbla: Caribbean Women and Literature.* Lawrenceville, N.J.: Africa World Press, 1990.

Davies, Paul, et la., eds. *The Bedford Anthology of World Literature: The Twentieth Century, 1900–The Present, Volume 6.* New York: Bedford/St. Martin's, 2002.

Dawes, Kwame, ed. *Talk Yuh Talk: Interviews with Anglophone Caribbean Poets.* Charlottesville: University Press of Virginia, 2001.

Demetz, Peter. *After the Fires: Recent Writing in the Germanies, Austria, and Switzerland.* New York: Harcourt Brace Jovanovich, 1986.

———. *Postwar German Literature: A Critical Introduction.* New York: Pegasus, 1970.

Doherty, Justin. *The Acmeist Movement in Russian Poetry: Culture and the Word.* Oxford: Oxford University Press, 1995.

Deshpande, Gauri, ed. *An Anthology of Indo-English Poetry.* Delhi: Hind Pocket, 1974.

Dharwadker, Vinay, and A. K. Ramanujan, eds. *The Oxford Anthology of Modern Indian Poetry.* Delhi: Oxford University Press, 1997.

Dooling, Amy D., and Kristina M. Torgeson, *Writing Women in Modern China: An Anthology of Women's Literature from the Early Twentieth Century.* New York: Columbia University Press, 1998.

Dordevic, Mihailo, ed. *Anthology of Serbian Poetry: The Golden Age.* (19th– and 20th–Century Poets) New York: Philosophical Library, 1984.

Duke, Michael, ed. *Contemporary Chinese Literature: An Anthology of Post-Mao Fiction and Poetry.* Armonk, N.Y.: M. E. Sharpe, 1985.

Dunning, Stephen. "Why Do You Teach Poetry?" (Excerpt from 1966 essay) *English Journal* 96, no. 1 (Sept. 2006): 22. (Entire issue [96, no. 1] is devoted to strategies for teaching of poetry in schools.)

Ellison, David R. *Ethics and Aesthetics in Modernist Literature: From the Sublime to the Uncanny.* New York: Cambridge University Press, 2001.

Elsie, Robert, ed. *Anthology of Modern Albanian Poetry: An Elusive Eagle Soars.* Nottingham, U.K.: Forest Books, 1993.

Ernst, Josef. "Computer Poetry: An Act of Disinterested Communication." *New Literary History* 23 (Spring 1992): 451–465.

Fekkema, Douwe, and Elrud Ibsch. *Modernist Conjectures: A Mainstream in European Literature 1919–1940.* New York: St. Martin's Press, 1988.

Figgins, Margo A., and Jenny Johnson. "Wordplay: The Poem's Second Language." *English Journal* 96, no. 3 (Jan. 2007): 29–35.

Finkel, Donald, and Carolyn Kizer, trans. *A Splintered Mirror: Chinese Poetry from the Democracy Movement.* San Francisco: North Point, 1991.

Flores, Angel. *Spanish American Authors.* New York: H. W. Wilson Company, 1992.

———. *Spanish Poetry: A Dual-Language Anthology, 16th–20th Centuries.* New York: Dover, 1998.

Forbes, Peter. *Scanning the Century: The Penguin Book of the Twentieth Century in Poetry.* London: Puffin/Penguin, 2000.

Forché, Carolyn, ed. and intro. *Against Forgetting: Twentieth-Century Poetry of Witness.* New York: W. W. Norton, 1993.

Forrest-Thompson, Veronica. *Poetic Artifice: A Theory of Twentieth-Century Poetry.* Manchester, U.K.: Manchester University Press, 1978.

Fowlie, Wallace. *Poem and Symbol: A Brief History of French Symbolism.* University Park: Pennsylvania State University Press, 1990.

Franco, Betsy. *Conversations with a Poet. Inviting Poetry into K-12 Classrooms.* Katonah, N.Y.: Richard C. Owen, 2005.

Franco, Jean. *An Introduction to Spanish-American Literature.* Cambridge: Cambridge University Press, 1994.

Gander, Forrest, ed. *Mouth to Mouth: Poems by Twelve Contemporary Mexican Women.* Bilingual Spanish/English. Translated by Zoe Anglesey. Minneapolis: Milkweed Editions, 1993.

Garton, Janet, ed. *Contemporary Norwegian Women's Writing: An Anthology.* Norwich, U.K.: Norvik Press, 1996.

Gies, David T., ed. *The Cambridge History of Spanish Literature.* Cambridge: Cambridge University Press, 2005.

Gifford, Henry. *Poetry in a Divided World.* Cambridge: Cambridge University Press, 1986.

Gikandi, Simon. *Writing in Limbo: Modernism and Caribbean Literature.* Ithaca, N.Y.: Cornell University Press, 1992.

Glad, John, and Daniel Weissbort. *Twentieth-Century Russian Poetry.* Iowa City: University of Iowa Press, 1992.

Gonzales, Mike, and David Treece, eds. *The Gathering of Voices: Twentieth-Century Poetry of Latin America.* London: Verso Books, 1992.

Gross, John, ed. *The Modern Movement.* London: Harvill Press, 1992.

Hamilton, Ian. *The Oxford Companion to Twentieth-Century Poetry.* Oxford: Oxford University Press, 1994.

Handal, Nathalie, ed. *The Poetry of Arab Women: A Contemporary Anthology.* New York: Interlink Books, 2001.

Hasan-Rokem, Galit, Tamar S. Hess, and Shirley Kaufman, eds. *The Defiant Muse: Hebrew Feminist Poems from Antiquity to the Present. A Bilingual Anthology.* Foreword by Alicia Suskin Ostriker. New York: Feminist Press of the City University of New York, 1999. London: Loki Books in association with the European Jewish Publication Society and the Arts Council of England, 2000.

Hassan, Wail S. "World Literature in the Age of Globalization: Reflections on an Anthology." *College English* 63, no. 1 (Sept. 2000): 38–47.

Hawley, John C., ed. *Writing the Nation: Self and Country in the Postcolonial Imagination.* Amsterdam: Rodopi, 1996.

Heywood, Christopher. *A History of South African Literature.* Cambridge: Cambridge University Press, 2004.

Hofmann, Michael, ed. *Twentieth-Century German Poetry: An Anthology.* New York: Farrar, Straus and Giroux, 2006.

Hsu Kai-yu, ed. *Literature of the People's Republic of China.* Bloomington: Indiana University Press, 1980.

Huynh, Sanh Thong. *An Anthology of Vietnamese Poems: From the Eleventh through the Twentieth Centuries.* New Haven, Conn.: Yale University Press, 1996.

Irele, F. Abiola, and Simon Gikandi, eds. *The Cambridge History of African and Caribbean Literature.* Cambridge: Cambridge University Press, 2004.

Jayyusi, Salma Khadra. *Anthology of Modern Palestinian Literature.* New York: Columbia University Press, 1992.

———. *Modern Arabic Poetry: An Anthology.* New York: Columbia University Press, 1987.

———. *Trends and Movements in Modern Arabic Poetry.* 2 vols. Leiden, the Netherlands: Brill, 1977.

Kac, Eduardo, ed. *New Media Poetry: Poetic Innovation and New Technologies, Visible Language.* Vol. 30, No. 2. Providence: Rhode Island School of Design, 1996.

King, Bruce. *Modern Indian Poetry in English.* Delhi: Oxford University Press, 1987.

Klein, Leonard S. *Latin American Literature in the 20th Century.* New York: Frederick Ungar, 1986.

Koriyama, Naoshi, and Edward Lueders, compilers and trans. *Like Underground Water. The Poetry of Mid-Twentieth-Century Japan.* Port Townsend, Wash.: Copper Canyon Press, 1995.

Kristeva, Julia. *Revolution in Poetic Language.* New York: Columbia University Press, 1984.

Kumar, Santosh, ed. *The Fabric of a Vision: An Anthology of World Poetry.* Allahabad, India: Cyberwit.net Press, 2001.

————. *The Golden Wings: An Anthology of World Poetry.* Allahabad, India: Cyberwit.net Press, 2002.

Lau, Joseph, and Howard Goldblatt, eds. *Columbia Anthology of Modern Chinese Literature.* New York: Columbia University Press, 1995.

Lawall, Sarah, et al., eds. *The Norton Anthology of World Literature. Volume F: The Twentieth Century.* New York: W. W. Norton Co., 2003.

Lazarus, Neil, ed. *The Cambridge Companion to Postcolonial Literary Studies.* Cambridge: Cambridge University Press, 2004.

Lee, Peter H., ed. *A History of Korean Literature.* Cambridge: Cambridge University Press, 2004.

Lefevere, André. *Translating Literature: Practice and Theory in a Comparative Literature Context.* New York: Modern Language Association, 1992.

Lorenz, Dagmar C. G., ed. *Contemporary Jewish Writing in Austria: An Anthology.* Lincoln: University of Nebraska Press, 1999.

Madureira, Luís. *Cannibal Modernities: Postcoloniality and the Avant-Garde in Caribbean and Brazilian Literature.* Charlottesville: University of Virginia Press, 2005.

Makoto Ueda, ed. *Modern Japanese Tanka: An Anthology.* New York: Columbia University Press, 1996.

Mapanje, Jack, ed. *Gathering Seaweed: African Prison Writing.* Oxford: Heinemann Educational Publishers, 2002.

Marinetti, F. T. *The Futurist Cookbook.* Edited by Lesley Chamberlain, translated by Suzanne Brill. San Francisco: Bedfore Arts, 1989.

McCann, David R., ed. *The Columbia Anthology of Modern Korean Poetry.* New York: Columbia University Press, 2004.

McClatchy, J. D., ed. *The Vintage Book of Contemporary World Poetry.* New York: Random House, 1996.

McDuff, David, ed. and trans. *Ice Around Our Lips: Finland-Swedish Poetry.* Newcastle upon Tyne, U.K.: Bloodaxe Books, 1989.

McKendrick, Jamie. *The Faber Book of Twentieth-Century Italian Poems.* London: Faber & Faber, 2004.

McNerney, Kathleen, and Cristina Enríquez de Salamanca, eds. *Double Minorities of Spain: A Bio-Bibliographic Guide to Women Writers of the Catalan, Galician, and Basque Countries.* New York: Modern Language Association, 1995.

Mead, Philip, and John Tranter. *The Penguin Book of Modern Australian Poetry.* Melbourne, Australia: Penguin Books, 1991; Newcastle upon Tyne, U.K.: Bloodaxe Books, 1994.

Messerli, Douglas. *Language Poetries: An Anthology.* New York: New Directions, 1987.

————. *The PIP Anthology of World Poetry of the 20th Century: Volume 1.* Copenhagen and Los Angeles: El-E-Phant Books/Green Integer, 2004.

————. *The PIP Anthology of World Poetry, No. 7: At Villa Aurora: Nine Contemporary Poets Writing in German.* Copenhagen and Los Angeles: El-E-Phant Books/Green Integer, 2006.

Metcalf, John. *Salutation: Anthology of World Poetry.* (Grades 10–12) Toronto: Ryerson Press, 1970.

Milosz, Czeslaw, ed. and intro. *A Book of Luminous Things: An International Anthology of Poetry.* San Diego, Calif.: Harcourt Brace, 1998.

————. *Postwar Polish Poetry: An Anthology.* Berkeley: University of California Press, 1983.

Mishra, Vijay. *Devotional Poetics and the Indian Sublime.* Delhi, India: D. K. Print World, 1999.

————. *Literature of the Indian Diaspora.* Routledge Research in Postcolonial Literatures. London: Routledge, 2007.

Mitler, Louis. *Contemporary Turkish Writers: A Critical Bio-Bibliography.* Bloomington: Indiana University Press, 1988.

Moore, Gerald, and Ulli Beier. *The Penguin Book of Modern African Poetry.* 4th ed. London: Penguin, 1998.

Nemet-Nejat, Murat, ed. *Eda: An Anthology of Contemporary Turkish Poetry.* Bilingual Edition. Hoboken, N.J.: Talisman Books, 2004.

Ngara, Emmanuel. *Ideology and Form in African Poetry: Implications for Communication.* London: James Curry, 1990.

Niebylski, Dianna C. *The Poem on the Edge of the Word: The Limits of Language and the Uses of Silence in the Poetry of Mallarmé, Rilke and Vallejo.* New York: Peter Lang, 1993.

Ojaide, Tanure, and Tijan M. Sallah, eds. *The New African Poetry: An Anthology.* Boulder, Colo. and London: Lynne Rienner, 2000.

O'Sullivan, Vincent. *An Anthology of Twentieth Century New Zealand Poetry.* New York: Oxford University Press, 1987.

Owen, Stephen. "The Anxiety of Global Influence: What is World Poetry?" *New Republic* (Nov. 19, 1990): 28–32.

————. "Stepping Forward and Back: Issues and Possibilities for 'World' Poetry." *Modern Philology* 100 (2003): 532–548.

Padgett, Ron, ed. *World Poets*. 3 vols. New York: Scribner, 2000.

Paine, Jeffery, with Kwame Anthony Appiah, Sven Birkerts, Joseph Brodsky, Carolyn Forche, and Helen Vendler, eds., in collaboration with Agha Shahid Ali, Bei Dao, Anita Desai, Edward Dimock, Edward Hirsch, Garrett Hongo, Denise Levertov, Perry Link, Donald Keene, and Burton Raffel. *The Poetry of Our World: An International Anthology of Contemporary Poetry*. New York: HarperCollins/Perennial, 2001.

Palmowski, Jan. *Oxford Dictionary of Twentieth-Century World History*. Oxford: Oxford University Press, 1998.

Perloff, Marjorie. *21st-Century Modernism: The 'New Poetics.'* (Blackwell Manifestos.) Oxford: Blackwell, 2002.

———. *Radical Artifice: Writing Poetry in the Age of Media*. Chicago: University of Chicago Press, 1991.

———. *Wittgenstein's Ladder: Poetic Language and the Strangeness of the Ordinary*. Chicago: University of Chicago Press, 1999.

Picchione, John, and Lawrence R. Smith, eds. *Twentieth-Century Italian Poetry: An Anthology*. In Italian, with introduction and notes in English. Toronto: University of Toronto Press, 2003.

Pilling, John. *A Reader's Guide to Fifty Modern European Poets*. London: Heinemann and Barnes and Noble, 1982.

Preminger, Alex, Terry V. F. Brogan, and Frank J. Warnke, eds. *The New Princeton Encyclopedia of Poetry and Poetics*. Princeton, N.J.: Princeton University Press, 1993.

Raizen, Esther, ed., trans., and intro. *No Rattling of Sabers: An Anthology of Israeli War Poetry*. Austin: University of Texas Press, 1995.

Ramraj, Victor J., ed. *Concert of Voices: An Anthology of World Writing in English*. Peterborough, Ont.: Broadview Press, 1995.

Roberts, Neil, ed. and intro. *A Companion to Twentieth-Century Poetry*. Oxford: Blackwell, 2001. An excellent collection of particularly useful scholarly essays, defining a wide array of topics, including movements, themes, national literatures, criticism.

Robinson, Peter. *Twentieth Century Poetry: Selves and Situations*. Oxford: Oxford University Press, 2005.

Robinson, Roger, and Nelson Wattie, eds. *The Oxford Companion to New Zealand Literature*. Oxford: Oxford University Press, 1998.

Rosenberg, Donna. *World Literature: An Anthology of Great Short Stories, Drama and Poetry*. Lincolnwood, Ill.: NTC Publishing Group, 1992.

Rosenthal, Peggy. *The Poets' Jesus: Representations at the End of a Millennium*. Oxford: Oxford University Press, 2001.

Rothenberg, Jerome, and Pierre Joris. *Poems for the Millennium: The University of California Book of Modern and Postmodern Poetry. Volume One: From Fin-de-Siècle to Negritude*. Berkeley and Los Angeles: University of California Press, 1995.

———. *Poems for the Millennium: The University of California Book of Modern and Postmodern Poetry. Volume Two: From Postwar to Millennium*. Berkeley and Los Angeles: University of California Press, 1998.

Rowe, William. *Poets of Contemporary Latin America: History and the Inner Life*. Oxford: Oxford University Press, 2000.

Sabir, Rafiq, Kamal Mirawdeli, and Stephen Watts, eds. *Modern Kurdish Poetry: An Anthology & Introduction*. Uppsala, Sweden: Endangered Languages and Cultures, ELC (No. 2), 2006.

Sato, Hiroaki, ed., and Burton Watson, trans. *From the Country of Eight Islands: An Anthology of Japanese Poetry*. New York: Columbia University Press, 1986.

Smith, Lawrence R., ed. and trans. *The New Italian Poetry: 1945 to the Present: A Bilingual Anthology*. Berkeley and Los Angeles: University of California Press, 1981.

Smith, Stan. *Inviolable Voice: History and Twentieth-Century Poetry*. New York: Humanities Press, 1982.

Sonntag Blay, Iliana L. *Twentieth-Century Poetry from Spanish America*. Lanham, Md.: Scarecrow Press, 1998.

Spears, Monroe. *Dionysus and the City: Modernism in Twentieth-Century Poetry*. Oxford: Oxford University Press, 1970.

Stewart, Frank, Arthur Sze, and Michelle Yeh, eds. *Mercury Rising: Contemporary Poetry from Taiwan*. Honolulu: University of Hawaii Press, 2003.

Sumari, Anni, and Nicolaj Stochholm, eds. *The Other Side of Landscape: An Anthology of Contemporary Nordic Poetry*. Buffalo, N.Y.: Slope Editions, 2006.

Susko, Mario, ed. *Contemporary Poetry of Bosnia and Herzegovina*. Sarajevo: International Peace Center/PEN Club of Bosnia and Herzegovina/Graphics Publishing House "OKO," 1993.

Tapscott, Stephen, ed. *Twentieth-Century Latin American Poetry: A Bilingual Anthology.* Austin: University of Texas Press, 1996.

Thackston, Wheeler M. *A Millennium of Classical Persian Poetry: A Guide to the Reading & Understanding of Persian Poetry from the Tenth to the Twentieth Century.* Bilingual edition. Bethesda, Md.: Ibex, 1994.

Treece, David. *Exiles, Allies, Rebels: Brazil's Indianist Movement, Indigenist Politics, and the Imperial Nation-State.* Westport, Conn.: Greenwood Press, 2000.

Valaoritis, Nanos, ed. *Twentieth-Century Greek Poetry.* Hoboken, N.J.: Talisman House, 2004.

Van Doren, Mark, ed. *An Anthology of World Poetry.* New York: Harcourt, Brace, 1936.

Van Wyhe, Tamara L. C. "Remembering What Is Important: The Power of Poetry in My Classroom." *English Journal* 96, no. 1 (Sept. 2006): 15–16.

Wachtel, Michael. *The Cambridge Introduction to Russian Poetry.* Cambridge: Cambridge University Press, 2004.

Wainwright, Jeffrey. *Poetry: The Basics.* London: Routledge, 2004.

Wang Ping, ed. *New Generation: Poems from China Today.* Brooklyn, N.Y.: Hanging Loose Press, 1999.

Washburn, Katharine, and John S. Major, eds. *World Poetry: An Anthology of Verse from Antiquity to Our Time.* New York: W. W. Norton, 1997.

Watts, Jane. *Black Writers from South Africa: Towards a Discourse of Liberation.* New York: St. Martin's Press, 1989.

Weeks, Ruth Mary. *World Literature.* New York: Scribner, 1938.

Weissbort, Daniel, ed. *Looking Eastward: Modern Poetry in Translation.* Toronto: Zephyr Press, 2004.

———. *The Poetry of Survival: Post-War Poets of Central and Eastern Europe.* London: Penguin/Puffin (reprint ed.), 1993.

Willbanks, Ray. *Australian Voices: Writers and Their Work.* Austin: University of Texas Press, 1991.

Willhardt, Mark, with Alan Michael Parker, eds. *Who's Who in Twentieth-Century World Poetry.* 2d ed. London: Routledge, 2002.

Yeh, Michelle, ed. and trans. *Anthology of Modern Chinese Poetry.* New Haven, Conn.: Yale University Press, 1992.

Zavala, Iris M. *Colonialism and Culture: Hispanic Modernisms and the Social Imaginary.* Bloomington: Indiana University Press, 1992.

Zwart, Martijn, and Ethel Grene, eds. *Dutch Poetry in Translation: Kaleidoscope: From Medieval Times to the Present.* Wilmette, Ill.: Fairfield Books, 1998.

R. Victoria Arana

APPENDIX II

WINNERS OF THE NOBEL PRIZE IN LITERATURE

Awarded to novelists, playwrights, essayists, and poets. (Names of poets with individual entries in this volume are in **boldface** type.)

2007 - Doris Lessing
2006 - Orhan Pamuk
2005 - Harold Pinter
2004 - Elfriede Jelinek
2003 - J. M. Coetzee
2002 - Imre Kertész
2001 - V. S. Naipaul
2000 - Gao Xingjian
1999 - Günter Grass
1998 - José Saramago
1997 - Dario Fo
1996 - **Wisława Szymborska**
1995 - Seamus Heaney
1994 - Kenzaburo Oe
1993 - Toni Morrison
1992 - **Derek Walcott**
1991 - Nadine Gordimer
1990 - **Octavio Paz**
1989 - Camilo José Cela
1988 - Naguib Mahfouz
1987 - **Joseph Brodsky**
1986 - **Wole Soyinka**
1985 - Claude Simon

1984 - **Jaroslav Seifert**
1983 - William Golding
1982 - Gabriel García Márquez
1981 - Elias Canetti
1980 - **Czesław Miłosz**
1979 - **Odysseus Elytis**
1978 - Isaac Bashevis Singer
1977 - **Vicente Aleixandre**
1976 - Saul Bellow
1975 - **Eugenio Montale**
1974 - Eyvind Johnson, **Harry Martinson**
1973 - Patrick White
1972 - Heinrich Böll
1971 - **Pablo Neruda**
1970 - Aleksandr Solzhenitsyn
1969 - Samuel Beckett
1968 - Yasunari Kawabata
1967 - Miguel Angel Asturias
1966 - Samuel Agnon, **Nelly Sachs**
1965 - Mikhail Sholokhov
1964 - Jean-Paul Sartre
1963 - **Giorgos Seferis**
1962 - John Steinbeck
1961 - Ivo Andrić
1960 - **Saint-John Perse**
1959 - **Salvatore Quasimodo**
1958 - **Boris Pasternak**
1957 - Albert Camus
1956 - **Juan Ramón Jiménez**
1955 - Halldór Laxness

1954 - Ernest Hemingway

1953 - Winston Churchill

1952 - François Mauriac

1951 - Pär Lagerkvist

1950 - Bertrand Russell

1949 - William Faulkner

1948 - T. S. Eliot

1947 - André Gide

1946 - Hermann Hesse

1945 - **Gabriela Mistral**

1944 - Johannes V. Jensen

1943 - The prize money was allocated one-third to the Main Fund and two-thirds to the Special Fund of this prize section.

1942 - The prize money was allocated one-third to the Main Fund and two-thirds to the Special Fund of this prize section.

1941 - The prize money was allocated one-third to the Main Fund and two-thirds to the Special Fund of this prize section.

1940 - The prize money was allocated one-third to the Main Fund and two-thirds to the Special Fund of this prize section.

1939 - Frans Eemil Sillanpää

1938 - Pearl Buck

1937 - Roger Martin du Gard

1936 - Eugene O'Neill

1935 - The prize money was allocated one-third to the Main Fund and two-thirds to the Special Fund of this prize section.

1934 - Luigi Pirandello

1933 - Ivan Bunin

1932 - John Galsworthy

1931 - Erik Axel Karlfeldt

1930 - Sinclair Lewis

1929 - Thomas Mann

1928 - Sigrid Undset

1927 - Henri Bergson

1926 - Grazia Deledda

1925 - George Bernard Shaw

1924 - Władysław Reymont

1923 - William Butler Yeats

1922 - Jacinto Benavente

1921 - Anatole France

1920 - Knut Hamsun

1919 - Carl Spitteler

1918 - The prize money was allocated to the Special Fund of this prize section.

1917 - Karl Gjellerup, Henrik Pontoppidan

1916 - Verner von Heidenstam

1915 - Romain Rolland

1914 - The prize money was allocated to the Special Fund of this prize section.

1913 - **Rabindranath Tagore**

1912 - Gerhart Hauptmann

1911 - Maurice Maeterlinck

1910 - Paul Heyse

1909 - Selma Lagerlöf

1908 - Rudolf Eucken

1907 - Rudyard Kipling

1906 - Giosuè Carducci

1905 - Henryk Sienkiewicz

1904 - Frédéric Mistral, José Echegaray

1903 - Bjørnstjerne Bjørnson

1902 - Theodor Mommsen

1901 - Sully Prudhomme

APPENDIX III

POETS BY REGION

AFRICA

Abani, Chris (Nigeria b. 1966)
Achebe, Chinua (Nigeria b. 1930)
Anyidoho, Kofi (Ghana b. 1947)
Awoonor, Kofi Nyidevu (Ghana b. 1934)
Breytenbach, Breyten (South Africa b. 1939)
Brutus, Dennis (South Africa b. 1924)
Cheney-Coker, Syl (Sierra Leone b. 1945)
Chipasula, Frank Mkalawile (Malawi b. 1949)
Chinweizu (Nigeria b. 1943)
Chirikure, Chirikure (Zimbabwe b. 1962)
Clark-Bekederemo, John Pepper (Nigeria b. 1935)
Dadié, Bernard Binlin (Ivory Coast b. 1916)
Diop, David (Senegal 1927–1960)
Hove, Chenjerai (Zimbabwe b. 1954)
Kunene, Mazisi (Zulu/South Africa b. 1930)
Marechera, Dambudzo (Zimbabwe 1952–1987)
Mugo, Micere M. Githae (Kenya b. 1942)
Neto, Antonio Agostinho (Angola 1922–1979)
Ojaide, Tanure (Nigeria b. 1948)
Okara, Gabriel (Nigeria b. 1921)
Okigbo, Christopher (Nigeria 1932–1967)
Osundare, Niyi (Nigeria b. 1947)
p'Bitek, Okot (Uganda 1931–1982)
Peters, Lenrie (Gambia b. 1932)
Sallah, Tijan (Gambia b. 1958)
Saro-Wiwa, Kenule Beeson (Nigeria 1941–1995)

Senghor, Léopold Sédar (Senegal b. 1906)
Serote, Mongane Wally (South Africa b. 1944)
Soyinka, Wole (Nigeria b. 1934)
Zimunya, Musaemura Bonas (Zimbabwe b. 1949)

ASIA

Bei Dao (Zhao Zhenkai) (China b. 1949)
Bose, Buddhadeva (India 1908–1974)
Das, Jibanananda (Bengal, India 1899–1954)
Das, Kamala (Malabar, Kerala, India b. 1934)
Duo Duo (Li Shizheng) (China b. 1951)
Dharker, Imtiaz (India/Scotland [Muslim] b. 1954)
Ezekiel, Nissim (India [Jewish] 1924–2004)
Faiz Ahmed Faiz (Pakistan 1911–1984)
Gu Cheng (China 1956–1993)
Guo Moruo (China 1892–1978)
Han Yongun (Korea 1879–1944)
Hagiwara Sakutaro (Japan 1886–1942)
lqbāl Muhammad (India 1879–1938)
Kalia, Mamta (India b. 1940)
Kim Chi-ha (Korea b. 1941)
Kim Su-young (Korea 1921–1968)
Kolatkar, Arun Balkrishna (India b. 1932)
Ma Anandamayee, Shree Shree (India 1896–1981)
Mahapatra, Jayanta (India b. 1928)
Miyazawa Kenji (Japan 1896–1933)
Nasrin, Taslima (Bangladesh b. 1962)
Ramanujan, Attipat Krishnaswami (India 1929–1993)

Shin Kyong-nim (Korea b. 1935)
Shu Ting (Gong Peiyu) (China b. 1952)
Suh Jung-ju (Korea 1915–2000)
Tagore, Rabindranath (India 1861–1941)
Takamura Kōtarō (Japan 1883–1956)
Tamura Ryūichi (Japan 1923–1998)
Tanikawa Shuntaro (Japan b. 1931)
Thiên, Nguyên Chí (Vietnam b. 1939)
Yosano Akiko (Japan 1878–1941)
Yun Dong-ju (Korea 1918–1945)

AUSTRALIA AND NEW ZEALAND

Baxter, James K. (New Zealand 1926–1972)
Keane, Jayne Fenton (Australia b. 1971)
Murray, Leslie Allan (Australia b. 1938)
Wright, Judith (Australia 1915–2000)

MIDDLE EAST

Adonis (Ali Ahman Said) (Syria/Lebanon b. 1930)
Amichai, Yehuda (Israel b. 1924)
Baraheni, Reza (Iran b. 1935)
Bialik, Hayyim Nachman (Russia/Israel 1873–1934)
Chedid, Andrée (Lebanon b. 1920)
Darwish, Mahmud (Palestine b. 1942)
Farrokhzad, Forugh (Iran 1933–1967)
Gibran Khalil Gibran (Lebanon 1883–1931)
Hikmet, Nazim (Turkey 1902–1963)
Ibrahim, Muhammed Hafiz (Egypt 1871–1932)
Mansour, Joyce (Egypt and France 1928–1986)
Tchernihovsky, Shaul (Crimea/Ukraine/Israel 1875–1943)
Tuqan, Fadwa (Palestine b. 1917)
Youssef, Saadi (Iraq b. 1934)
Yushij, Nima (Yush, Iran 1895–1960)

CARIBBEAN

Brathwaite, Edward Kamau (Barbados b. 1930)
Césaire, Aimé (Martinique b. 1913)
Cliff, Michelle (Jamaica b. 1946)
Depestre, René (Haiti b. 1926)
Glissant, Édouard (Martinique b. 1928)
Goodison, Lorna (Jamaica b. 1947)

Guillén, Nicolás (Cuba 1902–1987)
Morejón, Nancy (Cuba b. 1944)
Perse, Saint-John (Marie-René-Auguste-Alexis Léger) (Guadeloupe 1987–1975)
Salkey, Andrew (Jamaica 1928–1995)
Senior, Olive (Jamaica b. 1943)
Walcott, Derek (Saint Lucia b. 1930)

SOUTH AND CENTRAL AMERICA

Alegría, Clara Isabel (El Salvador b. 1924)
Belli, Carlos Germán (Peru b. 1927)
Belli, Gioconda (Nicaragua b. 1948)
Borges, Jorge Luis (Argentina (1899–1985)
Bopp, Raul (Brazil 1898–1984)
Cabral de Melo Neto, João (Brazil b. 1920)
Cardenal, Ernesto (Nicaragua b. 1925)
Cadenas, Rafael (Venezuela b. 1930)
Dabydeen, David (Guyana b. 1955)
Damas, Léon-Gontran (French Guiana 1912–1978)
Darío, Rubén (Nicaragua 1967–1916)
Drummond de Andrade, Carlos (Brazil 1902–1987)
González Martínez, Enrique (Mexico 1871–1952)
Harris, Wilson (Guyana b. 1921)
Huidobro, Vicente (Chile 1893–1948)
Ibarbourou, Juana de (Uruguay 1895–1979)
Lihn, Enrique (Chile 1929–1988)
Lima, Jorge de (Brazil 1895–1953)
Meireles, Cecília (Brazil 1901–1964)
Meneses, Vidaluz (Nicaragua b. 1944)
Mistral, Gabriela (L. Godoy y Alcayaga) (Chile 1889–1957)
Neruda, Pablo (Chile 1904–1973)
Nervo, Amado (Mexico 1870–1919)
Pacheco, José Emilio (Mexico b. 1939)
Parra, Nicanor (Chile b. 1914)
Paz, Octavio (Mexico 1914–1998)
Storni, Alfonsina, (Argentina 1892–1938)
Vallejo, César (Peru 1892–1938)
Zamora, Daisy (Nicaragua b. 1950)

EUROPE

Akhmatova, Anna (Russia 1889–1966)

Alberti, Rafael (Spain b. 1902)
Aleixandre, Vicente (Spain 1898–1984)
Apollinaire, Guillaume (France 1880–1918)
Aragon, Louis (France 1897–1982)
Artaud, Antonin (France 1896–1948)
Bachman, Ingeborg (Austria 1926–1973)
Benn, Gottfried (Germany 1886–1956)
Bjørnvig, Thorkild (Denmark b. 1918)
Blaga, Lucian (Romania 1895–1961)
Blok, Aleksandr (Russia 1880–1921)
Bobrowski, Johannes (Germany 1917–1965)
Bouchet, André du (France 1924–2001)
Boye, Karin (Sweden 1900–1941)
Brecht, Bertolt (Germany 1898–1956)
Breton, André (France 1896–1966)
Brinkmann, Rolf Dieter (Germany 1940–1975)
Brodsky, Joseph (Russia 1940–1996)
Cavafy, Constantine P. (Greece 1863–1933)
Celan, Paul (Romania 1920–1970)
Cendrars, Blaise (France 1887–1961)
Char, René (France 1907–1988)
Christensen, Inger (Denmark b. 1935)
Çirak, Zehra (Turkey/Germany b. 1960)
Claudel, Paul (France 1868–1955)
D'Annunzio, Gabriele (Italy 1863–1938)
Diego, Gerardo (Spain 1896–1987)
Domin, Hilde (Germany b. 1912)
Dupin, Jacques (France b. 1927)
Éluard, Paul (France 1895–1952)
Elytis, Odysseas (Greece 1911–1996)
García Lorca, Federico (Spain 1898–1936)
George, Stefan (Germany 1868–1933)
Giuliani, Alfredo (Italy b. 1924)
Goll, Yvan (Isaac Lang) (France 1891–1950)
Guillén, Jorge (Spain 1893–1984)
Gustafsson, Lars (Sweden b. 1936)
Haavikko, Paavo (Finland b. 1931)
Herbert, Zbigniew (Poland 1924–1998)
Holub, Miroslav (Czechoslovakia 1923–1998)
Jacobsen, Rolf (Norway 1907–1994)
Jiménez, Juan Ramón (Spain 1881–1958)
Kling, Thomas (Germany 1957–2005)
Kurghinian, Shushanik (Armenia 1876–1927)
Lalic, Ivan (Yugoslavia 1931–1996)
Lasker-Schueler, Else (Germany 1869–1945)

Machado, Antonio (Spain 1875–1939)
Mandelstam, Osip Yemilyevich (Poland 1891–1938)
Martinson, Harry (Sweden, 1904–1978)
Mayakovsky, Vladimir (Russia 1893–1930)
Miłosz, Czesław (Poland b. 1911)
Montale, Eugenio (Italy 1896–1981)
Noailles, Anna de (Romania/Greece/France 1876–1933)
Nordbrandt, Henrik (Denmark b. 1945)
Pasolini, Pier Paolo (Italy 1922–1975)
Pasternak, Boris (Russia 1890–1960)
Pavese, Cesare (Italy 1908–1950)
Pessoa, Fernando (Portugal 1888–1935)
Pignotti, Lamberto (Italy b. 1926)
Popa, Vasko (Yugoslavia 1922–1991)
Prévert, Jacques (France 1900–1977)
Quasimodo, Salvatore (Italy 1901–1968)
Rilke, Rainer Maria (Austria/Hungary/Germany 1875–1926)
Ritsos, Yannis (Greece 1909–1990)
Saba, Umberto (Italy 1883–1957)
Sachs, Nelly (Germany 1891–1970)
Sanguineti, Edoardo (Italy b. 1930)
Seferis, George (Greece 1900–1971)
Seifert, Jaroslav (Czechoslovakia 1901–1986)
Södergran, Edith (Finland 1892–1923)
Szymborska, Wisława (Poland b. 1923)
Tabidze, Titsian (Georgia 1893–1937)
Tadić, Novica (Montenegro/Serbia b. 1949)
Trakl, Georg (Austria 1887–1914)
Tranströmer, Tomas (Sweden b. 1931)
Tsvetaeva, Marina (Russia 1892–1941)
Tzara, Tristan (Romania/France 1896–1963)
Ungaretti, Giuseppe (Italy 1888–1970)
Utler, Anja (Schwandorf) (Germany b. 1973)
Valéry, Paul (France 1871–1945)
Vesaas, Tarjei (Norway 1897–1970)
Volponi, Paolo (Italy b. 1924)
Voznesensky, Andrey (Russia b. 1933)
Yevtushenko, Yevgeny (Russia b. 1933)

Gaelic Language

Dhomhnaill, Nuala Ní (Ireland b. 1952)

SPECIAL TOPICS

Arab rap and hip hop culture
colonialism, poetry and
ecopoetics
écriture

field poetics
French rap
modernism, poetry and
Negritude Movement
poetry beyond the page

LIST OF CONTRIBUTORS

Dvir Abramovich (University of Melbourne, Australia)

Rochelle Almeida (New York University)

R. Victoria Arana (Howard University, Washington, D.C.)

Shushan Avagyan (Illinois State University)

Jennifer Perrine (Drake University, Iowa)

Sandra Beasley (American Scholar, Washington, D.C.)

Geraldine Cannon Becker (University of Maine, Fort Kent)

Joseph Becker (University of Maine, Fort Kent)

Wendy Belcher (University of California, Los Angeles)

Olaf Berwald (University of North Dakota, Grand Forks)

Jacob Blakesley (University of Chicago)

Ben Bollig (University of Westminster, U.K.)

Heather Brady (Monmouth College, Illinois)

Sabrina Brancato (Johann Wolfgang Goethe University, Frankfurt)

Tom Bristow (Edinburgh University, Scotland)

Philip Christensen (SUNY-Suffolk)

Patrick L. Day (University of Wisconsin, Eau Claire)

Emily S. Davis (University of California, Santa Barbara)

James Davis (Howard University, Washington, D.C.)

Analisa DeGrave (University of Wisconsin, Eau Claire)

Yasmin DeGout (Howard University, Washington, D.C.)

Kevin De Ornellas (University of Ulster, U.K.)

Tom Dolack (University of Oregon, Eugene)

Thomas Eder (University of Vienna, Austria)

Winter Elliott (Brenau University, Gainesville, Georgia)

Osita Ezeliora (University of Witwatersrand, Johannesburg, South Africa)

Alex Feerst (Macalester College, Minnesota)

Christophe Fricker (St John's College, Oxford University)

Ferial Ghazoul (American University of Cairo, Egypt)

Rebecca Gould (Columbia University, New York City)

Heike Grundmann (University of Munich, Germany)

Jihee Han (Gyeongsang National University, Seoul, South Korea)

Takao Hagiwara (Case Western Reserve University, Ohio)

Anett Jessop (University of California, Davis)

Eugene Johnson (Queen's University, Canada)

Kelly Josephs (Rutgers University, New Jersey)

Jayne Fenton Keane (Queensland, Australia)

Karen Keck (Texas Tech University, Lubbock)

Robin Kemp (Kennesaw State University, Georgia)

Stacey Kidd (University of Utah, Salt Lake City)

Daniela Kukrechtova (Brandeis University, Waltham, Massachusetts)

Yianna Liatsos (University of Oklahoma, Norman)

Ursula Lindqvist (University of Colorado, Boulder)

Rupendra Guha Majumdar (University of Delhi, India)

Sean McDonnell (University of California, Davis)

Alexander B. McKee (University of California, Santa Barbara)

Rini Bhattacharya Mehta (University of Illinois, Urbana-Champaign)

Amelia Mondragón (Howard University, Washington, D.C.)

Debali Mookerjea-Leonard (James Madison University, Virginia)

Enrique Morales-Diaz (Hartwick College, New York)

Paul Munn (Saginaw Valley State University, Michigan)

A. Mary Murphy (University of Calgary, Canada)

Luciana Namorato (University of Oklahoma, Norman)

Ram Shankar Nanda (Sambalpur University, India)

Shonu Nangia (Louisiana State University, Alexandria)

Jan H. K. Nielsen (University of Washington, Seattle)

Oyeniyi Okunoye (Obafemi Awolowo University, Nigeria)

Annette Olsen-Fazi (Texas A&M International University, Laredo)

Ted Olson (East Tennessee State University)

Firat Oruc (Duke University, Durham, North Carolina)

Friederike Pannewick (University of Oslo, Norway)

Daniel Pantano (University of South Florida, Tampa)

Jennifer Perrine (Drake University, Iowa)

John Peters (University of North Texas, Denton)

Chris Picicci (University of Oregon, Eugene)

Masood A. Raja (Florida State University, Tallahassee)

James C. R. Redman (University of Utah, Salt Lake City)

Eric Reinholtz (University of Southern California, Los Angeles)

Michele Ricci (Oberlin College, Oberlin, Ohio)

Maria Roof (Howard University, Washington, D.C.)

Michaela Schrage-Frueh (University of Mainz, Germany)

Xuemei Shan (Xinjiang University, China)

J. Shantz (University of Toronto, Canada)

Renee Silverman (Oberlin College, Oberlin, Ohio)

George Syrimis (Yale University, New Haven, Connecticut)

Alina Sokol (Dartmouth College, Hanover, New Hampshire)

Steven Teref (Columbia College, Chicago)

Mercedes Tibbits (Howard University, Washington, D.C.)

Josephine von Zitzewitz (St John's College, Oxford University)

Peter C. Weise (Boston University)

Donald Wellman (Daniel Webster College, New Hampshire)

Sonia Wichmann (University of California, Berkeley)

INDEX